RAISING KEYNES

Raising Keynes

A Twenty-First-Century General Theory

STEPHEN A. MARGLIN

Harvard University Press

CAMBRIDGE, MASSACHUSETTS

LONDON, ENGLAND

2021

First printing

Library of Congress Cataloging-in-Publication Data

Names: Marglin, Stephen A., author.
Title: Raising Keynes : a twenty-first-century general theory / Stephen A. Marglin.
Description: Cambridge, Massachusetts : Harvard University Press, 2021. |
Includes bibliographical references and index. |
Identifiers: LCCN 2020019316 | ISBN 9780674971028 (cloth)
Subjects: LCSH: Keynes, John Maynard, 1883–1946. | Keynesian economics. |
Industries—Self-regulation. | Economics, Mathematical.
Classification: LCC HB99.7 .M344 2021 | DDC 330.15/6—dc23
LC record available at https://lccn.loc.gov/2020019316

For Emmanuelle, Suzanne, Oriah, Jordan,
Micah, Nasia, Mira, Yael, Noah, and Gabriel,
the next generation

CONTENTS

PART IV Building Blocks

PART V Fiscal Policy in Theory and Practice

PART VI Keynes in the Long Run

NOTATION

Chapter 1

P = Nominal price of output

W = Nominal wage rate

P/W = Real price, the ratio of the nominal price of output to the nominal wage

Y = Output = Income (in real terms)

W/P = Real wage, the ratio of the nominal wage to the nominal price of output

L = Labor

Chapter 2

E = Expenditure (real)

ρ = Interest rate

I = Investment

Chapter 3

$I(\rho)$ = Investment as a function of the (hurdle) rate of interest = I_D, desired investment

c = MPC = Marginal propensity to consume

C = Consumption (real)

C_D = Desired consumption

MEC = Marginal efficiency of capital = rate of interest associated with any given level of desired investment

M_1 = Transactions demand for money

$\bar{M}_1$ = Supply of money for transactions

α = Ratio of transactions demand for money to nominal value of output

A = Wealth (nominal)

M_2 = Asset demand for money

$\bar{M}_2$ = Supply of money in market for financial assets

β = Ratio of asset demand for money to nominal value of wealth

K = Capital stock (real)

$\bar{B}$ = Stock of bonds in the hands of the public

P_B = Price of bonds

R = Bond coupon = Periodic payment due until bond is redeemed

M = Total demand for money

$\bar{M}$ = Money supply

V = Income velocity of money = $1/\alpha$ if we ignore the asset demand for money

$\bar{M}/P$ = Money supply (real)

$Y = F(K, L)$ = Output as function of capital and labor inputs (production function)

$F_L \equiv \partial Y/\partial L$ = Marginal productivity of labor

$L = L(P/W)$ = Supply of labor in terms of time worked

$LS(P/W) = F(K, L(P/W))$ = Supply of labor in terms of output produced

$GS(P/W)$ = Supply of goods

Derivatives indicated by $'$

Chapter 5

Q = Quantity

$D(P)$ = Quantity demanded as a function of price

$S(P)$ = Quantity demanded as a function of price

$\dot{X}$ = Rate of change of the variable X with respect to time

$S^{-1}(Q)$ = Supply price associated with the quantity Q = Marginal cost of Q

$D^{-1}(Q)$ = Demand price associated with the quantity Q

E_D = Desired expenditure

θ_i = Speed of adjustment

Chapter 7

ρ_{WHEAT} = Own rate of interest for wheat

ρ_{OIL} = Own rate of interest for oil

$\phi_{W/O}$ = Rate of change of the price of wheat relative to the price of oil

ϕ = Rate of change of the price level

ρ_{REAL} = Real rate of interest

$\rho_{NOMINAL}$ = Nominal rate of interest

ρ_R^B = Real interest rate on bonds

ρ_R^M = Real interest rate on money

ρ_N^B = Nominal interest rate on bonds

ρ_N^M = Nominal interest rate on money

c_1 = Propensity of wealth holders (creditors) to consume out of income

c_2 = Propensity of businessmen (debtors) to consume out of income

s_1 = Propensity of wealth holders (creditors) to save out of income

s_2 = Propensity of businessmen (debtors) to save out of income

a = Propensity to consume out of wealth

a_1 = Propensity of wealth holders (creditors) to consume out of wealth

a_2 = Propensity of debtors to consume out of (negative) wealth

α_i = Conditions on elements of Jacobian matrix required for stability

γ_i = Proportion of income received by creditors ($i = 1$) and debtors ($i = 2$)

Chapter 8

Y_i = Income of Type i agents, $i = 1$ (creditors), $= 2$ (debtors)

Y_I = Industrial output = Industrial Income

Y_A = Agricultural output

$\tilde{Y}_A$ = Agricultural income

Y_A^S = Agricultural output for crops consumed domestically and exported

Y_A^0, Y_A^1 = Part of Y_A^S consumed domestically (in Figure 8.10)

C_I = Consumption of industrial output

γ_{ij} = Propensity to consume goods produced in sector j from income resulting from production in sector i, $i = A$ (agriculture), $= I$ (industry)

I_i = Investment demand in sector i

P_i = Nominal price of goods produced in sector i

Chapter 9

$Y_{FE} = Y(K, LS(P/W))$, Output at full employment (labor supply is assumed to be independent of P/W in Figure 9.4)

$C_{D\,FE}$ = Desired consumption at full employment

S = Aggregate saving

Π = Total profits

$r = \Pi/K$ = Rate of profit

s_π = Propensity to save out of profits

s_w = Propensity to save out of wages

Chapter 10

q = quasi-rent on investment, the annual flow of returns net of operating costs other than interest

Ω = Subjective probability of being able to utilize additional capacity

ψ = Functional relationship between investment demand and the annual return on investment. The general functional form is $I = \psi(q - \rho)$

$\psi(q - \rho) = \psi(\Omega(Y)[Y/K - (P/W)^{-1}L/K] - \rho)$ is the functional form of investment demand for capital widening

$\psi(q - \rho) = \psi((P/W)^{-1} MP_K/MP_L - \rho)$ is the functional form of investment demand for capital deepening

λ_1 = Coefficient of K^ζ in constant-elasticity-of-substitution production function

λ_2 = Coefficient of L^ζ in constant-elasticity-of-substitution production function

$\sigma = 1/(1 - \zeta)$ = Elasticity of substitution between capital and labor

Chapter 11

θ_Y = Speed of adjustment of output (income) when desired investment and desired saving are different

θ_ρ = Speed of adjustment of the interest rate when desired investment and desired saving are different

D_A = Demand for financial assets corresponding to the capital stock

S_A = Supply of financial assets corresponding to the capital stock

ρ_s = Short-term interest rate, assumed to be the rate on 3-month Treasury bills in empirical analysis

ρ_s^* = Normal short-term rate of interest

ρ_{coup} = Coupon yield = ratio of periodic payment to bond price

ρ_{mat} = Yield to maturity = rate of discount which makes the stream of bond payments (including redemption value) equal to the current bond price

ρ_{hold} = Holding yield = sum of coupon yield plus the percentage change in bond price

Chapter 12

M = Money in asset portfolios

M^* = Demand for money or bills in asset portfolios (in the mathematical appendix)

$\bar{M}$ = Supply of money, endowment to agent

$E(\dot{P}_B)/P_B$ = Expected value of the bond-price change (in continuous time) as a percentage of the price, abbreviated to $E(\dot{P})/P$ in the empirical appendix

$E(\Delta P_B)/P_B$ = Expected value of the bond-price change (in discrete time) as a percentage of the price

$E(P_{B,t})$ = Demand price at time t of bonds on the part of agents characterized by normal reversion and risk neutrality

$E(\rho_{\text{coup},t})$ = Coupon yield at time t assuming bond price is equal to the demand price

B_{CORP} = Quantity of corporate bonds demanded

$\bar{B}_{\text{CORP}}$ = Endowment of corporate bonds

P_{CORP} = Price of corporate bond

ρ_{CORP} = Yield on corporate bond

P = Bond price (in the empirical appendix)

$\rho_{\text{mat}}(m,t)$ = Yield to maturity of a bond with maturity m at time t

$\rho_{\text{hold}}(m,t)$ = Holding yield on a bond of maturity m at time t

$\rho_{\text{mat}}(\infty)$ = Limiting yield to maturity as bond maturity increases without limit

ρ_s^* = Normal short-term rate of interest

ρ_s = Short-term rate of interest

θ = Speed of adjustment of short-term rate of interest to normal short-term rate

θ_B = Rate of change of bond price

$\alpha(m)$ = Risk premium as a function of the time until the bond matures

$m^{-1}\int_0^m \alpha(\tau)d\tau$ = average risk premium for bonds with maturities ranging from 0 to m

ρ_s^{R*} = Real normal short-term interest rate

$\hat{\rho}_s^R(\tau)$ = Estimated real short-term interest rate at time τ

$\rho_{m\text{CORP}}$ = Yield to maturity on corporate bond

U_1 = Marginal utility of (expected) wealth

U_2 = Marginal utility of holding bills (money)

ρ_{mat}^R = Real yield to maturity

$\hat{X}$ = Estimated value of X

B^* = Demand for bonds

n = Number of agents, each having the same endowment of bills ($\bar{M}$)and the same endowment of bonds ($\bar{B}$)

$m(P_B, \rho_s)$ = Number of agents desiring to hold only bills, as a function of the price of bonds and the bill rate

Chapter 13

ε = Elasticity of transactions demand with respect to ρ_s

f = bank fee per conversion of bills to money (and vice versa), assumed to be independent of transaction size

m = number of conversions between bills and money by agents who hold bills to earn interest but need money to settle accounts

TC = total cost of holding money including foregone interest on bills

Chapter 14

C_A = Additional consumption demand from wealth

Y_{FE} = Aggregate demand required for full employment, which is assumed to be a fixed level of output, in effect assuming a vertical labor-supply schedule

G = Government expenditure on the purchase of goods and services

t = Tax rate, assumed to be a constant fraction of income

Chapter 15

CO = The fraction of new spending which displaces existing production

$m = 1 - CO$ = The fraction of new spending that results in new production

v = The first-round MPC, the fraction of income spent by the direct beneficiaries of government transfers or tax cuts

g = The rate of growth of output and income

μ = The propensity to consume out of permanent income

Y^P = Permanent income

ϕ = Rate of growth of permanent income

η = Speed of adjustment of permanent income to actual income

E = Transfer payments by states, chiefly Medicaid

R = Non-ARRA (American Recovery and Reinvestment Act) state revenues

A = Transfers from federal government to states under ARRA

$L = R + A - (G + E)$ = Saving (negative sign means dissaving) by states

$O = G + E$ = State outlays

N = Number of observations

z = Ratio of estimated regression coefficient to standard error of the estimate

Chapter 16

X^* = Optimal value of $X = C, I, G$

$\zeta = Y/Y_{FE}$ = Ratio of output to full-employment output

t_0 = Upper limit on tax rate

t_1 = Tax rate consistent with the specified level of consumption and full employment

ρ_h = Hurdle rate for investment, assumed fixed by central bank

D = Government debt in nominal terms

P = Price level

d = Ratio of the primary deficit to GDP (the primary deficit leaves out interest on the debt)

ρ = Rate of interest on government debt (conceptually distinct from the hurdle rate ρ_h; in practice an average of rates on debts of different maturities)

g = Rate of growth of nominal GDP

$\gamma = D/PY$ = Ratio of government debt to nominal GDP

Chapter 17

g = Rate of growth of real output

$v = \Delta K/\Delta Y$ = Incremental capital:output ratio

s = Propensity to save, assumed to be constant

$g_w = s/v$ = (for Harrod) The warranted rate of growth of *output*, the value of g for which $I_D = S_D$

$g_n = \Delta N/N$ = Rate of growth of population and labor force

$g_w = \Delta I_D/I_D$ = (for Domar) The change in desired investment as a percentage of desired investment

$s = \Delta S_D/\Delta Y$ = (for Domar) Ratio of change in desired saving to change in income

$v = \Delta K/\Delta Y$ = (for Domar, as for Harrod) The incremental capital:output ratio, but it is determined differently. For Domar it is the multiplier process that fixes the value of ΔY

$Y = F(K, L)$ = Output as a function of capital and labor inputs, assumed to exhibit constant returns to scale

$k = K/L$ = Ratio of capital to labor input

$f(k) \equiv F(K/L, 1)$ = Output per unit of labor as a function of the capital:labor ratio

$f(l) \equiv F(1, L/K) =$ Output per unit of capital as a function of the labor:capital ratio

$I_D = \psi(\rho_h) =$ Investment demand per unit of capital as a function of the hurdle rate of interest (in the long run, with l as the state variable rather than Y)

$S_D =$ Desired saving per unit of capital (in the long run, with l as the state variable rather than Y)

$L_S/N = \phi(P/W) =$ Ratio of labor supply to population as a function of the real price

$g_w^i =$ (for Robinson) Warranted rate of growth of capital stock, $i = 0, 1$

$r_w^i =$ (for Robinson) Rate of profit at the warranted rate of growth, r_w^i corresponding to $g = g_w^i$, $i = 0, 1$

Chapter 18

$I_D =$ Investment demand per unit of capital (no subscript in mathematical appendix)

$S_D =$ Desired saving per unit of capital (no subscript in mathematical appendix)

$E =$ energy

$Y = F(K, L, E) =$ Production function with three arguments, capital, labor, and energy

$P_E =$ Nominal price of energy

$\xi = P_E/P =$ Real price of energy

$l = L/K =$ Labor per unit of capital

$e = E/K =$ Energy per unit of capital

$Y/K = F(1, l, e) = f(l, e) =$ Output per unit of capital as a function of l and e

$h(l, \xi) = \max_e \left[f(l, e) - \xi e \right] = f\left(l, e(l, \xi)\right) - \xi e(l, \xi)$, where $e(l, \xi)$ is the amount of energy per unit of capital which, for given l and ξ, maximizes the expression $f(l, e) - \xi e$

$h_i = \partial h/\partial i$, $i = l, e, \xi$

$h_{ij} = \partial^2 y/\partial j \partial i$, $i, j = l, e, \xi$

$e_i = \partial e(l, \xi)/\partial i$, $i = l, \xi$

$r = \Pi/K = f(l, e) - (P/W)^{-1} l - \xi e = h(l, \xi) - (P/W)^{-1} l =$ Rate of profit

$MP_L = h_l =$ Marginal product of labor

$MP_K = h - h_l l =$ Marginal product of capital

$X_i = \partial X/\partial i$, $X = I, S$; $i = P/W, l, \eta$

$s_w =$ Propensity to save of workers

$K_\pi =$ Capital stock owned by capitalists

$\delta = K_\pi/K =$ The fraction of the capital stock owned by capitalists

$L =$ Employment

$\eta = L/LS =$ Employment as a fraction of the labor supply

$n =$ The sum of the population growth rate and a normal rate of immigration into the capitalist sector of the economy at full employment

RAISING KEYNES

PROLOGUE

What Is This Book About?

The orthodox equilibrium theory of economics has assumed, or has
at least not denied, that there are natural forces tending to bring the
volume of the community's output, and hence its real income, back to
the optimum level whenever temporary forces have led it to depart
from this level. But . . . the equilibrium level towards which output
tends to return after temporary disturbances is not necessarily the
optimum level, but depends on the strength of the forces in the
community which tend towards saving.

—JOHN MAYNARD KEYNES

The most shocking view in *The General Theory* was the allegation that
economic equilibrium need not produce full employment. Economists like Schumpeter found this to be simply incredible. Smith's
Invisible Hand was brought under direct attack. This was revolution,
not evolution.

—PAUL SAMUELSON

This book presents a macroeconomic theory that builds on the central vision
of Keynes's *General Theory of Employment, Interest and Money,* namely, that a
capitalist economy is not self-regulating; there is no endogenous mechanism,
no invisible hand, that guarantees full employment even in the most favorable
case of a competitive economy in which there are neither frictions nor imperfections. In Keynes's vision, aggregate demand is a determinant of how the
level of output and employment adjusts to a variety of shocks. In my render-
ing of Keynes, the adjustment mechanism not only determines the trajectory of the economy outside of equilibrium it also determines the equilibrium
itself.

And none of the putative guarantors of full employment operate in real
time as they do in a static comparison of equilibrium positions—not a reduction of the cost of production via a decrease in the money wage; not a reduction of the price level and a consequent decrease in the interest rate and an

increase in investment, via a decrease in the transactions demand for money; not an increase in the real purchasing power of money and an associated increase in consumption demand consequent upon a fall in the price level. In real time these mechanisms are more likely to contribute to unemployment than to cure it.

Why is it important to elaborate a theory based on the centrality of the adjustment process in the context of a competitive economy? Why not continue to rely on mainstream theories based on imperfections and frictions, especially since we know that frictions and imperfections are endemic?

The first reason is that the focus on imperfections and frictions leads naturally to a focus on policies that will remove these imperfections and frictions, policies that will make the economy more closely resemble the textbook model of perfect competition—and a rejection of policies that adjust aggregate demand to the full-employment potential of the economy. This is not hypothetical: the push toward deregulation at the end of the twentieth century, particularly financial deregulation, contributed to the financial crisis of 2008 and the ensuing Great Recession. And deregulation was promoted on the basis of the idea that regulation above and beyond the self-regulation of the market gets in the way of good economic performance. The hostility to aggregate-demand management stems in large part from a failure to understand the argument why aggregate demand matters.

The second reason for assuming an idealized economy is that a focus on imperfections and frictions limits the applicability of aggregate demand to the short run; New Keynesians, like Monetarists, New Classicals, and Real Business-Cycle theorists, regard the long run as a period in which time dissolves whatever warts might mar capitalism in the short run, particularly price and wage rigidities. By situating the argument in a perfectly competitive economy, it becomes possible to address the question of whether there is a long-run trade-off between price stability and growth built into the structure of a market economy. (The answer is yes, there is.)

Making the argument that unemployment can exist even under conditions of perfect competition requires us to rescue Keynes's insight about aggregate demand from his friends as well as from his foes, for the friends (the Keynesians of Axel Leijonhufvud's *Keynesian Economics and the Economics of Keynes*) bear much of the responsibility for the distortion of Keynes's message. Friendly criticism of *The General Theory*, following the lead of Franco Modigliani (1944), attributed unemployment to nominal-wage rigidity, arguing that wage flexibility would make the rate of interest and investment demand a mechanism for adjusting aggregate demand to the needs of full employment. Less friendly criticism from the likes of Gottfried Haberler (1939, 1941) and Arthur Pigou (1943) made the "real-balance" effect, the adjustment of the purchasing power of money and consumption demand, the mechanism for doing the heavy lifting for restoring full employment after a shock to demand. For Milton Friedman (1970) the real-balance effect was the killer argument against *The General Theory*.

Without some exegesis of both *The General Theory* and the dispute that followed about the nature of Keynes's message, it is impossible to understand the real lesson of the dispute, namely, the limitations of comparative statics for describing and assessing how a capitalist economy works. Keynes and his critics were talking past each other, in the sense that the critics relied on static models in which "change" involves a comparison of equilibrium positions that exist outside of time, while Keynes's idea of change is a movement in real time. The critics were right in the context of comparative statics; Keynes was right in the context of real-time changes, and right about the consequent need for dynamic models.

This is not an exercise in the history of thought. I have neither the training nor the inclination for such an exercise. Nor do I attempt to provide insight as to what Keynes "really" meant, an enterprise I regard as a search for the holy grail. I can hope that this is the book that Keynes would have written if he had had eighty years to think about his project, to bone up on mathematics unavailable to him in the 1930s, to digest the criticisms that were offered on all sides, and, not least, to observe the changes in the economy that have taken place since *The General Theory* was published. But I intend the book to stand on its own, whatever Keynes might have thought of it.

While sharing Keynes's vision of how capitalism works, this book recognizes and attempts to fill major gaps in his argument, gaps that ultimately led to the eclipse, indeed the demise, of *The General Theory*. This requires five important innovations:

1. This book provides a dynamic model that concretizes Keynes's intuition about how capitalism operates left to itself: even with flexible wages and prices, a capitalist economy normally does not move to a full-employment equilibrium.

2. I extend the Keynesian vision to the long period, in which neither the capital stock nor the labor force is fixed. If there is a long-run tendency to full employment, it is because in the long run the labor force is endogenous. The central role of aggregate demand is not limited to the short period, as most present-day Keynesians believe. In the long run, as in the short run, there is a trade-off between price stability and employment. Farewell to the vertical Phillips curve.

3. Rightly understood, Keynes's theory of liquidity preference provides a theory of spreads between various interest rates, while leaving the level

of interest rates indeterminate. Building on Keynes, I provide a coherent theory of interest in which it is only when an institution like a central bank anchors the spread that the interest rate becomes determinate.

4. I relate the theory of employment and interest to a theory of money. A theory of money is necessary for the theory of interest and employment, which makes its absence from *The General Theory* all the more surprising—even though Keynes's complete title is *The General Theory of Employment, Interest and Money.*

5. Generalizing Abba Lerner's theory of functional finance, this book provides a framework for fiscal policy that takes account not only of the choice facing governments with respect to the level of employment but also the choices about the composition of aggregate demand, how much private consumption and investment, how much infrastructure, education, health care, and the like, goods which the government typically has a preponderant role in providing. It is this second set of issues that raises the issue of the public debt, but the real issue is very different from the noise that has substituted for reasoned political debate.

Because so much of this book is devoted to the elaboration and criticism of models, I should perhaps say something up front about what models are good for—and their limits. For me (and, I suspect, for Keynes, but no matter) models are ways of organizing one's thinking, not machines for prediction. At a practical level, Keynes's conception of capitalism provided a way of thinking about the economy in which the greatness of the Great Depression was not the surprise that it was for the mainstream. An updated version of Keynes's vision will clarify the role of aggregate demand in bringing about and prolonging the global recession that came in the wake of the financial crisis of 2008—and for thinking about the policies appropriate for the next recession, not to mention policies for demand management for growth.

Indeed, Keynes provided not only diagnosis but medicine, a framework for organizing appropriate policy responses to economic shocks. Keynes was more successful in this than he was in providing a new way of thinking about how the economy works because the policy message survived the distortions of *The General Theory* perpetrated by friends as well as enemies. For a variety of reasons, the policy message could be, and was, acted upon more effectively in the United States than in Europe after the fall of Lehman Brothers in September 2008. To be sure, the United States fiscal response would have been more successful if Keynes's way of thinking about the economy had prevailed so that there was a general receptivity to activist fiscal policy. And the European monetary response would have been more effective if Keynes rather than Friedman had been the guiding light of the European Central Bank.

The problem is not that macroeconomists failed to predict the financial crisis. I don't believe that any model inspired by Keynes's vision, certainly not my models, would have done any better. The failure of macroeconomics is that it provided no plausible way of understanding the recession that followed—not for nothing called the Great Recession. Here the contrast with a macroeconomics building on Keynes is dramatic.

I do not deny the technical strides in mainstream macroeconomics since Keynes's day. But the gain in technical sophistication has been achieved at a steep price. The currently dominant approach to macroeconomic modeling, so-called dynamic, stochastic, general-equilibrium (DSGE), obscures key insights of *The General Theory*, in particular that aggregate demand matters even in the absence of frictions and rigidities. To make progress in macroeconomics requires us to take a step backward in order to undo the damage done by an "equilibrium discipline" (Lucas 1977) that identifies equilibrium with market clearing, a key feature of the DSGE approach in all its avatars.

The Plan of the Book

This book is not an easy read. It necessarily contains sustained and detailed theoretical argument, and parts of the argument are accessible only with some mathematics and econometrics. But these more technical parts are set apart from the main text in appendices and serve to supplement a self-contained narrative that is accessible to readers with a minimal background in economics and even less background in math.

Part I, "Background: The Rise and Fall," provides an overview of the history of the central message of *The General Theory*, that aggregate demand is a separate force influencing output and employment. It also sketches the views that Keynes opposes, and why these views had no place for aggregate demand in their picture of the economy.

Chapter 1 lays out the strategy and structure of Keynes's argument and provides an overview of the theoretical criticisms that emerged in the decade after publication. In addition to the professional critique of Keynes, there was a political reaction, a reading of Keynes as the useful idiot of a communist conspiracy that was supposed to be undermining capitalism from within at the same time as the masters of this conspiracy in the Kremlin were extending the borders of the Soviet empire in Europe and Asia. These criticisms had little to do with the theoretical opposition to Keynes, but political opposition shaped how Keynes's message was received by the public. Finally, events— first profit squeeze in the late 1960s, then the oil shocks of the 1970s—conspired with theoretical critique and political opposition to derail Keynes altogether. There was by this time a lot of accumulated bath water that deserved to be thrown out the window; alas, the baby was also thrown out.

Chapter 2 examines the mainstream economics that formed the context for *The General Theory*. The focus is on why the economics profession had no need for aggregate demand, thinking that wage and price flexibility were not only necessary but also sufficient to guarantee full employment, and how this view has changed—and how it has not changed—over time.

Part II, "Keynes Defeated: Static Models and the Critics," lays out two static models that are more or less explicit in *The General Theory;* chapter 3 elaborates a "first-pass" model based on a given interest rate and a "second-pass" model based on a given money supply. The first shows how the interest rate connects financial markets to the real economy of output and employment, and it provides a vehicle for arguing the scope and limits of monetary policy. The second-pass model is intended to show the limits of the invisible hand in guiding the economy to full employment; it replaces a given interest rate with a given money supply and allows the interest rate to be determined by economic forces. In terms of the logical progression of the argument for what ails capitalism and how to fix it, the second model should precede the first, but the first-pass model makes it easier to understand how the parts of Keynes's theory intertwine and provides a basis for understanding the policy implications of *The General Theory*.

Chapter 4 presents the arguments of the early critics who honed in on an assumption Keynes considered mere scaffolding, to be torn down after the edifice of *The General Theory* was built: the assumption of rigid money wages. Franco Modigliani argued in terms of the responsiveness of the interest rate and investment to the level of wages (through the impact of money wages on the price level), and Gottfried Haberler and Arthur Pigou argued in terms of the impact of prices on consumption via the real-balance effect. Analyzing different parts of Keynes's theoretical apparatus, Modigliani and Haberler (and Pigou) reached mutually reinforcing conclusions, namely, that even on Keynes's own terms, his pessimistic conclusion about the possibility of capitalism to sustain full employment relied critically on the assumption of wage rigidity. Keynes, no doubt kicking and screaming in his grave, was reduced to a sophisticated theorist of sand in the wheels, in this sense no different from the myriad economists who had argued that the problems of capitalism are rigidities, frictions, and imperfections, and can be cured by remaking the economy in the image of textbook accounts of perfect competition.

All this is prologue, but essential prologue, for it establishes the need for addressing real-time changes in a more appropriate framework than the comparative-statics analysis in which both the models of *The General Theory* and the models of the critics were cast. Part III, "Keynes Vindicated: A Theory of Real-Time Changes," sets out a "third-pass" model that starts from the adjustments economic actors make outside of equilibrium. This model determines equilibrium from these disequilibrium actions. The novelty of my approach is its reliance on the signals—plural—that producers receive outside of equilibrium and how these signals are processed. In contrast with the single signal, namely, price, that guides production at a market-clearing equilibrium, away from equilibrium producers receive two signals, a price signal that contains information about the profitability of production at the margin and a quantity signal that contains information about how fast goods are moving off (or piling up on) their shelves. And, unlike the situation of competitive producers at a market-clearing equilibrium, producers have two decisions to make, one on how much to change the price they charge, the other on how much to change the quantity they produce. How the signals are processed determines the trajectory of the economy out of equilibrium—not only the disequilibrium trajectory: the trajectory determines the equilibrium.

An important characteristic of the equilibrium is that while, absent technological progress, the real price, P/W (the inverse of the real wage), does not change over time, both the numerator and the denominator are in flux. In a depression setting, money wages and money prices are both falling. In the comparative-statics context of chapter 4, lower wages and prices are key both to Modigliani's argument that investment demand would increase sufficiently to get the economy to full employment (barring a liquidity trap or completely inelastic investment demand) and to Haberler's and Pigou's argument that consumption demand would rise to the occasion. In real time, these results no longer hold. Modigliani's full-employment (and market-clearing) equilibrium may not be stable. And fractional-reserve banking may make Modigliani's argument moot because falling prices may have no impact on investment demand. And there is an additional argument, namely, that a falling price level in real time may actually drive up the relevant interest rates (the Fisher effect, after Irving Fisher [1896]). The Haberler–Pigou road to wealth and prosperity fares just as badly: this road may be so littered with the corpses of defaulting debtors that it becomes impassable.

A fair verdict has to reverse the judgment of the comparative-statics analysis of chapter 4. Far from undermining Keynes's argument about the limits of the invisible hand, not to mention the limits of the visible hand of monetary policy, once we shift to the real-time framework of chapter 7, the considerations raised by Modigliani, as well as the considerations raised by Haberler and Pigou, actually support the arguments of *The General Theory*.

The final chapter of this part of the book, chapter 8, examines data from the Great Depression. The idea is to test the theory elaborated in the previous three chapters against the view championed by Friedman that a relatively mild downturn morphed into the Great Depression because of bad policy decisions by the Federal Reserve. It will probably not surprise anybody that I come down on the side of *The General Theory*.

The experience of agriculture highlights Fisher's (1933) debt-deflation theory of depression as a complement to *The General Theory*. In terms of output and employment, U.S. agriculture suffered no depression at all: 1932 was as good as 1929. The considerable pain suffered by farmers was due rather to a fall in the prices they received relative to the prices they paid and to the huge burden of real debt (the flip side of the real-balance effect) and the corresponding burden of interest payments (the Fisher effect) caused by the falling price level.

Part IV, "Building Blocks," examines the various elements of *The General Theory* in the light of critiques that have been developed over the years. Separate chapters are devoted to the theory of consumption and the theory of investment, and two chapters are devoted to the most novel and controversial element, the liquidity-preference theory of interest.

Chapter 9 examines the claim that rational actors will determine today's consumption and saving on the basis of their long-term resources. This underlying assumption of DSGE models builds on Modigliani's life-cycle hypothesis and Friedman's permanent-income hypothesis. One implication of these theories is that the marginal propensity to consume is low—zero in the limit—when income changes are viewed as transitory. This result is important for policy purposes since, were it true, it would eviscerate countercyclical fiscal policy intended to compensate for changes in private demand.

My view is that Modigliani and Friedman at best explain the behavior of a small fraction of the population, upper middle-class professionals who fulfill the psychological and cognitive prerequisites of Modigliani–Friedman optimization, not to mention that this group has the financial cushion that makes it feasible to optimize today's consumption in terms of the agent's long-term resources rather than in terms of her current income. For the rest of the population—both the 1 percent, the rich and superrich, and the vast majority of working folk—other paradigms are more relevant.

We are actually in better theoretical shape in talking about how the 80 to 90 percent or so of the population whose lives are so insecure that rational consumer choice is not rational: lagged adjustment to changes in income was posited by both Keynes and Paul Samuelson (1943) as the explanation of why the short-term marginal propensity to consume is likely to be smaller than the long-term propensity. As for the 1 percent, we know very little about the determinants of their consumption and saving decisions—except that they are even less likely to operate according to the dictates of Modigliani–

Friedman optimization than are people who have to work for a living. This chapter concludes with an analysis of the implications of taking class seriously as a determinant of consumption and saving, as in the so-called Cambridge saving theory, a revival of the classical view that the source of saving is the surplus that remains after wages and other costs are paid.

Chapter 10 deals with investment demand. As for consumption and saving, *The General Theory* offered a highly simplified model of investment, one that abstracts from all its determinants except the rate of interest. This chapter attempts to fill in some of the more important gaps, beginning with the relationship of the interest elasticity of investment demand to the durability of projects. This relationship provides an important clue to why monetary policy has been focused on residential construction, rather, than, say, on business investment to upgrade the laptops of their employees.

A second topic of this chapter is the evolution of Keynes's investment model, taken over without much modification from Irving Fisher (1930), to subsequent investment theories, specifically, to so-called Q-theory developed by James Tobin (William Brainard and Tobin 1968; Tobin 1969). In the Fisher–Keynes approach, the focus is on project evaluation, on whether or not future revenues of particular investments justify the requisite capital outlay. Q-theory shifts the focus to make versus buy, to a decision whether to direct capital outlays to the purchase of existing capital or to building anew. As long as the focus is on individual projects, this shift in focus can illuminate the dynamics of investment demand, at least in limited areas where make and buy are real options; residential housing once again comes to mind.

The scope for extending Q-theory beyond individual projects to the analysis of strategic decisions is much more limited. Tobin (and Keynes before him) sought to relate investment demand to stock market valuations, but this relies on make versus buy being an option with regard to creating new capital or buying an existing company. I have read that Microsoft did just this, having decided to compete with Google in the search-engine business. But this appears to be the exception to the rule: in carrying out strategic visions, new investment and the purchase of existing companies are not generally alternatives, so the level of the Dow Jones Industrial Average wouldn't seem to be very relevant to investment decisions.

The major innovation of this chapter is the analysis of the impact of the real price P/W on investment demand. The real price has opposite effects on investment demand depending on whether the proposed investment is "capital widening," that is, intended to expand capacity, or "capital deepening," intended to substitute capital for labor (or other inputs). A higher real price has a positive effect on capital-widening investment, but a negative effect when investment is capital deepening. This difference is important because it plays a role in answering the question of whether or not high (real) wages are good for employment and output, a question that the emphasis on aggregate demand brings to the fore even if Keynes himself paid it little attention. This question is a principal concern of the long-run model developed in chapter 18. Whether or not a high real price increases investment depends on where the economy is in the business cycle, since capital deepening will form a larger part of total investment demand when there is considerable slack than when the economy is bursting at the seams.

The final topic in chapter 10 is the psychological aspect of investment demand, why there is an irreducible element of what Keynes called "animal spirits" in investment decisions. And why this matters.

Chapters 11 and 12 critically assess Keynes's liquidity-preference theory of interest. Liquidity preference is an alternative to the mainstream idea that interest rates are determined by thrift and productivity, as reflected in desired saving and desired investment. The mainstream relies on a rapid adjustment of price (the interest rate) to bring desired investment and saving into line. Keynes argues that because the interest rate is kept busy adjusting asset demands and supplies, it will adjust with glacial slowness to differences in desired saving and investment; it is left to output to do the heavy lifting of adjusting desired saving and investment.

To regard the investment-saving nexus as the site of interest-rate determination is simply a category mistake. Alas, this mistake is not just a chapter in the history of thought. No less an economist than Larry Summers repeats the error:

> Just as the price of wheat adjusts to balance the supply of and demand for wheat, it is natural to suppose that interest rates—the price of money—adjust to balance the supply of savings and the demand for investment in an economy. (2016, p. 3)

Chapter 11 translates Keynes's somewhat confused statement of liquidity preference into a coherent model. In this model, following Keynes, the only assets are cash and bonds. The bond yield is assumed to provide a reference rate of interest (what I call the "hurdle rate") for private investment, which is in effect to assume the bonds are comparable in terms of default risk and duration to the class of investment projects under consideration. Chapter 11 shows that the argument of *The General Theory,* even if confused, is logically consistent on its own premises. In this argument the hurdle rate is determined as the equilibrium rate in the market for bonds.

The problem with this theory is not its logic but its premises. In particular, chapter 12 focuses on Keynes's assumption that the alternative to placing wealth in bonds is to hold wealth as cash. Once we no longer *assume* that the alternative to bonds is cash, the theory outlined in chapter 11 has to be modified: the hurdle rate, as the equilibrium in the bond market, will depend on the rate of interest on the asset (say, 3-month T-bills) that is the short-term riskless alternative to bonds.

How is the short-term rate determined? *Not* in the market for bonds and bills: there are not enough degrees of freedom. In principle the difficulty is the standard difficulty of general-equilibrium models: n goods (here $n = 2$) determine $n - 1$ relative prices. One price must be assumed, with the result that only the spread between the two interest rates (the T-bill rate and the hurdle rate) is determined by the market.

In a pure market economy, this leaves the hurdle rate indeterminate. In the world in which we live, central banks resolve the indeterminacy. By fixing the short-term rate, a central bank anchors the spread.

The empirical appendix to chapter 12 reconciles the argument of this chapter with the empirical literature that purports to find no confirmation of liquidity-preference theory in actual interest-rate data. My contention is that the vast amount of research on the so-called "expectations hypothesis" has failed to come to grips with Keynes. The data, I argue, actually confirm Keynes's view of the sources of liquidity preference and in this respect validate the theory.

The final chapter in this part of the book, chapter 13, reprises the importance of what is assumed about the nature of money. While Keynes understood that, whatever its history, money was no longer tied to a commodity— gold, silver, or cowrie shells—his theory of liquidity preference was based on implicit acquiescence to a commodity theory of money. Keynes intended liquidity preference to be an alternative to the mainstream theory of interest as the outcome of the interplay of desired investment and desired saving, and accordingly the theory has to provide the level of the hurdle rate along with the spread between the hurdle rate and the short-term rate. But without a central bank to anchor the short-term rate of interest, the only way that this can happen is if the liquid asset in wealth portfolios is literally cash. Because cash carries a zero rate of interest, the spread is necessarily equal to the hurdle rate. This story makes sense if we are in a world of commodity money, but not otherwise.

If we assume that money is not a commodity, but a creation of the banking system, then the absence of a monetary authority to anchor the spread leaves the level of the hurdle rate up in the air. Indeed, capitalism left to its own devices lacks a theory of the interest rate, which has as its counterpart the indeterminacy of equilibrium in the realm of employment and output. In other words: we can calculate the hurdle rate appropriate for any level of employment, but there is no reason to think the market will oblige by selecting the corresponding short-term rate. With no anchor to the spread, there is a continuum of asset-market equilibria and no way to ensure that asset markets will settle on the particular combination of long and short rates consistent with full employment and asset-market equilibrium.

The next section of this book, Part V, "Fiscal Policy in Theory and Practice," examines the main policy lesson of *The General Theory*. Chapter 14 lays out the basis for countercyclical fiscal policy as a means of maintaining aggregate demand at full-employment levels in the face of fluctuations in private demand. This chapter explores how tax and expenditure policies combine with the overall size of the government budget to provide stabilization of demand, in particular, how this is largely accomplished without legislative or executive action, operating independently of which party controls Congress or the White House. Rather "automatic stabilization" is built into the government budget through differences in the way outlays and taxes respond to fluctuations in output and income. This chapter also explores the limits to automatic stabilization, which in turn explains the need for discretionary fiscal policy in the case of severe downturns, whether the purpose of augmenting aggregate demand is acknowledged, as in the case of the Obama stimulus, or unacknowledged, as in the case of the Reagan tax cuts.

The following chapter explores the Obama stimulus in some detail, as a case study in discretionary fiscal policy. Chapter 15 provides a bridge between the theory of the multiplier and the multiplier in practice and a detailed analysis of the most controversial part of the Obama stimulus, the roughly $250 billion, some one-third of the total, that went to the states. Though several researchers have found that these grants increased state spending significantly, an influential study by John Cogan and John Taylor (2012) argued that the states pocketed the money, using it to shore up their balance sheets rather than for additional spending. This chapter supports the view that the stimulus did in fact stimulate state spending. Not only is the Cogan–Taylor analysis faulty on its own terms, but complementing econometrics by interviews with state officials provides strong evidence that grants to states were spent rather than hoarded.

The final chapter of this part, chapter 16, extends the analysis of fiscal and monetary policy to the question of the size of government. How big the government should be depends on how much society values the goods and services government provides—infrastructure, military power, education— relative to the goods provided privately—consumption and investment in factories, machinery, residential housing. This choice has implications for long-run deficits and the national debt, in contrast with countercyclical policies that can in principle balance out deficits in lean years by surpluses in fat years. In spirit this is Abba Lerner's "functional finance," in which causality runs from decisions about government expenditures and revenues to implications for deficits and debt. The contrast is with "sound finance," in which balanced budgets constrain the management of aggregate demand.

Part VI, "Keynes in the Long Run," extends the analysis from the short period, in which the capital stock is assumed to be fixed, to a longer period characterized by the recognition that investment not only contributes to aggregate demand but also shapes the capacity of the economy to supply goods and services. Chapter 17 sketches the early attempts to translate the vision of *The General Theory* to the long run, focusing on the separate contributions of Roy Harrod (1939, 1948) and Evsey Domar (1946, 1947), whom misunderstanding has joined at the hip in the so-called Harrod–Domar theory. The contribution of Robert Solow (1956) was to derail the attempt to construct a theory of the long run in which aggregate demand plays a role analogous to its role in the short run. Again, misunderstanding has played a big role: Solow is widely thought to have demonstrated the irrelevance of aggregate demand in the long run, but the fact is that he simply assumed away the whole issue—as he himself recognized. This chapter concludes with an analysis of the rearguard action of Joan Robinson (1962) to keep aggregate demand in the long-run picture.

Chapter 18 lays out a series of long-run models that build on Robinson. An important theoretical innovation is to modify the standard assumption that the labor force is exogenously given by population growth. Instead, the labor force available to the capitalist sector of the economy is assumed to be virtually unlimited, with domestic sources such as household labor and agricultural labor supplemented by immigration when kitchen and farm prove insufficient.

If the supply of labor is endogenous, a substitute has to be found for the marginal-productivity theory of wages. In the models of this chapter, unemployment remains a driver of money wages, as in the short run, but the focus of wage dynamics is on a conventional wage, determined, à la Karl Marx and his classical predecessors, by social norms and class power.

Coupled both with the distinction between saving responding to profit and saving responding to income and with the distinction between capital widening and capital deepening, these models provide a framework for answering the question of whether high real wages are good for capitalism. The answer is yes if the positive impact on consumption demand outweighs the negative impact on investment demand. The yes is likely to be more solid in slack times, when investment is more heavily weighted toward capital deepening. Indeed, when there is considerable slack in the economy and capital widening is unprofitable, high real wages are likely to be a positive for investment as well as for consumption, since a high real wage increases the profitability of capital deepening.

Chapter 19 tests the empirical implications of the model against a half century of U.S. data on inflation and employment. Just as the depression-oriented short-run model elaborated in Chapter 6 is characterized by equilibria at which money prices and wages fall at the same percentage rate, with the result that the real price is stationary over time, so the long-run model of chapter 18 is characterized by equilibria at which price and wage inflation take place at the same rate. Is higher inflation the price of greater output and employment? As long as the economic change is demand driven, the model implies a positive relationship between inflation and employment; that is, it implies the familiar Phillips-curve result. Supply-side shocks are more complicated—depending on the adjustment mechanism that is assumed—as are changes in the conventional wage. Not to keep the reader in suspense, I conclude that the data are consistent with the implications of the long-run models presented in chapter 18, particularly the contention that aggregate demand matters in the long run as well as in the short run. This chapter concludes with a discussion of why inflation at rates that characterized the United States over the half century between 1970 and 2020, or even the more elevated rates that characterized the period between 1970 and 1990, have been generally held to be an evil on a par with the black plague.

A short epilogue concludes the book.

— I —

Background

The Rise and Fall

— 1 —

INTRODUCTION

Is This Resurrection Necessary?

> I believe myself to be writing a book on economic theory which will
> largely revolutionize—not, I suppose, at once but in the course of the
> next ten years—the way the world thinks about economic problems.
> —JOHN MAYNARD KEYNES TO GEORGE BERNARD SHAW,
> JANUARY 1, 1935

Right after Lehman Brothers went belly-up in the fall of 2008, I overheard several younger members of my department earnestly arguing in the foyer of the Littauer Building, the home of the Harvard Economics Department.[1] The subject was the likely effect of the emerging financial crisis on the real economy, so-called—the economy of output, consumption, investment, and employment. Opinions were divided, but the consensus was clearly that the financial mess should have little or no impact. After all, the productive capacity of the economy was unaffected by the fall of Lehman Brothers; why should production, and hence income take a hit? And if production and income remained unaffected, why should employment and consumption or investment be affected? Shades of 1930 to 1933: I daresay that when the Littauer Building was still a gleam in the eye of Lucius Littauer, faculty and students were having the same debate and were reaching the same conclusions.

Well, not exactly. As 1930 turned into 1931 and 1931 into 1932, it became less and less possible to deny the reality of the Great Depression and harder and harder to avoid the connection between finance and physical reality. The stock market had crashed in the fall of 1929, and at first the downturn in the real economy—which had in fact preceded the stock market crash by a few months—seemed no worse than earlier detours on the road to ever greater prosperity. But by 1932 the financial structure and the real economy were both in shambles. In the early 1930s banks failed at double, then triple, the rates of the 1920s, with losses to depositors reaching more than six times the average of the 1920s (FDIC [n.d.]). The real economy of the early 1930s was a shadow of the Roaring Twenties. Employment decreased by more than 20 percent between 1929 and 1933, gross domestic product by more than 25 percent.[2] Economists and historians continue to sort out cause and effect in the relationship between money and finance on the one hand and production, income, and employment on the other and to assess the role of government policies in alleviating or contributing to the agony of the Great Depression. But there is an important difference in the discussion then and now: in the early 1930s no framework existed within economics for integrating money, finance, and the real economy, a gap filled by John Maynard Keynes's *General Theory of Employment, Interest, and Money* only in 1936.

"Keynes" and "Keynesian" evoke and provoke. There is the impact on economic theory: what was Keynes's contribution? Was, as some have maintained (see for instance David Laidler [1999]), *The General Theory* old wine in new bottles? Did Keynes really have anything new to say, or were latter-day critics right to relegate him to a formalizer of sand in the wheels? What about policy? What were the policy implications of *The General Theory,* and why did these ideas fall into desuetude? Are there good grounds for rejecting Keynes as a policy guru? In sum, why has Keynes gone from being the prophet of a new economics to oblivion—and back?

The short answer is that the critics won the day for good reasons and bad ones. They had the better of the argument once it was formalized in the only framework available to economists in the years following the publication of *The General Theory.* I demonstrate this in chapters 3 and 4.

But Keynes was aware of the need for a different framework, one that could cope with real-time adjustment, even though, like Moses, he was unable to enter the promised land. When what Joseph Schumpeter called the preanalytic vision behind the theory is formalized in the appropriate framework, which this book does in chapters 5 to 7, the critiques offered by friend and foe turn out to support Keynes rather than to undermine him.[3] The rest of this chapter sketches fuller answers to these questions by assessing Keynes's contribution in *The General Theory* and the reactions from both the economics profession and the larger society. The rest of the book fills in the sketch.

Why Was/Is *The General Theory* Important?

Prior to the publication of *The General Theory,* Keynes had been writing for more than five years about the need for more activism on the part of governments, particularly his own and the government of the United States. Indeed, Britain had never really enjoyed the pre-Depression boom, a fact that Keynes attributed to the misguided exchange-rate policy he had opposed since the mid-twenties. In the context of the General Election held in May 1929—well before the U.S. stock market crash and the ensuing collapse—Keynes had advocated public works to stimulate the British economy (Keynes and H. D. Henderson, "Can Lloyd George Do It?", abridged as "A Programme of Expansion" in Keynes 1931a, pp. 118–134).

A major goal of *The General Theory* was to provide a framework for such policy initiatives, a framework for integrating private initiative and collective action—government intervention—to make effective use of the available resources. *The General Theory* was, after all, conceived in the womb of the Great Depression and motivated by the need to make sense of the most glaring economic disaster in the history of capitalism.

If this had been Keynes's only goal he most likely would have located the argument in the specifics of the British economy of the 1920s and 1930s, taking for granted the overwhelming importance in manufacturing and transportation of large-scale monopolistic and oligopolistic industries with substantial control over prices and wages. This was of course in stark contrast to the assumptions of a competitive economy, in which firms were subservient to the market, prices and wages being set by the interaction of demand and supply and taken by each participant as beyond his control.

Had he situated his argument in the realities of the economy of his day, Keynes could have appealed to the theory of monopoly or the newfangled theories of monopolistic competition, to which his own protégée, Joan Robinson, along with Harvard's Edward Chamberlin, was a leading contributor. But for the purpose of converting the economics profession to a new point of view, the reality of the twentieth century was less important than the received doctrines of competitive economics. Shortly after the publication of *The General Theory,* Keynes wrote to the Swedish economist Bertil Ohlin, "The reference to imperfect competition is very perplexing. I cannot see how on earth it comes in. Mrs Robinson, I may mention, read my proofs without discovering any connection" (Keynes 1973b, p. 190).

Paradoxically, to have focused too closely on reality would have diverted attention from the central question of whether any new theory was necessary. If the problem lay in monopoly or other departures from the ideal of perfect competition, wasn't the solution simply to make the world resemble more closely the perfectly competitive model? This is the enduring mantra of mainstream economics, as central to Adam Smith's attack on mercantilism in the late eighteenth century as it has been to the neoliberal project of dismantling government "interference" and unleashing capitalism that emerged in the late twentieth century.

In the 1930s, almost to a man (precious few economists were women), economists believed that slumps were limited in duration and severity by a self-correcting market mechanism; that slumps were salutary in purging the economy of excesses that inevitably accompanied booms; and—most important—that anything the government might do in the way of positive action would most likely make matters worse. The minority of economists who believed in activist government as the counterweight to a flailing private sector had no coherent framework in which to express their analysis and conclusions. By situating the argument of *The General Theory* in a competitive economy, Keynes sought to convince his fellow economists that the problem of unemployment had deeper causes than frictions and imperfections and that attempts to address unemployment by making the economy more like the textbook were doomed to fail.

The basis of the idea that a market system has a built-in mechanism for avoiding lengthy, deep slumps is that the very existence of involuntary unemployment will induce an adjustment of wages, an adjustment that ends only when the demand for labor on the part of profit-maximizing firms is equated with the supply of labor provided by utility-maximizing households. Frictions apart, the only obstacle to full employment recognized by orthodoxy was the undermining of competition by the market power of some actors (trade unions have long been a favorite bogeyman of economic orthodoxy) or the intervention of the state (unemployment insurance and other income-support measures of the welfare state are other bogeymen). Imperfectly competitive labor markets may permanently prevent the wage rate from settling at a point where there is a job for every willing worker, but the cure is implicit in the diagnosis. More and better (read more competitive) markets were—in 1936 as in 2020—the cure for market failure. It was literally unthinkable for an orthodox economist that there could be a systemic failure of a *competitive* market system, one which could lead to prolonged, profound, and painful unemployment. Any economist who thought so branded himself a Marxist or some other stripe of heretic.

By contrast, frictions and imperfections, just as they are in 2020, were the stuff of normal economics. So much so that by 1936, when *The General Theory* was published, there was little need and equally little appetite for a new theory of unemployment based on frictions or other market imperfections. Only three years earlier, the "prof," Arthur Pigou, had laid out the argument in a well-received book called *The Theory of Unemployment*.[4] Nor, as I have mentioned, was there any lack of policy recommendations for government intervention to fight frictional unemployment, including public works.

The conflict over whether the problems of capitalism were superficial or systemic was not a new one; neither was it limited to academic economists. Before World War I, three economic visions contended with each other in the United States. The orthodox Republican view, which came into its own in the 1920s, was that the government should stay out of the way of an economy that had delivered, and would continue to deliver, the goods—literally. Two competing visions took a less rosy view of unbridled capitalism. On the one hand was the vision proclaimed by Theodore Roosevelt as the New Nationalism during the electoral campaign of 1912: big business dominated the economic landscape because of its efficiency, and the role of government was to provide a countervailing power. On the other hand, against the New Nationalism, was Woodrow Wilson's New Freedom: big business dominated because of its predatory power, and the role of government was to level the playing field so that small business had a fair chance.

The Depression gave new point to these competing visions of the nature of the economy and the appropriate role for the government. With a third of the industrial labor force unemployed and a corresponding amount of capital underutilized, the issue was no longer whether an economy dominated by big business deployed labor and capital efficiently; it was now a question of whether any sort of market economy could and would mobilize resources effectively. If the Republican vision was momentarily sidelined, echoes of the debate between followers of the first Roosevelt and followers of Wilson could be heard in the debates about policies that Franklin Roosevelt should follow to combat the Depression.

Keynes recognized that any argument for government intervention to steer the economic ship had to be grounded in a convincing argument as to why the ship could not steer itself. *The General Theory* thus had to do more than show how unemployment might persist in the workings of the actual economy, 1930s capitalism warts-and-all. As long as no one could be sure whether the problem was capitalism or the warts, it was impossible to counter the reigning orthodoxy, which held that it would be enough for the government to remove the warts.

For Keynes nothing less than an all-out attack on the received doctrine, one that went well beyond the superficialities of frictions and market structure, would do. Given the hegemony of the belief in the fundamental resilience and beneficence of markets, it had to be shown that even competitive markets were defective when it came to providing jobs.

In a BBC broadcast in 1934, when he was a year away from finishing *The General Theory*, Keynes pinpointed the fundamental difference between an approach to the Depression based on frictions and imperfections and an approach based on more fundamental defects in the market system:

> On the one side were those who believe that the existing economic system is, in the long run, a self-adjusting system, though with creaks and groans and jerks, and interrupted by time-lags, outside interference and mistakes . . .

> The strength of the self-adjusting school depends on its having behind it almost the whole body of organized economic thinking and doctrine of the last hundred years . . .
>
> If the heretics on the other side of the gulf [among whom Keynes included himself] are to demolish the forces of nineteenth century orthodoxy . . . they must attack them in their citadel. (Keynes 1934, p. 850)

The heretical view did not for a moment deny the existence of imperfections, but in this view the role of monopoly and its attendant frictions was, to say the least, exaggerated. The problem of capitalism lay much deeper.

In short, to accomplish the constructive goal of providing a framework for economic policy, Keynes had first to achieve the critical goal of showing that a capitalism resembling the idealized version of the textbooks could still fall short of providing jobs for willing workers, could carry on indefinitely with idle men and idle plant. For this reason Keynes eschewed appeal to theories of monopoly, oligopoly, or monopolistic competition. His very title, emphasizing the greater generality of his theory compared to the reigning orthodoxy, precluded the appeal to the kinds of imperfection that the orthodox readily recognized and just as readily deplored.

Keynes saw himself, then, as faced with a twofold task, persuading his fellow economists to abandon old ways of thinking about how markets work and laying out the framework for a new way of approaching the policy problem of maintaining full employment. Keynes had no doubt which part was more challenging. As he puts it in the preface to *The General Theory,*

> The composition of this book has been for the author a long struggle of escape, and so must the reading of it be for most readers if the author's assault upon them is to be successful,—a struggle of escape from habitual modes of thought and expression. The ideas which are here expressed so laboriously are extremely simple and should be obvious. The difficulty lies, not in the new ideas, but in escaping from the old ones, which ramify, for those brought up as most of us have been, into every corner of our minds. (p. viii)

To compound the difficulties which *The General Theory* presented, Keynes had in mind a revolution not only in economic policy and in economic theory, but also in economic method. This third revolution involved nothing less than changing the analytic framework from a static conception of equilibrium based on equality of demand and supply to a dynamic framework based on how the economy adjusts when not in equilibrium. This was not so much a rejection of equilibrium but a reconceptualization of its meaning and role.

At the very outset of *The General Theory,* in the preface, Keynes writes,

> My so-called "fundamental equations" [in Keynes's earlier book, *A Treatise on Money*] were an instantaneous picture taken on the assumption of a given

output. They attempted to show how, assuming the given output, forces could develop which involved a profit-disequilibrium, and thus required a change in the level of output. But the dynamic development, as distinct from the instantaneous picture, was left incomplete and extremely confused. This book, on the other hand has evolved into what is primarily a study of the forces which determine changes in the scale of output and employment as a whole. (p. vii)

However, the methodological content of that revolution was never well understood by the economics profession. Perhaps not by Keynes himself; he had the intuition but lacked the tools to carry through this part of his program.

The economics profession, as it has evolved over the eighty-plus years since the publication of *The General Theory*, has long since come to possess the tools, but has never developed the intuition. This book attempts to fill that gap, to marry formal models to Keynes's intuition, to deploy the tools necessary to understand what Keynes was about.

In a word, *The General Theory* is methodologically based on differences between three concepts: the price mechanism, equilibrium, and market clearing.

The price mechanism is the process that is supposed to bring about equilibrium, to adjust intentions of agents so that at the end of the day (or week or year or whatever time period might be posited) these intentions are in balance with one another.

Equilibrium describes the balance. It characterizes a situation where forces tending to move the economy in one direction are just counterbalanced by opposing forces.

Market clearing describes a situation where demands and supplies just equal. *It is neither a necessary nor a sufficient condition for equilibrium.*

Mainstream economics, viewed in the lens of Keynes, makes two mistakes. First it uncritically identifies market clearing with equilibrium, when market clearing is only one of many possible ways in which opposing forces might be in balance. Second, the profession emphasizes equilibrium and treats the price mechanism, the adjustment process, as simply an adjunct to equilibrium. Elementary texts dismiss the price mechanism with a paragraph of hand-waving, with a just-so story of how excess demand or excess supply is eliminated. Graduate texts are no better. A leading text devotes fewer than ten pages (out of one thousand) to the price mechanism, justifying this imbalance with a frank admission:

We have, so far, carried out an extensive analysis of equilibrium equations. A characteristic feature that distinguishes economics from other scientific fields is that, for us, the equations of equilibrium constitute the center of our discipline. Other sciences, such as physics or even ecology, put comparatively more emphasis on the determination of dynamic laws of change. In contrast, up to now, we have hardly mentioned dynamics. The reason, informally speaking, is that economists are good (or so we hope) at recognizing a state of equilibrium but are poor at predicting precisely how an economy in disequilibrium will evolve. (Mas-Colell, Whinston, and Green 1995, p. 620)

The stakes are high: as we shall see, Keynes's contention that a capitalist economy left to its own devices will not gravitate to full employment cannot be demonstrated on the basis of static equilibrium. Quite the contrary. As I indicated at the outset of this chapter, on that playing field the critics won.

Nor can anything more than a partial case be made for the limits of monetary policy as a tool of economic management—though this case is particularly relevant for severe downturns like the Depression or the long slump that followed the financial crash of 2008. To deliver the knockout blow to the complacent theory of a self-adjusting economy or an economy steered by monetary policy alone, it is necessary, as Keynes intuited, that we focus on the process of adjustment, and this is necessary whether the goal be to understand the limits of laissez-faire or the limits of central banks.

Chapters 3 and 4 tell the story of what happens when the adjustment process is ignored. Keynes introduces a fixed money wage as a simplifying assumption to facilitate his narrative. Franco Modigliani, a Nobel Laureate known all his life as a Keynesian, took this feature of Keynes's exposition and made it central to the analysis. In Modigliani's words,

> It is usually considered as one of the most important achievements of the Keynesian theory that it explains the consistency of economic equilibrium with the presence of involuntary unemployment. It is, however, not sufficiently recognized that, except in a limiting case to be considered later, this result is due entirely to the assumption of "rigid wages." (Modigliani 1944, p. 65)

Thus Keynes becomes a theorist of sand in the wheels: get rid of the friction of rigid money wages and all will be well in the economy.

Modigliani demonstrates the existence of a full-employment equilibrium in a model based on Keynes's theoretical apparatus—without the assumption of a fixed money wage. In effect, his analysis says that if we start from a particular level of the money wage and the outcome involves involuntary unemployment, reduce the money wage and recalibrate the equilibrium. Run the movie again, or more accurately, take another snapshot. His contention is that if we do this repeatedly, we will find a money wage for which the equilibrium is consistent with full employment.

The important distinction is that Modigliani's approach does not literally imply changing the wage: it is not about change in the sense of the wage first being at one level, say $20 per hour, and then being reduced to $15 per hour. Modigliani's logic of "change" rather invites us to imagine a series of planets that are identical in all but one respect: the level of the money wage. The literal contention is that if we go down the list of these planets, comparing their static equilibria, we will find one in which the wage meets Goldilocks, neither too high nor too low, but just right for full employment. No change, in the sense of movement in real time, is involved. On the Goldilocks planet, the money wage is now, always has been, and always will be at the level necessary for a full-employment equilibrium.

Contrast Keynes's own approach. When he finally drops the assumption of a fixed money wage (chapter 19 of *The General Theory*), the discussion is all about what happens when the wage starts out at one level and then falls, perhaps but not necessarily under the pressure of the unemployed competing for jobs. It is all about *change* in the sense of adjustment. To be sure, the discussion is not very satisfying, especially to the twenty-first-century reader. Lacking the tools for a formal mathematical argument, Keynes falls back on a catalog of the advantages and disadvantages for employment of reducing money wages.

The difference is between comparative statics (the study of equilibria on different planets) and dynamics (the study of adjustment when the economy starts from a disequilibrium position). It is not clear why the mainstream has paid so little attention to dynamics. As Mas-Colell, Whinston, and Green argue, dynamics is much harder, but economists do not always shy away from difficult problems.

Difficulties aside, one reason for avoiding these issues is that such theorizing as has been done tends to undercut rather than reinforce the basic arguments of mainstream theory. All theory is by its very nature unrealistic, if for no other reason than that it must be a map which simplifies the territory. But the theoretical assumptions we need to make about dynamics in order for static equilibrium to be a plausible way of characterizing an economy render the theoretical assumptions required for the existence of equilibrium the very essence of realism. It is no wonder that the few studies that have addressed the problem have sunk like stones in the sea of economic theory (for example, F. Fisher 1983).

A second reason is the nature of the difficulties that economists would encounter were they to take dynamics seriously. The very multiplicity of plausible adjustment mechanisms would make it necessary for economists to dirty their hands in the messy complexities of how agents actually behave in real life, an investigation of distinctly lower status that blurs the line between economics, a discipline aspiring to the status of science, and anthropology, forever tainted in the eyes of most economists by its reliance on interpretation. Indeed, you can count on one hand the serious studies during my lifetime of how agents actually set wages and prices (for example, Bewley 1999; Blinder et al. 1998.)

A third reason for the neglect of dynamics, and I must be more tentative here, is the comfort that economists may have drawn from Paul Samuelson's "correspondence principle." As developed by Samuelson in the 1940s, the correspondence principle establishes a relationship between static properties of equilibrium and the dynamics of adjustment when equilibrium is disturbed (Samuelson 1947). Specifically, the correspondence principle relates these static properties to the question of whether the equilibrium is stable or unstable, stability characterizing the situation where disequilibrium adjustment will lead back to the original equilibrium and instability the situation in which the trajectory leads ever further away. The analysis provides legitimacy, at least under certain circumstances, for analyzing change without ever addressing the adjustment process, instead simply comparing static equilibria as if they were a set of observations from different planets.

The relationship between static equilibrium and dynamic adjustment has not gone completely unnoticed in the attempt to figure out Keynes's message. Samuelson's own attempt (1947, pp. 276–283) represents one such effort, not one, I should add, that appears to have advanced our understanding. More promising was Don Patinkin's magisterial *Money, Interest, and Prices: An Integration of Monetary and Value Theory,* the leading text for graduate students in the heyday of Keynesian macroeconomics. Indeed, Patinkin makes disequilibrium the key to Keynes's argument that laissez-faire, even bolstered by monetary policy, cannot be relied on to propel the economy to full employment.

But Patinkin frames the argument against laissez-faire in terms of the political unacceptability of the wage (and price) adjustments that might be necessary to achieve full employment, not the difference between the existence of a full employment equilibrium and the nonexistence of a path from the here of unemployment to the there of full employment. (See Patinkin 1965 [1956], secs. XIII:3 and XIV:1.) When it comes to the efficacy of monetary policy, Patinkin does distinguish between there and getting there, but the argument is that getting there might mean a slow and bumpy ride. Only by stepping outside his models does Patinkin find reasons—perverse behavior of expectations and redistribution of income accompanying changes in the price level—for arguing that the problem is worse than a slow and bumpy ride: as the Maine farmer, after reflecting on the matter for some time, told the tourist asking directions to another town, "You can't get there from here." Says Patinkin, in summary:

Keynesian economics is the economics of unemployment *dis*equilibrium. It argues that as a result of interest-inelasticity, on the one hand, and distribution and expectation effects, on the other, the dynamic process of [a capitalist economy left to its own devices]—even when aided by monetary policy—is unlikely to converge either smoothly or rapidly to the full-employment equilibrium position. Indeed, if these influences are sufficiently strong, they may even render this process unstable. In such a case the return to full employment would have to await the fortunate advent of some exogenous force that would expand aggregate demand sufficiently. (1965 [1956], pp. 337–338)

Samuelson had begun to deploy the tools for analyzing disequilibrium. But by the time the tools were adequately developed, the profession had moved on. As Milton Friedman, another Nobel Laureate, who became the personification of the anti-Keynes, put it in 1970 (p. 207),

Keynes's basic challenge to the reigning theory can be summarized . . . As a purely *theoretical* matter, there need not exist, even if all prices are flexible, at *long-run equilibrium* position characterized by "full employment" of resources . . .

[This] proposition can be treated summarily because it has been demonstrated to be false. Keynes's error consisted in neglecting the role of wealth in the consumption function or, stated differently, in neglecting the existence of a desired stock of wealth as a goal motivating savings. All sorts of frictions and rigidities may interfere with the attainment of a hypothetical long-run equilibrium position at full employment; dynamic changes in technology, resources, and social and economic institutions may continually change the characteristics of that equilibrium position; but there is no fundamental "flaw in the price system" that makes unemployment the natural outcome of a fully operative market mechanism.

Friedman notwithstanding, Keynes was right: there *is* a flaw in the price system. A major purpose of this book is to lay it bare.[5]

The General Theory of Employment, Interest and Money is a theory of how monetary and real factors jointly determine real output and employment along with the level of prices and wages. "A monetary economy," according to Keynes, "is essentially one in which changing views about the future are capable of influencing the quantity of employment" (*The General Theory*, p. vii). This does not on its face sound like a revolutionary manifesto, but it is. Economists would not have been surprised to learn that changing views about the future might influence the *composition* of output and employment. If people were more optimistic about the future, more inclined to put resources into improving or expanding the capital stock, investment and saving would be

expected to increase at the expense of consumption. But the idea that changing views about the future might affect the level of output and employment
today was in fact quite novel. There might be frictions in the adjustment process, but the composition of output could adjust without compromising, at
least not compromising for long, the ability of a free-market system to accommodate the supply of labor. The idea that views of the future might have an
impact on the current level of employment and output flew in the face of the
most basic and revered lessons of economics.

That this could happen because of money compounded the heresy. From
David Hume on, money was considered to be a veil that obscured the workings of the real economy. The classical dichotomy put on one side "real" quantities like the number of hours required to produce a ton of steel, or the quantity of goods a worker received for an hour's work, or the physical output of
the economy; the real side was separate from the side of "nominal" quantities,
like the quantity of money in circulation, the price of a ton of steel, or the
money-wage rate.[6] According to the classical dichotomy, real magnitudes
were determined by other real magnitudes, nominal magnitudes by other
nominal magnitudes. (My colleagues debating the impact of the fall of the
House of Lehman on September 15, 2008, were in fact debating the classical
dichotomy.) The so-called quantity theory of money, according to which the
quantity of money determines the price level, but not the level of production,
is a corollary of the classical dichotomy.[7]

All this *The General Theory* rejected. Changing views about the future
would change people's willingness to hold money, which in turn would affect
interest rates. That interest rates would change in response to views about the
future was all well and good: from Adam Smith on, precisely the role of the
interest rate was to equalize the desire to save with the desire to invest. But in
the received doctrine, the interest rate operated solely on the real side of the
economy. For Keynes the interest rate was two headed, one head on the
nominal side of the classical divide, influenced by the stock of money and liquidity preference, the other on the real side, influencing investment demand,
and thereby aggregate demand. The rate of interest affected not only the composition of output but also its level. *Through aggregate demand, the monetary
side of the classical divide affects output and employment.* This is the principal
take-away of *The General Theory*. Not for nothing was the full title *The General Theory of Employment, Interest and Money.*

So the seemingly innocuous idea that the essence of a monetary economy
is that changing views about the future could affect the level of output and
employment turns out to have far-reaching implications. On the side of theory, the time-honored view that—frictions apart—laissez-faire would lead to
full employment goes by the board. On the policy side, the government must
assume the role of steering the economy to full employment, and a purely

monetary policy geared to controlling the level of the short-term rate of interest might fall short. On the methodological side, a new approach was called for, one that eschewed the static equilibrium analysis based on equality of demand and supply in favor of a dynamic focus on the process of adjustment.

The General Theory: Strategy and Structure

How to present the new ideas in a way that was not only intelligible but would clear the mind of old ways of thinking? The positive goal of providing a new account of how the economy actually operates and the negative goal of demolishing the old argument that a wart-free capitalism would provide full employment were complementary—but hardly identical. Indeed the two goals could and did get in the way of each other.

The strategy of exposition Keynes adopts is first to lay out the critical monetary and real determinants of employment and output, then to show how the monetary and real elements of the economy are linked, finally to remove an important part of the scaffolding needed to erect his theoretical edifice. We shall examine this scaffolding in detail beginning in chapter 3. For now a broad-brush summary will suffice. A first pass at modeling the economy is based on

- a fixed money wage;
- a given rate of interest;
- the relationship between the rate of interest and the amount of expenditure people are willing to make on renewing and expanding the stock of real capital (plant, equipment, infrastructure, housing);
- the relationship between people's incomes and how much they are willing to spend on consumption goods;
- and finally, the relationship between the rate of interest and how people allocate their wealth among various assets, including money, as well as the relationship between the level of output and the money required to finance the transactions associated with this level of economic activity—though little attention is paid to the relationship between output and money, the transactions demand for money, presumably because it was well understood and accepted.

In order to determine the price level, which according to the preface to *The General Theory,* is what makes the theory *general,*[8] Keynes appends

- a conventional supply curve based on profit maximization, a relationship between the level of prices (given the money wage) to the level of output.

Two important assumptions distinguish this first-pass model from the revisions that are introduced later in the argument. First of all is the fixed money wage, taken as an essential element of the theory by later commentators, beginning, as we have seen, with Franco Modigliani—despite Keynes's insistence that a fixed money wage is a "simplification, with which we shall dispense later, . . . introduced solely to facilitate the exposition" (*The General Theory*, p. 27). Second is the assumption of a given rate of interest. By specifying the rate of interest along with the money wage, Keynes can argue that the level of output and employment is determined solely on the demand side, supply entering only to determine the price level and, given the level of money wages, the real wage as well (*The General Theory*, pp. 27–32). The link with the monetary side of the economy at this point is therefore quite one-sided: the given rate of interest determines the amount of money agents will hold as an asset, and the level of output determines the amount of money required for transactions.

Several points are worth making here. First, Keynes, as I have noted, does not bake the cake; he only provides the list of ingredients. Nowhere in *The General Theory* does Keynes present his argument in the form of a system of equations that economists of the twenty-first century, or indeed, economists of the younger generation in 1936, would recognize as a model. Second, reviewers paid no attention to this model, presumably because of its self-evidently provisional nature. Chapter 3 of the present book fills in this first-pass model, not out of antiquarian concern with the details of *The General Theory*, but because the first-pass model is the best starting point for understanding the new policy framework that Keynes intended. Moreover, the first-pass model provides a basis for the methodological revolution that Keynes also intended, replacing static equilibrium by a dynamic adjustment process.

After laying out the first-pass model, Keynes turns his attention to exploring the psychological underpinnings of the key elements of the theory, the propensity to consume, the demand for physical investment, and the liquidity-preference relationship between the demand for money as an asset and the rate of interest that obtains in the money market. Having done so, he is in a position to put these three relationships, along with the transactions-demand for money, together in the form of a second-pass model, one that starts not from a given rate of interest but from a given money supply.

In Keynes's second-pass model, also laid out in chapter 3, the relationship between the rate of interest and the amount of money that people are willing to hold in cash or cash equivalents (like checking accounts and other liquid assets)—the theory of liquidity preference—replaces the assumption of a fixed interest rate. Since the overall supply of money is now fixed, the rate of interest becomes one of the unknowns in the system of equations that encapsulate the underlying behavioral relationships.

Once again, Keynes tells us what goes into the model, but he does not formalize the model (*The General Theory*, chap. 18), a pity, because he might have discovered that the demand and supply sides of the second-pass model are now interconnected. He simply repeats the assertion that employment and output are determined on the demand-side alone, while dropping an assumption—a given interest rate—crucial to that result. It is not true that "if we take as given the factors specified above [propensity to consume, investment-demand, and liquidity preference, along with a given money wage and a given money supply], these variables determine the national income (or dividend) and the quantity of employment" (*The General Theory*, p. 247)—unless the price level also is taken as given. But we can't fix the price level and hold onto the idea that the price level is determined by the goods-supply schedule, an assumption that Keynes makes early on, in the context of his first-pass model, and never abandons.

What we get from the relationships and parameters that characterize the second-pass model is a downward sloping aggregate-demand schedule, demand as a function of the price level, rather than the vertical schedule that falls out of the first-pass model—a big difference: once the AD schedule is downward sloping rather than vertical, it is no longer true that the only role for supply-side conditions is to determine the price level and the real wage. Demand *and* supply—Alfred Marshall's famous scissors—determine both quantity and price.

Once again there is a bit of paradox in the sequel to *The General Theory*. The second-pass model was formalized by John Hicks (1937) soon after the publication of *The General Theory*, but in the next two decades the goods-supply equation was dropped from Hicks's model, and the standard representation of Keynes's theory assumed fixed money wages and prices. By the 1960s this modified version of Hicks, the so-called IS-LM model, became canonical textbook Keynes. Missing was any recognition that with given prices and wages the model determined one point on the entire AD schedule rather than an equilibrium level of output and employment.

Indeed, the very language of Keynesian models from the 1950s through the 1970s is misleading: whereas the LM schedule is (correctly) presented as representing equilibrium in financial markets given the price level—clearing the money market in the jargon—the IS schedule is wrongly presented as clearing the goods market. It does nothing of the sort. An equation characterizing equilibrium of desired saving and desired investment, the condition of simply being on the AD schedule, was read as if it were characterizing balance between aggregate demand and goods supply: it may be that the word "supply" led to confusion between the supply of saving and the supply of goods (not to mention the supply of labor). In the textbook IS-LM analysis, what Keynes claimed made *The General Theory* a general theory—that it determines output, employment, *and prices*—had gone missing.

The coexistence of first- and second-pass models is one of the sources of the confusion about the message of *The General Theory.* There are two models because of the dual purpose of the book, to provide both a theory of how the financial and real sectors of the economy actually intertwine and a theory of why even an idealized capitalism would fail to provide for the full use of capital and labor. The first-pass model, precisely because it does not assume a fixed money supply, is a better starting point for understanding how the economy actually works, while the second-pass model is not quite up to the job of laying bare the failure of an idealized capitalism to settle at a full-employment equilibrium.

The Taming of *the General Theory:* How the Economics Profession Dealt with the New Ideas (or, with Friends like Modigliani . . .)

The General Theory was initially met by incomprehension, in large part due to the difficulty and opacity of the argument, not to mention the gaps to which I have alluded. Indeed, *The General Theory* divided the economics profession. Older, established economists had difficulty with the new framework and concepts introduced to make the case for a central role of aggregate demand, and even more difficulty with the policy implications: the necessity for governments to maintain aggregate demand in the face of a scarcity of private demand. (There were notable exceptions. Alvin Hansen, once a pillar of pre-Keynesian orthodoxy, became a leading exponent of Keynesian theory and even more so of its implications for activist economic policy.)

The young were equally baffled by the argument, even if more open to its policy implications. Samuelson describes this generational disconnect in these terms:

> The *General Theory* caught most economists under the age of 35 with the unexpected virulence of a disease first attacking and decimating an isolated tribe of South Sea islanders. Economists beyond 50 turned out to be quite immune to the ailment. (1946, p. 187)

For Samuelson, money-wage rigidity coupled with involuntary unemployment was the hardest pill to swallow. Samuelson later recalled,

> What I resisted in Keynes the most was the notion that there could be equilibrium unemployment. I'd argue with Bob Bryce [a fellow graduate student

at Harvard who had attended Keynes's lectures in Cambridge, England], and discuss with Leontief [professor at Harvard and later winner of the Nobel Prize for his work on input-output analysis], that first chapter where workers react differently to an increase in money wages from the way they react to a change in real wages that comes from inflation.

Samuelson was never persuaded. He simply put the matter to one side:

> The way I finally convinced myself was to just stop worrying about it. I asked myself: why do I want to refuse a paradigm that enables me to understand the Roosevelt upturn from 1933 to 1937? It's . . . completely untrue that the New Deal didn't work until World War II came and bailed it out. Some of the highest rates of real increase in and highest levels of plant and equipment capital formation are in the period 1934 to 1937. I was content to assume that there was enough rigidity in relative prices and wages to make the Keynesian alternative to Walras operative. (Colander and Landreth 1996, pp. 159–160)

Samuelson's generation was not unduly troubled by the inconsistency between the standard competitive model and the models implicit in *The General Theory*. They were all too ready to accept that, as in Modigliani's telling, money-wage rigidity was not merely an expositional device, but a critical assumption. In Samuelson's words:

> We [young Keynesians] always assumed the Keynesian unemployment equilibrium floated on a substructure of administered prices and imperfect competition. I stopped thinking about what was meant by rigid wages and whether you could get the real wage down; I knew it was a good working principle, a good hypothesis to explain that the real wage does not move down indefinitely so long as there is still some unemployment. Thus I assumed a disequilibrium system, in which people could not get on the supply-of-labor curve. (Colander and Landreth 1996, pp. 160–161)

For Modigliani, Keynes's conclusions about the limits of the market system depend critically on a rigid money wage that prevents the labor market from clearing. Once the level of output is determined, the assumption of profit maximization fixes the ratio of prices to wages, but this says nothing about the absolute levels of prices and wages. Without money-wage rigidity there is nothing to anchor the price level! This matters because the price level affects real aggregate demand: the lower the price level, the less money is needed for transactions at any given level of output, so—assuming the money supply is fixed—more money spills over into asset markets. Absorbing the extra cash requires a lower interest rate, for the amount of cash agents wish to hold varies inversely with the interest rate; in its simplest form liquidity preference is a trade-off between the higher returns available from relatively illiquid financial assets and the greater security of holding wealth in the form of cash or near-equivalents. But if the interest rate varies directly with the price level, investment demand varies in the opposite direction, since the lower the rate of interest the more attractive are investment opportunities. Finally, higher investment demand means higher aggregate demand.

In short, once we drop the assumption of a given money wage, the level of aggregate demand depends indirectly on the money wage via the effect of the money wage on the price level. The lower the money wage, the greater the level of aggregate demand and, in consequence, the greater the level of employment and output. What then determines the money wage? Modigliani's answer is to assume full employment: or, more precisely, to fix the wage so that the interest rate and investment demand are just what are required to provide a job for every willing worker!

It may be surprising that the two models, Keynes's and Modigliani's, lead to such different results. After all, doesn't Modigliani's model simply do what Keynes promised: to drop the scaffolding of a fixed money wage once the building blocks of his theory were in place? In fact, the meaning of equilibrium is very different in the two models. Keynes's second-pass equilibrium is contingent and historical, starting from a given money wage: in chapter 19 he asks what happens when the wage *falls*. The question of what happens if the money wage *changes* is, I have suggested, different from the question of the existence of a market-clearing money wage (and associated price level) in a model that abstracts from time and history. Modigliani's equilibrium is ahistorical, timeless, with nothing to fix even a starting point for the evolution of nominal wages and prices. It is, as it were, an equilibrium in the mind of God.

Equilibria in the mind of God have their uses, but it is also useful to bear in mind their limits. In an interview with David Colander in the mid-1980s, Paul Samuelson recounted Edwin Bidwell Wilson's take on equilibrium (Wilson was a physicist whose lectures on mathematical economics Samuelson had attended in the 1930s):

> You leave your car in the MIT parking lot overnight. The rubber tire is a membrane which separates the inside of the tire from the atmosphere, and because of this stiff wall there's an equilibrium difference in pressure. Wilson would say, "Come back a thousand years later, and that tire will be flat." That was not strict equilibrium. It's just a very slowly adjusting disequilibrium. (Colander and Landreth 1996, p. 163)

Modigliani's conception of equilibrium does not invite us to examine the process of adjustment, to investigate the consequences of moving from one price level to another. By contrast, these consequences are crucial for Keynes, which is why examining an economy's trajectory starting from a given wage is fundamentally different from analyzing an equilibrium in which the wage rate is completely up for grabs, with no past and no future, existing timelessly in the mind of God.

The concept of a historically contingent equilibrium becomes especially important in the context of *The General Theory* because of the volatility of the underlying behavioral relationships. An important innovation of *The General Theory*, amplified in a response to critics in *The Quarterly Journal of Economics* in 1937, is Keynes's insistence on the role of uncertainty—as distinct from risk—as a destabilizing factor in the economy. Keynes did not invent the distinction between risk and uncertainty, risk referring to situations in which a probability distribution of outcomes can be deployed, uncertainty referring to situations in which probability distributions are irrelevant, where one must rely on some combination of hunch and convention. Uncertainty is essential to Keynes's argument that the underlying schedules constituting his theory are themselves subject to sudden and violent disruption, which—given the adjustment mechanism posited by his theory—means that a capitalist economy is subject to ups and downs in equilibrium levels of output and employment.

The volatility of equilibrium, the property of being subject to violent disturbances, is quite distinct from whether the equilibrium is stable in the sense that there are self-correcting forces within the system that can be counted on to guide the system to a new equilibrium if a random shock uproots the economy from its old equilibrium. It is the volatility of the underlying schedules, perhaps more than any other consideration, that has led some of Keynes's followers to reject equilibrium altogether as a way of characterizing economic outcomes.

Paul Davidson (1991) distinguishes between ergodic and nonergodic characterizations of the economy, that is, between economic environments characterized by stable probability distributions (risk) and economic environments characterized by the absence of stable probability distributions (uncertainty). For Davidson, equilibrium analysis may make sense in an ergodic environment but not otherwise, and the world we live in is otherwise. Robert Skidelsky's (2009) retrospective on Keynes and *The General Theory* is another example of rejecting equilibrium as inconsistent with uncertainty.

For my own part, I do not doubt that uncertainty is an important part of Keynes's argument: it can lead to volatile investment demand, volatile liquidity preference, and even a volatile consumption function. But this does not persuade me that uncertainty requires us to dispense altogether with equilibrium. In fact, I see no alternative to equilibrium—conceived of as the potential outcome of a dynamic process—as an organizing principle for the argument of *The General Theory*.

As far as the economics profession is concerned, Modigliani hit a home run. As Samuelson made clear, the first generation of American Keynesians had early on accepted the idea that rigidities were central to the argument of *The General Theory*. Rigidities, like the poor, would always be with us, so if Keynes provided a good map for finding our way in a rigid world, that was enough. One ought not to worry about whether *The General Theory* was sufficiently general.

The first generation, whom I have referred to as "Young Keynesians," sought to integrate Keynes into the mainstream canon through what Samuelson, *primus inter pares,* called the neoclassical synthesis. The neoclassical synthesis, in Samuelson's hands, described a situation in which the government managed aggregate demand to bring about full employment, mostly through fiscal policy, and thus created an environment in which the old verities and virtues of a market system as a device for allocating resources among competing uses came into their own.[9] Active government was in this view the precondition for the market system to function efficiently, at least in the short run.

The neoclassical synthesis was undoubtedly useful in maintaining the professional respectability of the Young Keynesians as they matured into Older Keynesians, however much it damaged Keynes's legacy. Had he survived the end of World War II by more than several months—he died in April 1946— Keynes might have said that with friends like Modigliani, who counted himself and was counted by others a Keynesian, he didn't need enemies.

How wrong he would have been! The argument to which Milton Friedman appeals as the Keynes slayer (1970) is not Modigliani's, but one formulated originally by hostile critics of Keynes, in particular by Gottfried Haberler (1939, 1941) and independently by Pigou (1943). In brief, the "real-balance effect" as the Haberler–Pigou argument came to be called, hinges on the wage-price nexus. As wages vary so will prices; if wages and therefore prices fall, the money that people hold as part of their asset portfolios will increase in purchasing power regardless of what happens to real income. Eventually, the holder of even a single dollar or euro, indeed of even a single yen, will become richer than Croesus, and her consumption demand will increase without bound. However much aggregate demand is needed for full employment, it will be forthcoming in a world of flexible prices and wages. As we shall see in chapters 4 and 7, the operation of the real-balance effect is very different in the comparative-statics of timeless comparisons from its operation in a world of real-time changes. Because of its asymmetric impact on debtors, the real-balance effect goes from being a killer argument against *The General Theory* in chapter 4 to being a pillar of support in the dynamic context of chapter 7.

As time went on, Keynes came in for treatment harsher than being reduced to a theorist of short-run frictions. Under the banners of rational expectations and real business cycles, the old neoclassical ("classical" in Keynes's language) orthodoxy was revived as New Classical theory. In a competitive market system, equilibrium, as for Pigou, is determined jointly by the goods-supply function of profit-maximizing businesses and the labor-supply function of utility-maximizing households. Re-outfitted in the garb of fancy mathematics, this new dispensation eliminated aggregate demand in the context of calculating, self-interested agents, reducing Keynes from a theorist of short-run frictions and rigidities to a theorist of a world where most of the people were being fooled all of the time, which is emphatically not the world of orthodox economic theory.

The conversion was rapid. And, as these things go, enduring. It was only after the financial crisis erupted in 2008 that New Classical theory lost its hold on the economics profession. In Friedman's intellectual progeny, Robert Lucas, Finn Kydland, Edward Prescott, and Thomas Sargent, to name only those who were recognized with Nobel Prizes for their contributions, economics came full circle, to where it had been when Pigou and his ilk had argued that unemployment was incompatible with a system of competitive markets, arising only because of the intemperate meddling of trade unions and governments.

The conflict between Keynes and orthodoxy over the ability of the invisible hand to ensure full employment, I should emphasize, is not just an issue of abstract theory. The self-regulating economy is the philosophy behind the policies of deregulation that were inflicted on the economy prior to the crash of 2008 and that bear at least some of the responsibility for the crash.[10]

Economists in 2020 are not of one mind about the short run. There are two camps: the partisans of more or less extreme versions of New Classical theory, for whom aggregate demand never matters, and the partisans of one or another version of so-called "New Keynesian" theory, the theory embraced by the heirs of Samuelson and his generation, for whom frictions are the core of the argument that aggregate demand does indeed matter in the short run. The long run is another story: it is generally agreed that the long run is a country in which the writ of Keynes does not run.

Throughout the evolution of economics after Keynes, from Samuelson and Modigliani on, there is a thread that unites the friends and enemies of *The General Theory:* the pull toward a unified economics that synthesizes macro and micro, the economy as a whole with the actions of separate individuals. We can see this early on in Samuelson's neoclassical synthesis (note 9 above) and in Modigliani's and Friedman's attempts to put the theory of consumption on a rational basis (Modigliani and Brumberg 1954; M. Friedman 1957)—read, on a basis of fully informed individuals calculating and maximizing long-term utility subject to a long-term budget constraint—as against what the profession saw as the ungrounded assumption of Keynes's "psychological law" disposing people to consume a fraction of whatever income comes their way. (For more on the rational consumer and his discontents, see chapter 9.)

This *Gleichschaltung* begins long before its latest and most complete manifestation in the guise of New Classical economics. Nor, as I have indicated, is it limited to the avowed enemies of Keynes. Indeed, the assumption that informs mainstream macroeconomics in 2020, whatever its stripe, is that macro behavior must be grounded in the individual—not any individual, but the "rational" individual who is formed by the microeconomic texts.

The Taming of *The General Theory:* **The Political Response to Keynes (Or, To Every Action . . .)**

But I get ahead of my story. At the end of World War II, the economists susceptible to the blandishments of Keynes were no longer graduate students and young instructors. Economists steeped in *The General Theory* began to fill the professorial ranks of colleges and universities and, even where not numerically preponderant, dominated in terms of energy, commitment, and the confidence of the bearers of a new dispensation. Samuelson himself, always a step ahead, was already a tenured professor at MIT.

The new prominence and even ascendance of Keynes invited reaction and retaliation. Keynesian is a plastic word, which can mean anything from the actual content of *The General Theory* to a conception of the economy in which the state takes responsibility for a large measure of economic activity, particularly for the provision of social insurance against the loss of income because of old age and retirement, disability, and unemployment due to a failure of aggregate demand. Only the last of these, unemployment insurance, could be considered Keynesian in the sense of relating to the message of *The General Theory,* though in point of fact unemployment insurance was initiated in Britain in 1911, in Italy in 1920, and in Germany in 1927—long before Keynes began to formulate the ideas and concepts that formed the backbone of his *magnum opus* (Social Security Board 1937).

It was natural that after the sacrifices of World War II there would emerge a strong sentiment for an enhanced role for the government as a means of preventing, to the extent possible, the calamity of depression, as well as for mitigating the effects of downturns to the extent prevention failed. But the sentiment was hardly universal, and many regretted the passing of a society based, at least in their perception, on "rugged individualism," with its implications of self reliance, personal responsibility, and minimal government.

The very idea that unemployment could be the result of a systemic failure of demand rather than the personal choice or at least the responsibility of the individual who found himself out of work was anathema to the creed of rugged individualism. The idea that a failure of private demand might require deficit spending, and in the worst of circumstances, deficit spending as far out as the eye could see, compounded the original sin of *The General Theory.*

And there was worse. One justification of economic inequality had long been—and still is—that the rich, freed from the immediate pressures of consuming enough to hold body and soul together, were the source of capital accumulation, the benefits of which eventually trickled down to the lowliest worker. Keynes himself put this justification forward in the opening pages of *The Economic Consequences of the Peace,* the book that in 1919 had transformed him from middling civil servant—he resigned his position at the Treasury in protest over the Treaty of Versailles—into public intellectual.

The General Theory turned this argument on its head. In a world in which aggregate demand was problematic, attempts to save more meant less spending on consumption, hence less output, income, and employment:

> In contemporary conditions the growth of wealth, so far from being dependent on the abstinence of the rich, as is commonly supposed, is more likely to be impeded by it. One of the chief social justifications of great inequality of wealth is, therefore, removed. (p. 373)

This "paradox of thrift," as it came to be called, meant not only the loss of a justification of inequality but also an argument for greater equality: if workers and middle income folks were prepared to spend more of their income, then transfers to them from the rich would add to aggregate demand and reduce unemployment.

This was not an argument Keynes himself urged on his readers. *The General Theory* makes no more than passing reference to the positive effects of a more equal distribution of income on the overall propensity to consume (for example, in chapter 22, as a counterweight to a low investment demand). In fact, in Keynes's own models the distribution of income between wages and profits is not an exogenous variable, determined outside the system, but the consequence of the interplay of aggregate demand and aggregate supply; distribution is a thermometer, not a thermostat. Nonetheless, the idea was there for so-called left Keynesians to add to the reasons why more income equality would be better than less—and one more reason for the right to oppose Keynes and all he appeared to stand for.

In the end, however, Keynes was opposed, even vilified, not so much because of his specific doctrines but because he was a convenient focus for the anxieties attendant to the transformation of the American economy, polity, and society during a decade and a half of depression and war. Keynes was lumped together with radical socialists and other opponents of "free enterprise," all seen as witting or unwitting agents of Soviet communism in its bid for global hegemony. In this view of the world, communists were everywhere, particularly in the government and the universities, and economists who did not toe the free-enterprise line might be the advance party of the conspiracy, or at least were doing the work of softening up the country for the communists. The indiscriminate nature of the attack on the "enemies" of capitalism is striking: both the Veritas Foundation, which led the charge in its pamphlet, *Keynes at Harvard,* and the young William Buckley, fresh from four years as an undergraduate at Yale, Harvard's traditional Ivy League rival (Buckley 1951), even attacked Schumpeter as a fellow traveler of Keynes and the communists who would destroy the capitalist system. In point of fact, Schumpeter was an implacable foe of Keynes and champion, albeit despairing champion, of rugged individualism.[11]

The cutting edge of the attack on Keynes was the attempt to purge college campuses of the baneful influence of teachers and textbooks that promulgated the view from *The General Theory.* The campaign of alumni and other stalwarts of rugged individualism was successful in attacking the first text to frame itself in the Keynesian message, Lorie Tarshis's *Elements of Economics.* Paul Samuelson was more careful and in his own words, lawyer-like (Colander and Landreth 1996, p. 172), and his *Economics* escaped the purges.

But the economics profession had learned its lesson. I have argued that the internal attractions of assimilating Keynes to the mainstream, stripping *The General Theory* of its most radical implications, had an intellectual appeal all on its own. But this appeal was strengthened by the survival advantages of a Keynesian economics that, far from reducing the mainstream to a special case of a more general theory, reduced *The General Theory* to a special case of sand in the wheels. Theoretical accommodation served both intellectual and political purposes.

The Taming of *The General Theory:* Theory and Reality (Or, the Supply Side Comes into Its Own)

With the passage of time there was trouble in another quarter: economic events forced a reconsideration of the role of aggregate supply. Here Keynes's followers, as distinct from Keynes himself, had gone too far. In a short space of time, the couple of decades separating the mid-1930s from the mid-1950s, aggregate demand went from invisibility to a one-man show in the drama of output determination.

As we have seen, in their enthusiasm for the IS-LM apparatus, Keynesian economists lost sight of the supply side, confusing the supply of saving with the supply of goods. Until the 1970s made it impossible to ignore the supply side of output determination, the consensus reflected in Samuelson's neoclassical synthesis was that demand management was the necessary and sufficient condition for getting to full employment. As full employment was approached, the supply of labor would begin to matter, and once there, Keynes's economics would become irrelevant. In short, demand *or* supply rather than demand and supply: up to full employment, Keynes's first-pass model without any qualification, or the second-pass model as told by IS-LM, with fixed prices as well as fixed wages; once full employment was attained, aggregate demand could be ignored.

With the profit squeeze of the late 1960s, and even more so with the oil shocks of the 1970s, the neoclassical synthesis had to be expanded to allow a role for aggregate supply in the determination of output, regardless of whether the economy was at full employment. In 2020, the New Keynesian view is that both aggregate demand and aggregate supply matter in the short run, a period defined not so much by a particular amount of calendar time, but as the time in which rigidities constrain the adjustment of demand and supply.

As far as the long run is concerned, the Old Keynesians surrendered before the New Keynesians were out of diapers. In the Keynesian consensus, aggregate demand does not vanish once we leave the short run, but it becomes irrelevant—except for the determination of the price level. As James Tobin, who did as much as any American to develop postwar Keynesian economics, put it, "According to the synthesis of classical and Keynesian macroeconomics reached by 1960, Keynesian macroeconomics is short-run. It does not pretend to apply to long-run growth and development" (1992, p. 392).

This book rejects this "Keynesian" consensus: in the story told in chapters 18 and 19, the principle idea of *The General Theory*—that aggregate demand exerts an independent influence on economic outcomes—applies in the long run as well as in the short run.

Economic Policy after *The General Theory*

Keynes intended *The General Theory* to provide the underpinnings of a new framework for policy, but little is actually said on policy in its pages. The policy implications of *The General Theory* are nonetheless far-reaching. The major theoretical conclusion was that once undergoing a shock that moves it away from full employment, an economy might remain mired in depression indefinitely. The economy would reach an unemployment equilibrium, equilibrium in the sense of a position at which the forces moving the economy one way or the other are just balanced. A full-employment equilibrium might exist in the mind of God or his mainstream votaries, but no way exists to get from the here of unemployment to the there of full employment. Not only would the "self-correcting mechanism" of the market fail, but under certain circumstances, it might be impossible for monetary policy alone to move the economy to full employment.

The government would have to take more direct action. Keynes does not prescribe fiscal policy, deficit spending, or any other unorthodox measure; the most specific he gets is a general argument for government policies to influence both the demand for investment and the propensity to consume, in order to equalize investment and saving at a high level of employment. To this end Keynes speaks of the need for a "somewhat comprehensive socialization of investment" (*The General Theory,* p. 378).

But this in itself was not a new departure. Keynes had for a long time advocated more government activism to address the depression, and, as I noted earlier, even before the Great Depression began, he was an advocate of public works as a means of creating employment—and so deficit spending.

Clarity is important here. One can find arguments for public works to combat unemployment long before Keynes—I have found one from 1829—but not arguments based in a framework of the economy in which unemployment is something other than a transient curse. A new framework is what *The General Theory* provided, and this framework is at the same time its major virtue and a major cause of the opprobrium heaped on Keynes from the right.

With regard to fiscal policy, it was not Keynes who drew the most radical conclusions from *The General Theory,* but Abba Lerner, a young disciple. The basic idea of what Lerner called "functional finance," in opposition to the bedrock prescription of "sound finance" that the budget should be balanced at all costs, was that government finance should serve the goal of full employment, injecting demand into the economy when private demand is slack, withdrawing demand when private demand is greater than the capacity of the economy at full employment (1941, 1943, 1944). The point was to manipulate aggregate demand so that it would achieve the magic of simultaneously intersecting with both goods supply and labor supply. Fiscal policy became not one weapon in the arsenal of government intervention, but the only weapon when monetary policy fell short as a means of stimulating (or, indeed, limiting) aggregate demand to the necessary degree.

Countercyclical fiscal policy, which is to say government expenditures ramped up during periods of recession or depression, tax rates reduced, the opposite in times of boom—all this was bad enough. At least there was the prospect that over the cycle, taking good times with the bad, the government budget might remain in balance, deficits in slumps being offset by surpluses in booms. But Lerner and others, especially Alvin Hansen (1938), went much further: full employment might require a continuing and growing deficit to offset a continuing decline in opportunities for productive and profitable investment in the private sector. This vision of "secular stagnation," buttressed by appeals to Keynes's own authority, held out the prospect not only of the "euthanasia of the entrepreneur" (Keynes's phrase) but also of a growing public sector and, worse, a growing public debt. *The General Theory* really did lead to thinking the unthinkable.

Keynes's influence on policy formulation has waxed and waned; it took the crash of 2008 to realize how profoundly, in the end, Keynes affected the political climate in which fiscal policy is determined, not to mention actual policies themselves. "Well I guess everyone is a Keynesian in a foxhole," said Robert Lucas in October 2008, as much as anyone the father of the New Classical counterrevolution (Fox 2008a), though he quickly added, "but I don't think we are there yet" (2008b). The Obama stimulus of approximately $800 billion over two years speaks volumes about the change in public opinion, even though the effects of the stimulus are hotly contested. For all the yammering of the right (and, for that matter, the center and even Obama himself) about the unsupportable debt, educated opinion has shifted markedly since the Great Depression, and to a large part this shift is due to the impact of *The General Theory*.

The difference between the editorial stance of the *New York Times* during the Great Depression and its editorial stance during the Great Recession is illuminating. During the presidential election campaign of 1932 and the run-up to the inauguration of Roosevelt, the *Times* reiterated the view that the best thing the federal government could do for the American economy was to get its own fiscal house in order. Echoing Adam Smith's famous dictum, "What is prudence in the conduct of every private family, can scarce be folly in that of a great kingdom," (1937 [1776]), editorials bemoaned the deficit. Under the title, "Balancing the Federal Budget," the *Times* offered this analysis:

> [The] possibility that the deficits for two years [fiscal 1932 and 1933, which is to say the period from July 1931 through June 1933] may have been underestimated only strengthens the argument for increased taxation made by [Secretary of the Treasury] Mellon. At best the Government must borrow heavily during the next six months. . . . In these circumstances it is important for the Government to give evidence to present holders of its securities and to those to whom it hopes to sell new issues that the budget will be balanced at the earliest practicable date. As Secretary Mellon said: "This is es-

sential not merely for maintaining unimpaired the credit of the Government but also for reinvigorating the entire credit structure of the country." (January 14, 1932, p. 20)

Just before the presidential election, the *Times* reiterated its stand under the banner "Federal Budget Still Unbalanced":

> It is clear that further action must be taken when Congress reconvenes, both to reduce costs and to provide more dependable sources of revenue. (November 4, 1932, p. 18)

After the election of Roosevelt, the *Times* trumpeted the "Sound Advice" (this is the headline) that financier Bernard Baruch had offered the Senate Finance Committee:

> He pointed out that the Government's credit is good only so long as its professed intention to balance the budget is believed. He also pointed out that its ability to provide relief is in the long run dependent on its credit. . . .
>
> Such testimony as Mr Baruch gave in Washington . . . supports the hope that under President Roosevelt a new Congress, meeting in special session, will at last move boldly to bring the Federal budget into balance and remove all doubt of the Government's credit. (February 16, 1933, p. 18)

On the eve of the inauguration of the new president, the advice was the same ("Roads to Recovery"):

> The national budget was first thrown out of balance in January 1931—twenty-five months ago. It has never been in balance since that time. . . . During all this time public confidence has been disturbed by the failure of the Government to put its financial affairs in order. (March 2, 1933, p. 16)

Arthur Krock, the perennial if not immortal columnist for the *Times* (he retired only in the 1960s after writing his column for more than thirty years), had previously been a deficit hawk, but softened a bit after the new president entered office, accepting the distinction made by the Roosevelt administration between the regular budget, which Krock (and the Roosevelt people) maintained had to be kept in balance, and the emergency budget, which required deficits in the interest of recovery. He was especially reassured by the president's apparent commitment to wind down the emergency budget as soon as possible:

> So determined is the President that the extraordinary budgeting shall be prudently retired, that he has notified Congress he will recommend a sufficient tax if that body fails to produce it. (May 19, 1933)

By July, the editorial page of the *Times* was echoing Krock:

> The Administration argues, with much force, that it is fair to draw a distinction between charges which constitute a lasting burden on the Treasury and emergency expenditures which can be shut off when the need for them has passed. (July 10, 1933, p. 12)

But even softened, the editorial position of the *Times* in the depths of the Depression is very different from its position as the Great Recession unfolded. Under the title "The Truth About the Deficit," the *Times* had this to say a year into Obama's tenure:

> Americans should be anxious, for reasons including the huge deficit. But the cold economic truth is this: At a time of high unemployment and fragile growth, the last thing the government should do is to slash spending. That will only drive the economy into deeper trouble. (February 7, 2010)

Of course the *Times,* while an important voice, has no monopoly of public opinion, and the reaction to deficit spending was building both in the United States and abroad from the moment the ink dried on the Obama stimulus legislation. The G-20 summit in June 2010 revealed the deep divisions among the governments of the world's largest economies with regard to the proper role of deficit spending in restoring prosperity, and the divisions are no less profound within nations. Although there were many reasons why the American electorate repudiated the Democrats in the 2010 midterm elections, there is no way that the results can be read as a ringing endorsement of the Obama stimulus—nor for that matter the results of the 2012 elections, even though Obama was returned to office. Keynesians would (and did) argue that the stimulus prevented the recession from turning into a depression of the order of the 1930s, but this argument did not resonate with the general public. Once again, concerns for the deficit and the burden of the debt took center stage, and these concerns, along with the political limitations of counterfactual arguments, appeared, for the moment at least, to have tipped the balance in favor of "sound finance." Under President Trump, the pendulum has again swung, with former deficit hawks in the Republican Party quiet about the deficit projections accompanying the tax cut enacted in 2017. The important point for purposes of this book is that the Keynesian voice is part of the debate, a difference not only from the dark days of the Great Depression but also from more recent times when Keynes's theory was considered anachronistic and Keynesian policies irrelevant.

There was more unsettling news in *The General Theory* than the implications for the government deficit. John Maynard Keynes legitimized ideas that had previously belonged to the underground of economics, chiefly the idea that there could be too much saving. Myron Watkins, who in 1933 surveyed the heretical responses to the Great Depression in the prestigious *Quarterly Journal of Economics,* spoke for the mainstream when he characterized the belief that more spending might promote prosperity as the hallmark of ignorance if not perversity. "More puerile nonsense than this would be hard to imagine," Watkins wrote as the Great Depression entered its fourth year (Watkins 1933, p. 524).

As long as Keynes's ideas remained in the realm of theory, none of this mattered very much. Franklin Roosevelt might have been a practicing Keynesian in countenancing budget deficits during most of the time he was president, but in this respect he was Molière's Monsieur Jourdain, who spoke prose for forty years without knowing it. His budgets were unbalanced because, as Arthur Krock discovered, there was no way to balance the budget and still pay for federal programs deemed essential to recovery (and later essential to the war effort).

Paradoxically, the first policy use of Keynesian ideas and concepts was not in formulating policies for recovery but in planning for World War II. Both in Britain and in the United States, the framework of Keynes's first-pass model proved serviceable in estimating the gap that had to be covered by taxation or other means to keep aggregate demand to a level consistent with the availability of goods after the needs of the military and essential government services had been met. Keynes's pamphlet *How to Pay for the War* was a direct application of the framework elaborated in *The General Theory,* if to a very different goal in a very different context.

As an end to the war became something more than a dim light on a far shore, economists' attention turned to planning for peace and demobilization. The discussion was largely in Keynes's terms, the propensity to consume, the demand for investment, the multiplier, all paraphernalia of *The General Theory.* Followers of Keynes divided sharply in their forecasts of the likely outcome of the withdrawal of the huge stimulus to aggregate demand from war expenditure. Many predicted gloom and doom, even a depression of the order of the 1930s. Keynes himself was more sanguine, at least about the immediate postwar period, despite his sense that over the long-term investment opportunities would dry up: he foresaw a boost to consumption demand from the large holdings of cash, bank deposits, and government bonds on the part of the public, coupled with the backlog of unmet needs and wants—for housing, automobiles, and other consumer durables—that had been built up during the war, along with the new programs of social insurance that made saving for a rainy day or retirement less of a priority. The discussion is interesting in its own right, but the main lesson here is the extent the framework of *The General Theory* had permeated into the economist's consciousness.[12] The stage was set for the postwar ascendency of visions, theories, and models inspired by *The General Theory*.

The theoretical reaction to Keynes that culminated in the ascendency of New Classical economics had its counterpart in economic policy. The consensus about the long run implies that demand management can affect only the price level, the real economy being determined, as my younger colleagues in Littauer averred on that fall day in 2008, by the real variables that operate on aggregate supply. Even in the short run, where New Keynesians sought to carve out a theoretical role for government intervention, it was argued that practical limitations (see chapter 14, p. 538) made it impossible to deploy countercyclical monetary policy effectively, and even more difficult to deploy fiscal policy. In any case, temporary infusions of demand through countercyclical monetary and fiscal policy could have only a very limited impact by virtue of their temporary nature.

Central banks around the world adopted the New Classical view to a greater or lesser degree, with the European Central Bank the most influential voice for the new anti-Keynesian orthodoxy. The ECB (n.d.) offered the following rationale for making price stability the primary objective of monetary policy:

> The **natural role of monetary policy** in the economy is to maintain price stability. . . . Monetary policy can affect real activity only in the shorter term. . . . But ultimately it can only influence the price level in the economy (emphasis in original).

The ECB website amplified:

Long-run neutrality of money

It is widely agreed that in the long run—after all adjustments in the economy have worked through—a change in the quantity of money in the economy will be reflected in a change in the general level of prices. But it will not induce permanent changes in real variables such as real output or unemployment.

This general principle, referred to as "the long-run neutrality of money", underlies all standard macroeconomic thinking. Real income or the level of employment are, in the long term, essentially determined by real factors, such as technology, population growth or the preferences of economic agents.

Inflation—a monetary phenomenon

In the long run a central bank can only contribute to raising the growth potential of the economy by maintaining an environment of stable prices. It cannot enhance economic growth by expanding the money supply or keeping short-term interest rates at a level inconsistent with price stability. It can only influence the general level of prices.

Ultimately, inflation is a monetary phenomenon. Prolonged periods of high inflation are typically associated with high monetary growth. While other factors (such as variations in aggregate demand, technological changes or commodity price shocks) can influence price developments over shorter horizons, over time their effects can be offset by a change in monetary policy.

The ECB website made note of the sand in the wheels that may cause unemployment but was unequivocal about the "hierarchy of objectives":

In the actual implementation of monetary policy decisions aimed at maintaining price stability, the Eurosystem should also take into account the broader economic goals of the Community. In particular, given that monetary policy can affect real activity in the shorter term, the ECB typically should avoid generating excessive fluctuations in output and employment if this is in line with the pursuit of its primary objective.

Post-2008 Europe is reaping the whirlwind: the continuing story about the southern rim of the European economy is one of unemployment and stagnation. It is true that following the accession of Mario Draghi, the ECB looked for ways to stimulate the economy, but the constraints embodied in its founding documents drastically impeded its efforts. And precious years were lost before the ECB even attempted to intervene.

No greater tribute could have been paid to the power of economic theory than the ECB's mission statement quoted above.[13] Samuelson had a point when he observed, "Let those who will write the nation's laws, if I can write its textbooks" (widely cited in his obituary; see, e.g., Henderson 2009). However, the textbook to which the ECB looked for guidance was likely to have been inspired more by Milton Friedman and Robert Lucas than by Keynes, or by Samuelson for that matter.

The chapters that follow are not an attempt to represent Keynes, though I sometimes joke that I am channeling him. Nobody will ever know what Keynes "really" meant, and in any case I agree with those who have argued that Keynes's intuition ran way ahead of his ability to set out logically tight arguments. This is a book that Keynes might have written if he had had eighty years to think about his ideas, to digest the criticisms and the changes that were taking place as he was originally formulating his arguments, not to mention the changes since—and if he had the tools available to us in 2020. In any case, I am willing to assert that it is the book he should have written.

At some points I diverge from the arguments of *The General Theory*. The complete title is *The General Theory of Employment, Interest and Money*. There is, I have suggested, not one theory of employment, but at least two. One—the second-pass model—is designed to investigate and ultimately to demolish the claim that a competitive capitalist economy is self-regulating, that competitive capitalism left to itself will provide jobs for all willing workers. Another—the first-pass model—is designed to investigate the possibilities and limitations of using monetary policy to steer capitalism to the goal of full employment that eludes it when left to its own devices. This model sets the stage for a theory of fiscal policy—even if *The General Theory* fails to provide the theory.

There is also a theory of interest, perhaps the most innovative of the novelties of Keynes's theory. This theory of interest, however, is incomplete at best; moreover, its incompleteness contributes to the failure of *The General Theory of Employment* to carry the day in theoretical debate.

But there is no theory at all of money. What is implicitly assumed about money is at odds with Keynes's own stated position (in his earlier work, *A Treatise on Money*), and is at the very least anachronistic if not altogether wrong. And the absence of a theory of money is at least part of the reason why *The General Theory of . . . Interest* is incomplete (or wrong) and in turn why Keynes's theory of employment has had such rough sailing.

The chapters that follow lay all this out.

— 2 —

WHAT WERE THEY THINKING?

Economics Before The General Theory

> With perfectly free competition among workpeople and labour
> perfectly mobile . . . there will always be at work a strong tendency for
> wage-rates to be so related to demand that everybody is employed.
> Hence, in stable conditions every one will actually be employed. The
> implication is that such unemployment as exists at any time is due
> wholly to the fact that changes in demand conditions are continually
> taking place and that frictional resistances prevent the appropriate
> wage adjustments from being made instantaneously.
>
> —ARTHUR PIGOU

> In a perfectly flexible economy where money costs and prices quickly
> adjust themselves to changed circumstances, there could be price
> level fluctuations, profit fluctuations, or fluctuations in the real
> income of labor, but there could not be substantial fluctuations of
> employment or production. Our system rests upon the assumption of
> the existence of price flexibility and cannot operate smoothly without
> it. But in fact the price structure is shot through with rigidities, and
> even, as in the case of tax rates and freight rates, with perverse flexi-
> bilities.
>
> —JACOB VINER

It is sometimes asserted that mainstream economists had no theory of output as a whole before Keynes. Indeed, at one point, Keynes himself appears to have held this view (Keynes 1937a, p. 223). The mainstream may have had the wrong theory and lacked a clear exposition, but that is altogether different from having no theory. For the mainstream a full-employment equilibrium was the normal level of output.

Specialists on business cycles or on money and banking implicitly shared the view that a full-employment equilibrium is the normal state of economic activity around which business fluctuated, but they paid more attention to the ups and downs of the economy around this normal state, which is to say, with the causes of booms and the remedies for slumps. Rich and varied as these literatures were, the question of how the normal, full-employment, level of output is determined seems never to have been addressed! (See David Laidler [1999] for an informative discussion of these ideas in the context of the theory Keynes was to produce in *The General Theory*. John Hicks [1967] provides an insightful account of the history of monetary thought and practice).

Rather, the determination of the normal level of overall output emerged from what has come to be called microeconomics, from the supply-demand constructions based on Alfred Marshall's partial equilibrium analysis, or for the more adventurous, from the general equilibrium constructions of Léon Walras. In microeconomics full employment was and still is the norm, the equilibrium to which an economy gravitates, a position at which the economy would remain if it were not disturbed by the factors that were at the heart of the specialist literatures on cycles and money. Fluctuations were understood to be temporary departures that need not interfere with our understanding of the underlying tendency of the economy, at least of a perfectly competitive economy, to provide jobs for all willing workers as well as to maximize profits for business. Even when the possibility of deviations from full employment was recognized, as in Keynes's *Treatise,* the principal concern was with price movements.

Keynes took Arthur Pigou's *Theory of Unemployment,* published in 1933 in the early stages of the long pregnancy leading to *The General Theory,* as the paradigm of mainstream ("classical" in Keynes's terminology) theory. Or perhaps it is more fair to say that Keynes creates a composite Pigou to stand for the mainstream position, which, as Keynes himself acknowledges, is difficult to pin down. But no matter. Whether or not the mainstream of Keynes's day held so clear a view of the determination of employment and output, there is no question that the view Keynes attributed to Pigou is the prevailing mainstream view in 2020. Look no further than your favorite textbook. If your text is Mankiw's *Principles of Economics* (eighth edition), check out chapter 18, particularly figure 4 on page 370. If you prefer *Economics: Principles and Policy* by Baumol, Blinder, and Solow (fourteenth edition), read chapter 19, especially figure 2 on page 397. Prefer Frank and Bernanke, *Principles of Economics* (third edition)? See chapter 14, especially the "recap" at the bottom of page 404. Finally, try Krugman and Wells, *Economics* (fifth edition), chapter 19, figure 19-6 on page 544.

Each of these texts provides its version of Figure 2.3(a) below, which is a two-schedule summary of Pigou's theory, one schedule depicting the supply of goods that producers find profitable to provide at various prices, the other the amount of labor that households find advantageous to provide at different wages.[1] "Prices" and "wages" here mean real magnitudes, prices relative to wages, and wages relative to prices. Although Keynes (*The General Theory,* chap. 2) disagreed with the idea that labor supply is a function of the real wage (or price), he had no quarrel with the idea that producers maximize profits by equating real marginal cost to the real price—in Keynes's terminology the price in wage units—or flipping the equation, equating the marginal product of labor to the real wage.

Strong assumptions are required to aggregate the myriad goods and services that are produced into a single good, "output." But if we are willing to swallow other assumptions that the mainstream makes in order to tell its story about how the market guarantees a job for every willing worker—or for that matter Keynes's story about how it doesn't—assumptions about aggregation shouldn't deter us. To keep the story as simple as possible, for the most part we ignore land and other primary resources, so that output can be taken to be a function of the stock of capital and the flow of labor into the productive apparatus.

The goods-supply (GS) schedule is the economy-wide real marginal-cost schedule, as shown below in Figure 2.1, in which the vertical axis is the price level relative to money wages, P/W, and the horizontal axis measures real output, Y. Marginal cost is simply $(W \times \Delta L)/\Delta Y$ in terms of money, or $\Delta L/\Delta Y$ in real terms, that is, in terms of labor per unit of output; thus the profit-maximizing level of output is given by $P = (W \times \Delta L)/\Delta Y$, or $P/W = \Delta L/\Delta Y$.

The second schedule is the labor-supply (LS) schedule, determined in

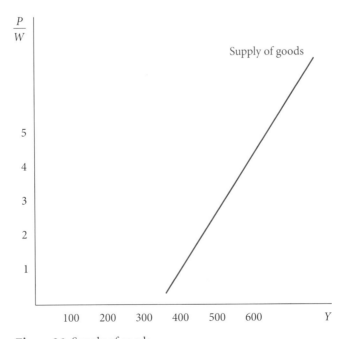

Figure 2.1 Supply of goods.

mainstream theory by individuals (or households) optimizing among alternative combinations of labor and leisure. The vertical axis measures the real wage rate, W/P, and the horizontal axis measures the level of employment, L. The LS schedule slopes upward or "backward" according to which of two contradictory effects dominates, the substitution effect of higher wages making leisure more costly or the income effect of higher wages making leisure more affordable. When these two effects are exactly in balance, the LS schedule is vertical, defining a single level of full employment. Otherwise, every point on the LS schedule corresponds to a different level of "full" employment, since this schedule is defined by the number of hours (or days or weeks) workers wish to work at various levels of (real) wages. Figure 2.2 depicts a situation in which the substitution effect dominates.

Figure 2.3(a) transposes the GS schedule from the space of $Y \times P/W$ to the space of $L \times W/P$.

The GS schedule becomes a demand-for-labor schedule because, in the short run, the capital stock is fixed and output varies with the level of employment: profit maximization can be equally well described in terms of increasing output to the point that the real marginal cost is equal to the real price of goods ($P/W = \Delta L/\Delta Y$) or adding labor to the point that the marginal productivity of labor falls to the real wage ($W/P = \Delta Y/\Delta L$). The intersection of the demand and supply schedules determines both the equilibrium real wage and the equilibrium level of employment.

In Figure 2.3(a) the determination of output is described in terms of an equilibrium level of employment that both provides full employment (the optimal amount of work in the sense of balancing workers' desire for the

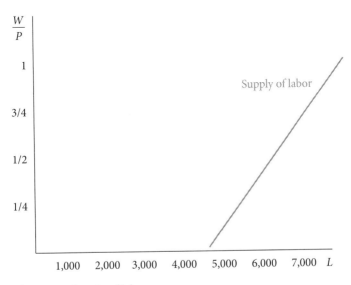

Figure 2.2 Supply of labor.

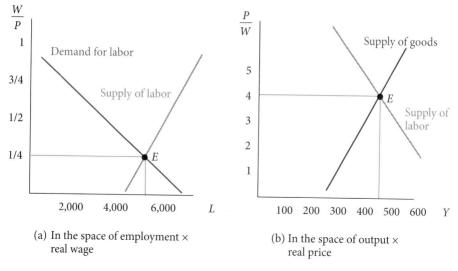

(a) In the space of employment ×
    real wage

(b) In the space of output ×
    real price

Figure 2.3 Equilibrium in terms of employment and output, I.

goods that their wages can buy and the leisure they enjoy) and maximizes
profits for producers.

The same result is described in Figure 2.3(b) in terms of the level of output.
Just as Figure 2.3(a) transposes the GS schedule into a labor-demand schedule, Figure 2.3(b) transposes the supply of labor into a supply of output, the
amount of output that workers optimally balancing leisure and labor would
produce. Equilibrium exists at the real price for which the two levels of supply, the supply of output that is optimal for workers (labeled "Supply of labor"
even though it is output that is supplied) and the supply of output that maximizes profits for producers (labeled "Supply of goods"), coincide.

Three salient results emerge from this simple construction, the results that
distinguished the mainstream from what Keynes would propose in *The General Theory*. First of all, there is no such thing as involuntary unemployment
in equilibrium. Second, there is no role for aggregate demand. As can be seen
by comparing Figures 2.3(a) and 2.3(b), the demand for labor reflects only the
profit-maximizing supply of goods; it is derived from the supply conditions of
producers, not from demand for consumption or investment. Finally, the
mainstream results reflect the classical dichotomy, according to which only
real variables matter to the determination of equilibrium output and income.

Let us look at these results in order. The mainstream equilibrium, whether
characterized in terms of employment or output, is at a point at which every
worker can work as much as she wishes at the going real wage. She may
choose to work more or less—this is a voluntary decision—but nobody is out
of work because she can't find a job. Only if the real wage is too high, which is

to say the real price is too low, say $W/P = 1$ (and $P/W = 1$), can we speak of involuntary unemployment. In this case, the supply of labor would exceed the demand, the profit-maximizing supply of goods would fall short of the supply of goods that workers would choose. If employers were to prevail in such a situation, producing only as much output as maximized profits, there would not be a job for every willing worker. This is shown in Figure 2.4, where the amount of unemployment at F in panel (a) is approximately 4,000 ($= 8,000 - 4,000$) and the amount of lost output at F in panel (b) is 200 ($= 650 - 450$). Not only is the cause of unemployment—too high real wages—clear from the diagram, so is the cure: eliminate the obstacles that prevent the real wage from adjusting profit maximization and worker optimization to each other.

Trade unions were always a prime suspect in the search for rigidities that prevented the adjustment mandated by mainstream theory. But the logic did not compel union bashing. As chapter 1 noted, any systemic rigidity that gets in the way of price and wage adjustment, any element of monopoly, be it on the side of capital or the side of labor, could be the culprit.

The second implication of the theory is that there is no role for aggregate demand in determining the level of output and employment. There is a demand schedule in the left-hand panels of Figures 2.3 and 2.4, but it derives from producer optimization, like the GS schedule in the right-hand panels, not the "final" demand that comes from the desires of consumers, businessmen, governments, and foreigners for consumption, investment, public spending, and exports.

The third lesson of the mainstream story—really an assumption rather than

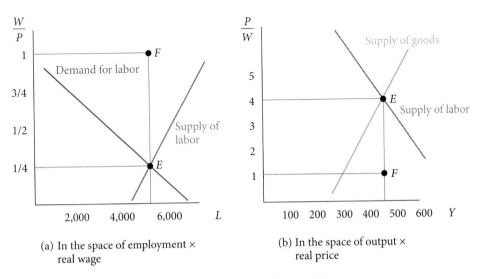

(a) In the space of employment ×
real wage

(b) In the space of output ×
real price

Figure 2.4 Equilibrium in terms of employment and output, II.

a theorem—is that equilibrium depends on real variables only. Except for a short period in which adjustment takes place, a higher or lower nominal price level leaves the volume of employment and output unaffected.

Jacob Viner and the Depression: Diagnosis and Cure in Search of an Analytic Framework

Chapter 1 noted that the absence of a theory hinging on aggregate demand did not prevent arguments for deficit spending or other policies. How did deficit spending fit into a purely supply-side framework? The answer is "not well." In fact, a purely supply-side framework deprived these arguments of a coherent theoretical basis. Jacob Viner's policy interventions in the early 1930s are a case in point.

Viner, a stalwart of the University of Chicago economics faculty and a teacher of both Paul Samuelson and Milton Friedman, became a leading critic of Keynes's *General Theory*. Indeed, he was the one participant in a symposium published by the *Quarterly Journal of Economics* in the fall of 1936 to whom Keynes replied at length and the one whose intervention Keynes acknowledged to be "the most important" (Keynes 1937a, p. 210). Most perceptive in his analysis of individual trees, Viner never could see Keynes's forest. Viner's own espousal of deficit spending, even the intellectual apparatus behind his prescription, had much in common with *The General Theory*—except for lacking a theoretical framework in which deficits made sense.

Like the majority of the profession, Viner understood the Depression in terms of an imbalance between costs and prices. Without a framework that allowed a separate and distinct role for aggregate demand, Viner could think only in terms of supply-side remedies. So, as long as the United States was on the gold standard, Viner, lecturing at the University of Minnesota in February 1933, could envisage a solution only in terms of what he called "balanced deflation" (1933a), which is to say, getting costs to fall to the same degree as prices. Hardly a month had passed, however, before Franklin Roosevelt, in one of his first acts as president, had effectively taken the United States off the gold standard, which allowed a new remedy, inflation, to accomplish the supply-side goal of restoring the price:cost balance. Some months later, in a paper presented at the Institute of Public Affairs at the University of Georgia (1933b), Viner expanded a remedy offered as a hypothetical aside in February (1933a, pp. 25–27) into the centerpiece of his policy prescription: the goal remained to find the right balance between prices and costs, but the solution now lay in expansionary monetary policy.

Figure 2.4 can be deployed to clarify Viner's basic argument. Imagine what happens when the economy is out of equilibrium, as in Figure 2.5, and there are no obstacles to adjustment of the wage rate.

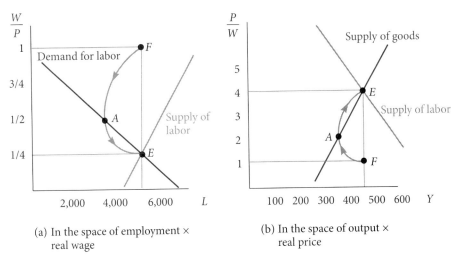

Figure 2.5 Equilibrium in terms of employment and output, III.

Suppose the economy is displaced from the initial equilibrium E, pictured in the right-hand panel as $<450, 4>$, to a new position $F = <450, 1>$. For present purposes it doesn't matter what causes the displacement; we can assume either a monetary or a real shock that causes the price level to fall while leaving the money wage unchanged. In either case, the disequilibrium reflects Viner's imbalance between prices and costs: we may suppose that prices have fallen by a factor of four while wages remain unchanged. At F marginal cost exceeds price, and the marginal product of labor falls short of the real wage. What happens now?

One story goes like this: producers respond to the shortfall of (real) price relative to (real) marginal cost by reducing output. It no longer pays to produce at the level 450 because reducing output will lower costs more than it does returns. At the same time unemployed workers, competing for jobs, drive money wages down and thus the real price up. Together, these two arguments imply a trajectory that initially moves the economy from F to the northwest, as the arrow indicates. (The equivalent trajectory in the left-hand panel is to the southwest, the change in employment being governed by a comparison of the marginal product of labor with the real wage and the change in the real wage being governed by the level of unemployment.)

We can identify two phases in the trajectory of output and real price. First, a depression phase in which output (and employment) fall even as the real price begins to recover; second, a period of recovery of output once the real price has risen to the point that it exceeds marginal cost. The economy bottoms out at A, which marks the transition from the first to the second phase. Recovery is complete when the original equilibrium E—characterized by both

profit maximization and full employment—is reached. Observe that equilibrium money prices and wages are four times lower at the end of the story than
at the beginning. Prices were assumed to fall to one-quarter of their original
level as the economy moved from E to F, and the return to E is accomplished
by reducing the wage rate by the same percentage amount. This is the essence
of "balanced deflation."[2]

Viner has sufficient faith in the market to trust that equilibrium will be restored sooner or later, but the Depression has taught him that "later" can be
too long a time:

> I still believe that even if nothing is done costs will eventually probably fall
> sufficiently to restore a profit margin. But I am becoming more and more
> convinced that there is serious risk that they won't do so quickly enough to
> forestall wholesale economic collapse, if reliance is placed wholly on the
> self-acting processes of recovery. (1933a, p. 10)

Speeding up a process that a competitive economy would follow anyway
thus spares people pain and suffering. In February 1933, Viner looked to
Washington to take action to bring about balanced deflation—for instance,
enforcing antitrust legislation to force down the prices of raw materials such
as steel, which Viner sees as being maintained by "quasi-monopolistic organi-
zation" (1933a, p. 14). He also suggests that even though the pressures of the
market have corrected President Hoover's misguided attempts to maintain
money wages at pre-Depression levels, some wages—particularly the wages of
railway workers and government employees—must come down in order to
reduce freight charges and taxes.[3]

Once the dollar was no longer linked to gold, a new possibility for jump-
starting the recovery process exists. Since the key to moving the economy is
the ratio of real prices to real marginal costs, instead of relying on the "natural" forces of the market to reduce wages, prices can be artificially raised to
accomplish the rebalancing necessary for industry to reverse course:

> Now that we are off [the gold standard], we have a freedom which, if prop-
> erly exercised, gives us ground for hope that with the aid of monetary mea-
> sures we may be able to end the depression within a reasonable length of
> time.
>
> The theory behind inflation as a remedy for the depression consists sim-
> ply in the proposition that if you can get prices up, and if costs do not go up
> simultaneously or do not go up in the same proportion, profit margins will
> reappear for business and business men will then be willing to use such
> spendable funds as they still own, and will be willing to ask and be success-
> ful in persuading the bankers to create new spendable funds, to be used in
> buying raw materials, hiring labor, and so on. This process of putting pur-

chasing power into circulation will operate to increase the total volume of money income, prices will rise, but in less proportion than business expenditures, and the result will be an increased physical output, which will mean an increased employment of the productive factors. (1933b, p. 123)

Among the measures Viner advocates is deficit spending on the part of the federal government. In a passage that eerily anticipates Keynes, Viner writes,

> If the government were to employ men to dig ditches and fill them up again, there would be nothing to show afterwards. But, nevertheless, even these expenditures would be an indirect contribution to business recovery. Their major importance would not be in the public works or the unemployment relief which immediately resulted, but in the possibility of hope that a substantial expenditure would act as a priming of the business pump, would encourage business men by increased sales, make them more optimistic, lead them to increase the number of their employees, and so on. (1933b, p. 130)

There is a step missing in the argument. How exactly is the purchasing power created by public works going to stimulate private-sector production and sales? The answer is easy with aggregate demand in the picture as a force driving output, mysterious at best without aggregate demand. To assume that the inflow of money from expanding government payrolls *directly* increases private-sector sales and employment undercuts the premise of Viner's argument for balanced deflation or inflation—namely, that the underlying cause of the Depression is the relationship of prices to costs. Viner can't have it both ways—first, arguing that the problem lies in an unfavorable price:cost ratio and second, arguing that "substantial [government] expenditure" will prime the business pump, leading to an expansion of sales and employment—at least not without an intermediate step in which the inflow of government money first raises prices without raising costs, producers then responding to a more favorable price:cost structure by increasing output. Such an intermediate step would, however, tacitly admit aggregate demand into the picture through the back door.

Viner is trapped by a purely supply-side perspective. Lacking any way of integrating deficit spending into a supply-side story, Viner's argument for deficit spending failed to gain traction. Three years later, Keynes makes virtually the same argument—and it makes perfect sense within the framework of *The General Theory*:

> If the Treasury were to fill old bottles with banknotes, bury them at suitable depths in disused coalmines which are then filled up to the surface with town rubbish, and leave it to private enterprise on well-tried principles of *laissez-faire* to dig the notes up again . . . , there need be no unemployment

and, with the help of the repercussions, the real income of the community, and its capital wealth also, would probably become a good deal greater than it actually is. It would, indeed, be more sensible to build houses and the like; but if there are political and practical difficulties in the way of this, the above would be better than nothing. (*The General Theory*, p. 129)

Making Aggregate Demand Disappear

Robert Malthus, nineteenth-century population theorist and interlocutor of David Ricardo, was rare among economists before Keynes in maintaining the importance of aggregate demand. The economics profession has ever since worked very hard to divest itself of Malthus's insight. There are in fact two ways of making demand go away, but one of the two, which depends on *assuming* full employment (see chapter 4, esp. Figure 4.9), was a reaction to Keynes. The pre-Keynesian way is to argue that the case of output as a whole differs from the market for a single good because supply creates its own demand: aggregate demand is thus identically equal to what is supplied.

The kernel of truth in the argument lies in an elementary fact of national income and product accounting: income and output are two ways of looking at the same thing. We can see this most easily in the simple case in which no material inputs or services are purchased from upstream suppliers. In this simplest of cases, production involves the sweat of the worker's brow (and the entrepreneur's) in combination with the services of machines and the gifts of nature embodied in land and other natural resources. When these "factors of production" produce a dollar's worth of output, a dollar's worth of income is also generated—wages to workers, rents to landlords, interest to bondholders and banks, and profit to the entrepreneur. (Profit can be looked at as the balancing item that ensures the sum of income generated to the owners of land, labor, and capital will just equal the value of the product.)

So output—supply—is equal to income. How does this ensure that the *demand* for output is equal to supply, which is to say that the expenditure on output is equal to the income generated by its production? The equality between the output of apples and the income generated in the production of these apples does not ensure that the demand for apples necessarily equals the supply; orchard workers or owners may choose to spend their incomes on other goods. But looking at output as a whole, this imbalance does not arise: if workers choose all of a sudden to spend less on apples, then they will spend more on something else, maybe pears. Or bicycles. Or laptop computers. In *total*, demand must equal income, and therefore output—and therefore can be ignored.

There is a difficulty with this argument. What if agents wish to save some of their income, for a rainy day, for retirement, or to make a major purchase (like a house) at some point in the future? Isn't saving a diversion from spending? Keynes seized upon what he perceived to be the weak link in the relationship between income and expenditure:

> An act of individual saving means—so to speak—a decision not to have dinner to-day. But it does not necessitate a decision to have dinner or to buy a pair of boots a week hence or a year hence or to consume any specified thing at any specified date. Thus it depresses the business of preparing to-day's dinner without stimulating the business of making ready for some future act of consumption. (*The General Theory*, p. 210)

This sounds plausible, but mainstream economics had long since taken account of Keynes's objection and had posited a mechanism for transforming saving—abstaining from consumption—into investment—additions to the stock of goods (machines, buildings, infrastructure) used to produce goods and services in the future. Indeed, Adam Smith may have been the original source of the argument that a general deficiency of spending, or to see matters from the other side, a general glut of production, was impossible in a market system. As Smith put it,

> Whatever a person saves from his revenue he adds to his capital, and either employs it himself in maintaining an additional number of productive hands, or enables some other person to do so, by lending it to him for an interest, that is, for a share of the profits. As the capital of an individual can be increased only by what he saves from his annual revenue or his annual gains, so the capital of a society, which is the same with that of all the individuals who compose it, can be increased only in the same manner. . . . What is annually saved is as regularly consumed as what is annually spent, and nearly in the same time too. . . . That portion which [an individual] annually saves . . . is consumed by labourers, manufacturers, and artificers, who reproduce with a profit the value of their annual consumption. (1937 [1776], p. 321)

Keynes associated the view that supply creates its own demand not with Smith but with David Ricardo, the great English economist of the first half of the nineteenth century, and with Jean-Baptiste Say, the nineteenth-century French economist, whose eponymous Law embodied the conventional wisdom.[4] A clear statement of this view, due to John Stuart Mill, is cited by Keynes in *The General Theory* (p. 18):

> [If we could] suddenly double the productive powers of the country, we should double the supply of commodities in every market; but we should, by the same stroke, double the purchasing power. Everybody would bring a double demand as well as a supply: everybody would be able to buy twice as

much, because everyone would have twice as much to offer in exchange. (Mill 1909 [1848], bk. 3, chap. 14, para. 2)[5]

This view was dominant as Keynes's *General Theory* was taking shape. In 1933, a journeyman economist, Myron Watkins, summed up conventional economic wisdom in the prestigious *Quarterly Journal of Economics:*

> The whole joint product of industry in any period is the same as the aggregate income of the community during that period; it cannot be more and it cannot be less. The aggregate income of the community represents the total available purchasing power of the community, nothing more and nothing less; . . . an addition to the community's stock of capital assets, through savings from whatever type of current income derived and in whatever volume effected, constitutes a demand for a corresponding part of current production. It follows that the total available purchasing power of the capitalistic community must be exactly equal to the joint product of industry, however swiftly the latter may be increased and however *inequitably* it may be distributed . . .
>
> [T]he erroneous assumption that production and consumption must somehow be kept "in balance," . . . rests, in turn, upon the naïve belief that income which is not "consumed," but "saved," does not constitute a demand for the current output of industry. More puerile nonsense than this would be hard to imagine, and were it not for the frequency and volubility with which such ideas are put forward, even occasionally—alas!—by economists with a respectable reputation, . . . the space of a professional journal would not need to be encumbered with their refutation. (1933, pp. 523–524)

Say's Law is summarized in Figure 2.6. Output and expenditure are defined in real terms and are independent of prices and wages, hence independent of the real price. The result is that, defining the level of aggregate demand as the level of output for which expenditure and output are equal, the entire shaded area of Figure 2.7 represents the AD "schedule," combinations of real price and output for which expenditure and output are equal. According to Figure 2.7, output and expenditure are equal at *every* level of output, for *every* level of the real price. Since this equality holds everywhere, it necessarily holds when production is at full-employment levels of output or at profit-maximizing levels of output. That is, aggregate demand overlaps with the LS schedule and the GS schedule. This is shown in Figure 2.8. The result is paradoxical: since every point in Figure 2.7 is a point on the AD schedule, the AD schedule is superfluous and can be ignored when it comes to characterizing equilibrium.

How do Smith, Ricardo, Say, and Mill, not to mention Dr. Watkins, know this? What assures that for every individual who decides to go without dinner today there will be another individual who will step forward to use the re-

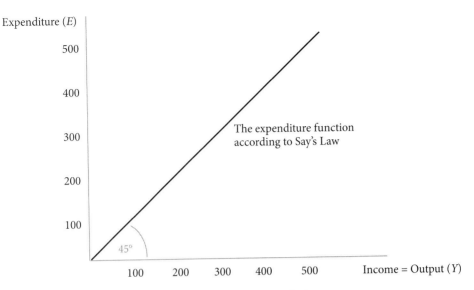

Figure 2.6 Say's Law: expenditure = income at every level of output.

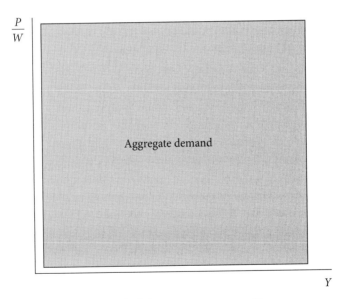

Figure 2.7 Say's Law: output = expenditure.

sources thus freed to fashion kitchen utensils for tomorrow's dinner, so that expenditure is always equal to income? How do they know that If Millie saves one dollar of her income and thus breaks the chain of income and spending, the link is restored by Mollie, who borrows the dollar to add to the capital stock, in short, that the saving done by all the Millies is spent by all the Mollies?

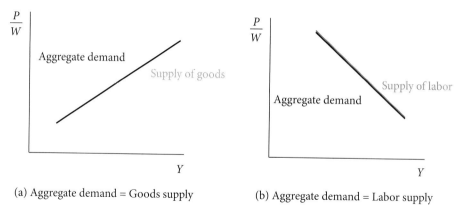

(a) Aggregate demand = Goods supply   (b) Aggregate demand = Labor supply

Figure 2.8 Aggregate demand, goods supply, and labor supply.

The key, or so most "respectable" economists thought, was that the interest rate guaranteed equilibrium between the demand for investment and the supply of saving—not that the past tense is appropriate: in the words of Robert Frank and Ben Bernanke,[6]

> Desired saving is equated with desired investment through adjustments in the real interest rate, which functions as the "price" of saving. The movements of the real interest rate clear the market for saving in much the same way that the price of apples clears the market for apples. (2007, p. 639)

Frank and Bernanke are hardly alone. Larry Summers (2016) explains why low interest rates are evidence for a lack of investment demand in exactly the same manner:[7]

> Just as the price of wheat adjusts to balance the supply of and demand for wheat, it is natural to suppose that interest rates—the price of money—adjust to balance the supply of savings and the demand for investment in an economy. (p. 3)

This may be the natural supposition, at least for a mainstream economist, but not for Keynes.

Equilibrium vs. Equilibrating: Prices and the Price Mechanism

The problem is confusion between an *equilibrium price* and an *equilibrating price mechanism*. To rely on the saving-investment equilibrium requires more than the supposition that investment demand and saving supply are equal. This argument also requires that if either the investment-demand schedule or the saving-supply schedule shifts, then (1) the shift has no impact on the other schedule, and (2) the interest rate adjusts the levels of investment demand and supply saving to a new equilibrium. The basic diagram is given below in Figure 2.9. Suppose we start out at a point with the rate of interest equal to ρ_0 and the level of investment and saving equal to I_0. There is nothing in Figure 2.9 with which Keynes would have any reason to take issue. For Keynes, as well as for the lineage of Smith, the demand for investment depends on the rate of interest, and while Keynes did not emphasize the influence of the interest rate on the supply of saving, there is nothing in *The General Theory* that rules out a role for the interest rate as one of the determinants of saving. Indeed, the *only* diagram in the book is one that relates *both* saving and investment to the rate of interest, introduced on page 180 precisely to make the present point![8]

The difference between Keynes and Smith is not about the interest rate characterizing an equilibrium between saving supply and investment demand. It is about the interest rate as a mechanism for bringing about equilibrium. Suppose there is a shock to the economy that moves the investment-demand schedule downward, as in Figure 2.10. (Imagine it is September 2008, and Lehman Brothers is going under; entrepreneurs worry about future economic prospects, and those who remain optimistic can't get credit for their projects.) How does the mainstream, from Smith to Knut Wicksell to Bernanke and Summers, see the consequences?

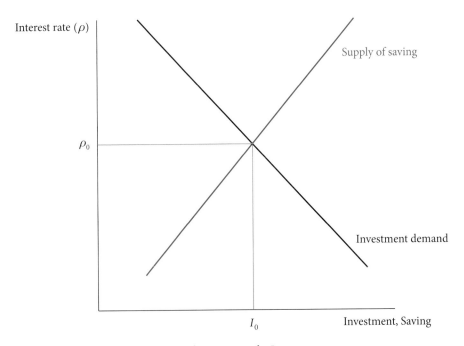

Figure 2.9 Investment demand and saving supply, I.

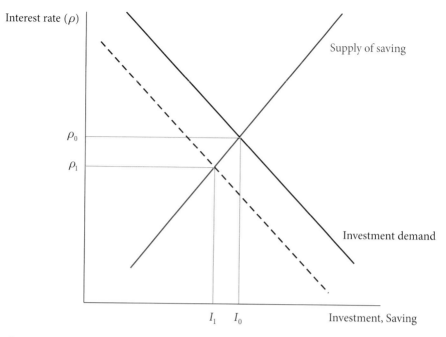

Figure 2.10 Investment demand and saving supply, II.

In the mainstream view, the existing interest rate, ρ_0, will no longer clear the market, but no matter, except for those troublesome rigidities that might rear their heads in the short run. Although the composition of output will change—there will be more consumption and less saving and investment—there is no overall, macro, impact on the economy. Because the supply of saving at ρ_0 exceeds the demand for investment, the interest rate will fall. At ρ_1 where the new investment-demand schedule, the dashed line, intersects the saving-supply schedule, saving will again equal investment at the new (lower) level I_1. The rate of interest adjusts the amount of saving in the economy as well as the quantity of investment so that they are once again in equilibrium, the price mechanism working as microeconomics teaches that it operates in the apple market. In the end, there is less investment (and saving) but more consumption. Aggregate demand is unaffected.

We shall explore Keynes's own model presently. For now it is enough to observe that the Keynesian mechanism that brings investment demand and saving supply into line is the level of production itself. A shift in the investment-demand schedule leads to a shift in the saving-supply schedule: the two schedules are not independent. And (to a first approximation) there is no impact on the rate of interest. Keynes's argument is that the interest rate *mechanism* equilibrates the so-called money market (shorthand for intertwined markets in which the *stocks* of financial assets are traded). This mechanism is thus not available to equilibrate *flows* of investment and saving. Yes, in equilibrium, for Keynes as well as for the mainstream, the quantity of investment demanded and the quantity of saving forthcoming are equal, so Say's Law holds in the sense that expenditure is equal to income, but this is not as an identity that is true for any level of output. The picture is in Figure 2.11. There are two points at which saving and investment are equal: the old equilibrium between desired saving and investment at I_0 and the new equilibrium at I_2, the intersection of the displaced saving-supply schedule, the red-dashed line, and the new investment-demand schedule. A key difference from the mainstream is that the new intersection of investment and saving schedules does not correspond to a higher level of consumption; the level of consumption *falls,* along with the level of output and income.

From the point of view of *The General Theory,* relying on the rate of interest to equalize saving and investment is not like relying on the price of apples to equalize demand and supply in the apple market, the analogy proposed by Bernanke and Frank, but like relying on the price of pears to do the job. If there is a shift in the apple-supply schedule, then within the space of apple demand and supply versus apple price, we rely on a movement *along* the apple-demand schedule to restore the balance between demand and supply.

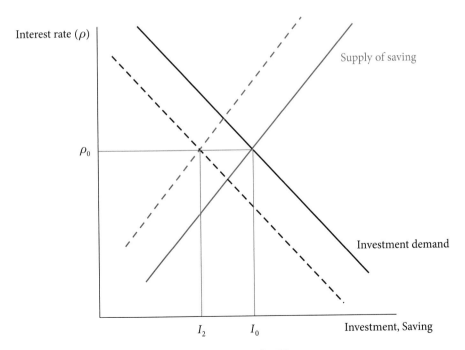

Figure 2.11 Investment demand and saving supply, III.

But if we focus on the price of pears, adjustment comes about mainly through a shift *in* the apple-demand schedule rather than through the price mechanism. Similarly, the adjustment of saving to a shift in the investment-demand schedule comes about through a shift in the saving schedule rather than movement along the original saving schedule.

Formally, it is a matter of adjustment speeds: for the mainstream the interest rate responds quickly to a difference in the demand for investment and the supply of saving, so there is no reason to suppose that output need respond and that the saving schedule need shift when the investment schedule shifts, as it does in Figure 2.11. For Keynes, however, the interest rate, busy equilibrating demands and supplies in markets for financial assets, moves at a glacial rate in response to discrepancies between desired investment and saving; output does the heavy lifting in bringing investment and saving into line. For Keynes,

> The rate of interest is not the "price" which brings into equilibrium the demand for resources to invest with the readiness to abstain from present consumption. It is the "price" which equilibrates the desire to hold wealth in the form of cash with the available quantity of cash. (*The General Theory*, p. 167)[9]

This is as much an empirical as a theoretical proposition. As I argue more fully in chapter 11, one can imagine a world in which the interest rate adjusts desired saving and investment as the mainstream argues. This is a world where there is no market for financial assets apart from current flows, reflected in so-called "on-the-run" bonds, because bonds are always held to maturity. (Viner [1936] suggested this possibility in his critique of *The General Theory* in the *Quarterly Journal of Economics* symposium that I alluded to earlier in this chapter.) In this case, the interest rate would have nothing else to do but adjust desired investment and saving, at least if we assume that bonds are issued only to finance investment. Say's Law would hold, and aggregate demand would be irrelevant for the real economy. No Keynes, and no *Raising Keynes*.

But this is not the world that we inhabit, and it has not been since the dawn of capitalism. The relative magnitudes of asset-market turnover and saving and investment make the mainstream view untenable: the average *daily* volume of domestic bonds in the United States was over $750 billion in 2017 (Securities Industry and Financial Markets Association 2018), whereas the gross *annual* flow of investment (and saving) was just over $3 trillion. Assuming 250 trading days in the year, the ratio of annual volume of bond trading to investment is approximately 60.[10]

In the passage quoted above, Keynes in effect assumes the limiting case, a zero speed of adjustment of the interest rate to flow discrepancies between desired saving and investment. A reasonable simplifying assumption, I would argue, in view of the relative magnitudes of the stocks and the flows.[11]

In 2020, it would be hard to find a defender of the doctrine that supply creates its own demand in exactly the sense of Mill.[12] I expect that Bernanke and Summers would prefer Knut Wicksell as their patron saint, situating their argument in a world in which a "natural" rate of interest emerges from the interplay of the demand for investment and the supply of saving (Wicksell 1958). But Wicksell's logic is essentially no different from Say's and Mill's.

In the final analysis, for all the attention Say's Law received in *The General Theory* and in the post–*General Theory* literature, it turns out to be a bit of a red herring in the sense that it is neither necessary nor sufficient for a full-employment equilibrium. It is not necessary because Modigliani's model shows how full employment is possible in the framework of *The General Theory,* without Say's Law; not sufficient because of the indeterminacy of equilibrium with which it leaves us, as we shall see in just a moment.

First, note that Say's Law is a silent partner in the adjustment story represented in Figure 2.5. Nowhere did the story rely on Say's Law for determining the level of output! Instead, the story, at least the story I told on Viner's behalf, has the adjustment of output depend on the ratio of price to marginal cost, and the adjustment of money wages depend on the level of unemployment. Because there is nothing in the story about the adjustment of nominal prices, the adjustment of money wages is also the adjustment of real wages and real prices.

This story gets the economy to a full-employment, profit-maximizing equilibrium without specifically invoking Say's Law. But Say is nonetheless having his say, by eliminating aggregate demand from any role in moving the economy. To see this, suppose we try a different story, one in which businesswomen adjust prices rather than output. Operating in the framework of Figure 2.5(b), imagine that when the economy is to the left of the GS schedule, businesses reduce prices to stimulate sales. Conversely, when to the right of the GS schedule, businesses raise prices. This would in effect make the actions of business symmetric with the actions of labor, who respond to unemployment by reducing money wages.

The problem with this story is that we are left with *no* story for output adjustment; indeed, Say's Law precludes any story, since wherever output happens to be, it will remain. Indeed, Say's Law suggests that recovery could stall out somewhere before full employment is reached. Suppose the economy happens to find itself at *B* in Figure 2.12. Being to the left of both the GS and LS schedules, both prices and wages are falling. If it so happens that prices and wages are falling at the same percentage rate, the real price will not move.

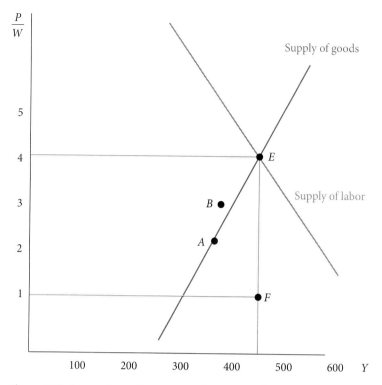

Figure 2.12 Incomplete adjustment: at *B,* prices and wages fall at the same rate.

At the same time, Say's Law guarantees that output won't move! So here, unless we bring in aggregate demand as a separate determinant of output, we have no mechanism whatsoever for moving the economy. Say's Law effectively narrows the adjustment process down to a single algorithm, the one I have attributed to Viner.

Reading Keynes through Mainstream Lenses: The Eclipse

If the 1950s and 1960s were the time in which *The General Theory* was reduced from a general to a special theory, the 1970s were the time in which the frontal attack on Keynes emerged from the shadows. Attacks on Keynes were nothing new—witness the inroads of Milton Friedman's "permanent income hypothesis" (1957) and Franco Modigliani's "life cycle hypothesis" (Modigliani and Brumberg 1954; Ando and Modigliani 1963) into the naïve version of Keynes's consumption function that made income the unique determinant of consumption, about which more in chapter 9—but the success of the attacks of the 1970s was unprecedented.

The ground was prepared by the overreliance of 1960s Keynesians on a simple version of *The General Theory* in which demand alone determined (real) output and income, and the role of supply considerations was limited to determining the price level. This view found empirical support in the work of A. W. Phillips (1958), whose eponymous curve documented an inverse relationship between the level of unemployment and the rate of inflation. An oversimplified reading of *The General Theory* transformed Phillip's empirical regularity into a causal relationship that eliminated the supply side from the picture.

The idea of a trade-off between unemployment and price stability worked tolerably well for more than three decades after the publication of *The General Theory,* but only because this was a period in which aggregate demand was relatively volatile and supply relatively stable. It was once again Milton Friedman who, in his presidential address to the American Economic Association in 1968, planted doubts about the plausibility of a stable Phillips curve in the presence of persistent price inflation. But the mortal blow to the Phillips curve as a causal relationship was dealt by events, not by theory. The 1970s saw supply-side convulsions, mainly oil-price shocks, that led to "stagflation"—higher prices coupled with higher unemployment—the opposite of the Phillips-curve relation. It became clear that the economy could not be modeled in terms of demand varying against the backdrop of fixed supply.

By itself, this need not have led to an eclipse of Keynes's theory. To be sure, supply had to be given its due, and the shift to the aggregate-demand/aggregate-supply framework dates from this period, even though its first use goes back at least to the late 1940s.[13] There were promising new developments dating from Robert Clower's important essay on the relationship between the framework of *The General Theory* and Walrasian general equilibrium (1984 [1963]). Axel Leijonhufvud's *Keynesian Economics and the Economics of Keynes* (1968) argued for a return to the source, to *The General Theory,* which had been misunderstood and distorted by a generation of disciples and critics. This call was not heeded, but the 1970s saw a flowering of innovative approaches, summarized in Mauro Boianovsky and Roger Backhouse (2003).

But in the end these attempts did not save the baby from being thrown out with the bathwater. The neoclassical revival carried the day, to the point that both Keynesians and anti-Keynesians noted the absence of young Keynesian economists from the academy after the 1970s (Blinder 1988, p. 278; Lucas 2013).

The new data with which the old theory had to cope were the final blow, but the counterrevolution had been long in the making. The doubts sown by Modigliani's 1944 article were multiplied by a new insistence on anchoring economic behavior in the rational, calculating, self-interested individual, *homo economicus.* Money-wage rigidity could not easily be reconciled with competitive markets, in which everybody acts in terms of calculation of his or her own advantage.[14]

Robert Lucas coupled competitive markets with the "rational expectations" argument that economic actors all share a correct idea of how the economy works and do not make systematic mistakes in predicting the future—they might be wrong individually, but their errors would cancel each other out, so that the average prediction would hone in on the true values of future output, employment, interest rates, and so forth. In this case, everybody would agree on the equilibrium, and nothing would prevent the economy from moving at once to a new rational-expectations equilibrium if something upset the old one.

The crucial point is that the equilibrium exists not only in the mind of Lucas and God (interchangeable for many economists who came of age in the 1980s) but also in every agent's mind as well. No need at all, therefore, for a dynamic theory of adjustment, the third pillar of the Keynesian revolution. For Lucas and his followers, there was no question about which model of the economy was the correct one: in this crucial respect there was no advance from Pigou's day, in which perfect competition ruled the roost. The only way for aggregate demand to play a role in this world would be if a large fraction of economic agents were to act "irrationally," that is, if most of the people were fooled most of the time.[15]

The rational-expectations equilibrium perspective was ramped up a notch in the "real business cycle" theory put forth by Finn Kydland and Edward Prescott (1982). Kydland–Prescott is the classical dichotomy in overdrive: the shocks that move equilibrium are technological in nature, and aggregate demand has no influence, not even in the short run.

The formalism of real business cycle theory was new, but the ideas were not. As I observed in the previous chapter, "New Classical" economics, the economics of Friedman, Lucas, Kydland, and Prescott, had come full circle, back to the economics in which unemployment was the result of frictions, rigidities, and other imperfections.

The New Classicals and the New Keynesians remain divided to this day— but only on the short run, where the New Keynesians appeal to one form or another of inflexibility to argue somewhat defensively, at least until the 2008 crisis, for the efficacy of monetary and (to a lesser extent) fiscal policy. As far as theory is concerned, a well-established consensus conceding the long run to an anti-Keynesian view of the world is the common face of mainstream economics. At least in terms of consistency, it must be admitted that the New Classicals would appear to have the better of the argument. I have never heard a convincing story why frictions, rigidities, and other imperfections would characterize the short period but can be counted upon to disappear in the long run. One simply has to have faith that (unnamed) forces must be at work to undermine all imperfections. In the long run, the arc of the universe bends not only toward justice, as Martin Luther King supposed, but also toward perfect competition. It is just that these forces work slowly enough that the short period is blemished.

This book takes issue both with the idea that rigidities are responsible for a main result of *The General Theory*—the possibility of an unemployment equilibrium—and with the related idea that the writ of Keynes does not run when we move from the short period to the long. We turn now to Keynes's first-pass model.

— II —

Keynes Defeated

Static Models and the Critics

— 3 —

THE DETERMINATION OF OUTPUT AND EMPLOYMENT

First and Second Passes at Equilibrium

> Given the propensity to consume and the rate of new investment, there will be only one level of employment consistent with equilibrium. . . . There is no reason in general for expecting it to be *equal* to full employment. The effective demand associated with full employment is a special case, only realised when the propensity to consume and the inducement to invest stand in a particular relationship to one another. This particular relationship, which corresponds to the assumptions of the classical theory, is in a sense an optimum relationship. But it can only exist when, by accident or design, current investment provides an amount of demand just equal to the excess of the aggregate supply price of the output resulting from full employment over what the community will choose to spend on consumption when it is fully employed.
>
> —JOHN MAYNARD KEYNES

Keynes's first goal, as we have seen, was to establish that even in the absence of frictions, a capitalist economy might not settle down at a point where every willing worker had a job, and the productive apparatus of the economy was fully utilized. The style of *The General Theory,* if not the argument, is of a bygone era and was uncongenial even in 1936 to the twenty-somethings who would become the backbone of the Keynesian Revolution. The big difference between Keynes, between the rhetorical style of his generation, and the style of subsequent generations is that there are no models in today's sense of the term. Indeed, in the twenty-first century, economics students find *The General Theory* unrecognizable as economic argument. What passes for a model is no more than descriptions of how variables relate to one another, a list of ingredients without the recipe for baking them into a cake. Our task here is to bake the cake, or rather to bake a couple of cakes based on alternative ways of putting the ingredients together.

Stripped to its essence, the theory developed in *The General Theory* hinges on five relationships: (1) the relationship between the rate of interest and investment demand; (2) the relationship between the level of output and desired saving; (3) the relationship between the level of output and the transactions demand for money; (4) the relationship between the asset demand for money (what Keynes called the speculative demand) and the rate of interest;[1] (5) finally, the relationship between goods supply and the real price. (Keynes uses the term "wage units" for real price.)

The first and the third of these relationships could not have upset the most orthodox reader of *The General Theory;* the first is the standard stuff of received doctrine, in the form of Irving Fisher's theory of investment, and the third is the so-called quantity theory of money, which remains a part of the monetary side of *The General Theory,* but not the whole. Neither is the second relationship necessarily controversial, though it would be challenged by Milton Friedman (1957) and Franco Modigliani (Modigliani and Brumberg 1954; Ando and Modigliani 1963). In 1936 it would have been argued that the dependence of saving on income is irrelevant because, as was pointed out in chapter 2, the interest rate does the heavy lifting in equilibrating investment demand and the supply of saving. Similarly, the fifth relationship is unremarkable: the basis of supply decisions in a competitive economy is profit maximization, and the supply schedule is the schedule of the real marginal cost of output.

This leaves the fourth relationship, what Keynes calls the liquidity-preference theory of interest. It is in fact the interrelationship between liquidity preference and the theory of investment demand that is the principal innovation of *The General Theory.* The financial and real sectors of the economy are linked by the two-sided nature of interest, one side its role in the financial sector via liquidity preference and the other its role in the real sector via its impact on investment demand. Together with the other relationships, the dual role of interest leads to a central role for aggregate demand in determining the level of output and employment.

As those who have followed the history of *The General Theory* from its birth know, the translation of the key relationships into models is not as straightforward as it might appear if we start looking back from 2020, or from even a few years after publication. In the first place, besides what I have identified as key relationships, there are less important relationships. For example, relatively early on, the post–*General Theory* literature started taking output to be a single, homogeneous good, in keeping with the macro orientation of Keynes's project. But the first reviews (for example, James Meade [1937]) paid considerable attention to the relationship between the output of investment goods and the output of consumption goods, as well as to their relative prices.

It was by no means obvious which were the core relationships and which were peripheral to Keynes's argument.

Then there is what is left out. For now we shall stay squarely in the short run, a period in which we do not need to concern ourselves with the growth of either the capital stock or the labor force. So there is nothing about these relationships in the list. This simplifies our task. Furthermore, instead of relating wages and labor supply, as in the mainstream theory sketched in the previous chapter, Keynes simply posits a fixed money wage. Despite his insistence that this is an assumption made merely to simplify the exposition, the basis of Modigliani's (1944) contrary assertion was that money-wage rigidity is essential to Keynes's argument. We shall turn to Modigliani's argument in chapter 4.

There remains the problem of moving from theory to model. The difficulty is that there are more variables than there are relationships. This means that some of the relevant variables have to be specified in advance, predetermined. Transactions demand and liquidity preference together specify a relationship between the amount of money required to grease the wheels of commerce and satisfy the asset demands of wealth holders on the one hand and output and interest rates on the other. But this leaves us in the dark as to whether the relationships specify a demand for money based on levels of output and interest, or levels of output and interest based on a supply of money.

Since Keynes's monetary theory is an outgrowth of the quantity theory, albeit with significant modification, we might hope that the earlier theory would provide some guidance. Alas, this is not to be. Despite Milton Friedman's assertion that the quantity theory is and always has been a theory of money demand, there is considerable ambiguity about whether the M in $MV = PY$ represents demand or supply.

In point of fact, Keynes presents ingredients for two models. A first-pass model, which we shall investigate now, assumes a given rate of interest, derives the corresponding level of output, and then calculates money demand from the needs of businessmen and wealth holders. A second-pass model, which we shall develop later in this chapter, reverses the causality, taking the money supply as given and deriving from it both output and interest rate.[2]

Baking the First-Pass Cake: The Real Side

We consider each of the five relationships—investment demand, supply of saving, transactions demand for money, asset demand, and goods supply—in turn. The relationship between the rate of interest and investment demand, $I = I(\rho)$, Keynes's "marginal efficiency of capital," is shown in Figure 3.1. The higher the rate of interest—seen here as a cost of investing in plant, equipment, structures—the lower is the level of investment. At a rate of interest equal to ρ_0, the corresponding level of investment is 100.

The easiest way to think about the "marginal efficiency of capital" schedule is to imagine an array of potential investment projects, ranked by their respective rates of return.[3] For each value of the rate of interest, ρ, the corresponding amount of investment demand is the total capital cost of all projects with rates of return at least equal to ρ. The marginal efficiency of capital is the rate of return on the marginal project.

The rate of interest ρ is the hurdle rate that projects must meet or surpass to be worth undertaking. If ρ is the rate at which businessmen discount investment returns, projects will normally have positive present values if their rates of return exceed ρ. For a rationally calculating, profit-maximizing, businessman, the rate of interest is the opportunity cost of capital. He makes a comparison of the return on capital expenditure and the return on a bond yielding the going rate of interest and opts for the subset of projects with higher returns than are available in the bond market. In Keynes's words:

> There is always an alternative to the ownership of real capital-assets, namely the ownership of money and debts; so that the prospective yield with which the producers of new investment have to be content cannot fall below the standard set by the current rate of interest. (*The General Theory*, pp. 212–213)

Or, equivalently (for our purposes at least), a businesswoman can be assumed to be comparing the returns of capital expenditure over and above operating

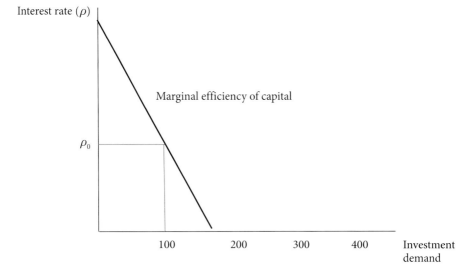

Figure 3.1 Investment demand as a function of the rate of interest.

costs with the interest and principal payments she has to make on loans she incurs for the sake of investment.

The second relationship, that between saving and output, is more novel—not, I have observed, in asserting that the level of desired saving depends on the level of output, but in asserting the importance of this relationship. Equality of desired saving and investment means that the circular flow from output and income on the one hand to expenditure on the other is uninterrupted: any leakage from the circuit running from output and income to consumption expenditure is made up by expenditure on new capital goods, that is, by investment. But what guarantees the equality of desired investment and desired saving, and therefore of income and expenditure, is not the interest rate. Instead, it is the level of income itself. Keynes, as we saw in the last chapter, rejects the mainstream theory, whereby desired saving and desired investment are quickly if not immediately equated by the interest rate, arguing instead that it is the dependence of saving on income that ensures the equality of saving and investment. Say's Law becomes an equilibrium condition for expenditure and income that is satisfied by a unique level of output rather than a relationship between expenditure and income that holds for any level of output.

We start from Figure 3.2, which depicts the relationship between real income and real expenditure. Assume that out of every dollar of income $0.75 is spent on consumption goods. In Keynes's terminology, the marginal pro-

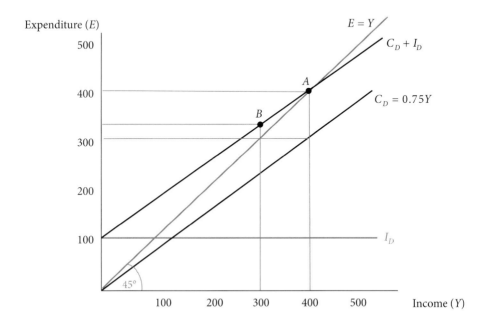

Figure 3.2 Consumption and investment determine aggregate demand.

pensity to consume is 0.75. This relationship is represented by the schedule $C_D = 0.75Y$, the consumption function in Keynesian jargon. The gap between income and consumption expenditure is given by the distance between the 45-degree line—on which expenditure and income are equal—and the consumption function. Investment constitutes additional expenditure, here assumed to be 100, independent of the level of income. The schedule labeled $C_D + I_D$, the expenditure function, represents for each level of income the amount that would be spent. Aggregate demand is given by the point on this schedule where there is no leakage from the circular flow, or more accurately, where leakages from consumption expenditure are just matched by injections of investment demand. Graphically, this occurs where the expenditure function crosses the 45-degree line, at $A = <400, 400>$.

Aggregate demand is thus a stationary, or equilibrium, level of expenditure and income, the level of income at which Say's Law holds. At any other point, where expenditure and income are not equal, the dynamics of the system will force a change in both. Suppose that economy were at $B = <300, 325>$, where 300 is being produced and distributed as income, but 325 is being spent on consumption and investment together. What happens as a result of this imbalance? The first result will be that goods will fly off of the shelves faster than they are being replaced. What happens next? The logic of Keynes's previous book, *A Treatise on Money*, was that prices will rise.

But a group of young faculty members at the University of Cambridge—the "circus"—who had gathered to digest and analyze the *Treatise* suggested that there was more to the story—as did Richard Kahn (1931) in his pioneering article on the multiplier, the indirect repercussions on employment of government spending.[4] A key passage reads:

> At normal times, when productive resources are fully employed, the supply of consumption goods in the short period is highly inelastic. . . . But at times of intense depression when nearly all industries have at their disposal a large surplus of unused plant and labour, the supply curve is likely to be very elastic. The amount of secondary employment is then large and the rise of prices is small. (p. 182)

In the *Treatise* Keynes had glimpsed the possibility that an imbalance between expenditure and income would lead to a change in employment and output. His parable of a "banana economy" argued that, in the absence of a corresponding expansion in investment expenditure, a thrift campaign would lead to a downward spiral in employment and output that would end only when the balance between desired saving and investment was restored or the economy bottomed out at zero:

There will be no position of equilibrium until either (*a*) all production ceases and the entire population starves to death; or (*b*) the thrift campaign is called off or peters out as a result of the growing poverty; or (*c*) investment is stimulated by some means or another so that its cost no longer lags behind the rate of saving. (1930, vol. 1, p. 178)

Missing from Keynes's parable is the analysis of the process by which a fall (or a rise) in output and income is self-limiting, in the sense that the change in output would itself correct the imbalance between investment and saving.[5]

As we shall see, there are at least two different ways of thinking about how an excess of expenditure relative to output drives changes in output. One is "Marshallian," in which output responds to a more favorable relationship between prices and costs (Viner's thinking, as reconstructed in chapter 2). A second, "Walrasian," way of thinking is that when inventories are drawn down to satisfy higher expenditure, the first response is to replenish inventories.

We shall examine both these stories in some detail in chapter 5, in preparation for the dynamic models laid out in chapters 6 and 7. For now, suffice it to say that the Marshallian story is a better fit with the story Keynes tells in his banana parable, a story continued by Joan Robinson (1933a, 1933b). Keynes sees the collapse of the banana economy beginning with a situation in which "the selling price of bananas [has] fallen and not their cost of production" (1930, vol. 1, p. 177). Robinson's starting point for an increase in output is a situation in which "prices are in excess of costs" (1933b, p. 24). In both these stories the imbalance of expenditure and income changes prices, and the imbalance between prices and costs changes output.

Nonetheless, when expenditures and incomes are out of line, the assumption that the impact on output is direct and immediate makes for an easier story of adjustment.[6] In Figure 3.2, let us suppose for concreteness that when *E* equals 325, orders increase by the full amount of the shortfall in goods, 25. This leads to greater production (325 in place of 300), greater incomes (325), and more spending on consumer goods ($243.75 = 0.75 \times 325$ in place of $225 = 0.75 \times 300$). But this is only the beginning. There is still a shortfall, since spending, including spending on investment as well as on consumption, is now $343.75 (= 243.75 + 100)$, whereas production is only 325. So the process repeats with businesses increasing orders by 18.75 to make up for the shortfall. And the new, higher, level of output and income leads to even more spending.

There are in effect an infinite number of rounds of additional expenditure and income, but each adds progressively less to the total because at each round a proportion, in our case one-quarter, of the newly generated income escapes the circular flow, ending up as saving. If we ignore the time dimension, and conflate all these rounds into a moment of time, or if we imagine that the original injection of spending is repeated over and over again, we will find that the process converges to the equilibrium $A = <400, 400>$, where expenditure and income are equal, and there is no pressure of sales to expand output further.

It is important to be clear what an equilibrium like A represents—and what it does not represent. It *is* a point of rest with respect to the balance of expenditure and income; that is, it represents the level of aggregate demand—the level of income at which Say's Law holds—corresponding to the given assumptions about consumption, saving, and investment. It is *not* an equilibrium for the economy, or for the "goods market," as a generation of Keynes's followers (myself included once upon a time) were wont to label it, at least not without assuming very special circumstances. For we have, so far, said nothing about supply.

Equivalently, aggregate demand is the level of income and output at which desired saving S_D and desired investment I_D are equal, as in Figure 3.3. This follows directly from the definitions of expenditure and income. In our model expenditure is equal to desired consumption plus desired investment: $E = C_D + I_D$. Since by definition $S_D = Y - C_D$, $Y = E$ implies $I_D = S_D$ and vice versa.

This equilibrium condition is different from the definitional identity $I \equiv S$,

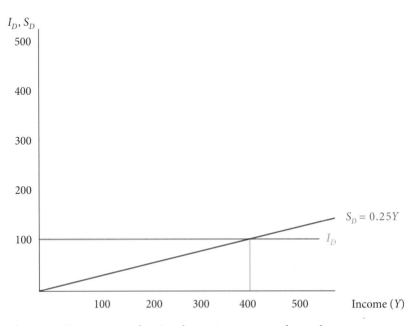

Figure 3.3 Investment and saving determine aggregate demand.

which follows from three accounting facts: output is the sum of consumption and investment, income is the sum of consumption and saving, and output is equal to income. Algebraically, we have $Y = C + I$ and $Y = C + S$, so $I = S$ whatever the level of Y.

Except at equilibrium, actual investment (I), which includes changes in inventories whether desired or not, will differ from desired investment (I_D), which includes only desired changes in inventories. This difference is crucial, at least for the Walrasian story. In a Walrasian world, moving from B to A hinges on unintended reductions in inventories triggering the expansion of output; the opposite, an unintended accumulation of inventories as expenditure falls short of income, moves the economy downward.

Figure 3.3 facilitates two important insights into Keynes's conception of aggregate demand: the central role of investment demand and the concept of the multiplier. Consider Figure 3.4, which reproduces Figure 3.3 with the addition of a second investment schedule, represented by the dashed line at 125. The construction of Figure 3.4 tells us that an increase in investment demand of 25 increases aggregate demand by 100, from 400 to 500. The original impulse is *multiplied* by 4.

How does this work? The basic idea is the same as the idea behind the adjustment process in Figure 3.2, from the disequilibrium B to the equilibrium A. The original increase of expenditure of 25—let us say, to build a factory—is

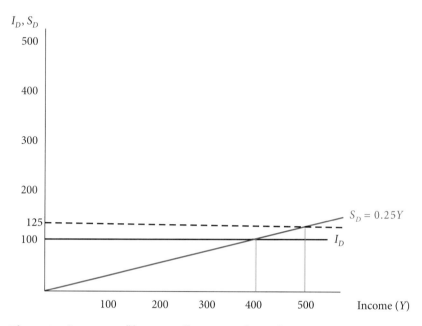

Figure 3.4 Investment "determines" aggregate demand.

in turn partially spent on consumption by the workers, managers, and business owners, who receive wages, salaries, and profits from the new construction activity. This leads to additional production to provide the newly demanded consumption goods and services. This new activity in turn creates new income and new demand. Since there are no supply constraints (yet), the process is limited only by "leakages" from the chain of spending, in the present simplified case, leakages into saving. Formally, we have the change in Y (ΔY) equal to

$$25 + (0.75 \times 25) + (0.75 \times 0.75 \times 25) + \cdots,$$

which, as a geometric sum, adds to 100. In general, if the spending by income recipients out of each additional dollar of income is a uniform amount, which we shall denote MPC, for *m*arginal *p*ropensity to *c*onsume, we have

$$\Delta Y = 1 + MPC + MPC^2 + MPC^3 + \cdots = \frac{1}{1 - MPC}.$$

Here the original impulse, the additional investment, is assumed to be 1 rather than 25.

If—and this is a big if—the propensity to consume is given, then we can interpret investment as driving aggregate demand and determining saving. Since aggregate demand is the point at which $I_D = S_D$, the level of I_D must also be the level of S_D. Thus, for a given level of investment, the level of output and income must be just enough to generate this level of desired saving—and no more. Change I_D and S_D changes by the same amount because the level of income adjusts to produce the required change in desired saving.

Putting together the investment demand function and the saving function in Figure 3.5, we have the real side of the first-pass model, that is, a relationship between the interest rate and the level of output.

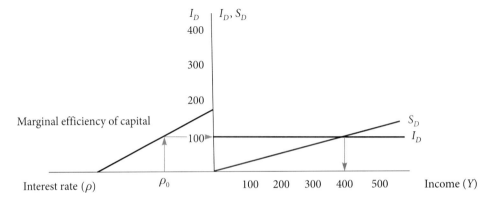

Figure 3.5 Aggregate demand for given interest rate.

Baking the First-Pass Cake: The Financial Side

The other side of Keynes's first-pass model is the relationship between the interest rate, the level of output, and the demand for money. For Keynes the demand for money comes from both the transactions associated with any given level of real output and the desires of agents to hold assets in liquid form. Transactions are assumed to require a proportionate amount of money, M_1, the constant of proportionality depending on both the price level P and a variety of institutional factors summarized in the parameter α, which is the inverse of the output-velocity of money:[7]

$$M_1 = \alpha PY.$$

As far as transactions are concerned, Keynes did not stray from the orthodox view reflected in the quantity theory of money.

With regard to the second source of the demand for money, *The General Theory* breaks new ground: Keynes creates his novel liquidity-preference theory of interest from the assumption that there is a relationship between the interest rate ρ and the amount of money, M_2, agents wish to hold in their portfolios of assets:

$$M_2 = \beta(\rho)A.$$

$\beta(\rho)$ is agents' desired ratio of liquid assets, M_2, to total nominal wealth, A. The picture is in Figure 3.6.

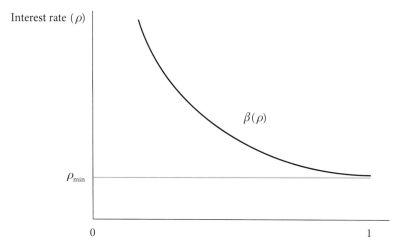

Figure 3.6 Liquidity preference as a function of the interest rate.

The liquidity-preference schedule $\beta(\rho)$ has two salient properties. First, desired cash is inversely related to the rate of interest. For Keynes, interest is the reward for giving up immediate access to wealth, so that the higher the interest rate, the less desirable, relatively, is liquidity. Second, the proportion of wealth agents wish to hold in liquid form goes to 100 percent at a positive rate of interest, ρ_{min}, rather than at $\rho = 0$. This second condition is the form the so-called liquidity trap takes in a model in which the only financial assets are bonds and cash. We take up both aspects of the liquidity-preference schedule, the downward slope and the positive minimum interest rate, in chapters 11 and 12.

Following Keynes, at least for now, we assume that wealth consists of two parts, bonds reflecting the nominal value of the capital stock, PK, and the amount of money in wealth portfolios, M_2. We assume bonds are consols (after their origin as "consolidated annuities" in eighteenth-century Britain), commitments to pay a fixed yearly nominal sum, R, forever. For this commitment to be invariant in real terms with respect to the price of goods and real capital, we assume that the number of bonds $\bar{B}$ varies proportionately with P. That is, we assume the rentier claim on real income, $R\bar{B}$, is independent of the price level, which is the appropriate normalization in the comparative-statics framework of this chapter and the next. For simplicity, assume there is one bond for each dollar's worth of capital, so that $\bar{B} = PK$.

There is another price to reckon with, the price of bonds P_B. In general, the bond price is a decreasing function of the rate of interest, but with the assumption that bonds are consols, the relationship between P_B and ρ is a particularly simple one, namely, $P_B = R/\rho$, so that the relationship is the rectangular hyperbola in Figure 3.7.

With assets limited to bonds and cash we have

$$A = P_B(\rho)\bar{B} + \bar{M}_2 = P_B(\rho)PK + \bar{M}_2,$$

where $\bar{M}_2$ is the quantity of money available for wealth portfolios. For equilibrium the demand for money must be equal to the supply, which is to say,

$$M_2 = \beta(\rho)\left[P_B(\rho)\bar{B} + \bar{M}_2\right] = \beta(\rho)\left[P_B(\rho)PK + \bar{M}_2\right],$$

$$M_2 = \bar{M}_2 = \frac{\beta(\rho)}{1 - \beta(\rho)}P_B(\rho)\bar{B} = \frac{\beta(\rho)}{1 - \beta(\rho)}P_B(\rho)PK.$$

We put asset and transactions demands together in Figure 3.8, in which the second quadrant combines Figures 3.6 and 3.7 to produce the liquidity-preference schedule. The first quadrant pictures transactions demand. Given the level of aggregate demand $Y = 400$ and interest rate ρ_0, we have $M_1 = 300$ and $M_2 = 200$. In consequence $M = 500$.

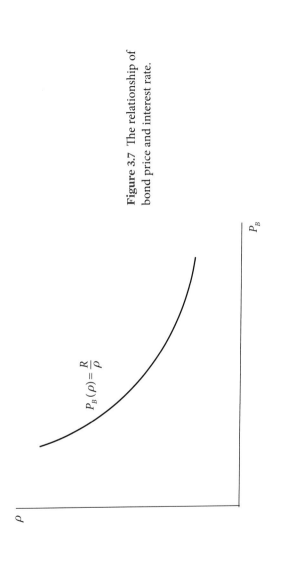

Figure 3.7 The relationship of bond price and interest rate.

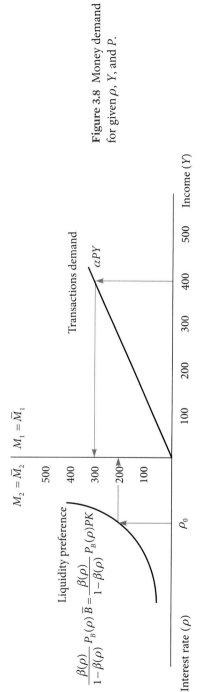

Figure 3.8 Money demand for given ρ, Y, and P.

Baking the First-Pass Cake: Combining the
Real and the Financial Sides of the Model

We now can put the real and financial sides of aggregate demand together in the form of a single diagram with four quadrants: flip Figure 3.8 on the horizontal axis and marry it to Figure 3.5 to obtain Figure 3.9. Figure 3.9 maps a given interest rate, in this case ρ_0, to corresponding demands for real output and money, $Y = 400$ and $M = 500$.

Figure 3.9 holds the price level as well as the wage level constant. What happens if we vary the price level, while holding the wage constant in money terms? If the price level increases from P_0 to P_1 as in Figure 3.10, the dashed lines represent the new transactions-demand and liquidity-preference schedules. At the higher price level, the same interest rate and aggregate demand generate a higher money demand, M_1 increasing from 300 to more than 350, and M_2 increasing from 200 to 300.

In the first-pass model, price changes do not affect the real side of the picture—desired consumption, saving, and investment. For this reason, if we relate aggregate demand to the price level, as in Figure 3.11, we find that the AD schedule is a vertical line. Here we start from a given interest rate (and ignore various complications that will be introduced in later chapters), so output is determined solely by aggregate demand and is independent of the price level.

But we are not free to vary the price level arbitrarily; in the first-pass model the price level is determined as part of the equilibrium configuration by a GS schedule. Indeed, in the first-pass model this is the *only* reason that goods supply matters. By virtue of the assumption of perfect competition, the supply curve, as we have seen, is simply the economy's marginal-cost curve. In Figure 3.12, which adds a GS schedule to the AD schedule of Figure 3.9, the equilibrium price level is 3.5. Observe that by fixing the nominal wage rate ($W = W_0$), the nominal price level P fixes the real price.

There is some irony in this representation of the economy in the light of the transformation of Keynes by friends and enemies from critical theorist to theorist of one more version of sand in the wheels. In the mainstream view, the AD schedule has a negative slope and the aggregate-supply schedule is vertical—except in the short run, when sand gets in the wheels. In Figure 3.12 the AD schedule is vertical, and the GS schedule has a positive slope. In contrast with the mainstream view, in which supply rules the roost and demand matters only to determine the price level, supply here matters only to determine prices, the nominal price level and the real wage. Output is determined solely on the demand side!

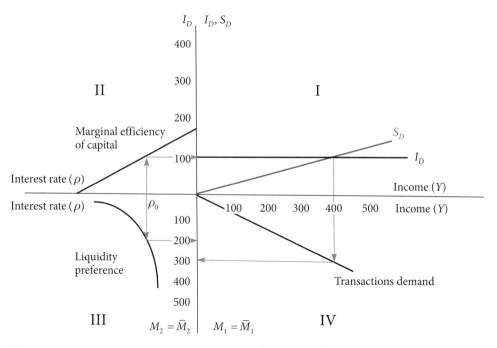

Figure 3.9 Aggregate demand and money demand determined by the interest rate.

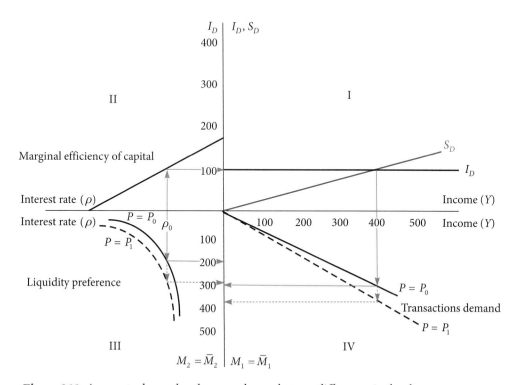

Figure 3.10 Aggregate demand and money demand at two different price levels.

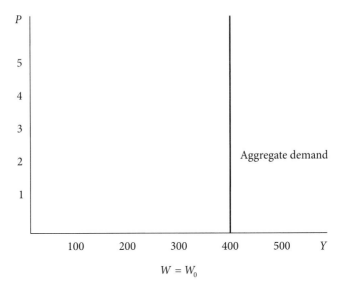

Figure 3.11 Aggregate demand at a given interest rate.

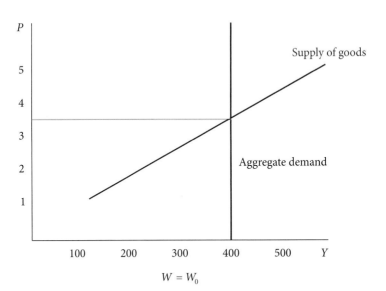

Figure 3.12 Aggregate demand and goods supply at a given interest rate.

Unemployment in the First-Pass Model

The equilibrium in Figure 3.12 determines a level of employment—the number of workers required to produce 400 units of output—but it says nothing about the level of unemployment. In fact, *The General Theory* begins with a somewhat convoluted definition of involuntary unemployment, which we shall examine in the first appendix to this chapter. Suffice it to say here that Keynes rejects the core idea of the mainstream LS schedule, which is that the supply of labor, and hence full employment, depends on the real wage.

Whatever the merits of Keynes's strictures on the mainstream depiction of the supply of labor, his critique does not fit very well with his avowed purpose of meeting mainstream economics on its own turf as far as the structure of markets is concerned. For that reason I shall out-Keynes Keynes in assuming that there is no money illusion and no concern with relative wages so that, as the mainstream argues, the supply of labor depends on the real wage.

It is not clear how much importance Keynes attached to his own characterization of unemployment despite the prominence he gives to laying it out. In any case, the cutting edge of his characterization, namely, that unemployment can exist without any pressure on money wages, is a provisional assumption, scaffolding rather than part of the building, which allows him to lay out the core ideas of *The General Theory*. He clearly states his intention to abandon this assumption when the building is complete and the scaffolding no longer necessary. In his own words:

> We shall assume that the money-wage and other factor costs are constant per unit of labor employed. But this simplification, with which we shall dispense later, is introduced solely to facilitate the exposition. The essential character of the argument is precisely the same whether or not money-wages, etc., are liable to change. (*The General Theory*, p. 27)

This is not quite accurate. In one sense the argument needs serious recasting, a major purpose of this book! Reconstructing (or constructing) a general theory that reflects Keynes's intuition but is intelligible to present-day students of economics is better served by sticking to the standard definition of unemployment, competitive labor supply and all. It may bear repeating that this is not to deny the existence of rigidities and other imperfections in the labor market, but to make it clear that Keynes's insights about the role of aggregate demand do not depend on imperfections. In this framework, unemployment will exist if the equilibrium of aggregate demand and goods supply in Figure 3.12 lies to the left of the supply of labor.

Figure 3.13 adds the supply of labor (in terms of the goods the labor will produce) at the price 3.5, one point on the LS schedule. At $P = 3.5$ and $W = W_0$ (in other words, at the real price $3.5/W_0$), workers are ready, willing, and able to produce 500. The output gap between the AD = GS equilibrium and full employment is 100 ($= 500 - 400$).

In the first-pass model there is no mechanism that automatically leads to full employment. Indeed, even if the economy happens to find itself at full employment, it will not stay there. Suppose the economy is initially at $F = $ <450, 4> in Figure 3.14. At this point there is both full employment and profit maximization, but the economy will move away from this point to the AD-GS equilibrium, $E = $ <400, 3.5> as long as aggregate demand remains at 400. Expenditure falls short of income and output when $Y = 450$, and one way or another this sets in motion a decline in output.

The assumption of a given money wage $W = W_0$ precludes the reaction that the mainstream relies upon to sustain its version of equilibrium, namely, a fall in money wages whenever unemployment is present. It is true that at the AD-GS equilibrium the marginal disutility of labor for the unemployed is less than the going real wage $W_0/3.5$, but nothing follows from this inequality. With aggregate demand driving the economy, full-employment equilibrium is possible only if aggregate demand can be expanded to the level at which the GS schedule and the LS schedule intersect. Figure 3.14 shows the new AD schedule as a dashed line. The real wage at F is lower than the real wage at E, but this change is the consequence of the movement from E to F rather than a cause—a thermometer rather than a thermostat.

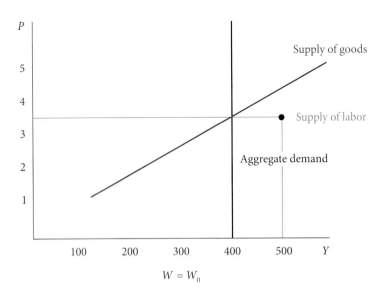

Figure 3.13 Aggregate demand, goods supply, and labor supply.

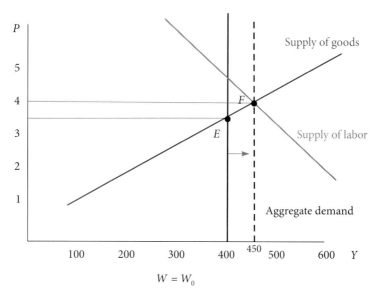

Figure 3.14 Aggregate demand, goods supply, and labor supply: moving to full employment.

Figure 3.15 indicates the changes in the interest rate, investment, and money required for the full-employment equilibrium at F in Figure 3.14: the interest rate has to be ρ_1 in order to coax out investment demand equal to 112.5, which is the amount of investment needed to generate a demand for output equal to 450. At the higher level of output, the real marginal cost is also higher, so the price level has to be higher to ensure that producers are maximizing profits. Both because prices are higher and because output is higher, transactions require a greater amount of money, and the lower rate of interest and the higher price level also drive up the asset demand for money. Money demand totals almost 900, with M_1 just shy of 400 and M_2 near 500.

Monetary Policy and Its Limits

We can, in the spirit of comparative statics, imagine a planet on which the central bank sets the interest rate at ρ_1 and fixes the money supply to accommodate money demand at this interest rate. Here the possibility of full employment depends on whether the central bank has sufficient flexibility with regard to ρ and on whether investment demand is sufficiently responsive to ρ—in Keynes's terms, upon liquidity preference and the marginal efficiency of capital. Because of the liquidity trap the central bank cannot drive the interest rate below $\rho_{\min}$, which could prevent the necessary expansion of in-

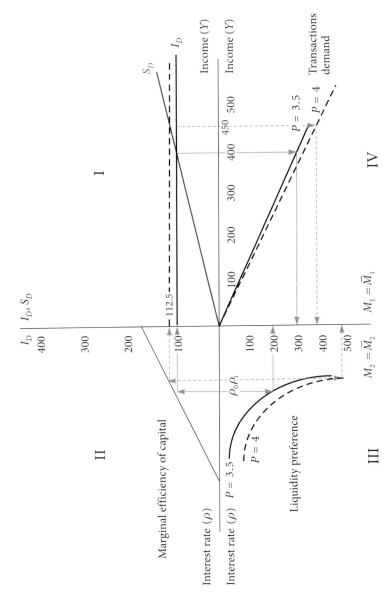

Figure 3.15 Interest, investment, aggregate demand, and the price level: moving to full employment.

vestment demand—so could the inelasticity of the marginal-efficiency schedule: even at a zero rate of interest, there could be insufficient investment demand.

Figure 3.16 shows both possibilities. As the liquidity-preference schedule is drawn, ρ_{min} is too high for investment demand compatible with full employment. With $\rho = \rho_{min}$ investment demand is only 60, which, given a multiplier of 4, generates aggregate demand of 240.

Even if there were no liquidity trap and the interest rate could be driven to zero, the demand for investment may be too low to generate the aggregate demand corresponding to a full-employment level of output and income: in Figure 3.16 investment demand is only 80 at $\rho = 0$, and aggregate demand is 320.

Keynes himself thought a floor to the hurdle rate of more theoretical than practical significance. "Whilst this limiting case might become practically important in future, I know of no example of it hitherto" (*The General Theory,* p. 207). Both in *The General Theory* and in later writings, Keynes put more emphasis on the inelasticity of the marginal efficiency of capital schedule. He didn't go quite as far as stagnationist Keynesians (like Alvin Hansen) who thought that capitalism was on the verge of exhausting its possibilities for profitable private investment even at very low rates of interest, thinking that it would take decades rather than years for the stagnationist vision to be realized (*The General Theory,* chap. 24, sec. 2).[8]

The policy takeaway is that eliminating involuntary unemployment might require the government to go beyond monetary policy in order to compensate for the limits of private investment demand. Although Keynes had long advocated deficits—we have seen that he was hardly alone in this—in *The General Theory* he is vague about the means, saying only,

> I expect to see the State . . . taking an ever greater responsibility for directly organizing investment; since it seems likely that the fluctuations in the market estimation of the marginal efficiency of different types of capital . . . will be too great to be offset by any practicable changes in the rate of interest. (p. 164)

Indeed, although the term "fiscal policy" occurs several times in *The General Theory,* there is no systematic discussion of the implications of the overall argument for taxing and government spending.[9] The theoretical justification for using fiscal policy to compensate for shortages in private demand was conceived in the womb of *The General Theory,* but—see chapter 14—it was Abba Lerner rather than Keynes who spelled out the radical implications of *The General Theory* for fiscal policy.

Besides the doubt it casts on the efficacy of monetary policy, the first-pass

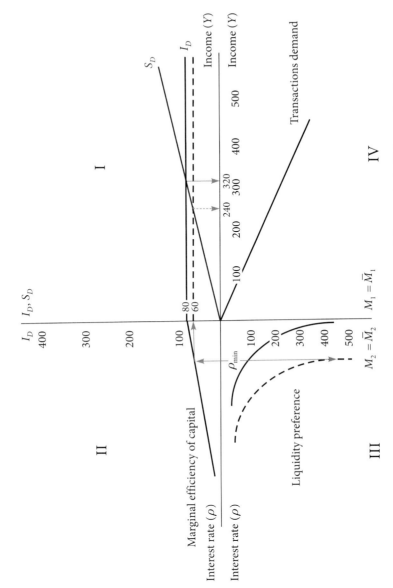

Figure 3.16 Aggregate demand limited by liquidity preference and the marginal efficiency of capital.

model lays out a very different approach from the mainstream story about the determination of output and employment, in which supply-side factors are no longer in the driver's seat. Keynes's first-pass model is one in which the starring role goes to aggregate demand, to the point that supply matters only in determining the price level. Full employment may be achievable but it requires the visible hand of government to manage demand; the self-correcting market mechanism is permanently AWOL.

The Second-Pass Model: Capitalism Left to Its Own Devices

Keynes's critical intention went beyond providing an apparatus for showing the possibilities and limitations of monetary policy. He intended no less than the overthrow of basic mainstream doctrine that a capitalist economy left to itself would reach an equilibrium in which each and every market—including the labor market—would have a willing buyer for every willing seller, an equilibrium in which involuntary unemployment was impossible. The first-pass model doesn't accomplish this, for it takes as given two parameters—the interest rate and the money wage—whose flexibility the mainstream considered essential in leading the economy to full employment. Keynes obliges with a second-pass model, in which the money supply rather than the interest rate is given. For now, the money wage is still assumed to be given; for Keynes this remains a "simplification . . . introduced solely to facilitate the exposition" (*The General Theory*, p. 28).

The change involved in relaxing the assumption of a fixed interest rate is enough to complicate the determination of output and employment: although Keynes claims that the demand side of the model continues to determine the levels of output and employment in the second-pass model (*The General Theory*, p. 247), we shall see that this result no longer holds. The consequence of reversing the direction of causality in the liquidity-preference schedule is that aggregate demand varies with the price level, and equilibrium output and employment are jointly determined by aggregate demand and goods supply.

The easiest way to enter into the logic of the second-pass model is to view the equilibrium represented in Figures 3.9 and 3.12 in reverse. Instead of fixing the interest rate and deducing the implications for money *demand,* we fix the money *supply* and examine the consequences for the interest rate, along with output, prices, and wages.[10]

Go back to Figure 3.9 and the arrows that run from the interest rate ρ_0 to the components of the overall money demand $M_1 = 300$ and $M_2 = 200$. The first question in constructing the second-pass model is how to go in the opposite direction, how to determine the interest rate, and therewith investment demand and output, starting from an exogenously given money supply.

The first problem is that money is money. How do we know the market will break up a given total, like 500, into the appropriate components, money for transactions ($M_1 = 300$) and money as an asset ($M_2 = 200$)? More generally, for an arbitrary total money supply, how do we know what the appropriate division is between money to facilitate transactions and money to hold as an asset?

We shall deploy Hicks's (1937) IS-LM model to answer these questions. The key insight behind IS-LM is that financial and real variables provide separate and distinct relationships between the interest rate and the level of income (output), both of which have to be satisfied to establish the level of aggregate demand.

Look first at the financial relationships that connect the transactions demand to income and the asset-market equilibrium to the interest rate. Assume the total money supply is given as 500. Figure 3.17 reproduces the relevant parts of Figure 3.9 with one modification: although we continue to measure asset money in quadrant three from "north" to "south," in quadrant four we measure transactions money from bottom to top, south to north. The point $M_1 = \bar{M}_1 = 0$ corresponds to the point $M_2 = \bar{M}_2 = 500$ in quadrant three. In effect, we deduct money required for transactions from the overall money supply to find the money available for holding as an asset. This allows us to trace out the relationship between the interest rate and the level of aggregate demand consistent with financial equilibrium, that is, consistent with the total demand for money (asset + transactions) being equal to total supply.

Divide the total money supply, $\bar{M} = 500$, into $\bar{M}_1 = 300$ and $\bar{M}_2 = 200$. Now ask what the implications of this division are for the interest rate and the level of income, that is, what levels of the interest rate and the level of income are compatible with this division and thus with each other? Going up the vertical axis from $\bar{M}_1 = 0$ to $\bar{M}_1 = 300$, we follow the horizontal arrow to its intersection with the transactions-demand schedule: $\bar{M}_1 = 300$ supports an income of 400. At the same time, $\bar{M}_1 = 300$ leaves 200 to satisfy the demand for money as an asset. We move to the left from $\bar{M}_2 = 200$ to the point of intersection with the liquidity-preference schedule, namely $\rho = \rho_0$. Translating this through quadrant two, we can finally relate the rate of interest and the level of aggregate demand to one another in quadrant one. Specifically, the division of the money supply into $\bar{M}_1 = 300$ and $\bar{M}_2 = 200$ corresponds to the point $<400, \rho_0>$ in the space of $Y \times \rho$. (We actually knew this already since this composition of money demand emerged in the first-pass model from the assumption $\rho = \rho_0$, which led to an aggregate demand of 400.)

Now keep the money supply constant but change the composition of demand. For example, set $M_1 = 200$ and $M_2 = 300$. This generates a second point in quadrant one, as shown in Figure 3.18.

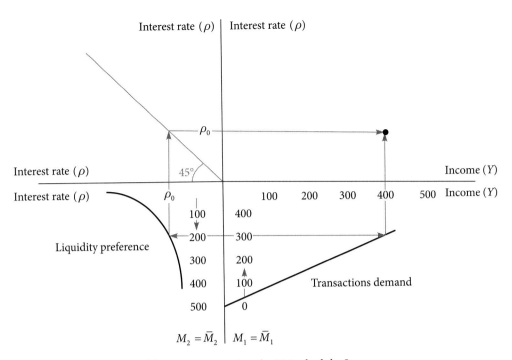

Figure 3.17 Financial equilibrium: constructing the LM schedule, I.

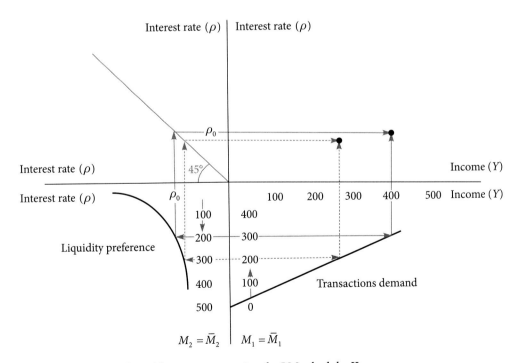

Figure 3.18 Financial equilibrium: constructing the LM schedule, II.

If we vary the composition of the money supply continuously, always holding the total constant at 500, we generate a continuous schedule in quadrant one, each point on the schedule reflecting the combination of ρ and Y corresponding to a particular composition of the money supply. This is the LM schedule, shown in Figure 3.19. The LM schedule traces out the requirement of financial equilibrium in this very simple model: namely, that money demand, $M_1 + M_2$, equals money supply, $\bar{M}$,[11] which is to say

$$\bar{M} = \alpha PY + \frac{\beta(\rho)}{1 - \beta(\rho)} P_B(\rho)\bar{B} = \alpha PY + \frac{\beta(\rho)}{1 - \beta(\rho)} P_B(\rho)PK.$$

Let us look next at the real side of the model, the relationship between the interest rate and aggregate demand, as mediated by the marginal efficiency of capital. In Figure 3.20, quadrant three shows the marginal efficiency of capital schedule; in particular, the interest rate ρ_0 corresponds to an investment demand of 100, which in turn corresponds, in quadrant four, to an aggregate demand of 400. The correspondence is reflected in quadrant one, which relates the interest rate to aggregate demand. Raising the interest rate produces a new, lower, level of investment demand and income, as Figure 3.21 shows.

Just as we varied the composition of money demand to obtain the LM

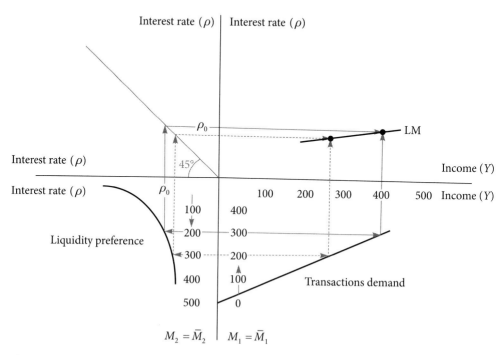

Figure 3.19 Financial equilibrium: constructing the LM schedule, III.

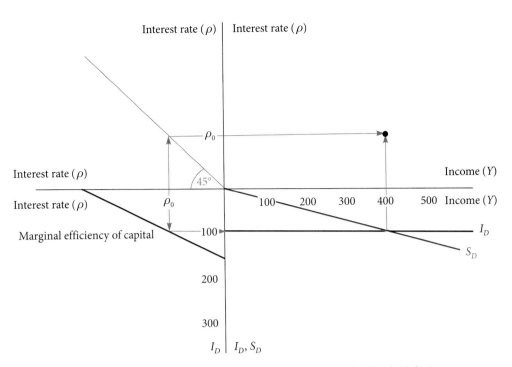

Figure 3.20 Equilibrium of expenditure and income: constructing the IS schedule, I.

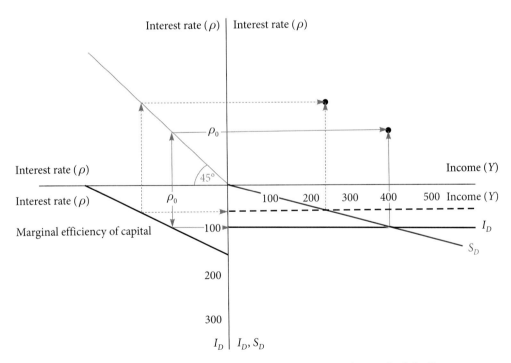

Figure 3.21 Equilibrium of expenditure and income: constructing the IS schedule, II.

schedule, we can vary the interest rate to obtain the IS schedule, which is the set of combinations of interest rate and real output for which investment demand and the supply of saving are equal:

$$I(\rho) = sY.$$

Figure 3.22 traces this out graphically.

Now superimpose the first quadrant of Figure 3.19 on the first quadrant of Figure 3.22. We obtain the IS-LM diagram, pictured in Figure 3.23, which has served as the alpha and omega of Keynesian economics for generations of undergraduate economics majors. The intersection of the two schedules, the point $<400, \rho_0>$ defines aggregate demand for the given price level. To be sure, we don't learn much from the diagram; we already learned earlier in this chapter that the combination of $Y = 400$ and $\rho = \rho_0$ is compatible with a money supply of 500 divided as $M_1 = 300$ and $M_2 = 200$. Indeed, with the interest rate fixed exogenously, as it is when the central bank is assumed to be in control, the IS-LM analysis is superfluous. Now it becomes important precisely because we start not from the interest rate but from the money supply. And this makes a difference when we come to the next question: what happens when we vary the price level?[12]

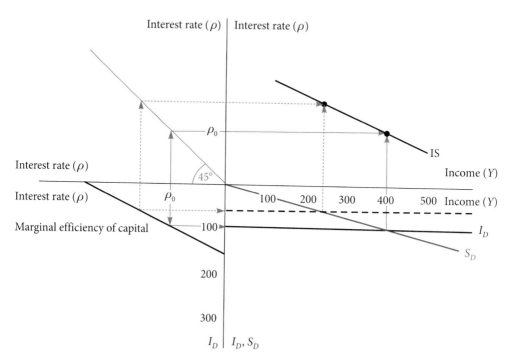

Figure 3.22 Equilibrium of expenditure and income: constructing the IS schedule, III.

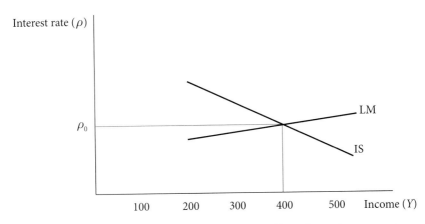

Figure 3.23 Expenditure-income and financial equilibria determine aggregate demand.

Since the price level has no impact on real investment demand, it makes no difference to aggregate demand what the price level is when the interest rate is fixed exogenously—the first-pass model—changes in the price level simply translate into changes in the amount of money required to support the level of income corresponding to the given interest rate. But in the second-pass model, the interest rate is free to take on different values, and increasing the price level has the same effect as decreasing the money supply. Or rather, *may* be equivalent, depending on what is assumed about the wage level.

We start, with Keynes, assuming that the nominal wage is fixed, $W = W_0$. Then the liquidity-preference and transactions-demand schedules in Figures 3.10, 3.11, and 3.12 shift with an increase in P from P_0 to P_1 to produce a new LM schedule, the dashed curve in quadrant one of Figure 3.24.

For any given level of income, more money is necessary to carry out transactions. Hence less is available to hold as wealth. For agents to be content with holding the reduced amount of money in their portfolios, interest rates must be higher; this change is represented by a move along the liquidity-preference schedule. Additionally, at least in a comparative-statics framework, a higher price level implies a higher nominal stock of bonds (each with a par value of one dollar), which is reflected in a shift of the liquidity-preference schedule from the solid to the dashed curve.

Observe that the interest rate lives a double life: it is a real variable in relation to investment demand and a nominal variable relative to the asset demand for money. In its first incarnation it is independent of the price level. Saving too is determined in real terms, in the present model by real income alone. Hence the IS schedule is unaffected by a change in the price level.

The result is that we can superimpose the IS schedule from Figure 3.22 to

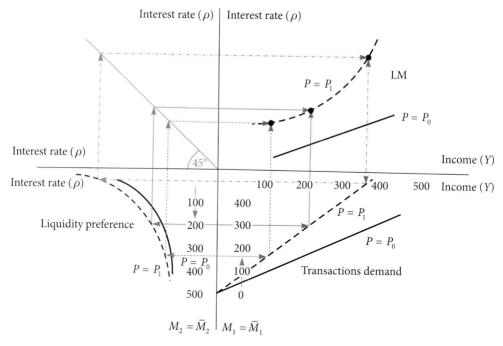

Figure 3.24 Financial equilibrium: constructing the LM schedule for different price levels.

obtain a new aggregate-demand equilibrium. In Figure 3.25 the interest rate ρ_1 and the level of income 360 correspond to the price level $P = P_1 = 4.8$, while the interest rate ρ_0 and $Y = 400$ correspond to the price level $P_0 = 3.5$.

Evidently, the relationship between the price level and aggregate demand when the interest rate is held constant is different from the relationship between price and demand when the money supply is held constant. In the first case, the price level, varying with money demand, has no impact on aggregate demand, at least not until we introduce considerations that go beyond Keynes's first- and second-pass frameworks, hence the vertical AD schedule in the first-pass model.

By contrast, in the second case, with the money supply fixed, there is an inverse relationship between the price level and aggregate demand: *the lower are prices, the less is the amount of money required for transactions, hence the more is available to satisfy the demand for money as an asset, hence, in turn, the lower the interest rate and the higher is investment demand.* This relationship, first noted by Keynes in chapter 19 of *The General Theory* (p. 266), would come to be known simply as the "Keynes effect." It is represented by a shift along the liquidity-preference schedule as the amount of money in asset portfolios varies.

In Figure 3.24 there is also a "bond effect," the shift *in* the liquidity-preference schedule. This shift reflects a changing quantity of bonds as the value of the capital stock varies with the price level.

Figure 3.26 assumes the price level varies continuously and maps the IS-LM equilibria in $Y \times \rho$ space of Figure 3.25 to $Y \times P$ space. In Figure 3.26 the point <400, 3.5> corresponds to <400, ρ_0> in Figure 3.25, and <360, 4.8> corresponds to <360, ρ_1>.

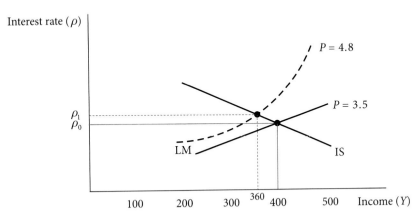

Figure 3.25 Expenditure-income and financial equilibria determine aggregate demand: as the price level rises, the equilibrium level of income—the level of aggregate demand—falls.

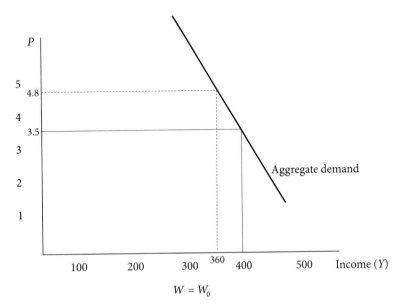

Figure 3.26 Aggregate demand schedule determined by varying P while holding $\bar{M}$ constant.

Equilibrium requires that the economy be not only on its AD schedule but also on its GS schedule. Figure 3.27 shows the AD-GS equilibrium at E. Unemployment exists as long as the labor supply at the equilibrium real price would produce more output than is produced at E. Here, the full-employment level of output is 500, and the output at the AD-GS equilibrium is 400. In Keynes's story, there is no reason why a capitalist economy will provide a job for every willing worker even if we swap the first-pass model for the second-pass model.

The lesson of both the first- and the second-pass models is that eliminating unemployment requires an appropriate interest rate to coax out the requisite level of investment demand and hence aggregate demand. This, according to Keynes, is beyond the capacity of a capitalist economy left to its own devices, that is, a capitalist economy without the hand of a central bank at the monetary tiller. And even the most steady hand may not be enough.

What happens if we drop the "scaffolding" of a fixed money wage? The following chapter explores Franco Modigliani's (1944) argument that flexible money wages can do the job of adjusting investment demand to the requirements of full employment. And, for good measure, we explore the fallback argument, due originally to Gottfried Haberler (1939, 1941), that in the event investment demand proves unresponsive, flexible wages can adjust *consumption* demand to the needs of full employment. Together these arguments constitute a powerful critique of Keynes's theoretical claims—or so mainstream economics has believed for more than half a century.

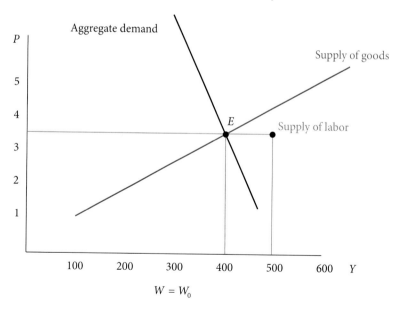

Figure 3.27 Aggregate demand–Goods supply equilibrium: the supply of labor is a nonbinding constraint.

APPENDIX 1: KEYNES'S DEFINITION(S) OF UNEMPLOYMENT

As for the creation of Eve in Genesis, there are two accounts of the meaning of involuntary unemployment in *The General Theory*:

> Men are involuntarily unemployed if, in the event of a small rise in the price of wage-goods relatively to the money-wage, both the aggregate supply of labour willing to work for the current money-wage and the aggregate demand for it at that wage would be greater than the existing volume of employment. (p. 15)

> An alternative, though equivalent, criterion is that . . . aggregate employment is inelastic in response to an increase in the effective demand for its output. (p. 26)

The first definition says that if the real wage goes down because of an increase in the price level relative to the money wage, both the supply of labor and the demand for labor would be higher than the amount of employment at the original real wage. The second, if we insert the adverb "completely" before inelastic, is tautological: full employment is reached when there is no possibility for expanding output and employment.

The first definition is problematic for several reasons, one being that it is based on a counterfactual. Apparently, we can't tell if there is involuntary unemployment without asking what *would* happen if the real wage were to change. This is odd enough. But for Keynes's readers it must have been even more odd to distinguish between a change in the real wage that takes place because the price level changes and a change that takes place because the money wage changes.

One reason for distinguishing between the effect of price changes and the effect of wage changes is money illusion: workers focus on their money incomes rather than on their real incomes. The problem with money illusion from a mainstream point of view is that a canon of orthodoxy is the ability of economic agents to see through the "veil" of money and determine their actions on the basis of real rather than monetary values. According to the classical dichotomy, it shouldn't matter whether the real wage changes because of a change in the price level or because of a change in the wage rate. One of the early charges leveled at the argument of *The General Theory* was precisely that it hinges on money illusion.

In point of fact, Keynes does not rely on money illusion, but rather on the importance of relative wages. Any single group of workers will resist wage cuts because this puts them at a disadvantage relative to their fellow workers. But the same workers will accept price increases that reduce real wages because all are hit equally, at least up to the point that the "reduction proceeds so far as to threaten a reduction of the real wage below the marginal disutility of the existing volume of employment" (*The General Theory*, p. 14). That is, employed workers customarily enjoy a rent because the marginal disutility of labor is usually less than, rather than equal to, the going real wage.

This leads to the paradoxical result that there usually exists some unemployment in the sense that, at the going real wage, workers would prefer to work more. Moreover, Keynes's reasoning leads to the conclusion that the only reason workers do not accept pay cuts is because "reductions of money-wages . . . are seldom or never of an all-around character" (*The General Theory*, p. 14).

The focus on relative wages and the existence of wage rents need not lead to the conclusion that workers are concerned with money wages rather than real wages, or that they respond differently to wage cuts and price increases. We can define labor supply as the amount workers wish to work at the going real wage (or real price, as in the models of this chapter), provided we stipulate that changes in the money wage, like changes in the money price, affect all workers equally, which is to say that wage changes are *not* piecemeal. At any real wage, unemployment exists if the actual level of employment and output is less than the labor supply at that real wage. When unemployment exists, the marginal disutility of labor is less than the real wage.

This definition is compatible with Keynes's second definition of full employment in terms of a completely inelastic response of output and employment to aggregate demand. The only additional assumption we have to make is to rule out compulsory overtime and the like so that the LS schedule becomes an absolute limit on the amount of employment.

Keynes may believe that he needs to focus on relative wages to explain money-wage rigidity, but this is true only if money-wage rigidity is essential to his argument. This Keynes denies, with the result that his definition of involuntary unemployment in terms of an asymmetry between the effect of a wage cut and the effect of a price rise adds nothing but confusion. It is no wonder there remained doubts about Keynes's theory even among those who accepted the policy implications.

APPENDIX 2: DO INTEREST RATES ADJUST SAVING AND INVESTMENT?

We can now revisit the question of the role of the interest rate in equilibrating the demand for investment and the supply of saving and compare the mainstream position examined in the previous chapter with Keynes's own position. The mainstream position, before Keynes and afterward, has been that desired investment and desired saving constitute the two blades of a Marshallian scissors exactly analogous to the textbook model of a competitive market. And the rate of interest is the price that brings investment demand (Keynes's marginal efficiency of capital) and saving into equilibrium.

We start from the equilibrium $<I_0, \rho_0>$ in Figure 3.28 and suppose that the equilibrium is disturbed by a collapse of investor confidence. If the apple analogy suggested by Frank and Bernanke (2007, p. 639)—"the movements of the real interest rate clear the market for saving in much the same way that the price of apples clears the market for apples"—were valid, we would expect that the excess supply of saving at the original equilibrium interest rate, ρ_0, would drive the rate of interest down as savers competed with each other to place their funds now that fewer borrowers are in the market. This process would continue until the interest rate coaxed out sufficient investment to match the desired saving. In Figure 3.28 the new equilibrium interest rate is ρ_1. (For simplicity, saving is depicted as completely inelastic with respect to the rate of interest, a simplification that does not affect the logic of adjustment.)

The General Theory offers a different analysis. To a first approximation, the impact of a decrease in investment demand will fall on saving itself: the saving schedule will move inward to accommodate the new, lower, investment demand at the original rate of interest, ρ_0. The picture is given in Figure 3.29.

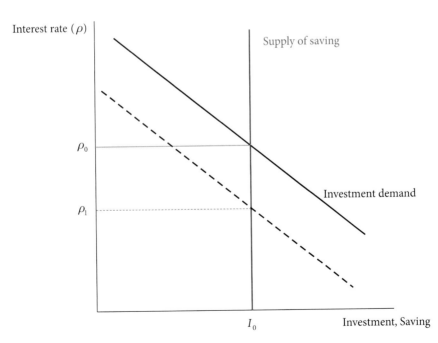

Figure 3.28 Investment demand and saving supply: equilibrium restored by a change in the interest rate.

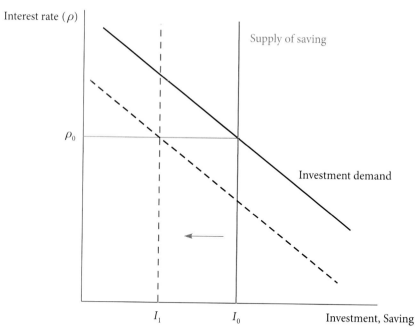

Figure 3.29 Investment demand and saving supply: equilibrium restored by a shift in the saving schedule.

In Keynes's story, the downward shift in the investment schedule constitutes a reduction in aggregate demand, and the level of output falls in response. The fall continues until desired saving, responding to the level of output and income, falls to the new level of investment demand. End of story—at least in the first-pass model.

Things are more complicated in the second-pass model. With a fixed money supply, there is a secondary effect because the price level falls and more money spills over into the demand for financial assets. We can trace the effects of the downward shift in the investment-demand schedule in the third quadrant of Figure 3.30. This shift translates into a fall in the level of output that equilibrates desired saving and investment in the fourth quadrant, and a downward shift in the IS schedule in the first quadrant. As investment (and saving) fall from I_0 to I_1, income falls from Y_0 to Y_1.

This, however, is still an approximation. For not only does the IS schedule shift but there is a shift *along* the LM schedule (and, before we are done, a shift *in* the LM schedule itself, as the price level responds to the change in the level of economic activity).

The shift along the LM schedule takes place because at a lower level of economic activity, less money is needed for transactions and more money is thus

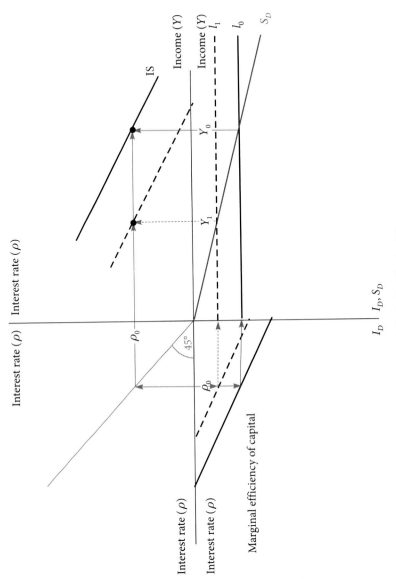

Figure 3.30 A decrease in investment demand shifts the IS schedule.

available to satisfy asset demands. But with more money chasing the same amount of financial assets, the prices of bonds will rise and the interest rate will fall. This effect is shown in Figure 3.31.

In this figure the money released to the asset market by a reduction in income and output from Y_0 to Y_1 is willingly held by agents only if the rate of interest falls from ρ_0 to ρ_1. This fall in the interest rate stimulates movement along the investment-demand schedule and thus leads to higher output and income. For financial markets to be in equilibrium and expenditure to be equal to income, both the LM and the IS schedules must be satisfied, as in Figure 3.32 at the point $<Y_2, \rho_2>$.

We now have to modify Figure 3.29 to take account of these changes in the financial sector. In place of the equilibrium $<I_1, \rho_0>$, we have the equilibrium $<I_2, \rho_2>$ in Figure 3.33.

But we are still not done. The process by which the economy moves from one equilibrium to another will be explored in detail in chapters 5, 6, and 7; for now, suffice it to say that we have dealt with only half of the process, the demand side. Indeed, not even: we have only examined the relationship of two points, each on a separate AD schedule but each assuming the same price

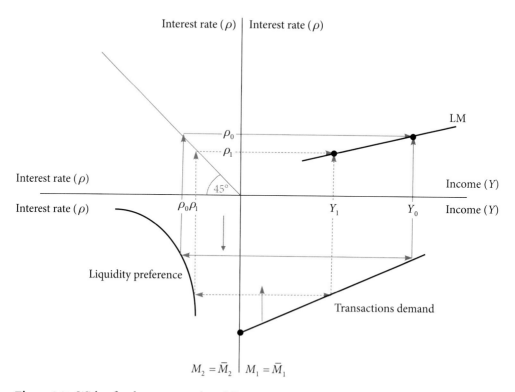

Figure 3.31 With a fixed money supply, a fall in income decreases the equilibrium interest rate.

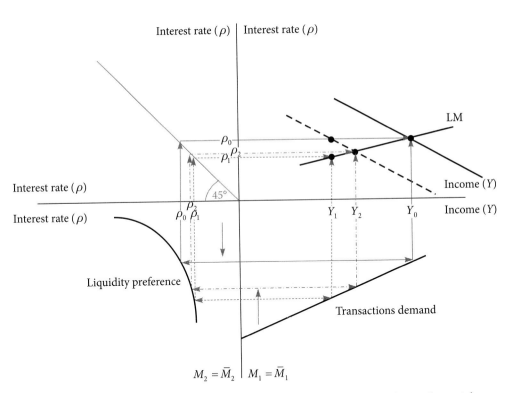

Figure 3.32 A lower interest rate stimulates investment demand, a partial offset to the initial decline.

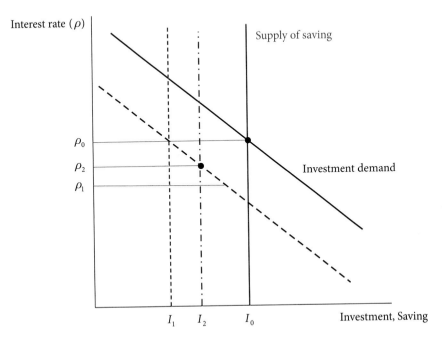

Figure 3.33 Shift in investment demand and induced shifts in supply of saving.

level. If we repeat the exercise while allowing the price level to vary, the entire AD schedule shifts in line with the assumed shift in the investment-demand schedule. The dashed line in Figure 3.34 represents the new AD schedule.

But what determines the price level? To answer this question we need to bring in the supply side. By superimposing a GS schedule on Figure 3.34, we can see that there is a further effect on the equilibrium level of output and income via the effect of a lower price level on the real money supply and hence on the interest rate and investment demand. As the level of output falls, the price level falls with marginal cost, and at the lower price level the transactions demand for money falls; the interest rate must fall to accommodate the greater volume of asset money relative to the stock of bonds. Figure 3.35 shows the new AD-GS equilibrium (Y_3) in the space of $Y \times P$, and Figure 3.36 the new equilibrium (I_3) in $I \times \rho$ space. The rate of interest ρ_3 in Figure 3.36 corresponds to the price level P_3 associated with the new equilibrium at Y_3 in Figure 3.35.

Keynes vs. the Mainstream on Interest Rates, Saving, and Investment: A Summing Up

The key difference between the mainstream story and Keynes's story is the difference between a movement along a given saving schedule in the mainstream story and a shift in this schedule in *The General Theory* story. The

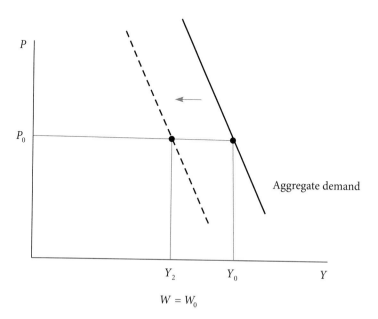

Figure 3.34 A fall in investment demand shifts aggregate demand downward.

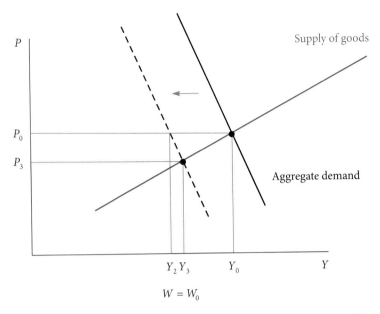

Figure 3.35 Taking into account the supply-side consequences of a fall in investment demand, I: in the space of income × prices.

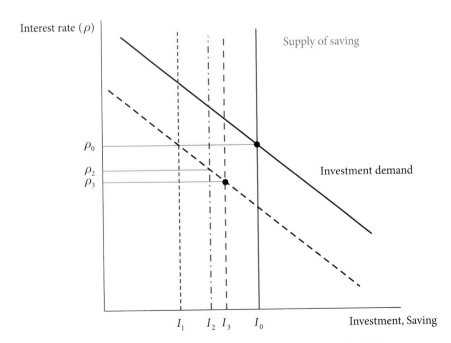

Figure 3.36 Taking into account the supply-side consequences of a fall in investment demand, II: in the space of investment and saving × interest.

mainstream relies on interest-rate adjustments, whereas, to a first approximation, Keynes relies on output adjustment.

If we go beyond the first approximation, the interest rate also adjusts in
Keynes's story, albeit with two important differences from the mainstream.
The first is that a shifting IS schedule and a stationary LM schedule—not a
shifting investment demand and a stationary saving supply—drive interest-
rate changes. The second is that even after all adjustments to a change in investment demand are made, IS-LM equilibrium moves in the same direction
as the original change; consequently aggregate demand moves in the same
direction.

The first-pass model is characterized by two equations on the real side and two equations on the financial side. The real-side equations are (1) the equality of investment demand and desired saving

$$I(\rho) = sY,$$

which defines the AD schedule, and (2) profit maximization, which defines the GS schedule

$$Y = GS\left(\frac{P}{W}\right)$$

by the first-order condition of equality between price and marginal cost

$$\frac{P}{W} = \left(F_L\right)^{-1}.$$

$F_L \equiv \partial Y/\partial L$ is the marginal productivity of labor, derived from the production function $Y = F(K, L)$. Differentiating the price = marginal cost condition with respect to P/W gives

$$GS' \equiv \frac{dY}{d\left(\dfrac{P}{W}\right)} = -\left(F_{LL}\right)^{-1}\left(F_L\right)^3,$$

which is positive since $F_{LL} \equiv \partial^2 Y/\partial L^2 < 0$. The models of this chapter also take the money wage as given: $W = W_0$.

On the money side the two equations are the demand (1) for money for transactions

$$M_1 = \alpha PY$$

and (2) for the demand for cash in wealth portfolios

$$M_2 = \frac{\beta(\rho)}{1 - \beta(\rho)} P_B(\rho)B_N = \frac{\beta(\rho)}{1 - \beta(\rho)} P_B(\rho)PK.$$

Causality runs from the interest rate and the money wage, $\rho = \rho_0$ and $W = W_0$, to the equilibrium level of output, Y_0, determined by aggregate demand, and to the equilibrium price level, P_0, determined jointly by aggregate demand and goods supply. The price level and the level of output together determine the transactions demand for money, M_1, and the price level together with the rate of interest determine the asset demand for cash. Total demand is $M \equiv M_1 + M_2$.

Unemployment is measured by the gap between (1) the level of output that would be produced if all workers available at the equilibrium real wage W_0/P_0 were employed and (2) the level of output at the equilibrium of aggregate demand and goods supply: the output gap is

$$LS\left(\frac{P}{W}\right) - Y_0,$$

where $LS(P/W)$ is the level of output that workers would like to produce at the real price P/W. That is,

$$LS\left(\frac{P}{W}\right) = F\left(K, L\left(\frac{P}{W}\right)\right),$$

with $L(P/W)$ the amount of labor workers wish to supply at the price P/W, assumed to depend on the utility of goods and the disutility of work.

The Second-Pass Model

This model builds on the first-pass model but reverses the causality between money and interest. The interest rate is determined endogenously by equating the total demand for money M to an exogenous supply $\bar{M}$. We have

$$I(\rho) = sY,$$

$$Y = GS\left(\frac{P}{W}\right),$$

$$M \equiv \alpha PY + \frac{\beta(\rho)}{1 - \beta(\rho)} P_B(\rho)PK = \bar{M}.$$

Once again, $W = W_0$, and equilibrium unemployment is given by the output gap $LS(P_0/W_0) - Y_0$. As observed in the text, this system of equations, unlike the first-pass system, is not decomposable, and the level of output is not determined by aggregate demand alone. The interest rate in the aggregate-demand equation now depends, via the money equation, on the unknowns Y and P.

The IS-LM construction in the text varies P parametrically to derive aggregate demand from the intersection in $Y \times \rho$ space of the IS schedule, defined by $I = S$, and the LM schedule, defined by $M \equiv \bar{M}$. The negative slope of the IS schedule is confirmed by differentiating with respect to Y:

$$\frac{d\rho}{dY} = \frac{s}{I'},$$

with $I' \equiv dI/d\rho$. The derivative $d\rho/dY$ is negative because I' is negative. Similarly, differentiating the LM schedule gives

$$\frac{d\rho}{dY} = -\frac{\alpha}{\left(\dfrac{\beta' P_B}{(1-\beta)^2} + \dfrac{\beta P_B'}{1-\beta} \right) K},$$

which is positive since $\beta' \equiv d\beta/d\rho$ and $P_B' \equiv dP_B/d\rho$ are both negative. Differentiating the IS and LM schedules with respect to P shows that the AD schedule slopes downward in $Y \times P$ space. We have

$$I' \frac{d\rho}{dP} = s \frac{dY}{dP}$$

and

$$\alpha Y + \alpha P \frac{dY}{dP} + \frac{d\rho}{dP} \left(\frac{\beta' P_B}{(1-\beta)^2} + \frac{\beta P_B'}{1-\beta} \right) PK + \frac{\beta}{1-\beta} P_B K = 0.$$

Substituting $(s/I')(dY/dP)$ for $d\rho/dP$ gives

$$\frac{dY}{dP} = -\frac{\bar{M}}{P^2 \left[\alpha + \dfrac{s}{I'} \left(\dfrac{\beta' P_B}{(1-\beta)^2} + \dfrac{\beta P_B'}{1-\beta} \right) K \right]}.$$

Since both the numerator and the denominator are positive—I', β', and P_B' are all negative—we have $dY/dP < 0$.

— 4 —

EQUILIBRIUM WITH A GIVEN
MONEY SUPPLY

Critical Perspectives on the Second-Pass Model

> It is usually considered as one of the most important achievements
> of the Keynesian theory that it explains the consistency of economic
> equilibrium with the presence of involuntary unemployment. It is,
> however, not sufficiently recognized that, except in a limiting case to
> be considered later, this result is due entirely to the assumption of
> "rigid wages."
>
> —FRANCO MODIGLIANI

> When prices and wages fall, more and more money is released from
> transaction duties. Idle funds grow in terms of money and still faster
> (without any limit even if the quantity of money remains unchanged
> or decreases) in real terms. . . . When money hoards (inactive depos-
> its, Mr KEYNES' M_2) have reached a certain level people will stop
> saving (that is, in this case, they will cease to add to their hoards).
> That amounts to saying that the rate of saving is not only an increas-
> ing function of the level of (real) income, but also a diminishing
> function of the wealth the individual holds.
>
> —GOTTFRIED HABERLER

> Shortfalls in overall demand would cure themselves if only wages and
> prices fell rapidly in the face of unemployment.
>
> —PAUL KRUGMAN

Has Keynes made good on the claim that, with a given money supply, a competitive market economy may be at equilibrium but not, in the absence of activist monetary or fiscal policy, able to provide a job for every willing worker?
The equilibrium level of output in Figure 3.27 is 400, and the unemployed
workers would add 100; so the economy, according to Keynes, is at equilibrium but not at full employment.

However, anyone steeped in mainstream microeconomic theory would have difficulty accepting the aggregate demand-goods supply intersection at E as a true equilibrium. Figure 3.27 assumes a given money wage; what if the money wage were lower? Before we examine this question in the framework of the second-pass model, it serves as a useful benchmark to put the question in the framework of the first-pass model.

In this case, the supply side determines only the price level; the level of the money-wage rate makes no difference at all for the level of output. Suppose we compare, as in Figure 4.1, two equilibria, one (E) for the original wage W_0, the second (E') for a wage half as great, $0.5W_0$. All that changes is the price level. With the wage $0.5W_0$ instead of W_0, the equilibrium price level is 1.75 instead of 3.5.

In order to increase employment and output, it is necessary to stimulate aggregate demand. Moving the AD schedule from $Y = 400$ to $Y = 450$, as in Figure 4.2, leads to full employment, whether the wage is W_0 or $0.5W_0$. Once again, all that changes is the equilibrium price level, which is 4 if the wage is W_0 and 2 if the wage is $0.5W_0$.

The second-pass model behaves quite differently. With the addition of the LS schedule, the model, like its first-pass counterpart, is overdetermined, but with this key difference: the AD schedule is now downward sloping, as in Figure 4.3.

On the assumption that the wage rate is fixed, at most two of the three rela-

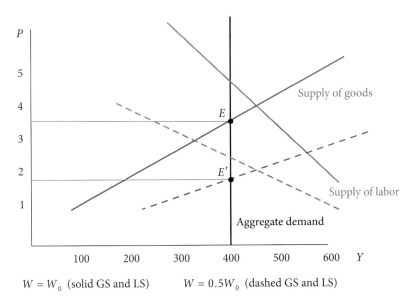

$W = W_0$ (solid GS and LS) $W = 0.5W_0$ (dashed GS and LS)

Figure 4.1 Aggregate demand, goods supply, and labor supply in the first-pass model, I.

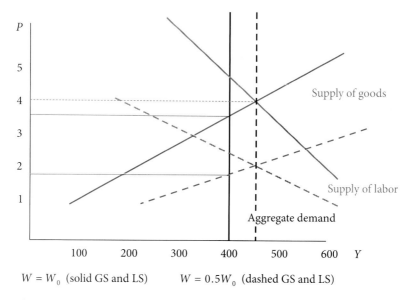

Figure 4.2 Aggregate demand, goods supply, and labor supply in the first-pass model, II.

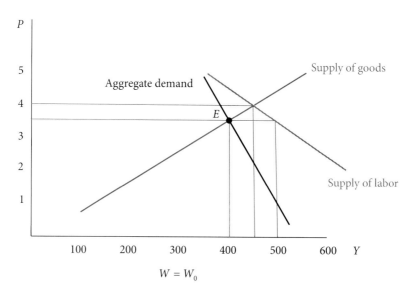

Figure 4.3 An overdetermined system, I.

tionships pictured in Figure 4.3 can be satisfied for any combination of Y and P, barring a serendipitous coincidence. Keynes's case for privileging the AD = GS equilibrium over the other two possibilities is that the LS schedule does not exist; he rejects the argument that a labor-market equilibrium requires that the wage rate be equal to the marginal disutility of labor (see appendix 1 to chapter 3).

If however we stipulate that changes in money wages are general rather than piecemeal, Keynes's reason for suppressing the LS schedule loses its force. And if we are really trying to situate the argument in an economy without frictions and imperfections, we have no good reason to ignore the existence of the LS schedule.

Enter Franco Modigliani. Modigliani allows the money wage to vary (in God's mind) while holding the money supply constant. What appears to be a minor change in the model dramatically changes the main result: in Modigliani's version of the second-pass model, barring a liquidity trap or a completely inelastic investment demand in the neighborhood of a zero interest rate, equilibrium requires full employment. Since the only thing Modigliani does to Keynes's second-pass model is to substitute an LS schedule for a fixed money wage, it is an easy leap to the conclusion that the reason why Keynes obtains an unemployment equilibrium is money-wage rigidity.

Observe, first of all, that, although Modigliani comes to the same conclusion as the composite "classical" economist whom Keynes identified with Pigou, he comes to this conclusion by a different, "Keynesian," route. Modigliani does not assume the classical dichotomy that allows the economy to be analyzed with money playing no more of a role than a medium of exchange and a unit of account. Modigliani's is a money economy, like Keynes's, complete with investment demand depending on an interest rate that clears the market for financial assets. Like Keynes, he locates the determination of the hurdle rate of interest on the financial side of the model, not in the investment-saving nexus.

It is through the dependence of the interest rate on the supply of money available for financial markets that Modigliani is able to restore the pre-Keynesian invisible hand. The key to Modigliani is that a lower money wage is associated with lower levels of prices, a smaller transactions demand, more money in wealth portfolios and, therefore, a lower interest rate and a higher level of investment—the Keynes effect.

Modigliani accepts the mainstream view that the level of employment is determined by the intersection of GS and LS schedules, both of which depend on the real price, P/W. In other words, GS and LS schedules jointly determine both the equilibrium level of output (employment) and the real price. But the real price is a ratio, P/W; so once the money-wage rate is freed from its moorings, the price level is also free to vary.

What then determines the price level (and, consequently, the wage level)? Modigliani assumes that the nominal price of output settles at the level at which the interest rate coaxes out just the right amount of investment, namely, the investment that generates aggregate demand equal to the output determined by the intersection of GS and LS schedules.

The logic is straightforward. First, Y and P/W are determined by the intersection of GS and LS schedules so that full employment obtains and the *real* price is determined. But P and W are separately up for grabs. To determine P we turn to the investment-saving nexus, $I(\rho) = sY$, and the money demand–supply relationship, the equation $M_1 + M_2 = \bar{M}$. With Y now a known quantity, the relationship $I(\rho) = sY$ determines I and ρ. Once we know ρ, the nominal price level falls out from the equations relating transactions demand to real output, $M_1 = \alpha PY$, and financial–market demand to the rate of interest,

$$M_2 = \frac{\beta(\rho)}{1 - \beta(\rho)} P_B(\rho)PK.$$

We have money supply equal to money demand,

$$\bar{M} = \alpha PY + \frac{\beta(\rho)}{1 - \beta(\rho)} P_B(\rho)PK.$$

Since the money supply is given, we can derive P from this equation as

$$P = \frac{\bar{M}}{\alpha Y + \dfrac{\beta(\rho)}{1 - \beta(\rho)} P_B(\rho)K}.$$

Now that we have P, we can determine W from the equilibrium real price P/W.

Graphically, shifts in the GS and the LS schedules resolve the overdetermination in Figure 4.3. In Figure 4.4, the quantity of goods supplied for $P = 1$ on the dashed schedule, namely $Y = 400$, is the same quantity that is supplied for $P = 3.5$ on the solid schedule because both of these prices correspond to the same real price. If we assume $W_0 = 1$, then in both cases $P/W = 3.5$. The same is true for labor supply: $Y = 500$ in both cases.

Alternatively, we can picture the GS and LS schedules in relation to the price level assuming the real-price level, $P/W = 3.5$, is fixed—as in Figure 4.5.

Evidently, there are two different concepts of the "price level" at work, which suggests an inherent ambiguity. Up to now we have represented the

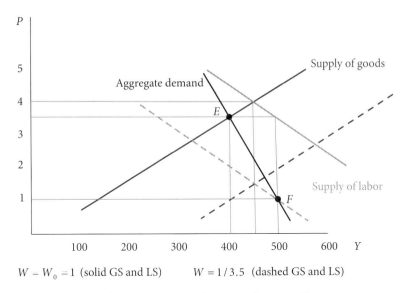

Figure 4.4 An overdetermined system, II.

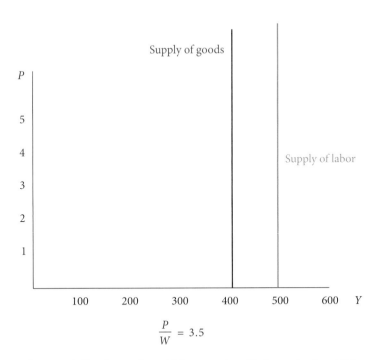

Figure 4.5 Goods supply and labor supply with the *real* price at 3.5.

price level as P varying relative to a fixed money wage, W_0, or in the case of Figures 4.1, 4.2, and 4.4, two different money wages, W_0 and $W_0/3.5$. By contrast, in Figure 4.5, the nominal price level varies while the real price is fixed, which is to say that the wage rate is assumed to vary in the same proportion as all other prices.

The price level is a composite, an index of the money values of the goods and services that the economy produces. Varying the price *level* evidently means varying all prices proportionately. The ambiguity stems from how we conceptualize labor, whether as different in kind from other goods and services, or as simply one more commodity. Treating labor differently, the price level measures prices independently of wages; treating labor the same as other commodities, with its nominal price—the money wage—varying in strict proportion to other prices, the price level measures what we will call the absolute price level, the price level on the assumption that the real price (and the real wage) is fixed.

Because the AD schedule is independent of the wage level, it is easy to move between the two diagrams, Figures 4.4 and 4.5.[1] Figure 4.6 superimposes the AD schedule on Figure 4.5; the points E and F represent the same combinations of prices, wages, and outputs that are represented by E and F in Figure 4.4.

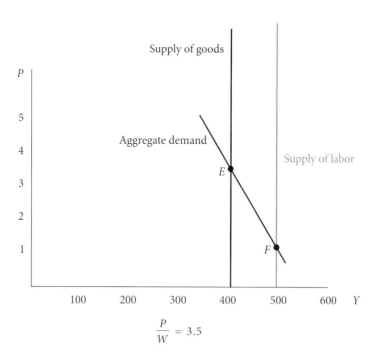

Figure 4.6 Equilibrium holding the *real* price at 3.5.

But what has been accomplished? Simply specifying a wage rate differing from the original one, or specifying a particular real price, leaves us with the same problem of overdetermination as before. In both Figure 4.4 and Figure 4.6, we still have three relationships to be satisfied by two variables.

Since in Modigliani's model the real price is a variable, and the full-employment, profit-maximizing level of output is associated with a specific real price, we can choose both an absolute price level P, on which aggregate demand depends, and a real price level P/W, on which full employment and profit maximization depend. All we have to do is to vary the money-wage rate. In the present case, at a *real* price $P/W = 4$, we have goods and labor supplies in sync with one another—meaning we have both full employment and profit maximization—at an output of 450. To achieve both, the *nominal* price level has to be set at the level that generates an aggregate demand of 450. Figure 4.7 represents the required nominal price level as 2, which is to say that the wage level is 0.5. The ambiguity of Figure 4.3 is resolved because the schedules converge on a single equilibrium; G is a point of serendipity at which the economy is simultaneously on its AD, GS, and LS schedules.

The same result can be pictured in the context of a variable absolute price level. Figure 4.8 assumes $P/W = 4$, which makes the GS and LS schedules coincide. This is of course the vertical aggregate-supply schedule reproduced in

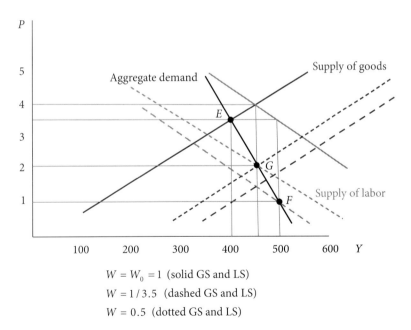

$W = W_0 = 1$ (solid GS and LS)

$W = 1/3.5$ (dashed GS and LS)

$W = 0.5$ (dotted GS and LS)

Figure 4.7 Aggregate-demand, goods-supply, and labor-supply schedules for three different wage rates.

virtually every elementary text as representing long-run supply conditions. It would no doubt help students if they were told that this supply schedule comes from going back to the old, pre-Keynesian, view of output being determined by profitability (the GS schedule) and workers' goods-leisure preferences (the LS schedule)! As it is, most students—and perhaps their teachers too—are in a fog about what assumptions must be made to make the supply schedule vertical, and how it is that labor and goods supplies, conceptually distinct, come together in a single schedule. The key is to *assume* full employment and profit maximization, so that instead of two separate supply schedules, we have a single "aggregate" supply, which is at one and the same time the supply of goods reflecting profit maximization and the supply of labor required to produce those goods. Superimposing aggregate demand on Figure 4.8, the serendipity of a full-employment equilibrium is reflected in the point G in Figure 4.9.

Observe that we have come full circle. With a given money supply, but the price level *and* the wage level variable, there exist prices and wages compatible with full employment. Moreover, supply conditions uniquely determine the level of output. Aggregate demand has no bearing on equilibrium output, entering the picture only to determine nominal prices and wages. Keynes seems to have unleashed a tempest in a teapot, at least insofar as the question is

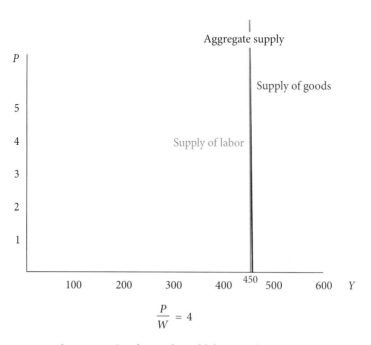

Figure 4.8 Goods supply and labor supply, $P/W = 4$.

the existence of full-employment equilibrium in a competitive economy un-
marred by imperfections and frictions—except for one, or rather two, special
cases.

In chapter 3 it was observed that investment demand can be insufficient to
reach a full-employment equilibrium either because the interest rate cannot
be brought to a sufficiently low level regardless of how much money is available to satisfy the asset demand for money—the liquidity trap—or because
even at a zero hurdle rate of interest an inelastic investment-demand schedule provides too little investment demand. Figure 4.10, which reproduces a
slightly modified Figure 3.16, shows both cases; in the liquidity-trap case, investment demand is limited to 60 and aggregate demand to 240, and, in case
of an inelastic investment schedule, maximum investment demand is 80 and
the corresponding aggregate demand is 320.

The consequences for aggregate demand are shown in Figure 4.11. In both
cases even a price level near zero would not lead to sufficient aggregate demand to employ the available work force. So, even after Modigliani, *The General Theory* retains some relevance as an argument about the limits of the
self-regulating mechanism of the market as well as the limits of monetary
policy. But this can provide little comfort for Keynes, for the special cases are
limited to a floor on the hurdle rate of interest, which he specifically dis-

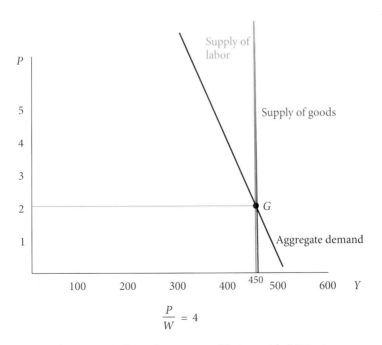

Figure 4.9 Full-employment equilibrium with $P/W = 4$.

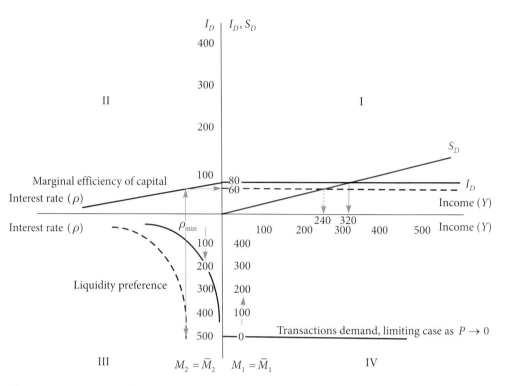

Figure 4.10 Aggregate demand limited by liquidity preference and the marginal efficiency of capital.

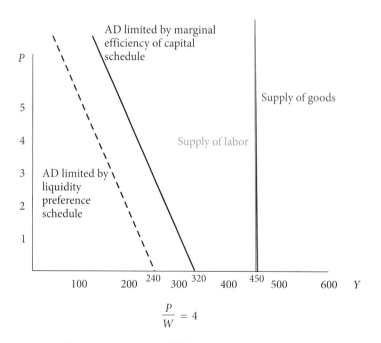

Figure 4.11 Limits to full-employment equilibrium.

avowed as a theoretical possibility with no historical traction, and stagnation of investment demand, which he thought to be a distant prospect rather than an immediate threat.

What are we to make of Modigliani's critique? In one sense there is nothing new in Modigliani's claim that there is a money-wage rate that is consistent with full employment, at least apart from the exceptional circumstances pictured in Figure 4.11. Keynes, had he lived long enough and found the time to answer Modigliani, might have claimed that Modigliani exaggerated the differences between them. As Keynes puts it immediately after introducing the Keynes effect,

> We can, therefore, theoretically at least, produce precisely the same effects on the rate of interest by reducing wages, whilst leaving the quantity of money unchanged, that we can produce by increasing the quantity of money whilst leaving the level of wages unchanged. (*The General Theory,* p. 266)

Keynes goes on to note that the same limitations that apply to monetary policy—a floor to the hurdle rate or an inelastic investment-demand schedule—might prevent a lower wage from having the desired effect on employment:

> It follows that wage reductions, as a method of securing full employment, are also subject to the same limitations as the method of increasing the quantity of money. The same reasons as those mentioned above, which limit the efficacy of increases in the quantity of money as a means of increasing investment to the optimum figure, apply *mutatis mutandis* to wage reductions.

The key point is that the money wage operates on aggregate demand in the same way as the money supply—in reverse. To be sure, the effects are diagrammed differently in the space of price level and real output. In the case of an increase in the money supply, aggregate demand moves outward, as in Figure 4.12. By contrast, reducing the money wage is depicted as a move *along* the AD schedule as the GS (and LS) schedules move downward with the money wage, as in Figure 4.13. But the effect on output is the same, and for the same reason: a larger nominal money supply increases the real supply of money $\bar{M}/P$, and so does a lower nominal wage via its effect on the price level. Since the LM schedule is defined by the equality of money demand and money supply, the equation for the real money supply, $\bar{M}/P$, is

$$\frac{\bar{M}}{P} = \alpha Y + \frac{\beta(\rho)}{1 - \beta(\rho)} P_B(\rho)K.$$

Raising $\bar{M}$ moves the LM schedule in the same direction as reducing P. In short, both wages and money supply operate on the rate of interest, and the

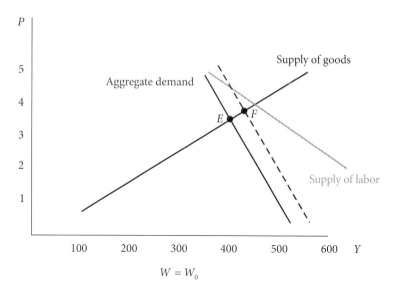

Figure 4.12 Aggregate demand, goods supply, and labor supply: increasing the money supply.

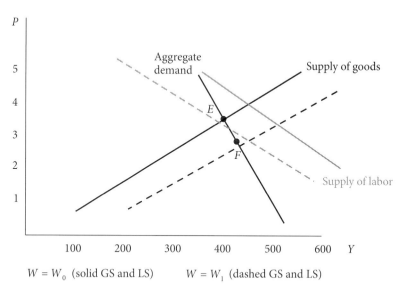

Figure 4.13 Aggregate demand, goods supply, and labor supply: reducing the real wage.

rate of interest operates on aggregate demand. We are a long way from the mainstream emphasis on a direct line of causality running from the real wage to employment and output, the mechanism of chapter 2.

It may be satisfying from the point of view of intellectual history that Keynes saw that the nominal wage and the money supply operate in the same way, through the interest rate.[2] But there is nonetheless a crucial theoretical difference between the two: wage-rate adjustment is supposed to operate automatically, whereas changing the money supply requires the visible hand of a central bank. Given this difference, it is not surprising that Modigliani's argument had an important effect on the evolving discussion of what were and what were not the essential assumptions of *The General Theory*. Modigliani's 1944 paper inflicted a grievous wound to the claim that *The General Theory* disproved the automatic tendency of a competitive market economy to provide a job for every willing worker. The wound continues to cause pain, as the Krugman epigraph to this chapter indicates.

Is Modigliani's Critique Compatible with Endogenous Money?

Modigliani claims that a competitive market economy has an equilibrium at a full-employment level of output. In making this claim Modigliani assumes, along with Keynes, a fixed money supply. What is the status of this assumption? Is it merely part of the scaffolding? Or is this assumption essential to the conclusion that a full-employment equilibrium exists if only we allow wages and prices to vary? Specifically, what happens to aggregate demand if we assume fractional-reserve banking, so that the money supply can vary endogenously even in the absence of a central bank?

Since the IS schedule is determined by real variables, the answer lies in the behavior of the LM schedule. As a benchmark, look again at the LM schedule when there are no banks and money is simply a predetermined quantity of Venetian gold ducats. In the simplest version, there are two classes of economic agents: households and restaurateurs. Households account for all the net wealth in the economy and deploy their money in two ways. They lend money to restaurateurs (perhaps themselves, wearing different hats) for working capital to carry out the transactions necessary in the restaurant business—buying the ingredients for tonight's dinner. The rest of their money forms the liquid part of their wealth. The other part of their wealth is a stock of bonds issued by restaurants as the financial counterpart of the stock of physical capital—structures, furnishings, equipment.

Assuming $P = 0.75$ and $\alpha = 1$ (α^{-1} is the transactions velocity of money), every ducat's worth of the flow of output requires a stock of 0.75 ducats. If

$Y = 400$, 300 ducats are required to grease the wheels of commerce. If $\bar{M} = 500$, and $M_1 = 300$, there are 200 ducats available to satisfy the asset demand for money. For financial markets to be in equilibrium, the interest rate must be equal to ρ_0, as we observed in constructing the LM schedule from transactions- and asset-demand schedules. The relevant graphs are reproduced in Figure 4.14. Liquidity preference is given by the solid curve in the third quadrant.

We assume the real capital stock is 1,333, so that with $P = 0.75$, the nominal value of bonds is 1,000. Assume that the bond coupon is equal to the interest rate, $R = \rho_0$, so that $P_B(\rho_0) = 1$.

If we posit a different output level, or a different price level, the economy will need more or less gold to carry out its transactions, and there will be correspondingly fewer or more ducats to satisfy asset demand. The consequence is that the interest rate that equilibrates financial markets will be higher or lower. If, for example, $Y = 266.67$, with $\alpha = 1$ and $P = 0.75$, the economy will need only 200 ducats for commerce. For households to be willing to hold the remaining 300 ducats as part of their asset portfolios, the interest rate has to be lower, ρ_1 in the diagram. With R fixed, the bond price will be higher. If we assume that $\rho_1 = \rho_0/1.2$, the bond price increases to $P_B(\rho_1) = 1.2$.

If the price of output (and capital) is 1.0 instead of 0.75, one ducat is needed to finance one unit of output, and 400 ducats are required to sustain an output

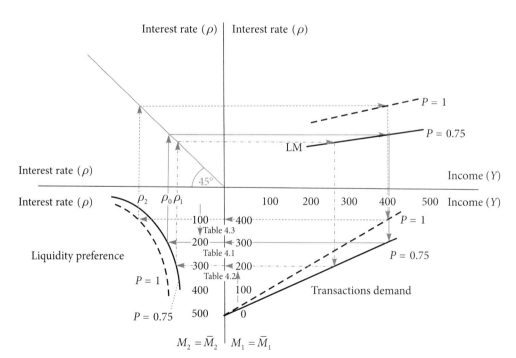

Figure 4.14 Financial equilibrium: constructing the LM schedule, I.

of 400. In this economy only 100 ducats are left over to satisfy asset demand, necessitating a higher interest rate, ρ_2. The transactions-demand schedule in Figure 14.4 shifts from the solid to the dashed line.

With a higher price level, there is not only a shift along the original liquidity-preference schedule because more ducats are required to grease the wheels of trade, there is also a shift of the liquidity-preference schedule because at a higher price level the nominal value of fixed capital is higher and, correspondingly, given R, there must be a larger stock of bonds. But since R is fixed, a higher interest rate means a lower bond price—say, $P_B(\rho_2) = 0.675$. The market value of bonds is now 900. As a result of the shifts of the transactions-demand and liquidity-preference schedules, the LM schedule also shifts; the dashed line replaces the solid line.

Tables 4.1, 4.2, and 4.3 summarize the three snapshots of the economy. For accounting purposes, restaurants are treated as entities for which assets and liabilities balance—so that their net worth is zero.

Table 4.1 $Y = 400$; $P = 0.75$; $\alpha = 1$; $\rho = \rho_0$; $P_B = 1$

Households			Restaurants			
Liquid Assets (Gold Ducats)	Nonliquid Assets (Bonds—Market Value)	Nonliquid Assets (Loans to Restaurants for Working Capital)	Working Capital (Gold Ducats)	Fixed Capital	Loans to Finance Working Capital	Quantity of Bonds
200	1,000	300	300	1,000	−300	−1,000

Table 4.2 $Y = 266.7$; $P = 0.75$; $\alpha = 1$; $\rho = \rho_1 = \rho_0/1.2$; $P_B = 1.2$

Households			Restaurants			
Liquid Assets (Gold Ducats)	Nonliquid Assets (Bonds—Market Value)	Nonliquid Assets (Loans to Restaurants for Working Capital)	Working Capital (Gold Ducats)	Fixed Capital	Loans to Finance Working Capital	Quantity of Bonds
300	1,200	200	200	1,000	−200	−1,000

Table 4.3 $Y = 400$; $P = 1$; $\alpha = 1$; $\rho = \rho_2 = \rho_0/0.675$; $P_B = 0.675$

Households			Restaurants			
Liquid Assets (Gold Ducats)	Nonliquid Assets (Bonds—Market Value)	Nonliquid Assets (Loans to Restaurants for Working Capital)	Working Capital (Gold Ducats)	Fixed Capital	Loans to Finance Working Capital	Quantity of Bonds
100	900	400	400	1,333	−400	−1,333

All this is straightforward—except for transactions money. Bonds are the counterpart of physical capital, structures, furnishings, machinery, and so forth. Indeed, the separation of wealth management from restaurant operation was introduced precisely to create a role for bonds as financial assets. This separation logically obliges household balance sheets to take account of the cash lent to restaurants for working capital, that is, for transactions purposes. Tables 4.1, 4.2, and 4.3 classify these loans as *nonliquid* financial assets of the lenders, which is to say assets akin to bonds, except perhaps for the length of time for which working capital is borrowed and lent. At the same time we assume that these loans have no impact on wealth management. They exist in a kind of limbo.[3]

Commercial loans apart, there is no conceptual difficulty in assuming an exogenous money supply of 500 that gets distributed between transactions demand and asset demand with the interest rate adjusting to clear financial markets according to the relative supplies of liquid and nonliquid assets. But what happens if the Venetian money supply does not consist only of gold ducats? Can we, in the context of a fractional-reserve banking system, sustain the assumption of an exogenous money supply when part of it is money created by the banks? Suppose that instead of 500 gold ducats there are only 200 coins in existence. Suppose further that households deposit these coins in banks, all of which operate under laws (or customs) that require them to hold reserves of at least 0.4 gold ducats for each ducat of deposits.

When fully loaned up, the banks can maintain deposits equal in value to 500 ducats against the reserves of 200 gold ducats. *In this context, to argue that the money supply is fixed at 500 is to argue that banks will always be fully loaned up—and that they have no way around reserve requirements.*

There are now three types of players to contend with: in addition to households and restaurateurs, there are bankers, who act as intermediaries between the original two groups. Households and restaurateurs may be the same people wearing different hats, but this assumption undermines one of the purposes of a banking system, which is to form a bridge between households with assets to deploy and businesses who need access to these assets to carry on their businesses. If we are going to assume the existence of banks, it now makes more sense to think of wealth holders and restaurateurs as two different groups of people.

What happens to the three snapshots in Tables 4.1, 4.2, and 4.3 under the new dispensation? If $P = 0.75$ and $Y = 400$, then the total transactions demand will again be 300 ducats. The 200 ducats that represent the deposits of households satisfy their demand for liquid assets. In this case, fractional-reserve banking changes very little. $P_B = 1$ and $\rho = \rho_0$ in Table 4.4, just as in Table 4.1.

And we can tie up the loose end of commercial lending: the anomalous status of working capital disappears when banks are assumed to be intermediaries between households and business. Commercial loans now reflect money created by the banking system, so-called inside money, that is an asset of the banks and a liability of the restaurants. Its net contribution to wealth is zero.

Now construct Table 4.5 with $Y = 266.67$ and $P = 0.75$, as in Table 4.2. Transactions demand is 200 ducats, 100 ducats less than in Table 4.4 (and Table 4.1). At $\rho = \rho_0$ total money demand, $M_1 + M_2$, is now 400 rather than 500. What happens to the money *supply* now depends on the banks. One possibility is that bankers actively seek outlets for their unused lending capacity of 100 ducats, which is to say that banks enter the market for bonds. To induce wealth holders to part with their bonds, the bond price must rise. Asset-market equilibrium is still achieved by balancing liquidity and yield, and the equilibrating mechanism is still the interest rate, reflected in the price of bonds. But the equilibrium rate of interest must be lower in Table 4.5 than in Table 4.2 if wealth holders' liquidity preferences are unchanged. For, having sold bonds worth 100 ducats to the banks, they now have a smaller number of bonds, but, as in Table 4.2, 300 ducats in cash. The value of their bonds must be less than 1,200 ducats. Why? Because if wealth holders possess 1,200 ducats worth of bonds, then the total value of all bonds, including the banks' share, would have to be 1,300, and so the price of bonds would be 1.3 ($= 1,300/1,000$). But with $P_B = 1.3$, the interest rate would be lower than ρ_1, which is the interest rate associated with $P_B = 1.2$ in Table 4.2. This contradiction—the composition of wealth is the same in the two cases—means that the value of wealth holders' bonds cannot be 1,200 in both cases.

If the market value of bonds in wealth holders' hands is less than 1,200, say 1,150, then the ratio of their liquid wealth (300) to their bond wealth (1,150) is higher in Table 4.5 than in Table 4.2. Compared with Table 4.2, the interest rate is lower, $\rho = \rho_3 = \rho_0/1.25$, and the price of bonds is higher, $P_B = 1.25$. Banks now own bonds with a market value of 100 ducats.

The novelty lies in the entry of banks into the bond market, which moves the liquidity-preference schedule (see Figure 4.15, where the new schedule is shown with dots). A real-time story—the entry of banks into the bond market increases the overall demand for bonds and leads to a higher bond price and a lower interest rate—is tempting. But in a comparative-statics framework, all we can say is that an asset-market equilibrium with fewer bonds in the hands of wealth holders requires a higher bond price and a lower yield than an equilibrium in which there are more bonds in the possession of wealth holders.

Assume now $Y = 400$ and $P = 1$, so that one ducat of transactions demand accompanies each unit of output. There is now no way to meet the demand generated by $Y = 400$ unless households are willing to accept lower levels of liquid assets in their portfolios. In effect, households have to be willing to buy 100 ducats of commercial loans from the banks.

Here we face the same question that was elided in the previous financial model, without banks: how do we classify the 100 ducats of commercial loans owned by households? Again, we have two alternatives: either we classify these loans as illiquid financial assets or we consider these loans to be like cash. There are real-world analogies for both classifications. Assume that in both cases the banks securitize these loans, in one case as a CDO (for collateralized debt obligation), in the other as the assets of a money-market fund. In the first scenario, CDOs average out the idiosyncratic risk of individual loans but leave households with important systemic risks. This scenario would make the CDO more like a bond than like cash. In the alternative scenario, we suppose that the residual systemic risks are small enough that the loans can be packaged in a liquid form—a money-market fund—that households treat like cash. In this case we can imagine the money-market fund selling shares to households and using the proceeds to buy commercial paper issued by restaurateurs.

Either way, we assume that the issuers of notes against working capital, the restaurants, maintain their bank deposits—their obligation to pay money for the ingredients in tonight's dinner is not changed. What then is the money supply? Under narrow definitions that limit money to cash and demand deposits, the money supply remains 500, 400 ducats of business deposits and 100 ducats of deposits belonging to households. But if the assets sold by banks to households end up in money-market funds, a broader definition of money would also include the 100 ducats households are now assumed to lend indirectly to restaurants as working capital. Despite the reserve requirement of 40 percent, 200 gold ducats get multiplied into 600 ducats!

We can summarize the three snapshots of the financial markets in the following tables. It is now bank intervention in asset markets that moves the economy along the liquidity-preference schedules in quadrant three of Figure 4.14; households respond to bankers' initiatives—at least if we step out of the comparative-statics mold temporarily to tell a story of change in real time. In this story the negative relationship between the proportion of bonds in households' portfolios and the interest rate is the complement of banks' pursuit of profits.

The common feature of these snapshots is that in all cases banks are fully loaned up. The LM schedules corresponding to Tables 4.4, 4.5, and 4.6 are shown in Figure 4.15. The new feature is the dotted liquidity-preference schedule, which corresponds to a goods-price level of 0.75 and the sale of bonds by households to banks (Table 4.5). Table 4.7 is represented in Figure 4.16, with a definition of the money supply that includes the money-market funds.

How do we know that banks are always fully loaned up? The answer is that we must assume this to be the case, that idle reserves are anathema. Without this assumption the equilibrium condition $\bar{M} = M_1 + M_2$ tells us nothing about whether money demand accommodates itself to money supply, as

Table 4.4 $Y = 400$; $P = 0.75$; $\alpha = 1$; $\rho = \rho_0$; $P_B = 1$

Households			Banks				Restaurants			
Bank Deposits	Nonliquid Assets (Bonds—Market Value)	Commercial Loans	Nonliquid Assets (Bonds—Market Value)	Commercial Loans	Reserves	Bank Deposits	Bank Deposits	Fixed Capital	Commercial Loans	Quantity of Bonds
200	1,000	0	0	300	200	−500	300	1,000	−300	−1,000

Table 4.5 $Y = 266.67$; $P = 0.75$; $\alpha = 1$; $\rho = \rho_3 = \rho_0/1.25$; $P_B = 1.25$

Households			Banks				Restaurants			
Bank Deposits	Nonliquid Assets (Bonds—Market Value)	Commercial Loans	Nonliquid Assets (Bonds—Market Value)	Commercial Loans	Reserves	Bank Deposits	Bank Deposits	Fixed Capital	Commercial Loans	Quantity of Bonds
300	1,150	0	100	200	200	−500	200	1,000	−200	−1,000

Table 4.6 $Y = 400$; $P = 1$; $\alpha = 1$; $\rho = \rho_2 = \rho_0/0.675$; $P_B = 0.675$

Households			Banks				Restaurants			
Bank Deposits	Nonliquid Assets (Bonds—Market Value)	Commercial Loans	Nonliquid Assets (Bonds—Market Value)	Commercial Loans	Reserves	Bank Deposits	Bank Deposits	Fixed Capital	Commercial Loans	Quantity of Bonds
100	900	100	0	300	200	−500	400	1,333	−400	−1,333

Table 4.7 $Y = 400$; $P = 1$; $\alpha = 1$; $\rho = \rho_4 = \rho_0/0.8$; $P_B = 0.8$

Households			Banks				Restaurants			
Bank Deposits	Nonliquid Assets (Bonds—Market Value)	Commercial Loans	Nonliquid Assets (Bonds—Market Value)	Commercial Loans	Reserves	Bank Deposits	Bank Deposits	Fixed Capital	Commercial Loans	Quantity of Bonds
100	1,067	100	0	300	200	−500	400	1,333	−400	−1,333

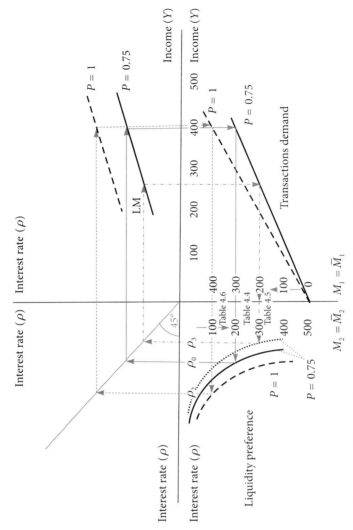

Figure 4.15 Financial equilibrium: constructing the LM schedule, II.

we have been assuming, or money supply responds passively to changes in money demand.

Instead of assuming that banks are always at the upper limit of deposit: reserve ratios, suppose that banks focus exclusively on providing short-term working capital, never venturing into the bond market. Then the money supply rather than its composition will change with the volume of loan demand. When commercial-loan demand is lower, banks simply curtail their operations and hold excess reserves rather than replace these loans with purchases of bonds. We then have Table 4.8 in place of Table 4.5. In Table 4.8 there is no change in the public's holdings of liquid and illiquid assets relative to the original position in Table 4.4, no change in bond prices and interest rates. In this case the aggregate money supply, $\bar{M}$, as well as its composition, fluctuates with the level of output and prices; when transactions demand is lower, the reserve ratio will be higher and the money supply lower. Now ρ_0 balances the advantages of bonds and bank deposits for wealth holders independently of transactions demand: the result is the horizontal LM schedule in Figure 4.17.

With a higher price level, say $P = 1$, and with the stock of bonds higher in the same proportion, we have the results in Table 4.9. In order for households to absorb the larger stock of bonds, a lower bond price—a higher interest rate—is required. Since M_2 is unchanged, the market value of bonds has to be

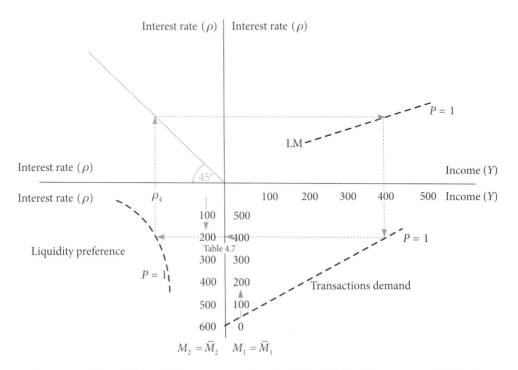

Figure 4.16 Financial equilibrium: constructing the LM schedule with money-market funds.

Table 4.8 $Y = 266.67$; $P = 0.75$; $\alpha = 1$; $\rho = \rho_0$; $P_B = 1$

	Households			Banks				Restaurants			
	Bank Deposits	Nonliquid Assets (Bonds—Market Value)	Commercial Loans	Nonliquid Assets (Bonds—Market Value)	Commercial Loans	Reserves	Bank Deposits	Bank Deposits	Fixed Capital	Commercial Loans	Quantity of Bonds
	200	1,000	0	0	200	200	−400	200	1,000	−200	−1,000

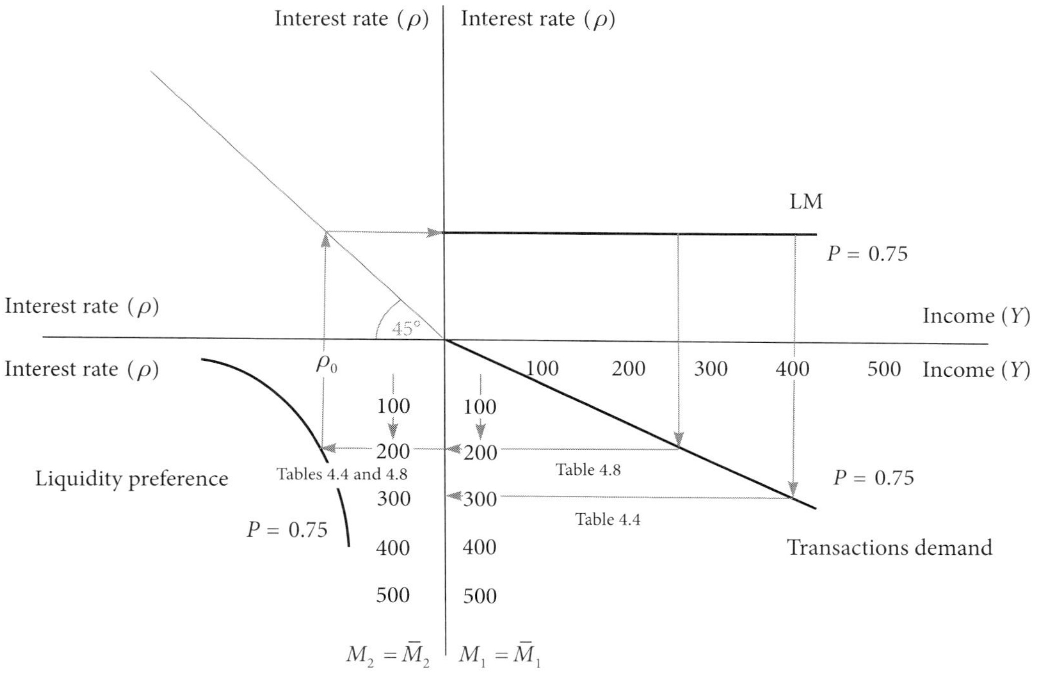

Figure 4.17 Financial equilibrium: constructing the LM schedule with endogenous transactions money, I.

lower than in Table 4.8, while the higher interest rate translates into a lower price of bonds. Observe that the higher price level shifts the LM schedule upward in Figure 4.18.

So even though fractional-reserve banking flattens out the LM schedule when banks respond passively to the transactions demand for money, the key difference between the second-pass and the first-pass models holds: aggregate demand continues to be a downward sloping function of the price level. Accordingly, there will be a full-employment equilibrium if the money-wage rate is up for grabs—at least barring the two exceptional cases that cancel the negative relationship between the price level and aggregate demand.

The causality is different. There is no Keynes effect; the smaller transactions requirements of a lower price level do not release money that is incorporated into asset portfolios. That avenue is closed off by the firewall between the two kinds of money, implicit in the assumption that the supply of money is the sum of a given amount of portfolio money and an amount of transactions money determined by output and the price level. It is, rather, the assumption that a change in the price level is accompanied by a change in the same direction of the stock of bonds that is responsible for the shift in the LM schedule. The result, a downward-sloping AD schedule, is the same because both the bond effect and the Keynes effect change the proportion of cash and bonds in the same direction, the bond effect by a positive relationship between the price level and the stock of bonds, the Keynes effect by a negative relationship between the price level and the stock of portfolio money.

Chapter 7 shows that there is no bond effect when changes in prices take place in real time. The consequences of assuming the money supply adjusts to transactions demand turn out to be different in the context of the disequilibrium dynamics explored in the next three chapters. And if we go the next step and assume that transactions demand and asset demand are complementary rather than competitive uses of money, the complications are even more serious. As we shall see in chapter 13, in the absence of a central bank, the interest rate will in general be indeterminate!

The Real-Balance Effect

In a comparative-statics framework, Modigliani's argument leaves one part of Keynes's edifice standing—some would say the most important part—in allowing for the exceptions of a liquidity trap (the floor on the hurdle rate) or an inelastic investment-demand schedule. An attack from another quarter, in the form of a critique based not on the effect of the price level on the interest rate and investment demand, but on the effect of the price level on consumption demand, did not leave Modigliani's exceptions standing.

Table 4.9 $Y = 266.67$; $P = 1$; $\alpha = 1$; $\rho = \rho_5 = \rho_0/0.6$; $P_B = 0.6$

	Households			Banks				Restaurants			
	Bank Deposits	Nonliquid Assets (Bonds—Market Value)	Commercial Loans	Nonliquid Assets (Bonds—Market Value)	Commercial Loans	Reserves	Bank Deposits	Bank Deposits	Fixed Capital	Commercial Loans	Quantity of Bonds
	200	800	0	0	266.67	200	−466.67	266.67	1,333	−266.67	−1,333

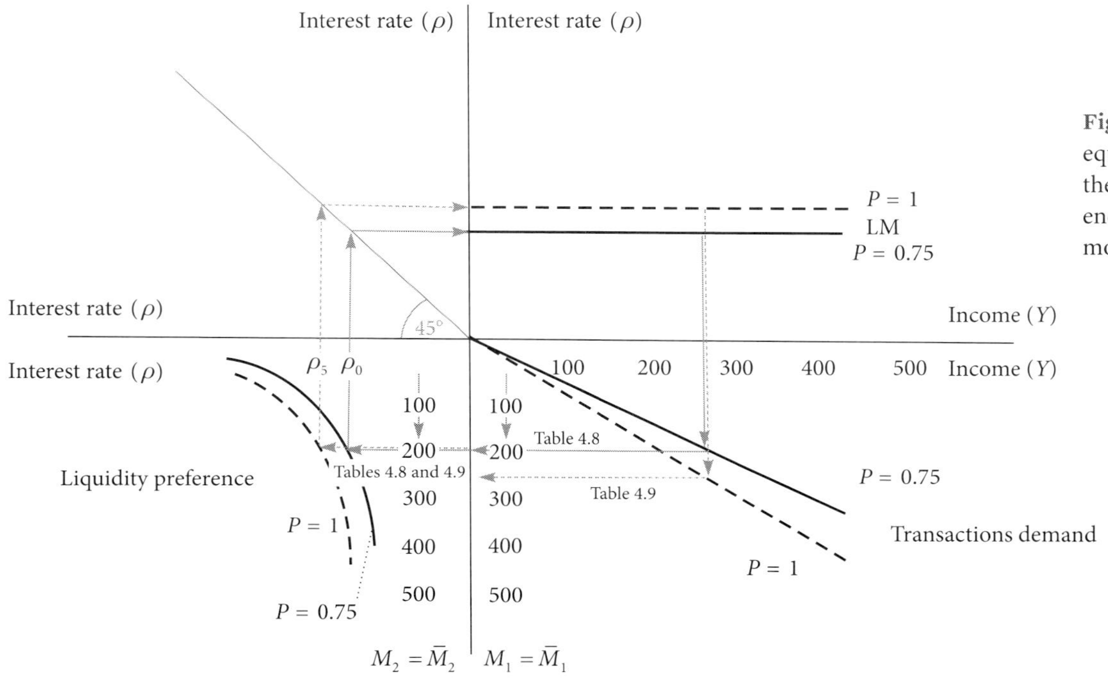

Figure 4.18 Financial equilibrium: constructing the LM schedule with endogenous transactions money, II.

Keynes always recognized the simplifications involved in making consumption depend solely on income, but what he regarded as a modest qualification became in the hands of his critics a weapon to knock down the entire enterprise of *The General Theory*. Keynes's consumption function was based on the view that

> The expenditure on consumption in [real] terms . . . depends in the main, on the volume of output and employment. (p. 96)

This justifies

> summing up the other factors in the portmanteau function "propensity to consume." (p. 96)

The takeaway, which serves as the basis for the simple consumption function deployed in the first- and second-pass models, is that

> Men are disposed, as a rule and on the average, to increase their consumption as their income increases, but not by as much as the increase in their income. (p. 96)

(Keynes stresses that the marginal propensity to consume is likely to decline with income, a complication we shall ignore until chapter 9.)

Keynes acknowledges that "other factors are capable of varying [the propensity to consume]," and he warns us parenthetically that "this must not be forgotten" (p. 96). In particular, he has already pointed to the impact of wealth on consumption, particularly surprise changes in wealth:

> The consumption of the wealth-owning class may be extremely susceptible to unforeseen changes in the money-value of its wealth. This should be classified amongst the major factors capable of causing short-period changes in the propensity to consume. (pp. 92–93)

And he reiterates that one reason for the propensity to consume to vary is that

> A decline in income due to a decline in the level of employment, if it goes far, may even cause consumption to exceed income . . . by some individuals and institutions using up the financial reserves which they have accumulated in better times. (p. 98)

As we shall see in chapter 9, the mainstream, under the tutelage of Milton Friedman (1957) and Modigliani (in a series of papers, beginning with Modigliani and Brumberg [1954]), turned Keynes's views on consumption inside out. What was for Keynes a qualification of the idea that the main determinant of consumption is income became in the "permanent income hypothesis" and the "life-cycle hypothesis" a radically different view of consumption in which wealth was the dog and income the tail.

For present purposes we need not go so far. The real-balance effect attacked Keynes not on the general grounds that consumption depends on total wealth rather than on income, but on the specifics of the supposed impact of the price level on consumption through its effect on the cash component of wealth. The opening salvo was fired by Gottfried Haberler, a leading business-cycle theorist whose 1936 *summa* of pre-Keynesian views, *Prosperity and Depression,* was rendered obsolete by *The General Theory* even as the ink was drying on the pages of the two books. A second edition of *Prosperity and Depression,* published in 1939, added a long chapter on *The General Theory* and the ensuing discussion, in which Haberler hinted at what was to become the real-balance effect. But it was in the third edition, published in 1941, that Haberler fleshed this argument out. A generation later the real-balance effect became, as I observed in chapter 1, the killer argument for an increasingly vocal anti-Keynesian mainstream and the source of increasing bewilderment to the shrinking band of brothers (and at least one sister) who had actually read and digested *The General Theory.*

What is the real-balance effect? To answer this question, we must back up and examine how wealth impacts consumption and saving. The simplest way is to redraw the consumption and saving functions of the last chapter, replacing the zero intercepts by nonzero intercepts—positive in the case of consumption, negative for saving—as in the right-hand panels of Figures 4.19 and 4.20.

Wealth is assumed here to change both the amount of consumption and saving that take place in the absence of any current income and the marginal propensities to consume and save, that is to say, both the intercepts and the slopes of the consumption and saving functions. What matters here is the intercept: with a positive intercept, even people with no income can—temporarily at least—consume, which is to say that they can save a negative amount. And the more wealth, the more consumption is possible.

The key to the real-balance effect is that some fraction of wealth is held in the form of money, and the purchasing power of this money varies inversely with the price level. Imagine that the price level is so low that a single thin dime will buy a life of luxury, and you happen to find an old dollar bill stashed in a dresser in the attic. Surely your consumption level will be much higher than if you find that dollar bill with prices what they are today.

Graphically, the intercept in the right-hand panels of Figures 4.19 and 4.20 varies with the price level; the level of consumption at a zero level of income increases and the level of saving decreases as the price level falls. Regardless of what happens to marginal propensities, any amount of aggregate demand can be generated by varying the price level. Haberler puts it like this:

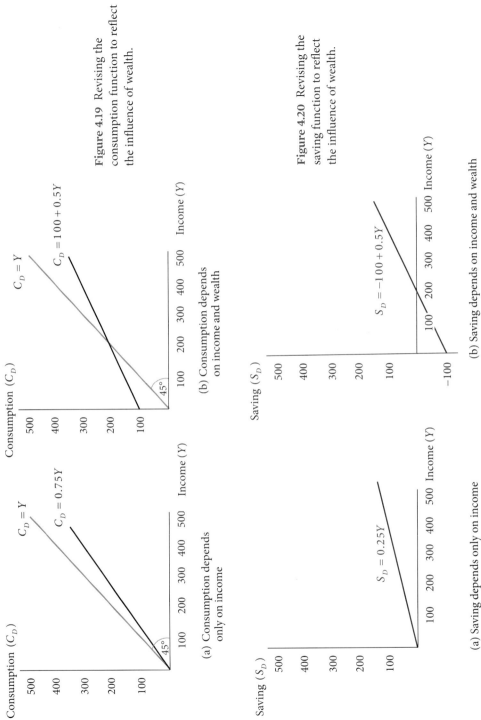

Figure 4.19 Revising the consumption function to reflect the influence of wealth.

(a) Consumption depends only on income

(b) Consumption depends on income and wealth

Figure 4.20 Revising the saving function to reflect the influence of wealth.

(a) Saving depends only on income

(b) Saving depends on income and wealth

Pari passu with the fall in prices, existing money hoards (M_2) rise in real value and, sooner or later, the point will be reached where even the most cautious individuals will find an irresistible temptation to stop hoarding and to dishoard. (1939, p. 403)

In the 1941 edition, Haberler expands on this theme (the relevant passage quoted as an epigraph to this chapter):

When prices and wages fall, more and more money is released from transaction duties. Idle funds grow in terms of money and still faster (without any limit even if the quantity of money remains unchanged or decreases) in real terms. It was argued [in the passage cited above] that sooner or later when money hoards (inactive deposits, Mr KEYNES' M_2) have reached a certain level people will stop saving (that is, in this case, they will cease to add to their hoards). That amounts to saying that the rate of saving is not only an increasing function of the level of (real) income, but also a diminishing function of the wealth the individual holds. (pp. 408–409)

Pigou (1943, 1947) independently developed the same idea, and Don Patinkin (1948) extended the argument to include government debt.

In the context of comparative statics, the real-balance effect means that the lower the price level, the greater aggregate demand—*with no upper limit on the level of demand.* Unlike the AD schedules in Figure 4.11, the AD schedule in Figure 4.21(a) will always intersect the aggregate-supply schedule provided the absolute price level can be brought arbitrarily close to zero. The same result is shown in Figure 4.21(b), with the price level varying with the money wage at different levels. Because the level of wealth, and hence the level of consumption demand, becomes infinite as the price level goes to zero, there is no need to qualify the argument that the economy is self-regulating. Neither a liquidity trap nor inelastic investment demand matters in this context.

We can see this by examining what happens to the various components of real wealth as the price level falls. Consider first the case in which there are no banks and money is specie. Nominal wealth is

$$P_B(\rho)\bar{B} + M_2 + M_1 \quad + \quad -\bar{B} + PK - M_1 + \text{Working Capital.}$$
$$\text{(Households)} \qquad\qquad\qquad \text{(Firms)}$$

Since $\bar{B} = PK$ and M_1 = Working Capital, the assets (PK + working capital) of firms and their liabilities ($\bar{B} + M_1$) are exactly equal regardless of the price level. So net financial wealth is equal to the assets of households,

$$P_B(\rho)PK + M_2 + M_1.$$

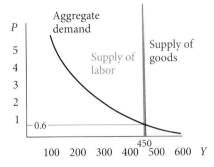

(a) Real price fixed at full-employment
   equilibrium level

$$\frac{P}{W} = 4$$

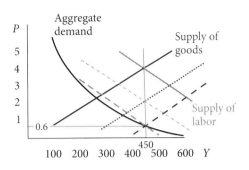

(b) Alternative levels of the
   money wage

$W = W_0 = 1$ (solid GS and LS)

$W = 0.5$ (dotted GS and LS)

$W = 0.15$ (dashed GS and LS)

Figure 4.21 No limits to full-employment equilibrium: aggregate demand with a real-balance effect.

Real wealth, which along with real income is now assumed to determine real consumption, is obtained by dividing financial wealth by the price level. We have

$$P_B(\rho)K + \frac{M_2}{P} + \frac{M_1}{P}.$$

As the price level goes to zero, this expression becomes infinite.

In a regime of fractional-reserve banking, the calculations are different. We have

$$\underset{\text{(Households)}}{P_B(\rho)\bar{B} + \bar{M}_2} \; + \; \underset{\text{(Banks)}}{M_1 + \bar{M}_2 - M_1 - \bar{M}_2} \; + \; \underset{\text{(Firms)}}{-\bar{B} + PK - M_1 + \text{Working Capital.}}$$

Once again we can ignore firms, because their assets and liabilities match. Bond liabilities ($\bar{B}$) are equal to the value of physical capital (PK), and borrowing from banks (M_1) is equal to working capital.

We can ignore banks as well, because their liabilities and assets also match. For the banks, commercial lending to restaurants for working capital (M_1) is an asset, while the deposits of these same restaurants are a liability (M_1 in red). Likewise, the deposits of wealth holders ($\bar{M}_2$ in red) are a liability for the banks balanced by their reserves ($\bar{M}_2$ in black).

In other words, as was pointed out by Michał Kalecki early on in the debate (1944, p. 132) that followed Pigou's formulation of the real-balance effect, so-called inside money created by the banking system does not constitute wealth from the vantage point of the economy as a whole: every ducat of M_1 in black is exactly offset by a ducat of M_1 in red. We are left with household wealth, which now includes only asset money. The result is the same as without banks; real wealth

$$\frac{P_B(\rho)\bar{B} + \bar{M}_2}{P} = P_B(\rho)K + \frac{\bar{M}_2}{P}$$

becomes infinite as P goes to zero—and so does aggregate demand.

Taking Stock

Is the Haberler–Pigou–Patinkin real-balance argument the stake through the heart of *The General Theory?* Yes and no. On its own terms, yes. Already disposed to interpreting Keynes's economics in terms of rigidities and frictions, mainstream economists did not have to accept the practical relevance of the real-balance effect. All they had to do was to agree that, in a world without imperfections, cash holdings would become more and more important for consumption spending at lower and lower levels of prices—and eventually provide enough demand to fully employ the labor force regardless of how low investment demand might sink. Milton Friedman was reflecting a consensus in 1970 when he wrote that because of the real-balance effect there was, as a matter of theory, no fatal flaw in the price system:

> [According to Keynes] as a purely *theoretical* matter, there need not exist, even if all prices are flexible, a *long-run equilibrium* position characterized by "full employment" of resources . . .
>
> [This] proposition can be treated summarily because it has been demonstrated to be false. Keynes's error consisted in neglecting the role of wealth in the consumption function or, stated differently, in neglecting the existence of a desired stock of wealth as a goal motivating savings.[5] All sorts of frictions and rigidities may interfere with the attainment of a hypothetical long-run equilibrium position at full employment; dynamic changes in technology, resources, and social and economic institutions may continually change the characteristics of that equilibrium position; but there is no fundamental "flaw in the price system" that makes unemployment the natural outcome of a fully operative market mechanism[6] (pp. 206–207).
>
> [5] Keynes, of course, verbally recognized this point, but it was not incorporated in his formal model of the economy. Its key role was pointed out first by Haberler (1941, pp. 242, 389, 403, 491–503) and subsequently by Pigou (1947), Tobin (1947), Patinkin (1951), and Johnson (1961).

[6] This proposition played a large role in gaining for Keynes the adherence of many noneconomists, particularly the large band of reformers, social critics, and radicals who were persuaded that there was something fundamentally wrong with the capitalist "system." There is a long history of attempts, some highly sophisticated, to demonstrate that there is a "flaw in the price system" (the title of one such attempt [Martin 1924]), attempts going back at least to Malthus. . . . But, prior to Keynes, these attempts had been made primarily by persons outside of the mainstream of the economics profession, and professional economists had little trouble in demonstrating their theoretical flaws and inadequacies. Keynes's attempt was therefore greeted with enthusiasm. It came from a professional economist of the very highest repute, regarded, and properly so, by his fellow economists as one of the great economists of all time. The analytical system was sophisticated and complex, yet, once mastered, appeared highly mechanical and capable of yielding far-reaching and important conclusions with a sminimum of input; and these conclusions were, besides, highly congenial to the opponents of the market system. Needless to say, the demonstration that this proposition of Keynes's is false, and even the acceptance of this demonstration by economists who regard themselves as disciples of the Keynes of *The General Theory,* has not prevented the noneconomist opponents of the market system from continuing to believe that Keynes proved the proposition, and continuing to cite his authority for it.

The main problem is that, like Modigliani, Haberler et al. relied on a comparative-statics argument. None of these authors directly addresses the issue of what happens when prices fall, as distinct from what happens when prices are at a lower rather than a higher level *and always have been.*

Keynes finally addresses the effects of real-time changes in the nominal wage in chapter 19 of *The General Theory.* The problem is that he never formalized this third pass at a critique of self-regulation in the form of a model. Without the framework of a model, it was easy to ignore this chapter altogether; it became possible for mainstream economists to disregard Keynes's clear statements about the provisional nature of the assumption of a given money wage and to focus on this assumption as the distinguishing feature of *The General Theory.* Chapters 6 and 7 of this book provide the missing model, after what may appear to be a digression but is not: in chapter 5 we explore the dynamics of adjustment. We start with the simple demand-supply models of the nineteenth-century pioneers of neoclassical economics, Alfred Marshall and Léon Walras.

Modigliani transforms Keynes's second-pass model by dropping the assumption $W = W_0$ and replacing it with the assumption that in equilibrium workers are on their supply schedules. $L = L(P/W)$ coupled with $Y = F(K, L)$ implies $Y = F(K, L(P/W)) \equiv LS(P/W)$. This adds a fourth equation along with the additional unknown W. The complete system is

$$I(\rho) = sY, \tag{4.1}$$

$$Y = GS\left(\frac{P}{W}\right), \tag{4.2}$$

$$M \equiv P\alpha Y + \frac{\beta(\rho)}{1 - \beta(\rho)} P_B(\rho)PK = \bar{M}, \tag{4.3}$$

$$Y = F\left(K, L\left(\frac{P}{W}\right)\right). \tag{4.4}$$

As outlined in the text, the solution is particularly easy since the system can be solved sequentially. The goods-supply and labor-supply equations, (4.2) and (4.4), allow us to solve for P/W and Y. Once Y is known, equation (4.1) determines ρ, and, finally, equation (4.3) determines P and hence W.

A solution is not guaranteed. Liquidity preference may prevent the value of ρ that emerges from the second step from satisfying the money equation. Even if there is no lower limit on ρ in equation (4.3), inelastic investment demand may preclude equality of investment and saving at the full-employment, profit-maximizing equilibrium of the subsystem formed by equations (4.2) and (4.4).

The real-balance effect remedies both the problem of a liquidity trap and the problem of inelastic investment demand. Replace the fixed-parameter saving function $S = sY$ in equation (4.1) by

$$S = S\left(\text{income, wealth}\right) = S\left(Y, \frac{M_2 + P_B(\rho)PK}{P}\right)$$

and suppose that wealth has a negative impact on saving, so that

$$S\left(0, \frac{M_2 + P_B(\rho)PK}{P}\right) < 0.$$

Suppose also that the derivative of saving with respect to wealth is negative and bounded away from zero. Then as $P \to 0$, real wealth, and therefore consumption demand, increase without bound. So aggregate demand increases without bound as $P \to 0$ regardless of what happens to investment demand.

The saving function $S(Y, (M_2 + P_B(\rho)PK)/P)$ reflects the assumption that wealth consists of portfolio cash and bonds, $M_2 + P_B(\rho)PK$. Cash for transactions is assumed to be inside money created by the banking system, so that as $P \to 0$, $M_1 \to 0$. The effect of real cash balances on aggregate demand does not depend on whether we assume banks are always fully loaned up; since we are assuming that $M_1 = P\alpha Y$ and $M_2 = \bar{M}_2$, we have $M_1 + M_2 = \bar{M}$ and $M_2 \to \bar{M}$ as $P \to 0$.

But the choice of assumption about banking does affect the shape of the LM schedule. If we assume that transactions money is created by the banking system to meet the demand αPY, and the amount of portfolio cash is fixed exogenously, then we have two demand = supply equations in place of the single money equation, (4.3):

$$M_1 \equiv \alpha PY = \bar{M}_1, \tag{4.3a}$$

$$M_2 \equiv \frac{\beta(\rho)}{1 - \beta(\rho)} P_B(\rho)PK = \bar{M}_2. \tag{4.3b}$$

$\bar{M}_1$ is now an unknown, determined by P and Y, whereas M_2 is determined by $\bar{M}_2$. Equation (4.3b) represents the LM schedule in Figure 4.17. It is horizontal because the level of ρ that emerges from equation (4.3b), given P, is independent of Y. It is still the case, that, as P falls, the level of Y determined by the intersection of the equations (4.1) and (4.3b) rises, which is to say that the AD schedule is downward sloping in $Y \times P$ space. The demonstration mimics the derivation of dY/dP in the mathematical appendix to chapter 3 and is omitted here.

— III —

Keynes Vindicated

A Theory of Real-Time Changes

— 5 —

THE PRICE MECHANISM

Gospels According to Marshall and Walras

When . . . the amount produced . . . is such that the demand price is greater than the supply price, then sellers receive more than is sufficient to make it worth their while to bring goods to market to that amount; and there is at work an active force tending to increase the amount brought forward for sale. On the other hand, when the amount produced is such that the demand price is less than the supply price, sellers receive less than is sufficient to make it worth their while to bring goods to market on that scale; so that those who were just on the margin of doubt as to whether to go on producing are decided not to do so, and there is an active force at work tending to diminish the amount brought forward for sale. When the demand price is equal to the supply price, the amount produced has no tendency either to be increased or to be diminished; it is in equilibrium.

—ALFRED MARSHALL

Let us take, for example, trading in 3 per cent French Rentes [consols] on the Paris Stock Exchange and confine our attention to these operations alone . . .

The three per cents, as they are called, are quoted at 60 francs. At this price, brokers who have received some orders to sell at 60 francs and other orders *at less* than 60 francs, will offer a certain quantity of 3 per cent Rentes . . . *Per contra*, the brokers who have received some orders to buy at 60 francs and others *at more* than 60 francs will demand a certain quantity of 3 per cent Rentes, when 60 francs is quoted . . .

[Let us assume that] demand is *greater than* the offer . . .

The brokers with orders to buy can no longer find brokers with orders to sell. This is a clear indication that the quantity of three per cents demanded at 60 francs is greater than the quantity offered at that price. Theoretically, trading should come to a halt. Brokers who have orders to buy at 60 francs 05 centimes *or who have orders to buy at higher prices* make bids at 60 francs 05 centimes. They raise the market price . . . In consequence of a two-sided movement, the difference between effective demand and effective offer is reduced . . . A new stationary state is thus found at a higher price.

—LÉON WALRAS

Keynes's critical endeavor in *The General Theory* was to establish that a perfectly competitive market system would not normally provide full employment if left to its own devices. Whether or not Keynes succeeded depends not only on whom you ask but also on how you pose the question.

Keynes intends his second-pass model to provide the background for answering a question about dynamics. This question begins with supposing an economy to be at full employment. The economy then suffers a shock that drives the unemployment rate into double digits—not unlike what happened after the stock market crash of 1929 or the financial crisis of 2008. Keynes's question is whether the market mechanism left to itself—with output, prices, and money wages responding to the new conditions—will return the economy to full employment, or instead whether the economy will settle at an unemployment equilibrium.

Keynes's answer is that the economy is not guaranteed to return to full employment even if we give it all the time in the world and assume away frictions and imperfections that interfere with the working of competitive markets. In short, Keynes is arguing for the existence of an unemployment equilibrium, using the second-pass model as scaffolding on which to tell a story about changing money wages.

But Modigliani, Haberler, et al. are asking a different question: if both the price level *and* the wage level can be chosen and the money supply is exogenously fixed, are there levels of money wages and prices and output and employment that satisfy AD, GS, and LS schedules? That is, do there exist levels of output and employment for which expenditure equals income, producers maximize profits, and a job is available for every willing worker? Here the question is whether or not there exists a full-employment equilibrium. The answer to this question is also yes.

The problem is that the two ways of asking about full employment—whether a full-employment equilibrium exists, and whether once disturbed, a competitive market economy will return to full employment—are not two versions of the same question. By distinguishing the two questions, I mean to highlight the difference noted in chapter 1 between an equilibrium in the mind of God and an equilibrium in a world in which people are situated in and encumbered by history. In the one case, the equilibrium exists independently of how and indeed whether an economy might reach it; in the second case, existence and adjustment are inexorably linked. The first question, whether or not a full-employment equilibrium exists, is the question that economists have imputed to Keynes, at least since Modigliani's 1944 article. The second question, this book argues, is Keynes's own question.

To answer Keynes's question requires detailed attention to the price *mechanism*—how adjustment takes place when the economy is not in equilibrium—

instead of following the usual practice (my own past practice included) of treating dynamics as an afterthought. There are two reasons why the usual practice won't do. The more general reason, one which goes far beyond the purposes of this book, is that models which ignore the adjustment process make unreasonable demands on agents in terms of the knowledge they have about the economy.

A standard trope of mainstream economics, going back to Adam Smith, asserts the contrary, not only that markets are self-regulating but that this self-regulation makes very minimal demands on agents' knowledge. They need to know very little about the economy: indeed nothing but the vector of equilibrium prices and their own consumption preferences and production possibilities. Choices of optimal plans in terms of the self-interest of each promote the well-being of all, at least in the limited sense of Pareto efficiency.

But this in itself tells us little about knowledge requirements when the data change, when, say, investment demand or saving desires change. What do agents do then? To move immediately to a new equilibrium requires first of all that every agent knows what the equilibrium looks like. Each must possess a comprehensive understanding of how the economy works in order to calculate, à la Modigliani or Haberler, what the new configuration of equilibrium prices will be, a much harder task than simply figuring out one's own reaction to this price vector. If investment demand falls or the desire to save increases, then for a change in the interest rate to stimulate enough investment or for a change in household wealth to stimulate sufficient consumption to get to a new full-employment equilibrium, the price level must fall. This much follows from the qualitative structure of the argument. But—here is the rub—to determine the new equilibrium configuration of prices, agents must have complete knowledge of the production possibilities and preferences of all agents, for these are the data that will determine the price vector at the new equilibrium. And, in addition, each agent must have confidence that other agents are making the same calculations *and* are prepared to act on them.

This part of the problem is not specific to Keynes and his critics. The world imagined by Kenneth Arrow and Gerard Debreu (1954; see also Arrow 1963–1964; Debreu 1959) sharpens our understanding as well as our wits, but it diverts attention from some of the more significant issues we face in unraveling the mysteries of markets. By collapsing time into a form of product differentiation, the Arrow–Debreu framework makes it difficult to think about what happens outside of equilibrium. In a very real sense, the Arrow–Debreu framework sets too easy a task for economists at the same time it makes life so much easier for economic agents.

Even if we assume that the equilibrium price vector is known to agents, the demands made by the Arrow–Debreu framework on agents' knowledge are hardly negligible: agents must know their own production possibilities and consumption preferences from the get-go. A more realistic assumption is that when the clock starts running, each consumer knows whether or not her marginal rate of substitution of apples for nuts exceeds the ratio of the price of nuts to the price of apples, but not the utility-maximizing allocation of her food budget. Each producer may know whether or not the marginal productivity of labor exceeds the wage, but not the precise point at which the two are equal. In short, producers and consumers may have sufficient knowledge to proceed in the direction of equilibrium but not enough knowledge to go there directly; agents know which way is up but little more. As consumers adjust in the direction of increasing utility, and producers adjust in the direction of more profit, they will presumably learn more and more about their utility and production functions. A world of experiential knowledge is necessarily a world of learning by doing, in which, faced with new data, agents adjust slowly because of the very nature of their knowledge. (See below, chapters 9 and 10, and Marglin 2008, chapters 7–9, for more extensive discussion of the assumption of knowledge and rationality in economics.)

To a mainstream economist, this looks like a rigidity, a friction imposed on the competitive model, à la Guillermo Calvo (1983), that arbitrarily restricts the ability of agents to adjust. This is a misunderstanding. Calvo-type limits on the frequency of adjustment *are* arbitrary, introduced into the New Keynesian version of dynamic, stochastic, general equilibrium precisely as a form of sand in the wheels. My conception of agency, by contrast, involves no constraints other than those of being human and therefore operating with limited knowledge and limited cognitive power. The local, experiential, nature of knowledge makes it impossible to go to the utility- and profit-maximizing equilibrium all at once. It is a stretch to cast an inherent limitation of human beings—the boundedness of rationality—as a friction.

There is a second reason, one specific to the introduction of aggregate demand into the story, why adjustment is important: in my interpretation of Keynes, the basic model of the economy is overdetermined. In contrast with just-determined models, we can't even define equilibrium apart from the adjustment process. Even if we wished to sidestep the whole question of dynamics by invoking assumptions that get the economy to equilibrium without the trouble and bother of disequilibrium, we don't have this option—whatever we might choose to assume about the knowledge of economic agents. Figure 5.1 pictures the simplest model. As we shall see, once we take all three schedules—AD, GS, and LS—into account, where the economy comes to rest cannot be disentangled from the process it follows outside of equilibrium.

Despite its importance, adjustment processes get short shrift from economists. Most think that the problem has been adequately covered if a brief

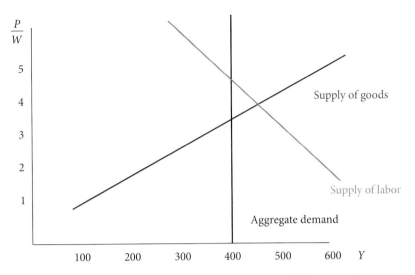

Figure 5.1 Aggregate demand, goods supply, and labor supply.

discussion of adjustment is tacked onto a demonstration of the existence of equilibrium. Neglect begins early on. In elementary texts, how the economy gets to equilibrium is usually covered (or covered up) in a few paragraphs. Greg Mankiw's *Principles of Economics* explains, "The price of any good adjusts to bring the quantity supplied and quantity demanded into balance" (2018, p. 78). It is tempting but wrong to put this down to Mankiw's conservative bias; a leading "liberal" text, *Economics,* written by William Baumol, Alan Blinder, and John Solow, says the same thing: "In a free market, the forces of supply and demand generally push the price toward its equilibrium level, the price at which quantity supplied and quantity demanded are equal" (2020, p. 66). Graduate texts do better, but not much better: as I observed in chapter 2, one leading text devotes no more than ten pages out of a thousand to the question of stability of equilibrium (Mas-Colell, Whinston, and Green 1995), the term of art for whether the economy gets to equilibrium, or more accurately, whether the economy will find its way back to equilibrium if it is dislodged by a shock to demand or supply.

On second thought perhaps we shouldn't be surprised. As Mas-Colell and his co-authors note (1995, p. 620) there is relatively little to say about what happens outside of equilibrium—and much of what can be said is quite damaging to mainstream theory. (See, for example, the illuminating but dead-end investigation by Frank Fisher [1983].) Even when the road to equilibrium lies in virtual space, with neither production nor exchange taking place to complicate matters, very special assumptions are required to guarantee that once disturbed, equilibrium will be restored. Such a guarantee is provided by assuming that all goods are substitutes for one another in the sense that if the price of, say, apples rises, more pears will be demanded. (This may be a reasonable assumption about apples and pears, but not necessarily about apples and piecrusts.)

More problematic is the assumption that time stands still while the economy is groping its way to equilibrium (Walras's word for his timeless-groping process is *tâtonnement*): in order to maintain the fiction of fixed demand and supply curves, the fiction that none of the data change, no transactions take place while trial prices are adjusted. The assumption of virtual adjustment is not indispensable, but it certainly makes the problem of disequilibrium more tractable.

There is another problem, noted by Tjalling Koopmans (1957) and Kenneth Arrow (1959) six decades ago: even in a world where all goods are substitutes and time conveniently stands still outside of equilibrium, we have trouble telling a story consistent with the basic assumptions of perfect competition once we give up the fiction of an "auctioneer" who stands outside the market. This auctioneer was implicitly assumed (by Léon Walras [1954 (1874)], about whom more below) to maintain the idea that agents always take prices as given and adjust quantities accordingly. But as Koopmans and Arrow pointed out, without the auctioneer the assumption that prices change in response to disequilibrium shortages and surpluses requires that one agent or another is not taking prices as given. She thus acts more like a monopolist than a perfect competitor.

Two Stories about Disequilibrium Adjustment

There are many stories we can tell about what happens outside of equilibrium, but two stories are enough to illustrate the multiplicity of options. One is a story generally attributed to Léon Walras, the nineteenth-century pioneer of general equilibrium theory. For Walras, demand and supply are determined by price, and equilibrium is a matter of finding prices for which the quantities demanded and supplied are equal. The Walrasian story also gives an account of how demand and supply adjust out of equilibrium, and how in turn prices adjust to shortages and surpluses.

The alternative is a Marshallian story, after Walras's British contemporary (and Keynes's teacher), Alfred Marshall, whose *Principles of Economics* went through eight editions between 1890 and 1920 and dominated English-speaking economics for long after. Marshall, unlike Walras, took quantity as the independent variable and price as the dependent. (Marshall's preeminence perhaps explains why contemporary economists, following Walras in making price the independent variable, nevertheless use the horizontal axis for quantity and the vertical axis for price, against the grain of mathematical convention.) In Marshall's story, and Keynes's for that matter, the "demand price" associated with a given quantity is the price at which that quantity will be demanded; the "supply price" is the price at which the quantity will be forthcoming from producers. By the same token, the disequilibrium adjustment process is different *chez* Marshall: quantities adjust according to the difference between demand and supply prices, instead of prices adjusting according to the difference between quantities demanded and supplied.

Both Walras and Marshall discuss disequilibrium adjustment, and both tell real-time stories, but it is fair to say that Walras's is more problematic. Walras explains his dynamics in terms of the order books that stockbrokers maintain on their clients' behalf. Suppose there are two groups of brokers, one of which has clients who in the aggregate wish to buy one thousand 3 percent *rentes* at 61 francs, two thousand at 60, three thousand at 59, the other with clients who have placed orders to sell one thousand *rentes* at 59, two thousand at 60, and three thousand at 61.

If the market opens at 61, offers to sell will outweigh offers to buy in the ratio 3:1. Similarly, if the market opens at 59, offers to buy will swamp the market. In the first case, there will be an excess supply of two thousand *rentes,* and in the second case, a shortage of two thousand *rentes.* In both cases, according to Walras, the price will respond, falling in the first case and rising in the second. The price will come to rest only when demand and supply are in balance, in the present case at 60. The picture is given in Figure 5.2.

Although Walras suggests the process takes place in real time, on the trading floor (1954 [1874], lesson 5, sec. 42, pp. 84–86), his story makes more sense as a virtual, premarket, process than as real-time, market, dynamics. In real time, what happens when the price is, say, 61, and supply exceeds demand? How many *rentes* are sold and at what price? What happens to the subsequent demand and supply of *rentes* at 60 if trades take place at an opening price of 61 (or 59)? If either demand or supply changes, does 60 remain the equilibrium price?

It is not that these questions cannot be answered but that the story quickly gets very complicated. By assuming the adjustment process takes place before markets open, before trade takes place, it becomes possible to stipulate that nothing at all happens out of equilibrium. If adjustment takes place outside of time, we need not even ask how quantities adjust, because the only quantities that matter are the equilibrium quantities.

Nor need we be too fussy about how prices change. We can imagine a Walrasian auctioneer who first chooses a price at random ("by chance," or perhaps "haphazardly" better conveys the meaning of *au hasard* in this context, but "at random" is the usual translation), then adjusts the price according to the difference between demand and supply, continuing the adjustment of price until the equilibrium is reached.

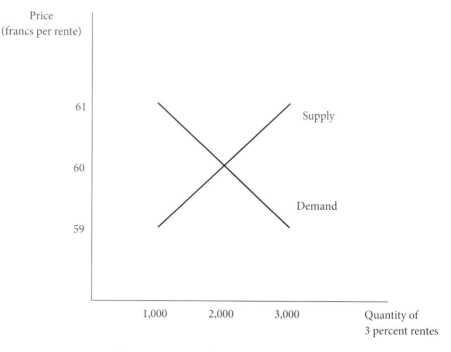

Figure 5.2 Demand and supply à la Walras.

Even as a virtual adjustment, there is no guarantee that the process will converge to equilibrium. If the auctioneer is guided only by the size of excess demand or supply, she could as well take the traders away from equilibrium as toward equilibrium. Starting from, say, a price of 60.25 francs per *rente,* she might overshoot the mark, responding to the oversupply by reducing the price to 59.50 francs, then overshooting again by raising the price to 60.75 francs. Only if the adjustment of price takes place in sufficiently small steps and the auctioneer is guided by the difference between the quantity demanded and the quantity supplied at each trial price, can we be sure that, as Figure 5.2 is drawn, the process will converge to the equilibrium at $<Q = 2{,}000, P = 60>$.

Marshall, for all the inevitable abstraction of a simple model, has a more convincing real-time story. He asks us (1920 [1890], p. 348) to imagine a fish market in an era with no refrigeration (refrigeration introduces the complexity of storage and inventory). The supply for the day is determined by the day's catch, which is the result of both systematic factors (the size of the fishing fleet, the quality of the fishing grounds, and so forth) and random factors (weather, etc.). To keep matters at their simplest, however, we abstract from the random factors and assume only an initial arbitrariness in the first day's catch, assumed to be 1,500 pounds in Figure 5.3. The equilibrium price on day 1 is the price that clears the market, namely $5.50 per pound.

Note the difference between the schedule labeled "Supply" and the schedule "Supply on day 1." The upward-sloping supply schedule tells us the price required to coax out a given supply on a consistent basis, for example, a price of $4.50 to elicit a supply of 1,500 pounds per day, or a price of $5.00 to get fishermen to bring 2,000 pounds to market. On the assumption that fishing is perfectly competitive, the supply price is the marginal cost of a pound of fish. The actual supply on day 1, by contrast, is accidental, arbitrary; a result, we might suppose, of the fishermen's initial ignorance of market conditions.

But on day 2 the fishermen have more information, namely, the market price on day 1. How many fishermen set forth tomorrow depends on the relationship between today's temporary equilibrium price—which in Marshall's story is always the demand price—and the supply price associated with today's catch—the marginal cost of fish. If the demand price exceeds the supply price, as it does in Figure 5.3 ($5.50 vs. $4.50), then fishermen can expect a windfall profit for going out to sea (that is, a return over and above the minimum required to coax them out of their homes), and the quantity of fish brought to market will increase. Depending on how strongly fishermen react to the difference between demand and supply prices, the day-2 catch may fall short of the equilibrium $<Q = 2,000, P = 5>$ or it may, like the Walrasian auctioneer's price, overshoot the mark. But if we imagine a market that adjusts by small steps, and if the adjustment is always proportional to the gap between demand and supply prices, and if demand and supply schedules do not

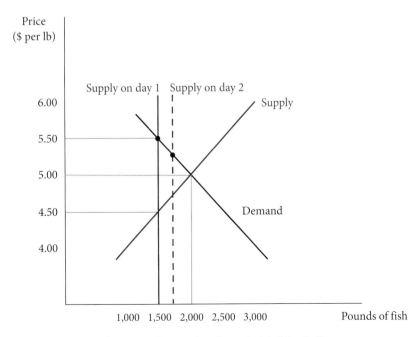

Figure 5.3 Demand and supply à la Marshall.

change, then, as Figure 5.3 is drawn, the process will converge to the equilibrium at <2,000, 5>.

Observe that Marshall's story does not address the Koopmans–Arrow paradox that price-taking agents have to change prices in order to get to equilibrium. Rather, Marshall finesses the contradiction by assuming that the economy is always in a temporary equilibrium at which the day's catch equals demand; he never tells us how the market arrives at the temporary equilibrium price. In his own words,

> It may so happen that the stock to be sold is practically fixed. This, for instance, is the case with a fish market, in which the value of fish for the day is governed almost exclusively by the stock on the slabs in relation to the demand: and if a person chooses to take the stock for granted, and say that the price is governed by demand, his brevity may perhaps be excused so long as he does not claim strict accuracy. (1920, p. 348)

We can tell a Walrasian fish story too. Instead of an arbitrary initial *quantity,* imagine an arbitrary initial *price,* say $5.50. Assuming this price will hold for the day, fishermen set forth. How much fish do they catch? If we abstract from random factors like the weather, then according to Figure 5.4, the supply will be 2,500 pounds. But at a price of $5.50 per pound, consumers are willing to purchase only 1,500 pounds. With no refrigeration, we must assume the rest gets tossed back into the sea, or perhaps onto a compost heap. Or we can assume that the leftover 1,000 pounds gets sold at knockdown prices, presumably somewhere between $5.50 and $4.50 per pound.

As in the Marshallian story, there is new knowledge that will likely affect the price on day 2. The question is how. We can continue to suppose that the fishermen as a group, led by the unlucky ones who couldn't find buyers at $5.50, lower the price. (Perhaps the elders get together over beer in the evening—where are the anti-trust police?—and decide on the next day's price.) However they resolve the Koopmans–Arrow paradox, we assume that on day 2 all the fishermen converge on a common price, say $5.25. The supply of fish falls to 2,250 pounds and the demand increases to 1,750 pounds, assuming once again that underlying demand and supply schedules do not change from one day to the next. Still, fish are in excess supply, and we can assume that the price will fall further. The end, once again, is equilibrium at <2,000, 5> if the price response is proportional to the gap between supply and demand and the steps are small enough.

The two stories are, in a sense, mirror images, the Walrasian story hinging on prices responding to the difference between quantities demanded and supplied at given prices, the Marshallian story hinging on quantities responding to the difference between demand and supply prices. In the Walrasian case, the quantity supplied responds to price, in the Marshallian, price responds to

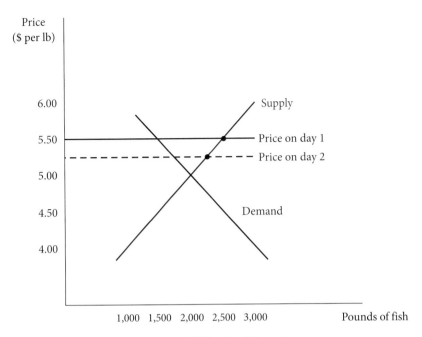

Figure 5.4 A Walrasian fish market.

the quantity supplied. The Walrasian story traces out a sequence of daily equilibria on the supply schedule; the Marshallian story, a sequence on the demand schedule.

Observe that in the Marshallian case the signals agents receive from one
day to the next are signals about profitability. The temporary equilibrium tells
producers whether the price of fish exceeds or falls short of marginal cost,
hence whether it pays to expand or contract production. In the Walrasian
case the signal is very different, reflecting how fast fish are selling relative to
the catch. The balance between quantity demanded and quantity supplied
tells producers whether to reduce or to increase price.

One way of marrying the two stories is to assume that, after experiencing a
Marshallian day-1 equilibrium, producers respond on day 2 à la Walras, taking the market-clearing price on day 1, $5.25, as given and delivering the as-
sociated quantity of fish, 2,500 pounds. This becomes the supply on day 2, and
the new Marshallian temporary equilibrium requires a dramatic fall in price,
to $4.25. The new price coaxes out a much-reduced supply on day 3, and so it
goes. Since the successive steps can no longer simply be assumed to be small,
there is no guarantee that the process converges to the demand-supply equilibrium. Convergence depends on the relative elasticity of the demand and
supply schedules.[1]

We can also tell a slightly different Walrasian story that gives the same pattern of price and quantity as the Marshallian-adjustment process. Suppose

that fishermen set the price each day and deliver the quantity of fish demanded at the day's price, $D(p)$. They continue to adjust the price according
to the difference between the day's production and the quantity that would
maximize profits at the day's price, that is, according to the difference $D(p)$ −
$S(p)$. When $S(p)$ exceeds $D(p)$, as in Figure 5.5, fishermen reduce prices in
order to sell more fish the next day.

Qualitatively, the path this modified Walrasian story charts is observationally equivalent to the original Marshallian story, the daily equilibria now tracing out a path on the demand schedule rather than on the supply schedule.
But the signaling is very different.

The Walrasian story pictured in Figure 5.5 may be less convincing than the
Marshallian one, but this is as much due to our following Marshall in his
choice of example than because the (modified) Walrasian process is inherently less plausible than Marshall's: we may find it hard to imagine fishermen
providing fish to order. But consider, say, a competitive handloom-weaving
industry, with weavers making a homogeneous product. We can certainly
imagine producers setting a quantity for the day with the price adjusting to
clear the market, but it would make as much, if not more, sense to imagine
producers setting a price for the day and producing however much buyers
order at that price, then adjusting tomorrow's price on the basis of the distance they end up from their supply schedules. If demand is slack and many

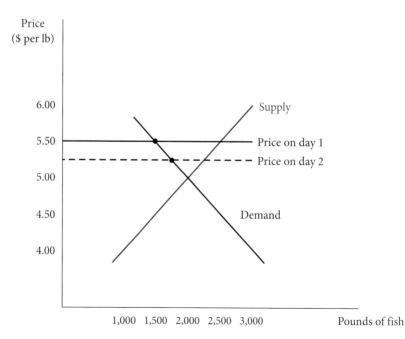

Figure 5.5 A modified Walrasian fish market.

looms are running for less time than the weavers wish, it is plausible that they will respond by reducing prices; by the same token, if the looms are humming and weavers are obliged to work into the night to fill customers' orders, in the next period they well might raise prices to take advantage of the favorable market, recognizing that this action will discourage demand.

Evidently, there are a variety of stories we can tell about adjustment, some of them more appealing than others (all of them of course just-so stories if for no other reason than that they assume small-scale production is the rule). Because all the stories limit producers to a single signal, they share a common problem. They all limit the trajectory of output and price to a dynamic in which the adjustment process keeps production on one of the two schedules—the demand or supply schedule—which define the system. For this reason neither Walras nor Marshall gives us any way of handling disequilibrium when the economy is away from *both* demand and supply schedules.

To see the problem, we ask a simple question, one we shall again ask when we apply the argument to Keynes's *General Theory*: what happens when an equilibrium configuration like <2,000, 5> ceases to be an equilibrium because one of the schedules moves? Suppose, as in Figure 5.6, a supply shock shifts the supply schedule upward and to the left (imagine an increase in the price of the coal on which the fishermen depend to run their boats' engines).

If, out of habit, fishermen continue to provide 2,000 pounds of fish, Mar-

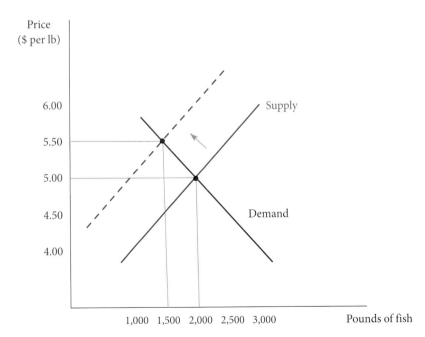

Figure 5.6 Disequilibrium caused by a supply shock.

shall's story can be invoked to explain how the economy might move from the old equilibrium to the new one at <1,500, 5.50>: on day 1 of the new dispensation, the market clears at the old equilibrium price and quantity—remember that the day's supply is perfectly inelastic, equal to 2,000 whatever the price—but this price is now below marginal cost, which is well over $6.00. So on day 2 fishermen cut back production, and the economy moves toward the new equilibrium.

Walras is, as it were, at sea, at least if we stick to the original Walrasian dynamic. There is no provision in this story for producing anywhere but on the supply schedule; we simply don't have a story to go with <2,000, 5> as a disequilibrium phenomenon. To be sure, we would face a similar problem with the Marshallian story if, instead of a supply shock, the economy were to suffer a demand shock; the Marshallian story always assumes the economy is on the demand schedule.

Hybrid Stories

We can solve the problems associated with starting from a point away from the demand and supply schedules by constructing a hybrid "Marshallian" process in which quantity adjusts according to Marshall's story and price according to Walras's.[2] The advantage of the hybrid is that producers can be assumed to process all the information at their disposal, one signal reflecting (marginal) profitability and the other about how fast goods are piling up or moving off the shelves. The difference between price and marginal cost drives quantity adjustment, and the difference between quantity demanded and quantity supplied drives price adjustment. Instead of forcing the system onto the demand or supply schedule even when it is not in equilibrium, we can now say what happens when the starting point $<Q_0, P_0>$ is not on either schedule.

As is the case with pure Marshall and pure Walras, the demand and supply schedules together define equilibrium: the demand schedule represents complete adjustment of fish production to demand, with the result that price does not change when the fish economy is on the demand schedule, and the supply schedule represents adjustment of marginal cost and price, so that quantity does not change when the economy is on the supply schedule. The labels $\dot{P} = 0$ and $\dot{Q} = 0$ on the two schedules in Figure 5.7 identify the schedules as, respectively, stationary loci of prices and quantities. $\dot{P}$ is the rate of change of price with respect to time, and $\dot{Q}$ is the rate of change of quantity.[3]

If the starting point is $<Q_0, P_0>$, output *expands* in response to the positive difference between price P_0 and marginal cost $S^{-1}(Q_0)$. At $<Q_0, P_0>$ price *falls* because the quantity demanded, $D(P_0)$, is less than the quantity produced, Q_0.

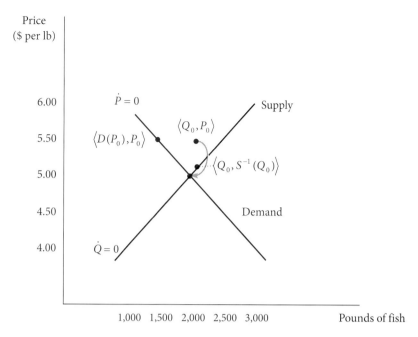

Figure 5.7 Disequilibrium adjustment as a hybrid Marshallian process.

As I indicated when I first told Walras's story, the unlucky suppliers who do not find ready buyers at the price P_0 scramble to unload their goods, driving the price down today, with tomorrow's price set after work, over beer in the pub. In neither case do we assume that the price falls to the level that clears the day's market, as in the pure-Marshallian story; a portion of the catch simply goes unsold. The result is to move the economy in the direction of the arrow, with price falling and quantity initially increasing. Once price falls to marginal cost, the trajectory changes course, with quantity falling.[4]

If we wish to add a dose of realism to the proceedings, we might take note of the likelihood that some producers will be luckier than others: the lucky ones, who are able to sell the day's catch at the price P_0, are receiving an entirely positive message from the market, in that they can both sell their catch and expand their operations profitably. Of course the unlucky ones, who are left with fish on their hands, are receiving a negative signal, but hope springs eternal: perhaps they will have better luck in finding customers tomorrow; and if they do, it will have paid them to expand their operations. All we need assume is that the positive, profitability, signal dominates with regard to quantity adjustment, while the negative, sales, signal dominates with regard to price, price-cutting by the unlucky fishermen perhaps forcing the hands of all the rest. Once again, convergence to equilibrium—stability—is guaranteed by assuming that adjustment takes place in small steps, continuously in the limit, and that prices respond positively to $D(P_0) - Q_0$, while quantities respond positively to $P_0 - S^{-1}(Q_0)$.[5]

We can also imagine an alternative hybrid, a "Walrasian" process, in which price and quantity adjustment are inverted, making price adjustment depend on the distance the actual quantity is from the quantity producers would like to provide, while the distance between actual production and the quantity demanded drives changes in output. The supply schedule becomes a stationary locus of price, and the demand schedule a stationary locus of quantity. In Figure 5.8 price adjustment is governed by $Q_0 - S(P_0)$ and quantity adjustment by $Q_0 - D(P_0)$.[6]

The economy now moves southwest rather than, as in Figure 5.7, southeast. Since the actual provision of fish on day 1 is below the level fishermen would choose to supply at the price P_0, they will lower the price of fish on day 2 in order to expand the market. At the same time, output falls in response to the discrepancy between actual production, Q_0, and the quantity consumers will purchase at the going price when they equate marginal rates of substitution with relative prices.

A key difference between the two adjustment processes is that, in the first, Marshallian, process, discrepancies between production and demand drive price changes, whereas in the second, Walrasian, process, the same discrepancies drive output changes. One signal, two different responses. This is not to

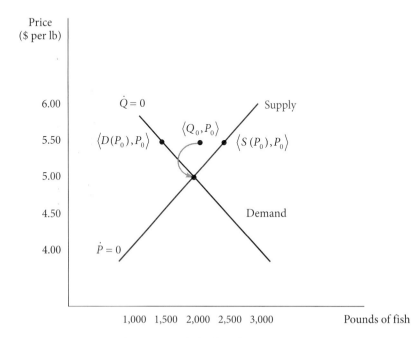

Figure 5.8 A hybrid Walrasian process.

say that quantities are unchanging in the Marshallian case or prices are unchanging in the Walrasian case. Profit maximization also enters the picture, driving quantity changes in the hybrid version of Marshall's story while driving price changes in the hybrid version of Walras's.

Why don't price and quantity go immediately to equilibrium? What accounts for the gradualness of the adjustment process? Here is where I depart from the equilibrium discipline that Lucas (1977) successfully urged upon the economics profession. My assumption, as I indicated in the beginning of this chapter, is that agents possess only local knowledge; at a point like $<Q_0, P_0>$ producers know the direction in which to change price and quantity, but *not by how much*. They know, for instance, that price exceeds marginal cost, $P_0 - S^{-1}(Q_0) > 0$, or that the current level of production is less than the amount they would optimally provide at the going price, $S(P_0) - Q_0 < 0$, but they do not know the equilibrium values of Q and P. Though they cannot go immediately to the equilibrium, they can move on a trajectory that will eventually bring the economy to equilibrium.

Alternative names for Marshallian and Walrasian processes are provided by John Hicks (1974). He distinguishes between "flexprice" and "fixprice" models, the first being more or less the Marshallian process, the second the Walrasian process. Hicks's terminology is misleading: in both cases prices are flexible, the difference lying in what drives prices and what drives quantities. In both flex- and fixprice adjustment, agents receive information of two kinds. One kind is information about how fast goods are moving off producers' shelves, based on the difference between actual output and how much consumers are willing to buy at the current price, $Q_0 - D(P_0)$. A second kind is how profitable business is, based (in the flexprice model) on the gap between the actual price and marginal cost or (in the fixprice model) on the gap between actual output and profit-maximizing output at prevailing prices. The difference between flex- and fixprice models lies in how the information is processed.

Information processing out of equilibrium is different from information processing in a competitive equilibrium. At equilibrium all that perfectly competitive producers need to know are price and (marginal) cost. The Koopmans–Arrow paradox is that perfect competition, if it means price-taking behavior, can exist only in equilibrium, where sales information becomes redundant. Out of equilibrium this information is not redundant: how fast goods are moving off the shelves is essential knowledge. The situation is even more complicated in overdetermined models, like the ones we shall encounter in the next chapter: the relevance of both kinds of information, signals about profitability and signals about market conditions, does not disappear in equilibrium.

Macrodynamics à la Viner

All this is preamble. Our real interest here is not in fish or cloth, but in the macroeconomy, a highly simplified version of the economy characterized by a single good that can be used interchangeably for consumption and invest-ment. But the preamble is essential, because macro-adjustment stories simply take elements from the basic Marshallian and Walrasian micro stories. For example, the story told by Jacob Viner, or more accurately, the story I imputed to him in chapter 2, is one of Marshallian adjustment, in which profitability drives output, and the GS schedule is a locus of stationary output. In the right-hand panel of Figure 2.5, reproduced below as Figure 5.9, the trajectory from F to E is one in which output is driven by profitability and the real price is driven by labor-market conditions. At F the vertical difference between real marginal cost, 4, and the real price, 1, drives output, causing the economy to contract. At the same time, in the labor market, money wages are driven by the difference between the supply of and the demand for labor. In response to unemployment, the money wage and hence the real wage fall, which is to say

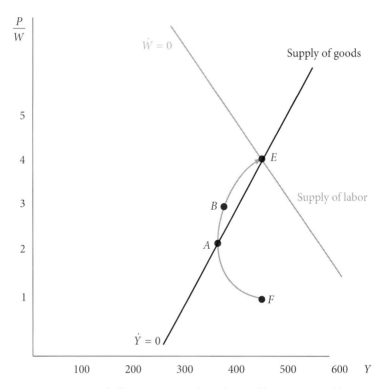

Figure 5.9 A Marshallian trajectory from disequilibrium to equilibrium with the price of output fixed.

the real price rises. Once the real price has risen enough for the economy to reach A, where price and marginal cost are equal, contraction gives way to expansion even as the real wage continues to fall and the real price continues to rise in response to unemployment. (As in fish or cloth markets, whether or not the trajectory converges directly to equilibrium depends on the values of adjustment parameters.) Money prices play no role in this story. The real price of output rises because the money wage falls, not because the nominal price of output rises.

The polar opposite of a fixed money price is a fixed money wage. Adjustment of the real price must now depend on nominal price adjustment. We suppose prices adjust in the manner of Walras, according to the gap between actual output and the profit-maximizing level of output at the going real price. And we continue to assume that output adjustment is Marshallian, responding to the gap between price and marginal cost. Then the GS schedule is at one and the same time the locus of stationary output and the locus of stationary real price. Every point on the GS schedule in Figure 5.10 is an equilibrium. The particular point to which output and the real price will gravitate (A in the figure) depends on the speeds of adjustment. Reaching full employ-

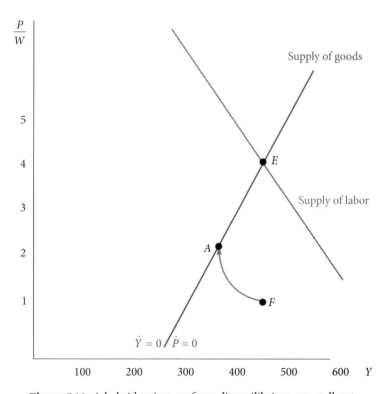

Figure 5.10 A hybrid trajectory from disequilibrium can stall out.

ment in this case would happen only if the price level adjusted infinitely more rapidly than output.[7]

If we try to tell a pure-Walrasian story, in which the GS schedule is a locus *only* of stationary prices, the economy will move only if we assume that output and employment respond to differences between the marginal disutility of labor and the current real wage. This is admittedly a bit odd, for it presupposes that workers rather than capitalists determine the level of economic activity. But economics is full of odd assumptions; even Nobel Laureates have been known to express indifference to the realism of their assumptions. In this case, the trajectory would follow a very different path from that in Figures 5.9 and 5.10, with employment, output, and the nominal price *rising* until full employment is reached at *B*, as in Figure 5.11.

As the economy continues from *B* until *E* in Figure 5.11, output exceeds capacity and gradually falls as the continuing rise in the price level finally brings the economy back to equilibrium at *E*.

Observe that Say's Law plays no role in either the Marshallian or the Walrasian story. Say's Law provides no theory of how output changes; it is if anything a theory of why output does *not* change. Demand is the dog which isn't barking.

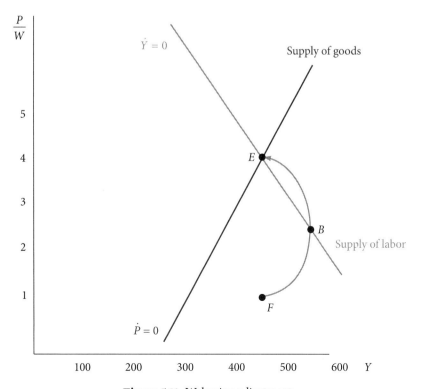

Figure 5.11 Walrasian adjustment.

Macrodynamics in *The General Theory*

The story in which output is driven by the relationship of actual output to the quantity demanded is one that has been told over the years to make Keynesian dynamics plausible. One textbook even makes it an essential part of the Keynesian story. In Robert Frank and Ben Bernanke's telling, an adjustment process based on meeting the demand determined by (temporarily) fixed prices—think handloom weavers producing to order—uniquely characterizes disequilibrium in Keynes's view of the world. They call this a "key assumption of the basic Keynesian model" (2007, p. 722).

Frank and Bernanke are mistaken. It is not this particular version of how aggregate demand matters that is essential to *The General Theory,* but the fact that aggregate demand matters at all. Aggregate demand may find a clearer, more direct, expression in a Walrasian, fixprice, version of adjustment, in which the GS schedule is a locus of stationary prices. But, as will be shown in chapter 6, *The General Theory* can be laid out in a Marshallian, flexprice, framework, in which goods supply is a locus of stationary output; moreover, despite the emphasis on the Walrasian story in the exegesis of *The General Theory,* Keynes's intellectual debts likely disposed him in toward a Marshallian understanding of adjustment. The struggle to escape the old, of which Keynes was excruciatingly aware, perhaps made a Walrasian framework more inviting but not necessarily easy to embrace.[8]

What happens if Keynes's economy is not at equilibrium? Suppose the interest rate and consequently investment demand are fixed, and we begin at a position to the left of the equilibrium, say $A = <300, 3.5>$ in Figure 5.12, which reproduces Figure 3.13 (without the point on the LS schedule).

In deriving the AD schedule from agents' consumption and investment propensities, chapter 3 argued the fixprice case that the excess of expenditure over income will deplete inventories and lead businesses to increase orders. With a propensity to consume equal to 0.75 and investment equal to 100, producers respond positively to the difference between output (300) and expenditure, which at $Y = 300$ is $325 = (0.75 \times 300) + 100$. Initially the expenditure-income gap leads to an increase in demand of 25; but this is only the beginning of the process: production responds to expenditure, which leads to an equal increase in income and a further increase in spending. The process of demand expansion continues until income and expenditure are in balance, namely at $Y = 400$.

If we begin at a level of output to the right of the AD schedule, we simply apply the logic of expansion in reverse. At $B = <500, 3.5>$, spending is only $475 = (0.75 \times 500) + 100$, and goods pile up on merchants' shelves. This leads to a cutback in orders and a reduction in output, and the downward spiral continues until expenditure and income are in balance, once again at $Y = 400$.

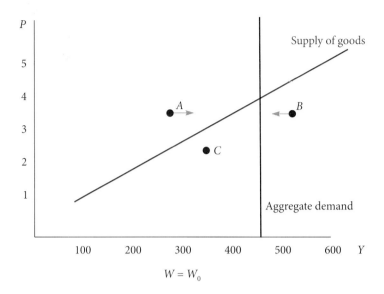

Figure 5.12 Aggregate demand and goods supply at a given interest rate.

In effect, we constructed the AD schedule out of a story in which the balance between the quantity produced and the quantity demanded drives output adjustment. However, as a story of adjustment of the economy as a whole, this argument is at best incomplete: businesses are assumed to increase or decrease production without any attention to whether the change in output is profitable. What has happened to the logic of goods supply based on profit maximization, an assumption implicit not only in Jacob Viner's mainstream approach but also in Keynes's explicit adoption of the "classical" postulate that the real wage is equal to the marginal productivity of labor (*The General Theory*, pp. 17–18)?

In the present case, it might be argued that there is no difference between assuming that inventory changes drive output and assuming that profitability drives output. Given the price $P = 3.5$ (a real price of $3.5/W_0$), it is profitable to expand production when expenditure exceeds income, as at A in Figure 5.12. And it is profitable to contract output when expenditure falls short of income, as at B. Profitability and inventory changes point in the same direction.

However, at a point like C, the two signals lead to different actions. The excess of marginal cost over price signals producers to contract output, while the shortfall of output relative to aggregate demand signals them to expand production.

There is another problem. Neither of these signals necessarily says anything about how the price level changes. Businesses may receive two signals—one about whether goods are flying off the shelves or accumulating in the back-room, the other about whether or not it is profitable to expand or contract output—but so far they take action in only one dimension, output. This leaves open the question of how prices change, and without an answer to this question we cannot characterize the path from a disequilibrium starting point.

It should be clear by now that the question is not whether producers, even competitive producers, change prices, but how and when they do so. What information guides price changes; what information guides output changes?

Output first. In the present case, if we wish to stick with the fixprice story that inventory changes drive output, output increases when $Y - AD$ is negative, and output falls when $Y - AD$ is positive. If demand drives output, we must look to the supply side for a signal to drive prices. Adapting the Walrasian process depicted in Figure 5.8, we assume that prices change according to the difference between the actual level of production and the level that would maximize profits at the present level of prices, which is to say according to the difference $Y - GS(P/W)$. At A in Figure 5.12, $Y - GS(P/W)$ is negative, so producers cut prices to increase sales; at B and C, $Y - GS(P/W)$ is positive, so producers raise prices to reduce the volume of output. Figure 5.13 illustrates the adjustment process initiated by a downward shift in aggregate demand, which makes the original equilibrium E untenable. Initially, only output changes because producers are still on their supply schedules at E even after

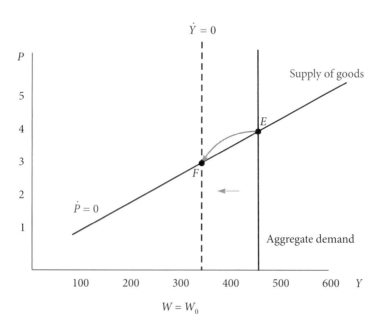

Figure 5.13 Walrasian adjustment in the first-pass model.

the downward shift in demand. But as time goes on, the gap between actual output and profit-maximizing output, $Y - GS(4)$, leads producers to decrease prices in the hope of increasing sales. As shown, the adjustment process converges to a new equilibrium, at which both output and prices are lower.

Of course, we are not confined to a Walrasian story. Marshallian flexprice adjustment marries the idea that output changes are driven by the relationship between price and marginal cost with the idea that imbalances between expenditure and income drive prices. This requires a different story about what happens when inventories fall below, or rise above, planned levels: instead of triggering orders for additional goods or triggering a cutback in orders, the inventory signal triggers price changes, prices rising in response to goods flying off the shelves, prices falling in response to goods piling up. In Figure 5.14 the starting point E is the same as in Figure 5.13, but the trajectory to the equilibrium at F is different. Initially, prices fall because a fall in expenditure leaves output piling up on producers' shelves; producers maintain the initial level of output because price and marginal cost are equal. But in time, as prices fall below marginal costs, producers begin to scale back output.

Observe that the economy's trajectory from E to F need not be the direct path in Figure 5.14. As was observed in note 6, it is possible for the economy

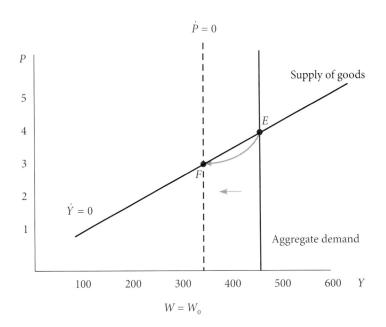

Figure 5.14 Marshallian adjustment in the first-pass model.

to follow a path of damped oscillations—ever smaller cycles around the equilibrium point. In the present case the approach to equilibrium will follow such a path if prices adjust much more rapidly than output. The picture is in Figure 5.15.

Finally, we should note the possible asymmetry between how the economy adjusts when desired expenditure (E_D) exceeds output (Y) and what happens when expenditure falls short. In the first case, goods are flying off the shelves, but once inventories are depleted, actual expenditure (E) cannot exceed Y. In the second case ($E_D < Y$), E can be less than Y. The reason is that including unwanted inventory accumulation in income as well as in output is problematic (despite the practice of the National Income and Product Accounts).

Sole proprietors such as fishermen would presumably not include unwanted inventories in calculating their incomes. It doesn't matter in the partial-equilibrium case because the income of fishermen can be assumed to have a negligible impact on the demand for fish. But if all output and income were generated by sole proprietors, the valuation of unwanted inventories would matter a lot because of the circular relationship between output, income, and expenditure. In this case we would need to take account of a possible gap between income and output.

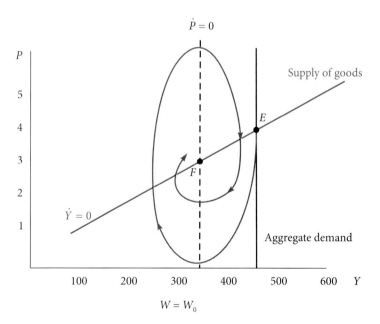

Figure 5.15 Marshallian adjustment in the first-pass model: damped cycles.

To do this, write $E = \min(E_D, Y)$ and reformulate the relationship between output and expenditure as

$$E = cE + I \qquad\qquad \text{with } E = E_D \text{ if } E_D < Y,$$

$$E = cE + I \qquad\qquad \text{with } E = Y \text{ if } E_D > Y,$$

where $c = 1 - s$ is the marginal propensity to consume. So

$$E = \frac{I}{1 - c} \qquad\qquad \text{if } E_D < Y,$$

whereas

$$E = cY + I \qquad\qquad \text{if } E_D > Y.$$

Instead of Figure 3.2, reproduced below as Figure 5.16, we have the expenditure function in Figure 5.17.

However, Keynes's focus, and ours, is on a capitalist economy rather than one composed of sole proprietors. The difference is that under capitalism goods are produced by means of wage labor. In this case it is more reasonable to assume that output is equal to income, and expenditure is equal to a fraction of income, c in the present case, regardless of whether inventory accumulation is desired or inadvertent. If goods are produced, wages must be paid whether or not the goods are sold. The only part of the link between output

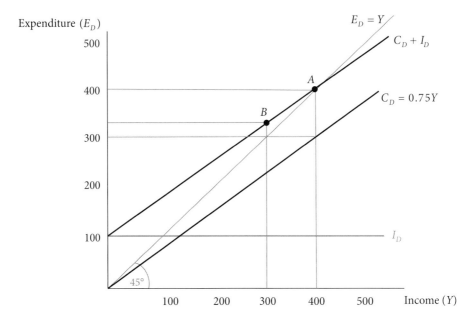

Figure 5.16 Consumption and investment determine aggregate demand.

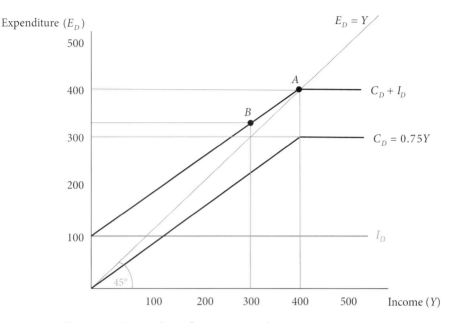

Figure 5.17 Expenditure function in a sole-proprietor economy.

and income that might be broken by excessive inventories is the profit link. It would be a very unwise producer who would count the bird in the bush alongside the bird in hand. So the slope of the expenditure function in Figure 5.17 might be less steep to the right of $E = Y$, but it would not be perfectly flat. If we focus on qualitative results, we can continue to use the assumption built into Figure 5.16, namely, that income and output are identical regardless of whether $E_D < Y$ or $E_D > Y$.

A Summing Up

How do economies adjust when not at equilibrium? What knowledge do agents mobilize? And how do they act on their knowledge? This chapter provides a framework for answering these questions by retelling stories that Alfred Marshall and Léon Walras offered their readers a century and a half ago. The stories may not be as different as I make out here (see note 3), but the point of emphasizing the differences is to make clear that there is more than one way to process the information that disequilibrium generates. Indeed, the starting point for understanding disequilibrium adjustment is that the information available to agents is much richer than in the simple tale of competitive markets at equilibrium, in which price-taking behavior is the defining characteristic—a good thing too, since it is also the case that the agents need much more information in order to adjust behavior in ways that might propel the economy toward equilibrium.

Out of equilibrium, agents not only have information on the profitability of production, as they do at equilibrium, but they also can observe, and act on, information about how fast goods are moving off their shelves. They need this additional information because they have to make two decisions rather than one. Not only must agents make choices about how much to produce, as they do on the basis of equilibrium prices, they also must make decisions about prices. Price-taking behavior is all well and good as a characterization of equilibrium, but it doesn't fit very well with stories about disequilibrium. Unless the problem is finessed, as Marshall did by assuming the economy is always in (temporary) equilibrium even as the equilibrium shifts, somebody has to decide whether and by how much to change prices.

Dynamics do not matter so much in standard demand-supply models—where demand curves slope downward and supply schedules edge upward—or, for that matter, in Keynes's first-pass model. But this is not the case when we graft an LS schedule onto the first- (and second-) pass models of *The General Theory*. The model becomes overdetermined—too many relationships for the number of variables—and the language of static equilibrium cannot even account for equilibrium. The first casualty is the identification of equilibrium with market clearing. In its more general sense of a balance of forces moving quantities and price, equilibrium survives, but only as the outcome of one adjustment process or another; different adjustment processes produce different equilibria. Nor does adjustment always lead to equilibrium. We have no choice but to examine dynamics directly.

In continuous time the hybrid Marshallian adjustment process is

$$\dot{P} = \theta_1 (D(P) - Q),$$
$$\dot{Q} = \theta_2 \left(P - S^{-1}(Q) \right).$$

The Jacobian is

$$J = \begin{bmatrix} \theta_1 D' & -\theta_1 \\ \theta_2 & -\theta_2 S'^{-1} \end{bmatrix},$$

with $D' \equiv (dD/dP)$ and $S'^{-1} \equiv (dS/dP)^{-1} = dS^{-1}/dQ$. The trace

$$tr\ J = \theta_1 D' - \theta_2 S'^{-1}$$

is negative, and the determinant

$$det\ J = -\theta_1 D' \theta_2 S'^{-1} + \theta_1 \theta_2$$

is positive, so the equilibrium is stable. Whether the approach to equilibrium follows a path like the one in Figure 5.7 (that is, the equilibrium is a node) or like the one described in note 5 (where the equilibrium is a focus) depends on the sign of the discriminant,

$$\left(\theta_1 D' + \theta_2 S'^{-1} \right)^2 - 4\theta_1 \theta_2.$$

If demand is inelastic and supply elastic (D' small and S' large), $\theta_1 D' - \theta_2 S'^{-1}$ will be small in absolute value. In consequence, the discriminant will be negative, and the equilibrium is a focus.

The mathematics is similar for alternative adjustment assumptions, and so is omitted here.

Macrodynamics à la Viner

The text proposed alternative adjustment processes for the pre-Keynesian model. The first assumes that the price level is fixed and adjustment of the real price takes place via changes in the nominal wage rate. The wage rate moves inversely with unemployment, measured here by the output gap

$$F\left(K, L\left(\frac{P}{W}\right)\right) - Y.$$

Output follows the logic of profit maximization and increases when the real price exceeds real marginal cost, decreasing when $P/W < F_L^{-1}$ with $Y = F(K, L)$ and $F_L \equiv dY/dL$. The system of adjustment is given by

$$\frac{\left(\frac{P}{W}\right)^{\bullet}}{\frac{P}{W}} = \frac{\dot{W}}{W} = \theta_1\left[F\left(K, L\left(\frac{P}{W}\right)\right) - Y\right],$$

$$\dot{Y} = \theta_2\left[\frac{P}{W} - F_L^{-1}\right].$$

We have the Jacobian

$$J = \begin{bmatrix} \theta_1 F_L L' & -\theta_1 \\ \theta_2 & \theta_2 F_L^{-3} F_{LL} \end{bmatrix},$$

where $L' \equiv dL(P/W)/d(P/W)$. The trace is negative and the determinant positive ($F_{LL} \equiv \partial^2 F/\partial L^2 < 0$). So the equilibrium is stable.

If we take the wage as fixed, and assume Walrasian price adjustment—the price level adjusts according to the distance between output and the GS schedule—the two adjustment equations become

$$\frac{\left(\frac{P}{W}\right)^{\bullet}}{\frac{P}{W}} = \frac{\dot{P}}{P} = -\theta_1\left[GS\left(\frac{P}{W}\right) - Y\right],$$

$$\dot{Y} = \theta_2\left[\frac{P}{W} - F_L^{-1}\right].$$

Now the Jacobian is

$$J = \begin{bmatrix} \theta_1\left(F_{LL}\right)^{-1} F_L^{3} & \theta_1 \\ \theta_2 & \theta_2 F_L^{-3} F_{LL} \end{bmatrix},$$

since

$$GS' = -\left(F_{LL}\right)^{-1} F_L^{3}.$$

The trace is negative, but $det\,J = 0$. This means that each and every point on the GS schedule is an equilibrium. The adjustment process stalls out once Y approaches $GS(P/W)$.

Finally, the adjustment depicted in Figure 5.11 is characterized by

$$\frac{\left(\dfrac{P}{W}\right)^{\displaystyle\cdot}}{\dfrac{P}{W}} = \frac{\dot{P}}{P} = -\theta_1\left[GS\left(\frac{P}{W}\right) - Y\right],$$

$$\dot{Y} = \theta_2\left[LS\left(\frac{P}{W}\right) - \frac{P}{W}\right],$$

where $LS(P/W) = F(K, L(P/W))$. The Jacobian is

$$J = \begin{bmatrix} \theta_1\left(F_{LL}\right)^{-1}F_L^{\;3} & \theta_1 \\ \theta_2(LS' - 1) & 0 \end{bmatrix},$$

so both the trace and the determinant are negative.

Macrodynamics in the First-Pass Model

Flexprice adjustment gives the system

$$\frac{\dot{P}}{P} = \theta_1[E - Y] = \theta_1[I(\rho) + cY - Y] = \theta_1[I(\rho) - sY],$$

$$\dot{Y} = \theta_2\left(\frac{P}{W} - F_L^{\;-1}\right).$$

Prices are driven by the balance between expenditure and income, which is to say the balance between investment demand $I(\rho)$ and desired saving sY, and output is driven by the balance between the real price P/W and the real marginal cost $F_L^{\;-1}$. The Jacobian is

$$J = \begin{bmatrix} 0 & -\theta_1 s \\ \theta_2 W^{-1} & \theta_2 F_L^{\;-3}F_{LL} \end{bmatrix}.$$

The trace is negative and the determinant is positive, guaranteeing a stable equilibrium. Once again the equilibrium can be either a node or a focus, depending on the sign of the discriminant

$$\left(-\theta_2 F_L^{\;-3}F_{LL}\right)^2 - 4\theta_1 s\theta_2 W^{-1}.$$

With relatively slow price adjustment this discriminant is positive, and the equilibrium will be a node, as pictured in Figure 5.14. If price adjustment is very rapid compared to output adjustment, the discriminant will be negative, and the equilibrium a focus, as in Figure 5.15.

Fixprice adjustment is governed by

$$\frac{\dot{P}}{P} = -\theta_1 \left[GS\left(\frac{P}{W}\right) - Y \right],$$

$$\dot{Y} = \theta_2 [I(\rho) - sY].$$

We have

$$J = \begin{bmatrix} \theta_1 \left(F_{LL} \right)^{-1} F_L^{\ 3} & \theta_1 \\ 0 & -\theta_2 s \end{bmatrix}.$$

Once again the trace is negative and the determinant is positive.

With fixprice adjustment the discriminant

$$\left(\theta_1 \left(F_{LL} \right)^{-1} F_L^{\ 3} + \theta_2 s \right)^2$$

is positive, and the approach to equilibrium is as pictured in Figure 5.13.

— 6 —

THE GENERAL THEORY WITHOUT RIGID PRICES AND WAGES

My so-called "fundamental equations" [in Keynes's earlier book, *A Treatise on Money*] were an instantaneous picture taken on the assumption of a given output. They attempted to show how, assuming the given output, forces could develop which involved a profit-disequilibrium, and thus required a change in the level of output. But the dynamic development, as distinct from the instantaneous picture, was left incomplete and extremely confused. This book, on the other hand has evolved into what is primarily a study of the forces which determine changes in the scale of output and employment as a whole.

—JOHN MAYNARD KEYNES

The real significance of the Keynesian contribution can be realized only within the framework of dynamic economics. Whether or not an underemployment equilibrium exists; whether or not full employment equilibrium always will be generated in a static system—all this is irrelevant. The fundamental issue raised by Keynesian economics is the stability of the dynamic system: its ability to return automatically to a full-employment equilibrium within a reasonable time (say, a year) if it is subjected to the customary shocks and disturbances of a peacetime economy. In other words, what Keynesian economics claims is that the economic system may be in a position of underemployment disequilibrium (in the sense that wages, prices, and the amount of unemployment are continuously changing over time) for long, or even indefinite, periods of time.

—DON PATINKIN

Very likely Keynes chose the wrong battleground. Equilibrium analysis and comparative statics were the tools to which he naturally turned to express his ideas, but they were probably not the best tools

Portions of this chapter were previously published in "The General Theory after 80 Years: Time for the Methodological Revolution," in *Keynes, Geld, und Finanzen,* ed. H. Hagemann, J. Kromphardt, and M. Marterbauer (Marburg: Metropolis, 2018), pp. 27–55; and in "Raising Keynes: A General Theory for the 21st Century," *EconomiA* 19 (January–April 2018): 1–11.

for his purpose . . . Keynes's comparative statics were an awkward
analytical language unequal to the shrewd observations and intuitions
he was trying to embody.

—JAMES TOBIN

Keynesian macroeconomics neither asserts nor requires nominal
wage and/or price rigidity. It does assert and require that markets not
be instantaneously and continuously cleared by prices. That is a much
less restrictive assumption, and much less controversial. It leaves
plenty of room for flexibility in any commonsense meaning of the
word.

—JAMES TOBIN

As Tobin says, it all depends how you understand the word "rigid." When
Franco Modigliani reduced the difference between Keynes and the mainstream to the assumption of rigid money wages (1944), at least rigid meant
what the dictionary says it means: "inflexible," "fixed."[1] And it is in this sense
that the models I develop to represent *The General Theory* do not assume rigidities; rather, prices and quantities respond flexibly to economic pressures.

But there is another, more contemporary sense of nominal rigidities, in
which rigid is not opposed to flexible. Rather, an economy with rigidities is
one which does not move *immediately* to equilibrium. In this sense, the absence of rigidities means there is no need to bother with adjustment at all. The
very need for adjustment "proves" the existence of rigidities. This is merely
part of the "discipline imposed by equilibrium theory," to use Robert Lucas's
phrase (1977, p. 12).

There is nothing but respect for language to prevent us from labeling gradual adjustment of prices and wages a case of nominal rigidities. But whatever
we might think in a general way of the discipline of equilibrium and the prospect of dispensing with disequilibrium altogether, it is not available in the
present context. Here we can't even define equilibrium apart from the dynamic processes that drive the economy when it is not in equilibrium.

Where Do We Start? The Choice of Models

I have observed that Keynes lists the ingredients only for two models, a first-
pass model, in which the interest rate is fixed, and a second-pass model, in
which the money supply is fixed. He conspicuously fails to provide a corresponding list to accompany chapter 19 of *The General Theory*, where he finally
drops the assumption of a fixed money wage. Without even a list of ingredi-

ents, there can be no recipe, no model. This chapter attempts to provide not only the ingredients but also the instructions for cooking, in short, the missing third-pass model.

Which model, the first- or the second-pass model, do we build on? It is tempting to build on the second-pass model for reasons internal and external to *The General Theory*. The internal reason is that this is the model sketched in chapter 18, immediately before the discussion of changing wages. Moreover, a model with a fixed money supply may seem more suitable to a discussion of the ability of the invisible hand to guide the economy to full employment. The external reason is that the assumption of a given money supply became integral to the presentation and understanding of *The General Theory* almost immediately, with the publication of Hicks's IS-LM exegesis (1937).

But the second-pass model is better understood as an attempt at a bare-bones refutation of the classical dichotomy than as a way of thinking about the economy Keynes was trying to analyze. Once it is accepted that aggregate demand matters, it is not clear that it makes sense to hold the money supply constant while varying the price level—except in a world in which money is limited to specie. Once the money supply is defined to include bank deposits, fractional-reserve banking makes the money supply endogenous, because money created by the banks (as distinct from the monetary base) is determined by the behavior of the banking system. As was observed in chapter 4, with the money supply endogenous, varying the price level can change not only the demand for money but also the supply. If the price level falls dramatically, it's hard to imagine banks not curtailing the supply of loans for transactions purposes (and hence the supply of money) in line with the much reduced value of collateral, not to speak of reduced demand. The question then becomes this: What do the banks do with the (potential) money; that is, what happens to the pyramid built on the monetary base? Chapter 4 pointed out that it takes a strong assumption about bank behavior to ensure that banks will replace commercial loans with purchases of other assets (bonds in our models). And that assumption is even stronger in the dynamic context in which changes in prices and output are at issue, not different levels of prices and outputs. We return to this point in chapter 7.

Treating the money supply as fixed may be a legacy of the quantity theory situated in the gold standard or some other form of commodity money. Here the regnant beliefs about the metallic origins of money on the part of Keynes's contemporaries may have swayed Keynes to assume a simple monetary system based on a fixed amount of currency or specie.[2] Absent such an intention, the exercise of assuming away the central bank and other elements of a modern economy would likely have appeared pointless to someone as deeply involved in contemporary finance and financial institutions as was Keynes.

If the existence of a central bank is assumed, as in the summary in chapter 18 of *The General Theory* (see p. 247), a natural way to characterize the money supply is that the central bank controls interest rates and varies the supply of bank reserves (or overdrafts) as the interest rate requires. But even if we leave out the central bank, it still makes sense to start from a given interest rate, as in the first-pass model, for this modeling strategy allows us to treat the interest rate separately from the price level. Like Keynes, we can vary the interest rate after the basic contours of the model are established. Unlike Keynes we shall do this with the help of a formal model, not on the basis of informal discussion of the complications introduced by varying wages and prices.

The First-Pass Model Augmented by a Labor-Supply Schedule

There is one important, indeed fundamental, difference between the model laid out in this chapter and Keynes's first-pass model: how labor supply figures in the picture. For purposes of the present argument, the labor market is assumed to be competitive in the textbook sense of the term, with the supply of labor—full employment—defined by how much employment workers desire at the going wage. The money wage adjusts in response to the difference between actual employment and the supply of labor. This is not the whole story of wage dynamics—see chapter 18—but wages do appear to respond to the existence of massive involuntary unemployment. During the Great Depression, hourly wages in U.S. manufacturing declined by more than 20 percent from their 1929 level to their level in 1932. Agricultural wages declined by even more, almost 30 percent.[3] And, as we shall see in chapter 19, the rate of unemployment appears to exercise a continuing influence on the rate of inflation.

The consequence of introducing labor supply is to overdetermine the model. Figure 6.1 presents aggregate demand, goods supply, and labor supply in a model in which the interest rate is fixed and the AD schedule is a vertical line. Two AD schedules, corresponding to two different interest rates, are shown. For the AD schedule represented by the solid line, there is an equilibrium $<Y = 450, P = 4>$, at which all three schedules are satisfied. Otherwise, as for the dashed AD schedule at $Y = 250$, there is no equilibrium at which the economy is on its AD schedule as well as on its GS and LS schedules.

If the existence of involuntary unemployment puts downward pressure on wages, we have to redefine the vertical axis: it will no longer do to assume $W = W_0$. We have a choice. We could, as in the construction of equilibrium in the contemporary AD-AS framework of mainstream texts, assimilate the

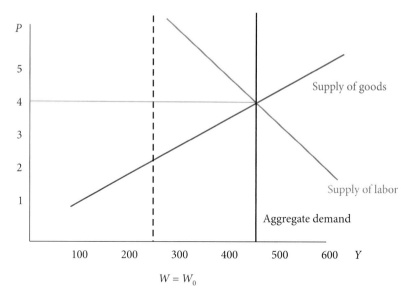

Figure 6.1 Aggregate demand, goods supply, and labor supply.

wage as just one more price, as in Figures 4.8 and 4.9. But this would presuppose the answer to the central question of what happens when the model is overdetermined; we would simply be assuming that workers are fully employed at the same time businesses are maximizing profits.

Instead of fixing the relative price of goods and labor at the full-employment, profit-maximizing level, we make the real price, P/W, a state variable of the model. As in Keynes's model, the price of goods is determined endogenously, and, as in the standard AD-AS model, the money-wage rate is also determined endogenously—but, unlike the AD-AS model, not by assuming full employment.

Serendipity, reflected in the solid AD schedule, apart, a conventional equilibrium does not exist in an overdetermined model. As I have already noted, we cannot even talk meaningfully about equilibrium without specifying the process that the economy follows outside of equilibrium.

The emphasis on dynamics, on the real-time trajectory of the economy, has many other implications, starting with the measure of economic activity on the horizontal axis of Figure 6.1. It becomes problematic to take the LS and GS schedules as given once and for all so that the full-employment, profit-maximizing level of output is constant over time. Moreover, if we assume that the process of adjustment takes place in real time, and that investment generates new productive capacity, the relationship between employment and output necessarily changes over time. If investment adds, say 2 percent to the capital stock each year, then after five years the capital stock will have grown by more than 10 percent, after ten years by more than 20 percent. Similarly with labor, if the labor force grows every year, then the full-employment level of output will increase accordingly.

In the case of the Great Depression, investment dried up so the capital stock did not grow very much. But a growing labor force, not to mention technological progress, made for a dramatic change in the relationship between unemployment and output: both the U.S. labor force and labor productivity grew by about 1 percent per year on average between 1929 and 1936.[4] The result was that although output returned to its pre-Depression level by the time *The General Theory* was published, unemployment was at 17 percent, fourteen percentage points higher in 1936 than in 1929.

Keynes's assumption that investment depends only on the current rate of interest is also more problematic in the dynamic context than in a static context. If we are interested in comparative statics, all the effects of the path that the economy followed to get to its present state can be understood as background to the relationship of investment to the current rate of interest. But path dependence plays a central role in the context of models that unfold over time: the investment-demand schedule is what it is today because of what happened yesterday. To assume away the influence of the past on investment as simply "background" means, among other things, that the investment schedule reproduces itself from one moment to the next, which is to say that what appears profitable to undertake today is unaffected by the projects taken up yesterday or the day before. The economy, as it were, never uses up opportunities, for investment opportunities always come back today even if they were exploited yesterday.[5]

There is another issue that takes on new meaning in the context of real-time adjustment: namely, the dependence of investment demand on P/W. The higher the real price of goods, the lower is the real wage and the higher is the rate of profit, and profits and wages influence different kinds of investment very differently. One might expect that investment undertaken to augment capacity would react favorably to increases in P/W and consequent increases in profits, whereas investment to cut operating costs by reducing labor inputs would react unfavorably to the same increase in P/W. For investment demand to be invariant with respect to P/W, as in Figure 6.1, it would take the unlikely coincidence that changes in capacity-increasing investment and labor-saving investment just balance each other out.

A similar logic leads to questioning the assumption that the propensity to save is independent of the distribution of income, reflected in the price level in Figure 6.1. Moreover, the propensity to save out of current income depends not only on today's income but on yesterday's saving and income, not to mention tomorrow's.

This said, we have plenty on our plate without taking into account just yet either the endogeneity of labor and capital or the influence of P/W on investment and saving. We will return to these issues in chapters 9, 10, 17, and 18, but for the present we continue to assume the AD schedule is vertical and that the capital stock and the labor force are fixed.

How Disequilibrium Unfolds

The basic model of the economy is given in Figure 6.2, which reproduces Figure 6.1 with a single change: the vertical axis no longer measures the nominal price with a fixed money wage. Instead, since the money wage is now a variable, the vertical axis measures the real price, P/W.

When the story opens, whether by design of the central bank, the cunning of the invisible hand, or dumb luck, aggregate demand serendipitously aligns with the intersection of goods and labor supply to produce the full-employment equilibrium $<Y = 450, P/W = 4>$.[6] Then the unthinkable happens—the end of a housing bubble, the discovery that collateralized debt obligations are toxic assets, a financial meltdown. What was thought to be risk, subject to the laws of probability, turns out to be radically uncertain. Financing becomes problematic, investment prospects appear less bright, households begin to worry about the future. There is a drying up of capital expendi-

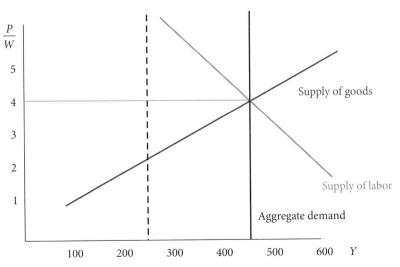

Figure 6.2 Aggregate demand, goods supply, and labor supply in the space of output × real price.

ture, or a retrenchment in consumer spending, perhaps both. As a result of this shock, the AD schedule moves to the left, to become the dashed line at $Y = 250$. What happens now?

Despite the upheaval, inertia may keep the economy for the moment at the original equilibrium $<Y = 450, P/W = 4>$, as my young colleagues supposed it would that fateful day in September 2008, when Lehman Brothers crashed (see chapter 1). But for how long? The Keynesian argument is that with the crisis of confidence comes a sharp pullback of expenditure. If output continues at its old pace, goods begin to pile up in shops and warehouses.

The next page of the story depends on the dynamics of the economy: what does a shortfall in expenditure relative to output communicate to sellers of goods and services? As we saw in the previous chapter, there are at least two possible answers, a Marshallian (flexprice) one and a Walrasian (fixprice) one.

In a Marshallian world, the world in which Keynes was raised and in which he remained most comfortable, we would expect prices to fall in response to the shortfall of expenditure. The AD schedule becomes a locus of stationary prices, $\dot{P} = 0$. Although this is not the assumption conventionally made in telling Keynes's story, we shall go along with it for the moment in a spirit of being more loyal to Keynes's teacher, Marshall, than was Keynes himself.

We can find a justification for the flexprice hypothesis in Keynes's work, but tellingly not in *The General Theory,* rather in the *Treatise.* In his banana parable (see chapter 3), Keynes argues,

> A thrift campaign leads to an overproduction of bananas . . .
>
> Since bananas will not keep, their price must fall. Thus as before, the public will consume the whole crop of bananas, but at a reduced price-level. . . . Since wages are still unchanged, only the selling-price of bananas will have fallen and not their cost of production; so that the entrepreneurs will suffer an abnormal loss. (1930, vol. 1, p. 177)

If prices fall *and nothing else happens,* the economy moves vertically downward and is no longer on either the LS or the GS schedule. Suppose the economy comes to a momentary rest at $<Y = 450, P/W = 3>$, as in Figure 6.3.

There is now involuntary unemployment because (by assumption) more work is desired at the new, higher, real wage; workers find themselves to the left of their supply schedule. (Recall that in the absence of money illusion, the fall in the price level has the same impact on the supply of labor as a corresponding rise in the nominal wage.) At the same time, producers are supplying more than the quantity of goods that maximizes profits since they are to the right of *their* supply schedule. Equivalently, since the supply curve reflects the marginal cost of output, producers comparing goods prices with marginal

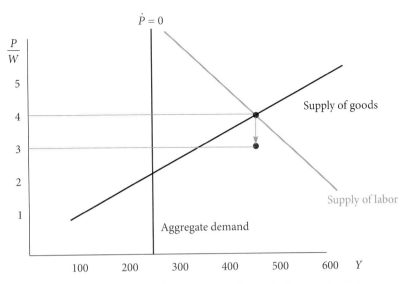

Figure 6.3 Flexprice adjustment to a shortfall of expenditure, I.

costs realize that, at the margin, costs are greater than revenues. Keynes continues the parable:

> The continuance of this will cause entrepreneurs to seek to protect themselves by throwing their employees out of work or reducing their wages. But even this will not improve their position, since the spending power of the public will be reduced by just as much as the aggregate costs of production. (1930, vol. 1, p. 177)

What happens next depends on the combined force of the *three* processes at work in the economy. Because we are to the right of the AD schedule, prices continue to fall. The effect of disequilibrium in the labor market is to put downward pressure on wages as workers compete over jobs, the LS schedule being a stationary locus of money wages, $\dot{W} = 0$. If wages are falling less rapidly than prices, the real price continues to fall, which is to say $(P/W)^{\bullet} < 0$. Output also falls, because real marginal cost exceeds the real price. For Marshall the GS schedule is a locus of stationary output, $\dot{Y} = 0$, as was the fish-supply schedule in chapter 5.

If wages are falling more slowly than prices, the economy moves to the southwest, as indicated in Figure 6.4. Both money prices and money wages are declining, the first because of the shortfall of expenditure relative to income, the second because of the shortfall of jobs relative to the supply of labor.

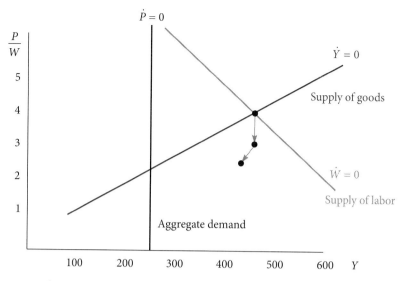

Figure 6.4 Flexprice adjustment to a shortfall of expenditure, II.

In Figure 6.4 the second step is pictured as a decline in P/W, but depending on the relative speeds of adjustment of wages and prices, it is possible that P/W will rise or, indeed, that P/W will not change at all. How do we chart the evolution of prices and output?

Equilibrium in an Overdetermined System: The Stationary Real-Price Locus

Consider Figure 6.5. On any line that we might draw between the AD schedule and the LS schedule within the shaded area, there is at least one point at which the relative rates at which prices and wages decline are equal, so that the ratio P/W remains constant over time. How do we know this? Because at point A the price level is stationary while the wage is falling, whereas at point B the price level is falling while the wage is constant. Thus if we go from A to B, the percentage rate at which the price level changes goes from zero to a negative number, and the rate at which the wage changes goes from a negative number to zero. At some point on any path between A and B, prices and wages are falling at the same percentage rate. In Figure 6.5 this point is labeled C. (Think of two cars travelling on the same road, one increasing its speed, the other one slowing down. If the first car is accelerating from 0 to 50, and the second is decelerating from 50 to 0, there is some point at which the two vehicles are necessarily traveling at the same speed.)

What is true of the line segment labeled AB is true of any other line segment connecting the AD and LS schedules in the shaded area, for instance the

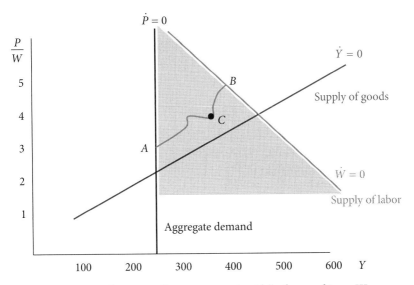

Figure 6.5 Flexprice adjustment to a shortfall of expenditure, III.

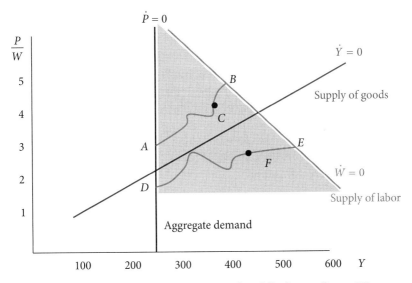

Figure 6.6 Flexprice adjustment to a shortfall of expenditure, IV.

line segment *DE* in Figure 6.6. Here the point where the cars are going at the same speed is labeled *F*. Now connect the dots: *C* and *F* and all the other points at which the percentage rates of change of wages and prices are equal trace out a schedule, or locus, of stationary real prices, as in Figure 6.7.

The intersection of the stationary real-price schedule, labeled $(P/W)^\bullet = 0$, and the GS schedule is the equilibrium. It is not, of course, a market-clearing equilibrium in which aggregate demand equals goods supply and labor supply, as at the serendipitous equilibrium $<Y = 450, P/W = 4>$ in Figure 6.2. But it is an equilibrium in the sense that there are no forces internal to the model to propel either P/W or Y away from the point E in Figure 6.8. *The downward pressure on prices just balances the downward pressure on wages. Both are falling at the same percentage rate, so the ratio of the two does not change.*

Several things are worth mentioning here. First, the equilibrium, as advertised, is an equilibrium with involuntary unemployment: E lies to the left of

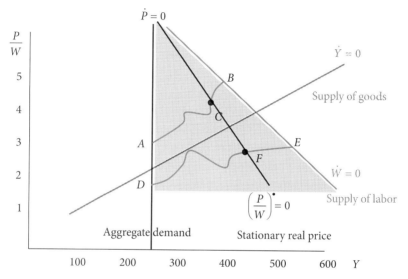

Figure 6.7 Flexprice adjustment to a shortfall of expenditure, V.

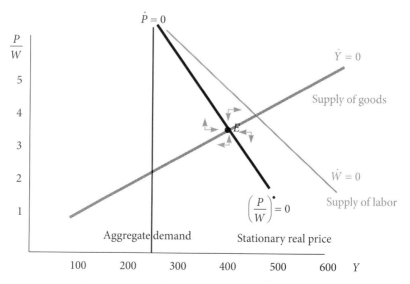

Figure 6.8 Equilibrium with flexprice dynamics.

the LS schedule. Second, the model is one of flexible wages (and prices), at least in the sense of flexibility before the idea took root that a nonrigid economy would go to equilibrium immediately, instead of gradually adjusting to imbalances. Third, we need not suppress the standard assumption that unemployment puts downward pressure on money wages; here unemployment not only coexists with flexible money wages but also drives money wages and partially drives real wages. In Figure 6.8, labor supply is a full and equal partner in determining how the economy moves when not in equilibrium, and the equilibrium is sensitive to any displacement of the economy relative to the LS schedule in the same way that it is sensitive to displacement away from the AD and GS schedules. Fourth, the equilibrium is stable—see the mathematical appendix—so that after a displacement of the AD schedule, as in Figure 6.2, the economy finds its way to the new equilibrium at E in Figure 6.8. Starting from any point in Figure 6.8, the length and the direction of the vertical arrow are determined by the distance from $(P/W)^{\bullet} = 0$ and the speeds of adjustment of prices and wages; likewise, the horizontal arrow by the distance from $\dot{Y} = 0$ and the speed of adjustment of output. Together, the two arrows indicate the trajectory of P/W and Y.[7] Finally, the exact position of the stationary real-price schedule depends on the relative speeds of adjustment of prices and wages. The AD schedule is itself one limiting case, in which prices react infinitely more rapidly than wages; at the other extreme, the LS schedule is a limiting case in which wages react infinitely more rapidly. The two cases are laid out in the two panels of Figure 6.9. Panel (a) in effect captures

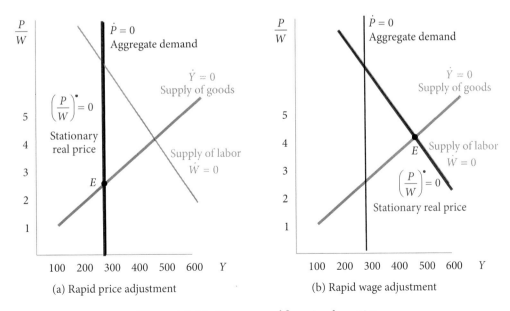

Figure 6.9 Limiting cases of flexprice dynamics.

Keynes's first-pass model, in which money wages adjust so slowly that we are back in the fixed-wage model and the LS schedule is redundant, real output being determined by aggregate demand, and the real-price level being determined by goods supply. Panel (b) is the mainstream case, in which the AD schedule is irrelevant, equilibrium being determined by the conditions of goods supply and labor supply.

Observe that unless prices adjust infinitely more rapidly than wages, equilibrium will be characterized by the indefinite accumulation of unwanted inventories.[8] At E in Figure 6.8, expenditure falls short of output and income; inevitably, goods pile up on producers' and merchants' shelves, and price reductions do nothing to alleviate the problem. The imbalance between expenditure and income persists because the real price remains constant, percentage reductions in money wages just matching (percentage) reductions in money prices. Attempts by producers to cut real prices are frustrated by workers' attempts to cut real wages.

There are two possible escape routes. One is that producers take account of ever-increasing inventories by raising the speed of adjustment of prices. If this action is not countered by workers, the effect will be to move the stationary-price locus ever closer to the AD schedule, a process for which the limiting case is Figure 6.9(a). The result is to eliminate the excess inventories by restoring the first-pass equilibrium. A second possibility is that producers will reduce output in response to inventory accumulation. This second possibility brings us to an alternative adjustment process, which I have identified with Walras rather than Marshall.

Alternative Dynamics, Alternative Equilibrium

Producers get two signals from the market. The first comes from the AD schedule, which represents an equilibrium between output and expenditure. Inventories and order books play a central role in the story: as order books shorten and inventories pile up, Marshallian producers respond by cutting prices, while, conversely, increasing backlogs and inventory depletion lead them to increase prices. The second signal comes from the GS schedule, which represents an equilibrium between marginal cost and price. If price exceeds marginal cost, Marshallian producers find it profitable to expand production; if price falls short of marginal cost, it is profitable to contract output.

In the alternative—fixprice or Walrasian—story, the reaction to market signals is reversed. An imbalance between expenditure and output triggers production adjustments; an imbalance between actual output and desired supply triggers price adjustments. Hence the immediate impact of shifting the AD schedule in Figure 6.10 is the opposite to the Marshallian case: the AD

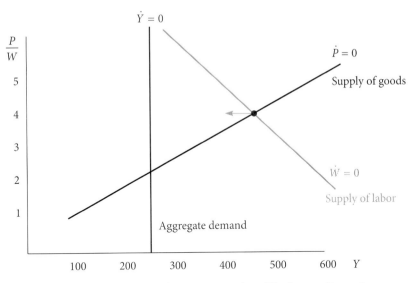

Figure 6.10 Fixprice adjustment to a shortfall of expenditure, I.

schedule is now a locus of stationary output, while the GS schedule becomes a locus of stationary (money) prices.

I have not been able find any reference to fixprice dynamics in *The General Theory*—nor for that matter anywhere else in the corpus of Keynes's work. But this was how my generation learned Keynesian economics. My own introduction, Paul Samuelson's *Economics* (1955) put the argument this way:

> Suppose income were higher than the intersection point [of the saving and investment schedules that determine aggregate demand]. Then . . . businessmen would be unable to sell enough to justify their current level of output. So they would contract their production and lay workers off. (p. 116)

As I have previously noted, Robert Frank and Ben Bernanke's introductory text goes even further:

> The basic Keynesian model is built on a key assumption . . . that firms do not continuously change their prices as supply and demand conditions change. Rather, over short periods firms tend to keep their prices fixed and *meet the demand* that is forthcoming at those prices. (2007, p. 722)

Nothing is said about prices and wages in either text, but in a flexible world, price and wage changes will follow. If we suppose once again that a negative demand shock moves the AD schedule to the left from serendipity, the shortfall of expenditure leads to a contraction of production, moving the economy in the direction of the arrow in Figure 6.10. At this point, workers, as before, are to the left of their supply schedule, with the result that money wages fall.

There is a new element: producers, who also find themselves to the left of and above their (goods) supply schedule, reduce prices in order to increase sales. Both prices and wages fall, but since we don't know anything about the relative speeds of adjustment, once again we can't say which is falling more rapidly. Hence we can't say whether the ratio of prices to wages, P/W, is rising or falling. At least not without more information.

As in the Marshallian case, the additional information is reflected in the locus of stationary real prices. The logic should now be familiar: somewhere between the GS schedule, which is now associated with stationary money prices, and the LS schedule, which continues to be a locus of stationary money wages, lies a schedule along which prices and wages are falling at the same percentage rate, so that the ratio of prices to wages remains constant. The construction of this schedule can be seen in Figure 6.11.

The points C and F are points at which money prices and money wages fall at the same relative rate. The stationary real-price locus, again labeled $(P/W)^{\bullet} = 0$, connects all such points. With this information, we can map out the trajectory the economy will follow, as well as the equilibrium to which this trajectory leads. Figure 6.12 shows the resulting stationary real-price schedule and the accompanying equilibrium at E. The vertical and horizontal arrows once again indicate the trajectory of the economy starting from different points on the diagram.

Initially, in contrast with flexprice adjustment, the real price does not change; the beginning point is on both the GS and the LS schedules, so nei-

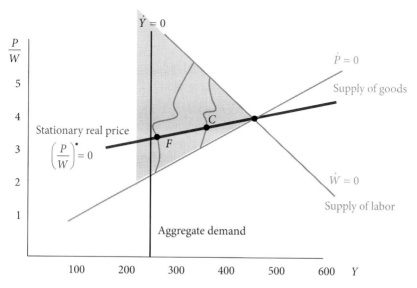

Figure 6.11 Fixprice adjustment to a shortfall of expenditure, II.

ther *P* nor *W* changes. But once the economy begins to contract, it finds itself above the stationary real-price locus, and the real price falls. If wages are adjusting more rapidly than prices, the stationary real-price locus slopes downward, as in Figure 6.13; in this case, the real price climbs along the trajectory to *E*.

Once again, the adjustment process has two limiting cases, one in which

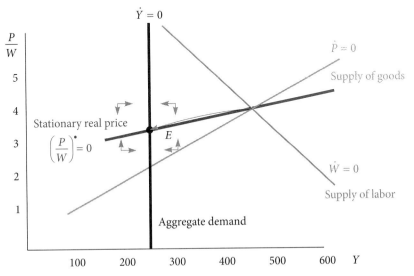

Figure 6.12 Fixprice adjustment to a shortfall of expenditure, III.

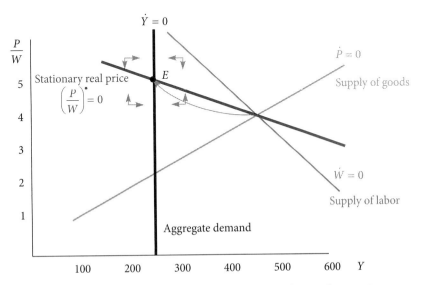

Figure 6.13 Fixprice adjustment to a shortfall of expenditure, IV.

price adjustment is infinitely more rapid, the other in which wages adjust infinitely more rapidly. The two cases are shown in the two panels of Figure 6.14. In both cases the equilibrium level of output is completely determined by the vertical AD schedule. Different speeds of adjustment affect only the equilibrium real price.

By comparing limiting cases, we gain a new perspective on the role of assumptions about the relative speed of adjustment of money wages and prices. With the relative speed of wage adjustment going to zero, as depicted in Figure 6.15, we are once again back to Keynes's first-pass model—a fixed money wage *is* the limiting case of rapid price adjustment. In the limiting case in which wages do not adjust at all, it turns out not to matter for equilibrium whether the rest of the model is determined by flexprice or fixprice dynamics; we have the same equilibrium in both cases. The LS schedule becomes irrelevant and we can ignore dynamics, at least in the sense that the equilibrium does not itself depend on the dynamic specification.

The two limiting cases of rapid wage adjustment are also revealing. In the first panel of Figure 6.16, the mainstream model comes into its own. With prices responding relatively slowly to aggregate demand, money-wage adjustment becomes, in the limit, real-wage adjustment, which obviates Keynes's stricture (see note 9) against confounding the determination of money wages and real wages. The equilibrium in both panels is a full-employment equilibrium.

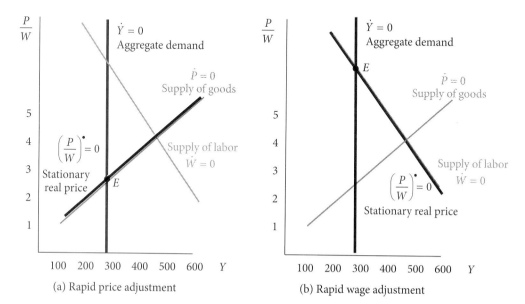

Figure 6.14 Limiting cases of fixprice dynamics.

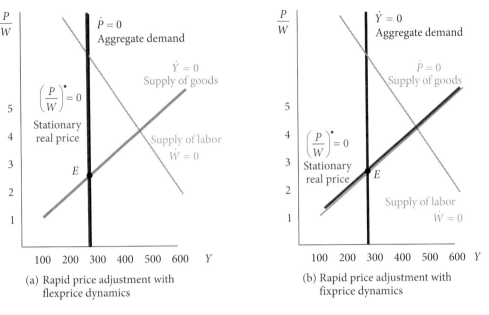

Figure 6.15 Limiting cases of rapid price adjustment.

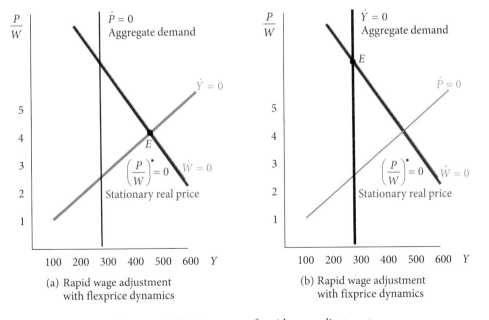

Figure 6.16 Limiting cases of rapid wage adjustment.

In Figure 6.16(a), the Marshallian case, aggregate demand plays no role in determining the real variables of the economy—output and the real price—its influence being limited to money prices. In Figure 6.16(b), aggregate demand and labor supply jointly determine equilibrium. In this case, aggregate demand matters for the real side of the economy; it is the goods-supply equation that becomes ineffectual except for determining the price level. Because wage adjustment is (by assumption) so rapid, producers' attempts to affect real prices by changing money prices are completely subverted by wage adjustments. Real-wage adjustment effectively resists any attempt to dislodge employment from the LS schedule.

Table 6.1 summarizes the four limiting cases, two "Keynesian" cases of rapid price adjustment, and two cases of rapid wage adjustment, one reflecting Modigliani's version of the second-pass model and one a hybrid of Keynes and the mainstream, in which "real wage resistance" (Joan Robinson's term [1962]) makes the LS schedule a full partner with aggregate demand in determining the equilibrium configuration.

The mainstream may see confirmation in Table 6.1: both the (first-pass) Keynesian formulation (ignoring the LS schedule) and the mainstream formulation (ignoring the AD schedule) turn out to be limiting cases of a more general model. But there is really not much comfort for orthodoxy. Between the limiting cases is a vast middle ground, in which equilibrium is determined jointly by the adjustment of prices, wages, and output. *And this middle ground belongs to Keynes.* Every equilibrium, apart from the two limiting cases of rapid wage adjustment, is an equilibrium with unemployment, the main critical point of *The General Theory.*

The limiting cases suggest that Keynes's rejection of the classical dichotomy takes place at two levels. Besides the complex argument in terms of monetary influences on the rate of interest, there is the simpler and more direct argument that the classical dichotomy is belied by the very fact that wage bargains are struck in money terms, with real wages emerging only as the price level is determined along with the level of output. Only in the limiting case in which money wages adjust infinitely faster than prices is revising the money-wage

Table 6.1 Limiting-Case Determinants of Equilibrium

	Flexprice	Fixprice
Rapid Price Adjustment	Keynesian	Keynesian
	AD and GS	AD and GS
Rapid Wage Adjustment	Mainstream	Real-Wage Resistance
	GS and LS	AD and LS

bargain tantamount to revising the real-wage bargain. In this limiting case, the classical dichotomy holds its own; in all other cases, wage bargains are nominal variables with real consequences.

Differences between Flexprice and Fixprice Models

In both models producers attempt to maximize profits, but—unlike Marshallian producers—Walrasian producers are frustrated by the market. Instead of expanding output in response to differences between price and marginal cost, producers respond to supply conditions by changing prices. They attempt to sell more goods by reducing prices, expecting larger quantities of goods to be demanded at lower prices. But they do not succeed for the same reason that, as Keynes argues, workers cannot fix real wages:[9] attempts to lower the real price of goods are frustrated because slack labor markets counter price reductions with wage reductions.

Another difference between the two models is that in the fixprice model equilibrium is conceptually closer to the vision captured in Keynes's first-pass model, output being determined solely by the AD schedule. This is true regardless of the speeds of adjustment of wages and prices.

It is also the case that the fixprice equilibrium does not carry with it the indefinite commitment to unwanted inventories. The equilibrium now lies on the AD schedule, along which output and expenditure are equal; the only inventories accumulated in equilibrium are desired inventories, those necessary to facilitate an orderly process of manufacture and distribution.

Finally, a difference between fixprice and flexprice models with empirical bite is the cyclical behavior of the real price. In flexprice models the real price moves procyclically (and the real wage contracyclically) if fluctuations are caused by demand shocks; this is because the stationary real-price locus moves procyclically against a stationary GS schedule. By contrast, in fixprice models the vertical AD schedule moves relative to a stationary real-price locus that slopes upward or downward depending on the relative speeds of adjustment of nominal prices and wages. If wages adjust more rapidly, then the stationary real-price locus slopes downward, and the real price moves *contracyclically* and the real wage *procyclically*.

These results undo an implication of the first-pass model that was from the get-go a troubling issue for Keynes and his followers—namely, the implication that demand changes cause money prices to adjust in the same direction as output, so that, with a fixed money wage, real wages and output move in opposite directions. A young American, John Dunlop (1938), and a young Canadian, Lorie Tarshis (1939), launched their academic careers by casting empirical doubt on the proposition of a negative relationship between real wages and output. (Subsequent research has generally led to the conclusion that fluctuations in real wages are mildly procyclical.) In reply, Keynes (1939) pointed out that the negative relationship between wages and economic activity was a consequence not of *The General Theory* but of Marshallian assumptions to which the economics profession had generally assented. The assumption of diminishing marginal productivity is built into the neoclassical production function, and therefore so is increasing marginal cost. The assumption of price-taking producers, for whom profit maximization implies equality between marginal cost and price, and the assumption that equilibrium is characterized by profit maximization are part and parcel of perfect competition.

One way out of the problem is to replace the assumption of perfect competition by an assumption of monopolistic competition or oligopoly. This chapter shows another way: drop restrictions imposed by assuming a fixed money wage, even though this complicates the idea of equilibrium. The argument developed in this chapter does not guarantee procyclical behavior of real wages, but it changes the question from the slope of the GS schedule into one of how adjustment takes place.

Conclusions

Despite the considerable ground this chapter has covered, the conclusions are relatively simple and straightforward. In the first place, one makes enormous progress in understanding Keynes's *General Theory* by jettisoning the static framework in which the argument has been normally framed, at least since Hicks's classic statement (1937). Building on Hicks, Modigliani (1944) formalized Keynesian economics in a way that reduces Keynes's contribution to nothing more than the replacement of the standard mainstream assumption of flexible money wages with the assumption of rigid money wages. Keynes's exposition gave ammunition to this point of view, and even if Keynes's commitment to rigid money wages was, as he claimed, no more than an expositional strategy, it became problematic in the light of the subsequent turn that both his followers and his critics took.[10] I would certainly agree with the critics that, to say the least, the argument of chapter 19 in *The General Theory,* in which the assumption of a given money wage is finally relaxed, is hardly a model of clarity. Lacking even a list of ingredients for a model comparable to Keynes's first- and second-pass models, the chapter was all the more easily ignored.

By recasting the argument in dynamic terms and redefining equilibrium in terms of equal rates of price and wage changes, we can incorporate the two elements that determine neoclassical equilibrium, an LS schedule and a GS schedule, and the two elements that (taking the rate of interest as given) determine equilibrium in Keynes's own model, the GS schedule and the AD schedule. The problem then is that the combined model is overdetermined: there are three relationships, the AD schedule, the GS schedule, and the LS schedule, but only two state variables, P/W and Y.

Robert Clower believed that the existence of these three schedules in a single model implied a contradiction with Walrasian theory:

> Either Walras' law is incompatible with Keynesian economics, or Keynes had nothing fundamentally new to add to orthodox economic theory. (1984 [1963], p. 41)

Walras' law is an equilibrium condition that holds only when producers and workers are (or assume they are) on their respective supply schedules. In the models of this chapter, even at equilibrium workers are not on their supply schedules, and producers may or may not be, except in some limiting cases. Walras's law is not compatible with equilibrium, but adjustment along Walrasian lines is perfectly compatible with the theory. Keynes had plenty "to add to orthodox economic theory"; he simply lacked the tools to articulate his message.

The present framework allows us to get beyond the pervasive view that nominal rigidities are the essence of Keynes's theory. No more than Keynes is it my intention to deny nominal rigidities; the point is rather that eliminating these rigidities would not eliminate the central causal role of aggregate demand, which is the core theoretical construction of Keynes's *General Theory*. Rigidities stemming from monopolistic competition, trade unions, menu costs, to mention only a few of the usual suspects, exist, but these do not get at the heart of the problem.

Specifying the dynamic-adjustment process involves two assumptions. First, an assumption about relative adjustment speeds in the labor and goods markets, and, second, an assumption about how producers respond to the dual signals they receive whenever they are not on the stationary loci of prices and output.

The crucial role of relative adjustment speeds of wages and prices becomes clear if we look again at the two limiting cases of the flexprice and fixprice models. In both models, when prices adjust rapidly and wages slowly, the equilibrium approaches the equilibrium in Keynes's first-pass model.

At the other extreme, when wages adjust infinitely more rapidly than prices, the dynamic model approaches either the mainstream model, in which aggregate demand doesn't matter, or a hybrid model of real-wage resistance, in which goods supply doesn't matter. In both these cases, full employment reigns at equilibrium.

In between these two extremes, equilibrium is characterized by unemployment, and relative speeds of adjustment determine how much. The in-between models formalize Keynes's vision about capitalism left to its own devices: there is no endogenous mechanism by which the economy sooner or later gets to full employment.

The second assumption, how producers process the dual signals they receive from goods markets when they are not on the AD and GS schedules, is more complex. In contrast to behavior at a demand = supply equilibrium, producers cannot in general be price takers who decide how much to bring to market at a price dictated by the market. They have two decisions to make, not one, and they receive two signals, not one. The first signal is the profitability of expanding or contracting output, measured either by the vertical distance from the supply curve, which reflects the difference between price and marginal cost, or by the horizontal distance, which reflects the amount by which producers would have to increase (or decrease) production in order to maximize profits. The second signal is whether it is easy or difficult to find buyers for a given level of output, whether products are accumulating on sellers' shelves or warehouses or flying out the door faster than they can be restocked.

By the same token, producers have two decisions to make, what to do about prices and what to do about output. The two dynamic systems, flexprice and fixprice, differ in the assumptions about how the signals are processed: does an accumulation of unwanted inventories trigger a reduction in prices (the flexprice reaction) or a reduction in output (the fixprice reaction)? Does a lack of profitability at the margin trigger a reduction in output (the flexprice reaction) or an increase in price (the fixprice reaction)?

Once dynamics become the focus of the model—we ought to begin with dynamics, with process, whether we are operating in a just-determined or an overdetermined system, but we are compelled to do so in the second case—it becomes essential to investigate the institutional basis of dynamic systems instead of requiring merely that the dynamics exhibit a surface plausibility. The question of whether producers react to disequilibrium by changing price or quantity, or rather how do changes in price and quantity interact, is hardly a new one, but it takes on a new importance once we commit ourselves to a dynamic view.

APPENDIX: A BRIEF HISTORY OF STATIONARY REAL-PRICE EQUILIBRIA

The possibility of an equilibrium at which prices and wages are falling at the same rate was noted by perceptive readers of Keynes, but they didn't know what to make of it other than to reject the idea on empirical grounds. Haberler seems to have been the first, at least the first to take notice in print of this possibility:

> A logical possibility would, of course, be that all money expressions (prices, wages, money values) fall continuously, while the real magnitudes including employment remain the same. That would be the implication of the assumption that the Keynesian relations remain unchanged in real terms in the face of such a situation. But this case is surely too unrealistic to be seriously contemplated.

This observation comes as a footnote to Haberler's discussion of the role of wage and price rigidity in Keynes and his predecessors:

> According to a widely held view, which can be described as a sort of simplified, popular Keynesianism, the possibility of underemployment equilibrium has been denied by the "classical" school and demonstrated by Keynes. The matter is, however, not so simple as that. This becomes quite clear if we reflect upon the intricate and crucial question concerning the role of wage (and price) rigidity in the Keynesian system. Keynes assumes that (money) wages are rigid downward. If this assumption, which is certainly not unrealistic, is rigidly adhered to, most of his conclusions follow: Underemployment equilibrium is then possible; an increase in the propensity to consume will then reduce unemployment and a decrease in the propensity to consume will produce unemployment (except if, as many classical writers assumed, the demand for idle funds, the liquidity preference proper, is entirely inelastic with respect to the rate of interest). But all this is entirely in accord with pre-Keynesian theory, although these conclusions certainly had not been generally realized and sufficiently emphasized before the appearance of *The General Theory*.
>
> If flexible wages—"thoroughgoing competition between wage earners" (in Pigou's words)—are assumed, the situation is radically changed. Obviously, underemployment equilibrium with flexible wages is impossible—wages and prices must then fall continuously, which can hardly occur without further consequences and cannot well be described as an equilibrium position. (1946, pp. 190–191)

Lawrence Klein made a similar observation in 1947:

> Within the framework of Keynesian economics wage flexibility does not correct unemployment and leads merely to hyper-deflation if carried to its logical conclusion. But in the real world one observes neither hyper-deflation nor full employment. The explanation is that wages are sticky; they are not flexible . . .
>
> When imperfections and rigid money wages are introduced into our

model of the Keynesian system, the results of under-employment equilibrium follow quite easily, providing a more realistic picture of how the economic system looks. But it is not true, as many have said, that the Keynesian equations in conjunction with a perfect, frictionless system will always yield a full-employment solution. Unemployment is extremely likely even under perfect competition. (p. 90)

Patinkin characterized Keynes's theory of unemployment as a process of slow disequilibrium adjustment, rather than as a stationary-price equilibrium:

Keynesian economics is the economics of unemployment *dis*equilibrium. It argues that as a result of interest-inelasticity, on the one hand, and distribution and expectation effects, on the other, the dynamic process of [a capitalist economy left to its own devices]—even when aided by monetary policy—is unlikely to converge either smoothly or rapidly to the full-employment equilibrium position. Indeed, if these influences are sufficiently strong, they may even render this process unstable. In such a case the return to full employment would have to await the fortunate advent of some exogenous force that would expand aggregate demand sufficiently. (1965, pp. 337–338)

The difference between Patinkin and Haberler is at least partly semantic: Patinkin, like Haberler, refuses to treat a situation in which prices and wages are falling as a true equilibrium. The crucial passage is

All, then, that Keynes means by the statement that the system may settle down to a position of "unemployment equilibrium" is that the automatic workings of the system will *not* restore the system to a position of *full-employment equilibrium*. He does not mean "equilibrium" in the usual sense of a term that nothing tends to change in the system. All that is strictly in equilibrium is the level—or, possibly, only the fact—of unemployment; but there is no equilibrium of the money wage rate. (1965, note K:3, pp. 643–644)

In an unpublished paper written in 1958, Clower echoes both Haberler and Patinkin:

Perhaps the most curious aspect of the matter is the fact that *if $\tilde{w}$ and $\tilde{p}$* [the money wage and the money price of goods] just happen to fall at the same rate over time then, starting from an initial position of Keynesian equilibrium (with excess supply in the labor market), the economy will remain "in equilibrium" indefinitely although prices and wages are constantly falling over time! Under these circumstances, it is perhaps natural to speak of the difference $\tilde{N}^s - \tilde{N}^d$ [labor supply less labor demand] as "involuntary unemployment"; but it [is] a curious of language to refer to the situation as a whole as one of equilibrium. (p. 13; quoted in Plassard 2018, p. 279–280)

In this paper Clower explores dynamics akin to the disequilibrium dynamics that characterize equilibrium in my models.[11]

As to whether or not "this case is surely too unrealistic to be seriously contemplated," as Haberler believed, see chapter 8. Klein, by the way, is inaccurate in assuming that the "logical conclusion" of an equilibrium with falling prices and wages is "hyper-deflation," if hyper-deflation means an increasing rate of deflation. The models in this chapter lead rather to a constant rate of deflation in a depression equilibrium. What Klein presumably meant was that the equilibrium entails prices and wages that approach zero as time goes to infinity. The point is that—contrary to the mainstream view—there are no *endogenous* forces in either the fixprice or the flexprice model that provide an antidote. In this sense, prices and wages falling forever is indeed a prediction of the model—chapter 8 examines how well it characterizes what actually happened during the Great Depression

Although I was ignorant of these earlier models, in the process of research and writing I came to know not only of Clower's 1958 model but also of three other attempts to model the dynamics of adjustment and the resulting equilibrium. The first is by Robert Solow and Joseph Stiglitz (1968). Though the details differ, the Solow–Stiglitz model is very similar to my own in that the equilibrium is characterized by a stationary real price as well as stationary output, along with nominal prices and wages changing at the same rate.[12]

James Tobin's 1975 article, from which I have included an excerpt in the epigraph to this chapter, is in some ways more like my model and in some ways less. In particular, Tobin explores alternative disequilibrium processes. A major difference is that Tobin pays scant attention to the labor market. And he characterizes equilibrium by a constant nominal price, so that the possibility of a self-sustaining depression (or boom) is tied to an unstable equilibrium. In this sense, the Tobin model is more like the dynamic version of Modigliani's 1944 model that I develop in the mathematical appendix to chapter 7—but with the Keynes effect replaced by the combined effects of real balance and Fisher effects.

Finally, in the 1980s Rodolphe Dos Santos Ferreira and Philippe Michel worked out a dynamic model that resolves the overdetermination in Figure 6.2 by introducing trade unions. In this model, unions intermediate between workers and employers, so that there are in effect two LS schedules, the (representative) worker's and the composite union's. The union LS schedule takes account of the level of employment and the corresponding real wage. The resulting unemployment equilibrium corresponds to the union labor supply, and in that sense reflects voluntary unemployment. Involuntary unemployment is either a disequilibrium phenomenon or it is the result of a union focus on relative wages that leads to abdication of overall wage setting to firms, which in this model vary wages in line with changes in unemployment rather than in response to its level. (Like Tobin's, the model of Dos Santos Ferreira and Michel is a version of Modigliani's variable wage model. At an equilibrium without involuntary unemployment, aggregate demand plays only the role of determining nominal price and wage levels.) This work circulated in draft form from at least 1987 but was published only in 2013. (See also Dos Santos Ferreira 2014.)

The third-pass model adds just one equation, representing the money-wage response to unemployment, to the dynamic version of the first-pass model considered at the end of chapter 5. The flexprice version of the complete model is

$$\frac{\dot{P}}{P} = \theta_1[I(\rho) - sY],$$ (6.1)

$$\dot{Y} = \theta_2\left(\frac{P}{W} - FL^{-1}\right),$$ (6.2)

$$\frac{\dot{W}}{W} = \theta_3\left[Y - LS\left(\frac{P}{W}\right)\right],$$ (6.3)

where $LS(P/W) = F(K, L(P/W))$. However, equilibrium is characterized not by stationary P and W, but by stationary P/W. From equations (6.1) and (6.3) we have

$$\frac{\left(\frac{P}{W}\right)^{\cdot}}{\frac{P}{W}} \equiv \left(\frac{\dot{P}}{P} - \frac{\dot{W}}{W}\right) = \theta_1[I(\rho) - sY] - \theta_3\left[Y - LS\left(\frac{P}{W}\right)\right].$$ (6.4)

The flexprice system is made up of equations (6.4) and (6.2). The equilibrium is stable since $tr\, J < 0$ and $det\, J > 0$, where

$$J = \begin{bmatrix} \theta_3\, LS' & -\theta_1 s - \theta_3 \\ \theta_2 & \theta_2 F_L^{-3} F_{LL} \end{bmatrix} = \begin{bmatrix} \theta_3\, LS' & -\theta_1 s - \theta_3 \\ \theta_2 & -\theta_2 (GS')^{-1} \end{bmatrix}.$$

The discriminant is

$$\left[\theta_3\, LS' + \theta_2 (GS')^{-1}\right]^2 - 4\left(\theta_1 s + \theta_3\right)\theta_2.$$

As note 7 in the text suggested, the path to equilibrium may be direct or convoluted—the equilibrium may be a node or a focus—depending on the sign of the discriminant, positive for a node and negative for a focus. The discriminant above is negative if θ_1 is large relative to θ_2 and θ_3; or if the elasticity of labor supply is high, so that LS' is large; or if the elasticity of goods supply is low, so that GS' is small. In these cases price adjustment will cause the economy to overshoot the equilibrium, but by progressively less over time.

The position of the stationary real-price locus depends on the relative speeds of adjustment of money prices and money wages. The higher the ratio θ_1/θ_3, the closer it is to the AD schedule. As this ratio increases, the response to any departure of expenditure from income gets larger and larger, so the stationary real-price locus is tied up ever more strongly with the AD schedule. The same logic in reverse means that as θ_1/θ_3 falls, the stationary real-price locus gets closer to the LS schedule.

In the limit as $\theta_1/\theta_3 \to \infty$, the stationary real-price locus fuses with the AD schedule, and the LS schedule drops out of the picture. We are back to the first-pass model. Conversely, as $\theta_1/\theta_3 \to 0$, equilibrium is determined by the LS and GS schedules; aggregate demand drops out of the picture.

Fixprice adjustment reverses the processing of the signals of demand pressure and profitability. We have

$$\frac{\dot{P}}{P} = -\theta_1 \left[GS\left(\frac{P}{W}\right) - Y \right], \tag{6.5}$$

$$\dot{Y} = \theta_2 [I(\rho) - sY], \tag{6.6}$$

$$\frac{\dot{W}}{W} = \theta_3 \left[Y - LS\left(\frac{P}{W}\right) \right]. \tag{6.7}$$

The stationary real-price locus is now

$$\frac{\left(\dfrac{P}{W}\right)^{\cdot}}{\dfrac{P}{W}} \equiv \left(\frac{\dot{P}}{P} - \frac{\dot{W}}{W} \right) = -\theta_1 \left[GS\left(\frac{P}{W}\right) - Y \right] - \theta_3 \left[Y - LS\left(\frac{P}{W}\right) \right]. \tag{6.8}$$

The Jacobian of the system composed of equations (6.6) and (6.8) is

$$J = \begin{bmatrix} -\theta_1 GS' + \theta_3 LS' & \theta_1 - \theta_3 \\ 0 & -\theta_2 s \end{bmatrix},$$

for which once again the trace is negative and the determinant positive. The discriminant is

$$\left(-\theta_1 GS' + \theta_3 LS' + \theta_2 s \right)^2,$$

which is necessarily positive; the equilibrium is invariably a node.

As in the flexprice case, the distance of the stationary real-price locus from the stationary nominal-price and nominal-wage schedules depends on relative speeds of adjustment of prices and wages. As $\theta_1/\theta_3 \to \infty$, the LS schedule drops out of the picture, and equilibrium is determined by the AD and GS schedules; as $\theta_1/\theta_3 \to 0$, the GS schedule drops out, and equilibrium is determined by aggregate demand and labor supply.

— 7 —

DYNAMICS VS. STATICS

Can the Economy Get from the Here of Unemployment to the There of Full Employment?

> The real source of trouble is the confusion between comparisons of equilibrium positions and the history of a process.
>
> —JOAN ROBINSON

> One of the ways in which history and historical time matter for macroeconomics is that they can affect the adjustment process very intimately. Financial and other commitments from the past, and expectations and apprehensions about the future, can easily interfere with the economy's ability to adapt to changes in aggregate demand and supply.
>
> —ROBERT SOLOW

> We find ourselves confronted with this paradox: in order for the comparative-statics analysis to yield fruitful results, we must first develop a theory of dynamics.
>
> —PAUL SAMUELSON

I can imagine a reader asking what has been accomplished by the long exploration of adjustment mechanisms in the previous two chapters. Yes, she might say, it has been shown that the adjustment process determines the equilibrium, but how important are the insights that emerge from this new way of looking at the economy? And, indeed, is it so new? The focus is still on *equilibrium,* to which the adjustment process eventually converges. Moreover, the analysis removes one rigidity—the money wage—only to replace it with another—a fixed interest rate.

There would be some truth in the criticism if we were at the end of the story rather than the middle. It might be helpful to recall Paul Samuelson's report of the musings of his teacher Edwin Bidwell Wilson on the relativity of equilibrium:

You leave your car in the MIT parking lot overnight. The rubber tire is a membrane which separates the inside of the tire from the atmosphere, and because of this stiff wall there's an equilibrium difference in pressure. Wilson would say, "Come back a thousand years later, and that tire will be flat." That was not strict equilibrium. It's just a very slowly adjusting disequilibrium. (Colander and Landreth 1996, p. 163)

The same might be said about an equilibrium at which both money wages and money prices continue to fall (or rise). Is such an equilibrium simply "a slowly adjusting disequilibrium," and what can be said about the continuing disequilibrium process? In particular, what happens to aggregate demand when the price level changes? In this chapter we examine four possible avenues by which price changes in real time may have a different impact from that of the virtual changes associated with comparative statics: the Keynes effect, the effect of fractional-reserve banking, the real-balance effect, and the Fisher effect.

The Keynes Effect in a World of Commodity Money

For starters, what happens to the interest rate and investment demand in a world of commodity money? We have seen in chapter 3 that a lower price level frees up money from its role in facilitating commerce and production and makes correspondingly more money available to satisfy the liquidity demands of wealth holders. These wealth holders willingly accommodate the extra cash only if the interest rate falls.

In chapter 6 I finessed this complication by assuming the interest rate is given, but is this a plausible assumption alongside an equilibrium at which the nominal price level is continually falling? In the laundry list of reasons Keynes provides in chapter 19 of *The General Theory* why (and why not) falling money wages might solve the problem of unemployment, he includes the effect of an accompanying fall in the price level. The resulting downward pressure on the rate of interest—the Keynes effect—is key to Modigliani's argument laid out in chapter 4.

So instead of a fixed interest rate, make the same assumptions that Modigliani made in constructing his version of the second-pass model, namely, a fixed money supply and the adjustment of the interest rate to the price level. But here we apply these assumptions in the context of money prices and wages that change in real time rather than varying on different planets.

How do we reflect this assumption graphically? The move from the first-pass to the second-pass model in chapter 3 involved a replacement of a vertical AD schedule with a downward-sloping one, but this modification won't work here. The reason is that the price variable is now the real price, not the nominal price, and it is the nominal-price level that influences the interest rate and investment demand via the Keynes effect. As the nominal price changes, the vertical AD schedule moves in $Y \times P/W$ space, rather than, as in the static second-pass model, a change in the nominal price causing a movement *along* the downward-sloping AD schedule.

Output thus chases a moving target as it is pulled from an original position of serendipity by a shock to aggregate demand. After its initial fall, the vertical AD schedule reverses course and moves to the right (lower prices, lower interest rate, more investment demand, more aggregate demand), in the direction of the full-employment equilibrium. In Figure 7.1, which assumes fixprice adjustment, the first impact of the shifting AD schedule is to slow down the contraction of the economy. As the price level continues to fall and the AD schedule continues to shift to the right, contraction turns into expansion; at point A the economy's trajectory is momentarily tangent to the moving AD schedule. The trajectory is vertical at this point, because expenditure is equal to income and there is no reason for the economy either to contract or to expand. (Similarly, the economy's trajectory is horizontal where it cuts the stationary price locus.)

The question is whether the economy converges to full employment, that is, whether the dynamic adjustment path approaches the equilibrium E that characterizes Modigliani's version of the second-pass model. This is the only possible equilibrium point in this model, because stationary output requires a

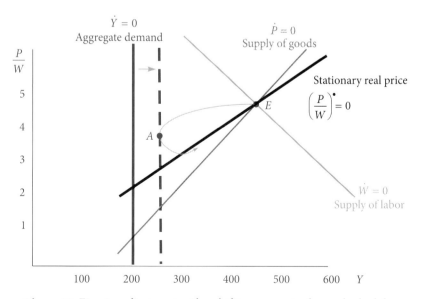

Figure 7.1 Fixprice adjustment with a shifting aggregate-demand schedule.

stationary interest rate, which in turn requires a stationary nominal price. So the only feasible equilibrium on the stationary real-price locus is the original starting point, E.

Convergence depends on how the adjustment process is specified. In the mathematical appendix to this chapter, the flexprice model is shown to converge to full employment however rapidly one variable or another responds to the pressure of disequilibrium. With fixprice models, convergence depends on parameter values. The economy does *not* return to full employment if (paradoxically) money wages adjust very quickly to unemployment compared with how rapidly money prices adjust to being off the GS schedule and if the high speed of wage adjustment is complemented by a low elasticity of labor supply. Under these conditions, the economy oscillates in an explosive orbit around the full-employment equilibrium, a possibility Keynes intuited but could not establish with the tools at his disposal: "If competition between unemployed workers always led to a very great reduction of the money-wage, there would be a violent instability in the price-level" (*The General Theory*, p. 253).[1]

The picture is in Figure 7.2. The explosive orbit is the trajectory of output and real price, the greyhound following the mechanical rabbit of aggregate demand. The invisible AD schedule is pulled forward by a falling price level and pushed back by a rising one, in an ever-widening orbit.

Alternatively, the economy might stall out because of a floor to the hurdle

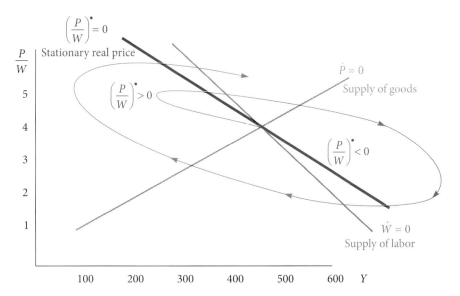

Figure 7.2 Fixprice adjustment with a shifting aggregate-demand schedule, unstable equilibrium.

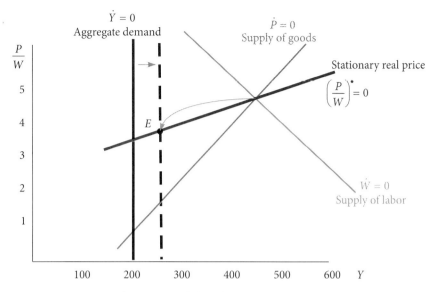

Figure 7.3 Fixprice adjustment with liquidity trap or inelastic investment demand.

rate of interest or because of inelastic investment demand—just as in Modigliani's version of the second-pass model. In these cases the rightward march of aggregate demand stops before it reaches the full-employment level of output, as shown in Figure 7.3 by the dashed AD schedule, with the equilibrium at E.

These dynamic results contradict Modigliani's static conclusions about the Keynes effect. Once serendipity is disturbed, the economy may, but it may not, return to full employment. Absent Modigliani's exceptional cases—a liquidity trap or an inelastic investment-demand schedule—it all depends on the adjustment process, on which information drives which changes (fixprice vs. flexprice). In the flexprice case, the equilibrium is always stable, but with fixprice adjustment, stability depends on how rapidly different variables (wages, prices, output) adjust.

Fractional-Reserve Banking in Real Time

I concluded in chapter 4 that in a static constant fractional-reserve banking did not affect the plausibility of Modigliani's critique of Keynes. Though the details of the argument change—a bond effect does the work of the Keynes effect—in a comparative-statics context, wart-free capitalism remains self-regulating even if the money supply is endogenous.

The analysis and conclusions are different if we examine real-time changes rather than comparative statics. In the spirit of chapter 4, I shall assume here that there is no central bank and that deposits of gold ducats by households constitute the reserves of banks. In the real-time context, endogenizing trans-actions money, M_1, while assuming an exogenous supply of asset money, M_2, in effect converts the second-pass model back into the first-pass model. As I shall demonstrate, the liquidity-preference schedule is invariant with respect to P, and therefore so is the interest rate. And so is the LM schedule. The re-sult is that the AD schedule is insensitive to the price level, just as in the first-pass model, and, indeed, as in the third-pass model developed in the previous chapter.

It turns out that there is a strong assumption about the very essence of money built into Modigliani's critique, albeit an assumption to which Keynes's argumentation gives some support, namely, that money is a commodity, the supply of which is fixed by nature, technology, and human ingenuity and ef-fort.[2] Once we depart from this assumption, Modigliani's results need not hold. The money supply may be a nonbinding constraint.

To see why, we return to the relationship between transactions money and portfolio money in a world of commodity money with no banking system at all and therefore no possibility of endogenous creation of money. The discus-sion of chapter 4 carries over from the comparative-statics framework to the real-time framework with one qualification, which turns out to matter when we drop the assumption that money consists of gold, silver, or cowrie shells. The dynamic picture of the financial sector is in Figure 7.4, which reproduces Figure 4.14, except that the liquidity-preference schedule does not shift when the price level shifts.

Why not? The difference between real-time changes and comparative-statics lies in what it makes sense to assume about the stock of bonds in the two cases. In both cases we assume the coupon (R) is fixed. In a comparative-statics framework, we assume that the quantity of bonds varies with the nominal value of capital, that is, with the price level; in other words, $\bar{B} = PK$. So, when the price level changes, the liquidity-preference schedule shifts. This shift takes place because we are considering separate planets that have each in its own way been the same since time immemorial. By assumption, planets have the same physical capital stock, so the appropriate assumption is that the planet with the higher price level has a larger number of bonds outstanding, the financial counterpart of the higher nominal value of its capital stock.

In a real-time context, there is no mechanism to change the quantity of bonds as the price level changes. Whatever happens to the price level, the stock of bonds remains $\bar{B} = P_0 K$, where P_0 is the price level when the story begins. Bond prices will change as the interest rate changes, but this is not the same thing as the quantity of bonds changing.

The real-time context transforms Tables 4.1, 4.2, and 4.3 of chapter 4 into the corresponding Tables 7.1, 7.2, and 7.3. The change is in the last cell of

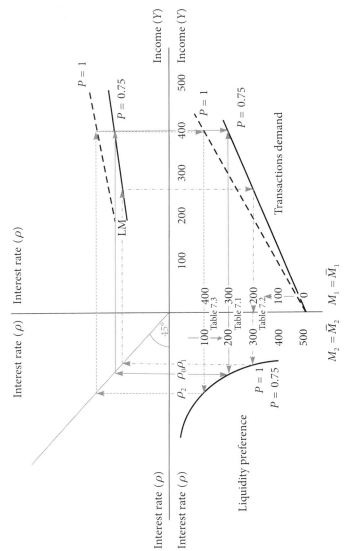

Figure 7.4 The LM schedule with commodity money.

Table 7.1 $Y = 400$; $P = 0.75$; $\alpha = 1$; $\rho = \rho_0$; $P_B = 1$

	Households			Restaurants		
Liquid Assets (Gold Ducats)	Nonliquid Assets (Bonds—Market Value)	Nonliquid Assets (Loans to Restaurants for Working Capital)	Working Capital (Gold Ducats)	Fixed Capital	Loans to Finance Working Capital	Quantity of Bonds
200	1,000	300	300	1,000	−300	−1,000

Table 7.2 $Y = 266.7$; $P = 0.75$; $\alpha = 1$; $\rho = \rho_1 = \rho_0/1.2$; $P_B = 1.2$

	Households			Restaurants		
Liquid Assets (Gold Ducats)	Nonliquid Assets (Bonds—Market Value)	Nonliquid Assets (Loans to Restaurants for Working Capital)	Working Capital (Gold Ducats)	Fixed Capital	Loans to Finance Working Capital	Quantity of Bonds
300	1,200	200	200	1,000	−200	−1,000

Table 7.3 $Y = 400$; $P = 1$; $\alpha = 1$; $\rho = \rho_2 = \rho_0/0.8$; $P_B = 0.8$

	Households			Restaurants		
Liquid Assets (Gold Ducats)	Nonliquid Assets (Bonds—Market Value)	Nonliquid Assets (Loans to Restaurants for Working Capital)	Working Capital (Gold Ducats)	Fixed Capital	Loans to Finance Working Capital	Quantity of Bonds
100	800	400	400	1,333	−400	−1,000

Table 7.3: there are now only 1,000 bonds (compared with 1,333 in Table 4.3) despite the increase in the nominal value of fixed capital. As a result, the interest rate ρ_2 that equilibrates financial markets is lower than the corresponding interest rate in Figure 4.14.

The consequence is that the only change in the demand for money is *along* the given liquidity-preference schedule, driven by changes in the bond price. For the moment this does not change the qualitative behavior of the LM schedule, namely, that it slopes upward and shifts upward with the general price level. The LM schedule continues to respond to the price level because a shift in the transactions-demand schedule is enough to move the LM schedule. A fixed money supply is still assumed, as in chapter 4, to be divided between transactions money and portfolio money, with more of the one meaning less of the other. Thus the intersection of a given IS schedule with the shifting LM schedule continues to produce a downward-sloping AD schedule in $Y \times P$ space, and Modigliani's conclusion, if not his argument, may survive—"may survive" rather than "survives" because the AD schedule is not stationary in $Y \times P/W$ space, and, as we have seen, may or may not return to a full-employment equilibrium.

In the comparative-statics context, it turned out not to matter very much whether or not banks are fully loaned up or hold excess reserves. Either way, the crucial element of the second-pass model holds: the LM schedule shifts with the price level, and consequently, the AD schedule slopes downward in $Y \times P$ space.

In real time, the position of the LM schedule is sensitive to whether or not banks are fully loaned up. The reason is that when banks have excess reserves the LM schedule is invariant with respect to the price level. As a reference point, recall the comparative-statics result, for which the relevant diagram is Figure 7.5 (Figure 4.18), in which the LM schedule is flat for a *given* price level but moves *with* the price level. In Figure 7.5 the LM schedule moves because the quantity of bonds shifts with the price level, so that the liquidity-preference schedule shifts, even though there is by assumption no link between M_1 and $\bar{M}_2$. Since $\bar{M}_2$ is unchanging, the rate of interest has to adjust to the higher quantity of bonds. With a higher rate of interest, the market value of bonds must be lower for agents willingly to hold the same amount of cash as at the lower price level. As observed in chapter 4, the bond effect and the Keynes effect both decrease the stock of bonds relative to portfolio cash at lower price levels, but by a different mechanism: the bond effect is the result of fewer bonds, the Keynes effect the result of more cash.

In real time, with the quantity of bonds fixed, the liquidity-preference schedule does not move, so the price of bonds and the interest rate remain unchanged when $\bar{M}_2$ is fixed. So Table 7.4 is the same as Table 4.8, but Table 7.5 differs from Table 4.9. As a result, the LM schedule does not change with the price level, as in Figure 7.6.

Now that the LM schedule is stationary, the AD schedule $Y \times P$ space is no longer downward sloping. Instead, it is vertical, just as it is in the first-pass model. Because interest and investment do not vary when prices change, aggregate demand is invariant with respect to the price level. There is neither a Keynes effect nor the substitute of a varying quantity of bonds. Unlike the picture presented in Figures 7.1, 7.2, and 7.3, the AD schedule in $Y \times P/W$ space remains stationary as the price level falls. The economy is constrained by liquidity preference even in the absence of a liquidity trap.

Fractional-reserve banking creates the possibility that money creation is endogenous. But there remains the possibility that banks are driven by market forces to utilize their reserves to the maximum possible extent, so that the theoretical possibility is a dead-end. Reserves would determine the money supply (via the money multiplier, 2.5 in chapter 4), to which money demand would adapt, just as commodity money regulates demand in a world without

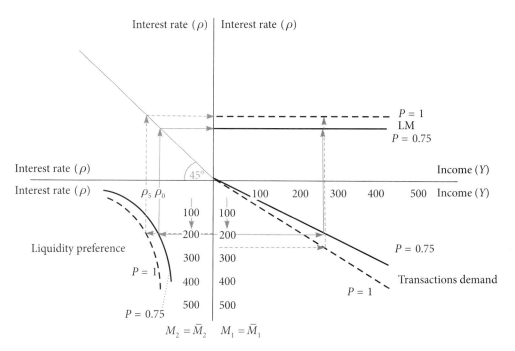

Figure 7.5 Financial equilibrium: constructing the LM schedule with endogenous transactions money, I.

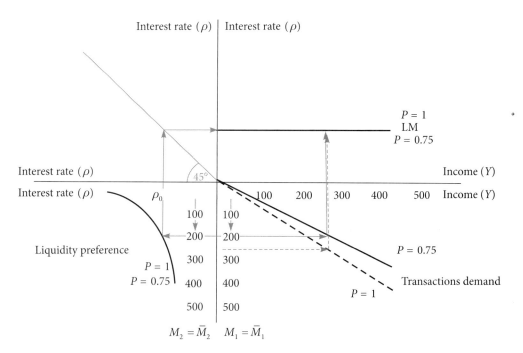

Figure 7.6 Financial equilibrium: constructing the LM schedule with endogenous transactions money, II.

Table 7.4 $Y = 266.67$; $P = 0.75$; $\alpha = 1$; $\rho = \rho_0$; $P_B = 1$

Households			Banks			Restaurants			
Bank Deposits	Nonliquid Assets (Bonds—Market Value)	Commercial Loans	Commercial Loans	Reserves	Bank Deposits	Bank Deposits	Fixed Capital	Commercial Loans	Quantity of Bonds
200	1,000	0	200	200	−400	200	1,000	−200	−1,000

Table 7.5 $Y = 266.67$; $P = 1$; $\alpha = 1$; $\rho = \rho_0$; $P_B = 1$

Households			Banks			Restaurants			
Bank Deposits	Nonliquid Assets (Bonds—Market Value)	Commercial Loans	Commercial Loans	Reserves	Bank Deposits	Bank Deposits	Fixed Capital	Commercial Loans	Quantity of Bonds
200	1,000	0	266.67	200	−466.67	266.67	1,333	−266.67	−1,000

banks. Chapter 4 did not try to resolve the tension between endogenous and exogenous money, but that irresolution should be reconsidered in a world of real-time changes.

In the comparative-statics context it was argued on the side of exogeneity that if banks lacked commercial-lending opportunities they would deploy reserves to purchase bonds, remaining fully loaned up one way or another. This assumption is more difficult to defend when change takes place in real time. In a comparative-statics context, bond prices, like everything else, never change even though the price of a bond is different on Planet A from what it is on Planet B. But in the context of real-time changes, the fear of losses on bonds can outweigh the lure of interest payments and lead bankers to hold idle reserves instead of bonds.

The danger of fluctuations in asset prices, not to mention the possibility of outright default, is the reasoning behind the "real-bills" doctrine, a variant of endogenous-money theory that its proponents thought would make the money supply respond to "legitimate" trade and insulate the financial system from aiding and abetting "illegitimate" speculation.[3] This is not the place to examine the history of monetary theory in general or the real-bills doctrine in particular.[4] For present purposes, the main problem with real bills as the basis of a theory of endogenous money is the implicit assumption of bank passivity. Even if banks have no other outlet for lending, they need not passively respond to demand for commercial loans. In the case of a downturn, with prices and output falling, expectations of a quick recovery may make the supply of transactions money less volatile than the demand, $M_1 = \alpha PY$, whereas if pessimism leads to expectations of continuing deflation, the supply may fall faster than the demand. The next chapter examines how expectations played out in the Great Depression.

The argument that fractional-reserve banking is compatible with a fixed money supply assumes not only that banks are fully loaned up but that reserves themselves are fixed. In chapter 4 gold ducats formed the base of the money supply; once deposited into the banking system by households, they remain there. In analyzing real-time changes this may be another inappropriate assumption. As prices fall, businesses and individuals who were struggling to meet their financial obligations even when prices were steady may go under. When they can't repay their loans, their creditors, including the banks that have provided working capital, also may go bust.[5] In the absence of deposit insurance (which was not introduced in the United States until 1934 and has never applied to large deposits), wealth holders may react to bank failures by withdrawing their deposits, changing the composition of the monetary base in favor of currency.[6] So the result of a decline in the price level may be a decline in reserves as well as a growth in excess reserves. The money supply may be endogenous simply because the public shifts from bank money to specie.

The Real-Balance Effect: Haberler, Pigou, and Patinkin—and Fisher

As laid out in chapter 4, the basic idea of the real-balance effect, also known as the "Pigou effect," starts from the assumption that the money supply, or at least a fraction of it, forms part of private wealth, so a nominally fixed money supply increases in purchasing power, in real value, as the price level falls. In principle, at least in the static context, there are no limits to the amount by which aggregate demand can expand, so aggregate demand can be whatever is required for full employment. In the context of chapter 4, critics like Milton Friedman could make this idea the killer argument against the theoretical claims of *The General Theory*. Even friends of *The General Theory* accepted the real-balance effect as disproving Keynes, at least at the theoretical level. Abba Lerner, someone who grasped *The General Theory* early and may have understood its implications for fiscal policy better than Keynes (see chapter 14), wrote

> There is a limit to hyperdeflations in that there is a certain amount of money in the economy which does not disappear in the course of the hyperdefla-tion and which becomes more and more valuable as prices fall. A great deal of money does disappear: much credit money, whether issued by banks or by others, may be destroyed, and therefore you could get wages and prices continuing to fall along with the terrible disruption of the economy. But there is a core of money which does not disappear—gold and the hard money provided by government. As the hyperdeflation proceeds, the value of the stock of money becomes so great and the people who own this money are so rich that this will overcome their tendency to hoard the increasingly valuable money. They will increase their demand for goods and services and this will put an end to the hyperdeflation and to the depression. (Lerner 1951, p. 205)

Paul Samuelson (1964, p. 333), while cautioning against any practical ap-plication of the real-balance effect, agreed that at a theoretical level Keynes lost the argument: "[The real-balance effect] did serve to save face and honor for the believers in the harmony of equilibrium."

At the same time, prominent Keynesians—James Tobin comes to mind—marveled at the pivotal role critics attached to the real-balance effect: "To an astonishing degree, the theoretical fraternity has taken the real-balance effect to be a conclusive refutation of Keynes" (1993, p. 59; see also Tobin 1980).

This raises an interesting question: how can grown-ups, all of them intelligent, all of them wise, all of them learned in the Torah of mainstream economics, all of them claiming to be scientific, disagree so fundamentally about the significance of the real-balance effect? The answer lies squarely in the difference between comparative statics and dynamics.

One preliminary: all would eventually agree with Lerner's stipulation that it is not the total money supply, but only outside money, the monetary base of bank reserves and currency, that is relevant for the real-balance effect. That is, inside money created endogenously by banks under a system of fractional-reserve banking is not included in the cash balances that are the basis of the real-balance effect. The reason is that inside money, money created by the banks in the process of making loans, is a wash, with one dollar of debt created for every dollar of credit. But this refinement affects only the quantitative importance of the real-balance effect, not its logic and therefore not the logical effect of letting the price level go to zero.

This logic is impeccable in the comparative-statics context. The progenitors of the real-balance effect, starting with Gottfried Haberler, cast their argument in dynamic language, in terms of what happens when the price level changes, but the symmetry assumed between creditors and debtors depends critically, if tacitly, on a comparative-statics context. In the timeless world of comparative statics, the burden of debt and the benefits enjoyed by creditors are the same now as yesterday, the same now as tomorrow.

Arthur Pigou, the real one (as distinct from the straw man Keynes created to represent the mainstream position on the supposed self-regulating property of capitalism), independently put forward the real-balance effect in a multipronged attack on Alvin Hansen's book *Fiscal Policy and Business Cycles* (1941). (The point of attack was Hansen's stagnationist view that a drying up of investment opportunities would lead to an excess of desired saving over investment demand at a full-employment level of output and that there would be no way of mopping up the excess saving other than for the government to match private surpluses with public deficits.) Pigou's argument (1943, esp. para. 10–11, pp. 349–350) is essentially Harberler's, and again, though the language is dynamic, the model itself, put forward in paragraph 11, is purely static. Pigou's model leads to the conclusion that there exists a price level at which aggregate demand will be whatever full employment requires—without the exceptions of an interest-rate floor and inelastic investment demand.

But there is nothing in Pigou's model about what happens along the way to get to this serendipitous state. Michał Kalecki, the economist credited by many with independently discovering the basic ideas of *The General Theory,* immediately pointed this out in a comment on Pigou's paper (1944). After observing that a fall in the price level would not increase the net value of real balances insofar as it acts on inside money, Kalecki goes on to make the crucial distinction between the static and dynamic contexts:

> The adjustment required would increase catastrophically the real value of debts, and would consequently lead to wholesale bankruptcy and a "confidence crisis." The "adjustment" would probably never be carried to the end. (p. 132)

The point is that in contrast with the static comparison of debts and credits at different price levels, the dynamics involve revaluation of debt. Debts taken on at one price level must be repaid with dollars earned at a lower price level. If a farmer borrows $10,000 to acquire land or equipment with wheat at $1.25 per bushel, and must repay the loan with wheat valued at $0.50, he must in effect pay back 2.5 times the number of bushels borrowed, 20,000 against 8,000. On an aggregate accounting, this is balanced by the creditor's windfall, but the real consequences are not symmetric unless the magnitude of the change is small. When the price level falls dramatically, the farmer may be driven to bankruptcy, while the creditor adds marginally to his consumption. As Kalecki concludes, "If the workers persisted in their game of unrestricted competition [driving down wages and prices], the Government would introduce a wage stop under the pressure of employers" (1944, p. 132).[7] In a world in which workers possess very little, it would necessarily be employers who are threatened with bankruptcy!

Keynes had in fact made a similar observation in his chapter 19 laundry list of objections to falling wages as a cure for unemployment:

> The depressing influence on entrepreneurs of their greater burden of debt may partly offset any cheerful reactions from the reduction of wages. Indeed if the fall of wages and prices goes far, the embarrassment of those entrepreneurs who are heavily indebted may soon reach the point of insolvency,— with severely adverse effects on investment . . .
>
> The method of increasing the quantity of money in terms of wage-units by decreasing the wage-unit increases proportionately the burden of debt; whereas the method of producing the same result by increasing the quantity of money whilst leaving the wage unit unchanged has the opposite effect. Having regard to the excessive burden of many types of debt, it can only be an inexperienced person who would prefer the former. (*The General Theory*, pp. 264, 268–269)

But, as is often the case with laundry, it is easy to lose one item or another on the list: Keynes's observation seems to have gone unnoticed by the various participants in the debate over real balances. And Keynes himself seems to have been unaware of Irving Fisher's pioneering work on the asymmetric impact of rising real liabilities and rising real assets. Fisher (1933) took this asymmetry to be *the* cause of depressions in general and the Great Depression in particular. It is worth quoting Fisher at length:

> Assuming . . . , that, at some point of time, a state of over-indebtedness exists, this will tend to lead to liquidation, through the alarm either of debtors or creditors or both. Then we may deduce the following chain of consequences in nine links: (1) *Debt liquidation* leads to *distress selling* and to (2) *Contraction of deposit currency,* as bank loans are paid off, and to a slowing down of velocity of circulation. This contraction of deposits and of their velocity, precipitated by distress selling, causes (3) *A fall in the level of prices,* in other words, a swelling of the dollar. Assuming, as above stated, that this fall of prices is not interfered with by reflation or otherwise, there must be (4) *A still greater fall in the net worths of business,* precipitating bankruptcies and (5) *A like fall in profits,* which in a "capitalistic," that is, a private-profit society, leads the concerns which are running at a loss to make (6) *A reduction in output,* in trade and in employment of labor. These losses, bankruptcies, and unemployment, lead to (7) *Pessimism and loss of confidence,* which in turn lead to (8) *Hoarding and slowing down still more the velocity of circulation.*
>
> The above eight changes cause (9) *Complicated disturbances in the rates of interest,* in particular, a fall in the nominal, or money, rates and a rise in the real, or commodity, rates of interest.
>
> Evidently debt and deflation go far toward explaining a great mass of phenomena in a very simple logical way. (pp. 341–342; emphasis in original)

Fisher tried to fit his trenchant insight into the only framework he knew, the quantity theory, but it didn't fit very well, and his analysis remained a scholarly footnote in the historiography of the analyses provoked by the Great Depression.

If we transpose the comparative-statics argument of chapter 4 to the context of real-time changes, it is easy to see how Fisher's observations impact the real-balance effect. Recall the expression for total wealth in a world of commodity money,

$$P_B(\rho)\bar{B} + M_2 + M_1 \quad + \quad -\bar{B} + PK - M_1 + \text{Working Capital.}$$
$$\text{(Households)} \qquad\qquad\qquad\qquad \text{(Firms)}$$

In the comparative-statics context, firms' assets and liabilities always match, and wealth reduces to household assets. Real wealth accordingly is

$$P_B(\rho)K + \frac{M_2}{P} + \frac{M_1}{P},$$

which, as we saw in chapter 4, becomes infinite as the price level approaches zero. Even though the real value of bonds increases only insofar as the price of bonds ($P_B(\rho)$) increases (because the issue of bonds is assumed to vary with the price level), the real value of both M_1 and M_2 becomes infinite regardless of what is assumed about interest rates and bond prices.

In the real-time context by contrast, $\bar{B}$ is fixed once and for all when bonds are first issued. Households are still getting ever richer in real terms with every fall in the price level. But the situation is very different for firms. PK, the dollar value of physical capital, declines with the price level, *while the dollar value of firms' liabilities ($\bar{B}$) remains fixed.*[8] Accordingly, the real value of firms' net assets

$$-\frac{\bar{B}}{P} + K$$

moves further and further into negative territory as the price level declines, and goes to $-\infty$ as P goes to zero, even as the real value of household wealth

$$\frac{P_B(\rho)\bar{B}}{P} + \frac{M_2}{P} + \frac{M_1}{P}$$

increases without bound. Provided P_B does not fall to zero, changes in P will raise the level of real household wealth by more than the decline in the net worth of firms because of the cash component of household wealth. If the change in P is small, so that we can assume a uniform propensity to consume for creditors and debtors, the overall real-balance effect will be positive. Overall wealth is

$$\frac{P_B(\rho)\bar{B}}{P} + \frac{M_2}{P} + \frac{M_1}{P} - \frac{\bar{B}}{P} + K,$$

which increases as P falls.

If the fall in P continues too long, however, the calculus changes. Firms will go into bankruptcy, which not only will diminish the bond wealth of households but will cause disruptions to production and therefore to incomes. The real-balance effect may cause the economy to spin even more out of control once debtors start going broke.

Fractional-reserve banking, and with it the distinction between outside and inside money, doesn't change the distinction between comparative statics and changes in real time. In the model of chapter 4, $\bar{M}_2$ is the outside money that constitutes the reserves of the banking system, and M_1 is created by the banks as the counterpart of commercial loans to finance working capital. Now nominal wealth is

$$P_B(\rho)\bar{B} + \bar{M}_2 \quad + \quad M_1 + \bar{M}_2 - M_1 - \bar{M}_2 \quad + \quad -\bar{B} + PK - M_1 + \text{Working Capital.}$$

(Households)	(Banks)	(Firms)

In the comparative-statics context, assets offset liabilities on the books of banks as well as on the books of firms, so that the qualitative effects of price-level changes do not differ from the simpler case of commodity money. Inside money, M_1, disappears from the calculation of real wealth.

In the real-time context, the results are different. In our simple model, banks are not the problem as long as they stick to commercial lending. Banks guided by the real-bills doctrine will remain solvent if they shrink their nominal lending, $M_1 = \alpha PY$, in line with declining price level; presumably working-capital requirements will vary inversely with prices. In reality, banks get into trouble if prices fall so rapidly that the value of collateral falls below the amount of the debt. The stock market crash of 1929 is a case in point, but stock-market debt was the antithesis of real bills.

The problem, as in the previous case of commodity money, is the part of firms' balance sheets that deals with fixed capital. A firm's financial position will suffer from a falling price level because the debt issued against its physical capital is assumed to be fixed in nominal terms. As before, the net position of firms in real terms is

$$-\frac{\bar{B}}{P} + K.$$

The net position of households differs from the commodity-money case only in the absence of M_1 in the formula for household real wealth,

$$\frac{P_B(\rho)\bar{B}}{P} + \frac{\bar{M}_2}{P}.$$

Apart from the implicit assumption that debtors value the bonds they owe in terms of their original value $(\bar{B}/P)$, whereas bondholders mark their bonds to market $(P_B(\rho)\bar{B}/P)$, the effects of real-time changes in the price level on the real value of debt and credit are symmetrical if we assume uniform propensities to consume out of wealth and income. In this case, the overall impact of the real-balance effect on aggregate demand remains positive since households also have a real cash balance, $(\bar{M}_2/P)$.

But this simplification obscures the same real-time issues that arise in the absence of fractional-reserve banking. Once changes in the price level become large, there is every reason *not* to assume that debtors and creditors have the same propensities to consume and save. Even if a uniform propensity to consume is a defensible assumption in a comparative-statics framework, in real time agents can be expected to respond differently to prosperity than to privation. If for no other reason, liquidity constraints are most likely to occur in times of deflation and a rising real burden of debt. If the propensity to consume is lower for creditors than for debtors, the positive multiplier for windfalls enjoyed by creditors may be overwhelmed by the negative multipliers attaching to rising real debt.

The above assumes that the debtors manage to survive economically. As prices continue to fall, survival becomes less and less likely. As noted, there is no limit to the real burden of debt as the price level goes to zero—except bankruptcy. At this point, the rising burden of debt is no longer offset by the increasing wealth of coupon clippers. And the ephemeral quality of the creditor's wealth is revealed the moment the debtor's IOU becomes worthless. The real-balance effect, far from being the savior of the system, turns out to be an agent of its destruction.

The problem does not stop with the destruction of the bond wealth of both lender and borrower. The creditor's cash hoard continues to increase in real value as P falls, but not by enough to counter the real effects of bankruptcy—not only the disruption of production at the site of the bankruptcy, but the whole chain of collateral damage, the effects on suppliers, customers, employees, as well as the banks, which discover that real bills do not insulate them from default.

The contagion caused by the ballooning of real debt has been understood by macroeconomists taking their cue from Fisher (1933) (see, for example, Bernanke 1983, 1995). The link to the real-balance effect, particularly how the growth of real debt vitiates Friedman's claim that the real-balance effect undermines the argument of *The General Theory,* seems to have eluded the post-Friedman generation.

Don Patinkin attempted to rescue the real-balance effect by shifting the focus from money to the qualitative differences between private and public debt. Patinkin argues that in a real-time context the real-balance effect is not only, or primarily, about cash balances, but about bonds, specifically about government bonds, which unlike private bonds do not, at least not in Patinkin's telling, pit creditor and debtor against each other:

> What constitutes the "cash balance" whose increase in real value provides the stimulatory effect of the Pigou analysis . . . [is] the net obligation of the government to the private sector of the economy. That is, it consists of the sum of interest- and non-interest-bearing government debt held outside the treasury and central bank. Thus, by excluding demand deposits and including government interest-bearing debt, it differs completely from what is usually regarded as the stock of money. (1948, pp. 550–551)

Patinkin's argument implicitly recognizes that for a falling price level to stimulate real consumption via an effect on wealth, there must be an asset that satisfies two conditions. First, the real value of the asset must vary in the opposite direction of the price level. Second, the asset must have no counterpart as a liability. The first condition means that most physical assets would not qualify: plant and equipment, houses, infrastructure—the money values of all such assets can be expected to vary more or less in line with the overall price level, so that their real values would, at least to a first approximation, be invariant with respect to prices.[9] Neither does working capital qualify. For similar reasons, equities would hardly be a candidate for inducing real-balance effects; a stock market boom might indeed stimulate consumption demand, and a crash might even provoke a crisis, but such movements are not consequences of changes in the *general* price level.

This leaves us with debt fixed in nominal terms. For present purposes we can rule out debt on working capital by assuming that it is sufficiently short term that a falling price level does not impair the capacity of firms to repay their loans, and that as loans are rolled over, the fall in demand for loans is matched by a fall in the supply of short-term credit.

There remain bonds, which satisfy the first condition of varying in real value inversely with the goods-price level. The problem with bonds is that they run up against the second condition, namely, that there be no liability corresponding to the asset. On the contrary, for every bond owner there is a debtor, and it has been observed that increases in the real value of bonds can have disastrous effects on borrowers, effects not likely to be offset by the addition to lenders' real wealth.

The one exception, the only asset that meets both of Patinkin's conditions, is a *government* bond, to which, indeed, he assimilates (outside) money, as a form of noninterest-bearing government debt. This seems more promising as a basis for the real-balance effect in real time, but the implicit assumptions in the argument cannot go unremarked.

The distinguishing feature of assets that lead to a real-balance effect is now bound up with the behavior of different classes of agents: governments, unlike private borrowers, are supposed to maintain the *status quo ante* in terms of taxing and spending even in the light of debilitating price changes. In Patinkin's words, "If we assume that government activity is not affected by the movements of the absolute price level, then the net effect of a price decline must always be stimulatory" (1948, p. 550).

To be sure, sovereign governments do not normally declare bankruptcy, but short of bankruptcy there are budgetary obstacles to maintaining the nominal value of government bonds. Again, the difference between the static and dynamic analysis is critical. In a static analysis, it is difficult to see any rationale for Patinkin's supposed insensitivity of the nominal stock of government debt to the level of prices. In a static model, real bonded indebtedness should in principle be independent of the price level, which is to say that nominal indebtedness *should* vary with the price level. If on Planet A the price level is and always has been 1 and the public debt is 500, on what grounds would the public debt in Planet B—identical in every respect to A except that the price level is and always has been 2—be anything but 1,000?

In the dynamic analysis, by contrast, it is more appropriate to assume that the quantity of government bonds is fixed once and for all when the debt is issued, just as we must assume for private debt. Patinkin's point is that unlike private debt, the resulting increase in the real public debt as P falls need not lead to adverse consequences for the economy. This is presumably what is meant by "[assuming] that government activity is not affected by the movements of the absolute price level." But if spending and taxation continue at the same levels in *real* terms, how does the government hold to its commitment to pay the interest and principal stipulated in *nominal* terms—which after all is the only basis on which the nominal value of government bonds can be maintained?

There is, to be sure, more than one way the government can uphold its nominal commitments, but not by business as usual, not by assuming that government activity is unaffected; for unless the government takes positive steps to counter the impact of a declining price level, tax revenues must decline along with the value of nominal output and income and, eventually, the value of property.

One thing the government can do is to raise taxes. But raising taxes will impose a drag on aggregate demand that will offset the stimulus of the rising real value of government bonds.[10] Or, more realistically, the government can allow the real-balance effect to work—by borrowing more in order to meet its interest obligations!

But think what this means: Patinkin's version of the real-balance effect now hinges on a commitment to deficit finance, and the proposition that there is no limit to the amount by which aggregate demand can be expanded via the real-balance effect turns out to be a proposition about the inability of unemployment to persist in the presence of sufficient fiscal stimulus. In this form, the real-balance effect may be alive and well. But it can hardly be what Milton Friedman (1970) had in mind when he dismissed Keynes's claim to have established the possibility of unemployment in a perfectly competitive economy:

> [The proposition that] as a purely *theoretical* matter, there need not exist,
> even if all prices are flexible, a *long-run equilibrium* position characterized

by "full employment" of resources . . . can be treated summarily because it has been demonstrated to be false. (pp. 206–207; see chapter 4 for the complete quotation)

Perhaps we are too quick to accept the assumption that government bonds do not pit the interests of debtors against the interests of creditors. The early years of the Roosevelt Administration provide considerable food for thought in this respect, particularly the "gold-clause" cases, *Perry v. United States* (294 U.S. 330, 1935) and *Norman v. Baltimore and Ohio Railroad Co.* (294 U.S. 240, 1935), which come within a whisker of a "natural experiment" with regard to the plausibility of Patinkin's behavioral assumptions.

These cases revolved around the constitutional legality of various congressional and presidential actions nullifying a standard clause in debt contracts—bonds, mortgages, etc.—that called for repayment in dollars reflecting the gold value of the dollar at the time the debt was contracted. A gold clause became part of bond boilerplate in the United States in the aftermath of the Civil War, when gold coins and "greenbacks" circulated side by side, both legal tender, even though greenbacks exchanged for gold at a discount.

Prior to 1933, the value of gold was $20.67 per troy ounce, but soon after his inauguration, President Roosevelt effectively broke the link to gold by forbidding U.S. citizens to own gold, and Congress by joint resolution abrogated the gold clauses in both private and public debts. These actions were further codified by various acts of Congress, culminating in the Gold Reserve Act of 1934. One purpose of all this legislation was to reduce the gold content of the dollar in an attempt to put a halt to the spiraling deflation. During 1933 the president was authorized to change the gold content of the dollar within certain limits, until under the authority of the Gold Reserve Act he fixed the price of gold to $35.00 per ounce, an increase of 69 percent over its pre-1933 level.

Creditors challenged the validity of the abrogation of gold clauses in both private *(Norman)* and public *(Perry)* obligations. The cases worked their way up through the courts and finally reached the Supreme Court in 1935. The Court held by a 5–4 majority that the government was acting legally if not morally in nullifying both private and public gold clauses. *Norman* did not touch Patinkin's version of the real-balance effect directly, because it involved a transfer of wealth between private creditors and private debtors. But it powerfully raised the question of the asymmetry between debtors and creditors. As Roosevelt was planning to inform the nation had *Norman* gone the other way,

If the letter of the law is so declared and enforced, it would automatically throw practically all the railroads of the United States into bankruptcy. . . .

The principle laid down today in the railroad case applies to every other corporation which has gold bonds outstanding, driving many another huge enterprise into receivership! It must be applied likewise to the obligations of towns, cities, counties, and states; and these units of government, now working bravely to meet and reduce their debts, would be forced into the position of defaulters. (quoted in Magliocca 2011, p. 33)

Even if we put to one side the asymmetrical effects of price changes on private debtors and creditors, there remains *Perry,* which involved the essence of the real-balance effect as interpreted by Patinkin, namely, the creation of private wealth to the detriment of the government's own balance sheet.[11] In the event, the Attorney General's argument to the Supreme Court made no mention of the benefits that might be enjoyed by allowing coupon clippers to prevail. Rather, he stressed the harm to the economy and the government.

Roosevelt himself was prepared to reject the Court's decision. Here are his intended words:

The actual enforcement of the gold clause against the Government of the United States will not bankrupt the Government. It will increase our national debt by approximately nine billions of dollars. It means that this additional sum must eventually be raised by additional taxation. In our present major effort to get out of the depression, to put people to work, to restore industry and agriculture, the literal enforcement of this opinion would not only retard our efforts, but would put the Government and 125,000,000 people into an infinitely more serious economic plight than we have yet experienced ...

To stand idly by and to permit the decision of the Supreme Court to be carried through to its logical and inescapable conclusion would so imperil the economic and political security of this nation that the legislative and executive officers of the Government must look beyond the narrow letter of contractual obligations. (quoted in Magliocca 2011, pp. 34–35)

This particular "fireside chat" was never given because the decisions in *Norman* and *Perry* went in the government's favor, but it reveals that Roosevelt was willing to suspend the constitutional order because of his perception of the catastrophic consequences of enforcing the law, a position not taken by any American president since Lincoln suspended *habeas corpus* during the Civil War. It apparently never occurred to any of the actors, certainly not to Roosevelt, that the increase in private wealth might have a salutary effect on the economy—or that (*pace* Professor Patinkin) the government's operations could not but be affected by an increase in the real value of its debt!

The Fisher Effect

Up to now we have been analyzing the effect on aggregate demand of price-level changes via two routes, the effect on investment demand of the interest rate, and the effect on consumption demand of wealth. It should now be clear that moving from a static to a dynamic context transforms anti-Keynesian arguments into much more tame, not to say lame, parodies of their static selves. Indeed, in a dynamic context, a lower price level is likely to depress demand rather than to increase it.

In this section we face a different challenge: the Fisher effect has no counterpart in the static context, for it is the effect of a *changing* price level on the interest rate—not a comparison of interest rates appropriate to two different price levels. The Fisher effect (I. Fisher 1896, 1930 [1907]) is the difference between the so-called real rate of interest and the nominal rate of interest, a difference that arises only if the price level is changing over time. Here "real" means what it has meant throughout this study, value in terms of goods and services, as distinct from value in terms of money: as its name suggests, the real rate of interest captures the time premium attaching to present *goods* over future *goods,* in contrast with the nominal rate of interest, which reflects the time premium of present *money* over future *money.*

In principle, as Fisher observed way back in 1896, there is a different interest rate for each and every good: the interest rate for wheat will be the same as the interest rate for oil if and only if the relative prices of wheat and oil do not change. In general

$$\begin{array}{ccc} \text{interest rate in} & = & \text{interest rate in} & - & \text{rate of change of price of} \\ \text{terms of wheat} & & \text{terms of oil} & & \text{wheat in terms of oil} \end{array}$$

$$\rho_{\text{WHEAT}} \quad = \quad \rho_{\text{OIL}} \quad - \quad \phi_{\text{W/O}},$$

where ρ_{WHEAT} is the wheat-specific rate of interest, what Keynes in his enigmatic chapter 17 calls the own rate of interest; ρ_{OIL} is the own rate of interest for oil; and $\phi_{\text{W/O}}$ is the percentage rate of change of the price of wheat in terms of oil, which is to say the difference between the rate of change of the dollar price of wheat and the rate of change of the dollar price of oil. In other words, the interest rate on two different goods will differ by the rate at which their relative price changes.

To understand the logic of this proposition, think of goods as potential stores of value. For oil and wheat to coexist as stores of value requires that agents be indifferent between holding wealth in the form of promissory notes in wheat and holding wealth in the form of promissory notes in oil. Ignoring storage costs and the like, and assuming price changes are known in advance, for the two forms of wealth-holding to be equivalent in agents' eyes, the wheat rate of interest—the premium on present wheat relative to future wheat—can differ from the oil rate of interest only by an amount equal to the rate at which the price of oil changes relative to the price of wheat.

We can also think of the equation $\rho_{\text{WHEAT}} = \rho_{\text{OIL}} - \phi_{W/O}$ as an equilibrium condition that must hold if investment takes place both by sacrificing some present oil for future oil and by sacrificing present wheat for future wheat. The right-hand side of the equation above is the return on an investment in oil, and the left-hand side is the return on an investment in wheat, both expressed in terms of wheat. The two investments must yield equal returns if the allocation of overall investment is in equilibrium, with both oil and wheat receiving positive doses of investment.

For example, suppose the oil rate of interest is 6 percent and the wheat rate of interest is 9 percent. If the relative price of the two goods is unchanging, all agents would prefer to hold wealth in the form of promises to pay wheat and to invest in wheat projects than to lend or invest in oil. For even if their ultimate goal is to consume oil, they can do better by swapping present oil for present wheat—let's assume that the prices start out at $1.00 per bushel of wheat and $1.00 per barrel of oil—and lending present wheat against future wheat. In this way, agents can reap 109 bushels of wheat next year for every 100 barrels of oil they hold at present. If relative prices are unchanging, they can then reswap the 109 bushels of wheat for 109 barrels of oil. By contrast, if they directly lend present oil against future oil, there will be only 106 barrels of future oil to show for every 100 barrels.

However, if (and only if) the price of wheat relative to oil falls by 3 percent—let's say oil remains at $1.00 while wheat falls to $0.97—the 109 bushels of wheat will only buy 106 barrels of oil next year, with the result that lending wheat versus lending oil is a wash, and agents will be indifferent between the two forms of wealth holding. A similar story can be told for investment that adds to the capacity to produce wheat or oil.[12]

The third-pass model developed in chapter 6 provides a special case of the general proposition encapsulated in the equation $\rho_{\text{WHEAT}} = \rho_{\text{OIL}} - \phi_{W/O}$—a special case in which bonds replace oil and "goods" replace wheat. If the nominal rate on bonds is ρ_{NOMINAL} and the percentage rate at which the price level is changing is ϕ, the real rate on bonds, ρ_{REAL}, is given by the formula

real rate	=	nominal rate	−	rate of change of price level
ρ_{REAL}	=	ρ_{NOMINAL}	−	$\phi.$

For example, if the nominal interest rate is 5 percent per year but prices are climbing at the rate of 4 percent, then the real interest rate is 1 percent. If $100.00 is lent at interest, it will return $105.00 at the end of the year, but a basket of goods that cost $100.00 at the beginning of the period will cost $104.00 at the end. The return in terms of goods will be the difference between the nominal return and inflation, namely $1.00. If the rate of inflation is 10 percent and the nominal interest rate is 5 percent, the real rate is −5 percent; a loan at 5 percent still returns the borrower $105.00, but that $105.00 will buy goods that were worth only $95.00 at the beginning of the period, 5 percent less than the original $100.00 could buy.

As in the generic example of wheat and oil, we can interpret the equation relating real and nominal rates of interest either as a definition of the return on bonds in terms of goods or as an equilibrium condition. As an equilibrium condition, the equation says that the return on real investment (the left-hand side of the equation) must equal the return on bonds (the right-hand side).

How should a changing price level modify our analysis of the relationship between the real and the financial sides of the economy? The answer to this question depends on whether the real rate determines the nominal rate or vice versa and thus goes to a fundamental difference between Keynes and the mainstream.

In the mainstream story based on the classical dichotomy, the real interest rate is determined in the real economy; it is the price that equilibrates the real supply of saving and the real demand for investment. In the equation $\rho_{REAL} = \rho_{NOMINAL} - \phi$, causality runs from ρ_{REAL} and ϕ to $\rho_{NOMINAL}$, which is to say that the real rate is the master, the nominal rate the slave. So, for the mainstream, the Fisher effect causes no revision of the theory of macroeconomic adjustment; there is no need to take account of price changes except in describing the nominal side of the classical dichotomy, namely, how the real interest rate is reflected in financial markets.[13]

This story breaks down completely when prices are falling: negative nominal rates may be required for the real rate to be the master. If, for example, $\rho_{REAL} = 2$ percent and $\phi = -5$ percent, then the nominal rate on bonds would have to be −3 percent. A zero-coupon bond[14] with a redemption value of $100.00 next year would have to sell at a premium today, at $103.00, the decline in value over the year reflecting the negative nominal interest on the bond.[15]

In stark contrast with the mainstream, the starting point for Keynes is the nominal rate of interest, determined in markets for financial assets: causality runs from $\rho_{NOMINAL}$ and ϕ to ρ_{REAL}. The framework of *The General Theory* thus requires a story about how the real rate of interest—not the nominal rate—is affected by changes in prices.

There are two ways of telling this story. The first allows us to continue to work with nominal interest rates and reflect price changes in terms of investment returns and investment demand. Consider an investment project which, for a sacrifice of $10.00 worth of goods today—say oil—gives back (net of operating costs) $1.50 worth of goods per year for the next ten years, 1.5 barrels at $1.00 per barrel. Paying back the cost of the project would require a level payment of $1.30 for principal and interest over the ten-year period to amortize the loan. Net of loan amortization, the project would return 0.2 barrels of oil per year, worth $0.20 per year, as in Table 7.6.

But if prices are changing over time, the numbers tell a different story. Suppose the price of oil is falling by 10 percent per year. Then the money value of the oil and the resulting profit would follow the trajectory in Table 7.7. This table suggests a simple approach to incorporating price level changes in the analysis: adjust the investment-demand schedule to reflect inflation or deflation in calculating project returns. In the present example, an attractive project under a regime of constant prices becomes a white elephant under a deflationary regime.

Instead of adjusting the investment-demand schedule, we can adjust the interest rate. We do all the calculations in real terms, but with this important difference: instead of assuming the real rate is unaffected by price changes, we adjust the hurdle rate used to determine which investment projects pass muster and which do not. The hurdle rate is now, as in the mainstream analysis, a real rate of interest, but in the framework of *The General Theory* this rate is determined jointly by financial markets and the rate of inflation or deflation: the equation $\rho_{REAL} = \rho_{NOMINAL} - \phi$ is read from right to left, with the real (oil) rate of interest the difference between a nominal hurdle rate and the rate of change of the price of oil.

Assume, as above, a nominal hurdle rate of 5 percent. If the price of oil falls by 10 percent each year, the hurdle rate calculated from the equation $\rho_{REAL} = \rho_{NOMINAL} - \phi$ is 15 percent. At this rate of interest, it takes about 2 barrels of oil to amortize the original 10 barrels of cost over ten years, a loss of 0.5 barrels per year given that production is 1.5 barrels.

There are two important points that emerge from Table 7.7. The first is the role of expectations. If, as in the oil example, the expected project life is ten years, then the relevant interest rate is the rate expected over the next ten years. Since investment by definition deals with costs incurred today for benefits in the future, the Fisher effect puts expectations front and center.[16]

The second point is the implications of the Fisher effect for liquidity preference. Absent the Fisher effect, we have thus far followed Keynes in dividing financial assets into two kinds: money (cash or cash equivalents such as demand deposits), for which the rate of interest is zero, and long term bonds, for which the interest rate is ρ. Once prices are assumed to change, money as well as bonds can deliver nonzero returns. If, for example, the price level is falling by 10 percent per year, money yields a 10 percent real return even though its nominal return is zero.

Table 7.6 Profit and Loan Amortization at 5 percent Interest

	Year									
	1	2	3	4	5	6	7	8	9	10
Nominal Project Returns	$1.50	$1.50	$1.50	$1.50	$1.50	$1.50	$1.50	$1.50	$1.50	$1.50
P&I	–$1.30	–$1.30	–$1.30	–$1.30	–$1.30	–$1.30	–$1.30	–$1.30	–$1.30	–$1.30
Net Cash Flow	$0.20	$0.20	$0.20	$0.20	$0.20	$0.20	$0.20	$0.20	$0.20	$0.20
Addendum: Allocation of Amortization between Interest and Principal; Principal Balance at Year End										
Interest	$0.50	$0.46	$0.42	$0.37	$0.33	$0.28	$0.23	$0.18	$0.12	$0.06
Principal Reduction	$0.80	$0.83	$0.88	$0.92	$0.97	$1.01	$1.07	$1.12	$1.17	$1.23
Principal Balance (End of Year)	$9.20	$8.37	$7.49	$6.57	$5.61	$4.59	$3.53	$2.41	$1.23	$0.00

Table 7.7 Profit and Loan Amortization at 5 percent Interest and 10 percent Deflation

	Year									
	1	2	3	4	5	6	7	8	9	10
Nominal Project Returns	$1.35	$1.22	$1.09	$0.98	$0.89	$0.80	$0.72	$0.65	$0.58	$0.52
P&I	–$1.30	–$1.30	–$1.30	–$1.30	–$1.30	–$1.30	–$1.30	–$1.30	–$1.30	–$1.30
Net Cash Flow	$0.05	–$0.08	–$0.20	–$0.31	–$0.41	–$0.50	–$0.58	–$0.65	–$0.71	–$0.77

Paradoxically, the variable governing asset demands remains the *nominal* rate of interest on bonds even though what matters to the agent is the difference between the real return on bonds and the real return on money. The paradox disappears once it is recognized that price-level changes affect bonds and money in exactly the same way because both money and bonds are denominated in nominal terms. Consequently, the difference between real rates is the same as the difference between nominal rates. Since the nominal rate on money is zero, the difference between real rates on bonds and money reduces to the nominal rate on bonds.

Algebraically we have the general formula for the fraction of wealth held in liquid form as a function of the difference between real rates, $\beta(\rho_R^B - \rho_R^M)$, in place of the original formulation, $\beta(\rho)$, where superscripts distinguish bonds and money, and subscripts distinguish real and nominal rates. Substituting from the general equation relating real and nominal rates gives

$$\rho_R^B = \rho_N^B - \phi$$

and

$$\rho_R^M = \rho_N^M - \phi = -\phi.$$

So $\beta(\rho_R^B - \rho_R^M)$ reduces to $\beta(\rho_N^B)$, which is the original formula for the demand for money as an asset.

As the oil example illustrates, the Fisher effect drives a wedge between the interest rate relevant for investment decisions and the rate relevant for financial market equilibrium. The first is the real rate, the second the nominal rate. That is, if returns are measured in real terms, investment demand is driven by the real rate,

$$I_D = I\left(\rho_R^B\right) = I\left(\rho_N^B - \phi\right),$$

while equality between the asset demand for money and its available supply depends on the nominal rate,

$$M_2 = \bar{M}_2 = \frac{\beta\left(\rho_N^B\right)}{1 - \beta\left(\rho_N^B\right)} P_B(\rho)\bar{B}.$$

The wedge between the two rates is the rate of change of the price level.

In terms of the basic four-quadrant representation of aggregate demand, the Fisher effect is reflected in a linear displacement of the vertical axis separating quadrants two and three. In Figure 7.7 the axis for quadrant three measures the nominal interest rate and for quadrant two the real interest rate. If the nominal rate is equal to ρ_0 and prices are falling at the rate ϕ, the corre-

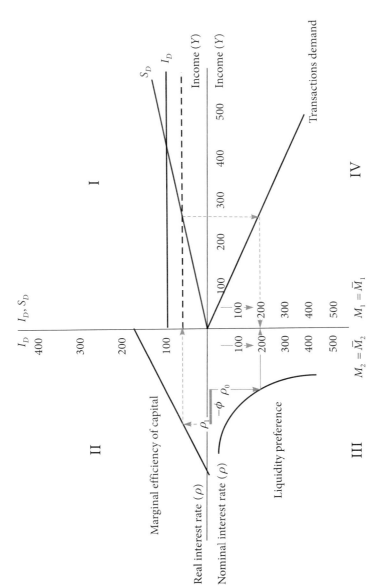

Figure 7.7 Aggregate demand determined by the real interest rate.

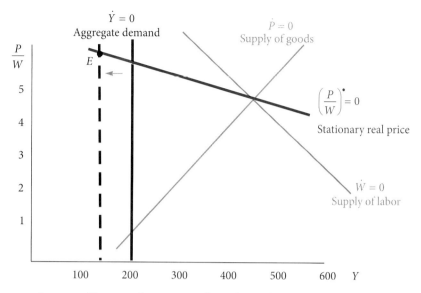

Figure 7.8 Fixprice adjustment: Fisher effect reduces aggregate demand.

sponding real rate is ρ_1. (We assume given endowments $\bar{B}$ and $\bar{M}_2$, so that the liquidity-preference schedule is stationary despite the assumption of a falling P.) In Figure 7.7 deflation displaces the investment-demand schedule downward from the solid line to the dashed line, and aggregate demand, instead of being 400, where a hurdle rate of ρ_0 would put it, is equal to 266.7.

The consequence of a real interest rate exceeding the nominal rate is that the economy is once again chasing a moving target of aggregate demand. The new complication is that the falling price level will have a knock-on negative impact on aggregate demand because, in the framework of *The General Theory*, a falling price level, $\phi < 0$, increases the real interest rate. Figure 7.8 illustrates the process assuming the nominal interest rate is fixed. The AD schedule moves to the left as output and prices fall. It is not necessarily the case that the process converges to a new equilibrium, but, as the mathematical appendix shows, the Fisher effect delays but does not derail the adjustment process—provided the propensity to save is sufficiently large and provided wages adjust more rapidly than prices.

By Way of Summary

Moving from comparative statics to real-time changes reverses the verdict on whether a capitalist economy can be self-regulating. In chapter 4 the verdict was against Keynes. Whatever the particular assumption we adopted about money and banks, the arguments of Modigliani and Haberler carried the day.

One way or another, wage and price flexibility assured the existence of a full-employment equilibrium.

But in a world of real-time changes, such as Keynes invites us to consider in chapter 19 of *The General Theory*, we get very different results. Even in a world of commodity money, there is no guarantee that Modigliani's full-employment equilibrium is stable: in contrast with the Eagles' "Hotel California," once you depart from full employment, you may be barred from ever returning.

If we accept that the framework of modern capitalism includes a fractional-reserve banking system, then the question of whether capitalism can be self-regulating becomes more complex. The key issue is whether banks remain fully loaned up when prices are falling. If banks do remain fully loaned up, the money supply is always a constant multiple of the reserve base,[17] and if the reserve ratio is fixed exogenously, so is the money supply. A world of fractional-reserve banking is then no different from a world of commodity money because banks simply multiply an exogenously given quantity of outside money.

If, however, the money supply is endogenous because the creation of money by banks varies directly with the price level, and there is no shifting between transactions money and asset money, then there is no Keynes effect. Moreover, unlike the case of comparative statics, there is no change in the quantity of bonds to accomplish the same result as the Keynes effect does, namely, to increase aggregate demand as the price level falls. Consequentially, there is nothing in the interest-investment nexus to propel the economy back to full employment after it has suffered a negative demand shock.

The killer argument against Keynes was supposed by Milton Friedman to be the real-balance effect because this argument, unlike Modigliani's, operates on the propensity to consume and is therefore not subject to the qualifications Modigliani was compelled to make for a liquidity trap and inelastic investment demand. Unlike the comparative-statics context, where one can finesse firms and banks and focus on the wealth of households, this is no longer possible when change takes place in real time. In real time, firm liabilities are fixed in nominal terms, while the value of firm assets varies with the price level. Price-level reductions, which are supposed in the comparative-statics context to drive household wealth and consumption demand ever upward, instead drive firms into bankruptcy and undermine the wealth of their creditors. Long before the bonanza of infinite wealth and unlimited aggregate demand materializes, the economy dissolves into catastrophe. Far from solving the problem of aggregate demand, the real-balance effect exacerbates it!

Finally, the Fisher effect piles on the bad news. A continuously falling price level increases real rates of interest and thus reduces investment demand. This reduces aggregate demand further and shifts the equilibrium to a lower level of output and employment.

All these effects, with the exception of the Keynes effect, have to do with the impact of real-time changes on the values of assets and liabilities. Considering how important the issue was to his purpose in writing *The General Theory,* it is curious how little attention Keynes pays to the interaction of the price level, debt, and aggregate demand. He appears content to argue that price flexibility is more of a problem than a solution. This argument is correct as far as it goes, but incomplete at best. In any case, there is no systematic treatment of the kind accorded to consumption, investment, and interest, and the anecdotal comments offered in his chapter 19 can hardly serve as a substitute.

In fact, as was noted in connection with the real-balance effect, it is not to Keynes but to Irving Fisher (1933) that one must turn for connecting aggregate demand to the nexus of prices, assets, and liabilities—except that Fisher had no place for aggregate demand in his conceptual framework, unquestionably a serious shortcoming; the solution, I have suggested, is to marry Fisher to Keynes.

In the context of real-time changes, none of the dynamic considerations discussed in this chapter is totally unambiguous, but, except for the Keynes effect, each is likely to depress aggregate demand as the price level falls. So the Keynes effect would not only have to survive the move from comparative statics to real time it would also have to work so well that it canceled out the others! It would take a tremendous act of faith *(credere quia absurdum)* to argue that wage and price flexibility vitiate the message of *The General Theory:* without this faith, it is not plausible that a market system left to itself will eliminate involuntary unemployment.

The first issue is the dynamic behavior of the Modigliani second-pass model. The focus is on the fixprice version of the model since this is the adjustment process that yields ambiguous results. (The mathematics is similar for the flexprice model.) We have the following system of equations:[1]

$$\frac{\left(\dfrac{P}{W}\right)^{\cdot}}{\dfrac{P}{W}} \equiv \left(\frac{\dot{P}}{P} - \frac{\dot{W}}{W}\right) = -\theta_1\left[GS\left(\frac{P}{W}\right) - Y\right] - \theta_3\left[Y - LS\left(\frac{P}{W}\right)\right], \quad (7.1)$$

$$\dot{Y} = \theta_2[I(\rho) - sY], \quad (7.2)$$

$$\frac{\dot{P}}{P} = -\theta_1\left[GS\left(\frac{P}{W}\right) - Y\right], \quad (7.3)$$

$$M \equiv M_1 + M_2 = \alpha PY + \frac{\beta(\rho)}{1 - \beta(\rho)} P_B(\rho)P_0K = \bar{M}. \quad (7.4)$$

For the sake of mathematical tractability I will assume that the adjustment of the interest rate to the price level in equation (7.4) is instantaneous. Equation (7.4) differs from its counterpart in chapter 4 because in a world of real-time change the quantity of bonds $\bar{B}$ is not assumed to change with the price level. Instead it is fixed once and for all at $\bar{B} = P_0K$, the value of the capital stock at the initial price level P_0. Differentiating equation (7.4) with respect to the price level gives

$$\rho' \equiv \frac{\partial \rho}{\partial P} = \frac{-\alpha Y}{\left(\dfrac{\beta'P_B}{(1 - \beta)^2} + \dfrac{\beta P_B'}{1 - \beta}\right)P_0K} > 0. \quad (7.5)$$

Here the impact of assuming $\bar{B}$ to be fixed is negligible because the fungibility of M_1 and M_2 means that ρ varies directly with the price of goods.

We have three state variables, (P/W), Y, and P, and three differential equations, equations (7.1), (7.2), and (7.3). The conditions for a stable equilibrium are correspondingly more complicated than in the two-equation systems that we have studied up to now. In general, if the Jacobian matrix is

$$J = \begin{bmatrix} j_{11} & j_{12} & j_{13} \\ j_{21} & j_{22} & j_{23} \\ j_{31} & j_{32} & j_{33} \end{bmatrix},$$

the stability conditions are

$$\alpha_1 = -\, tr\, J = -(j_{11} + j_{22} + j_{33}) > 0,$$

$$\alpha_2 = -(j_{13}j_{31} + j_{12}j_{21} + j_{23}j_{32} - j_{11}j_{22} - j_{11}j_{33} - j_{22}j_{33}) > 0,$$

$$\alpha_3 = -det\, J > 0,$$

$$\alpha_1\alpha_2 - \alpha_3 > 0.$$

Differentiating equations (7.1), (7.2), and (7.3) with respect to the state variables gives

$$J = \begin{bmatrix} -\theta_1 GS' + \theta_3 LS' & \theta_1 - \theta_3 & 0 \\ 0 & -\theta_2 s & \theta_2 I'\rho' \\ -\theta_1 GS' & \theta_1 & 0 \end{bmatrix},$$

so

$$\alpha_1 \;=\; \theta_1 GS' - \theta_3 LS' + \theta_2 s,$$

$$\alpha_2 \;=\; -\theta_1\theta_2 I'\rho' + \big(\theta_1 GS' - \theta_3 LS'\big)\theta_2 s,$$

and after simplification

$$\alpha_3 \;=\; -\theta_1\theta_2\theta_3 I'\rho'(GS' - LS'),$$

$$\alpha_1\alpha_2 - \alpha_3 = \big(\theta_1 GS' - \theta_3 LS' + \theta_2 s\big)\big(\theta_1 GS' - \theta_3 LS'\big)\theta_2 s - \theta_1\theta_2 I'\rho'\big[\theta_2 s + GS'\big(\theta_1 - \theta_3\big)\big].$$

The signs of the various terms guarantee that the expressions α_1, α_2, and α_3 are positive regardless of the magnitudes of the variables and parameters. The last expression, $\alpha_1\alpha_2 - \alpha_3$, is more problematic. If $\theta_1 > \theta_3$, then this expression also is positive and the system is stable, converging to the full-employment equilibrium E in Figure 7.1. But if $\theta_1 < \theta_3$, and if $\theta_1 GS'$ is not too large and $\theta_3 LS'$ is sufficiently small, then $\alpha_1\alpha_2 - \alpha_3$ will be negative, and the system will be unstable, as in Figure 7.2. To see this, suppose $0 < \theta_1 GS' \le \varepsilon$, $LS' \approx 0$. Then

$$\big(\alpha_1\alpha_2 - \alpha_3\big) \le \theta_1\theta_2\Big(GS's\big[\varepsilon + \theta_2 s\big] - I'\rho'\big[\theta_2 s - GS'\big(\theta_3 - \theta_1\big)\big]\Big),$$

which is negative if $\theta_3 - \theta_1$ is sufficiently large. These are the conditions stated verbally in the text (pp. 223–226).

Fractional-Reserve Banking

Real time makes an important difference for the impact of fractional-reserve banking on the ability of a capitalist economy to recover from a shock to output. With the quantity of bonds fixed once and for all, the price level has no impact on the rate of interest. In place of equation (7.4), we have

$$M_1 = \alpha PY, \tag{7.4a}$$

$$M_2 = \frac{\beta(\rho)}{1 - \beta(\rho)} P_B(\rho) P_0 K = \bar{M}_2, \tag{7.4b}$$

with M_1 determined by P and Y, and $\bar{M}_2$ determining ρ. The LM schedule becomes horizontal, as in chapter 4. The novelty is that the LM schedule is now invariant with respect to the price of goods because the bond issue is no longer assumed to vary with the nominal value of capital. Assuming that the LM schedule is characterized by equation (7.4b) breaks the link between the interest rate and goods prices. There is now neither a bond effect nor a Keynes effect. Aggregate demand is still characterized by $I(\rho) = sY$, but in place of the inequality in (7.5) we have $\rho' \equiv \partial\rho/\partial P = 0$. The AD schedule in $Y \times P/W$ space is once again vertical.

The Real-Balance Effect

The starting point for the real-balance effect is the argument, perfectly sensible in itself, that consumption and saving depend on wealth as well as on income. In place of the consumption function $C = cY$, we have in its simplest form $C = cY + aA$, where A here represents real wealth and a is the marginal propensity to consume from wealth. Since $S = Y - C$, in place of $S = sY$, where $s = 1 - c$, we have $S = sY - aA$. At lower and lower price levels, the cash component of wealth is worth more and more in real terms. This inverse relationship between A and P was the end of the real-balance story In chapter 4. Even if a liquidity trap drives ρ' to zero, or a lack of investment opportunities drives I' to zero, the AD schedule slopes downward so long as a is positive.

In chapter 4, bank lending and debt did not matter. In a comparative-statics framework, money creation and debt are always in balance, and nothing ever changes. It did not make any difference whether real balances included transactions money (as when households were assumed to lend directly to firms), or did not include transactions money (as when banks were assumed to finance trade by creating transactions money).

Here too bank lending is not central to the argument. There are two essential assumptions for the stunning reversal of the real-balance effect. The first is that the propensities to consume of debtors and creditors differ. The second is that as the real burden of debt increases, there comes a point where bankruptcy becomes the best of a bad lot of alternatives, if not the only way out of debt. The first idea can be reflected by simple modifications to the basic third-pass model.

To reflect different propensities to consume, assume two distinct kinds of agents: Type 1 are wealth holders, and Type 2 are business people whose physical capital is exactly equal to their debts when the story opens and $P = P_0$. Write desired expenditure as

$$C = C_1 + C_2,$$

$$C_1 = c_1 Y_1 + a_1 A_1 = c_1 Y_1 + a_1 \left[\frac{P_B(\rho)P_0 K}{P} + \frac{\bar{M}_2}{P} \right],$$

$$C_2 = c_2 Y_2 + a_2 A_2 = c_2 Y_2 + a_2 \left[K - \frac{P_B(\rho)P_0 K}{P} \right].$$

To simplify the calculations, I assume that debtors (Type 2) as well as creditors (Type 1) mark their bonds to market. Desired saving is

$$S = S_1 + S_2 = s_1 Y_1 - a_1 A_1 + s_2 Y_2 - a_2 A_2$$

$$= s_1 Y_1 - a_1 \left[\frac{P_B(\rho)P_0 K}{P} + \frac{\bar{M}_2}{P} \right] + s_2 Y_2 - a_2 \left[K - \frac{P_B(\rho)P_0 K}{P} \right].$$

Suppose $Y_1 = \gamma Y$, and $Y_2 = (1 - \gamma)Y$. Then aggregate demand is defined by equality between desired expenditure and income:

$$I(\rho) = s_1 \gamma Y - a_1 \left[\frac{P_B(\rho)P_0 K}{P} + \frac{\bar{M}_2}{P} \right]$$

$$+ s_2 (1 - \gamma)Y - a_2 \left[K - \frac{P_B(\rho)P_0 K}{P} \right].$$

(7.6)

In the absence of a Keynes effect, that is, with

$$M_2 = \frac{\beta(\rho)}{1 - \beta(\rho)} P_B(\rho)P_0 K = \bar{M}_2$$

and

$$\rho' = 0,$$

the effect of changes in the price level on aggregate demand is

$$\frac{\partial Y}{\partial P} = \frac{-\left(a_1 - a_2\right)\dfrac{P_B(\rho)P_0 K}{P^2} - a_1 \dfrac{\bar{M}_2}{P^2}}{s_1\gamma + s_2(1 - \gamma)}.$$

If $a_1 = a_2$, then a fall in the price level increases aggregate demand. But if $a_2 > a_1$ then the negative impact on the balance sheets of business can easily outweigh the positive effect on wealth portfolios.

The effects of bankruptcy are harder to model. If there were no fallout beyond the direct effects on the financial assets and liabilities of the debtor and creditor, bankruptcy might indeed have provided the salutary cleansing that Depression-era economists and politicians alike claimed for it.[2] The balance sheet of the creditor takes a hit, but this is offset by the improvement of the debtor's balance sheet. If it is true that the debtor's propensity to consume is higher than the creditor's, then bankruptcy would thus have a salutary effect on aggregate demand. Writing the market value of bonds as

$$P_B \bar{B} = P_B(\rho)P_0 K,$$

we have from equation (7.6)

$$\frac{\partial Y}{\partial\left(P_B \bar{B}\right)} = \frac{\left(a_1 - a_2\right)}{P\left[s_1\gamma + s_2(1 - \gamma)\right]}.$$

As the value of financial assets falls, aggregate demand increases.

The problem is of course the fallout beyond the contracting parties. As noted in the text, the contagion to suppliers, customers, employees, banks quickly erodes whatever relief bankruptcy provides.

The Fisher Effect

Again we focus on fixprice adjustment. The complete system is

$$\frac{\left(\dfrac{P}{W}\right)^{\textstyle\cdot}}{\dfrac{P}{W}} \equiv \left(\frac{\dot{P}}{P} - \frac{\dot{W}}{W}\right) = -\theta_1\left[GS\left(\frac{P}{W}\right) - Y\right] - \theta_3\left[Y - LS\left(\frac{P}{W}\right)\right], \quad (7.1)$$

$$\dot{Y} = \theta_2 \left[I \left(\rho - \frac{\dot{P}}{P} \right) - sY \right] = \theta_2 \left[I \left(\rho + \theta_1 \left[GS \left(\frac{P}{W} \right) - Y \right] \right) - sY \right], \quad (7.7)$$

where $\rho - \dot{P}/P$ is the real interest rate. The Jacobian becomes

$$J = \begin{bmatrix} -\theta_1 GS' + \theta_3 LS' & \theta_1 - \theta_3 \\ \theta_1 \theta_2 I'GS' & -\theta_2 \left(I'\theta_1 + s \right) \end{bmatrix}.$$

The trace and determinant conditions necessary and sufficient for a stable equilibrium are satisfied if $s > - I'\theta_1$ and $\theta_3 > \theta_1$. The first inequality is sufficient (but not necessary) for $tr\, J < 0$. The two inequalities together are sufficient (but again not necessary) for $det\, J > 0$. To see how the two inequalities together ensure that the determinant condition is satisfied, calculate $det\, J$ and simplify the expression to obtain

$$det\, J = \theta_1 \theta_2 \theta_3 I'(GS' - LS') + \theta_2 s(\theta_1 GS' - \theta_3 LS').$$

If $s > - I'\theta_1$, then

$$det\, J > \theta_1 \theta_2 \theta_3 I'(GS' - LS') - \theta_2 I'\theta_1(\theta_1 GS' - \theta_3 LS') = \theta_1 \theta_2 I'GS'(\theta_3 - \theta_1),$$

so $det\, J > 0$ if $\theta_3 > \theta_1$.

— 8 —

A DOSE OF REALITY

The Evidence of the Great Depression

Values have shrunken to fantastic levels; taxes have risen; our ability to pay has fallen; government of all kinds is faced by serious curtailment of income; the means of exchange are frozen in the currents of trade; the withered leaves of industrial enterprise lie on every side; farmers find no markets for their produce; the savings of many years in thousands of families are gone.

More important, a host of unemployed citizens face the grim problem of existence, and an equally great number toil with little return. Only a foolish optimist can deny the dark realities of the moment.

—FRANKLIN ROOSEVELT, FIRST INAUGURAL ADDRESS, MARCH 4, 1933

Many persons left their jobs for the more profitable one of selling apples.

—HERBERT HOOVER

Roosevelt puts some flesh on the bare bones of our models. Table 8.1 shows the changes in real U.S. gross domestic product by sectors from 1929 to 1933. One thing stands out from the economy-wide data: the massive decline in real GDP, led, as Table 8.2 shows, by private investment. By the time the economy reached bottom, output had fallen by almost one-fourth, and private investment by four-fifths. Investment in 1932 and 1933 was a shadow of its 1929 self.

The employment numbers in Table 8.3 bear out the GDP data. The major exception was the farm sector, where real output was higher in 1933 than in 1929 and employment was only marginally lower. Indeed, other data, presented in Table 8.4, suggest that farm employment in 1932 was higher than in 1929.

Whether or not total agricultural employment held its own, as Table 8.4 indicates, or decreased by 5 percent, as in Table 8.3, is not terribly important compared with the striking difference between the performance of agricul-

Table 8.1(a) Real GDP by Sector ($ billions at 1929 prices)

	Gross Domestic Product	Business	Nonfarm Business	Farm	Households and Institutions	Households	Nonprofit Institutions	General Government	Federal	State and Local
1929	103.60	89.40	80.50	8.90	9.00	7.40	1.50	5.20	1.10	4.10
1930	94.68	80.40	72.07	8.36	8.81	7.17	1.54	5.44	1.18	4.27
1931	88.54	74.42	64.95	10.12	8.51	6.85	1.56	5.54	1.13	4.41
1932	76.97	63.08	54.33	9.87	8.18	6.52	1.56	5.47	1.08	4.39
1933	75.98	61.76	53.32	9.40	8.10	6.47	1.53	5.77	1.33	4.42

Source: Bureau of Economic Analysis, *National Income and Product Accounts.*

Table 8.1(b) Real GDP by Sector (1929 = 100)

	Gross Domestic Product	Business	Nonfarm Business	Farm	Households and Institutions	Households	Nonprofit Institutions	General Government	Federal	State and Local
1929	100	100	100	100	100	100	100	100	100	100
1930	91	90	90	94	98	97	103	105	107	104
1931	85	83	81	114	95	93	104	107	103	108
1932	74	71	67	111	91	88	104	105	98	107
1933	73	69	66	106	90	87	102	111	121	108

Source: Bureau of Economic Analysis, *National Income and Product Accounts.*

Table 8.2 Real Gross Domestic Product (billions of chained dollars of 1937, scaled to
1929 price level)

	1929	1930	1931	1932	1933
Gross Domestic Product	104.6	95.7	89.5	78.0	77.1
Personal Consumption Expenditures	77.4	73.2	70.9	64.5	63.2
Goods	43.8	40.4	38.9	34.4	34.1
Durable Goods	9.8	8.2	7.0	5.4	5.3
Nondurable Goods	33.9	32.1	31.7	28.9	28.8
Services	33.6	33.0	32.1	30.2	29.0
Gross Private Domestic Investment	17.2	11.7	7.6	2.8	3.8
Fixed Investment	15.6	12.2	8.6	5.3	4.9
Nonresidential	11.6	9.7	6.5	4.1	3.8
Structures	5.5	4.7	3.0	1.9	1.4
Equipment	5.5	4.4	2.9	1.8	1.8
Intellectual Property Products	0.6	0.6	0.6	0.6	0.6
Residential	4.1	2.5	2.1	1.2	1.0
Change in Private Inventories	1.5	−0.6	−1.5	−3.4	−1.8
Net Exports of Goods and Services	0.4	0.2	0.0	0.0	−0.1
Exports	5.9	4.9	4.1	3.2	3.2
Goods	5.3	4.3	3.6	2.8	2.8
Services	0.6	0.5	0.5	0.4	0.4
Imports	5.6	4.8	4.2	3.6	3.7
Goods	4.5	3.9	3.3	2.8	3.0
Services	1.1	1.1	0.9	0.9	0.7
Government Consumption Expenditures and Gross Investment	9.6	10.6	11.0	10.7	10.3
Federal	1.9	2.1	2.2	2.3	2.8
National defense	1.0	1.1	1.1	1.1	1.0
Nondefense	0.8	0.9	1.0	1.1	1.6
State and Local	7.7	8.4	8.8	8.4	7.6
GPDI as Percentage of GDP	16.44	12.21	8.51	3.53	4.94

Source: Bureau of Economic Analysis, *National Income and Product Accounts.*

ture and nonagricultural business. A clue to this difference is provided by breaking down farm work between labor supplied by the farm household and that supplied by hired workers. It is clear that the reduction in total farm employment was limited to nonfamily workers; there were 5.5 percent more family workers on American farms in 1933 than in 1929.

Nominal output fell more sharply than real output because prices were declining as dramatically as was output. Tables 8.5 and 8.6 show nominal output and implicit price levels over the four years. In the nonfarm business sector, prices initially held their own. Even as nonfarm business output fell by more than 10 percent between 1929 and 1930, prices declined by barely 2 percent.

Table 8.3 Nonfarm and Farm Employment and Unemployment Rates

| | Civilian Labor Force | Employed | | | Unemployed | | | Federal Emergency Workers | Unemployed, Not Counting Federal Emergency Workers as Employed | |
| | | Total | Farm | Government | Number | Percentage of Civilian Labor Force | Percentage of Civilian Private Nonfarm Labor Force | Number | Percentage of Civilian Labor Force | Percentage of Civilian Private Nonfarm Labor Force |
	Table Ba470 (thousands)	Table Ba471 (thousands)	Table Ba472 (thousands)	Table Ba473 (thousands)	Table Ba474 (thousands)	Table Ba475 (percent)	Table Ba476 (percent)	Table Ba477 (thousands)	(percent)	(percent)
1929	47,757	46,374	10,541	3,065	1,383	2.90	4.05	0	2.90	4.05
1930	48,523	44,183	10,340	3,148	4,340	8.94	12.39	20	8.99	12.44
1931	49,325	41,604	10,240	3,563	7,721	15.65	21.74	299	16.26	22.58
1932	50,098	38,630	10,120	3,817	11,468	22.89	31.71	592	24.07	33.35
1933	50,882	40,247	10,092	5,361	10,635	20.90	30.02	2195	25.22	36.21

Source: Historical Statistics of the United States, Millennial Edition Online.

Table 8.4 Farm Labor: Family Workers and Hired Workers (thousands)

	Total Farm Employment Table K 174	Family Workers Table K 175	Hired Workers Table K176
1929	12,763	9,360	3,403
1930	12,497	9,307	3,190
1931	12,745	9,642	3,103
1932	12,816	9,922	2,894
1933	12,739	9,874	2,865

Source: Bureau of the Census 1975.

Table 8.5 Nominal GDP by Sector ($ billions)

	Gross Domestic Product	Business	Nonfarm Business	Farm	Households and Institutions	Households	Nonprofit Institutions	General Government	Federal	State and Local
1929	103.60	89.40	80.50	8.90	9.00	7.40	1.50	5.20	1.10	4.10
1930	91.20	77.30	70.40	7.00	8.50	6.90	1.60	5.40	1.10	4.20
1931	76.50	63.40	57.70	5.70	7.60	6.10	1.50	5.50	1.10	4.30
1932	58.70	47.00	43.00	3.90	6.60	5.20	1.40	5.20	1.10	4.10
1933	56.40	45.10	41.00	4.10	5.80	4.50	1.30	5.50	1.40	4.10

Source: Bureau of Economic Analysis, National Income and Product Accounts.

Table 8.6 Sectoral Price Levels, Implicit Deflators (1929 = 100)

	Gross Domestic Product	Business	Nonfarm Business	Farm	Households and Institutions	Households	Nonprofit Institutions	General Government	Federal	State and Local
1929	100	100	100	100	100	100	100	100	100	100
1930	96	96	98	84	96	96	104	99	93	98
1931	86	85	89	56	89	89	96	99	97	97
1932	76	75	79	40	81	80	90	95	102	93
1933	74	73	77	44	72	70	85	95	105	93

Sources: Tables 8.2 and 8.5, above.

Only when output continued its freefall did prices begin to fall at comparable rates.

Clearly there was something different about agriculture: prices fell dramatically from the beginning of the Depression, and continued to fall catastrophically until bottoming out in 1932. Table 8.7 summarizes the different behavior of the farm and nonfarm economies in terms of sectoral Fisher effects—rates of change of prices—for both nonfarm businesses and the farm sector. As Table 8.7 shows, after 1930, when price cutting became the norm, the Fisher effect became more significant in the nonfarm-business sector, even though deflation never became as calamitous as it was for farmers. Between 1930 and 1932 nonfarm businesses had some 10 percent per year tacked onto nominal interest rates because they were repaying in appreciated dollars. On the farm, debtors implicitly faced real interest rates as high as 33 percent per year even if they had been able to borrow at a zero nominal interest rate![1] The numbers in the example I gave in chapter 7 to flesh out the real-balance effect—a fall in the price of wheat from $1.25 per bushel to $0.50— were illustrative, not fanciful. In fact, wheat averaged $1.18 per bushel in the decade 1920 to 1929 and plummeted to $0.38 in 1931. Wheat was hardly exceptional: the price of cotton averaged $0.21 per pound in the 1920s, falling below $0.06 in 1931 (*Historical Statistics of the United States, Millennial Edition Online,* tables Da 719 and Da 757). At the end of this chapter, I return to the question of what distinguished agriculture from the rest of the economy.

Wages followed the same downward trajectory as prices. In fact, as Table 8.8 shows, money wages in manufacturing—whether measured by annual wages for full-time workers or by hourly wages—fell almost in lockstep with prices. As a result, real wages (reported in the last two columns of Table 8.8) remained virtually constant over the period 1929 to 1933, falling slightly for full-time employees, rising slightly on an hourly basis for manufacturing workers.

The toll of the Fisher and real-balance effects show up in mortgage delinquencies and business failures, shown in Tables 8.9 and 8.10. The two tables tell a similar story. The number of nonfarm mortgage foreclosures almost doubled between 1929 and 1932, and the number of corporate business fail-

Table 8.7 Percentage Change in the Price Level

	Gross Domestic Product	Nonfarm Business	Farm
1930	−3.67	−2.32	−16.26
1931	−10.31	−9.06	−32.74
1932	−11.73	−10.91	−29.87
1933	−2.67	−2.85	10.42

Source: Table 8.6, above.

Table 8.8 Money and Real Wages

	Avg. Annual Earnings, Full-Time Employees Table D 722	Avg. Hourly Earnings, All Manufacturing Table D 802	Avg. Annual Earnings, Full-Time Employees (1929 =100)	Avg. Hourly Earnings, All Manufacturing (1929 = 100)	Consumer Price Index (1929 =100) Table D 727	Avg. Real Annual Earnings, Full-Time Employees	Avg. Real Hourly Earnings, All Manufacturing
1929	$1,405	$0.56	100.00	100.00	100.00	100.00	100.00
1930	$1,368	$0.55	97.37	98.21	97.37	100.00	100.87
1931	$1,275	$0.51	90.75	91.07	88.65	102.37	102.73
1932	$1,120	$0.44	79.72	78.57	79.64	100.10	98.66
1933	$1,048	$0.44	74.59	78.57	75.37	98.97	104.25

Source: Bureau of the Census 1975.

ures increased by almost 50 percent over the same period. The liabilities of these failed businesses totaled over 1.5 percent of GDP in 1932, double the dollar amount of 1929, when prices were one-third higher. At the same time, instead of the steady growth in the number of active businesses characteristic of the 1920s, by 1933, voluntary attrition, as distinct from forced liquidation due to bankruptcy, led to the closure of 10 percent of the number of corporate businesses active in 1929. (I have not been able to find data on farm-mortgage foreclosures or noncorporate business failures.)

Finally, what happened to banks, to the money supply, to interest rates? The most obvious sign of distress was the precipitous rise in the number of bank

Table 8.9 Nonfarm Mortgage Foreclosures

	Number	Per 1,000 Mortgaged Structures
1926	68,100	3.6
1927	91,000	4.8
1928	116,000	6.1
1929	134,900	7.1
1930	150,000	7.9
1931	193,800	10.2
1932	248,700	13.1
1933	252,400	13.3

Source: Historical Statistics of the United States, Millennial Edition Online.

Table 8.10 Business Failures

	Active Firms (thousands)	Business Failures	
		Number	Per 10,000 Firms
1920	1,821	8,881	49
1921	1,927	19,652	102
1922	1,983	23,676	119
1923	1,996	18,718	94
1924	2,047	20,615	101
1925	2,113	21,214	100
1926	2,158	21,773	101
1927	2,184	23,146	106
1928	2,187	23,842	109
1929	2,203	22,909	104
1930	2,160	26,355	122
1931	2,127	28,285	133
1932	2,066	31,822	154
1933	1,986	19,859	100

Source: Historical Statistics of the United States, Millennial Edition Online.

failures. Again, outright failure is only part of the story: there were 40 percent fewer banks in 1933 than in 1929, weaker banks closing "voluntarily" or merging with more solid banks (Board of Governors of the Federal Reserve System 1943, table 1). Table 8.11 gives annual data for the relevant period, data which has to be understood against a baseline of failures of approximately five hundred per year over the decade following the end of World War I. These bank failures culminated in the Bank Holiday that set Roosevelt's New Deal in motion. (Roosevelt closed the banks by executive order thirty-six hours after assuming office; those deemed to be solvent reopened a week later.) In 1933 alone, the losses to depositors amounted to 1 percent of GDP. Bank failures were both cause and effect of the decline in the money supply, first gradual and then precipitous, over the period leading up to the crisis of 1933. Table 8.12 shows the course of GDP and summary monetary data from the end of the boom to the bottom of the Depression. The narrow measure of the money stock as currency plus demand deposits (M1, not to be confused with Keynes's M_1) declined, but not as rapidly as nominal GDP, with the result

Table 8.11 Bank Failures

	Number of Suspensions	Deposits of Suspended Banks ($ millions)	Losses to Depositors ($ millions)
1929	659	231	77
1930	1,352	869	237
1931	2,294	1,691	391
1932	1,456	725	168
1933	4,004	3,601	540

Source: Board of Governors of the Federal Reserve System 1943, sec. 7, table 66.

Table 8.12 Nominal GDP, Money Supply, and Implicit Velocity, All Data for June of Each Year except GDP ($ billions)

	Nominal GDP (calendar year)	Demand Deposits[1] Table 9	Currency in Circulation Table 9	Reserve Balances with Federal Reserve Banks Table 105	Monetary Base = Currency + Member-Bank Reserve Balances
1929	103.6	22.5	3.6	2.3	6.0
1930	91.2	21.7	3.4	2.4	5.8
1931	76.5	19.8	3.7	2.4	6.0
1932	58.7	15.6	4.6	2.1	6.6
1933	56.4	14.4	4.8	2.2	7.1

Sources: Bureau of Economic Analysis, National Income and Product Accounts; Board of Governors of the Federal Reserve System 1943.
  1. Demand deposits are adjusted to eliminate double counting of checks in process of collection.

that the income velocity of money, the ratio of GDP to $M1$, also declined, from almost four in 1929 to just under three in 1933.

The money supply shrunk for two reasons. The first is the shift from deposits to currency by people spooked by the increasing threat of losing their money to bank failure as the Depression deepened. This left the banks with lower reserves and a correspondingly reduced capacity to lend. But the reduced capacity to lend was likely less important than the reduced willingness to lend; excess reserves grew from 1931 on.

This brings us to the second reason, the decline in deposits associated with the decline in bank lending. The growth in idle reserves led to a sharp rise in the ratio of total reserves to total deposits and a correspondingly sharp fall in the money multiplier. The decline in the money multiplier becomes clearer from the more detailed data in Table 8.13 that exist for banks in the Federal Reserve System. These member banks, which accounted for close to 75 percent of total demand deposits at the outset of the Depression and almost 85 percent by the time the economy bottomed out, showed a steady rise in the ratio of reserves to deposits. Between 1929 and 1931, demand deposits declined slightly while total reserves increased. In June 1932 the picture was very different: as against the previous June, reserves declined by $340 million, even as required reserves were falling by $450 million. Excess reserves stood at $234 million in June 1932 and grew by more than $100 million over the next year. By June 1933 excess reserves were 20 percent of required reserves, enough to support some $3 billion of additional demand deposits at an average required reserve ratio of approximately 12 percent, more or less the amount by which demand deposits had declined since 1929.[2]

The asset side of the banks' balance sheets fills in the story. Tables 8.14 and 8.15 show both the decline and the change in the composition of bank assets, Table 8.14 in nominal terms, Table 8.15 in percentages of 1929 levels. "CIAC Loans" (commercial, industrial, agricultural, and consumer loans, excluding

Table 8.13 Deposits and Reserves of Member Banks of Federal Reserve System ($ millions)

June	Adjusted Demand Deposits Table 18	Time Deposits Table 18	Reserves at Federal Reserve Banks Table 105	Vault Cash Table 18	Required Reserves Table 105	Excess Reserves Table 105	Reserve Ratio (total reserves/ total deposits)
1929	16,324	13,168	2,314	433	2,275	42	0.078
1930	16,043	13,476	2,392	484	2,338	54	0.081
1931	15,208	13,247	2,404	519	2,275	129	0.084
1932	12,433	10,560	2,062	478	1,827	234	0.090
1933	12,089	8,890	2,160	405	1,797	363	0.103

Source: Board of Governors of the Federal Reserve System 1943.

Table 8.14 Nominal Output of Business Sector ($ billions) and Member-Bank Assets ($ millions)

As of June 30 Calendar Year	Nominal GDP, Business Sector	Total Loans + Investments	Total	Loans Open Market Paper	Loans on Securities	Real Estate Loans	Loans to Banks	CIAC Loans[1]	Investments Total	U.S. Government Obligations	Other
1929	89.40	35,711	25,658	447	9,759	3,164	670	11,618	10,052	4,155	5,898
1930	77.30	35,656	25,214	748	10,425	3,155	535	10,349	10,442	4,061	6,380
1931	63.40	33,923	21,816	885	8,334	3,218	457	8,922	12,106	5,343	6,763
1932	47.00	28,001	16,587	658	5,570	2,894	573	6,892	11,414	5,628	5,786
1933	45.10	24,786	12,858	594	4,704	2,372	330	4,857	11,928	6,887	5,041

Sources: Bureau of Economic Analysis, *National Income and Product Accounts,* for data on output of business sector; Board of Governors of the Federal Reserve System 1943, table 18, for Federal Reserve member-bank data.

1. CIAC loans are commercial, industrial, agricultural, and consumer loans not collateralized by securities.

Table 8.15 Indices of Nominal Output of Business Sector and Member-Bank Assets (1929 = 100)

As of June 30 Calendar Year	Nominal GDP, Business Sector	Total Loans + Investments	Total	Loans Open Market Paper	Loans on Securities	Real Estate Loans	Loans to Banks	CIAC Loans[1]	Investments Total	U.S. Government Obligations	Other
1929	100	100	100	100	100	100	100	100	100	100	100
1930	86	100	98	167	107	100	80	89	104	98	108
1931	71	95	85	198	85	102	68	77	120	129	115
1932	53	78	65	147	57	91	86	59	114	135	98
1933	50	69	50	133	48	75	49	42	119	166	85

Sources: Bureau of Economic Analysis, *National Income and Product Accounts,* for data on output of business sector; Board of Governors of the Federal Reserve System 1943, table 18, for Federal Reserve member-bank data.

1. CIAC loans are commercial, industrial, agricultural, and consumer loans not collateralized by securities.

loans against securities as collateral), are a rough empirical counterpart to Keynes's theoretical M_1. In 1929 CIAC loans constituted almost half of all loans. By 1933 CIAC loans had fallen by almost 60 percent, even more than the nominal value of output fell. Until 1932 the decline in the volume of CIAC loans was less rapid (in percentage terms) than the fall in output, but the decline in lending accelerated, so that between 1932 and 1933 CIAC loans fell by 30 percent while nominal output fell by "only" 5 percent; in other words, CIAC loans fell six times more rapidly than output between those two years. A plausible explanation is that banks tried to accommodate their customers as long as they could but then gave up.

The second largest category, "Loans on Securities," represents all lending against securities as collateral and thus includes both loans to stock-market brokers and dealers and CIAC lending against securities. The proportions changed dramatically during the Depression: with the collapse of the stock market, lending to brokers and dealers fell from 30 percent of all loans on securities in June 1929 to 20 percent of a much-reduced total in June 1933.

As was observed in chapter 4, for the money supply to remain constant in the face of a sharply contracting demand for transactions loans, banks would have to replace these loans with other financial assets purchased on the open market. Banks did expand their ownership of U.S. Treasury obligations, by a large percentage; however, the absolute increase, some $2.7 billion, only replaced a modest 20 percent of the decline of $12.8 billion in total loans and 40 percent of the decline in CIAC loans.

The breakdown of the U.S. public debt in Table 8.16, the breakdown of bank holdings of Treasury obligations in Table 8.17, and the path of interest rates together shed some light on why banks would prefer to maintain idle excess reserves rather than purchase Treasuries. The problem was not a shortage of Treasury obligations. From just over 15 percent in 1929, the ratio of the public debt to GDP rose to almost 40 percent by mid-1933. To be sure, this increase was largely because of the fall in GDP, but the outstanding debt rose by $5.6 billion, by one-third of its level in 1929. And banks held substantial portions of each class of debt, as Table 8.17 indicates.

But there were reasons for banks to avoid too much exposure to Treasury debt of all maturities. At the long end of the spectrum, bonds would suffer losses in capital values if and when interest rates recovered (as we shall see in chapter 11, this is one reason why wealth holders prefer cash and short-term Treasuries), especially in light of the fears of the financial community that continuing Federal deficits and mounting debt signaled runaway inflation in the offing. At the short end, Treasury obligations provided smaller and smaller nominal returns; by 1932 the return on short-term Treasuries had fallen so low that it hardly paid to own these securities. The middle offered both drawbacks, the possibility of a decline in capital values and very modest nominal returns.

Indeed, despite Keynes's oft-quoted observation that the liquidity trap was only a hypothetical possibility, Table 8.18 illustrates the phenomenon of a positive lower bound on the hurdle rate of interest for investment—here the yield on Baa-rated corporate bonds—when short rates are driven close enough to zero to be essentially equivalent to cash.[3]

Table 8.16 Federal Debt and Its Composition ($ millions)

As of June 30	Total Debt Outstanding	Long-Term Bonds (maturity greater than 5 years)	Treasury Notes (maturity 1–5 years)	Treasury Bills and Certificates of Indebtedness (maturity up to 1 year)
1929	16,931	12,125	2,254	1,640
1930	16,185	12,111	1,626	1,420
1931	16,801	13,531	452	2,246
1932	19,487	14,250	1,261	3,341
1933	22,539	14,223	4,548	3,063

Source: Board of Governors of the Federal Reserve System 1943, table 146.

Table 8.17 Federal Reserve Member-Banks' Holdings of U.S. Treasuries ($ millions)

As of June 30	Total	Bonds (maturity greater than 5 years)	Treasury Notes (maturity 1–5 years)	Treasury Bills and Certificates of Indebtedness (maturity up to 1 year)
1929	4,155	3,005	704	446
1930	4,061	3,340	463	259
1931	5,343	4,039	403	901
1932	5,628	4,163	503	962
1933	6,887	3,725	2,049	1,113

Source: Board of Governors of the Federal Reserve System 1943, table 20.

Table 8.18 Yields on Bonds and Short-Term Securities

June–July Average	Short-Term U.S. Government Securities (maturity 3–6 months) Table 122	Long-Term U.S. Government Bonds (due or callable after 12 years) Table 122	Baa-Rated Corporate Bonds Table 128
1929	4.68	3.67	5.32
1930	1.86	3.25	5.78
1931	0.48	3.14	7.22
1932	0.28	3.67	11.16
1933	0.13	3.21	6.85

Source: Board of Governors of the Federal Reserve System 1943.

These are of course nominal returns. Real returns, taking account of price level changes, were much higher on all classes of fixed-income securities, surpassing 20 percent on moderately risky Baa bonds in 1932. Nominal yields on Baa-rated corporate bonds actually rose through mid-1932, and they only began to return to anything like the pre-Depression normal after the first tentative beginning of recovery in mid-1933.

What Do the Data Tell Us?

The decline in nonfarm business output between 1929 and 1933 was the result of a massive failure of aggregate demand. The stock market crash of October 1929 is associated in the popular mind with the ensuing decline of output and employment, but there were clearly other forces at work, and economists have advanced various views as to the fundamental cause of the decline in demand. The fall in investment demand was most precipitous, but this does not automatically make it the *causa causans*. The real effects of the fall in demand were compounded by the accompanying fall in nominal prices and wages.

As Tables 8.1 and 8.6 show, the fall in prices and wages followed the decline in output, with nonfarm prices and wages holding fairly steady between 1929 and 1930 despite a significant fall in output. After 1930 the fall in prices and wages matched the fall in output, and prices and wages continued to fall into 1933 even as output was stabilizing. Output leading prices and wages down suggests that the nonfarm economy followed a fixprice-adjustment model. The fixprice story is made more plausible by the fact that inventories fell during the Depression, the opposite of what would have happened in a flexprice regime. In the fixprice model, a fall in aggregate demand leads to cutbacks in production, and the ensuing unemployment drives wages down; prices fall as business seeks to take advantage of lower costs. As we shall see below, these internal dynamics of the nonfarm business sector were compounded by the interplay between nonfarm business and the farm sector.

Nonfarm business thus followed the trajectory indicated in Figure 8.1, from a full-employment equilibrium at E to the unemployment equilibrium at F.

It is not clear whether the real economy of output and employment had reached this equilibrium when Roosevelt took office. Fortunately, the question was never put to the test; New Deal policy initiatives, particularly the break with gold early on, changed the dynamic of price and wage adjustment, and the economy began to recover from the Depression.

The monetary side of the Depression is explained by the joint effects of the fall in prices and output. Transactions demand, Keynes's M_1, declined with the nominal value of output, PY, and the money supply contracted in response. The fall in prices reduced the value of collateral and pushed many

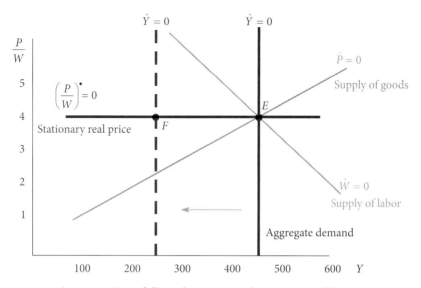

Figure 8.1 From full employment to a depression equilibrium.

businesses to the point of bankruptcy—and beyond. Business failures took a toll on banks, and both business and bank failures rose sharply as the Depression wore on. Banks became increasingly unwilling to lend, except to the federal government, which took a further toll on investment and aggregate demand.

Business default had two knock-on effects: first, it threatened the solvency of the banks themselves; second, even when the banks survived, they became more cautious as defaults and default risk increased, hence, though at the outset bank deposits remained relatively immune to the fall in the value of collateral, as banks were either unwilling to recognize publicly the threat to solvency or were trying to accommodate their customers—perhaps some of both. But as time went on and the economy failed to recover, bank deposits fell by more than strict proportionality with PY would have dictated. Table 8.14 bears this out: until 1932, CIAC loans fell less rapidly than output, but between 1932 and 1933 much more rapidly. A contributing factor to the decline in the money supply was the shift from bank deposits to cash, a reflection of the increasing systemic risk to which the banking system was subject.

Businesses that managed to stay current on their debt with respect to working capital still suffered from the increase in the real value of debt tied to equipment and structures. At the very least, this meant increased difficulties in servicing their debts, and for some businesses it was just too much. In chapter 7 this problem was formulated in terms of an increase in the real debt on fixed capital, $\overline{B}/P$. The (real) net worth of the representative firm was stated as

$$-\frac{\overline{B}}{P} + \text{Real Fixed Capital} - \frac{M_1}{P} + \text{Real Working Capital}.$$

Firms that managed to keep the last two terms in line with each other would still have had to deal with a growing wedge between the real debt and the real value of fixed capital.

Judging by the failure of interest rates to fall, the decline in M_1 did nothing for $\overline{M}_2$. On the contrary: the decline in business confidence increased liquidity preference, and the result was higher nominal interest rates, except for government obligations. The increase in the hurdle rate further dampened investment demand. Even more important than the rise in nominal interest rates was the Fisher effect, which implied a double-digit gap between real and nominal interest rates.

With one important amendment this interpretation of the data conforms to the vision if not the letter of *The General Theory*. The amendment concerns the role of debt and deflation. Both were very much in the public eye, topics of lively political debate, but Keynes did not pay a lot of attention to the price level and did not incorporate changing prices into the models of *The General Theory*.

If marginal for Keynes, debt and deflation were, as I emphasized in the previous chapter, central to Irving Fisher's theory (1933). In the end, however, Fisher supplements Keynes rather than providing an alternative. Fisher had no concept of aggregate demand and no argument for why equilibrium should be characterized by persistent deflation, nor did he provide a framework for how debt and default, caused by the persistent deflation, in turn fed back into the economy through their negative impact on aggregate demand.

Data often do not speak with great clarity, and the data of the Great Depression are a prime example. Even if we accept that the ultimate cause of the Depression remains a mystery, there are two alternatives to the dynamics of how it unfolded that are encapsulated in Figure 8.1. One deploys the static second-pass model; the other argues that all would have been well if incompetence at the Federal Reserve had not transformed the relatively mild, one might say routine, downturn of 1930 into the catastrophe of 1931 and 1932.

Keynes's own version of the second-pass model, to be sure, assumes a given money wage, leaving only the price level (and the real wage) to be determined by aggregate demand. This model clearly does not correspond to the reality of the Depression, characterized by falling prices and wages.

Modigliani's version offers more hope in this regard since it allows for a variable level of wages as well as prices. Indeed, for Modigliani a falling price level is the mechanism that ultimately restores full-employment equilibrium in the face of falling demand. In Modigliani's model a lower price level means that less money is needed for transactions; for the redundant money to be absorbed into asset portfolios, interest rates, including the hurdle rate, must fall. The stimulus to investment in turn boosts aggregate demand and restores full employment.

Modigliani got the first part right: falling wages and prices did reduce the transactions demand for money. But none of the rest followed. First, lower prices reduced not only transactions demand but also the supply of transactions money. As demand fell, banks simply created less money, and as Table 8.13 shows, excess reserves grew, as did the ratio of reserves to deposits. Not a dime moved into asset portfolios. The overall money supply, measured by the sum of demand deposits and currency in Table 8.12, contracted. Second, the hurdle rate of interest, proxied by the Baa bond rate in Table 8.18, rose due to a spike in liquidity preference. Third, the Fisher effect made a bad situation worse; as Table 8.7 shows, price declines added 9 percentage points to the real interest rate in 1931 and more than 10 percentage points in 1932.

Milton Friedman and Anna Schwartz (1963a) blame the ineptness of the Fed leadership. In summing up the lessons of their investigations, Friedman and Schwartz write,

> At all times throughout the 1929–33 contraction, alternative policies were available to the [Federal Reserve] System by which it could have kept the stock of money from falling, and indeed could have increased it at almost any desired rate. Those policies did not involve radical innovations. They involved measures of a kind the System had taken in earlier years, of a kind explicitly contemplated by the founders of the System to meet precisely the kind of banking crisis that developed in late 1930 and persisted thereafter. They involved measures that were actually proposed and very likely would have been adopted under a slightly different bureaucratic structure or distribution of power, or even if the men in power had had somewhat different personalities. (p. 693)

For Friedman and Schwartz, there is no question that earlier, pre-Fed, monetary arrangements would have prevented the disaster:

> If the pre-1914 banking system rather than the Federal Reserve System had been in existence in 1929, the money stock almost certainly would not have undergone a decline comparable to the one that occurred. (p. 693)

They also argued that the monetary contraction was not simply independent of declines in output and prices, it was the cause of these declines:

The contraction is additional strong evidence for the economic independence of monetary changes from the contemporary course of income and prices, even during the early phase of the contraction, from 1929 to 1931, when the decline in the stock of money was not the result of explicit restrictive measures taken by the System. (p. 694)

There are many holes in the Friedman–Schwartz story—some of which are explored in the appendix to this chapter. The most glaring one is the growth of excess reserves as the Depression deepened. For money demand to accommodate to money supply—the key assumption underlying Friedman–Schwartz—banks have to be fully loaned up or, equivalently, maintain a constant margin of excess reserves. The dramatic build-up of excess reserves in 1932, continuing into 1933—see Table 8.13, and Table 8.20 in the appendix—tells a different story. In 1933, Jacob Viner summed up the situation of the banks thus:

In the past three years the test of a successful banker has been the rate of speed with which he could go out of the banking business and into the safety-deposit business. Those bankers have survived who have succeeded in the largest degree and at the most rapid rate in converting loans into cash. That has been good banking from the point of view of the individual banker, or of his individual depositors; but from the social point of view it has been disastrous. (1933b, p. 130)

Federal Reserve policy may or may not have been inept; as Barry Eichengreen argues (2015), it is not clear that the Fed could have done much more than it did until Roosevelt cut the link to gold.[4] So even if Friedman is right that the Fed didn't do much to stop the rot, this failure hardly makes the Fed the cause of the Depression. The effectiveness of monetary policy in a period of slack demand has rightly been likened to pushing on a string.[5] The reason for this ineffectiveness is summarized in Figure 8.1, which reflects the theory developed in the third-pass model that I laid out in chapters 6 and 7. In this theory the central bank has little to no leverage on the hurdle rate of interest because of its limited control of the public's stock of short-term and long-term financial assets, and, given the rules and norms of twentieth-century banking, even less control over the public's liquidity-preference function.[6] The Fisher effect compounds the misery.

Why Was Agriculture Different?

An important qualification to the Keynesian account of the Great Depression is the anomalous behavior of the farm sector.[7] As was noted at the beginning of this chapter, agricultural production actually *increased* during the Depression. But this did not mean farmers escaped unscathed. Relative prices turned against agriculture, as Tables 8.6 and 8.7 indicate: compared with nonagricultural goods, the price level of farm products in 1932 was half what it was in 1929.

Equally, perhaps more, important, than the terms of trade, the fall in the nominal price level meant that debt quickly became unmanageable. As we have seen, real-balance and Fisher effects gave the nonfarm business sector a bad cold—farmers got pneumonia.

The relationship between farm prices and the output of the nonfarm business sector during both the Depression and the subsequent recovery is striking. Figure 8.2 plots nominal farm prices, and Figure 8.3 plots farm prices

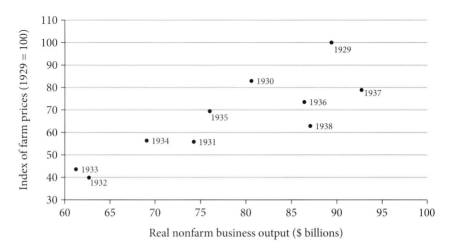

Figure 8.2 Farm prices vs. nonfarm output.

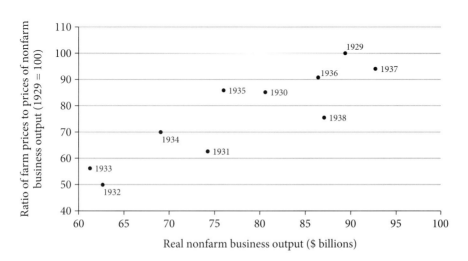

Figure 8.3 Relative prices vs. nonfarm output.

relative to nonfarm prices. The correlation is clearly strong in both cases, stronger for relative prices.

This much is well understood, but there remains the question of how to explain the correlation. How was it that real output and employment in agriculture actually rose during the Depression, and why were agricultural prices battered by the decline in nonfarm output?

The mainstream answer to these questions follows from its emphasis on frictions and rigidities: the resilience of agricultural output and the collapse of agricultural prices were due to the competitive structure of this sector. There is more than a germ of truth in this explanation. Unlike industry and transportation and large parts of wholesale and retail trade, which had become increasingly infected with the imperfections of monopoly and oligopoly, agriculture remained close to the economist's model of the price-taking producer.

Viner was one mainstream economist who saw the difference between farm and nonfarm sectors in these terms. In his lecture at the University of Minnesota in February 1933, he observed,

> Agriculture has in this depression been the only major portion of the national economy which has continued to operate and to produce to the limit of its capacity. There could be no business depressions if all sections of the national industry were as readily to adjust their demands to the level at which the market would absorb their full output. (1933a, p. 11)

Another was John Kenneth Galbraith though he was later to become a trenchant critic of mainstream economics. Prodigious author, senior official in the Office of Price Administration during World War II, adviser and ambassador under John F. Kennedy, Galbraith was trained as an agricultural economist and very likely his pre-Keynesian perspective on the causes of the Great Depression owed something to this training. In Galbraith's 1936 view (1981, p. 64), the problem was structural:[8]

> Free competition had given way to oligopoly and monopolistic competition, and because of the latter too many resources were being wasted on advertising and salesmanship. The shortfall in production from these defects caused the depression. . . . The remedy was more competition.

The mainstream view has changed little since the 1930s. Giovanni Federico (2005, p. 972) concluded his investigation into the causal role of agriculture in the Great Depression thus:

> The . . . most plausible hypothesis [why agricultural prices fell by so much more than non-farm prices] focuses on the asymmetry between agriculture and the rest of the economy. Agriculture was a competitive sector and, in the

peculiar conditions of the depression, its elasticity of supply was bound to be low. In fact the opportunity cost of farmers' labor was extremely low as it depended on the expected wages in other sectors. Real wages were rising, but the high rate of unemployment made the prospect of emigration to cities hardly attractive. Thus farmers were likely to go on producing as long as revenues covered their variable costs plus a minimum income for the purchase of indispensable consumer goods. In this situation, demand shocks caused prices to fall. In contrast, in the rest of the economy demand shocks caused a fall in output because prices were sticky. A long interpretative tradition, dating back to Keynes, attributes this feature to wage stickiness, determined by the power of trade unions, by the existence of welfare benefits or by the existence of long-term labor contracts. Another interpretation, first suggested by Steindl [no reference, presumably, Steindl 1952] and recently revived by Madsen [2004a, 2004b] blames limited competition in manufacturing.

Federico has it partly right: the supply elasticity of farm goods was indeed low, but the contrast with sticky prices elsewhere is misleading. He, along with Viner and Galbraith, were of course correct in observing that oligopoly and monopoly and all sorts of rigidities and frictions put more of a burden on output and employment adjustment in the event of a shock to the economy. But the argument of Keynes—the argument of this book—is that even in the case of perfect competition, output and employment will suffer along with prices. This didn't happen in agriculture.

Farm output, if not financial solvency, weathered the storm of the Depression[9] not because of the proximity of agriculture to the norms of competition, but because of its distance. The departure from the competitive model was not in the goods market, where farmers were indeed price takers, as the manual of perfect competition dictates, but in the labor market.

Consider how the competitive firm determines output and employment. In equilibrium it is a price taker both in goods markets and in labor markets. The competitive firm maximizes profits by producing, where real marginal cost $(MP_L)^{-1}$ is equal to the given real price (P/W) at Q_0 in Figure 8.4(a), and, equivalently, where the marginal productivity of labor is equal to the given real wage, at L_0 in Figure 8.4(b). Although farmers were price takers in product markets, family farms do not meet labor demands primarily by hiring workers—at least they didn't until the meaning of "family farm" changed fundamentally after World War II.

This is not to say that hired labor played no role. According to the Department of Agriculture data in Table 8.4, hired labor constituted some 25 percent of the U.S. farm labor force as the United States entered the Depression. The

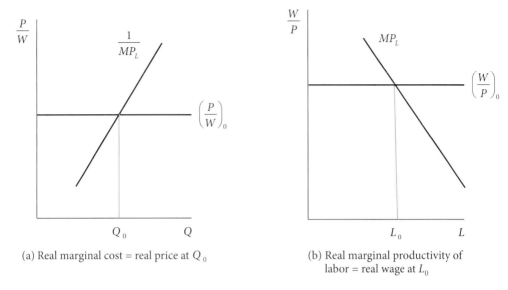

(a) Real marginal cost = real price at Q_0

(b) Real marginal productivity of labor = real wage at L_0

Figure 8.4 Profit maximization under perfect competition.

decline in hired labor between 1929 and 1933 was in fact smaller in percentage terms than the decline of nonfarm employment (15 percent vs. 25 percent), presumably because of the complementarity between hired labor and family labor. At peak times, especially at harvest, many family farms required extra help beyond what the family could mobilize on its own.[10]

The difference between hired labor and family labor is that it makes no sense to apply the rule of profit maximization—add labor only so long as the marginal productivity exceeds the real wage—to family members. Family members have to be fed, clothed, and sheltered whether they work or not. The cost of employing a family member is a fixed cost, not a wage bill that varies in proportion to the number of hours or days worked.[11]

Farm labor, both family labor and hired labor, had been a declining percentage of the total labor force since the early days of the Republic: as the World War I ditty went, "How can you keep 'em down on the farm after they've seen Paree?" But, as the economy weakened in 1930 and collapsed in 1931 and 1932, rising urban unemployment caused a hiatus in the steady flow from the farm. On this point I have no disagreement with Federico or others who oppose the flexible farm economy to the rigid nonfarm economy. If there was no work to be had in the city, many a young man simply went home.[12] As Robert Frost wrote in his poem "The Death of the Hired Man," "Home is the place where, when you have to go there, they have to take you in." And if there were more hands to feed, they might as well work.

Studying the very different context of subsistence peasant agriculture, the

Russian economist Alexander Chayanov (1966 [1925]) suggested a model that takes account of the distinctive features of family farms. Chayanov proposed replacing profit maximization by the criterion of maximum output. In the context of unlimited supplies of labor, which according to Chayanov characterized the relatively undeveloped economy of czarist Russia, this meant applying additional hours of labor until its marginal product fell to zero. The more general implication is that labor supply determines the marginal product of labor, as in Figure 8.5, rather than, as in Figure 8.4, the wage rate determining the marginal product of labor from the demand side.

At the aggregate level, the intersection between the MP_L schedule and the LS schedule in Figure 8.5 looks just like the picture of how the real wage is determined in the mainstream model: if we simply add up each farm's marginal productivity and LS schedules, we get an aggregate marginal-productivity schedule and an aggregate LS schedule that mirror the labor-demand and LS schedules of chapter 2. The real wage is determined by the marginal productivity of labor at full employment.

However, the two models are very different. In the Chayanov model, the marginal-productivity schedule is not a demand schedule in the sense of a schedule of how much labor will be employed at different wage rates. It can't be, for there is no wage rate in Chayanov's conception of the family farm. The relevance of productivity is limited to the case where the marginal productivity of labor goes to zero before utilizing the available labor. Moreover, in the mainstream model, the LS schedule reflects the disutility of labor, and unem-

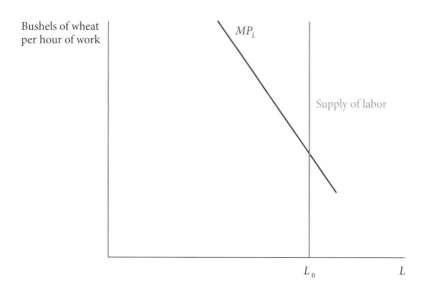

Figure 8.5 An alternative model of the family farm.

ployment leads to workers bidding down real wages as they compete for jobs. In Chayanov's model, by contrast, since there are no wages there can be no weighing of the disutility of labor with a real wage. Instead, labor supply directly drives family employment.

This difference between family farms and a capitalist enterprise makes it possible for a failure of demand in the capitalist sector to bring down farm prices while farm output hardly changes—and sow the seeds of bankruptcy and disaster. Consider an economy that includes a sector of family farms coexisting with a capitalist industrial sector.[13] The capitalist sector produces a dual-purpose good used for both consumption and investment, whereas the agricultural sector produces a single-purpose consumption good, food. We denote industrial output by Y_I, agricultural output by Y_A, agricultural income by $\tilde{Y}_A$. As we shall see, it is necessary to distinguish farm output and income because in this model falling prices mean rising agricultural surpluses that remain unsold. As noted at the end of chapter 5, an economy of sole proprietors—family farms fit the bill—drives a wedge between income and output.

Demand for industrial goods for consumption purposes, C_I, is given in nominal terms by

$$P_I C_I = \gamma_{II} P_I Y_I + \gamma_{AI} P_A \tilde{Y}_A.$$

Here, P_I and P_A are the prices of the two goods, γ_{II} is the propensity to consume industrial goods by the producers of industrial goods, and γ_{AI} is the propensity to consume industrial goods out of income from producing food. In real terms we have

$$C_I = \gamma_{II} Y_I + \gamma_{AI} \frac{P_A}{P_I} \tilde{Y}_A.$$

Demand for industrial goods for investment is the sum of the demands for additional capital for the capitalist sector and for additional capital for the farm sector:

$$I = I_I(\rho) + I_A(\rho).$$

Total demand for industrial goods is

$$Y_I = C_I + I,$$

so that

$$(1 - \gamma_{II}) Y_I = \gamma_{AI} \frac{P_A}{P_I} \tilde{Y}_A + I,$$

which is to say that saving out of income from producing industrial goods must be equal to the consumption of industrial goods by farmers plus investment. This equation defines an industrial-demand schedule that plays the same role here that the AD schedule plays in the one-sector economy.[14]

Analogously, the demand schedule in the agricultural sector is given by equality between agricultural income and desired food consumption,

$$P_A \tilde{Y}_A = P_A C_A = \gamma_{IA} P_I Y_I + \gamma_{AA} P_A \tilde{Y}_A,$$

so that

$$\tilde{Y}_A = \left(\frac{P_A}{P_I} \right)^{-1} \frac{\gamma_{IA}}{1 - \gamma_{AA}} Y_I.$$

Figure 8.6 reproduces the structure of Figure 8.1 to show a serendipitous full-employment equilibrium in the industrial sector at E and an unemployment equilibrium at F. The new element in Figure 8.6 is that the price on the vertical axis is the real price of industrial goods, and output on the horizontal axis is the output of industrial goods. Figure 8.7 shows the corresponding equilibria in the agricultural sector.

Initially, the agricultural economy is at E in Figure 8.7 because the industrial economy is at E in Figure 8.6. At this point, $\dot{P}_I = 0$, so the stationary relative-price locus, $(P_A/P_I)^\bullet = 0$, is identical to the stationary locus of the price of agricultural goods, $\dot{P}_A/P_A = 0$. Assuming flexprice adjustment in agriculture, $(P_A/P_I)^\bullet = 0$ is the food-demand schedule.

Why flexprice adjustment? The choice may appear arbitrary, especially having argued that fixprice equilibrium makes more sense in the macro model pictured in Figure 8.1. There is really no choice. The logic of the family-farm

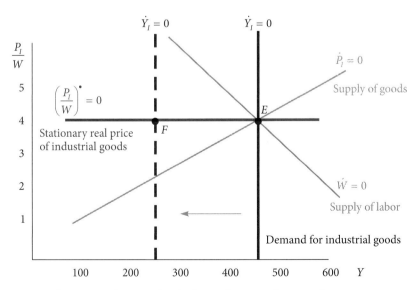

Figure 8.6 The capitalist (industrial) sector: fixprice adjustment.

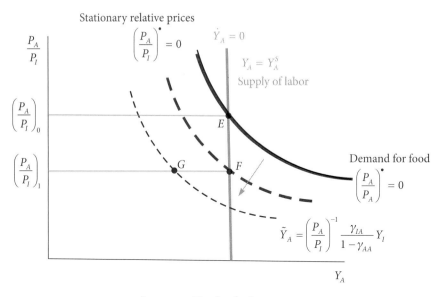

Figure 8.7 The family-farm sector.

model dictates flexprice adjustment because output is determined by the exogenously given supply of labor. Output cannot respond to a shortfall in expenditure, which explains why agricultural surpluses mounted during the Depression while inventories in the nonfarm business sector shrunk.[15]

Once the industrial economy moves away from E, the intersection of the demand and supply curves in Figure 8.7 no longer determines equilibrium relative prices. When industry is at F in Figure 8.6, the price ratio P_A/P_I can remain stationary only if P_A is falling at the same rate as P_I. But the price of farm output falls if and only if farm output is to the right of the demand schedule. So the new stationary-(P_A/P_I) locus, the red-dashed schedule in Figure 8.7, lies to the right of the black-dashed food-demand schedule, which is the stationary-P_A locus when the industrial economy is at F in Figure 8.6.

The reason for the distinction between farm income and output should now be clear. In Figure 8.7 the point F is the new equilibrium in the sense of stationary output and relative prices. At F, agricultural prices must be falling at the same rate as industrial prices at F in Figure 8.6, which implies an agricultural surplus that finds no market at the equilibrium $(P_A/P_I)_1$. Farm income is limited by what can be sold, represented by the point G. Mounting surpluses, empirically problematic as a description of the macro economy, as Table 8.2 shows, were part of the catastrophe that farmers experienced between 1929 and 1933.

Figure 8.7 determines equilibrium P_A/P_I for given Y_I, but in the demand equation in Figure 8.6, Y_I depends on P_A/P_I. We have to take the two demand equations together to determine both the level of industrial demand and the corresponding relative price of food. Rearranging the industrial-demand equation gives

$$Y_I = \frac{\gamma_{AI}}{1 - \gamma_{II}} \frac{P_A}{P_I} \tilde{Y}_A + \frac{1}{1 - \gamma_{II}} I,$$

and rearranging the agricultural-demand equation gives

$$\frac{P_A}{P_I} \tilde{Y}_A = \frac{\gamma_{IA}}{1 - \gamma_{AA}} Y_I.$$

Substituting from the agricultural equation into the industrial equation we have

$$Y_I = \frac{\gamma_{AI}}{1 - \gamma_{II}} \frac{\gamma_{IA}}{1 - \gamma_{AA}} Y_I + \frac{1}{1 - \gamma_{II}} I.$$

Collecting terms, we have an equation for industrial output as the product of the multiplier and the level of investment,

$$Y_I = \frac{1 - \gamma_{AA}}{\left(1 - \gamma_{II}\right)\left(1 - \gamma_{AA}\right) - \gamma_{AI}\gamma_{IA}} I.$$

We substitute back into the agricultural equation to obtain the value of farm income determined by the level of investment:

$$\frac{P_A}{P_I} \tilde{Y}_A = \frac{\gamma_{IA}}{\left(1 - \gamma_{II}\right)\left(1 - \gamma_{AA}\right) - \gamma_{AI}\gamma_{IA}} I.$$

Evidently, greater investment leads not only to greater industrial output but also to higher relative prices for farm goods. The corollary is that if investment dries up, as happened after 1929, not only will industrial output and prices fall; farm prices will also fall and fall harder than industrial prices.[16]

Observe that on present assumptions the level of farm output plays no role in the determination of industrial output. Changes in the level of farm output are cancelled out by offsetting changes in the ratio of agricultural to industrial prices, P_A/P_I: as we have seen, the equilibrium level of industrial output depends only on the level of investment and the multiplier.

This result depends on the assumption that the propensities to consume are fixed in both sectors. Truth to tell, the only defense of this assumption is tractability. In all likelihood, as relative prices vary, agents will vary the composition of their consumption baskets. It is reasonable to assume that industrial workers will purchase more from agriculture and less from industry as the relative price of food falls. Perhaps their overall consumption as a fraction of income will change too (Grigoli, Hermana, and Schmidt-Hebbel 2016).

Farmers will also react to relative price changes, but not necessarily in the same way. As the prices of farm products fall relative to the prices of industrial goods, farmers are worse off and the income effects may induce them to purchase less from industry, despite substitution effects working in the opposite direction. Again, their saving may or may not increase.

Different assumptions about how agents in the two sectors react to price changes will lead to different conclusions about the effect of changes in demand and supply. Of particular interest is causality running from agriculture to industry. The mathematical appendix to this chapter shows that the level of industrial output is sensitive to the level of agricultural output if we drop the assumption of fixed propensities to consume. The model in the mathematical appendix assumes instead that the fraction of income allocated to consumption of industrial goods—by capitalists, industrial workers, and farmers—is positively related to the relative price of food. For mathematical tractability I also assume that propensities to save do not change (in other words, that the fraction of income allocated to food goes down by exactly the same amount as the increase in the fraction devoted to industrial goods). A surprising result is that as Y_A^S increases, Y_I *falls;* the adverse effect on agricultural prices more than offsets the extra agricultural production.

This suggests that the increase in agricultural production in the 1920s, and the consequent deterioration of the terms of trade, may have contributed to the fall in industrial output from 1929 on,[17] as Jakob Madsen (2001) suggests. My own view is that causality running from industry to agriculture is more important, the fall in investment (and/or the propensity to consume) after 1929 producing the paradoxical result of more output in the agricultural sector. Indeed, the nadir of 1932–33 may have been an equilibrium: farm and nonfarm output, the real price of industrial goods, and the relative price of agricultural goods might have persisted indefinitely, with nominal prices (and wages) falling to ever-lower levels. Except that Franklin Roosevelt, inaugurated as president on March 4, 1933, took several actions that halted the downward spiral.

There has been relatively little analysis of how agricultural recovery influenced the return to prosperity. One exception is Peter Temin and Barrie Wigmore (1990), who consider devaluation of the dollar (see chapter 7 above) the lynchpin of the new economic regime, not only for its effects on commodity prices but, more generally, for its impact as a signal that change was the new order of the day. (The Temin–Wigmore argument was formalized by Gauti Eggertsson [2008].) Another exception is Joshua Hausman, Paul Rhode, and Johannes Wieland (2019), who focus more directly on the farm recovery as the engine of growth and recovery in the wider economy.

It is certainly the case that the Roosevelt administration's agricultural poli-cies assumed a negative relationship between Y_A^S and Y_I and attempted to har-ness this relationship to increase both agricultural and industrial incomes. Restricting agricultural production in order to raise prices and incomes was the clear intent of the Agricultural Adjustment Act, and the U.S. Department of Agriculture under Henry Wallace carried out the new policy with zeal.[18] Looking through the rearview mirror in 1936, Chester Davis, the head of the Agricultural Adjustment Administration, observed:

> We know that the country accepted this identification of the farm problem with the national problem. Rarely has an act of such moment encountered less opposition at its birth. Nonfarmers, as well as farmers, expected to bene-fit from it. Nonfarmers who thought the matter through believed that fairer prices to farmers would be bread cast upon the waters. They expected that the cost of the adjustment programs to them in the form of higher prices of food and fiber would be counterbalanced by increased industrial employ-ment and trade. (1936, p. 229)

The logic is the logic of immiserizing growth (see note 17)—the negative rela-tionship between Y_A^S and Y_I—but in reverse. If the decrease in Y_A^S is large enough, it could in principle propel the economy back to full employment, as in Figures 8.8 and 8.9. The increase in P_A/P_I more than makes up for the fall in agricultural production, driving demand upward in both sectors.

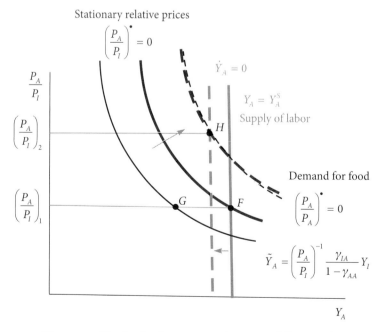

Figure 8.8 The family-farm sector adjusts to a fall in supply.

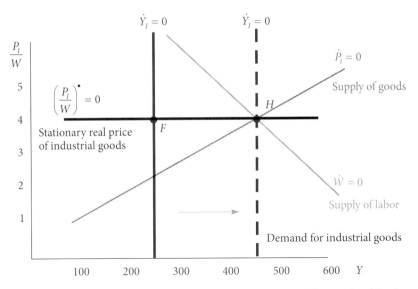

Figure 8.9 The industrial sector responds to a decrease in the supply of food.

There is one problem with this formulation of the relationship between agriculture and industry. In my story, agricultural prices are determined endogenously, which is tantamount to assuming a closed economy. This assumption, as I noted in note 13, describes the U.S. industrial economy of the interwar period accurately enough, and a large part of the agricultural economy was geared to the domestic market—think dairy farms, cattle ranches, and pig farms; orange groves, market gardens, and apple orchards. My calculations indicate that about 70 percent of agriculture was effectively insulated from foreign trade. But this still leaves a part of agriculture for which prices were determined in international markets. Half the cotton crop was exported in 1929 and over three-quarters in 1932.

As Temin and Wigmore (1990), Eggertsson (2008), and Hausmann, Rhode, and Wieland (2019) all note, the exchange rate was a critical determinant of dollar prices of exports. The United States effectively went off the gold standard in April 1933, and this had the immediate corollary of devaluing the dollar relative to other currencies. Export prices in terms of dollars rose accordingly, and agricultural exports were a large share of the total in this period; cotton alone accounted for 17 percent of total exports in 1932. Between April 1933 and February 1934, when a new gold parity was fixed at $35.00 per ounce, the price of cotton practically doubled in dollars but went up by only 15 percent in terms of sterling.[19] The price of wheat followed the same upward trajectory, increasing by more than 75 percent between April 1933 and February 1934 in dollars, while remaining flat in London. For the most part, goods that did not enter into international trade increased much less in value, if they increased at all. Milk was up almost 20 percent, but cattle were only 10 percent more expensive in February 1934 than in April of the preceding year; hog prices were unchanged. Corn was an exception: its domestic price rose more than the price of wheat even though little was exported—not even $3 million worth, out of a crop valued at more than $1.2 billion in 1933 (Bureau of the Census 1935).[20] Despite inflationary fears and scare tactics to induce consumers to buy before prices rose, the U.S. consumer price index rose less than 6 percent. (Food prices rose by just over 20 percent.)

A different model of price and output determination is required to account for export crops. We can still use the two-sector schema, but causality is different once agricultural prices are determined outside the model. In this case, the international price, along with the domestic demand schedule, determines the quantity consumed domestically, and the difference between total production and domestic consumption goes to export markets. In Figure 8.10, the price is initially fixed at $(P_A/P_I)_0$, and domestic consumption is determined by the equilibrium at E. Domestic consumption is Y_A^0, and exports plus additions to stocks are equal to $Y_A^S - Y_A^0$. Causality in this case runs in one direction, from the exogenously fixed export price to farmers' incomes to industrial demand. The only feedback from industry to agriculture is in determining how much of the crop is exported—what's left over after domestic demand is met.

In this model, devaluation increases the relative price of farm products to

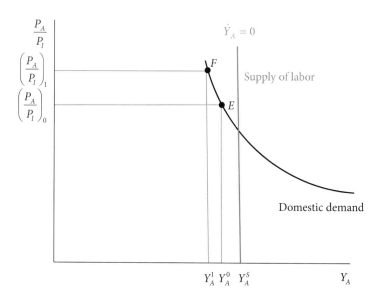

Figure 8.10 The export-crop sector.

$(P_A/P_I)_1$. The new equilibrium of domestic demand is at F. Industrial production increases in response to the additional demand coming from farmers, as in the closed-economy model. Exports also increase as a by-product of reduced domestic demand for agricultural products.

How well did the policies of devaluation and production restrictions succeed? The problem of assessing the role of crop restrictions, and more generally, the role of agricultural policy (counting devaluation as agricultural policy), is not only that other policies were in play. To compound the problem, Mother Nature collaborated with government in restricting output. The clouds of sand that covered the agricultural heartland and transformed it into the dust bowl had a silver lining.

Food for Thought

In the Great Depression, much more havoc was wrought by wage and price flexibility than by rigidity. Keynes came to this conclusion on theoretical grounds in chapter 19 of *The General Theory*, which is concerned with the pros and (mostly) cons of flexible prices and wages. He concludes with this observation:

> To suppose that a flexible wage policy is a right and proper adjunct of a system which on the whole is one of laissez-faire, is the opposite of the truth. It is only in a highly authoritarian society . . . that a flexible wage-policy could function with success. One can imagine it in operation in Italy, Germany or Russia, but not in France, the United States or Great Britain. (p. 269)

The mortgage-debt crisis brought on by the disastrous fall in prices, especially agricultural prices, points up the truth of the paradox that laissez-faire requires an authoritarian government. In fact, the democratic process in the United States responded quite sensibly to the intolerable position of mortgage debtors: the increasing debt burden led the Minnesota legislature to enact a statute allowing loan repayments to be postponed on the finding by a local judge of financial hardship—a perfectly reasonable reaction to hard times.

The problem was that the warp of American democracy on which the Minnesota legislature tried to weave debt relief was the Constitution of the United States, and on every traditional canon of constitutional interpretation—language, intent of the framers, and the spirit of the text—the Minnesota law was plainly unconstitutional. The founding fathers had deliberately constrained democracy in order to safeguard property rights. And so it was argued before the Supreme Court in the fall of 1933.

With respect to *language,* the relevant constitutional provision is clear:

it prevented states from enacting any law "abridging the obligation of contract." Moreover, this was the clear *intent* of the framers: the contract clause was a reaction to the agitation in many states—including the famous rebellion led by Daniel Shays in my backyard (Western Massachusetts)—to provide relief to debtors in the post-Revolutionary depression. Finally, the *spirit* of the provision was clearly directed against populist actions on the part of states, like the action of the Minnesota legislature to postpone debt repayment.

Nonetheless, in *Home Building & Loan Association v. Blaisdell* (290 U.S. 398, 1934), a very conservative, very originalist, U.S. Supreme Court, by a narrow vote of 5 to 4, upheld the Minnesota statute on the convoluted grounds that although the Depression did not create special state power, it might be the occasion for the exercise of such power.

The power at issue was the police power of the states. Police power? On second thought, quite right. The Minnesota legislature had good reason to fear riots and worse if hard-pressed debtors were not granted some relief.

In this regard authoritarian regimes clearly have a comparative advantage: they are not constrained in the use of repressive force in the way that democratic regimes are. In 1934 Germany, the cousins of the angry farmers who came together to disrupt foreclosure sales in Minnesota and throughout the Midwest would have found themselves in concentration camps if they had dared such a protest and lived to tell the tale. In the Soviet Union, peasants were starved to death for resisting foreclosure of another sort.

APPENDIX: MILTON FRIEDMAN AND ANNA SCHWARTZ ON WHAT MADE THE DEPRESSION GREAT

Friedman and Schwartz (1963a and 1963b) argue that the Fed could have prevented the downturn of 1930 from turning into the Great Depression. The best evidence that they can muster is their analysis of open market operations in 1932, when the Fed for a brief period actively purchased Treasury securities. In their view, this led to an expansion of the money supply, which in turn led to a recovery in industrial production. The rest of the story is that the Fed's failure to continue the program of buying Treasury securities aborted the recovery, thus reinforcing the argument that the money supply determines, rather than reflects, economic activity. By extension, all would have been well if the Fed had intervened earlier and consistently as it did briefly in 1932.

Friedman and Schwartz rely heavily on the timing of changes in the money supply relative to the uptick in industrial production:

The tapering off of the decline in the stock of money and the beginning of the purchase program were shortly followed by an equally notable change in the general economic indicators . . . Wholesale prices started rising in July, production in August. (1963a, p. 324)

They admit

There is, of course, no way of knowing that the economic improvement reflected the monetary improvement. But it is entirely clear that the reverse was not the case. Aside from the precedence in time of the monetary improvement, the program of large-scale open market purchases was a deliberative action undertaken by the Reserve System. And it was the major factor accounting for the monetary improvement. (p. 324)

Having feigned agnosticism, Friedman and Schwartz show their hand even more clearly in the next paragraph:

The timing relations, previous experience, and general considerations all make it highly plausible that the economic improvement reflected the influence of the monetary improvement, rather than the only other alternative—that it occurred shortly thereafter entirely by coincidence. We have observed that, in the past, an increase in the rate of monetary growth—in the present case, from rapid decline to mild decline and then mild rise—has invariably preceded a trough in general business. After three years of economic contraction, there must have been many forces in the economy making for revival, and it is reasonable that they could more readily come to fruition in a favorable monetary setting than in the midst of continued financial uncertainty. (p. 324)

This is thin gruel. "Past experience" is of very limited relevance, as are "general considerations." As Friedman and Schwartz were well aware, the Great Depression was unprecedented in the economic history of the United States. We are left with the fact that the episode of open-market purchases preceded the uptick in industrial production.

There is more than one problem with this timing argument. Federal Reserve numbers do indicate a sizeable increase in industrial production between July and October 1932 (Board of Governors of the Federal Reserve System [n.d.], pp. S-148–S-149), 19 percent without seasonal adjustment and 13 percent on a seasonally adjusted basis. Impressive at first sight but less impressive considering that in the first four months of 1931 there was a 10 percent increase in industrial production (3 percent with seasonal adjustment), an increase that appears to be unrelated to Federal Reserve policy. Wholesale prices too saw an upward spike, almost 9 percent between May and October 1932. As was the case for output, there was a milder spike in wholesale prices in the spring of 1931, prices rising by 2 percent between May and July (Federal Reserve Bank of St. Louis).

The possibility that there was nothing special about the uptick in the summer and fall of 1932 is reinforced by the revised series of the industrial-production index put together by Jeffrey Miron and Christina Romer (1990). Their series shows much more volatility in the monthly figures, with month-to-month *increases* of 10 percent or more in *every* year between 1929 and 1933. The only sustained increases (four months) were the periods January to April and September to December 1931. None in 1932!

Even without the Miron–Romer revisions, the fact that output and prices turned upward briefly on an earlier occasion makes pure coincidence a plausible explanation of the 1932 correlation between monetary expansion—or rather a slowdown in the rate of contraction—and the increase in real output and prices. Miron and Romer make us wonder if there is anything to explain.

But there is a more basic question. If we stipulate, as the lawyers say, that there were coincidental increases in the money supply on the one hand and prices and output on the other, what, we may reasonably ask, was the mechanism by which the progression "from rapid decline to mild decline and then mild rise" in the money supply turned the economy around?

Friedman and Schwartz's *Monetary History* presents no mechanism relating money to output and prices, but a mechanism is described in a paper of theirs (1963b) that can be read as the theoretical companion of the book. The basic idea outlined in the paper will be familiar: open-market purchases by the Federal Reserve lead to lower interest rates, and lower interest rates stimulate investment. The first step is an increase in the reserves of the banks:

> Although the initial sellers of the securities purchased by the central bank were willing sellers, this does not mean that they want to hold the proceeds in money indefinitely. The [central] bank offered them a good price, so they sold; they added to their money balances as a temporary step in rearranging their portfolios. If the seller was a commercial bank, it now has larger reserves than it has regarded before as sufficient and will seek to expand its investments and its loans at a greater rate than before. If the seller was not a commercial bank, he is not likely even temporarily to want to hold the proceeds in currency but will deposit them in a commercial bank, thereby, in our fractional reserve system, adding to the bank's reserves relative to its deposits. In either case, therefore, in our system, commercial banks become more liquid. (Friedman and Schwartz 1963b, p. 60)

The commercial banks will consequently increase the supply of money:

> Both the nonbank seller and commercial banks will therefore seek to read-
> just their portfolios, the only difference being that the commercial banks
> will in the process create more money, thereby transmitting the increase in
> high-powered money to the total money stock. (pp. 60–61)

More money means, for a given level of prices and output, more demand for
financial assets:

> It seems plausible that both nonbank and bank holders of redundant bal-
> ances will turn first to securities comparable to those they have sold, say,
> fixed-interest coupon, low-risk obligations. But as they seek to purchase
> these they will tend to bid up the prices of those issues [and thus reduce
> yields]. Hence they, and also other holders not involved in the initial central
> bank open-market transactions, will look farther afield. (p. 61)

And what do they find as their gaze widens?

> The banks . . . their loans; the nonbank holders . . . other categories of securi-
> ties—higher-risk fixed coupon obligations, equities, real property, and so
> forth. (p. 61)

The end result is greater investment:

> As the process continues, the initial impacts are diffused in several respects:
> first, the range of assets affected widens; second, potential creators of assets
> now more in demand are induced to react to the better terms on which they
> can be sold, including business enterprises wishing to engage in capital ex-
> pansion, house builders or prospective homeowners, consumers who are
> potential purchasers of durable consumer goods—and so on and on. (p. 61)

There is nothing theoretically problematic in the Friedman–Schwartz transmission theory. Their story actually fits Keynes's own second-pass model, as
well as Modigliani's version of this model. If the central bank is reducing the
money supply just when the sensible policy is expansion, we have a recipe for
disaster, not recovery. Here Friedman–Schwartz's monetarism does not contradict Keynes. On the comparative-statics interpretation provided by the
second-pass model, *The General Theory* is entirely consistent with the idea
that a combination of misguided policy and sheer incompetence caused the
Great Depression.

The third-pass, dynamic, model tells a very different story. The data for
deposits at all banks over the period June 1931 to December 1932 do indicate
that the decline that began in 1930 bottomed out, at least temporarily, in July

1932. But, as Table 8.19 shows, the composition of bank assets does not follow the Friedman–Schwartz story line. Holdings of U.S. government securities rose between June 1931 and June 1932. More to the point, the end purpose of the operation was foiled: loans continued south throughout this period, declining by 6.5 percent between June and December 1932. The more detailed data available for the member banks of the Federal Reserve System confirm this pattern. Table 8.20, like Table 8.19, shows that adjusted deposits (deposits net of interbank deposits) hit a floor in June 1932. On the liability side, the table makes it clear that the increase in investments after that date was due to a growing stake in U.S. Treasuries, a stake that continued to grow well after the Fed's open-market purchase program ended. No doubt the liquidity of the banking system improved, as indicated by the growth in excess reserves, which rose by $300 million between June and December 1932. Perhaps this was due, as Friedman and Schwartz suggest, to nonbank sellers of Treasuries depositing the proceeds of their sales into their bank accounts. In any case,

Table 8.19 Assets and Liabilities, All Banks ($ millions)

End of Month	Deposits	Adjusted Deposits	Total Investments	U.S. Government Obligations	Loans
Jun 1931	56,902	51,769	19,982	6,682	35,285
Dec 1931	49,509	45,925	18,651		31,395
Jun 1932	45,411	42,093	18,422	6,895	27,888
Dec 1932	45,886	41,752	19,060		26,109

Source: Board of Governors of the Federal Reserve System 1943, table 2.

Table 8.20 Assets and Liabilities, Member Banks of the Federal Reserve System ($ millions)

End of Month	Adjusted Deposits Table 18	Total Investments Table 18	U.S. Government Obligations Table 18	CIAC Loans[1] Table 18	Reserves at Federal Reserve Banks Table 105	Required Reserves Table 105	Excess Reserves Table 105
Jun 1931	31,338	12,106	5,343	8,922	2,404	2,275	129
Sep 1931	29,312	12,199	5,564	8,722	2,333	2,212	120
Dec 1931	27,391	11,314	5,319	8,126	2,069	2,010	60
Mar 1932					1,899	1,840	59
Jun 1932	24,717	11,414	5,628	6,892	2,062	1,827	234
Sep 1932	24,860	12,121	6,366	6,398	2,181	1,836	345
Dec 1932	25,020	12,265	6,540	5,970	2,435	1,909	526

Source: Board of Governors of the Federal Reserve System 1943.

1. CIAC loans are commercial, industrial, agricultural, and consumer loans not collateralized by securities.

the increased liquidity of the banking system did not lead to an easing of credit. CIAC loans continued to fall at virtually the same pace in the six months after June 1932, as in the six months before.

The open-market purchase program added U.S. Treasuries to the Federal Reserve's portfolio, almost $1 billion between March and June 1932 (Board of Governors of the Federal Reserve System [1943, table 91, p. 343]). But these additions did not in themselves contribute to the improved liquidity of the banks. Reserves hardly changed between December 1931 and June 1932. It was after the purchase program ended that bank reserves began to climb.

The remaining channel by which monetary easing might have contributed to recovery was via the interest rate. Here, as has already been noted, the evidence suggests a classic liquidity trap, at least in the sense of a floor to the hurdle rate when the T-bill rate hits the zero lower bound. Table 8.21 gives interest rates on a variety of instruments, both loans and investments. The main impact of the Fed's open-market purchases, not surprisingly, was on short-term Treasuries, the yield on which fell sharply in June 1932, as the bond-buying program topped out, and continued to fall through the summer. Yields on longer-term government bonds and on short-term commercial paper fell throughout 1932, but it is not clear how much the decline was the result of Fed intervention and how much had to do with the easing of fears about whether the United States would maintain its link to gold in the wake of Britain's decision to go off the gold standard in September 1931. There was much less of an impact on commercial loans and the moderately risky Baa-grade corporate bonds. Rates on both of these were much higher in June 1932 than they had been a year earlier, and even after these rates fell over the next six months, they remained higher than they had been in June 1931.

Table 8.21 Selected Interest Rates (percent per year)

Two-Month Averages (e.g., June and July)	Prime Commercial Paper (4–6 months New York) Table 120	Rates on Commercial Loans (avg. 19 cities) Table 125	Yield on Short-Term U.S. Government Securities (3–6 month Treasury Notes and Certificates) Table 122	Yield on Long-Term U.S. Government Bonds (due or callable after 12 years) Table 128	Yield on Baa-Rated Corporate Bonds Table 128	Yield on Aaa-Rated Corporate Bonds Table 128
Jun 1931	2.00	4.17	0.48	3.14	7.22	4.36
Sep 1931	2.57	4.19	1.08	3.44	8.56	4.77
Dec 1931	3.88	4.77	1.82	4.10	9.78	5.26
Mar 1932	3.57	4.88	1.68	3.80	9.65	5.08
Jun 1932	2.63	4.77	0.28	3.67	11.16	5.34
Sep 1932	2.07	4.58	0.02	3.43	7.74	4.67
Dec 1932	1.44	4.44	0.43	3.29	8.22	4.52

Source: Board of Governors of the Federal Reserve System 1943.

In the industrial sector of a two-sector model, desired expenditure is the sum of (1) consumption demand on the part of capitalists and workers in the industrial sector; (2) consumption demand on the part of farm families; (3) investment demand from both sectors. The demand schedule for industrial goods is defined by equality between income and expenditure:

$$Y_I = \gamma_{II} Y_I + \gamma_{AI} \frac{P_A}{P_I} \tilde{Y}_A + I(\rho).$$

Equivalently, the demand schedule is defined by the two-sector analog of $S = I$:

$$\left(1 - \gamma_{II}\right) Y_I = \gamma_{AI} \frac{P_A}{P_I} \tilde{Y}_A + I(\rho).$$

Assuming fixprice adjustment, the dynamics of the industrial sector are summarized by

$$\frac{\left(\dfrac{P_I}{W}\right)^{\bullet}}{\dfrac{P_I}{W}} \equiv \left(\frac{\dot{P}_I}{P_I} - \frac{\dot{W}}{W}\right) = -\theta_1\left[GS\left(\frac{P_I}{W}\right) - Y_I\right] - \theta_3\left[Y_I - LS\left(\frac{P_I}{W}\right)\right], \quad (8.1)$$

$$\dot{Y}_I = \theta_2\left[\gamma_{AI} \frac{P_A}{P_I} \tilde{Y}_A + \gamma_{II} Y_I + I(\rho) - Y_I\right]. \quad (8.2)$$

For agriculture we have expenditure equal to income when the consumption of agricultural goods by nonfarmers is equal to the saving of farm families:

$$\gamma_{IA}\left(\frac{P_A}{P_I}\right)^{-1} Y_I = \left(1 - \gamma_{AA}\right) \tilde{Y}_A. \quad (8.3)$$

But, unlike the industrial sector, flexprice adjustment is assumed to characterize agriculture. The adjustment equations are

$$\dot{Y}_A = -\theta_4\left(Y_A - Y_A^S\right), \quad (8.4)$$

$$\frac{\dot{P}_A}{P_A} = \theta_5 \left[\gamma_{IA} \left(\frac{P_A}{P_I} \right)^{-1} Y_I + \gamma_{AA}\tilde{Y}_A - Y_A \right]. \tag{8.5}$$

Combining equation (8.5) with the price-adjustment equation

$$\frac{\dot{P}_I}{P_I} = -\theta_1 \left[GS\left(\frac{P_I}{W} \right) - Y_I \right]$$

gives the adjustment equation for relative prices:

$$\frac{\left(\dfrac{P_A}{P_I} \right)^{\displaystyle \cdot}}{\dfrac{P_A}{P_I}} \equiv \left(\frac{\dot{P}_A}{P_A} - \frac{\dot{P}_I}{P_I} \right) = \theta_5 \left[\gamma_{IA} \left(\frac{P_A}{P_I} \right)^{-1} Y_I + \gamma_{AA}\tilde{Y}_A - Y_A \right] \\ + \theta_1 \left[GS\left(\frac{P_I}{W} \right) - Y_I \right]. \tag{8.6}$$

The complete system is made up of equations (8.1), (8.2), (8.3), and (8.4) plus (8.6).

At equilibrium, the variables are all stationary, and denoting

$$\Delta = (1 - \gamma_{II})(1 - \gamma_{AA}) - \gamma_{IA}\gamma_{AI};$$

we have, after substitution,

$$Y_I \frac{1 - \gamma_{AA}}{\Delta} I, \tag{8.7}$$

$$\theta_1 GS\left(\frac{P_I}{W} \right) - \theta_3 LS\left(\frac{P_I}{W} \right) = \left(\theta_1 - \theta_3 \right) Y_I, \tag{8.8}$$

$$\tilde{Y}_A = \frac{\gamma_{IA}}{\Delta} \left(\frac{P_A}{P_I} \right)^{-1} I, \tag{8.9}$$

$$Y_A = Y_A^S, \tag{8.10}$$

$$\tilde{Y}_A + \frac{\theta_1}{\theta_5} \left[GS\left(\frac{P_I}{W} \right) - Y_I \right] = Y_A. \tag{8.11}$$

Equation (8.11) explains the relationship between the food-demand schedule and the locus of stationary relative prices in Figure 8.7.

The stability conditions for a four-equation system are

$$\alpha_1 > 0,$$

$$\alpha_2 > 0,$$

$$\alpha_3 > 0,$$

$$\alpha_4 > 0,$$

$$\alpha_1 \alpha_2 - \alpha_3 > 0,$$

$$\alpha_3 (\alpha_1 \alpha_2 - \alpha_3) - (\alpha_1)^2 \alpha_4 > 0,$$

where the α's are the coefficients of the characteristic equation

$$\lambda^4 + \alpha_1 \lambda^3 + \alpha_2 \lambda^2 + \alpha_3 \lambda + \alpha_4 = 0$$

formed by the determinant of the Jacobian matrix

$$
\begin{bmatrix}
j_{11} & j_{12} & j_{13} & j_{14} \\
j_{21} & j_{22} & j_{23} & j_{24} \\
j_{31} & j_{32} & j_{33} & j_{34} \\
j_{41} & j_{42} & j_{43} & j_{44}
\end{bmatrix} =
$$

$$
\begin{bmatrix}
-\theta_1 GS' + \theta_3 LS' & \theta_1 - \theta_3 & 0 & 0 \\
0 & -\theta_2 (1 - \gamma_{II}) Y_I & \theta_2 \gamma_{AI} \dfrac{P_A}{P_I} & \theta_2 \gamma_{AI} \tilde{Y}_A \\
0 & 0 & -\theta_4 & 0 \\
\theta_1 GS' & \theta_5 \gamma_{IA} \left(\dfrac{P_A}{P_I} \right)^{-1} - \theta_1 & -\theta_5 (1 - \gamma_{AA}) & -\theta_5 \gamma_{IA} \left(\dfrac{P_A}{P_I} \right)^{-2} Y_I
\end{bmatrix}.
$$

Taking account of the zeros in *det J*, the coefficients of the characteristic equation are

$$\alpha_1 = -tr\, J = -(j_{11} + j_{22} + j_{33} + j_{44}),$$

$$\alpha_2 = j_{11}j_{22} + j_{11}j_{33} + j_{11}j_{44} + j_{22}j_{33} + j_{22}j_{44} + j_{33}j_{44} - j_{24}j_{42},$$

$$\alpha_3 = -(j_{11}j_{22}j_{33} + j_{11}j_{33}j_{44} + j_{11}j_{22}j_{44} + j_{22}j_{33}j_{44} - j_{11}j_{24}j_{42} - j_{33}j_{24}j_{42} + j_{41}j_{12}j_{24}),$$

$$\alpha_4 = det\, J = j_{11}j_{22}j_{33}j_{44} - j_{11}j_{24}j_{42}j_{33} + j_{41}j_{12}j_{33}j_{24}.$$

Fortunately, most of the terms disappear because of the zeros in the Jacobian, but the calculations are still formidable.

For this reason, we work with a simpler version of the model that takes the adjustment of farm output to the supply constraint to be instantaneous. This gives us the system formed by equations (8.1), (8.2), (8.3), (8.6), and (8.10). For this system the Jacobian is

$$J = \begin{bmatrix} j_{11} & j_{12} & j_{13} \\ j_{21} & j_{22} & j_{23} \\ j_{31} & j_{32} & j_{33} \end{bmatrix} = \begin{bmatrix} -\theta_1 GS' + \theta_3 LS' & \theta_1 - \theta_3 & 0 \\ 0 & -\theta_2(1 - \gamma_{II})Y_I & \theta_2 \gamma_{AI} \tilde{Y}_A \\ \theta_1 GS' & \theta_5 \gamma_{IA} \left(\dfrac{P_A}{P_I}\right)^{-1} - \theta_1 & -\theta_5 \gamma_{IA} \left(\dfrac{P_A}{P_I}\right)^{-2} Y_I \end{bmatrix}.$$

The stability conditions for this system are

$$\alpha_1 = -\,tr\,J = -(j_{11} + j_{22} + j_{33}) > 0,$$

$$\alpha_2 = -(\boldsymbol{j_{23}j_{32}} - j_{11}j_{22} - j_{11}j_{33} - j_{22}j_{33}) > 0,$$

$$\alpha_3 = -(j_{11}j_{22}j_{33} - j_{11}j_{23}j_{32} + \boldsymbol{j_{31}j_{12}j_{23}}) > 0,$$

$$\begin{aligned} \alpha_1\alpha_2 - \alpha_3 = &-\left(j_{11}^2 j_{22} + j_{11}^2 j_{33} + j_{22}^2 j_{11} + j_{22}^2 j_{33} + j_{33}^2 j_{22} + j_{33}^2 j_{11} + 2 j_{11}j_{22}j_{33} \right) \\ &+ j_{23}\left(\boldsymbol{j_{22}j_{32}} + \boldsymbol{j_{33}j_{32}} + \boldsymbol{j_{31}j_{12}} \right) > 0 \end{aligned}$$

once the zeros have been eliminated.

The signs of j_{12} and j_{32} are ambiguous, which in turn make the signs of the terms in boldface in the stability conditions ambiguous. If $j_{32} < 0$, which is to say,

$$\theta_5 \gamma_{IA} \left(\frac{P_A}{P_I}\right)^{-1} < \theta_1,$$

then $\alpha_2 > 0$. If, in addition, either $GS' \approx 0$ or $\theta_3 > \theta_1$, then $j_{31}j_{12}j_{23}$ is either very small (if $GS' \approx 0$) or negative (if $\theta_3 > \theta_1$), so $\alpha_3 > 0$. Finally, the same condition, small GS' or positive $\theta_3 - \theta_1$, ensures $\alpha_1\alpha_2 - \alpha_3 > 0$.

It should be emphasized that these conditions on j_{32}, j_{12}, and j_{31} are sufficient rather than necessary. The system will be stable even if $j_{32} > 0$, $j_{12} > 0$, and GS' is large, provided the centripetal forces represented by the (negative) diagonal elements of the Jacobian are stronger than the centrifugal forces represented by positive off-diagonal elements.

Finally, we have the comparative statics results associated with changes in the supply of agricultural output. Denoting $dy_{ij}/d(P_A/P_I)$ by γ_{ij}', and $d\Delta/d(P_A/P_I)$ by Δ', we differentiate equations (8.7)–(8.11) to obtain at the end of the day (actually many days),

$$\frac{dY_I}{dY_A^S} = \frac{\left[\gamma_{AA}'\Delta + \Delta'\left(1 - \gamma_{AA}\right) \right] I \dfrac{P_A}{P_I}}{\Delta^2 \tilde{Y}_A - \left(\gamma_{IA}' + \Delta'\gamma_{IA}\right)I - \left(\gamma_{AA}' - \Delta'\left(1 - \gamma_{AA}\right)\right)\dfrac{P_A}{P_I} \left(\dfrac{\theta_1}{\theta_5}\right) \left(\dfrac{\theta_3\left(GS' - LS'\right)}{\theta_1 GS' - \theta_3 LS'}\right) I},$$

$$\frac{d\left(\dfrac{P_A}{P_I}\tilde{Y}_A\right)}{dY_A^S} =$$

$$-\frac{\Delta^2 \dfrac{P_A}{P_I}}{\Delta^2\tilde{Y}_A - \left(\gamma_{IA}{}' + \Delta'\gamma_{IA}\right)I - \left(\gamma_{AA}{}' - \Delta'\left(1 - \gamma_{AA}\right)\right)\dfrac{P_A}{P_I}\left(\dfrac{\theta_1}{\theta_5}\right)\left(\dfrac{\theta_3\left(GS' - LS'\right)}{\theta_1 GS' - \theta_3 LS'}\right)I} \cdot$$

Assuming $\gamma_{II}{}' = -\gamma_{IA}{}' > 0$ and $\gamma_{AI}{}' = -\gamma_{AA}{}' > 0$, we have

$$\gamma_{AA}{}'\Delta + \Delta'\left(1 - \gamma_{AA}\right) = -\gamma_{II}{}'\left(1 - \gamma_{AA}\right)\left(1 - \gamma_{AA} - \gamma_{AI}\right) - \gamma_{AI}{}'\gamma_{IA} < 0$$

and

$$\gamma_{IA}{}' + \Delta'\gamma_{IA} = \left[\gamma_{IA}{}'\left(1 - \gamma_{AA}\right) + \gamma_{AA}{}'\gamma_{IA}\right]\left[1 - \gamma_{II} - \gamma_{IA}\right] < 0,$$

so that both dY_I/dY_A^S and $d([P_A/P_I]\tilde{Y}_A)/dY_A^S$ are negative. The economics is that as long as farmers and industrial workers and capitalists (1) increase their consumption of industrial goods when the relative price of agricultural goods rises and (2) decrease their consumption of agricultural goods by the same amount, a decrease in agricultural production (Y_A^S) will lead to an increase in industrial output (Y_I) and an increase in the real income of farmers ($[P_A/P_I]\tilde{Y}_A$, measured in terms of industrial goods). Both farmers and nonfarmers increase their demand for industrial goods as the terms of trade turn in favor of agriculture, but their reasons are different. It is plausible that income effects drive farmers, whereas substitution effects drive nonfarmers.

— IV —

Building Blocks

— 9 —

CONSUMPTION AND SAVING

> Aggregate income . . . is, as a rule, the principal variable upon which
> the consumption constituent of the aggregate demand function will
> depend . . .
>
> The fundamental psychological law, upon which we are entitled to
> depend with great confidence both a priori from our knowledge of
> human nature and from the detailed facts of experience, is that men
> are disposed, as a rule and on the average, to increase their consump-
> tion as their income increases, but not by as much as the increase in
> their income.
>
> —JOHN MAYNARD KEYNES

For Keynes, the "fundamental psychological law" that people spend some but
not all of any increases in income was the beginning rather than the end of
wisdom on consumption. This "law," however, soon morphed into highly simplified models in which income was the sole determinant of consumption,
models which were bound to be refuted by experience.

This transformation took place even though Keynes qualified his fundamental psychological law in many ways that in fact anticipated the arguments
of both friendly critics like Franco Modigliani and hostile ones like Milton
Friedman. On the one hand, he emphasized that the propensity to consume
was likely to be lower in the short run than over a longer period:

> [The tendency for consumption to change less than income] is especially the
> case where we have short periods in view, as in the case of the so-called
> cyclical fluctuations of employment during which habits, as distinct from
> more permanent psychological propensities, are not given time enough to
> adapt themselves to changed objective circumstances. For a man's habitual
> standard of life usually has the first claim on his income, and he is apt to save
> the difference which discovers itself between his actual income and the
> expense of his habitual standard; or, if he does adjust his expenditure to
> changes in his income, he will over short periods do so imperfectly. Thus a
> rising income will often be accompanied by increased saving, and a falling
> income by decreased saving, on a greater scale at first than subsequently.
> (*The General Theory,* p. 97)

In the longer run individuals would be subject to conflicting influences. Habit would play a smaller role as people adapt their standard of life to their incomes. So we should expect that the marginal propensity to consume will rise as we consider longer time periods. But Keynes offers an argument in the other direction:

> A higher absolute level of income will tend, as a rule, to widen the gap between income and consumption. For the satisfaction of the immediate primary needs of a man and his family is usually a stronger motive than the motives towards accumulation, which only acquire effective sway when a margin of comfort has been attained. These reasons will lead, as a rule, to a greater proportion of income being saved as real income increases. (*The General Theory*, p. 97)

Milton Friedman in particular, as we saw in chapter 4, chided Keynes for ignoring the role of wealth in determining consumption. On the contrary: Keynes is very clear that wealth forms a buffer that insulates consumption from variations in income, especially in the short period:

> A decline in income due to a decline in the level of employment, if it goes far, may even cause consumption to exceed income . . . by some individuals and institutions using up the financial reserves which they have accumulated in better times. (*The General Theory*, p. 98)

But *changes* in wealth may reinforce the effects of income changes even as *levels* of wealth have the opposite effect:

> The consumption of the wealth-owning class may be extremely susceptible to unforeseen changes in the money-value of its wealth. This should be classified amongst the major factors capable of causing short-period changes in the propensity to consume . . .
>
> If a man is enjoying a windfall increment in the value of his capital, it is natural that his motives towards current spending should be strengthened, even though in terms of income his capital is worth no more than before; and weakened if he is suffering capital losses. (pp. 92–93, 94)

The upshot of these qualifying observations is to change the consumption function from the simple linear form deployed so far, illustrated in Figure 9.1. Instead, we have two consumption functions, one for the short run and another for the long run, as in Figure 9.2.

In part stimulated by the accounting framework of Keynes's theory, economists began to compile and analyze data on consumption, saving, and income. In the United States, Simon Kuznets pioneered the collection of aggregate data, producing a comprehensive series of national income and product accounts that allowed historical comparisons on both an annual basis from 1919 to 1938 (Kuznets 1941a) and on a decadal basis from the late nineteenth century (1941b [quoted in Ezekiel 1942a, 1942b]). Mordecai Ezekiel (1942a, 1942b) analyzed the data collected by Kuznets and others over the period 1919 to 1940 and concluded that, as Keynes had suggested, over short periods the ratio of consumption to income tended to move inversely with income, higher at lower levels of income, lower at higher levels.

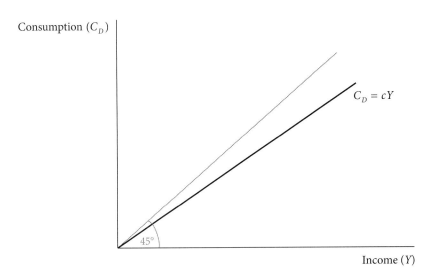

Figure 9.1 The relation between income and consumption, I.

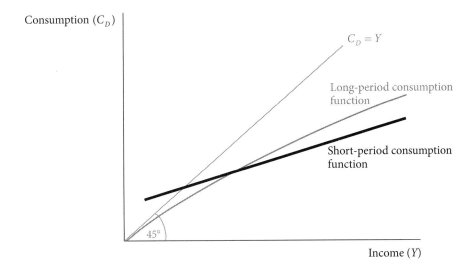

Figure 9.2 The relation between income and consumption, II.

But according to Ezekiel, the data only supported Keynes in part. For one thing, while the marginal propensity to consume was roughly constant, the short-period consumption function on the way up in the 1920s and in the post-1933 recovery lay below the corresponding function on the way down between 1929 and 1933; people appear to have maintained their standards of living in the face of an eroding economy, while rebuilding financially before spending on consumption as the economy recovered from a downturn (1942a, fig. 5, p. 32).

More important, over longer periods, Kuznets's data (1941b) did not support the idea of a secular decline in the propensity to consume, as the long-period consumption function in Figure 9.2 implies. Rather, over the period 1879 to 1928, decadal average rates of gross capital-formation in the United States remained remarkably constant, at about 20 percent of gross national product. Only the decade 1929 to 1938 witnessed a significant change: the capital-formation ratio fell to 15 percent (Ezekiel 1942b, table IV, p. 301). On this basis—without taking Ezekiel's dynamic modification into account—the relationship between short- and long-period consumption functions becomes that of Figure 9.3, with the long-run consumption function once again linear, and going through the origin if extrapolated backward.

The issues raised by the existence of two consumption functions were both theoretical and practical. Indeed, *The General Theory* challenged orthodox economics before it had much impact on the economy. It is ironic that it was in managing the economy during World War II, and even more so in the

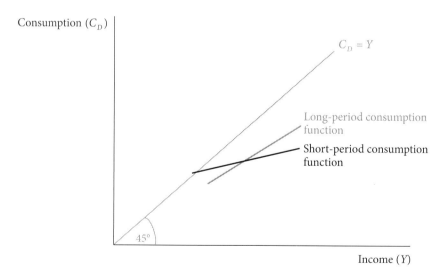

Figure 9.3 The relation between income and consumption, III.

planning of the postwar peacetime economy, that Keynesian economics came into its own—ironic because of the origins of *The General Theory* in a time of deep depression.

Samuelson on the Prospects for Full-Employment after World War II

Paul Samuelson's take on postwar opportunities and challenges is emblematic. Writing in 1943 he reflected the widespread concern that the economy would lapse into unemployment once the government was no longer spending vast sums on military procurement. In other words, would the private investment needed to match anticipated saving at full employment be forthcoming? If not, what could be done to prevent the calamity of renewed depression?

Samuelson was quick to dismiss the possibility of a redo of the collapse of 1929–1933. "Regardless of plans and intentions," he wrote, "any party in power would be forced by the mere sweep of catastrophic political events to provide sufficient demand to prevent this from happening" (1943, p. 28). Rather, Samuelson's concern was stagnation:

> The real danger lies in the possibility that we shall lag ever farther behind our true productive potential—that we shall be content with a half loaf instead of insisting upon the whole loaf which can be ours. The thing to fear is an ever-widening gap between our attained levels of output and employment and our true productive potential. (p. 28)

Samuelson, as was to become the norm, collapsed the LS schedule to a single level of output compatible with "full employment," a figure he estimated on the basis of the wartime economy. Using a highly simplified Keynesian framework, he calculated the amount of consumption demand that the economy would generate at full employment and, correspondingly, the full-employment amount of saving. Absent any other sources of spending, full-employment saving tells us how much investment demand is required for the economy to achieve its potential.

But which consumption function is relevant, the short-run or the long-run? In answering this question, Samuelson first makes the plausible argument that a long-run schedule like the one in Figures 9.2 and 9.3 is simply a locus of actually observed points on successive short-run consumption functions:[1]

> an enlarged scale of wants . . . causing an upward shift in the [short-run] consumption function at about the same rate as improvements in our pro-

duction potential [and] yielding a stable relation between percentage consumed out of national incomes corresponding to a given fraction of *full-
employment* income. (1943, p. 33)

Given the time frame, the long-run schedule may be of little relevance. It is
the short-run consumption function when the war ends that matters because
it is the immediate postwar period with the inevitable dislocations caused by
demobilization and its aftermath on which Samuelson focuses.

Figure 9.4 adds an assumption of full-employment output and income
($Y = Y_{FE}$) to the short-period consumption function of Figures 9.2 and 9.3.
The expenditure required to offset full-employment saving is given by the
vertical distance between the 45-degree line and the short-period consumption function, namely, $Y_{FE} - C_{D\,FE}$.

Samuelson poses the problem of achieving full employment in terms of a
list of potential offsets to full-employment saving, in which he includes not
only investment but also initiatives that the government might take to increase aggregate demand directly—government spending on goods and services—and indirect measures to redistribute income from people more likely
to save to people more likely to consume. That is, Samuelson's offsets include
measures to fill the gap $Y_{FE} - C_{D\,FE}$ both by mobilizing additional sources of
spending and by increasing $C_{D\,FE}$. Samuelson concluded not only that investment was likely to prove inadequate but that all the measures together were
likely to fall short.[2]

For our purposes, the most important of these offsets, the one around
which debate would coalesce, is the possibility that deferred demand, the con-

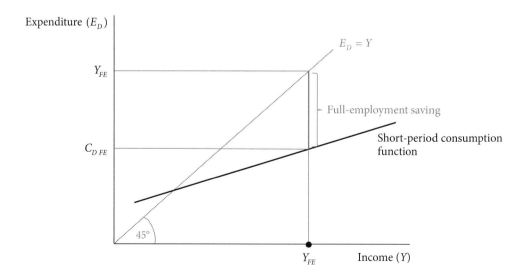

Figure 9.4 Full-employment saving.

sequence of the shortages of consumer goods because of the war effort, would provide additional consumption demand beyond the normal demand represented by the consumption function. Samuelson is far from sanguine about the quantitative boost that this will provide to ordinary consumption demand. In the event, the optimists (including Keynes, despite his reservations about the long-run prospects for self-sustaining demand) proved to have better crystal balls than the pessimists such as Samuelson. But this matters less than the importance that both sides attached to the role of wealth in consumption; as Samuelson notes, "*The real backlog of deferred demand . . .* will be accompanied by the financial means to make it effective" (1943, p. 46).

In 1943 the debate could still be framed in terms of consumption expenditure that ordinarily depends on income but may be influenced by other factors, including wealth and backlogs of unmet demands. Little more than a decade later this framework itself would be challenged. Instead of being an additional factor complementary to income, as Keynes originally argued, wealth was to become the central determinant of consumption.

Wealth, Consumption, and Saving: The Life-Cycle and Permanent-Income Hypotheses

Just as Keynes had charged his fellow economists with making a category mistake about interest-rate determination, the mainstream now returned the favor in arguing about how consumption and saving are determined. In effect, the mainstream charged Keynes with failing to understand that rational economic agents would allocate *stocks* of assets to *flows* of consumption, rather than basing current consumption flows on current income flows. The details, as we shall see, differ, but both Franco Modigliani's "life-cycle hypothesis" (Modigliani and Brumberg 1954) and Milton Friedman's "permanent-income hypothesis" (1957), attempt to correct Keynes's supposed mistake by assuming that agents determine current consumption and saving as part of a long-term consumption plan. The operative constraint is not current income but long-term wealth.

This theoretical argument received a boost from the studies of family-consumption data that were undertaken in the 1930s and the early postwar period. (Robert Ferber [1962] summarizes this literature.) Studies based on cross-sectional data (consumption and income data collected for different families at a single period of time) gave results qualitatively similar to the results gleaned from aggregate time-series data over short periods of time, namely, a positive increase in consumption as household income rose, but an increase that was modest in comparison with propensities to consume implicit in the long-run Kuznets data. If we scale the family-consumption data differently from the aggregate data, we can superimpose the family-consumption function on a long-term "Kuznets" consumption function along which the marginal propensity to consume is constant. The qualitative relation between the two consumption functions in Figure 9.5 is the same as in Figure 9.2.

Working from the same general premise, Modigliani and Friedman offer different, but mutually compatible, reasons why the long-run propensity to consume reflected in the aggregate data is greater than the propensity to consume reflected in the family data. Both the life-cycle and the permanent-income hypotheses start from the standard microeconomic theory of choice. In the simplest version, there are two commodities, say (with Greg Mankiw, *Principles of Economics* [2018]) pizza and cola, and the agent is a student with a snacks budget of, say, $1,000—provided by kind parents—which she can allocate as she pleases between the two goods. Figure 9.6 superimposes a budget constraint on a set of indifference curves.

As generations of students of introductory economics have learned, the consumer's optimum is where the budget constraint intersects with the highest attainable indifference curve, in the present case the indifference curve marked I_2. With smooth indifference curves, this optimum is characterized by equality between the slope of the indifference curve I_2 and the slope of the budget constraint. These slopes reflect the marginal rate of substitution of cola for pizza (the ratio of the marginal utility of pizza to the marginal utility of cola) and the ratio of the price of pizza to the price of cola. Optimization

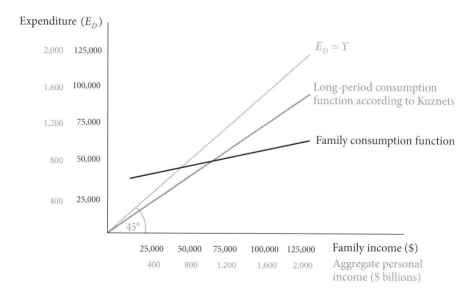

Figure 9.5 Aggregate and family consumption functions.

requires that the first, a subjective parameter that depends on the individual's utility function, be brought into line with the second, an objective parameter given by the market.

The beauty of the theory of consumer choice is its universality. We can go from pizza and cola to intertemporal consumption planning in a flash, simply by relabeling the axes and reinterpreting the budget constraint and the indifference curves. Figure 9.7 represents the intertemporal problem as the choice between consumption in two periods, present and future. The indifference curves are now the isoquants of a utility function reflecting the satisfaction associated with alternative consumption patterns over time, and the budget constraint now reflects the long-term resource—wealth—available to the agent. As before, the optimum is the point of tangency between the highest attainable indifference curve and the budget constraint, which reflects the adjustment of subjective marginal preferences, achieved by varying the consumption pattern, to the objectively given market prices.

The interpretation of preferences and prices changes. The marginal rate of substitution, given by the slope of the indifference curve, remains the relative marginal utility of the two goods, but now these goods are present and future consumption; the price ratio, given by the slope of the budget constraint, is the relative price of present and future consumption. The position of the bud-

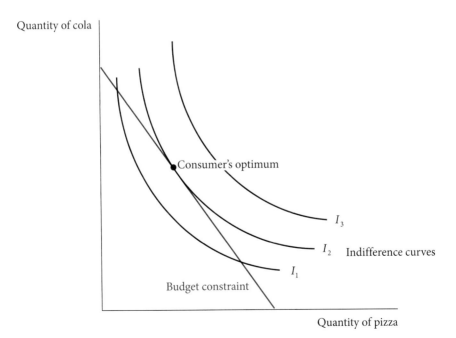

Figure 9.6 The rational consumer.

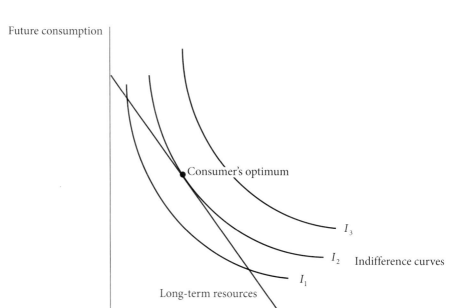

Figure 9.7 Optimal intertemporal choice.

get constraint is given by the agent's wealth. Its slope, the trade-off between the two goods, is given by the interest rate, since the price of present consumption relative to future consumption is one plus the market rate of interest between the two periods.

An important difference between Modigliani and Friedman is the time frame each has in mind when applying the future versus present model. For Modigliani, the future is the lifetime of an individual agent, who is assumed to maximize his or her utility with no thought for partner or progeny. Consider the simplest case, in which the rate of interest is assumed to be zero and indifference curves are assumed to be symmetric around the 45-degree line representing equal consumption, which is tantamount to assuming that the marginal utility of consumption in each period is the same when the level of consumption is unchanging over time. Suppose agents are supported by their parents until age twenty and continue their studies until age twenty-five, when they enter the workforce. (To keep matters simple, these agents receive full scholarships for tuition, books, and all costs associated with their studies, but they have to cover their living costs.) Once in the paid labor force, agents' earnings rise gradually from a beginning salary of $50,000 to a maximum of $121,500, when their careers end in retirement at age sixty. Agents live another twenty years. Nobody receives a pension; rather, everybody must save during his or her working life to provide twenty years' income in retirement.

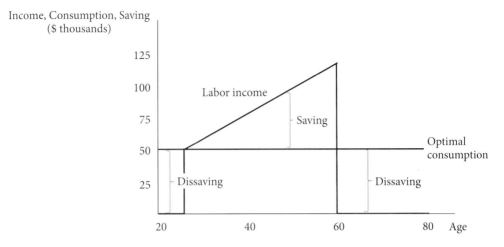

Figure 9.8 Income, consumption, and saving according to the life-cycle hypothesis.

Under the assumption that the marginal utility of income is constant over time when the level of consumption does not change, the optimum consumption plan is to consume the same amount in each period. Our assumptions about income, schooling, and retirement lead to an optimum consumption level of $50,000, as depicted in Figure 9.8. Saving is initially negative since as students aged between twenty and twenty-five agents must incur debt to support the optimum consumption plan. Positive saving—first to pay off student loans, then to provide for retirement—takes place when an agent enters the work force.

Modigliani's life-cycle agents do not provide for their survivors. Indeed, they have no motivation for saving other than to repay student debt and, later, to provide for their own retirement. If they plan properly, they die as paupers.

We can make the model more realistic by supposing that agents pay interest on student loans and earn a return on the assets they accumulate once these loans are paid off. Another dose of realism would be to replace the assumption of an earnings trajectory known with certainty by a set of probabilities with respect to earnings and interruption of earnings due to lay-offs, ill health, and other contingencies of work and life. We could also make life span a probabilistic variable rather than something known with certainty.

But the main lesson of the life-cycle hypothesis is clear even in a simple model without these complications: *lifetime earnings,* in this case $3 million, are the determinant of consumption at *each* point of time. The role of current income is that it contributes to one's lifetime earnings, not that it constrains today's consumption possibilities. Imagine, for example, that the agent is a sports star, for whom lifetime income is the same but the trajectory is the opposite of what is pictured in Figure 9.8.[3] Instead of a gradually rising income, this agent's peak income takes place the moment she enters the labor force, and declines gradually until retirement, as in Figure 9.9. If she has the same utility function as the agent depicted in Figure 9.8, she will choose the same consumption profile!

If we now plot either agent's consumption function against income, and superimpose this consumption function on an aggregate consumption function, we have the result depicted in Figure 9.10. Evidently, this is an extreme version of Figure 9.5, for here the family consumption function is flat, a result due, among other things, to the rather extreme assumption of a zero interest rate.[4] According to Modigliani's life-cycle hypothesis, the consumption function based on household budgets reflects the age distribution of the population, with the young and the elderly typically consuming more than they earn, and the middle-aged less.

In the life-cycle model, life-time saving is zero. How then is it possible for aggregate saving to be positive, as the long-run consumption function suggests? There are two possible sources of saving in this model, in the first place, population growth. If there are more thirty-somethings who are earning and saving than are necessary to balance the retired folk who are spending down their previous savings, net saving will be positive. (The dissaving of young adults is a complication, but one that doesn't change the basic picture.) Aggregate saving will be a weighted sum of individual saving distributed along the individual consumption function, with greater weight on savers than on dissavers simply because there are more savers when the population is growing.

The second path to positive saving in the life-cycle model is technological progress. Whatever we assume about how wages are determined, it is reasonable to assume that technological progress raises lifetime earnings. In this

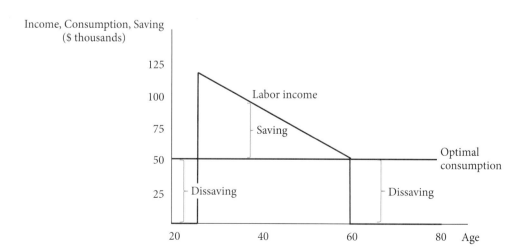

Figure 9.9 A sport star's optimum—according to the life-cycle hypothesis.

case, each cohort has a different consumption function, as in Figure 9.11, and each cohort saves accordingly.

The class of 1955 enters the paid work force in 1955 (at age twenty-five), and the class of 1975 does the same thing in 1975. Assume both cohorts are

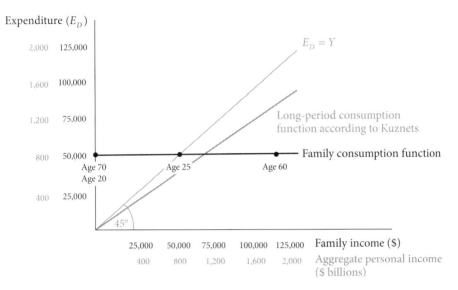

Figure 9.10 Aggregate and family consumption functions according to the life-cycle hypothesis, I.

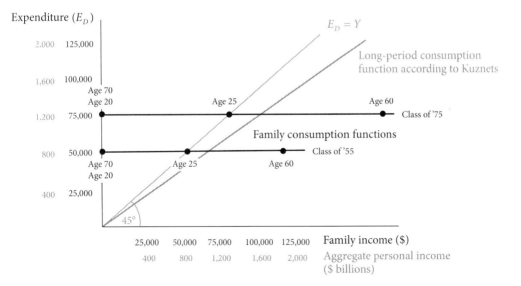

Figure 9.11 Aggregate and family consumption functions according to the life-cycle hypothesis, II.

the same size. In the year 2000, the positive saving of the class of 1975, now fifty years old, is based on a higher level of life-time income and will swamp the dissaving of the retirees of the class of 1955, now age seventy. Without technological progress (or population growth) and higher life-time earnings, earnings at age fifty would, as Figure 9.8 indicates, yield just enough saving to provide for about one year's retirement.

Milton Friedman's permanent-income hypothesis emphasizes a different aspect of lifetime optimization, namely, the difference in the effects on consumption of changes in income that are expected to be permanent from the effects of transitory changes, changes that are expected to be temporary. Friedman (1957) is deliberately vague about the time frame that distinguishes "permanent" from "transitory," but we can illustrate his argument within the life-cycle framework.

What happens to the consumption of the agent whose earnings profile is given in Figures 9.8 or 9.9 if she is laid off for a year at age forty-two?[5] Consumption will take a hit, but only a modest one. If she anticipates the loss, her lost income will be spread out over her entire adult life, so that 1/60 of the loss, approximately $1,500 ($85,714/60 = $1,429) will be felt each year. In Friedman's world, marginal propensities to consume when changes in income are transitory are determined by the ratio of the length of the transitory time period to the length of one's consuming life. In the present case, the one-year marginal propensity to consume is 1/60 when the loss is anticipated. Even If the loss is unanticipated, its effects will still be spread out over time. The optimal response to an unanticipated shortfall (or for that matter windfall) is to spread the effects out over one's *remaining* life span, in this case 37.5 years. Accordingly, the marginal propensity to consume will be 1/37.5.

In Modigliani's telling, the long-period propensity, the propensity to consume over one's whole lifetime, will be one. Friedman, however, is not committed to a lifetime horizon, and, accordingly, the permanent-income hypothesis leaves room for a long-run propensity to consume that is less than one; we can imagine saving taking place to provide for one's heirs, or to build a monument to oneself, or because of the inability to predict when one will die—if an agent is risk averse, she will err on the side of over-providing for her retirement.

In the permanent-income hypothesis, the long-run marginal propensity to consume is relevant for evaluating the impact of short-period changes in income if an unanticipated change in current income leads the agent to change her beliefs about the trajectory her income will follow in the future. If being out of work today leads her to believe she will suffer a permanent decline in income, the ratio of the change in current consumption to the change in current income—the short-run propensity to consume—will increase. If an agent receives an unanticipated increase in income that carries with it the expectation of permanence, as distinct from a windfall in the form of a one-time bonus, optimal consumption planning will lead the agent to spend according to her new evaluation of her long-term resources: her increased spending will be in line with her long-period propensity to consume, not with the short-period propensity associated with transitory income changes.

To see the rationale of distinguishing between permanent and transitory income, assume that five individuals are twenty-five years old and all initially expect to have the income trajectory depicted in Figure 9.8. Anna receives a jolt in the form of a one-year postponement of her starting date and takes a temporary job at half her expected starting salary, $25,000 instead of $50,000. Betsey has to settle for a lower-paying job in her chosen field, with a starting salary of $40,000, and her long-term income prospects fall proportionately. Carrie is luckier: she receives a one-time hiring bonus of $25,000. Delia is luckier still, starting her career at $75,000, which leads her to project higher incomes over her entire working life. Only Ellie is unaffected, remaining on the initial trajectory while all her friends are jostled by the winds of fortune. The position of each woman, in terms of her relationship between consumption and *current* income, is indicated by her initial in Figure 9.12. Anna and Carrie are on a consumption function reflecting transitory departures from the average (Ellie). The consumption function along which Betsey and Delia find themselves, by contrast, reflects changes in permanent income. The transitory-income consumption function evidently corresponds to the individual consumption function in the life-cycle analysis; the permanent-income consumption function corresponds to the aggregate function.

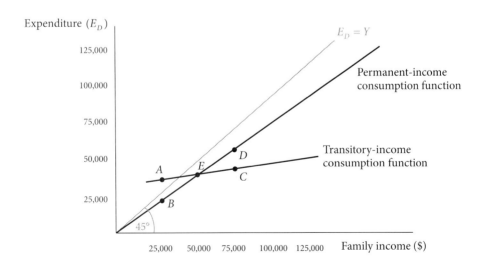

Figure 9.12 Responses to changes in permanent and transitory income.

As far as the aggregate relationship between consumption and income is concerned, individual good and bad luck cancels out, at least so it is assumed. If there are 160 million workers, the equilibrium E will also reflect the relationship between aggregate consumption and aggregate income, measured along the lower scale. For aggregate consumption and income to shift upward over time, we once again have to appeal either to population growth or to technological progress (or both). In this case, the permanent-income consumption function at the individual level coincides with the aggregate-consumption function, with the proviso that the two functions in Figure 9.13 are scaled differently.

The similarities of the two versions of optimal consumption trajectories are more important than the differences. The fundamental assumption is that consumption today (and every day) is based on optimization of long-term utility subject to a long-term resource constraint. This means that current income plays little to no role in determining current consumption, unless changes in current income are taken as harbingers of future changes. That is the key takeaway.

In any case, there is no fundamental incompatibility between the life-cycle and the permanent-income hypotheses. One can believe that the most important reason for saving is to allow for more or less constant consumption even though income varies sharply over one's lifetime, as the life-cycle hypothesis stresses, saving taking place to provide for a comfortable retirement (or to pay

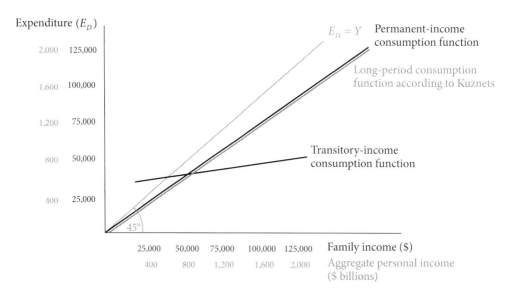

Figure 9.13 Aggregate and family consumption functions according to the permanent-income hypothesis.

off student debt). One can at the same time believe that saving is a shock absorber against unfavorable but transitory hits to income and a rainy-day fund when income gets a temporary boost, which is what the permanent-income hypothesis stresses.

What Accounts for the Triumph of Life-Cycle and Permanent-Income Thinking?

The two hypotheses, permanent income and life cycle, quickly carried the day as far as the economics profession was concerned. And while both have received considerable refinement over the years,[6] the original idea that wealth, not income, drives consumption has not been substantially modified; it remains the basis of mainstream thinking about the consumption function.

One might imagine that the life-cycle and permanent-income hypotheses supplanted the simple Keynesian consumption function because these theories were better at explaining the data. This is only partly true. The common core of these two theories is that they support the phenomenon of consumption smoothing. But other theories that lead to consumption smoothing have fallen by the wayside or never gained traction in the first place. Keynes himself offered reasons why consumption would change less rapidly in the immediate aftermath of an income change and only gradually catch up: in the excerpt from *The General Theory* quoted on the first page of this chapter, Keynes says, "A man's habitual standard of life usually has the first claim on his income."[7] Paul Samuelson echoes Keynes's observation in arguing that

> some time is required [for consumption] to become adjusted to increased levels of income so that in the short run consumption increases less with increased income than it does in the long run, saving taking up the slack. Moreover, when income drops, consumption is maintained at the expense of savings. According to this . . . point of view, the short-run marginal propensity to consume is less than the long-run marginal propensity to consume. (1943, p. 34)

Some years ago I tried to formalize this idea of delayed adjustment in what I called the disequilibrium hypothesis (Marglin 1984, chaps. 17–18; I guess I've always been attracted to disequilibrium). My formalization offered a theoretical argument for the relatively low propensities to consume implicit in family-budget studies—higher-income agents are more likely to be those who are in the process of adjusting to a change for the better in their economic status, and lower-income agents are more likely to be in the process of adjusting downward.

This theory accounted econometrically for the aggregate data at least as well as the life-cycle/permanent-income approach did. No surprise here because the very different theoretical bases of the two approaches are muted once the theories are formulated in a manner suitable for econometric comparisons; approaching the data from the point of view of disequilibrium adjustment and approaching the data on the basis of lifetime earnings or permanent income both lead to estimating equations that are consistent with observed parameter values even while differing radically on how the parameters are understood (see chapter 15). Neither was it surprising that no weakening of support for Modigliani's and Friedman's formulations followed from my efforts or the efforts of others working the same street before me, Tillman Brown (1952) and Hendrik Houthakker and Lester Taylor (1966), to mention only two studies.

The same fate befell theories that started life with more promise by virtue of appearing before there was a life-cycle or permanent-income hypothesis with which to compete. James Duesenberry's relative-income hypothesis (1949) is a case in point. Duesenberry explained the apparent contradiction between cross-sectional (family-budget) data and long time-series (aggregate) data by the role of relative income in determining the proportion of income that agents consume. The pressures to spend on lower-income households are greater not only because of absolute needs that exist independently of what anybody else might be consuming but also because richer individuals determine a standard of life that the relatively poor adopt for the sake of personal dignity. Richer folk, with fewer or no Joneses to keep up with, consume a relatively smaller part of their income.

Duesenberry's ideas took hold when he first published them but were soon eclipsed by Modigliani's and Friedman's. Duesenberry's theory has resurfaced from time to time, for example, in the work of Robert Frank (1999) and Juliet Schor (1998), but it has not challenged the hold of life-cycle and permanent-income reasoning on economists' thinking. As with the disequilibrium hypothesis, I think it's fair to say that the relative failure of relative income is not due to the econometrics.

What then does account for the success of the life-cycle and permanent-income hypotheses? I would argue that the main reason is the fit between these theories and the basic premises of mainstream economics, in particular, the key role of utility maximization subject to a resource constraint as the basis for all action. The attractiveness of these two theories is because of the aid and comfort they offer to the project of assimilating Keynes to mainstream economics and stripping *The General Theory* of its most subversive aspects.

From this perspective, empirical fit, while hardly irrelevant, is not decisive. Indeed, the theoretical apparatus of mainstream economics, in particular the pride of place accorded to the rational, utility-maximizing, agent, is not due to the role of this framework in predicting or accounting for behavior. In the context of so-called positive or descriptive economics, rationality is not so much an incorrect assumption as an irrelevant one. The relevant information about the demand for apples is contained in the demand schedule itself, not in the utility maximization that is supposed to underlie the demand schedule. Utility maximization adds very little empirically, especially once we move from an individual agent to total demand.

The apparatus exists rather to justify a particular, might I say peculiar, penchant of mainstream economics: the separation of efficiency from distribution and the emphasis on efficiency—distributional issues being regarded as political, philosophical, and thus distinguished from the "hard science" of economic efficiency. More specifically, the point is to justify capitalism as a self-regulating economy that maximizes efficiency when left to itself—the very argument that Keynes set out to demolish in *The General Theory*.

I mentioned earlier that the universality of the framework of constrained maximization is part of its appeal. In fact, this universality is an illusion. The model is plausible for pizza and cola because the budget constraint is well-defined—$1,000 per year, thanks to Mom and Dad—and the utility function can be assumed to exist on the basis of early trial and error before the history of rational choice begins.

Neither of these assumptions carries over to the context of long-term consumption planning. Consider the budget constraint, which in the life-cycle version of the story is an agent's lifetime earnings. Even if the agent starts her working life on a well-defined career ladder, how sturdy is the ladder? How high does it go? What if she gets stuck? Or falls off? Layoffs, illness, any number of factors can interfere with the steady progress assumed in Figure 9.8, or the steady decline in Figure 9.9.

Even if a lifetime budget constraint can be assumed, what about the indifference curves? George Akerlof has argued (2007) that the utility function consumers are supposed to maximize leaves out an important consideration, namely, norms of behavior. People save because it is the right thing to do, not because they have maximized a utility function whose arguments are consumption at different points of time. And people consume for the same reason. Adam Smith noted long ago that consumption follows social norms:

> By necessaries I understand, not only the commodities which were indispensably necessary for the support of life, but whatever the custom of the country renders it indecent for creditable people, even of the lowest order, to be without. A linen shirt, for example, is, strictly speaking, not a necessary of life. The Greeks and the Romans lived, I suppose, very comfortably, though they had no linen. But in the present times, through the greater part of Europe, a creditable day-labourer would be ashamed to appear in public

without a linen shirt, the want of which would be supposed to denote that disgraceful degree of poverty, which, it is presumed, no body can well fall into without extreme bad conduct. (1937 [1776], pp. 821–822)

I agree with Akerlof (and Smith) on the importance of norms but doubt that it is illuminating to incorporate norms into the utility function. This smacks of adding epicycles onto the Ptolemaic system. Yes, one can account for the phenomena by means of epicycles, but the fundamental thinking in terms of utility maximization is unaffected. As I argue in *The Dismal Science* (2008, pp. 71–73), an obligation to feed the hungry is fundamentally different from the warm glow you get from the look on a child's face after you have given her an ice-cream cone. Similarly, an obligation to save is different from the maximization of the utility of lifetime consumption.

Additionally, incorporating norms into the utility function reinforces the view that the utility function is a primitive of the argument, a given. This begs an important question. In the pizza-cola context, it is at least plausible to assume a prehistory of trial and error through which agents learn the contours of their utility functions. But what prehistory is available in the context of a lifetime consumption plan? Even believers in reincarnation do not generally believe that we can recall much from our past lives. Norms arguably fill the vacuum.

If norms are internalized cultural presuppositions, there is an obvious link to the social conditioning under which these norms are formed—and an important link from the budget constraint to the utility function. People who learn from experience that foresight pays off are more likely to believe in the virtue of the economist's formulation of consumption choice and to inculcate the virtue of constrained optimization in their offspring. People who learn from experience—the experience of parents, friends, neighbors, as well as their own—that they have little control over their own lives may react by trying obsessively to plan the areas of their lives where they do feel in control. More likely, in my view, they will react, as the origin myth of a weaving caste in the Indian state of Orissa suggests,

Niti araji, niti khāibi (I will earn every day, I will eat every day)
Jalāguḍi bate, bela cāhinbi (I will see the passage of time through the window)
(quoted in Marglin 1990, p. 272)

Different Strokes for Different Folks

Some of the problems articulated here can in theory be remedied, I have suggested, by recasting the framework in terms of probabilities. For instance, instead of lifetime earnings of $3 million, as in Figures 9.8 and 9.9, the individual might think in terms of a one-third probability of earning $2 million, a one-third probability of earning $3 million, and a one-third probability of earning $4 million.

But to think that recasting choice in probabilistic terms can rescue mainstream consumption theory is an illusion. Can people think in probabilistic terms when the uncertainties are enormous and the information sparse? More to the point, *do* people think in these terms? The salient difference between risk and uncertainty, brought to the fore by Frank Knight (1921), is precisely the difference between situations where the agent has enough information to think in probabilistic terms, Knight's risk, and situations more akin to asking the chances of surviving Niagara Falls in a barrel, uncertainty.[8]

No doubt some people do think in probabilities. People whose career paths are reasonably certain, for whom the threats of unemployment and illness are other people's problems (until these threats materialize in their own lives), people who can face the world with the confidence that comes from actually being in control of their own lives (or at least have the illusion of being in control). Duesenberry once quipped that the life-cycle hypothesis is exactly what one would expect from a middle-aged college professor, thus showing that some people's quips are as profound as other people's theories.

In point of fact, it is not only college professors who have a reasonably good idea of their future earnings and may have enough experience to weigh alternative lifetime consumption plans against one another—good enough that the constrained maximization framework of Figure 9.7 makes sense as a way of characterizing choice. Other professional women (and men), even those lacking formal tenure of the kind enjoyed by academics (or at least some of us), might also qualify.

But people lacking employment security and often lacking good health and the means to pay for prolonged illness might easily find rational consumption planning to be a bad joke, especially because their whole lives teach them that they have very limited control over how much they will earn over their lifetimes and, indeed, how much they will earn even over shorter periods that make the distinction between permanent and transitory income meaningful.

And then there are the very rich, the 1 percent upon whom the Occupy movement and the 2016 Democratic primary campaign of Bernie Sanders focused public attention. It is really a stretch to imagine the very rich planning consumption and saving in terms of trade-offs between the future and the present.[9] Once again, a Duesenberry story is apposite. The future Aga Khan once came up to the lectern after a class in which Duesenberry had presented the standard mainstream theory of consumer choice. "Sir," the young prince is reported to have asked, "that was very interesting. But how does it work without the budget constraint?"

A reasonable conclusion is different strokes for different folks: it is a mistake to look for a single explanation of consumption and saving. In the middle, maybe 10 to 25 percent of the population, is a professional class for which the standard mainstream choice model and its life-cycle or permanent-income corollary are a realistic basis on which to understand consumption and saving decisions. Below them on the socioeconomic scale are the vast majority of the population for whom the standard model makes no sense and for whom a simple disequilibrium-adjustment story seems to me to capture the process by which consumption is adjusted to income. For this, the working class, the simple Keynesian short-period consumption function, coupled with a long-term function à la Kuznets, is pretty much all we need, especially since working-class households possess relatively little wealth. At the top of the pyramid is a small class—the proverbial 1 percent. If we are honest, we must admit we know practically nothing about what motivates their consumption and saving decisions.

In the United States, I would suggest a cut-off between the working class and the professional middle class somewhere around $100,000 of family income. According to Emmanuel Saez (2014, slide 7), this cut-off was at approximately the 90th percentile of the income distribution in 2012; for that year, the Bureau of the Census (2019b, table A-2, p. 26) puts the $100,000 cut-off at approximately the 75th percentile. Saez calculates the income share of the segment of the population between the 90th and 99th percentiles at just under 30 percent, and the share of the top 1 percent at just over 20 percent, with an income floor of $400,000. If we use Saez's figure for the top-income share, the Bureau of the Census (2014, table 2, p. 9) data makes the segment between the 75th and 99th percentiles approximately 40 percent of overall income.[10] So the portion of income to which life-cycle/permanent-income logic might apply would be somewhere in the neighborhood of 30 to 40 percent. The rest of the population, those with incomes below $100,000 and those with incomes in excess of $400,000, obey different logics. Some 40 to 50 percent of income accrues to people below the $100,000 threshold, for whom the precariousness of their economic position imposes a different, Keynesian, rationality. Some 20+ percent of income accrues to the top 1 percent, whose affluence also mocks the rationality of the middle class.

The mainstream recognizes that one size does not fit all and that a large part of the population does not act according to any reasonable facsimile of life-cycle or permanent-income models. John Campbell and Greg Mankiw (1989) estimate the proportion of consumption based on wealth constraints and the proportion of consumption based on "rules of thumb," in which income rather than wealth is the driving force. They find the split to be roughly 50–50.

The standard explanation is that these households are "liquidity constrained," meaning that they are unable to access their wealth and convert it into consumption. Such households are perforce limited in their spending by current income and respond to income changes à la Keynes. Twenty-somethings, for example, might wish to draw on future labor income to smooth consumption in the manner of Figures 9.8 and 9.9. If indentured servitude were allowed, future labor income might be the basis for such loans; however, lacking acceptable collateral, these households may not be able to borrow in accordance with their optimal consumption plans.[11] In short, institutional constraints against slavery—a market imperfection if you will—may make it impossible to follow "optimal" consumption plans.

For the mainstream, it is acceptable to argue that agents would like to follow optimal consumption plans but are frustrated by government intervention that makes slavery illegal or tapping into equity difficult. The important point is that agents are *trying* to be good economic men and women. It is less acceptable to argue that agents aren't even trying to be rational, as rational is defined in the economic canon.

There is some hope: behavioral economics has made it possible to think the unthinkable and still be an economist in good standing. But the pace of change is glacial. Behavioral economics may be a big plus in describing economic reality, but it undermines the normative wing of economics, the wing that goes beyond trying to tell it like it is to make arguments that what is is the best of all possible worlds—or would be were it not for frictions and imperfections that can be addressed only by making the world more like the competitive model.

To be sure, what is at stake is not so much the specifics of the consumption function, but the larger issue of how to do macroeconomics. First of all, it doesn't matter very much empirically if we base the consumption function on the inability of consumers to access capital markets rather than on a totally different mindset from that implied by the utility-maximizing framework. Both "imperfections" are undoubtedly at play and reinforce each other rather than acting at cross purposes.

Even to the extent that Modigliani and Friedman got it right, the consequence is merely to reduce the short-term marginal propensity to consume, and thus the multiplier, relative to what might be expected in a Keynesian framework. But this doesn't matter all that much, first because there are more important reasons why multipliers that make sense in the simple Keynesian framework are likely to exaggerate actual multipliers once we factor in salient real-world features of the economy (see chapter 15). Second, the size of the multiplier indicates only the extent to which an initial shock to the economy or a government induced countershock is amplified by the internal workings of the economy. The logic of *The General Theory* does not depend on the size of the multiplier even if the size of the multiplier is critical in evaluating the effects of monetary and fiscal policy.

The Cambridge Saving Theory

Whereas class differences with respect to consumption propensities appeared to Keynes (and to Samuelson) the natural way to explain the cross-sectional evidence that the ratio of consumption to income declines with income, a key result of both life-cycle and permanent-income reasoning is that no such inference should be drawn from these cross-sectional studies. Class may determine the absolute amount of saving, but not the proportion of income saved. Redistribution of income from the rich to the poor (or vice versa) will not have any impact on aggregate demand! For Modigliani, higher savers are ordinary people nearer the peak of their earning power. They are not necessarily richer than anybody else in terms of their lifetime command over resources. For Friedman, higher savers may simply be people enjoying temporary windfalls, for example, farmers who reap bountiful crops while agricultural prices are high. The lean years will follow, just as surely as they did for Pharaoh in the land of Egypt.

An older view of consumption and saving assumed that working people simply lacked the economic capacity to save and that the rich were responsible for whatever saving the community was able to muster. In the nineteenth century, economists were not reluctant to associate the distribution of income with class: capitalists saved a substantial share of their profits, while workers, with meager wages, had all they could do to keep body and soul together. In the book that transformed him from middle-level civil servant to world-renowned public intellectual, *The Economic Consequences of the Peace*, Keynes himself made a class-based argument about saving, attributing the remarkable growth of capital and income between 1870 and World War I to a tacit social bargain that allowed capitalists to call a substantial part of the national product their own—on condition that they plowed it back into capital formation.

The class-based view of saving was revived by Cambridge economists— Nicholas Kaldor (1966), Luigi Pasinetti (1962), and Joan Robinson (1962, 1966)—following the lead of Michał Kalecki (1971 [1933]), whom, as noted on p. 235, some also credit with anticipating the essentials of *The General Theory*. In the simplest form of the "Cambridge saving theory," saving is proportional to total profit, $S = s_\pi \Pi$, s_π representing capitalists' propensity to save and Π total profits. Saving is now proportional to the rate of profit r since $\Pi = rK$, and in the short run K is given:

$$S = s_\pi r K.$$

The AD schedule is now defined by

$$I(\rho) = s_\pi rK.$$

We have

$$rK = Y - \left(\frac{P}{W}\right)^{-1} L,$$

and the equilibrium in $r \times I$ space that defines the AD schedule in the second quadrant of Figure 9.14 is unique. But in the space of $I \times Y$, for any given real price (P/W) there are in general two points at which saving and investment are equal. Observe that all the equilibria in the first quadrant correspond to the same rate of profit and the same rate of saving and investment: Y_1 and Y_4 are points where desired saving and investment are equal at the price level $(P/W)_2$, Y_2 and Y_3 with $(P/W) = (P/W)_1$. Multiple equilibria arise because at a given price level profits and therefore saving rise as long as the marginal productivity of labor exceeds the real wage, and then fall, while (in this simple case) investment demand is constant.

Figure 9.15 shows the implications for aggregate demand. For relatively high real prices, like $(P/W)_2$ and $(P/W)_1$, the two intersections of the desired-saving schedule and the desired-investment schedule in Figure 9.15(a) translate into two points on the AD schedule in Figure 9.15(b). At a low price, like $(P/W)_0$, there is no level of output that generates profit sufficient to balance the desired level of investment.

Observe that the GS schedule goes through the minimum point of the AD schedule. This is because, for any given real price, maximum saving corresponds to the point of profit maximization, which in turn defines the GS schedule. At the minimum of the AD schedule, there is only one level of output—namely, the profit-maximizing level—that generates enough profit and saving to cover the given amount of desired investment.

Class-based saving requires us to revisit the analysis of equilibrium. With flexprice adjustment, the story changes very little. In Figure 9.16, the logic of the equilibrium at E is the same as the logic laid out in chapter 6. The arrows indicate disequilibrium trajectories of real price and output.

The story changes somewhat more in a fixprice regime. There are now, as in Figure 9.17, two equilibria. But only the equilibrium at E is stable. If we start to the right of E', investment demand exceeds saving, and the economy is pushed further to the right. If we start to the left of E', saving exceeds investment, and the economy moves to the left.

There is also the possibility of an inflationary equilibrium, in which pressure in the labor market drives wages up, and producers find themselves in the happy position of too much demand, to which they respond directly (the

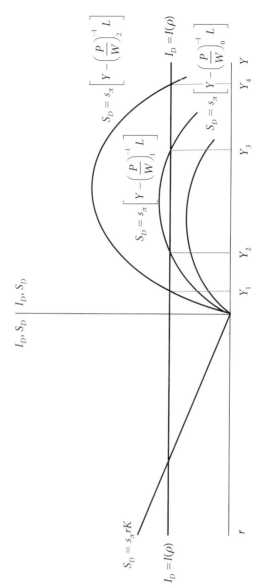

Figure 9.14 Aggregate demand determined by propensities to save and invest.

(a) Investment and saving holding real-price constant

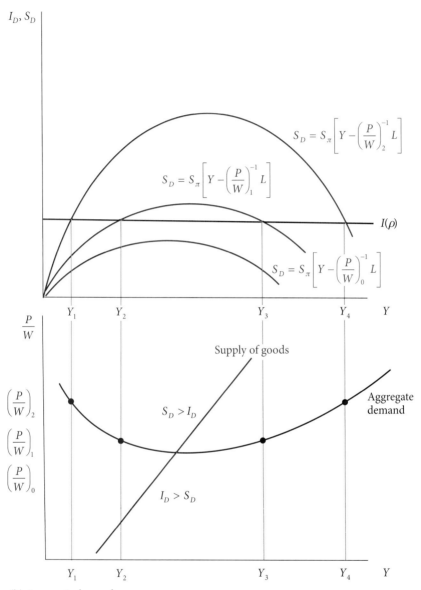

(b) Aggregate demand

Figure 9.15 Aggregate demand.

flexprice case) or indirectly (under a fixprice regime) by raising prices. The flexprice equilibrium in Figure 9.18 is stable regardless of adjustment speeds, whereas the fixprice equilibrium E in Figure 9.19 is stable only if prices and wages adjust faster than output. As in Figure 9.17, E' in Figure 9.19 is unstable. North- and southeast of E', the arrows take the economy to the east, further and further from E'. North- and southwest of E', the economy moves toward E. (See the mathematical appendix to this chapter for proofs.)[12]

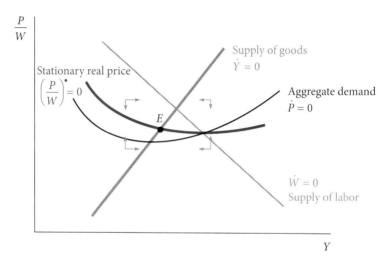

Figure 9.16 Equilibrium with saving determined by the Cambridge saving theory: flexprice adjustment.

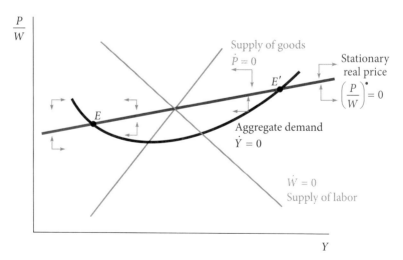

Figure 9.17 Equilibrium with saving determined by the Cambridge saving theory: fixprice adjustment.

In more general forms of the Cambridge saving theory, both capitalists and workers save, but their propensities to save are different, capitalists saving the fraction s_π, and workers saving the fraction s_w, with $s_\pi > s_w$. After some years of oblivion, this more general model may once again become relevant as a result of Thomas Piketty's (and his less well-known colleagues') investigations into inequality and its causes (Piketty 2014): Piketty's argument that the long-run tendency of capitalism is to produce greater and greater inequality is

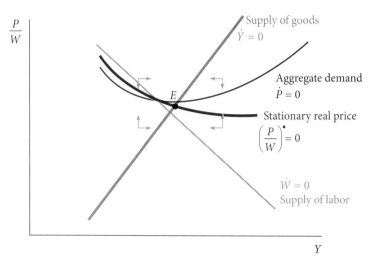

Figure 9.18 Inflationary equilibrium with saving determined by the Cambridge saving theory: flexprice adjustment.

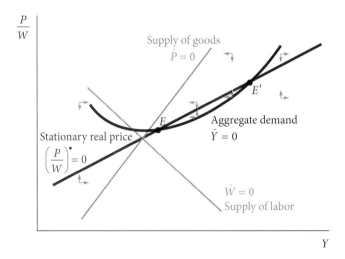

Figure 9.19 Inflationary equilibrium with saving determined by the Cambridge saving theory: fixprice adjustment.

made in the context of a two-class model in which there is saving both from capital income and labor income, that is, from profits and wages.[13]

I address this question in the mathematical appendix to chapter 18. The empirical richness of Piketty's *Capital in the Twenty-First Century* is well worth the price of admission. But Piketty's claims about the relationship between growth and distribution should be the beginning rather than the end of the discussion about inequality.

Conclusions

Wealth matters in the determination of consumption. Nobody disputes that. But to replace income by wealth as the most important determinant of consumption is, to say the least, an overreaction to the oversimplification of Keynes's argument in *The General Theory*. Even the mainstream is on board with this conclusion, although its path to a realistic assessment is made torturous by its insistence on liquidity constraints as the primary reason for income to play the primary role in the determination of consumption à la Keynes. This is a self-inflicted torture, one made necessary by the mainstream's allegiance to the utility-maximizing framework of the rational consumer, an allegiance in turn justified by the commitment to the idea that markets are efficient.

The path of wisdom is to acknowledge that one size does not fit all. A wealth-centered theory combining insights of the permanent-income and life-cycle hypotheses may be a good basis for understanding the consumption behavior of a minority that we can characterize as middle-class professionals—doctors, lawyers, academics, and the middle range of managers and technocrats in both the private and the public sectors.

The vast majority, what was once called the working class, is better characterized by a much simpler model, in which liquidity constraints play a role, but a supporting role. This class is driven by the uncertainty that surrounds both the intertemporal budget constraint and the intertemporal utility function, which makes it highly irrational to allow life-cycle or permanent-income considerations to dominate decision making. Instead, the majority operates according to simple rules of thumb that make income rather than wealth the most important variable driving consumption.

And then there are the rich and the super rich, the 1 percent. The fact is that we know almost nothing about what drives the consumption and saving decisions of this element of society. This gap in our knowledge would matter little were it not for the disproportionate amount of saving done by the 1 percent.

The one conclusion of the permanent-income and life-cycle hypotheses that can be most firmly rejected is the proposition that the long-run saving propensity is constant over the entire population, that rich and poor save the same proportions of their permanent or lifetime incomes. The contrary view is the basis of the Cambridge saving theory, which revives the nineteenth-century idea that saving comes disproportionately from the income of the rich, in a capitalist world from profits. For navigating the complexities of saving in a capitalist economy, the two-class model is a better vehicle than the mainstream vehicle of the representative consumer. The meaning of the working class in the context of two-class models may be different from its classical meaning in the works of Smith, Ricardo, and Marx, but the basic structure of the models does not change. Thanks to Thomas Piketty and his collaborators these models may come back into favor.

The new element in the story is the Cambridge saving theory. We now have flexprice adjustment characterized by the equations

$$\frac{\left(\dfrac{P}{W}\right)^{\bullet}}{\dfrac{P}{W}} = \theta_1 \left[I(\rho) - s_\pi \left(Y - \left(\frac{P}{W}\right)^{-1} L \right) \right] - \theta_3 \left[Y - LS\left(\frac{P}{W}\right) \right], \quad (9.1)$$

$$\dot{Y} = \theta_2 \left(\frac{P}{W} - F_L^{-1} \right). \quad (9.2)$$

The Jacobian is

$$J = \begin{bmatrix} -\theta_1 s_\pi \left(\dfrac{P}{W}\right)^{-2} L + \theta_3 LS' & -\theta_1 s_\pi \left(1 - \dfrac{\left(\dfrac{P}{W}\right)^{-1}}{F_L} \right) - \theta_3 \\ \theta_2 \left(\dfrac{P}{W}\right) & -\theta_2 (GS')^{-1} \end{bmatrix},$$

$$= \begin{bmatrix} -\theta_1 s_\pi \left(\dfrac{P}{W}\right)^{-2} L + \theta_3 LS' & -\theta_3 \\ \theta_2 \left(\dfrac{P}{W}\right) & -\theta_2 (GS')^{-1} \end{bmatrix},$$

since, by virtue of equation (9.2), $1 - (P/W)^{-1}/F_L$ vanishes in the neighborhood of equilibrium. We thus have $tr\, J < 0$ and $det\, J > 0$, so the equilibrium in both Figure 9.16 and Figure 9.18 is stable.

Fixprice dynamics are a bit more complicated. We have

$$\frac{\left(\dfrac{P}{W}\right)^{\bullet}}{\dfrac{P}{W}} = -\theta_1 \left[GS\left(\frac{P}{W}\right) - Y \right] - \theta_3 \left[Y - LS\left(\frac{P}{W}\right) \right], \quad (9.3)$$

$$\dot{Y} = \theta_2 \left[I(\rho) - s_\pi \left(Y - \left(\frac{P}{W} \right)^{-1} L \right) \right], \tag{9.4}$$

and the Jacobian is

$$J = \begin{bmatrix} -\theta_1 GS' + \theta_3 LS' & \theta_1 - \theta_3 \\ -\theta_2 s_\pi \left(\frac{P}{W} \right)^{-2} L & -\theta_2 s_\pi \left(1 - \dfrac{\left(\frac{P}{W} \right)^{-1}}{F_L} \right) \end{bmatrix}.$$

To the left of the intersection of the AD and GS schedules,

$$1 - \frac{\left(\frac{P}{W} \right)^{-1}}{F_L} > 0,$$

so $tr\, J$ is unambiguously negative. Provided $\theta_1 > \theta_3$, as in Figure 9.17, $det\, J > 0$, so that the equilibrium E is stable.

To the right of the intersection of the AD and GS schedules, the sign of $tr\, J$ depends on the speed of adjustment of prices and wages relative to the speed of adjustment of output. If θ_1 and θ_3 are large compared to θ_2, then $tr\, J$ will be negative despite the fact that $1 - (P/W)^{-1}/F_L$ is negative. With $\theta_1 > \theta_3$, $det\, J$ is positive if and only if the slope of the stationary-price locus (relative to the Y-axis) exceeds the slope of the AD schedule, which is to say,

$$\frac{\theta_1 - \theta_3}{\theta_1 GS' - \theta_3 LS'} > -\frac{\left(1 - \dfrac{\left(\frac{P}{W} \right)^{-1}}{F_L} \right)}{\left(\frac{P}{W} \right)^{-2} L}. \tag{9.5}$$

This explains why in Figure 9.19 E is stable, and why E' is unstable in both Figure 9.17 and Figure 9.19.

Observe that the condition $det\, J > 0$ precludes a stable inflationary equilibrium if wages adjust faster than prices. If $\theta_3 > \theta_1$, then the inequality (9.5) can't possibly hold, since the left-hand side is negative while the right-hand side is positive.

— 10 —

INVESTMENT

The level of output and employment as a whole depends on the amount of investment. I put it in this way, not because this is the only factor on which aggregate output depends, but because it is usual in a complex system to regard as the *causa causans* that factor which is most prone to sudden and wide fluctuation.

—JOHN MAYNARD KEYNES

In *The General Theory,* and in the macroeconomics that *The General Theory* spawned, investment means the commitment of abstract purchasing power to specific physical forms—plant, equipment, houses, infrastructure. It is that commitment that conceptually distinguishes investment from saving. In contrast with investment, saving constitutes *withholding* a commitment, namely, the commitment of resources to consumption.[1]

Though investment and saving are conceptually distinct, actual saving and actual investment are always equal, at least in a simple economy with no government expenditures and revenues and no foreign trade. The resources withheld from consumption are always equal to the commitment of resources to investment, provided we include the accumulation of inventories of final goods and goods in process as part of investment whether or not this accumulation is intended or is instead the result of a miscalculation on the part of producers. This is why saving and investment in national-income accounts are always equal, except for statistical errors that arise because of the different ways that realized investment and saving are measured.

Intended investment and saving are another matter. There is no reason why investment desires and saving desires should always coincide. This is especially the case in fractional-reserve banking systems: when banks can create claims on resources, investment does not depend on prior decisions about saving. Nonetheless, a condition of equilibrium between income and expenditure (again, absent government and foreign trade) is that desired saving and desired investment equal each other. That is, the amount of resources agents

Portions of this chapter were previously published in *The Dismal Science: How Thinking Like an Economist Undermines Community* (Cambridge, Mass.: Harvard University Press, 2008).

collectively wish to withhold from consumption and the amount they wish to commit to specific capital goods must be equal. Say's Law holds that this equality is true regardless of the level of income and output. In *The General Theory* this equality is the condition that defines the AD schedule.

This chapter is concerned with how the amount of resources people wish to commit to specific capital goods, how investment demand, is determined. The first question perhaps is why the demand for investment, the flow of new capital goods, attracts our attention (or Keynes's) at all. Why not focus on capital as a stock?

If capital were Lego sets and could be dismantled and put together in new forms at low cost, the action would be in a market for *stocks* of capital, not in a market for *flows* of investment. Each firm could adjust its capital stock as easily as it can adjust, or at least is assumed to be able to adjust, its labor force. The demand for *capital* would be determined by its marginal-productivity schedule, and the intersection with today's supply schedule would determine the current marginal productivity and *the* interest rate—in a world of Legos, the focus would be on short-run rates, because specific capital goods would exist only so long as these particular forms of capital are profitable for their owners.

This would still leave open the question of how the pace of capital accumulation is determined. In Lego world, today's investment demand would be infinitely elastic at an interest rate equal to today's level of the marginal productivity of capital. Logically, the rate of capital-stock growth must then be determined by the supply of saving.

This is precisely the model that Paul Samuelson proposed in the various editions of his elementary text, *Economics,* from the 1950s to the 1980s (I have consulted the second, third, and the eleventh—the last he authored by himself). In the eleventh edition he writes that net investment ceases when the interest rate is "low enough to choke off all desire to save, . . . low enough to make the community's average propensity to consume equal to 100 percent of income" (1980, p. 562).

As we shall see in chapter 17, this is also the model implicit in the canonical Solow growth model (1956). Observe that in the absence of any role for investment demand, there is no question of expenditure differing from income. We are back in the Garden of Eden with Jean-Baptiste Say.

Implicit in *The General Theory* view of investment demand as the critical element in determining the level of aggregate output is what I believe to be the correct intuition: that for the most part, once resources are committed to specific capital goods, these resources are frozen in place, a conception of the relationship between capital and investment captured by the ideas of vintage capital, irreversible investment, and putty-clay. In this view, investment is necessary for innovation as well as expansion. Indeed, any new product or new method, as well as additions to output, require a new commitment of resources to specific capital goods rather than simply a rearrangement of existing pieces of a Lego set.

This does not preclude markets in secondhand capital goods, nor does it preclude markets for financial assets—stocks, bonds, and the like—that correspond, at least dimensionally, to the agglomerations of capital goods. But, for the most part—we will consider exceptions down the road—the market in secondhand capital goods falls far short of what would be needed to make the world conform to the model of Lego capital. And the market for financial assets resembles a market for capital goods only dimensionally in that it is a market for stocks (like capital) rather than a market for flows (like investment). Indeed, when Keynes rejected the idea that interest rates are determined by demand and supply in a market for investment and saving, he carefully avoided any suggestion that interest rates are determined in *capital* markets understood as markets for physical capital goods. Rather

> The rate of interest is not the "price" which brings into equilibrium the demand for resources to invest with the readiness to abstain from present consumption. It is the "price" which equilibrates *the desire to hold wealth in the form of cash with the available quantity of cash.* (*The General Theory,* p. 167; emphasis added)

Investment, in this view, is the way agents compensate for the missing market, the one in which the price of capital—the interest rate—is theoretically determined by the demand for and supply of capital goods. This market is not temporarily absent without leave because of frictions or imperfections; it is permanently missing because the very nature of capital goods makes it extremely difficult to transform clay back into putty.

This said, in many ways the theory of investment is the least original element of *The General Theory.* Keynes builds up a demand schedule for investment, or more precisely, for the resources that investment requires, by assuming there exists an array of discrete projects offering higher or lower returns. In this, he follows Marshall and, even more closely, Irving Fisher. In the simplest case, projects offer a perpetual and constant annual return, net of operating costs, repairs, and maintenance. It simplifies the argument further, without any loss of generality, to assume that all projects entail the same original commitment, say, one dollar. In this case, projects can be ranked by their annual return, and the schedule in Figure 10.1 reflects, on the horizontal axis, the amount of investment yielding at least as much as the interest rate specified on the vertical axis. For example, the diagram says there are 100 one-dollar projects yielding at least ρ_0. At a level of investment of 100, ρ_0 is

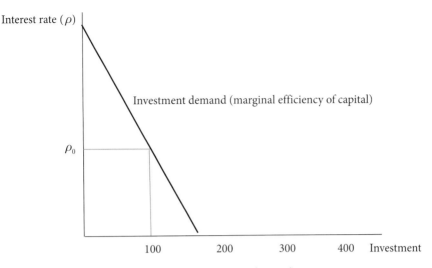

Figure 10.1 Investment demand.

Keynes's *marginal efficiency of capital,* though it would be more accurate to refer to ρ_0 as the marginal efficiency of *investment.*

The MEC schedule becomes an investment-demand schedule if we treat the vertical axis as the independent variable measuring a hurdle rate of interest. If the alternative to investing in the real economy of plant, equipment, infrastructure, houses is assumed to be holding a financial asset, the hurdle rate of interest is the return available in asset markets on securities with a pattern of returns comparable to the array of investment projects (and with the same degree of uncertainty). In the present case, the hurdle rate is the coupon yield on private-sector consols, bonds offering a perpetual fixed payment with no redemption date, with a default risk comparable to the probability of failure of potential investment projects. In the twenty-first century, preferred stock is the closest real-world analog of such obligations.

Suppose that the consol yield is ρ. Anyone with access to the array of projects whose returns are represented by the schedule in Figure 10.1 then has a choice between placing his one dollar in a consol yielding $\$\rho$ per year or undertaking a physical investment costing one dollar. How much investment will these agents undertake? If they are optimizing, they will choose projects for which the annual return exceeds the opportunity cost, which is to say projects for which the quasi-rent, q, the return net of variable costs for labor and other inputs associated with the project, is greater than (or, at the margin, equal to) ρ.

When $\rho = \rho_0$, all projects represented in the part of the MEC schedule lying above ρ_0 pass the test, so investment demand is 100. The MEC schedule, $I(\rho)$, is thus the bridge between the nominal economy of financial assets and the real economy of production, consumption, and investment.

Durability and the Elasticity of Investment Demand

What determines the slope of $I(\rho)$? Part of the answer, which is important for how the effects of monetary policy are distributed among various sectors of the economy, is investment durability. In this respect, investment in plant and equipment is no different from consumer durables. A sensible consumer will pay much less attention to the rate of interest on a car loan than she will to the rate of interest on a home mortgage.

Similarly for business: the rate of interest looms larger the more durable is a project. When a company is deciding whether or not to replace its employees' laptops, which might last for three years, the interest rate will not play much of a role in the decision. A decision about a new office building or new railway track, expected to last for thirty, forty, or more years, is exceedingly sensitive to the rate of interest.

We can formalize this intuition by assuming that instead of lasting forever, projects are "one-hoss shays" that operate for a finite amount of time and then collapse into worthless heaps of junk.[2] Assume as well that these investments, like perpetuities, throw off constant cash flows (net of all operating and maintenance costs). Instead of being equal to the hurdle rate, as is the case for perpetuities, this net cash flow now has to exceed the hurdle rate to allow for amortization of the cost of the investment. In place of the requirement for a perpetuity, $q - \rho > 0$, the project has to yield a discounted present value

$$Q = q\sum_{1}^{m}(1 + \rho)^{-\tau} = \frac{q}{\rho}\left[1 - (1 + \rho)^{-m}\right]$$

in excess of one dollar, the capital cost of the project. (The rate of return of a project is the value of ρ for which $Q = 1$.) The condition for an investment to be worthwhile, $Q > 1$, is equivalent to

$$q - \frac{\rho}{1 - (1 + \rho)^{-m}} > 0.$$

This formula generalizes the condition

$$q - \rho > 0$$

for projects that return q in perpetuity.

Since $[1 - (1 + \rho)^{-m}]$ increases as m increases, the required excess of the quasi-rent over the hurdle rate varies inversely with the durability of the investment. Table 10.1 compares the cash flow required to cover interest and principal when these charges are blended into a level payment for projects of different durabilities that require the same initial outlay of one dollar. For a three-year project, the required cash flow per dollar of investment changes modestly, from $0.33 to $0.40, as the hurdle rate varies from 0 to 10 percent, that is, by less than 25 percent. For longer-lived projects, the percentage change is much greater, more than 60 percent for the ten-year project, and 300 percent for the thirty-year project. (The absolute change in the quasi-rent is similar in the three cases, close to $0.07.) The impact on investment demand is pictured in Figure 10.2, which shows investment-demand schedules corresponding to the project durabilities in Table 10.1, with a perpetual return as a benchmark. (Figure 10.2 normalizes the amount of investment in projects of different durability so that for each class there are 1,000 units of investment when the hurdle rate is 0.01.)

The importance of durability in determining the interest elasticity of in-

Table 10.1 Required Quasi-Rent in Relation to Project Durability and Hurdle Rate

		Durability		
		3	10	30
	0.0	0.333	0.1	0.033
Hurdle Rate	0.05	0.367	0.13	0.065
	0.1	0.402	0.163	0.106

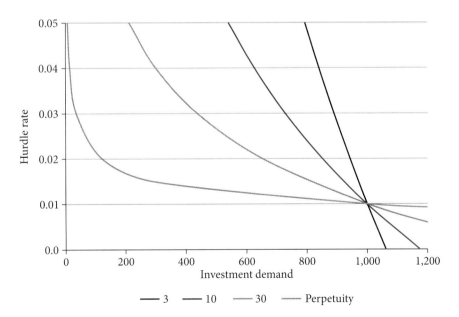

Figure 10.2 Investment demand for projects of varying durability (years).

vestment demand provides an important clue to how monetary policy operates, at least how it works through the interest-rate channel. Because changing the hurdle rate of interest disproportionately affects potential investment with a long pay-out period, monetary policy has historically focused on stimulating or contracting residential construction—housing being among the longest lived in the array of potential investment projects. The overreliance on monetary policy to bring the economy out of the recession of 2001 contributed to the housing boom of the first decade of this century. And this boom was the proximate cause of the financial crisis of 2008 and the ensuing recession.

Make vs. Buy and Tobin's Q

There is another way to look at investment decisions. According to William Brainard and James Tobin (1968, p. 104), "Investment is stimulated when capital is valued more highly in the market than it costs to produce it, and discouraged when its valuation is less than its replacement cost." At one level, the ratio of the value of new capital to its cost of production, which has been enshrined in the literature as Tobin's Q, contains no new information. If we continue to think in terms of projects with a capital cost of one dollar each, with Q the discounted present value of the quasi-rents, then the investment is profitable if $Q > 1$, and is unprofitable if $Q < 1$. But this is precisely the same information on which the investment-demand schedules in Figures 10.1 and 10.2 are based.

If this were all there were to Tobin's Q, no one would find very much value added in the concept. But Brainard and Tobin intend something more. Instead of a comparison of returns to a prospective project and its costs, they have in mind a *market* valuation of capital goods versus the cost of producing capital goods. This is an idea that Keynes had toyed with in his response to a symposium organized by the *Quarterly Journal of Economics* shortly after the publication of *The General Theory*:

> Capital-assets are capable, in general, of being newly produced. The scale on which they are produced depends, of course, on the relation between their costs of production and the prices which they are expected to realize in the market. Thus if the level of the rate of interest taken in conjunction with opinions about their prospective yield raise the prices of capital-assets, the volume of current investment (meaning by this the value of the output of newly produced capital-assets) will be increased; while if, on the other hand, these influences reduce the prices of capital-assets, the volume of current investment will be diminished. (1937a, pp. 217–218)

Lego capital offers an extreme version, in which the existence of a market for capital goods vitiates the idea of a downward-sloping investment demand. This idea evidently had some appeal for Tobin: his classic paper (1969, sec. 6) models a long run in which $Q = 1$ holds as an equilibrium condition, which makes sense for Lego capital. By contrast, in the short run, there are impediments to equating the cost of capital goods with their market values, and this discrepancy drives investment.

The original Brainard–Tobin model is more expansive. Instead of applying the theory at the level of individual capital goods, Brainard and Tobin apply Q to an ensemble of capital goods that constitutes an entire company:

> One of the basic theoretical propositions motivating the model is that the market valuation of equities, relative to the replacement cost of the physical assets they represent, is the major determinant of new investment. (Brainard and Tobin 1968, pp. 103–104)

Again, Keynes had had the same idea:

> The daily revaluations of the Stock Exchange, though they are primarily made to facilitate transfers of old investments between one individual and another, inevitably exert a decisive influence on the rate of current investment. For there is no sense in building up a new enterprise at a cost greater than that at which a similar existing enterprise can be purchased; whilst there is an inducement to spend on a new project what may seem an extravagant sum, if it can be floated off on the Stock Exchange at an immediate profit. Thus certain classes of investment are governed by the average expectation of those who deal on the Stock Exchange as revealed in the price of shares, rather than by the genuine expectations of the professional entrepreneur. (*The General Theory*, p. 151)

In this formulation, Q no longer represents the investor's calculation of the present value of a stream of future returns. It is now a market valuation of this stream, as reflected in the price of the shares of the company that owns a particular ensemble of capital goods. If you are thinking of entering an industry, one option is to buy up all the shares of XYZ, an existing company in the field. The other is to launch a whole new enterprise. If we normalize the cost of building new at one dollar, and the cost of the shares of XYZ as Q, we are formally in the same place: $Q > 1$ is the signal to invest, that is, to build new; $Q < 1$ is the signal not to invest, but to buy an existing company instead.

This decision is different from the decision that has engaged our attention until now. It is no longer a choice between undertaking a project or placing the same purchasing power in the market for financial assets. The choice now is to make or buy physical assets, with "make" implying a decision to undertake investment and "buy" representing a decision to take over an existing company.

There are certainly examples of this logic at work. When Microsoft finally looked at the search-engine business, it had the choice of acquiring an existing business or starting from scratch. In the event, neither option proved profitable because the Google train had long since left the station. When Amazon decided to enter the food-distribution business, it could have started from scratch to build a new supermarket chain. It decided instead to acquire Whole Foods.

In this world, the driving force of investment is the stock market. As Brainard and Tobin put it, and as subsequent commentators have understood the meaning of Q, "Investment is encouraged when the market yield on equity . . . is low relative to the real returns to physical investment (1968, p. 104)." A stock market boom stimulates investment because investment becomes cheaper than acquisition. By the same token, a slump makes investment less attractive because companies now become dirt cheap.

But is buying as realistic as the Brainard–Tobin version of Q-theory assumes? The question is how representative is Microsoft's choice about how to get into the search-engine business, or Amazon's choice about how to learn the ropes of the grocery business. The econometric evidence is mixed, researchers finding a strong influence of the stock market on investment or none, according to how they specify the model. My own view is that a coherent business strategy normally is not, and cannot be, pursued by acquisition; investment is the principal means by which new processes, methods, and products, as well as additional capacity to produce existing goods, are introduced. Investment is the way an actual economy compensates for the absence of a market in capital goods. The absence of this market, it bears repeating, is not the result of imperfections and frictions and thus cannot be brought into existence by the magic transition from the short run to the long run.

There are important exceptions. Warren Buffett's Berkshire Hathaway is one, perhaps *the* exception par excellence. Buffett apart, housing is an entire sector where making and buying are real options. New and existing homes are not perfect substitutes for one another but are close enough to make Q-theory relevant. And in fact, as a ratio of the value of residential housing to its replacement cost, Tobin's Q, correlates closely with residential construction, at least since the mid-1990s. Figure 10.3 shows the data from the early 1950s to 2019. Q-theory works here because it is applied to individual capital assets: when home prices are high relative to construction costs, new home construction is very profitable and the industry booms. When housing prices come down, residential construction comes down too.

We now have a second possible interest-rate channel through which mon-

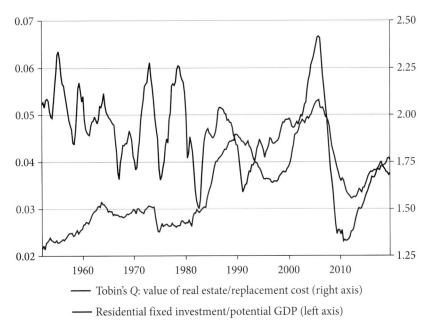

Figure 10.3 Tobin's *Q* and residential construction (1952–2019). *Sources:* BEA, Board of Governors, CBO. myf.red/g/pYZn

etary policy might drive the demand for residential construction. Prices of existing homes are sensitive to interest rates because of their durability, and new construction is sensitive to the price of existing homes relative to new construction. The idea, in other words, is that interest rates drive *Q*.[3]

Capital Widening vs. Capital Deepening

In chapters 3 to 9, and up to now in this chapter, investment demand depends only on the rate of interest. But I noted in chapter 3 that the effect on investment demand of the real price *P/W* would be addressed in due course. "Due course" is now.

The responsiveness of investment demand, and hence aggregate demand, to the real-price level—and hence to the distribution of income between profits and wages—depends on what kind of investment one has in mind, and the predominance of different kinds of investment will vary with the cycle. The first type is investment that adds to productive capacity, capital widening in an older literature.[4] For this type of investment, chapter 5 gives us a way of thinking about the decision that goes beyond a simple comparison of the anticipated return with the hurdle rate. There we explored how producers are guided by two different signals from the market, one about how quickly goods are moving off the shelves, the other about the profitability of selling more goods. The same two signals can be assumed to be at work in investment decisions. Capacity utilization provides information about how likely it is that additional goods will find a market. The more production presses on capacity, the more likely it is that new capacity can be profitably deployed. The real price provides additional information, information about how profitable additional production will be if it can be sold. This, as we shall see in chapters 18 and 19, is the type of investment on which growth models, including my own (Marglin 1984, chap. 20; Marglin and Bhaduri 1990; Bhaduri and Marglin 1990), typically have focused.

There is another kind of investment, investment that substitutes capital for labor (or other inputs), capital deepening. Capital deepening differs from capital widening in two ways. First, it is in principle less susceptible to the state of the market, to whether goods are moving quickly or slowly. The point of capital deepening is to cut costs, not to bring more goods to market; so its profitability does not depend on a growing demand. Second, since the name of the game is cutting costs, the higher the real wage (the lower the real price), the more profitable is capital substitution.

To capture the difference between these two basic types of investment, consider investment profitability in a highly simplified world in which capital is infinitely durable. The quasi-rent is the difference between (1) the gross return (equal to the sum of the marginal productivity of capital and the output attributable to any associated change in employment) and (2) the wages associated with the change in employment. The net return per unit of investment ($\Delta K = 1$) is the quasi-rent less the annual interest cost:[5]

$$q - \rho = MP_K + MP_L \frac{\Delta L}{\Delta K} - \left(\frac{P}{W}\right)^{-1} \frac{\Delta L}{\Delta K} - \rho.$$

In the mainstream conception of equilibrium, the above expression vanishes: the marginal productivity of capital (MP_K) is equal to the interest rate (ρ), and the marginal productivity of labor (MP_L) is equal to the real wage (W/P). In this book, there is no mechanism that brings capital productivity and the interest rate into equality once we leave the world of Lego capital. Moreover, the marginal productivity of labor and the real wage are equal only at a flexprice equilibrium. Otherwise, the change in labor input (ΔL) shows up in both the return and the cost of the investment, which is why the real price has opposite effects on capital widening and capital deepening.

For capital widening the generic formula for $q - \rho$ above becomes

$$q - \rho = \Omega(Y)\left(MP_K + MP_L \frac{\Delta L}{\Delta K} - \left(\frac{P}{W}\right)^{-1} \frac{\Delta L}{\Delta K}\right) - \rho,$$

where $\Omega(Y)$ is a parameter that varies from 0 to 1 as Y increases, the value of Ω reflecting the confidence that business has in its ability to sell additional output. If we assume that for capital widening the incremental labor:capital ratio is the current average labor:capital ratio,

$$\frac{\Delta L}{\Delta K} = \frac{L}{K},$$

we can rewrite the net return per unit of investment as

$$q - \rho = \left[\Omega(Y) \left(MP_K + MP_L \frac{L}{K} - \left(\frac{P}{W} \right)^{-1} \frac{L}{K} \right) - \rho \right].$$

With constant returns to scale

$$MP_K + MP_L \frac{L}{K} = \frac{Y}{K}$$

so

$$q = \Omega(Y) \left[\frac{Y}{K} - \left(\frac{P}{W} \right)^{-1} \frac{L}{K} \right] = \Omega(Y)r,$$

which is to say that the anticipated quasi-rent becomes the existing profit rate, r, multiplied by the probability of selling the additional goods, $\Omega(Y)$. The net annual return is

$$q - r = \Omega(Y)r - \rho.$$

For capital deepening, we assume that output is unchanged, which is to say,

$$MP_K \Delta K + MP_L \Delta L = 0,$$

so that

$$\frac{\Delta L}{\Delta K} = - \frac{MP_K}{MP_L}.$$

In this case the net annual return is

$$q - \rho = - \left(\frac{P}{W} \right)^{-1} \frac{\Delta L}{\Delta K} - \rho = \left(\frac{P}{W} \right)^{-1} \frac{MP_K}{MP_L} - \rho.$$

The quasi-rent q is the annual saving in wages, $-(W/P)\Delta L$, per unit of investment, ΔK. Since the amount of labor displaced by a unit of additional capital, $-\Delta L/\Delta K$, is equal to the inverse ratio of the respective marginal productivities, MP_K/MP_L, the quasi-rent increases with Y and decreases with (P/W).

In a world of perfect certainty, or in a world of Lego capital, where capital can be reshaped as new information becomes available, an excess of the quasi-rent over and above the hurdle rate of interest, $q - \rho > 0$, would call forth investment until the ratio MP_K/MP_L falls to the point at which $q - \rho = 0$. But in an uncertain world in which investment is irreversible, the most that we can assume is that investment demand is an increasing function of the annual return, $\psi(q - \rho)$. In this case the demand for capital-widening investment is

$$I\left(\frac{P}{W}, \rho\right) = \psi\,(q - \rho) = \psi\left(\Omega(Y)\left[\frac{Y}{K} - \left(\frac{P}{W}\right)^{-1}\frac{L}{K}\right] - \rho\right),$$

and the demand for capital deepening is

$$I\left(\frac{P}{W}, \rho\right) = \psi(q - \rho) = \psi\left(\left(\frac{P}{W}\right)^{-1}\frac{MP_K}{MP_L} - \rho\right).$$

In consequence, *the AD schedule is no longer vertical* in the space of real price and output even if we hold ρ constant. Its slope depends on the mix of the two kinds of investment as well as on the elasticity of substitution in production.

We will examine investment demand in more detail in chapter 18. For now, the important takeaway is that the equilibrium depends on whether investment tends to widen capital or deepen capital, which will depend importantly on where the economy is situated in the business cycle. The profitability of capital widening is influenced by investors' perceptions with respect to the market for additional output, captured here by the magnitude of the parameter $\Omega(Y)$. This parameter will be smaller to the point of vanishing when there is considerable slack in the economy; it will be close to one during a boom. So capital widening may be expected to be an important, if not necessarily the predominant, form of investment in prosperous times. During a recession, when $\Omega(Y)$ is a very small number, capital deepening may be the only game in town.

For each type of investment, we can derive the AD schedule by a construction analogous to the construction in Figure 9.15. Figure 10.4 constructs the AD schedule for capital widening. There is a critical difference between Figure 10.4 and Figure 9.15: for the AD schedule corresponding to the Cambridge saving theory, points above the schedule represent an excess of saving over investment and hence an excess of income over expenditure; points below reflect an excess of investment over saving. Here the situation is reversed. Above the AD schedule, desired investment exceeds saving, whereas below, saving exceeds investment. Consequently, the dynamics are very different in

(a) Investment and saving holding real-price constant

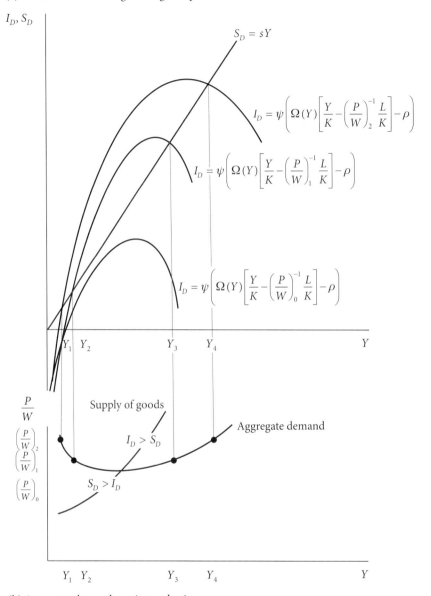

(b) Aggregate demand varying real price

Figure 10.4 Aggregate demand with capital-widening investment.

the two cases. Figures 10.5 and 10.6 depict flexprice equilibria, and Figures 10.7 and 10.8 depict fixprice equilibria. The stability of these equilibria depends on the relative speeds of adjustment of prices, wages, and output. In the flexprice case, stability is guaranteed if wages adjust much more rapidly than prices—the opposite of Keynes's assumption of a fixed money wage. Stable

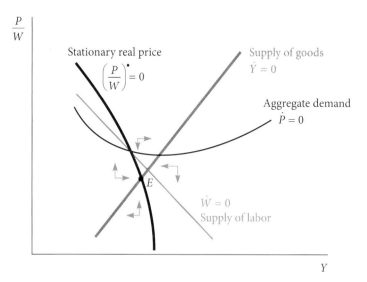

Figure 10.5 Deflationary equilibrium with capital-widening investment: flexprice adjustment.

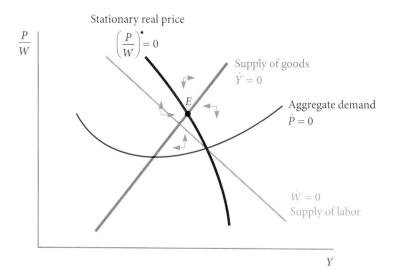

Figure 10.6 Inflationary equilibrium with capital-widening investment: flexprice adjustment.

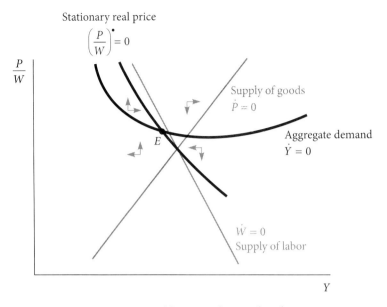

Figure 10.7 Deflationary equilibrium with capital-widening investment: fixprice adjustment.

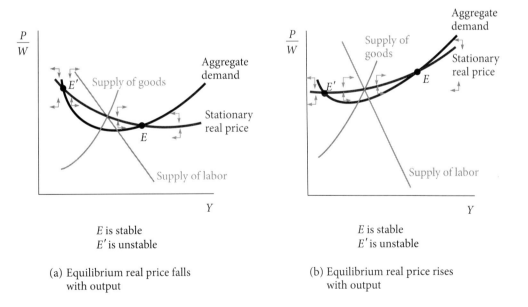

Figure 10.8 Equilibria with capital-widening investment: fixprice adjustment.

equilibrium in the fixprice case requires (1) that the slope of the AD schedule exceed the slope of the stationary-price locus (as it does at E in both Figure 10.7 and Figure 10.8 but not at E'), and (2) if the equilibrium entails deflation, that prices and wages adjust more rapidly than output. Details are in the mathematical appendix to this chapter.

An AD schedule corresponding to capital deepening is constructed along the same lines as in Figure 10.4. In Figure 10.9, investment demand and the

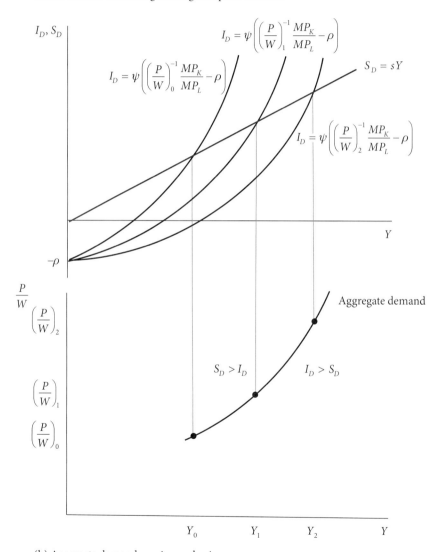

(a) Investment and saving holding real-price constant

(b) Aggregate demand varying real price

Figure 10.9 Aggregate demand with capital-deepening investment.

supply of saving are shown in panel (a), and the corresponding AD schedule is shown in panel (b).

The first question is why the investment-demand schedule slopes upward in Figure 10.9(a). We have assumed from the get-go that the marginal product of labor declines as more workers are employed with any given capital stock. And as the marginal product of labor declines, the marginal productivity of capital increases, thus giving a double boost to investment profitability.

But this is at best a partial answer: as the AD schedule in Figure 10.9(b) is drawn, investment profitability responds so strongly to the level of output that the slope of the investment-demand schedule increases with Y. The reason is an implicit assumption that technical possibilities for substituting capital for labor are limited, which formally is an assumption that the elasticity of substitution in production is less than one. This means that, as output expands, the ratio of MP_K to MP_L increases at a faster (percentage) rate than does the labor:capital ratio L/K. On this assumption, the marginal product of labor falls so rapidly (and the marginal product of capital increases so rapidly) that investment demand and hence aggregate demand respond more than proportionately to changes in output.[6]

Flexprice equilibria are depicted in Figures 10.10 and 10.11. The stability of the equilibria in these figures depends on the assumption that the GS schedule is steeper than the stationary-price locus.

The fixprice case is depicted in Figure 10.12. There are two equilibria: E' is unstable, and E is stable. As in Figure 9.19, stability depends on the relative slopes of the two schedules that determine the equilibria; in Figure 10.12, however, the stationary-price locus must be steeper than the AD schedule

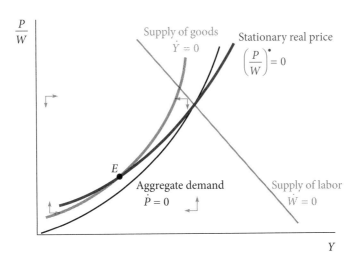

Figure 10.10 Deflationary equilibrium with capital-deepening investment: flexprice adjustment.

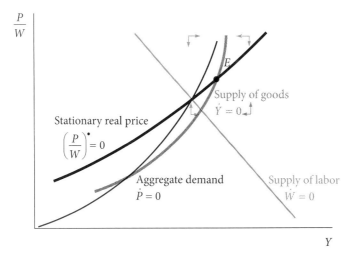

Figure 10.11 Inflationary equilibrium with capital-deepening investment: flexprice adjustment.

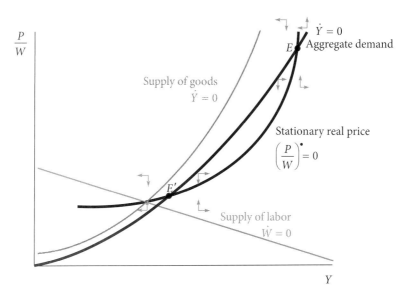

Figure 10.12 Multiple equilibria with capital-deepening investment: fixprice adjustment.

for a fixprice equilibrium to be stable. In addition prices must adjust faster than wages. Once again the details are in the mathematical appendix to this chapter.

Observe that the upward slope of the AD schedule does not contradict the assumption that capital-deepening investment demand is a decreasing function of the real price. This assumption is reflected in Figure 10.9(a), in which

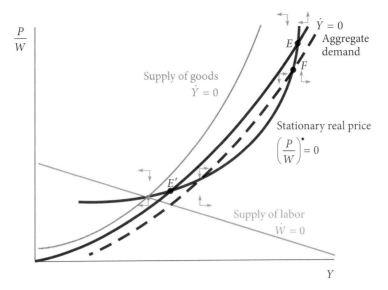

Figure 10.13 A shift in the aggregate-demand schedule due to a decrease in investment demand or an increase in desired saving.

investment-demand schedules associated with lower real prices reflect more demand at each level of output. The AD schedule in Figure 10.9(b) slopes upward only because this greater demand is absorbed by the available saving at lower levels of output. Even though the AD schedule slopes upward, shocks to aggregate demand shift equilibria as our intuition would suggest: a change in investment demand will lead to a change in output and employment in the same direction; a change in desired saving will lead to output and employment changes in the opposite direction. If an increase in the hurdle rate of interest displaces the investment-demand schedule $I_D = \psi(q - p)$ downward, or if the saving propensity increases, so that $S_D = sY$ is displaced upward, then the AD schedule moves downward, as in Figure 10.13. The (stable) equilibrium at E shifts downward to F, where output and the real price are both lower.

The Psychological Determinants of Investment:
Algorithm vs. Experience

I have followed Keynes (and Irving Fisher) in measuring an investment's attractiveness by the difference between its quasi-rent and the annual cost of interest and amortization, which, with our simplifying assumptions is equivalent to measuring investment worth by the difference between the discounted present value of its future returns and its initial cost. Alas, the formalism of the theory obscures its real content, or, perhaps I should say, lack of content. The problem is that the returns of any project, lying in the future, are not objectively given but are a subjective construction on the part of the investor. These returns depend on conjunctions of events about which the investor may have only vague notions and hunches, hardly the stuff of meaningful formal calculation. For Keynes, returns are vessels more or less filled according to the optimism or the pessimism of the investor herself. For Keynes, the "animal spirits" of investors play a crucial role in investment demand, and when investors' courage fails, so does investment demand. Indeed, one of *The General Theory's* most celebrated passages is a riff on animal spirits:

> There is the instability due to the characteristic of human nature that a large proportion of our positive activities depend on spontaneous optimism rather than on a mathematical expectation, whether moral or hedonistic or economic. Most, probably, of our decisions to do something positive, the full consequences of which will be drawn out over many days to come, can only be taken as a result of animal spirits—of a spontaneous urge to action rather than inaction, and not as the outcome of a weighted average of quantitative benefits multiplied by quantitative probabilities. Enterprise only pretends to itself to be mainly actuated by the statements in its own prospectus, however candid and sincere. Only a little more than an expedition to the South Pole, is it based on an exact calculation of benefits to come. Thus if the animal spirits are dimmed and the spontaneous optimism falters, leaving us to depend on nothing but a mathematical expectation, enterprise will fade and die. (pp. 161–162)

When animal spirits fail, all investors have to fall back on is the wisdom of the crowd. As Chuck Prince, erstwhile CEO of Citigroup, put it just before the economy began to unravel in 2007,

> When the music stops, in terms of liquidity, things will be complicated. But as long as the music is playing, you've got to get up and dance. We're still dancing. (quoted in Nakamoto and Wighton 2007)

Keynes anticipated this reliance on the wisdom (or folly) of the crowd. In his *Quarterly Journal of Economics* response to critics, he expanded on the role of animal spirits and what happens when animal spirits fail:

> We have, as a rule, only the vaguest idea of any but the most direct consequences of our acts . . .
>
>   By "uncertain" knowledge, let me explain I do not mean merely to distinguish what is known for certain from what is only probable . . . The sense in which I am using the term is that in which the prospect of a European war is

uncertain [Keynes was writing this in 1937], or the price of copper and the rate of interest twenty years hence, or the obsolescence of a new invention, or the position of private wealth-owners in the social system in 1970. About these matters there is no scientific basis on which to form any calculable probability whatever. We simply do not know. Nevertheless, the necessity for action and for decision compels us as practical men to do our best to over-look this awkward fact and to behave exactly as we should if we had behind us a good Benthamite calculation of a series of prospective advantages and disadvantages, each multiplied by its appropriate probability, waiting to be summed.

How do we manage in such circumstances to behave in a manner which saves our faces as rational, economic men? We have devised for the purpose a variety of techniques, of which much the most important are the three fol-lowing:

(1) We assume that the present is a much more serviceable guide to the future than a candid examination of past experience would show it to have been hitherto. In other words we largely ignore the prospect of future changes about the actual character of which we know nothing.

(2) We assume that the existing state of opinion as expressed in prices and the character of existing output is based on a correct summing up of future prospects, so that we can accept it as such unless and until something new and relevant comes into the picture.

(3) Knowing that our own individual judgment is worthless, we endeavor to fall back on the judgment of the rest of the world which is perhaps better informed. That is, we endeavor to conform with the behavior of the majority or the average. The psychology of a society of individuals each of whom is endeavoring to copy the others leads to what we may strictly term a *conven-tional* judgment. (1937a, pp. 213–214)

Not only do agents lack certainty about the returns of prospective investment projects, they cannot even attach objective probability assessments to the range of possible outcomes. The returns that govern profit calculations are embedded not in the investments themselves but in the heads, and as Keynes would have it, in the hearts of the investors. Profitability, like beauty, lies in the eye of the beholder.

Frank Knight (1921) distinguished uncertainty and risk on the grounds of whether meaningful probabilities can be calculated; for Knight, meaningful probabilities were associated with objective frequencies. As we saw in chapter 9, assimilating uncertainty to risk became part of the project of restoring the hegemony of mainstream microeconomics after *The General Theory*. This project was partly about coherence, to reconcile Keynes's macroeconomic arguments with the principles of microeconomics for the sake of a unified theory—or, failing reconciliation, to toss out Keynes's arguments as bathwater—even if this necessitated the demise of the baby as well.

The mainstream was also, perhaps more so, interested in restoring the legitimacy of the claim that markets work well for people, a central component of which was utility maximization—the "good Benthamite calculation" to which Keynes adverts in his 1937 discussion of uncertainty.[7] The problem for the mainstream was how people could possibly maximize utility when they can't calculate probabilities.

The first step in the assimilation process was to blur the Knightian distinction by transforming Knight's binary opposition into a continuum and observing that, at the risk end of the spectrum, we can never really know an empirical (as distinct from logical) probability distribution; we have only more or less relevant information on particular samples. By the same token, at the uncertainty end, we are never totally without information about the likelihood of alternative outcomes. Moreover, the essential (for Knight) institutional difference between risky and uncertain events—the difficulties of insurance in the case of uncertainty—is also blurred: markets exist in a wide range of situations that are closer to uncertainty than to risk; for instance, futures markets in commodities and the ad-hoc insurance contracts that have long been the specialty of Lloyd's of London.

The blurring in practice of the distinction between risk and uncertainty ignores the obvious in Knight's theory—that these categories are ideal types. (In this, Knight was likely influenced by the great German sociologist Max Weber.) The existence of mixed cases and fuzzy lines becomes the pretext for abolishing the distinction altogether. If one is disposed in that direction, it is an easy intellectual step from the fuzziness at the edges of the distinction to the idea that all probabilities are personal or subjective in nature.

Frank Ramsey (1980 [1926]) and Bruno de Finetti (1980 [1937]) provided axiomatic foundations for subjective probabilities, which captured the attention of both economists and statisticians in the wake of the seminal work on game theory by John von Neumann and Oskar Morgenstern (1944). These ideas took shape in the formal model of decision making elaborated by Jimmie Savage (1954), according to which optimal decisions are characterized by the maximization of expected utility, with the probability distribution given by the subjective evaluations of the decision makers in a way that parallels the utility function as the subjective valuation of different outcomes.

Savage had not even published his theory when Maurice Allais (1953) offered an example of a choice situation in which experimental subjects were inclined to violate the Savage axioms. (Savage himself was, on his own admission [1954], tempted, but upon reflection recanted intuition in favor of the axioms.) A few years later Daniel Ellsberg (1961) crafted an example to separate risk from uncertainty and found once again that Savage, along with many other distinguished economists and decision theorists, was disposed to reject Savage, whose axioms have no room for the "ambiguity"—Ellsberg's word—of pure uncertainty. Indeed, Keynes had anticipated Ellsberg, distinguishing ambiguity (which he called the "weight of an argument") from probability understood as degree of belief. However, Keynes went only half-way down the street of subjective probability theory: *A Treatise on Probability* (published in 1921 as a revised version of his fellowship dissertation of 1908) interpreted probability as degree of belief rather than relative frequency, but Keynes held to the view that degree of belief could be given an objective, interpersonal meaning as belief rationally justified by the evidence.[8]

Subsequent criticism, initiated by Daniel Kahneman and Amos Tversky (1979), has been even more damning, since it questions the very ability of people to make the kind of calculations required by probabilistic choice with any degree of consistency. For example, Tversky and Kahneman (1981) showed that decision makers respond to the way in which the problem is posed, a 90 percent chance of surviving a medical procedure eliciting a different response than a 10 percent chance of succumbing. The line of investigation begun by Kahneman and Tversky has gathered a substantial following within economics, its value recognized in the award of a Nobel Prize to Kahneman in 2002.[9]

Nonetheless, subjective probability has a firm hold on the economist's imagination. This, it should be understood, is not thanks to the predictive or normative power of the approach. The hidden agenda is to take human behavior, strip it of all its vagaries, conflicts, and contradictions, and then compress it within the confines of the maximization paradigm. In the positivist euphoria of the mid-twentieth century, the appeal of subjective probability was doubtless enhanced by its consistency, at least in Savage's version, with the axioms of revealed preference: in principle, subjective probabilities, like subjective utilities, could be recovered from choices and actions. But for this project to succeed, subjective probabilities have to be stable, rooted in a fundamental psychology that is resilient to changing facts on the ground. If probabilities change with the phases of the moon, it will be neither possible to recover these probabilities from agents' choices nor to characterize the choices people make as optimal in any but the most ephemeral manner. In the absence of stable subjective probabilities, the attempt to recover subjective probabilities from observed behavior would not contribute anything to the argument that markets work well for people. If one gives up on this argument—as well we should—it is hard to come up with any reason for maintaining the purity of economic man as a maximizing agent.[10]

I expressed my own view in the previous chapter: under conditions of uncertainty, consumption decisions are unlikely to rely very heavily on an apparatus of calculation and maximization. This is true in spades for investment decisions. Moreover, to the extent calculation governs investment, subjective probabilities are not likely to be stable. And without objective data on which to peg probabilities, individuals necessarily fall back on intuition, conventional behavior, authority—in short, on experience—to form subjective probabilities. Experience constitutes a different system of knowledge from the knowledge that drives maximizing behavior, what I call algorithm. It not only has a different epistemology, it also has different rules of transmission and innovation, not to mention a different implicit politics.

I have elaborated the contrast and complementarity of algorithm and experience in a variety of publications, most recently in my book on how economics has undermined community (2008). Suffice it to say that here the point of a systems-of-knowledge approach is not to deny a role for calculation, but to argue that a framework of calculation based on subjective probabilities should be understood as one cause of the vagaries of investment demand. And, thus, subjective probability actually creates a space for the elements that Keynes thought essential to understanding investment behavior, from the intuition of animal spirits to the conventional judgments of the crowd.[11]

The subjective element in investment calculation explains why investment demand, and hence aggregate demand, is likely to be volatile, more volatile than if it were grounded in objective data subject to rational calculation. Consider the expression for the annual return anticipated on capital widening:

$$q - \rho = \Omega(Y)\left[\frac{Y}{K} - \left(\frac{P}{W}\right)^{-1} \frac{L}{K} \right] - \rho.$$

In this expression the parameter $\Omega(Y)$, which measures the perceived probability of making use of new capacity, does not reflect a rational calculation of the state of the market, but is rather a reflection of hopes and fears. This parameter will respond to nonrational waves of optimism and pessimism that at one point in time buoy up investment demand and at another drive investment demand into the ground. Nor is the expression within brackets, the return on investment conditional on the new production finding a market, engraved in stone. As a projection into the future, $Y/K - (P/W)^{-1}L/K$ is a property of the investor's mind, not of the investment project.

In any case, the prospective annual return is not dispositive of the amount of investment demand. Twixt cup and lip is the function ψ relating the prospective return to some amount of new physical capital: ψ is not fixed by any objective data but rather embodies the animal spirits that Keynes invoked to explain the vagaries of investment demand.

I will give Keynes (almost) the last word:

> We have seen above that the marginal efficiency of capital [schedule] depends, not only on the existing abundance or scarcity of capital-goods and the current cost of production of capital goods, but also on current expectations as to the future yield of capital-goods. In the case of durable assets it is, therefore, natural and reasonable that expectations of the future should play a dominant part in determining the scale on which new investment is deemed advisable. But, as we have seen, the basis for such expectations is very precarious. Being based on shifting and unreliable evidence, they are subject to sudden and violent changes. . . .
>
> Often the predominant, explanation of the crisis is . . . a sudden collapse in the marginal efficiency of capital [schedule].
>
> The later stages of the boom are characterised by optimistic expectations as to the future yield of capital-goods sufficiently strong to offset their growing abundance and their rising costs of production and, probably, a rise in the rate of interest also. It is of the nature of organised investment markets, under the influence of purchasers largely ignorant of what they are buying and of speculators who are more concerned with forecasting the next shift of market sentiment than with a reasonable estimate of the future yield of capital-assets, that, when disillusion falls upon an over-optimistic and over-bought market, it should fall with sudden and even catastrophic force. (*The General Theory*, pp. 315–316)

The volatility of investment is central to understanding both the limits of self-regulation and the limits of monetary policy. In 1930, the first year of the Great Depression, fixed investment fell by 22 percent, from 15 percent of GDP to 13 percent of a much reduced level of output. In 2009, the first year of the Great Recession, fixed investment fell by 17 percent, from 16 to 14 percent of GDP.

The difference in what happened next lies in how the federal government responded to the decline in investment demand. Chapter 15 argues that the Obama stimulus, whatever its faults, made up for the shortfall in private demand, at least enough to stave off a repeat of the Great Depression. In 1932, fixed investment was 31 percent of what it had been in 1929. By 2011, fixed investment had recovered to 90 percent of its 2008 level.

Capital Widening: Flexprice Dynamics

We take up capital widening and capital deepening in turn. Flexprice dynamics for the capital-widening case are

$$\frac{\left(\dfrac{P}{W}\right)^{\cdot}}{\dfrac{P}{W}} = \theta_1\left[\psi\left(\Omega(Y)\left(Y - \left(\frac{P}{W}\right)^{-1}L\right)K^{-1} - \rho\right) - sY\right]$$

$$- \theta_3\left[Y - LS\left(\frac{P}{W}\right)\right], \tag{10.1}$$

$$\dot{Y} = \theta_2\left(\frac{P}{W} - F_L^{-1}\right). \tag{10.2}$$

At equilibrium the Jacobian is

$$J = \begin{bmatrix} \theta_1\psi'\Omega\left(\dfrac{P}{W}\right)^{-2}\dfrac{L}{K} + \theta_3 LS' & \theta_1\psi'\left\{\Omega'\left[\dfrac{Y}{K} - \left(\dfrac{P}{W}\right)^{-1}\dfrac{L}{K}\right] - s\right\} - \theta_3 \\ \theta_2 & -\theta_2(GS')^{-1} \end{bmatrix}.$$

Without further specification, the signs of both the trace and the determinant are ambiguous. A sufficient condition for a stable equilibrium, as in Figures 10.5 and 10.6, is that wages adjust much more rapidly than prices. If θ_3/θ_1 is sufficiently large, then both $\theta_1\psi'\Omega(P/W)^{-2}L/K + \theta_3 LS'$ and $\theta_1\psi'\{\Omega'[Y/K - (P/W)^{-1}L/K] - s\} - \theta_3$ will be negative and therefore $det\ J$ will be positive. The trace condition, $tr\ J < 0$, is also met if $\theta_1\psi'\Omega(P/W)^{-2}L/K + \theta_3 LS'$ is negative.

Capital Widening: Fixprice Dynamics

The fixprice case is characterized by

$$\frac{\left(\dfrac{P}{W}\right)^{\bullet}}{\dfrac{P}{W}} = -\theta_1\left[GS\left(\frac{P}{W}\right) - Y\right] - \theta_3\left[Y - LS\left(\frac{P}{W}\right)\right], \tag{10.3}$$

$$\dot{Y} = \theta_2\left\{\psi\left[\Omega(Y)\left(Y - \left(\frac{P}{W}\right)^{-1}L\right)K^{-1} - \rho\right] - sY\right\}, \tag{10.4}$$

$$J = \begin{bmatrix} -\theta_1 GS' + \theta_3 LS' & \theta_1 - \theta_3 \\ \theta_2\psi'\Omega\left(\dfrac{P}{W}\right)^{-2}\dfrac{L}{K} & \theta_2\left\{\psi'\Omega\left(1 - \dfrac{\left(\dfrac{P}{W}\right)^{-1}}{F_L}\right)K^{-1} + \psi'\Omega'\left[\dfrac{Y}{K} - \left(\dfrac{P}{W}\right)^{-1}\dfrac{L}{K}\right] - s\right\} \end{bmatrix}.$$

The condition $det\, J > 0$ requires

$$\frac{\theta_1 - \theta_3}{\theta_1 GS' - \theta_3 LS'} < -\frac{\psi'\left\{\Omega\left(1 - \dfrac{\left(\dfrac{P}{W}\right)^{-1}}{F_L}\right)K^{-1} + \Omega'\left[\dfrac{Y}{K} - \left(\dfrac{P}{W}\right)^{-1}\dfrac{L}{K}\right]\right\} - s}{\psi'\Omega\left(\dfrac{P}{W}\right)^{-2}\dfrac{L}{K}} \tag{10.5}$$

stated in the text as the requirement that the slope of the stationary-price locus be algebraically smaller than the slope of the AD schedule. When the equilibrium takes place on the upward-sloping part of the AD schedule, like E in Figure 10.8, the term

$$\psi'\left\{\Omega\left(1 - \frac{\left(\dfrac{P}{W}\right)^{-1}}{F_L}\right)K^{-1} + \Omega'\left[\frac{Y}{K} - \left(\frac{P}{W}\right)^{-1}\frac{L}{K}\right]\right\} - s \tag{10.6}$$

is necessarily negative, so the trace condition, $tr\, J < 0$, is satisfied.

For a deflationary equilibrium to be stable, θ_2 must be small relative to θ_1 and θ_3 since 10.6 is positive. Observe that a fixprice deflationary equilibrium is not possible if $\theta_1 > \theta_3$ since this would violate the condition $det\, J > 0$.

Why Does a Stable Capital-Widening Equilibrium Look like a Cambridge Saving Equilibrium but Behave Differently?

Qualitatively, the pictures for the Cambridge saving theory, Figures 9.16 to 9.19, are similar to the pictures for capital-widening investment, Figures 10.5 to 10.8. But the stability conditions are very different; under a fixprice regime the determinant condition on the slopes of the stationary-price locus and the AD schedule are opposite to one another.

Moreover a change in saving or investment affects the AD schedule in opposite directions. To see why, look at the difference between displacing the saving or investment schedules in Figure 9.15 and displacing these schedules in Figure 10.4: the same displacement shifts the intersection between desired saving and desired investment in opposite directions. But because of the difference in the stability conditions, the resulting displacement, from E to F, is in the direction of greater output in both cases, as Figure 10.14 shows.

We illustrate the general result by calculating the derivatives dY/ds for the case of capital widening in Figure 10.14(a) and dY/ds_π in Figure 10.14(b). The AD schedule in Figure 10.14(a) is given by

$$\psi\left[\Omega(Y)\left(Y - \left(\frac{P}{W}\right)^{-1}L\right)K^{-1} - \rho\right] - sY = 0.$$

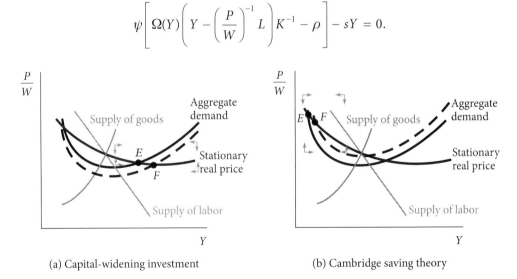

(a) Capital-widening investment   (b) Cambridge saving theory

Figure 10.14 Displacement of stable equilibrium by an increase in investment or a decrease in saving.

So, holding P/W constant,

$$\frac{dY}{ds} = \frac{Y}{\psi'\left\{\Omega\left[1 - \dfrac{\left(\dfrac{P}{W}\right)^{-1}}{F_L}\right]K^{-1} + \Omega'\left[\dfrac{Y}{K} - \left(\dfrac{P}{W}\right)^{-1}\dfrac{L}{K}\right]\right\} - s}.$$

That is, if s decreases, then Y will decrease if the AD schedule is downward sloping, so that the denominator on the right-hand side is positive, and Y will increase if the AD schedule slopes upward.

By contrast, the Cambridge saving theory generates an AD schedule from the equation

$$I(\rho) - s_\pi\left[Y - \left(\frac{P}{W}\right)^{-1}L\right] = 0.$$

We have

$$\frac{dY}{ds_\pi} = -\frac{Y - \left(\dfrac{P}{W}\right)^{-1}L}{1 - \dfrac{\left(\dfrac{P}{W}\right)^{-1}}{F_L}},$$

so that dY/ds_π is negative when the denominator is positive, which is to say, when the AD schedule lies to the left of the GS schedule and is downward sloping. When the AD schedule slopes upward, the denominator is negative, and dY/ds_π is positive.

The displacement of equilibrium is calculated by differentiating the entire system of equations. In the case of capital widening with a uniform propensity to save, the system is

$$-\theta_1\left[GS\left(\frac{P}{W}\right) - Y\right] - \theta_3\left[Y - LS\left(\frac{P}{W}\right)\right] = 0, \tag{10.7}$$

$$\psi\left(\Omega(Y)\left[Y - \left(\frac{P}{W}\right)^{-1}L\right]K^{-1} - \rho - sY\right) = 0. \tag{10.8}$$

From 10.7, we have

$$\frac{d\left(\dfrac{P}{W}\right)}{ds} = \left(\frac{\theta_1 - \theta_3}{\theta_1 GS' - \theta_3 LS'}\right)\frac{dY}{ds},$$ (10.9)

and from 10.8 we have

$$\left\{\psi'\Omega\left(1 - \frac{\left(\dfrac{P}{W}\right)^{-1}}{F_L}\right)K^{-1} + \psi'\Omega'\left[\frac{Y}{K} - \left(\frac{P}{W}\right)^{-1}\frac{L}{K}\right] - s\right\}\frac{dY}{ds}$$

$$+ \psi'\Omega\left(\frac{P}{W}\right)^{-2}\frac{L}{K}\frac{d\left(\dfrac{P}{W}\right)}{ds} - Y = 0.$$ (10.10)

Substituting from equation (10.9) into equation (10.10) and solving for dY/ds we obtain

$$\frac{dY}{ds} = \frac{Y}{\psi'\Omega\left(1 - \dfrac{\left(\dfrac{P}{W}\right)^{-1}}{F_L}\right)K^{-1} + \psi'\Omega'\left[\dfrac{Y}{K} - \left(\dfrac{P}{W}\right)^{-1}\dfrac{L}{K}\right] - s} + \dfrac{\psi\Omega\left(\dfrac{P}{W}\right)^{-2}\dfrac{L}{K}}{\psi'\Omega\left(1 - \dfrac{\left(\dfrac{P}{W}\right)^{-1}}{F_L}\right)K^{-1} + \psi'\Omega'\left[\dfrac{Y}{K} - \left(\dfrac{P}{W}\right)^{-1}\dfrac{L}{K}\right] - s}\dfrac{\theta_1 - \theta_3}{\theta_1 GS' - \theta_3 LS'}}.$$

At the equilibrium E in Figure 10.14(a), on the upward-sloping part of the AD schedule, the expression

$$\psi'\Omega\left(1 - \frac{\left(\dfrac{P}{W}\right)^{-1}}{F_L}\right)K^{-1} + \psi'\Omega'\left[\frac{Y}{K} - \left(\frac{P}{W}\right)^{-1}\frac{L}{K}\right] - s$$

is negative, and by virtue of inequality (10.5) we have

$$1 + \frac{\psi'\Omega\left(\dfrac{P}{W}\right)^{-2}\dfrac{L}{K}}{\psi'\Omega\left(1 - \dfrac{\left(\dfrac{P}{W}\right)^{-1}}{F_L}\right)K^{-1} + \psi'\Omega'\left[\dfrac{Y}{K} - \left(\dfrac{P}{W}\right)^{-1}\dfrac{L}{K}\right] - s} \cdot \frac{\theta_1 - \theta_3}{\theta_1 GS' - \theta_3 LS'} > 0.$$

So $dY/ds < 0$. That is, taking both the stationary-price locus and the AD schedule into account, the impact of a decrease in the saving propensity is to raise the equilibrium level of output. It follows from equation (10.9) that the impact on the real price is also positive.

With the AD schedule based on the Cambridge saving equation (which replaces equation [10.8]), the effect of displacing equilibrium is

$$\frac{dY}{ds_\pi} = -\frac{\dfrac{\left(Y - \left(\dfrac{P}{W}\right)^{-1}L\right)}{\left(1 - \dfrac{\left(\dfrac{P}{W}\right)^{-1}}{F_L}\right)}}{1 + \dfrac{\left(\dfrac{P}{W}\right)^{-2}L}{\left(1 - \dfrac{\left(\dfrac{P}{W}\right)^{-1}}{F_L}\right)}\dfrac{\theta_1 - \theta_3}{\theta_1 GS' - \theta_3 LS'}}.$$

At the stable equilibrium E in Figure 10.14(b),

$$\left(1 - \frac{\left(\dfrac{P}{W}\right)^{-1}}{F_L}\right) > 0,$$

so both the numerator and the denominator are positive. Thus in this case too $dY/ds_\pi < 0$; from equation (10.9) we also have $d(P/W)/ds_\pi < 0$.

Capital Deepening

The first order of business is the shape of the investment-demand schedule in Figure 10.9(a). We have

$$I = \psi\left(\left(\frac{P}{W}\right)^{-1}\frac{F_K}{F_L} - \rho\right).$$

We start from the production function $Y = F(K, L)$, which we assume reflects constant returns to scale and diminishing marginal productivities. We define $l \equiv L/K$ so that dividing through by K, we can work with $f(l) = F(1, L/K) = Y/K$. Differentiating $f(l)K = F(K, L)$ with respect to L and K, we have

$$f_l = F_L \text{ and } f - f_l l = F_K.$$

We now rewrite investment demand as

$$I = \psi\left(\left(\frac{P}{W}\right)^{-1}\frac{f - f_l l}{f_l} - \rho\right)$$

and obtain

$$\frac{\partial I}{\partial Y} = -\psi'\frac{f f_{ll}}{\left(f_l\right)^3 K}\left(\frac{P}{W}\right)^{-1}, \tag{10.11}$$

which is positive. ($f_{ll} < 0$ by virtue of diminishing marginal productivities.)

But whether $\partial I/\partial Y$ is itself increasing with Y or decreasing depends on the elasticity of substitution in production, σ. By definition, σ is the percentage-rate change in the labor:capital ratio corresponding to a one percent change in the ratio of factor marginal productivities, $(f - f_l l)/f_l$; that is,

$$\sigma = \frac{dl}{d\left[(f - f_l l)/f_l\right]}\frac{(f - f_l l)/f_l}{l}.$$

Expanding the derivative gives

$$\sigma = -\frac{f_l\left(f - f_l l\right)}{f l f_{ll}} = \frac{F_L F_K}{Y F_{LK}}.$$

Production functions with a constant elasticity of substitution have the generic form

$$F(K, L) = A\left(\lambda_1 K^\zeta + \lambda_2 L^\zeta\right)^{\frac{1}{\zeta}},$$

$$f(l) = A\left(\lambda_1 + \lambda_2 l^\zeta\right)^{\frac{1}{\zeta}},$$

with $\lambda_1 = 1 - \lambda_2$, and $\sigma = 1/(1 - \zeta)$. $\sigma \to 0$ as $\zeta \to -\infty$; $\sigma \to \infty$ as $\zeta \to 1$; and $\sigma < 1 \Leftrightarrow \zeta < 0$.

We can now determine the shape of the investment-demand schedule by rewriting equation (10.11) as

$$\frac{\partial I}{\partial Y} = \frac{I + \psi'\rho}{\sigma f_l l K}$$

and differentiating to obtain

$$\frac{\partial^2 I}{\partial Y^2} = \frac{1}{\sigma K} \frac{\dfrac{\partial I}{\partial Y} f_l l - \left(f_{ll} l + f_l\right)(I + \psi'\rho)\left(f_l K\right)^{-1}}{\left(f_l l\right)^2}$$

$$= \frac{(I + \psi'\rho)}{\sigma K^2 \left(f_l l\right)^2 f_l}\left(f_l \frac{1 - \sigma}{\sigma} - f_{ll} l\right). \tag{10.12}$$

The sign of $\partial^2 I/\partial Y^2$ depends on the elasticity of substitution. If $\sigma < 1$, then $\partial^2 I/\partial Y^2 > 0$, which is to say that the slope of the investment-demand schedule increases as Y increases, as is assumed in Figure 10.9(a).

Consequently, the AD schedule in Figure 10.9(b) is upward sloping. To see this, start from

$$\psi\left(\left(\frac{P}{W}\right)^{-1}\frac{f - f_l l}{f_l} - \rho\right) - sY = 0. \tag{10.13}$$

Differentiating equation (10.13) gives the slope of the AD schedule:

$$\frac{d\left(\dfrac{P}{W}\right)}{dY} = \frac{\dfrac{I + \psi'\rho}{\sigma f_l l K} - s}{\left(\dfrac{P}{W}\right)^{-2}\dfrac{f - f_l l}{f_l}} = \frac{P}{W}\frac{1}{f_l l K}\left(\frac{1}{\sigma} - \frac{sY}{I + \psi'\rho}\frac{f_l l}{f}\right).$$

Since $sY/(I + \psi'\rho)$ and $f_l l/f$ are both less than one, the entire expression exceeds one if $\sigma < 1$.

Flexprice-adjustment equations are

$$\frac{\left(\dfrac{P}{W}\right)^{\bullet}}{\dfrac{P}{W}} = \theta_1 \left\{ \psi\left(\left(\frac{P}{W}\right)^{-1} \frac{f - f_l l}{f_l} - \rho\right) - sY \right\} - \theta_3 \left[Y - LS\left(\frac{P}{W}\right)\right], \quad (10.14)$$

$$\dot{Y} = \theta_2\left(\frac{P}{W} - (f_l)^{-1}\right). \quad (10.2)$$

The Jacobian is

$$J = \begin{bmatrix} -\theta_1 \psi'\left(\dfrac{P}{W}\right)^{-2} \dfrac{f - f_l l}{f_l} + \theta_3 LS' & \theta_1 \left[\dfrac{I + \psi'\rho}{f_l lK}\left(\dfrac{1}{\sigma} - \dfrac{sY}{I + \psi'\rho}\dfrac{f_l l}{f}\right)\right] - \theta_3 \\[4ex] \theta_2\left(\dfrac{P}{W}\right) & -\theta_2 (GS')^{-1} \end{bmatrix}.$$

The trace is negative and the determinant is positive provided

$$\frac{\theta_1\left[\dfrac{I + \psi'\rho}{f_l lK}\left(\dfrac{1}{\sigma} - \dfrac{sY}{I + \psi'\rho}\dfrac{f_l l}{f}\right)\right] - \theta_3}{\theta_1 \psi'\left(\dfrac{P}{W}\right)^{-2}\dfrac{f - f_l l}{f_l} - \theta_3 LS'} < \frac{(GS')^{-1}}{\left(\dfrac{P}{W}\right)}.$$

That is, the stationary real-price locus must be less steep than the GS schedule, as it is at the equilibrium in Figure 10.10.

The adjustment equations for a fixprice regime are

$$\frac{\left(\dfrac{P}{W}\right)^{\bullet}}{\dfrac{P}{W}} = -\theta_1\left[GS\left(\frac{P}{W}\right) - Y\right] - \theta_3\left[Y - LS\left(\frac{P}{W}\right)\right], \quad (10.3)$$

$$\dot{Y} = \theta_2\left\{\psi\left(\left(\frac{P}{W}\right)^{-1}\frac{f - f_l l}{f_l} - \rho\right) - sY\right\}. \quad (10.15)$$

The Jacobian is

$$J = \begin{bmatrix} -\theta_1 GS' + \theta_3 LS' & \theta_1 - \theta_3 \\[3ex] -\theta_2 \psi'\left(\dfrac{P}{W}\right)^{-2}\dfrac{f - f_l l}{f_l} & \theta_2\left[\dfrac{I + \psi'\rho}{f_l lK}\left(\dfrac{1}{\sigma} - \dfrac{sY}{I + \psi'\rho}\dfrac{f_l l}{f}\right)\right] \end{bmatrix}.$$

The trace is negative provided that, compared to output, wages and prices adjust sufficiently rapidly (θ_1 and θ_3 both large), so that

$$\theta_2 \left[\frac{I + \psi'\rho}{f_l lK} \left(\frac{1}{\sigma} - \frac{sY}{I + \psi'\rho} \frac{f_l l}{f} \right) \right] < \theta_1 GS' - \theta_3 LS'.$$

The other condition for stability, $det\ J > 0$, will be met provided that (1) prices adjust more rapidly than wages ($\theta_1 - \theta_3 > 0$) and (2) the stationary price locus is steeper than the AD schedule,

$$\frac{\left[\dfrac{I + \psi'\rho}{f_l lK} \left(\dfrac{1}{\sigma} - \dfrac{sY}{I + \psi'\rho} \dfrac{f_l l}{f} \right) \right]}{\psi' \left(\dfrac{P}{W} \right)^{-2} \dfrac{f - f_l l}{f_l}} < \frac{\theta_1 - \theta_3}{\theta_1 GS' - \theta_3 LS'}.$$

In Figure 10.12, E, but not E', satisfies both (1) and (2).

— 11 —

THE THEORY OF INTEREST, I

Liquidity Preference in a World of Money and Bonds

> There is, I am convinced, a fatal flaw in that part of the orthodox
> reasoning which deals with the theory of what determines the level of
> effective demand and the volume of aggregate employment; the flaw
> being largely due to the failure of the classical doctrine to develop a
> satisfactory theory of the rate of interest.
>
> —JOHN MAYNARD KEYNES

Money, it is well known, serves two principal purposes. By acting as a
money of account it facilitates exchanges without its being necessary
that it should ever itself come into the picture as a substantive object.
In this respect it is a convenience which is devoid of significance or
real influence. In the second place, it is a store of wealth. So we are
told, without a smile on the face. But in the world of the classical
economy, what an insane use to which to put it! For it is a recognized
characteristic of money as a store of wealth that it is barren; whereas
practically every other form of storing wealth yields some interest or
profit. Why should anyone outside a lunatic asylum wish to use
money as a store of wealth?

Because, partly on reasonable and partly on instinctive grounds,
our desire to hold Money as a store of wealth is a barometer of the
degree of our distrust of our own calculations and conventions
concerning the future. Even tho this feeling about Money is itself
conventional or instinctive, it operates, so to speak, at a deeper level
of our motivation. It takes charge at the moments when the higher,
more precarious conventions have weakened. The possession of actual
money lulls our disquietude; and the premium which we require to
make us part with money is the measure of the degree of our disquietude.

The significance of this characteristic of money has usually been
overlooked; and in so far as it has been noticed, the essential nature
of the phenomenon has been misdescribed. For what has attracted
attention has been the *quantity* of money which has been hoarded;
and importance has been attached to this because it has been
supposed to have a direct proportionate effect on the price-level
through affecting the velocity of circulation. But the *quantity* of

hoards can only be altered either if the total quantity of money is changed or if the quantity of current money-income (I speak broadly) is changed; whereas fluctuations in the degree of confidence are capable of having quite a different effect, namely, in modifying not the amount that is actually hoarded, but the amount of the premium which has to be offered to induce people not to hoard. And changes in the propensity to hoard, or in the state of liquidity-preference as I have called it, primarily affect, not prices, but the rate of interest; any effect on prices being produced by repercussion as an ultimate consequence of a change in the rate of interest.

—KEYNES

The initial novelty [of *The General Theory*] lies in my maintaining that it is not the rate of interest, but the level of incomes which ensures equality between saving and investment. The arguments which lead up to this initial conclusion are independent of my subsequent theory of the rate of interest, and in fact I reached it before I had reached the latter theory. But the result of it was to leave the rate of interest in the air. If the rate of interest is not determined by saving and investment in the same way in which price is determined by supply and demand, how is it determined?

The resulting theory, whether right or wrong, is exceedingly simple—namely, that the rate of interest on a loan of given quality and maturity has to be established at the level which, in the opinion of those who have the opportunity of choice—*i.e.* of wealth-holders— equalizes the attractions of holding idle cash and of holding the loan.

—KEYNES

No part of *The General Theory* has caused readers more grief than Keynes's theory of interest. It is chock full of ambiguities and in the end—I will argue in the next chapter—is at best incomplete: it is not a theory of the rate of interest but a theory of interest spreads. Moreover, as the last epigraph to this chapter indicates, it is an afterthought. Having rejected the mainstream view that the rate of interest equilibrates desired saving and desired investment, Keynes had to offer an alternative.

Or did he? Could Keynes not have simply posited a central bank in control of the interest rate and done away with the need for a novel theory of interest? Yes and no. Yes, to the extent that his goal was to provide an operating manual for an economy in which the need for a governmental hand on the tiller is already recognized, as in the first-pass model elaborated in chapter 3. No, to the extent that the point was to demonstrate the need to steer the economy rather than to rely on putative self-regulating forces to maintain full employment. The theory of interest Keynes offers really comes into its own in the second-pass model, which was intended to serve the second of these two overlapping purposes—and of course in the third-pass model, which I intend to serve both purposes.

Keynes's interest theory departs dramatically from the mainstream: it rejects the idea that the interest rate is determined by the forces of productivity and thrift, the forces that govern the flows of desired saving and investment:

> The rate of interest is not the "price" which brings into equilibrium the demand for resources to invest with the readiness to abstain from present consumption. It is the "price" which equilibrates the desire to hold wealth in the form of cash with the available quantity of cash. (*The General Theory*, p. 167)

Keynes likely believed that, once stated, this dictum about where and how interest rates are determined—by demands and supplies in asset markets, not by investment and saving—is obvious. Probably the sheer size of asset markets, being markets in stocks, compared with the flows of investment and saving, was supposed to convince the reader. For me the stock versus flow argument is indeed persuasive, and even more persuasive is the volume in trading of financial assets relative to the volume of investment and saving. As chapter 2 noted, in 2017 U.S. saving and investment were approximately $3.4 trillion. By contrast, the *daily* volume of trading in bond markets was over $750 billion. Assuming 250 trading days, the annual trading volume works out to $187.5 trillion.

In any case, *The General Theory* offers no justification for the shift from investment and saving to asset markets. The result was a controversy, "liquidity preference versus loanable funds," that has never been fully settled. One reason is that loanable funds is a slippery concept. What are loanable funds, accumulated saving, that is, wealth, or current saving, this year's additions to wealth? If loanable funds are wealth, then there is no conceptual conflict with Keynes's foundational assumption that the interest rate clears the market for financial assets. If loanable funds correspond to current saving, then there is no daylight between the equilibrium in the loanable funds market and the equilibrium determined by desired saving and desired investment. Frictions, rigidities, and other imperfections apart, Say's Law is alive and well, and with it so is the rejection of a role for aggregate demand.[1]

The controversy over whether financial-asset markets or markets for saving and investment are the site for interest-rate determination can be understood as an argument about relative speeds of adjustment of the level of output and the rate of interest when saving and investment do not balance. If θ_Y is the speed at which output adjusts and θ_ρ is the speed at which the interest rate adjusts, the mainstream view is that we live in a world of the limiting case where $\theta_Y/\theta_\rho \to 0$. The interest rate does the heavy lifting of adjusting I_D and S_D. Keynes rather assumes the opposite limiting case, $\theta_Y/\theta_\rho \to \infty$. In *The General Theory* interest rates, kept busy adjusting asset demands and asset supplies, react with glacial slowness to imbalances between desired investment and desired saving. In consequence the heavy lifting is left to the adjustment of output. In the limiting case output adjusts so much faster to imbalances in saving and investment that we can ignore the interest rate as a factor in adjusting investment and saving. And focus entirely on asset markets.[2]

The saving-investment view of interest-rate determination, that is, the limiting case $\theta_Y/\theta_\rho \to 0$, is certainly a logical possibility. One way for this to happen is that there be complete segmentation between the flows of saving and investment and the stocks of financial assets. In this situation it is not a question of whether loanable funds or liquidity preference determines *the* interest rate; instead there are two interest rates, with loanable funds determining one in balancing flows of desired investment and saving, and liquidity preference determining the other in balancing demands and supplies for the stock of financial assets.

An extreme case of segmentation would be that there is no market for financial assets at all. This is perhaps the world that Adam Smith had in mind when he argued his version of Say's Law:

> Whatever a person saves from his revenue he adds to his capital, and either employs it himself in maintaining an additional number of productive hands, or enables some other person to do so, by lending it to him for an interest, that is, for a share of the profits. (1937 [1776], p. 321)

In principle, there need be no market for the bond that the entrepreneur issues to the saver. The saver may have no choice—and possibly no desire—but to hold the bond until it matures.

This would leave the rate of interest unemployed in asset markets, and so free to balance investment and saving. The grain of truth in this view was noted by Jacob Viner in his critique of *The General Theory*.

> There are, however, in every country large numbers of investors who have been taught to buy gilt-edge securities on the basis of their yield to maturity and to disregard the fluctuations in their day-to-day market values. (1936, p. 153)

Viner's observation is as valid in the twenty-first century as it was in the 1930s. In a world of cash and bonds, a financial planner might counsel her younger clients to hold portfolios that mature over the expected span of their golden years, with nary a side glance to cash.[3] These agents have no need for the liquidity that cash offers and no need for a bond market once they have made their initial commitments.

The disproportionate volume of trading in the most recently issued T-bonds, so-called "on-the-run" bonds, likely reflects the importance of Viner-type agents (or in 2020 the pension funds that act on behalf of these agents). Trading in newly issued, on-the-run, bonds with maturities from two to ten years dwarfed the volume of trading in off-the-run securities in Michael Fleming's data (2013), accounting for over 60 percent of *all* the trading in Treasury securities. Presumably, this disparity reflects a significant presence of agents who buy bonds when issued and hold them to maturity.

But the grain of truth in the difference in on-the-run and off-the-run trading does not really diminish the importance of the market in financial assets as the site for determining interest rates. Even the 40 percent of this volume that represents trading in off-the-run long-term bonds and short-term bills dwarfs saving and investment by a factor of more than twenty.[4]

If segmentation is a logical possibility, there is considerable evidence to the contrary. In the eighteenth century, at the dawn of financial capitalism, government bonds and shares in the companies that had monopolies over their countries' overseas trade—the Dutch and British East India Companies are the most famous—were frequently used as collateral for loans to finance new undertakings (Carlos and Neal 2011, *passim*). This would suggest a certain degree of integration of the market for existing assets with the market for new investment. Given this integration, it seems implausible that even in the 1700s capital markets were so compartmentalized that one interest rate (or, more realistically, one set of interest rates) was determined by the demand for investment and the supply of saving, and another was determined in bond and share markets.

Even if there were merit in the segmentation hypothesis as history, by the time Keynes wrote *The General Theory,* capital markets were highly integrated. To imagine capital markets so segmented that interest rates had no other role to play than to adjust the demand for investment and the supply of saving is out of touch with reality, Keynes's reality of the first decades of the twentieth century, not to mention the reality of the first decades of the twenty-first century.

But does it matter whether we focus on the investment-saving nexus or on the market for financial assets? Early on, Frank Knight dismissed the liquidity preference versus loanable funds controversy as a tempest in a teapot:

> It is self-evident that at any time (and at the margin) the rate of interest
> equates both the desirability of holding cash with the desirability of holding

nonmonetary wealth and the desirability of consuming with that of lending. (1937, pp. 112–113)

John Hicks agreed with Knight: *Value and Capital* argues that the choice between liquidity preference, with the interest rate being determined in markets for financial assets, and loanable funds, with the interest rate determined by the demand for investment and the supply of saving, is simply a matter of choosing a numéraire (1946 [1939], chap. 12).

A reviewer of a preliminary draft of this current book went even further. Since flows of investment and saving are simply changes over time in stocks of assets, the flows *must* be equal if asset markets are continuously in equilibrium. If $D_A = S_A$ continuously, where D_A and S_A are the demand for and supply of financial assets, then in a closed economy without government, $I_D = \dot{S}_A$ and $S_D = \dot{D}_A$. An implication of continuous equilibrium in asset markets is equality of demand for investment and the supply of saving.

Knight, Hicks, and my anonymous referee are undoubtedly correct. The simplified model of *The General Theory* view of adjustment to inequality between I_D and S_D presented in chapter 2 and the more complete model in the appendix to chapter 3 both end up with I_D and S_D equal at the equilibrium rate of interest.

But this misses the point. As Lawrence Klein pointed out long ago:

> Nothing has been proved by this argument. It does not tell whether the rate of interest is the mechanism which allocates funds into idle hoards as opposed to earning assets or which brings the supply and demand for [investment] into equilibrium. (1947, pp. 118–119)

I should be clear as to what is at stake. From one point of view, a lot. The implication of Keynes's dictum that interest rates are determined in asset markets is that the level of output rather than the rate of interest adjusts the demand for investment with the supply of saving. It is no exaggeration to say that this is the basis of his entire theory.

From a narrower perspective, not very much changes: that the rate of interest is determined in the market for stocks of financial assets hardly eliminates the possibility—nor does Keynes deny—that the rate of interest might influence flows of both investment and saving. Indeed, Keynes's theory of investment is taken over lock, stock, and barrel from Irving Fisher, and the rate of interest is *the* determinant of investment once the array of potential investment projects is given. (In one sense, Keynes, in emphasizing the psychological dimension of estimates of the returns of a given array of projects—animal spirits—departs significantly from Fisher.) And, while the influence of the rate of interest on saving is not emphasized, the only diagram in *The General*

Theory (p. 180) illustrates joint dependence of saving on the rate of interest and income.

Causality running *from* the rate of interest *to* investment and saving is not the sticking point between Keynes and the mainstream. The sticking point is rather the idea that causality runs in the other direction also, from saving and investment decisions to the rate of interest, with the rate of interest the adjustment mechanism for bringing saving and investment decisions into line with each other. For Keynes the arrow running from saving and investment decisions *to* the rate of interest is broken, so the rate of interest cannot harmonize investment and saving desires. As he puts it in the last epigraph to this chapter, the rate of interest becomes superfluous in bringing about equilibrium between investment and saving once the equilibrating function of the level of output is understood.

Liquidity Preference: The Basics

In addition to shifting the focus of interest-rate determination from flows of investment and saving to stocks of financial assets, Keynes offers a specific theory of asset-market equilibrium, his theory of liquidity preference. Chapter 3 summarized Keynes's theory of interest in a function $\beta(\rho)$ that relates the desire to hold cash as a fraction of total wealth to the rate of interest on bonds. Total nominal assets are A, the demand for money in wealth portfolios is M_2, and the interest rate on bonds is ρ. The demand for money as a fraction of total wealth, $M_2/A = \beta(\rho)$, is pictured in Figure 11.1. The demand for money in wealth portfolios is simply $M_2 = \beta(\rho)A$. Chapter 3 translated the relationship between desired cash holdings and total wealth into a relation-

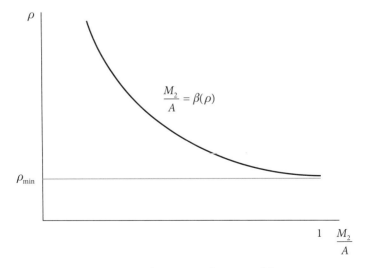

Figure 11.1 Liquidity preference as a function of the interest rate.

ship between desired cash and the value of bonds. If there is no government debt and no other financial asset (like equity), and we assume that physical capital is monetized in the form of bonds, then the stock of bonds, $\bar{B}$ (each with a par value of one dollar), corresponds to the nominal value of physical capital, PK. If each bond provides an annual payment of R, R is the interest rate on these bonds at par, but the interest rate consistent with equilibrium in the market for financial assets, ρ, is determined by the interaction of the value of bonds, $P_B\bar{B}$; the stock of money available for wealth portfolios, $\bar{M}_2$; and the liquidity-preference function $\beta(\rho)$. We have

$$A = P_B\bar{B} + \bar{M}_2 = P_B PK + \bar{M}_2.$$

For consols—bonds for which R is fixed in perpetuity—the relationship between the price of the bonds and the interest rate is particularly simple: the price of a consol is the ratio of R to ρ, $P_B(\rho) = R/\rho$, as in Figure 11.2.[5] If we put Figures 11.1 and 11.2 together, we can determine the interest rate that clears the market for financial assets. The demand for money as an asset, M_2, is given by

$$M_2 = \beta(\rho)\left[P_B(\rho)\bar{B} + \bar{M}_2 \right],$$

and asset-market equilibrium requires $M_2 = \bar{M}_2$ so that

$$M_2 = \bar{M}_2 = \frac{\beta(\rho)}{1 - \beta(\rho)} P_B(\rho)\bar{B}.$$

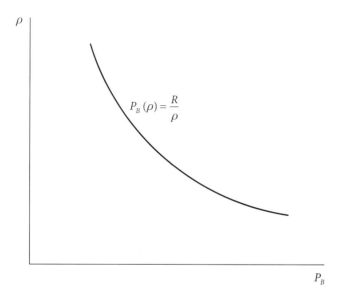

Figure 11.2 Bond price and interest rate.

Asset-market equilibrium is pictured in Figure 11.3, with the liquidity-preference schedule the locus of intersections of the money-demand and money-supply schedules.

The budget constraint requires that the sum of the demand for bonds ($P_B B$, as distinct from $P_B \bar{B}$) and the demand for money equals the sum of the endowments:

$$M_2 + P_B(\rho)B = \bar{M}_2 + P_B(\rho)\bar{B}.$$

So equality of the demand for and the supply of money implies equality of the demand for and the supply of bonds.

What happens when the price level of goods, P, changes? In the models deployed in this book, the price of physical capital changes in lockstep since capital is just a stock of congealed goods. In chapters 3 and 4, where the focus was on comparative statics, the appropriate assumption was that the quantity of bonds varies with the goods-price level. If two planets differ only in their respective goods-price levels, then the planet with the higher price level will have a proportionately larger volume of bonds outstanding.

In the dynamic context of chapters 5 to 8, where the focus is on real-time changes, there is no way for the number of bonds to vary as the goods-price level varies. The appropriate assumption is rather that the quantity of bonds is

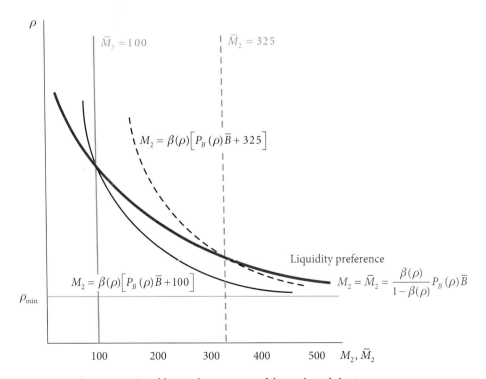

Figure 11.3 Equilibrium between portfolio cash and the interest rate.

fixed by the capital stock and the goods-price level at $t = 0$ and that it is invariant with respect to whatever goods-price level happens to obtain at any later time t.

Three questions present themselves. First, why is β positive rather than equal to zero? In other words, why do people hold any cash at all in their asset portfolios given that bonds pay interest and cash does not? (Why don't the schedules in Figures 11.1 and 11.3 coincide with the vertical axis?) Second, why is the amount of cash that agents wish to hold inversely related to the interest rate? (Why do the schedules in Figures 11.1 and 11.3 slope downward?) Finally, why does liquidity preference become absolute at a positive rate of interest ρ_{min}, so that the demand for cash becomes infinite at a positive rate of interest? (Why does the money-demand schedule reach its maximum of one in Figure 11.1 before approaching the vertical axis, and why does the rate of interest in Figure 11.3 approach a positive lower bound?)

Transactions, Precaution, Retirement, and Speculation

The fact that money is a medium of exchange explains why agents hold cash in anticipation of transactions. If you plan a trip to Mexico or India, you will need pesos or rupees. In the United States, we need dollars. We can't pay our bills with bonds or other assets. But money's role as the medium of exchange does not explain liquidity preference. The question here is a different one: why do agents hold cash in their asset portfolios, geared not to present transactions but to future ones.

One possible answer is the need for reserves against a rainy day; financial planners routinely advise clients to hold a precautionary cash reserve. But this is not an answer to the question posed in the epigraph to this chapter: *why does any sane person hold cash?* Why not bonds or other assets? Again, why is β positive?

The premise of the precautionary motive is that the time when cash is needed might be an extremely bad time to sell assets. As a Wells Fargo financial-planning website once put it,

> [since] the unexpected can always be expected, having a cash reserve ready is essential, [and] a good rule of thumb . . . is to have six to 18 months of cash to cover your living expenses and any other unexpected costs.

Wells Fargo advised its clients accordingly:

> In the Wells Fargo asset allocation strategy, across the board we hold a 3 percent allocation to cash . . .
>
> Cash is cash . . . If it's described as "like cash" then it's not cash, and that's how people got themselves in trouble before 2008. (Wells Fargo 2013)

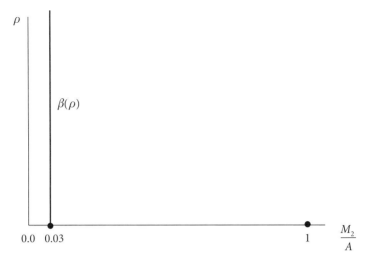

Figure 11.4 Precautionray demand for cash as a function of the interest rate.

As far as the precautionary motive is concerned, the Wells Fargo view is well-nigh universal.[6] I have never come across a financial planner who factored the rate of interest into his calculations of the appropriate size of a precautionary cash reserve, so that, if we represent Wells Fargo's 3 percent rule in Figure 11.4, we should see a vertical line, not a schedule along which the proportion of wealth held in liquid form varies inversely with the interest rate and reaches unity at a positive level of the interest rate.

The very lack of interest sensitivity makes the precautionary demand for cash more like the transactions demand. And indeed, Keynes merges the two, arguing,

> In normal circumstances the amount of money required to satisfy the transactions-motive and the precautionary-motive is mainly a resultant of the general activity of the economic system and of the level of money-income. (*The General Theory*, p. 191)

His formal statement of the demand for money echoes this assimilation of precautionary and transactions demands and their separation from what he calls the speculative demand on the basis of what drives the demand for money:

> Let the amount of cash held to satisfy the transactions- and precautionary-motives be M_1, and the amount held to satisfy the speculative-motive be M_2 ... Thus

$$M = M_1 + M_2 = L_1(Y) + L_2(r),$$

where L_1 is the liquidity function corresponding to an income Y, which determines M_1, and L_2 is the liquidity function of the rate of interest r, which determines M_2. (*The General Theory*, pp. 199–200)

Money held for precautionary reasons is technically part of wealth, as is transactions money to the extent it is not offset by debt. But money held for these reasons is fundamentally different from money held for speculative purposes. You and I hold small amounts of liquid assets to buy groceries and gas, and larger amounts to prepare for a rainy day on which our jobs disappear, illness strikes, or some other calamity occurs. And—a motive Keynes does not analyze—we hold bonds (and other financial assets) to provide for our retirement. In a cash versus bonds model, neither precaution nor retirement will lead us to be sensitive to the interest rate in designing the composition of our portfolios. Rainy-day funds will be entirely in cash, and retirement funds entirely in bonds, provided the bond maturities can be matched to an individual's expected time of retirement and life expectancy.

By contrast, Keynes's speculators derive a benefit in having liquid assets available to exploit targets of opportunity if and when they arise, like the opportunity to buy financial or physical assets on the cheap, or to stave off creditors if a business venture goes sour. Keynes's speculators are always calculating whether the interest potential on bonds is sufficient to induce them to limit access to their capital. Their answer—and therefore the composition of their portfolios—will depend on the return to illiquidity.

In this view, speculators drive the market since other agents will always choose *either* cash *or* bonds. Portfolios designed in the light of the precautionary motive will contain only cash. The retirement motive (or planning for a child's college education) produces Viner-type agents whose focus is on the wealth available at some well-defined period in the future; in the present model, with assets limited to cash and bonds, these agents will hold only bonds.[7]

Two Notions of Liquidity

There are two distinct reasons why cash is an attractive asset, not only when it comes to a reserve for emergencies but also when it comes to being prepared to deal with financial targets of opportunity. First, noncash assets may differ widely in their liquidity in the sense of the spread between bid and ask prices, that is prices that potential buyers are prepared to offer and prices that sellers are prepared to accept. (Call this "bid-ask" liquidity.) If you have to sell a boat, a second home, a rental property, or a factory to meet an unexpected need for cash, a relatively thin market may lead to a wide divergence between the prices offered and the prices you would expect if you weren't in a rush to sell. You know that if you wait, a buyer willing to pay the asking price, or very near, will very likely come forward, but you also know that you can't wait: you need the money now. This is why, as the Wells Fargo website (2013) put it, a cash reserve "prevents you from making short-term decisions with long-term assets."

But this reasoning doesn't apply to, say, U.S. T-bonds or shares of IBM stock. In the sense of the spread between bid and ask, these securities are extremely liquid. In September 2014, the bid-ask spread on 30-year T-bonds falling due ten years hence (in 2024) was $0.70 on a bond with a price tag of about $1,450, approximately one-twentieth of 1 percent of the price of the bond, and this spread was considerably higher than the spreads on recently issued, on-the-run, 10-year bonds. Moreover, these are retail spreads for relatively small purchases and sales.

There is, however, a second meaning of liquidity, namely, the possibility of a capital loss on the asset, and this less-intuitive meaning is the one that Keynes has in mind when discussing his theory of interest.[8] (Call this price-fluctuation liquidity.) If interest rates go up, the price of a bond with a fixed payment R will decline, and vice versa—even if we assume that it has zero default risk. So even though the market value at maturity is perfectly certain, a T-bond can fluctuate widely in value in the interim before it matures. It is perfectly liquid in the first (bid-ask) sense of liquidity but illiquid in terms of preservation of capital value. For this reason, wealth holders may be willing to forego the returns it offers, opting instead to hold cash.

There is an important difference between these two notions of liquidity, apart from the difference in relation to ordinary language. Bid-ask liquidity does not require that the value of an asset (measured by the average of bid and ask prices) vary over time for the bid-ask spread to be a factor, even a decisive factor, in portfolio management. An agent doesn't have to speculate about whether or not she will take a hit if she must quickly sell illiquid assets for which the bid-ask spread is great. She does not face a risk of capital loss but rather a virtual certainty.

Price fluctuations are another matter altogether. If we assume that gains and losses in capital value are equally likely, an agent who has to sell in a hurry is as likely to realize a windfall as to suffer a loss. Nonetheless, on standard models of utility maximization, in which wealth offers diminishing marginal utility, a gain of one dollar will count for less than the loss of one dollar. That is, agents will be risk averse, and their risk aversion may be sufficient to justify placing a portion of one's wealth in cash even in the absence of bid-ask liquidity concerns.

If average bond prices are not expected to be stationary, but rather to fall over time, wealth holders have another reason for holding cash. Assuming no default risk, it pays to forego bond interest today if tomorrow the bond can be bought at a discount to today's price, provided the expected reduction in price is greater than the foregone interest.

Default risk adds another dimension. Indeed, default risk is a special case of price fluctuations, in which the bond price falls dramatically, to zero in the limit.

To be sure, Keynes's first reason for liquidity preference is formally compatible with both bid-ask liquidity and price-fluctuation liquidity:

> A need for liquid cash may . . . arise before [a bond falls due . . . Consequently,] there is a risk of loss being incurred in purchasing a long-term debt and subsequently turning it into cash, as compared with holding cash. (*The General Theory*, p. 169)

The preference for cash comes from "the risk of loss" associated with long term debt, and loss can logically come about either from bid-ask illiquidity or price-fluctuation illiquidity. But in deference to the realities of bond markets, particularly the market for Treasuries, we can put bid-ask liquidity to one side in order to focus on price fluctuations. Keynes implicitly assumes—and we will too—that all financial assets are bought and sold in dense markets with only small spreads between bids and offers.[9]

The question then is how price fluctuations explain why the liquidity-preference schedules in Figures 11.1 and 11.2 slope downward, which is to say, why agents typically desire to hold a larger portion of their portfolios in cash the lower the interest rate.

Insurance and Risk Aversion

In *The General Theory* Keynes deploys an analogy between interest payments and insurance to explain why people might wish to hold increasing amounts of cash as interest rates fall:

> Every fall in [the interest rate] reduces the current earnings from illiquidity [that is, from holding wealth in the form of long term bonds], which are available as a sort of insurance . . . to offset the risk of loss on capital account. (p. 202)

The analogy suggests that it is risk aversion that makes price fluctuations problematic, for there is an obvious link between insurance and risk aversion.

But, as we shall see, the apparatus we develop to explain cash holdings in terms of risk aversion also helps to understand other motives for holding cash.

Understanding the idea of interest payments as insurance requires us to distinguish three measures of the return on bonds. The first is the *coupon yield*, $\rho_{coup} \equiv R/P_B$, measured by the ratio of the annualized periodic payment, the "coupon," R, to the price of the bond, P_B.[10] The second is the *yield to maturity*, ρ_{mat}, which is the solution to the following equation,

$$R \sum_{1}^{T} \left(1 + \rho_{mat}\right)^{-t} + \left(1 + \rho_{mat}\right)^{-T} = P_B,$$

that is, the yield to maturity is the discount rate that makes the present value of returns on a bond, including the return of principal (assumed here to be one) at maturity in year T, equal to the bond price today. In continuous time, the equation becomes

$$\int_0^T Re^{-\rho_{mat}t} dt + e^{-\rho_{mat}T} = P_B.$$

Finally, the *holding yield*, ρ_{hold}, the return on holding the bond for one time period, say one year, is the sum of the coupon yield and the percentage change in the price of the bond,

$$\rho_{hold} \equiv \frac{R}{P_B} + \frac{\Delta P_B}{P_B}.$$

In continuous time, the holding yield is the instantaneous return, which for convenience we continue to measure at an annual rate,

$$\rho_{hold} \equiv \frac{R}{P_B} + \frac{\dot{P}_B}{P_B}.$$

Evidently, the coupon yield, ρ_{coup}, and the yield to maturity, ρ_{mat}, are related. Indeed, consols have the convenient property that the coupon yield is exactly equal to the yield to maturity.[11] Since for all bonds the percentage change in the price of a bond is equal to the percentage change in its coupon yield, for consols the percentage change in the price of the bond is also the percentage change in the yield to maturity.

Why do we focus on the return from holding a bond for one year (or for an instant in continuous time)? Why one year (or one second) and not ten years? A short-term focus is not a self-evident given. Indeed, a more sophisticated model of speculation might take into account more explicitly the uncertainty surrounding the time when speculators might need to access their portfolios.[12]

But in order to get on with the story, we leave this point to one side. I shall simply follow Keynes and much of the subsequent literature, which implicitly assumes that speculators, who do not know when they might need to access their wealth, focus on the short term.

Suppose now that $\dot{P}_B/P_B$ (or $\Delta P_B/P_B$) is a random variable with mean zero, which is to say that capital gains and capital losses are equally likely. This assumption makes sense if we are dealing with consols and if there is no expectation that interest rates will change. Suppose further that the probability distribution of $\dot{P}_B/P_B$ is independent of P_B, and therefore of R/P_B (since R is fixed once and for all at the time bonds are issued). Since we are modeling portfolio choices, what matters are expectations; these expectations may or may not be based on frequency distributions of past performance and may be idiosyncratic or widely shared.

We can picture the resulting distribution of capital gains and losses in the first two quadrants of Figure 11.5. The third quadrant shows the breakeven coupon yield, the combinations of price changes, $\dot{P}_B/P_B$, and coupon yield, R/P_B, that makes the holding yield, ρ_{hold}, just equal to zero. For any level of the coupon yield, this schedule tells us the maximum rate at which the bond price can fall without making the holding yield negative.

This maximum rate determines the "uninsured" portion of the probability distribution, that is, the part of the probability distribution for which the loss

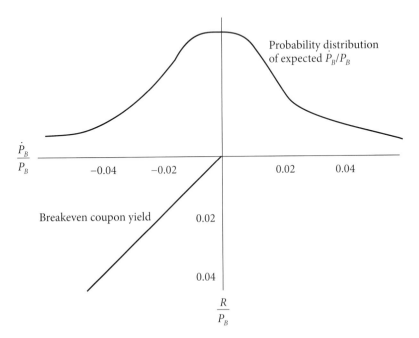

Figure 11.5 Coupon yield and "insurance" against holding yield loss, I.

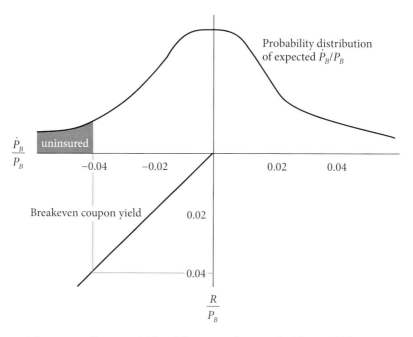

Figure 11.6 Coupon yield and "insurance" against holding yield loss, II.

of capital value exceeds the interest payment. For instance, with $R/P_B = 0.04$, the uninsured portion of the probability distribution is represented in Figure 11.6. For $R/P_B = 0.02$ the uninsured portion is as in Figure 11.7. The key point is that the lower the coupon yield, the larger is the uninsured zone. As long as bond-price changes stay to the right of this zone, holding bonds is superior to holding cash.

None of this matters to agents who are neutral with respect to risk. Given the assumed symmetry of the probability distribution around zero, gains are equally likely as losses, and no insurance is needed. But for risk-averse agents, the insurance buffer is important because it offsets the greater pain caused by loss in comparison with the pleasure of gain. Since higher coupon yields offer more protection against price fluctuations, it is plausible that wealth holders will wish to hold a smaller portion of their wealth in the form of cash when yields are higher.

This is as far as Keynes goes; the observation that higher coupon yields offer more protection against price fluctuations, like many of the trenchant observations in *The General Theory*, is not incorporated into a formal model relating liquidity preference to risk aversion. In fact it took twenty years for the model to appear in print, in a deservedly famous article by James Tobin (1958). Tobin's formalization allows us to derive a liquidity-preference func-

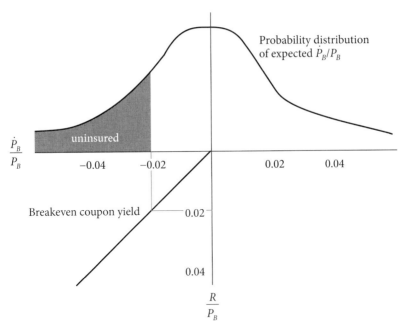

Figure 11.7 Coupon yield and "insurance" against holding yield loss, III.

tion $\beta(\rho)$ that answers the question of why this function slopes downward. I present a pre-Tobin version of Tobin's model in the mathematical appendix to chapter 12.

Liquidity Preference Without Risk Aversion: Reversion of Bond Yields to Normal

The risk-aversion story is lacking in one crucial respect: there is no guarantee of a liquidity trap. The ratio of money demand to money supply must, as has been observed, go to one as the bond price becomes infinite and the yield goes to zero. But a liquidity trap requires that the ratio of money demand to money supply goes to one *before* P_B becomes infinite and R/P_B goes to zero. There is nothing in the risk-aversion story that assures this result.

Keynes has another argument for liquidity preference that does imply a liquidity trap: namely, that agents do not necessarily expect bond prices and yields to be stationary over time. Instead, Keynes argues that there are reference prices and, correspondingly, reference yields, against which current prices and yields are judged to be high or low, with prices and yields expected to revert to these reference levels over time.

That is, unlike the case of pure risk aversion, expectations about bond-price fluctuations are not centered on zero. Rather the mean of the distribution of $\dot{P}_B/P_B$ may itself vary; in particular, it may vary with the coupon yield. If the current yield R/P_B is high relative to the reference yield, agents will expect it to come down, which is to say the mean of (anticipated) price changes is greater than zero, $E(\dot{P}_B) > 0.$[13] And vice versa: if the coupon yield is low, the same agent may expect the yield to rise and the price of the bond to fall. If $E(\dot{P}_B) < 0$, it may pay to defer purchasing the bond until it can be had more cheaply. "May pay," rather than "will pay," because the other side of the ledger is the loss in interest foregone while waiting for bond prices to fall.

Keynes's terminology in *The General Theory* for the reference rate is a "safe" level, though his definition of "safe" is somewhat circular; he refers to "what is considered a *safe* level of [the coupon yield], having regard to those calculations of probability which are being relied on" (p. 201). The important point is that, as the current rate fluctuates,

> If the general view as to what is a safe level of [the coupon yield] is unchanged, every fall in [the coupon yield] reduces the market rate relatively to the "safe" rate and therefore increases the risk of illiquidity [that is, the risk of holding bonds]. (p. 202)

The safe rate soon came to be called a "normal rate," normal in terms of agents' historical experience. As Keynes put it:

> *Any* level of interest which is accepted with sufficient conviction as *likely* to be durable *will* be durable; subject, of course, in a changing society to fluctuations for all kinds of reasons round the expected normal. (p. 203)

Figure 11.8 presents two distributions of $\dot{P}_B/P_B$, each corresponding to a different coupon yield. $R/P_B = 0.04$ is assumed to be the normal rate at which the probability distribution of $\dot{P}_B/P_B$, depicted by the solid curve, is equipoised between gains and losses, and so has its expected value at the origin. At $R/P_B = 0.03$, with the price of consols greater by one-third, price declines are perceived to be more likely than increases, and the probability distribution, represented by the dashed curve, moves to the left. The consequences for the amount of insurance provided by the coupon yield are evident in Figures 11.9 and 11.10.

As the breakeven coupon yield falls and the uninsured portion of the probability distribution increases in size, even risk-neutral agents will find it advantageous to put *all* their assets into cash at some point *before* the coupon yield falls to zero. This is in contrast to risk-averse agents facing a symmetric probability distribution (as in Figures 11.4, 11.5, 11.7, and 11.9), who will always hold some portion of their portfolios as bonds regardless of how high bond prices are.

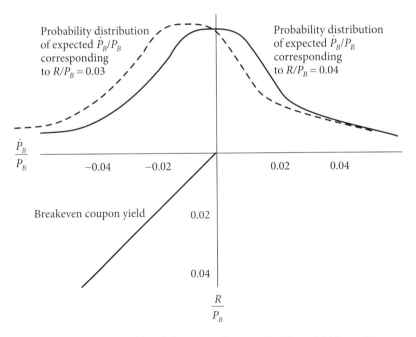

Figure 11.8 Coupon yield and "insurance" against holding yield loss with reversion to normal.

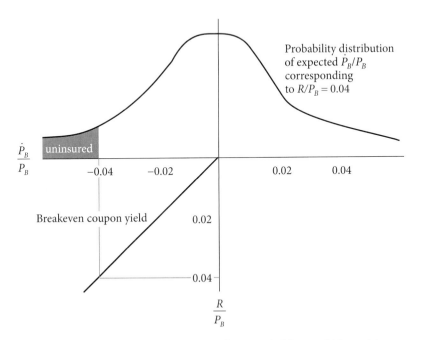

Figure 11.9 Coupon yield and "insurance" against holding yield loss with reversion to normal ($R/P_B = 0.04$).

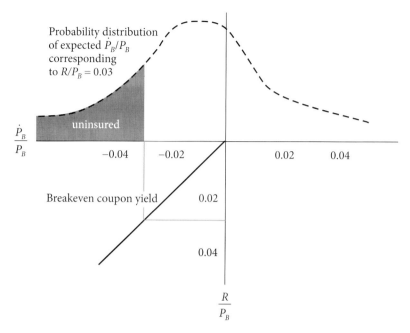

Figure 11.10 Coupon yield and "insurance" against holding yield loss with reversion to normal ($R/P_B = 0.03$).

In a world of risk-neutral agents, each has such a tipping point. In Keynes's words,

> Unless reasons are believed to exist why future experience will be very different from past experience, a long-term [coupon yield] of (say) 2 per cent. leaves more to fear than to hope, and offers, at the same time, a [coupon yield] which is only sufficient to offset a very small measure of fear. (*The General Theory*, p. 202)

In Figure 11.11, the tipping point is 1.5 percent, where the expected value of the change in price is just equal to the insurance provided by the coupon yield. Here a risk-neutral agent will be indifferent between bonds and cash.

If all risk-neutral agents have the same expectations, there is a unique equilibrium interest rate, that is, a unique interest rate that balances the demand for cash with the supply. With positive endowments of money and bonds, the only portfolio that is optimal for the agents and for which asset demands and supplies are equal is the knife-edge case shown in Figure 11.12; Figure 11.12(a) shows the demand for cash as a proportion of assets, and Figure 11.12(b) pictures the equilibrium interest rate, which is to say the bond yield at which the demand for money and its supply are equal. In a

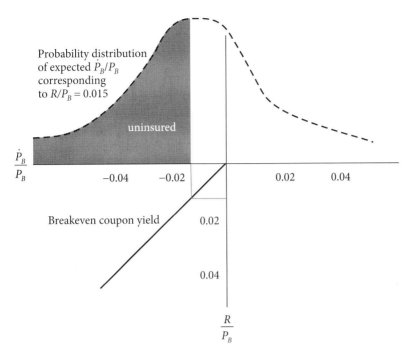

Figure 11.11 Coupon yield and "insurance" against holding yield loss with reversion to normal ($R/P_B = 0.015$).

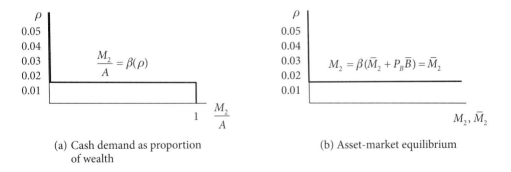

(a) Cash demand as proportion of wealth

(b) Asset-market equilibrium

Figure 11.12 Normal reversion and risk-neutral representative agents.

representative-agent, normal-reversion model, there is a liquidity trap—the horizontal segment of Figure 11.12(b)—but not a downward-sloping money-demand schedule.[14]

Observe that the very nature of a normal rate places a time limit on reversion to normal. The reason that speculators wish to hold cash is that the interest rate on bonds is (perceived to be) on an upward trajectory. But if this trajectory is expected to return the bond yield to normal rapidly, then the very basis of the argument—the positive gap between the normal rate and the actual rate—will soon be eliminated. If expectations of a relatively rapid increase in yield (and corresponding decrease in price) are disappointed, if the bond yield moves upward at a snail's pace or not at all, the gap between the actual yield and the normal yield remains. But, as Keynes says, any rate that persists long enough becomes normal, and a downward revision of the normal yield would also eliminate the gap between normal and actual.

Dennis Robertson saw reliance on reversion to normal as a flaw in the theory of liquidity preference:

> The rate of interest is what it is because it is expected to become other than it is; if it is not expected to become other than it is, there is nothing left to tell us why it is what it is—the organ which secretes it has been amputated, and yet it somehow still exists—a grin without a cat. (1937, p. 433)

And so it is—if liquidity preference rests *entirely* on reversion to normal. But reversion to normal is not an alternative to risk aversion; it is, rather, a complementary argument, one that delivers the missing piece—the liquidity trap—in the risk-aversion story.

Bulls and Bears

We do not need to rely on a combination of motives in order to end up with the liquidity-preference schedule of Figure 11.1: we can transform the flat segment of the money-demand schedule in Figure 11.12 into (almost) a continuously downward-sloping schedule and thus eliminate the knife-edge problem—*without* invoking risk aversion. But to do so we need another of Keynes's ideas, namely, that expectations are not uniform:

> Different people will estimate the prospects [for bond prices] differently and anyone who differs from the predominant opinion as expressed in market quotations may have a good reason for keeping liquid resources in order to profit, if he is right, from [lower bond prices later on] . . . The individual, who believes that future rates of interest will be above the rates assumed by the market, has a reason for keeping actual liquid cash, whilst the individual who differs from the market in the other direction will have a motive for borrowing money for short periods in order to purchase debts of longer terms. The market price will be fixed at the point at which the sales of the "bears" and the purchases of the "bulls" are balanced. (*The General Theory*, pp. 169–170)

The same agent can be a bull or a bear, depending on the bond yield. In Figure 11.12, which assumes that the mean of the distribution of bond-price changes is −1.5 percent, the agent is a bull at yields above 1.5 percent, desiring to hold all her wealth in the form of bonds. (Indeed, Keynes goes further; if she is "borrowing money . . . to purchase debts of longer terms," she is actually holding a negative portion of her wealth in cash!) She becomes a bear when coupon yields fall below 1.5 percent, cashing out her entire bond position to await lower bond prices.

At the same time, different individuals will evaluate the future differently and may have different probability distributions over $\dot{P}_B/P_B$. For one thing, they need not agree on the normal rate. But even if they share a view on what is the normal rate of interest, they need not agree on how fast today's rate will revert to normal.

Suppose there are two agents endowed with equal resources, $(\bar{M}_2 + P_B\bar{B})/2$, but heterogeneous beliefs; agent 1 has a tipping point between cash and bonds at 3.5 percent, agent 2 at 1.5 percent. Their individual money-demands, denoted M_{21} and M_{22}, are represented in Figure 11.13(a) and the aggregate schedule in Figure 11.13(b). The general formula for money demand in the aggregate is

$$M_2 = m\left(P_B\right)\frac{\bar{M}_2 + P_B\bar{B}}{2}.$$

For interest rates not equal to the tipping points, $m(P_B)$ represents the number of agents who desire to hold only cash; $m(P_B) = 0$ for $\rho > 0.035$, and $m(P_B) = 1$ when $0.035 > \rho > 0.015$. For $\rho = 0.035$, $m(P_B) = \beta_1 \le 1$, and for $\rho = 0.015$,

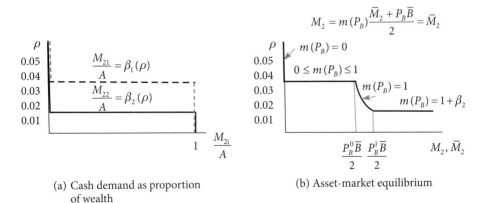

(a) Cash demand as proportion   (b) Asset-market equilibrium
      of wealth

Figure 11.13 Normal reversion with heterogeneous beliefs.

$m(P_B) = 1 + \beta_2 < 2$. At these tipping points, think of $m(P_B)$ as including fractional agents, the fraction equal to the proportion of the agent's wealth devoted to cash.

At equilibrium money demand and supply are equal:

$$M_2 = m(P_B)\frac{\bar{M}_2 + P_B\bar{B}}{2} = \bar{M}_2.$$

We have

$$M_2 = \bar{M}_2 = 0, \qquad\qquad \rho > 0.035$$
$$M_2 = \bar{M}_2 = \beta_1 P_B \bar{B}, \qquad\quad \rho = 0.035$$
$$M_2 = \bar{M}_2 = P_B \bar{B}, \qquad\qquad 0.035 > \rho > 0.015$$
$$M_2 = \bar{M}_2 = \frac{1 + \beta_2}{1 - \beta_2} P_B \bar{B}. \qquad \rho = 0.015$$

Observe that the equilibrium money supply corresponding to interest rates between 0.035 and 0.015 is equal to the value of the total endowment of bonds. This follows from the assumptions (1) that the two agents have equal endowments and (2) that in the interval (0.015, 0.035) one agent wants to hold only cash and the other only bonds. For this to be the case, the value of the bond endowment must equal the value of the cash endowment. The liquidity-preference schedule slopes downward in this interval because the value of bonds increases as the interest rate falls: the total value of bonds for $\rho = 0.035$ is $P_B^0 \bar{B} = R/0.035$; the value of bonds increases to $P_B^1 \bar{B} = R/0.015$ at $\rho = 0.015$.

The more diversity of beliefs, the smaller is each step in the aggregate money-demand schedule; as diversity increases, we obtain an aggregate schedule that more and more resembles the smooth schedule in Figure 11.1. Each step corresponds to a different division of bulls and bears, for, assuming risk neutrality, agents will generally allocate all or nothing of their portfolios to bonds according to whether their individual expected values of the holding yield on bonds are positive or negative; at each tipping point, at least one agent will be indifferent among alternative mixes of bonds and cash. A liquidity trap, the floor to the coupon yield, is encountered when there is so much cash in the hands of speculators and the price of bonds has reached such a high level that almost everybody has become a bear. The last holdout is willing to maintain a position in bonds, but she too would sell if the bond price got any higher, that is, if the yield got any lower. Since this would leave no one willing to hold bonds, her tipping point provides a floor to the bond yield.

Default Risk

There is one more argument that Keynes offers for liquidity preference, an argument that receives all too little attention relative to its intrinsic importance, especially at times of financial crisis. Up to now we have implicitly assumed that the default risk on bonds is the same as the default risk on money. The simplest assumption along these lines is that there is *no* default risk: bonds are issued by the government in its own currency, a currency over which the government has total control, and money consists of specie and bank deposits fully insured by the government.

Alternatively, we could simply ignore specie and assume (as Keynes does in *The General Theory*, p. 168) that bonds and bank deposits both carry a positive default risk, which just happens to be identical for the two assets. But if we drop this unrealistic assumption, and assume instead that bonds carry a greater default risk than bank deposits, we have yet another reason for liquidity preference. If money is free of default risk and the perceived default risk on bonds is 2 percent per year, and if this risk is independent of the coupon yield, then risk-neutral agents will display liquidity-preference schedules with the shape pictured in Figure 11.11—even though the reasoning is different.[15] In the present case, the expected holding yield on bonds will be 2 percent less than the coupon yield, and thus will be positive when the coupon yield exceeds 2 percent and will be negative when the coupon yield falls short of 2 percent. At 2 percent, risk-neutral agents will be indifferent between holding bonds and holding cash.

Once again, the assumption of heterogeneous beliefs transforms the aggregate liquidity-preference schedule. If different agents have different beliefs about default risk, the demand for money becomes a downward-sloping step function, as in Figure 11.13(b), and with enough heterogeneity the money-demand function morphs into the smooth money-demand function of Figure 11.3.

Conclusions

In its simplest version liquidity preference is the desire to hold cash rather than a less liquid form of wealth, bonds. It would hardly seem necessary to devote considerable space to analyzing this desire, except that for Keynes it is the basis of a new theory of interest. For Keynes, interest is not, as in mainstream economics, a reward for deferring consumption, and the rate of interest does not balance productivity and impatience. Interest is rather a reward for overcoming a preference for liquid assets. Liquidity preference is thus a theory of portfolio management, which with given endowments of financial assets gives us a theory of asset-market equilibrium. The interest rate, or more realistically complex of rates that emerges from equilibrium in markets for stocks of financial assets (bonds and money in the simplest version of the model), is the dog that wags the tail of investment and saving.

Liquidity preference cannot be reduced to a single cause. Keynes rather suggests three different motives—risk aversion, reversion to normal, and default risk—for wealth holders to hold a portion, or even all, of their wealth in cash despite the prospect of receiving periodic payouts of interest on bonds.

A risk-averse agent foregoes the returns on bonds because bond-price fluctuations can cause the agent to lose money if she is obliged to sell the bond before it matures. The possibility of making money, even if it balances the possible financial loss, does not offset the pain of loss. Risk aversion is another way of saying that equal probabilities of gains and losses do not cancel each other out because of diminishing marginal utility of wealth.

An altogether different reason for liquidity preference is embodied in an agent who believes the current bond yield is below normal and will gradually revert to normal. This agent may calculate that the potential loss in the value of the bond outweighs the periodic interest payment associated with the bond. She may decide to hold cash even though she is risk neutral.

Default risk is the final reason why agents might prefer barren cash to interest-paying securities. If the default risk exceeds the nominal return, holding bonds is a money-losing strategy, and agents will choose to hold cash instead.

This chapter explored how the various motives behind portfolio management animate the three characteristics of the liquidity-preference schedule: first, that the asset-demand for money is a smoothly decreasing function of the bond yield, which is to say that a small change in yield triggers a small change in money demand in the opposite direction; second, that the demand for money increases without bound as the bond yield falls; third, that there is a positive lower bound to the bond yield, a positive minimum below which the bond yield cannot fall.

It turns out—see the mathematical appendix to chapter 12—that none of the motives for holding cash—risk aversion, reversion to normal, or default risk—can by itself provide a justification for all three properties of the liquidity-preference schedule. Risk aversion does not necessarily give rise to a positive lower bound to the bond yield, a liquidity trap. Reversion to normal and default risk provide the basis for a positive lower bound to the bond yield, but when beliefs about the future course of interest rates are homogeneous, the liquidity-preference schedule consistent with either reversion to normal or default risk is hardly the smoothly declining schedule that liquidity-preference theory assumes. Rather, it is a flat line reflecting a tipping point at which a risk-neutral agent moves from a portfolio consisting of all bonds to a portfolio consisting only of cash. At the tipping point, she is indifferent between holding money and holding bonds.

The smooth downward-sloping equilibrium between money demand and money supply, with a positive lower bound to the bond yield, requires that agents differ in their beliefs about the normal bond yield, or in their perceptions of default risk. With heterogeneous agents, there will be bulls and bears, agents who believe current bond prices undervalue bonds and agents who believe that bonds are overvalued. The first group will put all their wealth into bonds, the second all their wealth into cash. When opinions differ widely, only a small fraction of wealth holders will be indifferent between bonds and cash, and small changes in the bond yield will lead to small changes in the proportions of bulls and bears. Even with (almost) all agents in one camp or the other, the equilibrium bond price will be an increasing function of the money supply, and this equilibrium price will have an upper limit.

Risk aversion, normal reversion, and default risk are not mutually exclusive reasons for liquidity preference. We can imagine a population consisting of both risk-averse and risk-neutral agents, of agents who believe that bond yields will revert to a normal level and agents who believe that bond yields follow a random walk so that the current yield is always "normal." Or we can simplify the argument by assuming identical risk-averse agents who also believe in reversion to normal but with heterogeneous beliefs about the level of the normal rate or the speed with which current rates will revert to normal. We can also imagine that bonds carry a default risk, so that even without reversion to normal, there will be a lower bound to the bond yield. With any of these assumptions, liquidity preference provides a logically consistent theory of interest, with the equilibrium bond yield a decreasing function of the money supply that approaches a finite floor as the money supply increases without bound.

This chapter would thus appear to vindicate Keynes vis-à-vis critics who challenged his assertion that liquidity preference determines the level of interest rates. We have not only an argument why asset-market equilibrium rather than equilibrium between the demand for investment and the supply of saving determines the rate of interest but also an explanation of the properties of the liquidity-preference schedule that characterizes the equilibrium.

Of course, liquidity preference is not the sole determinant of the interest rate that obtains when the economy is in equilibrium. For the equilibrium, we need to specify the other components of the model with which liquidity preference interacts. In the third-pass model developed in chapters 6 and 7, investment demand, the supply of saving, the transactions demand for money, the GS schedule, and the LS schedule complete the story.

A lesson of that model was that the *dei ex machinis* of the second-pass model, the Keynes and real-balance effects, may well exacerbate the problem of unemployment rather than curing it. Price and wage flexibility turn out to be part of the problem of depression, not the solution.

The question remains whether, like a fixed money wage, a world of bonds and cash is a simplifying assumption that can be amended once the structure of the argument is understood or a critical assumption on which Keynes's edifice depends. This question is explored in the next chapter.

APPENDIX: BOND COUPONS AS INSURANCE AGAINST PRICE DECLINES

Keynes implicitly makes a stronger assumption than is reflected in the section on Insurance and Risk Aversion, above. He argues that the insurance provided by the coupon yield ("running yield" in his terminology) varies in proportion to the square of the coupon yield and that this geometric relationship is the most important reason why any attempt to reduce the (long-term) interest rate is frustrated by liquidity preference. The full statement is,

> Every fall in [the running yield] reduces the current earnings from illiquidity, which are available as a sort of insurance premium to offset the risk of loss on capital account, by an amount equal to the difference between the *squares* of the old rate of interest and the new. For example, if the rate of interest on a long-term debt is 4 per cent., it is preferable to sacrifice liquidity unless on a balance of probabilities it is feared that the long-term rate of interest may rise faster than by 4 per cent. of itself per annum, i.e. by an amount greater 0.16 percent. per annum. If however the rate of interest is already as low as 2 per cent., the running yield will only offset a rise in it of as little 0.04 per cent. per annum. This, indeed, is perhaps the chief obstacle to a fall in the rate of interest to a very low level. Unless reasons are believed to exist why future experience will be very different from past experience, a long-term rate of interest of (say) 2 per cent. leaves more to fear than to hope, and offers, at the same time, a running yield which is only sufficient to offset a very small measure of fear. (*The General Theory,* p. 202)

Keynes does not make his reasoning explicit. But a rational reconstruction suggests that he is assuming that the distribution of the expected change in the coupon yield, $\dot{\rho}_{coup}$, rather than the expected *percentage* change in the coupon yield, $\dot{\rho}_{coup}/\rho_{coup}$, is invariant with respect to the coupon yield. Since

$$\frac{\dot{\rho}_{coup}}{\rho_{coup}} = -\frac{\dot{P}_B}{P_B}$$

the breakeven coupon yield is now given by the formula

$$\dot{\rho}_{coup} = \left(\frac{R}{P_B}\right)^2.$$

Thus, the boundary of the insured portion of the probability distribution moves in proportion to the square of ρ_{coup} (rather than in proportion to ρ_{coup}) as in Figure 11.14, which replaces Figures 11.6 and 11.7.

But two considerations have to be addressed before it can be agreed that this quadratic feature of the breakeven coupon yield can be considered to be "the chief obstacle to a fall in the rate of interest to a very low level." First, the boundary of the insured portion of the probability distribution is one element, but not the only one, in determining the size of the insured por-

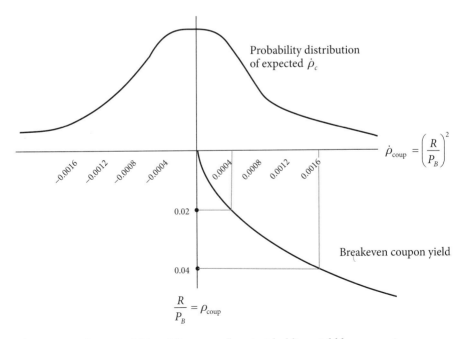

Figure 11.14 Coupon yield and "insurance" against holding yield loss assuming distribution of expected $\dot{\rho}_{coup}$ is invariant with respect to ρ_{coup}.

tion; different probability distributions will give different relationships of the size of the insured portion to its boundary. Second, if my reconstruction of Keynes's reasoning is accurate, the argument makes a strong assumption about the probability distribution itself. Since $\dot{\rho}_{coup} = -\rho_{coup}\,\dot{P}_B/P_B$, to assume the distribution of $\dot{\rho}_{coup}$ is independent of ρ_{coup} is to assume that the variance of the distribution of $\dot{P}_B/P_B$ varies inversely with ρ_{coup}, which is in turn to say that $\dot{P}_B/P_B$ varies *directly* with P_B. In other words, higher bond prices imply higher price volatility. Denoting variance by Var, we have $\mathrm{Var}(\dot{\rho}_{coup}) = \mathrm{Var}(-\rho_{coup}\dot{P}_B/P_B) = \rho_{coup}^2\mathrm{Var}(\dot{P}_B/P_B)$. Thus if $\mathrm{Var}(\dot{\rho}_c)$ remains constant as the coupon yield varies, then $\mathrm{Var}(\dot{P}_B/P_B)$ must fall with the coupon yield. Since the coupon is fixed, the bond price varies inversely with the coupon yield, so $\mathrm{Var}(\dot{P}_B/P_B)$ varies directly with the price of the bond.

This appendix demonstrates the key feature of the construction of Figure 11.3, namely, that, where the liquidity-preference and money-demand schedules intersect—which is to say where (asset) money demand and supply are equal—the liquidity-preference schedule

$$M_2 = \bar{M}_2 = \frac{\beta(\rho)}{1 - \beta(\rho)} P_B(\rho)\bar{B} \tag{11.1}$$

is flatter than the money-demand schedule

$$M_2 = \beta(\rho)\left[P_B(\rho)\bar{B} + \bar{M}_2 \right]. \tag{11.2}$$

Mathematically, since both $d\bar{M}_2/d\rho$ and $dM_2/d\rho$ are negative, this amounts to

$$\frac{d\bar{M}_2}{d\rho} < \frac{dM_2}{d\rho} \tag{11.3}$$

wherever $M_2 = \bar{M}_2$.

Differentiating (11.1) we have

$$\frac{d\bar{M}_2}{d\rho} = \frac{\beta'}{(1 - \beta)^2} P_B\bar{B} + \frac{\beta}{1 - \beta} P'_B\bar{B}, \tag{11.4}$$

and differentiating (11.2) gives

$$\frac{dM_2}{d\rho} = \beta'\left(P_B\bar{B} + \bar{M}_2 \right) + \beta P'_B\bar{B}, \tag{11.5}$$

where $\beta' = d\beta/d\rho$, and $P'_B = dP_B/d\rho$. Since the liquidity-preference schedule is defined by the locus of intersections between demand for money and supply, we can substitute the right-hand side of equation (11.1) for the left in equation (11.5). Collecting terms, we obtain

$$\frac{dM_2}{d\rho} = \frac{\beta'}{1 - \beta} P_B\bar{B} + \beta P'_B\bar{B},$$

thus

$$\frac{d\overline{M}_2}{d\rho} = \frac{1}{1-\beta}\frac{dM_2}{d\rho},$$

which guarantees that the inequality (11.3) holds.

A liquidity trap exists at $\rho = \rho_{\min}$ because $\lim\limits_{\rho \to \rho_{\min}} (d\overline{M}_2/d\rho) = \lim\limits_{\rho \to \rho_{\min}} (dM_2/d\rho) = -\infty.$

— 12 —

THE THEORY OF INTEREST, II

Liquidity Preference as a Theory of Spreads

To the extent that "money" includes deposit accounts bearing interest, the theory [of liquidity preference] becomes not a theory of the rate of interest but of the gap between different rates of interest, *viz.,* the yield on Government securities and the interest on bank deposits.

—DENNIS ROBERTSON, PERSONAL CORRESPONDENCE TO
KEYNES, FEBRUARY 3, 1935

It would be a mistake, which would be as damaging to further analysis of liquidity preference as it would be to classical doctrines, if it were thought that uncertainty and liquidity differentials are the *sine qua non* for the existence of a [positive] rate of interest. Such a view can be compared with a theory of land rent based upon differences in the quality of different kinds of land. I believe that the analogy is not a superficial one.

—PAUL SAMUELSON

I observed at the outset of the previous chapter that nothing caused the readers of *The General Theory* more grief than liquidity preference. It is thus not surprising that, from the very moment of publication of *The General Theory,* this part of Keynes's overall argument was subjected to intense criticism. Ultimately, liquidity preference provides only a partial explanation of the phenomenon of interest and the level of interest rates. For good reasons (see the epigraph to this chapter) and bad (see the quotation in the previous chapter), Dennis Robertson had strong reservations about liquidity preference, and this chapter at least partly vindicates his intuition: Keynes's theory tells us why bonds of different quality and maturity commonly offer different yields but not whether the overall level of yields is high or low.

We can see why by asking a simple question: if illiquidity were the sole determinant of interest, what would be the limiting value of the rate of interest as the term to maturity of a bond without default risk gets shorter and shorter? Keynes's answer has to be zero. But this is decisively disproven by the data on the rate charged for overnight loans between banks (in the United States the so-called Federal Funds rate, the name deriving from what is actually borrowed and lent: namely, funds on deposit with the Federal Reserve banks). Figure 12.1 shows the Fed Funds rate for the period 1954 to 2019. Only rarely during that time was the Fed Funds rate been below 2.5 percent—the eight years that followed the fall of Lehman Brothers are an obvious exception to this rule.

The basic problem is that the theory presented in the previous chapter is too simple: liquidity preference explains interest in a world with two assets, money and bonds, because the spread determines the interest rate on the bond. Given that the yield on money is zero, the spread between the yield on bonds and the yield on money *is* the yield on bonds, so in this special case, determining the spread is tantamount to determining the level of the (long-term) interest rate.

As a matter of principle, Keynes would no doubt agree with the need to generalize the argument to include short-term interest-bearing assets. But in *The General Theory* he offers only a fudge:

> We can draw the line between "money" and "debts" at whatever point is most convenient for handling a particular problem. For example, we can treat as money any command over general purchasing power which the

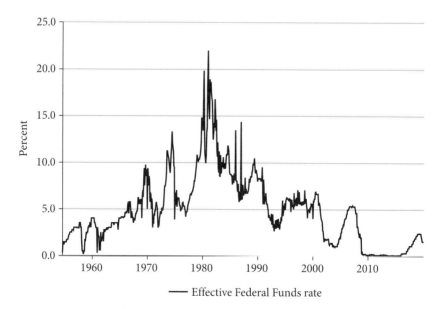

Figure 12.1 Fed Funds rate (1954–2019). *Source:* Board of Governors of the Federal Reserve System (U.S.). myf.red/g/pXAD

owner has not parted with for a period in excess of three months, and as debt what cannot be recovered for a longer period than this; or we can substitute for "three months" one month or three days or three hours or any other period . . . It is often convenient in practice to include in money time-deposits with banks and, occasionally, even such instruments as (*e.g.*) treasury bills. (p. 167n)

Treating "the line between 'money' and 'debts'" as a matter of convenience actually highlights the limitations of liquidity-preference theory. Allow money to include interest-bearing assets that dominate cash (by yielding a greater return without sacrificing liquidity) and it becomes clear that liquidity preference does not speak to the question of why interest exists or offer an explanation of the overall *level* of interest rates. Liquidity preference becomes a theory of interest-rate *differentials* or *spreads*.

But do interest-bearing bills dominate noninterest-bearing demand deposits and banknotes? The central issue is the relationship between money as a medium of exchange and money as a store of value. It is the second with which liquidity preference is concerned. For transactions, agents need cash, bank deposits, or other forms of legal tender, but this does not necessitate holding cash or deposits as a store of value. The last chapter noted that if you travel to Mexico, you will need pesos, and if you travel to India, you will need rupees, but this does not mean that you will necessarily hold pesos or rupees as part of your asset portfolio or that your holdings of foreign currencies will be sensitive to the exchange rate. Just so with wealth portfolios: your portfolio need not contain cash—dollar bills or noninterest-bearing demand deposits—even though when it comes time to paying your bills you have to pay with cash. For clarity, I shall (*pace* Keynes) limit the use of the term "money" to the medium of exchange, for which legal tender is of the essence. In wealth portfolios, money in this sense is replaced by short-term interest-bearing assets, like T-bills.

This separation of two textbook functions of money suggests that we can separate transactions demand for money from portfolio demand for short-term financial assets and thus ignore the costs of converting one into the other. The operative assumption is that decisions about the assets that go into wealth portfolios are separate from decisions about the assets held for transactions purposes. This means one of two things: either the amount of money agents hold for transactions purposes is interest insensitive *or* agents who engage in transactions do not hold asset portfolios.

Chapter 13 will return to the issue of whether or not transactions demand, and hence cash, is relevant to the determination of interest rates. For the moment we simply bracket this question and assume that interest rates are determined by liquidity preference and the public's holdings of a spectrum of interest-bearing financial assets.

Liquidity Preference Without Money

There is of course more than one short-term interest-bearing asset, and many of these assets are perceived as normally differing little in default risk. Over the period 1954 to 2019 the Fed Funds rate moved pretty much in tandem with rates on 3-month T-bills and 3-month commercial paper, as Figure 12.2 indicates. For brief periods, T-bills have sold at a premium (which is to say they yielded less than the Fed Funds rate and less than commercial paper), but for the most part the market has judged these three securities to be good substitutes for one another.[1]

What a difference a panic makes. Figure 12.3 shows the rates on these assets over the year following the collapse of Lehman Brothers. Fed Funds, T-bills, and commercial paper were no longer perceived to be substitutes for one another. In the immediate wake of Lehman's collapse, the Fed Funds rate was more than two percentage points above the 3-month T-bill rate, and then the market in commercial paper threatened to freeze up completely (see chapter

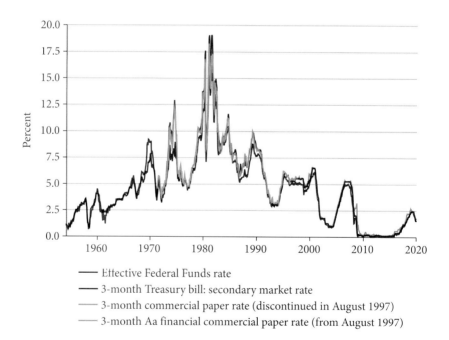

Figure 12.2 Short-term rates (1954–2019). *Source:* Board of Governors of the Federal Reserve System (U.S.). myf.red/g/pY1W

13, note 9). Liquidity preference with a vengeance! Only as the economy bottomed out in early 2009, and it became clear that the Great Recession would not repeat the descent into economic hell of the Great Depression, did financial paper once again become a plausible substitute for Fed Funds or T-bills. After June 2009, we see the old relationships among these three kinds of short-term assets.

If in normal times liquidity preference does not create much of a spread between high-grade short-term commercial paper and short-dated T-bills, the spreads between short-term and long-term rates, as well as the spreads between government and private long-term paper, are a different matter. We turn now to analyzing the difference it makes when the liquid alternative to long-term bonds is an interest-bearing short-term asset rather than cash.

Fortunately, we already have in hand an apparatus for modeling these spreads; the logic is the logic of the relationship between bonds and cash in the two-asset model studied in chapter 11. Figure 12.4 charts the relationship between 3-month and 10-year Treasuries. This figure has three notable features. First, the yield on T-bills is generally below the yield on 10-year bonds. Second, the spread is inversely related to the level of yields. Finally, there are occasions—early 2007 is a case in point—in which the spread is inverted, so that short-term bills yield more than long-term bonds. Both risk aversion

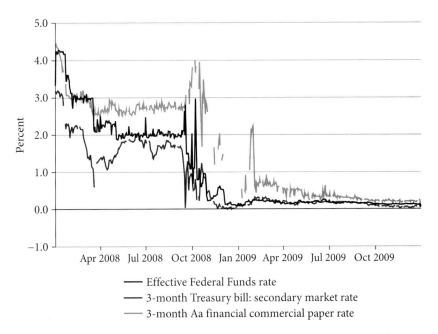

Figure 12.3 Short-term rates (2008–2009). *Source:* Board of Governors of the Federal Reserve System (U.S.). myf.red/g/pY22

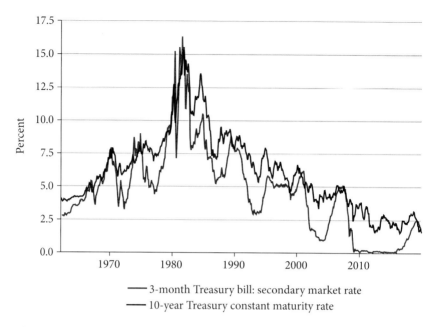

Figure 12.4 3-month Treasury bill and 10-year Treasury note (1962–2019).
Source: Board of Governors of the Federal Reserve System (U.S.). myf.red/g/pY2a

and the expectation of reversion to normal can explain a yield premium on longer-dated securities, but reversion to normal cannot by itself account for the tendency of bond yields to exceed bill yields. And as risk aversion was characterized in the previous chapter, it cannot account at all for the periods in which short-term bills yield more than long-term bonds.

Both risk aversion and reversion to normal become more complicated when cash is replaced by T-bills or other interest-bearing liquid assets. Consider risk aversion. Cash, paying no interest, has no interest-rate risk. By contrast, as an alternative to long bonds, bills are not immune to the possibility, indeed, the likelihood, that the interest rate will fluctuate over time. (Not within the lifetime of a single bill but over a succession of bills held as an alternative to bonds.) This is clear from Figures 12.1 to 12.4. Here the agent's time horizon becomes crucial. For investors with short time horizons, these fluctuations are of no concern; the nominal return on short-term bills, barring default, is certain. But if you have a long time horizon, if your portfolio is arranged to put your three-year-old through college fifteen years from now or to provide for your retirement twenty-five years hence, then the liquid asset may actually be riskier than the long bond, rather than the other way around, as it is when cash is the alternative to bonds.[2]

If long-horizon agents dominate, and they are motivated by risk aversion alone, we would expect bills to yield more than bonds to compensate for the extra risk. This might be temporarily upset by the belief that the bill rate is below normal so that bond prices are expected to fall, but the relationship between the bond yield and the bill rate would in this case follow a pattern opposite to the pattern in Figure 12.4. The actual pattern strongly suggests, even if it does not compel, the view that participants in asset markets generally have a short time horizon, so that risk aversion focuses on variations in wealth over a short period. There may indeed be agents with much longer horizons, but only on the relatively rare occasions when short rates exceed long yields are these agents obliged to balance risk and return. Otherwise, they get a free ride: they would be willing to give up returns in order to hold long bonds, but the market only occasionally compels them to do so.[3]

A short-period focus for risk averse agents provides an explanation of the relative rarity of inversions of the customary pattern of a yield premium on bonds. Even if people were to expect interest rates to go up or down with equal frequency, normal reversion would have to overcome risk aversion in order to wipe out the yield premium on bonds. This was a main point of John Hicks's exposition of liquidity preference in *Value and Capital*: "The short rate can only lie above the long rate if the short rate is regarded as abnormally high" (1946, p. 152).

Risk aversion and normal reversion work in combination to account for all three characteristics of Figure 12.4—provided we assume, first, that risk aversion is focused on the near term and, second, that over time the mean of the distribution of anticipated price changes, $E(\dot{P}_B)/P_B$, averages to zero. The yield on bills is generally below that on bonds because of risk aversion. The spread widens at low levels of interest rates because reversion to normal reinforces risk aversion and, even in the absence of default risk, the yield premium enjoyed by bondholders rises because of greater volatility in bond prices. The exceptional occasions when the term structure is inverted, like 2007, can be explained as times at which reversion to normal and risk aversion are working at cross purposes. Agents are willing to commit to long-term bonds during these periods because they believe on balance that long-term yields will fall; they are motivated to buy while bonds are perceived to be cheap. In this case, expectations of reversion to normal dominate the price-fluctuation risk of holding long-term bonds, and, unusually, agents have to be compensated in the form of higher returns, not for holding illiquid bonds, but for holding short-term paper. Here is where long-horizon agents become players in asset markets rather than passive free riders who enjoy lower risk and higher returns by specializing in long-dated bonds.

In the mathematical appendix to this chapter we derive the relationship between short- and long-term yields on the basis of risk aversion alone, assumed from here on in to focus on the variability of wealth in the short term. Then we examine the spread assuming risk-neutral agents who believe that present rates will revert to normal. Finally, we combine the two hypotheses, assuming that risk aversion and normal reversion operate at the same time. Here we summarize the results.

The Interest Rate Spread with Risk-Averse Agents

The simplest way to introduce interest-bearing securities into the picture is to have bills replace money in the agent's endowment. As in chapter 11, her endowment is $\bar{M}_2 + P_B\bar{B}$ but $\bar{M}_2$ now consists of a stock of Treasury (or commercial) bills rather than a sum of money.[4] The difference is that the short-term asset now offers a riskless return of $\rho_s \geq 0$, rather than strictly zero. The equilibrium spread between the bill rate ρ_s and the bond yield $\rho_{coup} = R/P_B$, pictured in Figure 12.5, has two noteworthy properties. A positive relationship between the bond yield and the bill rate replaces the negative relationship between the bond yield and the quantity of portfolio money. This change in the meaning of liquidity preference changes the meaning of a liquidity trap. Now a liquidity trap is a positive lower limit to the bond yield at the zero lower bound (zlb) of the bill rate.

This is analogous to the definition of the liquidity trap in a bonds versus cash model, but it is not the same thing. In chapter 11 we defined the liquidity trap in terms of the behavior of the bond yield as the cash endowment increases without bound, and we found that risk aversion by itself was no guarantee of a liquidity trap. Here the endowment of bills (and bonds) is assumed to be fixed;[5] what varies is the bill rate, and the liquidity trap is now defined as a positive lower bound to the bond yield as the bill rate approaches the zlb.[6]

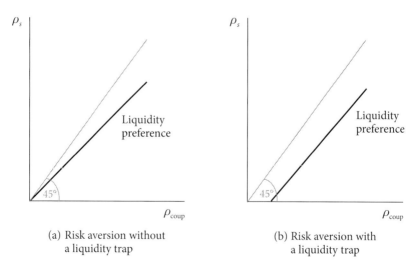

(a) Risk aversion without
a liquidity trap

(b) Risk aversion with
a liquidity trap

Figure 12.5 Liquidity preference without money, I: risk-averse agents.

Now, if risk aversion is the only game in town, a liquidity trap may or may not exist. As the liquidity preference schedule is drawn in Figure 12.5(a), the liquidity-preference schedule goes through the origin; assuming spreads are driven solely by risk aversion, and assuming the short-term rate is at the zlb, the bond price may have to become infinitely high, so that the bond yield falls to zero, before wealth holders will put all their eggs in the bill basket. It is also possible for the liquidity-preference schedule to exhibit a liquidity trap, that is, a positive intercept on the ρ_{coup}-axis, as in Figure 12.5(b). (See the mathematical appendix to this chapter for details.) In this case, desired bond holdings go to zero when the bond price passes a finite threshold.

The most important takeaway from substituting bills for cash as the liquid store of value is that we can infer from the assumption of asset-market equilibrium *only* the spread between the yields on the assets that comprise the market. Robertson's observation to this effect—see the first epigraph to this chapter—was correct in 1935, and Samuelson (quoted in the second epigraph) was right in 1947.[7]

In a way this should not be surprising. That liquidity preference determines only spreads is the counterpart of a more general limitation of market equilibrium, namely, that with n goods only $n - 1$ prices emerge, which is to say that only relative prices are determinate. In asset markets there are not enough degrees of freedom to determine the separate yields.

Nor is this result problematic in a world with central banks. For most of the last century, monetary policy has consisted of choosing the bill rate with an eye to fixing the bond yield. In other words, the central bank has taken on the task of anchoring the spread at the short end, leaving it to asset markets to determine bond yields and associated hurdle rates of return for new capital expenditure.

Reversion to Normal

But I get ahead of my story. Risk aversion is only one of the arguments for liquidity preference. What happens to normal reversion when we substitute interest-bearing short-term assets for cash? Little changes qualitatively, but the existence of bills as an interest-bearing alternative to cash makes it necessary to flesh out the normal-reversion argument.

In a model with cash and bonds, the short rate is the return on cash; it is fixed at zero and so cannot revert to anything else. Reversion in the cash-bond case necessarily refers only to the bond yield. In the present model, by contrast, reversion is fundamentally a property of the short-term bill rate, and we can derive the trajectory of the breakeven bond yield, the yield that makes an agent indifferent between bonds and bills, from the expected trajectory of short rates.

The starting point is that, in the absence of risk aversion, the willingness of agents to hold both bills and bonds requires the anticipated holding yield on bonds (ρ_{hold}) and the yield on bills (ρ_s) to be equal. In continuous time this indifference condition is

$$\rho_{\text{hold}} \equiv \frac{R}{P_B} + \frac{E\left(\dot{P}_B\right)}{P_B} = \rho_s,$$

where $E(\dot{P}_B)/P_B$ is the mean of the distribution of anticipated bond-price changes. If the above equality holds for the future as well as the present, we can infer a "demand price," $E(P_{B,t})$, for the bond at any time t from the solution to the integral equation:

$$E\left(P_{B,t}\right) = \int_t^\infty Re^{-\int_t^\tau \rho_s(x)dx}\, d\tau,$$

where

$$-\int_t^\tau \rho_s(x)\, dx$$

is the discount factor at time t for a future time τ, namely, the value at time t of one dollar available at time τ when the discount rate for each point in time between t and τ is given by the value of ρ_s. At $t = 0$, we have

$$E\left(P_{B,0}\right) = \int_0^\infty Re^{-\int_0^\tau \rho_s(x)dx}\, d\tau.$$

Whether or not it makes financial sense for the agent to hold bonds depends on how the actual price today compares with her demand price, that is, the price based on her view of expected reversion to normal. If the actual price exceeds the demand price, then she is better off putting her financial resources into short-term bills. If the actual price is lower than the demand price, it makes sense to buy bonds. If the two prices are exactly equal, she can expect capital losses to just offset the coupon and would logically be indifferent between bills and bonds.

In terms of yields, the demand price defines a coupon yield $R/E(P_{B,0})$ at which the agent will be indifferent between holding bonds and holding bills. She will put her whole wealth into bonds if the actual coupon yield exceeds $R/E(P_{B,0})$ and prefer bills if $R/E(P_{B,0})$ is above the actual.

In this model, reversion to normal of the bill rate drives the demand price of bonds and the corresponding yield. So how do we characterize the expected path of short-term rates? The simplest story is that the short rate is expected to make up the distance between the current rate ρ_s and the normal rate ρ_s^* at a speed proportional to the distance:

$$\dot{\rho}_s = -\theta\left(\rho_s - \rho_s^*\right).$$

In this formulation, the subjective elements of an agent's belief system reduce to two parameters, the normal bill rate (ρ_s^*) and the speed of adjustment (θ).

If the agent projects this process into the future, the expected future rate at time τ is given by a weighted average of the current rate and the normal rate, with the weight on the present declining as we move forward in time:

$$\rho_s(\tau) = \left(1 - e^{-\theta(\tau-t)}\right)\rho_s^* + e^{-\theta(\tau-t)}\rho_s(t).$$

Substituting into the equation for the demand price, we obtain

$$E\left(P_{B,0}\right) = \int_0^\infty Re^{-\rho_s^*\tau + \frac{\rho_s(0)-\rho_s^*}{\theta}(e^{-\theta\tau}-1)}\,d\tau,$$

and the critical value of the current coupon yield—the value below which the agent will hold only bills, and above which only bonds—becomes

$$E\left(\rho_{coup,0}\right) = \frac{R}{E\left(P_{B,0}\right)} = \left(\int_0^\infty e^{-\rho_s^*\tau + \frac{\rho_s(0)-\rho_s^*}{\theta}\left(e^{-\theta\tau}-1\right)}\,d\tau\right)^{-1}.$$

Figure 12.6 charts the relationship between ρ_s and $E(\rho_{coup,\,0})$ on the assumptions $\rho_s^* = 0.04$ and $\theta = 0.1$. If the current short-term rate is zero, Figure 12.6 says that the critical value of the long-term bond yield is 0.029. (The mathematical appendix provides a numerical solution to the equation that defines the schedule in Figure 12.6.) If $\rho_{coup} > 0.029$, the agent will commit her portfolio entirely to bonds; if $\rho_{coup} < 0.029$, entirely to bills. Evidently, if all agents are alike, the only long-term yield consistent with agents' holding both bills and bonds is $\rho_{coup} = 0.029$. At this coupon yield, all agents believe that capital losses will just cancel out interest earnings and are indifferent between alternative portfolio mixes of bills and bonds.

If agents have different beliefs about how rapidly ρ_s will revert to normal (or different beliefs about what constitutes normal, or both), then only a subset of agents need be equally comfortable with alternative portfolio mixes. Everybody else will specialize either in bonds or in bills. Figure 12.7 assumes five types of agents differing only in their assumptions about the speed of reversion to normal. Evidently, there is a liquidity trap, defined now as the existence of a positive floor to the (equilibrium) bond yield when the bill rate is at the zlb.

The relationship between bills and bonds is pictured in Figure 12.8, which resembles Figure 12.5 but with two differences. First, a liquidity trap is an essential part of the story. Even in the case in which the present ($t = 0$) value of

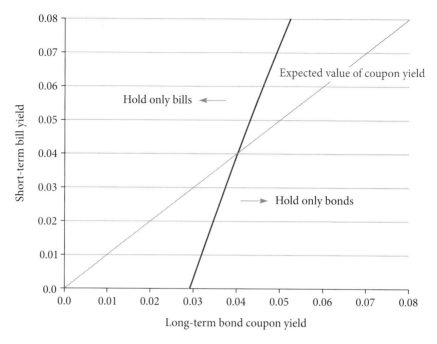

Figure 12.6 Term structure: expected short- and long-term rates with reversion to normal.

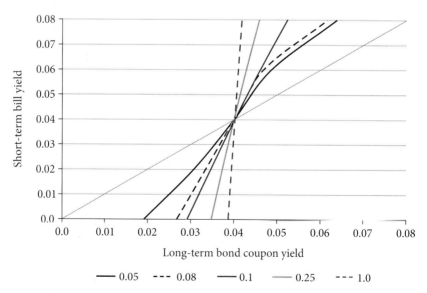

Figure 12.7 Term structure: relationship between short- and long-term rates with different adjustment speeds.

ρ_s is zero, the bond yield will be positive because it is an average of short-term rates over the life of the bond, and these rates are expected to be positive as the short rate reverts to normal.

Second, when the bill rate is above normal, the relationship between the bond yield and the bill rate is inverted. Unlike the risk-aversion case, in which the yield premium exists regardless of the level of interest rates, in the normal-reversion case short-term bill rates exceed the bond yield when the current bill rate is above the normal rate. Although short-horizon risk aversion cannot account for the inversion of short and long rates pictured in Figure 12.4, normal reversion can.[8]

Reversion to normal is a plausible reason for interest-rate spreads. But reversion to normal is no more adequate by itself than is risk aversion. For one thing, if reversion to normal were the sole force at work, we should expect that, over time, short-term rates would be distributed more or less symmetrically around the normal rate, so that the mean of the difference between the current short-term rate and the normal rate would be zero. This would imply that inversions of the yield premium would be common, not the relatively rare events they are in Figure 12.4. Moreover, a major implication of the absence of risk aversion is that *individual* portfolios are specialized to bonds or bills except when agents are on the margin and willing to hold both securities in combination. When all is said and done, the idea of portfolios consisting of only one kind of security is only marginally more palatable than the idea of

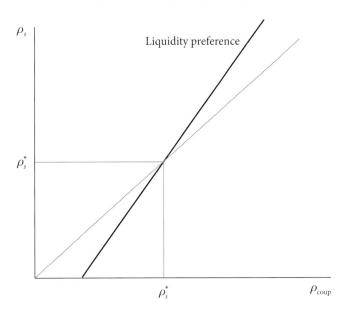

Figure 12.8 Liquidity preference without money, II: reversion to normal.

identical risk-neutral agents, which leads to demand oscillating wildly between short- and long-dated securities in response to small changes in the
spread. There may be wide diversity of opinion, but with risk-neutral agents
there is practically no diversification!

Combining Risk Aversion with Reversion to Normal in a Theory of Interest-Rate Spreads

Risk aversion and normal reversion are not mutually exclusive theories.
Rather, as in chapter 11, the two theories are complementary. Risk aversion
answers a question to which normal reversion provides no answer, namely,
why do agents diversify their holdings? And normal reversion answers a
question to which risk aversion provides no answer, namely, why does the
term structure sometimes exhibit an inversion of the usual positive spread
between long and short coupon yields?

Figure 12.9 combines these results, showing how normal reversion displaces the liquidity-preference schedule in Figure 12.5. Observe that at A,
corresponding to a bill rate equal to the normal rate, the two schedules intersect. At A an agent who believes that current rates always revert to normal has
no difference of opinion with an agent who does not believe at all in reversion
to normal; where $\rho_s = \rho_s^*$, both agents share the belief that $E(\dot{P}_B)/P_B = 0$. When
risk aversion and normal reversion are combined, the short-term rate must be

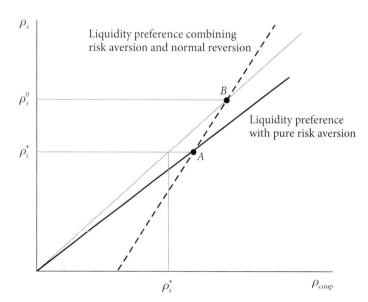

Figure 12.9 Liquidity preference without money, III: combining
risk aversion and normal reversion.

more than marginally greater than the normal rate for an inversion of the yield premium to take place. In Figure 12.9 only when the short rate exceeds ρ_s^0 is the bill rate higher than the bond yield.

The two extremes of pure risk aversion and pure normal reversion reduce to extreme assumptions about portfolio optimization. Pure risk aversion, without normal reversion, can be expressed as the assumption $E(\dot{P}_B)/P_B = 0$; pure normal reversion reduces to an assumption about the utility function, namely, $-U_2/U_1 = 0$. In this formulation, explored more fully in the mathematical appendix to this chapter, U_1 is the marginal utility of (expected) wealth, and U_2 reflects the marginal utility of holding wealth in liquid form. Normal reversion without risk aversion means that the marginal utility of liquidity is zero.

The empirical appendix to this chapter assesses the relative importance of risk aversion and normal reversion in determining the yield premium over time. The conclusion is that most of the time normal reversion is of relatively minor importance—but not all the time. At critical junctures—including the period since the financial crisis developed in the fall of 2008—normal reversion not only matters, it has been the dominant force driving interest-rate spreads, at least for spreads between Treasury securities.

Default Risk

Up to now we have considered two assets, one of which has price risk. But neither entails any default risk. T-bills and T-bonds are the canonical examples, though (as was observed at the beginning of the chapter) high-grade commercial paper as well as Fed Funds usually are interchangeable with short-term T-bills. Since our focus is ultimately on how the hurdle rate for private investment decisions is determined, we need to extend the story to take account of the possibility, always present in private undertakings, that the borrower may default.[9] The hurdle rate relevant for private investment is not the yield on Treasuries, but the yield on bonds issued by corporations with a risk of default comparable to the risk that a particular investment in physical assets will go sour.

How do we conceptualize the relationship between yields on Treasuries and yields on corporate bonds? The logic of this comparison is the same as the logic for comparing short- and long-term government obligations: agents are assumed to compare the expected holding yields on the two types of bonds, taking account of the impact of default on the expected change in bond price. Risk-averse agents presumably require a premium reflecting the greater price volatility associated with corporate bonds—once default risk is factored in.

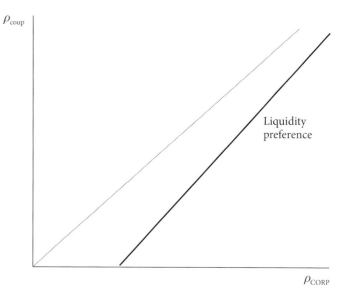

Figure 12.10 Liquidity preference without money, IV: optimizing between corporate and Treasury bonds.

Figure 12.10 summarizes the results of adding default risk to liquidity preference. The spread between Treasury and corporate bonds is assumed to be decreasing with the Treasury yield. This is intended to reflect the increase in both perceived and actual default risk at times of slack aggregate demand, when the Federal Reserve typically reduces Treasury yields but corporate default risk, and hence the spread $\rho_{CORP} - \rho_{coup}$, increases.

This is particularly salient at times of financial panic. From 1990 to 2007, the difference between the yield on corporate bonds and the yield between Treasuries of comparable maturity suggests an implicit default risk on the lowest investment-grade corporate bonds (Moody's Baa rating) of the order of 1.5 percent per year.[10] By contrast, in the year following the collapse of Lehman Brothers, the implicit default risk rose on average to 4 percent, peaking just above 5.5 percent in December 2008.

Figure 12.11 shows how the relationship between short and long Treasuries is modified by the addition of default risk. It is still theoretically possible to have an inverted term structure—possible for the corporate bond to have a lower yield to maturity than a short-term T-bill—though it takes a higher short-term rate to offset the higher price risk when default is part of the picture. In fact, even though the term structure of Treasuries exhibited inversion six times between 1962 and 2019, the short-term bill rose above the corporate bond yield only three times, and very briefly at that (in 1973, 1980, and 1981), as Figure 12.12 shows.

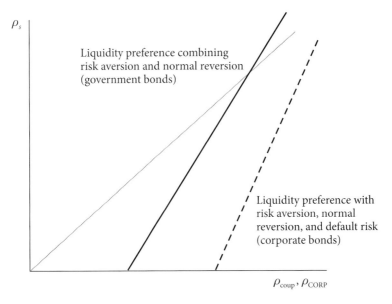

Figure 12.11 Liquidity preference without money, V: adding in default risk.

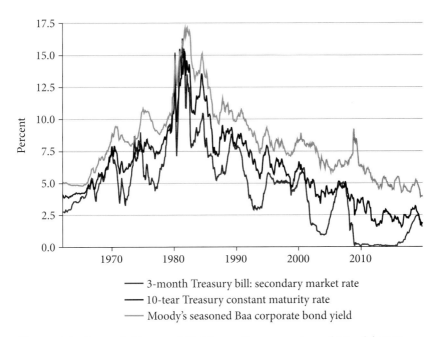

— 3-month Treasury bill: secondary market rate
— 10-tear Treasury constant maturity rate
— Moody's seasoned Baa corporate bond yield

Figure 12.12 3-month Treasury-bill, 10-year Treasury note, and Moody's BBB corporate bond index (1962–2019). *Sources:* Board of Governors, Moody's. myf.red/g/pY2y

Liquidity Preference and Monetary Policy
Innovations in the Great Recession

If we couple the construction of the liquidity-preference schedule in Figure 12.11 with the investment-demand and saving schedules, we can determine the hurdle rate of interest, the level of aggregate demand, and the demand for transactions money, as in Figure 12.13. Liquidity preference may provide only a theory of spreads, but with a central bank's hand on the steering wheel, a theory of spreads is all that is needed to determine aggregate demand: the central bank fixes the short-term bill rate—$\rho_s = 0.05$ in Figure 12.13—and bond markets take care of the rest.

The Federal Reserve's immediate response to the financial crisis and the ensuing recession was to reduce the bill rate to its lower bound of zero. This had only a modest effect on the hurdle rate because of both increased risk aversion—like investment demand, liquidity preference is based on expectations and highly volatile—and the expectation that interest rates would revert to normal: the spread between the T-bill rate and the corporate bond yield—see Figure 12.12—was more than 500 basis points throughout 2009. Given the endowments of bonds and bills in the hands of the public, the Fed could do little to change the spread.

These endowments are not immutable in theory and were not in practice. The Fed followed up its policy of setting the bill rate at zero by "quantitative easing," essentially swapping bills for the public's bonds, and by this means shifting the liquidity-preference schedule inward. (In actuality the swap was central-bank reserves for bonds; see chapter 13, note 10.) In the mathematical appendix to this chapter, it is shown that for changes in the endowments that are wealth preserving, that is, for which

$$M_2 + P_B B = \bar{M}_2 + P_B \bar{B} = \text{const.},$$

the relationship between the equilibrium bond price and the quantity of bonds in the hands of the public is negative when certain assumptions about risk preferences hold. Under these assumptions an increase in $\bar{M}$ and a corresponding decrease in $\bar{B}$ shift the liquidity-schedule inward, as in Figure 12.14.

A second novelty in Fed policy as recovery slowed was the commitment to maintain the short-term rate virtually at zero. Reversion to normal has been framed as a process in which the current value of the short-term interest rate is fixed by the central bank, and its expected evolution follows a path of gradual adjustment to normal. Under this assumption, the central bank may set ρ_s as low as it chooses, even at zero (as was effectively the case from the fall of 2008 to the end of 2015), but expectations embodied in θ determine the

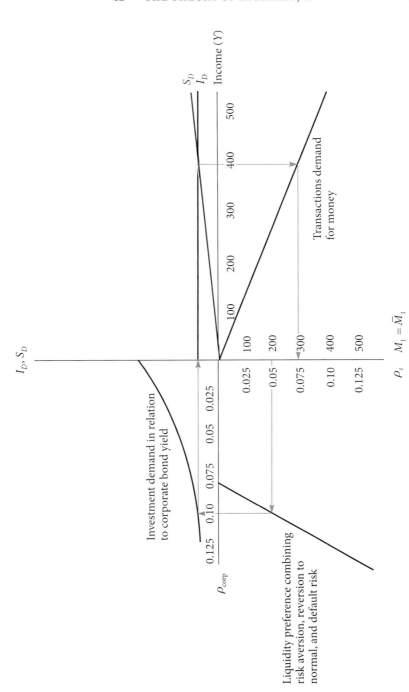

Figure 12.13 Aggregate demand and the transactions demand for money.

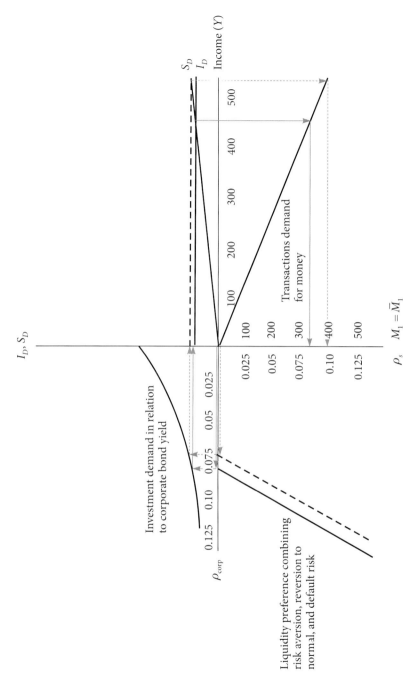

Figure 12.14 Aggregate demand and the transactions demand for money with quantitative easing.

bond yield. This is what makes a liquidity trap, defined as the level of ρ_{coup} (or ρ_{CORP}) associated with $\rho_s = 0$, possible.

However, θ is not etched in stone; θ is a variable under (partial) control of the central bank. A commitment to maintain ρ_s below the normal rate in effect reduces θ, and the longer the duration of its commitment, the lower the current bond yield. The effect is, like the effect of quantitative easing depicted in Figure 12.14, to shift the liquidity-preference schedule inward, with the difference that the shift is more pronounced the further the economy is from the normal rate.

The limit to the central bank's control over θ is the credibility of its commitment. In the limit, a credible commitment to $\rho_s = 0$ for the entire term of a T-bond drives θ to zero over this whole period. The result is that the price of the T-bond exceeds its par value, and the gradual fall in the price of the bond exactly offsets the coupon; the yield to maturity is zero. Observe that in contrast with a commitment to maintain $\rho_s = 0$ for a definite amount of time, a commitment that expires when a trigger is pulled (for example, the unemployment rate reaching 5 percent) leaves the path of θ uncertain because of the uncertainty as to when the gun will be fired.

Conclusions

This chapter addressed the major shortcoming of liquidity preference as a theory of interest: the alternative to holding bonds is not to hold cash or bank deposits, but short-term bills that normally offer an interest payment to their owners. The cash-bonds model, unlike the rigid money-wage model, turns out not to be a part of the scaffolding that can be jettisoned once the building is in place!

When all is said and done, Keynes's critics were right to question liquidity preference as a theory of interest. Liquidity preference is instead a theory of interest rate *differences*. In a world of money and bonds, liquidity preference provides a coherent and complete theory of the rate of interest, but only because a theory of differences between yields on the short-term asset (money) and the long-term asset (bonds) is necessarily a theory of the rate of interest on the long-term asset. The nominal return on money is by definition zero, so the difference between the two rates is simply the nominal return on bonds.

This result does not generalize to a more realistic world in which wealth holders choose among an array of assets of varying terms, yields, and default risks, an array in which, as a store of wealth, money is dominated by short-term bills. In this world, the writ of liquidity preference runs no further than the spreads between these various yields. In a world in which a central bank steers the economy by imposing a short-term interest rate, this limitation is not, in principle, a problem, because all that is needed is a theory of spreads.

As in the money-bonds world of the previous chapter, liquidity preference is a big tent in which risk aversion and reversion to normal as well as default risk all influence the structure of interest rates. And as in the simpler cash-bonds model, none of these motives for holding liquid assets is sufficient by itself to account for observed patterns of interest-rate structures. Short-horizon risk aversion leads to the prediction that interest-rate differentials do not depend on the existing short rate, and that bond yields will always be above short-term rates. As we shall see in the empirical appendix to this chapter, the data reveal some dependence of the spread on the level of the bill rate, something we can see in Figures 12.4 and 12.12.

Reversion to normal accounts for the widening of the difference between long and short yields at low interest rates, but by itself would predict that inversions of the term structure would be as frequent as the usual term structure, in which yields rise with bond term. Neither aversion to the risk of bond-price fluctuations nor reversion of interest rates to normal accounts for the persistent gap between yields on government securities and yields on corporate bonds of comparable maturity. Here, liquidity-preference theory has to appeal to another kind of risk, namely, the risk of default.

The various motives for holding more liquid assets are not mutually exclusive. We can imagine agents who embody both risk aversion and a belief in reversion to normal. Or we can imagine that some agents are risk averse without believing rates will revert to normal, and others are risk neutral while believing in reversion to normal. Either way, we will get a liquidity-preference relationship between short rates and long rates, and more to the point, between riskless short rates and the hurdle rate that governs investment decisions. Even if the short-term rate is equal to its zlb, the hurdle rate will be positive. And higher short-term rates generally correspond to higher long-term yields. Together these two results are the essence of liquidity preference.

It should come as no surprise that the liquidity-preference schedule, like the investment-demand schedule, is likely to be extremely volatile. The reason is the same here as in chapter 10: the central role of expectations and the fragility of the knowledge on which expectations are based.

We should expect risk aversion to vary over the cycle because both actual default rates and, more important, the fear of default rise in bad economic times. But risk aversion can, as we shall see when we examine the data, increase even with respect to T-bonds, a result that takes some explaining.

The impact of normal reversion also changes over the cycle. Most of the time, the data suggest, normal reversion is noticeable for its absence. Most of the time, agents have little clue as to which way interest rates will move. But sometimes normal reversion is the most important, if not the only, driver of interest-rate spreads. From the beginning of the financial crisis of 2008 until the end of 2015, interest rates had nowhere to go but up. In this period, the question was the speed with which interest rates would move, not the direction in which they would move. During that period, there was increasing speculation about whether the normal rate itself has changed. In 2020 we are still waiting for the answer.

MATHEMATICAL APPENDIX

Tobin's 1958 model quickly became the canonical model for analyzing liquidity preference in terms of risk aversion. In the intervening decades, there have been many modifications, but the basic ideas remain the same. Tobin assumes first that the distribution of price changes, $\Delta P_B/P_B$ (in a discrete time model), is independent of the price of bonds, as in Figure 11.4, and, second, that agents maximize a utility function based on the mean and the standard deviation of the one-period performance of portfolios that include bonds and cash. Tobin rationalized the emphasis on the mean and standard deviation in terms of quadratic expected utility à la von Neumann and Morgenstern (1944). John Campbell and Luis Viceira (2002, chap. 2) review alternative assumptions about the utility function and the distribution of returns that justify a focus on the short-term mean and variance.

In this section I follow Tobin and his heirs in focusing on risk aversion, but the main points of the argument can be made more transparently with fewer restrictive assumptions—in particular, without the assumption of von Neumann–Morgenstern utility and corresponding restrictions on the distribution of bond-price changes. The essential idea, laid out in chapter 11, is that money provides utility over and above its contribution to wealth because of the flexibility it provides to take on targets of opportunity in an uncertain world.

Here we suppose that agents choose a combination of money and bonds to maximize an (ordinal) utility function $U(E(A), M)$, in which A represents wealth, $E(A)$ represents expected value of wealth at the end of the year (the mean of the probability distribution of year-end portfolio values), and M (no subscript is necessary for present purposes) represents the money in the portfolio at the beginning of the year. Utility increases with $E(A)$, but for any given level of expected wealth, the greater the fraction of the portfolio in money, the greater is the level of utility. Utility increases with M because more money means less risk of fluctuations in wealth; the initial price of bonds P_B is assumed to be given, but the terminal price $P_B + \Delta P_B$ is a random variable.

Expected wealth is

$$M + \left(1 + \frac{R}{P_B} + \frac{E(\Delta P_B)}{P_B}\right) P_B B.$$

The utility function is

$$U(E(A), M) = U\left(M + \left(1 + \frac{R}{P_B} + \frac{E\left(\Delta P_B\right)}{P_B}\right) P_B B, M \right) \qquad (12.1)$$

where B and M are the agent's holdings of bonds and money.

Indifference curves associated with $U(E(A), M)$ are pictured in Figure 12.15. The positive relationship of utility to the portfolio's expected value and to the portion of the portfolio committed to money is reflected in the signs of the derivatives $U_1 \equiv \partial U/\partial E(A) > 0$ and $U_2 \equiv \partial U/\partial M > 0$.

To construct a liquidity-preference schedule along the lines of Figures 11.1 and 11.2, we need to impose restrictions on the indifference map: (1) indifference curves become *steeper* as we move upward, that is, holding the amount of portfolio money constant; (2) indifference curves *flatten out* if the agent increases her holdings of money while maintaining a given level of expected wealth; and, finally, (3) indifference curves become *less steep* when $E(A)$ and M increase at the same rate. Assumption (1) means that agents become more risk averse as their expected wealth increases relative to their money holdings. Assumption (2) implies that agents become less risk averse as their money holdings increase relative to their expected wealth. Together these two assumptions imply that the indifference curves are convex to the origin, so each one becomes less steep from northwest to southeast (in the direction of the

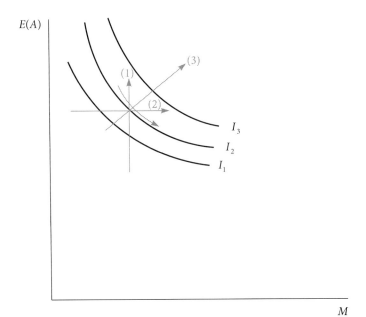

Figure 12.15 Liquidity preference as aversion to risk.

curved arrow).[1] Assumption (3) guarantees that the impact of additional wealth on the risk-return trade-off is smaller than the impact of additional liquidity, measured by an equal increase in M. These three assumptions are reflected in the changes in the slope of the indifference curves along the directional arrows (1)–(3) in Figure 12.15.

We obtain formal expressions for Assumptions (1)–(3) from the behavior of the slope as we move in one direction or another. Write the slope as

$$\frac{dy}{dx} = h(y, x) = h(E(A), M) = -\frac{U_2}{U_1}.$$

Assumption (1), that indifference curves become steeper as we move vertically in Figure 12.15, means that the derivative of h with respect to expected wealth is negative, which is to say

$$h_1 = -\frac{U_{21}U_1 - U_{11}U_2}{U_1^2} < 0. \tag{12.2}$$

An increase in the slope $-U_2/U_1$ holding $E(A)$ constant, Assumption (2), implies

$$h_2 = -\frac{U_{22}U_1 - U_{12}U_2}{U_1^2} > 0. \tag{12.3}$$

Convexity means that every indifference curve flattens out as we move along it in a southwest direction. This is to say

$$h_1 \frac{dy}{dx} + h_2 = \left(-\frac{U_{21}U_1 - U_{11}U_2}{U_1^2}\right)\left(-\frac{U_2}{U_1}\right) - \frac{U_{22}U_1 - U_{12}U_2}{U_1^2} > 0. \tag{12.4}$$

Assumption (1) implies that the first term in equation (12.4) is positive, and Assumption (2) implies that the second term is positive. Assumption (3) requires that h_1 be small in absolute value relative to h_2. Starting from any point in Figure 12.15, the slopes of successive indifference curves increase along the 45-degree line of equality between $\Delta(E(A))$ and ΔM:

$$h_1 + h_2 = -\frac{U_{21}U_1 - U_{11}U_2}{U_1^2} - \frac{U_{22}U_1 - U_{12}U_2}{U_1^2} > 0. \tag{12.5}$$

Optimization is constrained by wealth:

$$M + P_B B = A_0 = \overline{M} + P_B \overline{B}, \tag{12.6}$$

where $\overline{M}$ and $\overline{B}$ are, respectively, the agent's endowment of cash and bonds. The agent is assumed to maximize expression (12.1) subject to the portfolio composition possibilities reflected in equation (12.6).

The return on cash is by assumption zero, so that if the portfolio consists entirely of cash, expected wealth at the end of the year is the initial wealth $A_0 = \bar{M} + P_B\bar{B}$. To the extent the portfolio includes bonds, expected wealth increases by the expected holding yield, multiplied by the amount of the portfolio in bonds,

$$\left(\frac{R}{P_B} + \frac{E\left(\Delta P_B \right)}{P_B} \right) P_B B.$$

In the case of pure risk aversion, $E(\Delta P_B)/P_B = 0$, so the relationship between the expected value of the portfolio and the holdings of bonds and money is given by

$$E(A) = M + \left(1 + \frac{R}{P_B} \right) P_B B = A_0 + \frac{R}{P_B} P_B B = A_0 + \frac{R}{P_B}\left(A_0 - M \right),$$

and the problem is to maximize

$$U(E(A), M) = U\left(A_0 + \left(\frac{R}{P_B} \right)\left(A_0 - M \right), M \right). \tag{12.7}$$

In the text, cash is replaced by short-term bills as the alternative to bonds. This does not change the optimization problem, except that now we regard M as the desired holdings of bills, and $\bar{M}$ as the endowment of bills. Equation (12.6) continues to represent the budget constraint, but expected wealth and the utility function change because bills are assumed to yield ρ_s. Expected wealth is now

$$E(A) = \left(1 + \rho_s \right) M + \left(1 + \frac{R}{P_B} \right) P_B B = \left(1 + \rho_s \right) A_0 + \left(\frac{R}{P_B} - \rho_s \right)\left(A_0 - M \right),$$

and utility is

$$U(E(A), M) = U\left(\left(1 + \rho_s \right) A_0 + \left(\frac{R}{P_B} - \rho_s \right)\left(A_0 - M \right), M \right).$$

Figure 12.16 shows the menu of alternative portfolios of bills and bonds and the optimal portfolio at E.

In Figure 12.16 the optimal balance between return and risk is struck at E, with the demand for bills given by $M = M^*$, and the demand for bonds $P_B B^* = \bar{M} + P_B\bar{B} - M^*$. The first-order condition for an interior maximum is

$$\frac{R}{P_B} - \rho_s - \frac{U_2}{U_1} = 0,$$

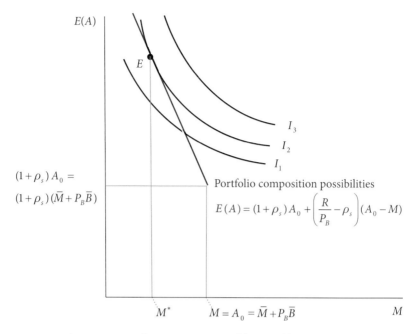

Figure 12.16 Balancing coupon yield, capital loss, and risk.

which can be rewritten as

$$\frac{R}{P_B} - \rho_s = \frac{U_2}{U_1}.$$

U_2/U_1 is a risk premium, the amount by which the expected yield on bonds must exceed the riskless return available on short-dated assets, "must" in the sense of the dictates of constrained maximization of the wealth holder's utility.

A change in the yield R/P_B changes the optimal balance of risk and return in two ways. If P_B rises, which is to say that the yield decreases, the value of the agent's endowment increases with the price of the bond to the extent that her endowment takes the form of bonds—a "wealth effect." At the same time, the reward for holding bonds decreases, a "substitution effect." The two effects are shown in Figure 12.17, the wealth effect by the shift in the position of the intercept of the schedule of portfolio possibilities, the substitution effect by the shift in the slope of this schedule.

At the two limits $\bar{B} = 0$ and $\bar{M} = 0$, portfolio possibilities shift as in Figure 12.18. F is the new equilibrium when the agent's endowment consists only of bills and F' is the new equilibrium when only bonds. Observe that in the second case the wealth effect is necessarily negative.

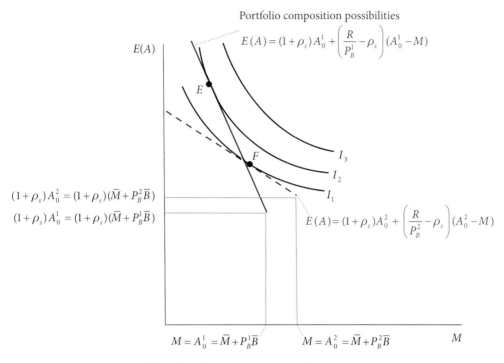

Figure 12.17 The effect of a change in the bond price and interest rate.

Even though the wealth effect can work against the substitution effect, the increase in the price of bonds from P_B^1 to P_B^2 generally leads to an increase in the portfolio demand for bills and a corresponding decrease in the demand for bonds. In addition to the restrictions on the indifference-curve slopes embodied in Assumptions (1)–(3), a sufficient condition for this result is that the return on the optimal holding of bonds be bounded by the expected value of the bond endowment,

$$\frac{R}{P_B} B^* < \left(1 + \frac{R}{P_B} \right) \bar{B}.$$

Otherwise, a (negative) wealth effect may swamp the substitution effect, and, consequently, the demand for money might decrease, as is the case in Figure 12.18 at the limit $A_0 = \bar{M}$, where the new equilibrium at F involves a lower demand for bills.

To see this, substitute from the portfolio constraint into the utility function to transform the optimization problem from a choice of B to a choice of M:

$$U\left(E(A), M \right) = U\left(\bar{M} + P_B \bar{B} + \rho_s M + \frac{R}{P_B}\left(\bar{M} + P_B \bar{B} - M \right), M \right). \quad (12.8)$$

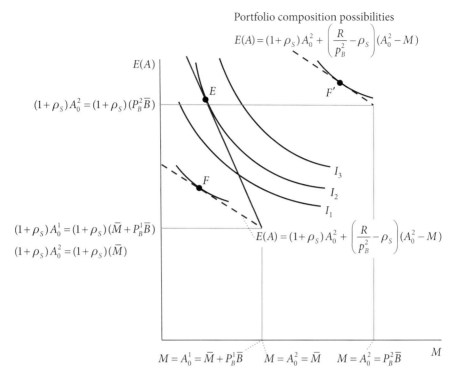

Figure 12.18 The effect of a change in the bond price and interest rate: two limiting cases.

The first-order condition for an interior solution remains the same, but now we write the first order condition as

$$H\left(M, P_B, \bar{M}, \bar{B}, \rho_s\right) \equiv \frac{R}{P_B} - \rho_s - \frac{U_2}{U_1} = 0. \tag{12.9}$$

With P_B given along with $\bar{M}$, $\bar{B}$, and ρ_s, we can solve equation (12.9) for the optimal amount of bills and write the solution as

$$M = M^*\left(P_B, \bar{M}, \bar{B}, \rho_s\right).$$

Taking the total derivative of the function

$$H\left(M^*\left(P_B, \bar{M}, \bar{B}, \rho_s\right), P_B, \bar{M}, \bar{B}, \rho_s\right) = 0$$

with respect to P_B tells us how the demand for bills ($M = M^*(P_B, \bar{M}, \bar{B}, \rho_s)$) is related to the price of bonds. We have

$$H_1 \frac{\partial M^*}{\partial P_B} + H_2 = 0,$$

so that

$$\frac{\partial M^*}{\partial P_B} = -\frac{H_2}{H_1}.$$

By virtue of equation (12.8), differentiating equation (12.9) with respect to M gives

$$H_1 = \left(\frac{U_{21}U_1 - U_{11}U_2}{U_1^2}\right)\left(\frac{R}{P_B} - \rho_s\right) - \frac{U_{22}U_1 - U_{12}U_2}{U_1^2},$$

$$H_2 = -\frac{R}{\left(P_B\right)^2} - \frac{\left(U_{21}U_1 - U_{11}U_2\right)\left[\left(1 + \dfrac{R}{P_B}\right)\bar{B} - \dfrac{R}{P_B}B\right]}{U_1^2}.$$

H_1 is positive because of Assumptions (1) and (2). Assumption (1) also ensures H_2 is negative if

$$\left(1 + \frac{R}{P_B}\right)\bar{B} - \frac{R}{P_B}B^* \geq 0.$$

The takeaway is that, unless the demand for bonds is large compared to the endowment, the wealth effects of bond-price changes dominate, and the demand for money or bills increases as the bond price rises and the bond yield falls.

Equilibrium in a Representative-Agent Model

Demand is of course just half the story of asset-market equilibrium; the other half is supply. In general, demand-supply balance in any market is an aggregative property and thus requires us to sum demands and supplies over all agents.

A representative-agent model (a model in which all other agents are clones of the representative) simplifies our task: the representative agent is a microcosm of the world, and the overall supply-demand equilibrium must be replicated at the level of the individual agent. With identical agents, not only must the agent's demand for bills and bonds add up to her total wealth, but each separate demand must be equal to the respective endowment, just as for the population as a whole. If endowments of bills and bonds are respectively $\bar{M}$ and $\bar{B}$, the agent's choice has to respect both the overall constraint

$$M + P_B B = A_0 = \bar{M} + P_B\bar{B}$$

and also the individual constraints $M = \bar{M}$ and $B = \bar{B}$. (Evidently if $M = \bar{M}$, the budget constraint guarantees $B = \bar{B}$, so we don't need to consider the second condition separately.)

With a given endowment $\bar{M}$, it is precisely the function of the interest rate to bring equilibrium about, which is to say that, *given the short-term interest rate ρ_s*, the equilibrium bond price P_B and interest rate R/P_B are endogenously determined by the endowments to equilibrate the demand for and supply of both bills and bonds.

The tangencies reflected in Figures 12.16 and 12.17 continue to play a role but are necessary rather than sufficient to characterize equilibrium. The tangency between an indifference curve and the portfolio constraint is now subject to the conditions $M = \bar{M}$ and $P_B = P_B(\bar{M}, \bar{B}, \rho_s)$. That is, the endowments $\bar{M}$ and $\bar{B}$ determine the bond price $P_B(\bar{M}, \bar{B}, \rho_s)$ that just makes the demand for bills equal to the supply. At the individual level, we have the demand function

$$M = M^* \left(P_B, \bar{M}, \bar{B}, \rho_s \right)$$

and equality of demand and supply

$$M = M^* \left(P_B \left(\bar{M}, \bar{B}, \rho_s \right), \bar{M}, \bar{B}, \rho_s \right) = \bar{M}.$$

With the agent representing the cosmos, market equilibrium

$$\sum M = \sum M^* \left(P_B, \bar{M}, \bar{B}, \rho_s \right) = \sum \bar{M}$$

reduces to the same relationship at the level of the representative agent

$$M = M^* \left(P_B, \bar{M}, \bar{B}, \rho_s \right) = \bar{M}.$$

Does an equilibrium exist? A simple fixed-point theorem shows that a sufficient condition for existence of equilibrium in this model is that the economy not be in a liquidity trap; that is, the condition $\rho_s > 0$ must hold. Construct the demand function by starting with a price P_B^1 such that $R/P_B - \rho_s = 0$. That is, $P_B^1 = R/\rho_s$. At this price, it does not pay to hold bonds, and with $B = 0$

$$M + P_B B = M = \bar{M} + P_B \bar{B} > \bar{M}.$$

Now consider the lower end of the price range. As $P_B \to 0$, we have

$$\lim_{P_B \to 0} M + \lim_{P_B \to 0} \left(P_B B^* \right) = \bar{M} + \lim_{P_B \to 0} P_B \bar{B} = \bar{M},$$

with the result

$$\lim_{P_B \to 0} M < \bar{M} \qquad \text{if } \lim_{P_B \to 0} \left(P_B B^* \right) > 0,$$

$$\lim_{P_B \to 0} M = \bar{M} \qquad \text{if } \lim_{P_B \to 0} \left(P_B B^* \right) = 0.$$

So we have

$$M = M^* \left(P_B^1, \bar{M}, \bar{B}, \rho_s \right) > \bar{M},$$

$$\lim_{P_B \to 0} M = \lim_{P_B \to 0} M^* \left(P_B, \bar{M}, \bar{B}, \rho_s \right) \le \bar{M},$$

and, since M is a continuous function of P_B, there must exist a price, $P_B = P_B^*$, for which $M = \bar{M}$. The picture in Figure 12.19 assumes

$$\lim_{P_B \to 0} M = \lim_{P_B \to 0} M^* \left(P_B, \bar{M}, \bar{B}, \rho_s \right) < \bar{M}.$$

Observe that this argument fails at the zlb. When $\rho_s = 0$, there is no finite bond price at which $R/P_B = 0$, so there may be no finite bond price P_B^1 at which the demand for bonds vanishes and M exceeds $\bar{M}$. Pure risk aversion is consistent with the absence of a liquidity trap since it may be the case that for $\rho_s = 0$ the equilibrium bond yield may also be zero, as in Figure 12.5(a).

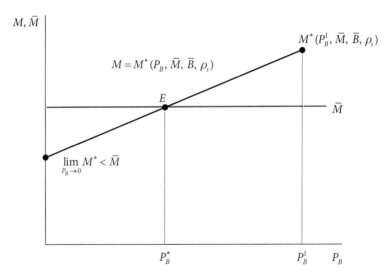

Figure 12.19 Equilibrium in a representative agent model.

The Impact of Bill Supply on the Price of Bonds

What happens when the endowment of bills increases? The bill supply and the demand for bills both increase, and the result of these two counteracting forces is ambiguous. In Figure 12.20 the equilibrium bond price rises, and the bond yield falls, but, as we shall see, this result is guaranteed only if ρ_s is small.

The math is as follows. If $M^* = \bar{M}$, then P_B is no longer a free parameter. Instead we have $P_B = P_B(\bar{M}, \bar{B}, \rho_s)$ such that

$$H\left(M^*\left(P_B\left(\bar{M}, \bar{B}, \rho_s\right), \bar{M}, \bar{B}, \rho_s\right), P_B\left(\bar{M}, \bar{B}, \rho_s\right), \bar{M}, \bar{B}, \rho_s\right) = 0.$$

If we differentiate this equation with respect to $\bar{M}$, we obtain

$$H_1\left(\frac{\partial M^*}{\partial P_B}\frac{\partial P_B}{\partial \bar{M}} + \frac{\partial M^*}{\partial \bar{M}}\right) + H_2\frac{\partial P_B}{\partial \bar{M}} + H_3 = 0.$$

Since

$$M = M^*\left(P_B\left(\bar{M}, \bar{B}, \rho_s\right)\bar{M}, \bar{B}, \rho_s\right) = \bar{M},$$

we have

$$\frac{\partial M^*}{\partial P_B}\frac{\partial P_B}{\partial \bar{M}} + \frac{\partial M^*}{\partial \bar{M}} = 1,$$

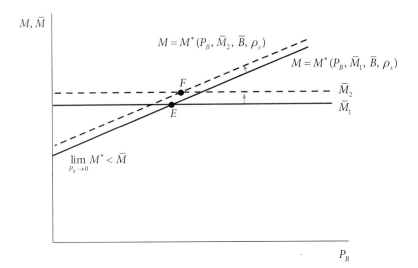

Figure 12.20 An increase in the supply of bills raises the equilibrium bond price.

so

$$\frac{\partial P_B}{\partial \bar{M}} = -\frac{H_1 + H_3}{H_2}$$

with

$$H_3 = -\left(\frac{U_{21}U_1 - U_{11}U_2}{U_1^2}\right)\left(1 + \frac{R}{P_B}\right).$$

The sum $H_1 + H_3$ is

$$H_1 + H_3 = -\left(\frac{U_{21}U_1 - U_{11}U_2}{U_1^2}\right)(1 + \rho_s) - \left(\frac{U_{22}U_1 - U_{12}U_2}{U_1^2}\right)$$

$$= -\left(\frac{U_{21}U_1 - U_{11}U_2}{U_1^2}\right) - \left(\frac{U_{22}U_1 - U_{12}U_2}{U_1^2}\right) - \left(\frac{U_{21}U_1 - U_{11}U_2}{U_1^2}\right)\rho_s. \quad (12.10)$$

The sign of the right-hand side of equation (12.10) is ambiguous since, by Assumption (3), the sum of the first two terms is positive, while Assumption (1) makes the last term negative. The ambiguity vanishes if ρ_s is small since the last term goes to zero with ρ_s. In this case we have

$$\text{sgn}\,\frac{\partial P_B}{\partial \bar{M}} = -\frac{\overset{+}{-}}{-} = +,$$

which is to say that the equilibrium bond yield is a decreasing function of the endowment of bills in the neighborhood of the zlb.

Equilibrium Spreads

For a given endowment of bills, we calculate the relationship between the bond price and the bill rate by taking the total derivative of $H(M^*(P_B(\bar{M}, \bar{B}, \rho_s), \bar{M}, \bar{B}, \rho_s), P_B(\bar{M}, \bar{B}, \rho_s), \bar{M}, \bar{B}, \rho_s)$ with respect to ρ_s and equating it to zero. This gives

$$H_2 \frac{\partial P_B}{\partial \rho_s} + H_5 = 0$$

since the stock of bills is constant and therefore

$$\frac{\partial M^*}{\partial P_B}\frac{\partial P_B}{\partial \rho_s} + \frac{\partial M^*}{\partial \rho_s} = 0.$$

The derivative H_5 is

$$H_5 = -1 - \frac{U_{21}U_1 - U_{11}U_2}{U_1^2} M,$$

which is negative. So

$$\text{sgn} \frac{\partial P_B}{\partial \rho_s} = \text{sgn}\left(-\frac{H_5}{H_2}\right) = -\frac{-}{-} = -,$$

and in turn the equilibrium bond yield is a positive function of the bill rate.

Quantitative Easing

In this chapter (see Figure 12.14) quantitative easing is represented as an exchange of the public's bonds for the monetary authority's bills. We have $M^*(P_B, \bar{M}, \bar{B}, \rho_s) = \bar{M}$ and $B = \bar{B}$, so

$$M^*\left(P_B, \bar{M}, \bar{B}, \rho_s\right) + P_B\left(\bar{M}, \bar{B}, \rho_s\right)B = \bar{M} + P_B\left(\bar{M}, \bar{B}, \rho_s\right)\bar{B}. \quad (12.11)$$

When the central bank buys bonds from the public, the corresponding change in the public's stock of bills is given by total differentiation of equation (12.11). Since $M^* = \bar{M}$ and $B = \bar{B}$, all terms but the derivatives of M^* and $\bar{M}$ cancel out on the two sides, and we are left with

$$\frac{\partial M^*}{\partial P_B}\frac{dP_B}{d\bar{B}} + \frac{\partial M^*}{\partial \bar{M}}\frac{\partial \bar{M}}{\partial \bar{B}} + \frac{\partial M^*}{\partial \bar{B}} = \frac{d\bar{M}}{d\bar{B}}.$$

Since $\partial \bar{M}/\partial \bar{B} = -P_B$ and $\partial \bar{M}^*/\partial \bar{B} = P_B \partial \bar{M}^*/\partial \bar{M}$, we can write $dP_B/d\bar{B}$ as

$$\frac{dP_B}{d\bar{B}} = \frac{\dfrac{d\bar{M}}{d\bar{B}}}{\dfrac{\partial M^*}{\partial P_B}}.$$

Because an increase in the availability of bonds must decrease the availability of bills, the numerator is negative. So the sign of the fraction depends on the denominator. Provided ρ_s is small, $\partial M^*/\partial P_B > 0$, and we have

$$\text{sgn} \frac{dP_B}{d\bar{B}} = \frac{-}{+} = -.$$

In the neighborhood of the zlb, as the stock of bonds in the hands of the public falls, the equilibrium price of bonds rises and bond yields fall.

　　The dynamics of bond-price adjustment lead to a more general result, which does not rely on ρ_s being small. Assume that P_B adjusts proportionately to the excess demand for bonds

$$\frac{\dot{P}_B}{P_B} = \theta_B \left(B - \bar{B} \right)$$

and thus negatively with the excess demand for bills

$$\dot{P}_B = -\theta_B \left(M^* \left(P_B, \bar{M}, \bar{B}, \rho_s \right) - \bar{M} \right).$$

$\dot{P}_B$ must increase when the supply of bonds in the hands of the public falls and the quantity of bills rises. We have

$$\frac{d\dot{P}_B}{d\bar{B}} = -\theta_B \left(\frac{\partial M^*}{\partial \bar{M}} \frac{\partial \bar{M}}{\partial \bar{B}} + \frac{\partial M^*}{\partial \bar{B}} - \frac{\partial \bar{M}}{\partial \bar{B}} \right) = -\theta_B \left(-\frac{H_3}{H_1} \left(-P_B \right) - \frac{H_4}{H_1} - \left(-P_B \right) \right)$$

and

$$H_4 = -\frac{\left(U_{21}U_1 - U_{11}U_2 \right) \left(1 + \dfrac{R}{P_B} \right) P_B}{U_1^2}.$$

Combining this equation with equation (12.10) eliminates $P_B H_3 - H_4$, giving the result

$$\frac{d\dot{P}_B}{d\bar{B}} = -\theta_B P_B.$$

The picture is in Figure 12.21. Suppose asset markets are originally in equilibrium, with $B = \bar{B}$ and $M = \bar{M}$. At this point $\dot{P}_B = 0$. Now let B and

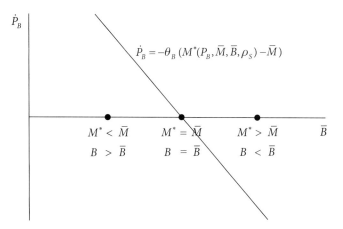

$$\dot{P}_B = -\theta_B \left(M^*(P_B, \bar{M}, \bar{B}, \rho_S) - \bar{M} \right)$$

| $M^* < \bar{M}$ | $M^* = \bar{M}$ | $M^* > \bar{M}$ | $\bar{B}$ |
| $B > \bar{B}$ | $B = \bar{B}$ | $B < \bar{B}$ | |

Figure 12.21 Disequilibrium price change ($\dot{P}$) as a function of the quantity of bonds in the public's hands ($\bar{B}$).

M remain fixed while $\bar{B}$ falls and $\bar{M}$ increases in accordance with the constraint

$$\bar{M} + P_B \bar{B} = \text{const.}$$

A fall in $\bar{B}$ drives up the price of bonds: to the left of the equilibrium $\dot{P}_B > 0$. The increase in P_B leads to a new, higher, level of M^* and a lower level of B, and eventually to a new equilibrium price P_B^* that exceeds the original price, and this independently of the size of ρ_s.

Bringing in Normal Reversion

When the current short-term rate is below normal, normal reversion simply reinforces risk aversion. The equilibrium condition is now

$$\frac{R}{P_B} - \rho_s = -\frac{E\left(\Delta P_B\right)}{P_B} + \frac{U_2}{U_1}.$$

The yield premium $R/P_B - \rho_s$ exceeds the risk premium U_2/U_1 by the absolute value of the expected capital loss, $-E(\Delta P_B)/P_B$. Compared with the case of pure risk aversion, in which $E(\Delta P_B)/P_B = 0$, the portfolio constraint shifts inward, as in Figure 12.22.

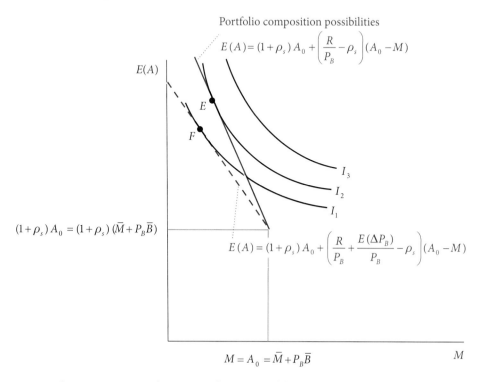

Figure 12.22 Normal reversion changes portfolio composition possibilities.

The more interesting case is when the current short rate exceeds the normal rate. In this case normal reversion and risk aversion are working against one another, since $-E(\Delta P_B)/P_B < 0$ and $-U_2/U_1 > 0$. If the expected capital gain is great enough, the combined force of normal reversion and risk aversion can be negative

$$\frac{R}{P_B} - \rho_s = -\frac{E(\Delta P_B)}{P_B} - \frac{U_2}{U_1} < 0.$$

That is, the yield premium $R/P_B - \rho_s$ can become negative at the optimum F in Figure 12.23.

FREE RIDING BY AGENTS WITH LONG HABITATS   An agent looking to the risk and return of her portfolio at retirement or when her last child is about to enter university will derive positive utility from bonds and will be averse to holding bills. Her indifference curves will have the shape in Figure 12.24, so provided the schedule of portfolio composition possibilities has a negative slope, the optimum will typically be a corner solution like E. Having a long "preferred habitat," she gets a free ride provided the yield premium $R/P_B - \rho_s$ is positive and the expected price change is non-negative. For an interior solution, in which the agent holds bills as well as bonds, the bill rate must ex-

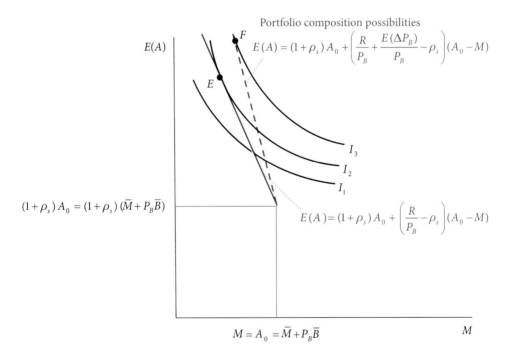

Portfolio composition possibilities

$E(A)$

$E(A) = (1+\rho_s)A_0 + \left(\frac{R}{P_B} + \frac{E(\Delta P_B)}{P_B} - \rho_s\right)(A_0 - M)$

$(1+\rho_s)A_0 = (1+\rho_s)(\bar{M} + P_B\bar{B})$

$E(A) = (1+\rho_s)A_0 + \left(\frac{R}{P_B} - \rho_s\right)(A_0 - M)$

$M = A_0 = \bar{M} + P_B\bar{B}$ M

Figure 12.23 A negative yield premium.

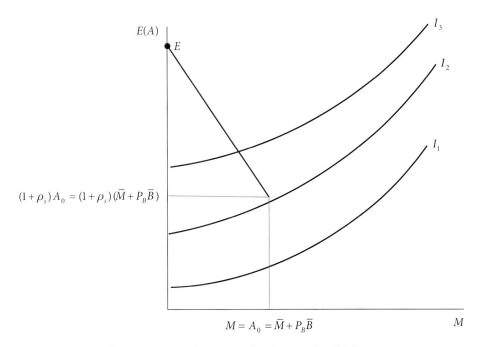

Figure 12.24 Equilibrium with a long preferred habitat.

ceed the bond yield by more than the expected increase in the bond price. The
first-order condition remains

$$\frac{R}{P_B} - \rho_s + \frac{E\left(\Delta P_B\right)}{P_B} + \frac{U_2}{U_1} = 0,$$

but U_2 is now negative.

WHAT IF AGENTS ARE RISK NEUTRAL?   In the absence of risk aversion,
the indifference curves become flat, reflecting the assumption that no disutility (or utility) attaches to owning bonds, which is to say that bills affect utility
only because they are part of wealth, not because of the added flexibility they
provide.

    With horizontal indifference curves, agents are driven to put all their eggs
in the bond or money basket according to the sign of

$$\frac{R}{P_B} + \frac{E\left(\dot{P}_B\right)}{P_B} - \rho_s,$$

the instantaneous holding yield on bonds minus the bill rate. Three possibilities are shown in the three panels of Figure 12.25.

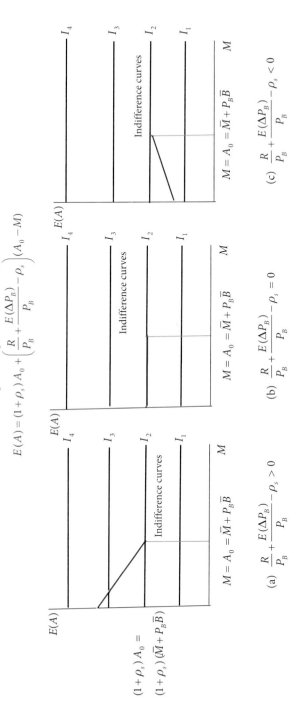

Portfolio composition possibilities

$$E(A) = (1+\rho_s)A_0 + \left(\frac{R}{P_B} + \frac{E(\Delta P_B)}{P_B} - \rho_s \right)(A_0 - M)$$

(a) $\dfrac{R}{P_B} + \dfrac{E(\Delta P_B)}{P_B} - \rho_s > 0$

(b) $\dfrac{R}{P_B} + \dfrac{E(\Delta P_B)}{P_B} - \rho_s = 0$

(c) $\dfrac{R}{P_B} + \dfrac{E(\Delta P_B)}{P_B} - \rho_s < 0$

Figure 12.25 Optimization with normal reversion and risk neutrality.

The main body of this chapter laid out the mathematics for calculating an agent's demand price for a bond on the assumption of continuous equality between the holding yield on a bond and the bill rate, depicted in Figure 12.25(b), coupled with the assumption of a simple linear reversion to normal of ρ_s,

$$\dot{\rho}_s = -\theta\left(\rho_s - \rho_s^*\right). \tag{12.12}$$

If the actual bond price is lower than demand price, then the agent will devote her portfolio entirely to bonds, as in Figure 12.25(a); if higher, to bills, as in Figure 12.25(c). Or, as expressed in Figure 12.6, if the actual coupon yield ρ_{coup} exceeds $E(\rho_{coup})$, where the expected coupon yield at $t = 0$ is

$$E\left(\rho_{coup,0}\right) = \frac{R}{E\left(P_{B,0}\right)} = \left(\int_0^\infty e^{-\rho_s^* \tau + \frac{\rho_s(t) - \rho_s^*}{\theta}\left(e^{-\theta\tau} - 1\right)}\, d\tau\right)^{-1}, \tag{12.13}$$

then the optimal strategy is to commit 100 percent to bonds, whereas if $\rho_{coup} < E(\rho_{coup})$, then the optimizing agent holds only bills.

If the evolution of the bill rate is governed by equation (12.12), we can calculate equation (12.13) by a formula derived in an old paper (Marglin 1970):

$$\frac{R}{E\left(P_{B,0}\right)} = \left\{\frac{1}{\rho_s^*}\left[1 + \sum_{n=1}^\infty \left[\left(\frac{\rho_s(0) - \rho_s^*}{\theta}\right)^{-n}\prod_{j=1}^\infty \left(\frac{\rho_s^*}{\theta} + j\right)^{-1}\right]\right]\right\}^{-1}.$$

THE RELATIONSHIP BETWEEN EXPECTED BOND-PRICE CHANGES AND THE BILL RATE   We continue to assume normal reversion and risk-neutral agents. Differentiating the equation

$$E\left(P_{B,t}\right) = \int_t^\infty Re^{-\int_t^\tau \rho_s(x)dx}\, d\tau$$

with respect to t, we have

$$E\left(\dot{P}_{B,t}\right) = -R + \rho_s E\left(P_{B,t}\right)$$

or

$$\frac{E\left(\dot{P}_{B,t}\right)}{E\left(P_{B,t}\right)} = -\frac{R}{E\left(P_{B,t}\right)} + \rho_s,$$

so

$$\partial \frac{\dfrac{E\left(\dot{P}_{B,t}\right)}{E\left(P_{B,t}\right)}}{\partial \rho_s(t)} = \frac{R}{E\left(P_{B,t}\right)^2} \frac{\partial E\left(P_{B,t}\right)}{\partial \rho_s(t)} + 1.$$

Since

$$E\left(P_{B,t}\right) = \int_t^\infty Re^{-\int_t^\tau \rho_s(x)dx}\, d\tau = \int_t^\infty Re^{-\rho_s^*(\tau-t)+\frac{\rho_s(t)-\rho_s^*}{\theta}\left(e^{-\theta\tau}-e^{-\theta t}\right)}\, d\tau,$$

we have

$$\partial \frac{\dfrac{E\left(\dot{P}_{B,t}\right)}{E\left(P_{B,t}\right)}}{\partial \rho_s(t)} = \frac{R}{E\left(P_{B,t}\right)^2} \int_t^\infty e^{\frac{1}{\theta}\left(e^{-\theta\tau}-e^{-\theta t}\right)}\, d\tau + 1,$$

and, setting $t = 0$,

$$\partial \frac{\dfrac{E\left(\dot{P}_{B,0}\right)}{E\left(P_{B,0}\right)}}{\partial \rho_s(0)} = \frac{R}{E\left(P_{B,0}\right)^2} \int_0^\infty e^{\frac{1}{\theta}\left(e^{-\theta\tau}-1\right)}\, d\tau + 1.$$

Since the right-hand side exceeds one, the expected *percentage* change in the bond price is in the same direction as a change in the bill rate, but greater than the absolute change in the bill rate.

Equilibrium with Normal Reversion and Risk Neutrality

Suppose there are n agents, each having the same endowment of bills and the same endowment of bonds. Each agent has her own forecast of the normal rate and the speed of reversion to that rate, so each has her own tipping point between bonds and bills. The total demand for bills is the sum of the individual demands

$$m\left(P_B, \rho_s\right)\left(\bar{M} + P_B\bar{B}\right),$$

where $m(P_B, \rho_s)$ is the number of agents desiring to hold only bills, and $\bar{M} + P_B\bar{B}$ is the value of the individual endowment.

When we include individuals on the margin of indifference, m can take on fractional values. Suppose we order individuals by the bond price that tips them from bonds to bills. If $m(P_B^0, \rho_s)$ maps to the interval between individual 20 and individual 21, this means that, when $P_B = P_B^0$, twenty agents desire to hold only bills and the twenty-first agent, who is indifferent between bills and bonds, is willing to hold any fraction of her wealth, from zero to one, in bills. Both elements of the demand for money, $m(P_B, \rho_s)$ and $(\bar{M} + P_B\bar{B})$, are increasing in P_B. Figure 12.26 shows the relationship between the price of bonds and the number of agents, including fractional agents, wishing to hold only bills, and Figure 12.27 shows the demand for bills as well as the aggregate supply, $n\bar{M}$. At the equilibrium E, one agent holds both bonds and bills.

The math is straightforward. Equilibrium is characterized by the equality

$$m\left(P_B, \rho_s\right)\left(\bar{M} + P_B\bar{B}\right) = n\bar{M}$$

or

$$mP_B\bar{B} = (n - m)\bar{M}. \tag{12.14}$$

As before, let

$$P_B = P_B\left(\bar{M}, \bar{B}, \rho_s\right).$$

Differentiate equation (12.14) with respect to $\bar{M}$. The result is

$$\frac{\partial m}{\partial P_B}\frac{dP_B}{d\bar{M}}\left(\bar{M} + P_B\bar{B}\right) + m\left(1 + \bar{B}\frac{dP_B}{d\bar{M}}\right) = n$$

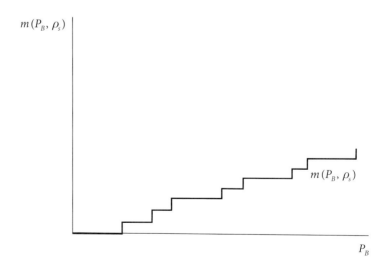

Figure 12.26 Number of agents desiring to hold bills in relation to bond price.

or

$$\frac{dP_B}{d\bar{M}} = \frac{n - m}{\dfrac{\partial m}{\partial P_B}(\bar{M} + P_B\bar{B}) + m\bar{B}}.$$

The expression on the right is positive unless everybody is 100 percent into bills, so just as in the case of pure risk aversion, the bond yield falls as the endowment of bills rises. This establishes the downward-sloping liquidity-preference function in the space of $\rho_{\text{coup}} \times \bar{M}$.

For given endowments of bonds and bills, the equilibrium bond price decreases (or at least does not increase) as the bill rate increases. Differentiating equation (12.14) with respect to ρ_s for fixed $\bar{M}$ and $\bar{B}$, we obtain

$$\frac{dP_B}{d\rho_s} = -\frac{\dfrac{\partial m}{\partial \rho_s}(\bar{M} + P_B\bar{B})}{\dfrac{\partial m}{\partial P_B}(\bar{M} + P_B\bar{B}) + m\bar{B}}.$$

Since $\partial m/\partial \rho_s \geq 0$ and $\partial m/\partial P_B \geq 0$, we have $dP_B/d\rho_s \leq 0$, so that the bond price cannot increase with the bill rate, and the bond yield is a nondecreasing function of the bill rate. Figure 12.28 shows the mappings $m(P_B, \rho_s^1)$ and $m(P_B, \rho_s^2)$ with $\rho_s^2 > \rho_s^1$. Figure 12.29 shows the two corresponding demand schedules.

What about the liquidity trap? The chapter 11 version of the liquidity trap

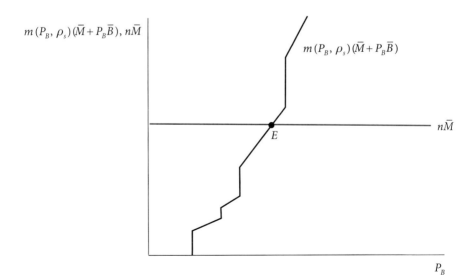

Figure 12.27 Demand and supply in bills market.

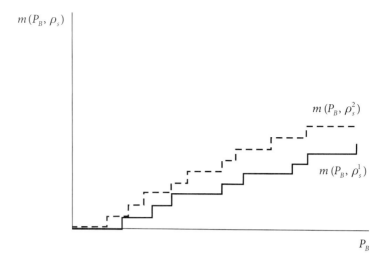

Figure 12.28 Number of agents desiring to hold bills as the bill rate varies.

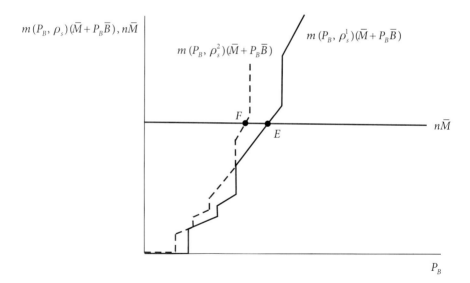

Figure 12.29 Demand and supply in bills market as the bill rate varies.

is a positive lower bound to the coupon yield ρ_{coup} and hence an upper bound to P_B as $\bar{M}$ increases without bound. Write the tipping-point price of the nth agent (the last agent to switch from bonds to bills as P_B increases) as P_B^n. Since for $P_B > P_B^n$ we have

$$m\left(P_B, \rho_s\right)\left(\bar{M} + P_B\bar{B}\right) = n\left(\bar{M} + P_B\bar{B}\right) > n\bar{M},$$

so that the demand for bills exceeds the supply. At the upper limit P_B^n we write m as $n - 1 + \beta_n$, where β_n is the proportion of bills in the wealth portfolio of the nth agent. The demand for bills is

$$\left(n - 1 + \beta_n\right)\left(\bar{M} + P_B^n \bar{B}\right).$$

Equation (12.14) becomes

$$\left(n - 1 + \beta_n\right) P_B^n \bar{B} = \left(1 - \beta_n\right)\bar{M}.$$

Demand and supply are maintained in balance as $\bar{M}$ increases because β_n increases in tandem. $\beta_n \to 1$ in the limit as $\bar{M} \to \infty$.

In this chapter, a liquidity trap exists if the equilibrium bond price remains finite when the bill rate is at its lower bound, $\rho_s = 0$. For a given endowment of bills and bonds, the proof of the existence of a liquidity trap in this sense parallels the proof of the existence of equilibrium in the risk-aversion case represented in Figure 12.19. For $P_B > P_B^n$, the demand for bills exceeds supply. At $P_B = 0$ there is no demand for bills. Since the mapping $m(P_B, 0)(\bar{M} + P_B\bar{B})$ is continuous, it must intersect the supply schedule somewhere on the interval $[0, P_B^n]$.

The Spread between Treasury Yields and Corporate Yields

Liquidity preference is supposed to lead to a theory of how the hurdle rate is determined, but so far I have limited my attention to T-bills and T-bonds. To finish the story, imagine a separate market in which Treasury and corporate bonds are traded.[2] Portfolio possibilities are given by

$$P_{CORP}B_{CORP} + P_B B = P_{CORP}\bar{B}_{CORP} + P_B\bar{B},$$

where P_{CORP} and B_{CORP} are prices and quantities of corporate bonds, and $\bar{B}_{CORP}$ is the endowment of corporate bonds. As before, P_B and B are the price and quantity of Treasuries, and $\bar{B}$ is the agent's endowment of Treasuries. Expected wealth is

$$E(A) = \left(1 + \frac{R_{CORP}}{P_{CORP}} + \frac{E\left(\Delta P_{CORP}\right)}{P_{CORP}}\right)P_{CORP}B_{CORP} + \left(1 + \frac{R}{P_B} + \frac{E\left(\Delta P_B\right)}{P_B}\right)P_B B$$

$$= P_{CORP}\bar{B}_{CORP} + P_B\bar{B} + \left(\frac{R}{P_B} + \frac{E\left(\Delta P_B\right)}{P_B}\right)P_B B$$

$$+ \left(\frac{R_{CORP}}{P_{CORP}} + \frac{E\left(\Delta P_{CORP}\right)}{P_{CORP}}\right)\left(P_{CORP}\bar{B}_{CORP} + P_B\bar{B} - P_B B\right).$$

With the utility function now

$$U\left(E(A), P_B B\right) = U\left(E(A), P_{CORP}\overline{B}_{CORP} + P_B\overline{B} - P_{CORP}B_{CORP}\right),$$

the first-order condition characterizing agents who hold both types of bonds is

$$\left(\frac{R}{P_B} + \frac{E\left(\Delta P_B\right)}{P_B}\right) - \left(\frac{R_{CORP}}{P_{CORP}} + \frac{E\left(\Delta P_{CORP}\right)}{P_{CORP}}\right) = \frac{U_2}{U_1}.$$

As before, U_1 reflects the marginal utility of expected wealth, but U_2 now measures the comparative safety of holding Treasuries relative to holding corporates. Assuming that the two types of bonds are of comparable maturities eliminates differences in price risk that are independent of default risk, so that the difference

$$\frac{E\left(\Delta P_B\right)}{P_B} - \frac{E\left(\Delta P_{CORP}\right)}{P_{CORP}}$$

measures the default risk on the corporate bond. Now the optimization condition is that the yield premium on corporate bonds

$$\rho_{CORP} - \rho_{coup} = \frac{R_{CORP}}{P_{CORP}} - \frac{R}{P_B}$$

is equal to the sum of the default risk and the illiquidity premium,

$$\frac{E\left(\Delta P_B\right)}{P_B} - \frac{E\left(\Delta P_{CORP}\right)}{P_{CORP}} + \frac{U_2}{U_1}.$$

In the absence of risk aversion, $U_2 = 0$, so the yield premium is exactly equal to the default risk. With risk aversion, the yield premium must be higher than the default risk to compensate for the aversion to loss.

What Do the Data Say?

This appendix examines the evidence for liquidity preference as a theory of how interest-rate spreads are determined by expectations of the course of future short-term interest rates. More specifically, the focus is on sorting out the relative importance of reversion to normal, risk aversion, and default risk in determining the spread between the hurdle rate of interest and the return on safe, short-term assets.

Near the end of the last century, John Campbell offered an authoritative assessment of the empirical state of play of interest-rate determination, based on his own joint work with Robert Shiller as well as on his comprehensive knowledge of a vast literature. Campbell argued that the data contradict a key provision of pure normal reversion (the "pure expectations hypothesis" in Campbell's terminology).[1] The hybrid hypothesis that both normal reversion and risk aversion are at work (Campbell's "expectations hypothesis") doesn't fare any better. Campbell regresses changes in bond yields on spreads between yields on bonds of various maturities and the short rate and finds

> In these regressions, the spread is scaled so that if the expectations hypothesis holds, the slope coefficient should be one. In fact, all but one of the slope coefficients are negative; all are significantly less than one, and some are significantly less than zero. When the long-short yield spread is high, the long yield tends to fall, amplifying the yield differential between long and short bonds, rather than rising to offset the yield spread as required by the expectations hypothesis. (1995, pp. 138–139)

Nobody to my knowledge has contradicted Campbell's assessment, and a more recent summary of the term-structure literature (Gürkaynak and Wright [2012]) affirms Campbell's position. Campbell is right that the data contradict the expectations hypothesis, in both its pure and hybrid forms, at least as the post–World War II literature has framed the argument. The problem is that Campbell and others neither offer nor test a theory of the expectations hypothesis, pure or hybrid, but rather a joint test of the expectations hypothesis and a very specific—and highly implausible—theory of how expectations are formed.

Beginning in the 1970s, the expectations hypothesis was married to rational expectations, an idea that would have been summarily rejected by Keynes.[2] In its new life the hypothesis being tested became a hypothesis not only that present spreads depend on future short rates but also that agents correctly predict the future (up to a random error). Framed this way, looking for confirmation of the expectations hypothesis is a fool's errand. It is hard to see how any agent—except perhaps Nostradamus—could correctly forecast future rates ten years into the future, as agents endowed with rational expectations must be assumed to do when they calculate expected yields on 10-year bonds.

As in the main body of this chapter, I assume that short and long rates relate to one another both through risk aversion and through expectations formed on the hypothesis that the short rate will revert to a normal rate taken for the purposes of this exercise to be fixed exogenously. These expectations are not "rational." Neither are they irrational. They simply are.

From Consols to Long Bonds, From Coupon Yields to Yields to Maturity

Before we turn to empirical tests of various aspects of liquidity-preference theory, the theory has to be modified to take account of an important difference between the models we have laid out in chapters 11 and 12 and the real world, namely, the virtual absence of consols from bond markets. In the United States, consols have never been a regular part of Treasury debt, though apparently some of the debt issued in connection with financing the Panama Canal, long since retired, took this form.[3] In the United Kingdom, the original home of the consol, this particular debt instrument has gone the way of the dodo (see chapter 11, note 5).

There is instead a spectrum of Treasury obligations of various finite maturities, running, in the United States, from one day to thirty years. Those with a term of more than a year are issued as "coupon" bonds, paying interest twice a year. Short (one year or less) instruments are bills issued at a discount to their value at maturity. Returns to obligations maturing at different times are conventionally summarized in a *yield curve,* representing the relationship between the yield to maturity and the bond's term. Figure 12.30 represents the yield curve for Treasury obligations in March 2014, when the short-term rate was virtually zero and the 30-year bond, maturing in March 2044, offered a yield to maturity of 3.6 percent.

By definition, the yield to maturity is the interest rate that just makes the present value of the bond's lifetime returns equal to the current price of the

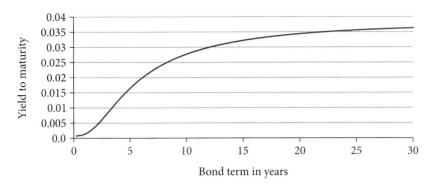

Figure 12.30 Yield curve (March 2014).

bond, P. In continuous time, assuming the bond is redeemed for $1.00 at time $t + m$,

$$P(m, t) = \int_{t}^{t+m} R e^{-\rho_{mat}(m,t)\cdot(\tau-t)} d\tau + e^{-\rho_{mat}(m,t)\cdot m}$$

$$= -\frac{R}{\rho_{mat}(m, t)}\left(e^{-\rho_{mat}(m,t)\cdot m} - 1\right) + e^{-\rho_{mat}(m,t)\cdot m},$$

where R is the (annualized) return, t is the calendar date at which the bond price is evaluated, and m is the term to maturity. For notational convenience, the subscript in the expression for the bond price is omitted in this appendix. The bond price is denoted by P or by $P(m, t)$, showing the functional dependence of the bond price on both the time to maturity (m) and the calendar date (t) when the extra detail is helpful. (The price of goods, which was previously denoted by P, does not enter the analysis here.)

For a consol, we can define the yield to maturity as $\rho_{mat}(\infty) = \lim_{m\to\infty}\rho_{mat}(m, t)$; the above equation reduces to

$$P(m, t) = \frac{R}{\rho_{mat}(\infty)}$$

so that

$$\rho_{mat}(\infty) = \rho_{coup} \equiv \frac{R}{P}.$$

That is, the limiting yield to maturity is equal to the coupon yield R/P.[4] By contrast, in the case of finite maturities, the two yields will generally differ. Only when the bond trades at par, that is, at its redemption value, $P = 1$, will the two conceptually distinct yields coincide in value.

Whatever the term to maturity, agents continue to anticipate the holding yield as the sum of the coupon yield and the expected (percentage) change in the bond's price,

$$\rho_{\text{hold}}(m, t) \equiv \frac{R}{P(m, t)} + \frac{E(\dot{P})}{P(m, t)}.$$

And market equilibrium, as characterized by equality between the expected holding yield on long bonds and the sum of the short rate plus a risk premium, U_2/U_1, continues to hold for finite-maturity bonds, except that U_2/U_1 now depends on the term to maturity, since the longer the life of the bond, the greater the expected variability of its price and the greater the sensitivity of utility to the value of bonds in the portfolio. Denoting the risk premium U_2/U_1 by $\alpha(m)$, we have the equilibrium condition for agents to hold both bonds and bills:

$$\frac{R}{P} + \frac{E(\dot{P})}{P} = \rho_s(t) + \alpha(m).$$

The spread between the coupon yield and the short-term rate continues to be equal to the difference between the risk premium and the change in price:

$$\frac{R}{P} - \rho_s(t) = \alpha(m) - \frac{E(\dot{P})}{P}.$$

When we were dealing with consols, this result made it easy to deal with the two polar cases where only risk aversion or only normal reversion is at play. The first assumption—no risk aversion—implies $\alpha = 0$, whereas the second assumption—no reversion to normal—implies $E(\dot{P})/P = 0$. The first of these two assumption carries over to a world of finite bond maturities: the absence of risk aversion implies $\alpha(m) = 0$ whatever the term of the bond. But the absence of reversion to normal does not imply $E(\dot{P})/P = 0$ when m is finite.

Unlike consols, every finite maturity bond is characterized by a terminal condition, namely, a condition that the price must approach the redemption value of the bond as we approach the redemption date.[5] Although this terminal condition is independent of whether risk aversion or normal reversion drives bond prices, its effect plays out very differently in the two cases.

In the case of pure risk aversion (no reversion to normal), expected bond price and yield will have the general shape of Figure 12.31. This figure assumes that the short-term rate is zero when the bond is issued (March 2014), and will continue to be equal to zero as far out as the eye can see (or rather the mind can imagine). On this assumption it represents the trajectory of the price and yields (both the coupon yield and the yield to maturity) of a 30-year bond with a par value of $1.00 and a coupon of $0.036.

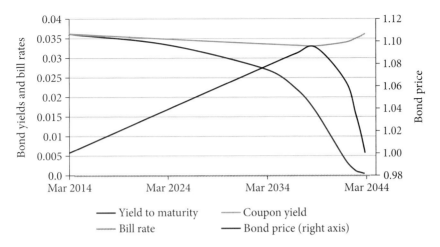

Figure 12.31 Bond yields, bond prices, and bill rates: risk aversion without reversion to normal.

How do we account for the shapes of the various schedules in Figure 12.31? Observe first that the yield-to-maturity schedule is the mirror image of the yield curve in Figure 12.30: the long bond starts life as a 30-year bond but over time morphs into bonds of successively shorter maturities. At every point in the bond's life, the condition of market equilibrium is that the holding yield $(R/P) + (E(\dot{P})/P)$ on the long bond equal the short rate ρ_s plus a risk premium $\alpha(m)$, where m is the time remaining until the bond matures.

In 2043 the 30-year bond issued in 2014 will be equivalent to a 1-year bill in price risk, and, therefore, equivalent in its return to a short-term bill issued in 2043 (apart from tax treatment and bid-ask liquidity considerations). This is to say that in 2043 the 30-year bond issued in 2014 requires a very small premium to offset its price volatility. With the 1-year bill rate expected to remain at the near-zero level obtaining in 2014, and with virtually no risk premium on the 2014 vintage bond ($\alpha \approx 0$), in 2043–44 the holding yield on this bond is now expected to be near zero. But this can only happen if the price is expected to fall by about as much as the coupon, namely, by about \$0.036. This tells us that the price in 2043 must be in the vicinity of \$1.036 since it is (by assumption) certain that the bond will be redeemed for \$1.00 in 2044.

What comes down must first have gone up. Long bonds, by assumption, start life at par, so the price of the 30-year bond issued in 2014 must rise early in its life to be able to come down at the end of its life. If, as expected, the bond price begins to rise upon issuance, both the yield to maturity and the coupon yield initially fall since the two yields start out life together.

Evidently, it is no longer the case that $E(\dot{P})/P = 0$. Rather, the expected value of bond-price changes with the remaining maturity of the bond. When risk aversion rules, price changes are expected to be positive at the beginning of the bond's life and negative at the end.

This contrasts sharply with the expected price behavior of the same 30-year bond in a world of reversion to normal, without risk aversion. Figure 12.32 shows the expected course of the yield to maturity, the coupon yield, and the price of the same 30-year bond issued at par with a coupon rate of 3.6 percent, along with the expected course of the short-term bill rate, under the assumption that the bill rate will revert to a normal rate of 6 percent at the rate $\theta = 0.25$, after an initial three-year period at zero and two more years of slower adjustment. The differences between Figures 12.31 and 12.32 evidently hinge on the different assumptions about the trajectory of the bill rate as well as on the relationship between the holding yield and the short rate. Because the short-term rate is expected to rise, the yield to maturity on the long bond must also rise as we approach the redemption date. The bond price must initially fall since market equilibrium continues to require

$$\frac{R}{P} + \frac{E(\dot{P})}{P} = \rho_s + \alpha(m).$$

But in the absence of risk aversion, $\alpha = 0$ for all m, not just at the short end of the term structure, so when the bond is issued at par, the expected bond price must fall in order to equalize returns on bills and bonds. As the price falls, the coupon yield rises because the coupon yield is the ratio of a fixed coupon to a varying price. Once the short-term rate catches up to the coupon yield, the downward price trajectory is reversed, and the price once again reaches par when the bond is redeemed.[6]

Observe that the yield curve, a static picture at one point in time, itself tells

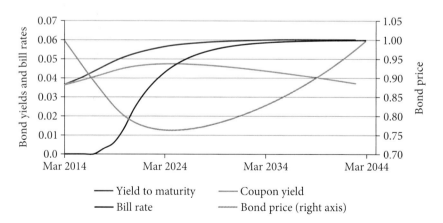

Figure 12.32 Bond yields, bond prices, and bill rates: reversion to normal without risk aversion.

us nothing, or rather very little, about the roles of risk aversion and normal reversion in the determination of the spread between long and short rates. The only difference between the two theories that might reveal itself in the yield curve is the incompatibility between pure risk aversion and a downward-sloping (inverted) yield curve. As has been observed, Hicks argued that a downward-sloping yield curve presupposes that "the short rate is regarded as abnormally high" (1946 [1939], p. 152).[7]

In any case, an upward-sloping yield curve is consistent both with risk aversion and with reversion to normal. To demonstrate this consistency, Figure 12.33 shows the actual yield curve for March 2014, alongside a hypothetical yield curve constructed on the basis of reversion of a zero-coupon bond (see below) to normal, with $\theta = 0.8$ and $\rho_s^* = 0.0385$. Evidently, the hypothetical yield curve does a good job of approximating the actual curve. If, however, we project the curves five years into the future, from 2014 to 2019, and assume that the actual 2014 curve is based solely on risk aversion, the resulting curves behave very differently. Pure risk aversion implies that the yield curve does not change over time (unless wealth holders become more or less risk averse); pure normal reversion implies that the yield curve flattens out. So, under the hypothesis of pure risk aversion, we would expect a 30-year bond issued in 2019 to have the same yield to maturity as one issued in 2014. Under normal reversion, the 30-year bond issued in 2019 is expected to yield the average of short-term rates forecast in 2014 for five to thirty-five years hence. Figure 12.34 pictures 2014 predictions for the two yield curves in 2019, both of them now hypothetical.

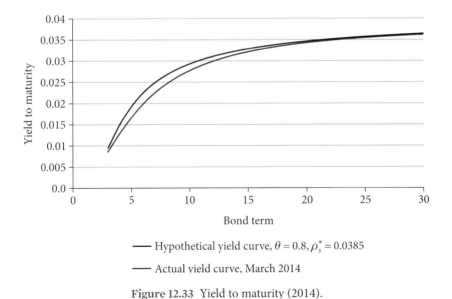

Figure 12.33 Yield to maturity (2014).

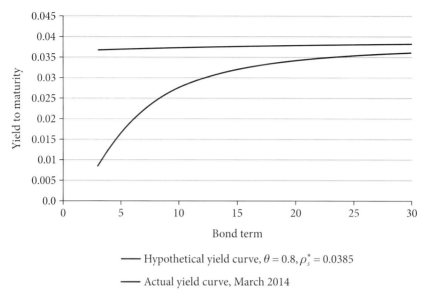

Figure 12.34 Yield to maturity (2019).

Sorting Out Risk Aversion and Normal Reversion in a World of Zero-Coupon Bonds

Coupon bonds are the real-world norm, but in exploring the implications of risk aversion and normal reversion, it is useful to assume that all bonds provide returns not by periodic payments of interest but by virtue of a difference between the lower price paid at the time of purchase and the redemption value when the bond matures (assumed to be one dollar). Such bonds, so-called zero-coupon bonds, are unavailable even in theory in a world of consols because nobody would hold a bond that offers no periodic payment and will never be redeemed. But in the real world of finite maturities, zero-coupon bonds have become the focus of both theoretical and empirical research because it is simpler to analyze a bond with only one payment than a bond with periodic payments and a final payment of a different amount. Real-world, m-year coupon bonds can be understood as composite securities put together from m zero-coupon bonds, each corresponding to a single payment of interest (assumed to take place once per year), with the last payment including the repayment of principal.[8]

One obvious difference between zero-coupon and ordinary bonds is that ordinary bonds generally begin their lives at par (and are referred to as "par bonds") and, as Figures 12.31 and 12.32 show, can be expected to fluctuate differently according to whether risk aversion or normal reversion is operating on bond prices. By contrast, the price of a zero-coupon bond increases over time regardless of whether risk aversion or normal reversion is the driving force. Or, rather, bond prices will be expected to increase. Actual bond prices may fall, but nobody will hold a zero-coupon bond that is expected to fall in price as long as holding money is costless. By contrast, yields to maturity, which differ from changes in bond prices when yields change over time, can be expected to rise or fall, depending on whether risk aversion or reversion to normal is calling the tune.

As is the case for par bonds, the trajectories of two zero-coupon bonds of the same maturity and the same initial yield to maturity—one reflecting normal reversion and the other risk aversion—must start out together and end at the same point. The difference between the price trajectories in Figures 12.31 and 12.32 translates into the difference in Figure 12.35. Both bonds start from a value of just over $0.30 when first issued, corresponding to a yield to maturity of 0.038. But the slope of the schedule depicting normal reversion is flat at the outset, and the schedule depicting risk aversion is flat when the bond matures.

To see why, start from the relationship between the price of a zero-coupon bond and the yield to maturity. By definition, the yield to maturity is the in-

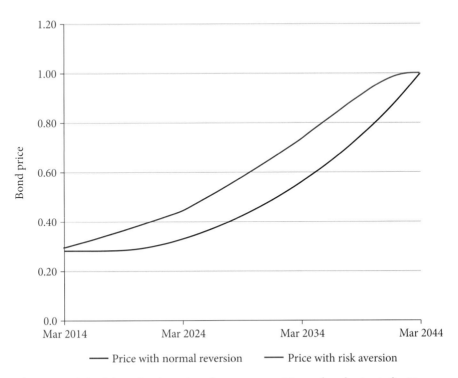

Figure 12.35 Anticipated trajectories of zero-coupon 30-year bond price in limiting cases.

terest rate that makes the return on purchasing the bond today equal to the value of the bond at maturity:

$$P(m,t)e^{\rho_{mat}(m,t)\cdot m} = 1.$$

Equivalently, the price today is equal to the present value of the redemption price, discounted at the yield to maturity,

$$P(m,t) = e^{-\rho_{mat}(m,t)\cdot m}.$$

The holding yield on the bond is just the (percentage) rate of price appreciation,[9]

$$\frac{\hat{P}}{P} = \rho_{mat} - \frac{d\hat{\rho}_{mat}}{dt}m,$$

where $d\hat{\rho}_{mat}/dt$ is the total derivative of ρ_{mat}, taking account of the interdependence between the remaining time to maturity m and the calendar time t, $m = T - t$, with T the redemption date:

$$\frac{d\hat{\rho}_{mat}}{dt}m = \frac{\partial\hat{\rho}_{mat}}{\partial t}m - \frac{\partial\hat{\rho}_{mat}}{\partial m}m.$$

The holding-yield condition is that the expected price increase be equal to the sum of the short rate and the risk premium

$$\frac{\hat{P}}{P} = \rho_{mat} - \frac{d\hat{\rho}_{mat}}{dt}m = \hat{\rho}_s(t) + \alpha(m).$$

The first-order differential equation

$$\frac{d\hat{\rho}_{mat}}{dt} - \frac{\rho_{mat}}{m} = -\frac{\hat{\rho}_s(t) + \alpha(m)}{m}$$

has the solution

$$\rho_{mat}(m,t) = m^{-1}\left(-\int\hat{\rho}_s(t)dt - \int\alpha(m)dt\right) + m^{-1}c$$
$$= m^{-1}\left(-\int\hat{\rho}_s(t)dt + \int\alpha(m)dm\right) + m^{-1}c.$$

To solve for the constant term, c, we take limits

$$\lim_{m\to 0}\rho_{mat}(m,t) = \rho_{mat}(0,T) = \lim_{m\to 0}\frac{-\hat{\rho}_s(t)(-m) + \alpha(m)m}{m} + \frac{c}{m}.$$

Since $\rho_{mat}(0,T) = \lim_{m\to 0}\hat{\rho}_s(t) = \hat{\rho}_s(T)$, we have $c = \lim_{m\to o}\alpha(m)m = 0$. Hence

$$\rho_{mat}(m,t)m = -\int\hat{\rho}_s(t)dt + \int\alpha(m)dm.$$

In words: the holding-yield condition implies that discounting at the yield to maturity is equivalent to discounting at the average expected short-term rate plus the corresponding risk premium. The relationship between bond price, yield to maturity, and short-term rates is

$$P(m,t) \equiv e^{-\rho_{mat}(m,t) \cdot m} = e^{-\int_t^{t+m} \hat\rho_s(t)d\tau + \int_0^m \alpha(\tau)d\tau} = e^{-\int_t^{t+m} \left[\alpha(m+t-\tau)+\hat\rho_s(\tau)\right]d\tau},$$

where $\alpha(m + t - \tau)$ is the risk premium at time τ, $(m + t - \tau)$ reflecting the time remaining until the bond matures, and $\hat\rho_s(\tau)$ representing the estimate of the short-term interest rate at τ. The holding-yield condition can be derived from this equation by taking total derivatives on both sides, but there is new information in the limits of integration. Take logarithms on both sides

$$\ln P(m,t) \equiv \rho_{mat} m = -\int_t^{t+m} \left[\alpha(m + t - \tau) + \hat\rho_s(\tau)\right]d\tau$$

and then take *partial* derivatives with respect to both calendar time t and maturity m. We obtain two new conditions that characterize the instantaneous relationship between the yield to maturity, forecasts of short-term rates, and the risk premium.

First we differentiate the discount factor $\rho_{mat} m$ with respect to t, holding m constant. The resulting partial derivative $\partial\hat\rho_{mat}/\partial t$ is the estimate of the rate of change over time of the yield to maturity on an m-period bond, holding maturity constant, that is, the rate of change of the constant-maturity yield:

$$\frac{\partial\hat\rho_{mat}}{\partial t} m = \alpha(0) + \hat\rho_s(t + m) - \alpha(m) - \rho_s(t) + \int_t^{t+m} \frac{\partial\alpha}{\partial t}\, d\tau.$$

The last term can be seen to be equal to $\alpha(m) - \alpha(0)$ by making the substitution $\omega = \tau - t$ and noting that

$$\int_t^{t+m} \frac{\partial\alpha}{\partial t}\, d\tau = -\int_0^m -\frac{d\alpha}{d\omega}\, d\omega = \alpha(m) - \alpha(0).$$

Thus the equation reduces to the *consistent forecasting condition*

$$\frac{\partial\hat\rho_{mat}}{\partial t} m = \hat\rho_s(t + m) - \rho_s(t),$$

which says that the anticipated change in the constant-maturity discount factor, $\rho_{mat} m$, must equal the difference between the expected gain at the end of the bond's life, $\hat\rho_s(t + m)$, and the loss at the beginning, $\rho_s(t)$.[10]

A second condition is obtained by differentiating $\rho_{mat} m$ with respect to maturity, holding time constant. The derivative $\partial\rho_{mat}/\partial m$ is the rate of change of the yield to maturity along the yield curve. (Since the yield curve is known to the agent, this is not an estimate; hence no hat.) This gives the *forward-rate condition*

$$\rho_{mat}(m, t) + \frac{\partial\rho_{mat}}{\partial m}\, m = \hat{\rho}_s(t + m) + \alpha(m).$$

The left-hand side is the forward rate implicit in the yield curve. The forward rate is the yield that an agent can obtain in the future if she enters into a swap in which she makes offsetting sales and purchases of bonds that mature at time $t + m$ and time $t + m + \varepsilon$. If time is divided into discrete periods, we can imagine an agent making a short sale of one bond maturing $m - 1$ periods hence and with the proceeds buying bonds maturing m periods hence. At the present time she need make no cash outlay; the cash outlay takes place $m - 1$ periods from now, when she must redeem the bond she sold short today. A market equilibrium in which agents hold both long- and short-term securities requires the forward rate to be equal to the expected short rate plus the risk premium.[11]

Why does the forward rate equal the sum of the yield to maturity, $\rho_{mat}(m, t)$, and the maturity-weighted change along the yield curve, $(\partial\rho_{mat}/\partial m)m$? An example might help. Suppose time is divided into discrete periods of one year each. Assume that for bonds with terms of zero to four years, the yield to maturity is 1 percent; that is, $\rho_{mat}(4, t) = 0.01$, and that the yield to maturity on 5-year bonds is 2 percent, $\rho_{mat}(5, t) = 0.02$. The agent of the previous paragraph—let's call her Naomi—sells a 4-year bond short and buys 5-year bonds. With continuous compounding, the bond she sells, with a redemption value of $1.00, nets her $0.961. This allows her to buy 1.062 5-year bonds, since the 5-years are worth $0.905 each.

The cost of the 5-year bond is offset for four years by the short sale of the 4-year bond. During this period Naomi has no money at risk and earns nothing. At the end of the fourth year, however, Naomi has to return the bond she borrowed to initiate the process, and to do so she has to lay out $1.00 to make the lender of the bond whole. At the end of year five, she receives $1.062 when it comes time to redeem the 5-year bonds. The net return of $0.062 can be broken down into a 1 percent yield (the yield on 4-year bonds), plus an additional 1 percent per year over five years, or 6 percent in all,

$$\rho_{mat}(4, t) + \left(\frac{\Delta\rho_{mat}}{\Delta m}\right)_{m=5} \times 5 = 0.01 + (0.01 \times 5),$$

which is precisely the formula on the left-hand side of the forward-rate condition.

Equilibrium requires that the forward rate equal the expected short rate at time $t + m$ *plus* a risk premium $\alpha(m)$. Why is a risk premium necessary to equilibrate expectations about future short rates and opportunities for future gain available with certainty today (assuming no default)? If the short rate expected in year five is say, 2 percent, how could Naomi's offsetting transactions yield 6 percent? After all, she lays out $1.00 at the end of year four and reaps $1.06 at the end of year five, a short-term return on a short-term investment. The answer is that, even though no cash is required of Naomi until year five, she is committed to the transaction from the get-go and thus runs the price risks that would accompany premature (literally) unwinding of her positions. This commitment, rather than the actual laying out of cash, is the reason for a risk premium in the first place.

The forward rate provides only upper bounds for $\hat{\rho}_s(t + m)$ and $\alpha(m)$, because it tells us only what the sum $\hat{\rho}_s(t + m) + \alpha(m)$ must be when Naomi is indifferent between committing to the (partially) offsetting purchase and sale today and holding short-term bonds in the future.[12] A given value of the forward rate is compatible with any combination of the expected short-term rate and the risk premium that sums to this value. That is, any given forward rate is compatible with a high value of $\hat{\rho}_s(t + m)$ and a low value of $\alpha(m)$, or vice versa. Of course, the total absence of risk aversion implies that the forward rate on long bonds must be exactly equal to the expected future short rate for the forward market to be in equilibrium. At the other extreme, the absence of expectations of reversion to normal means that the expected short rate is equal to today's short rate. In the example, a forward rate of 6 percent for year five is compatible with an expected short rate of 6 percent coupled with a risk premium of zero, or a risk premium of 0.06 coupled with an expected short rate of zero—or with in-between values that sum to 0.06.

If we combine consistent forecasting with the forward-rate condition, we obtain the holding-yield condition

$$\frac{\hat{P}}{P} = \rho_{\text{mat}}(m, t) + \frac{\partial \rho_{\text{mat}}}{\partial m}m - \frac{\partial \hat{\rho}_{\text{mat}}}{\partial t}m = \rho_s(t) + \alpha(m).$$

Rearranging terms, we obtain a relationship between the expected change in the yield to maturity (taking account of the change in term to maturity) and the spread between long-bond yield and short-term rate:

$$\frac{\partial \hat{\rho}_{\text{mat}}}{\partial t}m - \frac{\partial \rho_{\text{mat}}}{\partial m}m = \rho_{\text{mat}}(m, t) - \rho_s(t) - \alpha(m).$$

Analysis of this equation allows us to understand the very different ways that expectations have been understood to interact with interest rates. As I have argued in this chapter, Keynes's liquidity-preference theory is really a theory of how interest-rate spreads are determined by expectations about the future course of interest rates and risk aversion. So if causality is read as going from right to left, we have

$$\rho_{mat}(m, t) - \rho_s(t) = \frac{\partial \hat{\rho}_{mat}}{\partial t}m - \frac{\partial \hat{\rho}_{mat}}{\partial m}m + \alpha(m),$$

with the yield premium the dependent variable and the terms on the right-hand side the independent variables. The key to teasing out the separate impact of risk aversion from the separate impact of normal reversion is the behavior of $\partial \hat{\rho}_{mat}/\partial t$ and $\partial \hat{\rho}_{mat}/\partial m$, particularly how these terms relate to the current short-term rate of interest. If we combine the forecasting-consistency condition

$$\frac{\partial \hat{\rho}_{mat}}{\partial t}m = \hat{\rho}_s(t + m) - \rho_s(t)$$

and the forecasting equation

$$\hat{\rho}_s(\tau) = \left(1 - e^{-\theta(t-\tau)}\right)\rho_s^* + e^{-\theta(t-\tau)}\rho_s(t),$$

the solution to the differential equation

$$\rho_{mat}(m, t) + \frac{\partial \hat{\rho}_{mat}}{\partial m}m = \frac{\partial \hat{\rho}_{mat}}{\partial t}m + \rho_s(t) + \alpha(m)$$

becomes

$$\rho_{mat}(m, t) = m^{-1}\int_0^m \alpha(\tau)d\tau + \left(1 - \frac{1 - e^{-\theta m}}{\theta m}\right)\rho_s^* + \frac{1 - e^{-\theta m}}{\theta m}\rho_s(t) + m^{-1}c.$$

We solve for the constant term c by invoking the boundary conditions, $\rho_{mat}(0, t) = \rho_s(t)$ and $\alpha(0) = 0$.

The solution is $c = 0$, so the spread is given by

$$\rho_{mat}(m, t) - \rho_s(t) = m^{-1}\int_0^m \alpha(\tau)d\tau + \left(1 - \frac{1 - e^{-\theta m}}{\theta m}\right)\rho_s^* + \left(\frac{1 - e^{-\theta m}}{\theta m} - 1\right)\rho_s(t).$$

The two limiting cases of no risk aversion and no normal reversion are characterized by

$$\rho_{mat}(m, t) - \rho_s(t) = \left(1 - \frac{1 - e^{-\theta m}}{\theta m}\right)\rho_s^* + \left(\frac{1 - e^{-\theta m}}{\theta m} - 1\right)\rho_s(t)$$

$$\text{no risk aversion: } \alpha(\tau) = 0, \tau \in [0, m],$$

$$\rho_{mat}(m, t) - \rho_s(t) = m^{-1}\int_0^m \alpha(\tau)d\tau \quad \text{no normal reversion: } \theta = 0.$$

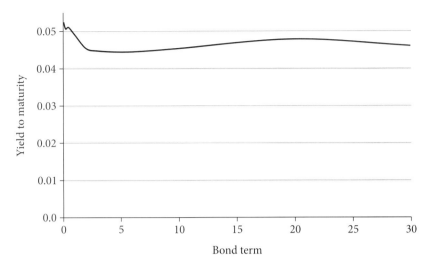

Figure 12.36 Yield curve (March 2007).

One consequence of assuming away normal reversion is to limit the yield curve to the general shape of Figure 12.30, with a positive yield premium, one that increases with the term to maturity. If we add the assumption of an upper limit to $\alpha(m)$ as $m \to \infty$, we obtain an asymptotic limit to the yield to maturity. The absence of normal reversion thus rules out inverted yield curves, yield curves along which the spread between long and short bonds falls with the maturity of the bond. Assuming agents are focused on short-term wealth, the fact that from time to time we actually observe inverted yield curves, as for example in early 2007 in Figure 12.36, implies that risk aversion is not the whole story.

Testing Whether Both Risk Aversion and Normal Reversion Matter

Which is it, risk aversion or normal reversion—or both? Testable differences between risk aversion and normal reversion follow from the implications of the two hypotheses for regressions of the yield premium on the short-term rateals

$$\rho_{\text{mat}}(m,t) - \rho_s(t) = a_0 + a_1 \rho_s(t) + \varepsilon.$$

In the absence of risk aversion, this regression should give

$$a_0 = \left(1 - \frac{1 - e^{-\theta m}}{\theta m}\right) \rho_s^* > 0,$$

$$-1 < a_1 = \left(\frac{1 - e^{-\theta m}}{\theta m} - 1\right) < 0.$$

And in the absence of normal reversion the resulting coefficients should be

$$a_0 = m^{-1} \int_0^m \alpha(\tau)d\tau > 0,$$

$$a_1 = 0.$$

In between the two limiting cases, we would expect

$$a_0 = m^{-1} \int_0^m \alpha(\tau)d\tau + \left(1 - \frac{1 - e^{-\theta m}}{\theta m}\right)\rho_s^* > 0,$$

$$-1 < a_1 = \left(\frac{1 - e^{-\theta m}}{\theta m} - 1\right) < 0,$$

with both the constant term (a_0) and the coefficient on the short rate (a_1) larger in absolute value the greater is m.

Regressing the spread $\rho_{mat} - \rho_s$ (or the bond yield ρ_{mat}) against the short-term rate is problematic if the error term ε is correlated with ρ_s. The standard remedy is to change the regression technique, to abandon ordinary least squares (OLS) in favor of two-stage least squares (TSLS). In the first stage of the process one or more new variables are used as instruments to replace actual observations of the independent variable (ρ_s) with synthetic observations that are stripped of the offending correlation with ε. For this process to provide statistically consistent estimates of the regression coefficients, the instrument(s) should meet two criteria, relevance and exogeneity. An instrument is relevant if it accounts for the variation in the independent variable; it is exogenous if it is uncorrelated with the error term.

The instrument deployed in the regressions that follow is the rate of inflation. This instrument is obviously relevant, but its exogeneity is less clear since it depends on what is assumed about the relationship between inflation and long-bond yields. For now I assume that inflation directly affects only the current short rate and that the direct effect feeds through to long-bond yields via expectations about future short rates, which are still assumed to be driven by the equation

$$\hat{\rho}_s(\tau) = \left(1 - e^{-\theta(t-\tau)}\right)\rho_s^* + e^{-\theta(t-\tau)}\rho_s(t).$$

The key point is that the *normal* rate of interest is assumed to be unaffected by the current inflation rate. On this assumption, the rate of inflation will not be correlated with the error term, so that the exogeneity condition is satisfied.[13]

Inflation (INF) is measured by the urban Consumer Price Index (CPI). These data, like interest-rate data, are reported on a monthly basis, but I use year-on-year changes in the index to eliminate noise in the monthly data. Separate regressions over periods of rising inflation and periods of falling inflation (before and after 1980) make it clear that the coefficient on inflation in the first-stage regression is markedly higher in the period after 1980. This makes sense if the short rate actually depends on a distributed lag of past and present inflation, since lagged inflation will be lower than current inflation in the first period and higher in the second. Without introducing an explicit lag function, this effect can be approximated by adding a dummy variable (DUMINF), which takes the value zero until June 1980 and is equal to the inflation rate thereafter.

The results of the first-stage regression of the short rate and the second-stage regression of the difference between the long rate and the short rate are reported below. TB3MS is the monthly return on 3-month T-bills in the secondary market rate, which I use as the measure of the short-term bill rate, ρ_s. YLDPREM is the difference between the yield to maturity of a zero-coupon 10-year T-note and the short rate, which represents $\rho_{mat} - \rho_s$.

$$TB3MS = .000949 + .697 \ INF + .405 \ DUMINF$$
$$\qquad\quad (.0002) \quad (.033) \qquad (.050)$$
$$R^2 = .57$$

$$YLDPREM = .00284 - .313 \ TB3MS$$
$$\qquad\qquad (.0009) \quad (.020)$$
$$R^2 = .38$$

Robust Standard Errors in Parentheses

Observations: 497 $F(2, 494) = 223.7$

Variable	Obs	Mean	Std Dev	Min	Max
YLDPREM	497	0.0015	0.0012	−0.0028	0.0036
TB3MS	497	0.0044	0.0027	0.0000083	0.0136
INF	497	0.0036	0.0025	−0.0017	0.0123

Interest and inflation are per month, so that 0.001 corresponds to 12 percent per year.

A couple of pictures will help us understand these results. Figure 12.37 is a scatter of the yield premium versus the short rate, along with the fitted values of the two-stage regression (and the OLS values for comparison). The next picture, Figure 12.38, shows the fitted equation with a plot of the yield premium against the estimate of the current short-term rate calculated in the first stage. The vertical lines in Figure 12.38 demarcate an interval of one standard deviation on each side of the mean of the fitted short-term rate. Figure 12.38 makes clear that the strength of the regression derives from the outliers, when estimated 3-month bill rates are more than one standard deviation away

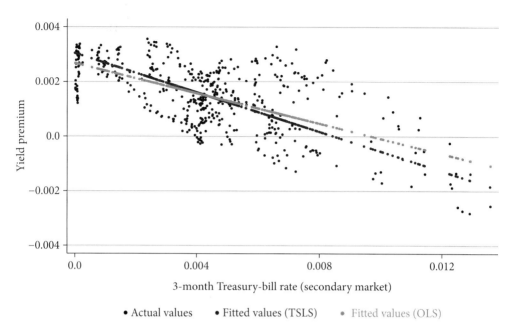

Figure 12.37 Yield premium on a 10-year Treasury note vs. actual 3-month Treasury bill rate.

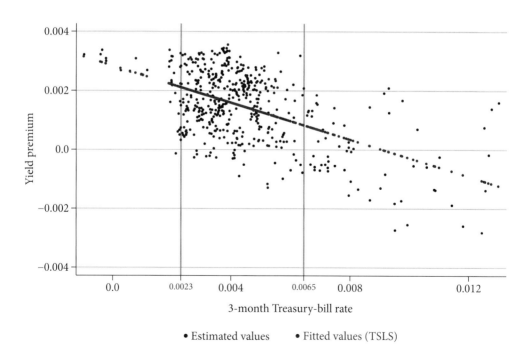

Figure 12.38 Yield premium on a 10-year Treasury note vs. estimated 3-month Treasury bill rate.

from the mean, that is, less than 0.0023 and greater than 0.0065. For if we repeat the regression limiting the sample to observations within the one standard deviation interval, the second-stage coefficient a_1 is closer to zero and
has a much smaller t-value. The coefficient goes from -0.313 to -0.185, and
its t-value falls from 15.6 to 4.2.

$$\text{TB3MS} = .0006 + .795 \text{ INF} + .401 \text{ DUMINF}$$

$$(.0003)\quad(.060)\qquad\quad(.068)$$

$$R^2 = .28$$

$$\text{YLDPREM} = .00237 - .185 \text{ TB3MS}$$

$$(.0002)\quad(.045)$$

$$R^2 = .15$$

Robust Standard Errors in Parentheses

Observations: 399 $F(2, 396) = 91.2$

These results support the plausible notion that both normal reversion and
risk aversion play a role in determining the spread between the long-bond yield
and the short-term rate. The negative coefficient on TB3MS supports a role for
normal reversion, while the fact that this result is driven mostly by the outliers suggests that most of the time normal reversion matters relatively little.[14]
We can exploit regression results for bond maturities other than ten years
to learn about the empirical relationship between risk aversion and the term
of the bond. Risk aversion predicts that $\alpha(m)$ increases with m because a
given change in the yield to maturity will cause the bond price to fluctuate
more the longer is the bond term. The result is that on theoretical grounds
$m^{-1}\int_0^m \alpha(\tau)d\tau$ should increase with m, reaching its maximum $\bar{a}$ as m goes to ∞.
So on this account alone, we would expect a_0 to be an increasing function of
m. But normal reversion makes the same prediction for the other part of a_0,
$[(1 - (1 - e^{-\theta m})/\theta m)]\rho_s^*$, at least in the range of m that is relevant for the value
of θ implicit in the estimate of a_1 (namely, $\theta = 0.0067$).[15] Since we can't sort out
the response of a_0 between its two components, there is not much to be
learned about $\alpha(m)$ from the relationship of a_0 to m.
On the other hand we can learn something from the ratio a_0/a_1. In the general case we have

$$\frac{a_0}{a_1} = -\frac{m^{-1}\int_0^m \alpha(\tau)d\tau + \left(1 - \dfrac{1 - e^{-\theta m}}{\theta m}\right)\rho_s^*}{\left(1 - \dfrac{1 - e^{-\theta m}}{\theta m}\right)} = -\frac{\theta\int_0^m \alpha(\tau)d\tau}{\left(\theta m - \left(1 - e^{-\theta m}\right)\right)} - \rho_s^*.$$

Both $\theta\int_0^m \alpha(\tau)d\tau$ and $\theta m - (1 - e^{-\theta m})$ increase with m, but the ratio can rise or
fall, depending on which term rises more rapidly. With $\theta \approx 0.007$, the elastic-

ity of the denominator with respect to m is approximately two, so a_0/a_1 rises or falls in absolute value according to whether the elasticity of the numerator $m\alpha(m)/\int_0^m \alpha(\tau)d\tau$ is greater or less than two. If $\alpha(m)$ were a linear function of m, then its elasticity would be just equal to two, so a_0/a_1 increasing in absolute value would indicate that $\alpha(m)$ has an increasing slope in $m \times \alpha(m)$ space; a decreasing absolute value suggests a decreasing slope.

In the event, Table 12.1 suggests that $\alpha(m)$ increases slowly at low levels of m, then almost but not quite linearly, more or less in line with the yield curve in Figure 12.30. On the left-hand side of the table, a_0/a_1 falls over intermediate

Table 12.1 Regressions of Yield Premium Against Short-Term Bond Rate

	Sample Period						
	1971–2012				1985–2012		
Maturity (years)	a_1	a_0	a_0/a_1	θ	a_1	a_0	a_0/a_1
1	−0.01052	0.00049	−0.04658	0.0018	0.04838	0.00023	0.00480
2	−0.07502	0.00097	−0.01296	0.0066	0.01068	0.00058	0.05399
3	−0.12564	0.00135	−0.01076	0.0076	−0.03432	0.00091	−0.02661
4	−0.16738	0.00167	−0.00998	0.0079	−0.07789	0.00123	−0.01573
5	−0.20247	0.00194	−0.00959	0.0078	−0.11854	0.00151	−0.01275
6	−0.23223	0.00218	−0.00937	0.0077	−0.15575	0.00177	−0.01138
7	−0.25755	0.00238	−0.00924	0.0075	−0.18931	0.00201	−0.01061
8	−0.27899	0.00256	−0.00916	0.0072	−0.21920	0.00222	−0.01012
9	−0.29726	0.00271	−0.00910	0.0070	−0.24552	0.00240	−0.00978
10	−0.31267	0.00284	−0.00907	0.0067	−0.26849	0.00256	−0.00955
11					−0.28837	0.00270	−0.00938
12					−0.30548	0.00282	−0.00925
13					−0.32012	0.00293	−0.00914
14					−0.33259	0.00301	−0.00906
15					−0.34317	0.00309	−0.00900
16					−0.35213	0.00315	−0.00894
17					−0.35970	0.00320	−0.00889
18					−0.36609	0.00324	−0.00884
19					−0.37148	0.00327	−0.00880
20					−0.37604	0.00329	−0.00875
21					−0.38043	0.00331	−0.00870
22					−0.38377	0.00332	−0.00866
23					−0.38663	0.00333	−0.00861
24					−0.38909	0.00333	−0.00857
25					−0.39124	0.00333	−0.00852
26					−0.39311	0.00333	−0.00847
27					−0.39477	0.00332	−0.00842
28					−0.39626	0.00332	−0.00837
29					−0.39761	0.00331	−0.00831
30					−0.39884	0.00329	−0.00826

bond maturities of one to five years and levels out when the regression is run for maturities of six to ten years.

The results of regressing the yield premium against the short rate over the full range of maturities are on the right side of Table 12.1.[16] The ratio a_0/a_1 does not change very much from the value on the left-hand side, at least for maturities in the seven to ten year range; a_0/a_1 falls relatively sharply when bond maturities range from three to six years, and then falls slowly. By contrast, at the short end of the spectrum a_1—contrary to the predictions of both risk aversion and normal reversion—is significant at the 99 percent level but has the wrong sign, which makes the ratio a_0/a_1 also have the wrong sign.

Is the Risk Premium Stationary?

So far it has been assumed that the risk premium depends only on the (remaining) term until the bond matures. Both theory and data suggest otherwise. Refet Gürkaynak and Jonathan Wright (2012) survey a larger literature on variable risk premia. The theory developed in chapter 11 and this chapter suggests specific reasons why the risk premium ought to vary.

One is variation in the relative supplies of bonds and bills. Suppose the bill rate is given, then the more bonds in the mix, the lower the price of bonds and the higher the yield. Conversely, the more bills, the lower the bill price and the higher the bill yield. Thus the yield premium ought to vary directly with the proportion of bonds in the mix of Treasury obligations. A convenient measure of the bond:bill ratio is the average maturity (AVGMAT) of Treasury obligations.

A second reason why the risk premium varies, namely, changes in the rate of unemployment, is less obvious. As a measure of business conditions, unemployment might be a reason for default rates to vary, but default is not an issue for Treasury obligations. However, as a proxy for the degree of uncertainty about the economic future, it is plausible for the unemployment rate to influence the degree of perceived liquidity risk through an effect on the volatility of bond prices. Liquidity preference as aversion to risk suggests that the more volatile are bond prices, the greater will be the risk premium.

We can test this relationship by asking whether or not the volatility of bond-price changes is systematically related to the unemployment rate. According to Figure 12.39, there is a clear relationship.

The vertical axis measures monthly price changes of zero-coupon bonds, estimated by the formula

$$\frac{\dot{P}}{P} = \rho_{mat}(m, t) + \frac{\partial \rho_{mat}}{\partial m} m - \frac{\partial \rho_{mat}}{\partial t} m,$$

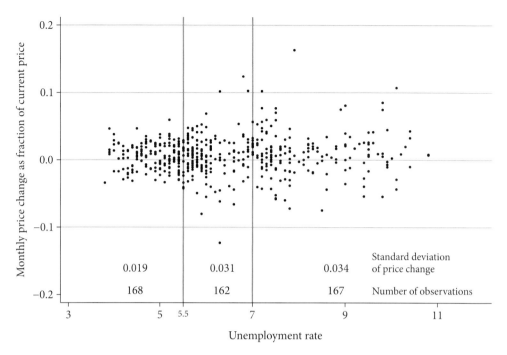

Figure 12.39 Change in price of a 10-year Treasury note (1971–2012).

in which the price change $\dot{P}/P$ and the shift in the yield curve $\partial\rho_{mat}/\partial t$ are actual rather than expected price changes. At low levels of unemployment, the standard deviation of bond-price changes is two-thirds its value at higher levels, so the unemployment rate makes sense as a proxy, if not a direct cause, of bond-price volatility.

If we linearize a risk-premium function that depends on the unemployment rate (UNRATE, measured as a percentage of the civilian labor force), the average maturity of Treasury obligations (AVGMAT, measured in months), and bond maturity ($\alpha(m)$), the risk premium becomes the sum of a constant term $\alpha(m)$ and linear terms reflecting the impact of the unemployment rate and the mix of bonds and bills:[17]

$$\alpha(m, \text{UNRATE}, \text{AVGMAT}) = \alpha(m) + b_1\text{UNRATE}(t) + b_2\text{AVGMAT}(t).$$

The differential equation relating the holding yield on the bond to the bill rate becomes

$$\frac{d\hat{\rho}_{mat}}{dt} - \frac{\rho_{mat}}{m} = -\frac{\rho_s(t) + \alpha(m) + b_1\text{UNRATE}(t) + b_2\text{AVGMAT}(t)}{m}.$$

And the solution becomes

$$\rho_{mat}(m,t) = m^{-1}\left(\int \hat{\rho}_s(t+m)dm + \int \alpha(m)dm\right)$$
$$+ b_1 \text{UNRATE}(t) + b_2 \text{AVGMAT}(t) + m^{-1}c.$$

As before, examination of the limiting case as $m \to 0$, gives $c = 0$. With short rates forecast by the equation

$$\hat{\rho}_s(\tau) = \left(1 - e^{-\theta(\tau-t)}\right)\rho_s^* + e^{-\theta(\tau-t)}\rho_s(t),$$

the yield premium is now related to the short-term bill rate by the equation

$$\rho_{mat}(m,t) - \rho_s(t) = m^{-1}\int_0^m \alpha(\tau)d\tau + \left(1 - \frac{1-e^{-\theta m}}{\theta m}\right)\rho_s^* + \left(\frac{1-e^{-\theta m}}{\theta m} - 1\right)\rho_s(t)$$
$$+ b_1\text{UNRATE}(t) + b_2\text{AVGMAT}(t).$$

Once again we use TSLS to estimate the equation for the yield premium, which is now

$$\rho_{mat}(m,t) - \rho_s(t) = a_0 + a_1\rho_s(t) + b_1\text{UNRATE}(t) + b_2\text{AVGMAT}(t) + \varepsilon.$$

The results are

TB3MS = .000974 + .661 INF + .453 DUMINF − .00176 UNRATE − .0000137 AVGMAT
(.0002) (.044) (.071) (.00006) (.000009)
$$R^2 = .58$$

YLDPREM = .00274 − .291 TB3MS + .000375 UNRATE + .0000228 AVGMAT
(.00009) (.019) (.00002) (.000002)
$$R^2 = .60$$

Robust Standard Errors in Parentheses
$F(4, 492) = 115.34$

Variable	Obs	Mean	Std Dev	Min	Max
YLDPREM	497	0.0015	0.0012	−0.0028	0.0036
TB3MS	497	0.0044	0.0027	0.0000083	0.0136
INF	497	0.0036	0.0025	−0.0017	0.0123
UNRATE	497	6.43	1.58	3.8	10.8
AVGMAT	497	56.22	12.41	29.0	74.0

The coefficient on the short-term rate hardly changes. But in place of the constant term

$$a_0 = m^{-1}\int_0^m \alpha(\tau)d\tau + \left(1 - \frac{1-e^{-\theta m}}{\theta m}\right)\rho_s^* = m^{-1}\int_0^m \alpha(\tau)d\tau - a_1\rho_s^* = 0.00274$$

we have

$$m^{-1}\int_0^m \alpha(\tau)d\tau + \left(1 - \frac{1 - e^{-\theta m}}{\theta m}\right)\rho_s^* + b_1 \text{UNRATE}(t) + b_2 \text{AVGMAT}(t)$$

$$= m^{-1}\int_0^m \alpha(\tau)d\tau - a_1\rho_s^* + b_1 \text{UNRATE}(t) + b_2 \text{AVGMAT}(t)$$

$$= .00274 + .000375 \text{ UNRATE} + .0000228 \text{ AVGMAT},$$

which fluctuates considerably around its mean, as Figure 12.40 shows. Without an assumption about the normal rate, we cannot sort out the stationary element of the risk premium $m^{-1}\int_0^m \alpha(\tau)d\tau$ from the normal-rate term $-a_1\rho_s^*$ because the constant 0.0274 is the sum of the two terms. If we resolve the ambiguity by assuming that the normal rate is equal to the sample mean of TB3MS, $\rho_s^* = 0.0044$ (0.053 on an annual basis), then we have

$$m^{-1}\int_0^m \alpha(\tau)d\tau = 0.00146,$$

which translates into an annual risk premium on the 10-year bond of 0.0175. This estimate is extremely close to the estimate of 0.0171 in John Campbell and Luis Viceira (2002, p. 73), whose model is built on very different assumptions from mine.

In any case, the fluctuations over time of the expression

$$m^{-1}\int_0^m \alpha(\tau)d\tau + \left(1 - \frac{1 - e^{-\theta m}}{\theta m}\right)\rho_s^* + b_1 \text{UNRATE}(t) + b_2 \text{AVGMAT}(t)$$

$$= .00274 + .000375 \text{ UNRATE} + .0000228 \text{ AVGMAT}$$

involve only the risk premium if we assume that the normal rate is unchanging. Observe that over time AVGMAT acts overall as a counterweight to UNRATE; as Figure 12.41 shows, average maturity peaks about the same time that the unemployment reaches its floor. But over certain intervals of time, UNRATE and AVGMAT reinforce each other in terms of their effects on the yield premium. This is the case in the periods 1979–1983, 1993–1996, and 2003–2007. These are also, it turns out, periods in which the changes in the risk premium reinforce the effects of changes in the short rate. In 2003–2007, for example, changes in UNRATE and AVGMAT together account for almost one-fourth of the total fall in the yield premium, and these changes partly explain the failure of long yields to respond to the dramatic increase in short rates over this period.[18] (The other part of the mystery is explained by expectations that short rates were, in Hicks's phrase, "abnormally high" and were therefore expected to fall—as indeed they did.)

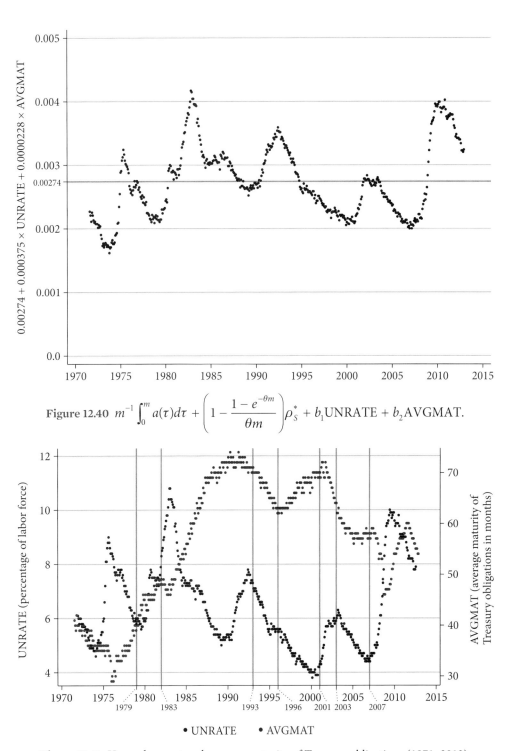

Figure 12.40 $m^{-1} \int_0^m a(\tau)d\tau + \left(1 - \dfrac{1 - e^{-\theta m}}{\theta m} \right) \rho_S^* + b_1 \text{UNRATE} + b_2 \text{AVGMAT}.$

• UNRATE • AVGMAT

Figure 12.41 Unemployment and average maturity of Treasury obligations (1971–2012).

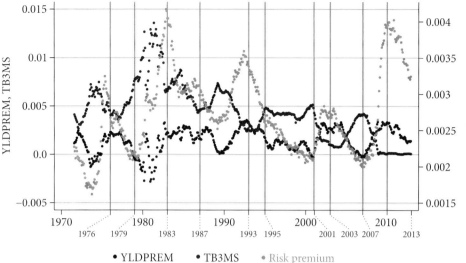

Figure 12.42 Short-term rate, yield premium, and risk premium.

Figure 12.42 graphs the short rate, the yield premium, and the risk premium, this last equal to the sum of the constant element, 0.00274, and the variable elements, 0.000375 UNRATE + 0.0000228 AVGMAT. The risk premium pulls the yield premium down between 2003 and 2007, reinforcing the effect of the rise in the short rate. In 1983 to 1987, however, the fall in the risk premium worked at cross-purposes with the decline in the short rate, so that the yield premium hardly budged. Since 2010, the risk premium has fallen as the economy has improved; and the yield premium has fallen even as the short rate has hovered near the zlb.

Bill Clinton's time as president was a period when changes in the risk premium both reinforced and counteracted the effect of the short rate on the yield premium. Over the eight years of the Clinton administration, the yield premium (on a monthly basis) fell by more than 0.003, almost 0.04 on an annual basis. Unemployment—proxying for bond-price variability—appears to have been driving the fall in the risk premium of approximately 0.0015, or 0.018 on an annual basis. But half of the reduction in both the risk premium *and* the yield premium took place in the first two years of Clinton's tenure, when the reduction in average maturity reinforced the fall in the unemployment rate, rather than, as in the period from 1995 to 2001, when the two variables moved in opposite directions. Table 12.2 summarizes the relevant data.

Table 12.2 Short Rate, Yield Premium, Unemployment, and Average Maturity (selected months)

Date	Levels				Changes			
	TB3MS	YLDPREM	UNRATE	AVGMAT	ΔTB3MS	ΔYLDPREM	ΔUNRATE	ΔAVGMAT
Jan 1976	0.00406	0.00228	7.9	29				
Jan 1979	0.00779	−0.00051	5.9	39	0.00373	−0.00279	−2.0	10
Jan 1983	0.00655	0.00226	10.4	48	−0.00124	0.00277	4.5	9
Jan 1987	0.00453	0.00164	6.6	64	−0.00203	−0.00063	−3.8	16
Jan 1993	0.0025	0.00334	7.3	70	−0.00203	0.00171	0.7	6
Jan 1995	0.00476	0.00171	5.6	65	0.00226	−0.00163	−1.7	−5
Jan 1996	0.00417	0.00064	5.6	62	−0.00059	−0.00108	0.0	−3
Jan 2001	0.00429	0.00019	4.2	69	0.00013	−0.00045	−1.4	7
Jan 2003	0.00098	0.00274	5.8	64	−0.00332	0.00255	1.6	−5
Jan 2007	0.00415	−0.00016	4.6	58	0.00318	−0.0029	−1.2	−6
Jan 2010	0.00005	0.00334	9.7	54	−0.0041	0.0035	5.1	−4
Dec 2012	0.00006	0.0014	7.9	54	0.00001	−0.00194	−1.8	0

How Does Inflation Bear on Interest-Rate Forecasts?

The results reported in this appendix depend not only on a theory of how the risk premium is determined but also on a theory of how short-term rates are forecast, particularly how inflation is incorporated into projections of the future course of interest rates. The data permit at least a limited test of my assumption about inflation, namely, that inflation works its way into long rates by a progressive ramping up of the short-term rate according to the formula

$$\hat{\rho}_s(\tau) = \left(1 - e^{-\theta(\tau - t)}\right)\rho_s^* + e^{-\theta(\tau - t)}\rho_s(t).$$

An alternative is that inflation-induced changes in the short rate are immediately incorporated into forecasts of the normal rate, which is to say that these changes are treated as permanent. (In this alternative a 2 percent increase in the current rate of inflation translates into the expectation that inflation will be 2 percent higher indefinitely.) The propagation of inflation in expected short-term rates is different under this assumption, with expected rates higher at each point in time by the amount of today's inflation. Denoting inflation at time t by $\text{INF}(t)$, and real rates by the superscript R, we have real normal and current rates given by

$$\rho_s^{R^*} = \rho_s^* - \text{INF}(t),$$

$$\hat{\rho}_s^R(\tau) = \hat{\rho}_s(\tau) - \text{INF}(t).$$

In real terms, the relationship between the expected short rate, the current rate, and the normal rate is now

$$\hat{\rho}_s^R(\tau) = \left(1 - e^{-\theta(\tau - t)}\right)\rho_s^{R^*} + e^{-\theta(\tau - t)}\rho_s^R(t),$$

whereas the nominal relationship does not change:

$$\hat{\rho}_s(\tau) = \left(1 - e^{-\theta(\tau - t)}\right)\rho_s^{R^*} + e^{-\theta(\tau - t)}\rho_s^R(t) + \text{INF}(t) = \left(1 - e^{-\theta(\tau - t)}\right)\rho_s^* + e^{-\theta(\tau - t)}\rho_s(t).$$

Since the real yield to maturity on the long bond is given by

$$\rho_{\text{mat}}^R(m, t) = \rho_{\text{mat}}(m, t) - \text{INF}(t),$$

the *real* yield premium and the *real* short rate are now driven by the same equation as in the regression reported earlier:

$$\rho_{\text{mat}}^R(m, t) - \rho_s^R(t) = \rho_{\text{mat}}(m, t) - \rho_s(t) = m^{-1}\int_0^m \alpha(\tau)d\tau + b_1\left(\text{UNRATE}(t)\right)$$

$$+ b_2\left(\text{AVGMAT}(t)\right) + \left(1 - \frac{1 - e^{-\theta m}}{\theta m}\right)\rho_s^{R^*}$$

$$+ \left(\frac{1 - e^{-\theta m}}{\theta m} - 1\right)\rho_s^R(t),$$

except that now the nominal interest rates on the right-hand side are replaced by real rates. On the left-hand side, the spread is the same whether expressed in real or nominal terms since inflation now affects the short rate and the long-bond yield equally.

We can rewrite the spread equation as

$$\rho_{mat}(m, t) - \rho_s(t) = m^{-1} \int_0^m \alpha(\tau) d\tau + b_1 \text{UNRATE}(t) + b_2 \text{AVGMAT}(t)$$

$$+ \left(1 - \frac{1 - e^{-\theta m}}{\theta m}\right) \rho_s^{R^*} + \left(\frac{1 - e^{-\theta m}}{\theta m} - 1\right) \rho_s(t)$$

$$- \left(\frac{1 - e^{-\theta m}}{\theta m} - 1\right) \text{INF}(t) = a_o + a_1 \rho_s(t) + a_2 \text{INF}(t)$$

$$+ b_1 \text{UNRATE}(t) + b_2 \text{AVGMAT}(t).$$

This leads to a straightforward test of the two hypotheses about how inflation affects the relationship between the short rate and the yield premium. On the hypothesis that the normal rate is independent of the rate of inflation and that inflation affects the adjustment to normal (H1), the test statistic is the coefficient a_2: the hypothesis is $a_2 = 0$. On the alternative hypothesis, inflation is immediately incorporated into forecasts, so that the expected real short rate is a weighted average of today's real rate and the normal real rate (H2), the test statistic is sum of the coefficients: according to H2, we expect $a_2 + a_1 = 0$.

The results of running a two-stage least-squares regression augmented by the addition of the variable INF are

TB3MS = .000974 + .661 INF + .453 DUMINF − .00176 UNRATE − .0000137 AVGMAT
   (.0002)   (.044)   (.071)   (.00006)   (.000009)
$$R^2 = .58$$

YLDPREM = .00269 − .219 TB3MS + .000374 UNRATE + .0000187 AVGMAT − .0712 INF
   (.00009) (.058)   (.00002)   (.000004)   (.049)
$$R^2 = .63$$

Robust Standard Errors in Parentheses
Observations: 497   F(4, 492) = 115.34

The standard errors of the estimated coefficient are consistent with H1 but not with H2. The data do not reject $a_2 = 0$ since the coefficient is .071 and the standard error is .05. But the data do reject $a_2 + a_1 = 0$ since the sum of these two coefficients is −.29 and the standard error of this sum is .02 (already estimated in the previous regression).

To summarize: the data are consistent with a theory of interest-rate spreads in which both normal reversion and risk aversion matter. Additionally, the data support the view that the risk premium is sensitive both to relative supplies of bonds and bills and to economic conditions, the second of these two influences being proxied by the unemployment rate. It is important to bear in mind that economic conditions enter the picture not because they affect default risk, as would be expected for private obligations, but because economic conditions correlate with the volatility of bond prices. Finally, of two models of how inflation affects interest-rate forecasts, the data are consistent with a model in which the normal rate is fixed in nominal terms but reject the alternative model in which reversion is determined by real rates. This supports, but does not prove, the assumption that inflation meets the exogeneity criterion in the TSLS regressions above.

The data also reinforce the commonsense view of the balance between normal reversion and risk aversion. Figure 12.38 suggests that when short-term rates are abnormally high or abnormally low normal reversion matters a lot. But it is the nature of abnormality that it be relatively rare.

Normal Reversion Matters a Lot, But Only Some of the Time

Experience says that most of the time, even if individual agents have strong views, there is not generally a strong consensus. But sometimes—like during the Great Depression, or in the wake of the Great Recession—agents have strong opinions *and* there is a strong consensus. In 2014 there was general agreement that short rates were going up—they had nowhere to go but up—but there was considerable disagreement about how rapidly interest rates would move. Even the members of the Federal Open Market Committee, who are presumably in a good position to know, and who had been uniform in their view that short-term rates would rise over the next few years, diverged widely with respect to the pace of the anticipated change. (They had been polling themselves at regular intervals since 2012 and continue to do so.) Figure 12.43 is an example, emerging from the FOMC meeting in September 2014 (p. 3, fig. 2). Figure 12.43 shows both the uniformity of views with respect to the *direction* of change and the divergence with respect to the *pace* of change. The so-called "dot plot," as the note to the figure explains, tells us where individual members of the FOMC believed the Federal Funds rate would be at year's end from 2014 through 2017, as well as in an unspecified "longer run," a period in which the normal rate might be expected to come into its own.[19]

Both the central tendency and the variation are interesting. Starting from the (September) 2014 rate of (near) zero, the median of the forecast for (December) 2015 was an annual rate of 1.375 percent; for (December) 2017 it was 3.75 percent.[20] But while everybody agreed that short-term rates would rise,

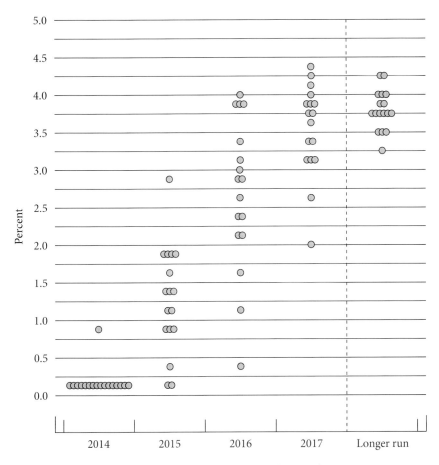

Figure 12.43 Appropriate pace of policy firming: midpoint of target range or target level for the Federal Funds rate. *Note:* Each shaded circle indicates the value (rounded to the nearest one-eighth percentage point) of an individual participant's judgment of the midpoint of the appropriate target range for the Federal Funds rate or the appropriate target level for the Federal Funds rate at the end of the specified calendar year or over the longer run.

there is a wide band around the median forecast. The Federal Reserve of this period was committed to keeping interest rates low until labor-market conditions improved, but views differed on what constituted sufficient improvement and how quickly improvement was likely to take place. And it is evident that the Fed was hardly unanimous with regard to its perceptions of the implications of an improving labor market for price stability—or, for that matter, its perceptions of the relative importance of the two elements of its dual mandate. Given these differences it is hardly surprising that the variability in individual forecasts increases as the time horizon lengthens.

The most interesting thing about the chart is its very existence. I don't have in mind the transparency of the FOMC, though that in itself reflects a historical sea change in the conduct of central banking, but rather that members had views about the course of future interest rates. If you had polled the FOMC in 2004, you well might have got similar answers to the polls in 2014; at that time, too short rates had nowhere to go but up. But in 1996 or 2006 I imagine that the FOMC would not have had any view at all, certainly not a firm view, as to where interest rates were going. Lesser mortals perhaps did, but they were paid to have firm views; nobody shells out good money for a forecaster to say "I don't have a clue which way interest rates will move." It is no wonder that for most of the observations in Figure 12.38—399 out of 497—the level of the short rate has relatively little predictive power with respect to the yield premium but that when short rates are abnormally high *or* abnormally low (as they were in 2015)—the other 98 observations—the short rate has considerable weight.

The Spread Between Treasury and Corporate Debt

To complement the analysis of the spread between returns on short- and long-term Treasury debt, we turn now to the spread between long Treasuries and long corporate debt. The principle difference between the two kinds of debt is default risk, totally absent in the analysis of Treasury debt and of varying importance in the analysis of corporate debt, intermittently the dominant factor, but hardly the only factor: analogously to the effect of the composition of Treasury debt on the spread between long and short Treasury yields, the relative amounts of Treasury and corporate debt ought to affect the spread between Treasury and corporate bonds (as Arvind Krishnamurthy and Annette Vissing-Jorgensen [2012] have argued).

The risk premium on corporate bonds relative to short-term T-bills can be written as

$$\alpha_C(m, \text{UNRATE}, \text{AVGMAT}, \text{DEFTRAIL}, \text{DELDEF}, \text{CORPFRAC})$$
$$= \alpha_C(m) + d_1\text{UNRATE}(t) + d_2\text{AVGMAT}(t) + d_3\text{DEFTRAIL}(t)$$
$$+ d_4\text{DELDEF}(t) + d_5\text{CORPFRAC}.$$

Two new variables measuring default risk are DEFTRAIL, the trailing 12-month default rate for all U.S. corporate bond issues (calculated by Moody's Analytics), and DELDEF, the first difference of this series.[21] DELDEF is arguably a better indicator of the current default rate than DEFTRAIL since DELDEF, measuring the difference between the most recent observation and the observation from one year further back, captures the momentum of default. The last variable, CORPFRAC, measures the volume of corporate bonds outstanding relative to the total bond volume, including securities issued by government agencies and government sponsored entities, as well as state and municipal bonds, but excluding the holdings of the Federal Reserve.[22]

The integral equation for the corporate-bond-yield premium over the T-bill rate is

$$\rho_{m\text{CORP}}(m,t) = m^{-1}\left(\int \hat{\rho}_s(t+m)dm + \int \alpha_C(m)dm\right) + d_1\text{UNRATE}(t) + d_2\text{AVGMAT}(t)$$
$$+ d_3\text{DEFTRAIL}(t) + d_4\text{DELDEF}(t) + d_5\text{CORPFRAC}(t) + m^{-1}c,$$

where $\rho_{m\text{CORP}}$ is the yield to maturity on corporate bonds that mature in m years. Once again we invoke limiting values of the left- and right-hand sides to fix c, and once again we have $c = 0$.

Alas, direct estimation of the coefficients is problematic because of the lack of a series of zero-coupon bonds comparable to the series that Houston McCulloch originally developed for Treasuries in the 1970s (1971, 1975).[23] In principle one could construct a zero-coupon corporate bond following the procedures that have been applied in the case of Treasuries, but in view of the considerable resources that would be necessary, I am taking the easier route of simply subtracting the equation for Treasuries

$$\rho_{\text{mat}}(m,t) = m^{-1}\left(\int \hat{\rho}_s(t+m)dm + \int \alpha(m)dm\right) + b_1\text{UNRATE}(t)$$
$$+ b_2\text{AVGMAT}(t) + m^{-1}c$$

from the equation for corporates. This gives

$$\rho_{m\text{CORP}}(m,t) - \rho_{\text{mat}}(m,t) = m^{-1}\int\left(\alpha_C(m) - \alpha(m)\right)dm + \left(d_1 - b_1\right)\text{UNRATE}(t)$$
$$+ \left(d_2 - b_2\right)\text{AVGMAT}(t) + d_3\text{DEFTRAIL}(t)$$
$$+ d_4\text{DELDEF}(t) + d_5\text{CORPFRAC}(t).$$

For this equation to generate unbiased estimates of the relevant parameters, it is necessary to assume that the difference between yields to maturity on zero-coupon and coupon bonds is the same, up to a random error, for Treasuries and for corporates. This seems plausible, but it must be recognized that there is no way to test this hypothesis short of constructing a time-series of zero-coupon corporate bonds and estimating the yields.

The data set now includes the yields on 10-year corporate bonds from the Treasury "High Quality Market" Corporate Bond Yield Curve (U.S. Department of the Treasury [n.d.]). Using quarterly data, the regression for the period 1984 to 2012 is

$$\rho_{mCORP}(m,t) - \rho_{mat}(m,t) = -.0005974 + .0001114 \text{ UNRATE}(t) - .0000119 \text{ AVGMAT}(t)$$
$$(.001369) \quad (.0000437) (.0000151)$$

$$+ .003932 \text{ DEFTRAIL}(t) + .0359 \text{ DELDEF}(t) + 0.004 \text{ CORPFRAC}(t)$$
$$(.00380) (.01014) (0.001)$$

$$R^2 = .54$$

Newey-West Standard Errors in Parentheses

Variable	Obs	Mean	Std Dev	Min	Max
$\rho_{mCORP}(m,t) - \rho_{mat}(m,t)$	116	0.0018	0.0006	0.0011	0.0042
UNRATE	116	6.1483	1.5071	3.9000	9.9333
AVGMAT	116	63.138	6.775	46.0	73.0
DEFTRAIL	116	0.0222	0.0158	0.0057	0.0829
DELDEF	116	0.00008	0.0055	−0.0264	0.0231
CORPFRAC	116	0.3558	0.0505	0.2710	0.4396

Yields are per month, data are quarterly.

The coefficient of UNRATE, the estimate of the difference $d_1 - b_1$, 0.0001114, taken together with the coefficient of UNRATE in the Treasury yield-premium regressions, 0.000375, implies that the effect of unemployment on corporate bonds is almost 0.0005. That is, an increase of one percentage point in the unemployment rate leads to an increase in the corporate-bond yield of 0.05 percentage points per month, or 0.6 percentage points on an annual basis. This suggests that if UNRATE is indeed a proxy for price variability, corporate-bond price variability should exhibit the same correlation with unemployment that shows up for Treasuries in Figure 12.39. But the data show no such correlation, as Figure 12.44 shows. Except for the two outliers in the 6 to 8 percent unemployment interval, the pattern of corporate-bond price changes does not show any sensitivity to the rate of unemployment. It may be that this is due to the truncated sample of 10-year corporate bond yields. The 497 observations in the (monthly) Treasury regressions include the high unemployment years of the 1970s and 1980s. In contrast, the data for 10-year corporates begins in 1984. More likely, the *current* unemployment rate is a better proxy for default risk than the *trailing* index of actual default over the previous twelve months: the coefficient on the index itself, the variable DEFTRAIL, is insignificant in the presence of UNRATE, but is significant ($t = 2.7$) when the unemployment variable is suppressed. By contrast, the coefficient on the change in the default index, DELDEF, is statistically significant whether or not the unemployment rate is included in the regression.

The interpretation of the unemployment rate as a proxy for default risk is plausible, but further investigation suggests this is not all there is to the story. If we replace the trailing index of default by the default risk over the subse-

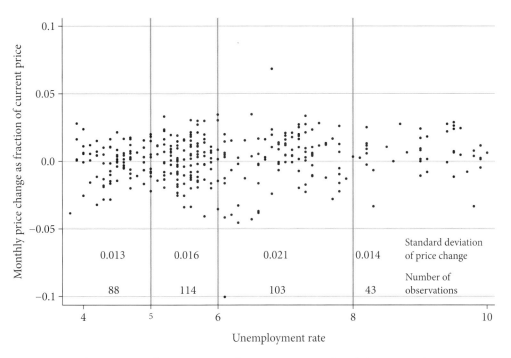

Figure 12.44 Change in price of 10-year corporate bonds (1984–2012).

quent year, DEF, and the change in the index by the change of the index over the next year, labeled DELDEF+1, both variables are significant, and the regression fit improves markedly:

$$\rho_{m\text{CORP}}(m,t) - \rho_{\text{mat}}(m,t) = .0006821 + .0001204 \; \text{UNRATE}(t) - .000012 \; \text{AVGMAT}(t)$$
$$(.0009217) \quad (.0000312) \qquad\qquad (.00000953)$$

$$+ .0093 \; \text{DEF}(t) + .0439 \; \text{DELDEF} + 1(t) + 0.00375 \; \text{CORPFRAC}(t)$$
$$(.00284) \qquad\qquad (.0102) \qquad\qquad\qquad (0.000866)$$

$$R^2 = .71$$

Newey-West Standard Errors in Parentheses

Variable	Obs	Mean	Std Dev	Min	Max
$\rho_{m\text{CORP}}(m,t) - \rho_{\text{mat}}(m,t)$	116	0.00085	0.00051	0.00026	0.00352
UNRATE	116	6.14828	1.50706	3.90	9.93
AVGMAT	116	63.1379	6.77507	46.0	73.0
DEF	116	0.02228	0.01573	0.00573	0.08293
DELDEF+1	116	0.00008	0.00549	−0.02637	0.02307
CORPFRAC	116	0.35576	0.05053	0.27097	0.43961

Yields are per month, data are quarterly.

An obvious problem with this regression is its reliance on the ability of agents to forecast default rates. As I indicated at the beginning of this appendix, I am not enamored of rational expectations, but the problem here is less acute than in forecasting interest rates over a much longer (ten-year) period. It is at least arguable that information about the likelihood of future defaults is available to bond-market participants, and in the absence of a time series of forecasts, relying on actual future defaults may be defensible. But in this case the unemployment variable becomes a supplementary indicator of default sentiment rather than a replacement for the actual default rate. We must now argue that the forward-looking default rate is simply grist for the mill of expectations, along with current unemployment, rather than arguing that agents actually know future default rates.

What Do the Numbers Mean?

The regressions in this appendix provide a quantitative estimate of the contribution of various factors—the short rate, unemployment, average maturity, default risk—to the desirability of T-bills relative to longer Treasury obligations and to corporate bonds. Of particular interest, given the focus of Keynes's *General Theory,* is the consequence for the liquidity trap, here meaning the spread between the short rate and the corporate bond yield when the short rate approaches the zlb.

In Tables 12.3 and 12.4 we compare predicted and actual spreads before the financial crisis unleashed by the fall of Lehman Brothers in September 2008 and three observations after the crisis began to unfold. Table 12.3 reflects trailing default risk and Table 12.4 future default risk.

The relationship between short and long Treasuries is the same in both tables. The T-bill rate falls from almost 4 percent per year in the fall of 2007 to 0.67 percent a year later, and then to almost zero (where it remained until the Federal Reserve began to raise rates in December 2015). Between fall 2007 and fall 2008, the spread between the 10-year Treasury and the 3-month bill widens by just over 150 basis points. According to the decomposition in both tables, this increase is driven in equal measure by unemployment, presumably a proxy for price volatility, and the decline in the bill rate, presumably an indicator of anticipated reversion to normal. The increase in the proportion of bills in the mix of Treasury debt (AVGMAT declines from 57.3 to 46 months) mitigates the rise in the spread: according to the regression coefficients the spread would have widened by 180 basis points without the decline in the average maturity of Treasury debt.

By contrast, default risk is the driver of the corporate-Treasury spread. As the federal deficit rises, the decrease in the relative volume of outstanding corporate debt softens the blow, but not by much.

Table 12.3 Estimated Spreads with Varying Unemployment and Default Risk (trailing default rates)

	Sample Mean	Observations	Fall 2007 (Oct–Dec)	Fall 2008 (Oct–Dec)	Winter 2009 (Jan–Mar)	Fall 2009 (Oct–Dec)	Cumulative (Fall 2007– Fall 2009)
TB3MS $= \rho_s(t)$ (percent, annual)	5.26	1971:6–2012:12	3.39	0.3	0.21	0.06	
UNRATE (percent)	6.43	1971:6–2012:12	4.8	6.87	8.27	9.93	
AVGMAT (months)	56.0	1971:6–2012:12	57.3	46.0	47.0	51.3	
DEFTRAIL (index)	0.022	1984:1–2012:12	0.006	0.025	0.041	0.083	
DELDEF (index)	0.00008	1984:1–2012:12	−0.0018	0.0068	0.0161	0.0046	
CORPFRAC (fraction)	0.356	1984:1–2012:12	0.437	0.403	0.412	0.407	
					Actual (percent, annual)		
YLDPREM $= \rho_{\mathrm{mat}}(m,t) - \rho_s(t)$	1.76	1971:6–2012:12	1.06	3.62	3.15	3.78	
$\rho_{m\mathrm{CORP}}(m,t) - \rho_{\mathrm{mat}}(m,t)$	1.02	1984:1–2012:12	1.44	4.22	3.72	1.49	
$\rho_{m\mathrm{CORP}}(m,t) - \rho_s(t)$	2.78	1984:1–2012:12	2.5	7.84	6.87	5.28	
					Estimates (percent, annual)		
YLDPREM $= \rho_{\mathrm{mat}}(m,t) - \rho_s(t)$	1.76	1971:6–2012:12	1.6	3.12	3.8	4.72	
$\rho_{m\mathrm{CORP}}(m,t) - \rho_{\mathrm{mat}}(m,t)$	1.02	1984:1–2012:12	1.15	1.89	2.58	2.42	
$\rho_{m\mathrm{CORP}}(m,t) - \rho_s(t)$	2.78	1984:1–2012:12	2.75	5.01	6.38	7.14	

Decomposition of Estimated Changes

$$\Delta[\rho_{\mathrm{mat}}(m,t) - \rho_s(t)] = -0.2909278\ \Delta\text{TB3MS} + 0.0003748\ \Delta\text{UNRATE} + 0.0000228\ \Delta\text{AVGMAT}$$

	Fall 2008	Winter 2009	Fall 2009	Cumulative
$\Delta[\rho_{\mathrm{mat}}(m,t) - \rho_s(t)]$	1.52	0.68	0.91	3.11
Contribution of ΔTB3MS	0.9	0.02	0.05	0.97
Contribution of ΔUNRATE	0.93	0.63	0.75	2.31
Contribution of ΔAVGMAT	−0.31	0.03	0.12	−0.16

Table 12.3 (continued)

	Sample Mean	Observations	Fall 2007 (Oct–Dec)	Fall 2008 (Oct–Dec)	Winter 2009 (Jan–Mar)	Fall 2009 (Oct–Dec)	Cumulative (Fall 2007–Fall 2009)
			Decomposition of Estimated Changes				
			$\Delta[\rho_{mCORP}(m,t) - \rho_{mat}(m,t)] = 0.0001114\ \Delta UNRATE - 0.0000119\ \Delta AVGMAT$ $+ 0.0039318\ \Delta DEFTRAIL + 0.0358872\ \Delta DELDEF$ $+ 0.0039981\ \Delta CORPFRAC$				
$\Delta[\rho_{mCORP}(m,t) - \rho_{mat}(m,t)]$				0.74	0.69	−0.16	1.27
Contribution of $\Delta UNRATE$				0.28	0.19	0.22	0.69
Contribution of $\Delta AVGMAT$				0.16	−0.01	−0.06	0.09
Contribution of $\Delta DEFTRAIL$				0.09	0.08	0.2	0.36
Contribution of $\Delta DELDEF$				0.37	0.4	−0.49	0.28
Contribution of $\Delta CORPFRAC$				−0.16	0.04	−0.02	−0.14

Table 12.4 Actual vs. Estimated Spreads (current and future default rates)

	Sample Mean	Observations	Fall 2007 (Oct–Dec)	Fall 2008 (Oct–Dec)	Winter 2009 (Jan–Mar)	Fall 2009 (Oct–Dec)	Cumulative (Fall 2007–Fall 2009)
TB3MS = $\rho_s(t)$ (percent, annual)	5.26	1971:6–2012:12	3.39	0.3	0.21	0.06	
UNRATE (percent)	6.43	1971:6–2012:12	4.8	6.87	8.27	9.93	
AVGMAT (months)	56.0	1971:6–2012:12	57.3	46.0	47.0	51.3	
DEF (index)	0.022	1984:1–2012:12	0.009	0.041	0.064	0.07	
DELDEF+1 (index)	0.00008	1984:1–2012:12	0.0033	0.0161	0.0231	−0.0127	
CORPFRAC (fraction)	0.356	1984:1–2012:12	0.437	0.403	0.412	0.407	
			Actual (percent, annual)				
YLDPREM = $\rho_{mat}(m,t) - \rho_s(t)$	1.76	1971:6–2012:12	1.06	3.62	3.15	3.78	
$\rho_{mCORP}(m,t) - \rho_{mat}(m,t)$	1.02	1984:1–2012:12	1.44	4.22	3.72	1.49	
$\rho_{mCORP}(m,t) - \rho_s(t)$	2.78	1984:1–2012:12	2.5	7.84	6.87	5.28	

Estimates (percent, annual)

$\text{YLDPREM} = \rho_{\mathrm{mat}}(m,t) - \rho_s(t)$	1.76	1971:6–2012:12	1.6	3.12	3.8	4.72
$\rho_{m\mathrm{CORP}}(m,t) - \rho_{\mathrm{mat}}(m,t)$	1.02	1984:1–2012:12	1.29	2.64	3.49	1.83
$\rho_{m\mathrm{CORP}}(m,t) - \rho_s(t)$	2.78	1984:1–2012:12	2.89	5.76	7.29	6.54

Decomposition of Estimated Changes

$$\Delta[\rho_{\mathrm{mat}}(m,t) - \rho_s(t)] = -0.2909278\ \Delta\text{TB3MS} + 0.0003748\ \Delta\text{UNRATE} + 0.0000228\ \Delta\text{AVGMAT}$$

$\Delta[\rho_{\mathrm{mat}}(m,t) - \rho_s(t)]$	1.52	0.68	0.91	3.11
Contribution of ΔTB3MS	0.9	0.02	0.05	0.97
Contribution of ΔUNRATE	0.93	0.63	0.75	2.31
Contribution of ΔAVGMAT	−0.31	0.03	0.12	−0.16

Decomposition of Estimated Changes

$$\Delta[\rho_{m\mathrm{CORP}}(m,t) - \rho_{\mathrm{mat}}(m,t)] = 0.0001204\ \Delta\text{UNRATE} - 0.000012\ \Delta\text{AVGMAT} + 0.0093002\ \Delta\text{DEF} + 0.0439496\ \Delta\text{DELDEF+1} + 0.0037535\ \Delta\text{CORPFRAC}$$

$\Delta[\rho_{m\mathrm{CORP}}(m,t) - \rho_{\mathrm{mat}}(m,t)]$	1.35	0.85	−1.67	0.54
Contribution of ΔUNRATE	0.3	0.2	0.24	0.74
Contribution of ΔAVGMAT	0.16	−0.01	−0.06	0.09
Contribution of ΔDEF	0.36	0.26	0.07	0.68
Contribution of ΔDELDEF+1	0.68	0.37	−1.89	−0.84
Contribution of ΔCORPFRAC	−0.15	0.04	−0.02	−0.13

The residuals in the regressions for the spread between corporate and Treasury are much larger in Table 12.3 than in Table 12.4. In fall 2008, the direness of the economic situation had yet to be reflected in the numbers: unemployment was less than 7 percent—it would rise to 10 percent before the end of the next year—and default rates had only begun to rise. In Table 12.3 the estimate of the yield premium on 10-year corporate bonds relative to Treasuries of the same maturity for this period is less than 45 percent of the actual premium, 1.89 percent annually versus 4.22 percent. This model does better by the following winter, but the estimate is still less than 70 percent of the actual. In Table 12.4 by contrast, the estimate for fall 2008 is 2.64, percent and for the winter of 2009 it is 3.49, respectively 63 percent and 94 percent of the actual.

Finally, the composition of the overall debt, both the relative size of corporate and Treasury debt and the average maturity of Treasury debt, is statistically significant in both of the equations for $\rho_{mCORP}(m,t) - \rho_{mat}(m,t)$, but the effects of CORPFRAC and AVGMAT are each relatively small; moreover, the two effects worked in opposite directions. The burgeoning Treasury debt between 2007 and 2009 reduced the fraction of corporate bonds by almost four percentage points, which in turn had the expected negative impact on the corporate-Treasury spread (the estimate is −.14 percentage points in Table 12.3 and −.13 percentage points in Table 12.4). This reduction was shaved by more than half by the shortening of the AVGMAT of Treasury debt from 57 to 51 months.

— 13 —

TAKING MONEY SERIOUSLY

The wild duck has dived down to the bottom—as deep as she can
get—and bitten fast hold of the weed and tangle and all the rubbish
that is down there, and it would need an extraordinarily clever dog
to dive after and fish her up again.

—JOHN MAYNARD KEYNES

We are a long way from the simple models of chapter 3. In those models the
interest rate is either fixed directly by the central bank or is determined by the
money supply and two sources of demand, a demand for money to grease the
wheels of commerce and industry and a demand for money as a constituent
of asset portfolios. In the first case, which I dubbed the first-pass model, aggregate demand alone determined the level of output, whereas in the second-
pass model, real aggregate demand depended on the nominal price of output,
and the equilibrium level of output depends not only on aggregate demand
but on supply conditions as well.

The first-pass model lays out the interconnections of the elements of
Keynes's vision in the simplest possible form, and serves to demonstrate both
the possibilities and the limits of monetary policy as a tool in the service of
full employment.

The second-pass model can be interpreted either as a slightly more con-
crete formalization of how monetary policy may or may not be sufficient to
direct the economy to a full-employment equilibrium or as a model of how a
capitalist economy left to its own devices may or may not spontaneously
achieve full employment. In the first interpretation, a central bank is assumed
to set the money supply. In the second, there is no central bank and we have
two choices. In the simplest model, the money supply is an exogenously given
supply of gold, silver or cowrie shells. In a more sophisticated financial world,
commodity money is but one form that money takes. The overall money supply is determined by a fractional-reserve banking system, which is free to
create money up to the maximum ratio of deposits to reserves permitted by
law or custom.

Even without the complications introduced with respect to propensities to
consume and save (chapter 9), investment demand (chapter 10), and the the-

ory of interest (chapters 11–12), the second-pass model foundered once we left the safe harbor in which money is a commodity. Once we assume that banks create money to fulfill the transactions demand, we no longer can count on a simple equation in which the transactions demand and the asset demand add up to a given supply. Crucially, it is no longer the case that monetary equilibrium requires more of one money demand to mean less money available to supply the other. A firewall now exists between the two kinds of money.

None of this turned out to matter very much in a comparative-statics framework. Even if transactions demand is passively satisfied by the banking system, so that transactions money and asset money are independent of one another, the volume of bonds (by assumption the only other financial asset) will vary with the price level of output. The result in chapter 4 was that the equilibrium interest rate, determined by the demand for and supply of financial assets, varied directly with the price level. Thus the essential quality of Keynes's second-pass model, the downward-sloping AD schedule, was preserved even though its *raison d'être* is now a bond effect, which makes the stock of bonds decrease with the price level, rather than the Keynes effect, which makes the stock of portfolio money increase as the price level decreases.

In a world of real-time changes, it makes no sense to assume that the volume of bonds will vary with the nominal value of capital. Rather, the appropriate assumption is that the volume of bonds is fixed once and for all. This seemingly small change makes a big difference. Now not only is the supply of asset money independent of the money demand (and supply) for transactions, but also the quantity of bonds is independent of the general price level. The consequence, as we saw in chapter 7, was that demands for financial assets become independent of the price of goods, and so does the interest rate. The AD schedule becomes vertical in the space of output versus price; the second-pass model collapses into the first-pass model. There is neither a Keynes effect nor a bond effect, one or the other a necessary condition for a downward-sloping AD schedule.

The purpose of this chapter is to revisit these results in the light of the theory of interest developed in the previous chapter. We begin with an issue that turns out to be central to the story but got virtually no attention in *The General Theory*.

The Missing Theory of Money

The title is *The General Theory of Employment, Interest and Money*. As we have seen, there is not one, but two theories of employment, one for a given interest rate, one for a given money supply.

What about the other two elements of the title, *interest* and *money?* The theory of interest is incomplete, and the theory of money is at best implicit.

There is a theory of the demand for money, and this theory is central to Keynes's argument. Reprised below, liquidity preference is Keynes's answer to the so-called quantity theory of money. The quantity theory (which, vampire like, is still with us) is not a theory of money at all; if truth in labeling prevailed, it would be called the quantity-of-money theory of prices. But Keynes is as remiss as the quantity theorists. Despite lots of talk about properties of money, including the impenetrable chapter 17 on own rates of interest, *The General Theory* offers no theory of how money comes to be or what it is.

The absence of a theory of money turns out to be an important reason why Keynes doesn't deliver on his promise to replace the conventional theory of interest, in which productivity and thrift rule the roost, by his own theory of liquidity preference. And this failure in turn supports the argument, which prevails to this day, that unemployment is the result of frictions and imperfections, problems that can be fixed by making the world more like the textbook heaven of deregulation and unfettered self-interest—or by just waiting for the long run, which magically dissolves all rigidities.

The theory of money is best approached through the theory of interest. Liquidity preference starts from the argument that the mainstream theory is built on a category mistake, namely, that the rate of interest is determined in a market for new capital goods in which demand comes from projects for adding to the capital stock (plant, equipment, housing, infrastructure), and supply comes from the willingness of the populace to abstain from consumption and thus provide resources for investment. For Keynes the locus of interest-rate determination is not to be found in the *flows* of investment and saving, the tail of asset markets, but on the dog itself, in markets for financial assets that correspond, dimensionally at least, to the *stock* of capital goods. The interest rate (singular for ease of exposition but plural in reality) that emerges from buying and selling in these markets becomes the "hurdle rate" for investment, separating the sheep from the goats among potential projects. Besides determining the demand for investment, the interest rate prevailing in the market for financial assets may also influence the supply of saving. But this is very different from arguing that interest rates are determined by investment demand and saving supply.

What does this have to with a theory of money?

As presented in *The General Theory*, there are two uses of money. One is to grease the wheels of commerce. This leads to a *transactions demand* for money, along the lines of the quantity theory that goes back to David Hume. The other use for money is to satisfy appetites for a store of value that can be reliably counted upon to meet future contingencies. This leads to a separate and distinct demand for money in wealth portfolios, which Keynes calls the *speculative demand*.

Why speculative? Keynes starts from a theory of wealth management in which portfolios are driven by two conflicting factors, return and risk. Returns matter for obvious reasons. Risk, or rather uncertainty, matters because agents might need cash to meet unpredictable contingencies of life.[1] Illness and job loss come to mind as the contingencies that most concern most people, but these are not the contingencies that Keynes would have had in mind if the theory was to apply to wealth management in the real world.[2] For the simple reason that few people, especially in his day, accumulate significant amounts of wealth, whereas for the people who do, questions like how to pay the doctor's bill or how to get along for a while without a salary are not uppermost in their minds as they think about how to deploy wealth. More important would be business losses, or for that matter business opportunities, situations where ready cash is necessary either to stave off serious reverses or to take advantage of extraordinary possibilities.

In making choices among the various forms in which to hold wealth, agents trade off the potential gains of holding assets that are expected to pay dividends, interest, or rents against the potential losses to which these instruments are subject. Losses are possible even if the asset is a long-term U.S. T-bond, which is perfectly safe in the sense of having no risk of default: bond prices go up and down as interest rates fall and rise. Given the potential for loss, economic actors might prefer to hold some or all of their wealth in the form of cash and forego the potential return on bonds and other assets, in order to ensure against loss if they need cash before the bonds mature. The possibility of default adds another degree of uncertainty, another reason for holding cash.

Keynes thus sees agents as necessarily speculating in two senses. First, they inevitably are speculating on the likelihood of the various contingencies that might force them to need cash; second, they must speculate on the prices they will receive for their assets if they have to cash out. In a simplified world in which a long-term T-bond stands in for the entire range of financial assets other than ready money, the second speculation is in part a gamble about the future course of interest rates and bond prices. Risk-neutral agents will not hold bonds if, averaging the probability of a capital gain and the probability of a capital loss, an expected loss in the value of a bond exceeds the coupon yield. But even if the probabilities of gain and loss cancel out, risk-averse agents will, in Keynes's theory, require compensation for holding long-term bonds; to a risk-averse agent, the damage caused by a loss outweighs the benefit of an equal gain. In return for foregoing liquidity, she will require a higher yield on the T-bond than she would if there were no possibility of changes in bond yields and bond prices. Risk aversion and the expectation that interest rates will revert to normal reinforce each other in creating a demand for liquidity when bond prices are expected to fall, but they work in opposite directions when bond prices are expected to rise. In any case, the higher the return on a bond, the more attractive it is. In a two-asset world, cash and long-term Treasuries, the speculative demand for money is an inverse function of the rate of interest on long bonds.

Different considerations govern the demand for money as a means of payment in business (and personal) transactions. The transactions demand is determined by the level of production and the price level. Higher levels of nominal economic activity mean either more transactions or more money per transaction (or both).[3]

The endowment of bonds and the nominal level of output determine the total demand for money. The other side of the coin, so to speak, is the supply of money. For any given supply of money, the rate of interest and the level of economic activity balance the overall demand for money and its supply. This is the essence of Keynes's theory of interest; its emphasis on balancing return against the risks associated with changing bond prices and yields explains why it is called the liquidity-preference theory of interest.

For Keynes, unlike the mainstream, money is not a veil, but an active component in determining how much is produced, consumed, and invested. The supply of money has a direct effect on the real side of the economy through its effect on interest rates and investment demand.

Three important conclusions follow. First, in a capitalist economy in which the supply of money is really and truly beyond human control, in an economy where nobody is at the monetary helm, there is no endogenous stabilizing mechanism that guarantees full employment. It is possible for the economy to settle down at a level of employment that leaves many willing workers without jobs. Second, control of the money supply is not only necessary but is usually sufficient to steer the economy to full employment. Third, there are exceptions to the usual case, a liquidity trap or an unresponsiveness of investment demand, that call for something more than activist monetary policy in order to keep the economy off the shoals of unemployment. (Keynes was vague about the "something more." *The General Theory* provides a glimpse of the promised land of fiscal policy as the additional tool, but a combination of Victorian virtue and his sense of the politically possible made Keynes shrink from its implications. Some years later, possibly under the tutelage of one of his acolytes, Abba Lerner, he overcame his inhibitions (see chapter 14, note 3).

There is an alternative to increasing the nominal money supply, which in theory can have the same positive effect on investment demand: reducing

nominal wages. Usually associated with Franco Modigliani's (1944) formalization of *The General Theory*, the argument was anticipated by Keynes:

> If the quantity of money is virtually fixed, it is evident that its quantity in
> terms of wage-units [that is, in real terms] can be indefinitely increased by a
> sufficient reduction in money wages. (*The General Theory*, p. 266)

At a lower level of wages, prices will also be lower, and less money will be required to facilitate the same level of production. Because the overall supply of
money is fixed, the money no longer needed for transactions must spill over
into the market for financial assets, that is, into the market for long-term
Treasuries. But agents are willingly holding the cash in their portfolios because the interest rate is what it is. They won't hold more unless the interest
rate falls. So to restore equilibrium between overall demand for money and
overall supply, the interest rate must be lower. There is thus a positive relationship between the overall price level and the rate of interest. This coupled
with the inverse relationship between the interest rate and investment demand implies that lower wages go along with greater aggregate demand, the
Keynes effect.

For Keynes, the Keynes effect showed the limitations of a policy of wage
reductions:

> It follows that wage reductions, as a method of securing full employment,
> are also subject to the same limitations as the method of increasing the
> quantity of money. (*The General Theory*, p. 266)

But wage reductions, like an increase in the quantity of money, "may exert an
inadequate influence over the long-term rate of interest" (p. 266). Moreover,
wage flexibility is a cumbersome and politically difficult way of achieving
what is more practically accomplished by deliberate monetary policy:

> A method which it is comparatively easy to apply should be deemed pref-
> erable to a method which is probably so difficult as to be impracticable.
> (p. 268)

Modigliani, as we saw in chapter 4, drew a different conclusion: wage and
price flexibility, Modigliani contended, up-ends Keynes's conclusion that even
a purely competitive capitalist economy, one free of the vices of frictions, imperfections, and inflexibilities, will provide full employment only under a
serendipitous constellation of economic forces. Specifically, Modigliani deployed the Keynes effect to argue that the same positive effects on demand
that can be accomplished by increasing the money supply can be accomplished by the invisible hand, without any top-down intervention, if the wage
level, and accordingly the price level, are sufficiently flexible.[4]

What Does Keynes's Liquidity-Preference
Theory Assume about Money?

Despite the lack of an explicit theory of money, an implicit theory is hard at work here—in two places. First, the supply of money is exogenous, either a fixed amount of a commodity given by the available resources and technology or a fixed amount dictated by the monetary authority. Second, the two uses of money, speculation and transactions, are assumed to compete for the available supply of money. One more dollar, euro, or yen greasing the wheels of commerce means one fewer available to satisfy the desire of wealth holders for a hedge against bond-price fluctuations.

There is more than one way to justify these two assumptions, but in the absence of an explicit theory of money, the justification must be inferred. In arguing about the capacity of capitalism to provide full employment without intervention from above, that is, in the absence of a central bank, the simplest assumption is that money is a commodity: gold, silver, or cowrie shells.

COMMODITY MONEY   With commodity money, the stock is fixed by the costs of finding, mining, and refining. And commodity money can be used for only one purpose at a time. A Venetian ducat used to pay for the fish needed for tonight's menu at the Poste Vecie cannot at the same time serve as an umbrella for a rainy day for the restaurant's owner or anybody else.

Commodity money fits the story that we learn from the texts, the one about money emerging spontaneously to allow trade to take place without the double coincidence of wants that makes barter efficient. Precious metals are uniquely positioned to act as money because they are, well, precious, and thus concentrate value, measured in terms of volume or in terms of weight. Precious metals are also durable and relatively easy to divide into smaller units, as needed. Abraham's hoard of silver could be easily divided to extract the four hundred shekels he needed to purchase Sarah's burial plot from Ephron the Hittite.

Commodity money thus fits neatly with the requirements of Keynes's liquidity-preference theory. It is both fixed in supply, and it can be used only for one thing at a time.

If money is not based on gold or cowrie shells, it is harder to justify either of these requirements. The problem is that, as history, the spontaneous evolution of precious metals into money has long since been discredited as at best incomplete and at worst a just-so story. Georg Friedrich Knapp published *The State Theory of Money* in 1905 (as *Staatliche Theorie des Geldes*). A. Mitchell Innes published "What is Money?" in 1913 and "The Credit Theory of Money" in 1914. Their titles tell us their respective emphases, each of which captures part of the critique of the commodity theory. Christine Desan's 2014 account of the evolution of English money from Anglo-Saxon times to the early modern period makes the limitations of the commodity theory clear and suggests that the questions raised by Knapp and Innes have been debated for centuries.

Keynes himself, in the *Treatise on Money,* recognized that the commodity-money story had long since passed its sell-by date. In the *Treatise* he invokes the authority of Knapp, but he had also read at least the first of Innes's articles, having reviewed it in the *Economic Journal* the year after it appeared in print.

According to Keynes,

> The right [to determine what constitutes money] is claimed by all modern States and has been so claimed for some four thousand years at least. It is when this stage in the evolution of Money has been reached that Knapp's Chartalism—the doctrine that money is peculiarly a creation of the State—is fully realised.
>
> Thus the Age of Money had succeeded to the Age of Barter as soon as men had adopted a money-of-account. And the Age of Chartalist or State Money was reached when the State claimed the right to declare what thing should answer as money to the current money-of-account . . . To-day all civilized money is, beyond the possibility of dispute, chartalist. (1930, vol. 1, pp. 4–5)

Chartalist money is fiat money. The state is centrally involved. A declaration like that of the U.S. government on every piece of our paper currency, "This note is legal tender for all debts, public and private," may not be necessary for fiat currency to be accepted as a means of payment or store of value, but it certainly helps—as does the state's ability to enforce its declaration.

With fiat money, the usual story is that the supply is fixed by the monetary authority, typically but not necessarily a central bank. Formally, money is still exogenous—we can ask what happens to various elements of the economy, including the rate of interest, at different levels of the money supply—but exogeneity doesn't mean the same thing anymore. A central bank is part of the financial, economic, and political system, and the substantive meaning of assuming that the money supply is determined outside the model is very different when the supply is fixed by economics and politics than when it is fixed by nature and technology.

FRACTIONAL-RESERVE BANKING   If the issue is the ability of a capitalist ship to right itself after a storm without the intervention of a helmsman, we have to take account of fractional-reserve banking. This question is prior to the role of the state, and thus prior to the introduction of a central bank, which is quintessentially a state institution (even when, like the Bank of England, it was legally a private entity for most of its history).

What happens if money is created out of whole cloth, as it is under fractional-reserve banking? (If you are devoted to the commodity theory, rephrase the question as What happens when commodity money is supplanted by, or if even that is too strong, supplemented by, fractional-reserve banking?)

How does fractional-reserve banking enter into Keynes's story about interest and employment? In a word, if a central bank changes the meaning of exogenous in "exogenous money supply," fractional-reserve banking delivers the first blow to the either/or conception of using money to satisfy transactions demand and using money to satisfy the appetites of wealth holders.[5]

Fractional-reserve banking is a system for creating money in the form of credit. It is like fiat money because it is divorced from a commodity base even when its issuers purport that it is as "good as gold" (or cowrie shells). It is *pseudo*-fiat money, because it does not require a state guarantee—though a state guarantee is certainly useful, and may be necessary, in encouraging wide acceptance. Fractional-reserve banking allows the supply of money to vary endogenously with demand via the creation and destruction of bank deposits, creation and destruction that are part and parcel of the expansion and contraction of bank credit. Key here is the acceptance of bank deposits (or bank notes) as a form of money, a way of discharging financial obligations. This is one reason a state guarantee is practically if not logically essential.

Fractional-reserve banking need not change the story that transactions demand and speculative demand are in competition with one another. But to ensure that the story holds, we have to make additional assumptions, strong assumptions that cannot be warranted in the name of expositional simplicity.

To see the difficulties, try to retell the story of the Keynes effect in a world with fractional-reserve banking. Output or the price level falls. Firms require less working capital to finance their on-going operations. Transactions demand falls, and, so, by the way, does the value of the collateral that firms must put up to cover their loans, especially if this collateral takes the form of physical goods (for example, the inventory of automobiles that car dealers pledge as collateral—or gondolas in Venice).

Now what happens? In the earlier story, "the money no longer needed for transactions must spill over into the market for financial assets, that is, into the market for long-term Treasuries." And this drives down interest rates, and so encourages investment. Something like this will happen in the present story *if* banks replace the working-capital loans they make to car dealers, restaurants, and others or their holdings of short-term commercial paper by adding to their portfolios of long-term T-bonds. That is, the reduction in transactions demand may be compensated by an increase in speculative demand *on the part of banks*.

In this case, the story goes through pretty much as before, though the mechanism is different. Banks operate on money demand, keeping the overall supply constant while varying the composition of demand. The crucial assumption here is that banks always attempt to deploy their assets so as to have no excess reserves, that they always try to stay fully loaned-up—and succeed in the attempt![6]

Without these assumptions the either/or conception of transactions money and speculative money breaks down. The consequence is that the theoretical equivalence of money-supply changes and changes in the price and wage levels can no longer be invoked, à la Modigliani, to argue for the self-regulating capacity of a capitalist economy. As Keynes wrote, somewhat cryptically, just before introducing the Keynes effect,

> If the quantity of money is itself a function of the wage- and price-level, there is indeed, nothing to hope for in this direction. (*The General Theory*, p. 266)

We can still write the equilibrium equation

$$M_1 + M_2 = \bar{M},$$

where M_1 represents transactions demand and M_2 asset demand, but $\bar{M}$ is no longer exogenous. Assuming banks operate under the same ideas of liquidity preference that Keynes attributed to nonbank agents, there may be no connection between transactions money and portfolio money. Instead of fungibility between the two kinds of money, the appropriate metaphor is a firewall: the supply of money is now determined by the transactions demand (for money as a means of payment, M_1) plus an exogenously given endowment of money (as a store of value, $\bar{M}_2$) in the hands of wealth holders

$$\bar{M} \equiv M_1 + \bar{M}_2.$$

Since $M_1 \equiv \bar{M}_1$, the equilibrium equation reduces to

$$M_2 = \bar{M}_2.$$

A change in M_1 is no longer automatically offset by an equal and opposite change in M_2.

In this story the supply of transactions money is endogenous, reacting to demand in a kind of inverse Say's Law, at least up to the point that banks reach the limits of reserve ratios and are fully loaned up. (For a comprehensive account of the financial side of an endogenous-money economy, see Marc Lavoie [2014, chap. 4.])

The supply of money for speculative purposes, that is, money as an asset in the portfolios of wealth-holding agents, requires a separate story. If Keynes's $\bar{M}_2$ is taken as given, the mechanism that produces the Keynes effect may completely break down even though liquidity preference may be alive and well in relating the speculative demand for money to the interest rate. (Whatever story we tell about M_2 and $\bar{M}_2$, it can hardly be argued that the logic of endogenous money creation for transactions purposes applies to the supply of money as a store of value.)

There is another complication introduced by fractional-reserve banking even if banks are fully loaned up: recall chapter 4, where we assumed a reserve ratio of 40 percent and bank reserves of 200 gold ducats representing the deposits of wealth holders. Banks initially made loans of 300 ducats based on these reserves, and the interest rate settled at a level that made wealth holders content with their division of wealth between bonds and bank deposits. Now suppose the price level increases and with it transactions demand, to, say, 400 ducats. How does money shift from asset markets to the market for working capital? How do banks make the additional loans?

The answer is they can't. Banks are fully loaned up, with loans and commercial paper equal to 300 ducats in their portfolios, and deposits of 500—300 corresponding to these loans, plus the 200 ducats of wealth-holder deposits.

Breaking the Rules to Create More Money

Banks can't make the additional loans—until someone thinks to change the rules of the game. Imagine that you own a bank, Banco Ziro, which is faced with the problem of being fully loaned up. (For the purposes of this exercise, assume Banco Ziro is a monopoly, which makes the accounting easier.) You realize that you can solve the shortage of money by selling loans worth 100 ducats to the wealth holders whose deposits form your reserves. How will that help? By getting 100 ducats off Banco Ziro's books, as in Tables 4.6 and 4.7. The trick is that this transaction leaves total deposits unchanged at 500, but instead of the original split between wealth holders (200) and restaurants (300), the split is now 100 and 400. The borrowers, the Venetian restaurateurs, still need to keep their money in the bank in order to settle their accounts with suppliers. For the settling of accounts it doesn't matter that their borrowing is now only partially mediated by the banking system.

You do have one obstacle, namely, that wealth holders might hesitate to take on these loans because they do not know the borrowers well enough to separate the sketchy from the solid. (This is normal; your business as a banker, after all, is to know your customer.) The solution proposed in chapter 4 was to consolidate the loans into a collateralized debt obligation, a CDO, which will eliminate much of the risk in each individual loan, not to mention—no coincidence—that CDOs can find a ready market where loans cannot, precisely because of the idiosyncratic risks, both known and unknown, of individual loans. Or, equivalently for present purposes, assume that a money-market fund accepts deposits and uses them to buy commercial paper issued by the restaurants. Once again, bank reserves are left untouched because businesses need deposit accounts to pay their bills.

Either way, Banco Ziro continues to have 200 ducats in reserves, against 500 in deposits. Of these deposits, 400 ducats correspond to the commercial loans and commercial paper held by the bank (300) and the money-market fund (100). The remaining 100 ducats are the liquid assets of wealth holders on deposit with the bank.

The question remains whether wealth holders treat their money-market assets (or CDOs) as liquid, or instead assimilate these assets to the inherently risky bonds in their wealth portfolios.

In chapter 4 I made a case both ways. On the one hand, these financial instruments, by construction, are short term in nature and therefore carry little price risk. On the other hand, money-market funds and CDOs carry some default risk even if this is minimized by risk pooling.

The other hand, that wealth holders treat these assets as risky bonds, is less disruptive to liquidity-preference theory. In this case, the theory actually continues pretty much unchanged, with higher interest rates the price that must be paid to wealth holders to induce them to give up 100 ducats of liquidity. But now we would need an additional asset class to reflect the intermediate position of the new assets between safe T-bills and long-term corporate bonds.

The first possibility, that the restaurateurs' debts are transformed into money-market funds offering liquidity similar to that of cash deposits, is also compatible with liquidity preference, superficially at least. It simply offers a free ride to the economy, allowing the banking system to mobilize the money supply toward satisfying transactions demand (up to 500 ducats in the present example) without compromising liquidity and thus without incurring any cost in the form of higher interest rates as the quid pro quo of reducing liquidity.

However, this "free ride" turns out to be in its own way subversive of the liquidity-preference edifice. The problem is that money-market funds normally pay interest, a (partial) pass-through of the interest paid by restaurateurs and other businesses. If these assets pay interest and have little to no price risk, why would anybody ever store their wealth in noninterest-bearing accounts?

One answer is default risk, but for purposes of this exercise we shall assume away this complication. Absent default risk, no one would ever hold noninterest-bearing deposits or cash *as a store of value* when equally liquid interest-bearing options are available. Checking deposits and cash still have their uses as means of payment, but that is not relevant to liquidity-preference theory, which is a theory of interest based on the relative benefits and costs of holding wealth in different forms.

A second possibility is that deposit accounts will begin to pay interest, in order to compete with the money-market funds—as indeed they did in reality, at least prior to the long reign of the zero lower bound (zlb) that began when Lehman Brothers crashed.

Fractional-reserve banking thus raises two problems for a theory of money. The first is whether, as is the case with commodity money, transactions and speculation are fungible, one more dollar dedicated to either of the two purposes meaning one dollar fewer for the other. If the money supply expands and contracts with transactions demand, then transactions and portfolio demands become separate, sealed, compartments, each reflecting a different use of money, the first money as a medium of exchange, a means of payment, the second money as a store of value.[7]

The possibility of transcending the limits of fractional-reserve banking by moving assets off the banks' books, as in the Banco Ziro example, is the second problem, namely, that transactions and portfolio demands are actually complementary activities, the same dollar serving the day-to-day needs of business at the same time it serves the liquidity needs of wealth holders—in this case, not only does the equilibrium equation become $M_2 = \bar{M}_2$. In addition with money serving two purposes at once, the overall equilibrium is characterized by an inequality

$$M \equiv M_1 + \bar{M}_2 > \bar{M},$$

where $\bar{M}$ represents the sum of the endowment of asset money and the amount of transactions money when this endowment forms bank reserves and banks are fully loaned up.

Why Would Agents Hold Money When There Are Safe Short-Term Bills Available?

The preceding section raises another money-theoretic question: what is the status of short-term credit in the theory of liquidity preference? As we saw in chapter 12, Keynes's own answer to this question was to assimilate cash and short-term safe assets: "We can draw the line between 'money' and 'debts' at whatever point is most convenient for handling a particular problem" (*The General Theory*, p. 167n). In other words, money is one end of a spectrum of short-term credit.

This view leads logically to the conclusion that as debt maturity shrinks to zero, the interest rate on this debt will similarly shrink to zero—the nominal rate of interest on cash. If interest "is the reward for parting with liquidity for a specified period" (*The General Theory*, p. 167), then, as the period goes to zero, the rate of interest must go to zero.

But experience says otherwise. As was observed in the last chapter, the Fed Funds rate, the rate charged by banks to one another for overnight loans of reserves at the Federal Reserve, is as close as we can get to the limiting case of a zero-duration loan. The fact is that it is rare for Fed Funds rates to be anywhere near zero, though someone whose memory goes back only to 2008 would not have that impression.

This would not matter if there were a good reason why money should be part of an agent's portfolio despite its having to compete with short-term financial assets that pay interest. Beginning with John Hicks (1946 [1939]), the "good reason" has been the cost of converting other stores of value into an acceptable medium of exchange. If transactions costs are high enough, then a portion of wealth should normally be allocated to money. At the margin agents will be indifferent not only between long bonds and short-term interest-bearing bills but also between these bills and the medium of exchange. Therefore, as in the cash-bonds model, the spread would be anchored by the zero return to money.

A problem with this line of argument, as Hicks recognized, is that transactions costs are likely to be proportional to the number of transactions rather than varying with the amount transacted. Size matters. In particular, holders of large amounts of wealth engage in transactions that are generally so large that the cost of transacting will not be an issue:

> Relatively large transactions can usually be made with very little more trouble than small transactions, but the total interest offered on a large sum is much larger than on a small sum; thus large capitalists will be tempted to buy bills much more easily than small capitalists. (1946 [1939], p. 165)

For "large capitalists," interest-bearing bills will always dominate cash, and will be preferred as long as the interest rate is positive. Hicks argued that if large capitalists called the tune, the demand for bills would drive their yield to zero, so that the distinction between bills and money would disappear:

> If . . . all traders reckon . . . a particular bill as perfectly safe, then there is no reason why that bill should stand at a discount. (p. 165)

In other words, short-term bills would yield nothing to their owners.

To avoid this conclusion, Hicks assumes that "small capitalists," for whom transactions costs are significant, also trade off liquidity against returns in markets for financial assets. There are not enough large capitalists to bid the price of bills up to par with money (and the interest rate down to zero), so the yield on bills normally remains positive. Hicks can therefore end where he started, with the argument that

> The imperfect "moneyness" of those bills which are not money is due to their lack of general acceptability; it is this lack of general acceptability which causes the trouble of investing in them, and that causes them to stand at a discount. (pp. 165–166)

Hicks elides the key issue: he simply asserts that in the absence of transactions costs, wealth holders would have such a large appetite for bills that yields would go to zero. Later theorists have attempted to provide a basis for substitution to take place between money and short-term assets. The *locus classicus* is the argument of William Baumol (1952) and James Tobin (1956). Baumol and Tobin develop a model in which agents' holdings of money for meeting transactions optimally vary with the rate of interest on short-term liquid assets.

The data do suggest that the interest rate on safe bills influences overall money demand.[8] But this does not establish that transactions demand affects the demand for portfolio assets because the interest sensitivity of transactions demand is a necessary rather than a sufficient condition for integrating transactions and speculative demands into a unified portfolio theory. It must also be the case that agents' holdings of money for transactions impact their wealth and hence their demands for various forms of wealth. Only if both these conditions—the interest sensitivity of transactions demand and substitutability between transactions money and speculative money—hold, would it make sense to consider the demand for transactions money along with the demand for interest-bearing assets in a unified theory à la Baumol and Tobin.

This theory evidently is more plausible for some agents than for others. Inconvenience and cost may be a factor in determining the money holdings of a majority of households without it mattering very much in the aggregate. One reason is that the majority of households account for little wealth, and even less financial wealth. Whatever the elasticity of their transactions demand with respect to the rate of interest on short-term bills, it wouldn't matter for portfolio demands because these households are not players in markets for financial assets. Even were we to suppose that households with modest means manage their wealth portfolios in terms of the risks and returns of various assets—a dubious assumption on behavioral grounds—the imperatives of convenience and cost would lead to a very inelastic demand for the medium of exchange unless the cost of transactions was extremely low or the interest rate extremely high. In plain English, the typical household will under normal conditions not vary its cash holdings in response to interest-rate variation.

This analysis does not apply to the important players in asset markets. For wealthy households, for nonprofits managing million- and even billion-dollar endowments, for insurance companies, pension funds, banks, and other financial institutions, the reasoning is exactly opposite to the reasoning for households who live paycheck to paycheck. For wealthy households, as well as for nonprofits and financial businesses, far from being the essential determinant of the separation of transactions and portfolio holdings, the costs and inconvenience of moving assets around are likely to be extremely small relative to the size of their portfolios. In the Baumol–Tobin model, the ratio of money holdings to income or wealth goes to zero as the denominator increases. These agents are the equivalent of Hicks's "large capitalists" for whom money is not a substitute for interest-bearing bills.

This leaves nonfinancial business. Businesses, especially businesses that depend on bank credit or on the issuance of commercial paper, have both motive and means for taking the interest rate into account in the management of current operations. The interest rate on short-term T-bills, or other instruments that approximate Hicks's safe bills, is reflected directly in the cost of borrowing for working capital. It is true that the cost impact is relatively modest compared with the impact of the interest rate on longer-term investment projects, but it can't be ignored. Even relatively small businesses deal in larger amounts of money than the average household, so the inconvenience and cost of transactions may not weigh as heavily as the interest cost of holding money balances. But this may matter less than the fact that businesses have ways of operationalizing a response to a change (say, an increase) in the interest rate, namely, pressuring financial managers to speed up action on accounts receivable and to slow down making good on accounts payable. These tactics are not generally available to households, and the difference between households and businesses in this and other respects supports the hypothesis that the behavior of nonfinancial business accords with the observed sensitivity of transactions demand to the interest rate on liquid assets.

Of all agent classes, nonfinancial business thus offers the best fit with the Baumol–Tobin argument that the demand for transactions money is sensitive to interest rates. I would go further and hypothesize that the (very modest) interest elasticity that shows up in the data (see note 7) is probably due to this class of agents. But to the extent that these agents are operating on borrowed funds, changes in transactions demand have *no* impact on wealth. No matter how much their transactions demand may respond to interest rates, there is no good basis for arguing the converse, that interest rates respond to transactions demand.

This compartmentalization implicitly assumes that nonfinancial businesses limit themselves to producing goods and services, distributing the fruits of enterprise, and investing in projects designed to enhance production or produce more cheaply in the future. If businesses are also important as holders of financial assets for the purpose of being able to strike at financial targets of opportunity as they arise—Apple with its mountains of offshore financial assets comes to mind, though its motive seems to be tax avoidance more than anything else—then the demand for transactions money for current operations would be thoroughly enmeshed with the demand for safe assets in their wealth portfolios. In this case, the interest sensitivity of transactions demand would in theory once again anchor the spread between various interest rates, and we would once again have a theory of the level of interest rates, including the hurdle rate, for investment demand. But it is difficult to imagine these firms, like the large capitalists of Hicksian theory, paying much mind to the costs of going back and forth between safe, liquid, stores of value and the medium of exchange.

In any case, combining wealth holding with business pursuits in a single portfolio is exceptional enough, I believe, that it makes sense to separate the two functions of money, medium of exchange and store of value. For wealth holders who are strictly portfolio managers, safe short-term bills will drive out cash and noninterest bearing checking deposits as a liquid store of value, relegating these forms of money to means of payment. Once short-term credit substitutes for checking deposits and cash as the liquid portfolio asset, we are firmly in the world we tentatively entered in chapter 4, where we considered the possibility of off-balance-sheet short-term assets answering to transactions demand and at the same time serving the liquidity demand of wealth holders. In the perspective of *The General Theory,* we can now answer the question that frames this section: Is credit money? For purposes of the theory of asset management, the answer hinges on whether credit instruments can be considered liquid assets. In my revision of liquidity-preference theory, short-term credit plays the role that Keynes assigns to money, an instrument that has little price risk and little perceived default risk.

And so it is in reality: T-bills exemplify this dual role, providing a safe asset (no default risk) and at the same time a liquid one (no price fluctuations), and so, at least most of the time, do money-market funds, repos, and other even more exotic financial instruments.[9] On the one hand, these instruments fund day-to-day business transactions and government operations; on the other hand, the same instruments provide liquidity that satisfies the portfolio demand of wealth holders.

What is Left of Liquidity Preference?

Once we drop the assumption of commodity money and replace it with the more realistic assumption of fractional-reserve banking and related forms of credit, we have to contend with both the endogeneity of money and the complementarity of speculative and transactions demands. What then is left of liquidity preference as a theory of interest? Surprisingly, everything that was there before.

Chapter 12 showed that liquidity preference could *never* be a theory of interest, even when the most favorable assumptions of commodity money were assumed to hold. Liquidity preference can never be more than a theory of interest-rate *differentials,* spreads between interest rates on obligations of different maturities and different default risks.

An exogenously given money supply, whether commodity money or fiat money, appears to transform a theory of spreads into a theory of levels only because of the addition of a crucial assumption, namely, that wealth portfolios include a zero-interest asset—cash or checking deposits. This assumption allows financial-market equilibrium to determine the levels of various bond rates, including the hurdle rate for investment, because it anchors spreads with an asset yielding a zero rate of interest.

In the world we actually inhabit, central banks substitute for commodity money in the sense that their control over short-term rates provides the anchor that cash does in Keynes's version of liquidity-preference theory. Indeed, if central banks did not exist, we would have to invent them just for the sake of economic theory. Alan Greenspan, Ben Bernanke, Janet Yellen, and, as of 2020, Jerome Powell are the helmsmen (and helmswoman!) who have anchored the spectrum of interest rates in this century.

The role of the modern central bank, up to the financial crisis of 2008, was precisely to fix the short-term interest rate and leave the rest to financial markets, where demands and supplies for a variety of assets determine the spectrum of interest rates. In theory, the actions of the central bank and the myriad agents acting in financial markets jointly produce a hurdle rate for investment and an accompanying level of aggregate demand consistent with full employment. In this world, liquidity preference is restored to a prominent role even if this role is not quite what Keynes thought it was.[10]

The present model implies a very different monetary regime from the regime assumed in the simple bonds-money model of chapter 11. Now the divorce between portfolios and transactions means that injections of money by the central bank do not affect asset markets directly: agents' portfolios are assumed to hold bills and bonds, and they have no reason to hold money. In a regime of reserve scarcity, the central bank's choice of a particular level of the short-term rate affects the amount of transactions money by varying the reserves held by banks. If the banking system is geared to providing working capital for commerce and industry, we can tell a plausible story of a fractional-reserve system in which banks create deposits that serve as the medium of exchange for transactions, up to the limit of the required reserve ratio. In return the banks acquire assets in the form of commercial loans or commercial paper. The transactions demand for money becomes the entire demand for money.

This is a key departure from *The General Theory*. Fractional-reserve banking erects a firewall between portfolios and transactions, and consequently $\bar{M}_1$ and $\bar{M}_2$ become apples and oranges even if the two assets are both denominated in dollars (or pounds, euros, and yen) and are identical in appearance; they are no longer the interchangeable parts of a homogeneous money supply. The existence of safe and liquid interest-bearing financial assets completes the divorce between money as a means of payment and money as a store of wealth. M_1 and $\bar{M}_1$ are demands for and supplies of money—cash or checking deposits—whereas M_2 and $\bar{M}_2$ are demands for and supplies of a short-term interest-bearing asset. M_1 and $\bar{M}_1$ are money as the asset that businesses (and households) need to settle debts incurred in carrying on the economic activities of producing and consuming. M_2 and $\bar{M}_2$ are money as a store of value in agents' wealth portfolios.

Until 2008, when the Fed started to pay interest on reserves, it relied on reserve scarcity to exercise its control over the short-term rate of interest. From 1994, when the Fed began to announce a target for the Fed Funds rate, it was able to vary the short-term rate without much actual change in the overall reserve position of the banks, relying on the effect of its announcements to accomplish the desired result (B. Friedman 1999; B. Friedman and Kuttner 2011).

It is not surprising that the Fed could change rates simply by announcing a new rate: like any monopolist, the Fed can set whatever price it chooses for its product (bank reserves) and therefore for close substitutes—provided it is prepared to supply the quantity demanded at that price. More surprising is that once the policy of announcing Fed Funds targets was put in place changes in the rate induced very little change in demand for reserves and so very little need for open-market operations to change the amounts of reserves.[11]

Since the 2008 meltdown the Federal Reserve has paid interest on reserves. Accordingly, for banks there is little reason to prefer comparable assets like T-bills or high-grade commercial paper. The new regime of paying interest has produced an unprecedented accumulation of excess reserves, just under $1.8 trillion in August 2018, down from a peak of almost $2.7 trillion in 2014. As in the pre-2008 period, the Fed simply announces a target rate for Fed Funds transactions, but now no change in reserves is needed to implement a change in the target rate.[12] The counterpart to the reserves on the liability side of the Fed's balance sheet is its holdings of Treasuries and mortgage-backed securities. Its holdings of all securities reached a peak of $4.5 trillion in early 2014, of which $2.5 trillion were T-bonds and $1.7 trillion were mortgages. By August 2018, the Fed's assets had come down much less than bank reserves: the Fed still owned $2.3 trillion worth of Treasuries and $1.7 trillion of mortgages, with total assets equal to $4.3 billion.

Real and Nominal Rates: Is Central Bank Freedom Limited by Necessity?

So far in this story the only limit to a central bank's power over the short-term rate is the zlb. This is actually a bit anachronistic. As long as cash, with its zero nominal holding yield, is an option, a zlb for bills makes perfect theoretical sense, but as long as there are costs to holding cash (storage, insurance, and the like), negative short rates become theoretically—and more important, practically—possible. The continuing recession in Europe led the European Central Bank to experiment with negative short-term rates in the form of charging banks interest on reserves. Indeed, for a large part of 2016, negative rates were not confined to the short end of the spectrum: ten-year government bond yields in Germany and Switzerland (and in Japan as well) also were negative.[13]

This does not mean a central bank can set short-term rates as far into negative territory as it might like, or that there are no limits on how far bond yields can fall. The costs of holding cash, even if not zero, limit the discretion of central banks as well as the possibilities for the market to drive bond yields down. Nothing short of a cashless economy or Silvio Gesell's stamped money (*The General Theory,* chap. 23) would remove the limit posed by the zero nominal yield of cash. Carrying costs shift the lower bound to the short rate into negative territory, but no further than the charge represented by these carrying costs.

More interesting is the question of the freedom of the central bank to control the *real* rate of interest, which differs from the nominal rate by the amount of inflation. The mainstream view is that at least in the long run, when frictions and imperfections are overcome, the real rate of interest (what Knut Wicksell [1936 (1898)] calls the "natural rate") is determined by forces of productivity and thrift. In the view put forward by Irving Fisher in 1896 and by Wicksell as well, a central bank can temporarily set the short-term rate of interest at a level incompatible with the natural rate, but economic forces will eventually make the central bank adjust to the natural rate. If, for instance, the central bank sets the short-term rate at such a low level that the bond yield—Wicksell's "money rate of interest"—is below the natural rate, economic activity will be stimulated. But with the economy normally at full employment, there would be no outlet for the stimulus other than to raise prices. Higher prices, however, would require more transactions money, and price inflation would eventually bump up against a fixed money supply (Wicksell 1936 [1898], pp. 116–117). Only by bringing the short rate, and thus the money rate of interest, into line with the natural rate can the inflationary pressure be relieved and transactions demand brought into line with the supply of money.

Twenty-first-century mainstream economics reflects the Fisher–Wicksell view that the real rate is determined by productivity and thrift and is in the long run independent of central bank policy. The difference from the older view is that the central bank is free to choose a short-term rate and the corresponding long rate. But the central bank's choice of interest rate is purely nominal, with only a transitory effect on the natural rate, that is, on the real rate. In consequence, the central bank is choosing a rate of inflation or deflation, which is the difference between the nominal rate chosen by the central bank (Wicksell's money rate) and the real rate (the natural rate) determined by desired investment and saving at full employment (the natural rate). In the equation linking real and nominal rates,

$$\rho_{\text{NOMINAL}} - \rho_{\text{REAL}} = \phi$$

where ϕ represents the rate of inflation, causality is read from left to right, from the real rate and the nominal rate to the rate of inflation.

Liquidity preference tells a different story. With the short-term rate fixed, the yield on a long-term bond is determined by a combination of risk aversion, reversion to normal, and default risk. With only bonds and bills available, portfolio choices are purely nominal, but nominal rates determine real rates. A rearrangement of the equation linking nominal and real rates, also read from left to right,

$$\rho_{\text{NOMINAL}} - \phi = \rho_{\text{REAL}}$$

implies a very different causality. Chapters 6 and 7 told the story and chapter 8 provided the numbers for the Great Depression: in this argument equilibrium rates of price (and wage) deflation are endogenously determined by aggregate demand, goods supply, and labor supply, and along with the nominal rate of interest, this equilibrium also determines the real rate of interest.

Money, Interest, and Output in the Revised Model

We can now pull all the strands of preceding chapters together. In the simplest case of investment demand depending only on the interest rate, and saving depending only on the level of output, aggregate demand is determined as in Figure 12.13, reproduced as Figure 13.1. The central bank sets the short-term

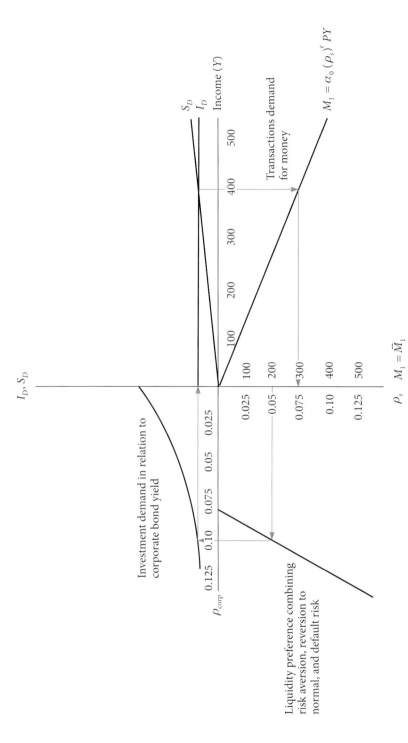

Figure 13.1 Aggregate demand and the transactions demand for money.

rate, and financial markets determine the hurdle rate. Aggregate demand corresponds to the level of output at which the supply of saving equals the resultant investment demand. More refined assumptions about investment and saving complicate the AD schedule, but the logic does not change. The AD schedule is of course just one of the elements of the revised model. In addition goods supply, labor supply, and the adjustment mechanism all enter into the determination of equilibrium.

Money exists in this model, but in a strict sense only as a medium of exchange. Paradoxically, we are back to a world in which the quantity equation holds, transactions demand being given by $M_1 = \alpha PY$, with α the inverse of the income velocity of money. The only amendment to the equation as pictured in the fourth quadrant of Figure 12.13 is that the parameter α is no longer a constant. If businesses weigh the costs and benefits of holding cash à la Baumol and Tobin, then the income velocity of transactions money depends on the bill rate

$$\alpha = \alpha_0 \left(\rho_s \right)^\varepsilon,$$

where α_0 is a constant and ε is the elasticity of transactions demand with respect to the bill rate.[14]

The quantity *equation* holds, but not the quantity *theory*. Causality does not run from M_1 to P or Y or ρ_s, but from PY and ρ_s to M_1. As J. Laurence Laughlin (1911) observed in debate with Irving Fisher on the operation of the quantity equation (see note 6), equilibrium between transactions demand and transactions supply is achieved because of the ability of the banking system to create money endogenously to satisfy transactions demand.

On the assumption of reserve scarcity, open-market operations target the supply of bank reserves to satisfy bank demands for reserves, which are a function of the public's demand for transactions money. The supply of reserves and the corresponding supply of transactions money must be consistent with the short-term rate, 0.05 in Figure 13.1.

What Happens If There Is No Central Bank? Money, Interest, and Output When Capitalism Is Left to Its Own Devices

The crucial issue is what we assume about money. The models of chapters 3 to 10 presupposed a world in which, *one way or another,* the rate of interest was determined by the demand for money and its supply. In all these models, money is money: there is no difference between money as a medium of exchange and money as a store of value. Chapter 11 developed Keynes's liquidity-preference theory along these lines and changed nothing essential in the models of previous chapters. But once money as a store of value becomes conceptually different from money as a medium of exchange, as in chapter 12, the stage is set for a very different assessment of how a capitalist economy functions when left to its own devices. Without a central bank to fix the interest rate on money as a store of value, that is, on short-term bills, this interest rate is indeterminate.

The result is that bond yields, including the hurdle rate for private investment, are also indeterminate, and so are the resulting levels of investment demand and aggregate demand. In effect we have an IS schedule but no LM schedule. So we can't pin down a point on the IS schedule to associate with each potential level of the price of goods.

The rate of interest turns out to be a conventional phenomenon rather than a reflection of market equilibrium. Many years ago, while trying to understand the psychology of Indian peasants encountering new agricultural technologies, I asked about local rates of interest charged by moneylenders. According to my informants, the annual interest rate, 18.75 percent, did not change from year to year or season to season or village to village. It may be that year after year in village after village 18.75 percent was the Goldilocks rate that just equalized the demand for the moneylender's services and their supply. But this is not how the villagers explained the uniformity. Rather, their explanation was that in British times, with the rupee divided into 16 annas and the anna into 4 paise, the conventional interest charge was one paisa of interest per month for one rupee of debt. One paisa per rupee works out to 1/64, or 12/64 on an annual basis (without compounding). Now 12/64 = 0.1875, a rate that compares favorably with the interest rates that U.S. households pay on their credit-card debt in 2020. Apparently, one paisa in the rupee was simply a convenient heuristic, a conventional rather than a market answer to balancing demands and supplies.

In any case, under a regime of capitalism left to itself, operating in a regime of fractional-reserve banking, there is no "natural rate of interest" that emerges from the free play of market forces and regulates the accumulation of capital. Asset markets are one equation short, and there is no plausible way of anchoring the spectrum of interest rates.

But there are at least two implausible ways. As chapter 10 noted, if capital were Lego sets and could be dismantled and put together in new forms at zero cost, we could imagine the hurdle rate being determined in a capital market. A firm could adjust its capital stocks just as it is assumed to adjust employment. The demand for *capital* (not investment!) would be determined by firms' marginal-productivity schedules; the intersection of the economy-wide demand schedule with the given supply-of-capital schedule would determine the current marginal productivity and *the* interest rate—in a world of Legos there would be no distinction between long and short run because specific capital goods would exist only so long as they are profitable for their owners.

This leaves open the question of how the pace of capital accumulation would be determined. If, as in this model, there is no investment demand per se, the rate of growth of the capital stock must be determined by the supply of saving. This is indeed the model that Paul Samuelson proposes in various editions of his elementary text (1948, 1955, 1980), and it is the model implicit in the canonical Solow growth model (1956) that we will consider in chapter 17. In Samuelson's or Solow's model, there is no investment demand and therefore no question of a distinct role for aggregate demand.

The alternative, equally implausible, is to assume that capital is not fungible but that saving and investment are insulated from markets for financial assets. Or even simpler, that there is *no* market for financial assets apart from the market for new issues that accompany the undertaking of new investment projects. We would be in a world where the dog's tail exists, but not the dog. Savers commit to capital formation in the same way that entrepreneurs do, or at least are supposed to do: once in, they are in for the duration.

This model is diametrically opposed to the model with fungible capital goods. In this case there is an investment-demand schedule that is regulated by the hurdle rate. The anchor comes from the other end of the spectrum, short-term interest rates adjusting (via liquidity preference) to the hurdle rate determined by the demand for investment and the supply of saving. In this case, unlike the case of Lego capital, an aggregate demand exists for output, but the price mechanism—the adjustment of the hurdle rate to the demand and supply of investment and saving—ensures that aggregate demand will not differ from aggregate supply.

In both cases we are thrust back into Jean-Baptiste Say's Garden of Eden, where aggregate demand is always equal to aggregate supply. Keynes's liquidity preference plays no role in the determination of aggregate demand, output, and employment.

In the real world, or rather in a world as real as can be imagined with capitalism left to its own devices, capital goods are not fungible and the hurdle rate of interest is the tail wagged by the market for financial assets. In this world we are left without *any* determinate theory of interest. Consequently, the level of aggregate demand and levels of output and employment are also indeterminate. Liquidity preference does not substitute for the neoclassical theory of interest even as it destroys this theory!

Keynes did not think his theory left the level of interest rates indeterminate,[15] but in a sense, the theoretical critique becomes even more devastating when the indeterminacy is recognized: capitalism left to itself is not a world of equilibrium with unemployment, but a world of drift. All we are left with is historical accident to determine the level of interest rates and the accompanying levels of capitalist economic activity.

Conclusions

There is no theory of money in *The General Theory*. Or, rather, there is no *coherent* theory of money. Given the existence of a central bank, Keynes undoubtedly thought of the money supply as fixed by the monetary authority, and the hurdle rate of interest responding, perhaps insufficiently, to the money supply. But his mechanism for transmission of monetary policy involves a substitution of money between different uses, which makes sense only if money can be used for only one thing at a time, transactions or as a store of wealth. And this in turn requires a homogeneity of the asset used as a medium of exchange and the asset used as a store of value.

The homogeneity and substitutability between store of value and medium of exchange make sense in a world of commodity money in which there are no interest-bearing short-term assets. It does not make sense in a world of fractional-reserve banking, in which banks create the bulk of transactions money in response to the public's demand for the medium of exchange, and in which there are alternative safe assets—safe in the sense both of being free of default risk and of being stable in nominal value. In this world, liquidity preference is a theory of spreads, which requires a monetary authority to anchor these spreads, as central banks have done by fixing the short-term rate.

For all the added complexity caused by recasting liquidity preference as a theory of interest-rate spreads, the basic message of *The General Theory* survives pretty well. At least if the question is one of how the economy works when the short-term interest rate is under the control of a central bank.

The results obtained in chapters 9 and 10 continue to hold. In particular, these chapters introduce the possibility of multiple equilibria and the possibility of instability. In some cases the instability depends not only on the adjustment process, but on parameter values, specifically, on the relative speeds of adjustment of prices, wages, and output.

Liquidity preference reverses the conventional view of the relationship between nominal and real interest rates. The conventional view is that the "natural" real rate is determined by the forces of productivity and thrift—the demand for investment and the supply of saving—and the nominal rate or the rate of inflation adjusts to the real rate. Keynes's view, which the modifications introduced in chapter 12 do not change, is that nominal rates are determined jointly by the central bank and liquidity preference. Together with investment and saving propensities and supply conditions, the nominal hurdle rate of in-

terest determines the levels of output and employment and the rate of inflation, and as part of this process the real rate of interest.

The incoherence of Keynes's monetary theory is in part due to the double
purpose of *The General Theory*. A model in which the central bank steers the
economy is conceptually clearer than a model of capitalism as a self-regulating
system: we face the inherent ambiguity of a counterfactual in specifying what
we mean by capitalism left to its own devices once we try to take account of
money and banking. The sticking point is how money is defined. The simplest
assumption is that money is a commodity, but with this definition we exclude
fractional-reserve banking and the creation of money by the banking system.
A central bank is clearly out of bounds, but fractional-reserve banking seems
well within the realm of possible capitalisms left to their own devices—as
does the existence of safe interest-bearing assets that dominate money in
wealth portfolios.

The two assumptions, commodity money or fractional-reserve banking
with safe interest-bearing assets, lead to very different results. With commodity money, the reasoning of *The General Theory* leads to a determinate level
(or schedule) of aggregate demand. With the other elements of the model,
goods supply and labor supply, we have a determinate equilibrium once we
specify the adjustment mechanism. The problem is that the equilibrium may
fall short of full employment (or, in theory at least, may lead to overfull
employment). In the revised model, with commodity money replaced by
fractional-reserve banking and a wedge between the medium of exchange
and the store of value, the problem is more profound. With a central bank,
aggregate demand responds to the short-term rate, and the overdetermination introduced by adding an AD schedule to the GS and LS schedules can be
resolved by focusing on the adjustment process. But without a central bank,
there is an equilibrium hurdle rate for each value of the bill rate, but no way to
anchor the spread, and therefore no determinate equilibrium. Without a central bank, the AD schedule is itself indeterminate, so specifying an adjustment process does not determine an equilibrium. The implication is even
more disturbing than Keynes imagined: not only might capitalism left to its
own devices fail to deliver jobs for all willing workers, the model is incapable
of determining how much employment will be generated by the economy
given the underlying data.

MATHEMATICAL APPENDIX

Baumol–Tobin

The Baumol (1952)–Tobin (1956) formula for the transactions demand for money is

$$M_1 = \left(\frac{fPY}{2\rho_s} \right)^{\frac{1}{2}},$$ (13.1)

where

> M_1 = the average holding of money for transactions purposes,
> f = bank fee per conversion of bills to money (and vice versa), assumed to be independent of transaction size,
> ρ_s = the bill rate, assumed to be riskless,
> P = price level,
> Y = real income.

Equation (13.1) is the first-order condition for an interior solution to the problem of minimizing the direct and indirect costs of holding cash instead of bills. The agent is assumed to have the option of holding some of her income in the form of interest-paying bills instead of noninterest-bearing cash. The downside of bills is that the bank charges a fee every time the agent makes a change in the composition of her portfolio. The cost of bank transactions is the direct cost, *fm,* where

> m = number of conversions between bills and money

plus the interest foregone for every dollar held as cash instead of bills, namely, $\rho_s M_1$. Total transactions costs are the sum of the two components

$$TC = fm + \rho_s M_1, \qquad\qquad m = 0, 2, 3, ...$$ (13.2)

The initial transaction is an exchange of money, the assumed means of payment for the agent's income *PY,* for bills. Hence, if there are any transactions at all, there must be at least two.

To make the math more manageable, we assume that exchanges of bills for money are of equal size and that the interval between them is constant and the same as the interval between the initial exchange of money for bills and the first conversion of bills into money. The money itself is assumed to be paid out at a constant rate between bank transactions. For the purpose of this exercise, assume saving is equal to zero, so that the entire income is spent over the year. On these assumptions, if PY, the agent's annual income, is paid in a lump sum at the beginning of the period, then her average holding of money is

$$M_1 = \frac{PY}{2m} \qquad \text{if } m \geq 2, \qquad (13.3)$$

$$M_1 = \frac{PY}{2} \qquad \text{if } m = 0. \qquad (13.4)$$

Substituting from equation (13.3) into (13.2) gives

$$TC = fm + \frac{\rho_s PY}{2m} \qquad \text{if } m \geq 2, \qquad (13.5)$$

$$TC = \frac{\rho_s PY}{2} \qquad \text{if } m = 0. \qquad (13.6)$$

If we treat m as a continuous variable, we can differentiate equation (13.5) with respect to m to obtain the first-order condition for an interior solution ($m \geq 2$) to the agent's cost-minimization problem

$$m = \left(\frac{\rho_s PY}{2f} \right)^{\frac{1}{2}}. \qquad (13.7)$$

Again substituting from equation (13.3), equation (13.7) gives the equation for the average money holding

$$M_1 = \left(\frac{fPY}{2\rho_s} \right)^{\frac{1}{2}}. \qquad (13.1)$$

The transactions fee f must be small relative to potential interest $\rho_s PY$ for the interior solution to dominate the corner solution ($m = 0$). In this case, dividing both sides of equation (13.1) by PY gives

$$\frac{M_1}{PY} = \left(\frac{f}{2\rho_s PY} \right)^{\frac{1}{2}}. \qquad (13.8)$$

So, as $PY \to \infty$, $M_1/PY \to 0$ and $m \to \infty$. At the other end of the spectrum— think of agents who are paid relatively small sums weekly or even monthly—

f is large relative to potential interest $\rho_s PY$. In this case, the corner solution ($m = 0$) will dominate.

   The important point is that, in both extreme cases, the lesson we draw is opposite to the usual lesson of the Baumol–Tobin framework. Optimal money holdings will not be sensitive to small changes in the bill rate. At $m = 0$ the interest rate would have to be sufficiently large to displace the optimum into the interior of the solution space before it can have any effect on money holdings. For an interior solution we have

$$\frac{\partial \left(\dfrac{M_1}{PY} \right)}{\partial \rho_s} \frac{\rho_s}{\dfrac{M_1}{PY}} = -\frac{1}{2} \frac{\rho_s}{PY}. \tag{13.9}$$

So, at the other end of the spectrum, as $Y \to \infty$, the elasticity of demand for cash goes to zero.

— V —

Fiscal Policy in Theory and Practice

— 14 —

FUNCTIONAL FINANCE AND THE
STABILIZATION OF AGGREGATE DEMAND

It is obvious that in the long run the budget must balance, but what is
the logical period?

—JACOB VINER

As soon as it is recognized as a duty of the government—perhaps
even the primary duty of the government—to ensure the maintenance of full employment, and that any so-called principle of "sound
finance" that might interfere with this task can have no possible
justification, the instruments by which full employment can be
maintained stand out clear and unmistakable.

—ABBA LERNER

The General Theory argues that a capitalist economy left to its own devices
may come up short in the jobs department *and* that there are limits to the
ability of monetary policy to steer the economy to full employment. Not only
might there be a liquidity trap that prevents the hurdle rate of interest from
falling to a level low enough to coax out investment demand sufficient for full
employment; but even if the hurdle rate could be driven to zero, the resulting investment demand might be insufficient. There is a third reason that
emerged from the study of investment demand in chapter 10. Since it is long-
term investment that responds most to the interest rate, residential construction becomes the swing element on which monetary policy operates. As long
as the swings are not enormous, the overweighting of one element of investment demand might not matter. But the reliance on monetary policy to bring
the economy out of the 2001 recession had unintended consequences both for
the price of the existing stock of housing and for new construction. The U.S.
and world economies reaped the whirlwind when the housing boom turned
to bust in 2007 and 2008.

All three of these arguments provide a theoretical justification for fiscal
policy. In the presence of a liquidity trap or inelastic investment demand, full
employment requires the active management of taxation and spending. Even

when the economy is not in extremis, the possibility that monetary policy will skew the composition of investment makes fiscal policy an appropriate complement for monetary policy at times when monetary policy alone would be sufficient to move the economy to full employment.

Keynes, as I have noted, has surprisingly little to say on the subject of fiscal policy. By my count the term appears seven times in *The General Theory;* all seven are in the context of how taxation might affect the propensity to consume.[1]

The most clear reference in *The General Theory* to fiscal policy is indirect:

> If the Treasury were to fill old bottles with banknotes, bury them at suitable depths in disused coalmines which are then filled up to the surface with town rubbish, and leave it to private enterprise on well-tried principles of laissez-faire to dig the notes up again (the right to do so being obtained, of course, by tendering for leases of the note-bearing territory), there need be no more unemployment and, with the help of the repercussions, the real income of the community, and its capital wealth also, would probably become a good deal greater than it actually is. It would, indeed, be more sensible to build houses and the like; but if there are political and practical difficulties in the way of this, the above would be better than nothing. (p. 126)

Keynes's point here is to emphasize the multiplier effects of government spending, and to argue that if there are no good projects on the table, the multiplier alone justifies unproductive spending; in the second and subsequent rounds of spending, the newly employed workers are producing useful goods.

Keynes's activist fiscal policy did not begin with *The General Theory.* I observed in chapter 1 that he had a long record of supporting government spending as a means of stimulating the economy, going back to the U.K. election campaign just before the Depression. Nor was Keynes alone in seeing government spending this way. Chapter 2 pointed out that Jacob Viner had used strikingly similar language in 1933, three years before the publication of *The General Theory.*[2] The difference between Keynes, on the one hand, and Viner and other proponents of activist fiscal policy, on the other, was that Keynes alone offered a framework in which the cause of unemployment—a failure of aggregate demand—and the limits of monetary policy—a liquidity trap and/or inelastic investment demand—are integrated, a framework in which activist fiscal policy then makes logical sense. In the absence of such a framework, the trained economist, who had mastered the art of seeing through common sense, was no more disposed to fiscal activism than any other solid citizen.

It is not surprising that Keynes became identified in the public mind with the idea of compensatory public finance, the idea that the government should lean against the wind if there is a shortfall or an excess of private expenditure relative to the supply of goods at full employment. And Keynes became identified also with an upsetting corollary: deficit finance and unbalanced budgets. Although it turns out that the logic of activist fiscal policy does not require deficit finance, there is a good reason for running deficits under conditions of slack private demand. Deficits provide more bang for the buck than a balanced-budget approach to compensating for a lack of private demand.

The fact is that Keynes, like Viner, does not appear to have challenged the idea that the government should balance its budget over time, though, again like Viner, he questioned the need to do so in every short period. But there is an important difference between Keynes and Viner. Viner never rejected the conventional logic that a government's budget, like that of a household or a business, must balance, at least in the long run. For Keynes the issue was not logic but practicality in the light of very strong public resistance to the idea of government debt growing without bound. It was not Keynes but one of Keynes's disciples, Abba Lerner, who laid out the logic of compensatory finance in its most provocative form, "functional finance," which Lerner deliberately contrasted with "sound finance" (1941, 1943, 1944).[3]

How Does Fiscal Policy Get the Economy to Full Employment?

Functional finance emerged from the discussion and debate about what the government could do to avoid a slump once World War II ended. Recall Figure 9.4, which summarizes Paul Samuelson's (1943) understanding of the problem. Figure 14.1 is adapted from Figure 9.4 with the consumption function simplified by assuming that the propensity to consume is constant. In this figure the LS schedule is collapsed into a vertical line representing a unique full-employment level of output, here represented by $Y_{FE} = 480$. The vertical distance between the 45-degree line and the consumption function represents the additional spending necessary for aggregate demand to equal the full-employment level of output. In a closed private-enterprise economy, that is, an economy without government or foreign trade, the spending gap consists of the saving that would be undertaken at full employment.

Samuelson's (and Keynes's) doubts and fears for the post–World War II economy revolved around whether private investment demand would be sufficient to offset the saving gap, 120 in this simplified example. One possible source of salvation, we saw in chapter 9, was the "wealth effect." Accumulated wealth and unfulfilled consumer demand, both the result of wartime restrictions on the production of consumer goods, might combine to shift the consumption function upward, at least temporarily, and narrow the spending gap.

But the pessimists doubted that this would be sufficient. If the stimulus to

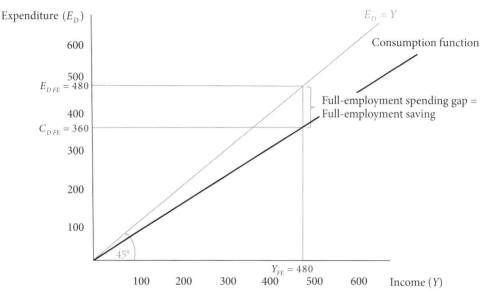

Figure 14.1 Full-employment spending gap, I.

consumption from the wealth effect (C_A) is 20 and investment demand (I_D) is 40, this still leaves a gap, as in Figure 14.2. The expenditure function, which is given by adding the additional consumption and investment to the original consumption function, now intersects the 45-degree line at $Y = 240$, reflecting the multiplier of 4 $(= 1/(1 - MPC) = 1/(1 - 0.75))$. This level of aggregate demand is only half what is required for full employment. With a multiplier of 4, the spending gap is now 60.

A Keynesian solution is for the government to substitute peacetime expenditure for military expenditure. If G, government expenditure on the purchase of goods and services, is 60, the expenditure function will be displaced upward, as in Figure 14.3. When $G = 60$ is added to $C_A + I_D = 60$, the additional spending closes the original gap, with aggregate demand equal to 480.

The impact of the additional spending is magnified by the multiplier. New government spending equal to 60 has an immediate impact since it represents an excess of total expenditure over total output and income. This excess increases the price level (with flexprice adjustment) or depletes inventories (fixprice adjustment), or some of both. The result is to increase production and thus income: under a fixprice regime producers respond directly to the new expenditure by replenishing inventories; under a flexprice regime the increase in prices leads to a positive gap between price and marginal cost, which in turn leads to greater production.

Expansion leads to a further increase in consumption demand, since three-

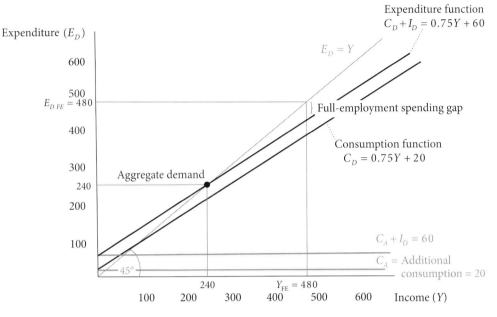

Figure 14.2 Full-employment spending gap, II.

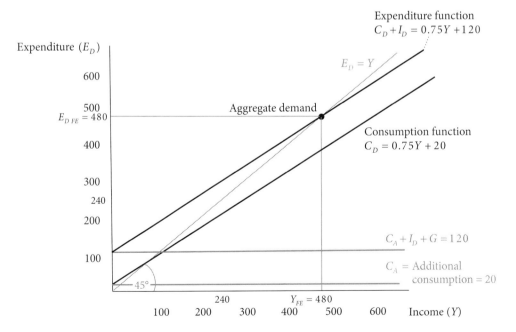

Figure 14.3 Full-employment aggregate demand with spending gap filled by government spending.

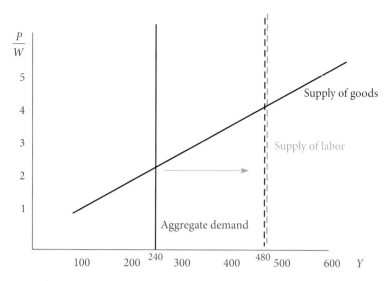

Figure 14.4 Government expenditure shifts aggregate demand.

quarters of each dollar of income is spent on consumption. If the economy is
on its AD schedule,[4] the process continues until "leakage" into saving, twenty-
five cents on the dollar, puts an end to further expansion of output. The multiplier, the ratio of the change in output to the original stimulus, is 4, so that
government purchases of goods and services equal to 60 leads to an increase
in aggregate demand of 240. Whether the adjustment regime is fixprice or flexprice, the new level of aggregate demand produces a full-employment equilibrium. The picture is in Figure 14.4, in which the AD schedule without
government spending is shown by the solid line, and the AD schedule with
$G = 60$ is shown by the dashed line.

From the perspective of traditional canons of government finance, there is
an obvious problem: the government runs a deficit as long as private demand
falls short of full-employment output. To match spending by taxation will reduce consumption demand and undermine the positive effect on aggregate
demand from G.

To see this, suppose that private consumption is determined by disposable
income, the amount left over after individuals meet their tax obligations. If
taxes are a constant fraction of income, t, consumption is now determined by
$(1 - t)Y$. Let $t = 0.2$. Then the consumption function is given by

$$C_D = 0.75(1 - 0.2)Y + 20 = 0.6Y + 20$$

and aggregate expenditure is

$$E_D = C_D + I_D + G = 0.6Y + 120 = 300.$$

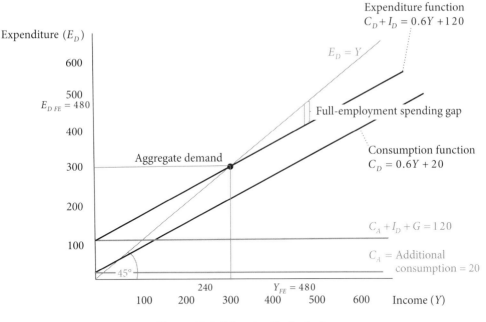

Figure 14.5 Balancing the budget.

The picture is in Figure 14.5. Taxation has the effect of reducing the marginal propensity to *spend*. Taxes, like saving, represent a leakage that reduces the multiplier, in this case from 4 to 2.5, with the result that the additional spending of 120 (as compared with Figure 14.1) leads to aggregate demand equal to 300 rather than to 480. In particular, the 60 of government spending leads to an additional 150 of output, rather than the 240 associated with $G = 60$ in Figure 14.3.

Three points are noteworthy. First, the government budget is balanced since $tY = G = 60$. Second, the new level of aggregate demand is well below the full-employment level of 480. At full employment there is once again a spending gap, now equal to 72. Third, government spending with a balanced budget still has a positive effect on output compared with no government spending (and no taxes). Instead of aggregate demand equal to 240, as in Figure 14.2, in Figure 14.5 aggregate demand is 300.

Alternative Fiscal Policies for Full Employment

Indeed, under the simplifying assumptions of the present model, the so-called "balanced-budget multiplier," the addition to aggregate demand resulting from an increase in government purchases of goods and services just balanced by an increase in taxation, is one. Why? The answer lies partly in the logic of the multiplier, and partly in the special assumptions of the present model. The logic of the multiplier is that taxation reduces spending by the same amount as the increase in spending by those who sell goods and services to the government.

So why isn't the multiplier zero? The reason is that the initial round of government spending involves the *purchase* of goods and services, the creation of new output, and this has no counterpart in the multiplier chain corresponding to taxation. It would be different if instead of purchasing goods and services government expenditure took the form of transfer payments, payments such as unemployment insurance, for which no output shows up on the other side of the ledger. In that case, the multiplier would indeed be zero.

This is the general logic, but the specifics of the model, particularly the assumption of a uniform marginal propensity to consume, play a role as well. As will be seen in chapter 15, if the marginal propensity to consume differs across the economy, the impact of taxation will depend in large part on the marginal propensity to consume of the taxpayers whose taxes are raised to balance government spending. And the impact of spending will depend on the propensities to consume of suppliers of goods and services to the government. The upshot is that the balanced-budget multiplier will be greater than one if the propensities to consume on the spending side are greater than the propensities to consume of taxpayers, less than one in the reverse scenario.[5] For present purposes, we ignore these complications and assume that the balanced-budget multiplier is precisely one.

The theory of fiscal policy developed by Lerner regards sound finance in the form of balanced budgets to be a hindrance to effective economic management, one to be done away with under the new dispensation of functional finance. Budget balance does indeed present a constraint on fiscal policy, but the constraint is not so simple: governments are not required to run a deficit to achieve the goal of full employment.

Continue to assume that the possibilities for expanding investment demand have been exhausted. $I = 40$ is the maximum that will be forthcoming when the central bank has done its all to lower rates. In this case, fiscal policy is the only remaining tool.

There is more than one fiscal policy that will lead to aggregate demand of 480. One possibility, as we have seen, is for the government to spend 60 while collecting no taxes. Another is to make use of the balanced-budget multiplier to arrive at an amount of spending that is both balanced by taxation and sufficient to raise demand to a level of 480.

To find the requisite rate of taxation and the corresponding level of government expenditure for a balanced-budget solution to the problem of inadequate private demand, we calculate the aggregate expenditure

$$E_D = C_D + I_D + G = 0.75(1-t)Y + 60 + G$$

with $E_D = Y = 480$ and $tY = G$. Solving the equations together gives $G = 240$, $t = 0.5$, and $C_D = 200$. The picture is in Figure 14.6.

The possibilities given by Figures 14.3 and 14.6 are only two of an infinite number of combinations of G and t that would give rise to a full-employment level of aggregate demand. Even though each is associated with a different level of government expenditure and taxation (hence a different level of the deficit) and a different value of the multiplier, all of these fiscal policies shift the level of aggregate expenditures from 240 to 480.

This raises a question about the necessity of rejecting sound finance in order to achieve the full-employment objective of functional finance. Why do we have to look beyond the balanced-budget configuration of taxes and spending represented in Figure 14.6? If there is a balanced-budget solution to the problem of unemployment, in what sense is sound finance a constraint on effective economic management?

The problem is that a balanced budget commits us to a particular size of the government budget. In the above numerical example, a balanced-budget path to full employment involves government expenditure (and taxes) of 300, while the deficit path involves expenditure of 60 (and taxes equal to 0). The deficit unleashes the full power of the multiplier, whereas a balanced budget prevents the multiplier from kicking in.[6]

The size of government is problematic for two reasons. One is the need to

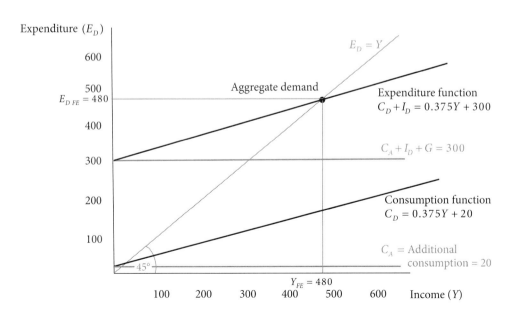

Figure 14.6 Balancing the budget at full employment.

balance the benefits of public and private expenditure. This problem will be addressed in chapter 16. The second problem is that a large government budget is difficult to manage once the context shifts from a one-time calculation of a full-employment saving gap to the calculation and recalculation of this gap in the context of fluctuating private demand. Even if the government had all the relevant information about economic conditions, it would be like turning a battleship around in a small harbor to continually adjust taxes and spending to the state of private demand. As in the analysis of equilibrium in the absence of government, real-time changes in budgets are different from comparative statics. In comparative-static comparisons of the positions of a battleship in the harbor, the battleship doesn't move, but moving is precisely the problem in the analysis of real-time changes.

Lack of information about the battleship complicates the problem of turning it around. Milton Friedman (1961) identified two issues. The first is a recognition lag, a delay in gathering and interpreting statistics that indicate the state of private demand. The second is an implementation lag, a delay in taking the steps to formulate and enact a plan to counter a shortfall or an excess of private demand relative to what full employment requires.

Both recognition and implementation lags present a problem for monetary policy as well as for fiscal policy, but implementation is orders of magnitude more difficult for fiscal policy. With monetary policy, the implementation problem is to form a consensus among twelve more or less like-minded professionals who make up the Federal Open Market Committee (the policy committee of the Federal Reserve). For fiscal policy, the problem is to form a consensus of two house of Congress and the executive branch, each with its own political agenda, indeed each with multiple conflicting agendas. Herding cats seems easy by comparison.[7]

In any event, post–World War II capitalism has relied more on changes in the deficit than on changes in the size of the government budget to regulate aggregate demand. Instead of changing expenditures and taxes in the same direction, as required to maintain a balanced budget, the Keynes–Lerner prescription for stabilizing aggregate demand envisages smaller swings in both expenditures and taxes—in opposite directions: *reducing* taxes and *raising* government expenditures when private demand slackens, and moving in the opposite direction when private demand strengthens.

This prescription has been followed to a great extent even by the fiercest ideological opponents of everything Keynes stood for. Even before the publication of *The General Theory*—see the data on the government debt during the Great Depression in Table 8.16—capitalist economies had incorporated one part of the Keynesian prescription for stabilizing aggregate demand into the very architecture of public finance, under the rubric of automatic stabilization.

Automatic Stabilization

Automatic stabilization has two components. First, expenditures tend to remain relatively stable over the cycle. Second, tax revenues tend to vary more or less proportionately with output as long as tax *rates* do not change. The consequence is that the deficit rises in slack times and falls in good times—*even if nobody has a hand on the tiller.* The consequences are clear in Figure 14.7. The only clues to the identity of the party or the president in power are the dates at the bottom of the graph. The deficit rose together with unemployment in every recession since 1970, and the deficit and unemployment fell together in every recovery.

It's not quite true that in practice nobody's hand was at the tiller—even though the helmsmen sometimes had very odd ideas on how to steer the economy. Discretionary fiscal policy, as distinct from automatic stabilization, is relatively rare for the same reasons that relying on the size of the budget is cumbersome. And in fact the U.S. government has used this option only in extremis. But automatic stabilizers were supplemented by Ronald Reagan's

Figure 14.7 Unemployment and the federal deficit (1948–2018). *Sources:* BLS, OMB. myf.red/g/pY6r

supply-side tax cuts in the early 1980s. And George W. Bush's supply-side tax cuts in the early years of this century led to the largest increase in the deficit since the Great Depression, at least until the Great Recession. More traditional, demand-oriented, tax cuts were put in place by Bush in 2008, at the end of his second term, as the downturn was getting underway. Both tax cuts and purchases of goods and services (principally by means of additional transfers to state governments) were a major piece of the Obama stimulus enacted in 2009.

Even without these extraordinary interventions, the very structure of taxation and spending should have meant that the ups and downs of private demand would not have had the same impact as in the pre–Great Depression era of small government. But did they do so in practice? If we look at the overall rate of unemployment, fluctuations do not seem to have moderated. Figure 14.8 suggests that post-Depression fluctuations have been as violent as the fluctuations between 1890 and 1930.

Appearances, however, are deceiving, because two contradictory forces are at work. On the one hand, the importance of agriculture in terms of both GDP and employment prior to the Great Depression dampened fluctuations in the unemployment rate. On the other hand, the role of government, as we have seen, has been increasing in importance since the Depression. This has to some extent offset the decline in the role of agriculture.

The reason why the decline in agriculture matters for the measurement of fluctuations is that the agricultural labor force is part of the denominator of the unemployment rate, but in the days when family farms dominated, agriculture—for reasons explored in chapter 8—did not function according to the

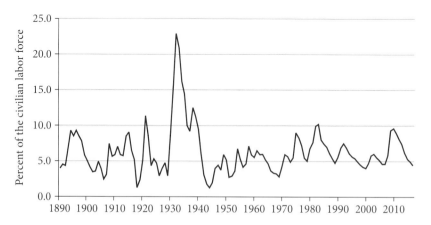

Figure 14.8 Unemployment. *Sources: 1890–1990, Historical Statistics of the United States;* post-1990: myf.red/g/pY6r

norms of capitalism. Indeed, if we define capitalism in terms of the predominance of wage labor, agriculture was not really part of the capitalist economy except as a reservoir from which to draw labor. For the same reasons, agricultural unemployment tended to be insignificant in bad times as well as in good times. So it makes sense to subtract agricultural employment from both the denominator and the numerator in calculating capitalist-sector employment and unemployment rates.

In the postwar period, government has, as we have seen, grown markedly. Like agriculture, government doesn't play by capitalist rules. Governments, especially state and local governments, do engage in layoffs, but unemployment is much rarer in this sector than in the private sector. If we are trying to understand differences over time in fluctuations of the unemployment rate under capitalism, it makes sense to subtract government employment from both the numerator and the denominator in calculating the unemployment rate.

If we eliminate both agriculture and government from the calculations and compute unemployment as a percentage of the nonfarm civilian labor force, we get unemployment rates that are consistently higher than the official series. More to the point, the unemployment rate fluctuates much less in the postwar period than in the pre-Depression period. Figure 14.9 plots the two series. If we focus on the capitalist-sector unemployment rate, as reflected in

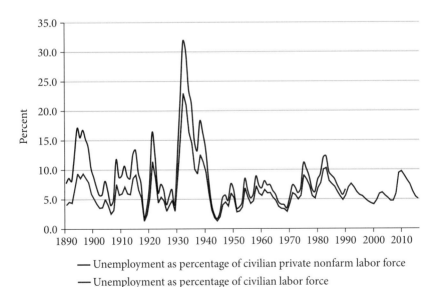

Figure 14.9 Two Measures of Unemployment. *Sources:* 1890–1990, *Historical Statistics of the United States;* post-1990: myf.red/g/pY6r

the unemployment rate as a percentage of the civilian nonfarm labor force, it is clear that there has indeed been a decrease in the volatility of unemployment.[8]

Summary: Functional Finance as a Tool for Stabilization

In principle, budget deficits are not necessary for managing aggregate demand with an eye to full employment. If society is indifferent to the size of government and if we abstract from the lags that prevent timely changes in the government's budget, aggregate expenditure can be increased or reduced by changing spending and taxes in the same direction, with the government budget always in balance.

But neither of these assumptions holds in practice. Recognition and implementation lags are endemic, and the size of government is a perennial issue. In practice, compensatory, countercyclical, variations in the deficit are a cornerstone of fiscal policy. Moreover, these changes in fiscal stance are built into the fiscal system via the inertia of tax *rates* and spending *levels*. Automatic stabilization is responsible for much of the observed correlation between the deficit and the unemployment rate, a correlation that transcends personal and partisan preferences. In point of fact, automatic stabilization has played a consistent if unsung role in mitigating the fluctuations in private demand.

To be sure, this success does not show up in the overall unemployment statistics, which suggest that the economy has been no less volatile since World War II than it was before the Great Depression. But unemployment relative to the nonfarm-private-sector labor force (as close as we can come to a measure of unemployment in the capitalist sector) tells a different story, namely that capitalism has become noticeably less volatile since the post–Great Depression regime of automatic stabilization was put in place.

In extremis, however, notably during the recession of the 1980s and the recession that followed on the financial crisis of 2008, automatic stabilization would have been insufficient. Ronald Reagan spoke the language of supply-side economics but took appropriate Keynes–Lerner measures to stimulate demand when the private sector faltered. When recession loomed again in 2001, George W. Bush undertook discretionary measures to stimulate demand, while covering his fiscal butt with Reagan's supply-side language. And he again deployed discretionary measures (this time abandoning the supply-side veneer) in 2008, in the face of the gathering storm that became the Great Recession.

It remained for Barack Obama to react with what, up to 2020, was the greatest peacetime fiscal stimulus in the history of the Republic, the American

Recovery and Reinvestment Act. The next chapter explores whether or not the Obama stimulus was successful.

There remains another question: what about the debt? The theoretical possibility of balancing the budget at full employment may not be practical, but nothing precludes balance over the cycle, with surpluses in the good years canceling out the deficits in lean times, a là Joseph in Pharaoh's Egypt. By varying the mix between the size of the government and the size of the deficit (and surplus), it is possible to keep the economy on an even keel of full employment—without a rising debt. If deploying fiscal policy to stabilize the economy at full employment does not explain the long-term rise in the national debt, what does? We shall return to this question in chapter 16 after we examine the Obama stimulus in chapter 15.

— 15 —

DID THE OBAMA STIMULUS WORK?

You know, you don't need to be an economist to know that jobs are the engine of our economy. And without jobs, people can't earn. And when people can't earn, they can't spend. And if they don't spend, it means more jobs get lost. It's a vicious cycle. And that's the vicious cycle we're in today. And it's one of the reasons that this bill is so desperately needed. We have to reverse that cycle.

But everyone knows that jobs are more than just about a job. They're about dignity. They're about respect. They're about being able to get up in the morning, look your child in the eye and say, "Everything is going to be okay; everything is going to be okay."

—VICE PRESIDENT JOE BIDEN, REMARKS AT THE SIGNING OF
THE AMERICAN RECOVERY AND REINVESTMENT ACT,
DENVER, COLORADO, FEBRUARY 17, 2009

And what we see with [President Obama's] plan is a lot of spending that I just don't think will work . . . We can't borrow and spend our way back to prosperity . . . Providing $300 billion of this package to states—$166 billion in direct aid to the states, another $140 billion in education funding—this is not going to do anything, anything to stimulate our economy.

—HOUSE MINORITY LEADER JOHN BOEHNER, ON
"MEET THE PRESS," JANUARY 25, 2009

In late 2008 and early 2009 the U.S. economy was hemorrhaging jobs at a rate unseen since the Great Depression. Indeed, the chart of unemployment from 2006 through 2009 in Figure 15.1(b) looks uncannily like a chart of unemployment over the years 1927 to 1930 in Figure 15.1(a). Fortunately, the subsequent history turned out very differently, as Figure 15.2 shows. Instead of plunging into depression, the economy gradually recovered after 2009. From early 2009 through early 2012, the ARRA (the American Recovery and Reinvestment Act) injected over $750 billion of spending and tax cuts in order to stimulate the U.S. economy, most of the money being spent between mid-

Portions of this chapter were previously published in Stephen A. Marglin and Peter Spiegler, "Unpacking the Multiplier: Making Sense of Recent Assessments of Fiscal Stimulus Policy," *Social Research* 80 (Fall 2013): 819–854.

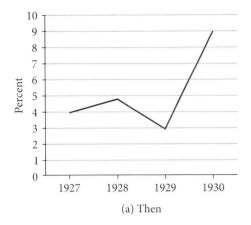

(a) Then

Figure 15.1(a) Unemployment in the Great Depression (1930).

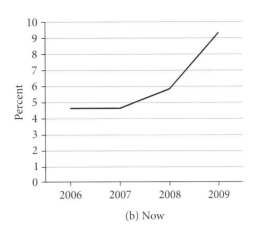

(b) Now

Figure 15.1(b) Unemployment in the Great Recession (2009).

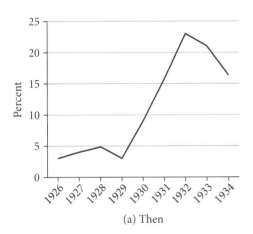

(a) Then

Figure 15.2(a) Unemployment in the Great Depression (1930–1934).

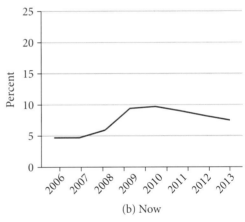

(b) Now

Figure 15.2(b) Unemployment in the Great Recession (2009–2013).

2009 and mid-2011. Its effects are still being debated. Did the ARRA stave off a slump that would have rivaled the Great Depression? Or was it a colossal waste? One node of the continuing dysfunction of U.S. politics is the polarization over this question.

In the case of the ARRA, there was in fact little additional spending by the federal government on direct purchases of goods and services; most of the stimulus took the form of transfer payments to individuals and tax reductions, both of which increased the disposable income of households and businesses. There were also sizeable transfers to state governments. Effectiveness thus boils down to two questions: first, to what extent did the recipients of transfers and tax breaks actually spend the money they received, rather than using it to shore up their finances, and, second, to what extent was their spending multiplied by a further chain of increased output, income, and spending?

I take up the second question, the size of the multiplier, first. Afterward, I address the question of whether there was anything to multiply by examining in some detail the most controversial part of the ARRA, the portion that went to the states (which I will here call the S-ARRA), that is, the transfers over and above the large amounts of financial aid routinely provided by the federal government over the last forty years of so-called fiscal federalism. The S-ARRA is of particular interest for two reasons. First, it comprises a substantial portion of the overall stimulus—roughly $250 million if we include supplemental Medicaid grants. Second, the fact that there are only fifty states allows us to explore the relevant behavioral and counterfactual conditions of the recipients of S-ARRA in relatively fine-grained detail.

The American Recovery and Reinvestment Act: A Brief Sketch

The official website of the stimulus program, www.recovery.gov, divided the stimulus into three roughly equal parts, as in Table 15.1.[1] Each of these categories includes a multitude of programs, of which the largest four in each category are listed. The largest single "Tax Benefit" program was an across-the-board tax cut enjoyed by over 116 million taxpayers, Making Work Pay, which provided a two-year $400 credit for an individual and an $800 credit for a couple with two working spouses, phasing out only at relatively high levels of $75,000 for an individual taxpayer and $150,000 for a couple filing joint returns. The total benefit amounted to $104.4 billion. At the other end of the spectrum were adjustments to the Alternative Minimum Tax Exemption totaling over $65 billion, which benefited only thirteen million taxpayers. Tax Benefits also included some $25.5 billion of tax breaks for students and $33 billion of tax breaks for businesses, including an adjustment to depreciation allowances totaling almost $24 billion.

"Entitlements," the smallest amount of benefits of the three parts in the table, was dominated by three programs: increases in the amount of Medicaid/Medicare covered by the federal government ($88.8 billion, all but $2 billion of which was Medicaid grants to states), extension of unemployment insurance ($61 billion), and family services ($38.4 billion, of which the lion's share was food stamps). One-time payments of $250 to social-security recipients in 2009 added another $13.2 billion of entitlements.

Table 15.1 Allocation of ARRA Funds through 2011

	Total Benefits ($ billions)
Tax Benefits	299.8
Making Work Pay	104.4
Increased Alternative Minimum Tax Exemption	65.0
American Opportunity Tax Credit	25.5
Special Allowance for Certain Properties Acquired in 2009	23.9
Entitlements	220.2
Medicaid/Medicare	88.8
Unemployment Insurance Programs	61.0
Food Stamps	31.1
Social Security One-Time Payments	13.2
Contracts, Loans, and Grants	225.8
Education	89.6
Transportation	33.3
Infrastructure	25.6
Energy/Environment	23.2

Source: American Recovery and Reinvestment Act website (www.recovery.gov), accessed February 25, 2012.

"Contracts, Loans, and Grants" consisted chiefly of grants to states and local governments (the vast majority to states) for a variety of purposes. Education accounted for $89.6 billion, and transportation for another $33.3 billion. Infrastructure ($25.6 billion) included grants from the Environmental Protection Agency to the states as well as supplements to the budgets of a variety of federal agencies, from the General Services Administration, responsible for the upkeep of federal buildings, to the Army Corps of Engineers, responsible for flood control on navigable rivers. Energy/Environment was also a hodge-podge, including $1.5 billion awarded to Savannah River Nuclear Solutions to clean up the Savannah River Site, where production for the military's nuclear arsenal took place during the Cold War, and a half-billion dollar loan guarantee for Solyndra, the solar-panel manufacturer that ARRA opponents love to hate—it went bust in 2011 despite the support of the federal government.

Unlike politicians, leading economists generally believed that the Obama stimulus succeeded in its stated goal of job creation. The University of Chicago's Booth School of Business periodically surveys a panel of prominent economists on policy questions. In early 2012, an overwhelming majority, more than 90 percent, concurred with the view that the ARRA had added jobs (ChicagoBooth 2012).[2]

John Taylor and John Cogan were at the forefront of the minority who believed that the ARRA was ineffective (Taylor 2011; Cogan and Taylor 2012).

In their view, the S-ARRA, like the rest of the ARRA, failed because state governments, like other agents, smooth expenditures over time à la Milton Friedman and Franco Modigliani (see chapter 9). As a result, any temporary fiscal stimulus will be largely, if not completely, saved rather than spent. In the Taylor–Cogan view, the stimulus did nothing more than provide debt relief— by substituting the debt of the United States for the debt of households, businesses, and state governments.

Chapter 9 argued that the premises and conclusions of the hypothesis of permanent-income/life-cycle expenditure smoothing are at best dubious for a large percentage of households. These are households that are liquidity-constrained or (for good reason) unable or unwilling to follow the mainstream logic of utility maximization that underpins the expenditure-smoothing argument.

Expenditure smoothing, rational or otherwise, is even less plausible for states. The second half of this chapter supports this contention with three separate investigations of the impact of S-ARRA. My conclusion is that states, like most households, are unable and/or unwilling to smooth expenditures in the face of fluctuating revenues.

To begin we focus on a more general question about the stimulus: how much bang was there for each buck? In the language of economics, how large was the multiplier?

The Multiplier in Theory

The multiplier is part and parcel of Keynes's *General Theory*, but it actually antedates *The General Theory* by several years. In a pamphlet co-authored with H. D. Henderson to support the Liberal Party's election campaign in 1929 (summarized in Keynes 1931a), Keynes argued that ripple effects from government spending would enhance the impact of the original outlay on the economy. In this connection he assigned his student, Richard Kahn, the task of quantifying these ripple effects. How much additional spending and income could be expected from an initial expenditure of one pound? What was the multiplier?

The basic idea, as we saw in chapter 3, is that a new purchase not only calls forth an immediate addition to production but also is an immediate increase in income for the producer, and therefore leads to a subsequent increase in his purchases. These purchases in turn represent new income for other producers, and new spending on their part. In principle, the chain continues indefinitely.

Then why isn't the multiplier infinite? Kahn's insight (1931) was that though the number of rounds might be infinite, each round of spending would be smaller because some of the income would "leak" into saving and imports, not to mention taxes. So from £1 of government spending, the workers, contractors, and other direct recipients of income might spend only half a pound, 50p (or 10 shillings as Kahn would have said), on domestically produced goods and services, creating only 50p of additional income. If in turn the recipients of this 50p also spend only half, the next round of spending will produce only 25p of new output and income.

In this analysis, the crucial determinant of the ripple effects is the proportion of new income that the typical individual spends on domestically produced goods and services—in Keynes' vocabulary, her marginal propensity to consume (*MPC*). The ultimate effect on output (ΔY) of an initial impulse—say an increase in government spending (ΔG)—is

$$\Delta Y = \Delta G + MPC\,\Delta G + MPC^2 \Delta G + MPC^3 \Delta G + \cdots$$
$$= \Delta G\left(1 + MPC + MPC^2 + MPC^3 + \cdots\right) = \frac{1}{1 - MPC}\,\Delta G,$$

and the multiplier is the ratio of the overall increase in output and income to the original injection of spending

$$\frac{\Delta Y}{\Delta G} = \frac{1}{1 - MPC}.$$

A reduction in taxes or an increase in transfer payments (social security, food stamps, unemployment insurance) also has a multiplier effect, but the tax multiplier is generally less than the spending multiplier because, as was observed in chapter 14, the first round does not involve the production of any goods or services. If taxes are cut by ΔT, and the recipients of the tax cut spend the same fraction of income as the average for the economy as a whole, then the direct spending is $MPC \times \Delta T$. This creates an equal amount of income and new spending of $MPC \times MPC \times \Delta T$. Taking all rounds of spending together we have

$$\Delta Y = MPC\,\Delta T + MPC^2 \Delta T + MPC^3 \Delta T + \cdots$$
$$= MPC\,\Delta T\left(1 + MPC + MPC^2 + MPC^3 + \cdots\right) = \frac{MPC}{1 - MPC}\,\Delta T$$

so that

$$\frac{\Delta Y}{\Delta T} = \frac{MPC}{1 - MPC}.$$

Simple models, with saving as the only leakage from successive rounds of spending, create the impression of very large multipliers. Saving equal to one-tenth of income would lead to a spending multiplier of ten and a tax multiplier of nine. Even if households were to save one-quarter of their incomes, the two multipliers would be four and three.

Observe that in both cases, the difference between the spending multiplier and the tax multiplier is one. Under the simplifying assumption of a uniform *MPC*, this result holds whatever the *MPC* might be. This is the so-called "balanced-budget multiplier" theorem, of which chapter 14 made extensive use.

The world is obviously a more complicated place than the stripped-down expositional models of this book, or for that matter the models of *The General Theory*. Not only are there leakages into saving, economic agents typically pay taxes, and the multiplier chain is also broken when income is spent on imports. (Imports add to domestic product only to the extent of processing and distribution expenditures within the importing country's national boundaries.) For these reasons empirical estimates of the multiplier are typically much lower than the multipliers suggested by a focus on saving alone. At two places in *The General Theory* (pp. 121–122 and pp. 127–128), Keynes estimates the multiplier as lying between 2 and 3 for a moderately open economy.

An example might help here. Imagine the chain of money income generated by a hypothetical injection of €1.00 of new spending that leads to the production and sale of €1.00 of new output. Assume that one-third of the sale proceeds end up as the return to capital (gross profit), and that, in the short run at least, *none* of capital's share is spent. (Investment plans have already been made, and extra profit ends up as retained earnings or is paid as taxes.) This leaves €0.67 to be distributed as wages. Assume that one-quarter of the wage share is paid as taxes, and three-quarters is disposable income. Thus of the original expenditure of €1.00, €0.50 ends up as the disposable income of households. Now assume that one-tenth of this disposable income is saved, and nine-tenths is consumed, that is, €0.45 spent on consumption. Of this, assume that three-quarters goes to domestic producers, and one-quarter goes for imports. So of the original €1.00 outlay, only 3/4 × €0.45, or €0.3375, is actually recycled into the economy. In this case the multiplier is

$$\frac{1}{1 - MPC} = \frac{1}{1 - 0.3375} = 1.51,$$

a far cry from the multiplier values implicit in the expositional models even though saving out of disposable income is one-tenth. The ratio of personal saving to disposable income turns out to exert relatively little influence on the multiplier compared with the division of income between labor and capital, tax rates, and the openness of the economy to imports.

There are two assumptions that require special scrutiny in evaluating expenditure and tax multipliers. The first deals with how much economic activity is displaced by government spending, the second with differences between the spending propensity of direct and indirect beneficiaries of stimulus. Mainstream theory, as we shall see in chapter 17, argues that crowding out takes place because government borrowing competes with investment demand for the available supply of saving, driving up interest rates and reducing the availability of credit. In Keynes's logic, there is no impact of government spending on investment via the interest rate or the credit channel; the pressure on resources is reflected in higher prices. In each case, under both mainstream and Keynesian reasoning, output would rise less than $1/(1 - MPC)$.

We can reflect crowding out in the multiplier formula by adjusting the multiplicand. If CO represents the fraction of new spending that displaces existing production and $m = 1 - CO$, initial spending of €1.00 now generates only €m of new output. Assuming subsequent rounds of spending are subject to the same degree of crowding out, the second round generates €$m \times (m \times MPC)$, the third round €$m \times (m \times MPC) \times (m \times MPC)$, and so on. The multiplier sum becomes

$$\frac{\Delta Y}{\Delta G} = m\left(1 + mMPC + m^2 MPC2 + m^3 MPC^3 + \cdots\right),$$

and the multiplier is

$$\text{Spending Multiplier with Crowding Out} = \frac{m}{1 - mMPC}.$$

Observe that m appears both in the numerator and in the denominator if, as we assume, crowding out is assumed to affect every round of spending equally.

The same logic applies to taxation and transfers. Recipients of tax breaks or enhanced entitlements may spend the increase in disposable income, but their spending may simply crowd out other spending. The tax multiplier becomes

$$\text{Tax Multiplier with Crowding Out} = \frac{mMPC}{1 - mMPC}.$$

The balanced-budget multiplier, the difference between spending and tax multipliers, now becomes less than one, approaching this upper limit only as crowding out goes to zero.

The logic of the tax multiplier breaks down if the spending of direct beneficiaries of the stimulus does not mirror the average spending pattern in the economy. Although we can justify using an economy-wide average for the second, third, and subsequent rounds of spending—there is no way of tracing out the expenditure of each income recipient in the chain—we can surely do better in measuring the impact on spending in the first round. The direct beneficiaries of a program to (say) rebuild the transportation infrastructure may include a large number of workers whose spending habits are markedly different from those of the general population. On the tax side, different kinds of tax cuts will produce very different responses from the beneficiaries. We now have the spending multiplier as

$$\text{Spending Multiplier with Crowding Out} = m\frac{1 + m(v - MPC)}{1 - mMPC},$$

where v is the first-round MPC, the fraction spent by the direct beneficiaries of government spending. The same logic applies to taxes and transfers. If v is the fraction spent by the direct beneficiaries of tax reductions, transfers, or grants, the tax multiplier becomes

$$\text{Specific Tax Multiplier with Crowding Out} = \frac{mv}{1 - mMPC}.$$

We can think of v as a valve controlling the flow of the initial stimulus into the economy. As might be expected, specific spending and tax multipliers are higher than their generic counterparts if $v > MPC$, and lower if $v < MPC$. At the lower limit, with $v = 0$, the valve is shut completely. The multiplier is zero, so spending increases income by m, and tax cuts do not increase income at all regardless of the size of the MPC.

Taylor and Cogan (Taylor 2011; Cogan and Taylor 2012) argued that $v = 0$ because agents follow the dictates of the mainstream theory of consumer choice and rationally smooth expenditures.[3] They reason that beneficiaries of tax rebates and transfers, recognizing the temporary nature of federal largesse, would treat the increase in disposable income as a one-time addition to their assets, to be doled out in little bits over the long-term future.

As chapter 9 observed, a rational individual will optimally insulate spending from fluctuations in income by lending in times of plenty and borrowing in times of dearth. Despite an array of refinements that have been added to the original work of Milton Friedman on the permanent-income hypothesis and by Franco Modigliani and associates on the life-cycle hypothesis, the essential kernel of both theories remains intact: rational agents smooth expenditures when income fluctuates.

A new wrinkle is that the same logic that applies to households also applies to state and local governments.[4] Cogan and Taylor note Edward Gramlich's pioneering work on the effects of federal grants on state budgets. Gramlich ends up skeptical of the efficacy of trying to stimulate the economy through grants to states, arguing, as do Cogan and Taylor a generation later, that grants end up fortifying state balance sheets (Gramlich 1978, 1979).

Before Gramlich, the terrain of how government spending is determined had been left mostly to students of politics. As early as the 1960s, Aaron Wildavsky argued the position that would later inform Gramlich's work: last year's expenditures are the primary determinant of this year's expenditures. An important difference between Wildavsky, on the one hand, and Gramlich, Taylor, and other economists who invoke expenditure smoothing, on the other, is that Wildavsky claimed no rational basis—on the contrary—for the workings of the budgetary process. (See Wildavsky 1964; Davis, Dempster, and Wildavsky 1966, 1974.) Nor did he apply his arguments to the operation of state and local government. His focus was rather on the process that determined agency budgets within the federal government. A crucial difference between the federal government and state and local governments is that no balanced-budget constraint operates at the federal level.

It was observed in chapter 9 that expenditure smoothing can take place for reasons that have nothing to do with the supposed rationality of basing expenditure on long-term resources rather than on current income. This idea, labeled the disequilibrium hypothesis in chapter 9, is like Wildavsky's theory in positing that agents are creatures of habit and inertia, which implies that adjustment of spending to income takes place only gradually. Applied to individuals, the disequilibrium hypothesis in its pure form is

$$\Delta C = \theta(Y - C_{-1}),$$

where θ is the speed of adjustment. We can combine the idea of disequilibrium with the more conventional Keynesian argument of consumption as a constant fraction of income, $C = \zeta Y$, where ζ is the marginal (and average) propensity to consume. In terms of changes,

$$\Delta C = \zeta \Delta Y = \zeta \frac{g}{1 + g} Y$$

with

$$\Delta Y = g Y_{-1}.$$

Adding the two expressions for ΔC, we have

$$\Delta C = \theta \left(Y - C_{-1} \right) + \zeta \frac{g}{1 + g} Y = \left(\theta + \zeta \frac{g}{1 + g} \right) Y - \theta C_{-1}.$$

As was also noted in chapter 9, this formulation can be made equivalent observationally to the permanent-income version of consumption smoothing. For a follower of Friedman,

$$C = \mu Y^{P}$$

and

$$\Delta C = \mu \Delta Y^{P},$$

where Y^P represents permanent income, and μ the propensity to consume out of permanent income. Permanent income is not directly observable, and we have some latitude in choosing the particular formula that we impute to agents for revising their notions of permanent income. For the sake of observational equivalence, assume a recursive formula that gives weight both to the current gap between actual income and last year's notion of permanent income, $Y - Y_{-1}^{P}$, and to the trend rate of growth of permanent income, ϕ:

$$\Delta Y^P = \eta \left(Y - Y_{-1}^{P} \right) + \phi Y_{-1}^{P}.$$

Together with the two equations above, this adjustment formula gives

$$\Delta C = \mu \eta Y + (\phi - \eta) C_{-1}.$$

In this case the permanent-income hypothesis and the disequilibrium hypothesis lead to the same equation, one which says that the change in consumption will depend on two variables, current income and lagged consumption. And both formulations have two parameters, μ and η, which can be estimated from the data.[5]

While the two formulations are econometrically identical, the interpretation of the parameters is very different, unsurprisingly in view of the very different premises of the two hypotheses. In the case of disequilibrium, the observed coefficient of lagged consumption is an estimate of the speed of adjustment θ to a gap between current income and last year's consumption. In the case of permanent income, the same coefficient $\phi - \eta$ is an estimate of the difference between the growth rate of permanent income and the rapidity with which the revision of permanent income takes place in response to a gap between actual income and lagged permanent income. By the same token, the interpretation of the coefficient of current income differs: in the one case, it is the sum of the adjustment-coefficient θ and the product $(\zeta g)/(1 + g)$; in the other case, it is the product $\mu \eta$.

Whichever interpretation one might prefer, there are good reasons to be skeptical about expenditure smoothing as a *general* assumption. First, many agents are simply unable to engage in expenditure smoothing, at least when incomes are falling. They have little or no saving and equally little access to credit markets. Chapter 9 noted the large literature on what are called in the jargon liquidity-constrained households. An equivalent liquidity constraint exists for the states to the extent that they are in fact bound by law or custom to cover current expenditures without borrowing.

Rational expenditure smoothing is especially suspicious. The economist's notion of rationality makes stringent demands on individuals with respect both to their intertemporal utility functions and to their intertemporal budget constraints. As observed in chapter 9, most people simply do not know enough about their future needs and wants, much less about their future incomes, for the standard theory of consumer choice to make sense. Instead, people fall back on habit, rules of thumb, and other perhaps less elegant but more realistic ways of coping. Moreover, real-world rationality may suggest a higher premium on solidarity and sharing than the economist's paradigm of individual choice allows. A poor person embedded in community may feel that sharing a tax rebate with her less fortunate neighbors, particularly the neighbor faced with eviction if the rent goes unpaid or a blackout if paying the electricity bill is put off, is a higher priority than replenishing her own bank account. She knows that someday it will be her turn to rely on the community (Stack 1975, quoted in Marglin 2008, p. 23). For a large segment of the population it seems more plausible to attribute consumption smoothing to disequilibrium adjustment than to a carefully thought out plan to balance long-term expenditure and long-term income.

It remains to be seen how much of the consumption-smoothing reasoning, of either permanent-income or disequilibrium inspiration, carries over to the states. This question goes beyond whether expenditure smoothing is a plausible behavioral assumption for private agents. There is also the question of the extent to which the constraints state governments face differ from those faced by households. One obvious difference is that as a practical matter we can take permanent income to be beyond the control of the household (even though in theory permanent income is not given—it is, rather, the outcome of a maximization process that trades off goods against leisure). But for states, permanent income is clearly endogenous. States, unlike households, have the power to levy taxes, so their maximization problem is more complicated than one of optimizing expenditures relative to an exogenously given income stream.

Multipliers for the Obama Stimulus

Theory and hypothetical examples, however, can take us only so far in estimating multipliers. Ideally, we would be able to settle disagreements over the appropriate value—actually *values*, see below—by appealing to data. Unfortunately, there are significant challenges to doing so. The greatest challenge is to isolate the effect of the stimulus from other macroeconomic activity—a standard difficulty of econometric analysis, but one that is made particularly acute in the case of estimating stimulus multipliers due to the paucity of relevant data. Not only are fiscal stimulus programs relatively rare, they are also idiosyncratic, responses to different kinds of economic stress. This turns a relatively small number of historical stimulus programs into an even smaller pool of different programs deployed under different circumstances (see note 4).

Concretely, this means that when we are prospectively assessing the wisdom of a particular stimulus program we cannot draw on a large sample of similar past episodes as a guide to its likely impact.

Notwithstanding, economists have deployed a variety of techniques to estimate multipliers. Valerie Ramey's (2011) review of the literature reports estimates from eighteen studies. She concludes:

> The range of plausible estimates for the multiplier in the case of a temporary increase in government spending that is deficit financed is probably 0.8 to 1.5 . . . If the increase is undertaken during a severe recession, the estimates are likely to be at the upper bound of this range.

To be sure, Ramey qualifies her conclusion by noting that

> there is significant uncertainty involved in these estimates. Reasonable people could argue that the multiplier is 0.5 or 2.0 without being contradicted by the data. (pp. 680–681)

The range of these estimates should not surprise us, especially if we take into account the problems attendant to the various estimation procedures. Peter Spiegler (Marglin and Spiegler 2013) has grouped these techniques under three rubrics: structural vector auto-regression (SVAR), dynamic stochastic general equilibrium (DSGE), and large-scale macroeconomic models (LSM).

Vector auto-regressions have been an important tool since the 1980s, beginning with a paper by Nobel Laureate Christopher Sims (1980) that offered this technique as an alternative to what Sims saw as a hodgepodge of ad hoc and sometimes inconsistent restrictions imposed on separate equations of a complex system. Vector auto-regressions were proposed as a way of letting the data speak for themselves by imposing only a minimal structure on how the variables interact. By its very nature, this virtue comes at the cost of ambiguity about causal relationships. SVAR models address this ambiguity by making assumptions about which variables are exogenous and therefore drivers of the system.

There remain problems. First, as a practical technique, SVAR requires us to limit the number of variables and is therefore not well suited to analyzing the impact of stimulus on different categories of beneficiaries. Second, it requires us to treat distinct episodes as sharing a common framework and therefore to suppress the idiosyncratic nature of stimulus; as Jonathan Parker (2011, p. 709) observed, "*By assumption,* the impulse response to an unexpected or exogenous increase in government spending is constrained to be the same independent of the state of the business cycle."

DSGE models go to the opposite extreme; they impose so much structure that multiplier estimates from these models make sense only to the extent that you buy into the model. DSGE models derive from the New Keynesian premise that a perfectly competitive economy will lead to a (Pareto) efficient allocation of resources. Recessions, unemployment, the space for stimulus are accounted for by grafting one or more imperfections on the textbook competitive model.

A relevant piece of the structure assumed in DSGE models is the reliance on a representative agent's consumption decisions based on intertemporal optimization à la Friedman and Modigliani. If this is the appropriate characterization, then the estimate of the multiplier resulting from an injection of stimulus reflects permanent-income/life-cycle consumption smoothing. Otherwise, the impact of stimulus is simply an unexplained correlation; it is reasoning in a circle to argue from parameter estimates to model validation. This is of course just one example of a general problem that Sims and others have noted: in Sims's words (2007, p. 153), "Making forecasts, policy projections, and (especially) welfare evaluations of policies with these models as if their behavioral interpretation were exactly correct is a mistake."

LSM models are the third way of estimating multipliers. These models have the virtue of nuance that both SVAR and DSGE models lack. That is, one can in principle estimate a variety of multipliers from the thousands of equations that these models typically mobilize to describe the economy. Both the federal government and private economists (for example, Alan Blinder and Marc Zandi [2010]) deployed LSM models to estimate the effects of the Obama stimulus. These models however do not escape the need for assumptions about the structure of the economy, and in their case, extremely detailed assumptions. The multiplier estimates that emerge are only as good as the assumptions are accurate.

A major problem with evaluating the usefulness of LSM models is that the same models were used *ex post* to evaluate the impact of the stimulus, thus the importance of independent analysis of the kind provided by Gabriel Chodorow-Reich et al. (2012), Daniel Wilson (2012), and others—including the present chapter.

One takeaway is that the multiplier is highly variable: different strokes not only for different folks, but for different types of stimulus and at different points in the economic cycle. A stimulus program targeted toward low-income people will give very different results from one directed toward upper-income groups, and the same target groups will react differently when the economy is in recession than in more prosperous times. A generic value of "*the* multiplier" that covers all situations at all times may be a legitimate simplification when introducing the idea for the first time but cannot be the stuff of policymaking.

This point is well understood by practitioners. In evaluating the Obama stimulus, the Congressional Budget Office, for example, used a variety of multipliers, and indeed a range of values rather than a single point estimate for each. The ranges varied from 0 to 0.4 for certain corporate tax breaks and 0.1 to 0.6 for tax cuts for high-income people, to 0.3 to 1.5 for tax cuts for middle-income folks and 0.4 to 2.1 for transfer payments such as food stamps and unemployment compensation. For payments to states to supplement education and Medicaid budgets, the CBO multiplier ranged from 0.4 to 2.1 (Congressional Budget Office 2012, table 2, pp. 6–7).[6]

The differences between the multiplier estimates for different elements of the stimulus does raise an obvious question: if the point was to add demand to a weakening private sector, and thereby to restore prerecession levels of employment and output, why would stimulus money take the form of tax breaks directed to corporations and high-income individuals? A much greater bang for the buck was available from tax cuts for middle-income people and transfers to the poor and unemployed, not to mention transfers to the states.

The likely answer is that tax breaks for the rich and tax breaks for corporations were never intended to stimulate. Perhaps as much as one-fourth of the total was the political price of stimulus, not stimulus itself. Tax breaks for the wealthy represent the price of getting action from a Congress dominated by special interests.[7]

Consider again the three-part division of the ARRA into Tax Benefits; Entitlements; and Contracts, Loans, and Grants in Table 15.1. A rough-and-ready division of Tax Benefits according to the specifics of the various programs makes it possible to identify eight programs that appear to benefit better-off segments of the population, listed in Table 15.2, along with the number of beneficiaries and the aggregate benefits of each. Table 15.2 also includes the two programs that benefit business, the last two items, which amounted to $43 billion. The total "stimulus" for the better-off segments of the economy totaled over $175 billion!

We suppose that the rest of the money included under Tax Benefits in Table 15.1, more than $120 billion, went to taxpayers who would not have operated by Friedman–Modigliani logic to the extent that those higher up the income distribution did. These programs included Making Work Pay, the $100+ billion program that was the centerpiece of the ARRA tax breaks for individuals; the Earned Income Credit ($5.1 billion); and the exclusion of a portion of unemployment benefits from taxable income ($6.3 billion).

It is undoubtedly an exaggeration to assume that not a penny of the $175+ billion benefiting the better-off was spent in the first round ($v = 0$), and to as-

Table 15.2 Tax Benefit Programs Chiefly Benefiting Better-Off Taxpayers

	Number of Taxpayers Benefiting (millions)	Benefits ($ billions)
Child Tax Credit	15.6	18.4
American Opportunity Tax Credit	10.2	25.5
First-Time Homebuyer Tax Credit	1.0	10.4
Extension of Alternative Minimum Tax Relief for Nonrefundable Personal Credits	13.0	4.4
Increased Alternative Minimum Tax Exemption	13.0	64.7
Residential Energy Credit	4.3	11.0
Business Incentives		34.5
Manufacturing and Economic Recovery		9.2
Total		178.1

Source: American Recovery and Reinvestment Act website (www.recovery.gov); data now stored at data.nber.org/data/ARRA.

sume that the entire addition to disposable income was spent ($v = 1$) when tax benefits flowed to the less well-off. But I can defend this generalization as much closer to the mark than assuming a uniform first-round *MPC*.

If we also assume that entitlements flow to the less well-off, and so are entirely spent, we are a long way toward assessing the impact of the ARRA on GDP. With the assumption that there is no crowding out, so that $m = 1$, the multiplier for tax benefits and individual entitlements depends only on the division between rich and poor, plus what is assumed about the average *MPC* in the economy. Here we assume $MPC = 1/3$, so that the tax/transfer multiplier appropriate to tax benefits and entitlements is

$$\frac{v}{1 - MPC} = 1.5v,$$

in line with the upper end of Ramey's plausible range and in line with the CBO estimates as well.

Table 15.3 summarizes a provisional reckoning. Observe that Table 15.3 shifts the $86.9 billion of Medicaid enhancements from the Entitlements row in Table 15.1 to the Contracts, Loans, and Grants row. The reason is that these grants were in fact grants to the states, not direct grants to individuals. As such they were fungible, and it is more reasonable to lump them together with other grants than to treat them like, say, food stamps or unemployment insurance, which were grants to individuals even though they flowed through the states. Although the states were bound by the terms of Medicaid grants to

Table 15.3 ARRA Spending and Impact, by Spending Category ($ billions)

	(1)	(2)	(3)	(4)	(5)	(6)
				Direct		
		Reallocating	First-Round	Spending of		Total
	Reported	Medicaid to	MPC	Recipients		Impact
	Spending	Grants	= v	= (3) × (4)	Multiplier	= (4) × (5)
Tax Benefits, upper-income recipients and business	178.1	178.1	0.0	0.0	0.0	0.0
Tax Benefits, lower-income groups	121.7	121.7	1.0	121.7	1.5	182.6
Entitlements	220.2	133.3	1.0	133.3	1.5	200.0
Contracts, Loans, and Grants	225.8	312.7	?	?	?	?
Total	745.8	745.8				?

Source: Column (1) from Table 15.2; remaining data, author's calculations.

maintain the programs in place before the financial crisis and ensuing Great Recession, the states did not have to come up with their own funds to meet the claims of a much enlarged program.[8]

We turn now to substituting numbers for the question marks in the bottom row of Table 15.3: how much of the money spent by the federal government under the heading of contracts, loans, and grants actually led to the purchase of additional goods and services?

What Did the States Do With the Money?

Indeed, the focus is a little narrower: I concentrate on what happened to the money the fifty states received. This limited focus makes sense because the data for the states is more tractable than for other entities (local governments and regional authorities, private businesses and nonprofits); moreover, according to my reckoning for the fiscal-year 2010, FY-2010, the year on which the cross-section analysis focuses, states received some 80 percent of the money under this category.

There are two issues. The first is the value of the MPC for all the spending after the first round. We shall continue to assume $MPC = 1/3$, and hence a multiplier of 1.5 for state outlays—even though the estimates implied by the cross-sectional analysis later in this chapter are somewhat higher. The second issue, on which the argument here focuses, is the first-round MPC, the v in the multiplier formulas developed earlier in this chapter. I offer three arguments why it is reasonable to suppose that the states spent *all* the money they received under S-ARRA programs, that is, $v = 1$.

The first argument examines the time-series evidence that John Cogan and John Taylor (2012) put forward in support of the hypothesis that state governments base their spending not on current revenues but on long-term resources, with the implication that for state governments $v = 0$. Far from offering independent support, the time-series evidence argues for expenditure smoothing only if one is already committed to that view.

A second line of inquiry examines the differential impact of the S-ARRA money on spending across the states. In conducting this exercise we are in effect starting from an agnostic position on whether the states could have found other funds in order to continue to spend as usual, and so might simply have substituted S-ARRA funds for drawing down their bank accounts or borrowing. This cross-sectional analysis leads to the conclusion that the S-ARRA money that went to the states was indeed spent.

The third approach is to see what the boots on the ground, state budget officers, have to say about the hypothesis that, absent the S-ARRA, states could have sustained prerecession levels of spending. These interviews lead to a clear conclusion: with very few exceptions, state budget officers say that their states could not have avoided spending cuts in the absence of the S-ARRA.

What Do Time-Series Regressions Say?

Cogan and Taylor (2012) use aggregate time series to investigate the impact of grants to states, complementing Taylor's earlier article (2011) that estimates the impact of the portions of the ARRA that involved tax reduction and transfers to individuals. All of this work finds that the stimulus had no impact on spending.

Cogan and Taylor's analysis is straightforward. The states had two options with respect to how they responded to S-ARRA grants. A state could have added to its expenditures or shored up its balance sheet. The funds, it is assumed, were fungible. Their point is that enhanced Medicaid reimbursement or education grants would not—and did not in fact—increase Medicaid spending or school spending if a state was planning to allocate its own money to these ends. The extra Medicaid or education dollars would then be allocated to other expenditures or to building up depleted assets or to reducing borrowing. (One possibility Cogan and Taylor don't seem to consider is the possibility of reducing taxes, or more realistically, raising taxes less than a state otherwise would have.[9] As we shall see, their intuition is sound here: though this is a possibility *a priori,* there is no support in the data for this option.)

Cogan and Taylor estimate the impact of the S-ARRA by regressing aggregate purchases of goods and services (G) and transfers (E) by states on non-

ARRA revenues (R) and ARRA grants (A), along with lagged values of the dependent variables:

$$G = a_0 + a_1 G_{-1} + a_2 R + a_3 A = 3.66 + 0.876 G_{-1} + 0.113 R - 0.097 A,$$

$$E = b_0 + b_1 E_{-1} + b_2 R + b_3 A = -6.1 + 0.743 E_{-1} + 0.056 R + 0.163 A.$$

From these two equations, Cogan and Taylor estimate aggregate saving—the addition to financial assets or the reduction in liabilities—on the part of the states (L) as the difference between revenues ($R + A$) and outlays ($G + E$):

$$L = -(a_0 + b_0) - a_1 G_{-1} - b_1 E_{-1} + (1 - a_2 - b_2) R + (1 - a_3 - b_3)\, A,$$

$$L = 2.442 - 0.876 G_{-1} - 0.743 E_{-1} + 0.831 R + 0.933 A.$$

I had questions about how Cogan and Taylor handled the data for these regressions, and my answers to these questions led to certain modifications, the most important of which was to collapse the distinction between transfer payments and purchases of goods and services.[10] After all these modifications, replacing G and E by the sum $O = G + E$ gives the result

$$O = a_0 + a_1 O_{-1} + a_2 R + a_3 A = -0.001 + 0.788 O_{-1} + 0.233 R + 0.049 A.$$
$$\phantom{O = a_0 + a_1 O_{-1}}(0.010)\quad(0.071)\qquad(0.109)\qquad(0.168)$$

This is to say that one dollar of S-ARRA funds only increased state-government outlays by a nickel, virtually identical to the Cogan–Taylor result that all but seven cents went to shore up state balance sheets. Newey-West standard errors (in parentheses below the coefficients) indicate that the coefficients on lagged outlays and revenues are significant at usual confidence intervals and that the coefficient on S-ARRA spending is statistically indistinguishable from zero.

The heavy lifting in all the estimating equations is done by the lagged dependent variables, a result certainly consistent with expenditure smoothing. But two qualifications are in order. First, as has been observed, expenditure smoothing may or may not mean that spending decisions are driven by long-term considerations in the manner of the permanent-income and life-cycle hypotheses. The coefficient on lagged outlays is consistent not only with long-term budgeting that smooths over revenue fluctuations, but also with the idea that lags occur because old habits die hard, and habit may be reinforced by institutional rigidities in the adjustment of spending to revenue.

To see this, look at the above equation rerun without the S-ARRA term and with the change in outlays as the dependent variable. We obtain

$$\Delta O = a_0 + a_1 O_{-1} + a_2 R = -0.001 - 0.204 O_{-1} + 0.224 R.$$
$$(0.009)\quad(0.048)\qquad(0.083)$$

As noted in the section titled The Multiplier in Theory, the disequilibrium interpretation of the coefficients is

$$\hat{\theta} = 0.204, \hat{\zeta} = 0.294,$$

and the permanent-income interpretation is

$$\hat{\mu} = 0.81, \hat{\eta} = 0.276.$$

These estimates assume that the rate of growth of nominal "permanent revenue" is equal to the trend rate of growth of nominal revenues over the sample period,

$$\psi = g = 0.072.$$

The constant term apart, the interpretation of the coefficients under the disequilibrium hypothesis is that outlays change by a bit over 20 percent of the gap between revenues and lagged outlays, with an additional immediate adjustment of almost 30 percent. Under the permanent-income hypothesis, the interpretation is that permanent income (revenues), Y^P, increases 7 percent every year and is further adjusted by just over one-fourth of the difference $(Y - Y^P_{-1})/Y^P_{-1}$, that is, 0.276 times the percentage gap between actual income and the lagged value of permanent income; the change in outlays is just over 80 percent of the change in permanent income.

A second, more important, qualification is the possibility that the coefficient of lagged outlay plays an outsize role in the regression because of serial correlation. Serial correlation in the data can generate the observed result that lagged outlay matters a lot even in the case where lagged outlay is actually irrelevant to current outlay. Suppose that in fact—a messenger from on high told me so—it is the other variables (ordinary revenues and S-ARRA revenues) that are driving expenditures. Nonetheless, a lagged dependent variable will still show up with a positive coefficient and bias the estimates of the true drivers downward, provided that in the correct specification (the one that the messenger vouched for) the independent variables and the error term are serially correlated (Achen 2001).

I analyze the data for serial correlation in the statistical appendix to this chapter. The results are consistent with the hypothesis that only revenues matter for expenditures, and the regression coefficients that emerge from the specification including lagged outlays are spurious. If we exclude lagged outlays, we obtain the following result:

$$O = a_0 + a_1 R + a_2 A = -0.008 + 1.094R + 1.630A.$$
$$\quad\quad\quad\quad\quad\quad\quad (0.012) \quad (0.095) \quad (0.213)$$

In this specification, the S-ARRA has a huge impact on spending. For every dollar of ARRA spending there is an additional $1.63 of outlay.

The upshot is that a high t-value for the coefficient of lagged expenditure does not provide independent support for expenditure smoothing. But we have to be careful in what we take away from this. That the high t-value on lagged outlays *could be* due to serial correlation does not prove that it *is* due to serial correlation. We cannot infer that there is no causal relationship running from expenditure smoothing (via a significant coefficient on lagged expenditure) to present expenditure, that is, we cannot infer that last year's expenditure does not drive this year's. Neither is there an implication that the alternative of basing present expenditure only on present revenues is the correct approach. All we can fairly say is that the impressive statistics that characterize the Cogan–Taylor regressions, either in their original form or in my modified form, add nothing to the argument for expenditure smoothing. The answer to the question of what effect the S-ARRA had on state expenditures is built into the regression assumptions.

What Can We Learn from Cross-Sectional Regressions?

In view of the indeterminacy of time-series regressions, it makes sense to see what is added by other approaches. In this section I deploy cross-sectional evidence to test the hypothesis that states spent the bulk of S-ARRA monies they received against the hypothesis that these monies had little or no effect on spending. This exercise provisionally commits us to the stipulation that the states had considerable latitude in this regard, that they could have maintained their actual expenditures if no ARRA monies had been forthcoming and, accordingly, that the S-ARRA money might simply have shored up their balance sheets.[11]

My conclusion is that even if states could have continued to spend without the S-ARRA, these grants had a considerable impact on spending. This result supports the results of previous cross-sectional tests, including the pioneering analyses by Chodorow-Reich et al. (2012) and Wilson (2012).

Before turning to the analysis, I need to say a few words about the data. In contrast with the time-series analysis of Cogan and Taylor (2012), the data here are restricted to state governments, leaving out the portion of S-ARRA grants channeled directly to local governments and other agencies at one remove from state governments.

There are several reasons for focusing on state governments. One is that the data are of better quality for the states than for the consolidated accounts of state and local governments; state government data are assembled from a survey of state governments, whereas local government data is collected through a sampling procedure and are therefore subject to sampling error. Another reason for focusing on the states has already been noted: the bulk of the ARRA monies in the S-ARRA—including both grants to government entities and contracts and loans to nongovernment entities—in fact went to the states. Substantial amounts of S-ARRA grants were in turn transferred by the states to localities as well as to higher educational institutions and other nonprofits, but for reasons exemplified by Medicaid grants, I regard these transfers as essentially equivalent to purchases of goods and services.[12]

For all the information that was available on the official website of the stimulus program, recovery.gov website, no breakdown of ARRA grants was provided between states, localities, universities and other nonprofits, and private businesses. For the portion of grants covered by the recipient-reporting requirement (Section 1512 of the ARRA), I separated state grants out by using a set of keywords like "department," "education," "executive office," "human services." For the programs not subject to Section 1512 reporting, the largest of which was Medicaid, I used the figures of the relevant federal departments. Because the quarterly listing of recipient reports lumped together disbursements through September 30, 2009, I also relied on reports of the Department of Education and the Department of Transportation to separate grants received by the states during FY-2009 from grants received during FY-2010.

Finally, a disclaimer. Since estimating the model, I have found errors in processing the raw S-ARRA data. These errors are small and do not affect the results, but it is possible there are errors that have gone undetected.[13]

The model is designed both to account for the impact of the S-ARRA on state expenditures, revenues, and borrowing, and to quantify the effects of these intermediate variables on output. The difficulties are obvious: all these relationships involve reciprocal cause and effect. For example, if the S-ARRA led to a decrease in taxes, this should in principle have stimulated the economy just as an increase in outlays does. At the same time, higher output will generate higher tax revenues. Output and revenue are thus simultaneously determined. The same story repeats itself with expenditure and output. As others have noted (Chodorow-Reich et al. 2012; Wilson 2012; Leduc and Wilson 2017; Feyrer and Sacerdote 2011; Conley and Dupor 2013), S-ARRA money may itself be influenced by the variables it is supposed, directly or indirectly, to explain. This leads to estimating parameter values by three-stage least squares (3SLS).

The endogenous variables are the change in outlays, that is, changes in state purchases of goods and services directly or indirectly (through transfers that are used for the purchase of goods and services), ΔO; non-ARRA revenues, R; S-ARRA grants, A; and gross state product, Y. All variables are measured per capita on the basis of state populations in April 2010.

The general idea of these regressions is that if the S-ARRA had an impact, it should show up in greater expenditures by states receiving more ARRA money and (or) by a reduction in taxation—both relative to baseline levels in the absence of S-ARRA funds. Hence there are two separate equations in which the change in expenditures and the change in non-ARRA revenues are the dependent variables. To estimate the impact of state-government spending requires another equation in which the dependent variable is the change in the state's gross product.

The basic cross-sectional model is

$$\Delta O = a_0 + a_1 R + a_2 O_{-1} + a_3 A + a'_1 Z_1 + \cdots + a'_n Z_n,$$

$$\Delta Y = b_0 + b_1 \Delta O + b'_1 Z_1 + \cdots + b'_n Z_n,$$

$$\Delta R = c_0 + c_1 \Delta Y + c_3 A + b'_1 Z_1 + \cdots + c'_n Z_n,$$

$$A = d_0 + d'_1 Z_1 + \cdots + d'_n Z_n,$$

where $Z_1, \cdots, Z_n$ is a set of exogenous variables that include the instruments for estimating S-ARRA grants and control variables relevant for determining the changes in outlays, production, and revenues.

Without the controls, variation across states of changes in spending in relationship to variations in non-ARRA revenues, prior levels of expenditure, and injections of S-ARRA money appear to confirm the time-series result that the S-ARRA had no statistically significant impact. With the change in outlays as the dependent variable, the time-series result is

$$\Delta O = a_0 + a_1 O_{-1} + a_2 R + a_3 A = -0.001 - 0.212 O_{-1} + 0.233 R + 0.049 A,$$
$$(0.010) \quad (0.071) \quad (0.109) \quad (0.168)$$

whereas 3SLS estimation of cross-sectional results for forty-five states—I omit Alaska as an outlier as well as the four states with fiscal years ending on dates other than June 30—gives

$$\Delta O = a_0 + a_1 O_{-1} + a_2 R + a_3 A = 137 - 0.311 O_{-1} + 0.270 R + 0.917 A.$$
$$(154) \quad (0.077) \quad (0.082) \quad (0.647)$$

The time-series and cross-sectional estimates are not inconsistent because the standard error on the coefficient of A is so much larger in the second equation.

The picture changes when we add financial and political controls: the impact of S-ARRA funds on state spending becomes significant both statistically and economically. And the coefficient on S-ARRA funds is 2.8 for the forty-five state regressions, which is to say that one dollar transferred to a state led to $2.80 of additional spending. When the states are separated by population, not only do the smaller states receive more S-ARRA funds per capita, but the estimates of the impact on state spending are markedly different for the smaller and larger states: the coefficient on S-ARRA funds for small states is more than 4.5, and the estimate for large states falls below one. The results are:

forty-five states

$$\Delta O = a_0 + a_1 R + a_2 O_{-1} + a_3 A + a'_1 Z_1 + \cdots + a'_n Z_n =$$
$$-323 - 0.065 O_{-1} + 0.015 R + 2.801 A + a'_1 Z_1 + \cdots + a'_n Z_n$$
$$(136) \quad (0.087) \quad (0.083) \quad (0.661)$$

twenty-two small states

$$\Delta O = a_0 + a_1 R + a_2 O_{-1} + a_3 A + a'_1 Z_1 + \cdots + a'_n Z_n =$$
$$-613 - 0.153 O_{-1} + 0.032 R + 4.58 A + a'_1 Z_1 + \cdots + a'_n Z_n$$
$$(180) \quad (0.152) \quad (0.125) \quad (0.826)$$

twenty-three large states

$$\Delta O = a_0 + a_1 R + a_2 O_{-1} + a_3 A + a'_1 Z_1 + \cdots + a'_n Z_n =$$
$$-233 - 0.141 O_{-1} + 0.181 R + 0.922 A + a'_1 Z_1 + \cdots + a'_n Z_n.$$
$$(165) \quad (0.106) \quad (0.115) \quad (0.484)$$

Notably, the impact of S-ARRA funds on state spending depends on whether the governor is a Democrat or a Republican, Republican states increasing spending by approximately fifty cents less per dollar of S-ARRA funds received.

The multiplier estimates—as reflected by the coefficient on ΔO in the equation in which ΔY is the dependent variable—are on the high side compared with other investigations. My estimates of the multiplier are 2.6 for the forty-five states, 2.8 for the twenty-two small states, and 4.7 for the twenty-three large states. To some extent the differences can be explained by the larger amount of spillovers from one state to another in smaller states.

In marked contrast with the time-series results, these findings are robust to how the relationship between spending and revenues and lagged expenditures is specified. In particular, the results are relatively little affected by whether or not we attach importance to expenditure smoothing.

What Did We Learn from State Budget Officers?

The econometrics adds to the consensus that the S-ARRA stimulated the economy. But I would be the last to claim that this analysis is conclusive. Not only because, as I have noted, there were errors in data processing, but because even regression results from a pristine data set are no better than the models used to interpret the data.

For this reason the quantitative analysis was supplemented by a direct examination of the plausibility of the counterfactual assumption on which the analysis was based, namely, that the states could have maintained expenditures despite the reduction in revenues and the reduction in Rainy-Day fund balances. Having risen by some 6 percent per year from FY-2003 to FY-2008, non-ARRA revenues fell by 3 percent in FY-2009 and barely recovered in FY-2010. Since upward pressure on expenditures intensified, Rainy-Day funds were bound to suffer. Here the aggregates are misleading since two states, Alaska and Texas, accounted for more than one-quarter of Rainy-Day assets at the end of FY-2008 and more than *half* of these assets when FY-2009 came to a close. As Table 15.4 shows, if we leave out these two states, Rainy-Day funds were practically exhausted by the end of FY-2010 and only began to recover in FY-2011, well after the ARRA spigot had been turned on.

To find out what the states did with the S-ARRA money, Peter Spiegler and I sent a questionnaire to all fifty state budget officers. The questions were framed to provide a basis for conversation without being so restrictive that they would prevent us from learning things about state-budgeting practice that we had not anticipated (Marglin and Spiegler 2013, pp. 842–844). Budget officers from twenty-nine states responded, and as near as we could tell these states did not differ systematically from the nonresponders.

Needless to say, this approach is unorthodox. Economists generally resist asking agents for information about why they do what they do or what they would have done if the circumstances had been different.[14] Often, there is good reason for this reluctance: there are too many agents, it is hard to get a representative sample, and agents may have trouble reconstructing the circumstances of their decisions well enough to answer, especially when the questions involve a counterfactual. Fortunately, none of these reasons apply to the case at hand. There are only fifty states, and state budget officers are a highly professional group of men and women. It thus seemed reasonable to ask these officers what they would have done had there been no ARRA funds to offset lost revenues and increased demands for expenditure that were the twin results of the Great Recession.

The responses to our questionnaire indicated that, aside from "fossil-fuel"

Table 15.4 Rainy-Day Fund Balances by Fiscal Year ($ millions)

	2008	2009	2010	2011
Rainy-Day Fund Balances, All States	32,943	29,006	21,034	24,651
Alaska	5,601	8,898	10,364	12,981
Texas	4,355	6,276	7,693	5,012
Rainy-Day Fund Balances, All Other States	22,987	13,832	2,977	6,658
Number of States with Zero Balance	5	10	15	17

Source: National Association of State Budget Officers, *The Fiscal Survey of States*, various years.

states, which generally rely on severance taxes on the extraction of natural resources rather than on income and sales taxes, internal funds[15] were insufficient to support operating expenditure at the level actually observed. Moreover, maintaining expenditure by shifting it to the capital budget was so limited that it would not have added significantly to the spending resources of the states. On the capital-expenditure side, the responses indicated that states were very limited in their ability to increase capital borrowing during the Great Recession, as their capital borrowing limit is tied to projected revenues.[16]

In short, it is implausible that states could have and would have increased net borrowing to fund spending at the levels observed *with* the S-ARRA. The collective view of the state budget officers was that the great majority of the states would have cut spending significantly without the S-ARRA. The evidence indicates that states not only *would* have done so but that in almost all cases they *could not* have done otherwise.

Conclusions

Did the stimulus work? The short answer is yes. If we fill in the blanks in Table 15.3, we can arrive at an estimate for the ARRA as a whole. Table 15.5 takes a conservative stance and estimates the first-round *MPC* of the states as one, a figure roughly two standard deviations below the point estimates of *A* in the cross-sectional regressions, and continues to assume a multiplier of 1.5, also a conservative figure relative to the cross-sectional estimates. On this basis we arrive at an estimate of $469 billion for the category of Contracts, Loans, and Grants.[17]

Table 15.5 ARRA Spending and Impact, by Spending Category ($ billions)

	(1)	(2)	(3)	(4)	(5)	(6)
	Reported Spending	Reallocating Medicaid to Grants	First-Round *MPC* = v	Direct Spending of Recipients = (3) × (4)	Multiplier	Total Impact = (4) × (5)
Tax Benefits, upper-income recipients and business	178.1	178.1	0.0	0.0	0.0	0.0
Tax Benefits, lower-income groups	121.7	121.7	1.0	121.7	1.5	182.6
Entitlements	220.2	133.3	1.0	133.3	1.5	200.0
Contracts, Loans, and Grants	225.8	312.7	1.0	312.7	1.5	469.0
Total	745.8	745.8				851.7

Source: Column (1) from Table 15.2; remaining data, author's calculations.

The overall impact of the ARRA up to December 2011 works out to $852 billion, a little more than 2 percent of GDP over the two and a half years between the summer of 2009 and the end of 2011. This is in line with the final estimate of the Council of Economic Advisers (2014). If the Obama administration can be faulted on its stimulus program, it is for failing to appreciate the gravity of the situation it inherited in January 2009, for lacking the courage or foresight to ask for more stimulus over a longer time period, for failing to argue forcefully enough that more of the stimulus should be directed to lower-income beneficiaries who would have been more likely to spend than to save.

Taken together, the available evidence suggests that state-government expenditure was significantly increased by the S-ARRA. Cogan and Taylor present time-series evidence that expenditure smoothing was responsible for the lack of an increase in spending beyond what non-ARRA revenues would have permitted. But this evidence requires a prior commitment to the idea that expenditure smoothing drives spending. Because of serial correlation in the data, roughly the same coefficients on lagged expenditure would show up even if no expenditure smoothing took place. So a high statistical significance for the coefficient of lagged expenditure and a correspondingly low significance for the coefficient of S-ARRA grants is not independent evidence for expenditure smoothing.

This chapter reinforces the consensus view with respect to the stimulus as a whole: both econometric analysis of cross-sectional state data and interviews with state budget officers suggest that the S-ARRA allowed the states to maintain spending programs that would have been drastically cut if the stimulus had not been enacted. A portion of the ARRA monies might have gone to shore up state balance sheets—as indeed was the intention of the ARRA legislation—but far less than Cogan and Taylor contend. My estimate, based on a conservative interpretation of the cross-sectional data, is that for FY-2010 the states on average spent all the S-ARRA money they received—and then some. Unsurprisingly, states with Democratic governors increased their spending more than states with Republicans in the statehouse.

Taylor rightly argues that much of the post-hoc vindication of the ARRA could have been—and in fact was—written before one dime of ARRA monies had been spent. But this is a case of the pot calling the kettle black: whatever the truth of the Cogan–Taylor hypothesis, their methodology guaranteed that the data on state and local governments would confirm expenditure smoothing. In contrast, the cross-sectional regressions presented here did not predetermine the outcome one way or another; the results could have been unfavorable to the hypothesis that the S-ARRA increased state-government spending.

Given the limits to what can be learned from any regression analysis, additional light on the question of causality was provided by state budget officers—the very individuals who would have been in the thick of cause and effect. Here too every attempt was made to frame questions in a way that would have permitted answers on both sides. There was a uniformity of responses—but *not* unanimity—with respect to how the S-ARRA actually affected expenditures, even when the respondents obviously differed in their evaluation of the ARRA as a policy. So, while it is true that the framework of analysis affects the results, it is not the case that all frameworks are created equal.

The final lesson is skepticism about the conventional distinction between positive and normative economics. Mainstream economists believe that description can be separated from values, the first representing science, the second ideology. But just as there are no facts without theory, there is no separate realm for description that does not embody values. Ideology ought not to be, as it is glossed in the *Cambridge Dictionary of Philosophy* (Audi 1999, p. 406), "a disparaging term used to describe someone else's political views which one regards as unsound." Acting on ideology is not a failing or disease of the Other, against which Taylor (or I) can claim immunity. As Joseph Schumpeter insisted (1949, p. 349), we all operate on the basis of assumptions that cannot be proved or disproved, and ideology is the coin of the vast realm of what is beyond our powers to confirm or deny. This does not mean there is nothing to discuss, nothing to learn. To the contrary. We may seek to transcend ideology, but we will never do so until we admit that it is the necessary starting point of any serious discussion about policy.

Regressions and Their Discontents

This appendix takes up three issues: first, the modifications of the Cogan–Taylor (2012) regressions and the reasons for these modifications; second, why lagged dependent variables may introduce spurious correlation; and, finally, the cross-sectional regressions summarized in the main body of this chapter.

Modifying Cogan–Taylor

A relatively inconsequential change is that I translated Cogan and Taylor's quarterly data to fiscal years, using the period July 1 to June 30 as the fiscal year, since this is the fiscal year for the overwhelming majority of the states.[1] The reason is that the fiscal year is the unit of time over which budget decisions are normally made (even though in an emergency like the one that followed the abrupt downturn of the economy in the fall of 2008, many states were obliged to make midcourse adjustments).

More important, I excluded the imputed value of capital services in the National Income and Product Accounts. NIPA calculations of state government purchases include these imputations, which lead to overstating purchases G and understating transfers E. This modification has a big impact on individual regression coefficients but does not change the qualitative results that Cogan and Taylor obtain. The key result is that the coefficients of S-ARRA grants in the two estimated equations imply a larger negative impact of the S-ARRA on G, which is not offset by a larger positive impact on E; the overall impact of the S-ARRA on the states' net addition to their financial assets (L) remains *positive*. Indeed, my time-series estimates suggest that one dollar of S-ARRA money leads to an increase of net saving of $1.36—whereas Cogan and Taylor's estimate is that just over $0.90 of every dollar of S-ARRA grant money is saved. My results are summarized in the first three columns of Table 15.6.

A further modification of the regression procedure is more consequential: column (4) consolidates transfer payments and purchases of goods and ser-

Table 15.6 Regressions of Nominal Purchases and Transfers on Lagged Dependent Variables, Revenues, and ARRA

	(1)	(2)	(3)	(4)
		Dependent Variable		
	G	E	L	O
Constant	8.85	−1.595	−7.255	5.169
	1.944	1.622		2.435
G_{-1}	0.78		−0.78	
	0.032			
E_{-1}		0.854	−0.854	
		0.06		
O_{-1}				0.783
				0.04
R	0.198	0.054	0.748	0.269
	0.025	0.017		0.041
A	−0.586	0.226	1.359	−0.314
	0.057	0.065		0.108
Adj R^2	0.9996	0.999		0.9997
Frequency/	FY	FY	FY	FY
Time Period	1969–2011	1969–2011	1969–2011	1969–2011
N	43	43	43	43

Sources: Bureau of Economic Analysis; Department of Health and Human Services.
Note: Newey-West standard errors appear below coefficients.

vices into a single variable, "outlays," denoted by O and equal to $E + G$. At the state level it makes little sense to distinguish between the two because transfers by states differ in important ways from transfers from the federal government. Most direct federal transfers to individuals come with few or no strings attached—think social security—and it is reasonable to consider such transfers simply as putting more money in the pockets of recipients. Food stamps, for example, though nominally tied to the purchase of groceries, are in fact fungible since they free up cash for other purposes. Estimates suggest that only about $0.26 to $0.35 of each one dollar of food stamps generates additional spending on food (Mark Nord and Mark Prell [2011], p. 17). The remaining $0.65 to $0.74 simply replaces spending that the recipient would have made out of her own pocket, freeing up spending on other goods and services.

Unlike food stamps, social security, and other federal programs,[2] the bulk of transfer payments made by states and localities are not really payments to the nominal recipients—except by national income accounting convention. Medicaid, the largest single transfer program, appears in the national income accounts as a transfer payment to individuals, but the individual never sees any cash. The payments are actually made to vendors of medical goods and services—for visits to doctors, surgical procedures, prescription drugs—and are purchases of goods and services every bit as much as direct purchases by state governments. For the purpose of analyzing the impact of the S-ARRA, it makes little difference whether states purchase goods and services directly or indirectly.

Following this logic, the relevant dependent variable is total current outlays, the sum of current purchases of goods and services and transfer payments. The result, in column (4) of Table 15.6, with total outlays, $O = G + E$, as the dependent variable, is that the coefficient of S-ARRA grants on outlays becomes negative, lying between the two separate coefficients for purchases and "transfers." More important, this coefficient is insignificantly different from zero.

There remains a problem: the data are dominated by an upward trend in all the variables. These trends hide the complementary behavior of purchases and transfers, purchases of goods and services being correlated with fluctuations in revenues, and transfers being correlated with the upward trend in revenues. For this reason, there is a stronger correlation between revenues and total outlays than between revenues and either of the two components of outlays.

Normalizing the variables by dividing by potential GDP removes some of the problems of using the trend-dominated data in its raw form. In columns (1) and (2) of Table 15.7, the negative effect of the S-ARRA on states' purchases of goods and services remains significant, both statistically and economically, and is not offset by the positive stimulus to transfers. But the regression in which the dependent variable is total outlay (column [4]), suggests a negligible impact on spending overall—the coefficient on A is not only small, suggesting that less than a nickel of each S-ARRA dollar got spent, it is statistically indistinguishable from zero. This regression, like the regressions reported by Cogan and Taylor, suggests that the lion's share of S-ARRA grants, the unspent $0.95, went toward increasing financial assets or reducing financial liabilities.

In short, all the modifications that I introduced into the Cogan–Taylor analysis do nothing to change their qualitative conclusions.

Spurious Correlation with Lagged Dependent Variables

Serial correlation in the data can generate the key result in the Cogan–Taylor regressions, namely, that lagged outlay matters a lot, and current revenues and S-ARRA funds matter hardly at all—even if lagged outlay is actually irrelevant to current outlay. Suppose that in the true specification revenues, including

Table 15.7 Regressions of Normalized Purchases and Transfers on Lagged Dependent Variables, Revenues, and ARRA

	(1)	(2)	(3)	(4)
		Dependent Variable		
	G	*E*	*L*	*O*
Constant	0.007	0.004	−0.011	−0.001
	0.010	0.004		0.010
G_{-1}	0.813		−0.813	
	0.084			
E_{-1}		0.980	−0.980	
		0.037		
O_{-1}				0.788
				0.071
R	0.098	−0.022	0.924	0.233
	0.078	0.035		0.109
A	−0.465	0.189	1.277	0.049
	0.081	0.113		0.168
Adj R^2	0.8101	0.982		0.9441
Frequency/	FY	FY	FY	FY
Time Period	1969–2011	1969–2011	1969–2011	1969–2011
N	43	43	43	43

Sources: Bureau of Economic Analysis; Department of Health and Human Services.

Note: Newey-West standard errors appear below coefficients.

S-ARRA funds, drive outlays, and lagged outlays are irrelevant. Lagged outlays still show up with a positive coefficient and bias the estimates of the true drivers downward if the independent variables, revenues and S-ARRA funds, and the error term are serially correlated (Achen 2001).

To see the effect of serial correlation in a simpler version of the present case, ignore the effect of the S-ARRA and suppose the correct specification is

$$O_t = a_0 + a_1 R_t + \omega_t.$$

In this regression both *R* and ω exhibit high serial correlation, with respective coefficients of 1.003 and 0.731. That is, if successive values of the independent variable and the error term are related by a first-order process, we have the results

$$R_t = \rho_1 R_{t-1} + \xi_t = 1.003 \ R_{t-1} + \xi_t,$$

$$\omega_t = \rho_2 \omega_{t-1} + \varepsilon_t = 0.731 \ \omega_{t-1} + \varepsilon_t.$$

If we substitute into the equation for O_t, we have

$$\omega_t = O_t - a_0 - a_1 R_t = \rho_2 \omega_{t-1} + \varepsilon_t = \rho_2(O_{t-1} - a_0 - a_1 R_{t-1}) + \varepsilon_t.$$

Since

$$R_{t-1} = (\rho_1)^{-1} R_t - (\rho_1)^{-1} \xi_t,$$

the equation for O_t becomes

$$O_t = (1 - \rho_2)a_0 + (\rho_1 - \rho_2)(\rho_1)^{-1} a_1 R_t + \rho_2 O_{t-1} + \varepsilon_t + \rho_2(\rho_1)^{-1} a_1 \xi_t.$$

The lagged dependent variable O_{t-1} sneaks in because of the serial correlation of the error term in the original equation and—when $\rho_1 > \rho_2$ and ρ_1 is close to unity—at the same time reduces the coefficient on the true explanatory variable R_t. In the case at hand, since $\rho_1 = 1.003$ and $\rho_2 = 0.731$, the estimated coefficient of R in this last equation is $(\rho_1 - \rho_2)(\rho_1)^{-1} a_1$, which is approximately one-quarter of its true value a_1. Table 15.8 presents the relevant data. The estimates of the constant term and the coefficient of revenues in column (2) are $\hat{a}_0 = -0.006$ and $\hat{a}_1 = 1.083$, with the result that the equation we derived for O becomes

$$\hat{O}_t = -0.001 + 0.294 R_t + 0.731 \hat{O}_{t-1} + \varepsilon_t + 0.789 \xi_t.$$

Observe that these numbers are close to what is reported in column (1) as the results of estimating the same equation by ordinary least squares,

$$O_t = b_0 + b_1 R_t + b_2 O_{t-1} + v_t,$$

for which $\hat{b}_0 = -0.001$, $\hat{b}_1 = 0.224$, and $\hat{b}_2 = 0.796$. Unsurprisingly, these coefficients differ little from the coefficients reported in column (4) of Table 15.7, which includes A as an explanatory variable.

The formulas for the limiting values of the direct estimates of the coefficients in column (1) are (Achen 2001, pp. 5–6)

$$\text{plim}\, \hat{b}_1 = \left(1 - \rho_1 \rho_2 \frac{1 - R^2}{1 - \rho_1^2 R^2} \right) a_1,$$

$$\text{plim}\, \hat{b}_2 = \rho_2 \frac{1 - R^2}{1 - \rho_1^2 R^2},$$

where R^2 is from the equation reported in column (2) of Table 15.8, and is equal to 0.7275.[3] Without knowing the true value of a_1 we cannot estimate the limiting value of $\hat{b}_1$; we can only estimate this limiting value conditional on the estimate $\hat{a}_1$. On this basis we have plim $\hat{b}_1 = 0.276$. In addition, on the assumption that the true coefficient of lagged expenditure is zero, we have

Table 15.8 Regressions of Total Spending with and without Lagged Dependent Variable

	(1)	(2)	(3)	(4)
		Dependent Variable		
	O	O	R	ω
Constant	−0.001	−0.006		
	0.009	0.012		
O_{-1}	0.796			
	0.048			
R	0.224	1.083		
	0.083	0.090		
R_{-1}			1.003	
			0.005	
ω_{-1}				0.731
				0.084
Adj R^2	0.944	0.721	0.999	0.498
Frequency/	FY	FY	FY	FY
Time Period	1969–2011	1969–2011	1969–2011	1969–2011
N	43	43	43	43

Sources: Bureau of Economic Analysis; Department of Health and Human Services.

Note: Newey-West standard errors appear below coefficients.

plim $\hat{b}_2 = 0.743$, which once again is close to the direct OLS (ordinary least squares) estimate of 0.796.

Estimating the Impact of the S-ARRA by Cross-Sectional Regressions

For now—I will modify the model as we proceed—the model is

$$\Delta O = a_0 + a_1 R + a_2 O_{-1} + a_3 A + a'_1 Z_1 + \cdots + a'_n Z_n + \varepsilon,$$

$$\Delta Y = b_0 + b_1 \Delta O + b'_1 Z_1 + \cdots + b'_n Z_n + \nu,$$

$$\Delta R = c_0 + c_1 \Delta Y + c_3 A + b'_1 Z_1 + \cdots + c'_n Z_n + \eta,$$

$$A = d_0 + d'_1 Z_1 + \cdots + d'_n Z_n + \mu,$$

where $Z_1, \cdots, Z_n$ are the exogenous variables, including both instrumental variables and other control variables.[4] Table 15.9 summarizes the data.

The first question is the extent to which cross-sectional evidence duplicates the Cogan–Taylor time-series results. I start with an OLS estimation of the outlay equation with all the Zs omitted. The first column in Table 15.10 pre-

Table 15.9 Summary Statistics

	Obs	Mean	Std Dev	Min	Max
Variable					
ΔO	46	139	203	−269	921
R	46	5,475	2,036	3,490	16,023
ΔR	46	30	226	−1160	427
O_{-1}	46	5,596	1,720	3,559	14,124
$R - O_{-1}$	46	−121	517	−907	1,899
A	46	308	82	158	599
ΔY	46	239	1,315	−5,249	2,150
Control Variables					
Med2008	46	910	260	460	1,483
Roads2008	46	108	182	2	816
Mine%2010	46	3	6	0	36
NF_{-1}	46	1,986	9,451	−3,641	60,584
ΔNF_{-1}	46	−323	681	−3,735	1,719
$Rainy_{-1}$	46	371	1,838	0	12,528
$\Delta Rainy_{-1}$	46	68	703	−584	4,642
$RepGov \times A$	46	142	177	0	599
DumRepGov	46	0.435	0.501	0	1
R_{-1}	46	5,445	2,096	3,425	16,174

Control Variables

   Med2008 = State payments to vendors for Medicaid, FY-2008.

   Roads2008 = Federal aid to state and local governments for highway trust fund, FY-2008.

   Mine%2010 = Percentage of gross state product due to mining and resource extraction, FY-2010.

   NF_{-1} = Net financial assets, end FY-2009.

   ΔNF_{-1} = Change in net financial assets, end FY-2009 minus end FY-2008.

   $Rainy_{-1}$ = Rainy-Day fund, end FY-2009.

   $\Delta Rainy_{-1}$ = Change in Rainy-Day fund, end FY-2009 minus end FY-2008.

   $RepGov \times A$ = Product of *DumRepGov* and A.

   DumRepGov = Dummy variable equal to 1 if the state house was occupied by a Republican at the beginning of FY-2010, equal to 0 if occupied by a Democrat.

   Except for *Mine%2010* and *DumRepGov*, all variables are expressed per capita of population (as of April 2010).

sents the results of this regression. The OLS results suggest that S-ARRA funds had a large impact on spending: the coefficient is close to one, and the *t*-statistic exceeds two. Nothing much changes if we take account of the endogeneity of S-ARRA money by instrumenting for A (column [2]). The coefficients change very little, and the standard errors increase only marginally. At a strict 5 percent significance level, the coefficient of A no longer passes muster, but $p = 0.058$ is very close.

The first-stage equation, deploying instruments similar in spirit to those devised by Wilson (2012) and Chodorow-Reich et al. (2012), yields an *F*-

Table 15.10 The Effect of S-ARRA on the Change in State Government Outlays between FY-2009 and FY-2010

	(1) OLS	(2) 2SLS(1) A Estimated in First Stage	(3) 2SLS(2) A and R Estimated in First Stage	(4) 3SLS	(5) 3SLS with controls	(6) 3SLS with controls	(7) 3SLS with controls	(8) 3SLS with controls	(9) 3SLS with controls	(10) OLS with controls
Constant	334.100 125.100	318.402 187.838	516.692 290.886	454.976 210.723	2.854 145.421	−304.127 128.075	−283.059 123.300	−318.612 137.660	−350.366 132.371	−13.923 124.856
R	0.190 0.059	0.186 0.093	0.296 0.124	0.325 0.103	0.119 0.055	0.044 0.076				0.175 0.076
ΔR								0.015 0.191		
O_{-1}	−0.274 0.067	−0.272 0.101	−0.379 0.139	−0.404 0.104	−0.216 0.061	−0.067 0.083		−0.018 0.027		−0.194 0.083
$R - O_{-1}$							0.051 0.074			
A	**0.961** 0.411	**1.049** 0.555	**0.404** 0.695	**0.535** 0.833	**2.365** 0.657	**2.365** 0.588	**1.913** 0.432	**2.323** 0.711	**2.138** 0.467	**1.265** 0.394

Table 15.10 (continued)

	(1) OLS	(2) 2SLS(1) A Estimated in First Stage	(3) 2SLS(2) A and R Estimated in First Stage	(4) 3SLS	(5) 3SLS with controls	(6) 3SLS with controls	(7) 3SLS with controls	(8) 3SLS with controls	(9) 3SLS with controls	(10) OLS with controls
Control Variables										
NF_{-1}						0.009	0.005	0.011	0.007	0.005
						0.008	0.007	0.010	0.007	0.008
ΔNF_{-1}						0.171	0.189	0.199	0.213	0.112
						0.068	0.057	0.053	0.043	0.068
$Rainy_{-1}$						−0.215	−0.209	−0.208	−0.209	−0.168
						0.082	0.077	0.083	0.080	0.084
$\Delta Rainy_{-1}$						0.420	0.436	0.408	0.447	0.279
						0.174	0.167	0.191	0.172	0.184
RepGov × A					**−0.231**	**−0.437**	**−0.441**	**−0.449**	**−0.471**	**−0.300**
					0.149	0.135	0.133	0.137	0.132	0.143
R^2	0.373	0.372	0.3126	0.280	0.294	0.523	0.561	0.512	0.513	0.552
N	46	46	46	46	46	46	46	46	46	46

Note: Standard errors appear below coefficients.

value of 28. Like them, I looked to the three areas that constituted the bulk of S-ARRA aid to the states. I was unable to find a good instrument among the obvious candidates in education spending, but FY-2008 payments by the states to vendors of Medicaid services *(Med2008)* and federal aid for roads in FY-2008 *(Roads2008)* proved serviceable for health care and highway spending.

To capture the particularities of states that rely directly or indirectly on extraction of natural resources for tax revenues, I added a variable representing the percentage of gross state product due to resource extraction *(Mine%2010)*. This variable was one of several with which I experimented to capture the special features of these states. As Figure 15.3 shows, there is a great difference among the states in this dimension, and I thought this instrument would capture the drop in the prices and production levels of oil, natural gas, and coal as well as the differential impact of these declines on the economies of the several states.

Something else must be at work. Despite steep declines in both production and prices in the second half of calendar 2008 (the first half of FY-2009), prices fell relatively modestly fiscal year to fiscal year, 12 percent for gas and

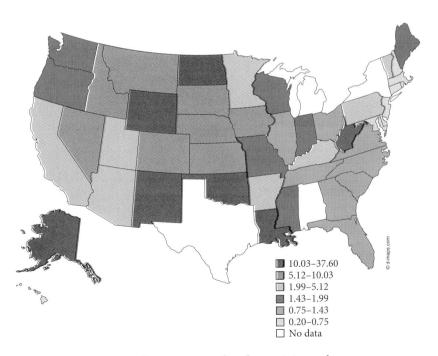

Figure 15.3 Percentage of state gross product from mining and resource extraction (2010).

8 percent for oil, while production was almost flat, as Figures 15.4(a) and 15.4(b) indicate.

Although endogenizing S-ARRA by itself has little effect, the coefficients change much more if we also treat non-ARRA revenue as endogenous (column [3] in Table 15.10). In particular, the coefficient of A falls to 0.4. In this case, the results are qualitatively similar to the time-series results, with similar coefficients on revenues and lagged expenditures. Table 15.11 compares column (4) of Table 15.7 with column (4) of Table 15.10. (The first regression is rewritten so that the dependent variable is ΔO rather than O.) The coefficient on S-ARRA funds is greater in the cross-section than in the time series, but in both cases the standard error on the coefficient of A is sufficiently high that we cannot reject the Cogan–Taylor view that the true value of the coefficient is zero. Observe that in the cross-sectional case, unlike the time-series case, serial correlation cannot be behind the high t value of the coefficient of O_{-1}.

Introducing control variables makes a big difference to the coefficient on S-ARRA funds. In column (5) of Table 15.10, the coefficient increases markedly, to 2.37, and it becomes statistically significant ($z = 3.6$). The imprecision of the estimate in column (4) appears to be at least partly the result of lumping states with Republicans in the state house with states with Democratic governors. For when we separate the two by means of a dummy variable (equal to 1 for Republican states and equal to 0 for Democratic states), we find a negative impact of Republican control on the amount of S-ARRA revenue that is translated into state government outlays and a larger and more precise estimate of the coefficient of A. The negative coefficient of $RepGov \times A$

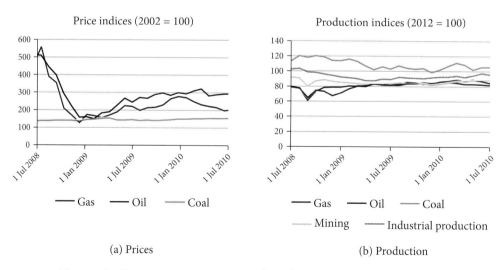

(a) Prices   (b) Production

Figure 15.4 Energy extraction: prices and production (FY-2009 and FY-2010).

Table 15.11 Comparison of Time-Series and Cross-Sectional Regressions with Expenditure Smoothing

	Time Series	Cross-Section
	Dependent Variable	
	ΔO	ΔO
Constant	−0.001	454.976
	0.010	210.723
O_{-1}	−0.212	−0.404
	0.071	0.104
R	0.233	0.325
	0.109	0.103
A	**0.049**	**0.535**
	0.168	0.833
R^2	0.2140	0.280
Frequency/ Time Period	FY 1969–2011	
Coverage		States with FY ending June 30
N	43	46

suggests that Republicans can be taken at their word: they will cut expenditures when they get the chance.

Introducing two kinds of financial controls, net financial assets and Rainy-Day funds, increases the precision of the estimate of the influence of political party and (except for column [8]) reduces the standard error of the estimate of the impact of S-ARRA funds on outlays. This combination of a large value of the coefficient and a high level of statistical significance is robust to the precise specification of the model, as columns (5) to (9) show.[5]

Apart from the Rainy-Day fund, all the coefficients have the expected sign. It turns out that the anomaly is due to Alaska, which is an extreme outlier in many respects. On a per-capita basis, its 2008 Rainy-Day fund was eighteen times the size of the Rainy-Day fund of the next highest state (Wyoming, also a natural-resource rich state). Its net financial assets per capita were more than three times the assets of the next state (also Wyoming), and its revenues and expenditures more than one and a half times the next state's (again Wyoming). If we omit Alaska, the summary data are given in Table 15.12.

The financial controls now make more sense, as Table 15.13 shows. Except for the last regression, *levels* of neither net financial assets nor the Rainy-Day fund are significant, while the *changes* in both variables have a positive sign. Since ΔNF_{-1} includes $\Delta Rainy_{-1}$, the coefficient of the change in Rainy-

Table 15.12 Summary Statistics (omitting Alaska)

	Obs	Mean	Std Dev	Min	Max
Variable					
ΔO	45	149	196	−248	921
R	45	5,241	1,287	3,490	9,658
ΔR	45	34	227	−1160	427
O_{-1}	45	5,407	1,156	3,559	8,933
$R - O_{-1}$	45	−166	422	−907	1634
A	45	302	70	158	521
ΔY	45	316	1,220	−5,249	2,150
Control Variables					
Med2008	45	898	250	460	1,483
Roads2008	45	92	149	2	691
Mine%2010	45	3	6	0	36
NF_{-1}	45	683	3,404	−3,641	18,552
ΔNF_{-1}	45	−247	451	−1,744	1,719
$Rainy_{-1}$	45	101	143	0	706
$\Delta Rainy_{-1}$	45	−33	138	−584	315
$RepGov \times A$	45	132	165	0	521
DumRepGov	45	0.422	0.499	0	1
R_{-1}	45	5,207	1,348	3,425	10,818

Day funds is approximately three times higher than the coefficient on the change in other net financial assets, that is, net financial assets excluding Rainy-Day funds. (Rewrite the control variable ΔNF_{-1} and $\Delta Rainy_{-1}$ as $[\Delta NF_{-1} - \Delta Rainy_{-1}]$ and $\Delta Rainy_{-1}$, and recalculate the two coefficients as they appear in the table, call them $a'_{\Delta NF-1}$ and $a'_{\Delta Rainy-1}$, as the coefficients a'_1 and a'_2 of $[\Delta NF_{-1} - \Delta Rainy_{-1}]$ and $\Delta Rainy_{-1}$. We have $a'_1 = a'_{\Delta NF-1}$ and $a'_2 = a'_{\Delta NF-1} + a'_{\Delta Rainy-1}$.) Roughly speaking, for every dollar that a state's Rainy-Day fund declines between FY-2008 and FY-2009, its outlays decline by $0.50, while for every dollar that non-Rainy-Day net assets decline, outlays decline by $0.15. This is not surprising unless, like Cogan and Taylor, you believe in the complete fungibility of state funds.[6]

Observe that the financial coefficients do not strongly support Friedman–Modigliani expenditure smoothing even if—given the large standard errors for the level variables—it is not rejected by the data. An agent who optimizes according to permanent-income logic bases outlays on total wealth, which is to say, on net financial assets (if we suppose the states to take revenues as given). The higher the level of net assets, the greater should be the level of outlays. $Rainy_{-1}$, by this logic, should be completely fungible with other assets, so its coefficient should be zero. By contrast, changes in net financial assets or

Table 15.13 The Effect of S-ARRA on the Change in State Government Outlays Between FY-2009 and FY-2010 (omitting Alaska)

	(1) OLS	(2) 2SLS(1) A Estimated in First Stage	(3) 2SLS(2) A and R Estimated in First Stage	(4) 3SLS	(5) 3SLS with controls	(6) 3SLS with controls	(7) 3SLS with controls	(8) 3SLS with controls	(9) 3SLS with controls	(10) OLS with controls
Constant	83.745	105.195	65.698	136.960	−95.181	−323.106	−279.347	−306.450	−326.057	−12.947
	122.833	157.736	182.005	153.691	132.463	135.740	130.859	141.565	137.643	126.792
R	0.263	0.266	0.255	0.270	0.187	0.015				0.173
	0.053	0.072	0.116	0.082	0.052	0.083				0.080
ΔR								0.058		
								0.197		
O_{-1}	−0.274	−0.300	−0.292	−0.311	−0.245	−0.065		−0.047		−0.193
	0.067	0.072	0.108	0.077	0.054	0.087		0.030		0.085
$R - O_{-1}$							0.038			
							0.083			
A	**0.990**	**0.890**	**1.077**	**0.917**	**2.006**	**2.801**	**1.855**	**2.655**	**2.004**	**1.277**
	0.350	0.628	0.753	0.647	0.544	0.661	0.451	0.722	0.485	0.413

Table 15.13 (continued)

	(1) OLS	(2) 2SLS(1) A Estimated in First Stage	(3) 2SLS(2) A and R Estimated in First Stage	(4) 3SLS	(5) 3SLS with controls	(6) 3SLS with controls	(7) 3SLS with controls	(8) 3SLS with controls	(9) 3SLS with controls	(10) OLS with controls
Control Variables										
NF_{-1}						0.008	0.006	0.010	0.005	0.005
						0.009	0.008	0.010	0.008	0.009
ΔNF_{-1}						0.156	0.202	0.162	0.221	0.111
						0.071	0.061	0.058	0.045	0.070
$Rainy_{-1}$						0.061	−0.106	0.075	−0.058	−0.135
						0.248	0.231	0.236	0.221	0.273
$\Delta Rainy_{-1}$						0.364	0.371	0.333	0.380	0.275
						0.179	0.177	0.194	0.182	0.190
RepGov* × *A					**−0.165**	**−0.463**	**−0.429**	**−0.451**	**−0.462**	**−0.303**
					0.130	0.143	0.139	0.138	0.137	0.147
R^2	0.511	0.508	0.510	0.508	0.458	0.406	0.522	0.443	0.487	0.595
N	45	45	45	45	45	45	45	45	45	45

Note: Standard errors appear below coefficients.

in Rainy-Day funds should have no impact on outlays. Since the year-on-year change between FY-2008 and FY-2009 is already included in the level at the end of FY-2009, both ΔNF_{-1} and $\Delta Rainy_{-1}$ should have zero coefficients.

For our purposes, the financial variables are not ends in themselves, but means to accurate measurement of the effects of the S-ARRA, as reflected in the coefficient of A and the coefficient of $RepGov \times A$. Evidently, omitting Alaska does not change the results qualitatively. The coefficient of A is insignificant until we add control variables. Once we add controls, the effect per dollar of S-ARRA funds in states with Democratic governors lies between $1.85 and $2.80 (omitting Alaska); in Republican states, the amount is about $0.45 less. Within these limits, the estimate depends on how revenues and lagged expenditures are supposed to affect the change in expenditures. Irrespective of the precise specification, the coefficient of A remains statistically significant, with z approximately equal to four in all cases. Of course there is a wide band on these estimates, and using a conservative lower bound fixed at two standard deviations from the point estimate would move the estimates closer to one.

I turn now to the other parts of the overall model, the impact of the S-ARRA on output and income, and its impact on tax revenues. S-ARRA revenues are supposed to affect output through the demand effect of additional state government outlays, whereas the impact on tax revenues has two potential channels, the first a direct one running from S-ARRA grants to changes in tax policy, the second via taxation of output at existing rates. Table 15.14 presents the complete model, with results for all forty-five states in columns (1), (2), and (3). Column (1) reproduces the results of column (6) in Table 15.13 and so needs no further comment. The coefficient of ΔO in the output equation (column [2]) is the multiplier. Its value of 2.6 is somewhat higher than the consensus range, but not implausibly so. Daniel Shoag, whose work I shall examine shortly, estimates the state-outlay multiplier to be greater than three in slack times (2010, table 12). In principle, the coefficient of ΔO should underestimate the multiplier since it does not take account of spillovers of demand across state lines. We shall take up the question of spillovers momentarily.

The revenue equation in Table 15.14 (column [3]) is interesting for two reasons. First, the coefficient of S-ARRA funds, though it has the expected negative sign, is insignificant, a result that is robust to alternative specifications. The implication is that there is no clear impact of S-ARRA funds on taxes. This runs counter to my intuition, which is that, without S-ARRA funding, the states would have been obliged to enact more and greater tax increases than the $24 billion actually enacted (see note 1, above). The second point of interest is the coefficient of ΔY. If we interpret causality as run-

Table 15.14 Modeling the Effect of the S-ARRA on Outlays, Gross State Product, and Revenues

	(1) 3SLS with controls	(2) 3SLS with controls	(3) 3SLS with controls	(4) 3SLS with controls; small states	(5) 3SLS with controls; small states	(6) 3SLS with controls; small states	(7) 3SLS with controls; large states	(8) 3SLS with controls; large states	(9) 3SLS with controls; large states
					Dependent Variable				
	ΔO	ΔY	ΔR	ΔO	ΔY	ΔR	ΔO	ΔY	ΔR
Constant	−323.106	266.687	119.465	−612.635	211.849	39.070	−232.762	−179.840	258.492
	135.740	169.546	118.818	179.564	217.091	174.796	165.260	225.269	167.903
R	0.015			0.032			0.181		
	0.083			0.125			0.115		
ΔR									
O_{-1}	−0.065			−0.153			−0.141		
	0.087			0.152			0.106		
$R - O_{-1}$									
A	**2.801**		**−0.394**	**4.580**		**−0.072**	**0.922**		**−0.750**
	0.661		0.393	0.826		0.543	0.484		0.624
ΔO		2.616			2.826			4.675	
		0.756			0.711			1.622	

	(1)	(2)	(3)	(4)	(5)	(6)	(7)	(8)
Mine%2010	−125.652 19.868	−7.351 5.223		−153.223 20.639	−11.025 7.330		12.376 41.619	−5.585 7.397
ΔY		0.170 0.031			0.138 0.041			0.036 0.041
Control Variables								
NF_{-1}	0.008 0.009			0.012 0.010			0.040 0.019	
ΔNF_{-1}	0.156 0.071			0.053 0.124			0.016 0.081	
$Rainy_{-1}$	0.061 0.248			0.396 0.307			0.317 0.461	
$\Delta Rainy_{-1}$	0.364 0.179			0.356 0.203			0.057 0.486	
RepGov × A	**−0.463** 0.143			**−0.469** 0.189			**−0.412** 0.143	−0.183
R^2	0.406	0.388	0.574	0.510	0.680	0.779	0.456	0.053
N	45	45	45	22	22	22	23	23

Note: Standard errors appear below coefficients.

ning from output and income to tax revenues, the coefficient of ΔY suggests an implicit tax rate of 0.17, much higher than the actual average tax rate of about 0.1.

The coefficients of *Mine%2010* in both the output equation and the revenue equation are implausibly high, suggesting that a one percentage point increase in the contribution of mining to a state's output resulted in a loss of \$126 per capita, not to mention a \$7 loss in per-capita tax revenue (though the coefficient of *Mine%2010* in the revenue equation is statistically insignificant).[7] This reinforces the suspicion that *Mine%2010* is capturing something other than mining.

In order to test the hypothesis that demand spillovers are important, I ran the regression model reported in columns (1), (2), and (3) separately on the twenty-two states with the smallest populations (excluding Alaska) and the twenty-three largest states. Figure 15.5 shows the two sets. The small states, it will be noted, have quite diverse economies, and this variation appears to be driving the results of these regressions. The results are reported in Table 15.14, columns (4), (5), and (6) for the twenty-two small states, and columns (7), (8), and (9) for the large states. My expectation was that the multiplier would be larger for the larger states because spillovers would be smaller. The point estimates support this conjecture, but the multiplier for the large states exceeds four, and is thus implausibly large. (For small states the multiplier is

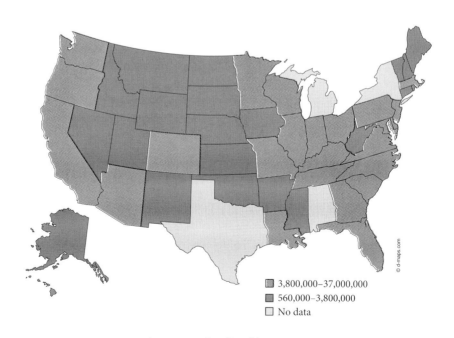

Figure 15.5 Small and large states.

less than three, still large but not implausibly so.) By the same token, the impact of one dollar of S-ARRA money on state-government outlays in the small states is estimated to be over four dollars, once again implausibly large. Interestingly, the effect of Republican governors seems to be the same in large and small states: the coefficients of *RepGov × A* differ by only 0.05 in the two samples. Finally, the differential impact of *Mine%2010* can be explained by underlying economic differences: states whose economies rely heavily on resource extraction are concentrated within the states with low populations, so that *Mine%2010* is significant in the small-state sample but not in the large-state sample.

Tables 15.15 and 15.16 present summary statistics for the two sets of states. Perhaps the most interesting information that emerges from a comparison of the two tables is the difference in the average size of S-ARRA grants: $333 per head in small states as against $272 in large states, a difference of approximately one standard deviation of the small-state distribution—not surprising, perhaps, when Wyoming, with a population of 500,000, and California, with a population north of 35 million, each has two senators.[8]

The other noteworthy difference between the two sets of states is the much greater variation in the small-state data. This is presumably why the small-state regressions produce much higher R^2 values.

Table 15.15 Summary Statistics, Small States (population < 3.8 million)

	Obs	Mean	Std Dev	Min	Max
Variable					
ΔO	22	181	248	−248	921
R	22	5,819	1,485	3,498	9,658
ΔR	22	12	303	−1160	427
O_{-1}	22	5,835	1,318	3,687	8,933
$R - O_{-1}$	22	−16	527	−907	1,634
A	22	333	70	220	521
ΔY	22	231	1,608	−5,249	2,150
Control Variables					
Med2008	22	930	280	460	1,483
Roads2008	22	172	183	34	691
Mine%2010	22	3	8	0	36
NF_{-1}	22	1,726	4,552	−3,641	18,552
ΔNF_{-1}	22	−241	610	−1,744	1,719
$Rainy_{-1}$	22	162	179	0	706
$\Delta Rainy_{-1}$	22	−51	188	−584	315
RepGov × A	22	167	181	0	521
DumRepGov	22	0.50	0.51	0	1
R_{-1}	22	5,807	1,580	3,425	10,818

Table 15.16 Summary Statistics, Large States (population > 3.8 million)

	Obs	Mean	Std Dev	Min	Max
Variable					
ΔO	23	118	125	−181	380
R	23	4,688	746	3,490	6,278
ΔR	23	56	119	−198	274
O_{-1}	23	4,997	808	3,559	6,377
$R - O_{-1}$	23	−308	218	−776	−6
A	23	272	57	158	401
ΔY	23	397	704	−1,128	1,419
Control Variables					
Med2008	23	867	219	510	1,461
Roads2008	23	16	8	2	33
Mine%2010	23	2	3	0	13
NF_{-1}	23	−314	1,127	−3,453	1,563
ΔNF_{-1}	23	−252	228	−642	243
$Rainy_{-1}$	23	41	52	0	188
$\Delta Rainy_{-1}$	23	−17	60	−133	141
$RepGov \times A$	23	99	144	0	401
DumRepGov	23	0.35	0.49	0	1
R_{-1}	23	4,632	739	3,473	6,187

One final exercise is worth reporting. In two papers, Daniel Shoag (2010, 2013) has proposed a clever way around the endogeneity problem in estimates of the multiplier associated with government spending: he uses "windfall" returns to state pension funds as an instrument for estimating purchases of goods and services by the state. Shoag argues that because state employees normally receive pensions based on some combination of years of service, average earnings, and peak pay—in 2008, 97 percent of state pension-fund assets were in so-called defined-benefit plans (Shoag 2010, p. 5)—the states rather than the pensioners are the residual claimants on pension-fund assets. As residual claimants, their current obligation to pay into their retirement fund is inversely related to the fund's performance, so that direct purchases of goods and services (education, highway maintenance) and indirect purchases (Medicaid "transfers") can be expected to vary positively with pension-fund performance.[9] Some portion of the difference in performance is explained by differences in the degree of risk a state is willing for its pension fund to take on. But controlling for asset allocation, idiosyncratic pension-fund performance (what Shoag calls windfalls) should be a reliable instrument for estimating the state-spending multiplier since it should be a good predictor of nonpension spending while being independent of differing economic conditions across the states.

Shoag finds support for this hypothesis in the data. In his earlier paper (Shoag 2010), he estimates that a dollar improvement in pension-fund performance is associated with $0.43 of increased government spending (2010, table 9) and that each dollar of additional spending increases personal income within the state by $2.12 (2010, table 12), and indeed by more than $3.00 in times of slack. This last estimate is consistent with the estimates in the cross-sectional regressions reported here. Shoag's later paper, which is limited to the postcrisis period, finds lower estimates of pension windfalls on government spending, $0.29, and of government spending on income, $1.43 (Shoag 2013, table 1).

I was unable to find an impact of pension-fund performance on state-government spending. When the controls included the change between end FY-2008 and end FY-2009 in per-capita pension-fund assets, expressed either as the per-capita change or the change as a percentage of FY-2008 assets, the coefficient of this variable had the wrong (negative) sign and was statistically insignificant. This was true independently of the particular specification of the relationship between non-ARRA revenues and lagged expenditures, on the one hand, and the change in expenditures, on the other. The FY-2009 level of pension-fund assets, either in combination with year-on-year changes or by itself, had the expected positive sign but was statistically insignificant.

— 16 —

FUNCTIONAL FINANCE AND THE
COMPOSITION OF AGGREGATE DEMAND

> A family which takes its mauve and cerise, air-conditioned, power-steered and power-braked automobile out for a tour passes through cities that are badly paved, made hideous by litter, blighted buildings, billboards, and posts for wires that should long since have been put underground . . . They picnic on exquisitely packaged food from a portable icebox by a polluted stream and go on to spend the night at a park which is a menace to public health and morals. Just before dozing off on an air mattress, beneath a nylon tent, amid the stench of decaying refuse, they may reflect vaguely on the curious unevenness of their blessings.
>
> —JOHN KENNETH GALBRAITH

> Equality of the marginal social benefits from the different directions of permissible spending is a necessary condition for the optimum use of the resources that can be employed . . .
>
> What many people find most disconcerting . . . is the complete disregard for, and even the absence of any reference to, the principle of balancing the budget.
>
> —ABBA LERNER

How large a role should the government play in the economy? Or, rather, what should be the composition of aggregate demand—how much private consumption, how much investment, how much devoted to the government purchase of goods and services? What is the right level of transfer payments? And how much of the government budget should be financed out of taxes, how much from debt?

We saw in chapter 14 that even if there are limits to how much investment is forthcoming, full employment can, in principle, be achieved without violating a commitment to sound finance, that is, while honoring the principle of a balanced budget. It is possible to do this not only over the cycle, in which surpluses in fat years balance deficits in lean ones, but, even if only in theory, at every moment of time.

We also saw that there are good reasons for rejecting this theoretical prescription in practice, including opposition to the enlargement of government that would likely take place if the commitments to full employment and sound finance were both honored at all times. Yet, it is a fact that the size of government has grown dramatically over the past century everywhere in the capitalist world. In the United States, the combined state and federal budget doubled in a single decade, total government expenditures rising from less than 10 percent of GDP just before the Great Depression to over 15 percent on the eve of World War II. Relative to the economy the combined government budget doubled again in the intervening years, reaching 33 percent of GDP in 2018. And the weight of the federal government in the mix doubled, from one-third in 1929 to two-thirds in 2018.

Growth in the size of government relative to GDP was a staple of the five decades from the 1930s through the 1970s, albeit the growth was in transfer payments rather than in the purchase of goods and services. Systemic deficit has characterized U.S. fiscal policy ever since. For a brief period, during Bill Clinton's presidency, the federal budget was in surplus, and the public debt actually came down, but otherwise the years between Ronald Reagan's tenure in the White House and 2018 saw a steady rise in the debt. Federal government debt held by the public climbed from 25 percent of GDP to 75 percent. We now have both large government and a large debt. Willy-nilly, we have embraced big government at the same time we have embraced continuing deficits.[1]

Determining the Optimal Size of Government

The size of government and continuing deficits are central to the controversy Abba Lerner raised in opposing functional finance to sound finance. The size of government purchases of goods and services and the volume of transfer payments at which Lerner's optimality condition "equality of the marginal social benefits from the different directions of permissible spending"—will only by chance be consistent with a balanced budget. And the size of the deficit will depend as well on the mix of private consumption and private investment.

The constraint posed by sound finance becomes clear if we pose the size of government as a choice problem in which the government acts as society's agent in selecting one out of all combinations of private consumption (C), private investment (I), and government purchases of goods and services (G), which I shall refer to for short as "collective goods."[2] In this exercise we ignore transfer payments (or, equivalently, consider transfers as negative taxes) even though to do so obscures the reason why government's presence in the economy has grown so large. Society is assumed to have a well-defined social-welfare function

$$W\left(\frac{C}{Y_{FE}}, \frac{I}{Y_{FE}}, \frac{G}{Y_{FE}}\right),$$

where Y_{FE} represents full-employment output, as in chapter 14 taken to be a unique level of output corresponding to a vertical LS schedule.

I do not mean to suggest that this abstraction represents the actual political process by which government budgets are determined in the United States or anywhere else. Not only does it ignore the problems of passing from individual utility to collective welfare, about which there is a vast "social-choice" literature;[3] even if these problems could be wished away, the most I can claim is that my model allows us to impute some measure of rationality to the "revealed preferences" of the U.S. government.

To represent social welfare in two-dimensional space, we shall for the moment assume that I is fixed. With $I/Y_{FE} = I_0/Y_{FE}$, the choice problem reduces to

$$\text{Max} = W\left(\frac{C}{Y_{FE}}, \frac{G}{Y_{FE}}, \frac{I_0}{Y_{FE}}\right)$$

subject to

$$\frac{C}{Y_{FE}} + \frac{G}{Y_{FE}} = 1 - \frac{I_0}{Y_{FE}}.$$

Graphically, we can represent the choice problem in Figure 16.1. The problem resembles the standard problem of a consumer maximizing her utility subject to a budget constraint, except that here the consumer is "society," and the "budget constraint" is given by full-employment output after providing for a stipulated amount of investment. The optimum configuration is $<C^*/Y_{FE}, G^*/Y_{FE}>$.

We can derive the tax rate t^* associated with the optimum from the consumption function. Ignore consumption out of wealth and assume a linear relationship between C and Y:

$$C = c(1 - t)Y,$$

with c the marginal propensity to consume out of disposable income $(1 - t)Y$. We then have

$$\frac{C^*}{Y_{FE}} = c(1 - t),$$

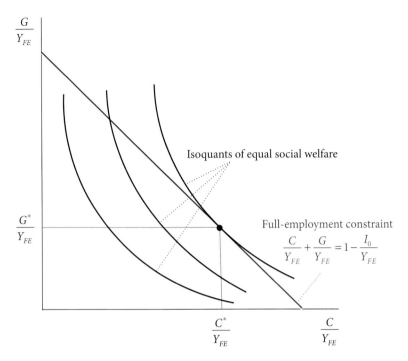

Figure 16.1 Maximization of social welfare subject to an investment constraint.

and if we solve this equation for the optimal level of the tax rate, we obtain

$$t^* = 1 - \frac{C^*}{cY_{FE}}.$$

The key point for the theory of functional finance is that only by chance will t^* be consistent with sound finance. That is, only by chance will t^* satisfy the equation $t^* = G^*/Y_{FE}$.

This is easily seen to be the case by superimposing the balanced-budget constraint, $G/Y_{FE} = t\zeta$, where $\zeta = Y/Y_{FE}$, on Figure 16.1, as in Figure 16.2. The horizontal intercept is given by setting $G/Y_{FE} = 0$, and therefore $t = 0$. Absent consumption out of wealth, output at the intercept is equal to the product of the multiplier and investment, so that

$$\zeta \equiv \frac{Y}{Y_{FE}} = \frac{1}{1-c}\frac{I_0}{Y_{FE}}.$$

We also have $C = cY$, which gives

$$c\zeta = \frac{C}{Y_{FE}} = \frac{c}{1-c}\frac{I_0}{Y_{FE}}.$$

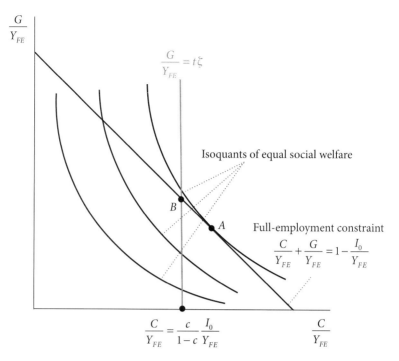

Figure 16.2 Maximization of social welfare subject to two constraints: full employment and sound finance.

As drawn in Figure 16.2, the sound-finance constraint is a vertical line. This follows from the logic of the balanced-budget multiplier: purchases of goods and services by the government add to output, but, when balanced by taxation, do not add to private consumption. (That is why the balanced-budget multiplier is one.)

Lerner's contention that sound finance should not be a constraint on fiscal policy—see the second epigraph to this chapter—is illustrated by the difference between the constrained optimum without the sound-finance constraint, point A, and the optimum with this constraint, point B: the sound-finance constraint requires society to settle for a lower level of welfare. Figure 16.3 represents the impact of sound finance by demarcating the subset of choices that are available—the shaded area of the diagram—when society commits to a balanced-budget constraint.

Balancing the budget is not all there is to the doctrine of "sound finance." Low taxes have been part of the sound-finance rhetoric since the barons of medieval England insisted that the king "should live on his own." And the low-tax party has become ever more vocal. Milton Friedman, for one, always insisted that achieving a balanced budget was less important than reducing spending and taxes:

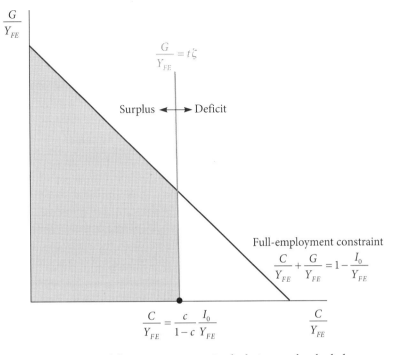

Figure 16.3 Sound finance restricts society's choices to the shaded area.

I have written repeatedly that while I would prefer that the budget be balanced, I would rather have government spend $500 billion and run a deficit of $100 billion than have it spend $800 billion with a balanced budget. (1983)

The usual justification is a supply-side argument about distortions introduced into supply schedules by high taxes, particularly disincentives to work and to invest.[4] The analytics of "starving the beast" as sound finance are in appendix 1, below.

We can also approach the choice problem by assuming that C is fixed and the full-employment trade-off is between private investment and collective goods, in other words, that the social-choice problem is to maximize

$$W\left(\frac{C_0}{Y_{FE}}, \frac{G}{Y_{FE}}, \frac{I}{Y_{FE}}\right)$$

subject to

$$\frac{I}{Y_{FE}} + \frac{G}{Y_{FE}} = 1 - \frac{C_0}{Y_{FE}}.$$

Fixing $C = C_0$ in turn fixes the tax rate at full employment, since

$$C_0 = c(1 - t)Y_{FE}$$

defines a tax rate t_1 that holds everywhere on the full-employment constraint in Figure 16.4. The policy tool controlling the mix of I and G for a given level of C is not the tax rate but the hurdle rate of interest ρ_h.[5] A higher level of ρ_h means less investment and thus more room for government expenditures. Observe that the full-employment constraint may not extend all the way down to the I-axis; there may be a nonzero minimum level of G required for full employment (for $C/Y_{FE} = C_0/Y_{FE}$) if either a liquidity trap or an inelastic investment demand is a limiting factor.

Although Figure 16.4, like Figures 16.2 and 16.3, reflects the balanced-budget constraint as a possible impediment to optimal choice, the constraint is now preventing choice to the *left* of the balanced-budget constraint. The shaded area once again reflects the choices remaining after the imposition of a balanced-budget constraint.

Finally, we can pose the choice problem as one of specifying a fixed level of government expenditure, $G/Y_{FE} = (G/Y_{FE})_0$, and optimizing among alternative feasible combinations of C and I, as in Figure 16.5. The novelty is that the

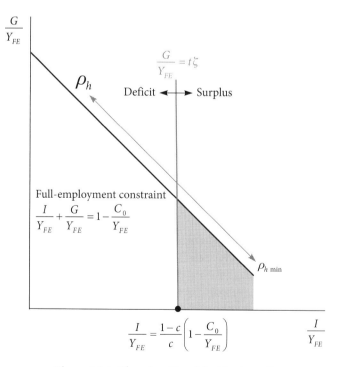

Figure 16.4 Choosing G and I with given C.

balanced-budget constraint is no longer vertical. Taking into account the change in the tax rate as Y increases, a change in investment drives output up by a multiplier of $1/(1-c)$, and each dollar of output leads to an increase of c dollars of consumption. The result is, as is shown in the mathematical appendix to this chapter,

$$\frac{dC}{dI} = \frac{c}{1-c}.$$

The relationship between the policy tools and the objectives is clear from Figure 16.5: the interest rate determines I, and the tax rate determines C.

We have in effect reformulated the determination of the optimal mix of aggregate demand as a problem of choosing two instruments, $\langle \rho_h, t \rangle$. Formally, the problem is

$$\underset{\rho_h, t}{\text{Max}} = W\left(\frac{C}{Y_{FE}}(t), \frac{G}{Y_{FE}}, \frac{I}{Y_{FE}}(\rho_h)\right)$$

subject to

$$\frac{C}{Y_{FE}} + \frac{G}{Y_{FE}} + \frac{I}{Y_{FE}} = 1.$$

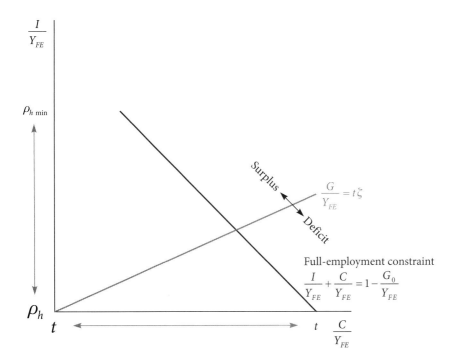

Figure 16.5 Choosing C and I with given G.

Evidently, functional finance is not about fiscal policy alone, or, rather, fiscal policy cannot be separated from monetary policy in the functional-finance framework.

In this framework we can understand a persistent deficit and a large government presence as a preference for private consumption (C) and collective goods (G), with relatively little weight on private investment (I). Opting for this mix of aggregate demand implies low taxes (to stimulate consumption) and a large government budget (to provide collective goods). Investment suffers as long as the economy's full-employment budget constraint is also satisfied.

Are Deficits Sustainable?

Functional finance requires us to address a long-standing debate about whether or not deficits are sustainable. Once we get beyond clichés,[6] two arguments for limiting deficits stand out. The first is that deficits lead to unsustainable debt.

That continuing deficits lead to growing debt is incontrovertible. That the debt is unsustainable is much more complex. The ratio of the nominal debt, D, to nominal GDP, and thus the sustainability of the debt, depends on four factors:

d = the ratio of the primary deficit to GDP (the primary deficit leaves out interest on the debt),

ρ = the nominal rate of interest on the debt (conceptually distinct from the hurdle rate ρ_h; in practice, an average of rates on debts of different maturities),

g = the rate of growth of nominal GDP,

t = taxes as a fraction of private income (GDP + ρD).

Imagine that deficits begin today, and that the primary deficit continues to be a constant proportion of GDP. Assume the rate of interest and the rate of growth are also constant over time. The mathematical appendix to this chapter shows that the ratio D/GDP converges to a finite limit provided the rate of growth of GDP is greater than the interest on the debt net of taxes. With continuous compounding of interest and growth, this limit is given by the following formula:

$$\lim \frac{D}{GDP} = d \, \frac{1}{g - (1 - t)\rho}.$$

The assumption that g exceeds $(1 - t)\rho$ is realistic for the United States over most of its history (see appendix 2, below). (The formula has to be modified if the interest on the debt is not included in personal income and taxed as such; see appendix 3.) If $(1 - t)\rho > g$, the debt ratio D/GDP becomes infinite over time.

Do Deficits Crowd Out Investment?

A second argument against functional finance is that long-term deficits crowd out investment. At full employment, there are evidently trade-offs between government expenditure, investment, and consumption, but this does not mean that deficits necessarily crowd out investment. With

$$C = c(1 - t)\left(Y + \rho\frac{D}{P} \right),$$

where P is the price level, the aggregate-demand equation

$$Y = I + G + C$$

becomes

$$Y = I + G + c(1 - t)\left(Y + \rho\frac{D}{P} \right)$$

or

$$I \quad + \quad G + \rho\frac{D}{P} - t\left(Y + \rho\frac{D}{P} \right) \quad = \quad (1 - c)(1 - t)\left(Y + \rho\frac{D}{P} \right),$$

which in words is

Investment   +   Deficit   =   Private Saving.

In the presence of government expenditure, taxation, and public debt, aggregate demand is no longer given by the equality of desired investment and saving, as in the models of chapters 3 to 10. The demand for private saving is now the sum of private investment demand and the government deficit, Investment + Deficit, whereas the supply of private saving is the saving propensity, $1 - c$, multiplied by the fraction of personal income left after the taxman has taken his bite, $1 - t$, multiplied in turn by the level of personal income, $Y + \rho(D/P)$.

If you take the right-hand side of the equation, Private Saving, as fixed, then a rise in Deficit on the left-hand side means that Investment must decline by an equal amount. Crowding out of investment is one for one.[7] In the mainstream story, however, consumption as well as investment will be crowded out if saving responds positively to changes in the hurdle rate of interest, now labeled ρ_h. Recall the picture from chapter 2, revisited in appendix 2 to chapter 3, and reproduced below as Figure 16.6. Introducing a deficit,

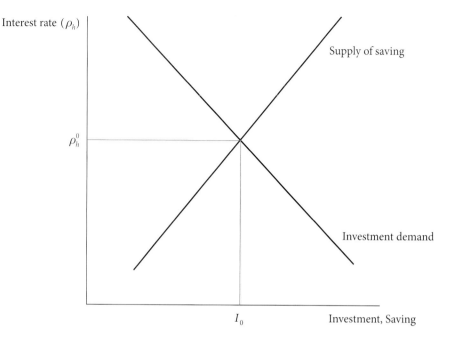

Figure 16.6 Investment demand and saving supply.

as in Figure 16.7, causes private investment to fall from I_0 to I_1, less than the amount of the deficit.

In a Keynesian approach to deficits, the economy's response will depend on the dynamics of adjustment, instead of the interest rate automatically rising to curtail investment demand to the extent necessary to accommodate the government deficit. To begin with, we will focus on fixprice adjustment and examine two different cases, the first with saving determined by the distribution of income between wages and profits, as in the Cambridge saving theory, and investment demand determined solely by the rate of interest; the second case assumes a uniform propensity to save with capital-widening investment. We then look at flexprice adjustment.

In the first case, the starting point is the serendipitous equilibrium at E in Figure 16.8. The mathematical appendix shows that this equilibrium is stable provided prices adjust more rapidly than wages. (We ignore the other equilibrium involving super-full employment because it is unstable regardless of adjustment speeds.) Assume that the government budget is in balance at E, government purchases of goods and services just equal to tax revenues.

Suppose now an increase in government purchases of goods and services or a decrease in the tax rate on profits moves the AD schedule upward, shifting the equilibrium from E to F. (For F to be stable requires not only that

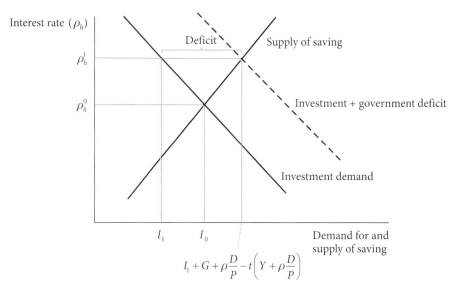

Figure 16.7 The mainstream view of crowding out.

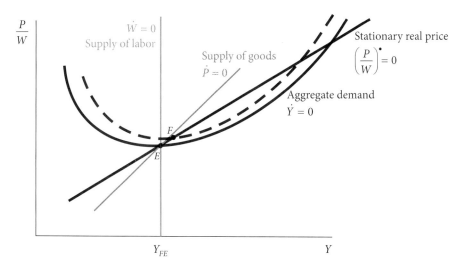

Figure 16.8 Fixprice response to an increase in G or a decrease in t with Cambridge saving.

prices adjust more rapidly than wages, as at E, but also that output adjusts more slowly than prices and wages.) The additional spending means an excess of expenditure over income, which has the immediate effect of making goods disappear from the shelves faster than they are being replenished. Under a fixprice regime, output and employment increase because of the additional

demand.[8] This expansion of output decreases profitability and private saving and so adds to the deficit. But there is an offsetting, positive, effect on
profits due to the increase in the equilibrium real price. The accompanying
redistribution of income from wages to profits more than offsets the negative impact of the increase in output. It is an increase in the rate of profit
rather than an increase in the rate of interest, and it is a reduction in consumption rather than a reduction in private investment, that accommodates
the deficit.

Instead of assuming that the distribution of income accommodates the
deficit, suppose the propensity to save is uniform across the population, and
that investment responds positively to the rate of profit, as described in chapter 10 for capital widening. Also assume that wages respond so much more
quickly than prices that the stationary real-price locus is practically vertical.
The picture is in Figure 16.9.

Once again, producers respond to the increase in expenditure by increasing
output. As output expands beyond the GS schedule, producers raise prices,
but only marginally. Workers, however, are more than able to demand higher
wages. So the real price falls. This combination of increasing output and falling real price continues until expenditure and income are in balance at H; the
real price and the profit rate continue to fall, and this in turn makes investment unattractive, with the result that output begins to contract. The adjustment process continues; depending on the relative speeds of adjustment of
wages and output, either the economy goes directly to F, as in Figure 16.9,

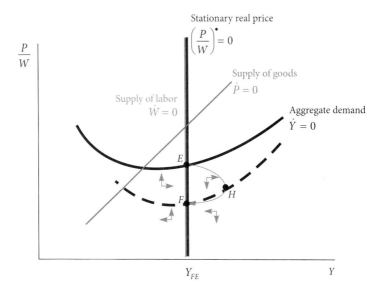

Figure 16.9 Fixprice response to an increase in G or decrease in t
with capital-widening and rapid wage adjustment, I.

or the economy approaches the new equilibrium with cycles that become smaller and smaller. The details are in the mathematical appendix.

The flexprice version of this case has a similar outcome but a different trajectory: the initial equilibrium in Figure 16.10 persists even as aggregate demand increases. In a flexprice regime, the response of producers to additional demand is to raise prices, but in the present case they do so very slowly, and workers in turn are able to nullify producers' attempts to raise real prices. Consequently, output does not change, and the new equilibrium at F coincides with the original equilibrium at E.

There is inflation and crowding out in all three deficit scenarios—at full employment increasing one component of aggregate expenditure must crowd *something* out—but there is nothing automatic about *what* gets crowded out. Investment demand is unaffected in Figure 16.8. (It may actually increase: if the nominal interest rate doesn't change, the real interest rate is reduced by the amount of inflation.) By contrast, investment falls in Figure 16.9, since the profit rate is lower at F than at E. Consumption rather than investment bears the brunt of the inflation. In the flexprice scenario in Figure 16.10, it is not clear what gets crowded out. Figures 16.9 and 16.10 both reflect the "forced saving" that Keynes relied on in the *Treatise on Money* to adjust expenditure to income, but Figure 16.10 does not answer the question of who is forced to do the saving.

Shrinking the government may also lead to a deficit that does not crowd out investment. Instead of assuming a change in government spending *or* a

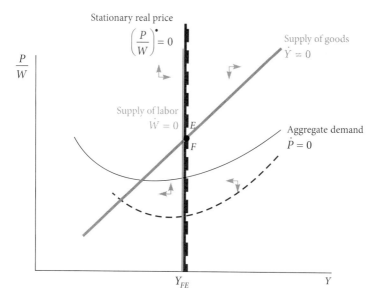

Figure 16.10 Flexprice response to an increase in G or decrease in t with capital-widening and rapid wage adjustment, I.

change in taxes, consider a decrease in government spending accompanied by a decrease in the tax rate, with the reduction in taxes tailored to generate just enough additional consumption spending to keep the economy on the full-employment frontier. In this case, the reduction in taxes must exceed the reduction in government purchases of goods and services. Paradoxically—the logic is the logic of the balanced-budget multiplier—this will increase the deficit but will not crowd out any private investment because private saving will increase by the same amount as the deficit. In the equation

$$I + G + \rho \frac{D}{P} - t\left(Y + \rho \frac{D}{P}\right) = (1 - c)(1 - t)\left(Y + \rho \frac{D}{P}\right),$$

the right-hand side is no longer fixed, and it is the accommodation of Private Saving to Deficit that prevents the crowding out of Investment. Differentiating this equation with respect to t tells what must happen to the tax rate, as well as to levels of consumption, the deficit, and private saving, for the economy to stay on the full-employment frontier when the level of government spending changes. We have

$$\frac{dt}{dG} = \frac{1}{c\left(Y + \frac{\rho D}{P}\right)},$$

$$\frac{dC}{dG} = -1,$$

$$\frac{d\text{Deficit}}{dG} = -\frac{1 - c}{c},$$

$$\frac{d\text{Private Saving}}{dG} = -\frac{1 - c}{c}.$$

The deficit increases as G falls, but this is entirely due to the decrease in taxes necessary to stimulate consumption. If taxes were not cut, the assumed decrease in government spending would depress the economy.

Rhetoric vs. Reason in Debating Fiscal Policy

In contrast with what happens at full employment, crowding out does not take place at all when the economy is operating inside the full-employment constraint. In this case, increasing the deficit may if anything crowd *in* investment demand. Moving from inside the choice set to the full-employment frontier will likely enhance the probability that new capacity will be utilized, and this will make capital widening more attractive. The mainstream logic reflected in Figures 16.6 and 16.7 is not only faulty but would be inapplicable in a stagnant economy even if it were correct for an economy operating on all cylinders.[9]

Rhetoric has more than made up for the gaps in the logic of the mainstream position. The blue-ribbon commission empanelled by the White House in the wake of the post-2008 debt explosion set the tone:

> Federal debt this high is unsustainable. It will drive up interest rates for all borrowers—businesses and individuals—and curtail economic growth by crowding out private investment. By making it more expensive for entrepreneurs and businesses to raise capital, innovate, and create jobs, rising debt could reduce per-capita GDP, each American's share of the nation's economy, by as much as 15 percent by 2035. (National Commission on Fiscal Responsibility and Reform 2010, p. 12)

The deleterious effects on investment and thus on growth became a central theme of the opposition to stimulus and deficits. Paul Ryan, then Chair of the House Budget Committee, began his alternative budget plan with a frightening picture of the future if deficits were to continue:

> The only solutions to a debt crisis would be truly painful: massive tax increases, sudden and disruptive cuts to vital programs, runaway inflation, or all three. This would create a huge hole in the economy that would be exacerbated by panic. (House of Representatives 2011, p. 21)

If the apocalypse doesn't materialize, deficits would kill the economy slowly:

> Even if high debt did not cause a crisis, however, the nation would still be in for a long and grinding period of economic decline if it stayed on its current path. A recent study completed by [Carmen] Reinhart and economist Ken Rogoff of Harvard confirms this common-sense conclusion. The study found conclusive empirical evidence that total debt exceeding 90 percent of the economy has a significant negative effect on economic growth.
>
> The study looked specifically at the United States, focusing on growth and inflation relative to past periods when this nation has experienced high debt levels. The study found that not only is average economic growth dramatically lower when gross U.S. debt exceeds 90 percent of the economy, but inflation also becomes a problem.
>
> Essentially, the study confirmed that massive debts of the kind the nation is on track to accumulate are associated with "stagflation"—a toxic mix of economic stagnation and rising inflation. (Ibid., p. 21)

If we look at the Reinhart–Rogoff study (2010), the "conclusive empirical evidence" is actually less than compelling. It is in fact not evidence at all. The key Reinhart–Rogoff chart, reproduced below as Figure 16.11, encapsulates the case that "economic growth [is] dramatically lower when gross US debt ex-

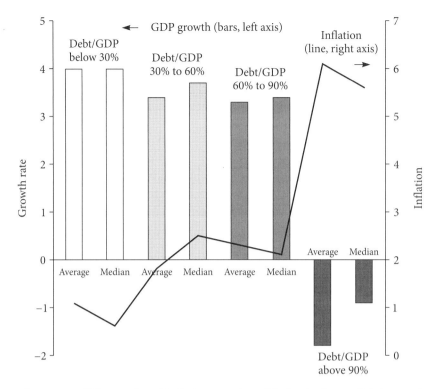

Figure 16.11 U.S. growth and inflation at various debt levels. *Source:* Reinhart and Rogoff 2010, p. 10.

ceeds 90 percent of the economy." The bars show mean and median growth rates for various ranges of the debt:GDP ratio. This ratio appears to have little effect on growth when it ranges between 0 and 0.9, especially in the range 0.3 to 0.9, where the debt ratio has spent most of the time since World War II. But once the debt:GDP ratio goes beyond 0.9, growth turns south, sharply.

Reinhart and Rogoff's data set consists of the entire historical record of U.S. debt and output, 216 observations in all. As Reinhart and Rogoff note

> The number of observations for the four debt groups are: 129 for debt/GDP below 30%; 59 for debt/GDP 30 to 60%; 23 observations for debt/GDP 60 to 90%; and 5 for debt/GDP above 90%, for a total of 216 observations. (2010, p. 10)

Look at Figure 16.12, which includes both the debt held by the public (the usual measure of the government debt) and the total debt including the portion held by the Social Security Trust Fund and the Federal Reserve. Total debt is Reinhart and Rogoff's preferred measure (though social-security debt is certainly a case of owing ourselves). The total-debt ratio is indeed in excess of 90 percent for five years (six by my count), but these constitute five or six

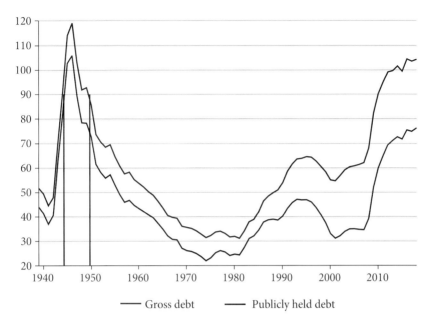

Figure 16.12 Debt as percentage of GDP (1939–2018). *Sources:* BEA, CEA, St. Louis Fed. myf.red/g/pYBJ

observations only because time is divided into years. If we divided time into days, we would have almost two thousand observations.

However many observations we reckon there are, there is only *one episode,* the last years of World War II and its immediate aftermath—1944 to 1949—bounded by the vertical lines in Figure 16.12. Real growth was low, even negative, after the war. The economy was demobilizing in 1945 and 1946, and there was a brief recession in 1949. Along with low growth, inflation was an inevitable result of financing the war with debt and utilizing price controls and rationing to balance demands and supplies of many goods. After years of privation during depression and war, people were flush with the wealth accumulated during the war, wealth on which there was little to spend. Responding to public pressure to remove price controls immediately after the end of hostilities but before conversion to peacetime production didn't help matters. Given these specifics, it is hard to see that this episode has any lessons for the consequences of peacetime deficits and debt, especially during periods of slack capacity utilization.[10]

Is There a Moral Argument Against Deficits?

There has been no shortage of argument about deficits that, Micawber-like, ignore the difference between governments and private entities. In two books,

Ben Friedman has presented a more challenging argument for reducing government deficit and debt, an argument that I applaud but ultimately reject. My applause is for Friedman's implicit endorsement of the basic premise of functional finance, namely, that the mix of aggregate demand is a matter of social choice that requires serious political deliberation:

> Citizens in a free society, and especially one as rich as ours, should have the right to choose how much of their income to devote to strictly private pursuits and how much of it to spend on public goods like defense or highways or parks or law enforcement. (1988, p. 24)

Friedman argues that there are moral reasons for choosing a high-investment aggregate demand, which means that either collective goods or private consumption has to give way. This has implications for the deficit.

The argument has two parts, made in two books separated by a decade and a half. *Day of Reckoning,* published in 1988 at the tail end of the Reagan administration, emphasizes what Friedman regards as a tacit but nonetheless morally binding intergenerational pact, one that Reagan broke by running deficits and piling up debt that shifted the composition of aggregate demand from investment to consumption:

> The radical course upon which United States economic policy was launched in the 1980s violated the basic moral principle that had bound each generation of Americans to the next since the founding of the republic: that men and women should work and eat, earn and spend, both privately and collectively, so that their children and their children's children would inherit a better world. Since 1980 we have broken with that tradition by pursuing a policy that amounts to living not just in, but for, the present. We are living well by running up our debt and selling off our assets. (p. 4)

> By now it is clear that this sense of economic well-being [enjoyed in the 1980s] was an illusion, an illusion based on borrowed time and borrowed money. Jobs are plentiful and profits are high because we are spending amply, but more than ever before what we are spending for is consumption. . . . Our after-tax incomes are rising because we are continuing to receive the usual variety of services and benefits from our government, but we are not paying the taxes to cover the cost. . . .
>
> The trouble with an economic policy that artificially boosts consumption at the expense of investment, dissipates assets, and runs up debt is simply that each of these outcomes violates the essential trust that has always linked each generation to those that follow. We have enjoyed what appears to be a higher and more stable standard of living by selling our and our children's economic birthright. (p. 5)

Our unprecedented splurge of consumption financed by borrowing has broken faith with the future. (p. 6)

Continued government spending not matched by the taxes to restrain private consumption is eroding the material basis for American society as we know it. What would America be like—what would Americans be like—without the fact, and consequently the idea, of progress? How long will it take before the rigidity, complacency, and mediocrity characteristic of economically stagnant societies set in? Which of our open and democratic institutions will survive the more fractious disputes over shares of a national product that is not increasing? (p. 10)

A policy that intentionally provides too little tax revenues to pay for the cost of government, as determined by the voters, while accumulating ever greater debt both at home and abroad amounts to willful bankruptcy: the deliberate curtailment of our economic growth for fear of how the next generation of Americans will use it. (p. 24)

We have "broken with . . . tradition," lived "an illusion based on borrowed time and borrowed money," followed "an economic policy that artificially boosts consumption," and by an "unprecedented splurge of consumption financed by borrowing . . . broken faith with the future." And it will lead, in the end, to the "rigidity, complacency, and mediocrity characteristic of economically stagnant societies," not to mention "willful bankruptcy."[11]

Friedman's *Moral Consequences of Economic Growth,* published in 2005 at the beginning of George W. Bush's second term, expands on a theme he only hints at in *Day of Reckoning:*

Periods of economic expansion in America and elsewhere, during which most citizens had reason to be optimistic, have also witnessed greater openness, tolerance, and democracy. (p. 9)

These positive externalities of growth mean that we must go beyond the calculus of private benefits and costs:

To the extent that economic growth brings not only higher private incomes but also greater openness, tolerance, and democracy—benefits that we value but that the market does not price—and to the extent that these unpriced benefits outweigh any unpriced harm that might ensue, market forces alone will systematically provide too little growth. (p. 15)

It helps to separate three major components of Friedman's argument. First, we owe future generations the same growth in material well-being that past generations (Friedman's and mine in particular) have enjoyed. Second, beyond the economic calculus, positive externalities for the social and political fabric of the nation mean that growth, and hence investment, are even more important than would be the case if we were to deliberate solely on the basis of our commitment to our progeny. Third, deficits undermine this moral commitment to the future.

Let me first address the last issue, the role of deficits. I agree with Friedman on two points. If we take full employment as a hard constraint, more of one thing must mean less of something else. More consumption—given the level of government spending—means less investment. In the model of this chapter, higher deficits brought about by lower tax rates and accompanied by higher interest rates are the only way of effectuating the substitution of consumption for investment while maintaining both full employment and the level of government spending. By the same token, if we hold consumption and the tax rate constant, more collective goods also mean less investment and a higher deficit.

But this does not imply the converse, namely, that deficits necessarily mean less investment. As we have seen, a higher deficit will also result from trading off government spending for private consumption when the tax rate (and private saving) adjusts to keep the economy at full employment. In this case, the trade-off involves no change in the level of investment. It is simply not true that "a policy that intentionally provides too little tax revenues to pay for the cost of government . . . while accumulating ever greater debt . . . amounts to . . . the deliberate curtailment of our economic growth."

My basic disagreement with Friedman is on causality, not on the facts. The 1980s did see a rise in consumption as a share of GDP, and a decline in investment, while government spending relative to GDP hardly budged. But this was not the inexorable logic of a deficit putting pressure on saving, and the rate of interest rising in response to this pressure. It was rather the result of two policy decisions, the decision to reduce taxes and the decision to maintain high real interest rates even after inflation had been tamed. With lower interest rates and a reduction in government spending—this was perhaps Reagan's plan—the government would still have incurred a deficit but a smaller one, with no impact on investment and growth.

The point is not to endorse either what actually happened in the 1980s or the alternative I am imputing to Reagan. From the point of view of functional finance, the conflation of the deficit with rates of investment and growth is the principal issue.

The moral imperative is less clear than Friedman suggests. I am sympathetic to the idea that the choice between consumption and investment is not simply a matter of taste, like the choice between vanilla and strawberry ice cream. And I accept the criticism that the framework laid out in Figures 16.1 to 16.5 elides moral issues.

And Friedman is of course correct that many of us are descended from immigrants who came to this country in part, if not entirely, for the opportunity to provide their children with better economic opportunities than existed in the old country. Our ancestors worked long hours at difficult and unpleasant jobs so that their offspring could have the opportunities that we have enjoyed. We no doubt have a moral debt to our own forefathers and foremothers, just as we owe a different debt to those who were brought here in chains and labored without any realistic hope that their children would do better.

But it is not clear to me that this adds up to a moral imperative to maintain a high rate of investment and growth. It is not at all clear what our debt to our ancestors implies about our debt to our own children, just as it is unclear what our debt to people who endured slavery and its aftermath implies about our debt to *their* children. I fully endorse Ta-Nehisi Coates's call for reparations to the descendants of slaves, defined as "the full acceptance of our collective biography and its consequences" (2014), but this is a matter of distributive justice rather than a reason for higher growth. On the count of obligation to our progeny, whether descendants of slaves, descendants of slaveholders, or neither of the above, the best I think Friedman can hope for is a Scotch verdict—unproven.

Does the verdict change when the externalities of growth are brought into the picture? I do not disagree with Friedman's assessment of American history, especially post–World War II history. The growth regime of the immediate post-war period combined a high rate of growth and a wide distribution of the fruits of growth, *and* saw the civil rights movement, second-wave feminism, and the beginnings of liberation from all kinds of gender stereotypes. Although, as Friedman acknowledges, none of these movements can be explained solely by economics, I would not disagree that economic prosperity played a role.

In the late 1970s and early 1980s this "Golden Age" came to a screeching halt. Ever since, the U.S. rate of growth has been much reduced and its benefits much more skewed toward the very rich. The slowdown of growth and the skewed distribution of its benefits fed the Bernie Sanders insurgency in the Democratic primaries of 2016 and was an element in the coalition that elected Donald Trump. Indeed the accession of Donald Trump to the White House is proof enough of Friedman's basic thesis:

> Rising intolerance and incivility and the eroding generosity and openness that have marked important aspects of American society in the recent past [Friedman wrote this in 2005!] have been, in significant part, a consequence of the stagnation of American middle-class living standards (p. 9)

Friedman is again right on the facts, and I agree with much of his analysis of how growth allows greater tolerance, openness, and civility (2005, chap. 4).

If we focus on comparing ourselves with our parents, then a growing economy can make us all winners. And when people are winning, there is much more to go around. Let growth grind to a halt, or just slow down, and we become more anxious about losing what we have. And difference becomes more threatening because it unmoors us from what we perceive, through rose-colored glasses, as a halcyon past. For Friedman these externalities clinch the argument for growth, and not incidentally the argument for capitalism as the engine of growth.

Capitalism has indeed proven itself the only economic system that has actually delivered sustained growth, and, ironically if not unsurprisingly, the failure to deliver ever-more prosperity for ordinary people has led to a call for an even heftier dose of the growth medicine. But perhaps this is the wrong takeaway. Maybe it is time to question the premise of an ever-higher standard of living as the moral basis for our economy, society, and polity. Is there no point at which we can say enough is enough?

When Will We Have Enough?

The short answer is that the more than half a billion residents of the United States, the European Union, Japan, and one or two other countries already have enough, and would have a lot left over if our wealth were distributed reasonably evenly. Given the standard of living already reached in these parts of the world, the further pursuit of consumption has real costs that outweigh the benefits that Friedman foregrounds.

The market system is unequaled as a device for ramping up production, consumption, and material wealth. Even without introducing Friedman's externalities into the reckoning, the good side of this is that enough economic growth provides the material basis for a dignified and meaningful life. With a large enough economic pie, we can meet our absolute needs—which is what Keynes (1931b) called the needs we have independent of what others consume—with very modest effort and time, freeing us from economic necessity and opening up possibilities for self-exploration and self-realization that have historically been available only to elites.[12]

But at the same time that capitalism is delivering the goods (literally as well as metaphorically), it is producing people. More specifically, markets produce precisely the attitudes, values, and beliefs that are necessary for success in the market—self-interest, a focus on the material as the measure of human value, limitless wants, an ideology of knowledge that denigrates experience in favor of algorithm (see chapter 10): we must become *homine economici* in order to succeed economically.

In short, along with "hard work, diligence, patience, discipline, and a sense of obligation" (B. Friedman 2005, p. 17), capitalism has relied on every man being for himself and leaving the hindmost to the devil. Community and spirituality, which require very different ways of relating than those cultivated by the market, are prime victims of economic growth. Market ways of thinking, being, and doing crowd out the ways of the community and the ways of the spirit.

There is another question: whether or not striving for more and more is desirable, is it feasible?

There are two threats to feasibility. A lack of *sources:* where will the world find the resources needed for the global economy to expand as it did in the twentieth century? And a problem of *sinks:* where do we throw the garbage, the waste products of growth? The most urgent problem is carbon emissions.

As part of its preparation for the Paris climate-change summit at the end of 2015, the International Energy Agency put forward a plan to augment the existing intentions of the various countries so that emissions would stay within the (relatively) safe boundary of 450 ppm CO_2 (International Energy Agency 2015). The problem is that the IEA plan relied heavily on untested technologies such as carbon capture and storage. If these technologies for decarbonization pan out, the world might escape the conflict between continued growth and a safe environment, at least as far as the climate-change boundary is concerned. If GDP growth can be decoupled from increased energy use or energy use decoupled from CO_2 emissions, we could hope to achieve emissions targets even with twentieth-century rates of economic growth.

However, the practical reality in 2020 is that decarbonization on the requisite scale would require global rates of improvement in energy systems several times faster than any historical experience. The major players—the United States, China, India, Japan, and the European Union—would have to go well beyond their declared intentions in 2015. China and the United States would have to reduce carbon intensity the most. For China almost 30 percent more than the plan its leaders presented to the Paris climate-change summit; more than 20 percent for the United States. And—most important—the optimists have to be right about the potential of technological fixes.

This was clear before the ink dried on the Paris Agreement. Hardly a year later, the United States had pulled out of the agreement altogether, and soon thereafter the Intergovernmental Panel on Climate Change had submitted a report calling global warming to be held to 1.5° Celsius (2018). Bigger technological fixes would be necessary.

Even if technology does rescue us on the climate-change front, the growth regime of the past remains problematic. Continued growth on a global scale at historical rates may sooner or later run into shortages of raw materials, or, equivalently, sharply increasing costs of raw-material extraction. Indeed, technological progress on energy efficiency and decarbonization may bring us more quickly to other ecosystem constraints.

Unlike climate change and other issues surrounding the detritus of growth, the problem of resource limitations has long been recognized; Thomas Malthus raised the first warning at the end of the eighteenth century—which brings up an enduring problem that reprises conflict about how to deal with climate change: the limits of technological fixes.

On the one side is the plain fact that the Earth is finite and so, therefore, are the resources available for expanding production and consumption. On the other side is the plain fact of technological ingenuity, which has confounded predictions of resource exhaustion since Malthus's day. Malthus took it as self-evident that under the most favorable circumstances, agricultural output could grow linearly, whereas population increases geometrically:

> Population, when unchecked, increases in a geometrical ratio. Subsistence increases only in an arithmetical ratio. A slight acquaintance with numbers will shew the immensity of the first power in comparison of the second. (1798, p. 4)

In the event, agricultural production has so outstripped population growth that the more than seven and a half billion of us in 2020 are better fed than the one billion souls alive in Malthus's own time, with a much smaller percentage of the world's labor and output. In much of the world, government policy is concerned with containing food surpluses, not in coaxing out enough to feed people.

For technological optimists, the lesson is obvious, and so are its applications: for one, the impending exhaustion of petroleum reserves is always impending, never realized. Table 16.1, produced by James Gwartney and his collaborators (n.d.) based on data from the website of the U.S. Energy Information Administration, illustrates how wild have been the miscalculations of those who ignore the prospects for technological improvement.

In 2013, the world had almost thirty times the reserves of a century ago,

Table 16.1 Estimated World Oil Reserves, Usage, and Years to Depletion at Current Usage Rates

Year of Estimate	Reserves (billion barrels)	Usage (billion barrels per year)	Years to Depletion
1920	60	6	10
1970	531	14.5	32
2000	1,000	26	38
2013	1,650	32.8	50

Source: From Gwartney, Stroup, Sobel, and Macpherson (n.d., p. 4).

having exhausted *all* the projected reserves of 1970 in the interim. Similar tables could probably be constructed for other major resources.

There is some irony in the fact that to respect the carbon boundary, it is likely that much of the existing petroleum reserves, not to mention reserves as yet undiscovered, will have to be left in the ground. But there can be little doubt that since Malthus's day the technological optimists have generally had the better of the argument.

Should the pessimists therefore concede? Can we stop worrying about resource limits? My own view is that, as Chou En-Lai is supposed to have said about whether or not the French Revolution was a good thing, "It's too early to tell." The pessimists argue that depleting resources in the hope that technology will save the day is a form of Russian roulette; just because the bullet is not in the chamber the first few times you pull the trigger, you have no guarantee that you are going to escape unscathed the next time. Indeed, if you play long enough, you are sure to lose.

We lack sufficient evidence to reject either the pessimistic or the optimistic argument. The important point is that we are in the grip of massive uncertainties—uncertainty about whether extraction technologies can evolve quickly enough to counter the increasing difficulties of access to resources, uncertainty about the true extent of reserves, uncertainty about the technologies for transforming resources into products. In fact, massive uncertainty is a common theme whether we are considering sources or we are considering sinks.

The question is what to do when you don't know and your probability assessments are shrouded in darkness. In one sense the problem is akin to the problem of determining whether or not to add capacity to manufacture a product for which the demand is highly uncertain. In this context Keynes observed (see chapter 10) that we must rely on the innate optimism of entrepreneurs, their willingness to take a chance when meaningful forecasts are nonexistent. But even the most optimistic among us might shy away from betting the planet on a technological fix or fixes that are at best in the planning stage and at worst a hope based on the assumption that technology always comes to the rescue.

Some have concluded that uncertainty is a good reason to do nothing, to wait until we know more, and then take action. This is a counsel of folly. Rather, prudence requires us to assume the worst with regard to the possibilities for sustainable growth. In countries such as the United States, this ecological argument is bolstered by the lack of any compelling need for more; quite apart from the question of feasibility, it is difficult to make an economic case for growth.

The logic of our planetary situation suggests that a new global polity may emerge in the coming decades—good or bad, beautiful or ugly. In one scenario, we will descend into a latter-day version of Hobbes's war of all against all, powerful nations fighting for access to the limited sources of materials and energy for growth and perhaps even for access to the limited sinks into which to throw out the garbage. In another scenario, we will go forward in appreciation of what unites us, building solidarity and equality, justice and compassion, quality of human life and ecological flourishing.

You would think this would be an easy choice.

Against these considerations, Ben Friedman's positive externalities constitute a weak case for growth. On the one hand, the moral obligation to provide a rising standard of living for future generations pales against the obligation to leave our children a livable planet. On the other hand, the positive externalities of growth, what Friedman offers, in the tradition of Bernard Mandeville's *Fable of the Bees* (1988 [1714]), is a consequentialist argument for an economy based on devil take the hindmost: the growth that such an economy can generate allows us to avoid confronting basic problems, for starters racism, sexism, homophobia. Mandeville, as his subtitle, *Private Vices, Publick Benefits,* indicates, discovered a moral *paradox,* not a moral argument.[13]

Ernest Gellner put it very well. In *Nations and Nationalism,* contemporary capitalism (what he calls industrial society to include the Soviet version of the modern economy) is presented as "the only society ever to live by and rely on sustained and perpetual growth" (1983, p. 22). For Gellner, growth is a means of "buying off social aggression with material enhancement" (p. 22). His characterization, "universal Danegeld," is apt. The important point is that the costs of universal Danegeld in deforming our humanity and threatening our sustainability are simply too high.

For all my disagreement with the particulars of Friedman's argument, I can still applaud his call for a national conversation on the appropriate mix of aggregate demand. Three decades on from when he wrote *Day of Reckoning,* it is high time for the reckoning.[14] And that reckoning will have to address the logic of debt sustainability in a low- or no-growth world. In the past, growth has held the debt:GDP ratio in check—see appendix 2—but in its absence the relationship between g and $(1 - t)\rho$ will not favor debt sustainability. We will have to find other means, for example, a progressively larger share of the debt ending up in the hands of central banks, or substituting collective consumption and higher taxes for private consumption, which may be desirable in its own right while at the same time keeping the debt in check.

What Happens When We Don't Owe the Debt to Ourselves?

There remains one more issue: the effect of deficits when we owe the resulting debt to foreigners. The data show clearly the increase in foreign holdings of

U.S. debt, already an issue for Ben Friedman in the 1980s—and certainly an issue for Keynes as he was contemplating the future of the British economy as World War II was winding down. As Figure 16.13 shows, as a percentage of the publicly held debt, foreign ownership rose from about 5 percent in 1970 to 20 percent at the end of the decade, declined in the 1980s as total debt was rising, only to resume its rise in the 1990s, reaching a maximum of almost 50 percent in 2014. (The foreign share of the debt has since come down modestly.)

Foreign ownership is a game changer. For Friedman the consequences cut to the heart of the role of the United States as a global power:

> World power and influence have historically accrued to creditor countries. It is not coincidental that America emerged as a world power simultaneously with our transition from a debtor nation dependent on foreign capital for our initial industrialization, to a creditor supplying investment capital to the rest of the world. But we are now a debtor again, and our future role in world affairs is in question. People simply do not regard their workers, their tenants, and their debtors in the same light as their employers, their landlords, and their creditors. Over time the respect, and even deference, that America had earned as world banker will gradually shift to the new creditor countries

Federal debt held by foreign and international investors
as a percentage of gross federal debt held by the public

Figure 16.13 Foreign held debt as percentage of publicly held debt (1970–2018). *Sources:* CEA, Treasury. myf.red/g/pYA9

that are able to supply resources where we cannot, and America's influence over nations and events will ebb. (1988, p. 13)

Contemporary deficit hawks have echoed Friedman's concerns. Again, Paul Ryan (before the leopard changed his spots in 2017):

> In the end, the debate about rising U.S. debt is not just about dollars and cents, but also about America's status as a world power and its freedom to act in its own best interests. If the nation stays on its current path, interest payments on the national debt will begin to exceed yearly defense spending just 11 years from now. In just 16 years, yearly interest expenses will be double national defense spending.
>
> If it stays on its current fiscal path, the United States will be unable to afford its role as an economic and military superpower. Other nations with very different interests will rush in to fill that role. Last year in *Foreign Affairs* magazine, financial historian Niall Ferguson surveyed some of the great empire declines throughout history and observed that "most imperial falls are associated with fiscal crises. All the . . . cases were marked by sharp imbalances between revenues and expenditures, as well as difficulties with financing public debt. Alarm bells should be ringing loudly . . . [for] the United States." (House of Representatives 2011, p. 21)

Friedman and pre-2017 Ryan may be right about the connection between foreign debt and empire, but foreigners may be forgiven for having doubts about the beneficence of U.S. dominance on the world stage.

Even some Americans have some doubts about our role as *the* economic and military superpower—I count myself among the doubters. This is not to advocate a retreat to isolationism but to argue for a more genuine multilateralism than we have contemplated since the end of World War II. Ecological constraints make a multilateral course of action all the more imperative.

In any case, whereas the problem of foreign ownership of the debt is real, its link to the *fiscal* deficit is tenuous. There is no question that it is in the power of government to decrease the trade deficit by decreasing the budget deficit—if we do not regard full employment as a binding constraint. Decreasing government purchases of goods and services, decreasing transfer payments (social security, food stamps, unemployment insurance, and the like), or increasing taxes will reduce disposable incomes, consumption spending, production, and hence imports. Unless other countries counter this move with policies designed to discourage imports from our country, our balance of payments will improve. But at what cost?

The more interesting, and one would hope, policy-relevant question is what happens when fiscal and monetary policies work in tandem to keep the economy on the full-employment frontier. In Friedman's telling, the link between the fiscal deficit and the trade deficit is a corollary of the impact of the deficit on interest rates: as interest rates rise, not only is investment crowded out but foreign funds are attracted to the United States, which drives up the exchange rate and increases imports (1988, pp. 10–11). The second part of the logic makes sense in a Keynesian perspective as well as in the mainstream view, but the first part is, as we have seen, problematic. One must embrace the mainstream view of crowding out to accept that an increase in the budget deficit automatically leads to an increase in the rate of interest.

In the Keynes–Lerner perspective of this chapter, the key point is that if the economy stays on the full-employment frontier, the composition of aggregate demand affects the trade deficit only to the extent that different components of demand entail different ratios of imports to domestic content. If consumption is more import intensive than government purchases of goods and services, then a substitution of private consumption for collective goods will increase both the budget deficit and the trade deficit. But if consumption is less import intensive, the budget deficit will increase while the trade deficit decreases.

Even if he has the causality wrong, Friedman still has an important point with regard to foreign ownership of U.S. assets: the share of foreign ownership of U.S. debt is the consequence of persistent trade deficits. This puts a very different light on the issue of foreign ownership. Evidently, if the United States runs current-account deficits, as it has done almost every year since 1970, its trading partners will end up owning more and more U.S. assets. Given this inescapable logic of accounting, the question becomes not whether foreigners will own U.S. assets but *which* assets.

I think most Americans, myself included, would agree with Friedman's preference for foreigners to own U.S. government bonds rather than the newspapers we read, the companies for which we work, or the houses in which we live (1988, pp. 12–13). But this need not lead us to share Friedman's view that original sin lies in the budget deficit. The rising share of debt owned by foreigners does not change the game for the better, but it is the least of evils in terms of how foreign-owned assets are deployed. By all means let us attack the current-account deficit, but until the attack is successful, we should be applauding a rising share of foreign ownership of the debt, not deploring it.

If it is public policy to contain the trade deficit, whether this be to preserve empire or to maintain U.S. ownership of U.S. assets, the effect is to add another consideration to the problem of choosing an optimal mix of aggregate demand. To the extent that the exchange rate responds to demands for U.S. financial assets and these demands are sensitive to the spread between U.S. and foreign interest rates, interest rates do double duty. Not only do interest rates regulate investment demand, they regulate the exchange rate, and thus the balance of payments.[15]

If we were to take a zero trade deficit as an absolute constraint, the hurdle rate would have to be set at a level that attracted just enough demand for the *stock* of U.S. financial assets for the exchange rate to balance the *flow* of exports and imports. In this scenario, the interest rate is no longer available as an instrument for determining investment demand. Respecting the zero trade-deficit constraint determines investment demand as a by-product.

Imagine, in line with Friedman's argument, a policy of trade-deficit reduction that is implemented by decreasing interest rates and the value of the dollar. The effect would be to raise investment demand and shift the full-employment constraint in $C \times G$ space inward at the same time as the sound-finance constraint is shifted outward. The picture is in Figure 16.14. As the two constraints shift, the optimum shifts from A to B.

The result is to reduce the budget deficit, but this is not the same thing as saying that the budget deficit causes the trade deficit. In this example, causality runs the other way, from a deliberate policy initiative to reduce the trade deficit to a reduction in the budget deficit. An increase in the budget deficit that results from lower government expenditure accompanied by lower taxes

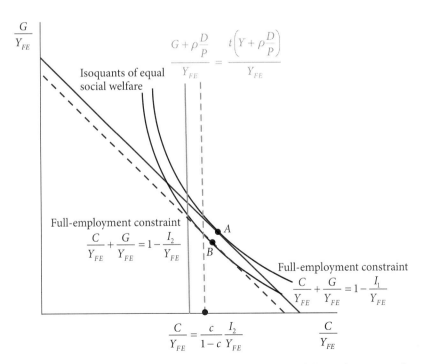

Figure 16.14 A balance-of-payments constraint shifts the full-employment and sound-finance constraints.

(rather than higher interest rates) would have no such effect. Indeed, a take-away from Figure 16.14 is that the logic of choice is unaffected. The new optimum at B still represents a mix of output that requires a budget deficit, and the trade-off between different components of the mix is unaffected.[16]

Summary

Functional finance has two components. Chapter 14 considered the problem of regulating aggregate demand countercyclically, exploring reasons why compensatory fiscal policy takes the form of adjusting the budget deficit rather than the size of the government sector. This chapter looks at the long-run issue of managing the composition of aggregate demand, in which the size of the government sector is central.

The obstacle posed by the constraint of a balanced budget is similar in the two cases. In the long run as over the business cycle, requiring a balanced budget removes a degree of freedom. In the long run, only if the stars align themselves can the economy achieve (1) an optimal combination of collective goods, private consumption, and private investment; (2) full employment of the available resources; and (3) a balanced budget. Lerner was right to argue that once the analogy between government debt and private debt is exposed as false, it is easy to see which of these three ought to give. We are left with an optimization problem of choosing instruments, the hurdle rate of interest ρ_h and the tax rate t, to maximize society's social-welfare function $W(C/Y_{FE}, G/Y_{FE}, I/Y_{FE})$, subject to the full-employment constraint $C/Y_{FE} + G/Y_{FE} + I/Y_{FE} = 1$.

Private consumption contributes to our immediate well-being. Private investment is valued for its contribution to the future availability of goods and services, for its contribution to growth. Government expenditure on collective goods is desired for its contribution both to investment and to consumption, through the provision of goods and services more effectively supplied collectively than privately, often (but not necessarily) because these goods and services are imbued with an essential characteristic of so-called public goods, namely, that your use is not rival to mine. All three—G, I, and C—provide social benefits; all three have opportunity costs. The trick is, as Lerner states in his epigraph to this chapter, to equalize the "marginal social benefits from the different directions of permissible spending."

In this framework, taxes exist not for achieving Mr. Micawber's definition of happiness but for regulating the level of private consumption. With the hurdle rate of interest regulating the level of investment, the level of government purchases of goods and services emerges as the consequence of the full-employment constraint.

Functional finance faces many challenges. First is the issue of debt sustainability. The bogeyman of insolvency turns out to be just that, a bogeyman, as long as we grant the assumption that agents consider government bonds to be part of their private wealth. The conditions for sustainability are complicated, involving the primary deficit, the rate of interest on government debt, the tax rate, and the growth rate of output. As appendix 2 shows, plausible numbers suggest a debt to GDP ratio that does not threaten the economy.

A second challenge is the mainstream contention that deficits crowd out private investment and thereby reduce growth. There is a certain truth to this charge, but not the truth based on the mainstream model, in which deficits raise the hurdle rate of interest for private investment. This model is based on the category mistake underlying Say's Law, namely, that the rate of interest is determined, à la Knut Wicksell, Ben Bernanke, and Larry Summers, by the demand for and supply of saving; whatever the limitations of the alternative of liquidity-preference theory, Keynes was on target in rejecting the Wicksellian model. At full employment, government expenditure has to crowd out something, but whether it is private investment or private consumption that gives way depends on how the instruments of taxation and monetary policy are deployed as well as on how the economy adjusts to shocks.

A third issue is the moral argument against deficits. The version offered by Ben Friedman does not appeal to false analogies between private debt and public debt, but rather to the effects of deficits on the mix of private investment and private consumption: given the level of government expenditure, the lower the tax rate, the higher is the deficit and the higher is the level of consumption relative to investment. For Friedman, high deficits threaten the basis of political and social stability in the United States, because the American Dream revolves around an increasing material standard of living, for which high rates of investment have been an essential ingredient.

Friedman raises an important question, one that Micawber-like noise has prevented us from discussing: to what extent is the American society and polity dependent on growth? Put another way, can we ever say enough is enough, and shift the focus of the American Dream to something other than ever-increasing material prosperity? This question becomes especially salient in the light of ecological constraints that humankind is wrestling with for the first time in our history. My own conclusion is that the moral imperative is for the rich nations of the world to slow down growth if not bring it to a complete stop. Depending on the mix of consumption and government spending, this may imply greater deficits as far out as the eye can see.

Finally, what happens when, as became more and more the case after 1980, we no longer owe the debt to ourselves? Even Abba Lerner, for all his commitment to functional finance, recognized that foreign debt is different from domestic debt (1944, p. 305). The impact of foreign ownership is to enlarge the scope of the social optimization problem to include trade-deficit reduction either as a goal or as a constraint. Optimization becomes more complex, but not different in kind.

And though what scares people—foreigners exercising influence if not control over domestic economic policy—turns out to be real enough, the solution of reducing the budget deficit is chimerical. It is the balance of payments that is the culprit, not the budget deficit. Indeed, as long as the United States continues to run trade deficits, foreigners will have a larger and larger claim on its assets. Holding government bonds is likely the most benign way they can deploy these claims!

Especially as we enter an era in which—whether or not by design—growth may be much less robust than in the past, we must hope that functional finance is an idea whose time has come. Both stabilizing the economy over the cycle and choosing an optimal mix of output are no more likely to be consistent with sound finance than in the past. And our margin for error may be much lower.

APPENDIX 1: SOUND FINANCE AS STARVING THE BEAST

If we add a maximum-tax constraint to Figure 16.3, that is, a constraint $t \le t_0 < t^*$, we further restrict the choice set. For any t we have

$$\zeta = \frac{\dfrac{I_0}{Y_{FE}} + \dfrac{G}{Y_{FE}}}{1 - c(1 - t)}$$

and

$$\frac{C}{Y_{FE}} = \frac{c(1 - t)\left[\dfrac{I_0}{Y_{FE}} + \dfrac{G}{Y_{FE}}\right]}{1 - c(1 - t)},$$

with the result that the slope of any tax-rate constraint as Y varies is constant

$$\frac{dG}{dC} = \frac{1 - c(1 - t)}{c(1 - t)}.$$

The horizontal intercept is inversely related to the tax rate

$$\frac{C}{Y_{FE}} = \frac{c(1 - t)\dfrac{I_0}{Y_{FE}}}{1 - c(1 - t)}.$$

The picture is in Figure 16.15. A tax-rate constraint, like a balanced-budget constraint, cuts down the feasible choice set, limiting the available options to the shaded area.

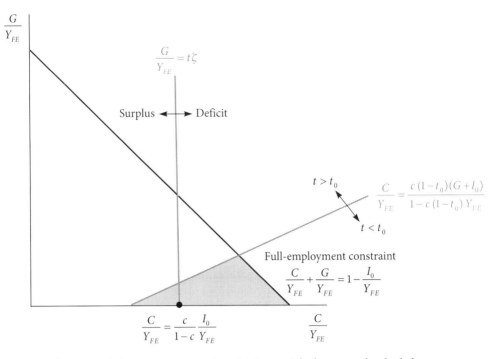

Figure 16.15 A maximum tax rate restricts society's choices to the shaded area.

The problem of achieving an optimal government budget is compounded by the simultaneous imposition of a balanced budget and a maximum tax rate. Under these circumstances, there may be *no* way even to reach full employment, much less a way to reach the unconstrained optimum. In the present case, the choice set that satisfies the balanced-budget constraint and the tax-rate constraint is limited to the shaded area in Figure 16.16; in this setting, full employment is a distant dream.

APPENDIX 2: THE EMPIRICS OF DEBT SUSTAINABILITY

The postwar period begins with a very high debt to GDP ratio, as Figure 16.12 shows. The ratio comes down gradually under Republicans and Democrats alike and reaches a low in the 1970s. Under Presidents Reagan and George H. W. Bush, the debt climbs again, but the 1980s trend is reversed under Bill Clinton. The presidency of George W. Bush saw a modest rise in the debt:GDP ratio until the black days of 2008, when the debt begins to rise sharply. This upward trajectory continued until 2011, with Barack Obama overseeing the sharpest rate of increase since the Great Depression and World War II. The debt:GDP ratio leveled out during Obama's second term.

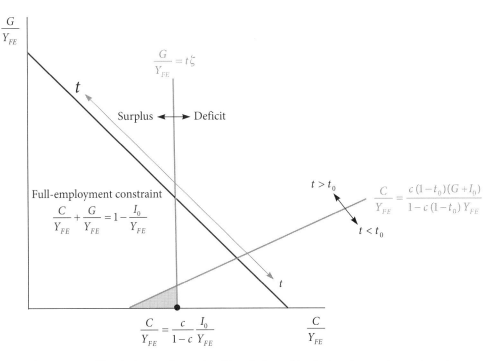

Figure 16.16 The choice set determined by a balanced budget and a maximum tax rate.

Inflation coupled with low interest rates whittled away at the debt in the second half of the 1940s—the high growth rates of nominal GDP in that period largely reflected rising prices rather than more output. Real output growth and low primary deficits (even some surpluses!) were the reasons the debt:GDP ratio declined from the 1950s to the 1970s. Higher interest rates and slower growth reversed the trend in the 1980s, but as interest rates came down and the primary surplus increased in the 1990s, the debt:GDP ratio once again fell. In the early years of the new century, higher inflation made up for some of the fall in the primary surplus, so the debt:GDP ratio remained relatively stable. In 2008 it all came apart. Despite the lowest rates of interest since the Great Depression, deficit, low growth, stable prices all combined to drive the debt:GDP ratio to levels not seen since the 1940s. Since then the only thing that changed is that the deficit declined markedly and the rate of growth of the debt:GDP ratio moderated. The ebb and flow of the various elements that determine the size of the debt relative to GDP are indicated in Figure 16.17.

Without claiming any powers of prediction, we can use the values of the relevant variables in Table 16.2 to see what might be in store for the U.S. economy with regard to the public debt. Table 16.2 provides values for the

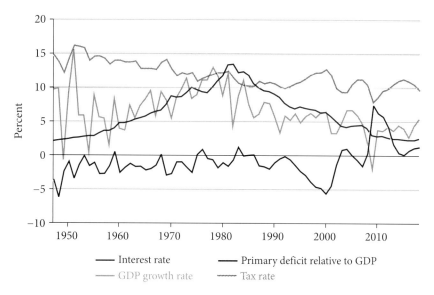

Figure 16.17 Determinants of debt sustainability (1947–2018). *Sources:* BEA, CEA, OMB. myf.red/g/pYzk

relevant variables and the limiting values for the debt:GDP and the debt-service:GDP ratios, if the data for any one year were reproduced from that year on, using the formulas

$$\lim \frac{D}{PY} = d \frac{1}{g - (1 - t)\rho}$$

and

$$\lim \rho \frac{D}{PY} = \rho d \frac{1}{g - (1 - t)\rho}.$$

(The formulas do not hold for 2009, when the economy contracted with the result that $(1 - t)\rho$ exceeded g.)

These figures do not—*pace* Professor Rogoff—suggest that debt unsustainability is a reason for Americans to stay awake at night—at least not as long as the numbers in Table 16.2 hold up. To be sure, the numbers for the first years of the Obama administration would have been reasonable cause for alarm *if* there were grounds to believe that the Great Recession and the American Recovery and Reinvestment Act would continue indefinitely: a debt to GDP ratio of eight or nine, as in the next-to-last column of Table 16.2, and debt service in excess of 25 percent of GDP (in the last column) is likely unsustainable. But even though growth remained anemic throughout the Obama years, the numbers in Table 16.2 for the period following 2011 are quite reassuring

Table 16.2 Limiting Values of Debt and Debt Service

	Ratio of Tax Revenues to GDP t	Ratio of Interest Payments to Debt ρ	Primary Deficit d	Growth Rate of Nominal GDP g	Limiting Ratio of Publicly Held Federal Debt to GDP D/PY	Limiting Ratio of Debt Service to GDP $\rho D/PY$
2009	0.078	0.035	0.078	−0.018	∞	∞
2010	0.085	0.032	0.075	0.038	9.039	0.290
2011	0.095	0.032	0.062	0.037	8.418	0.273
2012	0.097	0.029	0.047	0.042	2.959	0.086
2013	0.104	0.027	0.017	0.036	1.352	0.036
2014	0.108	0.027	0.012	0.044	0.608	0.016
2015	0.111	0.026	0.009	0.040	0.499	0.013
2016	0.108	0.025	0.014	0.027	3.204	0.081
2017	0.103	0.025	0.003	0.043	0.147	0.004
2018	0.095	0.026	0.026	0.054	0.829	0.022

Data source: Bureau of Economic Analysis (various dates). The primary deficit is measured by the difference between the total deficit and total interest payments.

(except perhaps for 2016, when economic growth ground to a halt). Even the 2018 spike in the deficit caused by the 2017 tax cut did not signal a huge problem with the debt, because growth picked up dramatically in 2018.

By comparison, in the Reagan era debt unsustainability was a serious issue: from 1982 until 1986 interest rates exceeded the growth rate of GDP, a reversal of the normal relationship that previously had happened only in times of recession and then only briefly. Only in the mid-1990s did the combination of steady growth, lower interest rates, a smaller deficit—leaving out debt service, the budget was in surplus from 1995 to the end of the century—reverse the growth of the debt. No wonder Ben Friedman (and many others) were concerned about the rising debt. But the problem was high interest rates, not the deficit.

APPENDIX 3: ARE GOVERNMENT BONDS PRIVATE WEALTH?
AND WHAT DIFFERENCE DOES IT MAKE FOR THE
SUSTAINABILITY OF THE DEBT?

If the government debt is not equal to zero, the condition for equality between real government expenditures and tax revenues—the balanced-budget constraint—is

$$\frac{G + \rho\dfrac{D}{P}}{Y_{FE}} = \frac{t\left(Y + \rho\dfrac{D}{P}\right)}{Y_{FE}},$$

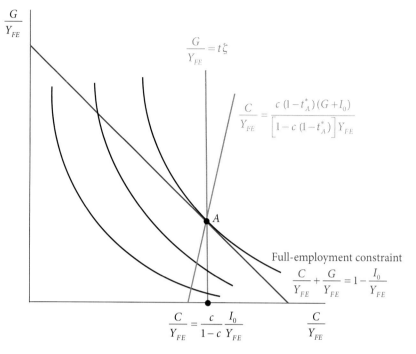

Figure 16.18 Serendipitous maximization of social welfare subject to full employment and sound finance.

where P is the price of goods. The question remains as to how private agents view their interest income $\rho(D/P)$ and their bond holdings D/P. In this appendix I address this question by exploring what happens when a serendipitous equilibrium, point A in Figure 16.18, is disturbed.

At A, the tax rate $t = t_A^*$, which characterizes the optimum $A = <C_A^*, G_A^*>$ given by the solution to the equation

$$\frac{C_A^*}{Y_{FE}} = \frac{c(1-t)\left(G_A^* + I_0\right)}{\left[1 - c(1-t)\right]Y_{FE}} = c(1-t).$$

Suppose there is a shock to confidence that reduces maximum investment demand I_1 below the initial level I_0. With $I_1/Y_{FE} < I_0/Y_{FE}$, the economy can continue to provide full employment only if consumption and government purchases of goods and services take up the slack.

The sound-finance constraint and the full-employment constraint adjust as in Figure 16.19. The dashed lines represent the new normal of an economy relying on increased level of government expenditure and private consumption to avoid long-term demand stagnation: as the full-employment constraint moves outward, the amount of income the economy can generate

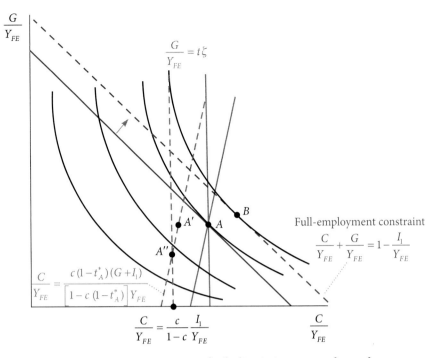

Figure 16.19 Consequences of a decline in investment demand.

without government expenditures and without taxation—the intercept of the sound-finance constraint—shifts inward, as does the constraint reflecting the tax rate at A. All this happens with the public debt still at zero.

What happens to the deficit and the debt depends on what fiscal policy the government follows (on the assumption that monetary policy has been deployed to its limits). If government adheres to the existing fiscal policy, which is to say the combination of G_A^* and the tax rate t_A^*, the equilibrium will shift from A to A'. This implies a reduction in C/Y_{FE}, but automatic stabilization limits the economic damage: A' is associated with a higher level of income and output—a higher level of government spending as well as a higher level of consumption—than A'', which maintains the tax rate t_A^* while continuing to enforce the sound-finance constraint.[17] At A', in contrast with A'', deficits will become the order of the day, and the debt will rise.

A' is superior to A'', but A' also shows the limits of automatic stabilization. The new optimum is at B, which is to say that in order to counter the shock to investment demand, government spending needs to be raised and/or the tax rate needs to be reduced.

What happens to the debt at $B = <C_B^*, G_B^*>$? Lerner's answer is that the debt itself will generate income to bondholders and taxes to the government's coffers, and in time this will solve the debt problem. If bonds form part of private wealth,[18] and private income in turn is the sum of output Y and the real value of the interest income on the public debt $\rho(D/P)$, then consumption is

$$C = c(1-t)\left(Y + \rho\frac{D}{P}\right),$$

and output is given by

$$Y = C + I + G = \frac{G + I + c(1-t)\rho\dfrac{D}{P}}{1 - c(1-t)},$$

so that for a given tax rate and given investment we have

$$\frac{C}{Y_{FE}} = \frac{c(1-t)\left(G + I_1 + \rho\dfrac{D}{P}\right)}{[1 - c(1-t)]Y_{FE}}.$$

The picture is in Figure 16.20. The sound-finance schedule continues to be vertical because the balanced-budget multiplier still holds. It is also independent of D/P. Along the sound-finance constraint

$$\frac{G + \rho\dfrac{D}{P}}{Y_{FE}} = t\frac{\left(Y + \rho\dfrac{D}{P}\right)}{Y_{FE}},$$

and consequently

$$Y = \frac{I_1}{(1-c)(1-t)} - \rho\frac{D}{P},$$

$$C = \frac{c}{1-c}I_1.$$

That is, changing the debt (like changing government purchases of goods and services) does not change consumption on the sound-finance constraint because the tax rate changes to offset any change in the debt.

Holding the tax rate constant at t_B^*, the consumption schedule moves to the right with the level of debt because, as the debt increases, private income and consumption go up; given the full-employment constraint, this means lower government spending. As the $t = t_B^*$ schedule moves to the right, t_B^* becomes progressively less optimal since the optimal consumption schedule must go through B. But for any given level of debt, achieving the optimal point B means a steeper consumption schedule—the solid line in Figure 16.20— therefore a tax rate t_B^{**} higher than t_B^*. Since G_B doesn't change, a higher tax rate means that the primary deficit declines over time.[19]

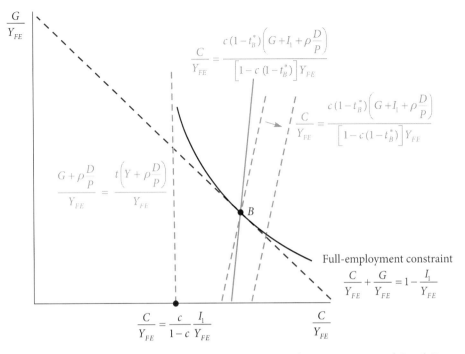

Figure 16.20 The evolution of the tax rate to maintain the optimum mix of C and G.

Lerner went further than asserting that the primary deficit would decline over time. In a 1943 article laying out the essence of functional finance, he argued that the process would end with a balanced budget:

As the national debt increases it acts as a self-equilibrating force, gradually diminishing the further need for its growth and finally reaching an equilibrium level where its tendency to grow comes completely to an end. The greater the national debt the greater is the quantity of private wealth. The reason for this is simply that for every dollar of debt owed by the government there is a private creditor who owns the government obligations (possibly through a corporation in which he has shares), and who regards these obligations as part of his private fortune. The greater the private fortunes the less is the incentive to add to them by saving out of current income. As current saving is thus discouraged by the great accumulation of past savings, spending out of current income increases (since spending is the only alternative to saving income). This increase in private spending makes it less necessary for the government to undertake deficit financing to keep total spending at the level which provides full employment. When the government debt has become so great that private spending is enough to provide the total spending needed for full employment, there is no need for any deficit financing by the government, the budget is balanced and the national debt automatically stops growing. (p. 49)

The idea of a self-correcting deficit requires that the propensity to consume rises with wealth because, in Lerner's words, there is "less . . . incentive to add to [wealth] by saving out of current income." This assumption runs counter to the usual hypothesis: as people become richer, the propensity to consume falls. So a rising propensity to consume is—to say the least—a strong assumption. Perhaps for this reason Lerner abandoned the whole line of argument in later expositions of functional finance.[20] It is a pity, since even without the controversial assumption of a rising propensity to consume (maybe *especially* without this assumption), the argument might have helped to cement the case for functional finance: in a growing economy, government debt may be part of the solution to the problem of inadequate aggregate demand.

Truth to tell, even if Lerner had assumed a constant propensity to consume, this line of thinking would have had rough going once the rational-expectations revolution had become the new orthodoxy. A corollary of rational consumer behavior, as it came to be understood in the post–World War II period (see chapter 9) was the polar opposite of the Lernerian argument that government debt is private wealth: so-called Ricardian equivalence, an argument identified with Robert Barro (1974, 1989), holds that the rational agent will understand that debt service (and principal payments for bonds with finite maturities) will require higher taxes in the future. This taxation will offset the nominal returns from holding debt. The upshot is that today's propensity to consume will adjust so that the effect of deficit-financed expenditure on demand is exactly the same as the effect of balanced-budget expenditure.

The logic of Ricardian equivalence is most clearly seen in the event that the government borrows to ransom King Richard from his Austrian captors. (In Ricardo's case it was to finance the Napoleonic Wars.) Let the ransom be £1 million and assume for simplicity that the Austrians are content to keep the £1 million in the bank—a simpler example for present purposes than a war because of the lack of repercussions of the additional spending, which allows us to focus on alternative financing arrangements. Barro's argument is that levying a tax of £1 million today has the same effect on aggregate demand as floating a consol in this amount and levying taxes every year to pay interest on the bonds. The bonds would carry a coupon of 5 percent, and would thus require a perpetual levy of £50,000 per year to pay the coupon.

According to Ricardian equivalence, agents would recognize the negative impact of debt service and understand that their real wealth today had been reduced by £1 million, so the effect of the two options would be identical. This position is easy to understand if the annual tax for debt service were applied only to the holders of the new bonds, but then of course nobody would buy the bonds: the tax would reduce the net return to zero, which would make the bonds worthless! But in Barro's world the effect on private wealth is the same if the additional taxes are spread over all forms of income. Even workers with no holdings of bonds or any other financial assets would take a hit to their wealth as defined by the life-cycle or permanent-income hypotheses—for these agents wealth is the present value of their future earnings net of taxes— and would act accordingly.

Whatever the merit of Barro's argument in the context of agents possessed of perfect foresight who optimize over an infinite future, there are many problems in applying his ideas to a world in which agents are finite in so many respects. One is the fundamental issue of knowledge and belief: do agents recognize the putative equivalence of taxation and borrowing? Ricardo himself had doubts on this score, which led at least one commentator to suggest that Ricardian equivalence should actually be called Ricardian nonequivalence:

> But the people who pay the taxes never so estimate them, and therefore do not manage their private affairs accordingly. We are too apt to think, that the war [with Napoleon] is burdensome only in proportion to what we are at the moment called to pay for it in taxes, without reflecting on the probable duration of such taxes. It would be difficult to convince a man possessed of 20,000 pounds, or any other sum, that a perpetual payment of 50 pounds per annum was equally burdensome with a single tax of 1000 pounds. (Ricardo 1810; cited in O'Driscoll 1976, p. 208)

If agents treat the income from government bonds as an addition to the income generated by the production of goods and services, there can of course be no equivalence between deficit financing and taxation.

Observe that the assumptions about information and information processing go beyond those that underlie the life-cycle and permanent-income hypotheses, namely, that consumption is based on wealth rather than on income. We can assume that agents base their consumption decisions on wealth without committing to the hyper-rationality of Ricardian equivalence; indeed, the idea of consumption smoothing, the essence of the shift from income to wealth as the driver of consumption, is perfectly consistent with the argument of functional finance. Debt service, ρD, represents the permanent-income proxy for bond wealth in the consumption function deployed in Figures 16.19 and 16.20.

The key difference between my version of Lerner and Barro's version of Ricardo is in the treatment of the propensity to consume out of disposable income and the treatment of the tax rate. For Barro, the propensity to consume is a choice variable rather than a behavioral parameter, and the tax rate does not affect the optimal consumption pattern. For Lerner, and in my models, the propensity to consume constrains tax-policy choices, and optimization dictates both government expenditures and tax revenues, with no presumption that the two will match—indeed, quite the contrary. This is transparently simple in the choice models in which investment is assumed to be fixed: the policy choice of an optimal level of consumption C^* together with the given propensity to consume c dictates the tax rate from the equation $C = c(1 - t)(Y + \rho(D/P))$, and the optimal level of government expenditure G^* determines the deficit or surplus from $G^* + \rho(D/P) - t(Y + \rho(D/P))$.

For all its abstract appeal—Ricardo was but the first of a long line of eminent economists who appreciated the intellectual attractiveness, indeed, beauty, of equivalence between taxation and debt finance—this idea is in the end a snare of abstract rationality against which, as I note in the Acknowledgments, Keynes warned us in the preface to *The General Theory*.

Sound Finance with G/Y_{FE} Fixed

To derive the slope of the sound-finance constraint, we calculate dC/dI, taking into account the relationship between the tax rate and the level of output. We have aggregate demand

$$Y = C + I + G$$

and the sound-finance constraint

$$G = tY.$$

We also have the consumption function

$$C = c(1 - t)Y.$$

Because G is fixed, t has to change inversely with Y,

$$0 = t + \frac{dt}{dY}Y,$$

so

$$\frac{dt}{dY} = -\frac{t}{Y}.$$

The slope of the sound-finance constraint is

$$\frac{dC}{dI} = \frac{dC}{dY}\frac{dY}{dI}.$$

Substituting for C and G in the aggregate-demand equation gives

$$Y = \frac{I}{(1 - t)(1 - c)}$$

and

$$\frac{dY}{dI} = \frac{1}{(1 - t)(1 - c)} - \frac{(1 - c)\dfrac{dt}{dY}\dfrac{dY}{dI}I}{[(1 - t)(1 - c)]^2},$$

so that substituting $-t/Y$ for dt/dY and solving for dY/dI we obtain

$$\frac{dY}{dI} = \frac{1}{1-c}.$$

From the consumption function we have

$$\frac{dC}{dt} = -cY,$$

$$\frac{dC}{dY} = c(1-t) - \frac{dC}{dt}\frac{dt}{dY} = c(1-t) - cY\left(-\frac{t}{Y}\right) = c.$$

The result is

$$\frac{dC}{dI} = \frac{dC}{dY}\frac{dY}{dI} = \frac{c}{1-c}.$$

The Debt:GDP Ratio Over Time

In continuous time the equation for the rate of change of the debt is the difference between total expenditures, the sum of debt service and spending on goods and services, $\rho D + PG$, and current receipts, $t(PY + \rho D)$

$$\dot{D} = \rho D + PG - t(PY + \rho D) = (1-t)\rho D + dPY.$$

The parameters $d = (PG - tPY)/PY, \rho, t$, and g are assumed to be constant over time. The rate of change of the debt ratio $\gamma = D/PY$ is

$$\dot{\gamma} = \left(\frac{D}{PY}\right)^{\bullet} = \left(\frac{\dot{D}}{D} - \frac{(PY)^{\bullet}}{PY}\right)\frac{D}{PY} = \left(\frac{\dot{D}}{D} - \frac{\dot{P}}{P} - \frac{\dot{Y}}{Y}\right)\frac{D}{PY} = \left[(1-t)\rho - g\right]\gamma + d.$$

For any time τ, the solution to this differential equation is

$$\frac{D}{PY} = \left(1 - e^{[(1-t)\rho-g]\tau}\right)\frac{d}{g - (1-\tau)\rho} + e^{[(1-t)\rho-g]\tau}\left(\frac{D}{PY}\right)_0,$$

where $(D/PY)_0$ is the initial debt ratio. It is clear that the ratio D/PY becomes infinite if $(1-t)\rho > g$, and converges to $d/[g - (1-t)\rho]$ if $(1-t)\rho < g$. Observe that the limiting debt ratio is independent of the initial debt level.

Crowding Out

The model underlying Figure 16.8, adapted from chapter 9, is

$$\frac{\left(\dfrac{P}{W}\right)^{\textstyle\cdot}}{\dfrac{P}{W}} = -\theta_1\left[GS\left(\frac{P}{W}\right) - Y\right] - \theta_3\left[Y - LS\left(\frac{P}{W}\right)\right],$$

$$\dot{Y} = \theta_2\left[I(\rho_h) + G - \left(s_\pi(1-t) + t\right)\left(Y - \left(\frac{P}{W}\right)^{-1}L\right)\right],$$

with the deficit assumed to be equal to zero. The Jacobian is

$$J = \begin{bmatrix} -\theta_1 GS' + \theta_3 LS' & \theta_1 - \theta_3 \\[2ex] -\theta_2\left(s_\pi(1-t) + t\right)\left(\dfrac{P}{W}\right)^{-2}L & -\theta_2\left(s_\pi(1-t) + t\right)\left(1 - \dfrac{\left(\dfrac{P}{W}\right)^{-1}}{F_L}\right) \end{bmatrix}.$$

At E in Figure 16.8, $1 - (P/W)^{-1}/F_L = 0$, so $tr\ J$ is unambiguously negative. Provided $\theta_1 > \theta_3$, as in Figure 16.8, we have $det\ J > 0$, so that this equilibrium is stable.

To the right of the intersection of the AD and GS schedules, the sign of $tr\ J$ depends on the speed of adjustment of prices and wages relative to the speed of adjustment of output. If θ_1 and θ_3 are large compared to θ_2, then $tr\ J$ will be negative despite the fact that $1 - (P/W)^{-1}/F_L$ is negative. With $\theta_1 > \theta_3$, $det\ J$ is positive if and only if the slope of the stationary-price locus (relative to the Y-axis) exceeds the slope of the AD schedule, which is to say,

$$\frac{\theta_1 - \theta_3}{\theta_1 GS' - \theta_3 LS'} > -\frac{\left(1 - \dfrac{\left(\dfrac{P}{W}\right)^{-1}}{F_L}\right)}{\left(\dfrac{P}{W}\right)^{-2}L}.$$

Crowding Out with a Uniform Saving Propensity and Capital-Widening Investment

From chapter 10, the fixprice case is characterized by

$$\frac{\left(\dfrac{P}{W}\right)^{\cdot}}{\dfrac{P}{W}} = -\theta_1\left[GS\left(\frac{P}{W}\right) - Y\right] - \theta_3\left[Y - LS\left(\frac{P}{W}\right)\right],$$

$$\dot{Y} = \theta_2\left\{\psi\left[\Omega(Y)\left(Y - \left(\frac{P}{W}\right)^{-1}L\right)K^{-1} - \rho_h\right] + G - (s(1-t) + t)Y\right\},$$

$$J = \begin{bmatrix} -\theta_1 GS' + \theta_3 LS' & \theta_1 - \theta_3 \\[2em] \theta_2\psi'\Omega\left(\dfrac{P}{W}\right)^{-2}\dfrac{L}{K} & \theta_2\left\{\begin{array}{l}\psi'\Omega\left(1 - \dfrac{\left(\dfrac{P}{W}\right)^{-1}}{F_L}\right)K^{-1} \\[1em] + \psi'\Omega'\left[\dfrac{Y}{K} - \left(\dfrac{P}{W}\right)^{-1}\dfrac{L}{K}\right] - (s(1-t)+t)\end{array}\right\} \end{bmatrix}.$$

The combination of a vertical LS schedule and the limiting assumption $\theta_1 = \varepsilon \approx 0$ means that the Jacobian takes the form

$$J = \begin{bmatrix} -\varepsilon\,GS' & \varepsilon - \theta_3 \\[2em] \theta_2\psi'\Omega\left(\dfrac{P}{W}\right)^{-2}\dfrac{L}{K} & \theta_2\left\{\begin{array}{l}\psi'\Omega\left(1 - \dfrac{\left(\dfrac{P}{W}\right)^{-1}}{F_L}\right)K^{-1} \\[1em] + \psi'\Omega'\left[\dfrac{Y}{K} - \left(\dfrac{P}{W}\right)^{-1}\dfrac{L}{K}\right] - (s(1-t)+t)\end{array}\right\} \end{bmatrix},$$

so that both the trace condition and the determinant condition are satisfied at E and F.

Whether the result is the trajectory in Figure 16.9, in which F is a node, or the configuration in Figure 16.10, in which F is a focus, depends on the sign of the discriminant. Ignoring terms in ε

$$\Delta = \left(\theta_2 \left\{ \psi'\Omega \left(1 - \frac{\left(\dfrac{P}{W}\right)^{-1}}{F_L} \right) K^{-1} + \psi'\Omega' \left[\frac{Y}{K} - \left(\frac{P}{W}\right)^{-1} \frac{L}{K} \right] - (s(1-t)+t) \right\} \right)^2$$

$$- 4\theta_3 \theta_2 \psi'\Omega \left(\frac{P}{W}\right)^{-2} \frac{L}{K}.$$

If $\Delta > 0$, which will be the case if θ_3 is small, then F will be a node, as in Figure 16.9. If $\Delta < 0$, which is to say θ_3 is large, then F will be a focus, as in Figure 16.21.

Flexprice adjustment is governed by

$$\frac{\left(\dfrac{P}{W}\right)^{\textstyle\cdot}}{\dfrac{P}{W}} = \theta_1 \left[\psi \left(\Omega(Y) \left(Y - \left(\frac{P}{W}\right)^{-1} L \right) K^{-1} - \rho \right) + G - \left[(s(1-t)+t) \right] Y \right]$$

$$- \theta_3 \left[Y - LS\left(\frac{P}{W}\right) \right],$$

$$\dot{Y} = \theta_2 \left(\frac{P}{W} - F_L^{-1} \right).$$

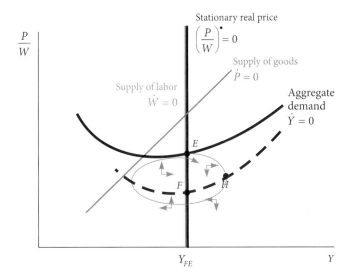

Figure 16.21 Fixprice response to an increase in G or decrease in t with capital-widening and rapid wage adjustment, II.

With $LS' = 0$ and $\varepsilon \approx 0$, the Jacobian is

$$J = \begin{bmatrix} \varepsilon\psi'\Omega\left(\dfrac{P}{W}\right)^{-2}\dfrac{L}{K} & \varepsilon\psi'\Omega'\left\{\left[\dfrac{Y}{K} - \left(\dfrac{P}{W}\right)^{-1}\dfrac{L}{K}\right] - s(1-t) + t\right\} - \theta_3 \\ \theta_2 & -\theta_2\left(GS'\right)^{-1} \end{bmatrix},$$

for which the trace is negative and the determinant positive.

— VI —

Keynes in the Long Run

— 17 —

FIRST STEPS INTO THE LONG RUN

Harrod, Domar, Solow, and Robinson

> When did the right stock of capital come into existence, and what mechanism, supposing that it did, keeps accumulation going at the right rate? The argument of the *General Theory*, which shows that there is no such mechanism in a private-enterprise economy, cannot be true at each moment of time and yet untrue "in the long run."
>
> —JOAN ROBINSON

Keynesian growth theory, like the son of upper-caste Hindus, is twice born, a fact that may account for the wrong turn taken as a teenager: in the hands of the mainstream, Keynesian growth theory abandoned the most distinctive feature of Keynes's revolution, the insistence on a role for aggregate demand in determining real economic outcomes. Joan Robinson's attempt to save Keynes from the mainstream misfired for the same reasons that Hicks's misfired—the absolute neglect of the supply side.[1] Furthermore, the entire exercise is characterized by the total absence of prices, rather odd for economic analysis of any kind, but perhaps the natural outcome of the tacit acceptance of a false premise, namely that *The General Theory* was all about a world with rigid prices and wages.

Chapter 6 touched on the dynamic questions of what happens when labor supply and the capital stock are growing over time. Despite investment and saving, despite population growth, the basic model of chapter 6 assumes that the capital stock and the labor force remain constant, so that equilibrium can be characterized by a stationary level of output and real price. This model is pictured in Figure 17.1.

Harrod: The Tension between Growth in Aggregate Demand and Growth in Labor Supply

The original attempt to take account of growth in the capital stock and labor force was Roy Harrod's "An Essay in Dynamic Theory." This essay was based, as Harrod tells us, on three propositions:

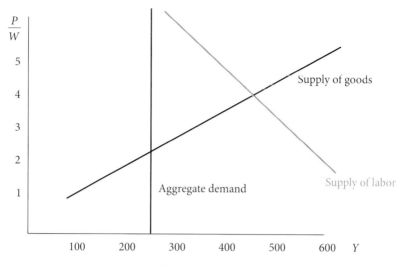

Figure 17.1 Aggregate demand, goods supply, and labor supply.

(1) that the level of a community's income is the most important determinant of its supply of saving; (2) that the rate of increase of its income is an important determinant of its demand for saving, and (3) that demand is equal to supply. (1939, p. 14)

These three propositions are summarized in the growth equation, $g = s/v$, which perpetuates Harrod's name—along with the name of Evsey Domar, the parent in the theory's other birth. For Harrod, g is the rate of growth of output (income); v is the incremental capital:output ratio, the stock of additional goods (plant, equipment, inventories of goods in process) for each additional unit added to the flow of output; s is the ratio of aggregate saving to aggregate output.

Like many important economic formulas—$I = S$ or $MV = PY$—the Harrod–Domar equation is an identity that acquires economic meaning only when we specify how the separate elements of the formula are determined. The tautology reveals itself immediately if we write out the various terms. Taking time to be made up of discrete periods (say, a year), we have $g = \Delta Y/Y$, $v = \Delta K/\Delta Y$, and $s = S/Y = \Delta K/Y$. So whatever the values of the individual terms, the equation $g = s/v$ must hold.

The tautology becomes a distinctive theory of growth when we distinguish the determinants of desired saving and desired investment. Following Keynes, Harrod's first proposition, at its simplest, is that desired saving is given by $S_D = sY$, with s a fixed parameter. Harrod's second proposition is a variation on Keynes: for Harrod it is not the interest rate but *expected* income growth that determines, along with v, the demand for additional capital. Denoting the expected change in income by ΔY_E, we can write investment demand as $I_D = v^{-1}\Delta Y_E$. (Here, as in most of the growth literature, the focus is on capital widening; capital deepening is ignored.) Harrod's third proposition requires $I_D = S_D$.

If we treat v as determined by technology, there is an immediate problem: there are two unknowns in the equation $I_D = S_D$, the level of income and the expected change. Harrod solves this problem by focusing on expectations that are in fact realized (rational expectations *avant la lettre*)—in Harrods's words expectations "which, if executed, will leave entrepreneurs in a state of mind in which they are prepared to carry on a similar advance" (1948, p. 82). If expectations are realized, we have $\Delta Y_E = \Delta Y \equiv Y - Y_{-1}$, and, assuming Y_{-1} is given, investment demand, like saving, depends on current income: $I_D = v\Delta Y = v(Y - Y_{-1})$.

The equality of desired saving and desired investment then determines Y and also converts the tautology $g = s/v$ into a relationship in which causality runs from right to left. The key is that at an income level where $I_D = S_D$ both investment intentions and saving intentions are realized. So the actual saving:income ratio $\Delta K/Y$ is equal to the desired ratio s. Harrod reserves the term *warranted rate of growth,* denoted g_w, for the particular value of g that corresponds to the values of s and v given respectively by consumer psychology and production technology.

Harrod notes two problems. First, the level of Y determined by equality of desired saving and investment is not a stable equilibrium. In Harrod's model there are no prices, so the only available adjustment mechanism is fixprice adjustment. If the economy finds itself at a point where I_D and S_D are unequal, fixprice adjustment leads the economy away from rather than toward the point where the equation $g_w = s/v$. To understand this strange result, consider first the simple textbook model of aggregate-demand determination laid out in chapter 3, reproduced below as Figure 17.2. Were output and income to exceed 400, desired saving would exceed desired investment, which is to say that aggregate expenditure would fall short of output and income. Inventories would pile up on store shelves, and, with fixprice adjustment, producers would get a strong signal to curtail output. Were output and income to fall short of 400, producers would get the opposite message: expenditure would exceed income and output, inventories would disappear and order backlogs would increase. Producers would increase output. (With flexprice adjustment, the process is more complicated, since in the first instance unwanted inventories trigger price changes rather than output changes, but since there are no prices in Harrod's world, this is a nonissue.) Thus, in Figure 17.2, as far as the demand side is concerned, 400 represents a stable equilibrium of desired saving and investment.

The picture is quite different in Harrod's case. Desired investment is no

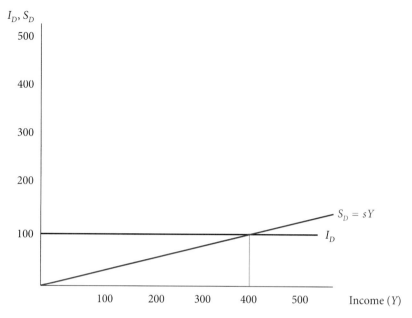

Figure 17.2 Investment and saving determine aggregate demand, I.

longer fixed in amount, but rather varies with the change in output this year relative to the previous year: v, by assumption, reflects a relationship between the amount of new capital that businesses must have to accommodate an expected change in output. With $I_D = v\Delta Y = v(Y - Y_{-1})$, we have Figure 17.3.

Here the equilibrium is unstable. If output exceeds 400, expenditure will *exceed* output and income, moving the economy further away from 400; if output falls short of 400, expenditure will fall short of output, and output will contract further.

It may appear that the instability is an accident of the draftsman's pen in making the investment schedule steeper than the saving schedule. To be sure, instability is the consequence of the fact that the investment schedule cuts the saving schedule from below rather than from above. But this is not the draftsman's fault. It is, rather, inherent in the logic of Harrod's I_D schedule. Since last year's output, Y_{-1}, is positive, the intercept of the investment schedule on the vertical axis must be positive, that is, $I_D = 0$ where $Y = Y_{-1}$ (unrealistically assumed to be at a level of 350, implying a warranted growth rate $\Delta Y/Y_{-1} = 50/350$, or approximately 14 percent). The investment schedule cannot cut the saving schedule from above, as would be necessary to ensure stability, without assuming that the previous period's income was negative!

Harrod's second problem is that the warranted rate of growth speaks to the demand side alone: g_w is the rate of growth that keeps the economy on the AD

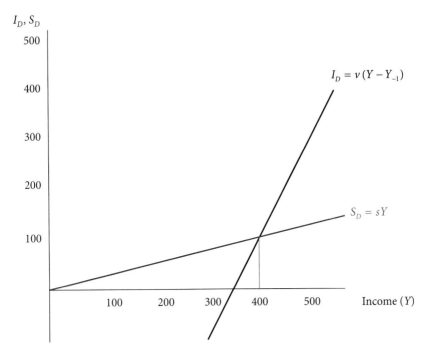

Figure 17.3 Investment and saving determine aggregate demand, II.

schedule. Supply enters the theory in what Harrod calls the *natural* rate of growth, g_n, the rate of growth determined by labor-force growth and technical change. If N denotes the size of the labor force and we ignore technological progress, we have $g_n = \Delta N/N$. Observe the conceptual difference: g_n has, in principle, nothing to do with g_w, which is the rate of growth for which desired investment and desired saving are equal. In effect, Harrod identifies the supply side with labor supply, assumed to be a constant fraction of an exogenously given population.

This may seem insufficient and even odd, but it is odd only with the benefit of twenty-twenty hindsight. For some years after the publication of *The General Theory*, the focus was on aggregate demand, and supply was brought in only in the form of additional constraints on output determination, such as an upper limit reflecting full employment. As noted earlier, price adjustment was ignored altogether.

Terminological confusion added to the problem. The terminology employed by Harrod (and others) distinguished the *demand* for investment from the *supply* of saving, a terminology that facilitated the belief that saving decisions formed the supply side of the economy rather than being an aspect of demand determination.

Be all this as it may, the distinction between warranted and natural rates of growth served Harrod's purpose of repositioning *The General Theory* in terms of a changing economy rather than in terms of a short-term static equilibrium. Since the natural rate g_n is determined independently of the warranted rate g_w, we have to take account of the interaction between the two rates.

If we were to take the warranted rate as the center of gravity of economic activity, as Keynes meant us to understand the corresponding notion of equilibrium in his own model, then $g_w < g_n$ would be a signal of economic stagnation. Saving and investment desires would be satisfied by a growth rate at which output is expanding less rapidly than the labor force, and if employment grows at the same rate as output, the imbalance between output growth and labor-force growth must mean growing unemployment. By the same token, $g_w > g_n$ would signal economic exhilaration. The economy would be straining at the bit, trying to grow faster than its labor resources allow.

But these are not the conclusions Harrod draws, and for good reason: the logic of taking the warranted rate as a center of gravity is built on the assumption that g_w represents a stable equilibrium of desired saving and desired investment. If, as in Figure 17.3, the equilibrium is unstable, then the implications of $g_w < g_n$, and $g_w > g_n$, are virtually the opposite of those of the previous paragraph. Consider: if $g_w < g_n$, then booms are at least possible. If the economy finds itself to the right of the level of output corresponding to g_w in Figure 17.3, then expansion will continue until the economy runs up against the labor constraint embodied in g_n. At this point, real expansion must give way to inflation, since the economy can no longer respond to an excess of expenditure over income by increasing output. (Needless to say, inflation is difficult to model without prices.) Of course, if the economy finds itself to the left of the point corresponding to g_w, there is nothing to stop it from running into the ground.

If, however, $g_w > g_n$, then sustained booms are not possible. A boom can take place only if the actual growth rate exceeds the natural rate, $g > g_n$. But $g > g_w > g_n$ will lead to an explosive increase in g that must end sooner rather than later in inflation without real growth, and $g_w > g > g_n$ means continuing decay. The natural rate g_n is a barrier to expansion if $g > g_w$ but no barrier to decline when $g < g_w$.

Clearly, the instability of the saving-investment equilibrium is central to Harrod's argument about the interaction of g_w and g_n. One way around the instability of g_w is to assume v to be a variable rather than a constant, to assume in effect that v is psychologically rather than technologically determined. In this interpretation, v reflects the decisions of capitalists about how much capital it is appropriate to add in the light of expectations about output, rather than positing a technologically *required* amount of capital per additional unit of output. Technology may still be an important factor in the determination of v, but that is hardly equivalent to making v into an aspect of the production function.[2] If v were to decrease with ΔY—not an implausible assumption—then we might have the picture represented in Figure 17.4, where the unstable equilibrium at 400 coexists with a stable equilibrium at 800. (Don't worry about the precise magnitudes; the stable equilibrium implies an enormous growth rate, even less plausible than the 14 percent growth rate implied by the equilibrium of Figure 17.3.)

Allowing v to vary with ΔY restores the intuitive association of $g_w < g_n$ with stagnation, and $g_w > g_n$ with exhilaration—the same result could be obtained by making the propensity to save, s, vary positively with the level of income—only if the level of output dictated by the natural rate of growth were to lie to the right of the first, unstable, saving-investment equilibrium. If the full-employment level of output, corresponding to g_n, were to lie to the left of $Y = 400$ in Figure 17.5, then even though $g_w > g_n$, the economy would find itself on a downward spiral; unable to sustain output in excess of the natural rate, the economy would end up in the centrifugal part of the diagram with nothing to cushion the fall. A qualitatively similar result obtains if we follow an alternative approach to making g_w stable by allowing growth expectations to be revised by experience.

Whether or not the warranted-rate equilibrium is unstable, the very opposition between warranted and natural growth rates highlights a problem that a simple comparative statics of aggregate demand obscures—and thus provides another reason for questioning the ability of a market system to provide full employment. Even if the economy were to manage to reach full employment at any given moment, there is no guarantee that the economy would evolve in precisely the way required to resolve the conflict between an equilibrium that satisfies the requirements of investors and savers and an equilibrium that satisfies the requirements of providing a job for every willing worker in the (growing) labor force.

We can summarize the results that emerge from Harrod's model in the form of the 2 × 2 matrix in Table 17.1, even though Harrod himself focused on only one column, the left-hand column, of the matrix. One way or another, the result, apart from a fortuitous equality between warranted and natural growth rates, is that the economy either strains at the bit, persistently to the left of its AD schedule, or ends up to the right of its AD schedule (or exactly on the schedule), but in either case further and further from the LS schedule. An economy that is perpetually straining at the bit, held back by inadequate labor-force growth, must eventually give itself over to flexprice adjustment, even though Harrod doesn't go there: since Harrod's economy cannot adjust forever to an excess of expenditure over income by increasing output, the re-

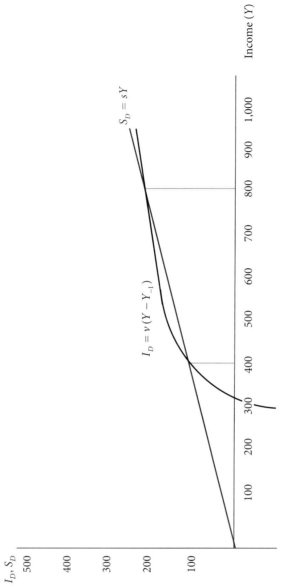

Figure 17.4 Investment and saving determine aggregate demand, III.

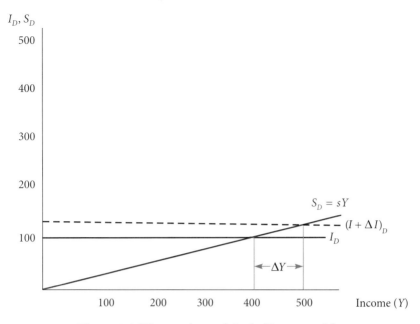

Figure 17.5 Warranted growth in the Domar model.

Table 17.1 Growth Determined by Warranted and
Natural Rates

	g_w unstable	g_w stable
$g_w < g_n$	$g \to g_n$ inflation or $Y \to 0$ unemployment	$g \to g_w$ unemployment
$g_w > g_n$	$Y \to 0$ unemployment	$g \to g_n$[1] inflation

1. Assuming g_n lies to the right of the unstable
equilibrium in Figure 17.3.

sult must be perpetual inflation, as the price level is the only means of adjusting excess demand. The other possibility is long-run unemployment, as the growth in output and capital, and hence of the demand for labor, lags behind the growth in the labor force. Harrod's economy left to itself offers no good outcome.

Observe that there is no role for goods supply based on profitability as a separate element of the model. Harrod implicitly assumes that actual output (and employment) grows at the warranted rate unless impeded by a lack of hands, that is, by a failure of the labor force to grow sufficiently rapidly to accommodate warranted-rate growth. There can't be a GS schedule based on profit maximization in the absence of a role for prices and wages.

Domar: The Tension between Growth in Aggregate Demand and Growth in Goods Supply

Goods supply is the heart of the alternative interpretation of the Harrod–Domar equation provided by Evsey Domar (1946, 1947). But it is not goods supply responding to profit maximization. For Domar, as for Harrod, there are no prices in the model and no profit maximization. Domar conceives of goods supply in terms of additions to productive capacity, and in this respect he is on the same page as Harrod. But capacity is no longer linked directly to labor-force growth.

Although Domar does not employ the terminology of warranted and natural rates, we can see both the similarities and the differences between his model and Harrod's by using the warranted/natural framework. In Domar's model, the relationship between the warranted rate, the propensity to save, and the capital:output ratio is, as in Harrod's model, $g_w = s/v$. But now $g_w = \Delta I_D/I_D$, and $s = \Delta S_D/\Delta Y$. That is, the warranted rate is the rate of growth of desired investment, now defined as a rate of growth of investment demand that is assumed to be given exogenously: think animal spirits and a given hurdle rate of interest. And the saving parameter is the *marginal* propensity to save. (The difference in the definition of saving disappears if we assume for simplicity that saving is a constant fraction of income, so that the marginal and average propensities to save are equal.)

The capital:output ratio, v, is formally the same ratio as it is in Harrod's approach, $\Delta K/\Delta Y$, but it has a different meaning. Here it is neither technologically nor psychologically determined; it is, rather, the multiplier process that fixes the value of ΔY: income must change to generate an amount of additional saving that matches the additional investment ΔI. The warranted-rate equation is now read from left to right, from the exogenously given growth rate of investment demand to the change in output, ΔY. As for Harrod, the key assumption is that desired investment and saving are equal.

The picture is in Figure 17.5. Assuming that the economy begins and ends on the AD schedule, the change in desired saving, ΔS_D, must be equal to the exogenous change in investment, ΔI_D. From the expression for s, we can calculate the required change in income, ΔY; s is simply the inverse of the multiplier. This fixes v, since $\Delta S_D = \Delta I_D$.

The natural rate of growth is also conceptually different. For Domar the natural rate of growth is the rate of growth of desired saving that results from full utilization of the capital stock. The capital:output ratio figures once again, but it is defined differently, this time as a technologically determined parameter relating additional capital, ΔK, to the additional output that can be generated if the new capital is fully deployed.[3] On standard mainstream assumptions we have

$$\Delta Y = MP_K \Delta K + MP_L \Delta L,$$

where MP_K and MP_L are the marginal products of capital and labor. If we set $\Delta L = \Delta N$, which is to say that the entire addition to the labor force is employed, we can solve for ΔY, which determines $v = \Delta K/\Delta Y$. The natural rate follows as

$$g_n \equiv \frac{\Delta S_D}{S_D} = \frac{\Delta(sY)}{sY} = \frac{s}{v} \equiv \frac{\dfrac{\Delta(sY)}{\Delta Y}}{\dfrac{\Delta K}{\Delta Y}}.$$

Besides the change in the meaning of v, the natural-rate equation differs from its warranted-rate counterpart because g_n is determined by v—the equation is read from right to left—opposite to the direction of causality in Domar's warranted-rate equation.

Domar's equilibrium, like Harrod's, is defined by equality of the warranted and natural rates of growth: for them both, this requires not only continuous equality of desired saving and investment but also continuing equality between the expansion of aggregate demand and the expansion of productive capacity. The differences lie in what drives aggregate demand and in what drives supply. Harrod endogenizes investment demand by making it depend on a capital:output ratio that is based on some combination of technology and the psychology of the businessmen and -women who undertake the investment. For Domar, investment demand is a black box.

With regard to supply, Harrod emphasizes labor-force growth, whereas for Domar the labor force is simply a background variable that affects the growth of capacity. If goods were produced by robots without involving any human labor, Domar's model would survive unscathed—we would simply set $\Delta L = \Delta N = 0$ in the equation for determining the expansion of productive capacity. The parameter v in the natural-rate equation would then be equal to the inverse of the marginal productivity of capital.

One equation, two very different interpretations. Nevertheless, there is an important common theme: even if the conditions for a serendipitous full-employment equilibrium were to be achieved at one point in time, there is no guarantee that the economy would grow in a way that maintained full employment. Both formulations point to the precariousness of macroeconomic equilibrium.

In the late 1940s, when Harrod and Domar launched Keynes into the long run, concern for maintaining full employment over time was a central question. But their mutual concern for the precariousness of sustained full employment faded away pretty quickly. For this there is an empirical reason: the robust performance of capitalist economies over the three decades following the end of World War II. At the level of theory, we have Robert Solow to thank—or to blame, as the spirit moves us.

Solow: Resolving the Tension between Growth in the Capital Stock and Growth in Labor Supply

Solow's contribution (1956) was in many ways a breath of fresh air. Confusion about the meaning of the Harrod–Domar equation was rampant. The very fact that the same equation was deployed without any self-consciousness to summarize two different theories is indicative.[4] And Solow's attempt at clarification is both elegant and convincing. Indeed, his paper marks a watershed in economics, from the discursive literary argumentation of Keynes and Harrod to the razor-sharp logic of calculus and allied mathematical tools, a major step in the mathematization of economics that has characterized the years since.

Solow addresses himself to the opposition between warranted and natural rates of growth, summarizing the problem in these terms:

> The characteristic and powerful conclusion of the Harrod–Domar line of thought is that even for the long run the economic system is at best balanced on a knife-edge of equilibrium growth. Were the magnitudes of the key parameters—the savings ratio, the capital-output ratio, the rate of increase of the labor force—to slip ever so slightly from dead center, the consequence would be either growing unemployment or prolonged inflation. In Harrod's terms the critical question of balance boils down to a comparison between the natural rate of growth which depends, in the absence of technological change, on the increase of the labor force, and the warranted rate of growth which depends on the saving and investing habits of households and firms. (1956, p. 65)

These are of course the results summarized in Table 17.1. But Solow sees the problem not as a problem of insufficient or excessive aggregate demand, as Harrod (and Domar too in his own way) do, but as the result of a very specific assumption about technology, an assumption that is inappropriate once we are no longer in the short run. Nor does Solow recognize that the instability of the aggregate-demand equilibrium in Harrod's model is only one reason for the precariousness of full employment. According to Solow

> Fundamental opposition of warranted and natural rates turns out in the end to flow from the crucial assumption that production takes place under con-

ditions of fixed proportions. There is no possibility of substituting labor for capital in production. If this assumption is abandoned, the knife-edge notion of unstable balance seems to go with it. (1956, p. 65)

For Solow, the "knife-edge" problem stems from the assumption that the demand for labor is constrained by the size of the capital stock: on the one hand, growing unemployment characterizes the economy when the growth of output and hence the growth of demand for labor fall short of the natural rate of growth, and, on the other hand, excess demand for labor and inflation characterize the economy when output and hence the demand for labor grow faster than the supply of labor. The weak link in this chain, Solow argues, is the link between output and the demand for labor. If it is possible to produce a given output with various combinations of labor and capital, there need be no rigid link between output and employment. In the limiting case of continuous substitution between capital and labor, we can characterize the relationship between output and inputs in terms of the so-called neoclassical production function, according to which substitution possibilities are reflected in the relative marginal productivities of the factors of production, which are assumed to vary smoothly with changes in factor proportions.

This gives Solow an extra degree of freedom to model the interaction of goods supply, labor supply, and aggregate demand. He could have used this degree of freedom along the lines of chapter 6, with explicit assumptions about the dynamics of goods supply, labor supply, and aggregate demand. Instead, following in the footsteps of Modigliani (1944), he simply *assumes* full employment and shows that adjustment of the capital:labor ratio will resolve any discrepancy between g_w and g_n. In effect, Solow eliminates the AD schedule in Figure 17.1, so that the problem becomes one of ensuring that the equilibrium of goods supply and labor supply evolves in a way that maintains a stationary capital:labor ratio. But like the models of Harrod and Domar, there are no prices in Solow's model; goods supply does not depend on profit maximization, and labor supply does not depend on utility maximization.

Along the way, Solow substitutes his own definition of the warranted rate of growth. Solow's warranted rate is the rate of growth of the capital stock, determined solely by saving propensities and the output:capital ratio. The important change here is not that capital replaces output, but that investment demand no longer plays any role. Solow keeps the definition of the natural rate as the rate of growth of the labor force, but with the assumptions of continuous substitution and full employment, the natural rate is now equal to the rate of growth of employment as well.

Solow takes it as his task to show that the automatic workings of the economy will bring the warranted and natural rates into line with one another—no booms or busts, no inflation or unemployment. To see how this happens, consider Figure 17.6, which reproduces Solow's Figure 1 (1956, p. 70). This figure relates warranted and natural rates to the capital:labor ratio.

We start with an aggregate production function $Y = F(K, L)$. Assume constant returns to scale, so that we can divide both sides of the equation by L to obtain a relationship between output per worker and capital per worker $Y/L = F(K/L, 1)$. Defining $k \equiv K/L$, and $f(k) \equiv F(K/L, 1)$, we can write this equation more compactly as $Y/L = f(k)$. In Solow's formulation, $g_w = \Delta K/K$ and, since $\Delta K = sY$, the growth of the capital stock per worker is given by the equation $g_w k = sf(k)$. In Solow's notation the natural rate of growth is n, so the growth of the capital stock per worker required for the capital:labor ratio to maintain stationary is $g_n k$.

The argument is that if $g_w > g_n$, the growth in the amount of capital at each worker's disposal ($g_w k$) must exceed the growth in the amount of capital needed to maintain the existing capital:labor ratio ($g_n k$). So k must be increasing over time. By the same token, if the inequality is reversed, and we start with $g_w < g_n$, k must be decreasing. The capital:labor ratio comes to rest only when $g_w = g_n$. In the picture, the gap between $g_w k$ and $g_n k$ becomes smaller as k moves from its initial position, k_0 or k_1; at the point k^*, k is neither increasing nor decreasing, which makes k^* an equilibrium to which the adjustment process converges.[5]

QED. Which was to be demonstrated.

Or was it?

One problem is that we have changed the meaning of the production function in applying it to the long run. In the short run, changes in the cap-

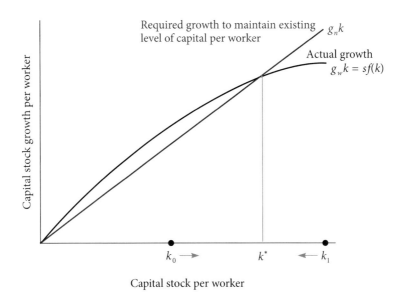

Figure 17.6 Warranted and natural rates in the Solow model.

ital:labor ratio have been assumed to be the result of changing the level of utilization of an existing capital stock. That is, the capital:labor ratio rises if there are fewer workers manning the machines, or if the workforce is on short time. The capital:labor ratio falls if more workers are employed, or if workers put in longer hours.

In the long run, the production function represents different technologies rather than different intensities of using an existing capital stock; a shift in the capital:labor ratio now represents a change in the technology by which goods and services are produced. The long-run production function raises fundamental issues: can we represent the distinct configurations of capital goods associated with different technologies in terms of an aggregate capital, K; what meaning attaches to this aggregate when the technology changes? The questions multiply: Can we order distinct technologies in terms of an overall quantity of capital? What is now the meaning of the marginal product of capital, and for that matter, the marginal product of labor? These are questions that have occupied some of the keenest minds of twentieth-century economics; even after the dust had settled, the mid-century "capital controversies" engendered no fewer than four entries in *The New Palgrave* published in 1987 (Eatwell, Milgate, and Newman). Nor is the subject over and done with; see David Rezza Baqaee and Emmanuel Farhi (2019) for more recent discussion.

For all its problems, I embrace the aggregate production function and its problematic deployment of an aggregate capital stock. For one thing, like Keynes, I am committed to engaging mainstream economics on its own turf, of which the aggregate production function is an important constituent. Perhaps more important is the plain fact that I do not know how to argue about the long run without an aggregate production function and its aggregate arguments.

Even within this framework, Solow is problematic. He does indeed dispose of one of Harrod's problems, but not the other. And not Domar's. Figure 17.6 speaks to the convergence of warranted and natural rates of growth under the assumption that saving at full employment determines investment and capital stock growth *but ignores the Keynesian problems of adjustment of aggregate demand that were at the heart of Harrod's and Domar's inquiries*—shades of J. B. Say.

Solow is aware both of what he accomplished and of what he had not accomplished. Concluding his seminal paper with a section titled "Qualifications," he begins with this observation:

> Everything above is the neoclassical side of the coin. Most especially it is full employment economics—in the dual aspect of equilibrium condition and frictionless, competitive, causal system. All the difficulties and rigidities which go into modern Keynesian income analysis have been shunted aside.

It is not my contention that these problems don't exist, nor that they are of no significance in the long run. (1956, p. 91)

But Solow did nothing to address these problems, and the legacy of the paper was to push the Keynesian issue of aggregate demand to the sidelines. The promise of a Keynesian theory of the long run that seemed well within reach to Harrod and Domar was never fulfilled.

A comparison of Harrod, Domar, and Solow brings to mind the Indian tale of the blind men, each of whom characterizes an elephant according to the part of the body he happens to touch: as a wall, a pillar, or a rope (to mention only three reports), corresponding to the elephant's side, leg, or tail. A nineteenth-century English retelling of the tale concludes

> And so these men of Indostan
> Disputed loud and long,
> Each in his own opinion
> Exceeding stiff and strong,
> Though each was partly in the right,
> And all were in the wrong![6]

Embedding Harrod, Domar, and Solow in a Common Model

The partial nature of each view emerges clearly if we embed Harrod, Domar, and Solow in the common framework of the model elaborated in chapter 6. The starting point is Figure 17.7, which appends stationary real-price schedules consistent with flexprice and fixprice dynamics to Figure 17.1. The long-run problem turns out to be the same as the short-run problem: the system is

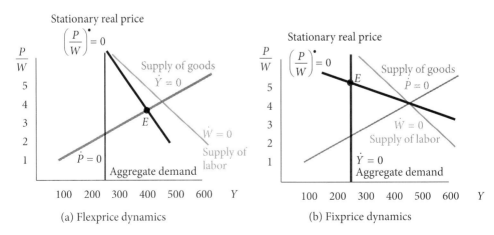

Figure 17.7 Equilibrium in the short run.

overdetermined, so even though Harrod, Domar, and Solow each finds a satisfactory solution to the problem he himself has posed, none of them solves
the problem that the others have posed.

À la Solow, we replace the short-run measure of economic activity, Y, with
a measure more suitable to an evolving economy. Our measure is the inverse
of Solow's k, namely, the labor:capital ratio $l \equiv L/K$. We now have $Y/K = f(l) \equiv$
$F(1, L/K)$.

Long-run equilibrium is defined as a state of affairs where both the real
price and the labor:capital ratio, and thus the output:capital ratio, are stationary. Unlike the level of output, which evidently must change over time as capital accumulates and employment increases, the labor:capital ratio and the
output:capital ratio can remain stationary even as the capital stock and labor
force evolve—at least as long as we ignore technological change.[7]

Figure 17.8 transposes Figure 17.1 to the new space of real price and
labor:capital ratio. Observe that the GS schedule now reflects a rising marginal cost. (The linear marginal cost curve that has been deployed up to now
has nothing to recommend it but the draftsman's convenience.)

The point of changing the state variable from Y to l is to avoid having to
deal with moving AD, GS, and LS schedules. We do not succeed completely

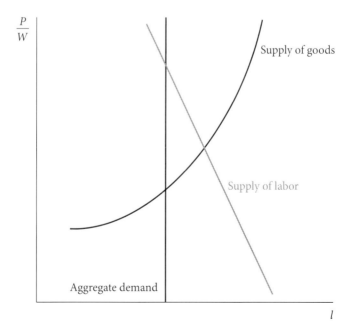

Figure 17.8 Aggregate demand, goods supply, and labor supply
in the space of $l \times P/W$.

until (in the next chapter) we modify the assumption that labor-force growth is exogenously given.

Consider first aggregate demand. In the context of an economy in which output grows over time, investment and saving must grow too. But if we assume that investment demand and saving supply *per unit of capital* are stationary over time, then aggregate demand per unit of capital will also be stationary. In the simplest version we assume that the hurdle rate of interest ρ_h is the sole driver of investment per unit of capital, which we (for now at least) denote $I_D = \psi(\rho_h)$. Similarly, the simplest saving schedule assumes that a constant proportion of all income is saved, so that we can write $S_D = sY/K$. Aggregate demand is defined by $I_D = S_D$ and is thus stationary provided that the investment-demand schedule, $\psi(\rho_h)$, and the propensity to save, s, do not change over time.

Observe that this definition of investment elides two problems at once. First, the instability of Harrod's equilibrium disappears once investment demand no longer depends on income, for it will be recalled that instability arose from the greater sensitivity of investment demand to output as compared with the sensitivity of saving. This does not, of course, mean that we are done with Harrod, for instability was only one of his issues. Even with this issue resolved, there remains the argument that the determinants of the warranted rate and the determinants of the natural rate are distinct and separate, and there is no mechanism for bringing the two rates into line with one another.

Second, Keynes's own problem of declining investment opportunities is also elided in this construction. Keynes saw the long run as providing an environment less and less favorable for investment, for which the only solution was a progressive diminution in the rate of interest, a diminution that would eventually lead to the "euthanasia of the rentier" (*The General Theory,* pp. 375–376). Keynes's view was developed by Alvin Hansen into a vision of the future in which capitalism is beset by a chronic failure of investment demand—what Hansen labeled secular stagnation. In turn, investment pessimism became the basis for Abba Lerner's theory of functional finance, which assigned to fiscal policy the primary role of compensating for the putative lack of investment demand, whatever the consequences for the government deficit and the national debt (Hansen 1938, 1941; Lerner 1944, chap. 24).[8]

Like aggregate demand, goods supply is invariant over time in the space $l \times P/W$ provided the production function does not change. (Remember, we are abstracting from systematic technological change, so the only thing that can change the production function is an isolated shock, something we consider in the next chapter.) The GS schedule, defined by equality between the real price and real marginal cost, requires $P/W = f'(l)^{-1}$, which, like the equation expressing the equality of desired saving and investment, is invariant over time.

This leaves the LS schedule. The natural assumption in the context of an evolving economy is that an underlying labor-supply function is fixed in the sense that, for a given real-price level, the *ratio* of desired employment (L_S) to the labor force (N) does not vary over time as a function of P/W. We write the functional relationship between L_S/N and P/W as $L_S/N = \phi(P/W)$. Denoting the ratio of labor supply to capital by $l_S \equiv L_S/K$, we have $l_S = \phi(P/W) \times N/K$. Since the ratio N/K enters into the determination of l_S, the LS schedule is not stationary over time unless the labor force and the capital stock are growing at the same rate.

If, as is characteristic of depressions, the rate of growth of the capital stock slows markedly so that N grows proportionately faster than K, the result will be that l_S grows for any given $\phi(P/W)$. This is to say that the LS schedule will move outward over the course of time; Figure 17.9 shows the evolution of a flexprice equilibrium, in which the original LS schedule (the solid line) morphs into the dashed one. Successive short-period equilibria are pictured on the assumption of flexprice adjustment. The later equilibrium F, reflects a higher labor:capital ratio, the result of the relative decline in the capital stock.

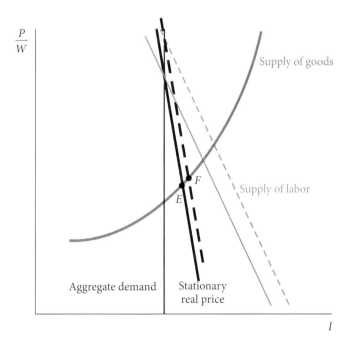

Figure 17.9 Evolution of flexprice equilibrium when labor force grows more rapidly than capital.

Note that moving from E to F reflects an economy that is getting poorer, not one in which more people are finding jobs.[9]

Observe that the process ends in disaster if it is allowed to continue unchecked: the labor:capital ratio increases without bound. Output per unit capital approaches a maximum if the limiting elasticity of substitution between capital and labor is less than one, and it increases without bound if this elasticity is greater than one. In both cases the increase in Y/K takes place because there is so little capital to go around; output per worker falls to zero, and the real price climbs higher and higher—the real wage goes to zero.

The alternative possibility is that the rate of growth of capital exceeds the rate of labor-force growth. This possibility is depicted in Figure 17.10, again under the assumption of flexprice adjustment. Here the results are topsy-turvy. As time passes and the original equilibrium E moves to F, labor becomes scarce, with employment eventually exceeding the labor supply! At F, money wages rise as a result of labor-market pressure, and prices rise because of an excess of expenditure over income. As long as investment per unit of capital exceeds population growth, the process continues, with not only a continually falling real-price level but also an ever-increasing rate of inflation.

Under a flexprice regime, there is a built-in potential check to an inflationary spiral but not to a deflationary spiral, the details of which are left to

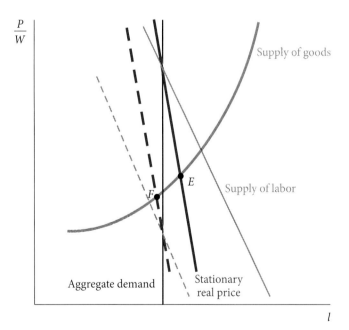

Figure 17.10 Evolution of flexprice equilibrium when labor force grows less rapidly than capital.

the appendix to this chapter. If the warranted rate of growth exceeds the natural rate, extending the model of chapter 6 to the long run provides a mechanism whereby a "quasi-warranted" rate of growth (quasi because investment intentions are partially frustrated by a lack of saving) falls until it is brought into line with the natural rate of growth. However, it is a one-way bridge. If the problem is a lack of demand, then the adjustment process does nothing to raise the rate of accumulation of productive capital. To be sure, the rate of growth of the total capital stock increases, but the increase takes the form of unwanted inventories that do nothing to resolve the tension between warranted and natural rates.

If we assume fixprice adjustment, the model of chapter 6 provides no way of reconciling warranted and natural rates. Figure 17.11 shows what happens when the warranted rate falls short of the natural rate and Figure 17.12 what happens when the warranted rate is higher than the natural rate.

With fixprice adjustment, equilibrium is always on the AD schedule, so expenditure and income are in balance, hence so are desired investment and desired saving. Movement of the LS schedule simply shifts the equilibrium along the (stationary) AD schedule, resulting in an ever-higher real price and an ever-higher rate of deflation when the labor force grows more rapidly than the capital stock (Figure 17.11), and a lower and lower real

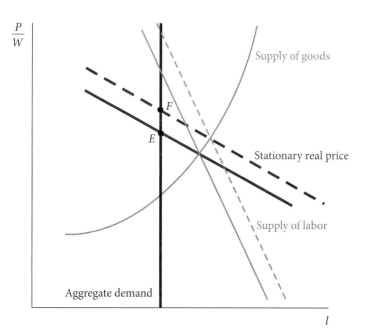

Figure 17.11 Evolution of fixprice equilibrium when labor force grows more rapidly than capital.

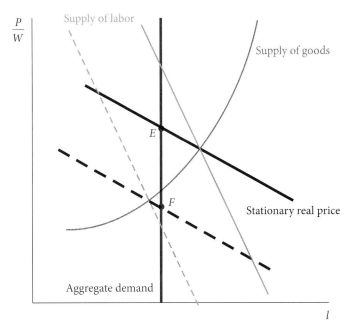

Figure 17.12 Evolution of fixprice equilibrium when labor force grows less rapidly than capital.

price and ever-greater inflation when the labor force grows less rapidly (Figure 17.12).

Taking all these results together, the model of chapter 6 does not hold out much hope for the economy's ability on its own to correct discrepancies between warranted and natural rates of growth. The consequence is to reinforce the pessimistic conclusions that Harrod and Domar drew from their respective analyses.

Bringing monetary policy into the picture does little to change this conclusion. Even if we assume away obstacles to successful deployment of monetary policy in the short period, the long run presents new challenges. Consider the serendipitous equilibrium in Figure 17.13. For l to equal l_0, a particular value of $\psi(\rho_h)$, and thus of ρ_h, is required. Barring a liquidity trap or highly inelastic investment demand, the central bank can put the right level of the hurdle rate into effect. But the corresponding warranted rate of growth is totally independent of the natural rate of growth. (This, of course, was Harrod's original point!) To bring the warranted rate into line with the natural rate may require more or less investment. Suppose $\psi(\rho_h) > g_n$, so that it is necessary to increase ρ_h as a way of scaling back aggregate demand to $l = l_1$. The new equilibrium, whether defined by a flexprice or a fixprice process, involves unemployment and continuing deflation. The price of dynamic equilibrium of warranted and natural rates is continuing economic slack. If, by contrast, $\psi(\rho_h) < g_n$, then the

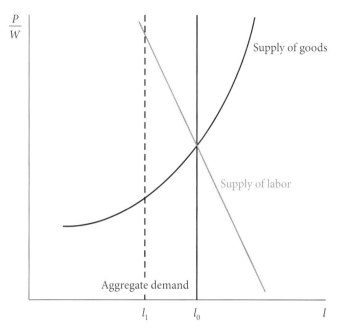

Figure 17.13 Serendipitous equilibrium not so serendipitous.

remedy is stimulus, monetary ease that reduces ρ_h and moves the AD schedule to the right. In this case, the price of dynamic equilibrium is continuing labor-market tightness (indeed, continuing overfull employment) accompanied by permanent inflation.

Toward a Keynesian Theory of the Long Run

Evidently, the two rates of growth, warranted and natural, can be aligned by appropriate intervention, but at a price: either chronic unemployment or endemic inflation. That at least is where Harrod's theory (and Domar's) leads us once we introduce prices and wages into their models. The historical record is somewhat more reassuring. Although the world has suffered bouts of both unemployment and inflation, neither seems as pervasive in post–World War II capitalism as pre-Solow apocalyptic visions suggested. So where did Harrod and Domar go wrong?

The error was to assume that the labor supply is exogenously given, a number of bodies independent of the needs of the economy. Like Solow's misplaced emphasis on factor substitution, exogenous labor supply was unhesitatingly (and unthinkingly) incorporated into the canon. Growth theory has seen many innovations since Harrod's time, but the assumption that the rate of growth must conform to the constraint of a labor force given by population growth has rarely been questioned. Harrod's 1939 assumption has cast a long shadow.

In this regard, Joan Robinson (1966 [1956], 1962) is exceptional. Robinson, Keynes's disciple and standard-bearer in Cambridge (as well as the theorist, along with Edward Chamberlin, of monopolistic competition), continued until her death to argue for a role for aggregate demand in analyzing the long run. But she and her followers were fighting a rearguard battle against an economics increasingly dominated by the mainstream view that the only possibility for aggregate demand to influence real outcomes lay in a short run characterized by frictions and rigidities.

Robinson's analysis contained three innovations, of which an endogenous labor force was one, but one easily lost sight of. First, in determining the rate of investment, she shifted the emphasis from the rate of interest to the return on capital. Instead of the equation $I_D = \psi(\rho_h)$, in which animal spirits combine with the hurdle rate of interest to drive investment demand, for Robinson investment demand is determined by the rate of profit, in the present notation, $f(l) - (P/W)^{-1}l$. In this spirit, chapter 10 developed an investment-demand function for capital widening, in which the *difference* between the rate of profit and the hurdle rate of interest drives investment demand:

$$I_D = \psi\left(1, \frac{P}{W}, \rho_h\right) = \psi\left(\Omega(l)r - \rho_h\right) = \psi\left(\Omega(l)\left[f(l) - \left(\frac{P}{W}\right)^{-1}l\right] - \rho_h\right).$$

Now, the rate of profit and the hurdle rate of interest both play a role in the determination of investment demand, but capital-stock adjustment does not bring the two variables into line with one another. As chapter 10 noted, things are different in a world of Lego capital, where every producer's capital can be adjusted in to bring about equality between the marginal productivity of capital and its rental cost. Once Lego capital is abandoned in favor of a more realistic putty-clay production function, the adjustment of the capital stock does not necessarily equalize marginal productivity and the rate of profit, or the expected profitability $\Omega(l)r$ and the interest rate, even in the long run.

A second innovation, one Robinson shared with other Cambridge economists working the Keynesian street, was to introduce class differences into consumption and saving.[10] Instead of the assumption of uniform propensities to consume and save for all types of income and all types of agents, the so-called Cambridge saving theory, explored in chapter 9, posits different consumption and saving propensities for profits and wages. In its simplest version, no wages are saved while a portion s_π of profits are saved. In consequence, the saving schedule provides a second relationship between growth and profit rates, namely $S_D = s_\pi r$.

The problems of aggregating the value of individual capital goods (see above, pp. 660–661) led Robinson to believe that a production function that assumes continuous substitution between inputs, the so-called neoclassical production function, is the root of all evil in mainstream economics. Whatever the merit of her antipathy, an antipathy which evidently I do not share, fixed-factor proportions make the depiction of equilibrium much easier. With l fixed, Robinson's version of Harrod's warranted rate of growth is a rate of capital-stock growth desired by savers (S_D) and investors (I_D), both dependent on the rate of profit. In Figure 17.14 (as in Figure 17.4) there are two rates of profit at which investment and saving desires coincide. The higher warranted rate, g_w^0, is stable, and g_w^1 is unstable.

The reasoning is the same as for Harrod's own model, with the rate of profit rather than the level of income driving adjustment outside of equilibrium. The investment function in Figure 17.14 assumes that successive increments of profitability call forth less and less additional investment. Eventually, increments in profitability call forth more saving than investment. Robinson does not justify this assumption, which plays the same role in her model that the lower responsiveness of investment to income, compared with the responsiveness of saving, plays in the version of Harrod's model in Figure 17.4. Formally, a sufficient condition for stability (but not a necessary one, as we shall see in the next chapter) is $\psi'\Omega < s_\pi$, where $\psi'\Omega$ represents the response of in-

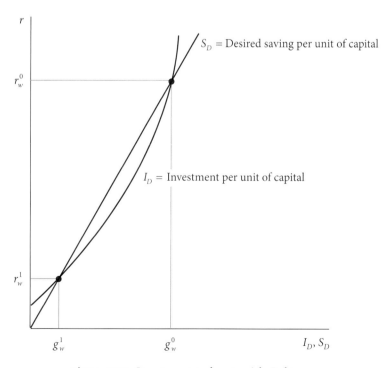

Figure 17.14 Investment and saving à la Robinson.

vestment demand to a change in the rate of profit when the labor:capital ratio is fixed.

In Robinson's formulation, the equilibrium real price and thus the distribution of income are determined by the rate of profit at the equilibrium levels of I_D and S_D. Substituting this rate of profit into the equation $r = f(l_0) - (P/W)^{-1}l_0$ allows us to solve for the real wage. The influence of the supply side is completely masked by assuming fixed proportions between capital and labor; $f(l)$ and l become parameters rather than variables.

Robinson's formulation of the warranted rate of growth can be understood in terms of the AD schedule in Figure 17.15, which we will formally derive in the next chapter. Take a vertical slice of Figure 17.15 at $l = l_0$. Varying P/W we can derive the relationship in Figure 17.14 between investment and saving and the rate of profit from $I_D = \psi(\Omega(l)r - \rho_h)$ and $S_D = s_\pi r$. The key is the equation $r = f(l_0) - (P/W)^{-1}l_0$.

This is aggregate demand with a vengeance! There is no supply-side equation in Figure 17.14.

Like Harrod, Domar, and Solow, Robinson in effect sees a portion of the elephant. Perhaps she sees more than her predecessors because of her third innovation: how she addresses the tension between the natural rate and the warranted rate. A variety of possible resolutions are cataloged in Robinson (1962), each with a colorful name (some samples: "golden age," when the warranted rate and the natural rate just happen to coincide; "bastard golden age," "creeping platinum age," and so forth). For my purposes, the interesting possibility is that the natural rate is not so natural, that labor-force growth is not given exogenously:

> Capitalist industry does not employ the whole work force in any country. Domestic service, paid or unpaid, jobbing work and small-scale trade, and,

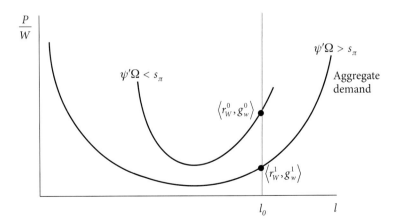

Figure 17.15 Generalizing investment and saving à la Robinson.

in most countries, agriculture, hold a reservoir of labour which fills up when regular employment is not expanding as fast as the population. (1962, p. 15)

The next chapter develops this idea more fully.

APPENDIX: INVENTORY ACCUMULATION AS A BRAKE ON OUTPUT

There is a peculiarity in the behavior of the economy under a flexprice regime. Take the simple case where the AD schedule is vertical. To the right of the AD schedule, it does not make sense to assume that all investment adds to the productive capital stock. Neither does it make sense to assume that the capital stock can continue to grow at a rate in excess of labor-force growth when the economy is to the left of the AD schedule.

To see this peculiarity more clearly, consider the inequality between expenditure and income at a deflationary flexprice equilibrium. At E in Figure 17.16 expenditure falls short of income and output. Consequently, as was noted in chapter 6, there is unwanted inventory accumulation. In the short period this need not complicate matters unduly, since it can be argued that producers factor in the possibility that they will be unable to sell all they produce. All that may be required to induce enough producers to take the chance associated with overproduction is a premium of price over marginal cost.

This assumption allows us to address the short-run problem of unwanted inventory accumulation by positing that goods supply involves a displacement of the GS schedule and hence a displacement of equilibrium from E to F. To the right of the AD schedule, where expenditure falls short of output,

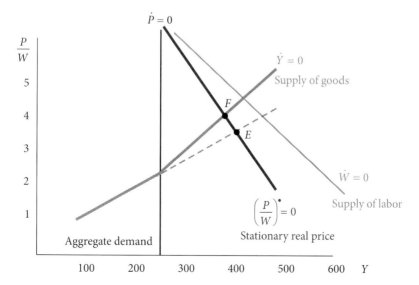

Figure 17.16 Taking account of unwanted inventories.

the premium is equal to the vertical distance between the solid GS schedule and the dashed marginal-cost schedule.

But in the longer run, the wedge between expenditure and output may undermine the very notion of equilibrium with unintended inventory accumulation. Implicitly—the time has come to make the assumption explicit—the model assumes that the accumulation of productive capital is determined by the *minimum* of desired investment and desired saving, which allows for inventory accumulation in situations where expenditure falls short of output. This is to say that total investment is always equal to desired saving, with any positive difference between desired saving and desired investment showing up as undesired investment in inventory. To the right of the AD schedule in Figure 17.16, the growth of unwanted inventory is equal to the gap $sY - \psi(\rho_h) K$, that is, to the gap between total saving and the addition to productive capital.

With flexprice adjustment this gap is a permanent feature of a deflationary equilibrium.[11] If the gap between desired saving and investment per unit of capital, $sY/K - \psi(\rho_h)$, relative to productive investment per unit of productive capital, $\psi(\rho_h)$, exceeds the ratio of unwanted inventories to the productive capital stock, then inventories will grow faster than productive capital. The presence of so much inventory must eventually defeat even the most optimistic producer calculating his chances of selling what he produces currently. If the gap is more modest, so that the ratio $[sY/K - \psi(\rho_h)]/\psi(\rho_h)$ is less than the ratio of unwanted inventories to the productive capital stock, then the inventory ratio will gradually diminish, and an equilibrium like F in Figure 17.16, at which businesses weigh profits against the likelihood of finding a market, may be sustainable.

Things are different when the economy operates to the left of the AD schedule. Here the problem is that expenditure can continue to exceed output only as long as businesses are willing and able to run down inventories. In a flexprice regime, prospective purchasers will eventually have to be turned away, and either consumption or investment will suffer. If we assume it is investment plans that are frustrated by inflation so that actual investment is constrained by saving, then the rate of growth of productive capital must slow down as inventories are depleted. The reversal of the inequality between desired investment and saving, $\psi(\rho_h) > sY/K$, implies a very different outcome from the previous case. Since the rate of accumulation of productive capital is falling, capital-stock growth will eventually come into equality with the exogenously given rate of growth of the labor force as the LS schedule moves to the right.

— 18 —

KEYNES IN THE LONG RUN

A Theory of Wages, Prices, and Employment

There are two propositions in the classical system which can be tentatively discarded. One is the population doctrine, the proposition that the supply of labour is infinitely elastic at a certain real wage, that wage being determined by what the labouring classes of the country regard as their minimum standard of living with sufficient firmness to influence their conduct in reproduction. This doctrine may still have relevance to large poverty-stricken areas of the world of to-day. It is one of the doctrines that may perhaps be regarded as valid in relation to certain circumstances although not universally valid. I am interested now particularly in the economies of the United States, Great Britain, Western Europe and other advanced countries. In this context we may regard the size of the population not, as in the old classical system, as a dependent but as an independent variable. To put the matter otherwise, changes in it may be regarded as exogenous changes.

—ROY HARROD

A long-run Keynesian theory is generally considered to be an oxymoron. The process of consolidating the Keynesian revolution made a role for aggregate demand contingent on one form or another of market imperfection or friction, and the resulting sand in the wheels was supposed to operate in the short term, not over the long run. By the late 1960s, when the neoclassical counterrevolution had begun in earnest, the Keynesians had already abandoned the long run to the neoclassicals. As chapter 17 argued, Robert Solow's 1956 essay, "A Contribution to the Theory of Growth," was widely understood to have demonstrated the irrelevance of aggregate demand, even though the "demonstration," as Solow himself recognized (p. 91), is simply an assump-

Portions of this chapter were previously published in "Generalizing Lewis: Unlimited Supplies of Labor in the Advanced Capitalist World," *Research in the History of Economic Thought and Methodology* 37A (2019): 165–171; and in "Wages, Prices, and Employment in a Keynesian Long Run," *Review of Keynesian Economics* 5 (Autumn 2017): 360–425.

tion. In the standard "New Keynesian" model, aggregate demand can have a transitory effect on the economy, but the effect dissipates as the economy returns to long-run equilibrium—an example is given at the end of the mathematical appendix to this chapter.

It can't be otherwise if we maintain the assumption of a fixed labor force, fixed not once and for all, but fixed by population growth. In this world there is a natural rate of growth, and we have two choices. One is to follow Solow and deny a role for aggregate demand. The other is to follow Joan Robinson in letting aggregate demand play a central role, with the result that—serendipity apart—the theory leads either to a "limping golden age" or even a "leaden age," characterized by perpetual growth of redundant labor, or to a "restrained golden age" or a "platinum age," characterized by rampant inflation (1962, pp. 51–59). Solow's route is unattractive for obvious reasons, and Robinson provides a way forward only if we generalize her insight that "capitalist industry does not employ the whole work force in any country" (1962, p. 15). In the models that follow, the tension between the rate of growth warranted by demand conditions and the rate of growth consistent with the supply side of the economy is resolved by reformulating the supply side, in particular the assumption that the labor supply is exogenously given.

Unlimited Supplies of Labor: The Road Not Taken

A key assumption of the models in this chapter is that capitalism operates in a world of unlimited supplies of labor. This assumption connects my model both to W. Arthur Lewis's seminal 1954 paper, and, in an odd way, to Harrod's pioneering attempt to apply Keynes's conceptual framework to a growing economy. Had they survived into the twenty-first century, it might not have surprised Harrod or Lewis that China has been able to sustain a remarkable rate of growth by virtue, among other things, of its huge agricultural sector from which to draw labor for industry. But neither thought the Lewis model of unlimited labor applicable to advanced capitalism. Lewis confined his argument to the poor "developing" world, and Harrod, as the epigraph to this chapter notes, discarded this hypothesis as irrelevant to the rich countries. For the rich countries, Harrod argued, it is more appropriate to take the labor supply as exogenously given. Harrod's choice has become the standard assumption about labor supply in growth models. In this respect, the present models constitute a road not taken.[1]

The idea of unlimited supplies of labor is counterintuitive because we normally focus on the supply of labor to an entire economy and society closed to immigration. In such a setting it is natural to think of labor supply in terms of population, and to think of population as given by the net reproduction rate.

The facts tell a different story. With the exception of Japan, labor supplies in the rich countries have been augmented by immigration for the better part of a century, and in the United States from the first permanent European settlement.

Moreover, there is no analytic reason to focus on the entire economy. Indeed, it is tendentious to argue that any single model can explain all economic behavior in all settings; and in practice, growth models implicitly assume that production is guided by profit maximization and that labor is a commodity, *wage* labor. In short, the focus of the present inquiry, like the focus of virtually all growth economics, is the behavior of a *capitalist* economy. What is novel in my approach is to take seriously the fact that the capitalist sector is always embedded in a larger economic formation, which includes sectors that follow a logic different from the logic of capitalism.

In particular, we can distinguish a "family-enterprise" sector, in which production is oriented toward the market but most if not all of the labor is supplied by family members who are not paid wages. The family farm—see chapter 8—is the most important case in point, and this is the sector that Lewis and other theorists of unlimited supplies of labor had in mind. But it is not the only source of labor supply for the capitalist sector. We can also distinguish a "household" sector, in which not only is wage labor minimal but production is for the immediate satisfaction of wants and needs, unmediated by the market. Food is prepared, clothes washed, children driven to football or piano practice—mostly by their mothers—with nary a dollar, euro, pound, or yen changing hands.

Both these sectors have historically been important constituents of the internal "reserve army." At the beginning of the last century, the agricultural sector, mostly family farms, contained some 40 percent of the labor force in the United States. By midcentury, 40 percent had fallen to 10 percent, and by 1970 to less than 5 percent. In the twenty-first century, agriculture's share of the labor force has never been above 2 percent (Federal Reserve Bank of St. Louis). Most of the rich capitalist world lagged behind the United States but eventually caught up. As late as 1960 some 30 percent of the labor force in both Japan and Italy and close to 25 percent of the French labor force were engaged in agriculture. By the beginning of this century, these countries more or less caught up with the United States; in none of them was agricultural employment more than 5 percent of the labor force (Bureau of Labor Statistics 2005, p. 30).

The household sector similarly provided a steady stream of recruits to the capitalist sector. Women didn't necessarily leave the kitchen altogether; most added paid labor to their domestic duties. Female participation rates rose in the United States from 35 percent in 1950 to 60 percent, declining slightly following the beginning of the recession in 2008. In the teens of this century, women's and men's participation rates have differed by hardly ten percentage points.

These internal recruits have complemented the external reserve army, the immigrant population that has served as a reliable if politically contentious source of labor, especially for those jobs that native populations have been reluctant to fill at going rates of pay. The time pattern of immigration into the United States is especially revealing. After an abrupt fall in the wake of World War I, a decline that lasted for almost half a century, immigration picked up around 1970, just as domestic agriculture dried up as a source of labor—see Figure 18.1.

Figure 18.2 shows the impact of the reserve army on the paid labor force in the United States. Whereas the native-born population grew at an annual rate of 1.3 percent over the twentieth century, paid private employment outside agriculture was able to grow half again as fast, at a rate of more than 2 percent.

The important point is that the reserve army is not a fixed body of men and women, the battalion of workers made redundant by progress in technique (or in our own day by outsourcing of whole sectors of the economy). Rather, the reserve army is constituted and reconstituted in terms of the needs of the capitalist economy: as one source of labor, domestic agriculture, dried up, other spigots were opened. In practical terms, labor supply is unlimited, not only in the poor countries, but in the rich countries as well.[2]

Figure 18.1 Sources of the Reserve Army in the twentieth century. *Source:* Statistical Abstracts of the United States.

What then determines the wage? The classical economists—Smith, Ricardo, and Marx—were on the right track in emphasizing subsistence as the determinant of wages, though they have been misunderstood by later generations who took subsistence to mean a minimal standard of living that would ensure the reproduction of the labor force. (This presumably was Harrod's understanding of the term and for him a reason to reject the whole idea of an unlimited labor supply.) Neither Smith nor Ricardo nor Marx conceived of subsistence solely in biological terms. For all three, there were historical, cultural, and institutional dimensions that entered the determination of real wages. Marx, not surprisingly, emphasized class power, but this emphasis did not preclude a recognition that class power is situated in a matrix of culture and history. Workers are better able to press their claims to the extent that public opinion is on their side. Subsistence, in short, is a social norm:[3]

> [The worker's] natural wants, such as food, clothing, fuel, and housing, vary according to the climatic and other physical conditions of his country. On the other hand, the number and extent of his so-called necessary wants, as also the modes of satisfying them, are themselves the product of historical development, and depend therefore to a great extent on the degree of civilisation of a country, more particularly on the conditions under which, and consequently on the habits and degree of comfort in which, the class of free labourers has been formed. In contradistinction therefore to the case of other commodities, there enters into the determination of the value of labour-power a historical and moral element. (Marx 1959 [1867], p. 171)

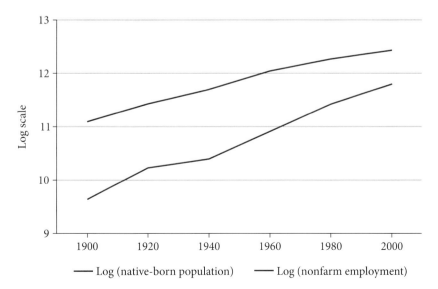

Figure 18.2 Growth of native-born population and nonfarm employment. *Source:* Gibson and Jung 2006.

To summarize: the long-run theory of labor supply proposed here reverses the mainstream relationship between the supply of labor and the real wage. Instead of an exogenous labor supply and an endogenous real wage, as the mainstream would have it, I here posit an endogenous labor supply. The equilibrium real wage is endogenously determined, but an ingredient of this equilibrium is an exogenous real wage that forms the basis of workers' monetary demands. To avoid confusion, I shall label this wage not a subsistence wage but a *conventional wage* (as did Lewis 1954, pp. 150, 172), conventional referring to both the customary elements and the contractual elements that enter into wage determination. In a dynamic setting the conventional wage is perhaps better understood as a target wage, the wage that the working class aims for in order to achieve norms of consumption conventionally conceived and understood if not unanimously agreed upon.

None of this is to say that productivity is irrelevant to wage determination. Productivity determines the size of the pie that the contending parties struggle over. Nineteenth-century British output had to be of a certain size before workers could obtain a share large enough to permit them to buy refined white bread rather than the coarse grains to which the lower classes had accommodated themselves in earlier times; twentieth-century American production had to be of a certain size before workers could successfully struggle for a share large enough to include an automobile or a mortgage payment as part of the wage packet. But a productive technology did not guarantee that either the nineteenth-century British pie or the twentieth-century American pie would be sliced in a way that would allow workers to achieve their aims. For this to happen, certain community standards, social norms, were essential.

These community standards underlie, for example, the very idea of a legal minimum wage—and the erosion of community underlies the erosion of the minimum wage in the United States since the 1970s. Nor is it just the minimum that is at issue. During this same period, there has been an ever-widening gap between workers in the middle of the wage distribution and the richest 1 percent of the income distribution, which includes both top managers and large stockholders. There is no longer even the pretense that we are all in it together, that the United States is a community when it comes to matters economic.

Not only is productivity relevant to wage determination, so are rates of price increases or decreases. Workers, as Keynes insists, may bargain in money terms, but they are bargaining about real wages, so that inflation or deflation plays an important role in determining money bargains.

Unemployment also matters. The ability of workers to achieve their ambitions in the sphere of wages, or to hold onto a level of real wages already achieved, depends on the state of the labor market. In the short period, in which wage claims are made (and contested), unemployment is a fact of life and may be the dominant fact, even if the labor force is endogenous in the long run.

Making the unemployment rate one among other determinants of changes in wages (rather than the sole determinant) resolves another problem. The idea that wages respond to unemployment, and unemployment alone, provides a tolerably good account of wage behavior during the period 1929 to 1933, but not since. Until the Depression bottoms out in 1933, changes in money wages are closely correlated with the unemployment rate, as Table 18.1 shows. But in 1933 wages stopped falling even though unemployment remained high. If we extend the table into the recovery, we find that wages pick up after 1933 even though unemployment never fell below 10 percent until the country entered World War II. Table 18.2 provides the extended data.

Table 18.1 Relationship between Unemployment Rate and Changes in Money Wages

	Unemployed, Not Counting Federal Emergency Workers as Employed (percent)	Year-on-Year Change in Hourly Manufacturing Wage (percent)
1930	9.0	−1.8
1931	16.3	−7.3
1932	24.1	−13.7
1933	25.2	0.0

Source: Historical Statistics of the United States, Millennial Edition Online.

Table 18.2 Relationship between Unemployment Rate and Changes in Money Wages (1930–1941)

	Unemployed, Not Counting Federal Emergency Workers as Employed (percent)	Year-on-Year Change in Hourly Manufacturing Wage (percent)
1930	9.0	−1.8
1931	16.3	−7.3
1932	24.1	−13.7
1933	25.2	0.0
1934	22.0	20.5
1935	20.29	1.9
1936	17.03	1.9
1937	14.32	12.7
1938	19.05	0.0
1939	17.17	1.6
1940	14.59	4.8
1941	9.94	10.6

Source: Historical Statistics of the United States, Millennial Edition Online.

Clearly a simple model of wages responding solely to the unemployment level will not do even if the long run is as limited as the transition from decline to recovery. The regression equation below, covering the period 1930 to 2011, adds labor's share of output, productivity growth, and the change in energy prices as explanatory variables, along with dummy variables meant to reflect changes in the conventional wage at three critical times in its evolution.[4] Unemployment still plays a role, but it has to share the stage with these other variables.

$$\frac{\Delta W}{W_{-1}} = 43.48 - 76.53\left(\frac{WL}{PY}\right)_{-1} + 0.4708\frac{\Delta Prod}{Prod_{-1}} + 0.1196\frac{\Delta P_E}{\left(P_E\right)_{-1}} - 0.3058\,\text{UNRATE}$$
$$(21.10)\quad(35.25)(0.1439)(0.0221)(0.1091)$$

$$+\;5.062\,\text{DUM1936} + 2.138\,\text{DUM1970} - 4.773\,\text{DUM1994}$$
$$(2.301)(0.9402)(1.037)$$

$$R^2 = 0.63$$

Newey-West Standard Errors in Parentheses
Observations: 82 (1930–2011) $F(7, 74) = 14.1$

Variable	Description	Mean	Std Dev	Min	Max
$\dfrac{\Delta W}{W_{-1}}$	Percentage Change in Nominal Wages	4.740	4.063	−13.210	17.539
$\left(\dfrac{WL}{PY}\right)_{-1}$	Labor Share of Output, Lagged One Year	0.560	0.018	0.514	0.596
$\dfrac{\Delta Prod}{Prod_{-1}}$	Percentage Change in Output per Employee Hour	2.215	2.391	−6.641	12.552
$\dfrac{\Delta P_E}{\left(P_E\right)_{-1}}$	Percentage Change in Price of Energy	4.641	11.852	−26.045	55.164
UNRATE	Unemployment Rate	7.241	4.849	1.200	24.900
DUM1936	= 0 prior to 1936, = 1 in 1936 and later years				
DUM1970	= 0 prior to 1970, = 1 in 1970 and later years				
DUM1994	= 0 prior to 1994, = 1 in 1994 and later years				

The conventional-wage share emerges from the model.[5] Money-wage dynamics, without the control variables, are given by

$$\frac{\Delta W}{W_{-1}} = \theta\left[\left(\frac{WL}{PY}\right)^{*} - \left(\frac{WL}{PY}\right)_{-1}\right],$$

where $(WL/PY)^*$ is the conventional wage, and θ is the speed of adjustment. Translating this formula into a regression equation we have

$$\frac{\Delta W}{W_{-1}} = a_0 + a_1 \left(\frac{WL}{PY} \right)_{-1} \equiv -a_1 \left[\frac{a_0}{-a_1} - \left(\frac{WL}{PY} \right)_{-1} \right] + \text{control variables.}$$

Thus the speed of adjustment, θ, is equal to $-a_1$, and the conventional wage share, $(WL/PY)^*$, is equal to the ratio $a_0/(-a_1)$. In the above regression, this ratio gives an initial value of the conventional wage share equal to 0.57 ($se = 0.033$, computed by the delta method). $(WL/PY)^*$ increases to 0.63 in 1936, and increases again to 0.66 in 1970. In 1994 the conventional-wage share falls to 0.6, close to its value in the early 1930s. We will revisit the determination of wage changes after the theoretical investigation in the remainder of this chapter and the empirical analysis in the next chapter.

The Checkered History of the Phillips Curve

One reason for moving beyond the short run is that the policy question that animated Keynes is not limited to the here and now, but is an issue for the long run as well. Can demand management improve the performance of the economy? Do changes in aggregate demand have long-run effects on employment and other variables? And, to go beyond Keynes, what is the impact of wages, or rather wage aspirations reflected in the conventional wage, on the level of economic activity?

Solow answered these questions by assuming aggregate demand away. Milton Friedman (1968) and Edmund Phelps (1968) took a different tack, arguing that aggregate demand would in the long run affect only the price level, as in Figure 4.9. The positive relationship between employment and inflation enshrined in the Phillips curve, understood by Keynesians to reflect the operation of aggregate demand, was dismissed by the counterrevolutionaries. The Phillips curve was now understood to be the result of misperceptions that would necessarily disappear as agents developed more sophistication about the economy. The implication was that demand cannot matter in the long run. Indeed, Friedman and Phelps predicted that periods of high inflation would not be accompanied by higher economic activity. In the long run there is no Phillips curve, no trade-off between economic activity and price stability. In this perspective, raising the conventional wage may lead to higher money wages, but this is necessarily an exercise in futility: higher money wages can mean only higher inflation, with no impact on employment and output. The classical dichotomy with a vengeance!

And the data do appear to bear out the prediction of no relationship between employment and inflation, at least not a simple one. Figure 18.3 plots
the data over more than half a century. Analyzing these data economists
have found, if anything, a negative relationship between real economic activity and inflation. Cross-sectional studies by Stanley Fischer (1993), Robert
Barro (1996), and others have found a significant negative correlation between growth and inflation. But since these results are dominated by high inflation rates, their relevance is perhaps limited to the relatively poor countries
where high inflation has been more common. More striking therefore are the
findings of Moshin Khan and Abdelhak Senhadji (2001), who separate poor
and rich countries and find that for the rich countries the threshold above
which inflation is associated with lower GDP growth is only 1 to 3 percent per
year. Other researchers, to be sure, have taken issue with these results, but
nobody to my knowledge has found the strong, positive relationship between
inflation and growth that the Phillips curve suggests.

None of this should surprise us. Once it has been determined that demand
does not matter in the long run, it makes sense to treat all observations symmetrically and look for supply-side effects.

Appearances notwithstanding, macroeconomists learned from the impact
of rising oil prices in the 1970s to sort out supply shocks from demand shocks
and thus to make sense of the data in terms of a Phillips curve along which
movements reflect demand shocks but which is itself moved by supply shocks
(see, among others, Robert Gordon [1984, 2013]). Sorting out demand and
supply shocks is central to my approach as well. But it will not do to lump
all supply shocks together since wage and price shocks may have different
impacts. This possibility is taken account of in this chapter: wage, price,

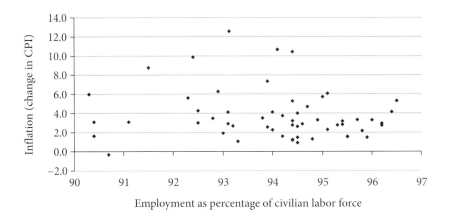

Figure 18.3 Employment vs. inflation (1956–2011).

and employment dynamics derive from the interaction of aggregate demand, profit maximization, and a conventional wage.

Are High Wages Good for Capitalism?

The relationship between wages, prices, and employment, specifically whether higher wages promote higher employment, has long been controversial. The question did not begin or end with Keynes, but *The General Theory* provided a framework in which it became possible to analyze the impact of the wage rate on aggregate demand. There is some irony here: in the main, *The General Theory* argues that the real wage rate is determined endogenously, a thermometer of economic conditions rather than a thermostat.[6]

Despite Keynes's own relative neglect of the issue, the potential for stimulating aggregate demand by redistributing profits and other forms of property income to wage earners became identified with *The General Theory*. With good reason: even though Keynes paid little attention to this issue, the importance of *The General Theory* framework to the macroeconomics of redistribution made Keynes a figure lionized by the social-democratic Left and despised by the Right. For the Left, it was a no-brainer. As long as the economy is operating at less than full employment, income redistribution amounts to a free lunch for the economy as a whole: shifting income from rich people with low propensities to consume to poor people with higher consumption propensities would boost aggregate demand. For the Right, redistribution was anathema, a threat not only to the free market but to social order and morality.

Among economists, the idea that redistribution could stimulate the economy came under attack from two sides. The permanent-income and life-cycle hypotheses (see chapter 9) challenged the idea that the propensity to consume is a function of income. And with the rise of supply-side economics, aggregate demand was relegated to being at best a short-run phenomenon of frictions and market imperfections, a fate for which Keynes's followers, especially in the United States, had helped to pave the way.

There was a minority view: the left Keynesians, who took inspiration from Joan Robinson and Michał Kalecki, continued to argue that aggregate demand was a problem that ran much deeper than frictions and imperfections, and Robinson, as I observed in chapter 17, devoted much effort to building long-run models in which outcomes depend on aggregate demand (1966 [1956], 1962). The distributional issue remained central in these models.

Bob Rowthorn (1982) formalized the argument that redistributing income from rich to poor would increase aggregate demand because the propensity to consume declines with income. A novel aspect of Rowthorn's argument was that higher consumption demand would be self-reinforcing through its effects on investment demand. Higher consumption demand implies higher employment, higher capacity utilization implies a higher rate of profit, and a higher rate of profit implies higher investment demand.

Amit Bhaduri and I challenged Rowthorn's logic, in particular, the impact of the wage rate on investment demand (Marglin and Bhaduri 1990; Bhaduri and Marglin 1990). We argued that the two factors that together determine the profit rate, namely, the share of profits in GDP and the rate of capacity utilization, should be treated separately because each has a distinct impact on investment demand. The profit share reflects the prospects for making money from new capacity, whereas the rate of capacity utilization reflects the likelihood of selling additional goods. When the profit share has a large positive effect on investment, the negative impact of higher wages on the profit share may outweigh the positive impact on capacity utilization via consumption demand. Our conclusion was that growth can be stimulated by higher wages under some circumstances, and by higher profits—lower wages—under others. Growth can be "wage led" or "profit led."

The intention was to change the debate about the impact of the wage rate on growth from one that focused entirely on consumption to one that included investment as well. Judging from the voluminous literature that has appeared since we published our papers, we succeeded. (See, for example, the symposium in the *Review of Keynesian Economics,* 2016 and 2017.)

Nonetheless, I have come to view our work as deficient, particularly in our focus on comparative statics and our corresponding neglect of dynamics. The version of our argument that appeared in the *Cambridge Journal of Economics* ends with the observation

> The recognition that quantities (capacity utilization) and prices (the real wage) may adjust simultaneously in a more general dynamic model raises a deeper conceptual issue regarding the interpretation of the IS-curve itself. It can be treated either as the locus of stationary capacity utilization . . . as has been implicitly assumed in our . . . analysis, or as the locus of stationary price level . . . Ultimately it boils down to one of the most important unsettled questions of modern macroeconomics: does excess demand for commodities lead primarily to quantity or to price adjustment? We cannot pretend to have an answer; but dynamic analysis cannot be undertaken without addressing this important, and as yet unsettled, question. (Bhaduri and Marglin 1990, p. 390)

I make no claim to be able to answer definitively the question of how prices and quantities adjust out of equilibrium. But the data on employment and inflation shed light on dynamics, especially if we separate wage and price adjustment rather than combining the two in the level of the mark-up.

There is another problem with the analysis Bhaduri and I offered in 1990: we lumped all investment together, implicitly assuming that investment takes place solely to expand capacity, an assumption that goes back to Roy Harrod (1939, 1948). Output-enhancing investment, capital widening in an older literature, is important, but it is not the only kind of investment. In addition to enhancing output, investment takes place in order to cut costs by substituting capital for labor, energy, or other inputs—capital deepening for short.

As chapter 10 observed, cost-cutting investment has a different logic from output-enhancing investment, in particular, a very different relationship to wages and profits. For output-enhancing investment, the lower the real wage, the better: lower real wages mean, *ceteris paribus,* higher profits. By contrast, cost-cutting investment, specifically labor-saving investment, ought to respond positively to higher wages: the higher the real wage, the greater the savings in labor costs from a given investment—hence the more profits.

The result is to make the distinction between wage-led and profit-led growth somewhat problematic. A lower real wage makes one kind of investment, capital widening, more profitable. But a lower real wage makes the other kind of investment, capital deepening, less profitable. In the one case, profit-led growth benefits from lower real wages, in the other, from higher real wages. The difference is that in the first case higher profitability as a stimulus to investment conflicts with higher real wages as a stimulus to consumption, whereas in the second case the stimulus to investment and consumption complement one another.

The different impact of capital-widening and capital-deepening investment is particularly important because the salience of the two types of investment is likely to differ markedly over the cycle. Over the decade 2008 to 2017, for example, there was considerable excess capacity and, consequently, relatively little demand for output-enhancing investment. A recession thus enhances the case for wage-led growth; wage-led growth becomes more attractive since high wages not only stimulate consumption demand directly but also stimulate the investment demand for capital deepening. If capacity utilization is at 90 percent, there may be little interest in output-enhancing investment, but cutting costs on 90 percent of maximum output is only 10 percent less worthwhile than cutting costs on 100 percent.

When bust is replaced by boom, capital widening becomes more important whether or not it takes center stage. In boom situations, the positive relationship between low wages and investment profitability bolsters the argument for profit-led growth.

The countercyclical response of overall investment to the real-wage rate has an important impact on the recurring effort to determine whether particular economies are wage or profit led. The search may reveal the economy to be a chimera. Any given economy may respond positively to high real wages in slack times and negatively in boom times; the average response over the cycle may be of limited interest.

A Long Run Model in the Spirit of *The General Theory*

The basic long-run model, depicted in Figure 18.4, takes the real price level P/W and the labor:capital ratio $l \equiv L/K$ as describing the state of the economy. (At any moment of time the capital stock is given, so in the short run, l is a measure of employment.) Formally we have

$$Y = F(L, K),$$

$$f(l) \equiv F\left(1, \frac{L}{K}\right).$$

In the simplest case, investment demand per unit of capital is a function of the hurdle rate of interest alone, $I_D = \psi(\rho_h)$; desired saving is a constant fraction, s, of income, and per unit of capital is $S_D = sf(l)$.

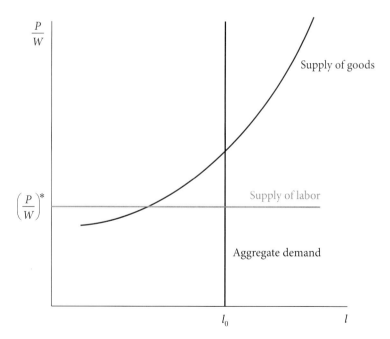

Figure 18.4 Aggregate demand, goods supply, and unlimited labor supply.

Figure 18.4 differs from the models of chapter 6 in how labor supply is represented. The same forces are at play in determining wage dynamics in the long run as in the short run, but in the short run the focus was entirely on unemployment; we ignored the conventional wage. In the long-run context, the emphasis is on the conventional wage: to keep matters simple we shall assume that the supply of labor is literally unlimited at the conventional real wage. This ignores the complication that, though the labor force is endogenous, it doesn't adjust instantaneously; the unemployment rate is an important variable in determining the creation and mobilization of one or another reserve army. (The mathematical appendix to this chapter lays out a model that incorporates both unemployment and the conventional wage as determinants of wages.)

Like the short-run models of previous chapters, the model in Figure 18.4 is overdetermined.[7] Any two of the three schedules are sufficient to determine employment and the real price. All three together make the usual concept of equilibrium insufficient. We can make sense of Figure 18.4 only if we shift the focus to the dynamics of adjustment.

With flexprice dynamics, the picture is in Figure 18.5. The equilibrium is at E, where both employment per unit of capital and the real price are stationary. E is an inflationary equilibrium, with prices and wages rising at the same

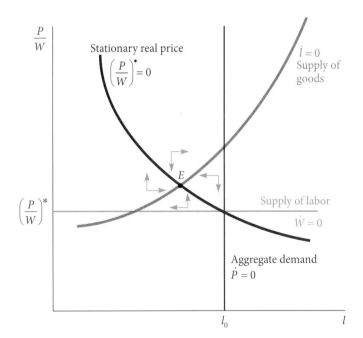

Figure 18.5 Equilibrium with flexprice dynamics.

percentage rate. Aggregate expenditure exceeds aggregate income, so prices rise. And because the equilibrium real wage is below the conventional wage, $P/W > (P/W)^*$, there is constant inflationary pressure on wages.

As in the short run, the alternative to flexprice adjustment is what Hicks (1974) called fixprice adjustment. In the long run as well as in the short run, this terminology is misleading since prices are not fixed; rather, the *direct* impact of an excess or a shortfall of expenditure relative to income is on output and employment. Prices (and wages) are affected indirectly. Prices are driven by the relationship between actual employment and the profit-maximizing rate of employment, that is, by the horizontal distance between today's level of employment and the GS schedule. Money wages continue to be driven by the gap between the actual real price and the conventional real price.

This process defines the equilibrium in Figure 18.6. Since the GS schedule is now a locus of stationary prices and the LS schedule is the locus of stationary money wages, the stationary real-price locus, $(P/W)^{\bullet} = 0$, lies between them.

As Figure 18.6 is drawn, the equilibrium, like the equilibrium in Figure 18.5, is characterized by inflation: producers raise prices because they are losing money at the margin, while workers, having to make do with less than the

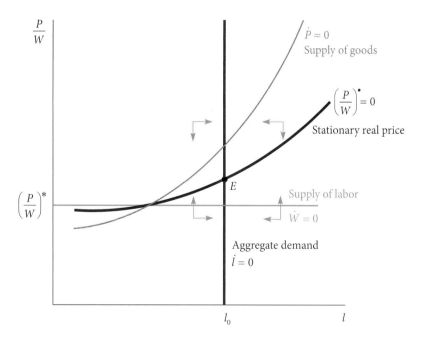

Figure 18.6 Fixprice dynamics.

conventional wage, put pressure on wages. At E, the pressure on prices and pressure on wages just balance, so that the real price remains stationary.[8]

Some Comparative Statics: Phillips and Anti-Phillips Curves

What happens when there is a shock to the system so that one or another schedule is displaced? Does the shift in the equilibrium produce a Phillips outcome, in which employment and inflation move in the same direction, or an anti-Phillips outcome, in which employment and inflation move in opposite directions?

Look first at what happens when aggregate demand changes, as in Figures 18.7(a) and 18.7(b). In both cases the increase in aggregate demand leads to an increase in economic activity accompanied by higher inflation, that is, a Phillips outcome.

Supply shocks are different, because demand and supply are not independent. As David Colander observed in 1995, a change in production conditions will not only shift the GS schedule but will normally move the AD schedule as well. A change in output is at the same time a change in income.

With flexprice dynamics, the results are ambiguous. An upward shift in the GS schedule produces a higher price level and higher inflation, but it may increase or decrease the level of employment depending on the relative speeds at which prices and wages adjust: a Phillips outcome, with higher employment and higher inflation, is a possible result of an upward shift in the supply schedule, but so is an anti-Phillips effect, coupling lower employment with higher inflation. In the case of fixprice dynamics, we always get a Phillips outcome since a leftward shift of the GS schedule means more workers are needed to produce the same output.

The simplest way of seeing this is to expand the production function to include a third variable, say, energy, denoted E. We write

$$Y = F(K, L, E)$$

and assume constant returns to scale, so that

$$\frac{Y}{K} = F(1, l, e) = f(l, e),$$

where $e = E/K$. We further assume that energy is purchased on a competitive market at the real price, $\xi = P_E/P$, where P_E is the nominal price of energy. The effects of a change in the price of energy depend on whether energy is produced domestically or imported. The simplest story is that energy is entirely imported and paid for by transferring goods abroad. $h(l, \xi)$ is then the

(a) Flexprice dynamics

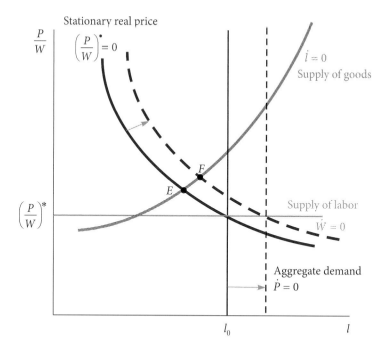

(b) Fixprice dynamics

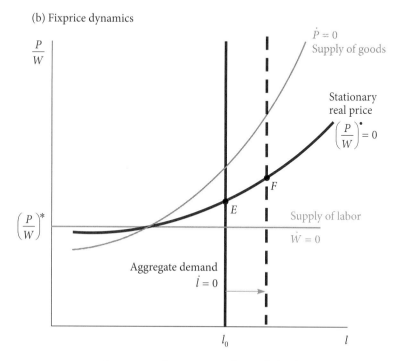

Figure 18.7 An aggregate-demand shock.

output:capital ratio net of the cost of energy. This assumption allows us to write

$$h(l, \xi) = \max_e \left[f(l, e) - \xi e \right] = f\left(l, e(l, \xi) \right) - \xi e(l, \xi),$$

where $e(l, \xi)$ is the amount of energy per unit of capital that, for given l and ξ, maximizes the expression $f(l, e) - \xi e$.

What happens when the real price of energy, ξ, changes? Figure 18.8 shows how an increase in ξ affects both goods supply and aggregate demand. Precisely how equilibrium shifts depends both on the adjustment process and on the relative speeds of adjustment.

With flexprice adjustment, there are contradictory forces at work, and the contradictions may be resolved in different ways. Two possibilities are shown in Figures 18.9 and 18.10. In Figure 18.9, the labor:capital ratio at F, the new equilibrium, is greater than at E, whereas in Figure 18.10, the new l is smaller than the old. In both cases the new real price is higher, which is to say that an increase in the price of energy leads to greater inflation, but the inflation is now "cost-push" with its origins on the supply side, as distinct from the "demand-pull" inflation caused by an increase in aggregate demand.

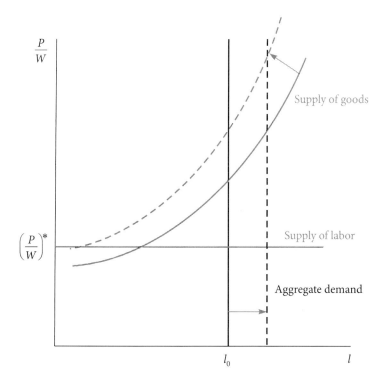

Figure 18.8 An increase in energy price.

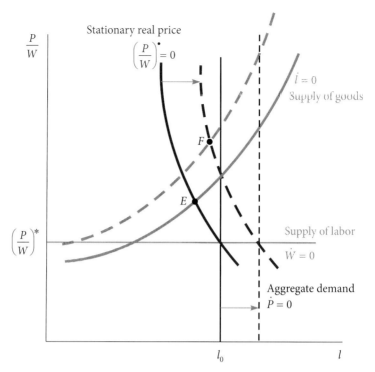

Figure 18.9 Increase in energy price with flexprice dynamics, I: sluggish wage adjustment.

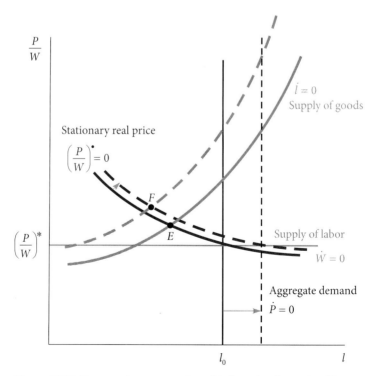

Figure 18.10 Increase in energy price with flexprice dynamics, II: rapid wage adjustment.

Why is the effect on output different in the two diagrams? The impact of the shift in the GS schedule is unambiguous: when the price of energy rises, the real marginal cost of output also rises (labor and energy are complements), and producers respond to the incentive to reduce output and employment.

The ambiguity is the result of contradictory effects on demand. The AD schedule moves outward since the higher energy price reduces real income and thus requires a greater income to generate sufficient saving to match the given level of investment demand. That is, output per unit of capital net of energy costs, $h(l, \xi)$, falls, and therefore so does saving. Because investment demand is assumed to be given, aggregate expenditure rises relative to income, and this causes the price level to rise. This makes production more profitable at the margin, which induces an increase in output and employment. However—this is the contradictory effect—the rise in prices reduces real wages. This leads to wage pressure that counters the positive effect of higher prices on output and employment. How these conflicting tendencies are resolved depends on the relative adjustment speeds of money prices and money wages.

Consider the limiting cases of rapid price adjustment and sluggish price adjustment (rapid wage adjustment). In the first case, which is Keynes's case of money-wage rigidity, and therefore real-wage flexibility, there is nothing to constrain the adjustment of the price level to an energy-price shock, and the workers' share of the burden is felt in lower real wages and higher inflation. Employment per unit of capital actually increases.

If wages adjust much more rapidly than prices, employment effects dominate. In the limit, the real wage is rigid, and the workers' share of the burden associated with a supply shock is through a reduction in employment per unit of capital. Once again, the rise in the price of energy leads to a permanently higher rate of inflation.

This analysis suggests a fissure in the working class with regard to a supply-side shock; if asked to choose between taking a hit in the form of reduced wages or in the form of reduced employment, all workers do not have the same interests. Those with secure employment, or with good job prospects in the face of job loss, might be expected to opt for rigid real wages. If these folks have their way, the stationary real-price locus will coincide with the conventional wage, and employment per unit of capital will bear the entire adjustment burden. Those at the margins with respect to employment opportunities might opt for rigid money wages. If they have their way the stationary real-price locus will coincide with the AD schedule, and the entire hit takes the form of lower real wages, employment being unaffected.

With fixprice dynamics, the picture is in Figure 18.11. An increase in the price of energy increases employment while lowering real wages and increasing the equilibrium level of inflation. Employment increases because more workers are required to produce the same output; with fixprice dynamics equilibrium is always on the AD schedule. Real wages fall because producing the new level of output at F is profitable only at a higher real price; inflation increases because workers increase the pressure on money wages as the real wage falls. With fixprice adjustment, the results are unambiguous: employment and inflation both rise in conjunction with a falling real wage. How much inflation rises and the real wage falls depends on the relative speeds at which prices and wages adjust. The more rapidly prices adjust, the greater the hit to inflation and the real wage.

The results of varying the conventional wage are similar to the results of a supply shock—without the ambiguity in the effect on employment that exists with flexprice adjustment. This is another case of cost-push inflation; indeed, wage pressure was practically synonymous with cost-push before the oil shocks of the 1970s.

As Figure 18.12(a) shows, in the flexprice case, an increase in the conventional wage, which is to say a fall in $(P/W)^*$, leads unambiguously to a reduction in employment per unit capital and an increase in inflation (except in the limiting case of rigid money wages); in the fixprice case, Figure 18.12(b), there is also an increase in the equilibrium rate of inflation, but employment is unaffected.

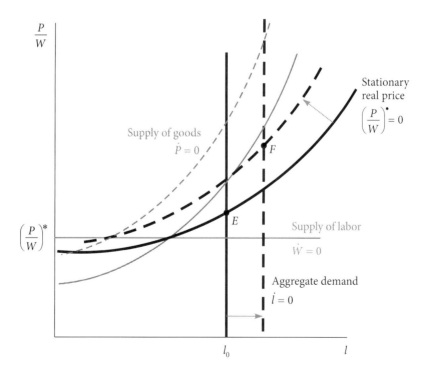

Figure 18.11 An energy-price shock with fixprice dynamics.

(a) Flexprice dynamics

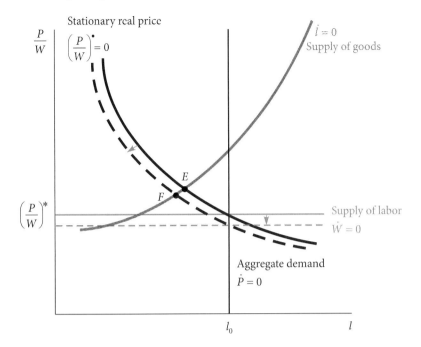

(b) Fixprice dynamics

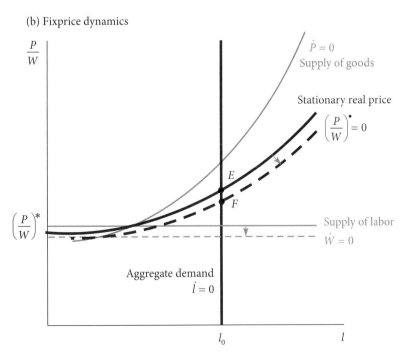

Figure 18.12 An increase in the conventional wage.

The fixprice result that employment is unaffected by a shift in the conventional wage is the result of a vertical AD schedule, the consequence of assuming, first, that saving is a constant fraction of income, and, second, that investment demand is exogenously given as a function of one variable, the hurdle rate of interest. As we relax these simplifying assumptions in the next section, we shall obtain different results.

The assumption of a uniform saving propensity makes it impossible to examine the left Keynesian view that higher wages are a boon to employment since this proposition rests on the assumption that the fraction of wages spent on consumption is higher than the fraction of profits. To see the distributional effect in action, we replace the assumption of a uniform propensity to consume with the assumption—itself highly simplified in the other direction—that all wages are consumed while only a fraction of profits are consumed, what was called in chapter 9 the Cambridge saving theory.

To see the effect of different assumptions about investment, we distinguish capital widening from capital deepening. Here, in contrast with chapter 10, we examine these different assumptions about investment in conjunction with the Cambridge saving theory. The mathematics is in the appendix.

Demand and Supply Shocks with the Cambridge Saving Theory and Capital-Widening Investment

As chapter 9 noted, a pre-Keynesian view of consumption and saving assumed that working people simply lacked the economic capacity to save and that the rich were responsible for whatever saving the community was able to muster. In the last chapter, we saw how Joan Robinson deployed this assumption along with an innovative characterization of investment demand as a function of the rate of profit. This section formalizes Robinson's argument—in a way she would likely deplore (given her aversion to a production function incorporating aggregate capital and continuous factor substitution)—in order to make clear the role of what is assumed about investment and saving in the analysis of the long run.

Saving first. Taking account of energy as well as capital and labor in the production function, we have the rate of profit as

$$r = \frac{\Pi}{K} = f(l, e) - \left(\frac{P}{W}\right)^{-1} l - \xi e = h(l, \xi) - \left(\frac{P}{W}\right)^{-1}$$

and the simplest version of the Cambridge saving theory on a per-unit of capital basis as

$$S_D = s_\pi r = s_\pi \left[h(l, \xi) - \left(\frac{P}{W}\right)^{-1} l \right].$$

This saving function is pictured in Figure 18.13, with the real price increasing from $(P/W)_1$ to $(P/W)_2$.

With respect to investment, we examine first the expansion of productive capacity—capital widening—which, as I have noted, is the nigh-universal assumption in the literature initiated by Roy Harrod in 1939. Capital widening responds positively to the real price as well as to the level of output, while capital deepening is relatively unresponsive to the level of economic activity and responds negatively to the real price. Taking account of energy and writing investment demand as a ratio to the stock of capital, capital-widening investment is

$$I_D = \psi\left(r, l, \frac{P}{W}, \rho_h, \xi\right) = \psi(\Omega(l)r - \rho_h) = \psi\left(\Omega(l)\left[h(l, \xi) - \left(\frac{P}{W}\right)^{-1} l\right] - \rho_h\right).$$

The argument of the investment function ψ is the anticipated annual return from a unit of investment that lasts forever. The gross return, what chapter 10 termed the quasi-rent, is the product of the subjective probability of finding a market for additional output, $\Omega(l)$, and the prospective rate of profit assuming the additional output can be sold, namely, $h(l, \xi) - (P/W)^{-1} l$. The net return is the difference between the quasi-rent, the probability-weighted profit, and the hurdle rate of interest. Figure 18.14 shows how capital-widening investment demand responds to the capital:labor ratio at two different levels of the real price.

Aggregate demand is defined by the equality of investment demand and desired saving, graphically determined by the intersection of the schedules in Figures 18.13 and 18.14. Figure 18.15(a) assumes that investment is more re-

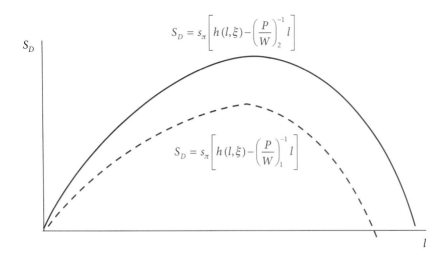

Figure 18.13 Cambridge saving at different real prices.

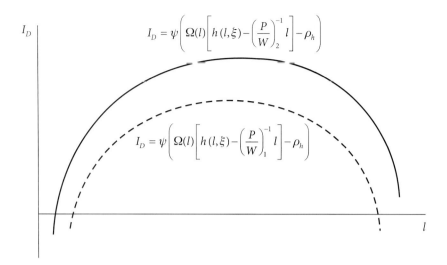

Figure 18.14 Capital-widening investment at different real prices.

sponsive to the rate of profit than is saving, $\psi'\Omega - s_\pi > 0$, at low rates of profit, whereas at higher rates of profit, it is the other way around, $\psi'\Omega - s_\pi < 0$. Note that the assumption that investment is more responsive at low rates of profit is necessary for the existence of the AD schedule; the intercept of the investment function in Figures 18.14 and 18.15(a) is negative, so if $\psi'\Omega - s_\pi < 0$ everywhere, investment never becomes equal to the amount of desired saving. The assumption that $\psi'\Omega - s_\pi$ is negative at higher rates of profit is not required for existence of the AD schedule, but it is, as we shall see, necessary for the left-Keynesian intuition that higher wages stimulate employment.

Figure 18.15(b) reflects the assumption that $\psi'\Omega - s_\pi$ switches sign: there are two distinct segments of the AD schedule, formed by the projection of the points of intersection of the investment and saving schedules in Figure 18.15(a) onto the space of $l \times P/W$.

Unsurprisingly, equilibrium is more complicated in this model. To streamline the argument we will focus on fixprice adjustment. Not only does this simplify, fixprice dynamics will prove, in the next chapter, to be more relevant empirically, just as in chapter 8.

The shape of the AD schedule gives rise to multiple equilibria, as in Figure 18.16. The equilibria at E' and F' are unstable. Southwest of F' the trajectory is downward, approaching the stationary-P/W locus as l falls to zero. This is secular stagnation with a vengeance: investment demand falls evermore short of saving with the capital stock per worker rising, not because of strong investment demand but because of ever-weaker demand for output and employment. Southwest of E' and northeast of F', the economy enters the orbit of

(a) Investment and saving holding real-price constant

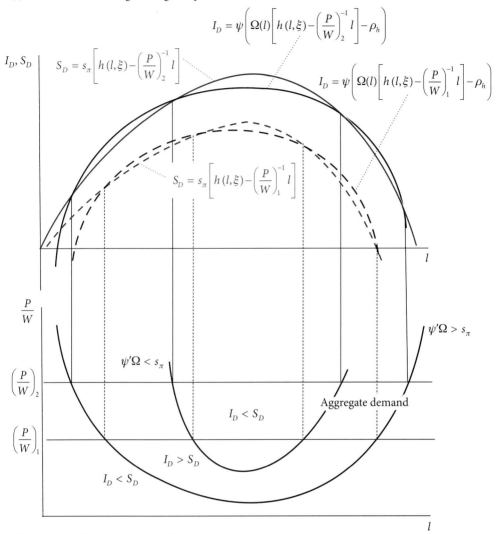

(b) Aggregate demand varying real price

Figure 18.15 Aggregate demand with Cambridge saving and capital widening.

E; northeast of E', the trajectory is toward F. The equilibrium at E is stable provided prices adjust more rapidly than quantities. The equilibrium at F is stable whatever the speeds of adjustment. Details are in the mathematical appendix.

The response to a demand shock or a price shock turns out to be the same for all stable equilibria. But the impact of a wage shock depends on whether

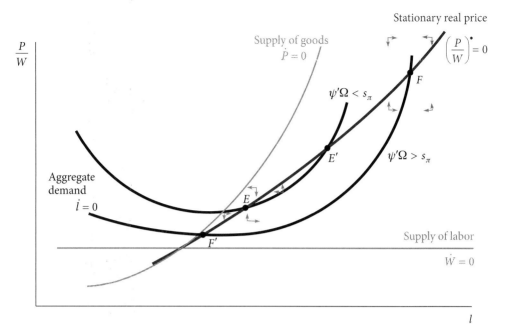

Figure 18.16 Equilibrium with Cambridge saving and capital widening.

or not investment is more responsive to profitability than is saving, that is, on which segment of the AD schedule the equilibrium lies. We take these changes one at a time.

Consider an increase in investment demand or a decrease in desired saving. The AD schedule shifts as in Figure 18.17. Starting from E or F, the new equilibrium is at E' or F'; employment increases along with the real price level and the rate of inflation.

Now suppose the price of energy increases, as in Figure 18.18. Net productivity—output per unit of capital net of energy costs, $h(l, \xi)$—decreases. This fall in productivity is reflected in the shift in the AD schedule. By itself, this shift would increase employment when saving is more responsive to profitability (starting from E) since more output and employment are required to generate saving, and would decrease employment when investment is more responsive (starting from F). But the increase in the price of energy also decreases profitability, which is reflected in the shift in the GS schedule. Starting from E (where $\psi'\Omega - s_\pi < 0$), the increase in employment puts pressure on prices, and the concomitant fall in profitability leads to a contraction of production and employment. Starting from F ($\psi'\Omega - s_\pi > 0$), the fall in employment reduces the pressure on prices, and employment rises. Figure 18.18 assumes this tension is resolved in favor of lower employment (at F'), but this result is by no means guaranteed.

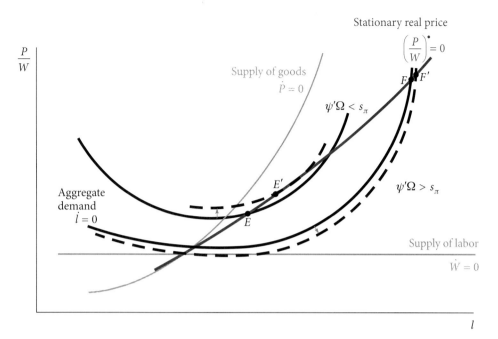

Figure 18.17 An increase in investment or a decrease in saving with Cambridge saving and capital widening.

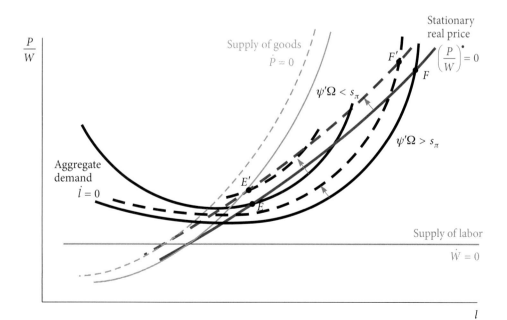

Figure 18.18 An increase in the price of energy with Cambridge saving and capital widening.

Similarly, the effect on the price level and inflation depends on the balance of the two opposing forces. Indeed, prices and employment can move in the opposite directions—stagflation—as in Figure 18.18. Or they can move in the same direction. Once again the details are in the mathematical appendix.

Consider now a change in the conventional wage. As Figure 18.19 shows, the effect of a higher conventional wage depends critically on the relative responsiveness of investment and saving to changes in profitability. In both cases, profitability falls as the conventional wage rises and greater pressure is put on wages. Starting from E, the effect of higher wages is reflected in lower profits and lower saving. Employment per unit of capital increases so that saving will continue to match the (relatively) fixed level of investment demand. Inflation also increases—overall, a Phillips outcome, in which inflation and employment move in the same direction.

If the starting point is at F, where investment is more sensitive to profitability than is saving, the higher conventional wage leads to *less* employment because of the negative impact on investment demand. Higher wages mean lower profits in this case as well, but lower profits discourage investment demand more than saving, and employment falls because of the reduction in aggregate expenditure. In this case, inflation also falls, once again a Phillips outcome.

Bhaduri and I highlighted this possibility as a counterpoint to the left-

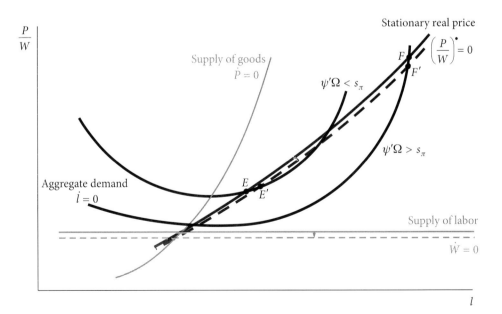

Figure 18.19 An increase in the conventional wage with Cambridge saving and capital widening.

Keynesian contention that higher wages are always good for employment (Marglin and Bhaduri 1990; Bhaduri and Marglin 1990). Our intention was not to offer a countervailing dogma, but to argue that the sensitivity of investment demand to profitability had to be taken into account to assess the impact of wages on employment. The contrast in Figure 18.19 between displacing the equilibrium at E and displacing the equilibrium at F makes this clear.

But there is more to the story. Once we drop the assumption that investment invariably takes place solely for the purpose of widening capital, sensitivity of investment demand to profitability may reinforce rather than undermine left-Keynesian policy views.

Capital Deepening

Capital deepening is in crucial respects opposite to capital widening. The prospective return to a single unit of investment is

$$\left(\frac{P}{W}\right)^{-1}\frac{MP_K}{MP_L} - \rho_h \equiv \left(\frac{P}{W}\right)^{-1}\frac{h - h_l l}{h_l} - \rho_h,$$

since the marginal product of labor is the derivative of $h(l, \xi)$ with respect to l

$$MP_L = h_l$$

and with constant returns to scale

$$MP_K = h - h_l l.$$

Investment demand becomes

$$I_D = \psi\left(\left(\frac{P}{W}\right)^{-1}\frac{h - h_l l}{h_l} - \rho_h\right),$$

with the ψ function, as before, reflecting the animal spirits of the business community.

Assuming that saving is a constant fraction of output (rather than of profit), the AD schedule can be derived in the same manner as we derived Figure 18.15. The picture is in Figure 18.20.

There is a new wrinkle that sets the long-run case apart from the short-run analysis of chapter 10. Unlike capacity-augmenting investment, which is assumed to maintain the labor:capital ratio unchanged, cost-cutting investment is specifically intended to reduce the labor:capital ratio. As shown in the mathematical appendix, the stationary-l locus must shift to take capital deepening into account. In a fixprice regime, the stationary-l locus is a rightward displacement of the AD schedule.

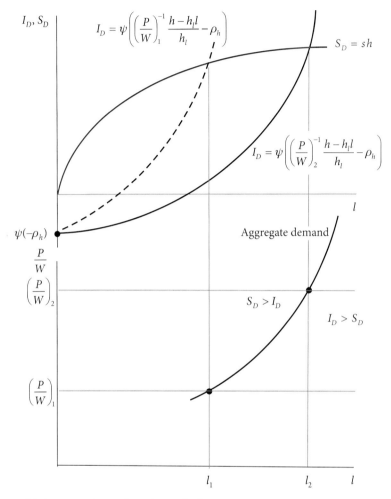

(a) Investment and saving holding real-price constant

(b) Aggregate demand varying real price

Figure 18.20 Aggregate demand with capital-deepening investment and uniform saving propensity.

The fixprice equilibria are pictured in Figure 18.21. The equilibrium E' is unstable and E is stable. Here the unstable equilibrium is more interesting than in other cases. If the starting point is to the left of E', the economy moves on a trajectory that follows the stationary-price schedule leftward. This trajectory involves ever-less employment per unit of capital. Real wages may initially rise or fall depending on the starting point, but eventually the real wage must rise. In a way this smacks of secular stagnation, in which a lack of ag-

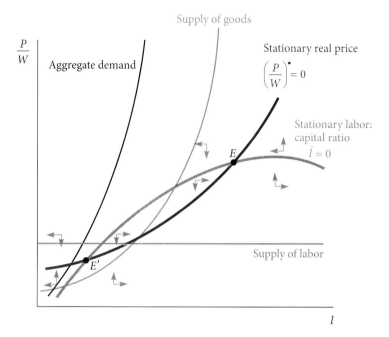

Figure 18.21 Equilibrium with capital-deepening investment and a uniform saving propensity.

gregate demand means that substituting capital to cut costs eventually takes a toll on employment. The saving grace is that stagnation does not imply falling living standards—at least not for the workers who retain their jobs.

The equilibrium at E is a bit strange: the boss's right hand does not know what the left hand is doing, and vice versa. The right hand is substituting capital for labor because it is cheaper to produce with more capital and less labor. At the same time, the left hand is hiring more workers because goods are flying off the shelves. (To the right of the AD schedule, expenditure exceeds income and output.) The two actions just balance each other at E, with the result that the labor:capital ratio does not change.[9]

More than one aspect of economic reality is hidden by consolidating all output into a single sector in which goods serve equally well for consumption and investment. Moreover, in the present model the demand and supply effects of capital deepening take place instantaneously (which is why the stationary-l locus lies to the right of the AD schedule). In reality, the supply side lags behind the demand effect, so capital deepening plays out differently in the short run and the long run.

In the short run, capital deepening, like capital widening, adds to demand: additional output and employment are required to put new plant and equipment in place. But unlike capital widening, which adds to productive capacity as the new capital comes on line, capital deepening leaves capacity unchanged while reducing employment. The specter of technological unemployment lurking behind capital deepening has haunted capitalism since the days of the Luddites.[10]

In the past, for the most part, successive waves of capital deepening, supported by capital widening, have managed to maintain the demand for labor overall even as particular workers in particular industries have suffered. But the question has resurfaced, even with some mainstream economists, whether the future of capital deepening is a threat at the macroeconomic level as well as the micro level. (See Daron Acemoglu and Pascual Restrepo [2018].)

The comparative statics of parameter changes are similar in most respects to what has already been encountered. Figures 18.22 through 18.25 show the effect of a higher level of investment demand (or a lower level of desired saving), the effect of a higher energy price, and, finally, the effect of a higher conventional wage.

As has been the case right along, an increase in investment demand or a decrease in desired saving, pictured in Figure 18.22, expands employment

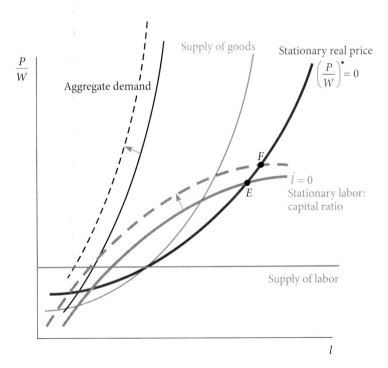

Figure 18.22 Capital-deepening investment: an increase in investment demand or a decrease in desired saving.

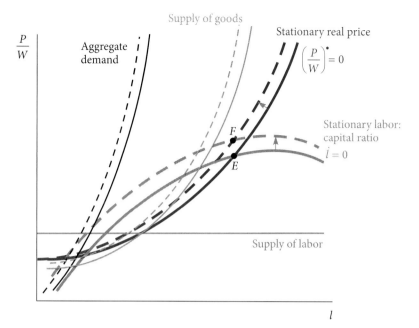

Figure 18.23 Capital deepening: an increase in the price of energy.

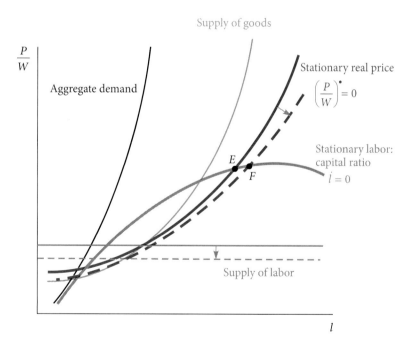

Figure 18.24 Capital deepening: an increase in the conventional wage, I.

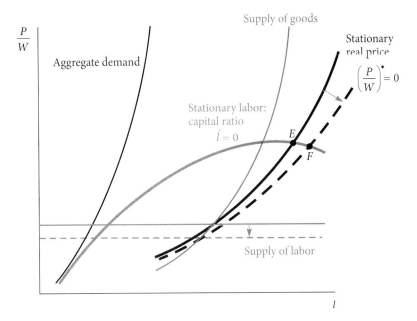

Figure 18.25 Capital deepening investment: an increase in the conventional wage, II.

and output and raises inflation. The effect of a higher price of energy also parallels earlier results. Both the real price and the level of employment can go up or down. And they can move in opposite directions, as in Figure 18.23, or in the same direction.

A change in the conventional wage, pictured in Figures 18.24 and 18.25, reflects a key difference between capital deepening and capital widening. When the purpose of investment is to substitute capital for labor, an increase in the conventional wage is unambiguously associated with a higher level of economic activity. The reason is that a higher conventional wage drives the equilibrium real wage up; a higher real wage means more investment demand because the higher the real wage, the more profitable it is to substitute capital for labor. This is of course the opposite of capital widening: when the purpose is to expand capacity, investment demand falls as the conventional wage rises and the profit rate falls. Since the mix of capital deepening and capital widening is likely to vary countercyclically, this difference is an important reason why the relationship between real wages and macroeconomic performance will vary over the cycle.

Observe that a higher conventional wage is not only expansionary, it is also inflationary, that is, the new equilibrium F in Figure 18.24 is associated with a higher level of inflation than is the original equilibrium E. Displacement of equilibrium on the falling portion of the stationary-l schedule, as in Figure

18.25, is more complicated, but the mathematical appendix shows that the overall effect is to increase the rate of inflation in this case as well.

Wages, Prices, and Employment: A Summary of Results

Tables 18.3 to 18.6 summarize the results of the previous sections.[11] A striking conclusion is that the positive relationship between employment and inflation embodied in the Phillips curve exists independently of how saving and investment are characterized.

A second result is the variability of the response to an exogenous price shock. An anti-Phillips, stagflationary, result, in which inflation and employment move in opposite directions, is one possibility, but Phillips-type movements, in which inflation and employment move in the same direction, are also possible. More surprising is the possibility that an increase in the price of energy can lead to higher employment.

Finally, results with respect to the conventional wage put left-Keynesian

Table 18.3 Fixed Investment with Saving a Fixed Fraction of Income

	Inflation	Employment
Investment↑ or Saving↓	↑	
		↑
Price of Energy↑	↑	
		↑
Conventional Wage↑	↑	
		0

Table 18.4 Cambridge Saving with Capital Widening: Saving More Sensitive to Profitability

	Inflation	Employment
Investment↑ or Saving↓	↑	
		↑
Price of Energy↑	?	
		?
Conventional Wage↑	↑	
		↑

Table 18.5 Cambridge Saving with Capital Widening: Investment More Sensitive to Profitability

	Inflation	Employment
Investment↑ or Saving↓	↑	
		↑
Price of Energy↑	?	
		?
Conventional Wage↑	↓	
		↓

Table 18.6 Capital Deepening with Saving a Fixed Fraction of Income

	Inflation	Employment
Investment↑ or Saving↓	↑	
		↑
Price of Energy↑	?	
		?
Conventional Wage↑	↑	
		↑

beliefs on the beneficial effects of high wages in perspective. If investment demand is confined to capital widening and saving depends on profits, the relationship between wages and employment depends on the relative responsiveness of investment and saving to profitability. A higher conventional wage is associated with greater aggregate demand and higher employment if saving is more responsive, but a lower conventional wage promotes employment if investment is more responsive. By contrast, the effect of the wage level on capital deepening is not at cross purposes with the effect on saving: a higher wage level stimulates capital deepening at the same time as it stimulates consumption demand. In both Tables 18.4 and 18.6 the effect is higher employment and higher inflation.

It remains to be seen how a Keynesian long-run model stacks up against the historical data for the U.S. economy. This is explored in the next chapter.

The basic flexprice model is

$$\frac{\left(\frac{P}{W}\right)^{\bullet}}{\frac{P}{W}} \equiv \left(\frac{\dot{P}}{P} - \frac{\dot{W}}{W}\right) = \theta_1[I - S] - \theta_3\left[\frac{P}{W} - \left(\frac{P}{W}\right)^*\right], \tag{18.1}$$

$$\dot{l} = \theta_2\left(\frac{P}{W} - (h_l)^{-1}\right), \tag{18.2}$$

and the fixprice version of the model is

$$\frac{\left(\frac{P}{W}\right)^{\bullet}}{\frac{P}{W}} = \theta_1\left[l - GS\left(\frac{P}{W}, \xi\right)\right] - \theta_3\left[\frac{P}{W} - \left(\frac{P}{W}\right)^*\right], \tag{18.3}$$

$$\dot{l} = \theta_2(I - S). \tag{18.4}$$

The novel element is the wage part of equations (18.1) and (18.3)

$$\frac{\dot{W}}{W} = \theta_3\left[\frac{P}{W} - \left(\frac{P}{W}\right)^*\right],$$

which says that workers are able to put pressure on money wages when the actual real wage is below the conventional wage, in other words, when $P/W > (P/W)^*$, and that employers have the upper hand when this inequality is reversed.

I and S denote, respectively, investment demand and desired saving per unit of capital. In the simplest case investment is a function of the hurdle rate alone

$$I = \psi(\rho_h), \tag{18.5}$$

and a uniform propensity to save gives the saving function

$$S = sh(l, \xi), \tag{18.6}$$

where $h(l, \xi)$ is the output:capital ratio, net of real energy costs, the assumption being that all energy is purchased abroad on a competitive market at an exogenously given nominal price P_E:

$$h(l, \xi) = \max_e[f(l, e) - \xi e] = f(l, e(l, \xi)) - \xi e(l, \xi). \qquad (18.7)$$

That is,

$$Y \equiv F(K, L, E),$$

$$\frac{Y}{K} \equiv F(1, l, e) \equiv f(l, e),$$

$$\xi \equiv \frac{P_E}{P},$$

$$l \equiv \frac{L}{K},$$

$$e \equiv \frac{E}{K},$$

$$h_l = f_l,$$

$$h_\xi = -e,$$

$$e_l = -f_{el}f_{ee}^{-1},$$

$$h_{l\xi} = f_{le}e_\xi = f_{le}f_{ee}^{-1},$$

$$h_{\xi l} = -e_l = f_{le}f_{ee}^{-1},$$

$$h_{ll} = f_{ll} + f_{le}e_l = f_{ll} - f_{le}^2 f_{ee}^{-1} = f_{ee}^{-1}\left(f_{ll}f_{ee} - f_{le}^2\right).$$

In equation (18.7), $e = e(l, \xi)$ is the amount of energy that, for given l and ξ, maximizes the expression $f(l, e) - \xi e$. We assume diminishing returns to each input, so that both f_{ll} and f_{ee} are negative. We also assume that energy and labor are complements, with the result that $f_{el}(=f_{le})$ is positive. h_{ll} must be negative; otherwise equality between the marginal productivity of labor and the real wage

$$h_l = f_l = \left(\frac{P}{W}\right)^{-1}$$

characterizes minimum rather than maximum profits. In other words, the assumption of an interior solution to the profit-maximization problem implies that diminishing returns to each input outweigh the complementarity of the two inputs.

With flexprice adjustment and investment and saving in the simple form of (18.5) and (18.6), we have

$$J = \begin{bmatrix} \theta_1\left(\dfrac{I_P}{W} - \dfrac{S_P}{W}\right) - \theta_3 & -\theta_1 S_l \\ \theta_2 & \theta_2 h_{ll}\left(h_l\right)^{-2} \end{bmatrix} = \begin{bmatrix} -\theta_3 & -\theta_1 sh_l \\ \theta_2 & \theta_2 h_{ll}\left(h_l\right)^{-2} \end{bmatrix}, \quad (18.8)$$

for which the equilibrium is stable, since $tr\,J < 0$ and $det\,J > 0$.

For the comparative statics of varying aggregate demand, goods supply, and the conventional wage, we calculate

$$\begin{bmatrix} \dfrac{\partial\left(\dfrac{P}{W}\right)}{\partial x} \\ \dfrac{\partial l}{\partial x} \end{bmatrix}$$

as the solution to the equation system

$$J \begin{bmatrix} \dfrac{\partial\left(\dfrac{P}{W}\right)}{\partial x} \\ \dfrac{\partial l}{\partial x} \end{bmatrix} = - \begin{bmatrix} \dfrac{\partial AA}{\partial x} \\ \dfrac{\partial BB}{\partial x} \end{bmatrix}. \quad (18.9)$$

Equation (18.9) is obtained by differentiating the system

$$AA \equiv \theta_1\left[\psi\left(\rho_h\right) - sh\right] - \theta_3\left[\dfrac{P}{W} - \left(\dfrac{P}{W}\right)^*\right] = 0, \quad (18.10)$$

$$BB \equiv \theta_2\left(\dfrac{P}{W} - \left(h_l\right)^{-1}\right) = 0, \quad (18.11)$$

with respect to the parameters $x = \rho_h, \xi$, and $(P/W)^*$. (We omit a calculation of the effect of changing the parameter s since the math is symmetrical with the corresponding operation with respect to ρ_h.) The solution to (18.9) is

$$\begin{bmatrix} \dfrac{\partial\left(\dfrac{P}{W}\right)}{\partial x} \\ \dfrac{\partial l}{\partial x} \end{bmatrix} = -J^{-1} \begin{bmatrix} \dfrac{\partial AA}{\partial x} \\ \dfrac{\partial BB}{\partial x} \end{bmatrix}, \quad (18.12)$$

where J^{-1} is the inverse of the Jacobian J.[1] In the 2 × 2 case

$$J = \begin{bmatrix} j_{11} & j_{12} \\ j_{21} & j_{22} \end{bmatrix},$$

we have

$$J^{-1} = \Delta^{-1} \begin{bmatrix} j_{22} & -j_{12} \\ -j_{21} & j_{11} \end{bmatrix},$$

where $\Delta = det\ J$. In the specific case of (18.6), we have

$$J^{-1} = \Delta^{-1} \begin{bmatrix} \theta_2 h_{ll}\left(h_l\right)^{-2} & \theta_1 sh_l \\ -\theta_2 & -\theta_3 \end{bmatrix}.$$

Differentiating equation (18.10) gives

$$\begin{bmatrix} \dfrac{\partial AA}{\partial p_h} \\ \dfrac{\partial BB}{\partial p_h} \end{bmatrix} = \begin{bmatrix} \theta_1 \psi' \\ 0 \end{bmatrix}, \quad \begin{bmatrix} \dfrac{\partial AA}{\partial \xi} \\ \dfrac{\partial BB}{\partial \xi} \end{bmatrix} = \begin{bmatrix} -\theta_1 sh_\xi \\ \theta_2 h_{l\xi}\left(h_l\right)^{-2} \end{bmatrix}, \quad \begin{bmatrix} \dfrac{\partial AA}{\partial\left(\dfrac{P}{W}\right)^*} \\ \dfrac{\partial BB}{\partial\left(\dfrac{P}{W}\right)^*} \end{bmatrix} = \begin{bmatrix} \theta_3 \\ 0 \end{bmatrix},$$

with the results

$$\begin{bmatrix} \dfrac{\partial\left(\dfrac{P}{W}\right)}{\partial p_h} \\ \dfrac{\partial l}{\partial p_h} \end{bmatrix} = -\Delta^{-1} \begin{bmatrix} \theta_1\psi'\theta_2 h_{ll}\left(h_l\right)^{-2} \\ -\theta_2\theta_1\psi' \end{bmatrix} = \begin{bmatrix} - \\ - \end{bmatrix}, \qquad (18.13)$$

$$\begin{bmatrix} \dfrac{\partial\left(\dfrac{P}{W}\right)}{\partial \xi} \\ \dfrac{\partial l}{\partial \xi} \end{bmatrix} = -\Delta^{-1} \begin{bmatrix} \theta_1\theta_2 s\left(h_l\right)^{-2}\left(-h_\xi h_{ll} + h_l h_{l\xi}\right) \\ \theta_2\left(\theta_1 sh_\xi - \theta_3\left(h_l\right)^{-2} h_{l\xi}\right) \end{bmatrix} = \begin{bmatrix} + \\ \pm \end{bmatrix}, \qquad (18.14)$$

$$\begin{bmatrix} \dfrac{\partial\left(\dfrac{P}{W}\right)}{\partial\left(\dfrac{P}{W}\right)^*} \\ \dfrac{\partial l}{\partial\left(\dfrac{P}{W}\right)^*} \end{bmatrix} = -\Delta^{-1} \begin{bmatrix} \theta_3\theta_2 h_{ll}\left(h_l\right)^{-2} \\ -\theta_3\theta_2 \end{bmatrix} = \begin{bmatrix} + \\ + \end{bmatrix}. \qquad (18.15)$$

These results confirm the graphical reasoning in Figures 18.7(a), 18.9, 18.10, and 18.12(a). The ambiguity in the response of employment to an energy-price shock is because the two terms in the expression $\theta_1 sh_\xi - \theta_3(h_l)^{-2} h_{l\xi}$

have opposite signs. Which dominates depends on the relative magnitudes of the adjustment speeds θ_1 and θ_3.

The effect on inflation of these shocks is more complicated. We have

$$\frac{\dot{P}}{P} = \theta_1 \left[\psi\left(\rho_h\right) - sh(l, \xi) \right]. \tag{18.16}$$

The complication is that for demand and energy-price shocks, the rate of price inflation, measured by the horizontal distance between the equilibrium and the AD schedule (along which $\dot{P}/P = 0$), moves not only because the equilibrium changes but also because the AD schedule itself shifts. The general formula is

$$\frac{d\left(\frac{\dot{P}}{P}\right)}{dx} = \frac{\partial\left(\frac{\dot{P}}{P}\right)}{\partial\left(\frac{P}{W}\right)} \frac{\partial\left(\frac{P}{W}\right)}{\partial x} + \frac{\partial\left(\frac{\dot{P}}{P}\right)}{\partial l} \frac{\partial l}{\partial x} + \frac{\partial\left(\frac{\dot{P}}{P}\right)}{\partial x}. \tag{18.17}$$

From equation (18.16) we have

$$\frac{\partial\left(\frac{\dot{P}}{P}\right)}{\partial\left(\frac{P}{W}\right)} = 0, \quad \frac{\partial\left(\frac{\dot{P}}{P}\right)}{\partial l} = -\theta_1 sh_l$$

and

$$\frac{\partial\left(\frac{\dot{P}}{P}\right)}{\partial\rho_h} = \theta_1\psi', \quad \frac{\partial\left(\frac{\dot{P}}{P}\right)}{\partial\xi} = -\theta_1 sh_\xi, \quad \frac{\partial\left(\frac{\dot{P}}{P}\right)}{\partial\left(\frac{P}{W}\right)^*} = 0.$$

Putting these results together with equations (18.13), (18.14), and (18.15), we have

$$\frac{d\left(\frac{\dot{P}}{P}\right)}{d\rho_h} = -\Delta^{-1}\theta_2\theta_1\psi'\theta_1 sh_l + \theta_1\psi' = -\Delta^{-1}\theta_1\theta_2\theta_3 h_{ll}\left(h_l\right)^{-2}\psi' = -,$$

$$\frac{d\left(\frac{\dot{P}}{P}\right)}{d\xi} = \Delta^{-1}\theta_2\left(\theta_1 sh_\xi - \theta_3\left(h_l\right)^{-2} h_{l\xi}\right)\theta_1 sh_l - \theta_1 sh_\xi = -\Delta^{-1}\theta_1\theta_2\theta_3 s\left(h_l\right)^{-2}\left(h_l h_{l\xi} - h_\xi h_{ll}\right) = +,$$

$$\frac{d\left(\frac{\dot{P}}{P}\right)}{d\left(\frac{P}{W}\right)^*} = -\Delta^{-1}\theta_1\theta_2\theta_3 sh_l = -.$$

Again, these results confirm the effects of parameter changes analyzed graphically in the text: the increase in aggregate demand in Figure 18.7(a), which we may imagine to be the result of a decrease in the hurdle rate of interest; the increase in the price of energy in Figures 18.9 and 18.10; and the increase in the conventional wage in Figure 18.12(a). All three of these parameter changes lead to an increase in inflation in line with the above formulas.

For the fixprice system (18.3) and (18.4), with investment and saving determined by (18.5) and (18.6), the Jacobian is

$$J = \begin{bmatrix} -\theta_1 GS_{\frac{P}{W}} - \theta_3 & \theta_1 \\ 0 & -\theta_2 sh_l \end{bmatrix},$$

and its inverse is

$$J^{-1} = \Delta^{-1} \begin{bmatrix} -\theta_2 sh_l & -\theta_1 \\ 0 & -\theta_1 GS_{\frac{P}{W}} - \theta_3 \end{bmatrix}.$$

As in the flexprice case, $tr\, J < 0$, and $det\, J > 0$, so the equilibrium is stable.

Comparative statics of demand, energy-price, and conventional-wage shocks are given by (18.12). In the fixprice case, we have

$$AA = \theta_1 \left[1 - GS\left(\frac{P}{W}, \xi \right) \right] - \theta_3 \left[\frac{P}{W} - \left(\frac{P}{W} \right)^* \right] = 0,$$

$$BB = \theta_2 \left[\psi(\rho_h) - sh \right] = 0,$$

and the derivatives are

$$\begin{bmatrix} \dfrac{\partial AA}{\partial \rho_h} \\ \dfrac{\partial BB}{\partial \rho_h} \end{bmatrix} = \begin{bmatrix} 0 \\ \theta_2 \psi' \end{bmatrix}, \quad \begin{bmatrix} \dfrac{\partial AA}{\partial \xi} \\ \dfrac{\partial BB}{\partial \xi} \end{bmatrix} = \begin{bmatrix} -\theta_1 GS_\xi \\ -\theta_2 s_\pi h_\xi \end{bmatrix}, \quad \begin{bmatrix} \dfrac{\partial AA}{\partial \left(\dfrac{P}{W} \right)^*} \\ \dfrac{\partial BB}{\partial \left(\dfrac{P}{W} \right)^*} \end{bmatrix} = \begin{bmatrix} \theta_3 \\ 0 \end{bmatrix},$$

so the fixprice counterparts of (18.13), (18.14), and (18.15) are

$$\begin{bmatrix} \dfrac{\partial \left(\dfrac{P}{W} \right)}{\partial \rho_h} \\ \dfrac{\partial l}{\partial \rho_h} \end{bmatrix} = -\Delta^{-1} \begin{bmatrix} -\theta_2 \theta_1 \psi' \\ -\left(\theta_1 GS_{\frac{P}{W}} + \theta_3 \right) \theta_2 \psi' \end{bmatrix} = \begin{bmatrix} - \\ - \end{bmatrix},$$

$$\begin{bmatrix} \dfrac{\partial\left(\dfrac{P}{W}\right)}{\partial\xi} \\[3ex] \dfrac{\partial l}{\partial\xi} \end{bmatrix} = -\Delta^{-1}\begin{bmatrix} \theta_2 sh_l\theta_1 GS_\xi + \theta_1\theta_2 sh_\xi \\[2ex] \left(\theta_1 GS_{\frac{P}{W}} + \theta_3\right)\theta_2 s_\pi h_\xi \end{bmatrix} = \begin{bmatrix} + \\ + \end{bmatrix},$$

$$\begin{bmatrix} \dfrac{\partial\left(\dfrac{P}{W}\right)}{\partial\left(\dfrac{P}{W}\right)^*} \\[5ex] \dfrac{\partial l}{\partial\left(\dfrac{P}{W}\right)^*} \end{bmatrix} = -\Delta^{-1}\begin{bmatrix} -\theta_2 sh_l\theta_3 \\[2ex] 0 \end{bmatrix} = \begin{bmatrix} + \\ 0 \end{bmatrix}.$$

With fixprice adjustment, price inflation is governed by

$$\frac{\dot{P}}{P} = \theta_1\left[l - GS\left(\frac{P}{W},\xi\right)\right],$$

and therefore

$$\frac{\partial\left(\dfrac{\dot{P}}{P}\right)}{\partial\left(\dfrac{P}{W}\right)} = -\theta_1 GS_{\frac{P}{W}}, \quad \frac{\partial\left(\dfrac{\dot{P}}{P}\right)}{\partial l} = \theta_1,$$

$$\frac{\partial\left(\dfrac{\dot{P}}{P}\right)}{\partial\rho_h} = 0, \quad \frac{\partial\left(\dfrac{\dot{P}}{P}\right)}{\partial\xi} = -\theta_1 GS_\xi, \quad \frac{\partial\left(\dfrac{\dot{P}}{P}\right)}{\partial\left(\dfrac{P}{W}\right)^*} = 0.$$

Consequently, inflation results are

$$\frac{d\left(\dfrac{\dot{P}}{P}\right)}{d\rho_h} = \Delta^{-1}\theta_1\theta_2\theta_3\psi' = -,$$

$$\frac{d\left(\dfrac{\dot{P}}{P}\right)}{d\xi} = -\Delta^{-1}\theta_1\theta_2\theta_3\left(sh_\xi + sh_l GS_\xi\right) = +,$$

$$\frac{d\left(\dfrac{\dot{P}}{P}\right)}{d\left(\dfrac{P}{W}\right)^*} = -\Delta^{-1}\theta_1\theta_2\theta_3 sh_l GS_{\frac{P}{W}} = -.$$

These results parallel the graphical results in Figures 18.7(b), 18.11, and 18.12. The novelties are that (1) the possibility of an energy-price shock leading to stagflation is eliminated—in the fixprice case both employment and inflation increase, and (2) the conventional wage has no bearing on the level of employment—in the fixprice case the conventional wage has no impact on investment or on saving and therefore no impact on aggregate demand.

Complicating Investment and Saving

At the price of mathematical complication, we can replace the simple investment and saving functions based on the hurdle rate of interest and a uniform propensity to save by investment functions that take account of capital widening, capital deepening, and the Cambridge saving theory. In its most general form, we can write investment as a function of P/W, l, and ρ_h, namely, $I(P/W, l, \rho_h)$, and saving as a function of P/W and l, $S(P/W, l)$. Specifically, we reflect capital widening in the investment equation

$$I = \psi\left(\Omega(l)r - \rho_h\right) = \psi\left(\Omega(l)\left[h(l,\xi) - \left(\frac{P}{W}\right)^{-1}l\right] - \rho_h\right), \quad (18.18)$$

and capital deepening in the equation

$$I = \psi\left(\left(\frac{P}{W}\right)^{-1}\frac{h - h_l l}{h_l} - \rho_h\right). \quad (18.19)$$

The simple version of the class-based theory of saving incorporated in the Cambridge saving theory is

$$S = s_\pi r = s_\pi\left[h(l,\xi) - \left(\frac{P}{W}\right)^{-1}l\right]. \quad (18.20)$$

As in the body of this chapter, we focus on the fixprice model summarized in equations (18.3) and (18.4). The stability conditions for various permutations of this model, as well as the conditions for the flexprice variant, are examined in my 2017 *Review of Keynesian Economics* paper in exhaustive, one might say excruciating, detail. Here I can be more selective, focusing on the difference between a relatively high responsiveness of investment to profitability, $\psi'\Omega - s_\pi > 0$, and a relatively high responsiveness of saving, $\psi'\Omega - s_\pi < 0$, as well as examining the difference between capital widening and capital deepening.

For (18.18) and (18.20) we have

$$
J = \begin{bmatrix} -\theta_1 GS_{\frac{P}{W}} - \theta_3 & \theta_1 \\ \theta_2 \left(\psi'\Omega - s_\pi \right) \left(\dfrac{P}{W} \right)^{-2} l & \theta_2 \begin{bmatrix} \psi'\Omega' \left(h - \left(\dfrac{P}{W} \right)^{-1} l \right) \\ + \left(\psi'\Omega - s_\pi \right) \left(h_l - \left(\dfrac{P}{W} \right)^{-1} \right) \end{bmatrix} \end{bmatrix}.
$$

The sign of j_{22} as well as j_{21} depends on whether the expression $\psi'\Omega - s_\pi$ is positive or negative. The slope of the AD schedule is given by the equation

$$
\left(\frac{d\left(\dfrac{P}{W} \right)}{dl} \right)_{AD} = - \frac{\theta_2 \left[\psi'\Omega' \left(h - \left(\dfrac{P}{W} \right)^{-1} l \right) + \left(\psi'\Omega - s_\pi \right) \left(h_l - \left(\dfrac{P}{W} \right)^{-1} \right) \right]}{\theta_2 \left(\psi'\Omega - s_\pi \right) \left(\dfrac{P}{W} \right)^{-2} l},
$$

and knowing the sign of $\psi'\Omega - s_\pi$ determines the sign of the denominator of the expression on the right-hand side. Whether a point is on the downward- or upward-sloping portion of the AD schedule determines the sign of the expression as a whole, numerator and denominator. Given the minus sign in front of the ratio, the numerator must be of the same sign as the denominator on the downward-sloping portion of the AD schedule and of the opposite sign on the upward-sloping portion. That is, the inequality $(d(P/W)/dl)_{AD} < 0$ holds on the downward-sloping portion, so $\psi'\Omega - s_\pi > 0$ implies that the numerator must be positive. On the upward-sloping portion we have $(d(P/W)/dl)_{AD} > 0$, so the implications of the sign of $\psi'\Omega - s_\pi$ for the numerator are reversed.

This information is crucial to determining the stability of equilibrium. Consider first the case where investment is less responsive than saving to changes in profitability, $\psi'\Omega - s_\pi < 0$. The condition $tr\, J < 0$ is satisfied at E in Figure 18.16 only if the adjustment speed of employment is slow relative to the adjustment speeds of prices and wages since

$$
\theta_2 \left[\psi'\Omega' \left(h - \left(\dfrac{P}{W} \right)^{-1} l \right) + \left(\psi'\Omega - s_\pi \right) \left(h_l - \left(\dfrac{P}{W} \right)^{-1} \right) \right]
$$

is necessarily positive. The determinant condition, $det\ J > 0$, is satisfied since the stationary real-price locus is steeper than the AD schedule. We have

$$\left[-\theta_1 GS_{\frac{P}{W}} - \theta_3 \right] \theta_2 \left[\psi'\Omega' \left(h - \left(\frac{P}{W}\right)^{-1} l \right) + \left(\psi'\Omega - s_\pi \right) \left(h_l - \left(\frac{P}{W}\right)^{-1} \right) \right]$$

$$> \theta_1 \left[\theta_2 \left(\psi'\Omega - s_\pi \right) \left(\frac{P}{W}\right)^{-2} l \right]$$

because

$$\left(\frac{d\left(\frac{P}{W}\right)}{dl} \right)_{\left(\frac{P}{W}\right)^{\cdot}=0} = \frac{\theta_1}{\theta_1 GS_{\frac{P}{W}} + \theta_3}$$

$$> - \frac{\theta_2 \left[\psi'\Omega' \left(h - \left(\frac{P}{W}\right)^{-1} l \right) + \left(\psi'\Omega - s_\pi \right) \left(h_l - \left(\frac{P}{W}\right)^{-1} \right) \right]}{\theta_2 \left(\psi'\Omega - s_\pi \right) \left(\frac{P}{W}\right)^{-2} l}$$

$$= \left(\frac{d\left(\frac{P}{W}\right)}{dl} \right)_{AD}^{\cdot}$$

In contrast, at F the trace condition is automatically satisfied since, with $\psi'\Omega - s_\pi > 0$, the inequality

$$\theta_2 \left[\psi'\Omega' \left(h - \left(\frac{P}{W}\right)^{-1} l \right) + \left(\psi'\Omega - s_\pi \right) \left(h_l - \left(\frac{P}{W}\right)^{-1} \right) \right] < 0$$

holds on the rising portion of the AD schedule. The condition $det\ J > 0$ is also satisfied because at F the AD schedule is steeper than the stationary real-price locus. That is,

$$\left(\frac{d\left(\frac{P}{W}\right)}{dl} \right)_{AD} > \left(\frac{dl}{d\left(\frac{P}{W}\right)} \right)_{\left(\frac{P}{W}\right)^{\cdot}=0}^{\cdot}$$

The effects of demand and supply shocks are the total derivatives of the equation system

$$AA \equiv \theta_1 \left[l - GS\left(\frac{P}{W}, \xi \right) \right] - \theta_3 \left[\frac{P}{W} - \left(\frac{P}{W} \right)^* \right] = 0,$$

$$BB \equiv \theta_2 \left\{ \psi \left[\Omega(l) \left[h(l, \xi) - \left(\frac{P}{W} \right)^{-1} l \right] - \rho_h \right] - s_\pi \left[h(l, \xi) - \left(\frac{P}{W} \right)^{-1} l \right] \right\} \theta_2 = 0,$$

with respect to the exogenous parameters $x = \rho_h, \xi,$ and $(P/W)^*$. We have

$$\left[\begin{array}{cc} -\theta_1 GS_{\frac{P}{W}} - \theta_3 & \theta_1 \\ \theta_2 \left(\psi'\Omega - s_\pi \right) \left(\frac{P}{W} \right)^{-2} l & \theta_2 \left[\psi'\Omega' \left(h - \left(\frac{P}{W} \right)^{-1} l \right) + \left(\psi'\Omega - s_\pi \right) \left(h_l - \left(\frac{P}{W} \right)^{-1} \right) \right] \end{array} \right]$$

$$\left[\begin{array}{c} \dfrac{\partial \left(\dfrac{P}{W} \right)}{\partial x} \\[4mm] \dfrac{\partial l}{\partial x} \end{array} \right] = - \left[\begin{array}{c} \dfrac{\partial AA}{\partial x} \\[4mm] \dfrac{\partial BB}{\partial x} \end{array} \right]$$

for which the solution is

$$\left[\begin{array}{c} \dfrac{\partial \left(\dfrac{P}{W} \right)}{\partial x} \\[4mm] \dfrac{\partial l}{\partial x} \end{array} \right] = -\Delta^{-1} \left[\begin{array}{cc} \theta_2 \left[\begin{array}{c} \psi'\Omega' \left(h - \left(\dfrac{P}{W} \right)^{-1} l \right) \\[2mm] + \left(\psi'\Omega - s_\pi \right) \left(h_l - \left(\dfrac{P}{W} \right)^{-1} \right) \end{array} \right] & -\theta_1 \\[10mm] -\theta_2 \left(\psi'\Omega - s_\pi \right) \left(\dfrac{P}{W} \right)^{-2} l & -\theta_1 GS_{\frac{P}{W}} - \theta_3 \end{array} \right] \left[\begin{array}{c} \dfrac{\partial AA}{\partial x} \\[4mm] \dfrac{\partial BB}{\partial x} \end{array} \right].$$

For $x = \rho_h$, we have

$$\left[\begin{array}{c} \dfrac{\partial AA}{\partial \rho_h} \\[4mm] \dfrac{\partial BB}{\partial \rho_h} \end{array} \right] = \left[\begin{array}{c} 0 \\[2mm] -\theta_2 \psi' \end{array} \right].$$

The results are

$$\frac{\partial\left(\dfrac{P}{W}\right)}{\partial \rho_h} = \frac{\theta_1 \theta_2 \psi'}{\Delta} = -,$$

$$\frac{\partial l}{\partial \rho_h} = \frac{\left(\theta_1 GS_{\frac{P}{W}} + \theta_3\right)\theta_2 \psi'}{\Delta} = -.$$

Combining the effects of interest-rate changes on real price and employment gives the impact on inflation

$$\frac{d\left(\dfrac{\dot P}{P}\right)}{d\rho_h} = \frac{\partial\left(\dfrac{\dot P}{P}\right)}{\partial\left(\dfrac{P}{W}\right)}\frac{\partial\left(\dfrac{P}{W}\right)}{\partial \rho_h} + \frac{\partial\left(\dfrac{\dot P}{P}\right)}{\partial l}\frac{\partial l}{\partial \rho_h} = \frac{\theta_1 \theta_2 \theta_3 \psi'}{\Delta} = -$$

since

$$\frac{\partial\left(\dfrac{\dot P}{P}\right)}{\partial\left(\dfrac{P}{W}\right)} = -\theta_1 GS_{\frac{P}{W}},$$

$$\frac{\partial\left(\dfrac{\dot P}{P}\right)}{\partial l} = \theta_1.$$

Monetary easing, reflected here by a reduction in ρ_h, stimulates the economy on a permanent basis, at least to the point beyond which the hurdle rate can no longer be reduced (a liquidity trap) or to the point that the responsiveness of investment demand ψ' goes to zero. These limits apart, monetary easing increases the labor:capital ratio as well as the inflation rate: the Phillips curve exists in the long run as well as in the short period.

Supply-side changes are more complicated. A change in the real price of energy gives the right-hand side of equation (18.12) as

$$\begin{bmatrix} \dfrac{\partial AA}{\partial \xi} \\[2mm] \dfrac{\partial BB}{\partial \xi} \end{bmatrix} = \begin{bmatrix} -\theta_1 GS_\xi \\[2mm] \theta_2 \left(\psi'\Omega - s_\pi\right)h_\xi \end{bmatrix}.$$

In consequence,

$$\frac{\partial\left(\dfrac{P}{W}\right)}{\partial\xi} = \frac{\theta_1\theta_2 \begin{bmatrix} \psi'\Omega'\left(h - \left(\dfrac{P}{W}\right)^{-1}l\right) \\ +(\psi'\Omega - s_\pi)\left(h_l - \left(\dfrac{P}{W}\right)^{-1}\right) \end{bmatrix} GS_\xi + \theta_1\theta_2\left(\psi'\Omega - s_\pi\right)h_\xi}{\Delta} = \pm,$$

$$\frac{\partial l}{\partial\xi} = \frac{-\theta_1\theta_2\left(\psi'\Omega - s_\pi\right)\left(\dfrac{P}{W}\right)^{-2}lGS_\xi + \left(\theta_1 GS_{\frac{P}{W}} + \theta_3\right)\theta_2\left(\psi'\Omega - s_\pi\right)h_\xi}{\Delta} = \pm,$$

$$\frac{d\left(\dfrac{\dot P}{P}\right)}{d\xi} = \frac{\partial\left(\dfrac{\dot P}{P}\right)}{\partial\left(\dfrac{P}{W}\right)}\frac{\partial\left(\dfrac{P}{W}\right)}{\partial\xi} + \frac{\partial\left(\dfrac{\dot P}{P}\right)}{\partial l}\frac{\partial l}{\partial\xi} + \frac{\partial\left(\dfrac{\dot P}{P}\right)}{\partial\xi}$$

$$= \frac{\theta_1\theta_2\theta_3\begin{bmatrix} GS_\xi\left[\psi'\Omega'\left(h - \left(\dfrac{P}{W}\right)^{-1}l\right) + (\psi'\Omega - s_\pi)\left(h_l - \left(\dfrac{P}{W}\right)^{-1}\right)\right] \\ +\left(\psi'\Omega - s_\pi\right)h_\xi \end{bmatrix}}{\Delta} = \pm.$$

Since $GS_\xi = -h_{l\xi}/h_{ll} < 0$, the signs of all these derivatives are ambiguous; the effects on demand and supply work in opposite directions. Suppose the effect of a change in the price of energy on the supply side is negligible, $GS_\xi \approx 0$. The demand-side effect on the real price and inflation is via $-h_\xi = e$; the strength of the effect depends on the energy-intensity of production, but in any case both the real-price level and the rate of inflation fall provided investment is more responsive than saving to a change in profitability, $\psi'\Omega - s_\pi > 0$. In this case, employment also falls because demand falls along with productivity and profitability. If $\psi'\Omega - s_\pi < 0$, then real price, inflation, and employment respond positively to an increase in the price of energy; now, the fall in productivity means that more workers are required to meet the relatively inelastic demand.

At the other extreme—when $e \approx 0$—supply-side effects dominate, and the decrease in profitability drives prices and production up when $\psi'\Omega - s_\pi > 0$, and down when the inequality is reversed. When both supply and demand are affected, the consequences for employment, the real price, and inflation cannot be determined on the basis of the qualitative structure of the model, but we can say that the stronger is the energy intensity of production, e, the more likely is an increase in ξ to increase employment, the real price, and inflation.[2] Except for the extreme cases $GS_\xi \approx 0$ and $e \approx 0$, there is no reason why employment and prices will necessarily move in the same direction: in the general case, the product

$$\frac{\partial\left(\dfrac{P}{W}\right)}{\partial\xi}\frac{\partial l}{\partial\xi}$$

is itself sign indefinite. Figure 18.18 pictures the stagflationary case in which prices and employment move in opposite directions.

The effect of a change in the conventional wage is more straightforward. We have

$$\frac{\partial\left(\dfrac{P}{W}\right)}{\partial\left(\dfrac{P}{W}\right)^{*}} = \frac{-\theta_3\theta_2\left[\psi'\Omega'\left(h - \left(\dfrac{P}{W}\right)^{-1}l\right) + \left(\psi'\Omega - s_\pi\right)\left(h_l - \left(\dfrac{P}{W}\right)^{-1}\right)\right]}{\Delta}$$

$$= \begin{matrix}+\\-\end{matrix} \text{ at } \begin{matrix}F \text{ in Fig. 18.16, } \psi'\Omega - s_\pi > 0\\ E \text{ in Fig. 18.16, } \psi'\Omega - s_\pi < 0\end{matrix},$$

$$\frac{\partial l}{\partial\left(\dfrac{P}{W}\right)^{*}} = \frac{\theta_3\theta_2\left(\psi'\Omega - s_\pi\right)\left(\dfrac{P}{W}\right)^{-2}l}{\Delta} = \begin{matrix}+\\-\end{matrix} \text{ at } \begin{matrix}F \text{ in Fig. 18.16, } \psi'\Omega - s_\pi > 0\\ E \text{ in Fig. 18.16, } \psi'\Omega - s_\pi < 0\end{matrix},$$

$$\frac{\partial\left(\dfrac{\dot{P}}{P}\right)}{\partial\left(\dfrac{P}{W}\right)^{*}} = \frac{\theta_1\theta_2\theta_3\left[\psi'\Omega'\left(h - \left(\dfrac{P}{W}\right)^{-1}l\right) + \left(\psi'\Omega - s_\pi\right)\left(h_l - \left(\dfrac{P}{W}\right)^{-1}\right)\right]\left[GS_{\frac{P}{W}} - AD_{\frac{P}{W}}\right]}{\Delta}$$

$$= \begin{matrix}\pm\\-\end{matrix} \text{ at } \begin{matrix}F \text{ in Fig. 18.16, } \psi'\Omega - s_\pi > 0\\ E \text{ in Fig. 18.16, } \psi'\Omega - s_\pi < 0\end{matrix}.$$

Where $AD_{P/W}$ is the inverse of $(d(P/W)/dl)_{AD}$. The sign of $\partial(\dot{P}/P)/\partial(P/W)^{*}$ evidently depends on the sign of $GS_{P/W} - AD_{P/W}$. We know this expression is negative at E because the stationary-price locus is steeper than the AD schedule:

$$\left(\frac{d\left(\frac{P}{W}\right)}{dl}\right)_{\left(\frac{P}{W}\right)^{\cdot}=0} = \frac{\theta_1}{\theta_1 GS_{\frac{P}{W}} + \theta_3} > -\frac{\theta_2\left[\begin{array}{c}\psi'\Omega'\left(h-\left(\frac{P}{W}\right)^{-1}l\right)\\ +\left(\psi'\Omega - s_\pi\right)\left(h_l - \left(\frac{P}{W}\right)^{-1}\right)\end{array}\right]}{\theta_2\left(\psi'\Omega - s_\pi\right)\left(\frac{P}{W}\right)^{-2}l} = \left(\frac{d\left(\frac{P}{W}\right)}{dl}\right)_{AD},$$

so

$$GS_{\frac{P}{W}} - AD_{\frac{P}{W}} < -\frac{\theta_3}{\theta_1}.$$

The takeaway is that an increase in the conventional wage, a decrease in $(P/W)^*$, can increase the equilibrium price level and inflation, and—as left-Keynesians have argued since the afternoon of the appearance of *The General Theory*—increase employment. The critical assumption is that in Figure 18.19 we start from E: saving is class-based and responds more to profitability than does investment.

Capital Deepening

In the long-run analysis of capital deepening, we cannot ignore the change in the labor:capital ratio due to the investment itself. Unlike capacity-augmenting investment, which is assumed to maintain the labor:capital ratio unchanged, cost-cutting investment is specifically intended to reduce the labor:capital ratio. As noted in the body of this chapter, this supply-side effect is supposed to take place instantaneously, at the same time as investment adds to aggregate demand. To capture the impact of capital deepening on supply, we start from the identity

$$i = \left(\frac{\dot{L}}{L} - \frac{\dot{K}}{K}\right)\frac{L}{K}$$

and the assumption that capital substitutes for labor

$$\left(h - h_l l\right)\dot{K} = -h_l \dot{L},$$

so

$$\frac{\dot{L}}{L} = -\frac{h - h_l l}{h_l}\frac{\dot{K}}{K}\frac{K}{L} = -\frac{h - h_l l}{h_l}\psi\left(\left(\frac{P}{W}\right)^{-1}\frac{h - h_l l}{h_l} - \rho_h\right)l^{-1}.$$

Assuming for this exercise that investment intentions are realized, which is to say,

$$\frac{\dot{K}}{K} = \psi\left(\left(\frac{P}{W}\right)^{-1}\frac{h - h_l l}{h_l} - \rho_h\right),$$

the supply-side effect is

$$\dot{l} = -\frac{h}{h_l}\psi\left(\left(\frac{P}{W}\right)^{-1}\frac{h - h_l l}{h_l} - \rho_h\right).$$

In the fixprice version of the model, with saving a constant fraction of total income, the stationary-l locus combining demand and supply effects is

$$\dot{l} = \theta_2\left\{\left[\psi\left(\left(\frac{P}{W}\right)^{-1}\frac{h - h_l l}{h_l} - \rho_h\right) - sh(l, \xi)\right] - \frac{h}{h_l l}\psi\left(\left(\frac{P}{W}\right)^{-1}\frac{h - h_l l}{h_l} - \rho_h\right)\right\}.$$

How to go from aggregate demand to stationary l is shown in Figure 18.26. In panel (a) investment demand

$$\psi\left(\left(\frac{P}{W}\right)^{-1}\frac{h - h_l l}{h_l} - \rho_h\right)$$

is replaced by

$$Z = \left(\theta_2 - \frac{h}{h_l l}\right)\psi\left(\left(\frac{P}{W}\right)^{-1}\frac{h - h_l l}{h_l} - \rho_h\right), \qquad (18.21)$$

and desired saving $sh(l, \xi)$ is replaced by $\theta_2 sh(l, \xi)$. The construction in Figure 18.26(b) follows from the fact that equation (18.21) has an interior maximum. To see this, set $\partial Z / \partial l$ equal to zero. This gives the following equation:

$$-\frac{\left(h_l\right)^2 l - h h_{ll} l - h_l h}{\left(h_l l\right)^2}\psi = \left(\frac{h}{h_l l} - \theta_2\right)\psi'\left(\frac{P}{W}\right)^{-1}\left(-\frac{h_{ll} h}{\left(h_l\right)^2}\right). \qquad (18.22)$$

Assuming a constant-elasticity production function,

$$f(l, e) = A(\lambda_1 + \lambda_2 l^\xi + \lambda_3 e^\xi)^{1/\xi} \qquad (18.23)$$

and combining equations (18.7) and (18.23), the elasticity of substitution σ is given by the equation

$$\sigma = \frac{1}{1 - \xi} = -\frac{f_l\left(f - f_l l\right)}{f l f_{ll}} = -\frac{h_l\left(h - h_l l\right)}{h l h_{ll}}.$$

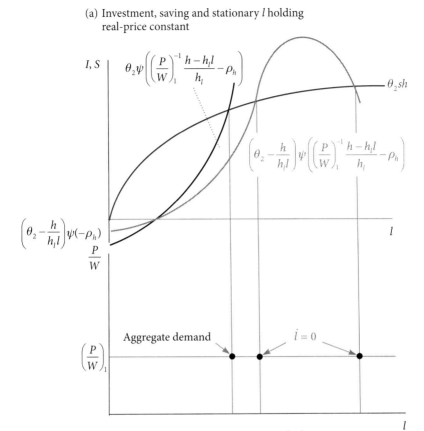

(a) Investment, saving and stationary l holding real-price constant

(b) Aggregate demand and $\dot{l} = 0$ for $\dfrac{P}{W} = \left(\dfrac{P}{W}\right)_1$

Figure 18.26 Aggregate demand and stationary l.

We have therefore

$$-\frac{h_{ll}}{(h_l)^2} = \frac{(1-\zeta)\lambda_1}{\lambda_1 h_l l + \lambda_2 h_l l^{\zeta+1}},$$

$$\frac{h}{h_l l} = \frac{\lambda_1 + \lambda_2 l^\zeta}{\lambda_2 l^\zeta}.$$

So equation (18.22) becomes

$$\frac{\zeta}{l}\psi = (1-\zeta)\left(\frac{\lambda_1 + \lambda_2 l^\zeta}{\lambda_2 l^\zeta} - \theta_2\right)\psi'\left(\frac{P}{W}\right)^{-1}. \tag{18.24}$$

We assume $\sigma < 1$ and consequently $\zeta < 0$. So if ψ' is bounded away from zero, the left-hand side of equation (18.24) falls from $+\infty$ to $-\infty$ as l goes from zero to ∞. The intercept of the right-hand side at $l = 0$ is negative, and the RHS goes to $+\infty$ as l goes to ∞, so there must exist an interior solution to this equation. The solution corresponds to a maximum of Z rather than a minimum because the LHS is falling and the RHS is rising, or at least is falling less rapidly. The shape of the stationary-l locus in Figures 18.21 to 18.25 follows from varying the real-price in Figure 18.26.

With price changes governed by

$$
\frac{\left(\dfrac{P}{W}\right)^{\!\bullet}}{\dfrac{P}{W}} = \theta_1\left[1 - GS\left(\frac{P}{W},\xi\right)\right] - \theta_3\left[\frac{P}{W} - \left(\frac{P}{W}\right)^{*}\right]
$$

and changes in the labor:capital ratio by

$$
\dot{l} = \left[\left(\theta_2 - \frac{h}{h_l l}\right)\psi\left(\left(\frac{P}{W}\right)^{-1}\frac{h - h_l l}{h_l} - \rho_h\right) - \theta_2 sh(l,\xi)\right],
$$

the Jacobian is

$$
J = \begin{bmatrix} j_{11} & j_{12} \\ j_{21} & j_{22} \end{bmatrix}
$$

$$
= \begin{bmatrix} -\theta_1 GS_{\frac{P}{W}} - \theta_3 & \theta_1 \\[2em] -\left(\theta_2 - \dfrac{h}{h_l l}\right)\psi'\dfrac{h - h_l l}{h_l}\left(\dfrac{P}{W}\right)^{-2} & \begin{aligned}&-\dfrac{(h_l)^2\, l - hh_{ll}l - h_l h}{(h_l)^2}\psi \\[0.5em] &+\left(\theta_2 - \dfrac{h}{h_l l}\right)\psi'\left(\dfrac{P}{W}\right)^{-1}\left(-\dfrac{h_{ll}h}{(h_l)^2}\right) - \theta_2 sh_l\end{aligned} \end{bmatrix}
$$

$$
= \begin{bmatrix} -\theta_1 GS_{\frac{P}{W}} - \theta_3 & \theta_1 \\[2em] -\left(\theta_2 - \dfrac{\lambda_1 + \lambda_2 l^{\xi}}{\lambda_2 l^{\xi}}\right)\psi'\dfrac{\lambda_1}{\lambda_2 l^{\xi}}\left(\dfrac{P}{W}\right)^{-2} & \begin{aligned}&\left[\dfrac{\xi}{l}\psi + (1-\xi)\left(\theta_2 - \dfrac{\lambda_1 + \lambda_2 l^{\xi}}{\lambda_2 l^{\xi}}\right)\psi'\left(\dfrac{P}{W}\right)^{-1}\right]\dfrac{\lambda_1}{\lambda_2 l^{\xi}} \\[0.5em] &-\theta_2 sh_l\end{aligned} \end{bmatrix}
$$

$$
= \begin{bmatrix} - & + \\ - & \pm \end{bmatrix}.
$$

The negative sign of j_{21} is the result of the inequality $\theta_2 > (\lambda_1 + \lambda_2 l^\varsigma)/\lambda_2 l^\varsigma$, which is necessary for the existence of an equilibrium that accommodates desired saving, desired investment, and the negative adjustment of l to investment, that is, for the existence of the stationary-l schedule. The sign of j_{22} is positive on the upward-sloping branch of the stationary-l schedule, negative on the downward-sloping branch.

Consequently, since stability requires both

$$tr \ J = -\theta_1 GS_{\frac{P}{W}} - \theta_3 + \left[\frac{\varsigma}{l}\psi + (1-\varsigma)\left(\theta_2 - \frac{\lambda_1 + \lambda_2 l^\varsigma}{\lambda_2 l^\varsigma}\right)\psi'\left(\frac{P}{W}\right)^{-1}\right]\frac{\lambda_1}{\lambda_2 l^\varsigma} - \theta_2 sh_l < 0$$

and

$$det \ J = \left(-\theta_1 GS_{\frac{P}{W}} - \theta_3\right)\left\{\left[\frac{\varsigma}{l}\psi + (1-\varsigma)\left(\theta_2 - \frac{\lambda_1 + \lambda_2 l^\varsigma}{\lambda_2 l^\varsigma}\right)\psi'\left(\frac{P}{W}\right)^{-1}\right]\frac{\lambda_1}{\lambda_2 l^\varsigma} - \theta_2 sh_l\right\}$$
$$+ \ \theta_1\left(\theta_2 - \frac{\lambda_1 + \lambda_2 l^\varsigma}{\lambda_2 l^\varsigma}\right)\psi'\frac{\lambda_1}{\lambda_2 l^\varsigma}\left(\frac{P}{W}\right)^{-2} > 0$$

on the upward-sloping branch of the stationary-l locus, prices and wages must adjust faster than employment, *and* the stationary real-price locus must be steeper than the stationary-l locus. Thus the equilibrium at E' in Figure 18.21 is unstable, whereas the equilibrium at E is stable provided the trace condition is satisfied. On the downward-sloping branch of the stationary-l locus, both stability conditions are satisfied since $j_{22} < 0$.

Comparative statics lead to the now familiar results that a reduction in the hurdle rate of interest promotes both employment and higher prices, whereas an increase in the price of energy leads to ambiguous results. A higher conventional wage—a lower $(P/W)^*$—leads to more employment, the same result that takes place when the impact on saving dominates the impact on capital-widening investment, but this result is achieved by a very different mechanism. The impact on inflation is in the same direction as the impact on employment.

We consider the comparative-statics of displacing ρ_h, ξ, and $(P/W)^*$ in order. We have

$$\begin{bmatrix} \dfrac{\partial\left(\dfrac{P}{W}\right)}{\partial x} \\[2em] \dfrac{\partial l}{\partial x} \end{bmatrix} = -\Delta^{-1}\begin{bmatrix} j_{22} & -j_{12} \\ -j_{21} & j_{11} \end{bmatrix}\begin{bmatrix} \dfrac{\partial AA}{\partial x} \\[1em] \dfrac{\partial BB}{\partial x} \end{bmatrix},$$

where now

$$AA = \theta_1 \left[l - GS\left(\frac{P}{W}, \xi\right)\right] - \theta_3 \left[\frac{P}{W} - \left(\frac{P}{W}\right)^*\right],$$

$$BB = \left(\theta_2 - \frac{h}{h_l l}\right) \psi\left(\left(\frac{P}{W}\right)^{-1} \frac{h - h_l l}{h_l} - \rho_h\right) - \theta_2 sh(l, \xi).$$

The results for monetary policy are

$$\frac{\partial\left(\frac{P}{W}\right)}{\partial\rho_h} = -\Delta^{-1}\theta_1\left(\theta_2 - \frac{\lambda_1 + \lambda_2 l^\varsigma}{\lambda_2 l^\varsigma}\right)\psi' = -,$$

$$\frac{\partial l}{\partial\rho_h} = -\Delta^{-1}\left(\theta_1 GS_{\frac{P}{W}} + \theta_3\right)\left(\theta_2 - \frac{\lambda_1 + \lambda_2 l^\varsigma}{\lambda_2 l^\varsigma}\right)\psi' = -,$$

$$\frac{d\left(\frac{\dot{P}}{P}\right)}{d\rho_h} = -\Delta^{-1}\theta_1\theta_3\left(\theta_2 - \frac{\lambda_1 + \lambda_2 l^\varsigma}{\lambda_2 l^\varsigma}\right)\psi' = -.$$

The results for an energy-price shock are

$$\frac{\partial\left(\frac{P}{W}\right)}{\partial\xi} = -\Delta^{-1}\left(-j_{22}\theta_1 GS_\xi + j_{12}\theta_2 sh_\xi\right) = \pm,$$

$$\frac{\partial l}{\partial\xi} = -\Delta^{-1}\left(-j_{21}\theta_1 GS_\xi + j_{11}\theta_2 sh_\xi\right) = \pm,$$

$$\frac{d\left(\frac{\dot{P}}{P}\right)}{d\xi} = -\theta_3\left(j_{22}\theta_1 GS_\xi + j_{12}\theta_2 sh_\xi\right) = \pm.$$

Finally, a change in the conventional wage gives

$$\frac{\partial\left(\frac{P}{W}\right)}{\partial\left(\frac{P}{W}\right)^*} = -\Delta^{-1}\theta_3\left\{\left[\frac{\varsigma}{l}\psi + (1-\varsigma)\left(\theta_2 - \frac{\lambda_1 + \lambda_2 l^\varsigma}{\lambda_2 l^\varsigma}\right)\psi'\left(\frac{P}{W}\right)^{-1}\right]\frac{\lambda_1}{\lambda_2 l^\varsigma} - \theta_2 sh_l\right\}$$

$$= \begin{array}{l} + \text{ if } \left(\dfrac{dl}{d\left(\frac{P}{W}\right)}\right)_{i=0} > 0 \\[2em] - \text{ if } \left(\dfrac{dl}{d\left(\frac{P}{W}\right)}\right)_{i=0} < 0 \end{array},$$

$$\frac{\partial l}{\partial \left(\dfrac{P}{W}\right)^{*}} = -\Delta^{-1}\theta_3\left[\left(\theta_2 - \frac{\lambda_1 + \lambda_2 l^{\zeta}}{\lambda_2 l^{\zeta}}\right)\psi'\frac{\lambda_1}{\lambda_2 l^{\zeta}}\left(\frac{P}{W}\right)^{-2}\right] = -,$$

$$\frac{d\left(\dfrac{\dot{P}}{P}\right)}{d\left(\dfrac{P}{W}\right)^{*}} = \Delta^{-1}\theta_3\theta_1\left(GS_{\frac{P}{W}}\,j_{22} + j_{21}\right) = -\theta_3\left(1 + \Delta^{-1}\theta_3 j_{22}\right)$$

$$= -\theta_3\left[1 - \frac{\theta_3}{\theta_3 + \theta_1\left(GS_{\frac{P}{W}} - \left(\dfrac{dl}{d\left(\dfrac{P}{W}\right)}\right)_{l=0}\right)}\right] = -.$$

The effect of a change in the conventional wage on employment is unambiguously positive. The change in inflation is unambiguously negative, but the algebra is more complicated. On the rising branch of the stationary-l locus in Figure 18.24, we can use the fact that j_{22} is positive, which makes $1 + \Delta^{-1}\theta_3 j_{22}$ positive, to conclude that inflation moves in the same direction as employment. At an equilibrium on the downward-sloping portion of the stationary-l locus, as in Figure 18.25, both j_{22} and j_{21} are negative, which ensures $GS_{P/W}j_{22} + j_{21} < 0$.

Extending the Cambridge Saving Theory: Mr. Piketty, Meet Mr. Pasinetti

Luigi Pasinetti (1962) extended the Cambridge saving theory to allow for workers' savings and consequent ownership of a share of the capital stock. Thomas Piketty's monumental study of wealth dynamics (2014) made Pasinetti newly relevant since Pasinetti provides a framework for assessing Piketty's claim that wealth distribution is driven by the relationship between the rate of growth g and the rate of profit r—more specifically, that the wealth dynamics resulting from an excess of r over g are responsible for the growing concentration of wealth. At one point, Piketty calls $r > g$ "the fundamental force for divergence" (p. 25); at another, "the central contradiction of capitalism" (p. 571). Here is his argument in a nutshell:

> When the rate of return on capital significantly exceeds the growth rate of the economy . . . , then it logically follows that inherited wealth grows faster than output and income. People with inherited wealth need save only a por-

tion of their income from capital to see that capital grow more quickly than the economy as a whole. (p. 26)

Piketty (2015, p. 49) makes it clear that the problem is not the inequality $r > g$ per se:

that $r > g$ is certainly not a problem in itself. Indeed, the inequality $r > g$ holds true in the steady-state equilibrium of the most common economic models, including representative-agent models where each individual owns an equal share of the capital stock.

Rather, the problem is that $r > g$ implies a growing concentration of wealth.

Piketty reaches this result with the help of two assumptions. First, r and g are treated separately rather than as joint outcomes of the growth process. Second, Piketty's focus is on the impact of $r - g$ on the fortunes of family dynasties, particularly its role in concentrating wealth by multiplying random shocks to accumulation, shocks that would otherwise dissipate over time (Piketty and Saez 2015, sec. 15.5, esp. sec. 15.5.4, pp. 1351–1356).

By contrast, in a Pasinetti framework the focus is on the interaction between steady-state r and g endogenously determined as outcomes of a growth model, and the emphasis is on what happens to the capitalist class as a whole rather on what happens to particular capitalists. In this framework we reach a conclusion opposite to Piketty's: there is *no* logical reason why inherited wealth should grow more rapidly than the capital stock or output, or faster than newly acquired wealth, even if the profit rate exceeds the growth rate.

To apply Pasinetti's generalized Cambridge saving theory to Piketty's argument requires us to redefine capitalists and workers because the traditional working class plays no role in Piketty's conception of wealth dynamics. Presumably, like workers in the original Cambridge theory, *chez* Piketty workers save nothing and accumulate no wealth. As far as saving is concerned, their place is taken by executives, managers, and technocrats, what Piketty calls a "patrimonial middle class" (2014, p. 373). Members of the PMC rely on work as well on accumulated capital for their income. The capitalists of the Cambridge saving theory are for Piketty rentiers whose wealth is inherited and who rely completely on profits for consumption and further accumulation. As an empirical shorthand we can identify Piketty's rentiers with the proverbial "1 percent" and the PMC with the next 9 percent down, or perhaps more accurately, we can identify the two groups with the top 0.1 percent and the next 9.9 percent.[3]

Pasinetti's extension of the Cambridge saving theory adds two assumptions, first, that "workers" (henceforth the PMC)[4] save a portion of their incomes, s_w, albeit a smaller portion than do "capitalists" (henceforth rentiers), that is, $s_w < s_\pi$; second, that, since members of the PMC save, they acquire a portion of the capital stock and therefore a portion of profits. The saving function for the rentier class is

$$S_\pi = \frac{\dot{K}_\pi}{K} = \frac{\dot{K}_\pi}{K_\pi}\delta = s_\pi\left[h(l,\xi) - \left(\frac{P}{W}\right)^{-1}l\right]\delta = s_\pi r\delta,$$

where $\delta = K_\pi/K$, the fraction of the capital stock owned by rentiers. The PMC saves both from its share of profits and from its labor income:

$$S_w = \frac{\dot{K}_W}{K} = s_w\left[h(l,\xi) - \left(\frac{P}{W}\right)^{-1}l\right][1-\delta] + s_w\left(\frac{P}{W}\right)^{-1}l = s_w r(1-\delta) + s_w\left(\frac{P}{W}\right)^{-1}l,$$

where $1 - \delta = K_W/K$ represents the PMC share of the capital stock.

Total saving is the sum of the saving of rentiers and the saving of the PMC:

$$\frac{\dot{K}}{K} = \frac{\dot{K}_\pi + \dot{K}_W}{K} = s_\pi\left[h(l,\xi) - \left(\frac{P}{W}\right)^{-1}l\right]\delta$$
$$+ s_w\left[h(l,\xi) - \left(\frac{P}{W}\right)^{-1}l\right][1-\delta] + s_w\left(\frac{P}{W}\right)^{-1}l. \tag{18.25}$$

The shares δ and $1 - \delta$ are determined endogenously since the relative amounts of saving of the two classes determines their relative shares. We have

$$\dot{\delta} = \frac{\dot{K}_\pi K - \dot{K}K_\pi}{K^2} = \left(\frac{\dot{K}_\pi}{K_\pi} - \frac{\dot{K}}{K}\right)\frac{K_\pi}{K} = \left(s_\pi r - g\right)\delta. \tag{18.26}$$

It is clear from equation (18.26) that an excess of $s_\pi r$ over g will increase the concentration of wealth in the hands of rentiers. But $s_\pi r > g$ is a much more stringent condition than $r > g$; the two conditions coincide only if $s_\pi = 1$. Chapter 9 suggested that we have no theory worth the name of the saving behavior of the very rich. The rich are different from the rest of us not only because they have more money, but there is no reason to believe that all or practically all of their income is saved.

Moreover, even if we amend Piketty's central contradiction to reflect the assumption that s_π is less than one, it is by no means clear that the inequality $s_\pi r - g > 0$ spells more and more concentration of wealth until rentiers end up owning all but a vanishing share of the capital stock. Wealth dynamics are endogenous to the model. It may be the case that $s_\pi r - g > 0$ on the transitional path to equilibrium, while the equilibrium value for δ (the value of δ at which $s_\pi r = g$ and $\dot{\delta} = 0$) is less than one. Indeed, $s_\pi r < g$ is compatible with equilibrium only if the rentier class ends up with a vanishing share of the capital stock, that is, with $\delta = 0$.

Substituting from equations (18.18) and (18.25) we obtain equation (18.27), and the complete dynamic fixprice system with capital widening is

$$\frac{\left(\dfrac{P}{W}\right)^{\bullet}}{\dfrac{P}{W}} = \theta_1\left[1 - GS\left(\frac{P}{W}, \xi\right)\right] - \theta_3\left[\frac{P}{W} - \left(\frac{P}{W}\right)^{*}\right], \tag{18.3}$$

$$\dot{I} = \theta_2(I - S) = \theta_2\left\{\begin{array}{l} \psi\left(\Omega r - \rho_h\right) - s_\pi r\delta - \\ s_w r[1 - \delta] - s_w\left(\dfrac{P}{W}\right)^{-1} I \end{array}\right\}, \tag{18.27}$$

$$\dot{\delta} = \left\{\left[(1 - \delta)s_\pi + \delta s_w\right]\left[h(l, \xi) - \left(\frac{P}{W}\right)^{-1} I\right] - s_w h(l, \xi)\right\}\delta. \tag{18.28}$$

The condition for a stationary value of δ requires special comment. For $\dot{\delta} = 0$, either $\delta = 0$, or $\delta = (s_\pi r - s_w h)/(s_\pi - s_w)r$. Evidently, $\delta > 0$ implies that the growth rate of rentier capital, $s_\pi r$, exceeds the growth rate of PMC capital, $s_w h$, associated with the PMC owning all but a vanishing share of the capital stock. A stationary $\delta > 0$ also implies that the growth rate of rentier capital is equal to the growth rate of the capital stock, in which case the growth rate in equilibrium must be less than the profit rate unless $s_\pi = 1$. Conversely, $\delta = 0$ implies $s_w h > s_\pi r$ since the growth rate of rentier capital, $s_\pi r$, is necessary less than the PMC saving rate, $s_w h$, when the patrimonial middle class owns the entire capital stock.

The conditions for stability are complicated, and to obtain definite results we have to make simplifying assumptions. The Jacobian of equations (18.3), (18.27), and (18.28) is

$$J = \begin{bmatrix} -\theta_1 GS_{\frac{P}{W}} - \theta_3 & \theta_1 & 0 \\ \theta_2\left[\psi'\Omega - \left(s_\pi - s_w\right)\delta\right]\left(\dfrac{P}{W}\right)^{-2} I & \theta_2\left\{\psi'\Omega'r + \left(\psi'\Omega - \left(s_\pi - s_w\right)\delta\right)\left[h_l - \left(\dfrac{P}{W}\right)^{-1}\right] - s_w h_l\right\} & -\theta_2\left(s_\pi - s_w\right)r \\ -\left\{\left[(1 - \delta)s_\pi + \delta s_w\right]\left(\dfrac{P}{W}\right)^{-2} I\right\}\delta & \left\{\left[(1 - \delta)s_\pi + \delta s_w\right]\left[h_l - \left(\dfrac{P}{W}\right)^{-1}\right] - s_w h_l\right\}\delta & -\left(s_\pi - s_w\right)r\delta \end{bmatrix}.$$

Writing

$$J = \begin{bmatrix} j_{11} & j_{12} & j_{13} \\ j_{21} & j_{22} & j_{23} \\ j_{31} & j_{32} & j_{33} \end{bmatrix},$$

it is clear that only the first of the four stability conditions

$$\alpha_1 = -tr\, j = -(j_{11} + j_{22} + j_{33}) > 0,$$

$$\alpha_2 = -(j_{13}j_{31} + j_{12}j_{21} + j_{23}j_{32} - j_{11}j_{22} - j_{11}j_{33} - j_{22}j_{33}) > 0,$$

$$\alpha_3 = -det\, J > 0,$$

$$\alpha_1\alpha_2 - \alpha_3 > 0$$

will be satisfied unless restrictions are imposed on the magnitudes of the j_{ij}'s. For starters, $-j_{13}j_{31} = 0$; $-j_{12}j_{21} < 0$ if $\psi'\Omega - (s_\pi - s_w)\delta > 0$; and $-j_{23}j_{32} < 0$ if at equilibrium δ is positive. Unless the off-diagonal elements of J are small relative to the diagonal elements, there is no guarantee that the centripetal forces making for stability will dominate the centrifugal forces.[5]

Assume that money wages adjust so slowly that we can take $\theta_3 \approx 0$, and that prices adjust very rapidly, which is to say that θ_1 is very large. Also assume $\Omega = 1$ so that $\Omega' = 0$. With these assumptions $h_l \approx (P/W)^{-1}$ and we have

$$J = \begin{bmatrix} -\theta_1 GS_{\frac{P}{W}} & \theta_1 & 0 \\ \theta_2\left[\psi' - \left(s_\pi - s_w\right)\delta\right]\left(\dfrac{P}{W}\right)^{-2}l & -\theta_2 s_w h_l & -\theta_2\left(s_\pi - s_w\right)r \\ -\left\{\left[(1-\delta)s_\pi + \delta s_w\right]\left(\dfrac{P}{W}\right)^{-2}l\right\}\delta & -s_w h_l\delta & -\left(s_\pi - s_w\right)r\delta \end{bmatrix}.$$

Now all four of the stability conditions are satisfied provided that both marginal saving propensities with respect to the rate of profit, the long-run propensity to save (s_π) and the short-run propensity to save $([s_\pi - s_w]\delta)$, exceed the marginal propensity to invest (ψ')

$$\alpha_1 = -trJ = -\left(j_{11} + j_{22} + j_{33}\right) = \theta_1 GS_{\frac{P}{W}} + \theta_2 s_w h_l + \left(s_\pi - s_w\right)r\delta > 0,$$

$$\alpha_2 = -(j_{13}j_{31} + j_{12}j_{21} + j_{23}j_{32} - j_{11}j_{22} - j_{11}j_{33} - j_{22}j_{33})$$

$$= -\theta_1\theta_2\left[\psi' - \left(s_\pi - s_w\right)\delta\right]\left(\dfrac{P}{W}\right)^{-2}l + \theta_1\theta_2 s_w h_l + \theta_1\theta_2 GS_{\frac{P}{W}}\left(s_\pi - s_w\right)r\delta > 0,$$

$$\alpha_3 = -\det J = -\theta_1\theta_2\left(\psi' - s_\pi\right)\left(\frac{P}{W}\right)^{-2}l\left(s_\pi - s_w\right)r\delta > 0,$$

$$\alpha_1\alpha_2 - \alpha_3 \approx \left(\theta_1\right)^2 GS_{\frac{P}{W}}\left\{\begin{array}{l} -\theta_2\left[\psi' - \left(s_\pi - s_w\right)\delta\right]\left(\frac{P}{W}\right)^{-2}l \\ +\theta_2 s_w h_l + \theta_2 GS_{\frac{P}{W}}\left(s_\pi - s_w\right)r\delta \end{array}\right\} > 0$$

for large θ_1.

The picture is in Figure 18.27.

The equilibrium E' is necessarily unstable, since along the lower portion of the aggregate-demand function, investment is more responsive to profitability than is saving, $\psi' - s_\pi > 0$, which violates the determinant condition $\alpha_3 = -\det J > 0$. This condition is satisfied at E, but stability also requires $\psi' - [s_\pi - s_w]\delta < 0$, namely, that the responsiveness of investment to the rate of profit be less than the response of saving. Stability also requires that the price level responds more rapidly to disequilibrium than does employment, which will be the case if θ_1 is sufficiently large. (Otherwise the economy will spiral outward from E in an ever-wider orbit.)

In the limiting case of instantaneous price adjustment, we have $h_l = (P/W)^{-1}$, and the profit rate is equal to the marginal productivity of capital:

$$r = h - h_l l. \tag{18.29}$$

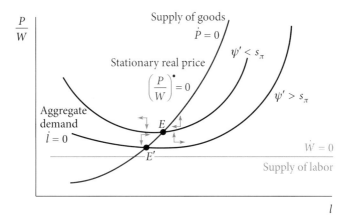

Figure 18.27 Equilibrium with Cambridge saving and capital widening: $\dot{\delta} = 0$ and $\delta > 0$, $\theta_3 = 0$ and $\theta_1 \to \infty$, $\Omega = 1$.

The fixprice model composed of equations (18.3), (18.27), and (18.28) then collapses into

$$\dot{l} = \theta_2 \left(I - S \right) = \theta_2 \left[\psi(r - \rho_h) - s_\pi r \delta - s_w r[1 - \delta] - s_w \left(\frac{P}{W} \right)^{-1} l \right], \quad (18.30)$$

$$\dot{\delta} = \left\{ \left[(1 - \delta)s_\pi + \delta s_w \right] r - s_w h(l, \xi) \right\} \delta. \quad (18.31)$$

Equations (18.30) and (18.31) essentially bring us back to Keynes's first-pass model with the modification that both investment and saving depend on the profit rate. Money wages are implicitly assumed to be fixed, and the GS schedule is smuggled in via equation (18.29). The novelty introduced by Pasinetti is that the saving function makes the distribution of wealth endogenous. The Jacobian is now

$$J = \begin{bmatrix} -\theta_2 \left\{ \left[\psi' - (s_\pi - s_w) \delta \right] h_{ll} l + s_w h_l \right\} & -\theta_2 (s_\pi - s_w) r \\ -\left\{ \left[(1 - \delta)s_\pi + \delta s_w \right] h_{ll} l + s_w h_l \right\} \delta & -(s_\pi - s_w) r \delta + \left[(1 - \delta)s_\pi + \delta s_w \right] r - s_w h \end{bmatrix}.$$

A sufficient condition for $tr\, J < 0$ is that the two diagonal terms be negative. The condition

$$-\theta_2 \left\{ \left[\psi' - (s_\pi - s_w) \delta \right] h_{ll} l + s_w h_l \right\} < 0 \quad (18.32)$$

has a clearer economic meaning if we make use of the relationship between output and the rate of profit

$$\frac{\partial h}{\partial r} = \frac{\dfrac{\partial h}{\partial l}}{\dfrac{\partial r}{\partial l}} = -\frac{h_l}{h_{ll} l}. \quad (18.33)$$

Substituting into equation (18.32), we can rewrite the trace condition as

$$\frac{\theta_2 h_l}{\dfrac{\partial h}{\partial r}} \left\{ \psi' - (s_\pi - s_w) \delta - s_w \frac{\partial h}{\partial r} \right\} < 0. \quad (18.34)$$

The expression inside the braces is the difference between the responsiveness of investment demand to a change in the profit rate and the *short-run* responsiveness of saving (short-run because δ is fixed). For the inequality (18.34) to hold, investment must be less responsive than saving.

The second diagonal element

$$-\left(s_\pi - s_w\right)r\delta + \left[(1 - \delta)s_\pi + \delta s_w\right]r - s_w h \qquad (18.35)$$

is unconditionally negative. If $\dot{\delta} > 0$, equation (18.28) implies

$$\left[(1 - \delta)s_\pi + \delta s_w\right]r - s_w h = 0.$$

If $\dot{\delta} = 0$, expression (18.35) reduces to $s_\pi r - s_w h$, which, as noted earlier, is necessarily the case when the PMC owns the entire capital stock.

The condition $det\ J > 0$ is satisfied if investment is less responsive to profits than is *long-run* saving. When $\dot{\delta} > 0$, $det\ J > 0$ if and only if $\psi' < s_\pi$. In this case, the growth rate of rentier capital is equal to the growth rate of the entire capital stock, and the responsiveness of saving to a change in r is simply s_π. When $\dot{\delta} = 0$, $det\ J > 0$ if and only if $\psi' < s_w(\partial h/\partial r)$. PMC capital is the entire stock of capital, and the responsiveness of capital-stock growth to profitability is given by $s_w(\partial h/\partial r)$.

Pictures may be helpful here. The vertical axis in Figures 18.28 and 18.29 measures the rate of profit. The horizontal axis measures the rate of growth of the capital stock, equal to rentier saving per unit of rentier capital, $s_\pi r$, when $\dot{\delta} > 0$, and equal to PMC saving, $s_w h$, when $\dot{\delta} = 0$. Figures 18.28 and 18.29 assume $\dot{\delta} = 0$.

In Figures 18.28 and 18.29, the global saving and growth rate is denoted

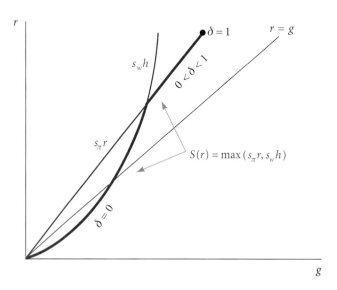

Figure 18.28 A two-class model of saving à la Pasinetti: $\sigma < 1$.

$S(r)$. We have $S(r) = \max(s_\pi r, s_w h)$. Why? The argument has two strands, both of which follow from equation (18.31): when $\delta > 0$ and is stationary, equation (18.31) guarantees both that the global saving rate is equal to $s_\pi r$ and that $s_\pi r > s_w h$; when $\delta = 0$, the same equation leads to the global saving rate being equal to $s_w h$, and $s_w h > s_\pi r$.

The relationship between the $s_\pi r$ and $s_w h$ schedules depends on the elasticity of substitution in production, σ. With production net of the cost of energy given by $h(l, \xi)$, defined by equation (18.7), the formula for σ can be expressed as on p. 728:

$$\sigma = -\frac{h_l\left(h - h_l l\right)}{h l h_{ll}}.$$

Substituting into equation (18.33) gives

$$\frac{\partial h}{\partial r} = \frac{\sigma}{\dfrac{h - h_l l}{h}},$$

which is to say that, given equation (18.29), the slope of $s_w h$ (with respect to the r-axis) is the ratio of the elasticity of substitution to the profit share. The opposite behavior of factor shares under the two regimes, $\sigma < 1$ and $\sigma > 1$, explains the divergent shapes of $s_w h$ in Figures 18.28 and 18.29. When $\sigma < 1$, we have

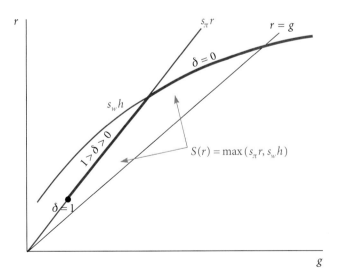

Figure 18.29 A two-class model of saving à la Pasinetti: $\sigma > 1$.

$$\lim_{l \to 0} \frac{h - h_l l}{h} = 0 \text{ and } \lim_{l \to \infty} \frac{h - h_l l}{h} = 1.$$

When $\sigma > 1$, these limits are reversed:

$$\lim_{l \to 0} \frac{h - h_l l}{h} = 1 \text{ and } \lim_{l \to \infty} \frac{h}{h} \frac{h_l l}{} = 0.$$

Hence $\partial h / \partial r$ goes from ∞ to zero when $\sigma < 1$, and from zero to ∞ when $\sigma > 1$. As a result, $s_w h$ exceeds $s_\pi r$ for small values of l and r in the first case, and $s_w h$ exceeds $s_\pi r$ for large values of l and r in the second.

Here's the economics. As the profit share approaches zero or one, the wage share approaches the opposite limit. So, as l and r increase, the decrease in the wage share concentrates wealth further in the hands of rentiers when $\sigma < 1$. But when $\sigma > 1$, the wage share increases with l and r, and this tips the balance toward the PMC with regard to ownership of capital. In this case, the higher is the rate of profit, the greater the equilibrium ($\dot{\delta} = 0$) share of capital held by the PMC.

The construction of Figures 18.28 and 18.29 reflects only saving, and the saving function plus the built-in supply-side assumptions do not by themselves determine equilibrium. We also need the investment function, as in Figure 18.30.

Two results emerge from the picture. First, as in Figure 18.27, there are two equilibria. The equilibrium at E' is necessarily unstable since the determinant condition, $\psi' < s_\pi$, is not satisfied. The equilibrium at E satisfies the determinant condition

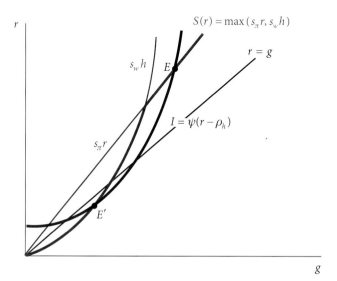

Figure 18.30 Equilibrium in a two-class model: $\sigma < 1$.

$$\psi' < s_\pi = \left(s_\pi - s_w \right) \delta + s_w \frac{h}{r}$$

but may violate the inequality

$$-\theta_2 \left\{ \left[\psi' - \left(s_\pi - s_w \right) \delta \right] h_{ll} l + s_w h_l \right\} l < 0, \qquad (18.32)$$

and, consequently, $tr\, J$ may not be negative. With $\sigma < 1$, $\partial h / \partial r$ is falling as r increases, so $h/r > \partial h / \partial r$. Thus at E, it is possible to have $det\, J > 0$ and at the same time $tr\, J > 0$.

This complication does not exist when $\delta = 0$ because long-run and short-run saving responses to the rate of profit are identical. For $det\, J$ to be positive when $\delta = 0$ we must have

$$\psi' - s_w \frac{\partial h}{\partial r} < 0,$$

which is exactly the same as the trace condition (18.32).

It is clear from Figure 18.30 that the equilibrium rate of profit may exceed the rate of growth of the capital stock without the shares of the capital stock changing, that is, with rentier capital growing at exactly the same rate as the overall capital stock. In the present model, the equilibrium distribution of wealth is endogenously determined by investment and saving, and δ can lie anywhere in the closed interval $[0, 1]$.

Change investment or saving, and the equilibrium will change, including the equilibrium distribution of capital. For instance, if the rate of interest ρ_h falls, investment demand will increase and so will the rate of growth, but the equilibrium rentier share of capital will increase. From the Jacobian, we have

$$\frac{\partial \delta}{\partial \rho_h} = -\frac{\psi'(\sigma - 1)s_w h}{\left(\psi' - s_\pi \right)\left(s_\pi - s_w \right) r^2},$$

which for $\sigma < 1$ and $\psi' < s_\pi$ is negative. That is, if the interest rate falls, the distribution of wealth shifts in favor of rentiers despite the higher rate of growth. The rate of profit rises by more than the rate of growth.

What happens when $\sigma > 1$? In Figure 18.31 the equilibrium at E is stable since the trace and determinant conditions are both satisfied. Observe that as in Figure 18.30, at E the rate of profit exceeds the equilibrium growth rate. And this is true despite the fact that rentiers own a vanishing share of the capital stock. With a lower interest rate, the investment function lies farther to the right, and it could be the case that the growth rate exceeds the profit rate at equilibrium. (This is *not* possible for the stable equilibrium in Figure 18.30.)

With a sufficiently low investment demand, the stable equilibrium will lie on the linear portion of the saving schedule, on which the rentier class owns a positive share of the capital stock. In this case, an increase in investment de-

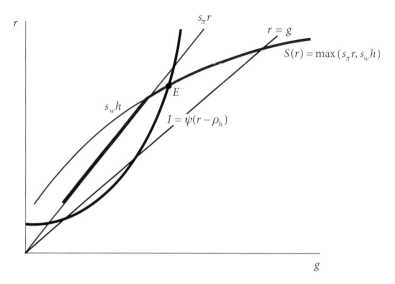

Figure 18.31 Equilibrium in a two-class model: $\sigma > 1$.

mand will, as in Figure 18.30, increase the rate of growth and the rate of profit, but the rentier share of capital will decrease; with $\sigma > 1$, $\partial\delta/\partial\rho_h$ is positive. The economics is that in Figure 18.31 an increasing wage share more than offsets the effect of a rising rate of profit, whereas in Figure 18.30 the profit share increases along with the rate of profit at higher levels of investment demand.

An obvious question is whether it is more likely that the elasticity of substitution is greater or less than one. In the second case, $\sigma < 1$, a higher equilibrium rate of profit will be associated with a greater concentration of wealth in the hands of rentiers, whereas in the first case, $\sigma > 1$, the opposite is true. In this case, if at equilibrium $\delta \in (0,1]$, a higher equilibrium rate of profit is associated with a lower rentier share of the capital stock!

Even so, Piketty believes that $\sigma > 1$, and justifies his belief on the grounds that "there are many different uses of capital in the long run" (2014, p. 221). The flexibility of capital surely has a bearing on the overall elasticity of substitution, but most empirical work suggests relatively low values of σ, well below one. (For a selective survey of the vast research aimed at estimating σ, see Robert Chirinko [2008]. Simon Koesler and Michael Schymura [2015] offer a more recent set of estimates by industry and geographical region.) In any case, an elasticity of substitution greater than one has an implausible feature: $\sigma > 1$ implies that it is possible to produce goods with only one factor of production, that we can make an omelet with our labor alone, without eggs. or, indeed, vice versa: with eggs that stir and then fry themselves. (The latter example is perhaps less far-fetched: it is the central assumption of the utopia—or dystopia—of complete automation.)

The inequality $r > g$ by itself tells us little about the dynamics of wealth distribution in a Pasinetti framework, but this ambiguity does not address the impact of a change in the rate of growth. Piketty assumes that the dynamics of g and r are independent of one another, and that, accordingly, an increase in the rate of growth decreases the concentration of wealth. In a Pasinetti framework, by contrast, the dynamics are intertwined.

Suppose, once again, a lower interest rate. Regardless of whether σ is less than or greater than one, with $\delta > 0$, higher investment shifts the equilibrium to the right:

$$\frac{\partial g}{\partial p_h} = \frac{\partial g}{\partial l} \frac{\partial l}{\partial p_h} = \frac{s_\pi \psi'}{\psi' - s_\pi} < 0.$$

The initial impact on employment and wages may increase the PMC's share of capital (temporarily in case $\sigma < 1$), but if we assume that wages adjust immediately, the rate of profit will rise by even more than the rate of growth—see Figures 18.30 and 18.31—so that the equilibrium difference between r and g also increases. With $g = s_\pi r$

$$\frac{\partial (r - g)}{\partial p_h} = \frac{\left(1 - s_\pi\right) \psi'}{\psi' - s_\pi} < 0.$$

Whether δ increases or decreases depends on the elasticity of substitution: $\sigma < 1$ implies an increase in the rentier share of wealth, and $\sigma > 1$ implies a decrease. The takeaway is that the effect of higher growth on the concentration of wealth is ambiguous.

I do not wish to leave the impression that my negative conclusions with respect to Piketty's "central contradiction of capitalism" are dispositive. The model I have elaborated to explore the equilibrium distribution of the capital stock is much too simple to draw any definitive conclusions from it. The analysis should be read rather as an invitation to consider the interactions of r and g and to focus on class dynamics rather than the dynamics of dynasties.

A More General Theory of the Long Run: Incorporating Unemployment as a Determinant of Labor Supply

The model elaborated in the body of this chapter can be made more plausible by incorporating the dependence of both wage dynamics and labor-supply dynamics on the rate of unemployment. Instead of wage dynamics that depend solely on the relationship between the actual real wage and the conventional wage

$$\frac{\dot{W}}{W} = \theta_3 \left[\frac{P}{W} - \left(\frac{P}{W} \right)^* \right],$$

assume that wage dynamics reflect the wage equation on page 681 in including unemployment as an independent variable:

$$\frac{\dot{W}}{W} = \theta_3 \left[\frac{P}{W} - \left(\frac{P}{W} \right)^* \right] - \theta_4 (1 - \eta), \qquad (18.36)$$

$$\eta = \frac{L}{LS} = \text{employment as a fraction of the labor supply}.$$

To keep the model tractable, I do not incorporate the price of energy, despite its significance in the wage equation of this chapter and the next.

The assumption that the labor supply is unlimited is replaced by the more realistic assumption that labor-supply growth depends on two factors: one a "natural" growth, nLS, the other a function of the unemployment rate. The natural rate is not quite as natural as it is in the Harrod tradition; the parameter n is the sum of the population growth rate and a normal rate of immigration—from both domestic and foreign sources—into the capitalist economy at full employment. Natural or not, this part of labor-force growth is assumed to be exogenous. The endogenous part of labor-supply growth is the variation in the rate of immigration due to job-market conditions: the unemployment rate $(1 - \eta)$ is assumed to proxy for how easy or difficult it is to find a job. We have

$$(LS)^{\bullet} = nLS - \theta_5 (LS - L)$$

and

$$\frac{(LS)^{\bullet}}{LS} = n - \theta_5 (1 - \eta).$$

With fixprice adjustment, the rate of capital accumulation is equal to the rate of investment as a ratio to the capital stock, $I = \dot{K}/K$, so

$$\frac{\dot{i}}{i} = \frac{\dot{L}}{L} - I$$

and

$$\dot{\eta} = \frac{\dot{L}}{L} - \frac{(LS)^{\bullet}}{LS} = \frac{\dot{l}}{l} + I - \frac{(LS)^{\bullet}}{LS} = \theta_2(I - S) + I - n + \theta_5(1 - \eta). \quad (18.37)$$

The complete model is

$$\frac{\left(\dfrac{P}{W}\right)^{\bullet}}{\dfrac{P}{W}} = \theta_1\left[1 - GS\left(\dfrac{P}{W}, \xi\right)\right] - \theta_3\left[\dfrac{P}{W} - \left(\dfrac{P}{W}\right)^{*}\right] + \theta_4(1 - \eta),$$

$$\dot{l} = \theta_2(I - S),$$

and equation (18.37).

We assume a Pasinetti saving function, but to keep the mathematics tractable we let the capital shares of the rentiers and the PMC, δ and $1 - \delta$, adjust instantaneously. This allows us to write the saving function as

$$S = \max(s_{\pi}r, s_{w}h).$$

Additionally, assume that investment responds positively to the real price P/W as a proxy for profitability and to η as a proxy for the pressure on capacity, but does not respond at all to changes in the labor:capital ratio l. With subscripts denoting the respective derivatives of the investment and saving functions, the Jacobian is

$$J = \begin{bmatrix} j_{11} & j_{12} & j_{13} \\ j_{21} & j_{22} & j_{23} \\ j_{31} & j_{32} & j_{33} \end{bmatrix} = \begin{bmatrix} -\theta_1 GS_{\frac{P}{W}} - \theta_3 & \theta_1 & -\theta_4 \\ \theta_2\left(I_{\frac{P}{W}} - S_{\frac{P}{W}}\right) & -\theta_2 S_l & \theta_2 I_{\eta} \\ \theta_2\left(I_{\frac{P}{W}} - S_{\frac{P}{W}}\right) + I_{\frac{P}{W}} & -\theta_2 S_l & (1 + \theta_2)I_{\eta} - \theta_5 \end{bmatrix}. \quad (18.38)$$

The analysis of stability is facilitated by subtracting the second row of the Jacobian (18.38) from the third, which gives us

$$J = \begin{bmatrix} j_{11} & j_{12} & j_{13} \\ j_{21} & j_{22} & j_{23} \\ j_{31} & j_{32} & j_{33} \end{bmatrix} = \begin{bmatrix} -\theta_1 GS_{\frac{P}{W}} - \theta_3 & \theta_1 & -\theta_4 \\ \theta_2\left(I_{\frac{P}{W}} - S_{\frac{P}{W}}\right) & -\theta_2 S_l & \theta_2 I_{\eta} \\ I_{\frac{P}{W}} & 0 & I_{\eta} - \theta_5 \end{bmatrix}.$$

This has the effect of replacing the state variable η and the adjustment equation

$$\frac{\dot{\eta}}{\eta} - \frac{\dot{L}}{L} \quad \frac{(LS)^{\cdot}}{LS}$$

by the state variable $K/LS = \eta/l$ and the adjustment equation

$$\left(\frac{K}{LS}\right)^{\cdot} = \left(\frac{\dot{\eta}}{\eta} - \frac{\dot{i}}{l}\right)\frac{\eta}{l} = \left(\frac{\dot{K}}{K} - \frac{\dot{LS}}{LS}\right)\frac{K}{LS}$$

or

$$\frac{\left(\dfrac{K}{LS}\right)^{\cdot}}{\dfrac{K}{LS}} = \left(\frac{\dot{\eta}}{\eta} - \frac{\dot{i}}{l}\right) = \left(\frac{\dot{K}}{K} - \frac{\dot{LS}}{LS}\right).$$

The stability conditions

$$\alpha_1 = -tr\,J = -(j_{11} + j_{22} + j_{33}) > 0,$$

$$\alpha_2 = -(j_{13}j_{31} + j_{12}j_{21} + j_{23}j_{32} - j_{11}j_{22} - j_{11}j_{33} - j_{22}j_{33}) > 0,$$

$$\alpha_3 = -\det J > 0,$$

$$\alpha_1\alpha_2 - \alpha_3 > 0$$

are satisfied if we make plausible restrictions on the values of the coefficients:

(1) $j_{33} = I_{\eta} - \theta_5 < 0,$

    growth of the capital stock responds more slowly than growth of the labor supply to changes in employment;

(2) $-\dfrac{j_{22}}{j_{21}} = \dfrac{\theta_2 S_l}{\theta_2\left(I_{\frac{P}{W}} - S_{\frac{P}{W}}\right)} > -\dfrac{j_{12}}{j_{11}} = \dfrac{\theta_1}{\theta_1 GS_{\frac{P}{W}} + \theta_3},$

    the slope of the AD schedule relative to the l-axis in $l \times P/W$ space is steeper than the slope of the stationary P/W schedule;

(3) $-\dfrac{j_{22}}{j_{23}} = \dfrac{S_l}{I_{\lambda}} > -\dfrac{j_{12}}{j_{13}} = \dfrac{\theta_1}{\theta_4},$

    the slope of the AD schedule in $l \times K/LS$ space is steeper than the slope of the stationary P/W schedule;

(4) θ_2 is small relative to other speeds of adjustment.

Condition (1) guarantees the trace condition, $\alpha_1 > 0$, since all the other terms in the trace are negative. Conditions (1) and (2) guarantee $\alpha_2 > 0$, since, given condition (1) the only expression of doubtful sign is $j_{13}j_{31} + j_{12}j_{21}$, and condition (2) ensures this expression is negative. Conditions (1), (2), and (3) together guarantee the determinant condition, $\alpha_3 > 0$, since, given condition (1), condition (2) ensures $j_{12}j_{21}j_{33} - j_{11}j_{22}j_{33} < 0$, and condition (3) guarantees $j_{31}j_{12}j_{23} - j_{13}j_{31}j_{22} < 0$. Finally, condition (4) guarantees $\alpha_1\alpha_2 - \alpha_3 > 0$. Observe that these conditions are sufficient rather than necessary for stability.

Consequences of Changes in Demand and Supply in the Long Run

Comparative-statics exercises confirm the main points of the simpler analysis without the adjustment of the labor supply. The equilibrium equations are now

$$AA \equiv \theta_1\left[1 - GS\left(\frac{P}{W}, \xi\right)\right] - \theta_3\left[\frac{P}{W} - \left(\frac{P}{W}\right)^*\right] + \theta_4(1 - \eta) = 0,$$

$$BB \equiv I - S = 0,$$

$$CC \equiv I - n + \theta_5(1 - \eta) = 0.$$

To find the effect of exogenous changes in demand or supply conditions, we differentiate the system of equations with respect to x, which can represent any of the exogenous parameters, $x = \rho_h, s_\pi, s_w, (P/W)^*, \xi$. For simplicity, the analysis is limited to the demand side; specifically, the effect of the hurdle rate on employment. Again, to keep the math simple, we limit ourselves to the case $0 < \delta \leq 1$, that is, the case where rentiers own a nonvanishing share of the capital stock. The result is the equation system

$$\begin{bmatrix} -\theta_1 GS_{\frac{P}{W}} - \theta_3 & \theta_1 & -\theta_4 \\ I_{\frac{P}{W}} - S_{\frac{P}{W}} & -S_l & I_\eta \\ I_{\frac{P}{W}} & 0 & I_\eta - \theta_5 \end{bmatrix} \begin{bmatrix} \dfrac{\partial\left(\frac{P}{W}\right)}{\partial x} \\ \dfrac{\partial l}{\partial x} \\ \dfrac{\partial \eta}{\partial x} \end{bmatrix} = -\begin{bmatrix} \dfrac{\partial AA}{\partial x} \\ \dfrac{\partial BB}{\partial x} \\ \dfrac{\partial CC}{\partial x} \end{bmatrix}. \qquad (18.39)$$

The generic inverse is

$$J^{-1} = \Delta^{-1}\begin{bmatrix} j_{22}j_{33} - j_{23}j_{32} & j_{13}j_{32} - j_{12}j_{33} & j_{12}j_{23} - j_{13}j_{22} \\ j_{23}j_{31} - j_{21}j_{33} & j_{11}j_{33} - j_{13}j_{31} & j_{13}j_{21} - j_{11}j_{23} \\ j_{21}j_{32} - j_{22}j_{31} & j_{12}j_{31} - j_{11}j_{32} & j_{11}j_{22} - j_{12}j_{21} \end{bmatrix},$$

where

$$\Delta = \det J = j_{11}\left(j_{22}j_{33} - j_{23}j_{32}\right) - j_{12}\left(j_{21}j_{33} - j_{23}j_{31}\right) + j_{13}\left(j_{21}j_{32} - j_{22}j_{31}\right).$$

For the coefficient matrix in the equation system (18.39), we have

$$\Delta = \left[-\theta_1 GS' - \theta_3\right]\left[-S_l\right]\left[I_\eta - \theta_5\right] - \theta_1\left[-I_p\theta_5 \underset{W}{} - S_p \underset{W}{}\left[I_\eta - \theta_5\right]\right] - \theta_4 S_l I_p \underset{W}{}.$$

We will assume $-(I_{P/W})\theta_5 > S_{P/W}[I_\eta - \theta_5]$, which is to say that $I_{P/W}$ is small relative to $S_{P/W}$. This assumption guarantees $\Delta < 0$.

For $x = \rho_h$, equation (18.39) becomes

$$\begin{bmatrix} -\theta_1 GS_{\frac{P}{W}} - \theta_3 & \theta_1 & -\theta_4 \\[2mm] I_{\frac{P}{W}} - S_{\frac{P}{W}} & -S_l & I_\eta \\[2mm] I_{\frac{P}{W}} & 0 & I_\eta - \theta_5 \end{bmatrix} \begin{bmatrix} \dfrac{\partial\left(\dfrac{P}{W}\right)}{\partial \rho_h} \\[4mm] \dfrac{\partial l}{\partial \rho_h} \\[4mm] \dfrac{\partial \eta}{\partial \rho_h} \end{bmatrix} = - \begin{bmatrix} 0 \\[2mm] I_{\rho_h} \\[2mm] I_{\rho_h} \end{bmatrix},$$

and from the inverse J^{-1} we have

$$\frac{\partial\left(\dfrac{P}{W}\right)}{\partial \rho_h} = \frac{\left(\theta_1 - \theta_5\right) - \theta_4 S_l}{\Delta}\left(-I_{\rho_h}\right) < 0 \text{ if and only if } \theta_1\theta_5 - \theta_4 S_l > 0,$$

$$\frac{\partial l}{\partial \rho_h} = \frac{\left[\theta_1 GS_{\frac{P}{W}} + \theta_3\right]\theta_5 + \theta_4 S_{\frac{P}{W}}}{\Delta}\left(-I_{\rho_h}\right) < 0,$$

$$\frac{\partial \eta}{\partial \rho_h} = \frac{\theta_1 S_{\frac{P}{W}} + \left[\theta_1 GS_{\frac{P}{W}} + \theta_3\right]S_l}{\Delta}\left(-I_{\rho_h}\right) < 0.$$

The effect on inflation of a change in the hurdle rate is given by

$$\frac{\partial\left(\dfrac{\dot{P}}{P}\right)}{\partial \rho_h} = \frac{\partial\left(\dfrac{\dot{P}}{P}\right)}{\partial\left(\dfrac{P}{W}\right)}\frac{\partial\left(\dfrac{P}{W}\right)}{\partial \rho_h} + \frac{\partial\left(\dfrac{\dot{P}}{P}\right)}{\partial l}\frac{\partial l}{\partial \rho_h} = \frac{\theta_1\theta_3\theta_5 + \theta_1\theta_4\left(GS_{\frac{P}{W}} + S_{\frac{P}{W}}\right)}{\Delta}\left(-I_{\rho_h}\right) < 0.$$

All of these derivatives are sign definite with the exception of $\partial(P/W)/\partial\rho_h$. A fall in the hurdle rate stimulates employment and inflation, but the real price level may fall or rise because the relative effect of greater investment on employment and on the labor force depends on relative adjustment speeds.

Consider the simpler case of assuming $S_{P/W} = I_{P/W} = 0$. We have

$$\Delta = \left[-\theta_1 GS_{\frac{P}{W}} - \theta_3 \right]\left[-S_l \right]\left[I_\eta - \theta_5 \right],$$

$$\frac{\partial l}{\partial\rho_h} = \frac{\left[\theta_1 GS_{\frac{P}{W}} + \theta_3 \right]\theta_5}{\left[-\theta_1 GS_{\frac{P}{W}} - \theta_3 \right]\left[-S_l \right]\left[I_\eta - \theta_5 \right]}\left(-I_{\rho_h} \right) = \frac{\theta_5}{S_l\left[I_\eta - \theta_5 \right]}\left(I_{\rho_h} \right),$$

$$\frac{\partial\eta}{\partial\rho_h} = \frac{\left[\theta_1 GS_{\frac{P}{W}} + \theta_3 \right]S_l}{\left[-\theta_1 GS_{\frac{P}{W}} - \theta_3 \right]\left[-S_l \right]\left[I_\eta - \theta_5 \right]}\left(-I_{\rho_h} \right) = \frac{1}{\left[I_\eta - \theta_5 \right]}\left(I_{\rho_h} \right).$$

In this simple case—shades of the first-pass model, except that investment as well as saving depends on income and employment—it is clear that whether l or η responds more vigorously to changes in the hurdle rate depends on the relative magnitudes of θ_5 and S_l. Since $l \equiv L/K$ and $\eta \equiv L/LS$, if $\theta_5 > S_l$, then the labor supply is responding more strongly than the capital stock. In case $\theta_5 < S_l$, η is responding more strongly than l, which is to say that the capital stock adjusts more rapidly than does the labor supply.

Observe that in this model, as in the other models elaborated in this chapter, shocks are permanent and have permanent effects. This is a principal difference between a Keynesian long run and the standard, New Keynesian, treatment of the long run, in which shocks are transitory however long a time it might take for their effects to dissipate. Greg Mankiw's simple New Keynesian model (2016, chap. 15) lends itself to a dynamic version suitable for comparison. Using Mankiw's notation

$\overline{Y}$ = Natural level of output
Y = Output
r = Real rate of interest
ρ = Natural rate of interest
ε = Demand shock
v = Supply shock
π = Rate of inflation
π^* = Target rate of inflation

the model is

$$\dot{Y} = \theta_1 [\bar{Y} - Y - \alpha(r - \rho) + \varepsilon],$$
$$\dot{\pi} = \theta_2 [Y - \bar{Y} + v],$$
$$\dot{r} = \theta_\pi [\pi - \pi^*] + \theta_Y [Y - \bar{Y}].$$

The equations for output and inflation are supposed to reflect the workings of the economy; the natural level of output is assumed to be fixed for simplicity. The adjustment of the interest rate is a central-bank reaction function à la Taylor (1993).

The Jacobian for this system is

$$J = \begin{bmatrix} -\theta_1 & 0 & -\theta_1\alpha \\ \theta_2 & 0 & 0 \\ \theta_Y & \theta_\pi & 0 \end{bmatrix}.$$

The system is stable if and only if the product $\theta_1\theta_Y$ is greater than the product $\theta_2\theta_\pi$.

The effect of a demand shock is given by inverting the Jacobian matrix to obtain

$$\begin{bmatrix} \dfrac{\partial Y}{\partial \varepsilon} \\ \dfrac{\partial \pi}{\partial \varepsilon} \\ \dfrac{\partial r}{\partial \varepsilon} \end{bmatrix} = -\Delta^{-1} \begin{bmatrix} 0 & -\theta_1\alpha\theta_\pi & 0 \\ 0 & -\theta_1\alpha\theta_Y & -\theta_1\alpha\theta_2 \\ \theta_2\theta_\pi & -\theta_1\theta_\pi & 0 \end{bmatrix} \begin{bmatrix} \theta_1 \\ 0 \\ 0 \end{bmatrix},$$

$$\frac{\partial Y}{\partial \varepsilon} = 0,$$

$$\frac{\partial \pi}{\partial \varepsilon} = 0,$$

$$\frac{\partial r}{\partial \varepsilon} = \frac{1}{\alpha}.$$

The result is that a demand shock has no permanent effect either on output or on inflation. The real rate of interest has to rise in order to curb demand and make room for the demand shock.

By contrast a supply shock has a permanent effect:

$$
\begin{bmatrix} \dfrac{\partial Y}{\partial v} \\[2ex] \dfrac{\partial \pi}{\partial v} \\[2ex] \dfrac{\partial r}{\partial v} \end{bmatrix} = -\Delta^{-1} \begin{bmatrix} 0 & -\theta_1 \alpha \theta_\pi & 0 \\ 0 & -\theta_1 \alpha \theta_Y & -\theta_1 \alpha \theta_2 \\ \theta_2 \theta_\pi & -\theta_1 \theta_\pi & 0 \end{bmatrix} \begin{bmatrix} 0 \\ \theta_2 \\ 0 \end{bmatrix},
$$

$$
\frac{\partial Y}{\partial v} = -1,
$$

$$
\frac{\partial \pi}{\partial v} = -\frac{\theta_Y}{\alpha \theta_\pi},
$$

$$
\frac{\partial r}{\partial v} = -\frac{1}{\alpha}.
$$

— 19 —

INFLATION AND EMPLOYMENT EMPIRICS IN THE KEYNESIAN LONG RUN

> The central forecast to which [M. Friedman's (1968) and Phelps's (1968)] reasoning led was a conditional one, to the effect that a high-inflation decade should not have less unemployment on average than a low-inflation decade. We got the high inflation decade, and with it as clear-cut an experimental discrimination as macroeconomics is ever likely to see, and Friedman and Phelps were right. It really is as simple as that.
>
> —ROBERT E. LUCAS, JR.

> The U.S. Phillips curve appears to be one of the most stable empirical macroeconomic relationships of the postwar era, one that shows no sign as of yet of being subject to Lucas's econometric critique
>
> —ROBERT GORDON

How do the models elaborated in the previous chapter stand up to the data? In particular, to what extent does this framework explain the ephemeral aspect of the Phillips curve that has led to the denial of the existence of a long-run trade-off between price stability and employment?

Were we living in a world without technological change, it would be reasonable to apply the theory developed in chapter 18 to data relating the labor:capital ratio to the real price of labor (or the real wage) and to translate demand and supply shocks into changes in the labor:capital ratio and changes in the real price. But in a world of changing technology, the labor:capital ratio will vary independently of demand and supply shocks and so will the real price. Without controlling for technology, it is pointless to look for an association between changes in the labor:capital ratio and changes in the real price.

The regression equation in chapter 18 controlled for technology by substituting a conventional wage *share* for the conventional wage *rate* in explaining wage changes over time. Here I follow a version of this strategy in replacing

Portions of this chapter were previously published in "Wages, Prices, and Employment in a Keynesian Long Run," *Review of Keynesian Economics* 5 (Autumn 2017): 360–425.

the labor:capital ratio by the employment ratio in explaining the rate of inflation. Despite the endogeneity of the labor force, it is fixed at each moment of
time and adjusts to demand only over time, as in the model elaborated in the
mathematical appendix to the last chapter.

The models of the text and the mathematical appendix to chapter 18 converge on one point: positive demand shocks, represented in the model by increases in investment demand or reduction in desired saving, lead to an increase in employment and an increase in inflation. In other words, according
to the theory, the Phillips curve should be reflected in the long-term data.

Beyond this prediction, the models suggest that there are a variety of plausible responses to supply shocks. Both a negative association between inflation and employment (anti-Phillips stagflation) and a positive association
(the Phillips relationship) are possible.

The challenge is then to make sense of the haphazard collection of points in
Figure 18.3, which shows the relationship between the employment ratio and
inflation in the United States over the period 1956 to 2011.[1] That figure does
not hold out much hope for a Phillips relationship until, as Robert Gordon
(1984, 2015) and others have argued, we separate demand and supply shocks.

We begin by looking at the data for the first years of this period, when
Keynesians believed all too easily that the world, like their models, could be
understood in terms of the behavior of demand, with nary a side glance at
supply. Figure 19.1 presents the subset of data from Figure 18.3 for the period
1956 to 1969. These data, especially for the earlier part of this period, do not
look very promising. We do not need a regression line to see that employment
and inflation do not move together until 1965.

However, we have not exploited one feature of the model laid out in chapter
6, namely, the different implications of the two adjustment processes for lags

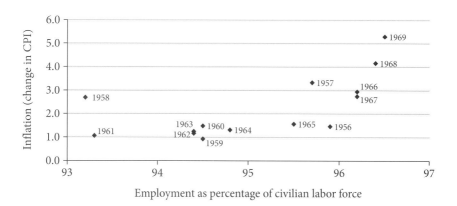

Figure 19.1 Employment vs. inflation (1956–1969).

between changes in employment and changes in the rate of inflation. Flex-price adjustment implies that prices move first, in response to positive difference between desired expenditure and output; employment adjusts later, when the rise in prices makes it profitable to expand production. We can capture this in a simple way by assuming that employment responds with a one year lag to inflation, with changes in the rate of inflation in turn triggered by a change in aggregate demand. Figure 19.2 presents the data for the period 1956 to 1969 with this lag structure. No improvement in the fit would be an overstatement.

However, if we assume fixprice adjustment and impose a lag structure that goes in the opposite direction—first comes the change in output and employment, then comes the change in the rate of inflation—the results look more promising. Figure 19.3 relates employment in year t to the rate of inflation in year $t + 1$. The fit is now very much in line with the prediction of the model

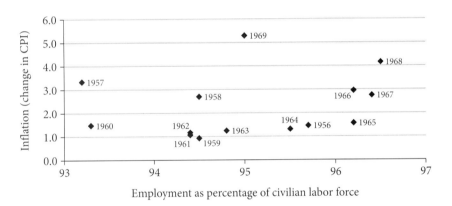

Figure 19.2 Employment(+1) vs. inflation (1956–1969).

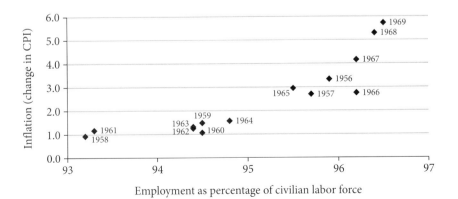

Figure 19.3 Employment vs. inflation(+1) (1956–1969).

for demand-driven changes, but the Phillips curve is really a curve rather than a linear relationship: higher levels of employment lead to more than proportionate changes in the rate of inflation. In fact, a log-linear specification does much better, as in Figure 19.4, in which one percentage point of additional employment leads to the same percentage increase in the inflation rate regardless of the employment ratio.

You probably know what happens when we extend the range of the data beyond the so-called Golden Age. Keeping to the lag structure suggested by fixprice adjustment, we have Figure 19.5, in which the years 1970 to 1975 have been added. The Phillips curve falls apart. Something other than aggregate demand is clearly in play.

If we take a somewhat longer view, we can make better sense of the data. Add the period through 1983, and the data sort themselves out differently. In Figure 19.6, there are two distinct Phillip curves covering, respectively, the

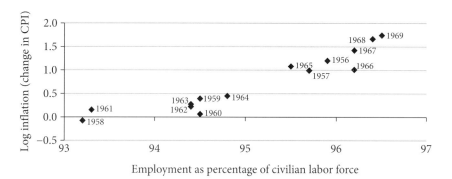

Figure 19.4 Employment vs. log (inflation[+1]) (1956–1969).

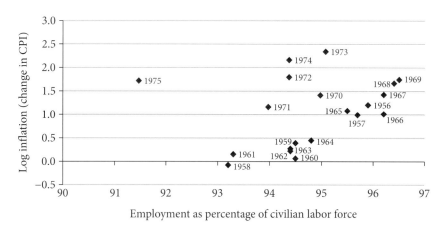

Figure 19.5 Employment vs. log (inflation[+1]) (1956–1975).

periods 1956 to 1969 and 1973 to 1983. The Phillips curve is somewhat flatter in the second period, but the more important distinction is that the intercepts are very different.[2] The Phillips curve has shifted.

Figure 19.7 brings the story up to the present century. In the figure there are important changes in the intercept, and the Phillips-curve trade-off increases moderately in the period 1997 to 2001. The period 1994 to 1996 is a transition period, like the period 1970 to 1972 in Figure 19.6, not belonging to either the era before or the era after.

Starting in the 1970s, changes took place that allowed any given employment ratio to be achieved at a progressively lower rate of inflation. For instance, in 1982, an employment ratio of just over 90 percent (an unemployment rate approaching 10 percent!) coexisted with an inflation rate of 3.1

Figure 19.6 Employment vs. log (inflation[+1]) (1956–1983).

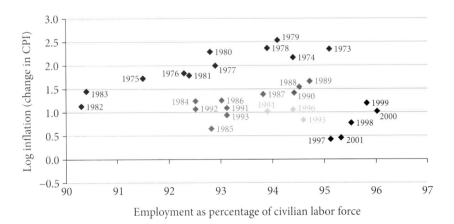

Figure 19.7 Employment vs. log (inflation[+1]) (1973–2001).

percent the next year (*exp*(1.13) = 3.1); approximately a decade later, in 1991, the employment ratio was over 93 percent, with the same rate of inflation; by the end of the century, in 2000, the employment ratio was just shy of 96 percent, with inflation even less than 3 percent. Indeed, Figure 19.8 suggests that by the late 1990s the relationship between employment and inflation was back to where it had been in the Golden Age of the 1950s and 1960s. To illustrate, the data points for 1956 and 1999 are virtually indistinguishable; in 1956 as well as in 1999, employment was just under 96 percent and inflation in both 1957 and 2000 was 3.3 percent.

Figure 19.9 brings the story into the second decade of this century. Something new has happened. Not only has the dispersion of the data increased, but the trade-off between employment and inflation has become much flat-

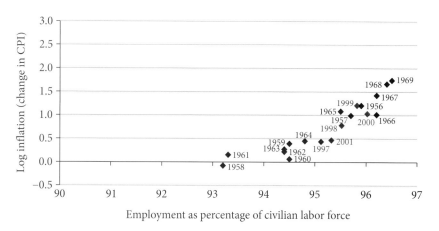

Figure 19.8 Employment vs. log (inflation[+1]) (1956–1969 and 1997–2001).

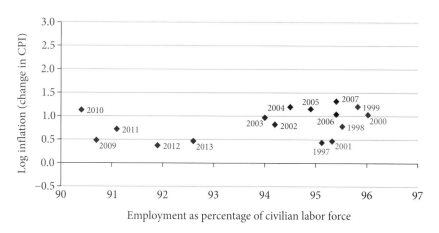

Figure 19.9 Employment vs. log (inflation[+1]) (1997–2013, excluding 2008).

ter.[3] If the data for the years 2002 to 2013 define a new Phillips curve, we could have been having much higher employment in this century without touching off much more inflation.

According to the theory laid out in chapter 18, the Phillips curve shifts over time because of supply shocks, which I model as changes in the real price of energy—the price of energy relative to the price of all goods other than energy and food. As Figure 19.10 shows, the real price of energy does indeed correlate with the observed shifts in the Phillips curve. The increase between 1973 and 1980 correlates with the upward shift in the Phillips curve in the 1970s, and the subsequent downward shift in the 1980s correlates with the downward shift of the Phillips curve in the later period.

Since the scatter of points in Figures 19.1 to 19.9 reflect both supply and demand factors, the visual appearance of the Phillips Curve relationship between inflation and employment in these diagrams is not an accurate representation of the relationship between inflation and aggregate demand. In the 1970s, when, as Figure 19.10 indicates, the real price of energy was on an upswing, aggregate demand would have had less effect on inflation than the observed data in Figures 19.6 and 19.7 suggest—regression lines summarizing the relationship between the two variables on the basis of the observed data would overstate the true relationship between aggregate demand and inflation. In the 1980s and early 1990s, when energy prices were falling sharply, aggregate demand would have had more of an effect on inflation than the data in Figure 19.7 suggest. For the period 2000 to 2008, similar to the 1970s in terms of the rising trajectory of energy prices, aggregate demand would have had even less influence on inflation than the data of Figure 19.9 indicate.

How do I account for the shifts in the Phillips curve during periods in which relative energy prices were flat, like the periods in Figure 19.10 shown in red and gray, 1970 to 1972 and 1994 to 1996? Here, I would argue, the driving force is wage shocks rather than price shocks. In these exceptional peri-

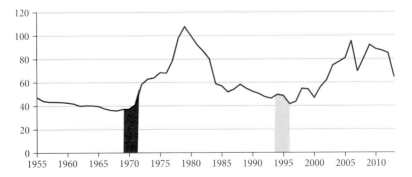

Figure 19.10 Energy price level as percentage of price level of all goods except energy and food (1982 = 100).

ods, employment and inflation appear to have been responding to changes in the conventional wage. The dummy variables DUM1970 and DUM1994 in the wage equation of chapter 18 were intended to capture this phenomenon, albeit in a somewhat stylized way by concentrating the effect into two years, 1970 and 1994. I interpret the positive coefficient on DUM1970 as reflecting the ability of American workers to raise the conventional wage (as a share of output) in the face of rising unemployment. In the second period, the negative coefficient on DUM1994 suggests that their children were unable to similarly defend themselves against the erosion of the conventional wage share even as unemployment was falling.

Why this difference between the two generations? In the late 1960s workers were riding high. Prosperity, strong unions, two terms of a Democratic Congress and administration, an economy relatively well insulated against low-wage competition from abroad—all combined to empower workers to press wage claims vigorously. By contrast, in the 1990s, while the economy was again prosperous, none of the other ingredients of working-class vigor was present. There was indeed a Democrat in the White House, but the Democratic Party had changed dramatically in a generation. With neither political party looking after their interests, workers had little power to prevent jobs from moving offshore and even less power to defend their wages. Unions had been in decline since the 1960s. The result was a fall in the conventional wage share, the culmination of trends and policies that had prevented real wages from rising very much over the previous two decades. The upside was a downward shift in the Phillips curve.

Here the specifics of the model come into play. In a fixprice regime in which capital widening is the dominant form that investment took, upward pressure on the conventional wage in the early 1970s is consistent with the observation of increasing inflation (and falling employment). And downward pressure on the conventional wage would have produced the opposite result in the 1990s.

To tie demand and supply together, consider the following regression, loosely based on the model formulated in the section "A More General Theory of the Long Run: Incorporating Unemployment as a Determinant of Labor Supply" in the mathematical appendix to chapter 18. This model incorporates the dependence of labor supply on the level of unemployment and the dependence of wage changes on the unemployment rate. But the empirics are still only loosely based on the theoretical model because, like the analysis of wage changes in the previous chapter, the regression analysis here also takes account of the reality of technical change and hence modifies the conventional wage: instead of a wage rate, the conventional wage is modeled as a wage share. Equilibrium is modeled as a relationship between nominal price inflation on the one hand and, on the other hand, wage inflation, technical change, and the change in the price of energy.

Assuming a stationary profit rate and ignoring capital deepening, the regression equation for price inflation is

$$\frac{\Delta P}{P_{-1}} = a_0 + a_1 \frac{\Delta W}{W_{-1}} + a_2 \frac{\Delta Prod}{Prod_{-1}} + a_3 \frac{\Delta P_E}{\left(P_E\right)_{-1}}.$$

The variables are defined below. In equilibrium the coefficients should be:

$a_0 = 0$.

$a_1 = 1$.

a_2 = reciprocal of wage share, with sign reversed, if *Prod* accurately measures technical change. a_2 will be smaller in absolute magnitude than the wage share if the measure of technical change overstates the true rate. This is likely the case here since *Prod* is actually a measure of output per employee hour, which includes the effects of capital deepening.

a_3 = the ratio of the share of energy in output to the labor share.

Ordinary least squares (OLS) regressions do not work in this situation since the error term is almost certainly correlated with the change in wages. Instead, we estimate the coefficients by means of two-stage least squares (TSLS). The model in the mathematical appendix to chapter 18 suggests the conventional wage share and the unemployment rate as instruments for estimating the change in wages in the first-stage equation. Additionally, three dummy variables reflect the changes in the conventional wage associated with the emergence of the U.S. economy from the Great Depression (dated 1936), the apex of working-class power (dated 1970), and the triumph of neoliberalism (dated 1994). The first- and second-stage regression results are, respectively,

$$\frac{\Delta W}{W_{-1}} = 43.48 - 76.53 \left(\frac{WL}{PY}\right)_{-1} + 0.4708 \frac{\Delta Prod}{Prod_{-1}} + 0.1196 \frac{\Delta P_E}{\left(P_E\right)_{-1}}$$
$$\quad\;\; (19.00)\quad(32.02)\qquad\qquad\quad(0.1330)\qquad\quad\;(0.0195)$$

$$- 0.3058\,\text{UNRATE} + 5.062\,\text{DUM1936} + 2.138\,\text{DUM1970} - 4.773\,\text{DUM1994}$$
$$\quad(0.1174)\qquad\qquad\quad(2.005)\qquad\qquad\quad(0.7530)\qquad\qquad\quad(0.8795)$$

$$R^2 = 0.63$$

$$\frac{\Delta P}{P_{-1}} = 0.1913 + 0.7465 \frac{\Delta W}{W_{-1}} - 0.4043 \frac{\Delta Prod}{Prod_{-1}} + 0.0925 \frac{\Delta P_E}{\left(P_E\right)_{-1}}$$
$$\qquad\quad(0.3035)\quad(0.0865)\qquad\quad(0.1401)\qquad\qquad(0.0223)$$

$$R^2 = 0.84$$

Robust Standard Errors in Parentheses

Observations: 82 (1930–2011) $F(7, 74) = 13.82$

Variable	Description	Mean	Std Dev	Min	Max
$\dfrac{\Delta P}{P_{-1}}$	Percentage Change in Consumer Price Index	3.263	3.955	−10.301	14.389
$\dfrac{\Delta W}{W_{-1}}$	Percentage Change in Nominal Wages	4.740	4.063	−13.210	17.539
$\left(\dfrac{WL}{PY}\right)_{-1}$	Labor Share of Output, Lagged One Year	0.560	0.018	0.514	0.596
$\dfrac{\Delta Prod}{Prod_{-1}}$	Percentage Change in Output per Employee Hour	2.215	2.391	−6.641	12.552
$\dfrac{\Delta P_E}{\left(P_E\right)_{-1}}$	Percentage Change in Price of Energy	4.641	11.852	−26.045	55.164
UNRATE	Unemployment Rate	7.241	4.849	1.200	24.900
DUM1936	= 0 prior to 1936, = 1 in 1936 and later years				
DUM1970	= 0 prior to 1970, = 1 in 1970 and later years				
DUM1994	= 0 prior to 1994, = 1 in 1994 and later years				

The regression coefficients all have the right sign, and, with the exception of the coefficient on wage changes in the second-stage equation, are of the magnitudes predicted by the model. The misbehavior of a_1 suggests that prices fail to adjust rapidly enough to achieve equilibrium in every year. Delay in adjustment is also reflected in Figures 18.3 to 18.9, in which price inflation is assumed to adjust with a one-year lag to the level of employment.

Observe that the first-stage equation is the same equation that was deployed in chapter 18 to explain wage changes, from which the conventional-wage share and its evolution over time were calculated.[4] At that point in the argument I could not motivate this equation, not yet having developed the long-run theory that was the subject matter of chapter 18 and its mathematical appendix.

Based on that theory, the two-stage regression describes an equilibrium between price inflation and wage inflation. Another interpretation presents itself if we regard the two-stage regression as a structural model of the relationship between wage and price dynamics. In this interpretation the first-stage regression captures the dependence of wage changes on the distance from the conventional wage share, unemployment, productivity growth, and energy-price changes; the second stage reflects the dependence of price inflation on wage inflation, productivity growth, and energy-price changes.

Whichever interpretation we adopt, the important takeaway from all this is, first, that there is indeed a trade-off between employment and output on the one hand and price stability on the other, not only in the short run but also in the long run. And, second, the starting point for the trade-off depends on supply conditions. Higher output due to greater demand must be paid for with higher inflation, but how much inflation is consistent with any given level of employment depends on the supply side, in my model reflected in the change in the price of energy and the level of the conventional wage.

Now we can see why Milton Friedman (1968) and Edmund Phelps (1968) were correct in predicting that high inflation would not see less unemployment, but Robert Lucas could still be stunningly wrong in theorizing that this meant the demise of the Phillips curve. As Lucas observed—see the epigraph to this chapter—the average rate of unemployment over the quarter century preceding Lucas's 1981 article did not depend very much on the level of inflation because, as the Phillips curves in Figure 19.6 show, the displacements due to supply-side shocks change the average rate of inflation more than the average rate of employment.

But there is no way that the analysis is as simple as Lucas claimed. The lack of correlation between the *average* rate of unemployment and the rate of inflation is totally consistent with the existence of a demand-induced trade off: within each of the two periods covered in Figure 19.6, higher employment goes along with higher inflation, even though across periods there is less difference between the average rate of unemployment (4.9 percent vs. 7.3 percent) than there is between the average rate of inflation (2.1 percent vs. 7.9 percent). Experience confirmed the letter of Friedman and Phelps, but not the interpretation that there is no Phillips curve in the long run.

There is an important corollary of more recent policy relevance. If I have the logic of investment demand right, it is precisely in times when the economy is in a deep slump, like the one that began in 2008, that higher wages will stimulate the economy, not only via higher consumption demand but also via the inducement that high wages provides for capital deepening. The presence of a large amount of unused capacity means that cost-cutting investment, if not the only game in town, is where most of the investment action is taking place. This is not to argue that shifting the conventional wage is a superior alternative to interventions to move the AD schedule, but rather that raising wages is another element in the toolbox of policy intervention—one which becomes more attractive when the limits of fiscal stimulus and monetary easing have been reached.

What's So Bad about Inflation?

In the theory developed in the previous chapter, higher levels of activity resulting from higher demand are always accompanied by higher rates of inflation. In recession this is hardly a downside, indeed, as the experience of the Great Depression illustrates all too vividly, the consequences of deflation can be even more catastrophic than the failure to make use of existing capacity. But what about the long run? What are the costs of inflation if we leave out the special case of an underperforming macroeconomy?

There is a disconnect between the man and the woman in the street and the economist. Economists tend to regard inflation as neutral between prices and wages, at least in the long run, and on this basis one can argue that inflation does not hurt the "representative agent," for whom all forms of income—profits, wages, rents—go up or down at the same rate. The man and the woman in the street differ, regarding inflation as a thief robbing them of their hard-earned wages.

In the mid-1990s, Robert Shiller documented the public fear and loathing of inflation in three countries: the United States, which has dealt with moderate inflation over most of the post–World War II period; Germany, where prices have been much more stable over this period, but second- and third-hand memories of the disastrous hyperinflation of the early 1920s are supposed to haunt public and policymakers alike; and Brazil, which for much of the second half of the twentieth century faced chronic inflation. Interviews with ordinary people revealed more similarities than differences among the three countries, as well as between older and younger respondents, despite the great differences in their actual experience of inflation. Among many surprising results, perhaps the most surprising was the strong preference voiced by the Americans and the Germans for relatively stable prices even at the cost of high unemployment. In these two countries, both those born before 1940, and presumably more sensitive to the evils of high unemployment as well as high inflation, and those born after 1940 preferred a hypothetical combination of annual inflation at a 2 percent rate coupled with 9 percent unemployment over a combination of an inflation rate of 10 percent per *month* coupled with 3 percent unemployment. The fraction of older German respondents who preferred the low inflation combination was two-thirds, while younger Germans opted five to one for this package. In the United States there was relatively little difference between the generations, with approximately three-quarters of both groups favoring low inflation even at the cost of high unemployment. Only the Brazilians, the one population with the more recent experience of very high inflation, were more or less evenly split between the two options (Shiller 1997, p. 27).

In Shiller's survey, the public was consistently at odds with economists over both the causes and the consequences of inflation. Much of the difference evidently lies in how the two groups perceive the effects of inflation on real incomes. Economists tend, I have noted, to conceptualize inflation as neutral between prices and wages, the second rising as rapidly as the first, so that inflation has no impact on the distribution of income (Shiller 1997, *passim,* esp.

p. 29). Noneconomists believe that their own real incomes are likely to suffer when inflation is high (Shiller 1997, p. 29).

Who's right? Greg Mankiw offered a perceptive comment on Shiller's essay (1997): supply shocks necessarily reduce the real income of some segment of the population, and inflation is simply one way of absorbing the hit. The real culprit is the supply shock, but to the extent the association between supply shocks and inflation holds, it is no wonder that the public associates price inflation with reductions in the real standard of living. In other words, it is reasonable to blame the messenger (inflation) for the message (the hit to real income) when the message is so frequently delivered by the same messenger.

Mankiw might have added that adverse demand shocks may also reduce real incomes; even positive demand shocks can have negative consequences somewhere along the line, especially when these shocks play out in terms of inflation. This is true whether the demand shock is the result of an expansion of the government's claim on resources (the *locus classicus* being the German hyperinflation of the 1920s, the result of the inability of the Weimar government to levy the taxes that would have been required to make reparations payments while maintaining price stability) or whether the demand shock is the result of expansion of private investment demand or, for that matter, consumption demand. The older term of art for the process by which the economy balances its books in accommodating a demand shock is "forced saving," *forced* highlighting the contrast between ordinary, voluntary saving and the involuntary nature of the reduction in real consumption that accompanies the failure of (some) money incomes to keep pace with rising prices.

In *A Treatise on Money* (1930), Keynes made important use of the concept of forced saving by workers whose wages fail to keep pace with prices; it is the mechanism by which resources are diverted from consumption to investment when investment demand runs ahead of profits. (By the time of *The General Theory,* having dropped the assumption of the *Treatise* that the normal state of the economy was one of full employment, Keynes was able to argue that no forced saving is necessary to accommodate an expansion of investment.)

Keynes already hints at forced saving in his polemic against the Versailles Treaty, *The Economic Consequences of the Peace.* No doubt heavily influenced by his experience as a middle-level adviser to the British Treasury during World War I, he defended capitalists against the charge of profiteering:

> "Profiteers," [quotation marks are Keynes's] are, broadly speaking, the entrepreneur class of capitalists, that is to say, the active and constructive element in the whole capitalist society, who in a period of rapidly rising prices cannot help but get rich quick whether they wish it or desire it or not. If prices are continually rising, every trader who has purchased for stock or owns property and plant inevitably makes profits. (1919, pp. 236–237)

Keynes expands on the process of forced saving in the context of wartime government finance in a lecture delivered at about the time he was putting the finishing touches on the *Treatise*. He explains how this mechanism worked to fuel inflation during World War I:

> When a government orders munitions of war at a rate faster than that of current savings as supplemented by taxation—the inevitable effect of such measures must be to cause prices to rise faster than wages. The government secures purchasing power for itself at the expense of the consumer, who is constantly finding that the real value of his income is less than he had supposed . . .
>
> The transference . . . puts some resources directly into the hands of the government. But to a very great extent the gains accrue in the first instance not to the government, but to business men, who, owing to this rise of price, are able to sell what they have produced at an unexpectedly high price which yields them a profit in excess of what they had anticipated. The selling price of their goods is rising all the time faster than their cost of production. That is to say, if this method of forced transference is adopted, the business men are made, in the first instance, the collectors—the agents, so to speak—for the government, to collect the purchasing power which has been thus forcibly diverted from the consumers . . . If, having allowed them to receive this additional sum, you then proceed to withdraw it from them through taxes and in fact treat them as having been agents for the government, then this device is far and away the most efficient that exists for collecting purchasing power from the consumers and transferring it into the hands of the government. (Lecture to the Royal United Service Institution, February 13, 1929, in Keynes 1981, pp. 785–786)

Economists today may be less convinced than Keynes that inflation hurts consumers, at least in the representative-agent model, but most are not ready to let inflation off the hook. Given the mainstream's concern (one might say obsession) with efficiency, a focus on the putative inefficiencies brought about by inflation is hardly surprising. Two favorites are "shoeleather" and "menu" costs, each a metaphor for a kind of wasteful activity imposed on economic agents by inflation. Shoeleather costs hark back to an era when depositors had to visit the bank to withdraw money or shift funds from interest-bearing accounts to demand deposits; they would use up more shoeleather in having to make more trips to the bank, trips they must make to avoid holding currency or noninterest-bearing checking accounts that are continually depreciating in value. Menu costs recall the same bygone era, for these costs were incurred because menus had to be reset in hard type as prices rose. The faster prices are rising, the more frequently menus have to be printed. Whatever the inefficiencies caused to previous generations by higher costs in terms of shoeleather and menus, neither of these can be considered formidable costs in the age of the computer, the internet, and the web.

Another inefficiency to which economists point—this time with more reason—is tax distortions, particularly in the treatment of capital gains. There is no question that, absent special provisions in the tax code, inflation causes people with significant capital gains to suffer at the hands of the taxman. Efficiency (and fairness as well) would arguably be served if the real gain could be separated from the nominal gain, so that the purely nominal part of capital gains could be exempted from taxation. In fact, it is extremely difficult to do so: I know of no country in which the tax code effectively separates out the real component of taxable gains and forgives the purely nominal component. In any case, this is a rather parochial interest in terms of the percentage of taxpayers seriously affected, and it is hard to make a popular case against inflation on these grounds, especially if, as in the U.S. Internal Revenue Code, there is a lower tax rate on capital gains on property held more than one year, as well as a very generous exemption for the sale of one's principal residence, the largest (and sometimes only) holding in most Americans' asset portfolios.

Although economists for the most part hold that inflation does not have much of an impact on the distribution of income, they charge that inflation redistributes *wealth* in an arbitrary fashion. Since inflation can never be entirely anticipated, debtors gain at the expense of creditors. But to argue, as two leading elementary texts do, that this redistribution is arbitrary is to stretch the definition of "arbitrary."[5] No doubt some creditors are people of modest means. But the plain fact is that the holdings of fixed-income securities—which are the assets most affected by inflation—are highly concentrated among the upper tiers of wealth holders. In consequence, any redistribution that results from the erosion of the real value of assets fixed in nominal terms is hardly arbitrary. It is another question whether such redistribution is fair— William Baumol, Alan Blinder, and John Solow may (or may not) be on the money when they write, "The gainers do not earn their spoils, and the losers do not deserve their fate" (2020, p. 477). But the redistribution is as systematic as can be. Wall Street has good reason to fear and loath inflation.

Keynes himself in his pre-Keynesian manifestation was partial to the view espoused by today's textbooks. Indeed, for the younger Keynes, inflation redistributed not only arbitrarily but apocalyptically. In a famous passage from *The Economic Consequences of the Peace* he wrote:

> Lenin is said to have declared that the best way to destroy the Capitalist System was to debauch the currency. By a continuing process of inflation, governments can confiscate, secretly and unobserved, an important part of the

wealth of their citizens. By this method they not only confiscate, but they confiscate *arbitrarily;* and, while the process impoverishes many, it actually enriches some. The sight of this arbitrary rearrangement of riches strikes not only at security, but at confidence in the equity of the existing distribution of wealth. Those to whom the system brings windfalls, beyond their deserts and even beyond their expectations or desires, become "profiteers," who are the object of the hatred of the bourgeoisie, whom the inflationism has impoverished, not less than of the proletariat. As the inflation proceeds and the real value of the currency fluctuates wildly from month to month, all permanent relations between debtors and creditors, which form the ultimate foundation of capitalism, become so utterly disordered as to be almost meaningless; and the process of wealth-getting degenerates into a gamble and a lottery.

Lenin was certainly right. There is no subtler, no surer means of overturning the existing basis of society than to debauch the currency. The process engages all the hidden forces of economic law on the side of destruction, and does it in a manner which not one man in a million is able to diagnose. (1919, pp. 235–236)

In the end, none of the economic reasons—the distortions caused by hyperinflation, the inefficiencies associated with more modest rates of inflation, the arbitrary redistribution of wealth—really explains the fear and the loathing of the public. Hyperinflation does distort the economy in major ways, but there is a missing step in the argument. I have never read a convincing defense of the argument that inflation is like pregnancy: there can be no such thing as a little bit, and initially modest rates of inflation, if not nipped in the bud, will escalate into hyperinflation. The other inefficiencies, shoeleather and menu costs, are anachronistic in the sense that they are based on obsolete technologies. The arbitrary redistribution of wealth turns out to be not so arbitrary after all, and this argument can easily explain why the very rich are sworn enemies of inflation—but it doesn't explain the attitudes of the rest of us.

I think Keynes was in touch with emotions that play a huge role in the public's dislike of inflation. Shiller reports a strong public identification with the idea that inflation undermines social cohesion and international prestige, and in the end can, if unchecked, lead to "economic and political chaos" (1997, pp. 37–46). But this is only part of the story. In a political system where money speaks loud and clear, and threatens to drown out every other voice, it is not credible that the very real economic interest of the creditor class in keeping prices in check plays no role in shaping political attitudes. Main Street may have its reasons, right or wrong, for disliking inflation, but central banks and finance ministers are more attuned to Wall Street in emphasizing price stability as the holy grail of economic policy.

Keynes for All Seasons

This chapter and the last develop and test a model that responds to Harrod's plea for a framework suitable for analyzing the economy over a period in which investment adds to the capital stock, and thus adds to the supply of goods while at the same time being a source of aggregate demand, indeed the key source of private demand so long as consumption is assumed to respond passively to income. As Harrod (1937) wrote in his review of *The General Theory,*

> The only criticism of Mr. Keynes which I venture to offer is that his system is still static . . . In the dynamic theory, as I envisage it, . . . our question will then be, what rate of growth can continue to obtain, so long as the various surrounding circumstances, including the propensity to save, remain the same? (pp. 85–86)

My theory immediately departs from Harrod and the ensuing literature in rejecting the idea of an exogenously determined labor force. This involves two major conceptual changes. First, we have to replace that mythical notion, "the economy," with the portion of the economy for which the essential features of wage labor and profit maximization are present. This is not to say that sectors like the household, the family farm, and the government—sectors in which one or the other distinguishing feature of capitalism is missing—are not worthy of study. Rather, these noncapitalist structures require a very different framework of analysis. One size does not fit all.

Second, we have to replace the idea that the labor force available to the capitalist sector is given by population, and, indeed, that population is given. Over the last several centuries, capitalist economies have grown much more rapidly than the larger economic structures in which they have been embedded. To do so, they have had to draw labor from noncapitalist parts of the economy. And when domestic sources of labor have not sufficed, permeable national borders (whatever the official stance of governments has been toward immigration) have filled the gap. Japan is the most notable exception to this dictum, relying only marginally on immigration, and at that only during its short-lived experiment with empire in the first half of the twentieth century. South Korea and China, each for its own reasons, have followed the path charted by Japan.

Like the short-run model developed earlier in this book, the long-run model is overdetermined because it has three independent schedules—aggregate demand, goods supply, and a conventional wage—but only two state variables, real price and the labor:capital ratio. As in the short run, equilib-rium cannot be defined apart from the dynamic process by which the econ-omy—strictly speaking, the capitalist sector—is assumed to adjust. The equi-librium associated with a flexprice process and the equilibrium associated with a fixprice process differ from one another, but both share the property that the equilibrium is characterized by a stationary labor:capital ratio and a stationary real-price level.

Deflation and stagnation are possible in the long run. But with rare excep-tions (the Great Depression of course, and, more recently, Japan again comes to mind), over several centuries the story of capitalism has been one of ex-panding output and ever-higher prices.

Interpreted through the lens of this model, the historical data for the U.S. economy from the 1950s to the 2010s suggest three important results. First, inflation responds with a lag to the level of economic activity, which implies that fixprice adjustment fits actual experience better than does flexprice ad-justment. With fixprice adjustment, the first response of the economy to dis-equilibrium caused by a demand shock is for output to adjust, with price ad-justments following as producers struggle to get back on their GS schedules, and money wages respond to the accompanying reduction in employment. (With flexprice adjustment, the sequence is the other way around: the first response is for prices to change, with output and wages both responding to the initial price change.) Second, aggregate demand shocks lead to a trade-off be-tween the rate of inflation and the level of demand, à la A. W. Phillips and his eponymous curve. Third, shocks to the GS schedule, emanating from changes in the relative price of energy, and to a lesser extent shocks to the conven-tional wage, shift the Phillips curve while changing the demand-side trade-off between inflation and employment relatively little. Only in this century does the *slope* of the Phillips curve change markedly, while during the whole pe-riod from 1956 to 2013 the Phillips curve *shifts* no fewer than five times.

One takeaway is that inflation is the price society pays for higher levels of economic activity. In contrast with the widespread view that inflation is the enemy of a thriving real economy, the theory presented here leads to the con-clusion that aggregate demand matters in the long run as well as in the short run, and that higher levels of aggregate demand produce higher levels of eco-nomic activity along with higher prices.

The implication is that monetary policy has real consequences in the long run as well as in the short run. This is of course contrary to the near unanimous view of the economics profession, which the late Fed Chair Paul Volcker summarized in these words:

> I know that it is fashionable to talk about a "dual mandate"—the claim that
> the Fed's policy should be directed toward the two objectives of price stabil-

ity and full employment. Fashionable or not, I find that mandate . . . illusory
. . . It is illusory in the sense that it implies a trade-off between economic
growth and price stability, a concept that I thought had long ago been re
futed not just by Nobel Prize winners but by experience. (2013, pp. 32–33)

The existence of a long-run trade-off between price stability and employment weakens the political argument for an independent central bank:
namely, that the central bank can and should be an apolitical institution because there is no reasonable alternative to a focus on price stability, so-called
inflation targeting (see, especially, Paul Tucker [2018].) If I am correct in
claiming that there is a conflict between employment and price stability, it becomes relevant to ask who benefits from different policies.

Clearly, the benefits of higher levels of economic activity and the benefits of
more stable prices are not shared evenly. Main Street may fear inflation, but
Main Street clearly benefits from high levels of economic activity. Wall Street
has good reason to be at best ambivalent about high levels of economic activity, but more than ample reason to loath inflation. And Wall Street has a much
easier time of getting itself heard in the halls of government, particularly in
the boardrooms of central banks.

Since the Great Recession, Europe has been mired in a recovery that has
moved at glacial speed, while an entire generation of Greeks, Italians, and
Spaniards are being sacrificed on the altar of fiscal rectitude, a pillar of which
is price stability. Keynes may have been right when he suggested, at the end of
The General Theory,

> The ideas of economists and political philosophers, both when they are right
> and when they are wrong, are more powerful than is commonly understood.
> Indeed, the world is ruled by little else. Practical men, who believe them-
> selves to be quite exempt from any intellectual influences, are usually the
> slaves of some defunct economist. (p. 383)

He may have been right as well to stress that "the power of vested interests
is vastly exaggerated compared with the gradual encroachment of ideas." But
the marketplace of ideas is a market far from the norm of perfect competition.
It welcomes those backed by purchasing power with open arms, while those
who challenge money power struggle to be heard. Other than the 1 percent,
all of us pay the price for this particular market failure.

EPILOGUE

Attack Them in Their Citadel

> Thus, if the heretics . . . are to demolish the forces of nineteenth-century orthodoxy, . . . they must attack them in their citadel . . .
> Only if they are successfully attacked in the citadel can we reasonably ask them to look at the problem in a radically new way.
>
> —JOHN MAYNARD KEYNES

Keynes wrote *The General Theory* to save capitalism from itself. Not the rugged individualism of every man for himself and devil take the hindmost, but a more humane, twentieth-century, version in which the state would provide the control and direction required for a prosperous economy while preserving individual liberty.[1]

The first step was to remove the rose-colored glasses through which economic orthodoxy had long viewed every man for himself. Among the supposed virtues of unfettered capitalism was the capacity to provide a job for every willing worker. This was an illusion, and a dangerous one at that, for it paralyzed governments from taking the actions necessary to correct the market failure that allowed the economy to get stuck far from full employment.

This was the heavy lifting of *The General Theory.* Once it was understood that the economy was not self-regulating, Keynes believed it would become legitimate for the government to keep the economy humming and the labor market at full employment. In the normal course of events, maintaining interest rates at sufficiently low levels would do the trick by making private investment sufficiently profitable to employ workers who would otherwise be redundant; in extremis, it would be necessary to use the government's power of the purse. Fiscal policy would complement monetary policy, and the need for more extensive state planning and control could be avoided.

The difference between the inaction of the U.S. Government in the early

Portions of this chapter were previously published in "History vs. Equilibrium One More Time: How Keynes's General Theory Foundered on the Rocks of Comparative Statics," *Review of Social Economy* 78, no. 1 (2020): 35–52.

1930s and its interventions in 2008 and 2009 are testimony to Keynes's success. The weakness of these interventions and the continuing commitment to austerity in Europe are testimony to Keynes's failure.

This book explains what Keynes got right and where he went wrong, and translates his vision into a theoretical basis for a macroeconomics for the twenty-first century. With Keynes, I set the argument in a framework of perfect competition. This may seem an unnecessary concession to the orthodoxy that Keynes was determined to bring down. Keynes understood—as did his contemporaries, at least the ones he took seriously—that the capitalist economy of his day, like the capitalist economy of ours, was riddled with imperfections. So why not assume these imperfections instead of assuming them away? The problem was and is the orthodox belief in a self-regulating economy. This belief is born of total immersion in the teachings of the classical economists and their modern heirs, epitomized from the mid-twentieth century on by the models of Kenneth Arrow and Gerard Debreu (Arrow and Debreu 1954; Arrow 1963–1964; Debreu 1959). A corollary of their world of perfect competition, in which there is indeed a job for every willing worker, just as there is a customer for every apple, is that lapses from full employment must be the result of imperfections, frictions, rigidities, warts on the body of capitalism. Once, over lunch, I described my project in this book to a colleague; his immediate response was "What's your imperfection?"

I guess the answer is people. As it has developed since the World War II era, orthodox economics has increasingly relied on an exaggerated degree of rationality and abundance of knowledge, not to mention an exaggerated degree of self-centered greed, to make its central point about the virtue of markets. In the hands of Robert Lucas and his New Classical colleagues, a consequence was that, if a full-employment equilibrium is disturbed by a shock to aggregate demand (or to supply, for that matter), economic agents possess the knowledge and calculating ability to move immediately to a new full-employment equilibrium. In this view any need to search for the new equilibrium reflects limited knowledge or limited cognitive ability, an imperfection or friction to the smooth functioning of the economy. Alas, this is an imperfection or friction that can be avoided only if people are more than the human beings we actually are, endowed with limited knowledge and limited cognitive power.

Orthodoxy has always recognized the problems caused by warts on the body of capitalism; indeed, orthodoxy has embraced the warts as impediments to the self-regulating abilities of the economy. At the same time, the perfection of the textbook economy, wart free, remains a principle, indeed a litmus test, of the canon. For the mainstream of the economics profession, these two propositions are not in conflict but rather serve as the basis for enlightened government policy: remove the warts, make the economy over in the image of the textbook. Period.

This is not mere theoretical speculation. The push to deregulate the economy, especially the financial sector, in the last decades of the twentieth century was founded on the idea that a competitive economy is self regulating. Alan Greenspan was shocked! shocked! shocked! when he discovered that bankers did not put aside enough capital to cushion themselves against the risks they took on in the run-up to the financial crisis of 2008.

Keynes assumed away imperfections to focus on the deeper problem of how aggregate demand enters into the determination of economic outcomes. The Achilles heel was that Keynes lacked the tools to make a convincing argument. This book makes up for that deficiency by recasting *The General Theory* in dynamic terms, that is, in terms of the adjustment process that takes place when equilibrium is disturbed. This leads to radically different results from the comparative-statics method of simply comparing equilibria.

I imply no criticism in suggesting that Keynes was biting off more than he could chew. The necessary mathematical techniques were not available even to the relatively small group of economists that was mathematically literate, a minority in which Keynes could count himself. But this was changing. After World War II, mathematics was clearly becoming the preferred language of economics, and in that generation there were plenty of economists with the requisite skill set. As I note in the appendix to chapter 6, by the 1960s there was a growing recognition of the inadequacy of comparative statics and the consequent need for an analysis of dynamics. Many economists—the names of Don Patinkin (1951 [1948], 1965 [1956]), Bob Clower (1958, 1960, 1984 [1963], and Axel Leijonhufvud (1968) come immediately to mind—recognized the problem; the first publication of a dynamic model appeared in 1968 (Solow and Stiglitz). There were at least two other attempts (Tobin 1975; Dos Santos Ferreira and Michel [1987]; and Dos Santos Ferreira and Michel [2013]), but it remains a mystery why Keynesians missed the opportunity to put Keynes on a dynamic footing. Most of the effort to update Keynes went in a different direction, typified by the models of Robert Barro and Herschel Grossman (1971, 1976) and Edmond Malinvaud (1977, 1980). In any case, by the 1970s the tide had turned against Keynes, and the clever young men (still not many women in the economics profession in the 1970s) were focused on demolishing his theory of economics and putting something new in its place. The 1970s saw the birth of the New Classical economics, an apt name for an approach that combined new heights of technical sophistication with old theories about the self-regulating nature of the economy.

The Keynesian project had run out of steam, and in 1979 it was pronounced dead by one of the leading architects of the New Classical school. In a talk to the annual management conference held at the Graduate School of the University of Chicago, Robert Lucas proclaimed,

> Keynesian economics is dead (maybe "disappeared" is a better term). I do not exactly know when this happened but it is true today and it was not true two years ago. This is a sociological not an economic observation, so evidence for it is sociological. For example, one cannot find a good, under-40 economist who identifies himself, works as "Keynesian." Indeed, people even take offense if referred to in this way. At research seminars people do not take Keynesian theorizing seriously any more—audience starts to whisper, giggles to one another. Leading journals are not getting Keynesian papers submitted any more. (2013, pp. 500–501; quoted in De Vroey 2016, pp. 210–211)

A prominent New Keynesian, Alan Blinder, echoed Lucas: "By about 1980, it was hard to find an American academic macroeconomist under the age of 40 who professed to be a Keynesian" (1988, p. 278).

For the anti-Keynesians this was Gresham's Law in reverse, good ideas driving out bad ones. The reality is more complicated: as I argue in chapter 1, the attack on Keynes was three pronged: in addition to the theoretical attack waged by Lucas and other New Classical economists, the stagflation of the 1970s was (mis)understood to be inconsistent with Keynesian theory. And politics influenced the receptivity to anti-Keynesian theories: particularly in the United States, Keynes was anathema on the right, which saw Keynesian policies as a stalking horse for an alien conspiracy intent on imposing socialism where God intended rugged individualism to thrive. The 1970s saw the collapse of the New Deal consensus in the United States and the eclipse of social democracy in Europe: the 1980s belonged to Reagan and Thatcher. Even where social democracy could claim a popular mandate, as in France, it was a shadow of its earlier self.

Theoretical issues plagued the development of Keynes's theory long before Lucas and friends appeared on the scene. Anticipating Lucas by a decade, Milton Friedman could write in 1970 that in the absence of imperfections there was nothing to Keynes's argument that a capitalist economy could not be self-regulating. "There is," Friedman concluded, "no fundamental 'flaw in the price system' that makes unemployment the natural outcome of a fully operative market mechanism" (p. 207).

Keynes Defeated: Static Models and the Critics

How could Friedman be so sure? To answer this question, we have to go back to the static structure of *The General Theory* and the ensuing critique. Keynes elaborated *The General Theory* in the context of a fixed money wage, an assumption that he regarded as scaffolding to simplify the exposition of a novel theory. It would be time enough to remove the scaffolding once the theoretical groundwork had been laid. And remove the scaffolding he did: chapter 19 is titled "Changes in Money Wages." But this chapter was bound to disappoint a reader looking for a unified theoretical argument. Instead, there are a series of separate reasons why reducing money wages would only exacerbate economic difficulties when aggregate demand is deficient. The orthodox argument for reducing money wages is for Keynes fallacious because it confuses money wages and real wages. The money wage may fall in the presence of unemployment (or by the fiat of an authoritarian ruler—Keynes contrasted the possibilities open to a Hitler, Mussolini, or Stalin with the possibilities available to leaders of the capitalist democracies), but the real wage is determined endogenously by the equilibrium price level corresponding to any given level of money wages. A fall in money prices will generally vitiate any direct stimulus to production from decreasing money wages.

Within Keynes's framework the only cogent reason for reducing money wages is an indirect effect on investment demand. Even though a fall in money prices defeats the hopes of those who mistakenly think that a reduction in money wages is tantamount to a reduction in real wages, it can have a positive effect on output and employment through its effect on the demand for money. The Keynes effect, as it came to be called, relies on three assumptions, the first and the third squarely orthodox, the one in the middle novel and controversial: (1) a fall in money prices reduces the amount of money required for transactions purposes; (2) this in turn makes more money available for wealth portfolios and causes interest rates to fall, a fall in interest rates being a necessary condition for wealth holders to hold the extra cash willingly; and (3) a fall in interest rates expands investment demand. Keynes considered the logic of this argument to be impeccable but doubted its practical value. Much simpler, less costly, and much less politically fraught—especially in a democracy—to expand the real money supply (the amount of money divided by the price level) by direct means rather than through the roundabout procedure of reducing money wages. Besides, the possibilities for expanding investment demand might be limited by a floor to the long-term interest rate that provides a hurdle for potential investment projects.

In 1944 Franco Modigliani published a formal model of the Keynes effect but drew opposite conclusions from Keynes's. For Modigliani, the lesson was that a fixed money wage was not scaffolding that could be removed once the building was erected. It was an essential assumption.

Modigliani casts his argument in the conventional form of comparative statics, in effect asking us to consider separate worlds that are identical in all but one respect. Population, conditions of production, preferences, endowments of resources (and money!) are all the same. Labor supply is determined by utility maximization, by workers who optimize in terms of leisure and goods. The supply of goods is determined by profit maximization on the part of capitalist producers. Aggregate demand is determined by consumption propensities and the demand for investment.

The only difference is the level of the money wage. Each planet has a different money wage. So changing the money wage has a different meaning from what it means in ordinary speech. It is not the case that the wage is $20.00 per hour today, and $10.00 per hour tomorrow. Planets are unchanging, the same today as yesterday and tomorrow. Change in this context involves traveling from world to world and observing the differences that result from different levels of the money wage.

If we temporarily suppress the labor-supply decision, as Keynes did for eighteen chapters, we will find that in worlds with lower money wages the equilibrium of aggregate demand and goods supply will involve greater employment and output. This is the consequence of coupling (1) the expansion of aggregate demand via the Keynes effect with (2) standard orthodox assumptions of profit maximization and diminishing marginal productivity of labor.

Now bring back the supply of labor. Because investment demand is low in a high money-wage world, the high wage AD-GS equilibrium provides less output and employment than the levels consistent with workers' labor versus leisure choices, which is to say less employment than is consistent with workers being on their supply curves. The opposite is true at low levels of money wages. So, as the money wage falls on our interplanetary travels, somewhere between very high money wages and very low money wages is the Goldilocks economy at which all three conditions—aggregate demand, goods supply, and labor supply—are satisfied. This is Modigliani's full-employment equilibrium.

Modigliani recognizes that the orderly succession from one world to another of greater output and employment associated with an AD-GS equilibrium may break down because of the second of the three assumptions behind the Keynes effect: more money available for wealth portfolios may not drive interest rates down sufficiently. If wealth holders cease to need an inducement to adjust their portfolios to the influx of cash released from transactions duties, there will be no effect on the interest rate and hence no effect on investment. So one of the main arguments of *The General Theory* remains even after Modigliani's criticism of the assumption of money-wage rigidity.

But it is another supposed effect of falling wages and prices, the real-balance effect, on which Friedman relied to reach his scathing conclusion that Keynes had failed in his attack on the citadel. This is the story of the effect of falling prices on consumption demand, making no assumption about investment demand. The real-balance effect begins with the determinants of consumption demand. In *The General Theory* Keynes argues that consumption depends primarily on income, with other factors playing smaller roles. Various critics—Gottfried Haberler (1939, 1941) was the first, though the real-balance effect is generally associated with another critic, Arthur Pigou (1943, 1947), and is often referred to as the Pigou effect—noted that wealth also affected consumption. Specifically, the cash component of wealth would become more valuable the lower the price level; with a low enough price level, a single rumpled dollar bill you find in your grandma's attic will buy the entire production of the nation! In these circumstances even if wages and prices move down in lockstep, the real-balance effect will ensure the self-regulating nature of the economy, whatever happens to investment demand.

Under the weight of the Keynes effect and the real-balance effect, Keynesians retreated to the position that after all it was the warts that were the problem. Paul Samuelson claimed that he and his Keynesian colleagues had always thought Keynes's argument rested on a bed of imperfections (see chapter 1 for the relevant quote; Colander and Landreth 1996, pp. 160–161). Be that as it may, by 1970 there was little opposition among Keynesians to Friedman's dictum that Keynes was merely a better expositor of sand in the wheels. Leijonhufvud's *On Keynesian Economics and the Economics of Keynes,* published in 1968, was important in emphasizing the distinction between Keynes and his followers in this regard. (I overstate the case: fundamentalist Keynesians, particularly the old guard who had been present at the creation in Cambridge, England, or arrived soon after, continued to argue that there was more to the message than messengers like Samuelson understood. Their efforts, joined by younger economists who would become "Post-Keynesians," met with little success in the mainstream Keynesian community.)

This retreat was a mistake; coupled with the new classical attack it has set macroeconomics back forty years. The basic problem was a misunderstanding about what the Keynes effect and the real-balance effect really mean. The misunderstanding lies in the difference between what Modigliani et al. thought they had proved and what they had really proved.

WHAT THEY THOUGHT   Suppose there is a shock to a full-employment equilibrium and the economy moves, temporarily at least, to a Keynesian unemployment equilibrium, that is, an equilibrium of AD and GS schedules at which aggregate demand is too weak for full employment. Unemployment will put pressure on money wages. If the money wage falls from $20.00 to $10.00, then the price level will fall *pari passu,* and if prices fall, then investment (Modigliani) or consumption (Haberler et al.) will increase, and a full-employment equilibrium will be attained.

WHAT THEY REALLY PROVED   If we consider a variety of planets that are identical except for the money wage, which varies on a continuum from zero to ∞, and we find the equilibrium for each of these worlds, there is one Gold-ilocks world in which full employment obtains, along with the economy being on its AD and GS schedules. None of these worlds has a history, so we can't properly speak of change in this context, at least not of change as Keynes conceived it, where one day the going wage is $20.00 per hour and the next it is $10.00.

There is a way, but it is a torturous one, of transforming change à la Modigliani and Haberler to change à la Keynes. Suppose all agents know that the Keynesian unemployment equilibrium is untenable because of the pressure on money wages to fall. And they know more: they each know the model that generates an AD-GS equilibrium for every world once the money wage for that world is known. So they know the money wage that corresponds to the Goldilocks, full-employment, economy. They can now recalibrate Goldilocks, taking account of the change in investment demand that triggered the move away from full employment. And they can take account of the real-balance effect, though that is somewhat more complicated because it requires agents to factor in the change in the value of debts and credits as the price level changes. If each agent accepts the "equilibrium discipline" that Robert Lucas introduced to the economics profession in 1977, and each agent believes that all the others do too, then the economy will move at once to the new Goldilocks configuration. Comparative statics morphs into dynamics, even if the dynamics is concentrated in the split second of time it takes these agents to calculate the new full-employment equilibrium. Big bang with a vengeance!

The torture lies in how much knowledge agents must be assumed to have. In fact, a great virtue of the decentralized market system is how *little* agents need to know. At a perfectly competitive equilibrium, a *homo economicus* or a *mulier economica* needs to know his or her own consumption preferences, his or her own production possibilities, and market prices—nothing else. But once equilibrium is displaced, those agents who needed to know so little at the original equilibrium need to be virtually omniscient to immediately find their way to a new one.

The equilibrium real wage presumably hasn't changed, because it depends only on goods supply and labor supply, and by assumption these have not changed. But nominal price and wage levels will be different, and the only way agents can know the new levels of nominal prices and wages is to know the AD schedule. And behind aggregate demand lie investment demand and liquidity preference, as well as consumption demand. In accord with the Keynes effect and the real-balance effect, both investment demand and consumption demand will change with the price level. Agents need to know the model for the economy to find the equilibrium for the economy once it's displaced.

This is not all. Agents need not only to know but to act. It makes sense to take actions based on the new Goldilocks only if each agent believes that others are going through the same process and are all going to make the same leap of faith.

In short, there is a possible theory of agent knowledge and behavior that makes comparisons across space relevant for comparisons over time. But the theory is on its face implausible. Whatever the merits of equilibrium discipline, it is a most egregious example of making the economy over in the mold of the textbook to assume that the agent as well as the theorist can (and should!) subject herself to the discipline of thinking only in terms of equilibrium. As I indicated earlier in this chapter, it is an odd use of the word "imperfection" to characterize human beings as imperfect because we do not possess the knowledge and cognitive power of gods.

Keynes Vindicated: A Theory of Real-Time Changes

Central to translating Keynes's vision into a theory for the twenty-first century is a dynamic alternative to omniscient agents finding their way back to equilibrium in a split second of ultrarationalism. To be sure, this alternative also makes considerable demands on agents once a full-employment equilibrium is displaced. They must now make decisions about prices and quantities, whether to change them or to stand pat, two decisions instead of the one that economic men and women make at a competitive equilibrium. Fortunately, agents have additional information at their disposal: they can observe not only whether they are making money but also whether goods are piling up unsold or flying off their shelves. And they need to know only at the margin. Boundedly rational consumers need to know only whether the marginal utility per dollar spent on pizza is greater than the marginal utility of a dollar spent on beer, and to adjust at the margin in accordance with this knowledge (unlike the omniscient consumer who knows her entire indifference map and therefore the optimum consumption bundle). Boundedly rational producers need to know only whether or not the real price exceeds the real marginal cost of production, and adjust at the margin (unlike the omniscient agent who knows her entire production possibilities and therefore knows the profit-maximizing level of output).

If we think of equilibrium as a combination of a real price and a level of output that do not change over time, the immediate problem is how to characterize the equilibrium when there are AD, GS, and LS schedules that must be satisfied. The mainstream solved (and still solves) the problem by ignoring aggregate demand, on the grounds that Say's Law guarantees that the economy will be on its AD schedule at any combination of real price and output—

except when imperfections muddy the waters. Consequently, equilibrium can be characterized in terms of goods supply and labor supply. Keynes provisionally jettisoned the LS schedule, in order to characterize equilibrium in terms of aggregate demand and goods supply, but he recognized that ignoring the LS schedule was not a satisfactory solution—hence, a whole chapter on what happens when the wage rate changes, not planet to planet but in real time on the particular planet we happen to inhabit.

We can take account of all three schedules if we are willing to drop the identification of equilibrium with the equality of supply and demand. Instead, a stationary real price is achieved by nominal prices and wages falling (or rising) at the same percentage rate. One way this can happen is that employers reduce prices in order to promote sales, while workers reduce wages in order to increase employment. If the percentage rates of price and wage reduction are the same, the real price will not change. Both workers and capitalists are frustrated: they are trying to change real wages and real prices, but their actions are offset by the actions on the other side. Everybody may be frustrated, but the economy is in equilibrium.

The resulting equilibria are different from the conventional supply equals demand equilibria in two important respects. First, equilibrium cannot be determined without specifying the adjustment process outside of equilibrium, and, second, there are consequently multiple equilibria. The determining factor is how producers process the two signals that the market sends them, one on profitability, the other on whether sales are running ahead of or behind production. For example, producers can respond to lagging sales by reducing prices or by cutting back on production. Similarly, producers can respond to negative profits at the margin by cutting output or by raising prices to discourage demand.

The story gets more complicated: once we leave the simplest models, it has to be demonstrated that a given process leads to equilibrium. This is not guaranteed, and indeed a dynamic version of Modigliani's model may or may not lead to equilibrium.

The difference between Keynes and the mainstream is the difference between night and day. An economy composed of omniscient agents who have internalized Lucas's equilibrium discipline will vindicate Modigliani, Haberler, Friedman, and the entire anti-Keynesian counterrevolution. If disturbed by a demand shock, the economy will find its way back to the original full-employment equilibrium. This economy is self-regulating, and the best the government can do to aid the process is—nothing.

An economy composed of agents with bounded knowledge and bounded rationality will perform very differently. This economy has the potential for prolonged and self-fulfilling depression, an economy characterized by equilibrium unemployment and continuing deflation. Wages and prices fall, but there is no Keynes effect: the lower price level does not drive down interest rates and stimulate investment. Nor do falling prices stimulate consumption via the real-balance effect.

The reason is that the Keynes effect does not work in real time as it is supposed to work in a comparative-statics framework. To be sure, a fall in prices leads to a reduction in transactions demand, but this does not lead to greater amounts of money pouring into wealth portfolios. "Money" turns out not to be homogeneous, and reductions in the demand for money to transact business are reflected in reductions in bank lending, not in an influx of money into wealth portfolios.

Instead of decreasing the rate of interest and increasing investment demand, the effect of falling prices is the opposite. The effective rate of interest for investment decisions is the real rate of interest, the sum of the nominal interest rate and the rate of deflation. (The impact of price changes on the effective rate of interest is called the Fisher effect, after Irving Fisher, who identified the wedge between real and nominal interest rates due to changing prices in 1896.) The greater the equilibrium rate of deflation, the less investment.

The real-balance effect is also undone by the change in prices: as prices fall, holders of cash or fixed-income securities prosper, as Haberler, Pigou, and especially Don Patinkin (1948) emphasized. But continuing deflation spells increasing hardship and possibly disaster for debtors. When the real debt reaches intolerable levels, the windfall to creditors is swamped by the wave of bankruptcies that wipe out the debtors. The real-balance effect is ashes in the mouths of every agent who took out loans in the good times and has to pay interest and principal fixed in nominal terms when her products bring in significantly less cash. Neither the Fisher effect nor the calamitous effect of deflation on debtors has any counterpart in the comparative statics of omniscient agents. Both effects depend on real-time changes in the price level that have no place in interplanetary comparisons.

The asymmetrical effects of falling prices on debtors and creditors was mentioned only in passing by Keynes. But it is the heart of Irving Fisher's 1933 contribution. Keynes couldn't fit debt and deflation into his static framework, and Fisher had no framework of aggregate demand into which to fit his "Debt-Deflation Theory of Great Depressions." A shame because the marriage of Fisher and Keynes, under the canopy of a dynamic theory, goes a long way to explaining the calamity of the Great Depression.

Agriculture is a case in point. In terms of employment and output, agriculture suffered no depression: both the number of people working on U.S. farms and the crops they produced were larger in 1933 than in 1929. But farmers suffered nevertheless. Coupled with the predominance of the family farm, the dynamics of adjustment led agricultural prices to fall much more than in the rest of the economy. Farmers who had taken out loans in the 1920s, when wheat was at $1.25 per bushel and cotton at $0.20 per pound, were obliged to pay back the interest and principal with $0.50 wheat and $0.07 cotton. The surprise is not that so many farmers went under but that so many remained solvent.

Building Blocks

Recasting the argument in a dynamic form is a main element in rescuing Keynes's vision. But it is not enough by itself. After more than eighty years of critical discussion, all the building blocks of *The General Theory* are in need of reevaluation. Most important is the most novel, Keynes's theory of interest. Keynes was surely right to argue that the rate of interest is not the "price" that balances desired saving and the demand for investment. If it were, the entire argument of *The General Theory* would fail, because the price mechanism—the interest rate—would always adjust to maintain equality between desired saving and investment and thus between aggregate demand and the level of output. In other words, Say's Law.

Instead, Keynes places the action of interest rate determination where it belongs: in markets for financial assets. The interest rate, he says, is the price of parting with liquidity, of giving up the advantages of holding cash, which an agent must sacrifice when she puts her wealth into bonds or other assets that fluctuate in value. Keynes's theory of interest is a theory of liquidity preference.

So far, so good. The problem with the theory is that it determines the spreads between the yields of different assets but not the level of interest rates. In Keynes's two-asset model, the spread is anchored by the assumption that the safe alternative to bonds is cash, which yields no interest. In this case the spread between the yield on cash and the yield on bonds is the yield on bonds.

But this is a special case. In reality, the relevant liquid alternative to bonds is not cash but assets such as short-term T-bills, which unlike cash normally pay interest. In this more general case, the spread between the liquid asset and other assets does not determine the level of interest rates.

So what does? Nothing, at least nothing inside the model. When Keynes asserted that a capitalist economy left to its own devices was not self-regulating, he meant that a competitive capitalist economy would likely settle at an equilibrium with less than full employment. Without a theory of interest, the level of investment demand is indeterminate and so, consequently, are the level of aggregate demand and the equilibrium.

This does not mean that the real world is in a state of perpetual drift, but that the model is incomplete. One way of closing the model to bring it more in line with reality is to introduce a central bank, whose function is precisely—or was before quantitative easing was added to the quiver of monetary-policy arrows—to fix the rate of interest on safe short-term assets like T-bills. Once this rate is determined, spreads translate into levels, and the indeterminacy disappears.

A chief result of liquidity-preference theory survives its reformulation as a theory of spreads, namely, the liquidity trap. But the meaning of the liquidity trap is different. In the context of agents who choose between cash and bonds, the liquidity trap refers to the behavior of the bond yield. In the context of agents who choose between bills and bonds, the reference is to the zero lower bound on the bill rate; the spread between bills and bonds at the zlb determines the effect on the bond yield. In both cases, however, the liquidity trap (not Keynes's terminology—see Ingo Barens [2018]) is a situation where a floor to the bond yield prevents sufficient investment demand for the economy to achieve a full-employment equilibrium; at this point the central bank of Keynes's day—a day that lasted until the adoption of quantitative easing in the wake of the financial crisis of 2008 and the ensuing Great Recession—has lost control over the economy.

Keynes's failure to provide a theory of interest reveals a deeper problem with *The General Theory*. The full title is *The General Theory of Employment, Interest and Money*, but, in fact, there is no theory of money. Most of the time money is what Milton Friedman later called helicopter money, money created by the central bank and deposited to the accounts of economic agents (Friedman 1969). At other points, though Keynes surely knew better, money is a commodity—gold, silver, or cowrie shells. At only one point in *The General Theory* (in the chapter on wage changes) does Keynes allude to the possible effects of the expansion and the contraction of the money supply by a fractional-reserve banking system.

The Keynes effect is a creature of this confusion. So is the identification of money as a means of payment (cash in the form of dollars, euros, or pounds) with money as a store of value (safe short-term assets such as T-bills) and the consequent argument that liquidity preference is a theory of the level of interest rates rather than a theory of the spread between interest rates.

Fiscal Policy in Theory and Practice

For Keynes, *The General Theory* was not an exercise in pure theory. It was intended to disarm the opposition to government intervention to manage aggregate demand, hence the need to make his readers understand, first, that the economy was not self-regulating, and, second, that there are limits to the effectiveness of monetary policy as a means of steering the economy to full employment.

This is the background for the essential policy innovation that emerges from *The General Theory,* the management of aggregate demand through the adjustment of taxation and government spending to the vicissitudes of private demand. The importance of *The General Theory* in this regard is not the development of a theory of fiscal policy. There is virtually nothing of the kind in the book, and what there is eerily resembles the observations of an economist who was to become a leading critic of book. Read the following passage from *The General Theory*

> If the Treasury were to fill old bottles with banknotes, bury them at suitable depths in disused coal mines which are then filled up to the surface with town rubbish, and leave it to private enterprise on well-tried principles of *laissez-faire* to dig the notes up again (the right to do so being obtained, of course, by tendering for leases of the note-bearing territory), there need be no more unemployment and, with the help of the repercussions, the real income of the community, and its capital wealth also, would probably become a good deal greater than it actually is. (p. 129)

and compare it with what Jacob Viner wrote three years *before* the publication of *The General Theory*

> If the government were to employ men to dig ditches and fill them up again, there would be nothing to show afterwards. But, nevertheless, even these expenditures would be an indirect contribution to business recovery. Their major importance would not be in the public works or the unemployment relief which immediately resulted, but in the possibility of hope that a substantial expenditure would act as a priming of the business pump, would encourage business men by increased sales, make them more optimistic, lead them to increase the number of their employees, and so on. (1933b, p. 130)

The difference between the two is that Viner had no theoretical framework in which his policy prescription made sense. (This is why Viner is forgotten except by specialists in the history of economic thought while Keynes is remembered not only by economists but by a much broader public.) In the context of *The General Theory,* the same advice makes eminent sense. Keynes's contribution to fiscal policy lay in providing a theoretical framework for the role of aggregate demand in the determination of equilibrium. *The General Theory* undermines the Micawber-like devotion to balanced budgets that characterized both the economics profession and "responsible" politicians.

It was left to Keynes's disciples (and critics) to develop a Keynesian theory of fiscal policy. A major role was played by Abba Lerner, whose 1944 book developed a theory of "functional finance," which he opposed to the "sound finance" of Mr. Micawber. The emphasis in functional finance is that taxation and spending should be in the service of stabilizing the economy at full employment, with the corollary that the deficit is irrelevant.

As a matter of theory, it is not the case that functional finance need lead to permanent deficits and a growing public debt. In principle, aggregate demand can be managed with a balanced budget if the size of the government budget is not a concern and we ignore the problems of ramping up and ramping down public expenditure in a timely manner. Even if these conditions are not met, as indeed they will not be met in practice, functional finance does not preclude balancing the budget over good times and bad. When the economy is booming, functional finance dictates a surplus to prevent aggregate demand from running ahead of capacity.

Stabilizing the economy in accord with the theory of functional finance has been a difficult sell, even though public opinion proved much more receptive to government deficits when the economy went south in 2008 than during the Great Depression. Nonetheless, whether or not politicians or economists acknowledge it, the U.S. government has been generally faithful to the dictates of functional finance. To a great extent this has been automatic, because taxation and transfer payments (think unemployment insurance) change more or less in line with economic activity, while government expenditure is relatively insensitive to the state of the economy.

But when automatic stabilization fails to do the trick, as in the recessions of the early 1980s and the early years of this century and, of course, during the Great Recession, the government has embraced stimulus in the form of a reduction of tax rates and an increase in spending. Ronald Reagan didn't acknowledge that his 1981 tax cuts were in the service of stimulating aggregate demand, nor did George W. Bush in the recession of 2001; the rhetoric was all about the supply side. In 2008 and 2009, both Bush and Barack Obama made no bones about the need to stimulate demand.

There remains some question about the effectiveness of the Obama stimulus. A part of the counterrevolution to Keynes was the argument that economic agents do not base expenditures on current income but rather on long-term resources. The permanent-income (M. Friedman 1957) and life-cycle (Modigliani and Brumberg 1954; Ando and Modigliani 1963) hypotheses formalized this idea with respect to individual consumers. According to permanent-income and life-cycle logic, rational agents engage in expenditure smoothing and have very muted responses to any change in disposable income perceived as temporary. In this view neither the adverse impact of a recession nor the attempt to offset this impact through discretionary fiscal policy has any impact on consumer spending.

There is no doubt that some households determine expenditures according to the dictates of permanent-income, life-cycle rationality. Chapter 9 argues that these households are likely to be a small proportion of the total, namely, middle-class professionals with stable job prospects and accordingly stable income trajectories. For the rest—the working class and the 1 percent (or maybe the 0.1 percent)—the assumptions underlying the so-called rational agent have minimal bearing on actual behavior. Most workers have too little idea of their future incomes and needs to undertake such planning, and at the other end of the spectrum there is no need for such planning.

The most controversial part of the Obama stimulus, however, was not the tax cuts and transfers to individuals, but the transfers to state governments. Did these transfers simply shore up state finances with no effect on spending, or did the states add to their overall expenditure? John Cogan and John Taylor (2012) applied the permanent-income/life-cycle argument to the states and hypothesized that the states would logically apply the corollary of expenditure smoothing. They find support for this hypothesis in time-series regressions.

The analysis in chapter 15 exposes flaws in Cogan and Taylor's time-series approach and, on the basis of both cross-sectional regressions and interviews with state budget officers, concludes that state governments actually spent the money they received. This analysis supports the conclusions of other economists (for example, Chodorow-Reich et al. 2012; Wilson 2012) who have analyzed the impact of the portion of the Obama stimulus channeled through the states.

A second aspect of functional finance normally gets short shrift but is in my judgment as important as the stabilization aspect: the appropriate level of government spending. Stabilization can be achieved by different combinations of the level of government spending with the size of the deficit or surplus. From the point of view of stabilization, these different combinations may be equivalent, but not from the point of view of social welfare. Once the level of output is fixed, government expenditure competes with consumption and investment for resources. The relevance for functional finance is that a good resolution of this competition may involve a government surplus *or* a government deficit. The difference from stabilization policy is that the surplus or the deficit is not cyclical in nature, but a permanent feature of the optimal configuration of government spending, private investment, and private consumption. So the question of the public debt inevitably raises its ugly head. My position is that a national discussion of our priorities is long overdue, but "sound finance" should not distort the argument.

Keynes in the Long Run

Even economists who accept the label of Keynesian find it something of an oxymoron to place "Keynes" alongside "long run." Limiting the relevance of Keynes to (at best) a short period makes sense if we accept a faulty premise and an illogical corollary. The premise is that the problem is the warts rather than the body of capitalism, and the corollary is that these warts are limited to the short run, magically disappearing with the passage of enough time. Accepting neither the premise nor the "corollary," I argue that Keynes is as relevant in the long run as he is in the short period. More specifically, *aggregate demand* matters in the long run as well as in the short run—not instead of supply, I hasten to add, but in addition.

The obvious objection to my view is that the unemployment rate shows no particular trend over time. If aggregate demand influences output and employment in the long run, what prevents growing unemployment when demand falls short, or growing pressure on capacity as the demand for labor squeezes the supply? It would be a remarkable coincidence if aggregate demand matters in the long run but just happens to stay in balance with the supply of labor so that the rate of unemployment displays no trend.

Implicit in this objection is the assumption that labor-force growth is given, the consequence of population growth and the exogenous forces determining participation rates. My assumption is rather that labor-force growth is endogenous, determined in the end by demand factors. Behind this assumption is a view of capitalism as embedded in a larger economy and able to draw on the "reserve armies" (to use Karl Marx's terminology) of other sectors as the need arises. Historically, the family farm and the kitchen have constituted principal reserve armies throughout the capitalist world. And when farmers and women have not been available in sufficient numbers, immigrants from the capitalist periphery have made up the difference, at least most of the time and in most places. (Japan is the most notable exception.) The key point here, and a difference at least in emphasis from Marx, is that the reserve army is not given once and for all but constituted and reconstituted over time in the service of capitalism. The resulting model may be seen as the offspring of a marriage between Keynes's *General Theory* and W. Arthur Lewis's 1954 "Economic Development with Unlimited Supplies of Labour," with the marriage consummated not on the bed of the poor, densely populated, countries that Lewis had in mind, but on the capitalist bed that was Keynes's focus.

Assuming the labor force is endogenous requires us to revisit the theory of wage determination. In analyzing the short run, I uncritically adopted a simple view of wage dynamics depending only on the level of unemployment. This simplification fits with the idea that the labor supply is exogenous, and a long-run theory need not dispute this as far as the short run is concerned. But the simplest long-run theory of wage determination consistent with an endogenous labor force is to ignore altogether the influence of unemployment on wages. Instead, wage dynamics are based on an exogenously given conventional wage. By conventional I mean what the classical economists, Adam Smith and David Ricardo, as well as Marx, meant by subsistence: not a minimum that holds body and soul together, but a social norm that reflects the economic, political, and social conditions of a time and place. In the mainstream literature, the same idea is captured by the concept of a target wage born of the aspirations of the working class and their power to achieve these aspirations, both existing in a matrix of culture and history.

The emphasis on a conventional wage does not mean that the current level of unemployment is irrelevant to wage dynamics, or, for that matter, to the evolution of the labor supply. But the mathematics are complicated when the level of unemployment is included, so the argument is placed in the mathematical appendix to chapter 18 rather than in the main body of that chapter.

The resulting model deploys the same dynamic structure as the short-run model used to understand depression economics, with this important difference: in the long run the interaction of aggregate demand, goods supply, and labor supply has historically led to inflation rather than deflation.

One virtue of the model is that it provides a unified framework for analyzing both demand shocks and supply shocks. This permits us to understand the confusion around the Phillips curve: specifically, does, or does not, a trade-off between employment and inflation exist in the long run? A long-run Keynesian model allows us to sort out movements along the Phillips curve from shifts in the Phillips curve. The conclusion is that, contrary to both New Keynesian and New Classical theories, the Phillips curve is, as Robert Gordon put it in the title of a 2013 working paper, alive and well—or at least was until the aftermath of the Great Recession.

A consequence is that the scope of monetary and fiscal policy is not limited to a short run in which imperfections temporarily open up a space for government to influence aggregate demand. In contrast with the New Keynesian view, monetary and fiscal policy can impact employment and output in the long run as well. Governments may choose not to push employment and output at the expense of price stability, but this is a political choice, not the consequence of a world in which inflation brings only pain without any gain.

My model also sheds new light on a perennial question that is as old as—indeed, older than—*The General Theory*: are high wages good for capitalism, more specifically, good for employment? Keynes did not spend much time on this question; in *The General Theory,* the *real* wage is endogenous, determined as part of the equilibrium configuration, so there is no way to even ask the question. This theoretical issue apart, Keynes thought redistribution to workers was indeed a means of increasing aggregate demand, since workers would likely consume more of their incomes than capitalists and other segments of the population. But he considered redistribution as a last resort; there were better means, like reducing the rate of interest, for stimulating aggregate demand.

Still the question has persisted, especially among left Keynesians and their social-democratic allies in politics. My answer, developed originally with Amit Bhaduri (Marglin and Bhaduri 1990; Bhaduri and Marglin 1990) and expanded here, is "it depends." In the model of chapter 18, the question is put as whether a higher conventional wage is associated with greater employment.[2] Against the positive impact on demand when workers have a higher propensity to consume than other agents must be weighed the effects of a higher conventional wage on investment demand. These effects are far from one-sided. A higher real wage means a lower profit share, but the impact of the profit share depends on the kind of investment. Lower profits make capital widening—investment that expands capacity—less attractive. But a higher real wage makes capital deepening—investment that substitutes capital for labor—*more* attractive. To complicate matters further, the balance of the two kinds of investment likely depends where the economy is in the business cycle. In boom times, with output pressing on capacity, capital widening will be more on point than in slack times, when there is considerable excess capacity. Capital deepening is less subject to swings in employment and output, so it will be relatively more important in slack times.

The implication is that in boom times, high real wages work in opposite directions on consumption and investment, and it is not possible on theoretical grounds to say which is more important. By contrast, in slack times, investment and consumption tell the same positive story about the effect of high wages. So, yes, "it depends," but in the conditions that persisted for most of the decade following the financial crisis of 2008, conditions that still persist in much of southern Europe, the model speaks clearly: a higher conventional wage would stimulate employment and output.

"It depends" also casts doubt on the idea that economies can be classified as wage led, where higher wages stimulate output and employment, or profit led, where lower wages (and higher profits) promote these goals. Timing is all: every capitalist economy is likely to be wage led in bad times and at least more likely to be profit led in boom conditions.

What Will It Take to Change Economics?

It takes new ideas, and this book has several worth pondering. First, the focus on real-time adjustment as the basis of equilibrium. Second, liquidity preference as a theory of interest-rate spreads. Third, the updating of the conception of money and the critical difference between money as a medium of exchange and money as a store of wealth. Fourth, the formulation of a model of the long run in which aggregate demand plays a critical role. Fifth, the recasting of Lerner's functional finance to separate stabilization from the composition of aggregate demand.

There is some creative destruction at work too. The focus on real-time adjustment exposes the shortcomings of the comparative-statics exercises on which rests the claim that unemployment is the consequence of frictions and rigidities. The mainstream theory of interest is seen to be based on a category mistake: there is no natural rate of interest determined by the interplay of investment demand and desired saving; indeed, there is no determinate level of interest rates unless we posit a central bank or its equivalent to anchor the spreads determined by liquidity preference. There may be a long-run tendency to full employment, or at least to an equilibrium rate of unemployment, but this is because in the long run the labor force is itself endogenous, not because there is an endogenous mechanism for adjusting the level of employment to an exogenously given labor force. There is a Phillips curve in the long run as well as in the short run, and the trade-off between employment and price stability requires political choices. Finally, while this book does not dispute the idea that a negative effect of high wages on investment might counter its positive effect on consumption, it adds some perspective by analyzing the difference between capital widening and capital deepening. Whereas capital widening creates a conflict between the impact of higher wages on investment and consumption, capital deepening reinforces the consumption argument for higher wages. The distinction between the two kinds of investment is especially important in thinking about wage policy in slack times, when capital deepening is likely to predominate.

Ideas are necessary, but not sufficient, especially if these ideas challenge the sacred proposition of economics, the beneficent invisible hand that guides the economy to an efficient allocation of resources unless it is undermined by imperfections, frictions, rigidities. Keynes carried the day, or rather the generation of 1936, because the new ideas of *The General Theory* made common cause with a newly ascendant political movement, the New Deal in the United States and social democracy in Europe. Even for those who understood little of the theory, the conclusions, especially the justification for an activist fiscal policy, fit well with the basic underlying philosophy that an important role for government was to address market failures. Not with more and better (read more competitive) markets, but with direct intervention; spending and taxing in the interest of stabilizing aggregate demand is a leading example. Indeed, outside the economics profession—and to some extent within it— "Keynesian" came to be identified with government intervention, including many forms of intervention to which Keynes was, at least until late in his life, at best cool, the welfare state a case in point.[3]

It is no coincidence that the dominance of Keynesian macroeconomics ended at the same time that the social-democratic and New Deal coalitions collapsed. Nor is the contemporaneous rise of New Classical economics and the rise of Margaret Thatcher and Ronald Reagan pure coincidence. New movements in economics and politics, both on the left and on the right, draw strength from one another. It is probably not too strong to say that the one is a precondition for the other.

The lack of success of the New Left in the 1960s supports this view. I was one of many of my generation who hoped that fundamental change would emerge from the civil rights movement, the anti- (Vietnam) war movement, May 1968 in France, and the hot autumn in Italy the same year. These movements did have lasting effects, but not the fundamental social change we hoped for. This is not the place, nor am I the person, to offer a full analysis of the failures of the 1960s. Nonetheless I think it's fair to say that one reason was the lack of any coherent set of ideas about the structures to be put in place; high on the list of what was missing was a new economics.

The abundance of new political movements in the second decade of the twenty-first century also illustrates my point. It is too early to tell if any of them, right or left, is more than a passing reaction to various (and deep) social ills. But I predict that if any of these movements shows staying power, it will be, at least in part, because it has forged an alliance with a new economics that feeds and is fed by the new politics.

In the meantime, those of us who challenge the reigning orthodoxy are planting seeds. Whether these seeds will germinate; if they germinate, whether they will grow; if they grow, whether the fruit will be sweet—depends on the soil, the weather, and the myriad other factors beyond our control. This book has planted a few seeds. I hope you will join me not only in praying for a good crop but in working to bring in the harvest.

Notes

References

Acknowledgments

Index

NOTES

Prologue

Epigraphs: Keynes 1973a, p. 406: "A note, probably written in 1932," according to Moggridge; Samuelson 1964.

Chapter 1

Epigraph: Keynes 1973a, p. 492.

1. Full disclosure: almost everybody in my department is younger than I am, but these people were really young, so young that I didn't even know them by name.
2. To put matters in perspective, at the worst of the Great Recession, the unemployment rate in the United States briefly touched 10 percent. In 1936, when John Maynard Keynes published *The General Theory,* the U.S. unemployment rate stood at 17 percent, almost double the 2009 rate. This represented a significant improvement over 1932 and 1933.

   At the lowest depths of the Great Depression, in 1933, official statistics recorded one out of four workers in the United States as out of work, but the official statistics underestimated the unemployment rate as a fraction of the wage-labor force. In the 1930s agriculture was a significant sector of the economy in terms of both employment and output, and because of the limited role of wage labor in pre–World War II agriculture, this sector did not suffer from unemployment in the same way as industry and commerce did. Until the 1950s American agriculture was dominated by the family farm, and family farms normally do not lay off family members as a way of absorbing economic shocks. The impact of the Great Depression on agriculture was not on employment and output but on prices and thus on farmers' money incomes and, even more so, on the real burden of debt that farmers carried. (More about this in chapter 8.) Leaving the agricultural sector out of the denominator, which makes sense if we are making comparisons between the Great Depression and the Great Recession, the 1933 unemployment rate in the United States was more like one in three; this is the ratio of the number of unemployed to the *nonagricultural* labor force, which was then only 75 percent of the total labor force, not the 98.5 percent it is in the twenty-first century.

   Among other capitalist countries, Germany suffered the most, with unemployment rates at the U.S. level. Nor was the calamity solely economic: the Great

Depression must take a good share of the blame for the political calamity named Adolf Hitler and indirectly for World War II.

3. Schumpeter (1954, p. 41) defines the pre-analytic vision in these terms:

    In order to be able to posit to ourselves any problems at all, we should first have to visualize a distinct set of coherent phenomena as a worth-while object of our analytic efforts. In other words, analytic effort is of necessity preceded by a preanalytic cognitive act that supplies the raw material for the analytic effort.

    Schumpter meant the distinction between vision and analysis as a general one but illustrates it with Keynes's *General Theory.*

4. Arthur Cecil Pigou was professor of political economy at the University of Cambridge from 1908 to 1943 and fellow of King's College, Keynes's university (and college), at a time and place when professor was a title mostly used in the singular: Alfred Marshall, teacher of both Pigou and Keynes, was the first professor of political economy, holding the chair from 1884 (when economics was still part of the field of moral sciences—it was established as a separate field in 1903) to 1908. Dennis Robertson, who had earlier been a close collaborator of Keynes but broke with him over *The General Theory,* succeeded Pigou as professor of political economy, serving in that capacity from 1944 to 1957. In the 1950s, the professorial ranks began to expand exponentially, and the British academic hierarchy came to resemble the American model, in which professors occupy the top floor of an academic apartment house rather than the pinnacle of a pyramid. (Thanks to Geoffrey Harcourt, personal communication on February 17, 2014, for setting me straight on the chronology of economics at Cambridge.)

5. Friedman adds a telling footnote after the sentence that ends in the assertion that Keynes's error lay in "neglecting the existence of a desired stock of wealth as a goal motivating savings":

    Keynes, of course, verbally recognized this point, but it was not incorporated in his formal model of the economy. Its key role was pointed out first by Haberler (1941, pp. 242, 389, 403, 491–503) and subsequently by Pigou (1947), Tobin (1947), Patinkin (1951), and Johnson (1961).

    All these references are to the so-called real-balance effect, which is a very peculiar, to say the least, application of the idea that Friedman did so much to promote, namely that wealth rather than income drives consumption. See below in this chapter and more extensively in chapters 4 and 7 for a discussion of the real-balance effect and chapter 9 for a discussion of wealth as a driver of consumption.

6. A search in J-Stor turned up classical or neoclassical dichotomy as early as 1936, but the term seems to have been first used in the sense of a division between real and nominal quantities by Don Patinkin in 1949.

7. "So-called" precisely because the quantity theory of money was not a theory of money at all, but rather a theory of the price level!

8. "Our method of analyzing the economic behavior of the present under the influence of changing ideas about the future is one which depends on the interaction

of supply and demand, and is in this way linked up with our fundamental theory of value. We are thus led to a more general theory, which includes the classical theory with which we are familiar, as a special case" (*The General Theory,* p. vii).

9. Samuelson's formulation, that full employment would "validate and bring back into relevance the classical verities" (1955, p. vi), echoed Keynes:

> If our central controls [over the level of investment] succeed in establishing an aggregate volume of output corresponding to full employment . . . , the classical theory comes into its own again . . . then there is no objection to be raised against the classical analysis of the manner in which private self-interest will determine what in particular is produced, in what proportions the factors of production will be combined to produce it, and how the value of the final product will be distributed. (*The General Theory,* pp. 378–379)

10. Some actually learned from that event. At a hearing of the House Committee on Oversight and Government Reform on October 23, 2008, Alan Greenspan, former head of the Federal Reserve, had this to say:

> Those of us who have looked to the self-interest of lending institutions to protect shareholders' equity—myself especially—are in a state of shocked disbelief . . .
>
> A Nobel Prize was awarded for discovery of the pricing model that underpins much of the advance in derivatives markets. This modern risk management paradigm held sway for decades. The whole intellectual edifice, however, collapsed in the summer of last year, because the data inputted into the risk management models generally covered only the past two decades, a period of euphoria . . .
>
> I made a mistake in presuming that the self-interest of organizations, specifically banks and others, were such is [sic] that they were best capable of protecting their own shareholders and their equity in the firms . . . (U.S. Government Printing Office 2008)

The chair of the committee, Representative Henry Waxman, had pressed Greenspan on his persistent and consistent championing of deregulation over a long career:

> You were, perhaps, the leading proponent of deregulation of our financial markets. Certainly you were the most influential voice for deregulation. You have been a staunch advocate for letting markets regulate themselves.

Waxman then cut to the chase: "My question for you is simple, were you wrong?" After Greenspan's less than convincing defense of the hands-off Fed, which emphasized that, for the most part, deregulation (or rather self-regulation) worked just fine, Waxman interrupted to ask: "Well, where did you make a mistake then?" Greenspan's response deserves to be quoted more fully. After acknowledging his mistake—see above—Greenspan went on to say,

> The problem here is something which looked to be a very solid edifice, and, indeed, a critical pillar to market competition and free markets, did break down. And I think that, as I said, shocked me. I still do not fully understand

why it happened and, obviously, to the extent that I figure out where it happened and why, I will change my views. If the facts change, I will change.
(Keynes is often cited as the source for the last sentence. Accused as he often was
of inconsistency, he was said to have replied on one occasion, "Sir, when I get new
facts, I may change my mind. What do you do?")

Greenspan's self-searching, such as it was, was echoed in the economics profession. But self-examination and self-criticism in the mainstream economics
profession lasted about ten minutes. After a brief dalliance with letting a hundred flowers bloom, the profession closed ranks, and it was back to business as
usual.

11. Schumpeter's sin apparently was twofold. First, as noted, he was pessimistic about
the prospects for capitalism, a thesis expounded in *Capitalism, Socialism and Democracy.* Second, he took Karl Marx seriously despite his rejection of Marx's fundamental doctrines. I have considerable personal experience with the taint that
comes from taking Marx seriously.

12. The controversy over postwar economic prospects provides a good illustration
of Keynes's view of models as mental constructions for organizing thought, as
against a mechanical view of models as mirrors, if not of nature, of economic
structures. Followers of Keynes who saw in the simple consumption function
of *The General Theory* a formula for prediction were misled: a fall in income
would in their view mechanically produce a proportionate decrease in consumption in line with the marginal propensity to consume. Others, like Keynes himself,
who did not take *The General Theory* model literally in its predicating consumer
spending on income, were mentally freer to take into account the special circumstances of the war and its legacy of both unprecedented liquid wealth and unprecedented unmet desires for goods.

13. Strangely, despite its policy shift, the mission statement remains basically unchanged. I consulted the ECB website again in the fall of 2015 and in the spring of
2020. Compared with 2009, the 2020 statement changed only the "hierarchy of
objectives": it now reads:

> To maintain price stability is the primary objective of the Eurosystem and of
> the single monetary policy for which it is responsible. This is laid down in
> the Treaty on the Functioning of the European Union, Article 127 (1).
>
> "Without prejudice to the objective of price stability," the Eurosystem
> shall also "support the general economic policies in the Union with a view to
> contributing to the achievement of the objectives of the Union." These in-
> clude inter alia "full employment" and "balanced economic growth."
>
> The Treaty establishes a clear hierarchy of objectives for the Eurosystem.
> It assigns overriding importance to price stability. The Treaty makes clear
> that ensuring price stability is the most important contribution that mone-
> tary policy can make to achieve a favourable economic environment and a
> high level of employment.

For the powers that be it is evidently less embarrassing to be consistently wrong
than to change their mind.

Chapter 2

Epigraphs: Pigou 1933, p. 252; Viner 1933a, p. 9.

1. Keynes's critique of Pigou in the appendix to chapter 19 of *The General Theory* attributes an explicit demand-supply model to *The Theory of Unemployment,* but on my reading of Pigou it is more accurate to say that this demand-supply model is implicit rather than explicit. *The Theory of Unemployment* focuses one-sidedly on the demand for labor that derives from profit maximization by producers. The supply schedule is hardly mentioned, and indeed Pigou's language often suggests that workers pick a point on the demand schedule even in the absence of monopoly or other restrictions that replace competition by concerted action; there are repeated references to the "real wage stipulated by workpeople." Nonetheless, Pigou's general argument can be understood only in the context of an LS schedule that would combine with the demand schedule to provide full employment were it not for disturbances to demand and various institutional impediments (trade unions, minimum wages, unemployment insurance, public sentiment about "what constitutes a reasonable living wage," p. 255) to workers' expressing their supply preferences. On page 252, in the passage quoted in the epigraph to this chapter, he comes reasonably close to the picture Keynes paints of him.

   Pigou is clearer in his 1927 discussion of what would later be termed structural unemployment ("structural" to distinguish it from "cyclical" unemployment):

   > Before the Great War there can be little doubt that wage-rates in Great Britain were adjusted in a broad way to the conditions of demand and supply . . . It was nowhere suggested that the general body of wage-rates had been forced up too high relatively to the openings for employment, in such wise that, even had no industrial fluctuations taken place, a substantial number of healthy persons seeking employment must have been always unable to find it. In the post-war period, however, there is strong reason to believe that an important change has taken place in this respect; that, partly through direct State action, and partly through the added strength given to workpeople's organisations engaged in wage bargaining by the development of unemployment insurance, wage-rates have, over a wide area, been set at a level which is too high in the above sense; and that the very large percentage of unemployment which has prevailed during the whole of the last six years is due in considerable measure to this new factor in our economic life. (p. 353)

   Pigou's 1933 treatise is indeed a curious book with a curious history. Apart from the question of whether or not it contains the demand-supply theory that Keynes attributes to it, it has the dubious distinction of being praised in the highest possible terms in the reviews that appeared just after publication, only to become in Keynes's new dispensation the epitome of all that was wrong with the old.

2. Figure 2.5 is not faithful to Viner in one respect because it identifies costs solely with wages. So what was for Viner an imbalance between producers' prices and costs, such as transportation and utilities, is pictured here as an imbalance be-

tween prices and wages. But the logic of Figure 2.5 is clearly Viner's: the cause of depression is that the prices businessmen receive for their outputs are well below the costs of their inputs, and the cure is to restore the balance between costs and prices.

3. Viner explicitly deplored President Hoover's exhortations to business to maintain money wages in the face of falling prices:

> At the beginning of the depression, Hoover pledged industry not to cut wages, and for a long time large-scale industry as a rule adhered to this pledge. There is not time for an adequate exposure of the errors of economic analysis from which this high-wage doctrine derives its plausibility. But its basic fallacy, to which, unfortunately, many of my professional colleagues have succumbed, can be made clear in a few words. All that is guaranteed by wages higher than employers can afford to pay and still give employment to the available supply of labor is unemployment. The doctrine asserts that high wages mean high purchasing power, but an unemployed laborer has no purchasing power at all, however high may be the wage rate he would get if he had a job. (1933a, pp. 12–13)

4. Whether or not J. B. Say is the author of Say's Law has been the subject of much argument. See William Baumol (1999) for a summary, and Alain Béraud and Guy Numa (2018).

5. Like Hume (see chapter 1), Mill qualified the bald statement quoted here to allow for short-run deviations from a fixed relationship between money and prices. And like Viner, Mill appears to view the problem caused by temporary deviations from Say's Law as one of unbalanced deflation—which makes sense in terms of the quantity theory that informed their thinking. Mill writes,

> It is also evident that this temporary derangement of markets is an evil only because it is temporary. The fall being solely of money prices, if prices did not rise again no dealer would lose, since the smaller price would be worth as much to him as the larger price was before. (1909, bk. 3, chap. 14, para. 4)

6. The same Bernanke who was the Chair of the Board of Governors of the Federal Reserve System from 2006 until 2014, that is before, during, and after the financial crisis of 2008–9 and the consequent recession. If the Frank–Bernanke claim were true, Bernanke would have had a much easier time as Fed Chairman!

7. This is a common trope in mainstream texts. See Mankiw (2018, chap. 26, fig. 1 and accompanying text, pp. 549–557).

> Both the Frank–Bernanke and the Mankiw texts distinguish between a "long run," in which the interest rate is determined by equilibrium between desired investment and desired saving, and a "short run," in which the interest rate is determined by the demand for and supply of money (Frank and Bernanke 2007, p. 772; Mankiw 2018, p. 742). The two texts root the distinction in terms of the rigidity of prices and wages in the short run versus flexibility in the long run. Presumably if prices and wages are flexible in the short run—as I shall assume when developing my preferred model in chapters 5 through 7—the long-run model applies in the

short run as well. (By the same token, if prices and wages are assumed to be rigid in the long run, the Frank–Bernanke and Mankiw short-run models would apply to the long run.)

Mankiw's text, the leading text in terms of market share, has a decidedly conservative bent. But the more liberal Baumol–Blinder–Solow (2020) text, while avoiding the idea that the interest rate equilibrates desired investment and saving in their discussion of macroeconomics, makes the same argument as Mankiw in its presentation of the theory of distribution (pp. 403–404).

The *Voluntary National Content Standards in Economics,* the codification of the mainstream consensus of what economics should be taught to U.S. schoolchildren, says high school graduates should know that "real interest rates rise and fall to balance the amount saved with the amount borrowed [for investment]. This affects the allocation of scarce resources between present and future uses" (Council for Economic Education 2010, p. 30).

8. If the interest rate has no impact on saving, the basic logic of Figure 2.9 is unchanged: "no impact" means only that the saving-supply schedule becomes vertical. Similarly, were we to assume that saving is interest-dependent but investment is given independently of the interest rate, the identical logic would still apply to the determination of equilibrium.

9. Peter Bauer, who later became a well-known opponent of all kinds of government intervention—he was made a life peer by Margaret Thatcher—published a review in German in 1938 of the English language discussion of *The General Theory.* This review, apparently for the first time in print, clearly indicated the difference between the role of stocks of financial assets in Keynes's theory of interest and the role of flows of investment and saving in the mainstream theory. Tibor Scitovsky (1940) analyzed the difference between the theories of Keynes and the mainstream in terms of stocks and flows. (I have not found an earlier English-language discussion in these terms, but I cannot rule out that one exists.) In an idealized world without government and foreign trade, the money market might be understood as a market in claims on the capital stock, but in fact the money market includes a variety of financial assets, chiefly government debt, that have no counterpart in physical capital.

10. A disproportionate amount of trading is in on-the-run Treasuries. Even allowing for this disproportion, it remains true that bond trading dwarfs current investment. See chapter 11 for more detail.

11. As far as I know, nobody has ever tested formally the extent to which interest rates adjust to desired investment and saving. The twentieth-century finance literature simply assumed that interest rates are determined in asset markets, without bringing in current rates of investment and saving. In this century there have been attempts to include macroeconomic variables in explaining the structure of interest rates—see Refet Gürkaynak and Jonathan Wright (2012, sec. 4.1) for a summary.

The contrast with mainstream macro is striking: in this literature, from introductory textbooks on up, interest rates are determined by the demand for investment and the supply of saving. at least in the pristine setting of the long run. The textbook waters are frequently muddied by the substitution of the term "loanable funds" for saving—see chapter 11, note 1.

12. But the same thing is accomplished through the assumption that goods supply and labor supply can be collapsed into an aggregate-supply schedule, which in the long run is vertical. See chapter 4.

13. An early, perhaps the first, exposition of the aggregate-supply schedule as the projection in $Y \times P$ space of the equilibrium of goods supply and labor supply is in Jacob Marschak's *Income, Employment, and the Price Level,* lectures given to graduate students at the University of Chicago in 1948 and 1949. Marschak's exposition is in the context of his elaboration of an aggregate-demand, aggregate-supply model based on the paper written by his PhD student Modigliani (1944), to which I have alluded earlier. This AD-AS model may be also be a first. AD-AS did not catch on for several decades, but once it did it became the gold standard for presenting (and circumscribing) Keynes. Marschak's lectures do not appear to have had much influence outside of Chicago. *Income, Employment, and the Price Level* was checked out of the Harvard library exactly once between 1963 and 2010.

14. In the 1970s and 1980s mainstream macroeconomists formalized nominal wage rigidity in terms of overlapping wage contracts (for example, Fischer 1977). Overlapping contracts prevent nominal wages from fully adjusting for a period defined by the longest extant contract. After this short run of nominal rigidity, wages become fully flexible over a longer period. Subsequently, John Taylor (1979, 1980) developed overlapping contract models in which rigidities could persist over a longer period.

15. Irrationally is in quotes because, as we shall see in chapter 9, it is an abuse of language to identify rationality with calculation and stigmatize the absence of calculation as irrationality.

Chapter 3

Epigraph: The General Theory, p. 28.

1. I depart from Keynes in what is included under transactions demand and what is included under asset demand. The division between a transactions demand determined by the level of output and the price level and an asset demand determined by the rate of interest leaves the precautionary motive for holding money—provision for a rainy day—somewhat in limbo. See chapter 11.

2. There is a theoretical equivalence between the first- and the second-pass models since in equilibrium there is a one-to-one correspondence between interest rate and money supply. But there is a crucial difference once we leave behind the simplifying assumption of a fixed money wage, one that Keynes does not appear to notice. He moves seamlessly from the first-pass model to the second-pass model when he takes stock of the argument (*The General Theory,* chapter 18) prior to taking on the question of what happens if money wages change.

3. We ignore the possibility of esoteric time-streams of investment returns and costs that can produce multiple rates of return.

4. The work of the circus and Kahn's article were not independent sources for the reconsideration of what happens when expenditure and income are out of balance. Kahn was not only a member of the circus, but the intermediary through whom Keynes was kept informed of the progress of the group's discussions and through whom Keynes suggested questions and issues for it to consider (Keynes 1973a, pp. 338–339). Kahn's multiplier article systematized an argument that Keynes and his collaborator H. D. Henderson had made on behalf of the Liberal Party in the 1929 election campaign (Keynes 1931a).

5. Two articles by Joan Robinson, also a member of the circus, published in February and October 1933 (1933a and 1933b) reflect the shift from emphasizing price effects to emphasizing quantity effects. In February, Robinson is still in the mode of the *Treatise,* with the primary impact of an imbalance between expenditure and income falling on prices, though there is a recognition of the possibility of an impact on output and employment. By October, the shift in emphasis is clear:

> When prices are in excess of costs windfall profits are earned by entrepreneurs, and however much of these profits the entrepreneurs spend the total of profits remains unchanged, since spending by one entrepreneur only serves to increase the windfall profits of others. This argument is valid upon the assumption that an increase in demand for consumption goods leads to no increase in their supply. Now to assume that the supply of goods is perfectly inelastic is a natural simplification to make, at the first step in the argument, if we are primarily interested in the price-level, but to make such an assumption when we are primarily interested in the volume of output is to assume away the whole point of the argument. (p. 24)

6. This indeed is the story by which my generation of economists was introduced to the concept of aggregate demand. It is only one story—see chapters 5 and 6—but for most of the economy it is likely the more relevant story empirically—see chapters 8 and 19.

7. If prices matter for the transactions demand for money, does the wage rate also matter? In principle, yes, but the influence is conventionally ignored. The simplest assumption is that wages are paid out of the proceeds of output sales, so that money is needed only to finance nonlabor inputs to the production process, not to finance wage payments.

8. Lawrence Klein (1947, esp. pp. 84–87) also emphasizes the inelasticity of investment demand as the primary reason for the existence of an unemployment equilibrium. See chapter 17, especially note 7, for a more extensive discussion of stagnation.

9. The discussion of fiscal policy is with respect to the factors that may affect the propensity to consume (*The General Theory,* pp. 94–95). The closest Keynes comes to endorsing deficit spending, to which his name is inseparably linked in the public imagination, is in the concluding section of chapter 10 in *The General Theory,*

where Keynes lays out the relationship between the propensity to consume and the multiplier. It is here one finds the ironic endorsement of unproductive public expenditure as better than no public expenditure at all, quoted at length in chapter 2.

10. Fixing the total money supply may seem the obvious modeling strategy for investigating whether laissez-faire will produce full employment. In fact, it is obvious only in the context of an economy where money consists exclusively of cash, an economy without banks or at least without fractional-reserve banking, a world of gold coins. As soon as we enter a world in which money is created endogenously by a fractional-reserve banking system, the assumption of a given money supply is hardly compelling. We return to the theoretical issue in chapters 4 and 7, and again in chapter 13. Endogenous money plays out differently in a *General Theory* based in comparative statics, as against a *General Theory* based in real-time adjustment. Chapter 8 examines the empirics of money-supply determination during the Great Depression.

11. Observe that if there is no asset demand for money, as the classical quantity theory of money assumes, the LM schedule becomes a vertical line: in the equation $MV = PY$, the quantity of money (M) uniquely determines the level of income (Y) once the income velocity of money (V) and the price level (P) are fixed. The LM schedule approaches this classical limiting case as the elasticity of the asset demand for money with respect to the interest rate approaches zero.

12. It should be noted that the IS-LM framework is being used off label. First, in Hicks's original version (1937), "output" is the *nominal* value of production in a two-sector model consisting of a consumption-goods sector and an investment-goods sector. Second, and more important, goods prices are not given exogenously but are determined endogenously by profit maximization. The intersection of the IS and LM schedules in this construction thus combines demand- and supply-side considerations and is an equilibrium for the economy as a whole.

The problem with Hicks's construction is the inherent ambiguity of the effect of a wage change on equilibrium. An increase in the money wage increases the equilibrium price level while decreasing the equilibrium level of real output. So nominal output can either rise or fall. In any case, what matters is the impact of wage changes on real output, about which Hicks's formulation in terms of nominal variables is unhelpful.

Subsequent expositors of Keynes modified Hicks's construction. The two-sector model was typically condensed into a single sector in which output is homogeneous, and the argument was formulated in real terms. Crucially, Hicks's endogenous determination of the price level was abandoned. Alvin Hansen, whose *Guide to Keynes* was the essential pony for economics students in the days when they were expected to read *The General Theory*, is a key link in the evolving construction of IS-LM. Hansen's IS-LM model has only one output, but Hansen does not make it clear whether output is measured in nominal or real terms. He doesn't have to choose because he treats the price level as given exogenously once and for all, in which case it simply doesn't matter whether we are dealing with nominal or real output. (Incidentally, Hansen is responsible for what became the standard nomenclature; for Hicks the schedules were labeled LL and IS.)

With a given price level, the intersection of the IS and LM schedules generates a single point on the AD schedule. In my own deployment of the IS-LM framework, below, the price level is exogenous but varies parametrically. With output defined in real terms, and with the simplifying assumptions that both the supply of saving and the demand for investment are independent of the distribution of income, the IS schedule is stationary with respect to the price level. In consequence, a varying price level moves only the LM schedule, and the shifting intersection with the stationary IS schedule traces out the AD schedule.

I am indebted to Ingo Barens for sending me back to the drawing board with respect to Hicks's 1937 paper and for pointing me to his unpublished papers (1997, 2001) that deal with the history of IS-LM post Hicks.

Chapter 4

Epigraphs: Modigliani 1944, p. 65; Haberler 1941, pp. 408–409; Krugman 2009, p. 182.

1. This is a strong assumption. Even with a uniform propensity to consume (an assumption examined in chapter 9), to assume money demand is independent of the wage rate ignores the possibility, indeed, the likelihood, that wages form part of the working capital that is financed by the transactions component of money demand—one more area in which we are obliged to suspend disbelief.

2. At one point in chapter 18 of *The General Theory,* Keynes takes stock of the argument up to the point before he departs from static equilibrium to ask what happens when the wage rate changes in real time. At this point he explicitly recognizes the possibility of a Modigliani-type outcome (as well as the possibility I examine in chapter 7 that dynamic fluctuations do not lead to full employment):

> If competition between unemployed workers always led to a very great reduction of the money-wage, there would be a violent instability in the price-level. Moreover there might be no position of stable equilibrium except in conditions consistent with full employment; since the wage-unit might have to fall without limit until it reached a point where the effect of the abundance of money in terms of the wage-unit on the rate of interest was sufficient to restore a level of full employment. At no other point could there be a resting-place. (p. 253)

The argument is confused (see below, chapter 7, note 1), but in any case this is less of a concession than a literal reading might suggest. Keynes is not arguing that a laissez-faire economy will actually reach full employment, à la Pigou and Viner. He rather treats the possibility that equilibrium exists only at full employment, along with the failure of the economy to achieve full employment in practice, as an argument why other factors generally intervene to prevent the necessary wage flexibility:

Whether or not [the idea that forces exist to limit fluctuations in money wages] is plausible *a priori,* experience shows that some such psychological law must actually hold. (p. 253)

For otherwise, as the previous quotation suggests, the economy would indeed come to equilibrium only at full employment. Here, as elsewhere in *The General Theory,* the argument is somewhat opaque because Keynes fails to make a clear distinction between static equilibrium and dynamic disequilibrium paths.

We shall return to this point in chapter 7. Here we focus on the statics of Modigliani's argument, in particular, how he arrives at a conclusion fundamentally at odds with Keynes.

3. This simply finesses the problem. We could take explicit account of commercial lending as a third financial asset or consider these loans to be like cash. At this point, introducing another financial asset would complicate the analysis more than is useful. Treating loans to restaurants like cash would require us to assume that working-capital loans have little default risk and are so short term that they hardly fluctuate in value as the interest rate on working capital varies. If both these assumptions hold, commercial paper is as good as gold (so to speak). But this raises the question of why anybody would ever hold cash as part of their wealth portfolio.

This is not a question we are ready to take up, but it is an important one. The problem is that even in a world of commodity money, the equation $\bar{M} = M_1 + M_2$ breaks down if the same coin can fulfill a transactions demand and serve as a liquid asset for households. In this case, rather than competing with each other, asset demand and transactions demand become complementary. Commercial loans transfer the usufruct of money from households to restaurateurs, but restaurateurs' obligations remain liquid assets in wealth portfolios. This point is developed below (p. 140) and in chapter 13. For now, we simply ignore the anomaly, which is why I say that these assets exist in a kind of limbo, counted as illiquid financial assets but not influencing wealth management.

An alternative way of dealing with commercial lending is to blur the line between wealth holding and business by assuming that households own and operate the restaurants, and we can therefore consolidate the two balance sheets. Transactions demand becomes simply a claim on household cash, and no lending is involved. But then households must be assumed to directly own the physical capital associated with the restaurant business, and there is no need for bonds to exist, so no balancing of financial assets.

Chapter 5

Epigraphs: Marshall 1920, p. 345; Walras 1954 [1874], pp. 84–85.

1. Nicholas Kaldor (1934, esp. pp. 133–135) gave the name "cobweb theorem" to this process, attributing the idea of such a recursive process to Henry Schultz and Umberto Ricci.

2. This moment may be as good as any to fess up that the opposition between Walras

and Marshall is almost certainly overdone to the point of being misleading. Although Walras lays out a "Walrasian" adjustment process early on in the *Elements* when he is concerned with a pure exchange economy, once production enters into the model, the adjustment process becomes the same as Marshall's—unless I am misreading Walras's lesson 21 (1954, sec. 208–220, pp. 243–254).

3. To simplify the mathematics, we assume changes take place continuously rather than once a day. The notation $\dot{P}$ and $\dot{Q}$ reflect this assumption. I will continue to tell discrete-time stories since periodic change is easier to grasp intuitively than is continuous change.

4. It may seem contradictory that a fall in price is accompanied by an increase in production. It is contradictory if we think about equilibrium responses to a change in demand, when prices and output move in the same direction. The response here is more akin to what happens when the supply schedule moves outward. The lure of profit drives quantity decisions—price exceeds marginal cost—while excess supply drives price down.

5. Whether the trajectory goes straight to equilibrium, as in Figures 5.7 and 5.8, or follows a more convoluted path depends on parameter values—see the mathematical appendix to this chapter. If demand is inelastic and supply elastic, the economy initially overshoots the equilibrium, and goes to equilibrium via a path of dampened oscillations around the equilibrium.

6. Alternatively, we can imagine consumers determining output adjustment by how the marginal utility of fish compares with its price. (The vertical distance between the starting point $<Q_0, P_0>$ and the demand schedule measures the initial difference between price and marginal utility.) If, as in Figure 5.8, price initially exceeds marginal utility, consumers will cut back on their fish orders. The trajectory is qualitatively the same as in Figure 5.8, but the logic is different, with producers no longer calling all the shots.

7. Evidently, the momentum of an increasing real price could be sustained beyond A by assuming that money wages respond negatively to unemployment at the same time as the nominal price level responds to profit maximization. This would lead to the expansion of output and eventually back to the full-employment, profit-maximizing equilibrium at E.

8. There is some evidence that this was so for the circus, the group of younger faculty members who served as a sounding board (and more) as Keynes was moving from *A Treatise on Money* to *The General Theory* (see the references in chapter 3 to the group).

Chapter 6

Epigraphs: The General Theory, p. vii; Patinkin 1948, pp. 562–563; Tobin 1975, pp. 195–196; Tobin 1993, p. 46.

1. Well, maybe it didn't. Modigliani defines "rigid wages" as an "infinite elasticity of the supply curve of labor when the level of employment is below 'full'" (1944, p. 65, note 23), whereas "flexible wages" is later defined as shorthand for "homo-

geneity of zero degree of the supply-of-labor function" (1944, p. 70, note 35). Since the supply of labor is, in Modigliani's telling, a function of the real wage, he presumably did not mean that the supply-of-labor function is homogeneous of degree zero, which is to say, that a doubling of the real wage would leave labor supply unaffected. Rather, he presumably meant that the supply of labor written as $L = L(W, P)$ is homogeneous of degree zero in the arguments W and P, which is to say that doubling W and P would leave the value of L unchanged. This is, to say the least, an odd definition of flexibility even if one accepts my clarification of what Modigliani intends in his definition of flexible wages.

2. The counterargument to the dominant view that money originated as convenience to simplify barter trade—the metallic theory—is that money originated as a way of facilitating taxation—the "chartalist," or state theory of money. The implication of the chartalist view is that money always has been fiat money, receiving its value from the ability of the state both to compel people to pay taxes and to fix the unit in which taxes are paid. For educating me on the chartalist alternative to the standard origins story, I am indebted to Christine Desan, especially to her 2014 book *Making Money;* see also L. Randall Wray (2014) and Pavlina Tcherneva (2007). An all but forgotten early twentieth-century statement of the chartalist view is Innes (1913, 1914). The standard reference is Georg Friedrich Knapp (1924 [1905]). Keynes fully accepted the chartalist view, paying homage to Knapp in the opening pages of *A Treatise on Money.* By contrast, *The General Theory* doesn't go into the consequences of chartalism for theorizing about the money supply. See chapter 13 below.

3. Keynes's take on this fact:

> It is not very plausible to assert that unemployment in the United States in 1932 was due either to labour obstinately refusing to accept a reduction of money-wages or its obstinately demanding a real wage beyond what the productivity of the economic machine was capable of furnishing. (*The General Theory,* p. 9)

This observation supports the idea that the assumption of a constant money wage was an expositional tactic rather than a basic assumption of the model. As we have seen, Keynes's protests to the contrary have not stopped the development of the idea that a fixed money wage and the irrelevance of the LS schedule are core assumptions of *The General Theory.*

4. Throughout this book, formal models do not take account of technical progress. Alexander Field (2011) has an informative account of technological change during the Great Depression.

5. Keynes emphasized the dependence of tomorrow's investment-demand schedule on today's investment: "A rate of investment, higher (or lower) than prevailed formerly, begins to react unfavourably (or favourably) on the marginal efficiency of capital if it is continued for a period which, measured in years, is not very large" (*The General Theory,* p. 251).

6. Observe that $P/W = 4$ in Figure 6.2 implies that $W_0 = 1$ in Figure 6.1.

7. Stability is no guarantee that the path to the new equilibrium is direct. The equilibrium may be stable but approachable only on a path of smaller and smaller os-

cillations around the equilibrium. Again, see the mathematical appendix to this chapter.

8. I owe this point to Peter Skott. Commenting on a workshop presentation of this model, Skott rightly took me to task for ignoring the consequences of inventory accumulation. See Chapters 8 and 17.

9. "There may exist no expedient by which labour as a whole can reduce its real wage to a given figure by making revised money bargains with the entrepreneurs" (*The General Theory,* p. 13).

10. A hedge is in order. There is some evidence in *The General Theory* that Keynes, likely because of the British experience during the Depression, saw money-wage rigidity as a fact of life. But he nevertheless recognized the need to modify this assumption if his theory was to live up to his claim that *The General Theory* was indeed more general than competing—mainstream—explanations of unemployment. And, as observed in note 3, he explicitly recognized that in the United States, money wages fell during the Depression.

11. Clower published a much shorter revision of this paper in the *Quarterly Journal of Economics* in 1960. The published version not only omits the paragraph quoted above, it also leaves out the dynamics that make Clower's 1958 paper an intellectual precursor of my own work. Thanks to Romain Plassard for his discussion of Clower's 1958 paper in his 2018 article "Clower's *Volte-Face* Regarding the 'Keynesian Revolution'" and for sharing the Clower paper with me.

12. However, the emphasis of the Solow–Stiglitz model was different; their purpose was to shed light on an important controversy of the 1960s, namely, the role of marginal productivity in determining the real wage, and the assumptions of their model are designed to this end. In particular, the assumption of a uniform saving propensity is replaced by the assumption of class-based saving, the Cambridge saving theory (see chapter 9). In its attempt to influence the marginal-productivity debate, the Solow–Stiglitz paper fails utterly: it miscasts marginal-productivity theory as simply the equality of marginal products with factor prices, in particular, the equality of the marginal productivity of labor with the real wage. This equality is an immediate corollary of profit maximization and competitive markets and applies to static *General Theory* models of chapters 3 and 4 as well as to the neoclassical alternative discussed in chapter 2. Marginal-productivity *theory* involves a stronger assumption, namely, that, in addition to profit maximization and competition, the real wage is endogenously determined by an exogenously given labor supply—in other words, the assumption that the real wage clears the (competitive) labor market. The difference between endogenous and exogenous determination of the real wage is discussed in chapter 18.

Chapter 7

Epigraphs: Robinson 1980, p. 57; Solow 1979, p. 345; Samuelson 1941, p. 102.

1. The passage concludes

> Moreover there might be no position of stable equilibrium except in conditions consistent with full employment; since the wage-unit might have to fall

without limit until it reached a point where the effect of the abundance of money in terms of the wage-unit on the rate of interest was sufficient to restore a level of full employment. At no other point could there be a resting-place.

Keynes's assertion is garbled. If there is "violent instability in the price level," so must there be violent oscillations in output and money wages. In this case there will be *no* stable equilibrium consistent with full employment. Keynes got oscillations in the price level right, but he was incorrect in conjecturing the existence of a stable equilibrium in the limiting case as $W \to 0$. In Figure 7.2 the money wage oscillates, like real output, along an ever-widening trajectory.

2. See chapter 13. In chapter 4, I noted Keynes's rejection of commodity money in the *Treatise*. Moreover, in chapter 18 of *The General Theory*, the money supply is assumed to be fixed by a central bank (p. 247) rather than by an exogenous supply of gold, and in chapter 19 he notes the possibility that the money supply is endogenous, and that this would undo the Keynes effect: "If the quantity of money is itself a function of the wage- and price-level, there is indeed nothing to hope in this direction" (p. 266). But beyond this passing comment, the idea of endogenous money is not developed.

Indeed, in the concluding section of *The General Theory*, Keynes suggests that the quantity of money might be limited by the availability of precious metals, for example in this passage:

Now, if the wage-unit is somewhat stable and not liable to spontaneous changes of significant magnitude (a condition which is almost always satisfied), if the state of liquidity-preference is somewhat stable, taken as an average of its short-period fluctuations, and if banking conventions are also stable, the rate of interest will tend to be governed by the quantity of the precious metals, measured in terms of the wage-unit, available to satisfy the community's desire for liquidity. (p. 326)

3. "The real bills doctrine is a rule purporting to gear money to production via the short-term commercial bill of exchange, thereby ensuring that output generates its own means of purchase and money adapts passively to the legitimate needs of trade." (Humphrey 1992, p. 3)

4. The real-bills doctrine bears some responsibility for the passivity not only of the commercial banking system but also of central banks during the Great Depression; see chapter 8, note 5.

5. The word bankrupt derives from the Italian *banca rotta,* describing the ritual by which bank failure was recognized and communicated: the *banca* (bench) where bankers conducted their business in the market place would be broken to signify a financial collapse.

6. Since the financial crisis of 2008, when the maximum was last raised, deposit insurance is limited to $250,000 per account in the United States.

7. Pigou revisited the real-balance effect some years later (1947). He came in the interim to recognize the difference between outside and inside money, though he never acknowledged Kalecki's priority in making this distinction. (Perhaps it was

mere forgetfulness. According to William Baumol [2000, p. 1n], "Dennis Robertson repeatedly told me how on passing Pigou's lair, the great man would regularly emerge, demanding 'Robertson—tell me, what is the Pigou effect?'").

More importantly, Pigou came to understand the difference between the comparative statics of real balances and the dynamics. His reversal is stunning:

> It is ridiculous to suppose that the public authorities would stand passive in the case of catastrophic disturbances. If a situation arose in which money income was being driven inexorably downwards in the way contemplated . . . no government would allow money wage rates to rush downwards very far . . . Thus the puzzles we have been considering . . . are academic exercises, of some slight use perhaps for clarifying thought, but with very little chance of ever being posed on the chequer board of actual life. (1947, p. 188)

8. The dollar value of firm liabilities actually rises if bonds are marked to market because $P_B(\rho)$ rises as the interest rate falls.

9. Not always. The dramatic changes in the real value of the housing stock, both up and down, are implicated in virtually every story about the causes of the Great Recession, as was the stock market crash in the story of the Great Depression.

10. Thus Keynes: "The effect of the lower price-level on the real burden of the National Debt and hence on taxation is likely to prove very adverse to business confidence" (*The General Theory*, p. 264).

11. This way of putting the issue reflects the government's position. The plaintiffs in *Perry* could have argued that the issue was whether the Supreme Court would allow the destruction of private wealth to the benefit of the government.

    Perry and *Norman* overlapped in many respects, but *Perry* raised the additional question of the constitutional meaning of the delegation to Congress in Article One, Section Eight, of the power to "borrow money on the credit of the United States" and the meaning of "the validity of the public debt" in Section 4 of the Fourteenth Amendment.

12. Observe that the formula $\rho_{\text{WHEAT}} = \rho_{\text{OIL}} - \phi_{W/O}$ gives an instantaneous relationship between own rates of interest on different goods. For finite periods, we must continuously compound interest and price changes, so that the one-year return of interest is $e^{\rho} - 1$ rather than ρ, and the annual change in prices is $e^{\phi} - 1$ rather than ϕ. The one-year formula relating the own rate of interest for wheat to the wheat rate of interest for oil is

$$e^{\rho_W} - 1 = (e^{\rho_O} / e^{\phi_{W/O}}) - 1 = e^{\rho_O - \phi_{W/O}} - 1.$$

13. I'm not sure what to make of Keynes's own account of the relationship between real and nominal interest rates. He argues:

> The expectation of a fall in the value of money stimulates investment, and hence employment generally, because it raises the schedule of the marginal efficiency of capital, *i.e.*, the investment demand-schedule; and the expectation of a rise in the value of money is depressing, because it lowers the schedule of the marginal efficiency of capital. (*The General Theory*, pp. 141–142)

So far, so good, though he is now expressing the marginal-efficiency-of-capital schedule in nominal terms rather than in real terms.

He goes on to make a distinction between anticipated and unanticipated price changes, and his argument becomes harder to follow. If a rise or a fall in prices is unanticipated, it will have no effect on expectations of returns, and so can be ignored. (At least for the time being, but presumably today's unanticipated price change will have an impact on expectations tomorrow.) If, however, price changes are anticipated,

> The prices of existing goods will be forthwith so adjusted that the advantages of holding money and of holding goods are again equalized, and it will be too late for holders of money to gain or to suffer a change in the rate of interest which will offset the prospective change during the period of the loan in the value of the money lent. (p. 142)

Keynes appears to be saying here that there cannot be inflation or deflation that is correctly anticipated by agents! I take up this question in chapter 13. On the fundamental question of whether real rates drive nominal rates, or vice versa, I am with Keynes and for vice versa.

14. A "zero-coupon" bond is a bond that pays no periodic interest, its yield being the annualized difference between the purchase price and the redemption value at maturity. T-bills are short-term, zero-coupon bonds. The empirical appendix to chapter 12 makes extensive use of zero-coupon bonds.

15. Negative bond yields have become a reality. Except for a short period during 2018, Swiss government 10-year bonds have been in negative territory continuously since 2015. The 10-year German *bund* danced around zero through much of 2016 and went negative in 2019. Even private companies have been able to borrow long term at negative rates.

There are obvious limits. Were nominal rates to spiral downward, the inconvenience of holding cash would eventually be outweighed by the nominal yield of zero on cash; cash would once again be king. To dethrone the king permanently, cash would have to lose value over time, like Silvio Gesell's stamped money. According to Keynes (*The General Theory,* pp. 353–358), Gesell, as a means of stimulating investment, proposed that a cost be imposed on holding money by a periodic requirement for stamps to be affixed to money to maintain its nominal value. The cost of a stamp would in effect impose a negative return on money held as a store of value. Ignoring the inconvenience of cash and the risk of bonds, to compete with stamped cash, bonds would need only to incur a smaller annual loss than the cost of a stamp. If the stamp for a one-dollar bill cost three cents, any negative bond yield closer to zero than −3 percent would be sufficient to drive people from cash to bonds.

16. Fisher himself was aware of the importance of expectations, and while a main point of his argument in *Appreciation and Interest* was to argue for the validity of the classical dichotomy in the long run, he recognized that in the short-run expectations play an independent role in determining real interest rates. He even

made expectations and their sluggish adjustment the centerpiece of his own theory of fluctuations (Dimand and Betancourt 2012).

17. Not quite always. See Tables 4.6 and 4.7 in chapter 4.

Chapter 7 Mathematical Appendix

1. Evidently, we could replace equation (7.1) by the wage equation

$$
\frac{\dot{W}}{W} = \theta_3 \left[Y - LS\left(\frac{P}{W} \right) \right],
$$

since equation (7.1) is obtained by subtracting the above equation from equation (7.3).

2. Joseph Schumpeter applied his ideas of creative destruction to find the silver lining in the Depression:

Now we have had combines and dry farming, more efficient methods of producing electricity, rayon and motors and radios, and a thousand similar things. This is really at the bottom of the recurrent troubles of capitalist society. They are but temporary. They are the means to reconstruct each time the economic system on a more efficient plan. But they inflict losses while they last, drive firms into the bankruptcy court, throw people out of employment, before the ground is clear and the way paved for new achievement of the kind which has created modern civilization and made the greatness of this country. (1934, p. 13)

According to Herbert Hoover (1952, p. 30), his Treasury Secretary, Andrew Mellon, advised:

Liquidate labor, liquidate stocks, liquidate the farmers, liquidate real estate . . . It will purge the rottenness out of the system. High costs of living and high living will come down. People will work harder, live a more moral life. Values will be adjusted, and enterprising people will pick up the wrecks from less competent people.

Both Laurence Ball (2018, chap. 12) and Barry Eichengreen (2015, p. 6) suggest that the same spirit animated the government's decision to allow Lehman Brothers to fail in 2008.

Chapter 8

Epigraphs: Roosevelt 1933; Hoover 1952, p. 195.

1. Creditors received no offsetting windfall unless they consumed wheat, cotton, and other farm products disproportionately. Their real returns were governed by changes in the overall price level, of the order of 10 percent annually over the critical period 1930 to 1932, not the 30+ percent premium that farmers paid.

2. In the first phase of the Depression, the shift in the composition of deposits in favor of time deposits reduced reserve requirements since time deposits carried a

much lower reserve requirement (3 percent) than did demand deposits (from 7 to 13 percent). By contrast, from 1931 on, deposits—both demand deposits and time deposits—and reserves contracted sharply, but deposits declined faster than reserves.

Reserve requirements on demand deposits also varied with bank location. Banks in central reserve cities were required to maintain a reserve ratio of 13 percent, banks in reserve cities 10 percent, and country banks 7 percent. All banks, irrespective of location, were required to hold reserves equal to 3 percent of time deposits (Goodfriend and Hargraves 1983, p. 11).

3. In his discussion of liquidity preference, Keynes says

> There is the possibility . . . that, after the rate of interest has fallen to a certain level, liquidity-preference may become virtually absolute in the sense that almost everyone prefers cash to holding a debt which yields so low a rate of interest . . . Whilst this limiting case might become practically important in future, I know of no example of it hitherto (*The General Theory*, p. 207).

Richard Sutch (2018) has argued persuasively that Keynes's meaning here of what came to be called the liquidity trap is not the meaning now ascribed to this concept, namely, the gap between the T-bill rate and the hurdle rate as the bill rate approaches its zero lower bound. See chapter 12.

4. For historical reasons peculiar to the United States, the Federal Reserve was not only a latecomer to the ranks of central banks, but only became a full-fledged central bank in stages, and the process was not complete when the Depression struck. (See Roger Lowenstein's account of the creation, 2015.) In the period from 1929 to 1933, the Fed was much more fragmented in its governance than the post-Depression Fed; much more power lay with the individual Federal Reserve Banks, twelve of them. The New York Fed was the most influential but lacked the power to force concerted action by the other banks. These institutional peculiarities compounded the constraint posed by the gold standard, though for the United States, as distinct from Great Britain, Germany, and Austria, the constraint was essentially psychological.

The psychology of central banking was shaped by the real-bills doctrine (see chapter 7). As Eichengreen points out (2015, p. 2):

> Central bankers, for their part, were in thrall to the real bills doctrine, the idea that they should provide only as much credit as was required for the legitimate needs of business. They supplied more credit when business was expanding and less when it slumped, accentuating booms and busts. Neglecting their responsibility for financial stability, they failed to intervene as lenders of last resort. The result was cascading bank failures, starving business of credit. Prices were allowed to collapse, rendering debts unmanageable.

5. For a more systematic view of the holes in Friedman and Schwartz's argument, a good starting point is Peter Temin's 1976 *Did Monetary Forces Cause the Great Depression?* Temin finds little support for Friedman and Schwartz in the data. He

favors what he calls the spending hypothesis, basically the failure of aggregate demand, not because the data overwhelmingly support this view but because it remains the plausible alternative after the shortcomings of the Friedman–Schwartz analysis are exposed. Eichengreen's 2015 account of how the Depression unfolded provides no more comfort for Friedman and Schwartz than does Temin.

6. This theory is modified in chapters 11, 12, and 13 in ways which give more agency to central banks in determining hurdle rates of interest.

7. Remember that we are not talking about the miniscule share of the U.S. economy of agriculture in 2020; agricultural employment came to almost 23 percent of total employment in 1929, and over 25 percent in 1932; and output was more than 10 percent of GDP in 1929, and close to 15 percent in 1933 (at 1929 prices).

8. In the summer of 1936, Galbraith was recruited to explain economics to Henry Dennison, one of a small number of businessmen who saw good in Roosevelt's New Deal. Dennison's idea was to collaborate with like-minded industrialists to write a book supporting FDR, and Galbraith was to provide the heavy economic artillery. The problem for Galbraith was that Dennison had his own ideas, which veered toward the unorthodox, especially in his intuitive grasp, *avant la lettre,* of the central idea of *The General Theory,* namely, the crucial role of aggregate demand. As Galbraith writes,

> In the very same weeks that I was writing my brief for my views on competition, I was reading *The General Theory.* As I did, I discovered that Keynes was with Dennison and not with me . . . I was shaken. This was not the primitive instinct of a businessman; this was the sophisticated case of a greatly renowned economist. (1981, p. 65)

Galbraith quickly came to embrace Keynes and *The General Theory* and later became an important advocate for demand management. But his conversion makes a main point of chapter 1 clearer, namely, that to justify active demand management nothing less than an all-out attack on the received doctrine, one that went well beyond the superficialities of frictions and market structure, would do. Given the hegemony of the belief in the fundamental resilience and beneficence of markets, it had to be shown that even competitive markets were defective when it came to providing jobs.

Keynes provided no explanation for the agricultural anomaly; indeed, he never took note of it. Likely this was because of the relative unimportance of agriculture to the British economy; Britain relied mostly on imports for food and fiber. One can only wonder whether the distinct behavior of a family-farm sector would have made more of an impression on Keynes if he had lived in the United States (or France), where the family farm persisted until mid-century.

9. Even though the Great Plains did not do so well when it came to the weather. The drought that began in 1933 gave rise to a new name for the region: Dust Bowl.

10. The figures in Table 8.1 likely overstate the role of hired help in the farm economy. The explanatory notes for this table state that to be counted as a family worker, the family member had to put in fifteen hours or more per week, whereas one hour

per week was sufficient to be counted as hired labor (Bureau of the Census 1975, p. 453).

The role of hired labor varied markedly from one part of the country to another. According to the reporting farmers on whom the Crop Reporting Board of the Department of Agriculture relied, between one-half and two-thirds of farm workers were hired hands in the states bordering on the Pacific (sometimes referred to in Board reports as the Far Western region, sometimes as the Pacific region); in other parts of the country, the figure was below one-third. See, for example, Crop Reporting Board, Bureau of Agricultural Economics, U.S. Department of Agriculture, "Farm Wage Rates and Related Data, April 1, 1933, with Comparisons" (USDA, Washington, D.C., April 11, 1933 [mimeo]), http://usda.mannlib.cornell.edu/MannUsda/viewDocumentInfo.do?documentID=1063 (accessed November 1, 2017).

11. As paraphrased by Lorie Tarshis, Keynes's lectures to Cambridge undergraduates during the years leading up to *The General Theory* made the essential institutional distinction:

> If we could have a society in which the employer would feel responsible for the employee, whether he was working or not, you wouldn't have to worry about unemployment. If the employer had to pay a worker's wage or salary whether there was work for him or not, he would be working. (Colander and Landreth 1996, p. 60)

12. Some excerpts from the Crop Reporting Board's summaries of farm-labor conditions:

> On April 1 [1930], all classes of [agricultural] wages . . . were at the lowest level since 1923. This is a reflection of the large supply of farm labor due to the small volume of industrial employment at the present time. ("Farm Labor and Wages, April 1, 1930, with Comparisons," April 9, 1930, p. 1)

> The supply of farm labor in per cent of normal was reported on January 1 [1932] 120.9%, and demand at 60.5%. Supply expressed as a per cent of demand was 199.8, which is the highest ratio recorded since the beginning of the record in 1918.
>
> Reports received by the Department particularly in the North Central States contain numerous instances where farm laborers are working for board and lodging alone. ("Farm Labor and Wages, January 1, 1932, with Comparisons," January 18, 1932, p. 1)

> Reports from crop correspondents indicated a supply of farm labor 125.8 per cent of normal on the first of the month [April, 1933] as compared with a supply 122.2 per cent of normal a year earlier. The larger supply was related, in turn, to the reduced level of employment in manufacturing industries. ("Farm Wage Rates and Related Data, April 1, 1933, with Comparisons," April 11, 1933 [mimeo], p. 5)

http://usda.mannlib.cornell.edu/MannUsda/viewDocumentInfo.do?documentID=1063 (accessed November 1, 2017).

While the Crop Reporting Board focuses on hired labor, the same process brought thousands of unemployed industrial workers back to the family farms they had left when factories were humming.

13. In principle, the economy is the world, because the essence of the model is the endogenous determination of the relative prices of agricultural and industrial goods. For this we need a closed economy. The actual economy of the pre–World War II United States was a mix: parts of the agricultural economy were very open—see below—whereas the industrial economy was virtually closed.

14. Once we disaggregate, even to the limited extent of a two-sector model, there is a demand schedule for industrial goods, and there is a food-demand schedule—see below—but there is no such thing as an AD schedule.

15. U.S. stocks of wheat at the end of the harvest season more than doubled between 1929 and 1932, from 28 percent of 1929 production to 50 percent of the slightly smaller production in 1932 (Bureau of the Census 1975, table K 509). Worldwide, wheat stocks increased from an average 13 percent of output over the years 1922 to 1929 to 18 percent over the years 1930 to 1932 (Farnsworth 1940, p. 63, for stocks; Federal Reserve Bank of St. Louis for production, https://fred.stlouisfed .org/series/A010131WA393NNBR, accessed May 23, 2019). The U.S. stock of cotton quadrupled between 1929 and 1932, rising from 15 percent of production to 75 percent (Bureau of the Census 1975, table K 556). Nineteen thirty-two is the appropriate reference year, because New Deal programs restricting output kicked in during 1933.

16. The same thing will happen if the propensity to save rises, which Peter Temin (1976) and Frederic Mishkin (1978) emphasize in their accounts of the downturn. The emphasis on falling consumption as the driver of the 1930 downturn is supported by Robert Shiller's account of the role of the stock market crash of 1929 on consumer psychology (2017, esp. pp. 988–994).

17. This is a form of "immiserizing growth" (Jagdish Bhagwati [1958]); Frederic Pryor (2007) provides an overview to a literature going back in its modern form to Harry Johnson (1955). The novelty of the present argument is twofold. Here growth is immiserizing all around, not just for the growing economy. Moreover, the institutional set-up is different.

18. The AAA was declared unconstitutional by the Supreme Court in 1936. It was revived in 1937 with a work-around to overcome the constitutional objection.

19. After a period of fluctuating gold prices and exchange rates, the Gold Reserve Act, signed into law by Roosevelt on January 30, 1934, authorized the president to fix a new parity. The price fixed by Roosevelt the next day, $35.00 per ounce, was 1.69 times the old parity. (It remained in effect until the United States broke the link to gold altogether in 1971.) The U.S. Treasury held a large share of the world's gold supply and was prepared to buy and sell gold to all comers—provided they were not domiciled in the United States Americans were prohibited from owning golds apart from ornamental and industrial uses.

20. Some if not all of the increase in the price of corn was weather related. Production in 1933 was almost 20 percent below 1932 (Bureau of the Census 1935, table 613).

Chapter 9

Epigraph: Keynes, *The General Theory,* p. 96.

1. For reasons that remain mysterious, Samuelson refuses to call this a long-run consumption function. A footnote offers this explanation:

   > Some might choose to interpret [this locus] as a very long-run consumption function, although I myself would not. Even if regarded as such, the fact that it does not show an increased percentage of saving as income rises does not in any way vitiate the application of the usual saving-investment analysis. It is necessary to emphasize this because in some quarters Prof. Kuznets's historical findings are taken as disproving the Hansen–Keynes long-run analysis [namely, a declining ratio of consumption to income]. (1943, p. 36)

2. Keynes differed. Though he believed that over a longer period of time the demand for investment would fall below full-employment saving, he viewed the immediate postwar period as one in which investment demand would outstrip full-employment saving ("The Long-Term Problem of Full Employment" and reply to Josiah Wedgewood, in Keynes 1980, pp. 320–325 and 350–351). To be sure, Keynes's focus was on the United Kingdom, and Samuelson's on the United States, but it is not clear that this is the source of the difference. Curiously, Samuelson punts on the question of deficit spending as a means of bridging the investment-saving gap, referring his readers to another article in the book (by Seymour Harris) on the public debt, while at the same time suggesting that "careful thought should be given to the alternative of the controlled issuance of noninterest-bearing debt" (1943, p. 43).

3. Evidently, a poorly paid sports star. No doubt because of gender: this sports star is assumed to be female.

4. If the rate of interest is positive instead of zero, consumption will optimally increase with time, in line with the rate of interest. Moreover, the consumption profile will depend on when income is earned as well as on total lifetime earnings.

5. Age forty-two is chosen for convenience because both the representative agent of Figure 8 and the sports star of Figure 9 have identical incomes in that year. Both are at the midpoints of their careers, earning approximately $86,000.

6. See especially Robert Hall (1978), who brought the argument into the rational-expectations framework.

7. For this reason Keynes was doubtful about the ability of temporary tax cuts to stimulate consumption. In arguing with James Meade in "The Maintenance of Full Employment" (the heading of his memo) about the potential role of countercyclical fiscal policy in postwar Britain, Keynes expands the point made in *The General Theory* about the role of habit:

   > People have established standards of life. Nothing will upset them more than to be subject to pressure constantly to vary them up and down. A remission of taxation on which people could only rely for an indefinitely short period might have very limited effects in stimulating their consumption. (Keynes to Meade, April 25, 1943, in Keynes 1980, p. 319)

For Keynes the unresponsiveness of consumption to temporary changes in disposable income was a reason to modify the "fundamental psychological law" of *The General Theory* "that men are disposed, as a rule and on the average, to increase their consumption as their income increases, but not by as much as the increase in their income" (p. 96). For Modigliani and Friedman, this unresponsiveness was a reason to jettison Keynes's framework.

8. In the interwar years of the twentieth century, probability was recast as subjective in nature rather than as an objective distribution based on empirical frequencies, precisely to overcome the risk-uncertainty distinction. Subjective probability caught hold from midcentury onward as a means of defending the identification of microeconomic general equilibrium with an efficient allocation of resources. It is another thing altogether to argue that people actually make decisions this way.

9. One percent of the population would be easy to ignore if we were interested only in the determination of aggregate consumption. However, the other side of the coin is saving, and this particular 1 percent does the lion's share of the personal saving.

10. Saez's data comes from Internal Revenue Service records, the Census Bureau's from household and family surveys. The data are not strictly comparable, hence the wide range in the estimates of income shares. Census Bureau data estimate the 2012 threshold of the top 5 percent at just over $190,000 for households, and at $210,000 for families. The 2012 share of the top 5 percent, according to Census Bureau data is just over 20 percent, whether for families or for households, slightly higher for households than for families (Bureau of the Census 2019a). This is the income share that Saez attributes, on the basis of IRS data, to the top 1 percent of the distribution.

11. Labor income apart, until the refi era, working-class households found it difficult to tap into their main source of wealth, namely, the equity in their homes, even if this was what their optimal consumption plan dictated. Exceptionally, during the housing boom that preceded the crash of 2008—to which mortgage refinancing was at the very least an important contributing factor—working-class as well as more affluent households were able to convert housing equity into cash and spend it on current consumption.

12. Assuming that changes in money wages are determined solely by an LS schedule dictates that inflation can occur only when there is excess demand for labor. The simplest assumption is that the overfull employment at the inflationary equilibria in Figures 9.18 and 9.19 is achieved through compulsory overtime. An alternative is to redefine the LS schedule as a stationary money-wage locus along which there is a positive rate of involuntary unemployment. The issue of wages and employment is at the heart of the theory of the long run presented in chapters 17, 18, and 19. (Observe that the possibility of an inflationary equilibrium does not require the complications introduced by the Cambridge saving theory; it exists in the simpler models of chapters 6 through 8, where saving depends only on income, not its distribution.)

13. To be sure, working-class saving is no longer identified with the traditional work-

ing class. That class is left out of the picture altogether, presumably on the grounds that, though far wealthier than the working class of Adam Smith's, David Ricardo's, or Karl Marx's times, it is still without the means to accumulate assets within the capitalist sector, managing at best gradually to become homeowners. "Workers" in a Piketty-type model are a "patrimonial middle class" (2014, p. 373), a class of executives, managers, professionals, and bureaucrats reminiscent of John Kenneth Galbraith's "technostructure" (1967). Capitalists, as in the original Cambridge model, are a class of rentiers who rely solely on profits for their income.

Chapter 10

Epigraph: Keynes 1937a, p. 221.

1. Keynes well understood the difference, as witness his remark:

    > An act of individual saving means—so to speak—a decision not to have dinner to-day. But it does not necessitate a decision to have dinner or to buy a pair of boots a week hence or a year hence or to consume any specified thing at any specified date. Thus it depresses the business of preparing to-day's dinner without stimulating the business of making ready for some future act of consumption. (*The General Theory,* p. 210)

    But he was wrong in thinking that this distinction by itself refuted Say's Law. See chapter 2.

2. "Have you heard of the wonderful one-hoss-shay,
    That was built in such a logical way?
    It ran a hundred years to a day, . . ."
    ("The Wonderful 'One Hoss Shay,'" by Oliver Wendell Holmes, 1858)

3. Alas, the data do not appear to support this hypothesis. Q is not correlated with interest rates, even after introducing appropriate controls. Moreover, the data suggest that, from the mid-1990s on, Tobin's Q substitutes for monetary policy rather than jointly determining residential construction. The visual impression that make versus buy became important only in the mid-1990s is borne out by time-series regressions: nominal mortgage rates are highly correlated with residential construction until 1995, and Q is not. After 1990, this situation is reversed: mortgage rates no longer appear to matter, whereas Tobin's Q seems to drive homebuilding single handedly.

4. The distinction between capital widening and capital deepening appears to have originated with Ralph Hawtrey (1937, p. 36):

    > The widening of the capital equipment means the extension of productive capacity by the flotation of new enterprises, or the expansion of existing enterprises without any change in the amount of capital employed for each unit of output. The deepening means an increase in the amount of capital employed for each unit of output.

5. I should perhaps make it clear that I posit this simple characterization of investment for one purpose only: to drive home the difference between capital deepening and capital widening.

6. Empirical estimates of the elasticity of substitution, conventionally denoted by σ, generally lie in a range well below one. A compelling theoretical argument for assuming $\sigma < 1$ is that the opposite assumption, $\sigma > 1$, leads to the odd result that only a single input, capital *or* labor, is required for production.

7. Behavioral economics has repeatedly shown that the maximization postulate is not only unnecessary but also counterproductive if all we wish to do is to describe how the economy actually works. And for almost half a century microeconomics has recognized that the assumption of utility maximization poses virtually no constraints on the shapes of individual demand functions.

8. Keynes was later persuaded otherwise, apparently by Ramsey.

9. If Tversky had not died, he would, I presume, have shared Kahneman's Nobel Prize. Allais also received a Nobel. Ellsberg narrowly escaped prison—not for his theory, but for leaking the Pentagon Papers.

   To be fair, some pioneers of decision theory—the names of Howard Raiffa and Savage himself spring to mind—never regarded consistency with the Savage axioms as innate. Generations of students have paid, and are still paying, good money to the leading business schools of the world to learn how to apply probabilities consistently. I do not wish even to hint that students don't get their money's worth, but I am very skeptical about how much their ability to deal with uncertainty is enhanced.

   For the purest of pure theorists, molded by Milton Friedman's positivism (1953), it does not matter whether individuals consciously calculate the subjective-probability distributions required by the theory. Just as with utility maximization uncomplicated by probabilities, "as if" behavior will do just fine.

10. High mainstream theory makes use of subjective probabilities with regard to the motives and choices underlying saving rather than investment. In fact, the most sophisticated theory, due to Kenneth Arrow and Gerard Debreu (1954), denies any role to the investor's state of mind. This theory teams up the states of mind of individuals as *consumers* with the idea of complete contingent markets. Decisions on saving require subjective probability calculations about the likelihood of different states of the world. These decisions are reflected in the purchase of consumption claims contingent on which potential state of the world is actually realized; saving thus does not require agents to hold physical capital to back their hunches about the future. In this model, investment responds to objective prices attached to goods in different states of the world, not to subjective utilities and probabilities. The assumption that these states are objectively describable removes all vagueness from future-project returns—the state of the world completely and uniquely determines investment returns—and the prices of contingent claims associated with particular states of the world guide the firm's investment decisions.

   Although the stock market, as Peter Diamond showed in a seminal paper half a century ago (1967), can in principle play the role of a universal contingent market, the number of companies that would be required to span the economically relevant states of the world is beyond the capacity of stock markets to list, financial experts to analyze, or computers to store in memory.

In practice, contingent markets are the exception rather than the rule, materializing only under unusual circumstances; otherwise opinions about the future are backed not by the purchase of contingent commodities but by commitments to particular forms of capital, by *investment*. In practice, firms' investment decisions are guided not by objective market prices but by prospective investment returns and associated hunches about the possibilities of realizing these returns, seen through a glass, darkly.

11. In this, Keynes had an unlikely ally. Well before Keynes extolled animal spirits in *The General Theory,* Joseph Schumpeter published *The Theory of Economic Development,* in which he wrote,

> As military action must be taken in a given strategic position even if all the data potentially procurable are not available, so also in economic life action must be taken without working out all the details of what is to be done. Here the success of everything depends upon intuition, the capacity of seeing things in a way which afterwards proves to be true, even though it cannot be established at the moment, and of grasping the essential fact, discarding the unessential, even though one can give no account of the principles by which this is done. Thorough preparatory work, and special knowledge, breadth of intellectual understanding, talent for logical analysis, may under certain circumstances be sources of failure. (1961 [1912], p. 85)

Chapter 11

Epigraphs: Keynes 1934, p. 850; 1937a, pp. 215–216; 1937b, p. 250.

1. Greg Mankiw characterizes the loanable-funds market as the financial market of a (simplified) economy to which "all savers go . . . to deposit their [current] saving, and all borrowers go to take out their loans . . . [Current] *saving is the source of the supply of loanable funds*" (2018, p. 549–550; italics in original). Loans in this model are for adding to the real capital stock, that is, for investment: *"investment is the source of the demand for loanable funds"* (2018, p. 550; italics in original). For Mankiw, "saving" is the excess over and above an agent's own investment, and "investment" is the excess over and above an agent's own saving, but it does no harm to assume that saving and investment are carried out by different agents, so that the investment on the part of savers is zero, as is saving on the part of agents who invest, that is, who add to the physical stock of capital.

Paul Krugman and Robin Wells (2018, pp. 706–715) generally agree with Mankiw's exposition of loanable funds. But when they discuss interest-rate equalization across national financial markets (pp. 711–714), they veer over toward the Keynesian notion of interest rates clearing markets for financial assets rather than flows of saving and investment.

William Baumol, Alan Blinder, and John Solow, wisely in my judgment, avoid the concept of loanable funds altogether in their text (2020), as do Robert Frank and Ben Bernanke (2007). At least neither textbook contains an entry for loanable funds in its index or glossary.

2. What about combining the two views by bringing saving and investment into the determination of interest rates in asset markets? Chapter 2 (note 11) observed that the separation between the finance literature, which focuses on asset markets as the site of interest-rate determination, and the macro literature, for which the saving-investment nexus is the focus, has been breached in this century (Gürkaynak and Wright 2012, sec. 4.1). A case can be made for bringing macro-economic variables into agents' demands for financial assets, but this is a far cry from investment and saving *determining* interest rates.

3. As we shall see in the next chapter, the calculations become more difficult when there are a variety of financial assets available. Young agents might opt for T-bills if bills pay a premium over the long-dated bonds that dovetail more closely with their retirement plans.

4. An analogy with the determination of exchange rates may be helpful. Are exchange rates determined by the balance of trade or by the balancing of asset portfolios? Once again, the statistics are orders of magnitude apart. Foreign trade, measured by exports, imports, or the balance of trade pale in comparison with the volume of transactions on foreign exchange markets. In 2010, U.S. exports and imports were of the order of $2 trillion, and the trade deficit of the order of $500 billion, while transactions of U.S. dollars against other currencies on the spot market alone averaged over $1 trillion per *day* for April of that year (data from Bank for International Settlements 2010, table E-1).

5. Consols, short for consolidated annuities, were first introduced in the mid-eighteenth century by the British government to consolidate the many outstanding debt issues into a single uniform security. Consols remained an important part of British public debt into the twentieth century. The last outstanding consols were redeemed in 2015 (HM Treasury and The Rt Hon George Osborne 2015).

6. Wells Fargo has since updated its recommendations. Its current website advises "investors to set aside the equivalent of at least 3 to 6 months of living expenses in an emergency fund." It also clarifies the meaning of cash:

> By "cash," we don't mean just dollar bills or even the money in your checking account. We use the term as shorthand for a spectrum of assets that have typically been very stable in value and can usually be liquidated quickly when you need to cover an expense. Short-term Treasury bills and money market funds are classic examples. (2019)

The latest guidelines make no reference to the 3 percent rule, perhaps because the bank's investment-advising section is trying to expand its client base: for 3 percent of wealth to cover six months of spending requires total wealth to be 16.7 times annual expenditure, which is true only of high-wealth individuals (and misers).

7. Keynes actually fudges the distinction between speculation and precaution. He includes holding cash against "unforeseen opportunities of advantageous purchases," in his characterization of the precautionary motive (*The General Theory*, p. 190), a reason my taxonomy attributes to speculation rather than to precaution, because it makes the demand for money sensitive to the interest rate.

In the end, the focus on speculation is not necessary to Keynes's argument. We could assimilate the precautionary motive, and the retirement motive as well, to speculation, and assume all three motives involve agents who are sensitive to a trade-off between the returns available from tying up their funds in illiquid assets and the potential for capital losses on these assets.

8. In the *Treatise on Money,* Keynes conflates bid-ask liquidity with price-fluctuation liquidity. One asset is more liquid than another if it is "more certainly realisable at short notice without loss" (1930, vol. 2, p. 67). "Short notice" invokes bid-ask liquidity, "without loss" price fluctuations.

9. In short, Keynes would have had no reason to deny the relevance of bid-ask liquidity, but would regard it as a friction of the kind he was at pains to minimize.

10. U.S. T-bonds and notes pay a semi-annual coupon, but it is simpler to assume the coupon is paid once a year.

11. Strictly speaking, the "yield to maturity" does not exist for a consol since consols never mature. The obvious substitute is the limiting value of the yield to maturity as the maturity date increases without bound.

12. People who hold wealth against a rainy day or to prepare for retirement face a similar issue of the choice of an appropriate horizon. For precautionary wealth holders, the issue is the same as for speculators: they don't know when they will need to tap into their wealth.

   Retirement poses a different issue if we suppose that people have a reasonably good idea of when they will retire, and at least probabilistic knowledge of the time span of their retirement. But in a model with only cash and consols, agents cannot tailor their portfolios to this knowledge. Consols, unlike bonds chosen with their maturity dates corresponding to the projected retirement period, involve the same price risks as they do for speculators. Like speculators, agents whose portfolios are geared to retirement may be assumed to trade the potential gains of holding consols against the variability of consol prices, but the holding yields would be measured over decades rather than over a year or instantaneously.

13. Again we confine ourselves to consols. For bonds with finite maturity dates, price fluctuations will not be centered on zero even without expectations of reversion to normal. See the empirical appendix to chapter 12.

14. A representative-agent model is one with identical agents—same preferences and same endowments. For some purposes, representative-agent models simplify the analysis greatly without much loss of generality. But here not: as the following section ("Bulls and Bears") shows, agent diversity makes the normal-reversion liquidity-preference schedule slope downward.

15. Two percent may seem a very modest annual risk, but over ten years it amounts to nearly a 20 percent probability of default. (The exact risk is $1 - (.98)^{10} = 0.18$ if default in any one year is independent of previous years.)

Chapter 12

Epigraphs: Robertson 1935, p. 499; Samuelson 1947, pp. 122–123.

1. Why aren't short-term bank loans included as substitutes for the short-term paper charted in Figure 12.2? The answer lies in the form of illiquidity introduced in

chapter 11 only to be put to one side, namely, bid-ask illiquidity. Bank loans are generally too idiosyncratic to command the dense markets necessary to eliminate this kind of risk. Securitization—see chapter 4—is a way of overcoming at least some of the idiosyncrasies of individual bank loans, but it is an imperfect way.

2. Jacob Viner (1936), in the critical passage on liquidity preference cited in chapter 11, likely had such agents in mind when he argued that holding long bonds through thick and thin would be the preferred strategy in the face of fluctuating yields. Franco Modigliani and Richard Sutch (1966) distinguished agents according to "preferred habitats," their way of characterizing the time horizons of different agents. Joseph Stiglitz (1970) developed a theoretical framework for analyzing portfolio management in the context of choosing an optimal consumption profile. In this framework, risk aversion can work both ways, leading to a premium on short-dated assets or on long-dated assets. John Campbell, working with various collaborators, revisited the problem of time horizon; see Campbell and Luis Viceira (2002).

3. If your inflation expectations exceed the expectations reflected in current bond yields, bills may be a better bet than bonds even if you have a long horizon.

4. Winston W. Chang, Daniel Hamberg, and Junichi Hirata (1983) hold the same view as I do with regard to the short-term options available to agents in choosing asset portfolios. Chang et al. demonstrate that with short-term riskless bills yielding a positive return, optimization precludes holding money. Their argument is limited to deriving asset demands as functions of interest rates; they do not investigate the properties of asset-market equilibrium, specifically the property that equilibrium determines the spread between bond and bill rates, not their levels. I am grateful to Korkut Alp Erturk for this reference.

   Subsequently, Ben Friedman referred me to earlier work by Albert Ando and Karl Shell (1975). Ando and Shell recognize that, from the point of view of a store of value, short-term bills dominate cash, but like Hicks (see chapter 13) they assume that at the margin this dominance is offset by the convenience/cost advantages of holding cash, given that as a medium of exchange cash dominates any other asset.

5. Until we take up the important monetary-policy response to the Great Recession, namely, quantitative easing.

6. Richard Sutch (2018) is exceptional in distinguishing the two definitions of the liquidity trap. I am persuaded by Sutch that confusion between these two definitions is responsible for the puzzlement surrounding Keynes's assertion that a liquidity trap—not Keynes's terminology—is of more theoretical than practical interest:

   Whilst this limiting case might become practically important in future, I know of no example of it hitherto. (*The General Theory,* p. 207)

   Since Keynes does not use the terminology of a liquidity trap, it is not precisely clear what he means by "this limiting case." But the context suggests, as Sutch argues, that he is referring to a floor to the hurdle rate of interest, not to the bill rate itself approaching zero. Readers who think of a liquidity trap in terms of the behavior of bond yields when the bill rate is at the zlb would necessarily be puzzled:

the short-term (U.S.) T-bill rate had reached the zlb in 1932, and except for a brief period in 1933 had stayed near zero while *The General Theory* was in preparation (and for many years thereafter).

7. Robertson's letter included a number of criticisms of *The General Theory* draft to which Keynes did respond, but he overlooked this one. To the best of my knowledge, Keynes never did counter Robertson on this point. Robertson went on to present other criticisms of the liquidity-preference theory of interest (for example, 1937), but none was as cogent and on the mark. Never acknowledged by Keynes and apparently forgotten by Robertson, Robertson's 1935 criticism seems to have surfaced only when Keynes's *Collected Works* was published in 1980.

8. Agents' time horizons are crucial here. It has been noted that in a world of long-horizon risk aversion, the short-term bill is more risky than the long-term bond. If long horizons dominated, we would expect an inverted yield curve to be the rule rather than the exception. If we assume away risk aversion, agents' time horizons no longer matter. If portfolio choice is grounded only in normal reversion, the issue becomes trading off the loss of principal against interest income, and the time horizon is irrelevant: long-horizon agents will make the same calculations as short-horizon agents.

9. It is not only private issuers of debt who may default but any issuer not in control of the currency in which the debt is denominated. U.S. states and municipalities, not to mention the otherwise sovereign countries that make up the Eurozone, are all subject to default risk. The contrast is with dollar bonds issued by the U.S. Treasury, or for that matter yen bonds issued by the Japanese government, or sterling bonds issued by the United Kingdom.

   A disclaimer is in order. In the summer of 2011, in order to extract concessions from President Obama, the Republican controlled House of Representatives delayed extension of the debt limit to the last minute, arousing fears of a default. The assumption that default is precluded if debt is issued in a currency controlled by the issuer needs to be qualified to exclude governments divided against themselves with at least one party playing with fire.

10. This difference varied between 1.2 and 2.8 percent, averaging just under 1.7 percent. I am here measuring default risk by the difference between yields to maturity on 30-year U.S. T-bonds and Moody's index of long-term Baa-rated corporate bonds. This index is based on seasoned bonds with remaining maturities of at least twenty years with maturities above twenty years (Federal Reserve Bank of St. Louis 2020). When I checked with Moody's Analytics in 2013 (personal communication, November 15, 2013), the average maturity of the index was twenty-eight years.

Chapter 12 Mathematical Appendix

1. This is to say that agents have less risk aversion the more their portfolios are committed to money, with expected wealth decreasing by just enough to offset the reduction in risk while maintaining the same level of utility.

2. This is a simplification of course. A more general formulation would be to treat all

bonds and bills as partial substitutes in a general-equilibrium framework. But the relatively small size of the corporate bond market justifies a sequential framework in which the Treasury yield is determined first. In 2018, the average volume of daily trading in Treasuries ($547.8 billion) was seventeen times the volume of corporate bond trading ($31.5 billion) (Securities Industry and Financial Markets Association 2020).

Chapter 12 Empirical Appendix

1. Campbell's negative conclusions themselves were hardly novel. A quarter century before Campbell, Ed Kane (1970) wrote

    It is generally agreed that, *ceteris paribus,* the fertility of a field is roughly proportional to the quantity of manure that has been dumped upon it in the recent past. By this standard, the term structure of interest rates has become . . . an extraordinarily fertile field indeed. (p. 361)

    In 1989 Kenneth Froot offered pretty much the same assessment, although his language was considerably less colorful:

    If the attractiveness of an economic hypothesis is measured by the number of papers which statistically reject it, the expectations theory of the term structure is a knockout. (p. 283)

    Nonetheless, the rigor and comprehensiveness of Campbell's analysis make his summary the obvious starting point for assessing the data.

2. It was hardly a shotgun wedding. One of the very first applications of rational expectations was to the relationship of long- and short-term rates (Sargent 1972). The fit between theorizing interest-rate forecasts and rational expectations must have appeared irresistible, love at first sight.

3. Some T-bonds issued in the nineteenth century were called consols, but these bonds were callable (redeemable at the discretion of the Treasury) and so were not really perpetual bonds. Some private railroad bonds issued in the nineteenth and twentieth centuries had maturity dates so far in the future that they might as well have been perpetuities. The West Shore Railroad, whose track was leased for 475 years by the New York Central in the nineteenth century (with an option to renew for another 500 years), issued bonds that were coterminous with the expiration of the initial lease in 2361. The Canadian Pacific Railway also issued perpetual debentures in the nineteenth century. According to the *Toronto Globe and Mail,* C$31 million were still outstanding in 2011 (Mittelstaedt 2012).

    Today the closest financial asset to consols is the preferred stock of public companies. Preferred stock is actually a conditional consol, for which the specified coupon payment can be omitted (or postponed) under certain circumstances.

4. In a world of consols, there is, strictly speaking, no yield to maturity because a consol never matures; hence the definition as a limit. In any case, we have no need for this concept when dealing with consols: the limiting value of the yield to maturity is equal to the coupon yield. In a world of finite-maturity bonds, the yield to maturity plays a separate and distinct role.

5. The analogous condition in the case of consols is a so-called transversality condi-

tion, an externally imposed limiting value for the price of the consol. Without such a transversality condition, there is nothing to prevent an infinitely long price bubble from equating the holding yield on a consol to any given value of the short-term interest rate, which is the optimality condition without a risk premium. For example, suppose the short-term interest rate is fixed at 5 percent. If a consol with a $5 coupon were priced at $200, giving it a coupon yield of 2.5 percent, it can offer a holding yield of 5 percent if it increases in value to $205. In subsequent years, the capital gain would have to be progressively greater than $5 for the holding yield to remain at 5 percent, but there is nothing to prevent this scenario other than the *assumption* that bubbles eventually pop. A transversality condition in effect rules out infinite bubbles.

6. It is of course possible that the expected price change is zero over time, but this requires a fortuitous combination of the rates of change of ρ_s and $\alpha(m)$. For $E(\dot{P})/P$ to equal 0, we must have

$$\frac{R}{P} = \rho_s + \alpha(m) = \text{const.},$$

which is to say that ρ_s must increase over time at exactly the same rate that $\alpha(m)$ is decreasing.

7. I say "might reveal itself" because I have been unable to prove Hicks's conjecture for coupon bonds, though it is clearly true for zero-coupon bonds, about which more below.

8. By separating the interest payments from the repayment of interest, bond dealers have created interest-only and principal-repayment (zero-coupon) bonds in derivatives markets. These derivatives are called STRIPs (for Separate Trading of Registered Interest and Principal of Securities).

9. "Hats" in general denote forecasts, as distinct from actual, unhatted, values.

10. The consistent-forecasting condition obtained by differentiating the definite integral is different from the corresponding derivative of the indefinite integral. The upper limit of integration introduces the term $\hat{\rho}_s(t + m)$. A similar change characterizes the forward-rate condition (below).

11. The forward-rate condition contains no new information since it can be derived from the holding-yield condition and the forecasting-consistency condition. The forward rate is conceptually different from the holding yield even though both reflect short-period returns from long bonds. The holding yield reflects the return to a commitment today with respect to the agent's portfolio over the next ε years, whereas the forward rate reflects a commitment m years hence to hold a bond maturing a further ε years in the future. If the forecast $\hat{\rho}_s(t + m)$ turns out to be accurate, today's forward rate for a point in time m years hence is equal to the holding yield on an $(m + \varepsilon)$-year bond at that future time.

12. When the forward rate is equal to zero, the yield curve itself tells us something about market expectations with respect to short-term rates. In this case equilibrium requires $\rho_s(t + m) + \alpha(m)$ to be equal to zero. With both $\rho_s(t + m)$ and $\alpha(m)$ constrained to be non-negative, this in turn implies $\rho_s(t + m) = \alpha(m) = 0$.

13. Later in this appendix, in the section titled "How Does Inflation Bear on Interest-

Rate Forecasts," we examine in more detail the nexus between the rate of inflation and interest-rate forecasting.

Given the attraction of the Taylor rule (the original statement is John Taylor [1993]), which emphasizes a trade-off between inflation and unemployment in setting the Fed funds rate, another obvious instrument for the bill rate is the unemployment rate. It makes little difference to the results to include this variable as an additional instrument. In fact I do so by default in later regressions, when unemployment is introduced as an explanatory variable for the risk premium α.

14. Though her concerns are very different, Yacine Ait-Sahalia's conclusions (1996) about the actual behavior of the seven-day Eurodollar deposit rate during the period 1973 to 1995 lead to similar results:

> The nonlinear mean-reverting drift pulls the rate back strongly into this middle region whenever it wanders outside (for example, below 4 percent in 1993 and early 1994 or above 17 percent in 1981 to 1982). This makes the process globally stationary . . . (p. 406)
>
> Loosely speaking, markets may become more nervous outside the central region, at both ends of the interest rate spectrum. Market participants may expect the Federal Reserve to credibly return the short-term interest rate to its middle range at some point, but are uncertain about the precise timing of the intervention. This rather speculative interpretation would also be consistent with the strong pull-back drift . . . at either end of the spectrum. (p. 407)

I am indebted to John Campbell for this reference.

15. Table 12.1 indicates the estimate of θ implicit in the value of a_1 is relatively stable with respect to the bond term, except for the shortest maturity of one year. When the bond maturity is between two and ten years, θ varies between 0.0066 and 0.0079, indicating an expectation that the gap between the normal short rate and the actual rate will close by 8 to 10 percent per year.

16. Bonds with maturities longer than ten years were issued in the 1970s, but the data for the full spectrum of maturities up to thirty years is available over from the 1980s.

17. UNRATE is the deviation from the mean unemployment rate (6.43 percent) and AVGMAT is the deviation from the mean average maturity (56.2 months) over the 497 observations.

18. Alan Greenspan, testifying before Congress in February 2005, referred to the failure of the long-bond yields to respond to the increases in short rates during 2004 as a conundrum:

> In this environment, long-term interest rates have trended lower in recent months even as the Federal Reserve has raised the level of the target federal funds rate by 150 basis points. This development contrasts with most experience, which suggests that . . . increasing short-term interest rates are normally accompanied by a rise in longer-term yields. For the moment, the broadly unanticipated behavior of world bond markets remains a conundrum. (Federal Reserve Board 2005)

19. There is also disagreement about what that normal rate might be. In Europe, with the yield on the German 10-year T-bond near zero (April 2015), there was evi-

dently a widespread belief that the new normal was significantly lower than historical experience would suggest. In mid-2014 the economist-journalist Anatole Kaletsky posted this question on his blog:

> What accounts for the rock-bottom levels not only of the overnight interest rates that central banks set directly, but also the long-term rates that depend on the willingness of pension funds, insurers and private investors to tie up their savings for 10 years or more in government bonds? (Kaletsky 2014)

In answering his question, Kaletsky offered as one possibility that the normal rate has fallen:

> If investors were absolutely confident that short-term rates set by the central banks would remain near zero for many years ahead, then the seemingly paltry returns—varying from 2.6 percent down to 0.6 percent—on 10-year bonds issued by the U.S., European and Japanese governments would seem generous. Rational investors would be happy to lock up their money for a decade at these rates.

In other words, reversion to normal is alive and well, but the normal rate itself is not what it used to be.

20. Estimates for 2017 were uniformly higher than what turned out to be the case. The actual Fed Funds rate at the end of 2017 was just below 1.5 percent.

21. These data were made available by Moody's Analytics by special agreement, and the results using these data are reproduced here by permission (Moody's Agreement No. 00043372.0).

22. CORPFRAC is measured by the ratio of two variables extracted from Flow-of-Funds data "Financial Accounts of the United States - Z.1," https://www.federal reserve.gov/releases/z1/20180607/html/default.htm#levels (accessed August 17, 2018). The numerator is Table L.213 Corporate and Foreign Bonds, line 1, Total liabilities. The denominator is the difference between total long-term debt and the long-term debt held by the Federal Reserve:

+ Table L.210 Treasury Securities, line 4, Other Treasury notes, bonds, and TIPS
− Table L.109 Monetary Authority, line 1, Other Treasury securities
+ Table L.211 Agency- and GSE-Backed Securities, line 1, Total liabilities
− Table L.109 Monetary Authority, line 1, Agency- and GSE-backed securities
+ Table L.212 Municipal Securities, line 2, State and local govt. liabilities
− Table L.212 Municipal Securities, line 3, Short term
+ Table L.213 Corporate and Foreign Bonds, line 1, Total liabilities

23. Refet Gürkaynak, Brian Sack, and Jonathan Wright re-estimated this series in 2006, and it is now updated on a continuous basis (https://www.quandl.com/data/FED/SVENY, accessed September 10, 2014).

Chapter 13

Epigraph: Keynes, *The General Theory,* p. 183—the wild duck was borrowed from Henrik Ibsen's play.

1. Predictable needs for cash—a new baby, children going to college, retirement— are another matter.

2. There is actually a third motive for holding money in *The General Theory*: the *precautionary demand* deals with the contingencies of ordinary life, like the ones mentioned above. As I noted in chapter 11, Keynes exhibits some ambivalence about where to place the precautionary demand relative to the transactions and speculative demands. In the end, the precautionary motive is assimilated to the transactions motive and plays no distinct role in the analysis of liquidity preference.

3. Does the money for transactions belong to the agents engaged in production, or is it borrowed from others, either in the commercial-paper market or in the form of bank loans? With the appropriate simplifying assumptions, it doesn't matter. The key assumption is that transactions money is unavailable to satisfy the speculative demand for money. The simplest story is that wealth holders and businessmen and -women are the same people, but they keep their asset money in one pocket and their transactions money in the other. Money deployed for transactions does not enter into wealth portfolios, and vice versa. Money shifts from one pocket to the other according to the needs of trade.

4. Keynes suspected, but could hardly articulate, much less demonstrate, that the virtues of price and wage flexibility might vanish completely if the framework of analysis were a dynamic one. Focusing on real-time change, as the models of chapters 6 and 7 do, rather than the static world of virtual change that was then (and continues to be) the playground of economic theory, in turn up-ends Modigliani.

5. There is a connection between central banking and fractional-reserve banking, but it is not a logical one. On the one hand, a central bank does not presuppose a fractional-reserve banking system—100 percent reserves are a logical possibility, but in practice the set of 100 percent reserve banking systems is an empty one. On the other hand, fractional-reserve banking does not logically require a central bank, nor does it in practice. Indeed, there was fractional-reserve banking long before central banks appeared in Europe or the United States. Neither, in principle, does fractional-reserve banking require the visible hand of the state.

6. One hundred years ago, economists were debating the impact on the quantity theory of the transition from cash money to bank-deposit money, a transition that was still under way in the United States despite the huge steps taken in this direction during the nineteenth century. At its annual meeting in 1911, the American Economics Association held a symposium on the causes of the changes in the price level experienced in the previous decade and a half. Differences of opinion hinged on assumptions about bank behavior with respect to reserves.

   Irving Fisher (1911, p. 38) emphasized the standard interpretation of the quantity theory, in which causality runs from the quantity of money, exogenously given, to the price level. J. Laurence Laughlin, a critic of the quantity theory, argued that causality actually ran in the opposite direction:

   > When the price is fixed, the credit medium by which the commodity is passed from seller to buyer comes easily and naturally into existence . . . That is, the quantity of the actual media of exchange thus brought into use is a result and not a cause of the price-making process. (1911, pp. 29–30)

Implicitly, Laughlin was making the case for endogenous money, by assuming that banks would vary reserve ratios according to the transactions demand for money rather than maintaining constant (fully loaned-up) ratios by moving in and out of speculative assets. Edwin Kemmerer, a third contributor, explicitly recognized the complication that fractional-reserve banking introduced into the quantity theory—only to dismiss it. Gold formed the basis of bank reserves and reserves were, he argued, exogenous. Profit maximization could be counted upon to ensure that reserves were always fully utilized:

> Banks do not make interest on money held in reserves, and accordingly take measures to invest such surplus money, keeping these reserves as low as is consistent with law and their ideas of safety. (1911, p. 56)

Consequently, though banks theoretically can vary reserve ratios, self interest would prevent them from doing so.

The Great Depression settled the question empirically. As was noted in chapter 8, excess reserves grew markedly in 1932 and 1933; in mid-1933 Jacob Viner saw these excess reserves as the result of a self-interested prudence on the part of bankers:

> In the past three years the test of a successful banker has been the rate of speed with which he could go out of the banking business and into the safety-deposit business. Those bankers have survived who have succeeded in the largest degree and at the most rapid rate in converting loans into cash. That has been good banking from the point of view of the individual banker, or of his individual depositors; but from the social point of view it has been disastrous. Which is preferable during a depression—a bank that continues to finance business and thus endangers its solvency, or a bank that acts on the principle that during an acute depression good banking means no banking? The latter have survived the crisis and now have the confidence of the public. They should now be able to serve effectively in taking care of the present needs of business if they are willing to return to the banking business. (1933b, p. 130)

7. Fractional-reserve banking has the potential to segment the demand for money into two noncompeting branches, but it doesn't necessarily do so. The intent of at least some of the framers of the Federal Reserve seems to have been to institutionalize this separation: through the discount window, the Federal Reserve Banks were to provide an "elastic currency" that would accommodate the needs of trade—transactions demand—hermetically sealed off from the speculative demands that operate in asset markets.

8. The Baumol–Tobin theory is consistent with a large amount of data supporting the idea that the demand for transactions money is sensitive to the interest rate, even if the elasticity of transactions demand turns out to be very low. My own regressions for the period 1959 to 2016, in which a narrow definition of money supply is deployed as a proxy for transactions demand, give similar results to those reported by Stephen Goldfeld and Daniel Sichel (1990), among others, for data covering shorter periods of time. Goldfeld and Sichel regressed the real money

supply on real GDP, inflation, and interest rates on time deposits and commercial paper, whereas I use the nominal 3-month T-bill rate along with the first two variables, but the difference in regressors has little impact on the empirical relationship between transactions-money demand and the short-term rate. Observe that for money supply to be a plausible proxy for money demand, it must be assumed that supply adjusts to demand, in other words, that the money supply is created endogenously.

Both my results and the Goldfeld–Sichel results point to considerable inconsistency in the impact of GDP and inflation over time on transactions demand. Most striking is the fall in the estimated interest elasticity of money demand from approximately 20 percent in the decade of monetary turbulence lasting from the mid-1970s to the mid-1980s, to approximately 1 percent in the decade following the financial turmoil of 2008. I would attribute this fall to the decline in the cost and inconvenience of moving between safe, interest-bearing, short-term assets and cash once we entered the age of electronic banking (the rise of money-market funds, daily sweeps from interest-bearing accounts to demand deposits, and the like).

9. In normal times high-quality commercial paper and the money-market funds that own this paper are also safe and liquid. A hallmark of financial crisis is that high-quality commercial paper loses its luster. One leading money-market fund, the Reserve Primary Fund, held close to $800 million of Lehman Brothers' commercial paper when the crash came. Immediately after Lehman's fall and the write-down of this paper (approximately 1 percent of the fund's assets), the Reserve Primary Fund "broke the buck"; it was forced to revalue its shares, normally priced at $1.00, at $0.97. A run on money-market funds followed, customers withdrawing some $350 billion over the next few days (Ball 2018, p. 44). The contagion was contained by a U.S. Treasury guarantee of money-market share prices put in place at the end of September 2008 (U.S. Department of the Treasury 2008) and the establishment of the Commercial Paper Funding Facility by the Federal Reserve in early October. At its peak in January 2009, the CPFF held some $350 billion of commercial paper, 20 percent of the total outstanding of $1.75 trillion, this total itself down from a peak of $2.2 trillion in August 2007 (Adrian, Kimbrough, and Marchioni 2011, charts 1, 6, and 7). The facility was wound down over 2009 and closed in early 2010.

Laurence Ball believes that the fall of Lehman Brothers could have been avoided. In his view the action, or rather, inaction of the Fed in allowing Lehman to go under resulted from the combination of Treasury Secretary Henry Paulson's desire to teach the markets a lesson and Fed Chair Bernanke's deference to the letter of the law and, more importantly, to Paulson. Coupled with the ignorance of who held how much Lehman paper, the judgment of the Treasury and Fed principals that the damage of a Lehman bankruptcy would be contained was—as the previous paragraph indicates—wildly off base.

Ball's account contrasts with the official story, or rather the story that officials later told to justify their actions (Bernanke 2015a; Geithner 2014; Paulson

2010): Lehman was insolvent as well as illiquid, leaving the government no choice when various attempts to arrange a takeover fell through. Ball goes through a detailed accounting of Lehman assets and liabilities to bolster his claim, but in the end he is unconvincing since so much of Lehman's assets took the form of securities for which there was effectively no market, so no way to establish *market* values.

There is a somewhat softer, but more convincing, version of Ball's claim, namely, that with nobody in a position to know the value of Lehman assets, it was impossible to say whether or not Lehman was solvent when it faced its terminal liquidity crisis. If this was the case, then it would have been possible to defend bailing Lehman out, and Ball's emphasis on the predilections of Paulson and Bernanke makes sense as the real reason for allowing Lehman to fail.

It is difficult to avoid the echo of Milton Friedman and Anna Schwartz (1963a), who see the Fed as the villain in the 1930s (see chapter 8, appendix). But in both cases, the Fed was an accessory rather than the perpetrator.

10. Of course, at times anchoring the spectrum, even at the zlb, fails to generate sufficient investment demand to make for a healthy economy. Having reached the zlb soon after the financial crash of 2008, the Federal Reserve had no room for maneuver with short-term rates. The Fed (and belatedly the European Central Bank) followed Keynes's advice in *The General Theory*:

> Perhaps a complex offer by the central bank to buy and sell at stated prices gilt-edged bonds of all maturities, in place of the single bank rate for short-term bills, is the most important practical improvement which can be made in the technique of monetary management. (p. 206)

Keynes's "complex offer" became actualized as quantitative easing (QE), in the event a very simple offer to purchase T-bonds and mortgage-backed securities issued by government-sponsored entities like Fannie Mae. Liquidity-preference theory predicts that, by increasing the supply of short-term debt relative to the supply of long-term debt in the hands of the public, the spread between the short and the long end of the spectrum will narrow, thereby reducing the hurdle rate. (See above, pp. 426–429.) QE seems to have done so, but it is questionable whether this contributed very much to stimulating investment demand. Remember, besides the level of the hurdle rate, the elasticity of investment demand is critical. Once the recovery from 2008 got underway, U.S. corporations sat on unprecedented piles of cash. The effective limit to investment demand would appear to be opportunity rather than the hurdle rate of interest.

11. Friedman and Kuttner explain the week-to-week inelasticity of demand by the intricacies of the lags in calculating reserve requirements. But, as they recognize, this explanation has no force for a longer period. Beyond a very short period, the relatively low elasticity of demand for reserves is better explained by the low interest elasticity of transactions demand (see note 8). If banks passively respond to borrowers who meet their credit standards, and if loan demand changes little when the interest rate changes, then reserves will not vary much in response to interest-rate changes.

12. In principle, the Fed announces a "corridor" rather than a single rate, with the rate paid on reserves as the floor, and the rate charged at the discount window as the ceiling. But given the large volume of excess reserves, the ceiling has been largely irrelevant. With a floor and a ceiling, the only impediment to controlling the Fed Funds rate is self-inflicted, namely, the Fed's acceptance of deposits from government-sponsored enterprises like the mortgage giants Fannie Mae and Freddie Mac. The Fed does not pay interest on these deposits, which gives the GSE's an incentive to undercut the interest rate paid by the Fed.

13. At the end of 2018, Swiss 10-year government bond yields were still in negative territory. The yields in question are yields to maturity, not coupon yields. See chapter 11 for an explanation of the difference, which is important for finite-maturity bonds but plays no role in a world of consols.

14. This supposes that transactions demand is given by the needs of business for short-term finance. It will not change things materially if banks also accommodate the needs of households for deposit accounts, or if banks also make longer term loans for investment in equipment, structures, and other long-term projects.

15. Maybe he did: "*Any* level of interest which is accepted with sufficient conviction as *likely* to be durable *will* be durable." (*The General Theory,* p. 203)

Chapter 14

Epigraphs: Viner 1933b, p. 129; Lerner 1944, p. 302.

1. Keynes's argument will surprise those who misunderstand Keynes as believing that the interest rate received by savers has no effect on how much is saved, for it is precisely this dependence that Keynes invokes in arguing that fiscal policy—in the form of taxation—will reduce saving and increase consumption. Keynes's argument is that taxation of capital income will reduce the incentive to save because it reduces the after-tax return (*The General Theory,* pp. 94–95, and chap. 24, *passim*).

2. Viner:

> If the government were to employ men to dig ditches and fill them up again, there would be nothing to show afterwards. But, nevertheless, even these expenditures would be an indirect contribution to business recovery. Their major importance would not be in the public works or the unemployment relief which immediately resulted, but in the possibility of hope that a substantial expenditure would act as a priming of the business pump, would encourage business men by increased sales, make them more optimistic, lead them to increase the number of their employees, and so on. (1933b, p. 130)

3. Lerner and others gave accounts of an interchange with Keynes that suggest that not only did Keynes find protracted deficit spending problematic from a practical point of view, but he also failed to grasp the logic of continual deficits. According to Lerner's own account, he was present at a lecture Keynes gave during one of his wartime visits to Washington. The subject was the ability of the U.S. economy to

sustain full employment after the end of hostilities and the end of the enormous military expenditure involved in the war effort (see chapter 9). Here is how Lerner recalled the exchange some years later:

> At a lecture to the Federal Reserve in Washington in 1944, [Keynes] showed concern that there might be "too much saving" after the war. When I pointed out that the government could always induce enough spending by incurring deficits to increase incomes, he at first objected that this would only cause 'even more saving' and then denounced as "humbug" my suggestion that the deficits required to induce enough total spending could always be financed by increasing the national debt. (I must add here that Evsey Domar, at my side, whispered: "He ought to read the *General Theory*" and that a month later Keynes withdrew his denunciation.) (Lerner 1978, p. 67)

Lerner's interpretation of Keynes's response suggests that Keynes was not entirely successful in his "long struggle of escape . . . from habitual modes of thought and expression." (*The General Theory,* preface, p. viii). In this view Keynes came around to the idea of a long-run budget deficit only after he read and digested *The Economics of Control,* in which Lerner lays out the theory of functional finance.

It is certainly true that Keynes wrote Lerner an effusive letter, worth quoting at length:

At sea, Septr 1944

My dear Lerner,

> Your book [*Economics of Control*] arrived in London whilst I was away at Bretton Woods. But now again I am on the sea for yet another visit to the USA, and the sea voyage has given me an opportunity to read it.

> It is a grand book worthy of one's hopes of you. A most powerful piece of well organized analysis with high aesthetic qualities, though written more perhaps than you see yourself for the cognoscenti in the temple and not for those at the gate. Anyhow *I* prefer it for intellectual enjoyment to any recent attempts in this vein . . .

> In the second of the two books which you have placed within one cover, I have marked with particular satisfaction and profit three pairs of chapters— chap 20 and 21, chap 24 and 25, and chap 28 and 29. Here is the kernel of yourself. It is very original and grand stuff. I shall have to try when I get back to hold a seminar for the heads of the Treasury on Functional Finance. It will be very hard going—I think I shall ask them to let me hold a seminar of their sons instead, agreeing beforehand that, if I can convince the boys they will take it from me that it is so . . .

> Yours ever

> Keynes

> (quoted in Colander and Landreth 1996, pp. 116–117)

But there is considerable evidence for the view that Keynes's skepticism about the feasibility of continued deficits was motivated not by a failure to understand the theory, but by practical considerations, including the difficulty of persuading people that a government's budget and debt are fundamentally different from the budget and debt of a business or of an individual. As David Colander (1984) notes, Keynes had much earlier, certainly before the seminar encounter with Lerner—the actual date of which is disputed—written to James Meade while both were occupied with war finance and postwar planning at the UK Treasury:

> I recently read an interesting article by Lerner on deficit budgeting, in which he shows that, in fact, this does not mean an infinite increase in the national debt, since in course of time the interest on the previous debt takes the place of the new debt which would otherwise be required. (He, of course, is thinking of a chronic deficiency of purchasing power rather than an intermittent one.) His argument is impeccable. [Not quite: see chapter 16, pp. 635–636.] But, heaven help anyone who tries to put it across to the plain man at this stage of the evolution of our ideas. (April 25, 1943, in Keynes 1980, p. 320; quoted in Collander 1984, pp. 1573–1574)

Robert Skidelsky (2000, p. 276) supports Colander's view, quoting Keynes's 1943 assessment that Lerner's conception of functional finance

> runs directly contrary to men's natural instincts . . . about what is sensible . . . spoiling a splendid idea by pretending it can be crudely put into force, and then refusing to look in the face of all practical difficulties.

4. As will be the case in general with fixprice adjustment. At a full-employment equilibrium, the economy is on the AD schedule in a flexprice regime as well.

5. In principle, there will also be differences in the propensities to consume in successive rounds of spending, on the one hand, and retrenchment, on the other. But in practice, the best the analyst can hope for is to be able to identify the first-round players, the taxpayers who are directly hit by the insistence on budget balance and the suppliers of goods and services to the government. She is not likely to do better than an economy-wide average for successive multiplier rounds.

6. To be sure, in these simple examples the only leakages from spending are taxes and saving. This simplification leads to an overestimation of the multiplier. See chapter 15.

7. Formulating monetary policy is not as easy as it sounds. Even after Lehman Brothers went under, the FOMC was still debating whether inflation or recession was the more serious danger. Janet Yellen, then the president of the San Francisco Fed, and, even more so, Eric Rosengren of Boston, stand out for their recognition of the looming danger of a recession. Favoring a signal in this direction, Rosengren said,

> The failure of a major investment bank, the forced merger of another, the largest thrift and insurer teetering, and the failure of Freddie and Fannie are likely to have a significant impact on the real economy. Individuals and firms will become risk averse, with reluctance to consume or to invest. Even if firms were inclined to invest, credit spreads are rising, and the cost and availability of financing is becoming more difficult. Many securitization vehicles are frozen. The degree of financial distress has risen markedly. Deleveraging is likely to occur with a vengeance as firms seek to survive this period of sig-

nificant upheaval. Given that many borrowers will face higher interest rates as a result of financial problems, we can help offset this additional drag by reducing the federal funds rate. I support [reducing] the fed funds rate 25 basis points. (Federal Open Market Committee 2008a, pp. 30–31)

In the event, the FOMC voted unanimously to do nothing (Rosengren was a non-voting member) but vowed to watch the economy closely.

The problem lay both in recognizing the new facts on the ground and in devising new instruments to deal with new problems, such as the freezing of the commercial-paper market (see chapter 13, note 9). Financial conditions continued to deteriorate after the September FOMC meeting, and three weeks later, in a highly irregular between-meetings conference call, the FOMC unanimously endorsed a joint action by the world's leading central banks to cut interest rates, including a 50 basis point (one-half percentage point) cut in the Federal Funds rate. Chairman Bernanke summarized the state of play:

On the economic growth side, what is particularly worrisome to me is that, before this latest upsurge in financial stress, we had already seen deceleration in growth, including the declines, for example, in consumer spending. Everyone I know who has looked at it—outside forecasters and the Greenbook producers here at the Board [of Governors of the Federal Reserve System]—believes that the financial stress we are seeing now is going to have a significant additional effect on growth. Larry [Slifman, a Fed staff member] gave some estimates of unemployment above 7 percent for a couple of years. So even putting aside the extraordinary conditions in financial markets, I think the macro outlook has shifted decisively toward output risks and away from inflation risks, and on that basis, I think that a policy move is justified.

I should say that this comes as a surprise to me. I very much expected that we could stay at 2 percent for a long time, and then when the economy began to recover, we could begin to normalize interest rates. But clearly things have gone off in a direction that is quite worrisome. (Federal Open Market Committee 2008b, pp. 13–14)

I suppose that for all the delay, this story actually illustrates the point made above, namely, that it is easier to form a consensus on monetary policy than on fiscal policy! No consensus was *ever* formed around President Obama's stimulus package—which received nary a Republican vote in the House of Representatives. In any case, the implementation lag was not due to the inherent difficulties of passing complex legislation. The American Recovery and Reinvestment Act (ARRA) was signed into law on February 17, 2009, within a month of Obama's inauguration. The problem was that the stimulus did not begin to take effect until six months later. (See chapter 15 for an analysis of the Obama stimulus.)

8. Christina Romer (1986) criticized this conclusion as an artifact of different methods of computing unemployment. The data in Figure 14.9 reflect the re-analysis of the data by David Weir (1992). See Susan Carter (2006, pp. 2-30 to 2-31) for an overview of the data. Thanks to Gabe Gold-Hodgkin for pointing me to Romer's article.

Chapter 15

Epigraphs: Biden 2009; Boehner 2009.

1. This website is no longer operative; the data are now stored at data.nber.org/data/ARRA/.

2. However, barely half agreed that the game was worth the candle. The doubters were either uncertain or disagreed with the statement

   Taking into account all of the ARRA's economic consequences—including the economic costs of raising taxes to pay for the spending, its effects on future spending, and any other likely future effects—the benefits of the stimulus will end up exceeding its costs. (ChicagoBooth)

   Two and a half years later, almost two-thirds (of a slightly larger pool) concurred with the conclusion that the benefits exceeded the costs, a significantly greater percentage, but still short of what might be expected if economics were, as its practitioners are wont to claim, a science like physics.

   The economics profession was hardly unanimous. An advertisement placed by the conservative Cato Institute in the *New York Times* and the *Wall Street Journal* on January 28, 2009, had as its central message "we the undersigned do not believe that more government spending is a way to improve economic performance." This ad was signed by some two hundred economists, including several Nobel Laureates (and future Laureates), http://object.cato.org/sites/cato.org/files/pubs/pdf/cato_stimulus.pdf (accessed February 2, 2016).

3. Cogan and Taylor were not the only dissenters from the consensus opinion of the economics profession that the ARRA created jobs and income. Before the ink was dry on the legislation authorizing the Obama stimulus, Robert Barro and John Cochrane separately argued that the multiplier would be zero. Barro (2009) focused on crowding out: if $m = 0$, then the multiplier is zero regardless of the value of the other parameters. Cochrane (2009) agreed with Barro on crowding out, but also argued that $v = 0$ on the grounds that any rational agent who receives a tax cut, transfer, or grant will take into account the debt that the federal government incurs to finance the stimulus, according to the "Ricardian Equivalence" theory developed by Barro in the 1970s and 1980s (Barro 1989)—see chapter 16, appendix 3. According to this theory, any new spending by stimulus recipients will be just cancelled out by spending reductions elsewhere in the economy.

   Crowding out is surely relevant to stimulus programs launched in times of high-capacity utilization. High-capacity utilization was the reality of World War II, one of the periods of rapid military mobilization on which Barro focused in order to avoid problems of data interpretation that arise when government expenditure and employment might be correlated but not because government expenditure is the cause of the increase in employment. Episodes of sharp increases in military spending avoid the econometric problem of spurious correlation, but they have little bearing on the Great Recession.

   Robert Gordon and Robert Krenn (2010) argue that the multiplier fell from two to one as slack was eliminated in the military build-up that took place between the fall of France in the spring of 1940 and the entry of the United States into World War II at the end of 1941. In that period, unemployment fell in half, from 15 percent to 7.5 percent.

By mid-2009, when the ARRA stimulus kicked in, the unemployment rate had climbed to almost 10 percent. There was, accordingly, plenty of spare capacity and an abundance of available labor. Crowding out was hardly an issue. (For a contrary view, see Timothy Conley and Bill Dupor [2013].)

4. This point was taken up by others and widely cited in the ensuing discussions of the fiscal multipliers and of the wisdom of fiscal stimulus policy. See, for example, Feyrer and Sacerdote (2011), Ramey (2011), Auerbach (2012), Jonas (2012), Conley and Dupor (2013), and Leduc and Wilson (2017).

5. If the trend rate of growth of actual income, g, is stationary, then $\phi = g$.

6. Similarly, the Blinder–Zandi (2010) multipliers are higher for programs aimed at those lower on the income scale—for example, 1.24 for a payroll-tax holiday versus 0.37 for making dividend and capital-gains tax cuts permanent. Romer and Bernstein (2009) used a disaggregated set of historical multipliers generated by the Federal Reserve Board/U.S. model and that of a private firm to estimate the impact of ARRA. Their overall multiplier was a weighted average of multipliers for the various parts of the stimulus program, reaching 1.57 after two years.

7. On another, more generous, reading, these tax breaks were not intended to stimulate spending directly, but rather to help private agents get their balance sheets in order after the excesses of the Bush years. Stimulus, or at least a substantial part of it, like the TARP (Troubled Asset Relief Program), was really about swapping high-quality federal government debt for the tarnished (if not absolutely toxic) debt of private individuals and businesses, as well as for the debt of state and local governments. A case can be made that these agents were not in a position to spend until their own financial houses were in order. This might qualify as indirect stimulus under an elastic definition of the term, but not stimulus as conventionally defined.

8. I return to the question of how to treat Medicaid below, in note 10.

9. According to the National Association of State Budget Officers (NASBO), in 2009 the states collectively enacted $24 billion of tax increases for FY-2010 (NASBO 2009, table 7, p. 18). Two states, California and New York, accounted for two-thirds of the total. The overall increase in expenditures in FY-2010 was $34 billion.

10. I explain why in the appendix to this chapter. The argument for collapsing the distinction between transfers and purchases of goods and services is illustrated by Medicaid. In the national income accounts, Medicaid shows up as a transfer payment to individuals (like social security). In fact, the recipient never sees any cash: Medicaid "transfers" are in fact payments to vendors of medical services.

11. This stipulation must be understood as provisional: the next section argues, on the basis of reports of state budget officers, that most states could not have maintained their actual spending without the ARRA.

12. Although the supplement published by the Bureau of Economic Analysis on the impact of the ARRA provides only aggregate data for state and local governments,

National Income and Product Accounts (NIPA) data break down federal grants between states and localities. These data show only a very modest increase in *total* federal grants to localities over the period of the ARRA. It follows that ARRA grants to the localities could not have been very large. This is confirmed by analysis of the detailed ARRA data on the recovery.gov website. My calculation is that, through the end of calendar 2011, if we add the total contracts, loans, and grants reported in line with Section 1512 of the Recovery Act, plus Medicaid, 85 percent went to state governments. The rest went to private nonprofit entities (like universities), to private businesses, as well as to local governments or their agencies.

13. Worse, I did not keep a careful record of all the transformations of the data, so that the only way to verify that the errors are small would be to build up the regression-data set from the original ARRA data.

14. There are a few notable exceptions. For example, H. D. Henderson's (1938) and Meade and Andrews' (1938) use of interviews with businessmen to explore the impact of the interest rate in the determination of investment, and Blinder et al. (1998) and Bewley (1999), who engage with relevant economic actors to explore the reasons behind the stickiness of prices and wages, respectively.

15. Internal funds are the sum of general budget-stabilization funds (including Rainy-Day funds) and special funds.

16. The fossil-fuel states are an exception to this, as they usually fund their capital expenditures from the operating budget. The question of whether they can engage in countercyclical capital borrowing, then, is not pertinent. North Dakota, enjoying a boom due to drilling and extracting oil and natural gas from the Baaken field, was in a class by itself. The unemployment rate never went above 4.2 percent and was under 4 percent for most of the period in question. North Dakota's response to our questions on the effect of the recession on state operations was in effect, "Recession, what recession?"

17. This assumes that the 20 percent of this category that did not go to state governments was also spent in its entirety.

Chapter 15 Empirical Appendix

1. Four states, Alabama, Michigan, New York, and Texas, start their fiscal years on other dates: Alabama and Michigan begin their fiscal year on October 1, as does the federal government. New York's fiscal year begins on April 1, and Texas's on September 1.

2. Food stamps, though administered by the states, is a federal program and is not part of any state's budget.

3. The value for R^2 differs slightly from the value reported for R^2 adjusted for degrees of freedom, reported at the bottom of column 2.

4. A logical case can be made for using the *difference* between FY-2010 and FY-2009 S-ARRA receipts rather than the FY-2010 *level* to measure the injection of ARRA money: FY-2009 revenues are already built into the level of FY-2009 state expenditures, so that what matters for FY-2010 is the additional input of S-ARRA funds.

Though this argument is plausible, there is good reason for rejecting it and using the level of FY-2010 ARRA money as the independent variable. The level of S-ARRA money received by a state in FY-2010 has virtually no correlation with the level received in FY-2009. (The correlation coefficient is 0.07.) This suggests that FY-2009 S-ARRA revenues did not serve as a meaningful baseline for FY-2010. This conclusion is supported by the fact that the regression coefficient on FY-2009 S-ARRA revenue is close to -1 in a first-stage regression of S-ARRA revenue on its instruments like the last one in Table 15.10—with the modification that the dependent variable is the difference between FY-2010 S-ARRA receipts and FY-2009 receipts. The independence of FY-2010 S-ARRA receipts from FY-2009 S-ARRA receipts makes intuitive sense because the relatively modest FY-2009 S-ARRA transfers to the states were largely determined by Medicaid reimbursement; a more complex allocation of S-ARRA funds among the states, evidently influenced by political bargaining during the legislative process leading up to the enactment of the ARRA, did not really kick in until FY-2010.

5. Experiments with alternative combinations of financial controls, omitting one or another of the measures of fiscal solvency, are not reported in Table 15.10, but the same pattern holds: coefficients in excess of 1.75, and z-values in excess of 3.

6. In a debate at Harvard University in February 2012 between Taylor, a former Undersecretary of the Treasury in the George W. Bush administration, and Larry Summers, former Treasury Secretary (under President Bill Clinton) and Obama adviser, Summers observed that constitutional or statutory balanced-budget requirements prevented the states from borrowing and smoothing expenditure. Taylor, in response, suggested that states could borrow on capital account to adjust their overall spending. In response to an email request for clarification, Taylor repeated that "borrowing for infrastructure investment is one means of flexibility" (Taylor, personal communication, February 29, 2012.)

7. By contrast, the ratio 7/126, which implies that tax revenues are 5.5 percent of mining income, is not unreasonable.

8. James Feyrer and Bruce Sacerdote (2011) make political clout in the federal legislative process, as measured by the average seniority of each state's house delegation, the instrument for explaining the distribution of ARRA moneys.

9. In theory, tax revenues rather than expenditures could be affected, but Shoag (2010, sec. 5.4) finds no effect on taxes, a finding similar to what my regressions on S-ARRA spending suggest.

Chapter 16

Epigraphs: Galbraith 1998 [1958], pp. 187–188; Lerner 1944, pp. 316, 318.

1. As a percentage of GDP, overall government purchases of goods and services actually declined significantly, from a peak of more than 30 percent of GDP during World War II to a range of 15 to 20 percent in the postwar years. The figure was 15 percent in 2018. The federal government's purchases of goods and services were about 5 percent of GDP in 2018, almost exactly where it was on the eve of the

military build-up in 1940. The increasing size of government is rather the result of the long-term increase in transfer payments (social security, grants to states, etc.). As a share of federal government expenditure, purchases of goods and services declined from just under 60 percent in 1940 to less than 25 percent in 2018. Over the same period, transfer payments rose from just over 20 percent to over 60 percent. (The remainder goes to pay interest on the public debt, some 10 percent of the federal budget in 1940 and 12 percent in 2018.)

These numbers are somewhat misleading. Transfers in the federal budget include payments to state and local governments under the rubric of fiscal federalism. The states and localities are thus a conduit for the federal purchase of goods and services. At an earlier time these transfers were not significant, but they became increasingly important, rising from less than 8 percent of federal expenditures in 1940 (3 percent during the height of the Cold War in the 1950s) to 13 percent in 2018. Transfers to states and their subdivisions show up in the National Income and Product Accounts either as direct purchases of goods and services by states and localities (as for highway construction or education) or as purchases by households (as for Medicaid). As chapter 15 noted, the states administer Medicaid and pay a share of its costs but receive transfer payments from Washington in support of their programs. In the NIPA tables, Medicaid is a transfer to households and a purchase of medical services by these households. Of course the households never see any money coming in or going out; it is purely an accounting convention to attribute Medicaid purchases to the private sector.

If we shift the 13 percent of its budget that the federal government transfers to the states into the category of purchases of goods and services, this category increases from about one-quarter of the budget to three-eighths in 2018. Transfers are reduced to about 50 percent of the budget.

Accordingly, a better picture of the relative roles of transfers and purchases of goods and services is obtained by consolidating government accounts. It is still the case that by 2018 the balance of expenditure had shifted markedly, but the difference between the consolidated account and the federal government account in isolation is quantitatively important. In 1952 the composition of overall government expenditure was broadly similar to the composition of the federal budget: close to 75 percent went to the purchase of goods and services, with 15 percent going to transfer payments and just under 10 percent to interest payments. In 2018 transfer payments and purchases of goods and services took about the same share of the consolidated government budget, just under 45 percent each. The remainder is interest on government debt.

2. The distinction between government purchases of goods and services and private purchases is not the same distinction as between private and public goods. In the private versus public distinction, private goods are those for which one more unit for me means one less for you—a loaf of bread—and public goods are those we consume simultaneously—the internet—in which there is no such trade-off between your consumption and mine (until a website crashes). There is no logical necessity for consumption and investment provided collectively by the govern-

ment to be identified solely and strictly with public goods, but there is an obvious affinity between public and collective, and the affinity is not purely semantic. Governments typically provide such goods as education, transportation infrastructure, and military, police, and fire protection, all of which have a large component of the public even if they don't fit the definition exactly.

The national income accounts categorize government purchases of goods and services, collective goods in my language, as consumption or investment. In actuality, most goods provided by the government defy being compartmentalized in this way, combining as they do elements of both consumption and investment.

3. In the field of economics, this literature dates from Kenneth Arrow (1963 [1951]).

4. Arthur Laffer (2004) and his eponymous curve is an extreme version. Laffer gives both Ibn Khaldun and Keynes authorial priority. I'm not sure what Ibn Khaldun had in mind, but Keynes clearly was not focused on supply. Early on in *The Means to Prosperity* (1933), Keynes writes,

> Nor should the argument seem strange that taxation may be so high as to defeat its object, and that, given sufficient time to gather the fruits, a reduction of taxation will run a better chance, than an increase, of balancing the Budget. (p. 7)

Laffer quotes this passage without, apparently, ever realizing that the whole pamphlet was about the effects of taxes on *demand*.

5. A crucial assumption here is that taxes are proportional to output. A tax levied on profits would change the story; in particular, investment would presumably become sensitive to the tax rate.

6. On the one hand, Mr. Micawber's "Annual income twenty pounds, annual expenditure nineteen six, result happiness. Annual income twenty pounds, annual expenditure twenty pound ought and six, result misery" (Charles Dickens, *David Copperfield*).

On the other hand, "We owe it to ourselves." Even in a closed economy, in which the entirety of the debt is held domestically, this simplification obscures the concentrated ownership of the public debt, the consequence of which is to place a disproportionate burden of debt service on the large majority who own a small to vanishing part of the debt. Sandy Hager (2016) explores the distribution of the ownership of the debt in the United States and finds that in 2015 the top 1 percent of the distribution owned about half of the privately held domestic share of the U.S. public debt.

7. See, for example, N. Gregory Mankiw (2018, pp. 72–74).

8. For the moment, we can assume compulsory overtime. (See chapter 9, note 12.) In the long-run context of chapters 18, 19 and 20, the result is an expansion of the labor force.

9. See the next chapter for a brief discussion of stagnation as a characterization of the long-run prospects for capitalism, a characterization that was in vogue in the wake of the Great Depression and, not surprisingly, revived in the wake of the Great Recession.

10. Priority for recognizing the peculiarities of the 1944 to 1949 U.S. debt episode

goes to John Irons and Josh Bivens (2010, p. 2). I am grateful to Michael Ash for pointing me to the Irons–Bivens paper and saving me the embarrassment of any claim to originality.

The Irons–Bivens argument should not be conflated with the discovery by Thomas Herndon, Michael Ash, and Robert Pollin of data errors that called other Reinhart–Rogoff conclusions into doubt (2014). Responding to Herndon et al., Rogoff argued that these errors did not vitiate the conclusions of their 2010 paper(s) or his later work, with Carmen Reinhart and Vincent Reinhart (2012). Rogoff (2013) emphatically disavowed any political motivation or interest: "Is our research politically motivated, as [Herndon *et al*] infer? No, we are centrists, our academic research has always been completely apolitical." Figure 16.11 does not appear in the published version of Reinhart and Rogoff's 2010 paper. Perhaps for reasons of space.

11. Friedman is not indiscriminate in his condemnation of deficits. When the economy is operating below its productive capacity, deficits may be appropriate to stimulate the economy. The problem comes when the deficit continues even after the economy has reached full employment. (1988, pp. 142–143)

For this reason, it is a bit inconvenient for Friedman's argument that most of the Reagan deficits took place when the economy was actually quite far from full employment, with an average rate of unemployment close to the average rate for the eight years following the financial crisis of 2008: the economy was not operating on the frontier of the choice space in Figures 16.1 to 16.5 but well in the interior. By the end of Reagan's second term, the unemployment rate was down to 5 percent, a rate that mainstream macroeconomists at that time considered to be full employment, the "non-accelerating inflation rate of unemployment" (NAIRU, for short). In any case, 5 percent was a great improvement over the average rate of unemployment during Reagan's tenure in office. But by 1989 the deficit had also come down sharply. The total deficit was 3 percent of GDP, and the primary budget was in surplus.

12. In this essay, "Economic Possibilities for Our Grandchildren," originally published in 1930 to cheer up his fellow Brits as the world was beginning to feel the shock of the Great Depression, Keynes distinguished between absolute needs and relative needs, the needs we must fulfill to keep up with the Joneses. The second class, he recognized, knows no bounds, but he evidently believed that relative needs can be ignored because they are important only while the economy is in the process of accumulating sufficient capital to satisfy absolute needs. Keynes's implicit corollary was that once this purpose has been fulfilled, relative needs will wither away.

It remains to be seen whether the genie of emulation will go back in the bottle once it is no longer functional to the project of creating the economic basis of a good and meaningful life. Max Weber's iron-cage metaphor certainly suggests otherwise (1930, pp. 181–182): the dignity threshold might be an ever-receding target. (Thanks to Will Rhatigan for bringing Weber to my attention in this regard. See Marglin 2008 [chap. 11], for a more extensive treatment of Keynes's argument.)

13. It was left to Adam Smith (1982 [1759], pp. 304, 312–313) to embrace consequen-

tialism fully as a moral argument. With some verbal sleight of hand, he was able transform vice into virtue and resolve the paradox. (See Marglin 2008 [chap. 6].)

14. Friedman published *Day of Reckoning* in 1988. In the intervening three decades, serious study has gone into providing the background for such a debate. Jon Bakija, Lane Kenworthy et al. (2016) provide a good introduction.

15. The argument is tricky. The claim is that the exchange rate determines the balance of payments, but not that the balance of payments determines the exchange rate. Keynes's liquidity-preference logic applies here. The starting point for liquidity-preference theory is that the interest rate is determined by stocks of various assets rather than flows of saving and investment. But even though investment and saving do not determine the rate of interest, the rate of interest (along with income) is a determinant of investment and saving.

    The same is true of exchange rates. These are determined by stocks of assets, not in markets for exports and imports of goods and services (flows). But exchange rates in turn (along with other variables) determine exports and imports and hence the balance of trade.

16. An alternative to imposing trade balance as a constraint is to incorporate the trade deficit as an argument of the social-welfare function. In this case, the beneficial effects of low interest rates on the trade deficit would be weighed against any putative welfare losses from driving investment beyond the socially desirable level.

    This trade-off could be avoided if it were possible to set the exchange rate independently of the interest rate. In this case, the addition of the new goal of controlling the balance of trade would be matched by the introduction of a new instrument (the exchange rate). The optimization problem would be more complex but no different in kind from the two-instrument, two-goal problem of choosing combinations of consumption, investment, and government spending subject to the full-employment constraint.

    It is debatable whether a country can determine its exchange rate even if it subordinates monetary policy to this goal. There are certainly examples of countries trying to do so and failing. But if any one country is able to do so, it would presumably be the United State. The dollar is the dominant reserve currency and, not coincidentally, U.S. resources for intervention in foreign-exchange markets are enormous.

17. The evolution from B to A'' captures the plight of the Eurozone under the impact of the 2008 financial crisis and the ensuing recession. The European Central Bank moved relatively quickly to reduce short-term interest rates, but the zero lower bound and inelastic investment demand prevented conventional monetary policy from restoring full employment in an increasingly beleaguered southern Europe. The short-term interest rate was reduced below zero in 2014, and quantitative easing was instituted early in 2015, but these unconventional forms of monetary policy were too little, too late.

    The functional-finance solution would have been an aggressive fiscal policy aimed at both higher government spending and higher consumption spending; it was a situation calling for a good measure of deficit finance. But, no institutions for delivering a Europe-wide deficit exist, and even if the institutions had been in place, from 2010 on the ideology of sound finance dominated German, and consequently, European politics (Bibow 2018).

During the teens of this century, sound finance, aka austerity, crippled the European economy. For the Eurozone as a whole, unemployment in 2014 was more than half again as high as it was in 2007, 11.6 percent against 7.2 percent. In Greece and Spain, unemployment reached levels not seen in the capitalist world since the Great Depression, with more than 25 percent of the labor force officially unemployed. As is usually the case, the young were hit especially hard: in both countries, unemployment rates among people under 25 topped 50 percent, and the figure doesn't include those who fled the land of their birth.

18. How does the acquisition of government bonds increase private wealth? There would be no change in private wealth were the exchange of cash for bonds simply an alteration of the composition of existing portfolios, as quantitative easing was modeled in chapter 12. Here private wealth portfolios grow, since agents are exchanging their current income for *newly issued* bonds.

19. Key to Lerner's story is the idea that public debt is private wealth. Here Lerner anticipates Don Patinkin's version (1948) of the real-balance effect. As chapter 7 noted, Patinkin's argument relies on deflation to raise the real debt:GDP ratio to whatever might be required for economic stimulus. Lerner argues for a falling primary deficit and hence a *falling* debt:GDP ratio.

20. This is surmise, hence "perhaps." Lerner's *Economics of Control,* published in 1944, contains no discussion at all of the effect of debt on private wealth. David Colander, who I believe knows the evolution of Lerner's views as well if not better than any other living soul, could not enlighten me on why the argument was dropped.

Chapter 17

Epigraph: Robinson 1962, p. 14.

1. Though in Hicks's case the problem was not in his original argument but in how the argument was understood, or rather misunderstood. See chapter 3, note 12.

2. Harrod's second proposition—that the rate of increase of income is an important determinant of the demand for saving [investment]—is actually quite vague. It is usually interpreted as providing a theory of investment demand based on a technological accelerator principle, but it is also consistent with a psychological basis for the incremental capital:output ratio. In the psychological interpretation, the key element is the optimism or the pessimism of businessmen and -women with respect to the durability of any expected increase in output. When animal spirits (to use Keynes's phrase) are strong, business will react enthusiastically to a given expectation of increased demand, but the same upsurge can trigger much less investment in a pessimistic climate in which the anticipated growth in output is not expected to be sustained. In chapter 10 we captured this by introducing Ω as a subjective measure of the probability of selling additional output.

The usual interpretation of v as a technologically determined parameter is more the product of subsequent theorizing than of a clearly stated view on Harrod's part. In a series of papers (see especially Besomi 2001), Daniele Besomi argues that subsequent theorizing misunderstood Harrod's concern in attributing to him a focus on the conditions of steady growth; in Besomi's view, Harrod's concern was rather with the trade cycle, and fluctuations in v were a critical piece of his story.

3. In fact, Domar has a moment of ambiguity where he toys with the idea that v may reflect investor psychology:

> In some problems $[1/v]$ may be interpreted as the minimum annual output per dollar invested which will make the investment worth undertaking. If this output falls below $[1/v]$, the investor suffers a loss or at least a disappointment, and may be unwilling to replace the asset after it has depreciated, (1947, p. 44)

But this interpretation goes against the grain of Domar's overall argument, which, when dealing with the natural rate of growth, emphasizes technological determination of v as a supply-side parameter.

4. A twenty-first-century reader might wonder why there was no apparent attempt by Harrod and Domar to sort out their differences, despite the fact that the two authors were developing their respective theories at pretty much the same time. Harrod's original paper was published in 1939 and Domar's in 1946, followed by a somewhat lengthier exposition in 1947.

Likely, the main reason was that World War II diverted attention and made scholarly communication across the Atlantic very difficult. Domar was evidently unaware of Harrod's contribution when he wrote his two papers. In the second of the two, there is a curious footnote, added after the paper was completed, in which Domar acknowledges Harrod's 1939 article as "[containing] a number of ideas similar to those presented here" (1947, p. 42n). In the preface to *Towards a Dynamic Economics,* Harrod, for his part, acknowledged being preoccupied by other duties during the war so that an apology was due "to those writers overseas whose recent contributions to the subject may appear to have been neglected in these pages" (1948, p. v).

5. This assumes that the elasticity of substitution in production does not exceed one, which guarantees that the slope of the production function $f(k)$, and hence $sf(k)$, is initially infinite and falls to zero as k increases. See the mathematical appendix to chapter 18 for a discussion of the elasticity of substitution.

6. http://en.wikisource.org/wiki/The_poems_of_John_Godfrey_Saxe/The_Blind _Men_and_the_Elephant

7. The reason for ignoring technological change is hardly that it is unimportant. Rather, the opposite: technological change is too important to be tacked on to a book that has as its purpose the fleshing out of a macro theory in the spirit of Keynes.

8. For an informative history of secular stagnation, see Roger Backhouse and Mauro Boianovsky (2016). This idea had a revival under the aegis of Larry Summers,

with Ben Bernanke, Robert Gordon, Paul Krugman, Ken Rogoff, and other prominent economists weighing in. (See Summers 2014, 2015; Bernanke 2015b; Gordon 2014, 2015, chaps. 17 and 18; Krugman 2014; Lo and Rogoff 2015.)

As with the blind men and the elephant, the participants in this debate stress
their differences, but there are basically two arguments: Krugman and Summers
offer reasons why investment demand might be deficient, whereas Bernanke and
Rogoff stress the reasons why saving might be excessive. Gordon's contribution to
the debate is to change the subject: his focus is not on aggregate demand, the focus of Hansen's original theory and of the other contributors to the revival, but
rather is about reasons why productivity growth can be expected to be lower in
the future than in the past. It is a supply-side riff on a demand-side debate.

My own take is that all the arguments are plausible—except for the argument
that the low level of real interest rates reflects the role of the interest rate in equilibrating the demand for investment with the supply of saving, relatively low rates
indicating low investment demand (Summers) or high savings (Bernanke). Both
Bernanke and Summers are stuck in a Wicksellian world (see chapter 2, note 7,
and the section titled "Real and Nominal Rates: Is Central Bank Freedom Limited
by Necessity?" in chapter 13).

But plausibility is not enough. Summers's brief for stagnation (or one or another of the variations on Summers's theme) may turn out to be prophetic—or it
may not, as Hansen learned when the post–World War II boom trumped his 1938
reasons for anticipating stagnation. Twenty-first-century stagnation may also turn
out to be one of those ideas that seems attractive at the time but whose time is yet
to come.

9. This is not just a theoretical possibility: over the four years of economic collapse
from 1929 to 1933, the U.S. labor force grew by 5 percent while the capital stock
actually shrunk! This would only have made matters worse for those lucky enough
to still be at work: equilibrium at F would imply a higher real-price level and thus
a lower real wage than equilibrium at E.

10. As noted above, the original source was likely Michał Kalecki, who in some ways
anticipated Keynes, and with respect to the theory of saving went back to the future in adopting the nineteenth-century class-based view of saving. See Kalecki
(1971 [1933]). See also Kalecki (1982 [1936]).

11. Unlike the fixprice model, where a gap between desired saving and desired investment is a disequilibrium phenomenon.

Chapter 18

Epigraph: Harrod 1948, pp. 19–20.

1. One exception is John Cornwall (1977, esp. chaps. 4 and 5). Another is Donald
Harris (1978, chap. 10, esp. pp. 273–276).

2. Figure 18.2 understates the historical contribution of the reserve army to the labor
force. The correct comparison with the growth of the paid labor force is not the
growth of the native-born population; at any given time the native-born popula-

tion includes children of immigrants, whom we might consider second-generation members of the reserve army. More appropriate than the growth of the native-born population as a standard of reference would be a hypothetical population based on the initial population at time zero and the hypothetical fertility of this population extrapolated over time.

This century may see the end of the labor-surplus economy. Even China, which in the twentieth century was the poster child for labor surplus, is approaching the time when the supply of workers from its hinterland will be exhausted (Fang Cai and Meiyan Wang [2011]). In 2016, the percentage of the Chinese labor force employed in agriculture was less than 30 percent (World Bank 2016). And, as of 2012, China's female participation rate was the highest in the world and close to the male participation rate, so there is not much left of that reserve army (Bureau of Labor Statistics 2012). China is unlikely to be willing or able to tap the reserves of foreign workers. According to World Bank data from 2016, India is much further behind in terms both of the ratio of employment in agriculture (approximately half the labor force) and female participation rates (barely one-quarter).

3. Arthur Pigou, who for Keynes epitomized the failings of the mainstream to understand the nature of unemployment under capitalism, endorsed the idea of a "subsistence" wage and the key role of public opinion in determining its level: "Public opinion in a modern civilised State builds up for itself a rough estimate of what constitutes a reasonable living wage" (1933, p. 255). This, for Pigou, was one reason why the real wage might persist at a level higher than the market-clearing wage, resulting in persistent unemployment.

The decline of unions is itself a consequence, at least in part, of the shift in public opinion against the working class. Richard Freeman and James Medoff (1984) argued that workers themselves were more likely to organize in unions to the extent the public had a favorable image of unions (cited in Surowiecki 2011).

There is a large literature on how norms enter into the determination of wages. Solow (1990) provides a good introduction and references to articles published in the 1980s, a (local) peak period of interest in the subject.

4. Olivier Blanchard and Larry Katz (1999) present a similar econometric analysis but with a very different interpretation of the variable that I interpret as a conventional wage.

5. The conventional wage is formulated as a *share* of product rather than as a wage *rate*. In the theoretical models of this chapter, we can assume the conventional wage is a fixed *rate* because there is no productivity growth to propel wage expectations. But this will hardly do for empirical analysis.

6. In discussing the (im)possibility of curing unemployment by reducing money wages, Keynes observes, "The transfer from wage-earners to other factors is likely to diminish the propensity to consume" (*The General Theory*, p. 262). This recognition of class-based differences in the propensity to consume is presumably the basis for his subsequent argument that an increase in overall consumption demand can be engineered by a deliberate policy of redistribution. Keynes saw no

immediate need for such a policy but argued that it might be necessary in a generation or two in order to counteract the effect of investment satiation (*The General Theory,* pp. 325–326, 374–377).

7. In the sections that follow, as in earlier chapters, the capitalist economy is assumed to be perfectly competitive in the sense that no agent has market power. Besides market power, real-world features such as frictions are notable for their absence in the model. The point, evidently, is not to provide a faithful description of the world as it is, but to forestall the argument that the results would not hold in the absence of one imperfection or another.

8. If the AD schedule lies to the left of the intersection of the GS and LS schedules, the stationary real-price schedule and AD schedule will intersect at a point where prices and wages are falling at the same rate, as in chapter 6. The distinction between inflation-with-growth and deflation-with-decline is not a theoretical distinction between the long run and the short run, but an empirical one; both are possible long-run outcomes. In fact, the history of capitalism has been mostly a history of rising output and inflation. The Great Depression and the Great Recession are exceptional in historical perspective.

9. What is at issue is the lack of coordination between different decisions, a phenomenon that we have encountered before, beginning with the first foray into dynamics in chapter 5. One way of understanding why the right and left hands appear at odds is that they might belong to different agents, for example, a capital-expenditure manager and a production manager.

　　The present formulation collapses two meanings of the production function. Chapter 17 noted the difference between the short-run function, which reflects varying intensities of utilization of an existing capital stock, and the long-run function, which reflects different production techniques. Presumably, the production manager is operating on the short-run function, whereas the capital-expenditure manager is thinking in terms of the long-run function. Adding the changes in the labor:capital ratio corresponding to the two distinct meanings of the production function is, to say the least, suspicious.

10. The original Luddites have got a bad rap for indiscriminately opposing labor-saving machinery. Oppose they did, but with considerable discrimination. Under the leadership of the mythical General Lud, these nineteenth-century English artisans demolished machinery that was destroying their trades. They had no argument with machinery that was compatible with artisanal production. On the Luddites as they really were, see E. P. Thompson (1963, pp. 521–602).

11. Flexprice results corresponding to Table 18.3 are omitted.

Chapter 18 Mathematical Appendix

1. Consider the generic case

$$\dot{u} = f(u,\, v,\, x)$$
$$\dot{v} = g(u,\, v,\, x).$$

At equilibrium $\dot{u} = \dot{v} = 0$, so

$$\begin{bmatrix} f_u \dfrac{\partial u}{\partial x} + f_v \dfrac{\partial v}{\partial x} + f_x \\ g_u \dfrac{\partial u}{\partial x} + g_v \dfrac{\partial v}{\partial x} + g_x \end{bmatrix} = \begin{bmatrix} 0 \\ 0 \end{bmatrix}$$

and

$$\begin{bmatrix} f_u \dfrac{\partial u}{\partial x} + f_v \dfrac{\partial v}{\partial x} \\ g_u \dfrac{\partial u}{\partial x} + g_v \dfrac{\partial v}{\partial x} \end{bmatrix} = - \begin{bmatrix} f_x \\ g_x \end{bmatrix}.$$

With

$$J = \begin{bmatrix} f_u & f_v \\ g_u & g_v \end{bmatrix}$$

we have

$$J \begin{bmatrix} \dfrac{\partial u}{\partial x} \\ \dfrac{\partial v}{\partial x} \end{bmatrix} = - \begin{bmatrix} f_x \\ g_x \end{bmatrix}$$

and

$$\begin{bmatrix} \dfrac{\partial u}{\partial x} \\ \dfrac{\partial v}{\partial x} \end{bmatrix} = -J^{-1} \begin{bmatrix} f_x \\ g_x \end{bmatrix}.$$

2. My *ROKE* paper (Marglin 2017) is in error on this point. The expression on page 391 for $\partial(P/W)/\partial\xi$ is the same as here, but I mistakenly assert that this expression is unambiguously positive.

3. Piketty (2014, pp. 346–347) identifies the patrimonial middle class as the 40 percent of the population between the top decile and the bottom half. Lumping four deciles together likely exaggerates the size of the group with significant wealth. If the top quarter of this group, that is, the decile lying between the 80th and 90th percentiles, possesses double the wealth of the average of the other three deciles and if the group as a whole owns 40 percent of total wealth, as in France in 2015 (Piketty 2020, fig. 4.2), then the three deciles lying between the 50th and 80th percentiles together hold only 24 percent of total wealth. Moreover, this wealth is mostly equity in their residences and other real estate (Piketty 2020, fig. 11.17). I haven't seen corresponding numbers for the United States, but I would be surprised if the qualitative pattern were different.

4. Observe that in the production function, *L* now represents executive, managerial, and technological labor. As I have noted, the traditional working class plays no role in the model; indeed, the simplest assumption is that this working class has been automated out of existence. More realistically, we could assume that a work-

ing class exists along with the PMC and the rentier class and that the PMC appropriates a percentage of total wages and salaries. The PMC's share of labor income plus its share of profits becomes the basis of its consumption and saving. The remainder of wages and salaries may be assumed to go to the rest of the working population, but the working class plays no further role in the analysis: by assumption, all its income is consumed. I do not think that greater realism in this regard would add much to the economics, but it would certainly complicate the mathematics.

5. For $\delta = 0$, the Jacobian is

$$
J = \begin{bmatrix}
-\theta_1 GS_{\frac{P}{W}} - \theta_3 & \theta_1 & 0 \\[2ex]
\theta_2 \psi' \Omega \left(\dfrac{P}{W} \right)^{-2} l & \theta_2 \left\{ \psi' \Omega' r + \psi' \Omega \left(h_l - \left(\dfrac{P}{W} \right)^{-1} \right) - s_w h_l \right\} & -\left(s_\pi - s_w \right) r \\[2ex]
0 & 0 & s_w h(l, \xi) - s_\pi r
\end{bmatrix}.
$$

This is essentially the model with a uniform propensity to save and capital widening, in which the condition for stability is that the stationary-price locus is flatter than the AD schedule.

Chapter 19

Epigraphs: Lucas 1981, p. 560; Gordon 1984, p. 42.
1. Inflation is measured by the consumer price index, which elides the relationship between wage changes and price changes. In the models of the previous chapter (and the mathematical appendix), this relationship is a simple one: these models assume an equilibrium in which the rate of price inflation and wage inflation are equal.
2. If we replace employment by capacity utilization (defined as the ratio of GDP to potential GDP), the slope of the Phillips curve changes very little over the sample until the first decade of the twenty-first century.
3. The year 2008 is omitted because inflation was negative and the log of the inflation rate therefore undefined. That year is literally off the chart. Evidently, including 2008 would increase the dispersion dramatically!
4. Standard errors are calculated differently in the TSLS procedure.
5. According to Mankiw, "Unexpected inflation redistributes wealth among the population in a way that has nothing to do with either merit or need" (2018, p. 645). According to Baumol, Blinder, and Solow, "Inflation redistributes income in an arbitrary way" (2020, p. 477).

Epilogue

Epigraph: Keynes 1934, pp. 850–851.
1. Rod O'Donnell (1999) and, more recently, James Crotty (2019) argue that Keynes's enlightened capitalism is really "liberal socialism," a term invoked by Keynes to

describe his economic philosophy in a 1939 interview with Kingsley Martin in the *New Statesman and Nation:*

> The question is whether we are prepared to move out of the nineteenth-century *laissez-faire* state into an era of liberal socialism, by which I mean a system where we can act as an organised community for common purposes and to promote economic and social justice, whilst respecting and protecting the individual—his freedom of choice, his faith, his mind and its expression, his enterprise and his property. (Keynes 1982, p. 500; quoted in O'Donnell, p. 164)

2. Note the resort to the language of comparative statics. No apologies: comparative statics is a useful tool when it does not force us to assume away essential differences between real-time change and ahistorical comparisons.

3. Maria Cristina Marcuzzo (2010) contrasts Keynes with Sir William Beveridge, whose eponymous Report laid the foundations for the post–World War II British welfare state. Crotty (2019, chap. 22) emphasizes Keynes's support for the Beveridge Report as evidence of his commitment to "liberal socialism."

   Crotty relies on a letter to Beveridge in which Keynes expresses "wild enthusiasm for your general scheme" (Keynes 1980, p. 204). However, most of his subsequent interventions—an entire chapter of the volume of Keynes's collected writings on his activities as adviser to the Treasury (Keynes 1980, chap. 4) is given over to Keynes's interactions with Beveridge and others during the drafting of the Report—concerned the financial details of unemployment insurance, children's allowances, and pensions. Robert Skidelsky, the magisterial biographer of Keynes, concludes,

   > The truth seems to be that he [Keynes] was not interested in social policy as such, and never attended to it. The sole question in his mind was whether the Exchequer could "afford" Beveridge. (2000, p. 270)

REFERENCES

Acemoglu, Daron, and Pascual Restrepo. 2018. "Artificial Intelligence, Automation and Work." MIT Working Paper 18-01, January.

Achen, Christopher H. 2001. "Why Lagged Dependent Variables Can Suppress the Explanatory Power of Other Independent Variables." Unpublished working paper, Department of Political Science and Institute for Social Research, University of Michigan.

Adrian, Tobias, Karen Kimbrough, and Dina Marchioni. 2011. "The Federal Reserve's Commercial Paper Funding Facility." FRBNY *Economic Policy Review* (May): 25–39. https://www.newyorkfed.org/medialibrary/media/research/epr/11v17n1/1105a dri.pdf (accessed December 2, 2018).

Ait-Sahalia, Yacine. 1996. "Testing Continuous-Time Models of the Spot Interest Rate." *Review of Financial Studies* 9:385–426.

Akerlof, George. 2007. "The Missing Motivation in Macroeconomics." *American Economic Review* 97:3–36.

Allais, Maurice. 1953. "Le Comportement de l'Homme Devant le Risque: Critique des Postulats et Axioms de l'Écôle Américaine" (Human Behavior Toward Risk: A Critique of the Postulates and Axioms of the American School). *Econometrica* 21:503–546.

Ando, Albert, and Franco Modigliani. 1963. "The 'Life Cycle' Hypothesis of Saving: Aggregate Implications and Tests." *American Economic Review* 53:55–44.

Ando, Albert, and Karl Shell. 1975. "Demand for Money in a General Portfolio Model in the Presence of an Asset That Dominates Money." Appendix to Ando and Franco Modigliani, "Some Reflections on Describing Structures of Financial Sectors." In *The Brookings Model: Perspective and Recent Developments,* ed. Gary Fromm and Lawrence Klein, pp. 560–563. Amsterdam: North Holland.

Arrow, Kenneth. 1959. "Toward a Theory of Price Adjustment." In *The Allocation of Economic Resources: Essays in Honor of Bernard Haley,* ed. Moses Abramovitz. Stanford: Stanford University Press.

———. 1963. *Social Choice and Individual Values.* 2nd ed. New York: Wiley. [First published in 1951.]

———. 1963–1964. "The Role of Securities in the Optimal Allocation of Risk-Bearing." *Review of Economic Studies* 31:91–96. [Originally published in French in 1953.]

Arrow, Kenneth, and Gerard Debreu. 1954. "Existence of Equilibrium for a Competitive Economy." *Econometrica* 22:265–290.

Audi, Robert, ed. 1999. *The Cambridge Dictionary of Philosophy.* 2nd ed. Cambridge: Cambridge University Press.

Auerbach, Alan. 2012. "The Fall and Rise of Keynesian Fiscal Policy." *Asian Economic Policy Review* 7:157–175.

Backhouse, Roger, and Mauro Boianovsky. 2016. "Secular Stagnation: The History of a Macroeconomic Heresy." *European Journal of the History of Economic Thought* 23:946–970.

Bakija, Jon, Lane Kenworthy, Peter Lindert, and Jeff Madrick. 2016. *How Big Should Government Be?* Oakland: University of California Press.

Ball, Laurence. 2018. *The Fed and Lehman Brothers: Setting the Record Straight on a Financial Disaster.* Cambridge: University of Cambridge Press.

Bank for International Settlements (BIS). 2010. "Triennial Central Bank Survey of Foreign Exchange and Derivatives Market Activity in 2010, Annex Tables." http://www.bis.org/publ/rpfxf10t.htm (accessed September 12, 2011).

Baqaee, David Rezza, and Emmanuel Farhi. 2019. "The Microeconomic Foundations of Aggregate Production Functions." *Journal of the European Economic Association* 17:1237–1392.

Barens, Ingo. 1997. "Destruction by Simplification: IS–LM after 60 Years." Presented at the 1997 Conference of the History of Economics Society, Charleston, June.

———. 2001. "Patinkin on Keynesian Economics and Hicksian IS-LM: The Neglected Supply Side of the Commodity Market." Presented at the Patinkin Conference, Lausanne, September.

———. 2018. "Robertson's 'Liquidity Trap' as an Answer to Keynes's 'Banana Parable,' or: Did the *General Theory* Really Have to be Written?" Presented at the 22nd Annual Conference of the European Society for the History of Economic Thought, Madrid, June 7–9.

Barro, Robert. 1974. "Are Government Bonds Net Wealth?" *Journal of Political Economy* 82:1095–1117.

———. 1989. "The Ricardian Approach to Budget Deficits." *Journal of Economic Perspectives* 3:37–54.

———. 1996. "Inflation and Growth." *Review,* Federal Reserve Bank of St. Louis (May–June): 153–169.

———. 2009. "Voodoo Multipliers." *Economists' Voice* 6 (2): article 5.

Barro, Robert, and Herschel Grossman. 1971. "A General Disequilibrium Model of Income and Employment." *American Economic Review* 61:82–93.

———. 1976. *Money, Employment and Inflation.* Cambridge: Cambridge University Press.

Bauer, Peter. 1938. "Die Allgemeine Theorie von Keynes und ihre Kritiker" (*The General Theory* of Keynes and Its Critics). *Zeitschrift für Nationalökonomie* 9:99–106.

Baumol, William. 1952. "The Transactions Demand for Cash: An Inventory Theoretic Approach." *Quarterly Journal of Economics* 66:545–556.

———. 1999. "Retrospectives: Say's Law." *Journal of Economic Perspectives* 13:195–204.

———. 2000. "What Marshall Didn't Know: On the Twentieth Century's Contributions to Economics." *Quarterly Journal of Economics* 115:1–44.

Baumol, William, Alan Blinder, and John Solow. 2020. *Economics: Principles and Policy.* 14th ed. Boston: Cengage.

Béraud, Alain, and Guy Numa. 2018. "Beyond Say's Law: The Significance of J.-B. Say's Monetary Views." *Journal of the History of Economic Thought* 40:217–241.

Bernanke, Ben. 1983. "Nonmonetary Effects of the Financial Crisis in the Propagation of the Great Depression." *American Economic Review* 73:257–276.

———. 1995. "The Macroeconomics of the Great Depression: A Comparative Approach." *Journal of Money, Credit, and Banking* 27:1–28.

———. 2015a. *The Courage to Act: A Memoir of Crisis and Its Aftermath.* New York: Norton.

———. 2015b. "Why Are Interest Rates so Low?" and "Why Are Interest Rates so Low, Part 2: Secular Stagnation." Ben Bernanke's Blog, March 30 and 31. http:// www.brookings.edu/blogs/benbernanke/posts/2015/03/30whyinterestratesso low?wpmm=1&wpisrc=nl_wonk; http://www.brookings.edu/blogs/benbernanke/ posts/2015/03/31whyinterestrateslowsecularstagnation.

Besomi, Daniele. 2001. "Harrod's Dynamics and the Theory of Growth: The Story of a Mistaken Attribution." *Cambridge Journal of Economics* 25:79–96.

Bewley, Truman. 1999. *Why Wages Don't Fall During a Recession.* Cambridge, Mass.: Harvard University Press.

Bhaduri, Amit, and Stephen Marglin. 1990. "Unemployment and the Real Wage: The Economic Basis for Contesting Political Ideologies." *Cambridge Journal of Economics* 14:375–393.

Bhagwati, Jagdish. 1958. "Immiserizing Growth: A Geometric Note." *Review of Economic Studies* 25:201–206.

Bibow, Jörg. 2018. "How Germany's Anti-Keynesianism Has Brought Europe to Its Knees." *International Review of Applied Economics* 32:569–588.

Biden, Joe. 2009. "Remarks by the President and Vice President at Signing of the American Recovery and Reinvestment Act, February 17, 2009." The White House, President Barack Obama. https://www.whitehouse.gov/the-press-office/ remarks-president-and-vice-president-signing-american-recovery-and-reinvest ment-act (accessed February 2, 2016; site now https://obamawhitehouse.archives .gov/the-press-office/remarks-president-and-vice-president-signing-american-re covery-and-reinvestment-act).

Blanchard, Olivier, and Larry Katz. 1999. "Wage Dynamics: Reconciling Theory and Evidence." *American Economic Review* 89:69–74.

Blinder, Alan. 1988. "The Fall and Rise of Keynesian Economics." *Economic Record* 68:278–294.

Blinder, Alan S., Elie R. D. Canetti, David E. Lebow, and Jeremy B. Rudd. 1998. *Asking About Prices: A New Approach to Understanding Price Stickiness.* New York: Russell Sage Foundation.

Blinder, Alan, and Marc Zandi. 2010. "How the Great Recession Was Brought to an End." http://www.economy.com/mark-zandi/documents/end-of-great-recession .pdf (accessed February 3, 2013).

Board of Governors of the Federal Reserve System. n.d. "Industrial Production, 1957–59 Base." Washington, D.C., pp. S-148–S-149. Retrieved from FRASER, http://fraser.stlouisfed.org/docs/meltzer/bogind62.pdf (accessed June 11, 2013).

———. 1943. *Banking and Monetary Statistics, 1914–1941,* Part 1. Washington, D.C. https://fraser.stlouisfed.org/title/38 (accessed May 24, 2020).

Boehner, John. 2009. Interview by David Gregory, *Meet the Press.* "'Meet the Press' Transcript for Jan. 25, 2009." NBC News. http://www.nbcnews.com/id/28841300/ns/meet_the_press/t/meet-press-transcript-jan/#.VrVB0vkrK00 (accessed February 5, 2016).

Boianovsky, Mauro, and Roger Backhouse. 2003. *Transforming Modern Macroeconomics: Exploring Disequilibrium Microfoundations, 1956–2003.* New York: Cambridge University Press.

Brainard, William, and James Tobin. 1968. "Pitfalls in Financial Model Building." *American Economic Review* 58:99–122.

Brown, Douglass V., Edward Chamberlin, Seymour E. Harris, Wassily W. Leontief, Edward S. Mason, Joseph A. Schumpeter, and Overton H. Taylor. 1934. *The Economics of the Recovery Program.* New York: McGraw-Hill.

Brown, Tillman. 1952. "Habit Persistence and Lags in Consumer Behavior." *Econometrica* 20:355–371.

Buckley, William. 1951. *God and Man at Yale.* Chicago: Henry Regnery.

Bureau of the Census. 1935. *Statistical Abstract of the United States, 1935.* Washington, D.C.: U.S. Department of Commerce. https://www.census.gov/library/publications/1935/compendia/statab/57ed.html (accessed October 7, 2018).

———. 1975. *Historical Statistics of the United States, Colonial Times to 1970.* Washington, D.C.: U.S. Department of Commerce.

——— (Carmen DeNavas-Walt and Bernadette D. Proctor). 2014. *Income and Poverty in the United States: 2013, P60-249.* Washington, D.C.: U.S. Department of Commerce. https://www2.census.gov/library/publications/2014/demographics/p60-249.pdf (accessed October 28, 2019).

———. 2019a. *Historical Income Tables: Income Inequality.* Washington, D.C.: U.S. Department of Commerce. https://www.census.gov/data/tables/time-series/demo/income-poverty/historical-income-inequality.html (accessed October 28, 2019).

——— (Jessica Semega, Melissa Kollar et al.). 2019b. *Income and Poverty in the United States: 2018, P60-266.* Washington, D.C.: U.S. Department of Commerce. https://www.census.gov/content/dam/Census/library/publications/2019/demo/p60-266.pdf (accessed October 27, 2019).

Bureau of Economic Analysis. various dates. *National Income and Product Accounts.* Washington, D.C.: U.S. Department of Commerce. https://apps.bea.gov/iTable/iTable.cfm?reqid=19&step=2#reqid=19&step=2&isuri=1&1921=survey (accessed various dates).

Bureau of Labor Statistics. 2005. *Comparative Civilian Labor Force Statistics, 10 Countries, 1960–2004.* Washington, D.C.: U.S. Department of Labor. http://www.bls.gov/fls/flslforc.pdf (accessed February 11, 2011).

———. 2012. *Charting International Labor Comparisons.* Washington, D.C.: U.S. Department of Labor. http://www.bls.gov/fls/chartbook/2012/chartbook2012.pdf (accessed November 27, 2016).

Cai, Fang, and Meiyan Wang. 2011. "Chinese Wages and the Turning Point in the Chinese Economy." *East Asia Forum,* January 29. www.eastasiaforum.org (accessed March 13, 2016).

Calvo, Guillermo. 1983. "Staggered Prices in a Utility Maximizing Framework." *Journal of Monetary Economics* 12:382–398.

Campbell, John. 1995. "Some Lessons from the Yield Curve." *Journal of Economic Perspectives* 9:129–152.

Campbell, John, and N. Gregory Mankiw. 1989. "Consumption, Income and Interest Rates: Reinterpreting the Time Series Evidence." In *NBER Macroeconomics Annual 1989,* vol. 4, ed. Olivier Jean Blanchard and Stanley Fischer, pp. 185–246. Cambridge, Mass.: MIT Press.

Campbell, John, and Luis Viceira. 2002. *Strategic Asset Allocation: Portfolio Choice for Long-Term Investors.* Oxford: Oxford University Press.

Carlos, Ann M., and Larry Neal. 2011. "Amsterdam and London as Financial Centers in the Eighteenth Century." *Financial History Review* 18:21–46.

Carter, Susan. 2006. "Labor Force." *Historical Statistics of the United States Millennial Edition Online,* pp. 2-3 to 2-35. Cambridge: Cambridge University Press. http://hsus.cambridge.org.ezp-prod1.hul.harvard.edu/HSUSWeb/essay/showessaypdf.do?id=Ba.ESS.02 (accessed December 24, 2017).

Chamberlin, Edward. 1962. *The Theory of Monopolistic Competition.* 8th ed. Cambridge, Mass.: Harvard University Press. [First published in 1933.]

Chang, Winston W., Daniel Hamberg, and Junichi Hirata. 1983. "Liquidity Preference as Behavior toward Risk Is a Demand for Short-Term Securities—Not Money." *American Economic Review* 73:420–427.

Chayanov, Alexander. 1966. *A. V. Chayanov on the Theory of Peasant Economy.* Ed. D. Thorner, B. Kerblay, and R. Smith. Homewood, Ill.: Irwin. [Chayanov's theory of a peasant economy was first published in 1925.]

ChicagoBooth. 2012. "Economic Stimulus." IGM Forum, February 15. http://www.igmchicago.org/igm-economic-experts-panel/poll-results?SurveyID=SV_cw5O9LNJL1oz4Xi.

Chirinko, Robert. 2008. "σ: The Long and Short of It." *Journal of Macroeconomics* 30:671–686.

Chodorow-Reich, Gabriel, Laura Feiveson, Zachary Liscow, and William Gui Woolston. 2012. "Does State Fiscal Relief During Recessions Increase Employment? Evidence from the American Recovery and Reinvestment Act." *American Economic Journal: Economic Policy* 4:118–145.

Clower, Robert. 1958. "Keynes and the Classics: A Reinterpretation." Robert Clower Papers, Box 4. David M. Rubenstein Rare Book and Manuscript Library, Duke University.

———. 1960. "Keynes and the Classics: A Dynamical Perspective." *Quarterly Journal of Economics* 74:318–323.

———. 1984. "The Keynesian Counter-Revolution: A Theoretical Appraisal." In

Money and Markets: Essays by Robert Clower, ed. Donald Walker, pp. 34–58. Cambridge: Cambridge University Press. [First published in 1963 as "Die Keynesianische Gegenrevolution: Eine Theoretische Kritik." *Schweizerische Zeitschrift für Volkswirtschaft und Statistik* 99:8–31.]

Coates, Ta-Nehisi. 2014. "The Case for Reparations." *The Atlantic,* June. www.theatlantic.com/magazine/archive/2014/06/the-case-for-reparations/361631/?wpisrc=nl_daily202&wpmm=1 (accessed February 11, 2019).

Cochrane, John. 2009. "Fiscal Stimulus, Fiscal Inflation, or Fiscal Fallacies?" www.faculty.chicagobooth.edu/john.cochrane/research/papers/fiscal2.htm (accessed June 24, 2012).

Cogan, John, and John Taylor. 2012. "What the Government Purchases Multiplier Actually Multiplied in the 2009 Stimulus Package." In *Government Policies and the Delayed Economic Recovery,* ed. Lee. E. Ohanion, John B. Taylor, and Ian J. Wright, pp. 85–114. Stanford, Calif.: Hoover Institution Press.

Colander, David. 1984. "Was Keynes a Keynesian or a Lernerian?" *Journal of Economic Literature* 22:1572–1575.

———. 1995. "The Stories We Tell: A Reconsideration of AS/AD Analysis." *Journal of Economic Perspectives* 9:169–188.

Colander, David, and Harry Landreth. 1996. *The Coming of Keynesianism to America.* Cheltenham, UK: Edward Elgar.

Congressional Budget Office. 2012. "Estimated Impact of the American Recovery and Reinvestment Act on Employment and Economic Output from October 2011 Through December 2012: A CBO Study." CBO Publication No. 4435. Washington, D.C.: United States Government Printing Office. Retrieved from http://www.cbo.gov/sites/default/files/cbofiles/attachments/02-22-ARRA.pdf.

Conley, Timothy G., and Bill Dupor. 2013. "The American Recovery and Reinvestment Act: Solely a Government Jobs Program?" *Journal of Monetary Economics* 60:535–549.

Cornwall, John. 1977. *Modern Capitalism: Its Growth and Transformation.* London: Martin Robertson.

Council for Economic Education. 2010. *Voluntary National Content Standards in Economics.* 2nd ed. New York: CEE.

Council of Economic Advisers. 2014. *The Economic Impact of the American Recovery and Reinvestment Act Five Years Later: Final Report to Congress.* Washington, D.C.

Crotty, James. 2019. *Keynes Against Capitalism: His Economic Case for Liberal Socialism.* New York: Routledge.

Davidson, Paul. 1991. "Is Probability Theory Relevant for Uncertainty? A Post Keynesian Perspective." *Journal of Economic Perspectives* 5:129–143.

Davis, Chester. 1936. "The Agricultural Adjustment Act and National Recovery." *Journal of Farm Economics* 18:229–241.

Davis, Otto A., M. A. H. Dempster, and Aaron Wildavsky. 1966. "A Theory of the Budgetary Process." *American Political Science Review* 60:529–547.

———. 1974. "Towards a Predictive Theory of Government Expenditure: US Domestic Appropriations." *British Journal of Political Science* 4:419–452.

de Finetti, Bruno. 1980. "Foresight: Its Logical Laws, Its Subjective Sources." In *Studies in Subjective Probability,* 2nd ed., ed. Henry Kyburg, Jr. and Howard Smokker, pp. 53–118. Huntington, N.Y.: Krieger. [Originally published in French in 1937.]

de Tocqueville, Alexis. 1969. *Democracy in America.* Trans. George Lawrence. Ed. J. P. Meyer. Garden City, N.Y.: Doubleday. [Original French publication in two volumes in 1835 and 1840.]

De Vroey, Michel. 2016. *A History of Macroeconomics from Keynes to Lucas and Beyond.* Cambridge: Cambridge University Press.

Debreu, Gerard. 1959. *Theory of Value.* New York: Wiley.

Department of Health and Human Services. various dates. *Medicaid Financial Management Report.* www.hhs.gov (accessed various dates).

Desan, Christine. 2014. *Making Money: Coin, Currency, and the Coming of Capitalism.* Oxford: Oxford University Press.

Diamond, Peter. 1967. "The Role of the Stock Market in a General Equilibrium Model with Technological Uncertainty." *American Economic Review* 57:759–776.

Dimand, Robert, and Rebeca Gomez Betancourt. 2012. "Irving Fisher's *Appreciation and Interest* (1896) and the Fisher Relation." *Journal of Economic Perspectives* 26:185–196.

Domar, Evsey. 1946. "Capital Expansion, Rate of Growth, and Employment." *Econometrica* 14:137–147.

———. 1947. "Expansion and Employment." *American Economic Review* 37:34–55.

Dos Santos Ferreira, Rodolphe. 2014. "Mr. Keynes, the Classics and the New Keynesians: A Suggested Modelling." *European Journal of the History of Economic Thought* 21:801–838.

Dos Santos Ferreira, Rodolphe, and Philippe Michel. 1987. "The Dynamics of Keynesian Price and Wage Adjustments." Bureau d'Économie Théorique et Appliquée, University of Strasbourg, Document 8702.

———. 2013. "Keynes' Wage-Price Dynamics." *Metroeconomica* 64:44–72.

Duesenberry, James. 1949. *Income, Saving, and the Theory of Consumer Behavior.* Cambridge, Mass.: Harvard University Press.

Dunlop, John. 1938. "The Movement of Money and Real Wages." *Economic Journal* 48:413–434.

Eatwell, John, Murray Milgate, and Peter Newman, eds. 1987. *The New Palgrave: A Dictionary of Economics.* London: Macmillan.

Eggertsson, Gauti. 2008. "Great Expectations and the End of the Depression." *American Economic Review* 98:1476–1516.

Eichengreen, Barry. 2015. *Hall of Mirrors: The Great Depression, The Great Recession, And the Uses—And Misuses—of History.* Oxford: Oxford University Press.

Ellsberg, Daniel. 1961. "Risk, Ambiguity, and the Savage Axioms." *Quarterly Journal of Economics* 75:643–669.

European Central Bank. n.d. "Objective of monetary policy." http://www.ecb.europa

.eu/mopo/intro/objective/html/index.en.html (accessed December 26, 2009 and April 26, 2020).

Ezekiel, Mordecai. 1942a. "Statistical Investigations of Saving, Consumption, and Investment. Part I: Saving, Consumption and National Income." *American Economic Review* 32:22–49.

———. 1942b. "Statistical Investigations of Saving, Consumption, and Investment. Part II: Investment, National Income and The Saving-Investment Equilibrium." *American Economic Review* 32:272–307.

Farnsworth, Helen. 1940. "'World' Wheat Stocks, 1890–1914 and 1922–39." *Wheat Studies of the [Stanford] Food Research Institute* 16:39–66.

Federal Deposit Insurance Corporation (FDIC). n.d. *A Brief History of Deposit Insurance in the United States, Prepared for the International Conference on Deposit Insurance,* Washington, D.C., September 1998. https://www.fdic.gov/bank/historical/brief/brhist.pdf (accessed May 24, 2020).

Federal Open Market Committee. 2008a. "FOMC Meeting Transcript, September 16, 2008." Federal Reserve Board. http://www.federalreserve.gov/monetarypolicy/files/FOMC20080916meeting.pdf (accessed February 24, 2014).

———. 2008b. "FOMC Conference Call Transcript, October 7, 2008." Federal Reserve Board. http://www.federalreserve.gov/monetarypolicy/files/FOMC2008 1007confcall.pdf (accessed August 18, 2015).

———. 2014. "Chair's FOMC Press Conference Projections Materials, September 17, 2014." Federal Reserve Board. https://www.federalreserve.gov/monetarypolicy/files/fomcprojtabl20140917.pdf (accessed March 27, 2019).

Federal Reserve Bank of St. Louis. 2020. "Moody's Seasoned Baa Corporate Bond Yield (DBAA)." https://fred.stlouisfed.org/series/DBAA (accessed May 12, 2020).

———. various dates. https://fred.stlouisfed.org/series (accessed various dates).

Federal Reserve Board. 2005. "Testimony of Chairman Alan Greenspan. *Federal Reserve Board's semiannual Monetary Policy Report to the Congress* Before the Committee on Banking, Housing, and Urban Affairs, U.S. Senate, February 16, 2005." https://www.federalreserve.gov/boarddocs/hh/2005/february/testimony.htm (accessed February 26, 2017).

Federico, Giovanni. 2005. "Not Guilty? Agriculture in the 1920s and the Great Depression." *Journal of Economic History* 65:949–976.

Ferber, Robert. 1962. "Research on Household Behavior." *American Economic Review* 52:19–63.

Feyrer, James, and Bruce Sacerdote. 2011. "Did the Stimulus Stimulate? Real Time Estimates of the Effects of the American Recovery and Reinvestment Act." *National Bureau of Economic Research Working Paper* #16759. http://www.nber.org/papers/w16759.

Field, Alexander. 2011. *A Great Leap Forward: 1930s Depression and U.S. Economic Growth.* New Haven: Yale University Press.

Fischer, Stanley. 1977. "Long-Term Contracts, Rational Expectations, and the Optimal Money Supply Rule." *Journal of Political Economy* 85:191–205.

———. 1993. "The Role of Macroeconomic Factors in Growth." *Journal of Monetary Economics* 32:485–512.

Fisher, Frank. 1983. *Disequilibrium Foundations of Equilibrium Economics.* Cambridge: University of Cambridge Press.

Fisher, Irving. 1896. *Appreciation and Interest.* New York: Macmillan.

———. 1911. "Recent Changes in Price Levels and Their Causes." *American Economic Review* 1:37–45.

———. 1930. *The Theory of Interest, as Determined by Impatience to Spend Income and Opportunity to Invest It.* New York: Macmillan. [Originally published in 1907.]

———. 1933. "The Debt-Deflation Theory of Great Depressions." *Econometrica* 1:337–357. Reprinted in *Review of the International Statistical Institute* 1 (January 1934): 48–65.

Fleming, Michael. 2013. "Information on Dealer Activity in Specific Treasury Issues Now Available." Posted on the Federal Reserve Bank of New York website, Liberty Street Economics, August 26. http://libertystreeteconomics.newyorkfed.org/2013/08/information-on-dealer-activity-in-specific-treasury-issues-now-available.html#.VAtXIvmwLYg (accessed August 26, 2013).

Fox, Justin. 2008a. "The Comeback Keynes." *Time,* October 23. content.time.com/time/magazine/article/0,9171,1853302,00.html (accessed January 10, 2011).

———. 2008b. "Bob Lucas on the Comeback of Keynesianism." *Time,* October 28. http://curiouscapitalist.blogs.time.com/2008/10/28/bob-lucas-on-the-comeback-of-keynesianism/#ixzz1AfQ4lkta (accessed January 10, 2011).

Frank, Robert. 1999. *Luxury Fever: Money and Happiness in an Era of Excess.* New York: Free Press.

Frank, Robert, and Ben Bernanke, with the assistance of Roger Kaufman. 2007. *Principles of Economics.* 3rd ed. New York: McGraw-Hill.

Freeman, Richard, and James Medoff. 1984. *What Do Unions Do?* New York: Basic Books.

Friedman, Benjamin. 1988. *Day of Reckoning: The Consequences of American Economic Policy.* New York: Random House.

———. 1999. "The Future of Monetary Policy: The Central Bank as an Army with Only a Signal Corps?" *International Finance* 2:321–338.

———. 2005. *The Moral Consequences of Economic Growth.* New York: Knopf.

Friedman, Benjamin, and Kenneth Kuttner. 2011. "Implementation of Monetary Policy: How Do Central Banks Set Interest Rates?" In *Handbook of Monetary Economics,* vol. 3B, ed. Benjamin M. Friedman and Michael Woodford, pp. 1345–1438. The Netherlands: North-Holland.

Friedman, Milton. 1953. "The Methodology of Positive Economics." In M. Friedman, *Essays in Positive Economics*, pp. 3–43. Chicago: University of Chicago Press.

———. 1956. "The Quantity Theory of Money—A Restatement." In *Studies in the Quantity Theory of Money,* ed. M. Friedman. Chicago: University of Chicago Press.

———. 1957. *A Theory of the Consumption Function.* Princeton: Princeton University Press.

———. 1961. "The Lag in Effect of Monetary Policy." *Journal of Political Economy* 69:447–466.

———. 1962. *Capitalism and Freedom.* Chicago: University of Chicago Press.

———. 1968. "The Role of Monetary Policy." *American Economic Review* 58:1–17.

———. 1969. "The Optimum Quantity of Money." In M. Friedman, *The Optimum Quantity of Money and Other Essays.* Chicago: Aldine.

———. 1970. "A Theoretical Framework for Monetary Analysis." *Journal of Political Economy* 78:193–238.

———. 1983. "Washington: Less Red Ink." *The Atlantic,* February. https://www.theatlantic.com/magazine/archive/1983/02/washington-less-red-ink/305450/ (accessed January 15, 2018).

———. 1987. "The Quantity Theory of Money." In *The New Palgrave: A Dictionary of Economics,* vol. 4, ed. J. Eatwell, M. Milgate, and P. Newman, pp. 3–20. London and Basingstoke: Macmillan.

Friedman, Milton, and Anna Schwartz. 1963a. *A Monetary History of the United States, 1867–1960.* Princeton: Princeton University Press.

———. 1963b. "Money and Business Cycles." *Review of Economics and Statistics* 45 (1), pt. 2, Supplement (February): 59–63.

Froot, Kenneth. 1989. "New Hope for the Expectations Hypothesis of the Term Structure of Interest Rates." *Journal of Finance* 44:283–305.

Galbraith, John Kenneth. 1967. *The New Industrial State.* Boston: Houghton-Mifflin.

———. 1981. *A Life in Our Times.* Boston: Houghton-Mifflin.

———. 1998. *The Affluent Society.* Boston: Houghton-Mifflin. [First published in 1958.]

Geithner, Timothy. 2014. *Stress Test: Reflections on Financial Crises.* New York: Crown.

Gellner, Ernest. 1983. *Nations and Nationalism.* Ithaca, N.Y.: Cornell University Press.

Gibson, Campbell, and Kay Jung. 2006. "Historical Census Statistics on the Foreign-Born Population of the United States: 1850–2000." Washington, D.C.: U.S. Bureau of the Census. https://www.census.gov/population/www/documentation/twps0081/twps0081.html (accessed May 25, 2020).

Goldfeld, Stephen, and Daniel Sichel. 1990. "The Demand for Money." In *Handbook of Monetary Economics,* vol. 1, ed. Benjamin Friedman and Frank Hahn, pp. 300–356. Amsterdam: Elsevier.

Goodfriend, Marvin, and Monica Hargraves. 1983. "A Historical Assessment of the Rationales and Functions of Reserve Requirements." *Economic Review,* Federal Reserve Bank of Richmond (March–April): 3–21.

Gordon, Robert. 1984. "Supply Shocks and Monetary Policy Revisited." *American Economic Review* 74:38–43.

———. 2013. "The Phillips Curve Is Alive and Well: Inflation and the NAIRU During the Slow Recovery." NBER Working Paper 19390. http://www.nber.org/papers/w19390 (accessed October 26, 2015).

——. 2014. "The Turtle's Progress: Secular Stagnation Meets the Headwinds." In *Secular Stagnation: Facts, Causes, and Cures,* ed. C. Teulings and R. Baldwin, pp. 47–60. London: CEPR Press.

——. 2015. *The Rise and Fall of American Growth.* Princeton: Princeton University Press.

Gordon, Robert, and Robert Krenn. 2010. "The End of the Great Depression 1939–41: Policy Contributions and Fiscal Multipliers." NBER Working Paper 16380. Cambridge, Mass.: National Bureau of Economic Research.

Gramlich, Edward. 1978. "State and Local Budgets the Day after It Rained: Why Is the Surplus So High?" *Brookings Papers on Economic Activity* 1978 (1):191–216.

——. 1979. "Macro Policy Responses to Price Shocks." *Brookings Papers on Economic Activity* 1979 (1):125–166.

Grigoli, Francesco, Alexander Hermana, and Klaus Schmidt-Hebbel. 2016. "The Impact of Terms of Trade and Macroeconomic Regimes on Private Saving." *Economics Letters* 145:172–175. http://dx.doi.org/10.1016/j.econlet.2016.06.020 (accessed November 29, 2017).

Gürkaynak, Refet, Brian Sack, and Jonathan H. Wright. 2006. "The U.S. Treasury Yield Curve: 1961 to the Present." Finance and Economics Discussion Series, Federal Reserve Board, Washington, D.C.

Gürkaynak, Refet, and Jonathan Wright. 2012. "Macroeconomics and the Term Structure." *Journal of Economic Literature* 50:331–367.

Gwartney, James, Richard Stroup, Russell Sobel, and David Macpherson. n.d. "Are We Running Out of Resources?" http://commonsenseeconomics.com/wp-content/uploads/CSE_H_Reading-Gwartney_Stroup_Sobel_Macpherson-Are_We_Running_Out_of_Resources.pdf (accessed March 14, 2016).

Haberler, Gottfried. 1939. *Prosperity and Depression: A Theoretical Analysis of Cyclical Movements.* Rev. ed. Geneva: League of Nations.

——. 1941. *Prosperity and Depression: A Theoretical Analysis of Cyclical Movements.* 3rd ed. Geneva: League of Nations.

——. 1946. "The Place of the *General Theory of Employment, Interest, and Money* in the History of Economic Thought." *Review of Economics and Statistics* 28:187–194.

Hager, Sandy. 2016. *Public Debt, Inequality, and Power: The Making of a Modern Debt State.* Oakland, Calif.: University of California Press.

Hall, Robert. 1978. "Stochastic Implications of the Life Cycle-Permanent Income Hypothesis: Theory and Evidence." *Journal of Political Economy* 86:971–987.

Hansen, Alvin. 1938. *Full Recovery or Stagnation?* New York: Norton.

——. 1941. *Fiscal Policy and Business Cycles.* New York: Norton.

——. 1953. *Guide to Keynes.* New York: McGraw-Hill.

Harris, Donald. 1978. *Capital Accumulation and Income Distribution.* Stanford, Calif.: Stanford University Press.

Harrod, Roy. 1937. "Mr. Keynes and Traditional Theory." *Econometrica* 5:74–86.

———. 1939. "An Essay in Dynamic Theory." *Economic Journal* 49:14–33.

———. 1948. *Towards a Dynamic Economics: Some Recent Developments of Economic Theory and Their Application to Policy.* London: Macmillan.

Hausman, Joshua K., Paul W. Rhode, and Johannes F. Wieland. 2019. "Recovery from the Great Depression: The Farm Channel in Spring 1933." *American Economic Review* 109:427–472.

Hawtrey, Ralph. 1937. *Capital and Employment.* London: Longmans, Greene.

Henderson, David. 2009. "Why Everyone Read Samuelson." *Wall Street Journal,* December 14.

Henderson, H. D. 1938. "The Significance of the Rate of Interest." *Oxford Economic Papers* 1:1–13.

Herndon, Thomas, Michael Ash, and Robert Pollin. 2014. "Does High Public Debt Consistently Stifle Economic Growth? A Critique of Reinhart and Rogoff." *Cambridge Journal of Economics* 38:257–279.

Hicks, John. 1937. "Mr Keynes and the Classics." *Econometrica* 5:147–159.

———. 1946. *Value and Capital.* Oxford: Clarendon Press. [First published in 1939.]

———. 1967. "Monetary History and Theory—An Attempt at Perspective." In J. Hicks, *Critical Essays in Monetary Theory,* pp. 155–173. Oxford: Clarendon Press.

———. 1974. *The Crisis in Keynesian Economics.* Oxford: Basil Blackwell.

Historical Statistics of the United States, Millennial Edition Online. n.d. Susan Carter and Richard Sutch, General Editors. Cambridge University Press. https://hsus .cambridge.org/HSUSWeb/HSUSEntryServlet (accessed various dates).

HM Treasury and The Rt Hon George Osborne. 2015. *Repayment of £2.6 Billion Historical Debt to Be Completed by Government,* March 27. https://www.gov.uk/gov ernment/news/repayment-of-26-billion-historical-debt-to-be-completed-by-gov ernment (accessed April 25, 2018).

Hoover, Herbert. 1952. *The Memoirs of Herbert Hoover.* Vol. 3, *The Great Depression 1929–1941.* New York: Macmillan.

House of Representatives, Committee on the Budget. 2011. *Path to Prosperity: Restoring America's Promise.* Washington, D.C.: United States Congress.

Houthakker, Hendrik, and Lester Taylor. 1966. *Consumer Demand in the United States, 1929–1970: Analyses and Projections.* Cambridge, Mass.: Harvard University Press.

Hume, David. n.d. "Of Money." In *Hume's Political Discourses: With An Introduction By William Bell Robertson,* pp. 27–39. London and Felling-on-Tyne: Walter Scott. [First published as *Political Discourses* in 1752.]

Humphrey, Thomas. 1992. "The Real Bills Doctrine." *Economic Review,* Federal Reserve Bank of Richmond (September–October): 3–13.

Innes, A. Mitchell. 1913. "What is Money?" *Banking Law Journal* 31 (May): 377–408.

———. 1914. "The Credit Theory of Money." *Banking Law Journal* 32 (February): 151–168.

Intergovernmental Panel on Climate Change. 2018. *Global Warming of 1.5°C: Summary for Policymakers.* http://www.ipcc.ch/ (accessed October 26, 2018).

International Energy Agency. 2015. *Energy and Climate Change.* Paris: International Energy Agency.

Irons, John, and Josh Bivens. 2010. "Government Debt and Economic Growth: Overreaching Claims of Debt 'Threshold' Suffer from Theoretical and Empirical Flaws." *Economic Policy Institute Briefing Paper #271,* July.

Johnson, Harry. 1955. "Economic Expansion and International Trade." *Manchester School of Economic and Social Studies* 23:95–112.

———. 1961. "The General Theory after Twenty-Five Years." *American Economic Review* 51:1–17.

Jonas, Jiri. 2012. "Great Recession and Fiscal Squeeze at U.S. Subnational Government Level." International Monetary Fund Working Paper WP/12/184. Washington: International Monetary Fund.

Kahn, Richard. 1931. "The Relation of Home Investment to Unemployment." *Economic Journal* 41:173–198.

Kahneman, Daniel, and Amos Tversky. 1979. "Prospect Theory: An Analysis of Decision under Risk." *Econometrica* 47:263–291.

Kaldor, Nicholas. 1934. "A Classificatory Note on the Determination of Equilibrium." *Review of Economic Studies* 1:122–136.

———. 1966. "Marginal Productivity and the Macro-Economic Theories of Distribution." *Review of Economic Studies* 33:309–319.

Kalecki, Michał. 1944. "Professor Pigou on 'The Classical Stationary State,' A Comment." *Economic Journal* 54:131–132.

———. 1971. "Outline of a Theory of the Business Cycle." In *Selected Essays on the Dynamics of the Capitalist Economy,* pp. 1–14. Cambridge: Cambridge University Press. [Originally published in Polish in 1933.]

———. 1982. "Some Remarks on Keynes's *General Theory.*" In Ferdinando Targetti and Bogulslawa Kinda-Hass, "Kalecki's Review of Keynes's *General Theory.*" *Australian Economic Papers,* pp. 244–260. [First published in Polish in *Ekonomista,* 1936.]

Kaletsky, Anatole. 2014. "Now May Not Be the Time to Buy Bonds." *Reuters,* June 6. http://blogs.reuters.com/anatole-kaletsky/2014/06/06/now-may-not-be-the-time-to-buy-bonds/ (accessed August 19, 2014).

Kane, Edward. 1970. "The Term Structure of Interest Rates: An Attempt to Reconcile Teaching with Practice." *Journal of Finance* 25:361–374.

Kemmerer, Edwin. 1911. "Money and Prices: Discussion." *American Economic Review* 1:52–58.

Keynes, John Maynard. 1914. "Review of A Mitchell Innes, 'What is Money?'" *Economic Journal* 24:419–421.

———. 1919. *The Economic Consequences of the Peace.* London: Macmillan.

———. 1921. *A Treatise on Probability.* London: Macmillan.

———. 1930. *A Treatise on Money.* London: Macmillan.

———. 1931a. "A Programme for Expansion." In *Essays in Persuasion,* pp. 118–134. London: Macmillan. [Condensed from "Can Lloyd George Do It?, a campaign tract written jointly with H. D. Henderson in support of the Liberal Party in 1929.]

———. 1931b. "Economic Possibilities for Our Grandchildren." In *Essays in Persuasion,* pp. 358–373. London: Macmillan. [First published in *The Nation and Athenaeum,* October 11 and 18, 1930.]

———. 1933. *The Means to Prosperity.* London: Macmillan. http://www.gutenberg.ca/ebooks/keynes-means/keynes-means-00-h.html (retrieved July 23, 2015).

———. 1934. "Is the Economic System Self-Adjusting?" *Listener* (November 21): 850–851. Reprinted, with editorial changes, as "A Self-Adjusting Economic System?" *New Republic* (February 20, 1935): 35–37.

———. 1936. *The General Theory of Employment, Interest and Money.* London: Macmillan.

———. 1937a. "The General Theory of Employment." *Quarterly Journal of Economics* 51:209–223.

———. 1937b. "Alternative Theories of the Rate of Interest." *Economic Journal* 47:241–252.

———. 1939. "Relative Movements of Real Wages and Output." *Economic Journal* 49:34–41.

———. 1940. *How to Pay for the War: A Radical Plan for the Chancellor of the Exchequer.* London: Macmillan.

———. 1973a. *Collected Writings of John Maynard Keynes.* Vol. 13, *The General Theory and After, Part 1, Preparation.* Ed. Donald Moggridge. London and New York: Macmillan and Cambridge University Press.

———. 1973b. *The Collected Writings of John Maynard Keynes.* Vol. 14, *The* General Theory *and After, Part II, Defence and Development.* Ed. Donald Moggridge. London and New York: Macmillan.

———. 1980. *Collected Works of John Maynard Keynes.* Vol. 27, *Activities 1940–6: Shaping the Post-War World: Employment and Commodities.* Ed. Donald Moggridge. London and New York: Macmillan and Cambridge University Press.

———. 1981. *Collected Works of John Maynard Keynes.* Vol. 19, *Activities 1922–9: The Return to Gold and Industrial Policy.* Ed. Donald Moggridge. London and New York: Macmillan and Cambridge University Press.

———. 1982. *The Collected Writings of John Maynard Keynes.* Vol. 21, *Activities 1931–9; World Crises and Policies in Britain and America.* Ed. Donald Moggridge. London and New York: Macmillan and Cambridge University Press.

Khan, Moshin, and Abdelhak Senhadji. 2001. "Threshold Effects in the Relationship Between Inflation and Growth." *IMF Staff Papers* 48:1–21.

Klein, Lawrence. 1947. *The Keynesian Revolution.* New York: Macmillan.

Knapp, Georg Friedrich. 1924. *The State Theory of Money.* Trans. H. M. Lucas and J. Bonar. London: Macmillan. [First published as *Staatliche Theorie des Geldes.* Leipzig: Duncker and Hublot, 1905.]

Knight, Frank. 1921. *Risk, Uncertainty and Profit.* Boston: Houghton Mifflin.

———. 1937. "Unemployment: And Mr. Keynes's Revolution in Economic Theory." *Canadian Journal of Economics and Political Science* 3:100–123.

Koesler, Simon, and Michael Schymura. 2015. "Substitution Elasticities in a Constant Elasticity of Substitution Framework—Empirical Estimates Using Nonlinear Least Squares." *Economic Systems Research* 27:101–121.

Koopmans, Tjalling. 1957. *Three Essays on the State of Economic Science.* New York: McGraw-Hill.

Krishnamurthy, Arvind, and Annette Vissing-Jorgensen. 2012. "The Aggregate Demand for Treasury Debt." *Journal of Political Economy* 120:233–267.

Krugman, Paul. 2009. *The Return of Depression Economics and the Crisis of 2008.* New York: Norton.

———. 2014. "Four Observations on Secular Stagnation." In *Secular Stagnation: Facts, Causes, and Cures,* ed. C. Teulings and R. Baldwin, pp. 61–68. London: CEPR Press.

Krugman, Paul, and Robin Wells. 2018. *Economics.* 5th ed. New York: Worth.

Kuznets, Simon, assisted by Lillian Epstein and Elizabeth Jenks. 1941a. *National Income and Its Composition, 1919–1938.* New York: National Bureau of Economic Research.

Kuznets, Simon. 1941b. "Capital Formation, Past and Present." Paper presented at the meeting of the American Statistical Association, December 1941.

Kydland, Finn, and Edward Prescott. 1982. "Time to Build and Aggregate Fluctuations." *Econometrica* 50:1345–1370.

Laffer, Arthur. 2004. "The Laffer Curve: Past, Present, and Future." Heritage Foundation Backgrounder #1765. http://www.heritage.org/research/reports/2004/06/the-laffer-curve-past-present-and-future (accessed July 23, 2015).

Laidler, David. 1999. *Fabricating the Keynesian Revolution.* Cambridge: Cambridge University Press.

Laughlin, J. Laurence. 1911. "Causes of the Changes in Prices Since 1896." *American Economic Review* 1:26–36.

Lavoie, Marc. 2014. *Post-Keynesian Economics: New Foundations.* Cheltenham, UK: Edward Elgar.

Leduc, Sylvain, and Daniel Wilson. 2017. "Are State Governments Roadblocks to Federal Stimulus? Evidence on the Flypaper Effect of Highway Grants in the 2009 Recovery Act." *American Economic Journal: Economic Policy* 9:253–292.

Leijonhufvud, Axel. 1968. *On Keynesian Economics and the Economics of Keynes.* New York: Oxford University Press.

Lerner, Abba. 1941. "The Economic Steering Wheel: The People's New Clothes." *University* [of Kansas City] *Review* (June): 2–8.

———. 1943. "Functional Finance and the Federal Debt." *Social Research* 10:38–51.

———. 1944. *The Economics of Control: Principles of Welfare Economics.* New York: Macmillan.

———. 1951. *Economics of Employment.* New York: McGraw-Hill.

———. 1978. "Keynesianism: Alive, If Not So Well." In *Fiscal Responsibilities in a*

Constitutional Democracy, ed. James Buchanan and Richard Wagner. Boston: Martinus Nijhoff.

Lewis, W. Arthur. 1954. "Economic Development with Unlimited Supplies of Labour." *Manchester School of Economic and Social Studies* 22:139–191.

Lo, Stephanie, and Ken Rogoff. 2015. "Secular Stagnation, Debt Overhang and Other Rationales for Sluggish Growth, Six Years On." BIS Working Papers No 482, January.

Lowenstein, Roger. 2015. *America's Bank: The Epic Struggle to Create the Federal Reserve.* New York: Penguin.

Lucas, Robert. 1977. "Understanding Business Cycles." *Carnegie-Rochester Conference Series on Public Policy* 5:7–29.

———. 1981. "Tobin and Monetarism: A Review Article." *Journal of Economic Literature* 19:558–567.

———. 2013. "The Death of Keynesian Economics." (A lecture delivered to the annual management conference held at the Graduate School of the University of Chicago in 1979.) In Lucas, *Collected Papers on Monetary Theory,* ed. Max Gillman. Cambridge, Mass.: Harvard University Press.

Madsen, Jakob. 2001. "Agricultural Crises and the International Transmission of the Great Depression." *Journal of Economic History* 61:327–365.

———. 2004a. "Price and Wage Stickiness During the Great Depression." *European Review of Economic History* 8:263–295.

———. 2004b. "The Length and the Depth of the Great Depression: An International Comparison." *Research in Economic History* 22:239–288.

Magliocca, Gerard. 2011. "The Gold Clause Cases and Constitutional Necessity." *Florida Law Review* 63:1–34.

Malinvaud, Edmond. 1977. *The Theory of Unemployment Reconsidered.* Oxford: Basil Blackwell.

———. 1980. *Profitability and Unemployment.* Cambridge: Cambridge University Press.

Malthus, Thomas. 1798. *An Essay on the Principle of Population, as It Affects the Future Improvement of Society.* London: Printed for J. Johnson, in St. Paul's Church-Yard.

Mandeville, Bernard. 1988. *Fable of the Bees, or Private Vices, Publick Benefits.* Vol. 1. Ed. F Kaye. Indianapolis: Liberty Classics. [First published in 1714; the Kaye edition was first published in 1924.]

Mankiw, N. Gregory. 1997. "Comment." In *Reducing Inflation: Motivation and Strategy,* ed. Christina Romer and David Romer, pp. 65–69. Chicago: University of Chicago Press.

———. 2018. *Principles of Economics.* 8th ed. Boston: Cengage.

Marcuzzo, Maria Cristina. 2010. "Whose Welfare State? Beveridge versus Keynes." In *No Wealth but Life: Welfare Economics and the Welfare State in Britain, 1880–1945,* ed. R. Backhouse and T. Nishizawa, pp. 189–206. Cambridge: Cambridge University Press.

Marglin, Stephen. 1970. "A Reformulation and Extension of Keynesian Theory." *Economic Journal* 80:910–931.

———. 1984. *Growth, Distribution, and Prices.* Cambridge, Mass.: Harvard University Press.

———. 1990. "Losing Touch: The Cultural Conditions of Worker Accommodation and Resistance." In *Dominating Knowledge: Development, Culture, and Resistance,* ed. F. Apffel-Marglin and Stephen A. Marglin, pp. 217–282. Oxford: Clarendon Press.

———. 2008. *The Dismal Science: How Thinking Like an Economist Undermines Community.* Cambridge, Mass.: Harvard University Press.

———. 2017. "Wages, Prices, and Employment in a Keynesian Long Run." *Review of Keynesian Economics* 5 (Autumn): 360–425.

Marglin, Stephen, and Amit Bhaduri. 1990. "Profit Squeeze and Keynesian Theory." In *The Golden Age of Capitalism,* ed. S. Marglin and J. Schor, pp. 153–186. Oxford: Clarendon Press.

Marglin, Stephen, and Peter Spiegler. 2013. "Unpacking the Multiplier: Making Sense of Recent Assessments of Fiscal Stimulus Policy." *Social Research* 80:819–854.

Margo, Robert. 1993. "Employment and Unemployment in the 1930s." *Journal of Economic Perspectives* 7:41–59.

Marschak, Jacob. 1951. *Income, Employment, and the Price Level: Notes on Lectures Given at the University of Chicago, Autumn, 1948 and 1949.* New York: Kelley.

Marshall, Alfred. 1920. *Principles of Economics: An Introductory Volume.* 8th ed. London: Macmillan. [First published in 1890.]

Martin, Percival. 1924. *The Flaw in the Price System.* London: King.

Marx, Karl. 1959. *Capital.* Vol. 1, *A Critical Analysis of Capitalist Production.* Moscow: Foreign Languages Publishing House. [Originally published in German in 1867.]

Mas-Colell, Andreu, Michael Whinston, and Jerry Green. 1995. *Microeconomic Theory.* New York: Oxford University Press.

McCulloch, J. Huston. 1971. "Measuring the Term Structure of Interest Rates." *Journal of Business* 44:19–31.

———. 1975. "The Tax-Adjusted Yield Curve." *Journal of Finance* 30:811–830.

Meade, J. E. 1937. "A Simplified Model of Mr. Keynes' System." *Review of Economic Studies* 4:98–107.

Meade, J. E., and P. W. S. Andrews. 1938. "Summary of Replies to Questions on Effects of Interest Rates." *Oxford Economic Papers* 1:14–31.

Mill, John Stuart. 1909. *Principles of Political Economy, With Some of Their Applications to Social Philosophy.* Ed., with an introduction, W. J. Ashley. London: Longmans Green. [First published in 1848.]

Miron, Jeffrey, and Christina Romer. 1990. "A New Monthly Index of Industrial Production, 1884–1940." *Journal of Economic History* 50:321–337.

Mishkin, Frederic. 1978. "The Household Balance Sheet and the Great Depression." *Journal of Economic History* 38:918–937.

Mittelstaedt, Martin. 2012. "Why CP's Old-Time Bondholders Have a Big Say in the Future." *Toronto Globe and Mail,* May 9. http://www.theglobeandmail.com/globe-investor/why-cps-old-time-bondholders-have-a-big-say-in-the-future/article4105862/ (accessed December 9, 2014).

Modigliani, Franco. 1944. "Liquidity Preference and the Theory of Interest and Money." *Econometrica* 12:45–88.

Modigliani, Franco, and Richard Brumberg. 1954. "Utility Analysis and the Consumption Function: An Interpretation of Cross-Section Data." In *Post Keynesian Economics,* ed. Kenneth K. Kurihara. New Brunswick, N.J.: Rutgers University Press.

Modigliani, Franco, and Richard Sutch. 1966. "Innovations in Interest Rate Policy." *American Economic Review* 56:178–197.

Nakamoto, Michiyo, and David Wighton. 2007. "Citigroup Chief Stays Bullish on Buy-Outs." *Financial Times,* July 9. http://www.ft.com/intl/cms/s/0/80e2987a-2e50-11dc-821c-0000779fd2ac.html#axzz3cQ8HaX00

National Association of State Budget Officers (NASBO). 2009. *The Fiscal Survey of States,* December. Washington, D.C.

———. 2012. *The Fiscal Survey of States,* Spring. Washington, D.C.

National Commission on Fiscal Responsibility and Reform. 2010. *Moment of Truth: Report of the National Commission on Fiscal Responsibility and Reform.* Washington, D.C.: The White House.

New York Times. 2010. "The Truth About the Deficit." An editorial from February 7. http://www.nytimes.com/2010/02/07/opinion/07sun1.html?scp=2&sq=+budget&st=nyt (accessed February 19, 2010).

Nord, Mark, and Mark Prell. 2011. "Food Security Improved Following the 2009 ARRA Increase in SNAP Benefits." ERR-116, U.S. Department of Agriculture, Economic Research Service, April. www.ers.usda.gov (accessed March 31, 2016).

O'Donnell, Rod. 1999. "Keynes's Socialism: Conception, Strategy and Espousal." In *Keynes, Post Keynesianism and Political Economy: Essays in Honour of Geoff Harcourt, Volume III,* ed. Claudio Sardoni and Peter Kriesler, pp. 149–175. New York: Routledge.

O'Driscoll, Gerald. 1976. "The Ricardian Nonequivalence Theorem." *Journal of Political Economy* 85:207–210.

Parker, Jonathan A. 2011. "On Measuring the Effects of Fiscal Policy in Recessions." *Journal of Economic Literature* 49:703–718.

Pasinetti, Luigi. 1962. "Rate of Profit and Income Distribution in Relation to the Rate of Economic Growth." *Review of Economic Studies* 29:267–279.

Patinkin, Don. 1948. "Price Flexibility and Full Employment." *American Economic Review* 38:543–564.

———. 1949. "The Indeterminacy of Absolute Prices in Classical Economic Theory." *Econometrica* 17:1–27.

———. 1951. "Price Flexibility and Full Employment." In *Readings in Monetary Theory,* ed. F. A. Lutz and L. W. Mints. Homewood, Ill.: Irwin. [Revised version of Patinkin (1948).]

———. 1965. *Money, Interest, and Prices: An Integration of Monetary and Value Theory.* 2nd ed. New York: Harper and Row. [First published in 1956.]

Paulson, Henry. 2010. *On the Brink: Inside the Race to Stop the Collapse of the Global Financial System.* New York: Business Plus.

Phelps, Edmund. 1968. "Money-Wage Dynamics and Labor-Market Equilibrium." *Journal of Political Economy* 76:678–711.

Phillips, A. William. 1958. "The Relation between Unemployment and the Rate of Change of Money Wage Rates in the United Kingdom, 1861–1957." *Economica* 25:283–299.

Pigou, Arthur. 1927. "Wage Policy and Unemployment." *Economic Journal* 37:353–368.

———. 1933. *The Theory of Unemployment.* London: Macmillan.

———. 1943. "The Classical Stationary State." *Economic Journal* 53:343–351.

———. 1947. "Economic Progress in a Stable Environment." *Economica* 14:180–188.

Piketty, Thomas. 2014. *Capital in the Twenty-First Century.* Trans. Arthur Goldhammer. Cambridge, Mass.: Harvard University Press.

———. 2015. "About Capital in the 21st Century." *American Economic Review* 105:48–53.

———. 2020. *Capital and Ideology.* Trans. Arthur Goldhammer. Cambridge, Mass.: Harvard University Press.

Piketty, Thomas, and Emmanuel Saez. 2015. "Wealth and Inheritance in the Long Run." In *Handbook of Income Distribution,* vol. 2, ed. Anthony Atkinson and François Bourguignon. Amsterdam: North Holland.

Plassard, Romain. 2018. "Clower's *Volte-Face* Regarding the 'Keynesian Revolution.'" *History of Political Economy* 50:261–287.

Pryor, Frederic. 2007. "Immiserizing Growth as Seen by Bhagwati, Samuelson, and Others." *Journal of Economic Education* 38:208–214.

Ramey, Valerie A. 2011. "Can Government Purchases Stimulate the Economy." *Journal of Economic Literature* 49:673–685.

Ramsey, Frank. 1980. "Truth and Probability." In *Studies in Subjective Probability,* 2nd ed., ed. Henry Kyburg, Jr. and Howard Smokker, pp. 23–52. Huntington, N.Y.: Krieger. [First published in 1926.]

Reinhart, Carmen, and Kenneth Rogoff. 2010. "Growth in a Time of Debt." NBER Working Paper 15639. [Condensed in *American Economic Review* 100 (2010): 573–578.]

Reinhart, Carmen, Vincent Reinhart, and Kenneth Rogoff. 2012. "Public Debt Overhangs: Advanced-Economy Episodes since 1800." *Journal of Economic Perspectives* 26:69–86.

Ricardo, David. 1810. "Essay on the Funding System." Supplement to the 4th, 5th, and 6th editions of *The Encyclopedia Britannica.* Online edition downloaded from www.amazon.com, August 17, 2015.

———. 1951. *On the Principles of Political Economy and Taxation.* Vol. 1 of *The Works and Correspondence of David Ricardo*, ed. Piero Sraffa with the collaboration of M. H. Dobb. Cambridge: Cambridge University Press. [*On the Principles of Political Economy and Taxation* was first published in 1817.]

Robertson, Dennis. 1935. Personal correspondence, to Keynes, February 3, 1935, commenting on a draft of *The General Theory.* In Keynes 1973a.

———. 1937. [Alternative Theories of the Rate of Interest, II.] In Bertil Ohlin, Dennis Robertson, and Ralph Hawtrey, "Alternative Theories of the Rate of Interest: Three Rejoinders." *Economic Journal* 47:423–443.

Robinson, Joan. 1933a. "A Parable on Savings and Investment." *Economica* (39): 75–84.

———. 1933b. "The Theory of Money and the Analysis of Output." *Review of Economic Studies* 1:22–26.

———. 1962. *Essays in the Theory of Economic Growth.* London: Macmillan.

———. 1966. *The Accumulation of Capital.* 2nd ed. London: Macmillan. [First published in 1956.]

———. 1969. *The Economics of Imperfect Competition.* 2nd ed. London: Macmillan. [First published in 1933.]

———. 1980. "History vs Equilibrium." *Collected Economic Papers.* Vol. 5. Cambridge: Basil Blackwell; and Cambridge, Mass.: MIT Press.

Rogoff, Kenneth. 2013. *FAQ on Herndon, Ash and Pollin's Critique of "Growth in a Time of Debt,"* October 1. Harvard University. https://scholar.harvard.edu/files/rogoff/files/faq_on_hap_update.pdf (accessed January 15, 2018).

Romer, Christina. 1986. "Spurious Volatility in Historical Unemployment Data." *Journal of Political Economy* 94:1–37.

Romer, Christina, and Jared Bernstein. 2009. "The Job Impact of the American Recovery and Reinvestment Plan." White House Council of Economic Advisers. Washington, D.C. http://otrans.3cdn.net/45593e8ecbd339d074_l3m6bt1te.pdf (accessed August 8, 2012).

Roosevelt, Franklin D. 1933. "Franklin D. Roosevelt's First Inaugural Address," March 4. National Archives Catalog. https://catalog.archives.gov/id/197333 (accessed September 28, 2018).

Rowthorn, Bob. 1982. "Demand, Real Wages, and Economics Growth." *Studi Economici* 18:3–53.

Saez, Emmanuel. 2014. *Income and Wealth Inequality: Evidence and Policy Implications.* Neubauer Collegium Lecture, University of Chicago. https://eml.berkeley.edu/~saez/lecture_saez_chicago14.pdf (accessed October 27, 2019).

Samuelson, Paul. 1941. "Stability of Equilibrium: Comparative Statics and Dynamics." *Econometrica* 9:97–120.

———. 1943. "Full Employment after the War." In *Postwar Economic Problems,* ed. S. Harris, pp. 27–54. New York: McGraw-Hill.

———. 1946. "Lord Keynes and the *General Theory.*" *Econometrica* 14:187–200.

———. 1947. *Foundations of Economic Analysis.* Cambridge, Mass.: Harvard University Press.

———. 1948. *Economics: An Introductory Analysis.* New York: McGraw-Hill.

———. 1955. *Economics: An Introductory Analysis.* 3rd ed. New York: McGraw-Hill.

———. 1964. "A Brief Post-Keynesian Survey." In *Keynes' General Theory: Reports of Three Decades,* ed. Robert Lekachman. New York: St Martins.

———. 1980. *Economics.* 11th ed. New York: McGraw-Hill.

Sargent, Thomas. 1972. "Rational Expectations and the Term Structure of Interest Rates." *Journal of Money, Credit, and Banking* 4:74–97.

Savage, Leonard J. 1954. *The Foundations of Statistics.* New York: Wiley.

Schor, Juliet. 1998. *The Overspent American: Upscaling, Downscaling, and the New Consumer.* New York: Basic Books.

Schumpeter, Joseph. 1934. "Depressions." In Brown, Chamberlin et al. 1934, pp. 3–21.

———. 1942. *Capitalism, Socialism and Democracy.* New York: Harper and Brothers.

———. 1949. "Science and Ideology." *American Economic Review* 39:346–359.

———. 1954. *History of Economic Analysis.* New York: Oxford University Press.

———. 1961. *The Theory of Economic Development: An Inquiry into Profits, Capital, Credit, Interest, and the Business Cycle.* Trans. Redvers Opie. Oxford: Oxford University Press. [First English publication in 1934. Originally published as *Theorie der Wirtschaftlischen Entwicklung,* Leipzig: Duncker and Hublot, 1912.]

Scitovsky [de Scitovszky], Tibor. 1940. "A Study of Interest and Capital." *Economica,* new series, 7:293–317.

Securities Industry and Financial Markets Association. 2018. Statistics. http://www.sifma.org/research/statistics/ (accessed October 6, 2018).

———. 2020. Statistics. http://www.sifma.org/research/statistics/ (accessed May 12, 2020).

Shiller, Robert. 1997. "Why Do People Dislike Inflation?" In *Reducing Inflation: Motivation and Strategy,* ed. Christina Romer and David Romer, pp. 13–65. Chicago: University of Chicago Press.

———. 2017. "Narrative Economics." *American Economic Review* 107:967–1004.

Shoag, Daniel. 2010. "The Impact of Government Spending Shocks: Evidence on the Multiplier from State Pension Plan Returns." Unpublished working paper.

———. 2013. "Using State Pension Shocks to Estimate Fiscal Multipliers since the Great Recession." *American Economic Review* 103:121–124.

Sims, Christopher. 1980. "Macroeconomics and Reality." *Econometrica* 48:1–48.

———. 2007. "On the Fit of New Keynesian Models: Comment." *Journal of Business and Economic Statistics* 25:152–154.

Skidelsky, Robert. 2000. *John Maynard Keynes vol. 3: Fighting for Britain, 1937–1946.* London: Macmillan.

———. 2009. *Keynes: The Return of the Master.* New York: Public Affairs, 2009.

Smith, Adam. 1937. *The Wealth of Nations.* Ed. E. Cannan. New York: Modern Library. [First published in 1776.]

———. 1982. *The Theory of Moral Sentiments.* Ed. D. Raphael and A. Macfie. Indianapolis: Liberty Classics. [First published in 1759.]

Social Security Board. 1937. *Unemployment Compensation: What and Why?,* Publication No. 14. Washington, D.C.: United States Government Printing Office. http://www.larrydewitt.net/SSinGAPE/UI1937book2.htm (accessed February 4, 2010).

Solow, Robert. 1956. "A Contribution to the Theory of Growth." *Quarterly Journal of Economics* 70:65–94.

———. 1979. "Alternative Approaches to Macroeconomic Theory: A Partial View." *Canadian Journal of Economics / Revue canadienne d'Economique* 12:339–354.

———. 1990. *The Labor Market as a Social Institution.* Cambridge, Mass.: Blackwell.

Solow, Robert, and Joseph Stiglitz. 1968. "Output, Employment, and Wages in the Short Run." *Quarterly Journal of Economics* 82:537–560.

Stack, Carol. 1975. *All Our Kin: Strategies for Survival in a Black Community.* New York: Harper Colophon.

Statistical Abstracts of the United States. various dates. https://www.census.gov/library/publications/time-series/statistical_abstracts.html (accessed various dates).

Steindl, Josef. 1952. *Maturity and Stagnation in American Capitalism.* Oxford: Blackwell.

Stiglitz, Joseph. 1970. "A Consumption-Oriented Theory of the Demand for Financial Assets and the Term Structure of Interest Rates." *Review of Economic Studies* 37:321–351.

Summers, Lawrence. 2014. "Reflections on the 'New Secular Stagnation Hypothesis.'" In *Secular Stagnation: Facts, Causes, and Cures,* ed. C. Teulings and R. Baldwin, pp. 27–46. London: CEPR Press.

———. 2015. "Demand Side Secular Stagnation." *American Economic Review* 105:60–65.

———. 2016. "The Age of Secular Stagnation: What It Is and What to Do About It." *Foreign Affairs* 95 (March–April): 2–9.

Surowiecki, James. 2011. "State of the Unions." *New Yorker,* January 17. http://www.newyorker.com/talk/financial/2011/01/17/110117ta_talk_surowiecki (accessed February 10, 2011).

Sutch, Richard. 2018. "Reading Keynes at the Zero Lower Bound: The Liquidity Trap, the Great Depression, and Unconventional Policy." *Journal of the History of Economic Thought* 40:301–334.

Tarshis, Lorie. 1939. "Changes in Real and Money Wages." *Economic Journal* 49:150–154.

———. 1947. *The Elements of Economics.* Boston: Houghton Mifflin.

Taylor, John. 1979. "Staggered Wage Setting in a Macro Model." *American Economic Review* 69:108–113.

———. 1980. "Aggregate Dynamics and Staggered Contracts." *Journal of Political Economy* 88:1–23.

———. 1993. "Discretion Versus Policy Rules in Practice." *Carnegie-Rochester Conference Series on Public Policy* 39:195–214.

———. 2011. "An Empirical Analysis of the Revival of Fiscal Activism in the 2000s." *Journal of Economic Literature* 49:686–702.

Tcherneva, Pavlina. 2007. "Chartalism and the Tax-Driven Approach to Money." In *A Handbook of Alternative Monetary Economics,* ed. Philip Arestis and Malcolm Sawyer. Cheltenham, UK: Edward Elgar.

Temin, Peter. 1976. *Did Monetary Forces Cause the Great Depression?* New York: Norton.

Temin, Peter, and Barrie Wigmore. 1990. "The End of One Big Deflation." *Explorations in Economic History* 27:483–502.

Thompson, E. P. 1963. *The Making of the English Working Class.* New York: Random House.

Tobin, James. 1947. "Money Wage Rates and Employment." In *The New Economics,* ed. Seymour Harris. New York: Knopf.

———. 1956. "The Interest-Elasticity of Transactions Demand for Cash." *Review of Economics and Statistics* 38:241–247.

———. 1958. Liquidity Preference as Behavior towards Risk." *Review of Economic Studies* 25:65–86.

———. 1969. "A General Equilibrium Approach to Monetary Theory." *Journal of Money Credit and Banking* 1:15–29.

———. 1975. "Keynesian Models of Recession and Depression." *American Economic Review* 65:195–202.

———. 1980. *Asset Accumulation and Economic Activity: Reflections on Contemporary Macroeconomic Theory.* Chicago: University of Chicago Press.

———. 1992. "An Old Keynesian Counterattacks." *Eastern Economic Journal* 18 (Fall): 387–400.

———. 1993. "Price Flexibility and Output Stability: An Old Keynesian View." *Journal of Economic Perspectives* 7:45–65.

Tucker, Paul. 2018. *Unelected Power: The Quest for Legitimacy in Central Banking and the Regulatory State.* Princeton: Princeton University Press.

Tversky, Amos, and Daniel Kahneman. 1981. "The Framing of Decisions." *Science* 211:453–458.

U.S. Department of the Treasury. n.d. "Corporate Bond Yield Curve Papers and Data." https://home.treasury.gov/data/treasury-coupon-issues-and-corporate -bond-yield-curve/corporate-bond-yield-curve (accessed September 7, 2014).

———. 2008. "Treasury Announces Temporary Guarantee Program for Money Market Funds," September 29. https://www.treasury.gov/press-center/press-releases/ Pages/hp1161.aspx (accessed December 2, 2018).

U.S. Government Printing Office. 2008. "The Financial Crisis and the Role of Federal Regulators." October 23. http://www.gpo.gov/fdsys/pkg/CHRG-110hhrg55764/ html/CHRG-110hhrg55764.htm (accessed July 11, 2015).

Veritas Foundation. 1960. *Keynes at Harvard.* New York: Veritas Foundation.

Viner, Jacob. 1933a. *Balanced Deflation, Inflation, or More Depression.* Lecture delivered on February 20, 1933, Minneapolis, Minnesota. Minneapolis: University of Minnesota Press.

———. 1933b. "Inflation as a Possible Remedy for the Depression." *Proceedings of the Institute of Public Affairs,* University of Georgia, 7th Annual Meeting, May 8–16, 1933, Athens, Ga.

———. 1936. "Mr. Keynes on the Causes of Unemployment." *Quarterly Journal of Economics* 51:147–167.

Volcker, Paul. 2013. "The Fed & Big Banking at the Crossroads." *New York Review of Books,* August 15.

von Neumann, John, and Oskar Morgenstern. 1944. *The Theory of Games and Economic Behavior.* Princeton, N.J.: Princeton University Press.

Walras, Léon. 1954. *Elements of Pure Economics, or The Theory of Social Wealth.* Trans. W Jaffé from the *Édition Définitive, Éléments de l'Économie Politque Pure,* Homewood, Ill., 1926. [First published in 1874.]

Watkins, Myron. 1933. "The Literature of the Crisis." *Quarterly Journal of Economics* 47:504–532.

Weber, Max. 1930. *The Protestant Ethic and the Spirit of Capitalism.* Trans. Talcott Parsons. New York: Scribner. [Originally published as "Die Protestantische Ethik und Der 'Geist' des Kapitalismus." *Archiv fur Sozialwissenschaft und Sozialpolitik* 20 (1905): 1–54; and 21 (1905): 1–110.]

Weir, David. 1992. "A Century of US Unemployment, 1890–1990: Revised Estimates and Evidence for Stabilization." *Research in Economic History* 14:301–346.

Wells Fargo. 2013. "How Much of Your Net Worth Should You Keep in Cash?" https://conversations.wfmagazines.com/create_wealth/investment_planning/article/how_much_of_your_net_worth_should_you_keep_in_cash/ (accessed August 5, 2013).

———. 2019. "How Much Cash Should I Hold in My Portfolio?" https://www08.wellsfargomedia.com/assets/pdf/personal/investing/investment-institute/how%20much%20cash.pdf (accessed May 12, 2020).

Wicksell, Knut. 1936. *Interest and Prices: A Study of the Causes Regulating the Value of Money.* Trans. Richard Kahn, London: Macmillan. [Originally published as *Geldzins und Güterpreise.* Jena: Gustav Fischer, 1898.]

———. 1958. "The Influence of the Rate of Interest on Commodity Prices." Trans. Sylva Gethin. In Wicksell, *Selected Papers on Economic Theory,* ed. Erik Lindahl. Cambridge, Mass.: Harvard University Press. [Originally published as "Penningeräntans Inflytande på Varuprisen." *Nationalekonmiska Föreningens Förhandlingar under Förra Halväret 1898,* pp. 47–70. Stockholm, 1899.]

Wildavsky, Aaron. 1964. *The Politics of the Budgetary Process.* Boston: Little Brown.

Wilson, Daniel. 2012. "Fiscal Spending Jobs Multipliers: Evidence from the 2009 American Recovery and Reinvestment Act." *American Economic Journal: Economic Policy* 4:251–282.

World Bank. 2016. *World Development Indicators.* Washington, D.C.: World Bank. http://databank.worldbank.org/data/reports.aspx?source=world-development-indicators (accessed November 27, 2016).

Wray, L. Randall. 2014. "From the State Theory of Money to Modern Money Theory: An Alternative to Economic Orthodoxy." Levy Economics Institute of Bard College, Working Paper 792. Annandale on Hudson, N.Y.

ACKNOWLEDGMENTS

My first debt is to the students to whom I presented my argument as it was developing. Their questions at some points, their incomprehension at others, and their encouragement at virtually every step were essential to this project. One of these students, Sam Harland, became an invaluable research assistant in my collaboration with Peter Spiegler assessing the Obama stimulus.

Duncan Foley read the entire manuscript in draft, and his questions and comments reflected the keen mind he has brought to economics for more than half a century. The book has benefited from his attention. Bob Rowthorn also read the manuscript, and made excellent points, unfortunately, for the most part too late in the process for me to incorporate them. Ben Friedman read the chapters on liquidity-preference theory, chapters 11 and 12. John Campbell read the empirical appendix to chapter 12. Both made helpful observations that saved me misunderstanding and error. Christine Desan prodded me, both in conversation and in her own writings, to explore the assumptions about money in *The General Theory,* and chapter 13 is much improved as a result. The assessment of the Obama stimulus in chapter 15 comes out of a project undertaken jointly with Peter Spiegler. It reflects his skepticism about the customary use of regression analysis to torture the data and the consequent need to supplement it with more humane methods of interrogation. Michael Ash made very helpful criticisms of an early draft of this chapter. I am also grateful to Professor Ash for pushing me to justify a fundamental assumption of this book: the importance of confronting mainstream economics on its most favorable turf, the field of perfect competition, rather than accepting that the ills of capitalism, particularly unemployment, are due to departures from the norms of perfect competition—frictions, rigidities, and the like.

My editor at Harvard University Press, Ian Malcolm, his assistant, Olivia Woods, and Cheryl Lincoln at Technologies 'N Typography helped transform a large and complicated manuscript into what we all hope is a readable book.

Michael Aronson, my longtime editor at Harvard University Press, retired in the middle of this project, but even after his retirement has given me unfailing support in many ways.

All of these people, I hope, have saved me from the fate that Keynes observed (in the preface to *The General Theory*) is too often the lot of theorists operating in isolation: "It is astonishing," he wrote, "what foolish things one can temporarily believe if one thinks too long alone."

INDEX

Abdelhak, Senhadji, 684

absolute needs, 324, 616, 847n12

Achen, Christopher, 563, 575–576

Adrian, Tobias, 835–836n9

Aga Khan, 327

aggregate demand (AD), 1–6; and adjustment process, 179–180, 210–211, 213, 220; and Cambridge saving theory, 330–336, 368–371, 698–701; and capital deepening, 356–359, 728–730; and capital widening, 349–356, 366–371, 699–701; and change in the price of energy, 691–695, 715–717, 718–719, 724–726; Dennison on, 817n8; as a determinant of equilibrium, 517, 519, 523; in Domar's model, 656–658, 661–662; in Dos Santos Ferreira and Michel's model, 218; empirical relationship with inflation, 755–764, 771, 790; as equality of expenditure and income, 81–85, 183–185; European Central Bank (ECB) on, 48; in first-pass model, 81–86, 90–92, 497; and fiscal policy, 12–13, 42–43, 531–543, 785–788, 790, 792; and Fisher effect, 250–252, 253–254, 259–260; in fixprice adjustment, 181–182, 204–211, 334–335, 354–356, 357–358, 497, 691–692, 702–711; in flexprice adjustment, 182–183, 197–204, 208–211, 334–335, 354, 357–358, 497, 691–692; and fractional-reserve banking, 135–145, 226–230, 257; and government debt, 635–638; in Great Depression, 274; in Harrod's model, 647–656, 661–662; and income distribution, 39, 330, 790–791; indeterminacy, 519–522, 523, 784–785; and interest rate, 28, 78, 92, 517–519; and investment demand, 110–118, 358–359; as locus of stationary labor:capital ratio (*l*), 664; as locus of stationary output, 204–205; as locus of stationary prices, 198; in long run, 13–14, 41, 664, 688–712, 771, 788–789, 791; mainstream view, 32, 54–55, 781–782; in Marschak's model, 804n13; in Modigliani's model, 33–34, 130–131, 224–226, 255–257, 276–277, 502; and money demand, 90, 119–120, 518–519; and money supply, 133–135, 193–194; and money wage, 133–135, 502, 777–781; in neoclassical synthesis, 36; and New Classical theory, 36–37; in New Keynesian theory, 37, 41; optimizing the composition of, 594–602, 612–623, 788; and paradox of thrift, 39; Patinkin on, 26–27, 216; and price level, 90, 104–107, 145, 223, 227, 230, 497; and real-balance effect, 36, 145–153, 154–155, 234–244, 253, 257–259; in Robinson's model, 670–673, 676; Samuelson on, 205; and Say's Law, 60–64, 68–69, 81, 378, 784; in second-pass model, 31, 99–108, 120–121; in Solow's model, 658–662; Temin on, 816–817n5; in third-pass model, 194, 203–204, 208–212, 219–221; as understood in the 1950s and 1960s, 40–41; in World War II and post-War planning, 46, 312–313

aggregate supply (AS), 39–41, 47, 71, 90, 129–131, 150, 521. *See also* goods supply; labor supply

Agricultural Adjustment Administration (AAA), 289

agriculture: in Great Depression, 8, 261–263, 266, 278–292, 300–304, 781–782, 797–798n2, 817–819nn7–15, 819nn17–18, 819n20; and measurement of unemployment, 540–541, 797n2; and reserve army, 677–678, 851–852n2

Ait-Sahalia, Yacine, 831n14

Akerlof, George, 325–326

Allais, Maurice, 363

Amazon, 349

goods supply (GS) *(continued)*
664–665; as locus of stationary output, 172–173, 176, 177, 199; as locus of stationary prices, 174, 177, 206, 690; in mainstream model, 37, 55–56, 163, 204, 781–782, 804n12; as marginal-cost schedule, 52, 664; in Marschak's model, 804n13; in Modigliani's model, 125–131, 154; in Passinetti–Piketty model, 739; and relative speeds of adjustment, 203–204, 207–211, 213; in second-pass model, 108; in Solow's model, 659
Gordon, Robert, 684, 754, 755, 790, 841–842n3, 850–851n8
Gramlich, Edward, 552–553
Great Depression, 4, 7–8, 17–18, 19, 21–22, 24, 39, 42, 43, 194, 196, 217, 233, 261–278, 365, 486, 538, 540, 544–545, 681–682, 764–765, 771, 797n2, 806n10, 810n4, 811n10, 812n4, 813n9, 815–816n2, 816n4, 846n9, 847n12, 853n8; agriculture in, 278–292, 300–305, 783, 797–798n2; Eichengreen on, 816–817n5; I. Fisher on, 236–237, 276, 783; M. Friedman and Schwartz on, 277–278, 293–299; mainstream views of, 46, 259, 815n2; *New York Times* on, 43–45; Roosevelt on, 244, 261; Temin on, 288, 290, 816–817n5, 819n16; Viner on, 56–60, 530, 801–802nn2–3, 833–834n6
Great Recession, 2, 4–5, 24, 45, 346, 365, 413, 426–429, 486, 516, 540, 544–545, 559–560, 568–569, 630, 772, 785, 787, 790, 797–798nn1–2, 802n6, 813n9, 827n5, 839–840n7, 841–842n3, 843n16, 846n9, 848–849n17, 853n8; *New York Times* on, 45
Green, Jerry, 23–25, 163
Greenspan, Alan, 514, 775, 799–800n10
Gresham's Law in reverse, 776
Grossman, Herschel, 775
Gürkaynak, Refet, 457, 477, 803–804n11, 825n23

Haberler, Gottfried: on real-balance effect, 2, 6, 7, 36, 108, 122, 144, 148–153, 160–161, 234–235, 252, 779–783, 798n5; on stationary real-price equilibria, 215–217. *See also* real-balance effect; stationary loci
Hager, Sandy, 846n6
Hamberg, Daniel, 827n4
Hansen, Alvin, 32, 43, 97, 235, 664, 806–807n12, 820n1, 850–851n8
Harcourt, Geoffrey, 798n4
Harris, Donald, 851n1

Harrod, Roy, 13, 647–664, 668, 669–671, 675–676, 679, 687, 699, 741, 770, 849–850n2, 850n4
Hausman, Joshua, 288, 290
Hawtrey, Ralph, 822n4
Helicopter money, 785
Henderson, H. D., 19, 548, 805n4, 843n14
Herndon, Thomas, 846–847n10
Hicks, John, 31, 51, 100, 175, 193, 212, 381, 415, 463, 480, 510–513, 647, 690, 806–807n12, 827n4, 830n7, 849n1
Hitler, Adolf, 777, 797–798n2
Hobbes, Thomas, 620
holding yield, 390–397, 400–401, 404–406, 418, 423, 435, 448–450, 460–464, 478, 826n12, 829–830n5, 830n11; on cash, 516; condition, 466–469, 830n11
Holmes, Oliver Wendell, 822n2
Home Building & Loan Association v. Blaisdell, 293
Hoover, Herbert, 58, 261, 802n3, 815n2
Houthakker, Hendrik, 324
Hume, David, 28, 499, 802n5
hurdle rate of interest, 10–12, 97, 125, 131–133, 225–226, 248, 252, 343–346, 349, 359, 417, 426, 430, 455, 456, 513, 514, 519, 520, 521, 522–523, 529, 600, 602, 603, 624, 625–626, 656, 664, 668, 670, 688, 698–699, 713, 718, 720, 724, 731, 749–751, 777, 786n3, 817n6, 827–828n6, 836n10; in Great Depression, 273, 276, 277, 298; as the interest rate on comparable bonds, 80, 273, 277, 343, 423, 499

Ibn Khaldun, 846n4
immiserizing growth, 289, 819n17
imperfections. *See* money-wage rigidity; monopolistic competition; monopoly; oligopoly; price rigidity; unemployment: insurance; unions; welfare state
income distribution, 328, 558, 680
inflation, 14, 33, 47–48, 71, 194, 247–248, 291, 331, 335, 339, 354, 358, 472–473, 484–486, 516–517, 522–523, 607, 614, 629, 652, 666–669, 674, 676, 680, 683–684, 689–691, 693, 695–696, 702, 704, 710–712, 717–720, 724–727, 731–733, 750–752, 771–772, 790, 821n12, 827n3, 830–831n13, 834–835n8, 839–840n7, 847n11, 853n8, 855n1, 855n3, 855n5; costs of, 767–768; and employment, 754–764; in Harrod's model, 655, 658–659; Keynes on, 767–769, 813–814n13; Mankiw